PICTORIAL FIELD

OF

THE CIVIL WAR

PICTORIAL FIELD BOOK

OF

THE CIVIL WAR

JOURNEYS THROUGH THE BATTLEFIELDS
IN THE WAKE OF CONFLICT

By BENSON J. LOSSING, LL.D.

WITH A NEW INTRODUCTION BY REID MITCHELL

ILLUSTRATED BY MANY HUNDRED ENGRAVINGS ON WOOD, BY LOSSING AND
BARRITT, FROM SKETCHES BY THE AUTHOR AND OTHERS

VOLUME III

THE JOHNS HOPKINS UNIVERSITY PRESS
BALTIMORE AND LONDON

Introduction © 1997 The Johns Hopkins University Press
All rights reserved
Printed in the United States of America on acid-free paper

Originally published in 1874 by T. Belknap
Johns Hopkins Paperbacks edition, 1997
06 05 04 03 02 01 00 99 98 97   5 4 3 2 1

The Johns Hopkins University Press
2715 North Charles Street
Baltimore, Maryland 21218-4319
The Johns Hopkins Press Ltd., London

Library of Congress Cataloging-in-Publication Data

Lossing, Benson John, 1813–1891
  Pictorial field book of the Civil War : journeys through the battlefields in the wake
of conflict / by Benson J. Lossing ; with an introduction by Reid Mitchell.
    p.   cm
  Originally published : Hartford : T. Belknap, 1870 (v. 2), 1874 (v. 3), 1876 (v. 1)
    ISBN 0-8018-5669-8 (pbk. : v. 1) — ISBN 0-8018-5671-X (pbk. : v. 2). —
ISBN 0-8018-5672-8 (pbk. : v. 3)
    1. United States—History—Civil War, 1861–1865—Miscellanea.
2. United States—History—Civil War, 1861–1865—Pictorial works. I. Title.
E468.L914 1997
973.7—dc21   97-12445
                                                                          CIP

A catalog record for this book is available from the British Library.

INTRODUCTION

 T the beginning of the third and last volume of his *Pictorial Field Book of the Civil War*, Ben Lossing faced a challenge: How does an author maintain narrative tension when he told readers in the previous volume that the two key turning points of the war occurred before this volume opens? Lossing seems never to have doubted that his account of the last years of the war would hold his readers' interest. Nowadays, what will help hold the reader's attention is the unexpectedness of what in his time was a conventional interpretation.

His military narrative was primarily different in emphasis from current Civil War histories. Lossing discussed what we think of as peripheral events in much greater detail than we are used to, and his judgment on various military figures often varies from ours. He preferred Fighting Joe Hooker, the failure of Chancellorsville, to George Gordon Meade, the victor of Gettysburg, and suggested that Hooker got a raw deal from the administration. (He made a good case, too.) Also, he held David Hunter and Ambrose Burnside in high regard. Hunter and Hooker were highly respected by the more radical Republicans. Lossing devoted as much attention to the battle of Knoxville as he did to the battle of Chickamauga. Bank's Red River Campaign, usually considered a poorly conceived Union fiasco, went uncriticized by Lossing.

At the end of his second volume, Lossing described the fall of Vicksburg, arguing that it was one of two key events in the Union victory, the other being emancipation. To begin the third volume, he had to backtrack to cover the battles of Chancellorsville and Gettysburg. Surely there are few volumes devoted to Civil War history that make less of the Gettysburg campaign. Lossing relegated the Gettysburg address to a footnote. Few accounts of Chancellorsville give so much weight to Stoneman's Raid and to operations around Suffolk. But these operations were successful: Lossing disliked writing about Union defeat.

Any Union victory seemed to Lossing to be well worth attention. According to Lossing, the battle of Bentonville, usually treated as a sad attempt by Joseph Johnston to try anything to slow the irrepressible progress of Sherman's army, not only could have resulted in a Confederate tactical victory, but it could have changed the course of the war. Lossing argued that Johnston could have destroyed Sherman's army and then marched north to join Lee around Richmond, where the Confederates could have crushed Grant's army as well. And he thought the battle was a near thing. It is impossible to think of any historian who would agree.

Of course, Lossing respected Johnston far more than he respected Robert E. Lee. As the first two volumes of the *Pictorial Field Book of the Civil War* demonstrate, Lossing felt nothing but contempt for Lee. He argued that the Confederate general leaned on Jackson and Longstreet, both of whom had minds superior to Lee's. Indeed, Lossing thought Longstreet's wounding at the Battle of the Wilderness was providential, as it turned over direction of that battle to Lee. Ever alert for signs of treachery, Lossing believed that Lee received copies of Grant's orders directly from Union headquarters, which seems to explain Lee's successes in the Wilderness Campaign at the same time it makes his failures more imponderable. One would like to know which former Confederate general told Lossing that Lee was "a greatly over-rated military leader—a man of routine—cold, undemonstrative, ambitious, the pet of the Virginians because he was a member of one of their 'first families'—without the moral courage to take the responsibility—so popular with the army that he might have ended the war any time after the taking of Atlanta." It sounds like Joseph Johnston, except that Johnston himself came from an old Virginia family.

Most of all, Lossing condemned Lee for prolonging the war after the November 1864 election, after which, Lossing believed, the inevitability of defeat must have been clear to both Lee and Jefferson Davis. Yet the two men, ambitious and careless of human life, continued the rebellion. Lossing even interpreted Lee's farewell order to the Army of Northern Virginia as malicious. The only romance around Lee to which Lossing succumbed was that of his men: even Lossing said they were sublime during the retreat from Richmond.

The argument against the idea that Lee, with his twisted sense of "duty," and Davis committed a crime by continuing the war long after it could be won has been resurrected in a recent book by Alan T. Nolan. In *Lee Considered* (1991), Nolan argues that historians have overlooked the hard questions about Lee—about his attitudes toward secession and slavery, his culpability for prolonging the war, his strategic vision. In many ways, Nolan's portrait of Lee is not so far removed from Ben Lossing's. But Lossing's interpretation, commonplace in the North after the war, has generally been forgotten. Northern admiration of Lee seems to have been one of the terms for sectional reconciliation. But Lossing denigrated Lee—hinting, for example,that he surely knew of the horrors of Andersonville and did nothing—and preferred Johnston, whom he praised for not following Lee's bad example at Appomattox when he surrendered his army at Durham Station, North Carolina.[1]

It would be hard to find another account of Sherman's March to the Sea and the subsequent march through the Carolinas as tame as Lossing's. For that matter, one could read Lossing through and have no idea of how ruinous Phil Sheridan was in the Shenandoah Valley. Lossing accepted Sherman's lie that Confederate General Wade Hampton burned Columbia, South Carolina. Lossing, who would have rejected the notion that the Civil War was the first modern war, wrote as if embarrassed by Union devastation. A man who dwelled on rebels' pillage as evidence of their depravity and the depravity of their cause, Lossing could not bring himself to celebrate the Union army's destructive war; and as he treated the cause of Union as sacred, he could hardly acknowledge the wreckage the federal armies left behind, even to deplore it. For Lossing, the Union had fought fair and won; the Confederacy had fought dirty and lost. This may be the only point in all three volumes at which it would be fair to accuse Lossing of out-and-out misrepresentation. George Ward Nichols's *The Story of the Great March*, which paints a much more vivid picture of the March to the Sea than Lossing does, was published in 1865. Lossing cited Nichols in his footnotes.[2]

Lossing took a providential view of the war. He said all contemplative Northerners could see that men were only the instruments for achieving the victory of "true principles," by which he meant emancipation. Lossing claimed that after Congress had adopted the thirteenth Amendment, the Union army always met with success—a sign of favor. Virtue, not innovations in war, led to victory.

In this volume Lossing returned to one of his preoccupations—conspiracy. In many ways the action of the volume takes place as much in the North as it does in the South. It is in the North that conspiracies are hatched to transform military victory into political defeat. The threat

---

[1] Alan T. Nolan, *Lee Considered: General Robert E. Lee and Civil War History* (Chapel Hill, 1991).
[2] George Ward Nichols, *The Story of the Great March* (New York, 1865).

from the Confederacy could be turned back. The more insidious threat lurked within the North itself. Lossing believed that the Peace Democrats conspired with the Confederacy against Union victory. He believed that the assassination of Lincoln was part of a Confederate conspiracy to disrupt the Union government. He charged that the death of so many prisoners of war in Confederate hands was willful. Even the Pope did not escape Lossing's ire.

To this day many historians, following contemporary usage, call the Peace Democrats "Copperheads"; for example, James M. McPherson uses the term throughout his *Battle Cry of Freedom*. According to Lossing, the Peace faction, with its ties to disgruntled conservatives among the officers of the Army of the Potomac, on the one hand, and to the Confederacy, on the other, prolonged the war by two years. Lossing claimed, for example, that General Steele's opposition to emancipation led to his poor performance in defending Arkansas. Furthermore, Lossing charged that the most treacherous Peace Democrats plotted a counter-revolution. For Lossing, the New York City draft riot in the summer of 1863 was no random outbreak. Traitors had plotted it to coincide with Lee's invasion of Pennsylvania. Had the Army of Northern Virginia achieved victory at Gettysburg, Lossing said, there would have been riots, ushering in counter-revolution, across the nation. He also believed that Confederate General Sterling Price and exiled Ohio politician Clement Vallandigham had plotted an uprising with the secret "Sons of Liberty" in the spring of 1864, which only Union General Rosecrans's diligence had forestalled.

A good republican of the 1860s, Lossing of course distrusted the Supreme Court. One of the most common misperceptions about the Civil War is that the Republicans, who fought for national supremacy, included the Supreme Court among strong federal institutions. For all practical purposes, they ignored it throughout the war. Until 1864, the Chief Justice was Roger B. Taney, notorious for the Dred Scot decision and Lincoln's would-be nemesis. Lossing argued that the Supreme Court and the principle of judicial review itself was a threat to democracy.

Like many another Northerner, Lossing believed that the assassination of Lincoln was not the work of a few pathetic souls but a conspiracy that answered to Jefferson Davis. Lossing saw it not as an act of vengeance but as a far-reaching plot designed to disorganize the national government. It seems never to have occurred to him to wonder why the Confederate plotters would wait until their armies had been defeated to strike this blow against the Union. The most Lossing could say was that the conspirators had hoped that "in some way" they would come to power in the confusion following the assassinations. While in captivity, Davis himself quite plausibly pointed out to a surgeon in the Union army that the assassination of Lincoln hurt ex-Confederates; he thought Andrew Johnson, a Southerner himself, had to advocate a harsh peace to survive politically. Davis was wrong, but his was a mistake that a number of Radical Republicans also made. Indeed, a later generation of conspiracy theorists argued that it was the Radical Republicans who had killed Lincoln for just this very reason.[3]

Lossing closed his Civil War volumes by discussing Confederate prisons. In no way did Lossing better characterize Northerners from his era than by his furious denunciations of the Confederacy's treatment of Union prisoners. The prisoner-of-war issue caused considerable bitterness in the North and in the South and led to acrimonious exchanges and misrepresentations on both sides.

Lossing estimated death rates in Civil War prisons as 17.6 percent for Confederate camps and "a little more than 11 percent" in Union ones. More recent estimates close the gap a little, estimating roughly 15.5 percent in Confederate prisons, and roughly 12 percent in Union prisons. Lossing found his estimated 6 percent difference between Confederate Union camp deaths highly significant, but even with his calculations another historian might consider the figures roughly comparable, given the Union's far-greater resources. The 3.5 percent difference indicated by more recent estimates hardly seems significant at all.

But as far as Northerners like Lossing were concerned, there was no comparison to make between Confederate and Union prisons. Lossing maintained that while the Union treated prisoners well, the record of Confederate prisons was "one of the darkest chapters in the history of human iniquity." According to Lossing, prisons in the North had been healthy, comfortable places, and prisons in the South were hellholes. Furthermore, the horrors of Confederate prisons were deliberate: the Confederacy had sought to ruin the health of the men they captured so that they could not return to service if they were exchanged, and Confederates often murdered their prisoners by deprivation and savage usages. During the war, Northern newspapers had been filled with stories of atrocities in rebel prisons: they would provide a generation of Republican politicians with materials for stump speeches. After the war, when a new recruit joined the postwar Grand Army of the Republic, the Union's premier veterans organization, he would dress as a prisoner of war and kneel before a coffin "labelled upon the lid, in a conspicuous manner, with the name and regiment of some soldier who died in Andersonville Rebel

---

[3] John J. Craven, *Prison Life of Jefferson Davis* (New York, 1866), 221–22.

Prison."[4] And even today it is hard to contemplate some of the photographs made of men held in Confederate prisons—some had been reduced to living skeletons.

For Lossing and others, the conspiracy they discerned in the Confederate prison system was part of a larger pattern. As Lossing himself said, what else could be expected from traitors but brutality? And as Lossing and others asked, what could be expected from slaveholders but treason and brutality? The United States Sanitary Commission, upon whose report on rebel prisons Lossing relied, argued "a too positive denial of humanity to another race, and a too positive contempt for a poorer class of their own race, have fostered those perverted principles, which would undermine a government filled with a more generous idea, and excite a hatred toward the people who would uphold it." Treason followed brutality. After the war, the Judge Advocate General of the U.S. Army, Joseph Holt, the man who prosecuted the commandant of Andersonville Prison, said that by looking at the cemeteries filled from Confederate prisons "we can best understand the inner and real life of the rebellion."[5]

When he described the bucolic conditions in Union prisons, Lossing probably did not know about the Union policy of retaliation, instituted in 1864. Those in authority, from the secretary of war down, said that the prisoners in Union hands should suffer the same treatment as those the Confederates held. Official retaliation largely meant short rations, so perhaps the higher death rate in Union prisons the winter of 1864–65 cannot be attributed entirely to the policy.

Lossing also probably failed to realize that conditions at the Elmira, New York, prison, the worst Union camp, rivaled Andersonville's and produced an even higher death rate. Prisoners suffered from exposure from sleeping in tents, even in the middle of winter, and receiving little clothing. Monotonous rations, limited to bread and water—a retaliatory measure—led to scurvy and disease in general. And, because much of Elmira was swamp at that time, illness was common. One Union inspector reported that "both the commanding officer and the medical officers" at Elmira "neglected the ordinary promptings of humanity in the performance of their duties toward sick men."[6]

---

[4] Stuart McConnell, *Glorious Contentment: The Grand Army of the Republic, 1865–1900* (Chapel Hill, 1992), 94.

[5] *Narrative of Privations and Sufferings of United States Officers and Soldiers while Prisoners of War in the Hands of the Rebel Authorities. Being the Report of a Commission of Inquiry Appointed by the United States Sanitary Commission* (Philadelphia, 1864), 97.

[6] Reid Mitchell, "'Our prison system, supposing we had any': The Confederate and Union Prison Systems," in *On the Road to Total War: The American Civil War and the German Wars of Unification, 1861–1871*, ed. Stïg Forest and Jörg Nagler (New York, 1997).

At the close of the war, Judge Advocate Holt hoped to convict Jefferson Davis of causing the deaths of Union prisoners of war. He also expected to try Davis for the assassination of Lincoln and interviewed witnesses who implicated the Confederate president in that crime. In the end, however, the federal government chose not to try Davis in either a military or a civil court. He was released on bail and never called back.

Lossing made it sound as if Davis had been mollycoddled. He wrote that "Davis was confined at Fortress Monroe, in a casemate—a comfortable prison—on a charge of being concerned in the murder of the President, and of treason, where he remained a long time, treated with the greatest kindness and consideration." Although in the absence of a conclusive trial Lossing was uncharacteristically circumspect in his accusations against Davis, he implied that the Confederate president, clearly guilty of treason, was guilty of the other crimes charged against him as well.

Perhaps it would have cheered Lossing to learn that the conditions of Davis's imprisonment were more severe than he indicated. At the beginning, the commandant of Fortress Monroe kept Davis shackled. The damp in his casemate cell threatened Davis's health. It seems from the account offered by John J. Craven, the Union officer who was his doctor, that Davis, as miserable as he was, understood the North's need to make him a criminal and that he himself knew how to play-act the martyr.

Ex-Confederates emphasized Davis's mistreatment. Indeed, it was probably his time in prison that reconciled many Southerners to Davis, as he had been widely unpopular at the war's end. Nonetheless, it is striking that the leader of one of the greatest armed rebellions in world history was let go scot-free, particularly in view of the hysteria that followed Lincoln's assassination. However much this may have disappointed Ben Lossing, sparing Davis was probably a wise decision: if prosecuted, Davis would have died with the same dignity and self-righteousness as John Brown did on the eve of the war and he would have became as great a martyr for his cause.

While there was much in Lossing's *Pictorial Field Book of the Civil War* that offended former Confederates, one relatively minor charge provoked an outcry from memorial organizations such as the Southern Historical Society. In his account of the battle of Gettysburg, Lossing claimed that the Confederates had employed both explosive and poisoned bullets. In January 1880, the Reverend Horace Edwin Hayden published an article on the subject in the *Southern Historical Society Papers*, the premier journal in which former Confederates presented their defenses against Yankee accusations, and their counteraccusations. Hayden presented many documents trying to show that the Confederates did not have such bullets; but then he went on to argue that the Union soldiers at Gettysburg did use them against Confederates. Lossing, he thought, had found Union bullets and misidentified them as Confederate.

Hayden concluded his article by questioning "whether as a historian Mr. Lossing is deserving even the notice of a novice in history; for while he is known to be a voluminous writer of American history, he is also known to be a writer of many and great inaccuracies." After listing some of these, Hayden continued. "But because Mr. Lossing's histories have flooded the North, and are largely accepted as authentic narrations of events, it is due the Confederates and the cause for which they so long and nobly battled, against such fearful odds, that the truth be made known, and Mr. Lossing's misstatements exposed."[7]

Of course, neither the Confederates nor the federals used explosive bullets at Gettysburg; such a charge is based on fantasy. What we should note here, however, was how similar the charges supporters of the Union and supporters of the Confederacy made against each other were. Explosive bullets were hardly the only subject on which both sides swapped nearly identical accusations.

The Confederate propensity for such charges and for shrill defensiveness is well known. Historians have long discussed "the Lost Cause." Generally less appreciated is what we might call "the Won Cause," the set of beliefs and legends that informed the North's vision of the Civil War. For anyone who cares to understand how the North understood our Civil War, Ben Lossing's *Pictorial Field Book of the Civil War* is a fine place to start.

---

[7] Rev. Horace Edwin Hayden, "Explosive or Poisoned Musket or Rifle Balls—Were They Authorized and Used by the Confederate States Army, or by the United States Army during the Civil War?—A Slander Refuted," *Southern Historical Society Papers* 8, no. 1 (1880): 18–28.

PICTORIAL FIELD BOOK

OF

THE CIVIL WAR

PREFACE.

HIS volume completes the Chronicle of the Civil War. It comprises a record of the events of the conflict from midsummer of 1863, until the close of the struggle, in the field, in the spring of 1865.

The second volume was ended with the record of the capture of Vicksburg and Port Hudson by the National armies, in July. This volume opens with an account of the movements of the Army of the Potomac in the winter and spring of 1863, which led to the Battle of Chancellorsville, and Lee's second invasion of Maryland that ended with the Battle of Gettysburg. It contains the story of the military and naval operations in the region of the Mississippi and the Gulf of Mexico, and all along the Atlantic coast, from Florida to the lower borders of Virginia, including the long siege of Charleston. Also, an account of the doings of the Anglo-Confederate pirate-ships, including those of the *Alabama*, and an account of her destruction. It also contains a record of the important movements in Eastern and Southeastern Tennessee. which were followed by Sherman's great march and series of con, flicts from Chattanooga, by way of Atlanta, to the sea, and thence through the Carolinas; and the expulsion of the Confederates from Tennessee, by Thomas.

It bears a record of the stirring events in the Red River region; in Texas; all along the Mississippi, and in the States whose borders are washed by its waters; at Mobile, and in the interior of the States of Mississippi and Alabama, and the final triumph of the National arms in all the vast region of the Republic southward of the Roanoke River and westward of the mountain ranges of Virginia, Tennessee, and North and South Carolina.

It contains a history of the great campaigns of the armies of the Potomac and the James, which ended in the capture of Richmond, the flight of the Conspirators, and the surrender of Lee ; also of the assassination of the President ; the surrender of the forces under Johnston and other leaders ; the flight and capture of the head of the Confederacy of traitors ; the closing scenes of the war ; the exchange and treatment of prisoners ; and the free-will offerings of the people in support of the Government. Also an outline sketch of the efforts of the loyal citizens to reorganize the Governments of States which had been disorganized by the Rebellion, and to restore the Union and re-establish it upon the sure foundations of Justice.

With a consciousness of fidelity to the laws of truth and righteousness, in the preparation of this work, the author offers it as his contribution to the historic records of his country.

B. J. L.

THE RIDGE, DOVER PLAINS, N. Y.

VOLUME III.

CHAPTER I.

CHAPTER II.

CHAPTER III.

CHAPTER IV.

CHAPTER V.

CHAPTER VI.

CHAPTER VII.

THE SIEGE OF CHARLESTON TO THE CLOSE OF 1863.—OPERATIONS IN MISSOURI, ARKANSAS, AND TEXAS.

CHAPTER VIII.

CIVIL AFFAIRS IN 1863.—MILITARY OPERATIONS BETWEEN THE MOUNTAINS AND THE MISSISSIPPI RIVER.

CHAPTER IX.

THE RED RIVER EXPEDITION.

CHAPTER X.

THE LAST INVASION OF MISSOURI.—EVENTS IN EAST TENNESSEE.—PREPARATIONS FOR THE ADVANCE OF THE ARMY OF THE POTOMAC.

CHAPTER XI.

ADVANCE OF THE ARMY OF THE POTOMAC ON RICHMOND.

CHAPTER XII.

OPERATIONS AGAINST RICHMOND.

CHAPTER XIII.

INVASION OF MARYLAND AND PENNSYLVANIA.—OPERATIONS BEFORE PETERSBURG AND IN THE SHENANDOAH VALLEY.

CHAPTER XIV.

SHERMAN'S CAMPAIGN IN GEORGIA.

CHAPTER XV.

CHAPTER XVI.

CHAPTER XVII.

CHAPTER XVIII.

CHAPTER XIX.

THE REPOSSESSION OF ALABAMA BY THE GOVERNMENT.

CHAPTER XX.

PEACE CONFERENCE IN HAMPTON ROADS.—THE CAMPAIGN AGAINST RICHMOND.

CHAPTER XXI.

CLOSING EVENTS OF THE WAR.—ASSASSINATION OF THE PRESIDENT.

CHAPTER XXII.

PRISONERS.—BENEVOLENT OPERATIONS DURING THE WAR.—READJUSTMENT OF NATIONAL AFFAIRS.—CONCLUSION.

VOLUME III.

THE CIVIL WAR.

CHAPTER I.

OPERATIONS IN VIRGINIA.—BATTLE OF CHANCELLORSVILLE.—SIEGE OF SUFFOLK.

HILE a portion of the National troops were achieving important victories on the banks of the Lower Missis-sippi,[1] those composing the Army of the Potomac were winning an equally important victory,[a] not far from the banks of the Susquehannah. We left that army in charge of General Joseph Hooker, after sad disasters at Fredericksburg, encamped near the Rappahannock;[2] let us now observe its movements from that time until its triumphs in the conflict at Gettysburg, between the Susquehannah and the Potomac rivers.

[a] July, 1863.

During three months after General Hooker took command of the army, no active operations were undertaken by either party in the strife, excepting in some cavalry movements, which were few and comparatively feeble. This inaction was caused partly by the wretched condition of the Virginia roads, and partly because of the exhaustion of both armies after a most fatiguing and wasting campaign. The Army of the Potomac, lying at Falmouth, nearly opposite Fredericksburg, when Hooker took the command, was weak and demoralized. Despondency, arising from discouragement on account of recent disasters, and withering homesickness, almost universally prevailed, and desertions averaged two hundred a day. The relatives and friends of the soldiers, at home, were equally despondent, and these, anxious for the return of their loved ones, filled the express trains with packages

---

[1] See the closing chapter of volume II.

[2] Page 497, volume II.

containing citizens' clothing, in which the latter might escape from the service. Great numbers fled in these disguises.

At the time we are considering (close of January, 1863), Hooker found the number of absentees to be two thousand nine hundred and twenty-two commissioned officers, and eighty-one thousand nine hundred and sixty-four

FREDERICKSBURG IN THE SPRING OF 1863.[1]

non-commissioned officers and privates.[2] These were scattered all over the country, and were everywhere met and influenced by the politicians opposed to the war. These politicians, and especially the faction known as the Peace Party, taking advantage of the public disappointment caused by the ill-success of the armies under McClellan and Buell in the summer and early autumn of 1862, had charged all failures to suppress the rebellion to the inefficiency of the Government, whose hands they had continually striven to weaken. They had succeeded in spreading general alarm and distrust among the people; and, during the despondency that prevailed after the failure of the campaign of the Army of the Potomac, ending in inaction after the Battle of Antietam,[3] and of the Army of the Ohio in Kentucky, when Bragg and his forces were allowed to escape to a stronghold near Nashville,[4] elections were held in ten Free-labor States, and, in the absence of the votes of the soldiers (two-thirds of whom were friends of the administration), resulted in favor of the Opposition. In these ten States Mr. Lincoln's majority in 1860 was 208,066. In 1862, the Opposition not only overcame this, but secured a majority of 35,781.

The expectation of conscription to carry on the contest, increased taxation, high prices of fabrics and food, and a depreciated currency were made powerful instruments in turning the public mind to thoughts of peace by means of compromise; especially when, after the Emancipation Proclamation was issued, the Peace Faction, assuming to speak for the entire Opposition, declared, with seeming plausibility, that "the war for the preservation

---

[1] This is from a photograph by Gardner, taken from the Stafford side of the Rappahannock, and showing the ruins of the railway bridge, near the spot where the troops crossed on the pontoon bridges, in December, 1861. See page 489, volume II.

[2] Testimony of General Hooker before the *Committee on the Conduct of the War*, April 11, 1865. The total of absentees doubtless included all the desertions since the organization of the Army of the Potomac, and the sick and wounded in the hospitals. It is estimated that 50,000 men, on the rolls of the army at the time we are considering, were absent.

[3] See chapter XVIII., volume II.   [4] See page 511, volume II.

of the Union had been perverted to a war for the negro." The political battle-cry of the Opposition, before the elections, was, " A more vigorous prosecution of the war !" Now the Peace Faction that gave complexion to the general policy of that Opposition, discouraged further attempts to save the Republic. In this they seem to have been encouraged by army officers, a large proportion of whom, in the Army of the Potomac, and especially of those of high rank, were, it is said, hostile to the policy of the Government in the conduct of the war:[1] The Emancipation Proclamation had quickly developed, in full vigor, the pro-slavery element among these officers, many of whom openly declared that they never would have engaged in the war had they anticipated this action of the Government. While the army was now at rest, the influence of these military leaders was powerful in and out of camp,[2] and, acting with the general despondency in the public feeling, had an ill effect, for a little while, upon the army.

Hooker's first care was to prevent desertions, secure the return of absentees, and to weed out the army of noxious materials. The express trains were examined by the provost-marshals, and all citizens' clothing was burned. Disloyal officers were dismissed so soon as they were discovered, and the evils of idleness were prevented by keeping the soldiers employed.

PICKET HUT.

Vigilance was everywhere wide awake, especially among the outlying pickets, whose rude huts of sticks, brush, and earth, at times white with snow, dotted the landscape for miles around the camp. Important changes were made in the organization of the army, and in the various staff departments; and the cavalry, hitherto scattered among the Grand Divisions,[3] and without organization as a corps, were consolidated, and soon placed in a state of greater efficiency than had ever before been known in the service. To improve them, they were sent out upon raids within the Confederate lines whenever the state of the roads would permit, and for several weeks the region between Bull's Run and the Rapid Anna was the theater of many daring exploits by the cavalry of both

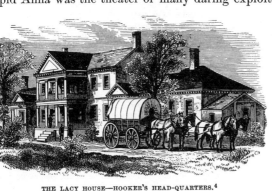

THE LACY HOUSE—HOOKER'S HEAD-QUARTERS.[4]

armies. Finally, at the middle of April, Hooker's ranks were well filled by the return of absentees, and at the close of that month, when he felt prepared for a campaign, his army was in fine spirits, thoroughly disciplined, and numbered one hundred and ten thousand infantry and artillery,

[1] Hooker's testimony before the *Committee on the Conduct of the War.*   [2] The same.
[3] See page 485, volume II.
[4] This is a view of the Lacy House, opposite Fredericksburg, from which Sumner observed the opera-

with four hundred guns, and a well-equipped cavalry force thirteen thousand strong. The leader of this fine army, like his immediate predecessor, was a zealous patriot and active soldier, and gave the tone of his own emotions to those of his troops.[1] "All were actuated by feelings of confidence and devotion to the cause," he said, "and I felt that it was a living army, and one well worthy of the Republic."[2]

Lee, meanwhile, had been assiduous in preparing his army for the spring campaign. He first turned his attention to supplies and equipment. His appeals to the people for the former were liberally answered. The arsenals at Richmond were kept busy in the re-equipment of his troops and the arming of new recruits. Much of his field artillery, which was inferior to that of Hooker, was replaced by new and improved guns. Careful attention was bestowed upon discipline. Prompt measures were taken to prevent

tions of his division on the 13th of December, 1862. See page 492, volume II. Here for awhile, after he took command, Hooker had his head-quarters. It was the property of Major J. Horace Lacey, who had been a major in the Confederate service. His mansion is one of the finest of the older houses in that region, and was built by William Fitzhugh, the father-in-law of the late Geo. W. P. Custis, the proprietor of Arlington House. See page 421, volume I. Major Lacey owned the land on which the Battle of the Wilderness was fought by Grant and Lee, in 1864.

[1] At this time General Hooker introduced the badge designation into his army with excellent effect. The idea originated with General Kearney at the battle of Fair Oaks. See page 411, vol. II. The occasion was as follows: It was impossible, at that time, for the common soldiers to renew their clothing, except by drawing

| 1 | 2 | 3 | 5 | 6 | 11 | 12 |

from the quartermasters the same as that used by enlisted men. Officers and men were thus dressed alike. To distinguish them apart, Kearney issued an order that the field and staff officers of his division should wear a red patch on the top of their caps, and the line officers the same in front. When General Birney succeeded the slain Kearney in command, he ordered that the wearing of these patches should be continued in memory of their gallant old commander, and that, for the same purpose, the rank and file should wear a red patch on the side of their caps; but none were entitled to wear the badge but those who had been in action with the division. General Hooker ordered each of the seven corps of the Army of the Potomac to be distinguished by a badge, as follows: The 1st, by a disk; the 2d, by a trefoil; the 3d, by a lozenge; the 5th, by a Maltese cross; the 6th, by a plain cross; the 11th, by a crescent; and the 12th, by a star.

Each corps had three divisions, and the badges, whose forms determined the corps, also designated the divisions, by colors. The badge of the first division of each corps was made of *scarlet* cloth; of the second, of *white;* and the third, of *blue*. These were all placed on the top of the cap. Those who wore hats placed the badge on the left side. The flags of each division head-quarters were designated as follows: 1st division, a white flag with a scarlet disk; 2d division, a blue flag with a white disk; and 3d division, a white flag with a blue disk. These flags were square. The brigade flags, bearing the different colored disks, were triangular in shape.

Additional honors were paid to General Kearney. It was agreed that all commissioned officers who had been in action under him should wear a "Kearney Decoration," which should consist of a golden Maltese cross, suspended by a red silk ribbon on the left breast of the dress coat. After the battle of Chancellorsville, General Birney caused several hundred bronze medals, patterned somewhat after this decoration, to be struck, to be awarded, as a sort of legion of honor, to such non-commissioned officers and privates of his division as especially distinguished themselves in that engagement.

KEARNEY DECORATION.

[2] Testimony before the *Committee on the Conduct of the War.*

desertions, and a conscription act, now put into rigorous operation, caused a rapid growth of his army in numbers.   In the space of three months "Stonewall" Jackson's corps alone increased from twenty-five thousand to thirty-three thousand men.[1]   Lee consolidated his artillery into one corps, and placed it under the command of General Pendleton, as chief.   He also gave a similar organization to his cavalry.   When April came, Lee found himself at the head of an army unsurpassed in discipline, and full of enthusiasm; yet it was divided, for, so early as February, he had sent Longstreet with two divisions to operate against General J. J. Peck in the vicinity of Suffolk, on the south side of the James River, and other troops were raiding with Imboden in West Virginia.   Yet he felt strong, with only about half the number of troops in hand commanded by his antagonist, for he had extended and strengthened his fortifications in rear of Fredericksburg, and constructed a system of elaborate works along his whole front reaching from Banks's Ford to Port Royal, more than twenty-five miles.[2]   Even with his superior force[3] Hooker could not hope to take these works, so he made preparations to force Lee out of them by turn-

CONFEDERATE GENERAL.[4]

ing the flank of the latter and threatening his rear.

We have remarked that the cavalry of both armies had been active for some weeks.   On the 10th of February[a] W. H. F. Lee, with his brigade, made an unsuccessful attempt to surprise and capture the National forces at Gloucester Point, opposite Yorktown; and at a little past midnight, a month later,[b] a small band of mounted men, led by the afterward famous guerilla chief, John S. Moseby, dashed into the village of Fairfax Court-House, took from his bed and carried away the commanding officer, Colonel Stoughton, and some others, and, with many horses and other property, hurried off in the direction of Hooker's army, cutting the telegraph wires on their way.   For this exploit Moseby

a 1863.

b March 8.

[1] *The Battle-fields of Virginia*, volume I.: *Chancellorsville*, by Captain Jed. Hotchkiss and Lieutenant-Colonel William Allan (officers of Lee's army), page 14.   This work contains carefully constructed maps, illustrative of the historical narrative.

[2] *Chancellorsville*, by Hotchkiss and Allan, page 15.

[3] Hooker's army was composed of seven *corps*, and comprised twenty-three *divisions*.   The First Corps was commanded by General J. F. Reynolds; the Second, by General D. N. Couch; the Third, by General D. E. Sickles; the Fifth, by General G. G. Meade; the Sixth, by General J. Sedgwick; the Eleventh, by General O. O. Howard, and the Twelfth, by General H. W. Slocum.   The division commanders were Generals J. S. Wadsworth, J. C. Robinson, A. Doubleday, W. S. Hancock, J. Gibbon, W. H. French, D. D. Birney, H. G. Berry, A. W. Whipple, W. T. H. Brooks, A. P. Howe, J. Newton, C. Griffin, G. Sykes, A. A. Humphreys, C. Devens, A. Von Steinwehr, C. Schurz, S. Williams, J. W. Geary, A. Pleasanton, J. Buford, and W. W. Averill.   The last three were commanders of cavalry under General G. Stoneman, who was the chief of the mounted men.

Lee's army was composed of two corps, the First commanded by General Longstreet, and the Second by "Stonewall" Jackson.   Of these General T. J. Jackson's entire corps, comprising the divisions of A. P. Hill, D. H. Hill, Trimble, and Early, and the divisions of Anderson and McLaws, of Longstreet's corps, were now present in front of Hooker.   Also the brigades of Fitzhugh Lee, and W. H. F. Lee, of Stuart's cavalry, with 170 pieces of artillery, making a total of a little more than 60,000 men of all arms.

[4] This shows the costume of a Confederate general, according to the regulations of their "War Department."   It was composed of a chapeau trimmed with gold lace, a gray coat with narrow buff collar and cuffs, blue pantaloons, and black leather sword-belt.   On the collar, within an embroidered wreath, a golden star.   On the coat two rows of gilt buttons, and sleeves trimmed with gold lace.

was publicly commended by General Stuart, and he was promoted to major of cavalry.[1]

A few days after Moseby's bold exploit, the first purely cavalry battle of the war occurred, not far from Kelly's Ford, on the Rappahannock, between

JOHN S. MOSEBY.

National troops, under General W. W. Averill, and Confederates under General Fitzhugh Lee. Averill was sent out to cut off Stuart and Lee, who, it was reported, were with a strong party enforcing the draft in Fauquier County.[2] In the face of brisk opposition from a small cavalry picket, Averill crossed the Rappahannock, and was push-

a March 17, 1863 ing on toward Culpepper Court-House,*a* when, about a mile from the ford, he encountered the forces of Lee. A desperate battle ensued, which continued until late in the evening, when Averill withdrew, and recrossed the river, followed by the Confederates to the water's edge. Averill lost about seventy-five men, and his antagonist about one hundred.

Early in April, notwithstanding the roads were yet heavy, Hooker deter-

[1] Moseby was a graduate of the University of Virginia, and a lawyer of some local repute. He had been one of Lee's most useful scouts for some time, and had proved himself to be a daring, dashing leader, who inspired his few followers with his own spirit. From the leader of a scouting party of a few men, he rose to the position of commander of a minimum regiment of adventurers, who, one of them said, Moseby himself declared, " could only be held together by the hope of plunder." See *Partisan Life with Moseby*, by John Scott. One of his most trusted and representative men seems to have been a Sergeant Ames, of the Fifth New York Cavalry, who deserted, Moseby's biographer, Marshall Crawford, says, " because he could not fight for the eternal negro." Moseby " took Ames to his bosom," and whenever any thing particularly revolting was to be done, the deserter appears to have been employed. His fitness for service with the guerrilla chief may be inferred from the fact, exultingly set forth in a history of Moseby's exploits by one of his followers (Major Scott), that when, on one occasion, the command encountered Ames's old regiment (Fifth New York), one of the latter recognized him in the hurly-burly, and pleasantly called out, " How are you, Sergeant Ames ?" " Well!" was the sergeant's reply, when, with his pistol, he shot his old friend dead. Moseby's military career, as described by his ardent friends, was more that of a highwayman, protected by the sanction of a pretended Government, under orders to harrass, pillage, and capture the enemy, than that of a soldier. Lee publicly commended him for his "activity and skill " in "killing, wounding, and capturing " during a brief period, " about 1,200 of the enemy, taking 1,600 horses and mules, 230 beef cattle, and 85 wagons and ambulances," with the loss of little more than twenty of his own men.

According to a statement to the author, by Colonel H. S. Gansevort, whose command was Moseby's most dreaded enemy in the region of Upper Virginia, east of the Blue Ridge, during the years 1863 and 1864, a large number of Moseby's men were volunteers from the regular Confederate cavalry, whose love of adventure and lust for plunder made them so much attached to their leader, that a threat to send one of them back to his regiment was sufficient to insure the good behavior of the recusant. The estimation in which Moseby was held by the Government is shown by the expressions of the Assistant Secretary of War, in the following account of an exploit in October, 1864 :—

" WAR DEPARTMENT, Washington,
" *October* 17, 9·40 P. M.

" Colonel Gansevort, commanding the Thirteenth New York Cavalry, has succeeded in surprising the rebel camp of the guerrilla and freebooter, Moseby, in the Blue Ridge Mountains, capturing his artillery, consisting of four pieces, with munitions complete.

" C. A. DANA, *Assistant Secretary of War.*"

[2] On the 28th of February, General Stuart asked Governor Letcher's leave to " collect together the militia of portions of Fairfax and Loudon (preparatory to the draft), which lay beyond the outposts."—*Autograph Letter of General Stuart.* Permission was given.

mined to march at once upon his foe, for the terms of enlistment of a majority of his men would soon expire. He directed[a] General Stoneman to proceed cautiously with his cavalry up the eastern side of the Rappahannock; cross above the Orange and Alexandria railway; strike and disperse Fitzhugh Lee's cavalry at Culpepper Court-House, estimated at two thousand men; push on to Gordonsville, and, turning to the left, strike the Fredericksburg and Richmond railway at Saxton's Junction,

[a April 12, 1863.]

JOSEPH HOOKER.

and destroy it, its bridges, stations, and rolling stock, with the telegraph wires along its line, so as to sever Lee's communication with Richmond. Hooker charged Stoneman to move with celerity, and to make his watchword and order, "Fight, *fight*, FIGHT!" He was instructed to harrass the retreating columns of the foe, for Hooker did not doubt that Lee would find it necessary to abandon Fredericksburg and fly toward Richmond. But his efforts were foiled, and his plans were modified by heavy rains, which so filled the Rappahannock that a division which had already crossed was recalled, and, on swimming horses, passed back to the left bank of the river.

Hooker paused for a fortnight, when he put his whole army in motion for the purpose of flanking Lee, drawing him from his defenses, and fighting him out of shelter. Ten thousand horsemen were prepared for a raid on the railways in Lee's rear, and on Monday, the 27th of April,[b] the turning column, composed of the corps of Meade (Fifth), Howard (Eleventh), and Slocum (Twelfth), was put in motion. Its destination was Chancellorsville, a point ten miles southwest of Fredericksburg, in Lee's rear. Stealthily the column moved up the Rappahannock, and crossed it[c] on a pontoon bridge at Kelly's Ford, twenty-seven miles above Fredericksburg, the march well masked by the passage of a heavy force below and near that city. The turning column pushed rapidly forward, and wading the Rapid Anna, armpit deep (the Fifth corps at Elly's Ford, and the Eleventh and Twelfth at Germania Ford), that night, in the light of huge bonfires, reached Chancellorsville on the afternoon of the 30th in excellent spirits, to find that the Confederate General, R. H. Anderson, had retired with his troops toward Fredericksburg that morning. It had been a most extraordinary march of thirty-seven miles in two days, with artillery and baggage, over heavy roads and across two rivers, with a loss of not more than half a dozen men. Meanwhile portions of Couch's corps (Second) had been waiting in concealment near Banks's and United States Fords, leaving the remainder, under General Gibbon, at Falmouth, in full view of the Confederates, so as to conceal the movement. So soon as the other three corps were making their way toward the Rapid Anna, the detachment of the Second crossed on a pontoon bridge, and marched rapidly on Chancellors-

[b 1863.]

[c April 28, 29.]

ville, where the reunited forces, about thirty-six thousand in number, exclusive of the artillery, and some detachments which had not arrived, bivouacked that night. General Pleasanton accompanied the infantry with one brigade of cavalry, and the remainder of the horsemen, under General Stoneman, pushed on toward Rapid Anna Station and Louisa Court-House.

From his head-quarters, near Falmouth, Hooker issued an exultant order,[a] such as the circumstances seemed to justify,[1] and, crossing the Rappahannock, he pushed on to Chancellorsville, where, in the spacious brick mansion of Mr. Chancellor, he made his head-quarters that night. Pleasanton's cavalry was thrown out upon the

[a] April 30, 1863.

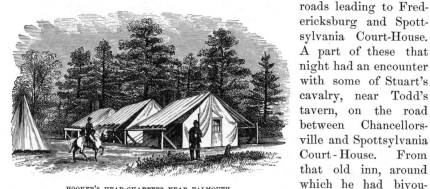

HOOKER'S HEAD-QUARTERS NEAR FALMOUTH.

roads leading to Fredericksburg and Spottsylvania Court-House. A part of these that night had an encounter with some of Stuart's cavalry, near Todd's tavern, on the road between Chancellorsville and Spottsylvania Court-House. From that old inn, around which he had bivouacked Fitzhugh Lee's brigade to watch the Nationals, Stuart set out with his staff for General Lee's head-quarters, when he encountered a regiment of Pleasanton's cavalry. He sent back to Todd's tavern for a regiment, and at the head of his staff gallantly attacked his foe. Ample assistance came, and after a sharp encounter in the bright moonlight the National force was broken and scattered.

While the movements on Hooker's right were so successfully performed, his left wing, under Sedgwick, composed of his own corps (Sixth), and those of Reynolds (First), and Sickles (Third), had as successfully masked the movement, for Lee, while watching the visible enemy in front of him, was not aware of the passage of the Rappahannock by the turning column, until the three corps were on their way toward the Rapid Anna. Taking position a little below Fred-

TODD'S TAVERN.[2]

---

[1] The following is a copy of the order: "It is with heartfelt satisfaction that the commanding general announces to the army that the operations of the last three days have determined that our enemy must either ingloriously fly, or come out from behind his defenses and give us battle on our own ground, where certain destruction awaits him. The operations of the Fifth, Eleventh, and Twelfth corps, have been a succession of splendid achievements."

[2] This is a view of Todd's tavern, as it appeared when the writer sketched it, in June, 1866. It was also the head-quarters of General Warren, and other officers, when the army under Grant was in that vicinity, in the spring of 1864.

ericksburg, Sedgwick caused pontoon bridges to be laid on the night of the 28th,[a] and before daylight Brooks's division crossed near the place of Franklin's passage,[1] and captured and drove the Confed- erate pickets there. Wadsworth's division also crossed. Breastworks were thrown up, and there was every appearance[b] of preparations for passing over a larger force. Pursuant to orders, Sickles now moved his corps stealthily away, and, marching swiftly, crossed the river at the United States Ford, and hastened to Chancellorsville.

  a April, 1863.

  b April 30.

  When Lee discovered Hooker's real intentions, he did not fly toward Richmond, as his antagonist supposed he would, but prepared to fight. He

FORD NEAR FALMOUTH.[2]

had called "Stonewall" Jackson's large force up from Moss Neck and its vicinity when Sedgwick made his demonstration, and now, with his army well in hand, from Hamilton's Crossing, on the railway, to the Rappahan- nock near the ford just above Falmouth, he determined to strike Hooker immediate and vigorous blows. His object was twofold: First, to secure the passage of the river at Banks's Ford, and thus widen the distance between Sedgwick and the main army ; and, secondly, to compel Hooker to fight in his disadvantageous position at Chancellorsville, which was in the midst of a region covered with a dense forest of shrub-oaks and pines, and tangled undergrowth, broken by morasses, hills, and ravines, called The Wilderness, and which extended from a little eastward of Chancellor's house to Mine Run on the west, and several miles southward from the Rapid Anna. With these designs, Lee left General Early, with about nine thousand men and thirty pieces of artillery, to hold his fortified position at Fredericks- burg against Sedgwick, and at a little past midnight on the first of May,[c] he put Jackson's column in motion toward Chancel- lorsville. It joined Anderson's (which, as we have observed, had fallen back from Chancellorsville on the approach of the National forces) at eight o'clock in the morning, near the Tabernacle Church, half way between

  c 1863.

---

 [1] See page 489, volume II.

 [2] This is a view of the Rappahannock just above Falmouth, as it appeared when the writer sketched it, in June, 1866, looking from the south side of the stream. The river is shallow here, with a rocky bottom, and broken by rocky islands. Near the white building seen on the left was Hooker's head-quarters tent (see page 24), at near the close of April. The river is always fordable here at low water.

Chancellorsville and Fredericksburg, where strong intrenchments were thrown up. There a plank road and a turnpike diverged, and met again at Chancellorsville. Along these Jackson ordered a general advance, Owen's cavalry leading. Jackson commanded in person the column on the plank road, and that on the turnpike was led by General L. McLaws.

Hooker had also disposed his army for battle. He was aware of the peril of fighting with the Wilderness at his back, and had directed his army to move out along the two roads just mentioned, and another leading to Banks's Ford, to give battle in the open country toward Fredericksburg. ^a May 1, 1863. In a circular issued that morning,^a he said head-quarters would be at the Tabernacle Church after the movement should commence; but Jackson was there before him, for Hooker's columns did not move until eleven o'clock. At that hour the divisions of Griffin and Humphreys, of Meade's (Fifth) corps pushed out on the left toward Banks's Ford, while Sykes's, of the same corps, supported by Hancock's division, and forming the center column, moved along the turnpike. Slocum's entire corps (Twelfth), with Howard's (Eleventh) and its batteries, massed in its rear, composing the right column, marched along the plank road.

The left column reached a point in sight of Banks's Ford without opposition, and the right column penetrated an equal distance eastward, without serious resistance. The center was not so fortunate. A little more than a mile in advance of the National works at Chancellorsville its cavalry met the vanguard of the Confederates, and a spirited contest ensued, in which the former were driven back. Then Sykes brought up his entire column, with artillery, and after a severe struggle with McLaws, whose force was deployed in line of battle across the turnpike, with Jordan's battery on the Mine road, he pushed his foe back. At about noon, he gained the advantageous posi-

GEORGE SYKES.

tion of one of the ridges, back of Fredericksburg, which are nearly parallel with the Rappahannock, and which commanded Chancellorsville and the surrounding country. Banks's Ford, which Lee had strenuously endeavored to cover, was now virtually in possession of the Nationals, and the distance between Sedgwick, opposite Fredericksburg, and the main army at Chancellorsville, was thereby shortened at least twelve miles. It now seemed as if a vigorous and general forward movement would give the Nationals a speedy and decisive victory, and possibly annihilate Lee's army. This movement some of the commanders were anxious to make, but circumstances compelled the chief to withhold his sanction. Slocum and Jackson had met on the plank road, and struggled fearfully, until at length the latter was making a serious movement on the flank of his antagonist, and strong columns were overlapping Sykes's flanks. Informed of this, and fearing his army might be beaten in detail before he could successfully resist the furious onset of Jackson, Hooker ordered its withdrawal behind his' works at Chancellorsville. The retreat was made in good order, the Confederates following close upon the rear of the Nationals. That night the respective chief commanders held councils of war, Hooker at his head-quarters in Chancellor's house, and Lee at his head-quarters under some pine trees where the Confederate line crossed the plank road.

Hooker's position for defense was a strong one. Around the Chancellor House was a small clearing, within a dense wood, filled, as we have observed, with a tangled undergrowth. In the woods he had constructed breastworks of logs, with trees felled in front so as to form a strong *abatis*. His cannon commanded these woods, and swept the approaching roads. The question at the council was, Shall we contract and strengthen our lines, and wait for an attack? or, Shall we assail the Confederate position in full force in the morning? General Warren, Hooker's senior engineer officer, and others, were in favor of the offensive. Hooker preferred the defensive attitude, and the latter was chosen. Preparations for a struggle in the morning were then made. The National line extended from the Rappahannock to the Wilderness Church, two miles west of Chancellorsville. Meade's corps, with a division of Couch's, formed the left; Slocum's and a division of Sickles's the center, and Howard's the right, with Pleasanton's cavalry near. The Confederate line extended from the Mine road on their right to the Catharine Furnace on the left, having the Virginian cavalry of Owen and Wickham on the right, and Stuart's and a part of Fitzhugh Lee's on the left, at the Furnace. McLaws's forces occupied the ridge on the east of the Big Meadow Swamp, and Anderson continued the line to the left of McLaws. Such was the general disposition of the opposing forces on the morning of the 2d of May.[a]   *a* 1863.

Lee was satisfied that his situation was a perilous one, and he was unwilling to risk the danger of making a direct attack upon Hooker. His chief counselor was the bold Jackson, who proposed a secret flank movement with his entire corps present, on the National right, so as to fall upon Hooker's rear. Lee hesitated, because he would have only the divisions of Anderson and McLaws left to oppose both Hooker and Sedgwick, should the latter cross the river and attack. To thus divide his army in the

ALDRICH'S HOUSE.[1]

presence of superior numbers might imperil its existence; yet, so much did Lee lean upon Jackson as adviser and executor, that he consented, and the bold movement was at once begun. With full twenty-five thousand men,

---

[1] This is a view of Aldrich's house, as it appeared when sketched by the writer, in June, 1866. It was used

Jackson turned off from the plank road at Aldrich's, not far from Chancellorsville, and moved swiftly and stealthily through the thick woods, with Stuart's cavalry between him and the Union lines, to the Orange plank road, four miles westward of Chancellorsville. At the same time Lee was attracting the attention of Hooker by vigorous demonstrations on his front, as if he was about to attack in full force.

The march of Jackson was not perfectly concealed. So early as eight o'clock in the morning,[a] General Birney, who was in command of Sickles's (First) division, between the Catharine Furnace and Melzie Chancellor's (Dowdall's tavern), discovered a portion of Jackson's column, under Rodes, crossing Lewis's Creek, and moving rapidly

DAVID D. BIRNEY.

southward. When informed of this, Sickles made a personal reconnoissance, and dispatched a courier to Hooker with the intelligence. The general impression among the commanders was, that Lee's army was retreating toward Richmond, and Hooker directed Sickles to ascertain the real character of the movement. For that purpose the latter pushed forward Birney's division, followed by Whipple's and Barlow's brigades of Howard's corps. Cannon were opened on the passing column, which threw it into some confusion, and expelled it from the highway; but it pressed steadily along the wood paths and a new road opened by it. Then Sickles directed Birney to charge upon it. He did so, and cut off and captured a Georgia (Twenty-third) regiment, five hundred strong, when Birney's farther advance was checked by Colonel Brown's artillery and a brigade under Anderson.

The National troops now held the road over which Jackson had been marching, and preparations were made for a vigorous pursuit of the supposed fugitives. Sickles asked for re-enforcements, when Pleasanton was sent with his cavalry, and Howard and Slocum each forwarded a brigade to help him. But before these forces could be brought to bear upon Jackson, near the Furnace, he had crossed the Orange plank road, and under cover of the dense jungle of the Wilderness, had pushed swiftly northward to the old turnpike and beyond, feeling his enemy at every step. Then he turned his face toward Chancellorsville, and, just before six o'clock in the evening,[b] he burst from the thickets with twenty-five thousand men, and like a sudden, unexpected, and terrible tornado, swept on toward the flank and rear of Howard's corps, which occupied the National right, the game of the forest—deers, wild turkeys, and hares—flying wildly before him, and becoming to the startled Unionists the heralds of the approaching

during the war as head-quarters by Generals Gregg and Merritt, and other officers of both armies. Near it the first skirmish at the opening of the battle of Chancellorsville occurred. It is rather a picturesque old mansion, on the south side of the plank road, about two miles southeast from Chancellorsville.

tempest of war.[1] These mute messengers were followed by the sounds of bugles; then by a few shots from approaching skirmishers; then by a tremendous yell from a thousand throats, and a murderous fire from a strong battle line.[2] Jackson, in heavy force, was upon the Eleventh Corps[3] at the moment when the men were preparing for supper and repose, without a suspicion of danger near. Devens's division, on the extreme right, received the first blow, and almost instantly the surprised troops, panic-stricken, fled toward the rear, along the line of the corps, communicating their emotions of alarm to the other divisions.

PLACE OF JACKSON'S ATTACK ON HOWARD.[4]

In vain the officers tried to restrain them, and restore order.[5] The high and commanding position at Talley's, with five guns and many prisoners, was soon in the hands of General R. E. Rodes, who was closely followed by Generals R. E. Colston and A. P. Hill. General Devens was severely wounded, and one-third of his division, including every general and colonel, was either disabled or captured. In the wildest confusion the fugitives rushed along the road toward Chancellorsville, upon the position of General Carl Schurz, whose division had already retreated, in anticipation of the onset, and the turbulent tide of frightened men rolled back upon General A. Von Steinwehr, utterly regardless of the exertions of the commander of the corps and his subordinate officers to check their flight. Only a few regiments, less demoralized than the others, made resistance, and these were

---

[1] See *Chancellorsville*, by Hotchkiss and Allan, page 48.

[2] Jackson formed his force in three lines of battle perpendicular to the turnpike, and extending about a mile on each side of it. Rodes occupied the front; Colston the next line, two hundred yards in the rear of Rodes, and back of this was A. P. Hill. Two pieces of Stuart's horse-artillery moved with the first line.

[3] Howard's corps (Eleventh), as we have observed, occupied the right of the army, and was composed of the divisions of Generals Devens, Carl Schurz, and Steinwehr. Devens was on the right, Schurz in the center, and Steinwehr on the left. Works for the protection of the corps were thrown up parallel to the plank road and the turnpike, facing southward. At the left of these was Steinwehr's division, joining Sickles. Devens, on the extreme right, was west of the intersection of the two roads mentioned, near Talley's house. The mass of his force occupied the works at that place. A portion of the brigades on the extreme right was thrown across the turnpike facing the west, and protected by slight breastworks and an *abatis*. Two pieces of artillery were on the plank road.

[4] This was the appearance of the spot when the writer sketched it, in June, 1866. The view is in a little intervale in The Wilderness, through which courses a small tributary of Lewis's Creek, and here it crosses the road.

[5] This was General Sigel's old corps, composed of 11,500 men, of whom 4,500 were Germans. Howard had recently taken command of the corps. He was censured at the time, and by General Hooker afterward in his testimony before the *Committee on the Conduct of the War*, for being so illy prepared for an attack in force. This censure seems to be unjust, for the Commander-in-Chief, and General Sickles who had commenced a pursuit of Jackson's column, appear to have been under the impression that the Confederates were retreating toward Richmond. On that afternoon, a short time before the attack, General Hooker wrote to Sedgwick, saying: "We know the enemy is flying—trying to save his trains. Two of Sickles's divisions are among them."—See Swinton's *Campaigns of the Army of the Potomac*, note, page 284. There appears no evidence of any lack of vigilance or skill on the part of Howard, either before or after the attack. No one seems to have suspected the bold and seeming reckless movement of Jackson until the moment when he burst upon Devens with almost the suddenness of a thunderbolt.

instantly scattered like chaff, leaving half their number dead or dying on the field.

While the divisions of Devens and Schurz were crumbling, Steinwehr quickly changed front and threw Buschbeck's brigade into works near Melzie Chancellor's (Dowdall's tavern), where some of Schurz's men were rallied, and for a brief space the advance of the Confederates was checked. But the halt was very short. Colston had joined Rodes, and the combined forces, with a terrific yell, charged upon and captured the works. In a few minutes almost the entire Eleventh Corps was seen pouring out of the woods in the deepening twilight, and sweeping over the dusty clearing around Chancellorsville in the wildest confusion, in the direction of the Rappahannock, strewing and blockading the roads with the implements and accouterments of war. These disordered the pursuing troops, and Rodes, when the darkness came on, finding himself entangled among felled trees, behind which was some National artillery, halted, and sent a request for A. P. Hill to be ordered to the front to take the advance, while the first and second lines should be re-formed.

In the mean time Hooker, apprised of the attack and the disorder on his right, had taken measures for checking the flight and recovering the field. The troops immediately at hand were his once own division, commanded by General H. G. Berry (the second of Sickles's corps), and French's brigade of Couch's corps. These were sent forward at the double-quick, and a courier was dispatched to Sickles, who had pushed some distance beyond the National lines, to inform him of the disaster to the Eleventh Corps, and his own peril, and to direct him to fall back and attack Jackson's left flank. Sickles was then in a critical situation, for the Confederates were in his rear and between him and the main army, while his artillery was behind him and exposed to capture, and Pleasanton, with two regiments of cavalry, were with the guns. These had been left behind, because artillery and cavalry could be of little service in the woods, and they were in a field at Hazel Grove. The circumstance proved to be a fortunate one, and probably saved Sickles and his two brigades from destruction or capture, for Pleasanton, by quick, skillful, and vigorous action, assisted the second division of the Sixth Corps, under Berry, in checking the pursuit long enough for Sickles to fall back in time to join in the conflict.

Pleasanton had just reached the artillery, when Jackson's pursuing column came thundering on after the flying Eleventh. Anxious to check the pursuers and save Sickles's cannon, he hurled one of his regiments (Eighth Pennsylvania, under Major Keenan) upon the Confederate flank. It was flung back terribly shattered. In the course of a few minutes Keenan was dead, and the ground was strewn with the greater portion of his men, slain or disabled. But they had checked the Confederates long enough for Pleasanton to bring his own horse-artillery, and more than thirty of Sickles's guns, to bear upon them, and to pour into their ranks a destructive storm of grape and canister shot. These were confronted by Confederate artillery on the plank road, under Colonel Crutchfield, who was soon wounded, and several of his guns were silenced, when desperate efforts were made by the Confederates to seize the National cannon. While this struggle was going on, General G. K. Warren, with the troops sent by Hooker, just mentioned, came to Pleasanton's assistance; and soon afterward Sickles, with his two brigades (Birney's and Whipple's), joined in the contest.

At this time Lee was making a vigorous artillery attack upon Hooker's left and center, formed by the corps of Generals Couch and Slocum, but the assailing force, whose heaviest demonstration was against General Hancock's front, was held in check by his skirmish line, under Colonel N. A. Miles.[1] And while Lee was thus failing, a heavier misfortune than he had yet endured befell him, in the paralysis of the right-arm of his power, by the fall of General Jackson. That officer, encouraged by the success of his first blow, was extremely anxious to press forward, and, by extending his lines to the left, cut off Hooker's communication with the United States Ford. While awaiting the arrival of General Hill to the front, he pushed forward with his staff and an escort on a personal reconnoissance, and when returning in the gloom to his lines, he and his companions seem to have been mistaken by their friends for Union cavalry, and were fired upon. Jackson fell, pierced by three bullets, and several of his staff were killed or wounded. Jackson was the superior of Lee as an executive officer, in moral force and in personal magnetism, and his loss to the Confederacy, and especially to the Army of Northern Virginia, as Lee's troops were called, was irreparable.[2]

Jackson had ordered a forward movement so soon as Hill should reach the front, and it was at the moment when that was accomplished that the notable leader was prostrated. Hill, also, was disabled by a contusion caused by the fragment of a shell while Jackson was on his way to the hospital, and the command of the corps devolved temporarily on Rodes, who, under the circumstances, thought it advisable not to attempt a forward movement in the night. General Stuart, whom Hill called to the command, agreed with him, and the Confederates occupied the night in defensive operations, and in preparations for renewing the struggle in the morning. Sickles, as we have observed, had reached Pleasanton at Hazel Grove, and at once attempted to recover a part of the ground lost by Howard. Birney's division, with Hobart Ward's brigade in front, charged down the plank road at midnight, drove back the Confederates, recovered some lost ground, and brought away several abandoned guns and caissons. Other attacks were made, but little more was accomplished, when Sickles, then reporting

---

[1] His troops consisted of the Fifty-seventh, Sixty-fourth, and Sixty-sixth New York Volunteers, and detachments of the Fifty-second New York, Second Delaware, and One Hundred and Forty-eighth Pennsylvania. See Hancock's Report.

[2] Jackson received three balls, one in the right hand and two in the left arm, by one of which the bone was shattered just below the shoulder, and an artery was severed. His frightened horse, now without guidance, turned and rushed toward the National lines, greatly imperiling the life of his rider, as he swept through the woods and underbrush. Jackson managed to turn him into the plank road, where he was checked by one of his staff (Captain Wilborn), who seized the bridle, and into his arms the general, exhausted by pain and loss of blood, fell. General Hill presently rode up, jumped from his horse, and stopped the flow of blood by bandaging the arm above the wound. Jackson was then placed on a litter, and conveyed to the rear in the midst of a storm of canister shot, which came sweeping down the road from two pieces of National cannon. One of the litter-bearers was shot dead. The wounded general was borne on to the Wilderness tavern (where the Confederates had established an hospital), attended by Dr. Hunter McGuire. There his arm was amputated. His wife was sent for, and two or three days afterward he was removed to Guiney's Station, nearer Richmond. There, at the Chandler House, he remained until his death, which was caused chiefly by pneumonia. That event occurred on Sunday, the 10th of May, 1863. "A few moments before he died," says an eye witness (Captain J. Hotchkiss), "he cried out in his delirium, 'Order A. P. Hill to prepare for action—pass the infantry to the front rapidly—tell Major Hawks——' then stopped, leaving the sentence unfinished. Presently a smile of ineffable sweetness spread itself over his pale face, and he said quietly, and with an expression as if of relief, 'Let us cross over the river, and rest under the shade of the trees.'"

directly to Hooker, was ordered to fall back and take position, and intrench in a new line formed by the chief, on heights between Fairview (a short distance west of Chancellorsville) and the Confederate lines in front of Dowdall's tavern. This was done at dawn on Sunday morning.

Hooker's situation was extremely critical, but with characteristic energy he had made new dispositions on Saturday night to meet the inevitable attack

HOOKER'S NEW LINE OF INTRENCHMENTS.[1]

on the morrow. When he heard of the southward march of Jackson's column on Saturday morning,[a] he called Reynolds's corps, more than twenty thousand strong, from Sedgwick. It arrived late that evening, and was received with joy, for it more than filled the space of the shattered Eleventh, and made Hooker's force full sixty thousand men, with whom to confront a little more than forty thousand men; yet his situation was perilous, and he knew it. He ordered Sedgwick to cross the river at once, and seize and hold the city and heights of Fredericksburg, and then, pushing along the roads leading to Chancellorsville, crush every impediment and join the main army as speedily as possible. He changed the front of a portion of his line so as to receive the Confederate attack, making a new line of battle, as we have observed, with more than thirty pieces of cannon, massed at Fairview, a little westward of his head-quarters. Sickles, connecting with Slocum on his left, occupied the intrenched line in advance of Fairview, which extended across the plank road, and included the elevated plateau at Hazel Grove. On the left of the line was a part of the Second Corps, and still further to the right, behind breastworks on the Elly's Ford road, was Reynolds's corps. On the National left, Meade's corps, with their faces toward Fredericksburg, joined Slocum's, Hancock's division being thrown back in a position to guard the communications with Banks's Ford; and on the extreme left the remains of Howard's corps were placed. The Confederates had also made dispositions for attack, in three lines: the first under Hill, the second under Colson, and the third under Rodes, with cannon massed on heights so as to command much of the

a May 2, 1863.

---

[1] This is a view of the line of intrenchments on the plank road, between Fairview and Melzie Chancellor's, as it appeared when the writer sketched it, in June, 1866. The works were constructed of logs and earth, breast high.

National line, and the open space around Chancellorsville. This disposition of his left wing being made known to Lee during the night, he directed Stuart to incline to the right, while McLaws and Anderson, under Lee's immediate command, should move to the left so as to form a junction of the separated army.

Such was the situation of the opposing forces on Sunday morning, the 3d of May, when, at dawn, Stuart advanced to the attack with the whole of Lee's left wing, under cover of artillery, and shouting, when he came in sight of the Nationals, " Charge, and remember Jackson !" He swung around his right, and seizing the elevation which the Eleventh Corps had been driven from on Saturday, he soon had thirty pieces of artillery in position there, and playing with destructive effect upon his antagonist. With a courage bordering on desperation, his men rushed down the road toward Chancellorsville, and charged heavily upon the National line fronting westward, composed of the corps of Sickles and the divisions of Berry and French, the last two supported by the divisions of Whipple and Williams. A severe struggle ensued. The right of the Confederates pressed back the Nationals and seized the commanding position at Hazel Grove, with four pieces of cannon, which were speedily brought to bear upon the Unionists with fearful effect. At the same time Stuart's left and center pressed heavily upon Sickles, who, when his ammunition began to fail, was driven back from the first line of works, and compelled to hold his position for a time with the bayonet. Around Fairview the battle raged furiously. The tide of success ebbed and flowed for more than an hour, while the result was doubtful. Sickles sent to Hooker for re-enforcements and ammunition, but when his messenger reached head-quarters he found the chief almost senseless, having been prostrated by a pillar of the Chancellor House, which had been struck by a cannon ball and thrown violently against him. The command had devolved on Couch (who withdrew head-quarters from the Chancellor House), and an hour —a most precious hour—passed by while the army was practically without a head. Sickles did not receive the needed re-enforcements. Meade was occupied by a force menacing his front. Reynolds was not called into action, and Howard's corps was unavailable. French had gallantly assailed Stuart's left, confused it, and captured several hundred of its men; but he was soon pressed back, and while Stuart was bearing heavily upon Sickles, Lee threw Anderson and McLaws upon Slocum and Meade. McLaws, press-

DARIUS N. COUCH.

ing along the plank road from the direction of Fredericksburg, attacked Meade, when the skirmish line of Hancock's division repulsed him, while Anderson, bearing heavily upon Slocum, succeeded in joining Stuart by a thin line.

Lee's head-quarters were now near Lewis's Creek, southwest of Chancellorsville, from which he issued orders for his united army to make a general advance. Sickles and Slocum were both forced back by an overwhelming pressure. Presently the line gave way, and the division of Hancock, and a portion of Slocum's corps, under General Geary, alone held the point of the line in front of Chancellor's house. These troops gradually fell back, and fought gallantly at the angle of the roads. This line, too, soon began to bend. The Confederates fell furiously upon it, and broke it, and at ten o'clock in the morning, after a struggle for six hours, they took possession of Chancellorsville. The mansion had been beaten into a ghastly ruin by the Confederate artillery. Couch had withdrawn the army to a position northward of it, where he formed a new line, of V or redan shape, along the

RUINS OF CHANCELLORSVILLE.[1]

roads leading to Elly's and United States Fords, the right resting on the Rapid Anna, the left on the Rappahannock, and the apex at Bullock's house. On this line were the fresh troops of Meade and Reynolds, which had not been called into the severe struggle during the morning. Hooker recovered, and resumed command at noon.

Lee's army was now united, and Hooker's was yet divided, Sedgwick and Gibbon, with an aggregate force of about thirty thousand men, being still near Fredericksburg. Hooker had vainly hoped for the appearance of these on Lee's flank and rear during the early morning struggle, and now they were separated from him by an army elated by victory. Lee, confident that he might capture or disperse the forces of his antagonist, was about to follow up his triumph by attacking Hooker in his new position, when news came from Fredericksburg which instantly arrested his operations in that direction. Sedgwick was seriously menacing his flank and rear.

So early as Saturday morning, Sedgwick had thrown his corps over the Rappahannock, at Franklin's crossing-place, and, after some skirmishing, had lain quietly until near midnight, when he received the order, already mentioned, to join the main army at Chancellorsville. He began the movement at

---

[1] This is a view of the ruins of the Chancellor House (called Chancellor's Villa, or Chancellorsville), as it appeared when the writer sketched it, in June, 1866.

once. General Warren arrived at two o'clock in the morning[a] to hasten it, but it was daylight before the head of Sedgwick's column entered Fredericksburg. He was soon afterward joined by General Gibbon, of Couch's corps, with about six thousand troops, who had been left at Falmouth, and had crossed on pontoons just below the rapids and ford at that place.

a May 3, 1863.

General Early, with his own division, and Barksdale's brigade of Mc-Laws's division, were on the heights to oppose Sedgwick. Barksdale occupied a position on Marye's Hill and behind a stone wall at the foot of it, precisely as he had done in December, when Burnside's troops were there repulsed.[1] On the crest were three companies of the Washington artillery, and Early occupied the range to the right of them. They felt quite secure in their advantageous position, and their sense of safety was increased when a portion of Newton's division, sent by Sedgwick to attack Barksdale, was repulsed, and driven back into the town in shattered columns. A flanking movement by General Howe on the left, and General Gibbon on the right, was equally unsuccessful, but not so disastrous, when Sedgwick determined to form powerful assaulting parties, and storm the Confederate works along their entire occupied line. Two storming columns were formed from Newton's division, one of four, and the other of two regiments;[2] and another, of four regiments, under Colonel Burham, of the Sixth Maine, was directed to move up the plank road, and to the right of the others, directly against the rifle-pits at the foot of Marye's Hill. General Howe, with three storming parties under the command, respectively, of General Neil and Colonels Grant and Seaver, was ordered to move simultaneously upon the Confederate works on the left, near Hazel Run.

The storming parties moved at near eleven o'clock in the morning. The onset was furious, and was gallantly resisted. Steadily the Nationals moved on, in defiance of a galling fire from artillery and small arms, driving Barksdale from his shelter at the stone wall, scaling Marye's Hill, seizing the rifle-pits and batteries, and capturing full two hundred prisoners, at the cost to Sedgwick of about a thousand men, the Sixth Maine first planting the National flag upon the captured works in token of triumph. Howe had, at the same time, carried the Confederate works on the left, under a heavy fire of artillery ; and in a short time after the movement began, the entire ridge was in possession of the Nationals, Early and his shattered columns were flying southward, and the plank road was opened to Sedgwick from Fredericksburg to Chancellorsville. This was the startling intelligence that reached Lee, just as he was about to attack Hooker in his new position.

Sedgwick immediately re-formed his brigades after his victory, and leaving Gibbon at Fredericksburg, marched along the plank road toward Chancellorsville. Lee, at the same time, ventured again to divide his army while in front of his foe, and sent General McLaws with four brigades to meet Sedgwick. Wilcox had already hastened from Banks's Ford, and throwing

---

1 See page 493, volume II.

2 The column of four regiments, on the right, was commanded by Colonel Spear, of the Sixty-first Pennsylvania, and was composed of his own regiment and the Forty-third New York, supported by the Sixty-seventh New York and Eighty-second Pennsylvania. The left column, of three regiments, was commanded by Colonel Johns, of the Seventh Massachusetts, and was composed of his own regiment and the Thirty-sixth New York.

his little force across the plank road, essayed to delay the progress of the
Nationals. He fell back while skirmishing, and finally made a stand at
Salem Church, on Salem Heights, toward which both Sedgwick and McLaws
had been hastening, and where the latter had already arrived, and was
forming a line of battle perpendicular to the road, and getting artillery in

SALEM CHURCH.

position. The church[1] was filled with Wilcox's
troops, and made a sort of a citadel, and so also was
a school-house near by.

Sedgwick advanced briskly, and before McLaws
could complete his battle-line, the former threw forward Brooks's division, which was moving up the
plank road, and on each side of it, the First New
Jersey on the right, and the brigade of General
Bartlett on the left. Newton's division followed, in
support of Brooks's, and Sedgwick's artillery was posted at a toll-gate in the
rear. A sanguinary conflict quickly ensued. Bartlett dashed forward, captured the school-house garrison, and, with furious onset, drove the Confederates, and seized the crest of the hill. The triumph and possession was
brief. Wilcox soon drove him back, released the school-house prisoners, and
seized their custodians, and, with General Semmes, pushed the Nationals
back to Sedgwick's reserves, near the toll-gate, where the well-served batteries of Williston, Rigby, and Parsons, under Colonel Tompkins, checked
the pursuers. The conflict had been short, sharp, and sanguinary, and
increased Sedgwick's loss in the morning at Fredericksburg to about five
thousand men. Wearied and disheartened, the National troops, like their
foes, slept on their arms that night, with little expectation of being able to
advance in the morning. Hooker, at the same time, seemed paralyzed in
his new position. His army was being beaten in detail, and the result of the
battle at Salem Church, only seven miles from him, had rendered a junction
of Sedgwick with the main army almost impossible. To make that impossibility absolute was now Lee's chief care.

Sedgwick found himself in a very critical situation on Monday morning.[a]
Lee, at an early hour, discovered that Hooker's position had
been much strengthened, and he considered it necessary to drive
Sedgwick across the Rappahannock, if possible, before making
another attack on the main body of the Nationals. For this purpose, Early,
who had concentrated his forces, changed front, and proceeded to attempt
the recapture of the Heights of Fredericksburg ; and Anderson's three remaining brigades were sent to re-enforce McLaws, on Sedgwick's front. Hooker,
apprised of Sedgwick's peril, desired him not to attack unless the main army
should become engaged ; to keep open his communications, with a view to
the salvation of his army, at all hazards ; and not to cross the Rappahannock, if he could avoid it. He was compelled to be governed by circumstances rather than orders. At an early hour in the day he was cut off from
Fredericksburg by Early, who had marched swiftly, and, with superior force,
had recaptured the heights there. At noon, Anderson arrived with his re-enforcements, and took position on Early's left, by which Sedgwick was inclosed

[a] May 4, 1863.

---

[1] A brick building on the south side of the plank road, about four miles from Fredericksburg.

on three sides. Every moment his position became more perilous. The day wore away with nothing more serious than skirmishing, until about six

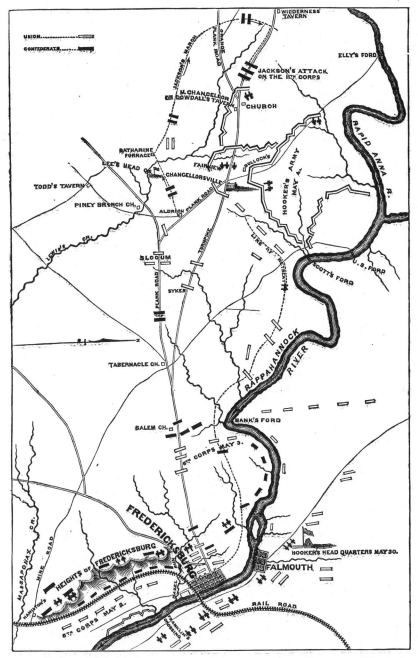

REGION OF MILITARY OPERATIONS FROM THE 27TH OF APRIL TO THE 6TH OF MAY, 1863.

o'clock, when the Confederates made a general attack. Sedgwick's forces, after a short but obstinate defense, gave way, and he retired toward Banks's

Ford, pursued as vigorously as the nature of the country (hilly, furrowed by ravines, and thick-wooded) allowed, until dark, when the chase ended. Before morning, Sedgwick, with the remnant of his corps, passed to the north side of the Rappahannock, over pontoon bridges, near Banks's Ford, under cover of thirty-two pieces of artillery. In the space of two days he had lost more than one-fifth of his entire command. Gibbon also withdrew from Fredericksburg to Falmouth that night, passing the river on pontoon bridges, just below the ford; and on Tuesday[a] Lee had only Hooker to contend with, and was free to concentrate all his forces against him. So he recalled McLaws and Anderson, to add strength to his main army, leaving Early and Barksdale to hold the line of the river from Fredericksburg to Banks's Ford, and prepared to strike Hooker a crushing blow before night. A heavy rain storm came on, which suspended operations, and caused a postponement of the forward movement until the next morning.

> [a] May 5, 1863.

Meanwhile Hooker had been busy in preparations to avoid or avert the blow. When, on Monday night, he was told of the situation of Sedgwick, then hovering on the bank of the Rappahannock, under the shelter of great guns, and utterly unable to co-operate with the main army, he determined to retreat across the river and save it. He conferred with five of his corps commanders[1] that night, when two of them (Couch and Sickles, whose forces, with Slocum's, had borne the brunt of the battle on Sunday) agreed with him, and one (Reynolds) did not express any opinion. Finding himself in accord with a majority of his active counselors, and with his chief of staff, General Butterfield, who was present, Hooker determined to retreat on the following day,[b] and made preparations accordingly.[2] The storm that restrained Lee favored Hooker, but it made the passage of the river a perilous task, for its banks were submerged at each end of his pontoon bridges, and the latter were in imminent danger of being swept away by the violent current at any moment. The passage, covered by Meade's corps, was safely made, however, without molestation, during the night, and, on the morning of the 6th,[c] the Army of the Potomac returned to its old quarters opposite Fredericksburg. On the same day the Confederate army resumed its former position on the heights in the rear of the city. The losses of each had been heavy. That of the Confederates was reported twelve thousand two hundred and seventy-seven, including about two thousand prisoners,[3] and that of the Nationals was

> [b] May 5.

> [c] May.

---

[1] Generals Meade, Reynolds, Howard, Couch, and Sickles. Slocum was not present, for the reason that the messenger who was sent failed to find him.

[2] In his testimony before the *Committee on the Conduct of the War* (volume I., 1865, pages 134 and 135), General Hooker said that General Reynolds, being very weary, threw himself on a bed, saying that "his opinion would be the same as General Meade's," and went to sleep; and that General Howard voted for an advance assigning as a reason that he felt that his corps (Eleventh), by its bad conduct, had placed the army in its perilous position, and that he "had to vote for an advance under any circumstances." General Meade was at first for an advance, because he did not believe a safe retreat across the river possible; but, according to the testimony of Generals Sickles and Howard (pages 135 and 136), he yielded his opinions to those of General Hooker, and acquiesced in his commander's decision. Couch and Sickles were decidedly in favor of a retreat. Howard was the only officer, at the close of the conference, who was decidedly in favor of an advance. The author of a history of the *Campaigns of the Army of the Potomac*, has recorded an error into which he was led, in saying, concerning the conference, that a majority of the corps commanders present "were in favor of an advance rather than a withdrawal," and giving as an inference, because the chief insisted on retreating, that "Hooker had lost all stomach for fight."

[3] Lee, in his report of the Battle of Chancellorsville (September 21, 1863), did not give an account of his

seventeen thousand one hundred and ninety-seven, including about five thousand prisoners. The latter left behind their dead and wounded,[1] thirteen pieces of artillery, about twenty thousand small arms, seventeen colors, and a large quantity of ammunition. Among their notable slain were Generals Berry and Whipple. Thus ended, in defeat and disaster to the Nationals, after a struggle of several days, the BATTLE OF CHANCELLORS-VILLE.[2]

While Hooker and Lee were contending, a greater portion of the cavalry of the Army of the Potomac, commanded by General Stoneman, was raiding on the communications of the Army of Northern Virginia with Richmond. Stoneman crossed the Rappahannock[a] with the main body at Kelly's Ford, and Averill (who had been ordered to push on through Culpepper Court-House to Gordonsville, and keep the Confederates in that direction employed, while detachments from the main column were destroying the railways running north from Richmond) passed the river with one division at the crossing of the Orange and Alexandria railroad. He soon encountered some of W. H. F. Lee's brigade, almost the only mounted force the Confederates could then spare to oppose Stoneman's ten thousand, but he pressed forward through Culpepper to the Rapid Anna, and no further. He failed to protect the right of the main column, and was recalled. Stoneman weeded his army of weak materials, and, with his best men and horses, in light marching order, pressed forward Buford was sent out to the left, and, skirmishing frequently with small bodies of cavalry, reached the Rapid Anna on the night of the 30th, and encamped near Raccoon Ford. Stoneman marched cautiously on, crossed the Rapid Anna at the same ford, and the whole force reached a point on the Virginia Central railway, a mile from Louisa Court-House, at two o'clock on the morning of the 2d of May.[b] Much of the railway in that vicinity was immediately destroyed, and at daylight Col-

[a] May 29, 1863.

[b] 1863.

losses, and it is only from those of his subordinates, published with his report in 1864, that the number, above given, has been ascertained. A Confederate surgeon at Richmond reported their loss, immediately after the battle, at 18,000 men; and in a congratulatory address to his troops, Hooker declared[c] that they had "taken 5,000 prisoners, 15 colors, captured and brought away 7 pieces of artillery, and placed *hors de combat* 18,000 of Lee's chosen troops." He also averred that they had inflicted "heavier blows than they had received." Lee, in a similar order, congratulated his troops on their "glorious victory;" told them that they were entitled to the praise and gratitude of the Confederate "nation;" that they should return their "grateful thanks to the only Giver of victory for the signal deliverance He had wrought, and appointed the following Sunday as a time for these united ascriptions of "glory due His name."

[c] May 6, 1863.

[1] The latter were recovered a few days afterward.

[2] The authorities from which this narrative of the Battle of Chancellorsville was drawn, are the reports of Generals Hooker and Lee, and their subordinate commanders; of the *Committee on the Conduct of the War*, volume I., 1865; history of *The Campaigns of the Army of the Potomac*, by William Swinton; *Chancellors-ville*, by Hotchkiss and Allan; and written and oral statements to the author by participants in the campaign.

As usual, in cases of disaster, there was much crimination and recrimination after the battle of Chancellors-ville, and men were blamed without sufficient cause. Among those who suffered the penalties of displeasure, was Brigadier-General Joseph W. Revere, who had been in the service of his country, without reproach, as a sailor and soldier, for thirty years. He commanded a brigade of the second division of Sickles's corps, in the battle on Sunday, the 3d of May. In the hurly-burly of that fight he found himself in the position of command-ing officer of his division, after the death of General Berry, and left to act in accordance with his own judgment, in the absence of orders from his superiors. That judgment led him to make a movement to another part of the field of action, where he thought he could be more useful. For this his corps commander relieved him from duty, and would not accept his offer to serve as a volunteer in any capacity. A week after the army recrossed the Rap-pahannock, he was tried by a court martial, found guilty of the charge of "conduct to the prejudice of discipline and good order," and dismissed from the service. It is the opinion of experts, who have well weighed the cir-cumstances and the testimony before the court, that General Revere acted the part of a true patriot and brave soldier in doing that for which he was condemned; that he was unjustly accused and illegally punished.

onel Kilpatrick, with his regiment, dashed into the little village of Louisa
Court-House, terrifying the inhabitants by his unexpected visit, and obtaining some supplies. After skirmishing with some of W. H. F. Lee's troops
that attacked them, the Nationals, toward evening, moved off to Thompson's Four Corners, where, at midnight, Stoneman gave orders for operations
upon Lee's communications by separate parties, led respectively by General
David McM. Gregg, Colonel Percy Wyndham, Colonel Hugh Judson Kilpatrick, and Colonel Hasbrouck Davis.

In the bright moonlight these expeditions started on their destructive
errands. Wyndham, with the First Maine and First New Jersey, pushed
southward to Columbia, on the James River, and on the morning of the
3d, destroyed canal boats, bridges, a large quantity of Confederate supplies
and medical stores; tried to demolish the massive stone aqueduct there
where the waters of the canal flow over the river, and then rejoined Stoneman.
Kilpatrick, with the Harris Light Cavalry (Sixth New York), reached Hun-
gary Station, on the Fredericksburg railway, on the morning of the 4th,
destroyed the depots and railroad there, crossed to the Brook turnpike, and,
sweeping down within two miles of Richmond, captured a lieutenant and
eleven men within the fortifications of the Confederate capital. Then he
struck the Virginia Central railway at Meadow Bridge, on the Chickahominy, destroyed that structure and some railway property,
and, dashing across the Pamunkey and the Mattapony the next   * May 5,
day,* went raiding through the country without molestation,   1863.
destroying Confederate property here and there, and reaching Gloucester
Point, on the York, on the 7th.

Meanwhile Lieutenant-Colonel Davis, with the Twelfth Illinois, swept
along the line of the South Anna to the Fredericksburg railway at Ashland,
where he intercepted an ambulance train filled with wounded soldiers from
Chancellorsville. These were paroled. Then the road and other railway
property was destroyed there, when Davis pushed on to Hanover Court-
House, on the Virginia Central railway, swept away the depot by fire, and
tore up the track in that vicinity. He then followed the line of the road to
within seven miles of Richmond, when he inclined to the left and started for
Williamsburg. Near the site of the White House[1] he met and skirmished
with Confederate cavalry, and being repulsed, he inclined still more to the
left, crossed the Pamunkey and Mattapony, and reached Gloucester Point
without further interruption. Gregg and Buford had, meanwhile, been raiding in the neighborhood of the South Anna, closely watched by Hampton
and Fitzhugh Lee. They burnt the bridges in their march. Dashing upon
Hanover Junction, they destroyed the railway property there, and damaged
the road. Finally the whole of Stoneman's command, excepting the forces
under Kilpatrick and Davis, was concentrated at Yanceyville, when it
marched northward, crossed the Rapid Anna at the Raccoon Ford, and on
Friday, the 8th of May, recrossed the Rappahannock at Kelly's Ford.
Much property had been destroyed during the raid, but the chief object of
the expedition, namely, the effectual destruction of Lee's communications
with Richmond, was not accomplished, and the week's work of the cavalry,

----

[1] See page 386, volume II.

as bearing upon the progress of the war, was of very little consequence.[1] The damages to the railways were repaired by the time the raiders had recrossed the Rappahannock. Had Stoneman's forces been concentrated, and their destructive energies been applied to the single object of Lee's direct communications, the Confederate army might, after its success at Chancellorsville, have fallen into the hands of the Nationals, for at that time its supplies came from Richmond, and it had not more than a few days' rations ahead at any time.

Let us now turn for a moment and view events of the greatest importance, which were occurring in Southeastern Virginia, at the time of the struggle at Chancellorsville.

We have observed (page 21) that Lee had sent Longstreet to command the troops operating against General John J. Peck, at Suffolk. Ever since the Confederates lost Norfolk,[2] and with it the mouth of the James River and the region bordering on the Nansemond and the Dismal Swamp, they had been devising measures for recapturing it, and the territory they had lost. To prevent this, and to establish a base for operations against the Weldon and Petersburg railway, a strong body of National soldiers was stationed at Suffolk, at the head of the Nansemond River, and upon a railroad branching to Weldon and Petersburg. This was an important military position, and became the center of stirring scenes in 1862 and 1863.

In September, 1862, Major-General John J. Peck was placed in command of nine thousand men at Suffolk, and at the same time Generals Pettigrew and French, with about fifteen thousand Confederates, were on the line of the Blackwater, menacing that post. Peck comprehended the great importance of his position, and immediately commenced the construction of a system of defenses for its protection.[3] The authorities at Richmond, believing he was preparing a base of operations for a grand movement against that city, in co-operation with the Army of the Potomac, caused the adoption of countervailing measures. A series of fortifications were erected from the line of the Blackwater to Fort Powhatan, on the James River, and late in February, 1863, General Longstreet was placed in command of all the Confederate troops in that region. He had then full thirty thousand troops, including those already on the line of the Blackwater, so posted that he could concentrate them all near Suffolk in the course of twenty-four hours.

Early in April, Longstreet prepared to make a sudden descent upon Peck. He determined to march with an overwhelming force, cross the Nansemond, capture or disperse the National garrison, and then, without further difficulty, seize Portsmouth and Norfolk, and seriously menace, if not actually

---

[1] In his report on the Battle of Chancellorsville, at page 15, Lee said: "The damage done to the railroad was small and soon repaired, and the James River canal was saved from injury." During the raid Stoneman and his command disabled but did not destroy Lee's communications, but they captured and paroled over 500 Confederate officers and soldiers; destroyed 22 bridges, 7 culverts, 5 ferries, 3 trains of railroad cars, and 122 wagons; burned 4 supply trains, 5 canal boats, 2 store houses, 4 telegraph stations, and 3 depots; broke canals in three places, and railways in 7 places; cut the telegraph wires in 5 places, and captured 356 horses and 104 mules. See Brackett's *History of the United States Cavalry*, page 311.

[2] See page 388, volume II.

[3] The first work constructed by him was begun on the 25th of September, and was named Fort Dix, in honor of the commander of the department. The position and names of the forts, and other fortifications and localities named in the text, may be observed by reference to the map on page 42, which is a careful copy, on a small scale, of one made by General Peck's engineers, and kindly lent by that commander to the writer.

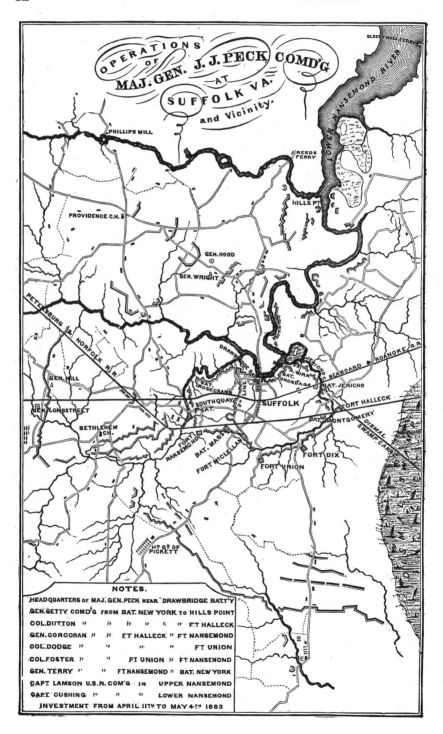

OPERATIONS OF MAJ. GEN. J. J. PECK COMD'G AT SUFFOLK VA. and Vicinity.

NOTES.

HEADQUARTERS OF MAJ. GEN. PECK NEAR DRAWBRIDGE BATT'Y
GEN. GETTY COMD'G. FROM BAT. NEW YORK TO HILLS POINT
COL. DUTTON   "   "   "   "   F.T HALLECK
GEN. CORCORAN "   "   FT HALLECK " FT NANSEMOND
COL. DODGE   "   "   "   "   FT UNION
COL. FOSTER   "   "   FT UNION   " FT NANSEMOND
GEN. TERRY   "   "   FT NANSEMOND " BAT. NEW YORK
CAPT LAMSON U.S.N. COM'G IN   UPPER NANSEMOND
CAPT CUSHING   "   "   "   LOWER NANSEMOND
INVESTMENT FROM APRIL 11TH TO MAY 4TH 1863

endanger Fortress Monroe. His first care was to conceal the facts of his own presence and his strength in numbers (then increased), and to weaken Peck's command. It was reported that he had gone to South Carolina, and D.-H. Hill was sent to attack Little Washington, and menace New Berne, in North Carolina, for the purpose of drawing some of the troops at Suffolk and at Fortress Monroe in that direction, while the bulk of Longstreet's army was in readiness along the Blackwater, and on the railway between Suffolk and Petersburg, for an immediate advance.

Longstreet thought his plan was working well, when spies informed him that General Foster, the successor of Burnside,[1] had ordered Peck to send three thousand soldiers to oppose Hill. Being in readiness, Longstreet at once crossed the Blackwater on pontoon bridges, and made a forced march on Suffolk[a] with about twenty-eight thousand men in three columns, under skillful commanders,[2] capturing the cavalry outposts of the Nationals on the way. Peck was ready for him, and Longstreet found in that officer an antagonist as vigilant and active as himself. He had watched the Confederates with sleepless scrutiny, and had penetrated their designs. He kept his superior informed of the increasing number of foes in his front, and had been re-enforced in March by a division under General Getty, making his whole force about fourteen thousand. Now he was about to comply, reluctantly, with a summons from Foster for three thousand troops to oppose Hill, when a Confederate mail, captured by General Viele, who was in command at Norfolk, informed him of Longstreet's plans, and the important fact that Hill's was only a co-operating movement.[3] The detachment was detained. Admiral Lee was asked, by telegraph, to send gun-boats up the Nansemond, and made a prompt and practical answer; and Longstreet quickly perceived that his attempt at a surprise was a failure. Then he determined to carry the works at Suffolk by assault.

Longstreet's first care was to drive away the half-dozen armed tug and ferry boats (commanded by Captains Lee and Rowe) which lay in the way of his crossing the Nansemond, there narrow and sinuous. For this purpose batteries were erected under cover of darkness, and opened upon them in broad daylight, which seriously wounded the little warriors afloat, but did not drive them far from the scene of conflict. And right gallantly did that little detachment of the National navy perform its part, and most usefully assist the land troops in a siege which continued twenty-four days. Longstreet recalled Hill from North Carolina, and the besiegers numbered about forty thousand. Gallant achievements were almost daily performed by both parties,[4] and the Confederates, with overwhelming numbers, tried in vain

[a] April 1863.

---

[1] See page 315, volume II.

[2] The Confederates were in four divisions, commanded respectively by Generals Hood, French, Pickett, and Anderson.

[3] Viele had ascertained that Longstreet was in possession of complete drawings of all of Peck's works, and had determined to get in his rear and surprise him.

[4] To General Getty was intrusted the river line below Onondaga battery (see map on page 42), the key of the position, extending about eight miles in length. During the siege General Getty stormed and carried, with the Eighth Connecticut and Eighty-ninth New York, aided by Lieutenant Lamson and the gun-boats, a Confederate battery on the west branch of the Nansemond. He captured 6 guns and 200 prisoners. General Peck mentioned with commendation Generals Corcoran, Terry, Dodge, and Harland, and Colonels Dutton and Gibbs, commanding front lines; Colonels Gurney and Waddrop, commanding reserves; Colonels Spear and Onderdonk, of the cavalry, and Captain Follet, chief of artillery. The forts were in charge of the following officers: *Fort Union,* Colonel Drake; *Nansemond,* Colonel Hawkins; *Halleck,* Colonel Sullivan; *Draw-bridge Bat-*

every skill and strategy of modern warfare to accomplish their object. Finally, on the day when Hooker and Lee had their severe battle at Chancel-lorsville,[a] Longstreet, foiled and disheartened, turned his back on Peck and retreated, pursued as far as the Blackwater by National troops under Generals Corcoran and Dodge, and Colonel Foster. Thus ended the remarkable SIEGE OF SUFFOLK, "which had for its object the recovery of the whole country south of the James River, extending to Albemarle Sound, in North Carolina; the ports of Norfolk and Portsmouth; eighty miles of new railroad iron; the equipment of two roads, and the cap-ture of all the United States forces and property, with some thousands of contrabands."[1]

[a] May 3, 1863.

The importance of the services of "the Army of Suffolk," as its com-manding officer styled it, seems not to have had due consideration hitherto. As an act of war, the holding of that position by the garrison against more than double its own number of assailants led by one of the best of the Con-federate officers, entitles the commanding general and his troops to the highest praise, and which he received from those most competent to judge.[2] But when we consider the grand object of the Confederates and the price at stake, and the fact that the holding of Longstreet south of the James, so that he could not re-enforce Lee, probably saved the Army of the Potomac, then one hundred and twenty-five thousand strong, from far greater disaster —possibly annihilation—at Chancellorsville, the value of the services of the gallant Peck and his brave soldiers may be appreciated, and should be fully recognized by the historian and the student.

---

tery, Colonel Davis; *Battery Mansfield*, Colonel Worth; the *Redan* and *Battery Rosecrans*, Colonel Thorpe; *Battery Massachusetts*, Captain Johnson; *Battery Montgomery*, Colonel England; *Battery Stevens*, Colonel Pease; *Fort Dix*, Colonel McEvilly.

[1] General J. J. Peck's Report, May 5, 1863.

[2] On the 15th of February, 1865, General Meade wrote to General Peck, saying: "That with the united force under your command, you should have held in check and defeated the designs of such superior numbers, is a fact of which you may well be proud, as the most practical proof of your own skill and the gallantry of your troops."

On the 1st of January, 1865, General Slocum wrote: "I think the gratitude of the nation is due to you and your gallant little army for the important services performed at Suffolk."

On the 30th of January, 1865, General Stoneman wrote: "I have always looked upon it as a most fortunate thing for us that you were enabled to hold Longstreet at Suffolk."

It has been asserted that Longstreet joined Lee at the battle of Chancellorsville. Lee, in his report of that battle, page 5, says: "General Longstreet, with two divisions of his corps, was detailed for service south of James River in February, and did not rejoin the army until after the battle of Chancellorsville."

CHAPTER II.

LEE'S INVASION OF MARYLAND AND PENNSYLVANIA.

LTHOUGH the Rappahannock was again flowing full and turbulent between the Army of the Potomac and the Army of Northern Virginia, and Hooker was in full communication with ample supplies, his forces were in a perilous situation. The enlistments of his nine months' and two years' men, to the number of almost thirty thousand, were expiring; and at the close of May,ᵃ his effective army did not exceed eighty-eight thousand ᵃ 1863. men. His cavalry had been reduced by one-third since March, and in every way his army was sadly weakened. Lee, meanwhile, had been re-enforced by the remainder of Longstreet's troops, which had been brought up from before the fortifications at Suffolk,[1] and the chief had reorganized his army into three corps, commanded respectively by Longstreet, A. P. Hill, and Ewell,[2] all able leaders, and each bearing the commission of Lieutenant-General.

Recent events had greatly inspirited the Confederates, and given a buoyant tone to the feelings of the army. Richmond seemed secure from harm for at least a year to come. Its prisons (especially the Libby, which became both famous and infamous during the war) were crowded with captives.

---

[1] See page 42.

[2] Probably at no time during the war was the Confederate army more complete in numbers, equipment, and materials, than at the middle of June, 1863, when, according to the most careful estimates made from the Confederate official returns, there were at least 500,000 men on the rolls, and more than 300,000 " present, and fit for duty." Full one-half of the white men of the Confederacy, eligible to military duty, were then enrolled for active service, while a large proportion of the other half were in the civil and military service in other capacities. Doubtless at least seven-tenths of the white adults were then in public service, while a large number of slaves were employed in various labors, such as working on fortifications, as teamsters, *et cetera*, for the cause of the conspirators. The following is the form of the voucher held by the "Government" as the employer of slaves for such purposes:—

" We, the subscribers, acknowledge to have received of John B. Stannard, First Corps of Engineers, the sums set opposite our names, respectively, being in full for the services of our slaves at Drewry's Bluff, during the months of March and April, 1863, having signed duplicate receipts.

FROM WHOM HIRED.	NAME AND OCCUPATION.	TIME EMPLOYED.	RATE OF WAGES.	AMOUNT FOR EACH SLAVE.	AMOUNT RECEIVED.	SIGNATURES.
J. G. Woodfire.	William, laborer.	22 days.	$16 a month.		$13 33	Joseph G. Woodfire.
William E. Martin.	Richard, "	37 "	" "	$19 75		
"	Henry, "	37 "	" "	19 75	39 46	W. E. Martin.

" I certify the above pay-roll is correct and just,
"JOHN B. STANNARD."

The above was copied from one of several in possession of the writer, taken from hundreds found in Richmond after the evacuation, and showing that thousands of slaves were employed on the fortifications in different parts of the Confederacy.

Charleston was defiant, and with reason. Vicksburg and Port Hudson, on the Mississippi, though seriously menaced, seemed impregnable against any force Grant and Banks might array before them; and the appeals of John-

LIBBY PRISON.[1]

ston, near Jackson, for re-enforcements,[2] were regarded as notes of unnecessary alarm.

The friends of the Confederates in Europe encouraged the latter with promises of aid. They were elated by the National disaster at Chancellorsville, and desires for the acknowledgment of the independence of the "Confederate States" were again strong and active. In England public movements in favor of the rebels were then prominent,[3] and these culminated in the spring of 1864 in the formation of a "*Southern Independence Association*," with a British peer (Lord Wharncliffe) as President, and a membership composed of powerful representatives of the Church, State, and Trade.[4] But the British Government wisely hesitated; and notwithstanding

---

[1] This was a large store and warehouse belonging to a man named Libby, who, it is said, was a friend of the Union, and the conspirators gladly ordered his property to be used for public purposes. It stands on the corner of Carey and Nineteenth Streets.

[2] See page 615, volume II.

[3] On the 26th of May a great open-air meeting was held at Sheffield, in England, at which Mr. Roebuck, M. P., was the chief speaker. The object of the meeting was to urge the British Government to recognize the independence of the Confederate States. On this occasion the following resolution, offered by the Rev. Mr. Hopp, was adopted "by an immense majority:" "Resolved, That in the opinion of this meeting, the government of this country would act wisely, both for the interests of England and those of the world, were they immediately to enter into negotiations with the great powers of Europe, for the purpose of obtaining the acknowledgment by them of the independence of the Confederate States of North America."

[4] This association was formed in Manchester in April, 1864, and the announcement of its organization, together with a list of its officers and members, was published in the *Manchester Guardian* on the 9th of that month. Nearly nine hundred names appeared in the list, representing the highest and most influential classes in England—members of the House of Lords, and of the House of Commons, not a few; baronets, clergymen, lawyers, magistrates, and merchants, prominent in all parts of the country, and representing immense wealth and social and political power. Of course the funds at the disposal of that association were immense, and no one doubts that these were used without stint in furnishing the Confederate armies, through blockade runners, with large supplies of clothing, arms, and munitions of war, and so prolonged the bloody strife. Collectively, these men were, in one sense, the British Government, for they represented the ruling classes, and, as such,

leaders of the Peace Faction in the city of New York had, six months before,[a] waited upon Lord Lyons, the British minister at Washington, with an evident desire to have his government interfere [a] Nov., 1862. in our affairs, and thus secure the independence of the Confederates,[1] and the emissaries of the conspirators were specially active in Europe, the British ministry, restrained by the good Queen, steadily refused to take decided action in the matter. Only the Pope of Rome, of all the rulers of the earth, acting as a temporal prince, officially recognized Jefferson Davis as the head of a real Government.[2] At the same time a scheme of the French Emperor for the destruction of the republic of Mexico, and the establishment of a monarch there of his own selection, pledged to act in the interest of despotism, the Roman Catholic Church, and the domination of the Latin race, was in successful operation, by means of twenty thousand French soldiers and five thousand Mexicans. In this movement, it is said, the con-

---

were professedly *neutral;* as individuals, acting as members of a private association, they were the British Government, *making deadly war* on the United States. Every right-minded Englishman condemned their iniquity, and none more keenly and effectively than the eminent Professor Goldwin Smith, in a *Letter to a Whig member of the " Southern Independence Association,"* in which he said at the beginning: "Your association wishes this country to lend assistance to the slave-holders of the Southern States, in their attempt to effect a disruption of the American commonwealth, and to establish an independent power, having, as they declare, slavery for its corner-stone. I am one of those who are convinced that, in doing so, she would commit a great folly and a still greater crime, the consequences of which would, in the end, fall on her own head."

[1] In the darkest hour of the war for the life of the Republic, when the loyal people of the country were despondent because of reverses suffered by their armies in the field during the summer and autumn of 1862, Lord Lyons, on his arrival in New York from a visit to England, found, he says, the " Conservative leaders" exulting in the success of the Opposition in the State, by whom Horatio Seymour had been elected Governor by a large majority. They felt assurance that they would henceforth have strength sufficient to check the government in its vigorous prosecution of the war, and believed that the President would heed the voice of warning given in the late elections. (See page 18.) " On the following morning, however," his lordship said, "intelligence arrived from Washington which dashed the rising hopes of the Conservatives," as the Democrats called themselves. It was announced that General McClellan, who " had been regarded as the representative of conservative principles in the army," had been superseded in command of the army, and suspended from active service. This was regarded as an evidence of the determination of the President to push straight forward in the course he had adopted for the suppression of the rebellion; and his lordship said that the "irritation of the Conservatives," seemed "to be not unmixed with consternation and despondency." "Several leaders of the Democratic party," he said, "sought interviews with me, both before and after the arrival of the intelligence of General McClellan's dismissal. The subject uppermost in their minds, while they were speaking to me, was naturally that of foreign mediation between the North and the South. Many of them seemed to think that this mediation must come at last, but they appeared to be very much afraid of its coming too soon. It was evident that they apprehended that a premature proposal of a foreign intervention would afford the Radical party a means of reviving the violent war spirit, and thus defeat their peaceful plans." Then they laid before his lordship " the plans and hopes of the Conservative party. At the bottom, I thought," continues his lordship, "I perceived a desire to put an end to the war, even at the risk of losing the Southern States altogether; but it was plain that it was not thought prudent to avow this desire. Indeed, some hints of it, dropped before the elections, were so ill received, that a strong declaration in the contrary sense was deemed necessary by the Democratic leaders. At the present moment, therefore, the chiefs of the Conservative party call loudly for a more vigorous prosecution of the war, and reproach the government with slackness as well as a want of success in its military measures." They expressed themselves determined to stand by " the South " in perpetuating slavery, and if their party should, as they hoped, speedily acquire the control of public affairs, " they would be disposed to accept an offer of mediation, if it appeared to be the only means of putting a stop to hostilities." They would prefer to have such proposition come from the great European powers conjointly, and Great Britain to appear as little prominent as possible.—*Dispatch of Lord Lyons to Lord John Russell, November* 17, 1862.

[2] In the autumn of 1862, Pope Pius the Ninth addressed a letter to the Archbishops of New York and New Orleans, enjoining them to employ their prayers and influence for the restoration of peace. These were published, and on the 23d of September, 1863, Jefferson Davis, in his official capacity, addressed a letter to " The Most Venerable Chief of the Holy See, and Sovereign Pontiff of the Roman Catholic Church," thanking him, in his own name and that of the Confederate States, for his " Christian charity and love," declaring that they then were and ever had been earnestly desirous that the " wicked war should cease." To this the Pope replied on the 3d of December, in a letter "To the Illustrious and Honorable Jefferson Davis, President of the Confederate States of America," expressing his gratification that Davis appreciated his letter to the archbishops, and to recognize that he and his people were animated by the same desire as himself " for peace and tranquillity." This was the only official recognition the Chief Conspirator ever received by the head of any Government.

spirators were the secret allies of the Emperor, it being understood that so soon as he should obtain a firm footing in Mexico he should, for valuable commercial considerations agreed upon, acknowledge the independence of the Confederate States, and uphold it by force of arms if necessary ; it also being understood that the Government which Davis and his fellow-conspirators were to establish at the close of hostilities, should in nowise offend Napoleon's ideas of imperialism.   Monarchical titles, distinctions, and privileges, were to prevail.   The slave-holding class were to be the rulers, and the great mass of the people were to be subordinated to the interests of that oligarchy.   Therefore the triumphal march of the French invaders toward the Mexican capital, in the spring of 1863, was hailed with delight by the authorities at Richmond.[1]   To them, and to the deluded people of the Confederate States, who did not penetrate the dark designs of the leaders, against their liberties, the skies never seemed brighter with promises of speedy success for their cause, and the establishment of a permanent empire, with slavery for its corner-stone.[2]   For in addition to the positive victory at Chancellorsville, the increase of Lee's forces, and the evident demoralization, for the moment, of the Army of the Potomac, the impression was universal in the Confederacy that the Peace Faction in the Free-labor States was a true exponent of the sentiments of the Opposition, and that a great majority of the people were eagerly awaiting an opportunity for revolting against the Government, because of its decided emancipation policy, its threat of conscription, the increase in the prices of food and fabrics, and the plain appari-

---

[1] Soon after the late civil war broke out, England, France, and Spain, entered into negotiations for a triple alliance, ostensibly for the purpose of compelling Mexico to pay its debts due to citizens of those countries, or punishing it for wrongs inflicted on those citizens.   The treaty was signed on the 21st of October, 1861.   Diplomatic relations with Mexico were broken off by those powers, and each ally sent a fleet with troops to the Gulf of Mexico, numbering in all 61 vessels and 38,000 men.   They appeared off Vera Cruz on the 8th of December, 1861, where they landed without much difficulty, the commanders assuring the Mexicans that there was no intention to interfere with their form of government, or to abridge their liberties.   It was soon discovered by the representatives of Great Britain and Spain that the French Emperor was playing falsely and selfishly in the matter, and in the spring of 1862 the British and Spanish troops left Mexico and returned home.

The real designs of Louis Napoleon were now made apparent.   His political design was to arrest the march of empire southward on the part of the United States.   His religious design was to assist the Church party in Mexico, which had been defeated in 1857, in a recovery of its power, that the Roman Catholic Church might have undisputed sway in Central America.   In a letter to General Prim, the Spanish commander, dated July 3, 1862, the Emperor, after saying that the United States fed the factories of Europe with cotton, and asserting that it was not the interest of European Governments to have it hold dominion over the Gulf of Mexico, the Antilles, and the adjacent continent, he declared that if, with the assistance of France, Mexico should have " a stable Government," that is, a monarchy, " *we shall have restored to the Latin race upon the opposite side of the ocean its strength and its prestige ;* we shall have guaranteed, then, security to our colonies in the Antilles, and to those of Spain ; we shall have established our beneficent influence in the center of America ; and this influence, by creating immense openings to our commerce, *will procure to us the matter indispensable to our industry.*"

Louis Napoleon supposed the power of the United States to be broken by the rebellion and civil war, and that he might, with impunity, carry out his designs against republican institutions in the New World, and establish a dependency of France in the fertile, cotton-growing regions of Central America.   His troops were re-enforced after the two allies withdrew.   They marched upon and seized the capital, and then, in accordance with a previous arrangement made with leaders of the Church party, the Austrian Archduke Maximilian was chosen Emperor of Mexico by a ridiculous minority of the people, known as the " Notables," and placed on a throne.   This movement was offensive to the people of the United States, for they saw in it not only an outrage upon a sister republic, but a menace of their own.   No diplomatic intercourse was held by them with Maximilian , and when the civil war was closed, in 1865, and it was seen that our Government was more powerful than ever, Louis Napoleon, trembling with alarm, heeded its warning to withdraw his forces, at the peril of forcible expulsion by our troops.   He was mortified and humbled, and, with a perfidy unparalleled in the history of rulers, he abandoned his dupe, Maximilian, and left him to struggle on against the patriots fighting for their liberties under the direction of their President, Benito Juarez, until the " Emperor " was finally captured and shot, leaving his poor wife, the " Empress " Carlotta, a hopeless lunatic in her home in Austria.

[2] For a year the subject of a seal for the Confederate States had been before the " Congress " at Richmond, and on the 27th of April, 1863, the " Senate," in which action upon the subject originated, amended a resolution

tion of an enormous and rapidly accumulating National debt. It was believed that a vigorous invasion of Maryland and Pennsylvania again would inaugurate a revolution in the Free-labor States, which would lead to a practical coalition between the Confederates and their political friends in the North, and a speedy peace on terms dictated, by the servants of Jefferson Davis, on the banks of the Susquehanna and the Ohio. Back of all this was a powerful and perhaps a prime motive for such an invasion, in the lack of subsistence for Lee's army, then to be obtained, it was believed, most speedily and abundantly from the herds and flocks and store-houses of more fruitful Maryland and Pennsylvania.[1] These considerations made the Confederate leaders audacious, and impelled them to attempt audacious achievements. At the time we are considering, the Army of Northern Virginia was in a condition of strength and *morale*, General Longstreet said, " to undertake any thing." [2]

Impelled by false notions of the temper of a greater portion of the people of the Free-labor States, and the real resources and strength of the Government, the conspirators ordered Lee to invade Maryland and Pennsylvania again. So early as the 28th of May Hooker suspected such movement, and so informed the Secretary of War. Earlier than this a benevolent citizen,[3] who had been much in the army for the purpose of comforting the sick and wounded, and had rare opportunities for obtaining information from Confederate councils, had warned the authorities at Washington, Baltimore, and Harrisburg, of the impending danger; but these were slow to believe that

of the " House of Representatives," and decided that the device for the seal should be as follows: " A device representing an equestrian statue of Washington (after the statue which surmounts his monument in the Capitol square at Richmond), surrounded with a wreath composed of the principal agricultural products of the Confederacy, and having around its margin the words, 'CONFEDERATE STATES OF AMERICA, 22D FEB., 1862,' with the following motto: 'DEO VINDICE,' "—God, the protector, defender, deliverer, or ruler. This was adopted by both " Houses," and then it was proposed to send some one through the lines to New York, to procure an engraving of the same on brass and steel. This was objected to, and the commission was finally given to an engraver in England. The writer was informed by Mr. Davis, of Wilmington, N. C., the Confederate " Attorney-General," that the engraving was not completed in time for use. It had just arrived at Richmond when the evacuation of that city occurred, in April, 1865, and no impression from it was ever made. *That pretended Government never had an insignia of sovereignty.* None of its officers ever bore a commission with its seal; and the writer was informed that many officers of high rank in the Confederate army never received a commission.

PROPOSED " CONFEDERATE STATES " SEAL.*

[1] To this necessity the Richmond journals pointed at that time, in guarded editorials, one of them closing with the remark: " We urge nothing, suggest nothing, hint nothing; only state facts."

[2] *Campaigns of the Army of the Potomac,* note 1, page 310.

[3] The informer was Clement C. Barclay, of Philadelphia, who gave the warning so early as the 20th of May, a notice of which, in a letter from Baltimore, was published in *The Inquirer,* of Philadelphia. " I am authorized to say," said the writer, " that Mr. Barclay has been in close counsel with our highest authorities here, and is more than ever convinced of the imperious necessity devolving on our people throughout the whole land to awake at once to a realizing sense of preparing to counteract the contingency of an invasion of Maryland and Pennsylvania by the rebel hordes. Mr. Barclay returns to Washington on important business, after which he proceeds immediately to Harrisburg, to confer with Governor Curtin upon matters of weighty moment, touching affairs in Pennsylvania. He is fully alive to the importance of his mission, and of his State

* This is copied from a rude wood-cut, at the head of a certificate of honorary directorship of a Confederate *Association for the Relief of Maimed Soldiers.* The object of that association was to supply artificial limbs gratuitously to soldiers who had lost them. A subscription annually of $10 constituted a member; of $300, a life member; and of $1,000, an honorary director.

Lee would repeat the folly of the previous year, because of his sad experience then; and preparations for invasion were deferred until the Confederate army, in full force, was pressing forward toward the Upper Potomac.

Lee's first step in this aggressive movement was to allure or drive Hooker from the Rappahannock. Leaving Hill's corps to occupy the lines at Fredericksburg, he put the remainder of his army in motion[a] westward toward Culpepper Court-House, where Stuart's cavalry was concentrated. Hooker, suspecting some important movement, threw Howe's division of the Sixth Corps over the river, at Franklin's Crossing, for observation. Hill's display of strength and numbers satisfied Howe that the Confederates were still in nearly full force on the heights, and he withdrew. Lee, who had halted his columns to await the result of this movement, now ordered them forward, and it was three days later before Hooker was certain that his antagonist was massing his forces toward the National right. Then, informed that Stuart was at Culpepper Court-House, he ordered Pleasanton, who was at the head of the cavalry, at Catlett's Station, to cross the Rappahannock at Beverly and Kelly's fords, with two of his divisions under Buford and Gregg, supported by two infantry divisions (Russell's, of the Sixth, and Ames's, of the Eleventh Corps), and push on toward Stuart's camp by converging roads. Accordingly, at dawn on the 9th,[b] Buford crossed at Beverly Ford, and immediately encountered a brigade of Confederate cavalry under the active General Sam. Jones. A sharp engagement ensued, when the Eighth New York, under Colonel B. F. Davis, was routed, and its commander was killed. A charge by the Eighth Illinois drove the Confederates, in turn, about two miles, when Jones was re-enforced by the brigades of Hampton and W. H. F. Lee. In the mean time Russell's infantry had come up and engaged the foe in front while Buford attacked their flank, when two Confederate regiments burst from the woods on the National flank, and placed the latter, commanded by Pleasanton in person, in great peril.

[a] June 3, 1863.

[b] June.

Gregg, who had crossed at Kelly's Ford, had been expected for several hours. He, too, had been fighting most of the morning with cavalry under General Robertson, whom he pushed back to Brandy Station, and gallantly took possession of the heights near there. At one o'clock he and Buford joined forces, when the Confederates recoiled; but Pleasanton, satisfied that the bulk of Lee's army was on his front, fell back, and at dusk recrossed the Rappahannock with a hundred prisoners, after a loss of about five hundred men. Stuart reported his loss at six hundred men, among whom was General W. H. F. Lee, wounded.

Pleasanton's cavalry reconnoissance developed the fact of Lee's grand movement, but so perfectly were his real intentions concealed, that while Hooker was expecting him to follow his route of the previous year,[1] and was watching and guarding the fords of the Rappahannock, he projected his left

---

losing no time in the organization of her militia, that she may be in readiness to meet any emergency. All the signs of the times, and very many indications, visible only to those who see behind the curtain in the arena of Secessionism, tend to show that the Confederates will, if they can, invade Maryland and Pennsylvania this summer."

Mr. Barclay urged the authorities of Pennsylvania to proceed at once to the "organization of the militia, so as to be in readiness to meet the emergency."

[1] See chapter XVII., volume II.

wing, under Ewell, through the Blue Ridge at Chester's Gap, and by way of Front Royal it crossed the Shenandoah River, and burst into the valley at Strasburg like an avalanche. That energetic leader moved with the divisions of Early and Edward Johnston rapidly down the Valley pike, and arrived before Winchester, where General Milroy was in command of about ten thousand men, on the evening of the 13th,[a] having marched from Culpepper, a distance of seventy miles, in three days. At the [a] June, 1863. same time Imboden, with his cavalry, was operating in the vicinity of Romney, to prevent Milroy from being re-enforced from the line of the Baltimore and Ohio railway. This was a bold movement on the part of Lee, for it made the actual line of his army, from Hill at Fredericksburg to Ewell at Winchester, full one hundred miles in length.

Although Milroy, since the first of the month, had felt a pressure from the foe stationed up the valley, and on the 12th had sent out strong reconnoitering parties to ascertain why it was increasing, it was not until the forenoon of the 13th that he was aware of any considerable force on his front. The revelation of that force so near was astounding, and the assurance of its overwhelming numbers, given by scouts and prisoners, would have justified him in retreating at once. But Milroy, brave even to rashness, resolved to fight before flying. He called in his outposts. Colonel McReynold's, with a brigade stationed at Berryville to watch the passes of the Blue Ridge and the fords of the Shenandoah, retreated before Rodes, and very soon Milroy had his forces, not more than seven thousand effectives, well in hand. While awaiting an attack, his foe was accumulating force on his front and flank, and on the evening of the 14th, after some skirmishing, the Confederates substantially invested the city and garrison. At one o'clock the next morning[b] Milroy, in compliance with the decision of a council of officers, resolved to retreat. He spiked his cannon, [b] June 15. drowned his powder, and was about to fly, when the Confederates fell upon him. Then began an unequal struggle, and an equal race, toward the Potomac. The fugitives were swifter-footed than their pursuers, and might all have escaped, had not Johnston's division, which had gained the rear of the post, stood in their way, four miles from Winchester. By these the flying troops were stopped, scattered, and many were made prisoners.[1] Most of those who escaped, crossed the Potomac at Hancock, and took refuge in Bedford County, Pennsylvania; and others fled to Harper's Ferry, where Milroy's wagon-train crossed the Potomac, and was conducted in safety to Harrisburg, by way of Hagerstown and Chambersburg. Milroy lost nearly all of his artillery and ammunition. Alarmed by the approach of the Confederates in such force, the garrison at Harper's Ferry, under General French, withdrew to Maryland Heights. The Shenandoah Valley was now clear of all obstacles to the march of the invading army.

Hooker, in the mean time, had been kept in the vicinity of the Rappahannock, partly by uncertainty concerning Lee's movements, and chiefly by directions from Washington;[2] but the moment he was informed of the

---

[1] Lee reported that in this affair his troops captured "more than 4,000 prisoners, 29 guns, 277 wagons, and 400 horses." These doubtless included 700 prisoners and 5 guns captured at Martinsburg by General Rodes.

[2] Hooker had been instructed by Halleck (January 31) to "keep in view always the importance of covering Washington City and Harper's Ferry." On the 5th of June, when he expected a movement of General Lee

presence of Ewell in the Shenandoah Valley, he called Howe across the river, and on the day when Milroy was driven from Winchester,[a] he moved rapidly northward, with his whole force, to Centreville and its vicinity, keeping his cavalry well to his left to watch the passes of the Blue Ridge, while intent, himself, upon covering Washington. The National authorities, as well as those of Maryland and Pennsylvania, had, meanwhile, become thoroughly aroused by a sense of danger. The Government had just created[b] two new military departments in Pennsylvania.[1] On the 12th, Governor Curtin, of that State, issued a call for the entire militia of the commonwealth to turn out to defend its soil, but it was feebly responded to; and on the 15th, the President called upon the States nearest the capital for an aggregate of one hundred thousand militia.[2]. This, too, was tardily and stingily answered, while uniformed and disciplined regiments of the city of New York so promptly marched toward the field of danger that the Secretary of War publicly thanked the Governor of that State for the exhibition of patriotism. Despondency had produced apathy, and it appeared, for the moment, as if the patriotism of the loyalists was waning, and that the expectation of the Confederates, of a general cry for peace in the Free-labor States, was about to be realized. Finally, when the Confederates were streaming across the Potomac, the number of troops that responded to the call was about fifty thousand, one-half of whom were Pennsylvanians, and fifteen thousand were New Yorkers.[3]

Lee had about a week's start of Hooker in the race for the Potomac, and when the latter disappeared behind the Stafford hills,[c] the occupants of Fredericksburg Heights marched for Culpepper. Longstreet, in position there, his ranks swelled by a part of Pickett's division, then moved along the eastern side of the Blue Ridge, and took possession of Ashby's and Snicker's Gaps, for the purpose of seriously menacing, if not actually attempting the capture of Washington, drawing Hooker farther from his supplies, and preventing the Nationals from darting through the Blue Ridge and striking the Confederates in the Valley, into which Hill, covered by Longstreet, speedily followed Ewell, and took position at Winchester. Hooker, meanwhile, was in the vicinity of Fairfax Court-House, expecting a direct attack from his adversary, and the cavalry of Pleasanton and Stuart had almost daily encounters. In one of these, near Aldie,[d]

[a] June 15, 1863.

[b] June 9.

[c] May 18.

[d] June 17.

---

toward the Potomac, he suggested, in a letter to the President, that in case he should do so, leaving (as he actually did) his rear resting on Fredericksburg, that it would be his "duty to pitch into" that rear, and desiring to know whether such an act would come within the spirit of his instructions. The President and General Halleck both disapproved the movement hinted at in the suggestion, and so, when Hooker found that Lee had stretched his army into a line a hundred miles long, and his rear was still at Fredericksburg, he was deprived of the privilege of cutting off the latter by a quick movement across the Rappahannock, and forcing his way between Hill and Longstreet, at Culpepper.

[1] The eastern, under General Couch, was called the Department of the Susquehanna, with head-quarters at Harrisburg; and the western, under General Brooks, the Department of the Monongahela, with head-quarters at Pittsburg. The Middle Department was under the command of General Schenck, head-quarters at Baltimore.

[2] Maryland was called upon for 10,000 men; Pennsylvania, 50,000; Ohio, 30,000; and West Virginia, 10,000.

[3] The Secretary of War and Governor Curtin called upon Governor Parker, of New Jersey, for troops, and he responded by issuing a call on the 16th. On the same day, General Sanford, of New York City, issued an order for the regiments of the First Division of that State to proceed forthwith to Harrisburg, "to assist in repelling" the invasion of Pennsylvania. In addition to these, about 1,800 volunteers from various parts of the State were organized and equipped, and sent to Harrisburg. On the 20th of June, about 50,000 men had responded to the President's call. New York had furnished 15,000; Pennsylvania, 25,000; New Jersey, 3,000; Delaware, 2,000; Maryland, 5,000. A patriotic appeal of Governor Bradford, of the latter State, fully aroused the loyal people to action.

at the Pass between the Bull's Run and Kittoctin mountains,[1] the position of Lee was partially revealed to Hooker, and caused the latter to send the Second Corps to Thoroughfare Gap, the Fifth to Aldie, and the Twelfth to Leesburg. In that encounter the Confederate cavalry was charged by Kilpatrick's brigade (First Maine, First Massachusetts, and a battalion of the Fourth New York), and driven back to Ashby's Gap, whence they had emerged. Two days earlier than this,[a] when Milroy's flying troops were crossing the Potomac at Hancock, a brigade of Confederate cavalry, fifteen hundred in number, under General Jenkins, detached from Ewell's corps, had dashed across the river at Williamsport, in pursuit of Milroy's wagon-train, swept up the Cumberland Valley to Chambersburg, in Pennsylvania, destroyed the railway in that neighborhood, and plundered the region of horses, cattle, and other supplies. Then, with fifty kidnapped negroes, they turned their faces toward the Potomac,[2] encamped at and held Hagerstown, in Maryland, and there waited for the advance of Lee's army.

[a] June 15, 1863.

Jenkins's raid was a reconnoissance for information. It satisfied Lee that very little opposition might be expected to an immediate invasion in force, and he determined to advance. By skillful movements he kept the Army of the Potomac in doubt, in the vicinity of Washington, while Ewell's corps pressed to the river, crossed it at Williamsport and Shepardstown into Maryland, on the 21st and 22d of June, moved directly on Hagerstown, yet held by Jenkins, and then up the Cumberland Valley to Chambersburg,[b] where General Knipe was in command. That officer fell back, and all Western Pennsylvania, up to its capital on the Susquehanna, appeared to be at the mercy of the invaders, for few troops had yet joined Couch or Brooks.[3] Still farther northward Ewell advanced in two columns, Rodes's division pushing on through Carlisle to Kingston,[c] within thirteen miles of Harrisburg, while Early's division marched up the eastern side of the South Mountain range, and through Emmettsburg, Gettysburg, and York, to the banks of the Susquehanna at Wrights-

[b] June 22.

[c] June 27.

---

[1] See map on page 586, volume I., and note 2, page 467, volume II.

[2] Drugs and other merchandise were purchased by the Confederates in Chambersburg, and paid for in Confederate scrip. During his stay there Jenkins lost some horses, and demanded their return or their reputed value ($900) in money. The scrip to that amount was tendered to him, and he dared not refuse the worthless paper, for fear of casting "discredit on the finances of his nation." He was compelled to "pocket the joke."

[3] There was great tardiness everywhere, especially in Western Pennsylvania. Homes in that region were most endangered, and men did not like to leave their families unprotected. Some were unwilling to take up arms, because they were opposed to the war, and did all they could to prevent their friends joining the defenders. These members of the Peace Faction were fearful of being retained in the field beyond the fall election, and thus be deprived of voting against the supply of further men or money for the war; and "some, also," says Professor Jacobs (*Rebel Invasion of Maryland and Pennsylvania*, page 10), "who were

PENNSYLVANIA COLLEGE.

brave and patriotic in words, could not make up their minds to expose themselves to the hardships of camp life, and to the perils of the battle-field." To this general hesitation there was a noble exception. At the time of Jenkins's raid, sixty students of Pennsylvania College, at Gettysburg, together with several from the Theological Seminary there, and a few citizens under Captain F. Klinefelter, a theological student, formed a company, and marched for Harrisburg on the 17th of June. These were the first to be "mustered into the service for the emergency."—See Jacob's *Rebel Invasion*, &c., page 10.

ville, opposite Columbia, levying contributions on the people, and destroying bridges along the line of the Northern Central railway, which connects that region with Baltimore. The great railway bridge that spanned the Susquehanna between Wrightsville and Columbia was fired by National troops at the latter place, under Colonel Frick, and was in flames when the Confederates came up.[1]

This sudden and formidable invasion created an intense panic, especially in Pennsylvania. Flocks and herds, horses and forage, accompanied by citizens who preferred peace to war, were hurried across the Susquehanna, for there was no longer any uncertainty; and the fact that Lee and his legions had flanked Hooker, and were on the soil of Pennsylvania, levying contributions on its citizens,[2] and threatening its political and commercial capital with seizure and plunder, was now the burning commentary of events on the wisdom and patriotism of Governor Curtin, and the folly of disregarding his timely warnings and appeals.[3] There seemed to be no power at hand adequate to stay the merciless tide of invasion, and for a moment it appeared probable that the Confederate footmen might have an undisturbed promenade between the Susquehanna and the Schuylkill, and that the horses of their cavalry might speedily be watered in the Delaware, and possibly neigh on the banks of the Hudson. Rumor and fear, magnifying and disturbing truth, made pale faces everywhere. Now the invaders

---

[1] As General Lee's errand was partly a political one, and there was a desire to conciliate all who were disposed for peace and friendship with the Confederates, he issued a stringent order on the 21st, directed to General Ewell, forbidding plunder and violence of every kind, directing payment to be made for all supplies received, and certificates to be given to those friends who should refuse compensation. At the same time he directed the orderly seizure, by proper authority, of all necessary supplies when owners refused to give or sell them. Also to seize *all* the property of any person who should conceal, or attempt to conceal, any property required by his army.

[2] In violation of the letter of Lee's order, commanders like Early proceeded to "live upon the enemy," and indulge their desires for plunder and destruction. When Early's corps approached York, the meek mayor, sympathizing, it was reported, with the Peace Faction, took the trouble to go several miles in the direction of the approaching invaders, to meet Early and surrender the borough to him, which, because of this mark of submission, was promised special immunity from harm. When the Confederate general occupied the town, his promise was broken, and he required the citizens to deliver, by four o'clock that afternoon, a large supply of food and clothing, and $100,000 in United States Treasury notes. Of the amount required, $28,000 were actually paid, and a larger portion of 200 barrels of flour, 40,000 pounds of fresh beef, 30,000 bushels of corn, and 1,000 pairs of shoes, and some other articles, "required for the use of Early's division," as the requisition said, were furnished.

Early also proceeded to the extensive iron works of Thaddeus Stevens, member of Congress, in that region, and, because of his eminent services in the National legislature, in providing means for crushing the rebellion, caused his property, to the amount of $50,000, to be destroyed. This was done by fire by the hands of some of Jenkins's cavalry. When the writer was at Marietta, in Georgia, in May, 1866, he met there a captain in that cavalry, by the name of Stevens, who boasted of being one of those who committed the sturdy old patriot's property to the flames. Early directed certificates to be given the citizens of York for property "contributed," well knowing that they were as worthless as the "Confederate scrip" which Lee ordered to be paid for supplies. No man knew better than did Lee, at that time, that a slip of soiled paper would have been as valuable to the citizens of Pennsylvania as the "money" he offered, "when any was offered;" and, in view of this fact, his assumed honesty in his order to Ewell of the 21st, cannot conceal the deliberate intention to plunder the people in an orderly manner.

The exhibition of ferocity on the part of the stay-at-home writers for the Confederate newspapers was sometimes sickening, but more often amusing. One of these, in the *Richmond Whig* of July 2, having heard that Lee was in Harrisburg, expressed a hope that he would set fire to all the anthracite coal-mines in Pennsylvania. He did not doubt Lee would do it, if the opportunity offered, and thereby all the coal would be "reduced to ashes!" "All that is needed," said the writer, "is to seize the anthracite fields, destroy the roads and the machinery of the pits, set fire to the mines and leave them. Northern industry will thus be paralyzed at a single blow."

[3] So early as the 15th of June, the Governor, through the newspapers and by placards headed with the words, in large letters, PENNSYLVANIA IN DANGER!—CITIZENS CALLED TO ARMS! informed the inhabitants of the peril that threatened them, and said, "Unless our people respond promptly, a large part of the State will be laid waste by the rebel invaders." He assured them that those who volunteered would be credited on the draft, then ordered; but it was difficult to arouse them to action.

were marching toward Pittsburg, and would scale the Alleghanies; then on Harrisburg, and would destroy the State buildings and archives; now on Philadelphia, to plunder its mansions and store-houses; and then on Baltimore and Washington, to proclaim Jefferson Davis the ruler of the Republic, with the power of a Dictator. Brooks cast up breastworks on the line of their expected approach to the mountains; Couch made intrenchments opposite Harrisburg, and some of his troops skirmished with the Confederate vanguard within four miles of the capital. Stockades and block-houses were constructed along the line of the Northern Central railway, between Baltimore and Hanover Junction; and at Philadelphia some pretty little redoubts were erected, at which the citizens laughed when the danger was over. That danger, so sudden and awful, seemed to have paralyzed efforts for any movement excepting in a search for safety of person and property. The contents of bank vaults were sent to points beyond peril; and valuable merchandise, household treasures, and bank deposits, were transported from Philadelphia

BLOCK-HOUSE.[1]

to distant places of safety,[2] while troops from farther north were hurrying through the city to meet the impending danger. But Philadelphia soon aroused from its stupor. Its mayor issued a stirring appeal to the citizens to " close their manufactories, workshops, and stores, before the stern necessity of common safety made it obligatory." The drill-rooms were soon crowded with volunteers from every class of citizens, and very speedily full regiments were organized and on their way to the field. "Even the clergy," said an eye-witness, " assembled, and to a man offered to drop both preaching and the pen, and take up either musket or spade."

---

[1] This little cut shows the form of block-houses erected along the line of the road, particularly at the bridge where the railway crossed Gunpowder Creek. These were built of stout hewn logs and pierced for musketry. At the dam of Jones's Falls Creek, about eight miles from Baltimore, where a reservoir, called Swan Lake, is formed, from which Baltimore is supplied with water, palisades, as seen in the annexed engraving, were erected across a road approaching from the westward. These were for the purpose of preventing the invaders, marching from that direction, striking the railway there, or cutting off the supply of water from the city.

PALISADES AT SWAN LAKE.

The alarm of the loyal people of Baltimore was also great. All the military and many citizens were made busy in erecting fortifications to defend the city against the invaders, while the Secessionists were joyful because of the prospect of soon welcoming to Baltimore what they were pleased to call " the deliverers of Maryland." Lines of intrenchments, with redoubts, were constructed, extending a long distance, so as to completely inclose the city on the land side. In that work the colored people, bond and free, bore the brunt of labor. A thousand of these were gathered by the police in one day and put into the ranks of workers.

[2] As an illustration of the sudden change from perfect confidence to wild alarm, the writer will mention the following occurrence: The Loyal League of Philadelphia had made extensive preparations for a magnificent celebration of the approaching anniversary of our National Independence. The writer was invited to be present as a guest. When the news came that Jenkins had been at Chambersburg and Ewell was in Maryland, he wrote to a leading citizen of Philadelphia, suggesting that the thousands expected at that celebration might be called to a defense of their homes rather than the pleasures of a festivity. In a letter on the 27th, that citizen repelled the idea of any peril, but on the 29th he wrote: " We are in danger. Heaven knows whether we are to be captured. All the town is excitement. We know not what to do!" And a friend who, in a letter two days before, declared there was no danger, wrote on that day, " I avail myself of your kindness to place under your care a box of merchandise, which you will please put in a dry place." Even the city of New York was considered unsafe in the last week in June, and for that reason precious things were sent from Philadelphia as far as the writer's home, more than seventy miles up the Hudson River.

The remainder of Lee's army, under Longstreet and Hill, crossed the Potomac on the 24th and 25th,[a] concentrated at Hagerstown, and pressed on in the path of Ewell toward the Susquehanna. In-

[a] June, 1863.

formed of this passage, Hooker put his own army in motion, and on the 26th and 27th crossed the river at and near Edwards's Ferry, one hundred thousand strong, having been re-enforced 'from the defenses around Washington, under General Heintzelman, and from Schenck's Middle Department.[1] Wishing still further to increase his army, and regarding the post at Harper's Ferry (then garrisoned, on Maryland Heights, by eleven thousand men, under General French) as of little account in the then state of affairs, asked the General-in-chief[a] (Halleck), " Is there any reason why Maryland Heights should not be abandoned after the public stores and

[b] June 26.

property are removed ?" Halleck did not approve of the abandonment of the post, and said so, when Hooker, who had the following day personally inspected French's position, again urged the abandonment of it, saying, the garrison was " of no earthly account " then, and that the stores were only " a bait for the rebels, should they return." [2] Expecting a compliance with his wishes, he advanced his army to Frederick, in a position to dart through the South Mountain passes, upon Lee's line of communications, or upon his columns in retreat, or to follow him on a parallel line toward the Susque-hanna. For this purpose he had ordered General Slocum to march his corps to Harper's Ferry to join General French, that their united forces might push up the Cumberland Valley and threaten Lee's rear.

But Halleck would not consent to the abandonment of Harper's Ferry, and the disappointed and irritated Commander of the Army of the Poto-mac telegraphed[c] to the General-in-Chief, saying, " My original instructions were to cover Harper's Ferry and Washington, I

[c] June 27.

have now imposed upon me, in addition, an enemy in my front of more than my numbers. I beg to be understood, respectfully, but firmly, that I am unable to comply with these conditions with the means at my disposal; and I earnestly request that I may be at once relieved from the position I occupy." His request was immediately granted, and, by an order issued on the same day, General George G. Meade was directed to assume the command of the army. General Hooker was ordered to Baltimore, there to await commands from the Adjutant-General. Three days passed by, and he heard nothing from Washington, when he proceeded to that city, and was at once arrested by order of Halleck, for visiting the capital without leave, in violation of a rule forbidding officers to do so. This was the end of General Hooker's services in the Army of the Potomac.

That change of chief commanders, in front of an enemy on the eve of an inevitable great battle, was a perilous thing, calculated to demoralize the best disciplined troops. But the Government trusted the men. The veterans of the Army of the Potomac knew, appreciated, and loved Hooker, and were

---

[1] General Heintzelman was in command of the Department of Washington, with about 36,000 men, and Schenck's Department east of the Cumberland, included the posts of Harper's Ferry and Winchester. It was not until Hooker was about to cross the Potomac that Halleck consented to let him have any troops from these Departments. Then he placed the forces in both at his disposal, but only nominally, for, as the text shows, when Hooker was about to use a portion of these troops in the grand movement against the invaders, Halleck interposed his authority and prevented such use.

[2] Hooker's telegraphic dispatch to Halleck, June 27, 1863.

sadly disappointed, for they knew less of Meade; but, impelled by the love of country, the shadow of regret soon passed from their brows, and they were ready and willing to trust and follow their new commander. To him General Halleck gave permission to use the garrison at Harper's Ferry, according to the dictates of his own judgment. In fact the army was placed under Meade's absolute control, with the assurance of the President that no exercise of executive authority or powers of the Constitution should interfere with his operations in the great emergency. With these extraordinary powers and responsibilities, General Meade prepared to meet General Lee in battle.

GEORGE G. MEADE.

On the day when Meade assumed the chief command,[a] Lee, who was about to cross the Susquehanna at Har-

[a] June 28, 1863.

risburg, and march on Philadelphia, was alarmed by intelligence of the presence of the Army of the Potomac, in augmented force, threatening his flank and rear, and the demonstrations on his front of the gathering yeomanry of Pennsylvania and troops from other States. He instantly abandoned his scheme of further invasion, and ordered a retrograde movement. Stuart on the same day crossed the Potomac at Seneca, with a large force of his cavalry, captured men and destroyed property near the river,[1] and, pushing on to Westminster, at the right of the Army of the Potomac, swept across its front to Carlisle, encountering Kilpatrick on the way, and then followed in the track of Ewell, toward Gettysburg. The latter had been directed to recall his columns, and take position near Gettysburg, the capital of Adams County; and Longstreet and Hill were ordered to cross the South Mountain range in the same direction, and press on by the Chambersburg road, leading through Gettysburg to Baltimore. The object was to keep Meade from Lee's communications, and to concentrate the Confederate Army for either defensive or offensive operations. Lee hoped to be able, by such concentration, to fall upon and crush the Army of the Potomac, and then march in triumph upon Baltimore and Washington. He was nervous about fighting so far from his base, so he chose the vicinity of Gettysburg for that concentration, because, in the event of defeat, he would have a direct line of retreat to the Potomac.

In the mean time General Meade had put his entire army in motion northward from Frederick, for the purpose of arresting the invasion, or meeting and fighting Lee; and General French was directed to evacuate Harper's Ferry, remove the public property to Washington, and occupy Frederick and the line of the Baltimore and Ohio railway. Meade moved on, but it was not until the evening of the 30th,[b] after two marches, that he received correct information of Lee's move-

[b] June.

---

[1] He burned 17 canal boats and a train of 178 army wagons, all laden with public stores.

ments, and his evident intention to give battle in full force. Satisfied of this, Meade issued a short but stirring address to his army,[1] and then sought a good position, where he might easily concentrate his troops, and engage advantageously in the great struggle which he knew was impending. He chose the line of Big Pipe Creek, on the water-shed between the Potomac River and Chesapeake Bay, southeast of Gettysburg, with the hills at Westminster in the rear. On the night of the 30th, he issued orders for the right wing, composed of General Sedgwick's (Sixth) corps, to take position at Manchester, in the rear of the creek; the center, consisting of Generals Slocum (Twelfth) and Sykes's (Fifth) corps, to move toward Hanover, in advance of the creek, and the left, nearest the foe, under General John F. Reynolds, formerly of the Pennsylvania Reserves, composed of his own (First), Sickles's (Third), and Howard's (Eleventh), to push on toward Gettysburg, and thus mask the forming of the battle-line on Pipe Creek. The Second Corps (late Couch's, and then under Hancock) was directed to take position, with the army head-quarters, at Taneytown, on the road from Emmettsburg to Winchester. Meade's cavalry, in the mean time, was diligently engaged on his front and flanks. Buford's division had moved north through Middleburg, and, at noon of the 29th,[a] occupied Gettys-

[a] June, 1863. burg. At about the same hour, Kilpatrick, with his command, while passing through Hanover, was suddenly and unexpectedly assailed by Stuart (then on his march for Carlisle), who led a desperate charge, in per-

SCENE OF CAVALRY BATTLE AT HANOVER.[2]

son, on the flank and rear of General Farnsworth's brigade, on the common near the railway at the eastern end of the village. A severe battle ensued in the town and on its borders, when General Custer, who had advanced to Abbottsville, returned, and the Confederates were repulsed with the loss of

---

[1] "The enemy are on our soil," he said; "the whole country now looks anxiously to this army to deliver it from the presence of the foe; our failure to do so will leave us no such welcome as the swelling of millions of hearts with pride and joy at our success would give to every soldier of this army. Homes, firesides, and domestic altars are involved. The army has fought well heretofore; it is believed that it will fight more desperately and bravely than ever, if it is addressed in fitting terms. Corps and other commanders are authorized to order the instant death of any soldier who fails in his duty at this hour."

[2] This is from a sketch made from the railway, by the writer, a few days after the battle, and represents the open common on the eastern end of the village, near that road. In the buildings, and also in the fence toward the right of the picture, a number of marks made by pistol-balls might then be seen. Here the battle began, and continued down the street seen near the center of the picture.

a flag and fifty men. Farnsworth lost about one hundred men. The gallant New York Fifth Cavalry, led by Farnsworth and Major Hammond, bore the brunt of battle, and won high commendation.

At this time Gettysburg was the focal point toward which the hostile armies were really tending, and circumstances speedily made the fields about that village the theater of a great battle,[1] instead of those along the line of Pipe Creek, where Meade expected to fight. Buford, as we have seen, entered Gettysburg on the 29th, and on the following evening, Reynolds, commanding the left, was ordered to advance upon it along the Emmettsburg turnpike. At that time the corps of Hill and Longstreet were upon the Chambersburg turnpike, west of Gettysburg, and Ewell was marching down from Carlisle, on the north.

At the hour when Reynolds was ordered to move on Gettysburg, the advance divisions of Hill were lying within a few miles of that town, after a reconnoitering party had ventured to the crest of Seminary or Oak Ridge, only half a mile northwest of the village. That night, Buford, with six thousand cavalry, lay between Hill and Gettysburg, and, at about nine o'clock the next morning,[a] he met the van of the Confederates, under General H. Heth,[2] on the Chambersburg road, near Wil-   [a] July 1, 1863.
loughby's Run, between Seminary Ridge and the parallel eminence a mile farther west. A skirmish ensued. Reynolds, who had bivouacked at Marsh Creek, a few miles distant, was then advancing with his own corps, followed by Howard's, and having those of Sickles and Slocum within call. The sound of fire-arms quickened his pace, and, at a little past ten o'clock, his advance division, under General Wadsworth, composed of the brigades of Generals Cutler and Meredith, passed rapidly through the village, and over the fields from the Emmettsburg road, under cover of Seminary Ridge, to the relief of Buford, who, by skillful maneuvering, and good use of his horse artillery, had kept the foe in check. Reynolds, who was with his advance, directed Cutler to place his brigade in position, with Hall's battery, on each side of the Chambersburg road and across a railway-grading at a deep cut near. Before this could be accomplished, the advancing Confederates were upon them, when a volley of musketry from the Fifty-sixth Pennsylvania, led by Colonel J. W. Hoffman, opened the decisive Battle of Gettysburg.[3] Meredith's "Iron Brigade" was immediately to

---

[1] Gettysburg lies on the northern slope of a gentle eminence, known as Cemetery Hill, because on its crown was a public burying-place. Half a mile west of the village is another eminence, called Oak Ridge, and sometimes Seminary Ridge, because a theological seminary of the Lutheran Church stands upon it. About a mile farther west, beyond Willoughby's Run, is a similar ridge, parallel with Oak Ridge. North of the town, also on a gentle slope, is the Pennsylvania College. Southeast from Cemetery Hill, between the Baltimore turnpike and Rock Creek, is Culp's Hill ; and beyond the creek, in that direction, is Wolf Hill, a rugged, wooded eminence. Two miles southwest of Cemetery Hill is a rocky peak, called Round Top, and near it a rocky hill of less altitude, called Round Top Ridge. This extends, in diminished altitude, to Ziegler's Grove, on Cemetery Hill. North of the town, the country is a rolling plain ; and, at a distance of about ten miles southwest of it, is seen the bold outline of the South Mountain range.

[2] Hill's corps consisted of the divisions of Heth, Pender, and Anderson, the first two containing 10,000 men each, and the last, 15,000. Longstreet's corps followed, with McLaws's division, 12,000, in advance ; Hood's, 12,000 ; and Pickett's, 7,000 ; the latter having the wagon-trains of the Confederates in charge. Two divisions of Ewell's corps (Rodes's, 10,000 strong, and Early's, 9,000) had encamped the previous night at Heidlersburg, nine miles from Gettysburg ; and his third division, under Edward Johnston, 12,000, was yet at Carlisle. At the hour when the van of each army met, the Union force near was less than 30,000 men, and that of the Confederates was over 70,000.

[3] Hoffman's regiment was in the second brigade of the first division of the First Army Corps, and was then under the command of Brigadier-General L. Cutler. The Fifty-sixth Regiment was the second in the column

charge into a wood on the left of the road, in rear of the Seminary, and fall upon Hill's right, under General Archer, then pressing across Willoughby's Run. Meanwhile a Mississippi brigade, under General Davis, assailed and flanked the three regiments of Cutler's brigade, on the Chambersburg road,

causing them to retire behind a wood on Seminary Ridge. This left Hall's battery uncovered, and the gunners were compelled to retire, leaving one cannon behind. The skirmishers of Cutler's other two regiments (Fourteenth Brooklyn and Ninety-fifth New York) were, at the same time, near the woods just spoken of, disputing the passage of Willoughby's Run. The "Iron Brigade" opportunely swept down in that direction, the Second Wisconsin, Colonel Fairchild, leading, and under the personal direction of Reynolds, struck Archer's flank, captured that officer and eight hundred of his men, and re-formed on

JOHN F. REYNOLDS.

the west side of the little stream. At the moment when the charge was made, Reynolds was anxiously observing the movement, having dismounted at the corner of the wood, when the bullet of a sharpshooter pierced his neck.[1] He fell forward on his face, and soon expired. His body was carried sorrowfully to the rear, and laid in the house of George George, on the Emmettsburg road, near the village.

General Doubleday had just arrived, and took Reynolds's place in command of the field, leaving his own division in charge of General Rowley. He ordered the "Iron Brigade" back to the woods, and

GEORGE'S HOUSE.

of Reynolds's advance division, and got into position a moment sooner than others, when the Confederates were seen within musket-range. The atmosphere was a little hazy. Hoffman turned to General Cutler, who was just behind him with a field-glass, and inquired, "Is that the enemy?" Cutler answered, "Yes," when Hoffman ordered his men to fire. Their volley was instantly followed by that of other regiments, and was returned in full measure by the foe, whose bullets killed and wounded many of the Fifty-sixth. So the BATTLE OF GETTYSBURG was begun.—See *Letter of General Cutler to the Governor of Pennsylvania*, November 5, 1863. The regimental flag of the Fifty-sixth Pennsylvania, bearing the disk badge of the First Army Corps, of red color, with seven holes in it, as evidences of the strife in which it was engaged, was presented to the Loyal League of Philadelphia, by Colonel Hoffman, on the 5th of December, 1863. In their house it is preserved as a precious memento of the gallantry of one of the most noted of the regiments of Pennsylvania. Under the leadership of Colonel (afterward General) Hoffman, it became perfect in discipline, and ever ready for daring service. In Pope's Army of Virginia, at Antietam, Fredericksburg, Chancellorsville, Gettysburg, and Grant's campaigns in 1864, it was always conspicuous. So much was the commander loved and honored by the officers and men of his regiment, that they presented him an elegant sword, in 1863, on which was inscribed the names of the battles in which the regiment had then been engaged, namely, Sulphur Springs, Gainesville, Manassas, South Mountain, Antietam, Union, Fredericksburg, Rappahannock, Chancellorsville, Beverly Ford, and Gettysburg.

STONE BARN.

[1] The Confederate sharpshooters had made a stone barn, near the western side of Willoughby's Run, and not far from the grove, at the edge of which Reynolds was making his observations, a sort of citadel, and it is believed that the bullet which slew the general went from that building. It was used, also, as a temporary hospital, and in it wounded Unionists, who had been made prisoners, were found after the Confederates fled from Gettysburg.

sent a force to attack Davis's flank, and save Hall's battery. These consisted of Cutler's two regiments, on the left of the road, which, with the Sixth Wisconsin, changed front and, led by Lieutenant Daws, charged upon Davis, who also changed front, and made a stand at the railway cutting. They not only saved the battery, but surrounded and captured Davis and his Mississippians, with their battle-flag. Meanwhile Cutler's other regiments, which had lost heavily in killed and wounded, had re-formed, and joined in the attack; and now, with his brigade unbroken, he took position farther to the right to meet the extension of the Confederate lines in that direction.

It was now meridian. The whole of the First Corps, under General Doubleday, was well posted on Seminary Ridge, and the remainder of Hill's was rapidly approaching. At the same time Rodes, with the advance division of Ewell's corps, had hastened forward from Heidlersburg, and, swinging round, took a commanding position on the ridge north of the town, connecting with Hill on his right, and seriously menacing the National right, held by Cutler. Doubleday sent Robinson's division to Cutler's aid, the brigades of Generals Baxter and Paul taking position on his right at the Mummasburg road. There a severe contest was sustained for some time, when three North Carolina regiments, under General Iverson, were captured.

The battle soon assumed far grander proportions. Thus far only the First Corps of the Nationals and the advance divisions of Hill's and Ewell's corps had been engaged. Howard's corps, animated by the sounds of battle in its front, pressed forward rapidly, and reached the field at a little past noon. Pender's division had been added to the strength of Hill's already in the struggle, and Early's division now joined that of Rodes. Howard, who had arrived in advance of his corps, had left General Steinwehr's division on Cemetery Hill, placed General Schurz, whose division was intrusted to General Schimmelpfennig, in temporary charge of the corps, and, ranking Doubleday, took the chief command of all the troops on the field of action. He placed the divisions of Barlow and Schurz to the right of the First Corps, to confront Early, and so, from the necessity of meeting an expected simultaneous attack from the north and west, the National line was lengthened and attenuated along a curve for about three miles. This was an unfortunate necessity that could not be avoided, for Howard had perceived the value of a position for the army on the series of ridges of which Cemetery Hill formed the apex of a redan, and

OLIVER O. HOWARD.

had determined to secure it, at all hazards, if his inferior numbers should be pressed back from the battle-line on the north and west of the town, which now seemed probable.

At this juncture, Rodes, near the northern extremity of **Seminary Ridge**, occupied the key-point of the entire field; and when, at about three o'clock in the afternoon, Early had pressed Barlow back, and there was a general advance of the Confederates, Rodes dashed through the weak center of the National line, and, aided by an enfilading battery, threw into confusion the right of the First and the left of the Eleventh Corps. Then the Nationals fell back in some confusion upon the village, in which they became entangled, when Early, dashing forward, captured about three thousand men, chiefly of the Eleventh Corps. The First Corps, whose left had been held firmly by Doubleday, now fell back. It brought away the artillery and ambulances from Seminary Ridge, and took position on Steinwehr's left and rear on Cemetery Hill, while the Eleventh

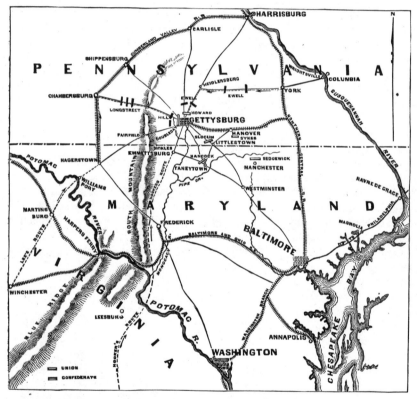

POSITION OF THE ARMY OF THE POTOMAC, JULY 1.

halted in its retreat on Steinwehr's right and front. Buford's cavalry had well covered the retreat, and when, toward sunset, Ewell's corps quietly occupied Gettysburg, and Hill's lay on Seminary Ridge, the sorely smitten Nationals were in a strong position on Cemetery Hill, anxiously awaiting the arrival of re-enforcements from the scattered corps of the Army of the Potomac, then on the way. So ended, in the defeat of the Unionists, the severe engagement[a] preliminary to the great Battle of Gettysburg, for the cautious Lee, ignorant of the number of the

* July 1, 1863.

troops of his adversary present or near at hand, prudently awaited the arrival of the rest of his army.[1]

When General Meade, at Taneytown, thirteen miles distant, heard of the death of Reynolds, he ordered General Hancock, the junior of Howard in rank, to leave his corps with General Gibbons, hasten to Gettysburg, and assume the chief command, at the same time giving him discretionary power to offer battle where the advance of the army then was, or to withdraw the troops to the line of Pipe Creek. Hancock arrived just as the beaten forces were hurrying toward Cemetery Hill. He was satisfied with the new position chosen by General Howard, and so reported to General Meade. After assisting in forming a new battle-line with the troops then present, and turning over the command to General Slocum, who arrived with his corps (Twelfth) from Littlestown at sunset, Hancock returned to head-quarters late in the evening.

Fortunately for the cause, Howard had called early upon Sickles and Slocum for aid, and both had promptly responded by moving forward. The former, with his corps (Third), was near Emmettsburg, where he had been halted in the morning by a circular letter from General Meade, ordering the advance to fall back, and the whole army to form a line of battle along the general direction of Pipe Creek, between Middleburg and Manchester.[2] Howard informed Sickles of the death of Reynolds, and the peril of the troops. Sickles was perplexed for a moment. It was full three o'clock in the afternoon when the astounding news reached him. He could not communicate with Meade, ten miles distant, without a delay that might be fatal to the National advance, so he took the responsibility of pressing forward. Just as Howard had gained position on Cemetery Hill, Sickles's van came up

and formed on the left, where it was joined by the whole corps before morning. Hancock, on his way back, met his own corps under Gibbons, which Meade had sent forward, and posted it a mile and a half in the rear of Cemetery Hill. When he reached head-quarters, at nine in the evening, he found

MEADE'S HEAD-QUARTERS.

Meade determined to make a stand at Gettysburg. He had given orders for the whole army to concentrate there, and was about leaving for the front. Both officers rode rapidly forward, and at one o'clock on the morning of the 2d,[a] Meade made his head-quarters at the house of Mrs. Lydia ₐ July, 1863. Leister, on the Taneytown road, a short distance in the rear of Cemetery Hill. Only the corps of Sykes and Sedgwick were then absent.

[1] See Lee's Report of the Battle of Gettysburg, July 31, 1863. In that report he says he had not intended to fight a general battle so far away from his base, but being "unexpectedly confronted by the Federal army, it became a matter of difficulty to withdraw through the mountains with the large trains."

[2] Meade was satisfied that the main object of his forward movement, namely, the arrest of the invasion, was accomplished, and proposed to take a defensive position and await further developments of Lee's plans.

The former, by a forced night march, arrived early in the morning, and the latter at two o'clock in the afternoon.[1]

Lee, too, had been bringing forward his troops as rapidly as possible. He made his head-quarters on Seminary Ridge, at the house of the venerable Mary Marshall, where the Chambersburg road crosses the eminence, and on the morning of the 2d of July, a greater portion of the two armies con-

fronted each other, both in a strong position, with the little village of Gettysburg, and a valley not a mile in width, between them. Meade's army lay along rocky heights, forming two sides of a triangle, with its apex at Cemetery Hill, near the town, its shorter line bending back south-easterly over Culp's Hill to Rocky Creek, and its longer line

CONFEDERATE HEAD-QUARTERS.[2]

bending back south-southwest to Round Top.[3] Howard's shattered corps, re-enforced by two thousand Vermont troops under General Stannard, occupied Cemetery Hill, supported by the divisions of Robinson and Doubleday, of the First, with Wadsworth's, of the same corps, on the right. This division joined Slocum's corps on Culp's Hill, which formed the right wing of the army. On the left of Howard, the corps of Hancock and Sickles occupied the irregular ridge from Zeigler's Grove, on Cemetery Hill, to Round Top, the latter forming the extreme of the left wing. Sykes's corps was held in reserve. Slocum's corps, re-enforced by Lockwood's Marylanders, twenty-five hundred strong, comprised about ten thousand men. Sedgwick, with over fifteen thousand men, was yet many miles away.

Lee's army then present occupied Seminary Ridge and the high ground to the left of Rock Creek, making an irregular curve along a line about five miles in length. His right, facing Sickles and Hancock, was composed of the divisions of Hood and McLaws, of Longstreet's corps. Hill's three divisions stretched from their left, so as to confront Howard on Cemetery Hill; and Ewell's, forming the left wing, occupied the village and its vicinity, the divisions of Early and Johnson extending so as to menace Wadsworth and Slocum on Culp's Hill. Stuart's cavalry had not yet arrived from Carlisle, and Buford's so roughly handled the day before, was recruiting its strength in the National rear. Such was the general disposition of the two armies on the morning of the 2d of July,[a] each having a large number of cannon in position.

a 1863.

---

[1] Sykes was not far from Hanover, twenty-three miles distant, when ordered to advance, and Sedgwick was at Manchester, more than thirty miles distant.

[2] This was the appearance of Lee's head-quarters when the writer sketched it, from the Chambersburg road, late in September, 1866. It was a substantial old stone house. Mrs. Marshall yet occupied it, and was then seventy-eight years of age.   [3] See note 1, page 59.

Both commanders were averse to taking the initiative of battle. Lee perceived the decided advantage in position which Howard had secured for the National army, it projecting like a wedge toward his center, with rocky acclivities along its front. Meade, feeling secure, had determined to leave to Lee the perilous movement of attack, if possible; and yet, early in the morning, observing Ewell stretching his line along the base of Culp's Hill, with batteries on heights in his rear, as if intending to attack, he was constrained to propose an offensive movement by Slocum with his own and the corps of Sykes, when Sedgwick should arrive. He finally sent orders for Slocum to attack without Sedgwick, but that officer considered it not advisable, and was supported in that opinion by General Warren, the Engineer-in-Chief. So the hours passed by with only a little skirmishing and now and then a shot from a battery, until late in the afternoon.

Lee, meanwhile, encouraged by the success of the previous day, and "in view of the valuable results that would ensue from the defeat of the army under General Meade,"[1] resolved to attack Sickles, who was holding the irregular ridge between Hancock and Round Top. Satisfied that a movement on him was in preparation, he had thrown a considerable portion of his corps forward to a slight elevation along the Emmettsburg road, his right, under General Humphreys, being several hundred yards in front of Hancock's left, with the line prolonged to the left by Graham's brigade of Birney's division, to a large peach-orchard belonging to John Scherfey, who lived near.[2] From that point Birney's line, formed by the brigades of De Trobriand and Ward, of his division, bent back obliquely toward Round Top, with a stony intervale behind it, and having some Massachusetts batteries on the extreme left. In this position Meade found Sickles between three and four o'clock in the afternoon. Sedgwick had arrived, after a march of thirty-five miles in nineteen hours, and been placed in reserve, and Meade had gone forward

SCHERFEY'S HOUSE.[3]

to superintend the posting of Sykes's troops on the left of Sickles, when he discovered the Third Corps well up toward the heaviest columns of the enemy, without flank supports. He deplored the perilous movement, and would probably have ordered Sickles back, had not the opening of the batteries of Lee and the pressing forward of his heavy columns to attack Sickles put an end to all deliberations. Meade could now do nothing better

---

[1] Lee's Report.

[2] General Birney sent out a regiment of sharpshooters, under Colonel Berdan, who advanced to a wood a mile beyond the Emmettsburg road, reconnoitering the Confederates. Berdan reported that the foe was moving in three columns, under cover of the woods, with the evident intention of turning the National left. It was this correct report which caused Sickles to advance his corps. The peach-orchard mentioned in the text was at an angle formed by the Emmettsburg road, and a cross lane from the Taneytown road, which entered it and ended there.

[3] Scherfey's was a brick house, on the west side of the Emmettsburg road, and, during the battle, was alternately in the possession of the National and Confederate troops. The family left the house when it was apparent that a battle was impending. The engraving is from a sketch made by the author in the autumn of 1866. The house, notwithstanding its exposed position, was very little injured.

than to give Sickles all possible support, for the battle was opened and the whole army was deeply concerned.

Lee had perceived this projection of Meade's left, and taken advantage of it. He had prepared to turn that flank of the National army, and now hoped to take its line in reverse, drive it from its strong position, and achieve a glorious victory. He directed Longstreet, his right-arm of dependence since Jackson's death, to make the attempt, while Ewell should attack Meade's right, and Hill menace his center, so as to prevent re-enforcements being sent to the left. Longstreet moved quickly and vigorously, under cover of heavy guns on Seminary Ridge and at other points. He sent his right division, under the dashing General Hood, to strike the salient of Sickles's bent line, at the peach-orchard, held by eight regiments of the divisions of Birney and Humphreys, and then to assail De Trobriand and Ward on the left, furiously. This was done effectively with the assistance of the left of McLaws, supported by Anderson. After a severe struggle, during which the tide of victory ebbed and flowed, the Confederates gained the key-point at the peach-orchard. Sickles, who was in the front of battle, had called for re-enforcements, when Meade ordered General Sykes to furnish them. General Barnes's division of the Fifth Corps was sent forward; but nothing could then save the left, which had been fighting gallantly against odds, from being pushed back by the pressure of more than twenty-five thousand men hurled vigorously upon it. After a hard struggle, Hood's right pushed for the wooded hollow, between the peak known as Round Top and a rocky eminence of less altitude, called Little Round Top, on which Birney's left had rested, but was then uncovered. To secure this hill was of infinite importance to both commanders, and for its possession a severe struggle ensued. Meade, as we have seen, ordered Sykes forward to assist Birney in saving it, if possible.[1] Warren had just reached its summit when Birney's line was bending and Barnes was advancing. He found the signal officers

SIGNAL-STATION ON LITTLE ROUND TOP.

at their rocky post folding their flags for flight. He ordered them to keep their signals waving, as if a host was behind them, and took the responsibility of detaching General Vinçent's brigade[2] and Hazlett's battery from Barnes's division, with the One Hundred and Fortieth New York in support, and hurrying them to the crown of Little Round Top. The cannon, dragged with great labor by hand up the steep, rocky acclivity, were speedily placed in battery behind hastily-thrown-up breastworks of stones. These forces were there just in time to save the ridge from seizure by Hood's

---

[1] Sykes was tardy in sending help to Sickles. Birney sent an officer to him to urge him to send forward a division at once, as the peril was imminent. Sykes said "he would be up in time: that his men were making coffee and were tired." It was an hour before they were up, when it was too late.—Birney's testimony before the *Committee on the Conduct of the War.*

[2] Composed of the Sixteenth Michigan, Forty-fourth New York, Eighty-third Pennsylvania, and Twentieth Maine.

Texans, who were at that moment scaling its rough slopes from the glen and among the huge masses of rocks on the bold western face of the hill. Never was there a wilder place for combat, and never was there a combat more fierce than was seen there, on that hot

THE DEVIL'S DEN.[1]

July evening, with blazing musketry, the clangor of steel as bayonets crossed in close and deadly strife, and hand-to-hand struggles with clubbed fire-arms and jagged stones. For half an hour this terrible conflict went on, when a charge from the Twentieth Maine, under Colonel Chamberlain, hurled the Texans from the hill. General Weed's brigade of Ayres's division of the Fifth Corps (to which Hazlett's battery belonged) had come up and taken position on Vincent's right, and the rocky citadel of the National left was secured, but at the cost of the lives of Generals Vincent and Weed, Lieutenant Hazlett, and scores of less prominent soldiers.[2]

During the struggle on the extreme left, there was also a fierce contest more toward the center, which assisted in securing Little Round Top to the Nationals. The brigades of Tilton and Sweitser, of Barnes's division, had been sent to the aid of Birney, and shared in the disaster that befell that line. When it fell back, the remainder of Sickles's corps (Humphrey's division and Graham's brigade) swung round back by the left, its right still clinging to the Emmettsburg road, the battery of Major McGilvray at the same time firing and falling back. Then Caldwell's division was advanced from Hancock's front to check the incoming Confederates, and a patch of open woods and wheat-fields, skirting a cross lane from the Taneytown to the Emmettsburg road, between the peach-orchard and Little Round Top, became a sanguinary battle-field. Caldwell advanced gallantly, with the brigades of Cross and Kelly in the front. Presently his second line, composed of the brigades of Brooke and Zook, were pushed forward. The strife was fierce, and in it Cross[3] and Zook were mortally wounded, and

---

[1] This little sketch shows a mass of rocks forming a sort of dark inclosure, which is called the Devil's Den. It gives a good idea of the masses of huge rocks among which the Confederates struggled up the steep slopes of Little Round Top. This heap was in front of Hazlett's battery, a little way down the hill.

[2] General Vincent was killed while urging on his men in the struggle, and General Weed was slain at Hazlett's battery, on the summit of Little Round Top. Seeing his commander fall, Lieutenant Hazlett hastened to his side. The expiring general seemed desirous of telling something, and, while Hazlett was bending over him with his ear near his lips, the bullet of a sharpshooter killed the lieutenant, and he fell upon the then dead body of his commander.

[3] This was the gallant Colonel Edward E. Cross, of the famous "Fighting Fifth" New Hampshire (see note 1, page 411, volume II.), who was now in command of a brigade. He was one of the most fearless and efficient officers in the army, and was greatly beloved by his troops. A few months before the battle of Gettysburg his regiment presented him an elegant sword, "as a token of their affection and admiration of his character as an officer, after eighteen months' service under his command." In a letter to the author, a month before the battle of Chancellorsville, speaking of an illustrated journal having an unpublished biographical sketch of him, he playfully said: "They are doubtless waiting, with commendable patience, for me to be killed. However, having received *nine* wounds in the present war, and three in other wars, I am not afraid of rebel bullets." He lived a few hours after receiving his fatal wound. His last words were: "I did hope I would live to see peace, and our country restored. I have done my duty. I think the boys will miss me. All my effects I give to my mother. Oh, welcome, Death! Say farewell to all." Then his mind wandered. He commenced giving commands, when he expired.

Brooke severely so. Firmly the Nationals held the line for some time against odds, assisted by the regulars, under General Ayres, on the left; but Caldwell was finally compelled to fall back, with a loss of nearly one-half his division. Ayres's was enveloped by the foe, but cut his way out gallantly. Then there was a renewed struggle for Little Round Top, when, at about six o'clock, six regiments of the division of Pennsylvania Reserves, of the Fifth 'Corps, led by the gallant General Crawford,[1] their commander, swept down the northwestern side of Little Round Top with a tremendous

shout, and drove the Confederates across the rocky intervale at its base and through the woods to the Emmettsburg road, taking three hundred of them prisoners. In this charge the Confederate General Barksdale was killed. Little Round Top was encircled by breastworks that evening, and twelve 30-pound Parrott guns were placed in battery on its summit, before morning.

VIEW ON LITTLE ROUND TOP.[2]

When the line of Humphreys and Graham swung round, the former, as we have observed, kept his right firmly on the Emmettsburg road. So soon as Sickles's left was disposed of, the victors hastened to strike this remainder, when Hancock sent to its support two regiments from Gibbons's division (Fifteenth Massachusetts and Eighty-second New York), and advanced Willard's brigade of Hays's division to fill a wide gap. At that moment Hill ceased threatening, and advancing in heavy force from Seminary Ridge, fell upon Humphreys and quickly pushed him back, with a loss of half his men and three guns. In this onset Willard was killed, and Sickles had a leg so shattered that he lost it. Birney then took command of the corps.

DANIEL E. SICKLES.

The Confederates, elated by their successes, dashed like turbulent waves up to the base of the ridge occupied

---

[1] See page 447, volume II.

[2] This is a view of the crest of Little Round Top, at the place of the battery, where General Weed and Lieutenant Hazlett were killed. In the distance is seen Zeigler's Grove, on Cemetery Hill, where Hancock's battery was placed; and near by, the village of Gettysburg and the plain over which the Confederates swept to their attacks.

by the Nationals, fighting most desperately, and throwing themselves recklessly upon supposed weak points of their antagonist's line.   In this encounter Meade led troops in person, and everywhere inspirited his men by
his presence.   Finally, just at sunset, a general charge was made, under the
direction of Hancock, chiefly by fresh troops under General Doubleday, who
had hastened to his assistance from the rear of Cemetery Hill.   These, with
Humphreys's shattered regiments, drove the Confederates back, and a portion of Doubleday's division, pressing up nearly to the opposing lines, recaptured four guns which had been lost.   At twilight, the battle on the left and
left center ended, when a new line was formed by the divisions of Robinson
and Doubleday, and troops from the Twelfth Corps brought up by General
Williams who was in temporary command of it, Slocum having charge of
the entire right wing.

When the sounds of battle were dying away on the National left, they
were suddenly renewed on the right.   Lee, as we have observed, had directed
Ewell to attack Slocum, simultaneously with Longstreet's assault on Sickles.
But it was sunset before he began.   Then he opened a heavy artillery fire
upon Howard's batteries in the field in front of the Cemetery, and under its
cover moved the corps of Early and Johnson to an attack.   The efforts of
the former were directed against Howard's right, and a body of troops,
known as the Louisiana Tigers, were ordered to storm the batteries on
Cemetery Hill, and attempt to break the National center.   Never was an
assault more gallantly made.   They charged up the slope in the face of a
heavy storm of canister and shrapnell shot, to the muzzles of the guns, pushing completely through one battery (Weidrich's) into another (Ricketts's),
and demanding the surrender of both.   The gunners fought desperately
with every missile at hand, and beat them back, until Carroll's brigade, sent
by Hancock to Howard's assistance, helped to repulse the Confederates and
secure the integrity of the National line.

In the mean time Ewell's left division, under Johnson, had pushed up
the little vale leading from Rocky Creek to Spangler's Spring, in the rear of
Culp's Hill, to strike the weakened right of the Nationals, which the divisions of Williams and Geary had occupied.   A greater portion of these
troops had been engaged in beating back the Confederates on the left, and
only the brigade of General Greene remained, with Wadsworth's division
within supporting distance on the left.   Johnson moved under cover of the
woods and the deepening twilight, and expected an easy conquest, by which
a way would be opened for the remainder of Ewell's corps to the National
rear; but he found a formidable antagonist in Greene's brigade.   The assault
was made with great vigor, but for more than two hours, Greene, assisted
by a part of Wadsworth's command, fought the assailants, strewing the
wooded slope in front of the works with the Confederate dead and wounded,
and holding his position firmly.   Finally his antagonist penetrated the works
near Spangler's Spring, from which the troops had been temporarily withdrawn, but, having been taught prudence by the events of the day, they did
not attempt to go farther.   So ended, at near ten o'clock at
night,[a] the second day of the battle, when nearly forty thousand   [a] July 2,
                                                                            1863.
men of the two armies, who were "effective" thirty-six hours
before, were dead or wounded.   The advantage seemed to be with the Con-

federates, for they held the ground in advance of Gettysburg occupied by the Nationals the previous day, and also that on which Sickles offered battle. "These partial successes," said Lee, in his report, "determined me to continue the assault next day."

When all was quiet, after the battle, General Meade and commanders held a consultation, when it was agreed to remain and accept battle again in the morning. The National line, with the exception of the small portion on the extreme right occupied by Johnson's men, was intact, and held its

DEFENSES ON CULP'S HILL.[1]

original and strong position on the rocky crests, from Wolf's Hill to Round Top. Slocum's corps was again concentrated on Culp's Hill, with a strong breastwork of logs and earth in front of it; and Shaler's brigade, of Sedgwick's corps, and Lockwood's Marylanders, were placed near it. Pickett, with three brigades (mostly Virginians), who came from Chambersburg, joined Longstreet early in the morning, when the batteries of the latter were advanced to the line of the Emmettsburg road, from which he had driven Sickles. Lee's general plan of attack was unchanged, excepting the employment of a portion of Hill's corps in support of Longstreet. He confidently expected Ewell would follow up his victory in the morning, when the National line might be assailed in front, flank, and rear.

Provision was made by Meade during the night to drive out the intruders on the National right, who had been strengthened for an early advance. A heavy artillery force was placed in that direction, and firing was commenced at four o'clock in the morning, under cover of which the divisions of Williams and Geary, and Shaler's brigade, moved to the attack. For four hours a desperate struggle went on, when, by a charge of Geary's division, the Confederates were driven, and the right flank was made secure. Meade, too quick for Lee, had foiled his efforts on the National right to obtain a victory. Ewell was repulsed and firmly held in check, and the Round Top was impregnable; so Lee determined to assail Meade's center with a force that should crush all opposition. The whole forenoon was spent in preparations for the move-

---

[1] On Culp's Hill, as on Round Top, piles of rocks, in several places, made natural defenses for the assailed Unionists. The above picture, made from a sketch drawn by the author a few days after the battle, shows the then appearance of the line of breastworks, of which some of the rocks were a part. This scene was at the point where the One Hundred and Fiftieth (Dutchess County) New York fought.

ment. Lee's superior artillery force was placed in advantageous positions, and at noon he had one hundred and forty-five cannon in battery along the line occupied by Longstreet and Hill. Meade, too, had been preparing for the expected shock of battle. General Hunt, his chief of artillery, had worked all night in arranging the great guns from Cemetery Hill to Little Round Top, where it was evident the blow was to be given, and he judiciously posted artillery in reserve under Colonel R. O. Tyler.[1]

At midday there was an ominous silence, during which General Lee entered Pennsylvania College building, which he was using for a hospital, ascended to the cupola, and, in violation of the acknowledged principles of honor in military life, stood under the sacred yellow flag which all civilized warriors respect as a protection to the sick and wounded, and where he was sure of safety from personal harm, and with his field-glass leisurely reconnoitered Meade's position.[2] His observations there determined him to aim his chief blow at Hancock's position on Cemetery Hill, and, giving the signal at one o'clock, one hundred and fifteen of his cannon opened a rapid cross fire upon the devoted point. Just behind it was Meade's head-quarters, where shot and shell made many a pit and furrow in the grounds around it, and endangered the life of every living thing connected with it.[3] A hundred National guns replied, and for the space of two hours the thunders of more than two hundred cannon shook Gettysburg and the surrounding country with their fearful detonations.

GEORGE PICKETT.

Then, like a stream of fiery lava, the Confederate infantry, in a line full three miles in length, preceded by a host of skirmishers, flowed swiftly over the undulating plain, threatening to consume every obstacle in its track. Behind this assaulting column was a heavy reserve. Pickett, with his Virginians, led the van in a charge upon Cemetery Hill, supported on his right by Wilcox's brigade, and on his left by a brigade of North Carolinians, of Heth's division, commanded by General Pettigrew; in all about fifteen thousand strong. The batteries had now ceased firing—Meade's first, because his available ammunition was failing, and there was a momentary lull in the tempest.

---

[1] The batteries of Bancroft, Dilger, Eakin, Wheeler, Hill, and Taft, under Major Osborne, were placed in the cemetery, where the kind and thoughtful General Howard had caused the tombstones, and such monuments as could possibly be moved, to be laid flat on the ground, to prevent their being injured by shot and shell. On the left of the cemetery, near Zeigler's Grove, were Hancock's batteries, under Woodruff, Brown, Cushing, Arnold, and Rorty, commanded by Captain Hazzard. Next to these, on the left, was Thomas's battery, with those of Thompson, Phillips, Hart, Rauth, Dow, Ames, and Sterling, under McGilvray, in reserve. On the extreme left were the batteries of Gibbs and Hazlett, the latter now commanded by Lieutenant Rittenhouse.

[2] Testimony of officers of the College.

[3] Samuel Wilkeson, then a correspondent of a New York journal, made the following record of the scene at head-quarters, of which he was an eye-witness: "Every size and form of shell known to British and to American gunnery, shrieked, whirled, moaned, and whistled, and wrathfully fluttered over our ground. As

The silence was soon broken by the awful roll of musketry. So compactly did the assailing force move, that its front did not cover more than two of Hancock's brigades, which were so reduced that they did not number, in the aggregate, more than six thousand men. Shot and shell from Hancock's batteries made fearful lanes through the ranks, yet they moved steadily on, and pressed up to within musket-range of the National line of infantry, where Gibbons was in command, Hancock being wounded. Half concealed, the infantry of the Second Corps kept silence. Suddenly Stannard's Ver- monters, of Doubleday's command, posted in a little grove, opened terrible volleys on Pickett's flank, doubling it a trifle. Yet he pressed onward, when the divisions of Hayes and Gibbons opened an appalling and contin- uous fire upon him. This was too much. Pettigrew's North Carolinians wavered a moment, fought well for awhile, and then gave way, when two thousand of them were made prisoners, and, with fifteen battle-flags, became trophies of victory for Hayes and his divisions.[1] Still Pickett moved on with his Virginians, and, with the greatest courage and fortitude, his men, following Generals Armistead and Kemper, scaled Cemetery Hill, burst through Hancock's line, and planted the Confederate flag on a stone wall. In this onset they drove back a portion of General Webb's brigade.[2] These were soon rallied, and, with other troops,[3] so effectively filled the breach that Pickett could go no further. At the same time Stannard's Vermont brigade, of Doubleday's division, opened a destructive fire on Pickett's flank, which broke the spirit of his men, and very soon twenty-five hundred of them were prisoners, and with them twelve battle-flags were captured.[4] Three-fourths of the gallant brigade were dead or captives. Wilcox, who failed to attack until Pickett was repulsed, met a similar fate in the loss of men, being also struck in the flank and ruined by Stannard's Vermonters.

---

many as six in a second, constantly two in a second, bursting and screaming over and around head-quarters, made a very hell of fire that amazed the oldest officers. They burst in the yard (see picture on page 63)—burst next to the fence, on both sides garnished, as usual, with hitched horses of aids and orderlies. The fastened animals reared and plunged with terror. Then one fell, and then another—sixteen lay dead and mangled before the firing ceased, still fastened by their halters. These brute victims of a cruel war touched all hearts. . . . . A shell tore up the little step at the head-quarters cottage, and ripped bags of oats as with a knife. Another car- ried off one of its two pillars. Soon a spherical case burst opposite the open door—another ripped through the low garret. . . . . Shells through the two lower rooms. A shell in the chimney that fortunately did not explode. Shells in the yard ; the air thicker and fuller, and more deafening with the howling and whirring of these infer- nal missiles."

It seems proper here to say that the correspondents of the public press, and the artists of the illustrated papers, justly rank among the heroes of the war. They braved every hardship and peril of the war—often under fire, and in the most dangerous positions during battles, in the business of their vocation as observers and recorders of events. And it is interesting to observe how accurate, as a general rule, were the descriptions of many of these Froissarts of the Civil War, even in the statistics of battles. They were generally able and con- scientious men, and to them the future historian and romancer must look for the most vivid and picturesque features of that great drama of the nineteenth century.

[1] These were mostly raw troops, and generally behaved well. They had been deceived, it is said, with the assurance that they would meet only Pennsylvania militia, but when the terrible fire was opened upon them, the fearful cry spread through their ranks, " The Army of the Potomac !"—See Dr. Jacobs's *Rebel Invasion of Maryland and Pennsylvania*, page 43, and Swinton's *Campaigns of the Army of the Potomac*, page 359. Pettigrew's brigade was terribly shattered when it gave way. Its commander was badly wounded, and all but one of its field officers were dead or maimed. It fell back under the command of a major. It was about 3,000 strong when it went into the battle, but only 800 answered to their names at roll-call the next morning.

[2] Sixty-ninth, Seventy-first, and Seventy-second Pennsylvania.

[3] The brigades of Hall and Harrow ; the One Hundred and Fifty-first Pennsylvania, and Twentieth New York, under Colonel Gates ; the Nineteenth Massachusetts, Colonel Devereux, and Wallon's Forty-second New York.

[4] General Garnett was killed, General Armistead was mortally wounded, and General Kemper was badly hurt.

At about this time, Meade, who felt anxious about his weaker left, had reached Little Round Top, and ordered Crawford to advance upon the Confederate right. The brigade of McCandless and a regiment of Fisher's pushed toward the Emmettsburg road, driving before them an unsupported battery upon a brigade of Hood's division, which made a feeble resistance and fled, leaving two hundred and sixty men (Georgians) as captives, with their battle-flag. In this sortie nearly the whole ground lost by Sickles the day before was recovered, with seven thousand small arms, a Napoleon gun, and the wounded Unionists, who had lain, uncared for, twenty-four hours.

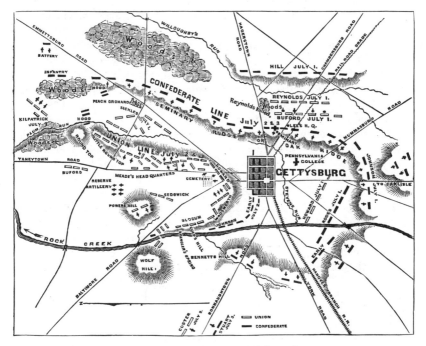

BATTLES AT GETTYSBURG, JULY 1, 2, AND 3.

Thus, at near sunset, ended in victory for the Nationals, the decisive BATTLE OF GETTYSBURG—a battle that had been fought by both armies with amazing courage and fortitude. The actors in it were chiefly of the artillery and infantry arms of the service. The cavalry force of each remained on the borders of the great conflict, yet, on the part of the Nationals, they rendered very important service in threatening the wings, the trains, and the communications of the opposing army, neutralizing the power of large bodies of infantry, and foiling Lee in his efforts to turn Meade's flanks. Buford, as we have seen, was in the National rear, while Kilpatrick and Gregg were on the flanks of the foe.[1] Specially important

---

[1] Kilpatrick, who had been out trying to intercept Stuart's cavalry on their way to join Lee, had a severe fight with them at Hunterstown, on the evening of the 2d of July. It was chiefly an artillery duel by the horse batteries of each. The Confederates were worsted, when Kilpatrick, according to an order, hastened to Two Taverns, on the Baltimore turnpike, in the rear of Meade's army. On the morning of the 3d, these troopers were on and near the Emmettsburg road, on the right and rear of the Confederates, and at eleven o'clock, made a

were the services of Merritt and Farnsworth, of Kilpatrick's command, on
the Confederate right, for they prevented Hood from turning
July, 1863. Meade's left during the terrible battle on the afternoon of the 3d.[a]

Both armies were severely shattered by losses and weakened by exhaustion,[1] but each rested on the night after the battle, in ignorance of the real
condition and destination of the other. Lee felt that his situation was a
perilous one,[2] and early in the evening he withdrew Ewell's division from
Gettysburg and the hills southeast of the town, and began preparations for
a retreat toward the Potomac, by way of the Cumberland Valley. During
that night and all the next day,[b] while his army remained on
[b] *July 4.* Seminary Ridge, he sent away as many of his sick and wounded
as possible, with his enormous wagon-train of baggage, stores, and plunder,
and troops of horses, mules, and cattle, captured in Pennsylvania.[3] These
took the Chambersburg and Hagerstown roads, and were followed on the
evening of the 4th by the whole army along the latter highway, by the
village of Fairfield,[4] carrying with them about four thousand prisoners.
A severe rain-storm had commenced at the close of the day, and the flight
was distressing to all who participated in it.

When it was made evident by the reports of cavalry scouts, on the night
of the 3d,[c] that Lee was about to retreat, General Meade was
[c] *July.* urged by some of his officers to make an immediate advance on
the Confederate army. Great responsibility makes men conservative and
cautious. It was only about twenty days since the command of the Army
of the Potomac, at a most critical time in its history, with all the inherent
responsibilities of the act, had been laid upon General Meade. This, and a
consideration of the shattered condition of that army after the great battle,
made him cautious and prudent, and he would not consent to a renewal
of the conflict at Gettysburg. So he lay there, quietly awaiting the development of the disposition and plans of his antagonist, until Sunday morning,
the 5th, when it was well known that Lee's whole army, excepting a few
pickets, was on its way toward the Potomac. Then, having been re-enforced

---

dash for the capture of their train. A heavy force of infantry was immediately sent to co-operate with some of
Stuart's cavalry in confronting this new danger, when Generals Farnsworth and Merritt, acting as if they had
heavy infantry supports, dashed forward over fences, and drove their foes back in much confusion. In the last of
the charges by which the result was reached, Farnsworth was slain, and with him many of his brave men. The
troops engaged in this affair, which greatly weakened the Confederate attack on Meade's lines, were the First
Vermont, First Virginia, and Eighteenth Pennsylvania Cavalry.

[1] When the battle ceased, the ammunition of the Army of the Potomac was becoming scarce; and of the
reserves, only a single brigade of Sedgwick's corps had not, in some way, participated in the battle. The Army
of Northern Virginia was equally exhausted. The National loss in men, from the morning of the 1st until the
evening of the 3d of July, was reported by Meade to be 23,186, of whom 2,834 were killed, 13,709 were wounded,
and 6,643 were missing. A greater portion of the latter were prisoners. Lee, as usual, made no report of his
losses. He spoke of them as "severe." A careful estimate, made from various statements, places the number
at about 30,000, of whom about 14,000 were prisoners. Generals Barksdale and Garnett were killed. Generals
Armistead, Pender, and Semmes were mortally wounded; Generals Hood and Trimble were severely wounded,
and Generals Anderson, Hampton, Heth, Jones, Pettigrew, Jenkins, and Kemper, not so badly.

[2] "Owing to the strength of the enemy's position, and the reduction of our ammunition," Lee said, in his
report, "a renewal of the engagement could not be hazarded, and the difficulty of procuring supplies rendered it
impossible to continue longer where we were."

Lieutenant-Colonel Freemantle, of the British army, who was with Lee, says, in his narrative (page 269), that
it was "difficult to exaggerate the critical state of affairs, as they appeared about this time," and declares that
"General Lee and his officers were evidently impressed with a sense of the situation."

[3] In his diary, July 4, Colonel Freemantle made the following record: "Wagons, horses, mules, and cattle,
captured in Pennsylvania, the solid advantages of this campaign, have been passing slowly along the road all
day; those taken by Ewell are particularly admired."

[4] See map on page 62.

the day before by the advance division of General Couch's militia, who had come up from the Susquehanna under General W. F. Smith, he ordered Sedgwick's comparatively fresh corps to commence a direct pursuit, and sent Kilpatrick to harrass the fugitives and destroy their train on the Chambersburg road. The greater part of the army remained to rest, and to succor the wounded and bury the dead.

Sedgwick overtook the rear-guard of the Confederates ten miles from Gettysburg, at the Fairfield Pass of South Mountain, and reported to General Meade that it was easily defensible by a small force, against him. Meade recalled Sedgwick, and determined to put his whole force in pursuit, in a flank movement, by way of Emmettsburg and Middletown, and the lower passes of the South Mountain range, through which he hoped to strike his antagonist's flank. He ordered General French at Frederick to send a force to Turner's Gap,[1] and with his main body to re-occupy Harper's Ferry. Leaving a brigade each of cavalry and infantry to harrass and delay the Confederate rear, he left Gettysburg, with a greater portion of the army, on the 6th, and crossed the mountains into the Antietam Valley. But he moved so cautiously and tardily that when, on the 12th,[a] he overtook Lee, the latter was strongly intrenched on ^{a} July, 1863. a ridge covering the Potomac from Williamsport to Falling Waters, waiting for the flood in the river, caused by the recent rains, to subside, and allow him to cross into Virginia. Unfortunately for Lee, General French had anticipated Meade's order, re-occupied Harper's Ferry, and sent a cavalry force to destroy the pontoon bridges which the Confederate commander had left, under guard, at Falling Waters. But for the accomplishment of this destruction, Lee's army might have passed over on the day of its arrival at Williamsport; but he was compelled to make preparations anew, and also to present a bold front to his pursuers. He showed so much strength when they approached, that Meade spent the 12th in intrenching and reconnoitering. He desired to attack Lee the next morning, but a majority of his commanders, whom he consulted late that evening, decided against it. Unwilling to take the responsibility, he allowed his army to remain inactive all the next day. That night,[b] Lee having constructed another bridge at Falling Waters, passed the corps of Longstreet and ^{b} July 13, 14. Hill quietly over it in the gloom, while Ewell's forded the river above Williamsport. The vigilant Kilpatrick had observed the movement toward the bridge, and struck Hill's rear-guard under the unfortunate Pettigrew, drove it to the river, killed one hundred and twenty-five of the men, and made fifteen hundred of them prisoners, with three battle-flags. Pettigrew was mortally wounded, and Major Webb, who led the Sixth Michigan Cavalry in a charge on the occasion, was killed. Kilpatrick's total loss was one hundred and five men. Thus ended, in utter discomfiture and repulse, Lee's formidable invasion of Maryland and Pennsylvania in the summer of 1863.[2]

---

[1] See page 471, volume II.

[2] In the preparation of this narrative of the events of the invasion, the writer has availed himself, in addition to personal observations, and the accounts, written and oral, given him by actors in the scenes, of the official reports of the opposing commanders and their subordinate officers; narratives of correspondents with the armies, and of Professor Jacobs and others who have published interesting monographs concerning the battle. Special acknowledgment is due to Colonel J. B. Batchelder, for his communications to the writer on the subject, and his admirable isometrical drawing of the battle-field of Gettysburg, whose accuracy is attested by General Meade and his fellow-commanders on that occasion. It is wonderfully minute in its

The writer visited the battle-ground at Gettysburg a week after the conflict, and again in the autumn of 1866, each time with traveling companions already mentioned in these pages. On the first occasion we encountered many difficulties after leaving Philadelphia, first in trying unsuccessfully to reach Gettysburg by way of Harrisburg, and then by detention in Baltimore, the Northern Central railway being in the exclusive service of the Government for some days after the battle. Having "friends at court," we gained, through them, permission to take passage in a Government train, which we did at ten o'clock on a pleasant morning, in company with Mr. Barclay, the philanthropist spoken of,[1] members, of both sexes, of the Sanitary and Christian Commissions,[2] and friends of slain and badly wounded soldiers.

On leaving Baltimore, we saw the evidences of the hasty preparations to repel the invaders;[3] and on the way to Hanover Junction we passed several of the block-houses constructed for the defense of the bridges on the railway.[4] We dined at the Junction, where lay the charred remains of a train of cars, destroyed by the invaders, and toward evening arrived at Hanover. There we tarried an hour, and the writer visited the scene of the cavalry fight on the 29th of June, and made the sketch on page 58. We reached Gettysburg at eight o'clock in the evening, and gladly accepted the kind hospitality of the family of a leading citizen (David M. McConaughy), whose services before the battle, in imparting information, were acknowledged by General Meade. He, like all other patriotic citizens of Gettysburg, had opened his house to the strangers who thronged the town; and on the following morning[a] he kindly accompanied us to the important points on the battle-field, of whose scenes he had been an eye and ear-witness. With him, in his light carriage, the writer was privileged to spend the entire day in an inspection of the theater of the drama chiefly within the National lines. We rode out on the Bounaughtown road, across Rock Creek, to the heights on which Ewell's guns were planted; and along a by-road we went down by the base of Wolf Hill,

[a] July 11, 1863.

A MONUMENT.[5]

recrossed the creek where the southern slopes of Culp's Hill touch it, and there began to see the evidences of the struggle of Slocum's corps with the foe on the right of the National line. Unexploded conical shells were half-buried in the oak-trees, whose branches were cut and bruised by others; and the trunks of nearly all were scarred so thickly with bullet-marks for ten or fifteen feet from the ground, that scarcely an inch together of the untouched bark remained. Over the rocky slope of Culp's Hill, up which the Confederates

details, showing the movements, even of regiments, during the conflict, and giving a perfect impression of the event. [1] See note 3, page 49.

[2] The blessed labors of the Sanitary and Christian Commissions everywhere, will be hereafter mentioned. We found the members of each in full force, when we were at Gettysburg, with supplies of every kind needful for the suffering bodies and minds of the soldiers. The Christian Commission distributed about a thousand boxes of stores and publications at Gettysburg. The Sanitary Commission was equally active there.

[3] See page 55. [4] See page 55

[5] This is a sketch of one of the monuments mentioned in the text. It was a rough piece of a sapling, with a figure 3 on a smooth spot, which referred to a registry made, that would indicate the number of bodies buried there. Great care was taken by the Unionists to have every one of the four thousand dead bodies found on the field, buried, and the places of burial indicated.

pressed in front of Slocum's lines, fragments of clothing, accouterments, shells, and fire-arms were strewed among many new-made graves, some in the form of trenches, in which a number of the dead were buried together, with some rude monument to mark the spot.

Passing over Culp's Hill among the *debris* of battle, along the line of breastworks depicted on page 70, we came to the open field where Wadsworth was stationed, between Culp's Hill and Cemetery Hill. There were the mounds of several batteries, and on the wooded slope in front were the marks of a severe struggle. Southward we could see Round Top, nearly three miles distant, and toward it we rode by way of the Cemetery, whose fences were gone and grounds were furrowed by shot and shell. There we saw the result of Howard's foresight and kindness, in the preservation of the monuments he had caused to be laid prone on the ground. One granite shaft, standing upright, had received a spent ball point-blank, which bruised but did not break the stone. In all that region the effects of the heavy cannonade on the 3d[1] were visible at every turn. The bodies of the slain soldiers were buried, but those of the horses, some untouched and some a-con-

SCENE NEAR THE TANEYTOWN ROAD.

suming by fire, were scattered thickly over the fields, especially where Hancock's batteries were, and along the Taneytown road, near Meade's headquarters. No less than eight dead horses were lying near a farm-house (Mr. Trossel's), as seen in the engraving; and during our ride within the Union lines we saw the remains of not less than two hundred of these noble brutes, many of them on fire, the smoke of which, with the effluvium of decomposition everywhere, filled the whole region of Gettysburg with unpleasant odors.

After sketching Meade's head-quarters,[2] we passed down the Taneytown road a short distance, and turned into a rough by-way that led over to the Emmettsburg road, at the northern slope of Little Round Top. From that eminence we had an excellent general view of the battle-field between it and Gettysburg. As we descended to the road, we saw the graves of several Massachusetts soldiers, at the heads of which their companions had placed small boards,

GRAVES ON THE FIELD OF GETTYSBURG.

with the name and regiment marked on each, and planted a small evergreen close by, a tender memorial of heavenly emotions in the midst of the hellish deeds of war. We passed on to the peach-orchard so prominent in the records of the battle, and then rode back to Gettysburg, observing the fields on our right, over which Pickett swept with his division to the attack of Hancock,[1] thickly strewn with the graves of men and horses, the former marked by small head-boards, and the latter distinguished by large mounds.[2]

Expecting to revisit Gettysburg soon, we did not then go over the Confederate line of battle. The remainder of the day was spent in visiting the head-quarters of the benevolent Commissions, already mentioned; the hospitals of the National wounded, in the town, and the College where the Confederate sick and wounded lay. Sad, indeed, were the sights that met us.

 Many, mostly young men, were maimed in every conceivable way by every kind of weapon and missile, the most fiendish of which was an explosive and a poisoned bullet, represented in the engravings a little more than half the size of the originals, procured from the battle-field there by the writer. These were sent by the Confederates. Whether any were ever used by the Nationals, the writer is not informed. One (figure *a*) was made to explode in the body *a* of a man, and the other (figure *b*) to leave a deadly poison *b* in him, whether the bullet lodged in or passed through him.[3]

Among the Confederates wounded at the College were boys of tender

---

[1] See page 72.   [2] See page 77.

[3] Figure *a* represents the explosive bullet. The perpendicular stem, with a piece of thin copper hollowed, and a head over it, of bullet metal, fitted a cavity in the bullet proper, below it, as seen in the engraving. In the bottom of the cavity was fulminating powder. When the bullet struck, the momentum would cause the copper inverted disk to flatten, and allow the point of the stem to strike and explode the fulminating powder, when the bullet would be rent into fragments which would lacerate the victim. In figure *b* the bullet proper was hollowed, into which was inserted another, also hollow, containing poison. The latter, being loose, would slip out and remain in the victim's body or limb, with its freight of poison, if the bullet proper should pass through.

It may be here remarked that wonder is often expressed because of the comparatively small loss of life in great battles. The explanation lies in the fact that a great proportion of the combatants are highly excited at the time of action, and as a general rule, when raising the musket to fire, bring it up with a jerk that makes the elevation of the piece, when fired, too great. The writer observed in the woods on Culp's Hill, between the lines of combatants, the bullet marks on the trees were thicker at a height above a man's head than below it. Again, in all armies there are a vast number of cowards and incompetents, who actually "lose their senses" in action, and perform accordingly. In a report of the number and condition of the small arms picked up on the field of Gettysburg, appears the curious fact, that of 27,554 gathered up, at least 24,000 were loaded. One-half contained two loads each, and many contained ten loads, showing that the bearers of them had loaded but did not fire. In some the balls were put in before the powder, and in many instances a large number of cartridges were found in one musket, having been put in without being torn. In one percussion smooth-bore

AUSTRIAN GUN AT GETTYSBURG.

musket were found 22 bullets, 62 buckshot, and a corresponding quantity of powder, mixed together. It has been estimated by experts, that a soldier in battle fires away, on an average, his weight in lead, before he kills a man.

WOUNDED CANNON AT GETTYSBURG.

The effect of blows upon fire-arms in battle is often very curious. Lieutenant C. A. Alvord, Jr., of General Caldwell's staff, who was in the Battle of Gettysburg, has in his possession an Austrian musket, which was struck by a cannon-ball while in the hands of a soldier, bent in the form seen in the engraving, and nearly every screw of the piece wrenched from its position, without being knocked from the hand of the bearer. The writer saw in the street at Gettysburg, a 12-pound brass cannon, with a bruise at the

age, and men who had been forced into the ranks against their wills ;[1] and a large portion of them were even then satisfied that on the part of the slave-holders, for whose special benefit the rebellion had been begun, it had been made, as thousands expressed it later in the contest, "The rich man's war and the poor man's fight." At a late hour we left these scenes of woe and returned to Mr. McConaughy's, where we passed another night, and departed for Baltimore the next morning on a cattle-train of cars, which bore several hundred Confederate prisoners, destined for Fort Delaware, on the Delaware River, which was used for the safe-keeping of captives

during a great portion of the war. We ar-rived in Baltimore in the evening in time to take the cars for Phila-delphia, whence the writer went homeward, reaching the City of New York when the great "Draft riot," as it was called, at the middle of July[a] was at

[a] 1863.

FORT DELAWARE.

its height, and a considerable portion of the city was in the hands of a mob.

The writer, with friends, revisited Gettysburg in September, 1866, and had the good fortune to go over nearly the entire ground on which the battle was fought, in the company of Professor Stoever, of Pennsylvania College, and the Rev. Mr. Warner, who had thoroughly studied the localities and incidents of the battle. Industry had changed the aspects of the theater of strife since our first visit, but many scars yet remained. Tradition had already treasured up a thousand touching stories of the conflict; and John Burns, a solitary "hero of Gettysburg," was yet a resident of the place, but absent at the time of our visit. It would be an interesting task to here record the many incidents of personal courage, sublime fortitude, holy self-denial, patient suffering, and Christian sympathy, at Gettysburg and else-

muzzle, and its ball about half-way out. It had been struck by a heavy solid shot, which made the piece recoil so suddenly and swiftly, that its own ball was made, by the momentum, to rush to the muzzle, where it was arrested by the crushed edge of the bore at that point.

[1] There were some Friends, or Quakers, from North Carolina, in the battle at Gettysburg, who were forced into the ranks, but who, from the beginning to the end, refused to fight. They were from Guilford County, which was mostly settled by their sect, and who, as the writer can testify by personal observation, presented the only region in that State where the evidences of thrift which free labor gave in a land cursed by slavery might be seen. These excellent people were robbed and plundered by the Confederates without mercy. About a dozen of them were in Lee's army at Gettysburg, and were among the prisoners captured there. They had steadily borne practical testimony to the strength of their principles in opposing war. They were subjected to great cruelties. One of them, who refused to fight, was ordered by his colonel to be shot. A squad of twelve men were drawn up to shoot him. They loved him as a brother, because of his goodness, and, when ordered to fire, every man refused. The remainder of the company was called up, and ordered to shoot the first twelve if they did not execute the order. The intended victim folded his hands, raised his eyes, and said, "Father, forgive them, for they know not what they do!" The entire company threw down their muskets, and refused to obey the order. Their exasperated captain, with a horrid oath, tried to shoot him with his pistol. The cap would not explode. Then he dashed upon him with his horse, but the meek conscript was unharmed. Just then a charge of some of Meade's troops drove the Confederates from their position, and the Quaker became a prisoner. He and his co-religionists were sent to Fort Delaware, when the fact was made known to some of their sect in Philadelphia. It was laid before the President, and he ordered their release.

where, related to the writer at different times; but it is not his province to do so in this chronicle.[1] Yet there is one incident, related by Professor Stoever, as coming under his own observation, which so vividly illustrates the character of a true man and Christian soldier, that it should not be left unrecorded, and is here given. When orders were issued for the army to pursue Lee,[2] General O. O. Howard, commanding the Sixth Corps, hastened to the bedside of Captain Griffith, one of his beloved staff-officers, who had received a mortal wound. After a few words, the General opened his New Testament, read the 14th chapter of John, and then, kneeling, commended his dying friend to God. An embrace and a hurried farewell followed, and so the friends parted, never to meet again on the earth. That night Captain Griffith died, and Howard, in pursuit of Lee, bivouacked in a drenching rain near the base of the South Mountain range.

Soon after the Battle of Gettysburg the State of Pennsylvania purchased seventeen acres of land adjoining the Evergreen Cemetery, on Cemetery Hill, near that village, for the purpose of a burial-place for all the Union soldiers who fell in that battle. On the 19th of November following, the ground was consecrated, with appropriate ceremonies, in the presence of the President of the United States, members of his cabinet, the governors of several States, generals of the army, and a vast concourse of other citizens. Edward Everett delivered an oration, and President Lincoln a brief but remarkable and touching dedicatory address.[3]

---

[1] After the Battle of Gettysburg, the body of a Union soldier was found in a secluded spot, partly reclining. In his cold hand was an ambrotype likeness of three little children, upon which his open, but then rayless eye had evidently been gazing at the last moment of his life. A notice of the fact was given in a Philadelphia paper. Public curiosity was excited, for there was no clew to the name of the soldier. Copies of the ambrotype were made. The touching story found its way through numerous newspapers, with a description of the soldier and the faces of the three children. By this means the widowed mother was informed of the fate of the husband and father. The soldier proved to be Sergeant Hunniston, of Portville, in Western New York, and to his afflicted family Dr. J. F. Bourns, of Philadelphia, conveyed the precious ambrotype, and some substantial presents from citizens of Philadelphia, early in January, 1864.

[2] See page 74.

[3] The following is a copy of Mr. Lincoln's remarks:—

"Fourscore and seven years ago our fathers brought forth upon this continent a new nation, conceived in liberty, and dedicated to the proposition that all men are created equal. Now we are engaged in a great civil war, testing whether that nation, or any nation so conceived and so dedicated, can long endure. We are met on a great battle-field of that war. We are met to dedicate a portion of it as the final resting-place of those who here gave their lives that that nation might live. It is altogether fitting and proper that we should do this. But in a larger sense we cannot dedicate, we cannot consecrate, we cannot hallow this ground. The brave men, living and dead, who struggled here, have consecrated it far above our power to add or detract. The world will little note or long remember what we say here, but it can never forget what they did here. It is for us, the living, rather to be dedicated here to the unfinished work that they have thus far so nobly carried on. It is rather for us to be here dedicated to the great task remaining before us, that from these honored dead we take increased devotion to that cause for which they here gave the last full measure of devotion; that we here highly resolve that the dead shall not have died in vain; that the nation shall, under God, have a new birth of freedom; and governments of the people, by the people, and for the people, shall not perish from the earth."

CHAPTER III.

POLITICAL AFFAIRS.—RIOTS IN NEW YORK.—MORGAN'S RAID NORTH OF THE OHIO.

 HE escape of Lee into Virginia, with the remainder of his army, his artillery, and spoils, was a great disappointment to the loyal people of the country, and the commander of the Army of the Potomac was freely charged with tardiness, over-cautiousness, and even incompetency—alleged causes for which Hooker had been relieved of command. General officers of merit, but of different temperament, who had urged him to more energetic action, added the weight of their opinions to the censorious judgment of the unknowing multitude; and criminations and recriminations followed, which were perfectly intelligible only to military experts. It is not the province of the writer to sit in judgment upon this matter, and he leaves the recorded facts with readers competent to do so.[1]

The public disappointment was of brief duration. The victory for the National cause was too decisive and substantial to allow regret to interfere with rejoicing. The battle had been won by Meade and his army, and that was quite sufficient for the contemplation of those who saw in men only the instruments for achieving the triumph of great and good principles—the principles enunciated in the golden rule. They saw in the discomfiture of the army of the conspirators against those principles a victory of righteousness over unrighteousness—of light over darkness—of democracy over an oligarchy—of God over Satan. They believed that the turning point in the war had been reached, and that the victories of Gettysburg and Vicksburg, occurring simultaneously in widely-separated regions of the Republic, were sure prophecies of the ultimate and perhaps speedy suppression of the rebellion. And so the President, as the representative of the Government and of the faith and patriotism of the loyal people of the country, called upon the latter, in a public proclamation,[a] to set apart a time in the near future,[b] "to be observed as a day for National thanksgiving, praise, and prayer," to Almighty God, "for the wonderful things he had done in the nation's behalf, and to invoke the influence of

[a] July 15, 1863.

[b] Aug. 6.

[1] On the 28th of August, an elegant sword was presented to General Meade by the officers of the division of Pennsylvania Reserves—a token of affection and esteem which had been ordered before the Battle of Gettysburg. The presentation ceremonies took place at the head-quarters of General Crawford, in Virginia, and the presentation speech was made by him. The handle of the sword was gold, inlaid with diamonds and rubies, and on the scabbard were inscribed the names of eleven battles in which the Pennsylvania Reserves had been engaged, from Mechanicsville to Gettysburg. A large number of officers of the army, the Governor of Pennsylvania, and several members of Congress, were present. A similar token of esteem had been agreed upon, to be presented to the now slain General Reynolds.

On the 26th of August, a horse and accouterments, sword and belt, were presented to General Sedgwick, commanding the Sixth Corps, by the officers of the second division of the Second Corps, which he had commanded. The ceremony was at Warrenton, and General Meade and staff participated in it.

His Holy Spirit, to subdue the anger which has produced and so long sustained a needless and cruel rebellion; to change the hearts of the insurgents;
to guide the counsels of the Government with wisdom adequate to so great a
national emergency, and to visit with tender care and consolation, throughout the length and breadth of our land, all those who, through the vicissi-
tudes and marches, voyages, battles, and sieges, had been brought to suffer
in mind, body, or estate; and finally to lead the whole nation, through paths
of repentance and submission to the Divine will, back to the perfect enjoyment of union and fraternal peace." [1]   And the Secretary of State, satisfied
                    that the rebellion would soon be crushed, sent[a] a cheering circular
a Aug. 12,   letter to the diplomatic agents of the Republic abroad, in which
   1863.
                    he recited the most important events of the war to that time;
declared that "the country showed no sign of exhaustion of money, material,
or men;" that our loan was "purchased at par by our citizens at the
average of $1,200,000 daily," and that gold was selling in our market at
23 to 28 per cent. premium, while in the insurrectionary region it commanded
twelve hundred per cent. premium." [2]

But while the loyal people were rejoicing because of the great deliverance
at Gettysburg, and the Government was preparing for a final and decisive

---

[1] On the day when the loyal people were assembled for the purposes set forth in this proclamation, so
glowing with the spirit of Christianity, an official address by the leader of the Conspirators, at Richmond, was
read to the soldiers of Lee's army, then confronting Meade's on the Rappahannock, in which the following
paragraph occurred: "Your enemy continues a struggle, in which our final triumph must be inevitable. Unduly
elated with their recent successes, they imagine that temporary reverses can quell your spirits or shake your
determination, and they are now gathering heavy masses for a general invasion, in the vain hope that by desperate efforts success may at length be reached. You know too well, my countrymen, what they mean by
success. Their malignant rage aims at nothing less than the extermination of yourselves, your wives, and your
children. They seek to destroy what they cannot plunder. They propose as spoils of victory that your homes
shall be partitioned among wretches whose atrocious cruelty has stamped infamy on their government. They
design to incite servile insurrection and light the fires of incendiarism whenever they can reach your homes, and
they debauch an inferior race, heretofore docile and contented, by promising them the indulgence of the evilest
passions as the price of their treachery. Conscious of their inability to prevail by legitimate warfare, not daring
to make peace, lest they should be hurled from their seats of power, the men who now rule in Washington
refuse even to confer on the subject of putting an end to outrages which disgrace our age, or listen to a suggestion for conducting the war according to the usages of civilization."

No man in the Confederacy knew better than Robert E. Lee, the willing associate of the Conspirators in
crime, the absolute untruthfulness of the charges with which that paragraph was burdened; yet, in obedience
to the diabolical spirit which incited the rebellion, he allowed his soldiers and the people to be thus deceived
and wronged, that he might, aided by a merciless conscription then in operation, fill his shattered army, and to
make the soldiers fight with the idea that they were contending with cruel savages, who deserved no quarter.
The raising of the black flag could not have been more wicked in intent.

Davis's address, countersigned by Judah P. Benjamin, was dated August 1, 1863. The allusion in the
closing sentence of the above paragraph is explained by the fact that, on the 4th of July, when Davis felt confident that Lee was victorious at Gettysburg, instead of preparing to fly before a conquering army, as he really
was, he sent Alexander H. Stephens, "Vice-President" of the Confederacy, to Fortress Monroe, with instructions to proceed to Washington and lay before the President "a communication in writing from Jefferson Davis,
Commander-in-Chief of the land and naval forces of the Confederate States, to Abraham Lincoln, Commander-
in-Chief of the land and naval forces of the United States." Stephens proceeded to Fortress Monroe in the flag-
of-truce boat, and said in a note addressed to Admiral S. H. Lee, "I desire to proceed directly to Washington in
the steamer *Torpedo*." Lee referred the matter to the Secretary of the Navy, who refused to allow Stephens to
go to Washington, the customary channels for communication being all that was needful.

Stephens's mission seemed to have a twofold object, namely, to seek, by an official reception at Washington, a recognition by the Government of the existence of a real government at Richmond; also if Lee (as it was
expected he would by the time Stephens should reach the capital) was marching in triumph on Philadelphia, to
demand peace upon terms of the absolute independence of the "Confederate States." A "Rebel War Clerk," in
his diary, under date of July 10th, wrote: "We know all about the mission of Vice-President Stephens. It was
ill-timed for success. At Washington news had been received of the defeat of General Lee." On the 16th he
recorded: "Again the *Enquirer*, edited by Mitchell, the Irishman, is urging the President to seize arbitrary
power." On that day news reached Richmond that Lee had been driven across the Potomac.

[2] According to a report of Memminger, the Confederate "Secretary of the Treasury," the Confederate debt,
on the 24th of August, 1863, was over $600,000,000, equally divided between Treasury notes, and bonds into which
currency had been funded.

struggle with its foes, leading politicians of the Peace Faction, evidently in affiliation with the disloyal secret organization known as *Knights of the Golden Circle*,[1] were using every means in their power to defeat the patriotic purposes of the loyalists, and to stir up the people of the Free-labor States to a counter-revolution. This had been their course for several months during the dark hours of the Republic, before the dawn at Gettysburg; and the more strenuous appeared the efforts of the Government to suppress the rebellion, the more intense was their zeal in opposing them.

This opposition was specially exhibited when the President acted in accordance with the law of Congress, passed in April, 1862, "for the enrollment of the National forces," and authorizing the Executive to make drafts, at his discretion, from such enrolled citizens for service in the army.[2] The President refrained from resorting to this extreme measure so long as the public safety would allow. Finally, in consequence of the great discouragements to volunteering produced by the Peace Faction, he issued a proclamation[a] for a Draft to begin in July, and caused the appointment of an enrolling board in every Congressional district. This
[a] May 8, 1863.
was made the pretext for inaugurating a counter-revolution in the Free-labor States, which the leaders of the rebellion had been promised, and which their dupes were expecting;[3] and organized resistance to the measure instantly appeared, general and formidable. The politicians of the Peace Faction denounced the law and all acts under it as despotic and unconstitutional, and a hitherto obscure lawyer, named McCunn, who had been elected to the bench in the city of New York by the Opposition, so formally decided. He was sustained by the decision of three respectable judges of the Supreme Court of Pennsylvania—Lowrie, Woodward, and Thompson—and, with this legal sanction, the politicians opposed the Draft with a high hand.

In the mean time the suspension of the privilege of the writ of *Habeas Corpus* and the practice of arbitrary arrests had become a subject for the bitter denunciations of the Peace Faction. They were specially excited to opposition by the arrest and punishment, under military authority, of C. L. Vallandigham, late member of Congress from Ohio, and the most conspicuous leader of the Opposition, in the West. This politician, possessing ability and pluck, was very busy in sowing the seeds of disaffection to the Government in the spring of 1863. On the 13th of April, General Burnside, then in command of a military department which included Ohio, issued a general order for the suppression of seditious speech and action, then seriously affecting the public service by discouraging enlistments. It declared that

---

[1] See page 187, volume I.

[2] So early as the 20th of August, 1861, General McClellan, then in command of the Army of the Potomac, had recommended such enrollment and conscription. The Act of April 18, 1862, provided for the enrollment of all able-bodied masculine citizens, including aliens who had declared their intentions to become naturalized, between the ages of eighteen and forty-five years; those between twenty and thirty-five to constitute the first class, and all others the second class. The President was authorized to make a draft from these after the 1st of July next succeeding (1862), the person so drafted not to serve in the armies for more than three years. A commutation of three hundred dollars might be received in lieu of such service; and the heads of executive departments, National judges, Governors of States, the only son of a widow, or of an aged and infirm father, dependent for his support on the labor of such son; the father of motherless dependent children under twelve years of age, or the only adult brother of such children, being orphans; or the residue of a family, of which two members might be in the service, were exempted. This Act was passed in each house of Congress by a party vote, the Republicans in its favor and the Opposition against it. It received in the Senate 35 yeas to 11 nays, and in the other House 115 yeas to 49 nays.

[3] See page 48.

persons who should "commit acts for the benefit of the enemies of our country should be tried as spies and traitors, and, if convicted, should suffer

CLEMENT L. VALLANDIGHAM.

death." "It must be distinctly understood," said the order, "that treason, expressed or implied, will not be tolerated in this department." In defiance of this order (whose specifications of offenses were clear[1]), Vallandigham continued his seditious speeches, and denounced the order itself.[2] He was arrested at his own house in Dayton, Ohio,[a] on a charge of having been guilty of treasonable conduct. He was tried by a courtmartial convened at Cincinnati,[b] over which Brigadier-General R. B. Potter presided;

[a] May 4 1863.

[b] April 22.

and was convicted, and sentenced[c] to close confinement in a fortress for the remainder of the war. This sentence was modified by the President, who directed him to be sent within the military lines of the Confederates, and, in the event of his returning without leave, to suffer the penalty prescribed by the court. Judge Leavitt, of the United States District Court of Ohio, refused an application for a writ of *Habeas Corpus* in his case, and the convict was passed by General Rosecrans toward the Confederate lines. Vallandigham being of use to the conspirators in Ohio, and none at all in their own dominions, his ungrateful "Southern friends," for whose cause he had labored, treated him with the indifference they would exhibit toward a poor relation.[3] Disappointed and disgusted, he soon left their society, escaped from Wilmington, and sailed to Nassau in a blockade-runner, and finally found his way to Canada, where he enjoyed congenial society among his refugee friends from the "Confederate States," with whom he was in sympathy. Meanwhile, the Democratic Convention of Ohio had nominated him for Governor.

[c] May 16.

The arrest of Vallandigham produced intense excitement throughout the country, and its wisdom and lawfulness were questioned by a few of the

---

[1] One specification was as follows: "The habit of declaring sympathies for the enemy will not be allowed in this department. Persons committing such offenses will be at once arrested, with a view to being tried as above stated, or sent beyond our lines into the lines of their friends."

[2] There appeared real fanaticism among the followers of this man, while he was engaged in this campaign against the Government. While he was riding in a procession at Batavia, in Ohio, some of his abject admirers took the more noble horses from his carriage, and drew the vehicle through the village themselves.—Letter of an eyewitness, a friend of the author.

[3] Lieutenant-Colonel Freemantle, of the British army, already mentioned, was then with the Confederate forces in Tennessee, below Murfreesboro'. In his Diary, under date of "May 28, 1863," he wrote: "When I arrived [at Wartrace], I found that General Hardee was in company with General Polk and Bishop Elliott of Georgia, and also with Mr. Vallandigham. The latter (called the Apostle of Liberty) is a good-looking man, apparently not much over forty, and had been turned out of the North three days before. Rosecrans had wished to hand him over to Bragg by flag of truce; but as the latter declined to receive him in that manner, he was, as General Hardee expressed it, 'dumped down' in the neutral ground between the lines, and left there. He thus received hospitality from the Confederates in the capacity of a destitute stranger. They do not in any way receive him officially, and it does not suit the policy of either party to be identified with one another. He told the generals that if Grant was severely beaten in Mississippi by Johnston, he did not think the war could be continued on its present great scale."—*Three Months in the Southern States*, page 137.

friends of the Government. When the news of his conviction and sentence was proclaimed throughout the land by the telegraph, Democratic politicians held meetings in several cities to express dissatisfaction with such proceedings. One of these, in the city of Albany,[a] New York (to which the Governor of the State, Horatio Seymour, addressed an impassioned letter[1]), in a series of resolutions, denounced the proceedings in Vallandigham's case as unlawful—"contrary to the spirit of our laws and the Constitution," and declared that they regarded "the blow struck at a citizen of Ohio as aimed at the rights of every citizen at the North." They implored the President to "reverse the action of the military tribunal;" and they sent the chairman of their meeting (Erastus Corning) to Washington City to lay their resolutions before the Executive. This was done. The gravity of the subject required serious consideration, and it was given. Then the President, in a long letter to the officers of the meeting,[b] ably defended the position taken by Congress and himself in the matter of the writ of *habeas corpus* and the arrest of seditious persons in time of rebellion, by citations of precedents found in our own history, and simple arguments based on the most tangible premises of common sense;[2] and closed with the assurance that he should continue " to do so much as might seem to be required by the public safety."

(margin note) May 15, 1863.

(margin note) b June 13.

---

[1] Mr. Seymour was an able public officer and an average statesman, with an irreproachable private character, and wide influence in society. He was one of the most conspicuous and uncompromising members of the Peace Faction; and was in full sympathy with the Conspirators concerning the doctrine of supreme State sovereignty, on which, if true, they justly founded their claim to the right of secession, and the severing of the bond which united them to the General Government, which was regarded by them as only " the agent of the States."* On that account his words had great weight with the vast majority of the Opposition party. His letter to the convention was therefore of great importance at that crisis, and was doubtless chiefly instrumental in fostering opposition to the war and to the measures used by the Government for carrying it on, which culminated, in the City of New York, a few months later, in a most fearful and bloody riot, as we shall observe presently. It was a highly inflammable missile, in which the Government was denounced as a despot, seeking " to impose punishment, not for an offense against law, but for a disregard of an invalid order, put forth in an utter disregard of principles of civil liberty;" and he told the people plainly that if the proceedings in Vallandigham's case were upheld by the Government and sanctioned by the majority, they were in a state of revolution. By implication, in carefully guarded language, he exhorted the people to resistance. He declared that the Governors and the courts of some of the great Western States had " shrunk into insignificance before the despotic powers claimed and exercised by military men;" and closed by saying: " The people of this country now wait with the deepest anxiety the decision of the Administration upon these acts. Having given it a generous support in the conduct of the war, we now pause to see what kind of Government it is for which we are asked to pour out our blood and treasure. The action of the Administration will determine in the minds of more than one-half of the people of the loyal States whether this war is waged to put down rebellion at the South, or to destroy free institutions at the North." The action of the Administration thenceforth, until the rebellion was crushed, was according to the rule in Vallandigham's case, and four-fifths " of the people of the loyal States " sustained it, in spite of the efforts of the Peace Faction to the contrary. The great body of the people of those States were sound friends of the Union.

[2] The question was raised, *Who* is authorized to suspend the privilege of the writ of *habeas corpus*, according to the provisions of the 2d clause of section 9, Article I. of the National Constitution ? The Opposition declared that only Congress, in regular session, could do so. The President and Congress declared that it was the right of the President to do so, if " rebellion or invasion," during the recess of Congress, should show that the public safety required it. On this subject, see able essays by Horace Binney, of Philadelphia, published at about that time, and replies thereto, both in pamphlet form. The President, in his letter, said : " By necessary implication, when rebellion or invasion comes, the decision is to be made from time to time; and I think the man whom, for the time, the *people* have, under the Constitution, made the Commander-in-Chief of their army and navy, is the man who holds the power and bears the responsibility of making it." Congress having justified the action of the President, and the people, by every demonstration of a desire to sustain the Government, having sanctioned the acts of Congress, the question of the constitutionality of the suspension of the writ of *habeas corpus* and of arbitrary arrests was settled, and all opposition thereto was consequently factious and seditious.

---

* An amusing illustration of action in accordance with this idea may be found in " Letters patent " of Jefferson Davis, dated 5th of June, 1863, revoking the authority of a British consul at Richmond. He said : " Whereas, George Moore, Esq., Her British Majesty's consul for the port of Richmond and State of Virginia, duly recognized as such by exequatur issued by a former Government [United States] which was, at the time of the issue, *the duly authorized agent for that purpose of the State of Virginia*," &c.

The Democratic Convention that assembled[a] at Columbus, Ohio, and nominated Vallandigham for the chief magistracy of the State,[1] also denounced the Government, and sent a committee[2] to the President to *demand* a revocation of the sentence of their candidate, "not as a *favor*, but as a *right*." They assumed to speak for a "majority of the people of Ohio." The President's reply[b] was brief and pointed. He defended the action of the Government, and, after telling them plainly that their own attitude in the matter encouraged desertion, resistance to the draft, and the like, and that both friends and enemies of the Union looked upon it in that light[3]—that it was a "substantial, and, by consequence, a real strength to the enemy"—he proposed to them to dispel it, if they were friends of their country, by publicly declaring, over their own signatures, that there was a rebellion whose object and tendency was to destroy the Union, and that, in their opinion, our army and navy were constitutional means for suppressing it; that they would not do any thing calculated to diminish the efficiency of those branches of the public service; and that they would do all in their power to provide means for the support of that army and navy, while engaged in efforts to suppress the rebellion; it being understood that the publication of the President's reply to them, with their affirmative indorsement of the propositions, should be, in itself, a revocation of the order in relation to Vallandigham. The Committee refused to "enter into any such agreement," giving, as a chief reason, that it was an imputation "on their own sincerity and fidelity as citizens of the United States." So the discussion, so far as the President was concerned, ended, and at the election for Governor of Ohio, a few months later, the assumption of the Committee, that they represented "a majority of the people" of that State, was rebuked by an overwhelming vote against Vallandigham. The majority of his opponent was over one hundred thousand, including that given by the Ohio soldiers in the field.

It was in the midst of the excitement caused by the arrest of Vallandigham, the harangues of Opposition speakers, and the passionate appeals of some Opposition newspapers to the instincts of the more disorderly classes of society, that the Draft was ordered. Then, as we have observed, the zeal of the Opposition against the measure became formidable and dangerous to the public welfare. Organized resistance to the Draft appeared in various parts of the country, and distinguished members of the Peace Faction were heard, on the National anniversary,[a] exhorting the

[a] June 11, 1863.

[b] June 29.

[a] July 4.

---

[1] See page 84.

[2] The following are the names of the Committee : M. Burchard, David A. Houck, George Bliss, T. W. Bartley, W. J. Gordon, John O'Neill, C. A. White, W. A. Fink, Alexander Long, J. W. White, George H. Pendleton, George L. Converse, Hanzo P. Noble, James R. Morris, W. A. Hutchins, Abner L. Backus, J. F. McKenney, P. C. DeBlond, Louis Schaefer.

[3] In a letter to the London *Times*, dated August 17, 1863, Mathew F. Maury, formerly Superintendent of the National Observatory at Washington, and one of the most unworthy of traitors to his country, said, in proof that there was no chance for the Union : "There is already a peace party in the North. *All the embarrassments with which that party can surround Mr. Lincoln, and all the difficulties that it can throw in the way of the war party in the North, operate directly as so much aid and comfort to the South.*" He then pointed to the apathy of the inhabitants of Western Pennsylvania (where the influence of the Peace Faction was powerful) at the time of Lee's invasion : "to the riots in New York, and to the organized resistance to the war in Ohio," in which Vallandigham was the leader, and said: "New York is threatening armed resistance to the Federal Government. *New York is becoming the champion of State Rights in the North, and to that extent is taking Southern ground.* . . . Vallandigham waits and watches over the border, *pledged, if elected Governor of the State of Ohio, to array it against Lincoln and the war, and to go for peace.* . . . Never were the chances for the South brighter."

people to stand firmly in opposition to what they called "the usurpations of the Government." The most conspicuous of these orators were ex-President Franklin Pierce,[1] and Governor Seymour, of New York, the former speaking to a Democratic gathering at Concord, New Hampshire, and the latter to the citizens of New York City, in the Academy of Music.

Mr. Pierce declared that the cause of the war was "the vicious inter-meddling of too many of the citizens of the Northern States with the con-stitutional rights of the Southern States." He spoke of "military bastiles," into which American citizens were thrust by the arbitrary exercise of power, and of "the mailed hand of military usurpation in the North, striking down the liberties of the people, and trampling its foot on a desecrated Constitu-tion." He lauded Vallandigham as "the noble martyr of free speech," and spoke in affectionate terms of Virginia, whose sons, by thousands, led by a dishonored scion of a once honored family of that commonwealth, were then desolating Pennsylvania with plunder and the tread of war, and drenching its soil with the blood of twenty thousand Union men in attempts to destroy the Republic. He declared "the war as fruitless," and exhorted his fellow-citizens, if they could not preserve the Union without fighting, to let it go. "You will take care of yourselves," he exclaimed. "With or without arms, with or without leaders, we will, at least, in the effort to defend our rights as a free people, build up a great mausoleum of hearts, to which men who yearn for liberty will, in after years, with bowed heads and reverently, resort, as Christian pilgrims, to the shrines of the Holy Land."[2] His hear-ers on that dismal day shouted applause, but the sons of New England showed their scorn for such disloyal advisers and evinced their own patriot-ism in trooping by thousands to the field of strife, to save their country from ruin at the hands of rebels and demagogues.

Mr. Seymour's speech was similar in tenor, but was more cautiously worded. It was able, and, viewed from his stand-point of political observa-tion, appeared patriotic. He opened with words of bitter irony applied to the struggling Government whose hands the Peace Faction were striving to paralyze, saying: "When I accepted the invitation to speak, with others, at this meeting, we were promised the downfall of Vicksburg, the opening of the Mississippi, the probable capture of the Confederate capital, and the exhaustion of the rebellion. By common consent all parties had fixed upon this day[a] when the results of the campaign should be known, to mark out that line of policy which they felt that our country should pursue. But in the moment of expected victory, there   [a] July 4, 1863. came the midnight cry for help from Pennsylvania, to save its despoiled fields from the invading foe; and, almost within sight of this great commer-cial metropolis, the ships of your merchants were burned to the water's edge." At the very hour when this ungenerous taunt was uttered, Vicksburg and its dependencies, and vast spoils, with more than thirty thousand Confed-erate captives, were in the possession of General Grant;[3] and the discomfited

---

[1] See notice of Mr. Pierce's letter to Jefferson Davis, note 1, page 215, volume I.

[2] Compare this last sentence with a paragraph on page 232, volume I. of this work, in which Judah P. Benjamin, the first Confederate "Secretary of War," eulogized the friends of the Conspirators, in the Free-labor States. His speech may be found in the *Congressional Globe*, January, 1861.

[3] See pages 628 and 630, volume II.

army of General Lee, who, when that sentence was written, was expected to
lead his troops victoriously to the Schuylkill, and perhaps to the Hudson,
was flying from Meade's troops, to find shelter from utter destruction, beyond
the Potomac.   And before the disheartening harangues of the Opposition
orators were read by the gallant soldiers on the banks of the Mississippi,
that great stream *was* opened, and the *Imperial* was making her way, without impediment, from St. Louis to New Orleans.[1]   Such was the commentary
on that speech; and the speedy response to it by the inhabitants of the city
of New York; to whom it was addressed, was the sending of thousands of
more troops to the field in defense of the Constitution and laws, and the life
of the Republic.

But there was an immediate response in the City of New York to the
utterances of leaders of the Peace Faction (of which those of Pierce and
Seymour were mild specimens), appalling but logical.   The Draft was about
to commence there.   Making that measure a pretext, as we have observed,
leading Opposition journals were daily exciting the subjects of it to resistance; and one went so far as to counsel its readers to provide themselves
with arms, and keep in every family "a good rifled-musket, a few pounds of
powder, and a hundred or so of shot," to "defend their homes and personal
liberties from invasion from *any* quarter."[2]   On the evening of the 3d of
July, a highly incendiary handbill, calculated to incite to insurrection, was
circulated throughout the city; and it is believed, that an organized outbreak
on the 4th had been planned, and would have been executed, had not the
news of Lee's defeat at Gettysburg, and Grant's success at Vicksburg, disappointed and dismayed the leaders.   Lee's invasion, as we have observed, was
a part of the programme of revolution in the Free-labor States, and so was
the raid of Morgan into Indiana and Ohio, at about the same time, which we
shall consider presently.   There can be no doubt that a sword, like that
which startled Damocles, hung by a single hair over the heart of the Republic at Gettysburg.[3]   Lee failed, and the nation was saved.   The grand
scheme of a counter-revolution in favor of peace and the independence of
the "Confederate States," assumed the lesser proportions of a riot in New
York City and outbreaks elsewhere, but its promoters were no less active in
preparations for another opportunity.

---

[1] See page 637, volume II.

[2] The *World* newspaper, quoted on pages 207 and 208 of the *Martyr's Monument.*

[3] An army chaplain from New York recorded that on that day, while on the steamer *Cahawba* with a large
number of Confederate prisoners, one of them, who seemed to be a shrewd politician, said: "Lee will not only
invade Pennsylvania and New Jersey, but New York also.   You will find war in the streets of your very city,
carried on by those who hate your Government and love ours.   You will be surprised at the number of friends
we have in your very midst; friends who, when the time comes, will destroy your railroads, your telegraph
wires, your government stores and property, and thus facilitate the glorious invasion now breaking you in
pieces."   Compare this with note 2, page 358, volume I.

At this time the Knights of the Golden Circle, who were numerous in the West, were very active.   They
held a meeting at Springfield, Illinois, on the 10th of June, when it was resolved to make the Draft the pretext
for a revolution, and measures were accordingly adopted.   They formed alliances with active members of the
Peace Faction throughout the country, and it was arranged that New York should take the initiative in the
revolutionary movement.   The plan was for each State to assume its "independent sovereignty."   New York
and New Jersey were to do this through their Governors; the rest of the States (excepting New England,
where there was no chance for success) were to be brought into the same attitude through the Knights of the
Golden Circle and the armed Peace Faction.   The argument to be offered was, that, the Government having
failed to suppress the rebellion, the Union was dissolved into its original elements, the States, and each of these
was left at perfect liberty to enter into new combinations.—Correspondent of the Chicago *Tribune*, August
5, 1863.

The riot in New York presented singular elements and phases. There were evidences of an organization in confusion, wildly led by perplexed leaders. When on Monday, the 13th of July, the Draft commenced in a building on the corner of Third Avenue and Forty-sixth Street, the spectators within were quiet and orderly, when suddenly a large crowd (who had destroyed the' telegraph wires leading out of the city) assembled in the street near, a pistol was fired, missiles were hurled at the doors and windows of the building wherein the Draft was going on, the rioters rushed in, the clerks were driven out, and the papers were torn up; a can of spirits of turpentine was poured over the floor, and very soon that building and adjoining ones were in flames. The firemen were not allowed to extinguish them, and the policemen who came were overpowered, and their Superintendent (Mr. Kennedy) was severely beaten by the mob. So began the tumult in which thousands of disorderly persons, chiefly natives of Ireland, and strangers,[1] were active participants, and who, for full three days and nights, defied all law. Like a plague the disorder broke out simultaneously at different points, evidently having a central head somewhere. The cry against the Draft soon ceased, when the shouts, "Down with Abolitionists! Down with Niggers! Hurrah for Jeff. Davis!" were heard. Hundreds of citizens, found in the streets or drawn out of large manufacturing establishments which were closed at the 'command of the mob, were compelled to fall into the ranks of the insurgents on peril of personal harm. Arson and plunder became the business of the rioters, who were infuriated by strong drink and evil passions; and maiming and murder was their recreation. The colored population of the city were special objects of their wrath. These were hunted down, bruised and killed, as if they had been noxious wild beasts. Neither age nor sex were spared. Men, women, and children, shared a common fate at the hands of the fiends. The Asylum for Colored Orphans, at the corner of Fifth Avenue and Forty-sixth Street, one of the noble city charities, in which about two hundred children without parents found a home, was first plundered and then laid in ashes, while the poor affrighted children, some beaten and maimed, fled in terror to whatever shelter they could find.

From Monday until Thursday the inhabitants of the great city were kept in mortal terror by the mob (which the organs of the Peace Faction spoke of as "a great uprising of the people"), for they were plundering and destroying almost without resistance. The Governor of the State interposed his authority as mildly as possible.[2] The troops at the service of General

---

[1] It is asserted, on what seems to be good authority, that large numbers of secessionists and rowdies had been for several days gathering in the city, at appointed places of rendezvous, chiefly from Baltimore, which, it is said, furnished about 3,000 of them.

[2] Governor Seymour had been in the city on the Saturday previous, and went, that evening, to Long Branch, a watering-place on the New Jersey shore, about two hours' travel from New York. The riot began on Monday morning. He returned to the city on Tuesday at noon, when the riot was at its height, and the mob were menacing the *Tribune* building, near the City Hall, with destruction. The rumor spread among the mob that the Governor was at the City Hall, when large crowds flocked thither. Mr. Seymour was politely introduced to them by the Deputy Sheriff, on the steps of the Hall, when, after being loudly cheered by the rioters, he addressed them as follows: "My Friends: I have come down here from the quiet of the country to see what was the difficulty—to learn what all this trouble was concerning the Draft. Let me assure you that I am your friend. [Uproarious cheering.] You have been my friends [cries of 'Yes,' 'Yes,' 'That's so,' 'We are and will be again '], and now I assure you, my fellow-citizens, that I am here to show you a test of my friendship. [Cheers.] I wish to inform you that I have sent my Adjutant-General to Washington, to confer with the authorities there, and to have this Draft suspended and stopped. [Vociferous cheers.] I now ask you, as good citizens, to wait for his return, and I assure you that I will do all that I can to see that there is no inequality

Wool, commander of the military district, were too few at the beginning to quell the riot. Others were summoned from the military posts in the harbor, and these, with the efficient Metropolitan Police, managed, by Thursday, to hold the mob in check. At that time the volunteer companies of the city were beginning to return from Pennsylvania,[1] and the leaders of the riot plainly saw that further resistance to authority would be dangerous. So the city, after a sacrifice of life estimated at full four hundred persons,[2] and a loss of property, for which it was compelled to pay, valued at $2,000,000,[3] became quiet and orderly. The Draft was temporarily suspended until further orders from Washington, and the Governor gave assurances that it would not be renewed in the State of New York until the question of its constitutionality should be decided by the courts. His political friends urged him to use the military power of the State in the maintenance of that position.[4]

Governor Seymour implored the President first to suspend the Draft because of alleged inequality in its operation, and to postpone it until the courts should pass judgment upon it. The Executive agreed to suspend it

DRAFTING.[5]

until a fair scrutiny of its operations could be had, but he refused to postpone it for adjudication, for the reason that precious time would thus be lost, and the National cause endangered, for the Confederates were then sweeping into their military ranks every able bodied man they could lay their hands on. It was obvious to all that compliance with the demands of the Governor would be the most speedy and efficient means for securing the triumph of the Conspirators; also, that the theory involved in that demand, when

and no wrong done any one. I wish you to take good care of all property, as good citizens, and see that every person is safe. The safe keeping of property and persons rests with you, and I charge you to disturb neither. It is your duty to maintain the good order of the city, and I know you will do it. I wish you now to separate as good citizens, and you can assemble again whenever you wish to do so. I ask you to leave all to me now, and I will see to your rights. Wait till my Adjutant returns from Washington, and you shall be satisfied."

And then the rioters cheered loudly, and went on plundering, burning, and murdering, while waiting for the return of the Adjutant, notwithstanding the Governor issued, on the same day, a proclamation against such disorderly conduct.

[1] See note 3, page 52.

[2] In his next annual message, Governor Seymour said the estimated number of the killed and wounded was 1,000.

[3] About twenty persons (twelve of them colored) were killed by the rioters. The remainder were slain by the military and police in the performance of their duty. They made exemplary work with the insurgents, firing directly among them, with deadly effect. Over fifty buildings were destroyed by the mob, and a large number of stores and dwellings, not burned, were sacked and plundered.

[4] " Governor Seymour," said the New York *Daily News*, "has pledged his word and honor (and the people of New York trust in and believe in him) that not one single drafted citizen shall be forced away from the State until the constitutionality of the conscription act shall have been decided." The *New York Express* said: "He is virtually pledged to call forth the entire militia force of the State of New York, to resist the kidnapping which Abolitionist howlers declare is inevitable, and we entertain no doubt that he will keep his word."

[5] This little picture represents the manner of drafting. The names of persons liable to the Draft or con-

put in practice, would be destructive of the sovereignty of the people, so clearly declared in the Preamble to the National Constitution. It would so subordinate the Legislative to the Judicial branch of the Government, that Congress, which is the direct representative of the people, would have its powers confined to the duty of simply suggesting laws for the Supreme Court to create by a judicial fiat. The theory was inconsistent with the principles of representative Government.

After proper investigation, the Draft went peaceably on; the armies were filled; the privilege of the writ of *habeas corpus* was suspended [a] throughout the entire Republic, and the war was prosecuted with vigor, in spite of formidable and organized opposition, which prolonged it. The Peace Faction, as essentially disloyal in theory and practice as were the armed Confederates, never represented the great mass of the Democratic or Opposition party in the Free-labor States. Its words and deeds were libels upon the genuine patriotism of the vast majority of the members of that party. Yet the influence of that active faction was such as to control the political action of the party, and to hold back thousands from the duty to their country which their patriotic instincts would have led them to perform. But in times of real, imminent danger to the sacred cause, they broke away from the thralls of the scheming demagogues who sought to make them instruments of mischief to their beloved country, and went nobly to battle. By that Peace Faction the war was prolonged at least two years, and, as a consequence, tens of thousands of precious lives, and tens of millions of treasure, were wasted. Its aims appeared no higher than the control of the powers and emoluments of public officers, and its loudest and most popular war-cry was, " Down with the Abolitionists! Down with the Negro!" That is to say, " Cursed be all Christian Philanthropists! Away with Justice and Humanity. Crucify them! Crucify them!" But the " common people " said " No;" and six months after the terrible " three days of July " in the City of New York, when no colored person's life was considered safe there, a regiment of Negro soldiers (Twenty-sixth United States Colored Troops), raised and equipped in the space of twenty days by the Loyal League of that city, marched down Broadway for the field, escorted by many of the leading citizens of the metropolis, and cheered by thousands who covered the sidewalks and filled windows and balconies. Everywhere the recruiting of this class of citizens was then going vigorously on. In that business Massachusetts had taken the lead, and Pennsylvania was a worthy imitator in zeal and success. When, late in 1864, the writer visited General Weitzel's (Twenty-fifth) corps, in front of Richmond, composed of colored troops, he found a large proportion of them from those States.[1]

We have alluded to Morgan's raid across the Ohio River, at about the time of Lee's invasion. The leader of it was the famous guerrilla chief, John

[a] August 19, 1863.

---

scription, were written on cards that were placed in the cylinder, made of tin, in which was a door. The drawing was public. A person, blindfolded, stood by the cylinder, and when it was turned several times, so as to mix the cards, he thrust in his hand and took out one. This was handed to the marshal, or his deputy, the name on the card distinctly spoken, and then recorded. This process was repeated, until the required number in the township or ward was drawn.

[1] So early as February, 1863, a few colored recruits were raised in Philadelphia, by Robert R. Corson and a few others, and sent to Boston to join the Fifty-fourth Regiment there. Such was the prejudice there against employing negroes in the army, that Mr. Corson was compelled to buy the railway tickets for his recruits, and get them into the cars, one at a time and place, to avoid creating excitement. From time to time this class of

H. Morgan, already mentioned.[1] The raid about to be considered had manifold objects in behalf of the Confederacy, namely, to prepare the way for
General Buckner, who was in East Tennessee on the borders of Kentucky,
to dash into that State and seize Louisville, and, with Morgan, capture and
plunder Cincinnati; to form a nucleus for an armed counter-revolution in the
Northwest, where the "Knights of the Golden Circle," and the "Sons of
Liberty," of the Peace Faction, were numerous, and to prevent re-enforcements from being sent from that region to Meade. Also for the purpose
of plunder for himself and followers. So early as the middle of June, a
pioneer party of about eighty Kentuckians crossed the Ohio into Indiana, at
Leavenworth, to test the temper of the people. They swept through two or
three counties in that region of the State, but were captured[a]
when making their way back, by the Leavenworth Home Guards,
under Major Clendenin, and the steamer *Izetta*. Morgan started
northward a little later,[b] with thirty-five hundred well-mounted men and six
guns. He crossed the swollen Cumberland River at Burksville,[c]
after some opposition from General Jacobs's cavalry,[2] and pushed
rapidly on to Columbia, where he was encountered[d] and kept in
check for three hours by one hundred and fifty of Wolford's
cavalry, under Captain Carter, who was killed in the affray. After partly
sacking the town, the raiders proceeded to destroy a bridge over the Green
River, at Tebb's Bend, where they were confronted[e] by two
hundred Michigan troops, under Colonel Moore, and, after a
desperate fight of several hours, were repulsed with a loss of more than two
hundred killed and wounded. Moore was intrenched, and lost only six
killed and twenty-three wounded.[3]

[a] June 19, 1863.

[b] June 27.

[c] July 1, 2.

[d] July 3.

[e] July 4.

---

recruits were thus sent out of the State for enrollment, the authorities of Pennsylvania refusing to accept them
as volunteers. Finally, at the middle of June, Governor Curtin forbade their being sent away. A new policy was begun. Major George H. Stearns was sent to Philadelphia with authority to raise colored troops. Mr. Corson, M. L. Hallowell, of the Society of Friends or Quakers, and Colonel Wagner, went to Chelten Hills, in the neighborhood of the city, and selected a spot for a recruiting station for colored troops, which was named Camp William Penn, by authority from Washington, to the command of which Colonel Wagner was appointed. Seventy-five men, whom Mr. Corson had recruited, were joined to the Third United States Colored Troops, and these, combined, pitched their tents, on the 20th of June, on the site of Camp William Penn, which became a great rendezvous for colored soldiers. A Supervisory Committee for recruiting colored soldiers was then appointed, and Mr. Corson was chosen general agent. Very soon the Government had at Camp William Penn barracks for 1,600 men, with every necessary appurtenance. A recruiting station was also opened in a large building on Chestnut Street,

BANNER OF THE THIRD UNITED STATES COLORED TROOPS.

in Philadelphia; and from the ladies of the city the colored troops received regimental banners, when about to take the field.

[1] See page 499, volume II.

[2] Morgan's artillery and baggage was crossed on hastily-constructed scows, and the troops swam their horses.

[3] Among the latter was a feminine soldier, a sprightly girl from Canada, only sixteen years of age, who served eighteen months in our service. She had been in seven different regiments, and participated in several battles. At Fredericksburg she was severely wounded. On account of the discovery of her sex, she was

From Green River Morgan moved rapidly upon Lebanon, then occupied by a thin regiment, under Colonel Hanson. His demand for a surrender being refused, the raiders tried for several hours to capture the place. Then they charged into the town, set it on fire, and captured Hanson and his men, with a battery. In this conflict Morgan's brother was killed. At dusk, the Confederates left the ruined village, pushed rapidly northward, by way of Bardstown, in a drenching rain, and, on the evening of the 7th,[a] their advance reached the Ohio, at Brandenburg, about forty *a July, 1863.* miles below Louisville. Morgan had fought and plundered on his way from Lebanon, and his ranks had been swelled by Kentucky secessionists to more than four thousand men, with ten guns. The advance of Rosecrans against Bragg at about this time had prevented the co-operation of Buckner, and Morgan determined to push on into Indiana and Ohio, in an independent movement.

At Brandenburg, Morgan captured two steamers[1] (*McCombs* and *Alice Dean*), and, on the 8th,[b] proceeded to cross the river upon them, *b July.* in spite of the opposition of some Indiana militia, and two gunboats that were patroling the Ohio. When his rear-guard was ascending the Indiana shore, and one of the steamers was a blazing ruin in the stream,[1] a force, equal to Morgan's, under General Hobson,[2] which had been pursuing, reached Brandenburg. Steamboats were procured, and, before daylight on the morning of the 9th, Hobson and his little army were on Indiana soil. At the same time, a greater portion of General Judah's division, stationed in the section of Kentucky between the Cumberland and Barren rivers, had been concentrated and put in motion for the capture of Morgan. These consisted chiefly of Indiana, Illinois, Michigan, and Kentucky cavalry, and went up the Ohio River in boats to intercept the raiders.

Morgan pushed northward to Corydon, the capital of Harrison County, before which he appeared on the afternoon of the 9th. There he was resisted by the Home Guards; but these were overpowered, the town was pillaged, citizens were murdered, three hundred horses were seized, and a new system of plunder was inaugurated, by demanding of the owner of each mill and factory one thousand dollars in currency, as a condition of the safety of his property from the flames. Having completed his work at Corydon, Morgan pushed on to Salem, the capital of Washington County, the next morning, captured between three and four hundred militia, pillaged the place, destroyed railway property, and received a thousand dollars each from three mill-owners. In this way he went on, from village to village, in the direction of Ohio, plundering, destroying, and levying contributions on the inhabitants almost without hinderance, until the evening of the 12th, when near Vernon, on the Madison and Indianapolis railway, he encountered stout resistance and defiance from about twelve hundred militia, under Colonel Lowe.

---

several times mustered out of the service, and then she would re-enlist in another regiment. Her name was Lizzie Compton.

   [1] The *McCombs* was first seized, and, while lying in the stream, gave a signal of distress, when the fine steamer, *Alice Dean*, appeared. The latter ran alongside the *McCombs*, when she was seized, and pressed into Morgan's service. When no longer needed she was burnt, with property valued at $60,000. The *McCombs* was not destroyed.

   [2] Composed of the forces of Generals Hobson, Wolford, and Shackleford, consisting of Ohio, Michigan, and Kentucky troops. These had formed a junction at Lebanon on the 6th, and, by order of General Burnside, Hobson was directed to assume the general command, and pursue Morgan until he was overtaken.

Morgan was now assured that Indiana was aroused because of his invasion. There was, indeed, a great uprising of the people, but not in a way the Conspirators had desired and hoped for. The victories at Gettysburg and on the Mississippi had made their friends in that region exceedingly circumspect, and the counter-revolution had been postponed to a more propitious time. It was now the spontaneous uprising of the loyal people. News of this sudden and formidable invasion had reached Indianapolis, the capital of the State, on the 9th.[a] Governor Morton[1] instantly issued a call for all the citizens to seize arms and turn out in a body to expel the intruders. The response was wonderful, and thrilled the loyal people of the country with joy, for it revealed the amazing latent power which the Government might, at any time, rely upon for help. Within forty-eight hours after the Governor's call was issued, sixty-five thousand citizens had tendered their services, and were hastening to military rendezvous. Party feeling was laid aside in the immediate presence of danger, and only the disloyal Peace Faction, which never, as we have observed, represented the great body of the Opposition, refused to respond. Within the space of three days, thirty thousand Indianians were organized and armed, and appeared in the field at various points.

[a] July, 1863.

Morgan was now alarmed. He moved quickly from the presence of Lowe's troops, under cover of darkness, and pressing on, his men in scattered detachments plundering as before, he concentrated his forces at Harrison, just within the borders of Ohio, preparatory to making his way back to Kentucky as quickly as possible. He knew that Hobson was in his rear, and Judah on his flank, and that thousands of armed Indianians were blocking every route, however circuitous, for a retrograde movement; so he determined to strike the Ohio at some point where he might cross over into Western Virginia, or Northeastern Kentucky, and make his way back to Tennessee with his plunder.[2]

When Morgan left Harrison, Hobson, who was pressing on in his track at the rate of forty miles a day (notwithstanding his inability to get fresh horses, because Morgan had seized them), had so gained upon the invader, that there was not more than half a day's march between them. Morgan quickened his pace, exchanged his jaded horses for fresh ones from the pastures of Ohio farmers, and plundered somewhat less for want of time. He swept around a few miles north of Cincinnati (where Burnside, like Wallace the year before,[3] had declared martial law,[b] and called upon the citizens to defend their homes[4]), and pushing on through the rich southern tier of counties in Ohio,[5] struck the river at Buffington Ford,

[b] July 13.

---

[1] See page 455, volume I.

[2] A commission appointed by the State of Indiana to consider the claims of citizens to payment for losses incurred by Morgan's raid, closed their labors in December, 1867, when they had audited claims to the amount of $415,000.

[3] See page 503, volume II.

[4] On Saturday and Sunday, the 11th and 12th of July, nearly 12,000 men were formed into regiments; and a call of Mayor Harris for 3,000 mounted volunteers, to intercept the raiders, was fully responded to within twenty-four hours. For want of horses, arms, and equipments, they were not ready for the field until Morgan had swept by.

[5] When they came to the Little Miami railway, east of Cincinnati, they obstructed the track, so that when a train came down, the locomotive was thrown from the road, wounding the engineer and killing the fireman. Then the raiders rushed from a wood near by, captured and paroled two hundred unarmed recruits, and burnt the train.

a short distance above Pomeroy, where the stream is divided by Buffington Island. His situation had been growing more critical every hour.
Governor Tod, of Ohio, like Governor Morton, of Indiana, had summoned
the people to arms, and the uprising of the loyal inhabitants was like that
of the sister State on the west, and with like effect upon the friends and foes
of the Government. The people did all they could to assist Hobson in his
wearisome chase, by harassing the raiders, obstructing the roads, and
removing or protecting Government property at different points. General
Judah, who had arrived at Cincinnati with most of his division, was sent
up the river with his command, in boats, to head off the invaders, and bodies
of militia were directed to move down from the north for the same purpose.
Gun-boats were also patrolling the Ohio to dispute his passage of it. Yet
Morgan moved on audaciously, plundering as he went, with a seeming assurance that he was invincible, until, at length, he made the fatal mistake of
turning from his line of march to Berlin, in Jackson County, where the Government had a large number of animals. There he was confronted by a
small force of militia, under Colonel Runkle, so well displayed, that, after
spending much precious time in real or feigned movements for attack,
Morgan thought it prudent to decamp, but only to find himself unexpectedly
involved in a net of difficulties. Union forces were concentrating upon him
from different points. Runkle was following him from Berlin; Hobson was
within a few hours' ride, on the west; three regiments from Scammon's
Kanawha division had come down from Parkersburg, and were watching for
him; General Judah, who had landed at Portsmouth, was moving up with
his whole division, from the southeast, and all the fords in that region were
watched by gun-boats.

Such was the perilous situation of Morgan and his men, when, on the 18th
of July, they reached the Ohio at Buffington Ford, and attempted to cross
the river, under cover of artillery. There a severe engagement occurred, on
the morning of the 19th, when General Judah's cavalry struck Morgan's
flank, the head of Hobson's column, under General Shackleford, struck his
rear, and two armed vessels, near, Buffington Island, opened upon his front.
Hemmed in on three sides, about eight hundred of the raiders surrendered,
and the remainder, leaving all their plunder behind them,[1] and led by Morgan, fled up the river, and attempted to cross to Belleville by swimming
their horses. The gun-boat *Moore*, Lieutenant-commanding Fitch, interfered, and after about three hundred had thus escaped, the remainder, still
led by Morgan, fled inland to McArthur, and, on a zig-zag line, pushed on in
a northeasterly direction, fighting squads of militia, burning bridges, and
plundering a little, until they were enveloped by militia and Home Guards,
near New Lisbon, the capital of Columbiana County, with Shackleford's
pursuing column in their rear, and compelled to surrender,[a] first
informally to Major Rae, of Shackleford's cavalry, and, half an   [a] July 26,
hour later, formally to Shackleford himself. Thus ended, in death   1863.

---

[1] This plunder consisted of lumber and pleasure-wagons; silks and other dry-goods of every kind, taken
from merchants; bags full of men's, women's, and children's clothing; jewelry, horses, and mules, and a large
amount of money.

At the opening of this battle the venerable Daniel McCook, the father of seven sons who were distinguished
in the Union army, was mortally wounded. One of his sons, General Robert L. McCook, had been brutally
murdered by a party of guerrillas, while sick, and riding in a carriage from Athens to Decherd, in Tennessee.

or captivity, the career of more than four thousand bold raiders, who entered the Free-labor States three weeks before, excepting a little more than three hundred, who escaped at Belleville, under Colonel Adam R. Johnson, and found refuge in Southwestern Virginia. Morgan and several of his officers were taken to Columbus, the capital of Ohio, and confined in felon cells in the Penitentiary, from which the leader and six of his captains escaped in November following, and succeeded in reaching the Confederate lines in Northern Georgia.[1]

This was one of the most daring, reckless, and foolish raids of the war; and the leader, instead of receiving an ovation, as he afterward did, at Richmond, as a *hero* worthy of honor, should have been cashiered as a freebooter, who had robbed friends and foes alike for his own benefit. Instead of assisting the Confederate cause, he damaged it most seriously by arousing to intense action the then comparatively half-slumbering martial spirit of the loyalists in the Ohio region, and lessening the chances for that counter-revolution which the Confederates so much desired and relied upon. As an exhibition of endurance in man and beast, that raid was wonderful, pursued and pursuers sharing alike in that respect. For three weeks the race had continued without cessation, at the average rate of thirty-five miles a day.

We have observed that the Conspirators, at this time, were sweeping into their military ranks every able-bodied man they could lay their hands on. By a law of the Confederate "Congress," passed in 1862, Davis was authorized to call into the military service all "white residents of the Confederate States between the ages of eighteen and forty-five years, excepting exempts." The first class, or those under thirty-five years of age, were called out in 1862. After the battle at Gettysburg, and the discomfiture of Lee, Davis issued an address to the people of the Confederate States,[a] calling out all who were liable to bear arms, between the ages of eighteen and forty-five years. It was supposed that this would summon to the field a little more than one hundred thousand men; but it was found that not more than ninety thousand remained subject to conscription. There were at least twenty thousand substitutes in the army, for planters and planters' sons were generally unwilling to take the field, excepting as officers; and it was reported that there were at least ten thousand fraudulent substitute papers held by persons not in service. And

a July 15, 1863.

The father, living in Cincinnati, heard that the murderer of his son was with Morgan, and, under the impulse of strong resentment, took his rifle and joined General Judah as a volunteer. He was shot, and died two days afterward.

[1] Morgan made his way from the prison, when he escaped, with Captain Hines, who left in his cell the following note, dated "Cell No. 20, November 20, 1863. Commencement, November 4, 1863. Conclusion, November 20, 1863. Number of hours of labor per day, three. Tools, two small knives. *La patience et amère, mais son fruit est doux.* By order of my six honorable confederates." This was an outline history of the method of their escape. They dug through the floors of their cells, composed of cement and nine inches of brickwork, into an air-chamber below, and then through the soft earth under the foundation walls of the penitentiary, making a passage into the yard. Captain Hines superintended this engineering. They had furnished themselves with a strong rope, made of bedclothes, with which they scaled the walls. They had, by some means, procured citizens' clothes, in which they escaped. Morgan and Hines went immediately to the railway station (one o'clock in the morning, November 28), and traveled toward Cincinnati. When near there, they went to the brake of the rear car, with it slackened the speed of the train, jumped off, made their way to the Ohio, and, crossing it in a skiff rowed by a boy, found shelter with sympathizing friends in Kentucky. The utter carelessness of the officer in charge of the prisoners, in not examining the cells, gave them the opportunity to escape. A reward of one thousand dollars was offered for Morgan, "dead or alive;" but the first positive news concerning him was an account of his ovation at Richmond. For a more minute account of this famous raid, see a volume entitled *Morgan and his Captors*, by Reverend F. Senour.

so loosely were military affairs managed, that deserters, stragglers, and absentees formed a very large proportion of the persons enrolled.

In view of these ugly facts and the discomfiture of the Confederate armies at nearly all points, Jefferson Davis issued another proclamation,^a in which he urged the immediate return to the army ^{a Aug. 1, 1863.} of all absentees, and alleged that if one-fourth or one-half of them should do so, there would be sufficient strength to achieve the independence of the Confederacy. He offered to grant full amnesty and pardon to all who should immediately return to the ranks, excepting such as had been twice convicted of desertion. He appealed to the women, asking them to "take care that none who owe service in the field shall be sheltered at home from the disgrace of having deserted their duty to their families, to their country, and to their God." But it had become a hard task to draw men back into the ranks by persuasion. No bounties seemed to have been offered after the passage of the Conscription Act in 1862, nor efforts made to fill up the ranks with volunteers. So the Conspirators used their usurped power with a high hand, and men and supplies were forced into the service at the point of the bayonet, as it were. An agent was appointed in every county to seize, if necessary, supplies for the use of the army; and at about the close of 1863, the "Congress" at Richmond passed an act which declared every white man in the Confederacy, *between the ages of eighteen and fifty-five years, to be in the military service, and subject to the articles of war and military discipline and penalties; and that upon failure to report for duty at a military station within a certain time, he was liable to the penalty of death as a deserter.* The history of civilized nations has no parallel to this despotic act. Davis and his fellow-conspirators had then reached a critical point in their wicked game, and seemed willing to sacrifice every man, ruin every family, waste all the property in the Confederacy, and see their section of the Republic converted into a wilderness[1] in a desperate effort to win, well knowing that failure would be ruin to themselves. They seemed to regard the "common people" as of no account, excepting as docile instruments for the aggrandizement of the slave-holding Oligarchy.

Let us now return to a consideration of the movements of the armies of Meade and Lee, which we left occupying opposite banks of the Potomac.[2] We will first turn aside for a moment to observe some operations on the Virginia Peninsula, designed to be co-operative with the Army of the Potomac.

It had been determined early in the campaign to menace Richmond by a reoccupation of the Peninsula which McClellan evacuated the year before. General Keyes, then in the Department of Virginia, under the command of General Dix, had been selected as the leader of the forces that were to effect it. He concentrated a considerable body of troops at Yorktown, and so soon as it was ascertained that Lee was moving toward the Potomac, Keyes was directed to make a demonstration on Richmond, then held by a few troops under Henry A. Wise. Colonel Spear, with his Eleventh Pennsylvania and detachments of Massachusetts and Illinois cavalry, about one

---

[1] See notice of the manifesto of Howell Cobb and Robert Toombs, note 2, page 471, volume II.
[2] See page 75.

thousand strong, made a sudden dash ᵃ upon White House,[1] drove the Confederates from the post, and pushed on to a point within ten miles of
ᵃ June 25, Richmond, alarming Wise, the citizens, and the Confederate author-
1863.
ities to such a degree, that orders were issued for the closing
of all places of business, and causing the Mayor to call upon the inhabitants
to "Remember New Orleans," and to array themselves in defense of their
homes. Turning northward, Spear galloped to Hanover Court-House and
beyond, destroying the railway and capturing General W. H. F. Lee,
wounded at Beverly Ford. Then sweeping through King William County, he
returned to White House, then held by Keyes, who, on the 1st of July, moved
five or six thousand troops toward the Chickahominy, under General Gettys,
with fifteen hundred cavalry in advance, with orders to push on north of
Richmond, destroy the railway bridge over the South Anna, and so cut
Lee's communications with the Confederate capital. This, and much more
that was expected, was not accomplished, and Keyes fell back, to the great
relief of the Confederates in and around Richmond.

When Lee escaped into the Shenandoah Valley, Meade determined to
follow him along the route pursued by McClellan in his race with the same
foe the year before, keeping close to the eastern slopes of the Blue Ridge,

and using its gaps as circumstances
might dictate. Only his cavalry
advance, under General Gregg, entered the Shenandoah Valley. That
leader crossed the Potomac at Harper's Ferry on the day when Lee
passed over above, and, pushing on
to Shepherdstown, he there encountered, fought and beat Confederate
cavalry under Fitzhugh Lee, each
party being dismounted, on account
of the ground being rough and
wooded, and each losing about one
one hundred men.

On the 17th and 18th of July,
Meade's army crossed the Potomac,
chiefly at and near Berlin, and

DAVID McM. GREGG.

moved rapidly southward by way of Lovettsville, Union, Upperville, and
Warrenton, seizing the gaps of the Blue Ridge on its way. Its route was
that which it had followed northward under Hooker a few weeks before. It
reached Warrenton on the 25th of July, after a detention at Manassas Gap,
where Meade had been led to expect an engagement of the two armies in large
force. At that time Meade had the start of Lee in the race toward Richmond, the latter having halted at Bunker's Hill and endeavored to recall or
distract his antagonist by a feint of recrossing the Potomac. He failed, and
pushed his columns rapidly up the Shenandoah Valley, to meet the dangers
which threatened his front and flank. He knew that a more vigilant and
active commander than McClellan was his competitor in the race for the

_____

prize of victory. His heavy columns pressed on near the mountain passes, and Buford, who, with his cavalry, had pushed well up into Manassas Gap, thought he discovered the presence of a greater part of Lee's army there and at Front Royal, and reported accordingly. Meade, believing it to be Lee's intention to press through the Gap, ordered a large part of his army to march upon it, at the same time directing French, with the Third (Sickles's) Corps, then guarding Ashby's Gap, to hasten forward to the support of Buford, who was calling for re-enforcements. This was done with so much rapidity, that the corps reached Piedmont before dark. Birney's division, temporarily under the command of General Hobart Ward, was sent immediately forward to Buford's aid, followed by the remainder of the corps, and on the following day [a] there was a warm engagement at Wapping's Heights, where the Third and Fourth Maine—Kearney's veterans—and the Excelsior (New York) Brigade, led by General   [a] July 24, 1863.
Spinola, gained renown by successful charges under the direction of General Prince, which drove the Confederates. The latter consisted of one of Ewell's brigades, which had been holding the Gap while a portion of Lee's army was passing by; and when, the next morning, the National troops pressed on to Front Royal, Lee's columns had all passed, and there was no foe to assail. Meade was disappointed. His detention at the Gap had given Lee a great advantage, who now swept rapidly around the right flank of the Army of the Potomac, through Chester Gap, and took position on the south side of the Rappahannock. Meade advanced slowly to that stream, when Lee retired to Culpepper Court-House. Then the opposing armies rested for some time.

Troops were now drawn from each army and sent to other fields of service. Bragg was then severely pressed by Rosecrans, in Tennessee, and Lee was ordered to detach Longstreet's corps [b] to his assistance. This reduc-   [b] September.
tion of his army compelled Lee to take a strictly defensive position. This fact was revealed by reconnoissances of Meade's cavalry, when the latter moved his whole army across the Rappahannock, [c] pressed Lee back,   [c] Sept. 16.
pushed two corps forward to the Rapid Anna, and occupied Culpepper Court-House, and the region between the two rivers just named. The Confederates had destroyed the bridges over all the streams behind them, but temporary ones were

JAMES LONGSTREET.

so quickly constructed, that Meade's advance was not checked.

Lee took a strong position on the south side of the Rapid Anna—too strong for a prudent commander like Meade to attempt to carry by direct assault; so he planned a flank movement, and was about to attempt its execution, when his army was suddenly reduced in numbers by the withdrawal of the Eleventh and Twelfth Corps (Howard's and Slocum's) for service elsewhere. These were placed under the command of General Hooker, and sent to re-enforce the Army of the Cumberland in Southeastern Tennessee and Northern Georgia. Meade was now, in turn, placed in a defensive position for awhile, but, finally, when new recruits came in, and troops, which had been taken from his army and sent to New York, to prevent interference with the draft, returned, at about the middle of October, he resolved to make an offensive movement.

A TEMPORARY ARMY BRIDGE.[1]

Meade's cavalry, meanwhile, had not been idle. On the 1st of August, Buford, with his division, crossed the Rappahannock River at Rappahannock Station, and with great gallantry pushed Stuart's cavalry back almost to Culpepper Court-House. So sudden and unexpected to Stuart was this dash of his foe across the river, and so vigorous was the assault and pursuit, that he and his staff came very near being captured at his head-quarters, on an eminence a short distance from Brandy Station. They were about to dine at a table sumptuously furnished by the family of Henry Miller, the owner of the house, when the near presence of their foe was announced. The daring leader and his followers instantly decamped, and left the dinner to be enjoyed by the Union officers. Buford pursued to the vicinity of Auburn, the residence of John Minor Botts,[3] where he was confronted by Stuart's strong infantry supports, and compelled to retreat, fighting as he fell back, when he, in turn, was re-enforced by the First Corps, and the pursuing foe halted. In that engagement Buford lost one hundred and forty men, of whom sixteen were killed.

STUART'S HEAD-QUARTERS NEAR BRANDY STATION.[2]

---

[1] This picture is given to illustrate the method of construction of those temporary bridges which the armies were continually erecting over small streams. This is a view of one over the Mattapony River.

[2] This is a view of the place, from the shaded lane in front, as it appeared when the writer visited and sketched it in October, 1866, when it was occupied by W. A. Stewart. The house was in a shattered condition, and bore marks of the battle near it. The porch had been torn away by a shell, and at the dark spot seen between the two windows in the sketch, was the fracture made by a round shot that passed through the house.

[3] Mr. Botts's beautiful seat, called Auburn, was about a mile from Brandy Station, on a very slight elevation,

A month later[a] General Kilpatrick crossed the Rappahannock at Port Conway, below Fredericksburg, drove the Confederates, and burned two gun-boats which they had captured on the Potomac and placed on the Rappahannock for future use. A little more than a fortnight afterward,[b] General Pleasanton, with the greater part of the cavalry of the Army of the Potomac, crossed the Rappahannock at the fords above Fredericksburg in three columns, commanded respectively by Buford, Kilpatrick, and Gregg, supported by the Second Corps, under General Warren. Stuart's cavalry were pressed back to the Rapid Anna with a loss, on his part, of two guns. It was this reconnoissance which revealed the fact of Longstreet's departure, when Meade was emboldened to cross the Rappahannock with his whole army.

> [a] Sept. 1, 1863.

> [b] Sept. 16.

General Meade, as we have observed, contemplated a forward movement early in October. On the 10th he sent Buford, with his cavalry division, to uncover the upper fords of the Rapid Anna, preparatory to advancing the First and Sixth Corps. Lee, having heard of the reduction of Meade's army by the sending away of two corps, was preparing for an offensive movement at the same time. He felt himself competent to cope with his antagonist, and proposed, it is said, the audacious measure of a direct march on Washington in full force, with a willingness to leave Richmond uncovered, if necessary, and exchange capitals.[1] Davis would not allow it, and Lee contented himself with an attempt to turn Meade's right flank, and get between him and the National capital. His chief object was to cripple Meade, and

with a little depression between his house and gentle cultivated ridges at a little distance. The writer and his friends already mentioned (Messrs. Buckingham and Young), visited this stanch Virginia Unionist, when on our way homeward from Staunton, mentioned on page 401, volume II. We had passed the preceding night and part of the day before at Culpepper Court-House and in visiting the battle-ground at Cedar Mountain. See page 448, volume II. At Culpepper Court-House we hired a carriage to convey us to Brandy Station, and our route lay across Mr. Botts's estate. We found him at home, and were very cordially received. The region just about him was a sort of neutral ground for some time, detachments from each army frequently meeting upon it and skirmishing. He told us that he had seen no less than nine of these engagements from his piazza. On one occasion his house was placed in great peril, between large bodies of the contending armies, who were about to fight. In front of his house General Rodes drew up fifteen thousand men in battle order, evidently with the design of bringing the mansion in range of the guns of the combatants, and thus effecting its destruction without its being done in evident wantonness. Botts went out to Rodes, told him that his house was filled with the women and children of the neighborhood (and his own family), who had sought shelter there, and warned him that, if these were all destroyed, the crime would rest forever as a stain on the Confederate general's name. Rodes was unwilling to incur the odium, and, changing his position, the mansion was saved.

AUBURN.

The reader is referred to page 94, volume I., for an extract of a letter from Mr. Botts, to "H. B. M.," of Staunton. At the time of our visit, he showed us another letter to him from the same writer, in which he denounced the rebellion as a crime, and declared that the traitors should be punished. He went into the war and had his skull fractured, and lost a little portion of his brain, that protruded, in one of the battles before Richmond. In his reply, Mr. Botts told him he believed his was the first case on record of a man being brought to his senses by having his brains knocked out.

[1] Statement of General Longstreet to the author of *Campaigns of the Army of the Potomac*, cited in note on page 377.

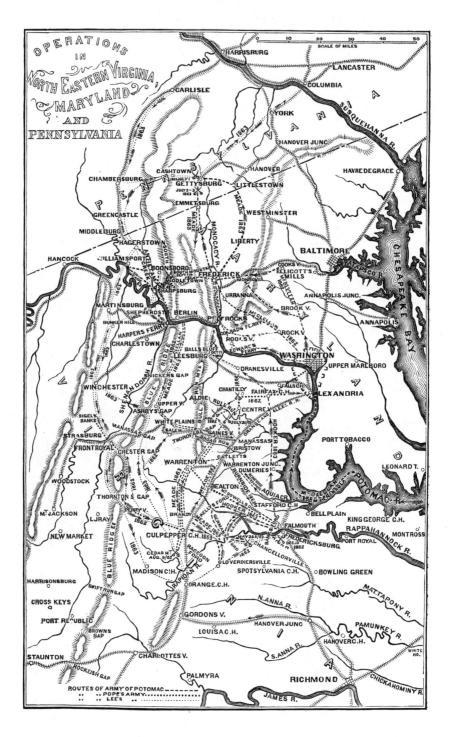

keep him, till winter, near Washington, so that more troops might be sent from Virginia to assist Bragg, Davis's favorite, then below Chattanooga, in need of help. So, on the day before Buford's cavalry marched on the Rapid Anna, Lee crossed it[a] in force, and along unfrequented and circuitous roads by way of Madison Court-House, and over Robertson's River, gained Meade's right before that commander suspected the movement. It was first revealed by an attack upon a portion of Kilpatrick's cavalry, who were holding the advanced posts on the National right. These were driven back on Culpepper by Stuart.[b] Satisfied that his right was turned, Meade instantly sent back his trains, and at a little past midnight[c] retreated across the Rappahannock, blowing up the bridge at Rappahannock Station, behind him. Lee advanced to Culpepper a few hours later, where he halted his main force, while Stuart followed as closely to Meade as Pleasanton, who covered the retreat, would allow. That night Pleasanton also crossed the river. · .

[a] Oct. 9, 1863.

[b] Oct. 10.

[c] Oct. 11.

Informed, on the morning of the 12th, that Lee had halted at Culpepper, Meade felt that his retreat might have been premature. Acting upon such presumption, he pushed the Second, Fifth, and Sixth Corps, with Buford's cavalry, back across the Rappahannock to the vicinity of Brandy Station. The mounted men pressed on toward Culpepper, where Meade intended to offer battle to Lee, but the latter had not waited for his antagonist. On that morning he had commenced another flanking movement to gain Meade's rear, and the two armies, for several hours, presented the appearance of a friendly countermarch on nearly parallel roads.

Meade was first advised of this new and dangerous movement of his foe by General Gregg, who had been watching the fords of the Upper Rappahannock with the Third Corps (French's) below him. Lee's van assailed Gregg and drove him back, and then the main column of the Confederates crossed the Rappahannock at Warrenton, Sulphur Springs, and Waterloo, where Jackson passed over the previous year when flanking Pope.[1] Meade at once, fell back, crossed the river, and continued his retreat to Catlett's Station. Fortunately Lee was ignorant of the real condition of Meade's army at that time, or he might, by turning aside, have demolished the Third Corps with his overwhelming force. Gregg was surrounded, attacked, and routed, at Jeffersonton, north of Hazel River, after a gallant fight,[2] with a loss of about five hundred men, most of whom were made prisoners.

Now[d] the veteran armies of the Potomac and of Northern Virginia commenced a third race northward, over nearly the same course pursued on former like occasions, Lee aiming to strike Meade's line of retreat along the Orange and Alexandria railway, and the latter using every energy to prevent him. Lee pressed on to Warrenton on the afternoon of the 13th, and prepared to advance from that point in two columns, his left under A. P. Hill, by the Warrenton turnpike to New Baltimore, and so on to Bristow Station, and his right, under Ewell, by way of Auburn Mills and Greenwich, for the same destination. This movement was begun on the morning of the 14th. Meanwhile there had been collisions.

[d] Oct. 13.

---

[1] See page 453, volume II.

[2] His command was composed of the Fourth and Thirteenth Pennsylvania, and First New York Cavalry, and Tenth New York Infantry.

Stuart, with about two thousand cavalry, was hanging closely upon the rear flank of Meade's army, picking up many stragglers. While eagerly pressing on, toward the evening of the 13th, he encountered the head of French's column, and was pushed toward Catlett's Station, near which he found himself, that night, in a perilous situation. The Second Corps, under General Warren, with Kilpatrick's cavalry, was at that time covering the National

HUGH JUDSON KILPATRICK.

rear, and when Lee reached Warrenton, this rear-guard was at Auburn, only a few miles eastward, with Caldwell's division and three batteries on the heights of Cedar Run, between them. Stuart had inadvertently got ahead of this covering force, and found himself hemmed in between the two National corps, with small chance to escape. His first impulse was to abandon his guns and all impediments to a speedy flight, and attempt to escape under cover of darkness, but he finally resolved to try another plan. So he hid his men in one of those dense thickets of small pine saplings which cover old fields in Virginia, and sent messengers through the Union lines to Lee, to ask for help. For this purpose, three men, dressed like Union soldiers, fell into the National line as it was moving, marched awhile, and then, dropping out, hurried to Lee. Relief for Stuart was immediately sent, and when the musketry of the skirmishers of the approaching re-enforcements were heard at dawn, the bold cavalry leader opened a cannonade from his concealment upon the rear of Caldwell's forces, who had bivouacked a little in front of this thicket. Caldwell, unexpectedly assailed, moved to cover on the opposite side of the hills, when he was attacked in like manner from the Warrenton road. This assault produced sufficient confusion in the Union ranks to allow Stuart to break through and escape. For a moment Warren's corps appeared to be in a very critical situation, surrounded and cut off, but it was soon found that the attacking party on the Warrenton turnpike was only the van of Ewell's column. These were repulsed by two regiments[1] thrown out by General Hayes from the north side of Cedar Run, and the way was cleared for the advance of the corps. Ewell was held in check until Warren's troops had crossed the Run and resumed their line of march (Caldwell covering the rear, and skirmishing almost continually) for the heights of Centreville, behind Bull's Run, the now prescribed destination of the Army of the Potomac, where Meade determined to offer battle.

Now the race for Bristow Station became hot, Lee pushing Hill and Ewell forward to gain that point before Meade should pass it. They failed. When Hill approached it, the entire Army of the Potomac had passed it,

---

[1] These were the One Hundred and Twenty-sixth New York and Twelfth New Jersey volunteers. In this encounter, Colonel Thomas Ruffin, the leader of Confederate cavalry, which charged furiously, was killed.

excepting Warren's corps, which was not then in sight of the Confederates. The Third Corps, in the rear of the troops that had passed, was just crossing Broad Run, and Hill pushed forward to attack it. At about noon, when he was preparing to charge, he was startled by the apparition of Warren's corps coming upon his rear. This had outstripped Ewell's, whose advance it had encountered in the morning near Auburn, and was now pushing forward expecting to meet Sykes's at Bristow Station. Warren was again in a critical situation. Hill quickly turned upon him, and almost instantly brought his batteries in full play upon this unexpected foe. Warren was surprised for a moment, but in the space of ten minutes the batteries of Brown and Arnold were playing upon Hill in response, and these, assisted by the infantry divisions of Hayes and Webb,[1] soon drove the Confederates, and captured six of their guns, which were instantly turned upon the fugitives. A flank attack by Heth's (formerly Pettigrew's[2]) was repulsed, with a Confederate loss of four hundred and fifty men made prisoners, with two battle-flags.

This was an effectual check upon Hill's advance, yet Warren was in great danger, for he found it unsafe to attempt to resume his march, and he stood at bay, skirmishing and maneuvering all the remainder of the afternoon. Just at sunset Ewell came up, and the Second Corps was actually confronted by nearly the whole of Lee's army; but before the latter was ready for an attack, Warren skillfully withdrew under cover of darkness, and joined the main army in the morning[a] on the heights of Centre- [a] October 15, 1863. ville. Warren's loss in the BATTLE OF BRISTOW STATION was about two hundred in killed and wounded. Among the former was Colonel James F. Mallon, of the Forty-second New York. General Posey, of Hill's corps, was mortally wounded.

At Bristow Station the great race ended. Lee was beaten. Meade was strongly posted on the Heights of Centreville, and was too near the defenses of Washington[3] to allow his competitor to gain his rear; so Lee, after pushing a thin line to Bull's Run to mask his designs, effectually destroyed the Orange and Alexandria railway, from Bristow to the Rappahannock, and then began a retreat[b] with his whole army. Meade [b] Oct. 18. followed him the next day, but could not touch him, excepting with his cavalry. These were almost continually engaged in spirited but not serious skirmishing, excepting in an encounter[c] on Broad Run, [c] Oct. 19. near Buckland's Mills, between the divisions of Kilpatrick and Hampton, the latter under the personal directions of Stuart. Kilpatrick was defeated by a stratagem. Stuart allowed him to flank Hampton, when the latter fell back, making way for Fitzhugh Lee to come down from Auburn, and fall on Kilpatrick's flank. This was done. At the same moment Stuart pressed his front, and Kilpatrick was driven back in some confusion, and a loss of over one hundred men made prisoners. The brunt of this heavy skirmish was borne by General Custer's brigade. On the following day, Lee crossed the Rappahannock, while Meade, in consequence of the destruction of the Orange and Alexandria railway, over which his supplies must pass, was unable to follow him further than Warrenton, for about three weeks.

---

[1] The brunt of the encounter fell chiefly on Webb's First and Third Brigades, and Hayes's Third.
[2] See page 72.   [3] See map on page 24, volume II.

In the audacious movement of Lee from the Rapid Anna to Bull's Run, and his retreat behind the Rappahannock, and the foiling maneuvers of Meade, each army lost, in killed and wounded, about five hundred men. The Confederates claimed to have captured two thousand prisoners, besides over four hundred taken by General J. D. Imboden, who, while in the Shenandoah, watching the gaps of the Blue Ridge, suddenly swept down upon Charlestown, not far from Harper's Ferry, on the day when Lee ᵃ October 18, began his retreat,ᵃ seized the post, and bore away prisoners and 1863. stores. He had scarcely secured these, when he was compelled to fall back, fighting a superior Union force which had come up from Harper's Ferry, all the way to Berryville. There, under cover of darkness, Imboden escaped with his prisoners and spoils.[1]

When the railway from Warrenton to the Rappahannock was repaired, Meade asked permission of the General-in-Chief to move rapidly upon Fredericksburg and seize the heights there, so as to make that point a base of operations against Richmond. Halleck opposed the project, and Meade was compelled to go forward from Warrenton in the beaten track, if at all. He did so early on the morning of the 7th of November, General Sedgwick, with the Fifth and Sixth Corps, composing the right wing, leading, followed by General French, with the First, Second, and Third Corps, composing the left wing. Sedgwick's column marched for the Rappahannock, at Rappahannock Station, and French's moved toward the same stream at Kelley's Ford. Lee, then in position near Culpepper Court-House, had outposts at these crossings.

At Rappahannock Station Sedgwick found the strong works thrown up previously by the Nationals on the north side of the river, and now covering a pontoon bridge, occupied by about two thousand men, of Early's division of Ewell's corps, under Colonel Godwin, composed of Hayes's Louisiana brigade, and Hoke's brigade of North Carolinians, just sent over. These works, consisting of a fort, two redoubts, and lines of rifle-pits, were on a ridge, with an open lowland traversed by a muddy ditch, and a dry moat, deep and broad, between them and the approaching Nationals. Sedgwick reached the vicinity at noon, and behind a hill, a mile away, he formed a battle-line, and then gradually advanced toward the river on each flank of

---

[1] Lee's failure now, as well as in his invasion of Maryland and Pennsylvania, to gain any positive advantages for the Confederate cause, military or political, produced much dissatisfaction, especially among those who hoped for a counter-revolution in the Free-labor States. " Alas!" they exclaimed, in substance, "the golden opportunity is passed. The elections in Ohio and Pennsylvania have gone for the war candidates. We must now rely on ourselves, under God, for independence, for Northern support is a delusion."—See *A Rebel War-Clerk's Diary*, ii. 80. Early in September, when Lee, driven from Maryland, was lying behind the Rappahannock, a Richmond paper said: " The success of the Democratic party would be no longer doubtful, should General Lee once more advance on Meade. General Lee must turn politician as well as warrior, and we believe he will prove the most successful politician the Confederacy ever produced. *He may so move and direct his army as to produce political results, which, in their bearing upon this war, will prove more effectual than the bloodiest victories.* Let him drive Meade into Washington, and he will again *raise the spirits of the Democrats*, confirm their timid, and give confidence to their wavering. He will *embolden the Peace Party* should he again cross the Potomac, for he will show the people of Pennsylvania how little security they have from Lincoln for the protection of their homes. It matters not whether the advance be made for purposes of permanent occupation, or simply for a grand raid ; it will demonstrate that, in the third year of the war, they are so far from the subjugation of the Confederate States, that the defense of Maryland and Pennsylvania has not been secured. A fall campaign into Pennsylvania, with the hands of our soldiers untied, not for indiscriminate plunder—demoralizing and undisciplining the army—but a campaign for a systematic and organized retaliation and punishment, would arouse the popular mind to the uncertainty and insecurity of Pennsylvania. This would react upon the representatives in Congress, strengthening the Democrats, and mollifying even to the hard shell of fanaticism itself."—*Richmond Enquirer*, September 7, 1863.

the works, with General David A. Russell's division of the Sixth Corps (the latter now commanded by General Wright) moving upon the center. The First Brigade, under Colonel P. C. Ellmaker, of the One Hundred and Nineteenth Pennsylvania,[1] was in the van of this division, and when, just before sunset, directions were given to storm the works, these troops gallantly performed the task. They moved forward in two columns, with one half of the Sixth Maine deployed as skirmishers. The Fifth Wisconsin, in solid column, pressed up close behind them, while the Twentieth Maine, of Upton's (Second) brigade, closed in on the left of the Wisconsin troops, and advanced in line with the Sixth Maine. The gallant Russell now ordered a charge on the strongest redoubt. There was an instant and grand response. With fixed bayonets the van of stormers rushed through a tempest of canister-shot and bullets, followed by the remainder of the First Brigade, and, after a struggle of a few minutes, the redoubt was carried. In that charge the slaughter of the Unionists was fearful, but their effort was entirely successful. At the same time two regiments of Upton's brigade,[2] after firing a single volley, charged the rifle-trenches, drove the foe, and sweeping down to the pontoon bridge, cut off the retreat of the garrison. Over sixteen hundred prisoners, with four guns, eight battle-flags, two thousand small-arms, and the pontoon bridge, were the fruits of the National victory in the BATTLE OF RAPPAHANNOCK STATION. The Union loss was about three hundred in killed and wounded.

While the right column was thus achieving victory, the left was no less successful, but without much struggle. The Third Corps, commanded by General Birney, reached Kelly's Ford while the right column was engaged above. Without waiting for the laying of a pontoon bridge, Birney's own division of that corps, under General Ward, waded across the river, and an attacking party under General De Trobriand,[3] under cover of batteries, carried rifle-pits and captured five hundred Confederates on the south side of the stream, with slight loss on the part of the victors. The pontoon bridge was then laid, and at dusk the Third Corps was all on the southern side of the Rappahannock, confronting the foe in force. Birney advanced early the next morning to the railway within two miles of Brandy Station, the Confederates falling back before him, when he was ordered to halt.

Lee, who was preparing to go into winter quarters near Culpepper Court-House, was alarmed by this unexpected and successful advance of his antagonist, and he prudently resolved to withdraw to a stronger position, for his force did not then exceed fifty thousand men, while Meade's was about seventy thousand. Fortunately for Lee, Meade, whose army was all on the south side of the Rappahannock on the morning of the 8th,[a] did [a] Nov., 1863. not immediately advance, and, under cover of the darkness that night, the Confederates withdrew beyond the Rapid Anna, leaving the Nationals to take quiet possession of the region the latter were occupying when the retreat toward Washington began.[4] The railway was soon com-

---

[1] Composed of the Fifth Wisconsin, Sixth Maine, and Forty-ninth and One Hundred and Nineteenth Pennsylvania.

[2] One Hundred and Twenty-first New York and Fifth Maine.

[3] Ward's Third Brigade, composed of Burdan's sharp-shooters, the Fortieth New York, First and Twentieth Indiana, Third and Fifth Michigan, and One Hundred and Tenth Pennsylvania.

[4] See page 103.

pleted to and across the Rappahannock to Brandy Station, and the last named place was made a general depot of supplies for the Army of the Potomac.

Meade lay quietly between the Rappahannock and the Rapid Anna until

CULPEPPER COURT-HOUSE.[2]

late in the month,[a] watching for a favorable opportunity to advance on his foe. It might have been more prudent for him to have gone into winter quarters, but the impatience and clamor of the public, because of the seeming unfruitfulness of the whole summer and autumn campaigns since the Battle of Gettysburg, and Meade's own eagerness to act, made him resolve to strike a blow so soon as a wise prudence would allow. So, when the bridge over the Rappahannock, which he destroyed on his retreat,[1] had been rebuilt, and his communication with his supplies and the capital were full and perfect, he planned a forward movement of great boldness, and proceeded to put it into execution.

[a] Nov., 1863.

The strength of Lee's army was now weakened by expansion over a large surface. His right, composed of Ewell's corps (was resting on the Rapid Anna at Morton's Ford (leaving all the lower fords of that stream uncovered), and extending to Liberty Mills, west of Orange Court-House; and Hill's corps was distributed in cantonments for winter, along the railway, from a little south of the latter point to Charlottesville, leaving wide gaps between the two corps. Lee had also constructed, for the defense of his right flank, a line of intrenchments along Mine Run, whose course is perpendicular to the Rapid Anna from Bartley's Run to its mouth, at Morton's Ford. Meade quickly perceived Lee's weak points, and determined to attempt to turn his right, and, sweeping around toward Orange Court-House, overwhelm Ewell, turn the works on Mine Run, and, thrusting his army between the two corps of his antagonist, destroy them in detail, and secure an effectual lodgment at Orange and Gordonsville. This movement would involve the perilous measure of cutting loose from supplies. Meade took the risk. Providing his troops with ten days' rations, he moved forward at six o'clock

---

[1] See page 103.

[2] This is a view of the building which gave name to one of the pleasantest villages in Virginia before the war broke out, and which was made famous by the stirring scenes of that war which occurred in its neighborhood. The old court-house walls and its whole external structure survived the war, but its interior was destroyed; and when, in October, 1866, the writer visited and sketched it, it was yet a mere shell, and presented the appearance given in the picture.

on the morning of the 26th,[a] leaving his trains parked at Richardsville, on the north side of the Rapid Anna. The plan of advance was for the corps of French, followed by Sedgwick, to cross the [a] Nov., 1863. river at Jacobs's Mill Ford, and march toward Robertson's tavern, on the Orange turnpike; while Warren's, destined for the same point, for the purpose of a junction with the others, should cross at Germania Ford. Sykes's, followed by two divisions of Newton's, was to cross at Culpepper Mine Ford, and march for Parker's store and Hope Church, on the Orange plank road. The right and left columns of the army would thus be placed in close communication, on parallel roads. Gregg, with his cavalry, was to cross at Elly's Ford and take position on the extreme left; and to the cavalry divisions of Custer and Merritt was assigned the duty of watching the upper fords of the Rapid Anna and the trains at Richardsville.

Meade had calculated the time of his march to the vicinity of Orange Court-House at not more than thirty-six hours, if all the prescribed movements should be made promptly. But the necessary conditions were not fulfilled. Instead of crossing the Rapid Anna that morning, and reaching Robertson's tavern and Parker's store that evening, so as to surprise the foe, nearly the whole day was consumed in the passage of the river, owing to the tardiness of French's troops, mistakes of engineers in the construction of the pontoon bridges, and the difficulties in getting the artillery up the steep banks of the stream at the fords. It was ten o'clock the next day[b] before any of the troops destined for Robertson's tavern reached that point, when the movement had become known [b] Nov. 27. to the foe, and Warren, who, with ten thousand men, followed by the reserve artillery, was in the advance, was confronted by the divisions of Early, Rodes, and Johnson, of Ewell's corps. Brisk skirmishing at once began, but Warren was ordered not to seriously engage the Confederates until French should come up. That officer had taken the wrong road in the morning, and had fallen in and skirmished with Johnson's division, of Ewell's corps, near the Widow Morris's. This, and other causes of delay, kept him back until night, when Warren was so hard pressed that Meade had been compelled to send troops from the left to his assistance. This failure of French to come up in time almost exhausted Meade's patience, for it frustrated all his plans. Lee had penetrated his designs, and had ample time to make dispositions accordingly. He withdrew Ewell's corps, called up Hill, and concentrated his whole army on the west bank of Mine Run, when he strengthened and so extended his fortifications along the line of that stream, that they crossed the two highways upon which Meade's army lay.

Lee's position was made a very strong one. His army was in a series of hills forming an irregular ridge, extending north and south about eight miles. On these hills the fortifications lay, the natural shape of the former making proper angles of defense. In the rear and on the flanks of this position was a tangled forest, similar to that of the Wilderness;[1] and a little more than a thousand yards in front was Mine Run, with marshy, abrupt, or timbered banks. In front of all was a strong *abatis*, made of a thick growth of pines.

---

[1] See page 25.

Sykes's corps coming up on the morning of the 28th,[a] Meade had his army then all in hand along a line not much exceeding five or six miles in length. Gregg was sent out to make observations. He skirmished with and drove back Stuart's cavalry, and ascertained the

[a] Nov., 1863.

ABATIS.[1]

general position of Lee's army along Mine Run. Warren, with his own and a part of Sedgwick's corps, took position on the left, near Hope Church,

GOUVERNEUR KEMBLE WARREN.

with instructions to feel the foe, ascertain how far southward his fortifications extended, flank them, and turn the Confederate right, if possible. The following day[a] was spent in reconnoitering; and at evening, Warren on the left, and Sedgwick on the right, reported that such was the position of the enemy, that an attack on his right and left wings would undoubtedly be successful. Meade thereupon ordered an attack to be made the next morning.

[b] Nov. 28.

To Warren was intrusted the task of opening the battle by the heaviest assault. He was re-enforced by troops from French's (Second) corps (which, with a part of Sedgwick's, occupied the center as a kind of reserve at first), which made his

---

[1] *Abatis*, an obstruction formed of felled trees, has been frequently mentioned in this work, and described in a note. This picture is intended to show to the uninformed the appearance of such obstructions in front of fortifications, and the difficulties they present to an assailant.

whole number about twenty-six thousand. He was directed to begin the assault at about eight o'clock in the morning,[a] when the batteries of the center and right were to open on the foe. Sedgwick [a] Nov. 30, 1863. was to strike Lee's left an hour later, when, it was hoped, Warren's attack would cause the weakening of that wing; and French, with his own broken corps and a part of the First, under Newton, who was only to menace at the beginning, was to advance and attack Lee's center when the assault on his right and left should be successful. The National cavalry was ordered to keep Lee's horsemen from Meade's communications.

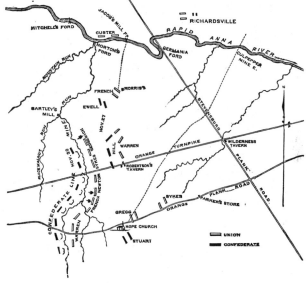

POSITION OF THE ARMIES AT MINE RUN, NOV. 30.

At the appointed hour, Meade's batteries on left and center were opened, and the skirmishers of the latter dashed across Mine Run, and drove back those of the Confederates. But Warren's guns were not heard. Sedgwick was in readiness, and anxiously waiting to perform his part, but Warren's guns were yet silent. The mystery was solved at a few minutes before nine o'clock, when Meade received a message from Warren, saying he had found Lee's position much stronger than he expected, and had taken the responsibility of suspending the attack. Meade hastened to the left, and found that his foe, informed of the massing of troops on his right, had concentrated his own forces there, men and guns, in formidable array. Meade was satisfied that Warren had behaved prudently, and he ordered a general suspension of operations for the attack. French and Sedgwick fell back, and Meade that day studied well the chances for success. He found that the opening of his batteries had given Lee hints to strengthen his defenses on his left, and he was doing so with energy. Indeed Lee's position was growing stronger every hour, while Meade's strength was diminishing, for his rations were nearly exhausted, and his supply-trains were beyond the Rapid Anna. To bring these over might expose them to disaster, for winter was at hand, and rains might suddenly swell the streams and make them impassable. Considering the risks, Meade determined to sacrifice himself, if necessary, rather than his army, by abandoning the enterprise at once. This he did. He recrossed the Rapid Anna,[b] without being fol- [b] Dec. 1, 2 lowed or molested, and went into winter quarters on his old camping grounds between that stream and the Rappahannock. He desired

to advance on Fredericksburg, seize the heights, and make his winter quar.
ters in that more advantageous position, but General Halleck would not
allow him to do so.[1]

So ended the campaign of the Army of the Potomac in 1863, and at
about the same time co-operating military operations in West Virginia were
closed, by the expulsion from that region of nearly all armed and organized
opponents of the Government.   But few military events, having an important bearing on the grander operations of the war, had occurred there since
the close of 1861.[2]   We have already mentioned the brilliant exploit of General Lander, in the vicinity of the Baltimore and Ohio railway,[3] early· in
1862.   Little was done there after that, except watching and raiding for
more than a year.   In May, 1862, General Heth was in the Greenbrier region,
and on the day when Kenly was attacked at Front Royal,[4] he marched upon
Lewisburg with three regiments, and attacked two Ohio regiments stationed
there, under Colonel George Crooke.   Heth was routed, and escaped by burning the bridge over the Greenbrier behind him, with a loss of over one hundred men (mostly prisoners), four guns, and three hundred muskets.   Crooke's
loss was sixty-three men.

After this there was comparative quiet in West Virginia, until the sum-
mer of 1863, when a raiding party, one thousand strong, under Colonel John
Tolland, composed of Virginia Union cavalry and the Thirty-fourth Ohio
infantry, left the Kanawha Valley, went southward to a point on the Coal
River, and then, turning more to the eastward, crossed over the rugged Flat
Top, and other mountains of the Appalachian range, and, on the 18th of
July, swept down upon Wytheville, on the Virginia and Tennessee railway.
They charged into the village, when they were fired upon from some of the
houses.   The leader was killed, and Lieutenant-Colonel Powell, of the Thirty-
fourth Ohio, was mortally wounded.   This unexpected resistance startled
the raiders, and, after firing the houses from which shots came, they hastily
retired, leaving their dead and wounded behind them.   After brief rest they
started for the Kanawha, under Lieutenant Franklin.   They suffered severely
from fatigue and lack of food among the almost uninhabited mountain ranges,
and at the end of a rough ride of about four hundred miles, going and
returning, during eight days, they lost eighty-two men and three hundred
horses.

A little later, General W. W. Averill started with his cavalry from Huttonsville, in Tygart's Valley,[5] and passing through several counties in the
mountain region southward, to Pocahontas, drove General W. S. (called
"Mudwall") Jackson out of that shire, and over the Warm Springs Mountain, in a series of skirmishes.   He destroyed the Confederate saltpeter works,
and other public property in that region, and menaced Staunton.   At Rock
Gap, near White Sulphur Springs, he was met by a much larger force than
his own, of General Sam. Jones's command, led by Colonel George S. Patten,
when a severe struggle for the pass ensued, which lasted a greater portion
of the 26th and 27th of August.[a]   Averill's ammunition began
to fail at noon of the latter day, when Patten was re-enforced.
Averill retreated, and made his way back to Huttonsville, weakly pursued

[a] 1863.

---

[1] See map on page 405, volume II.   [2] See page 104, volume II.   [3] See page 367, volume II.
[4] See page 391, volume II.   [5] See map on page 101, volume II.

by the Confederate cavalry. Averill's loss was two hundred and seven men, and a Parrott gun, which burst during the fight. The Confederate loss was one hundred and fifty-six men.

Much later in the year, Averill, still watching in West Virginia, made another aggressive movement. He left Beverly, in Tygart's Valley, early in November, with five thousand men of all arms, and, moving southward, again encountered "Mudwall" Jackson. He drove him until the latter was re-enforced by General Echols, who came up from Lewisburg, when the Confederates took a strong position on the top of Droop Mountain, in Greenbrier County. Averill stormed them there,[a] and pushed them [a] November 6, 1863. back into Monroe County, with a loss of over three hundred men, three guns, and seven hundred

SAMUEL JONES.

small-arms. Averill reported his own loss at "about one hundred, officers and men."

West Virginia was now nearly purged of armed rebels, and not long afterward, Averill started on the important business of destroying the communication between Lee and Bragg over the Virginia and Tennessee railway. With the Second, Third, and Eighth Virginia mounted infantry, the Fourteenth Pennsylvania (Dobson's battalion) Cavalry, and Ewing's battery, he crossed the mountains over icy roads and paths, in the midst of tempests a

W. W. AVERILL.

part of the time, and, on the 16th of December, struck the railway at Salem, on the headwaters of the Roanoke River. There he destroyed the station houses and rolling stock, and a large quantity of Confederate supplies ;[1] cut and coiled up the telegraph wires for half a mile ; and in the course of six hours tore up the track, heated and ruined the rails, burned five bridges, and destroyed several culverts in the space of about fifteen miles. This raid aroused all of the Confederates in that mountain region, and seven separate commands[2] were arranged in a line extending from Staunton

---

[1] He destroyed 2,000 barrels of flour, 10,000 bushels of wheat, 100,000 bushels of shelled corn, 50,000 bushels of oats, 2,000 barrels of meat, several cords of leather. 1,000 sacks of salt, 31 boxes of clothing, 20 bales of cotton, a large amount of harness, shoes, saddles, and tools, and 100 wagons.

[2] These were the commands of Generals Early, Fitzhugh Lee, Jones, Imboden, Jackson, Echols, and McCausland.

to Newport, to intercept the bold raiders on their return. Fortunately for them, Averill intercepted a dispatch from Jones to Early, which revealed the position and intention of some of the watchers. By this he was satisfied that Covington, on Jackson's River, between the commands of Jones and Jackson, would be the best place to dash through the Confederate line. He pushed on in that direction, and, as he approached Covington, the Eighth Virginia drove in the Confederate outposts, and secured the bridges there, which had been prepared for the flames, when the whole column, four miles in length, passed over the river, excepting one regiment, in spite of brisk opposition. Then Averill destroyed the bridges behind him, and the regiment that was cut off swam the stream and rejoined the command, with a loss of only four men drowned. Averill captured, during this *December 21, raid, about two hundred men. "My command," he said in his 1863.
report,[a] "has marched, climbed, slid, and swam,[1] three hundred and forty-five miles since the 8th instant." He reported his entire loss at "six men drowned, one officer and four men wounded, and ninety men missing."

A correspondent of the *Richmond Examiner* gave a spirited and somewhat comical account of this raid. "No language," he said, "can tell the sufferings of our men. They were in saddle day and night, save a few hours between midnight and day. They were beat up by the officers with their swords—the only means of arousing them—numb and sleepy. Some froze to death; others were taken from their horses, senseless. They forded swollen streams, and their clothes, stiff frozen, rattled as they rode. It rained in torrents, and froze as it fell. In the mountain-paths the ice was cut from the roads before they ventured to ride over. One horse slipped over the precipice. The rider was leading him; he never looked after him. The whole matter is summed up in a couple of sentences. Averill was penned up: McCausland, Echols, and Jackson at one gate; Lee and Imboden at the other. Some ass suggested he might escape, by jumping down the well, and coming out in Japan—that is, go to Buchanan.[2] Early ordered them to leave a gate open, and guard the well. He did not jump in."

Let us now return to a consideration of the military events west of the great mountain chain that separates the Atlantic States from those in the Valley of the Mississippi.

---

[1] "I was obliged to swim my command, and drag my artillery with ropes across Craig's Creek seven times in twenty-four hours," Averill said, in his report. A participant in the march said the creek was deep, and the current strong and filled with drifting ice.

[2] This allusion to Buchanan is explained by another paragraph in the writer's letter, when he relates the blunders of Early, "Major-General commanding," who believed a story told him, that Averill was marching on Buchanan instead of Covington. He acted accordingly, and ordered Lee and Imboden to march to Buchanan. This blunder left the "gate open" at Covington. The writer says no one should have believed a statement so absurd, "for it presupposed Averill had deliberately placed himself past escape."

CHAPTER IV.

CAMPAIGN OF THE ARMY OF THE CUMBERLAND FROM MURFREESBORO' TO CHATTANOOGA.

E left General Rosecrans and the Army of the Cumberland at Murfreesboro', after the Battle of Stone's River, at the beginning of 1863, where he established a fortified depot of supplies. General Bragg, his opponent, had taken a strong position north of the Duck River,[1] his infantry extending from Shelbyville to Wartrace, his cavalry on his right stretched out to McMinnville, and on his left to Columbia and Spring Hill, on the railway between Nashville and Decatur. General Polk's corps was at Shelbyville. Hardee's head-quarters were at Wartrace, and his troops were holding Hoover's, Liberty, and Bellbuckle Gaps. Bragg's main base of supplies was at Chattanooga, on the Tennessee River, with a large depot at Tullahoma.

In nearly these repective positions the two armies lay for almost six months, but not in idleness. Although Rosecrans had the most men, Bragg was his superior in cavalry, and this gave the latter a vast advantage, because of the relation of that arm of the service to his adversary's supplies. These were chiefly drawn from far-distant Louisville, over a single line of railway, through a country whereof a majority of the inhabitants were hostile to the Government. For that reason, Rosecrans was compelled to keep heavy guards at bridges, trestle-work, and culverts, to prevent their destruction by raiders and resident enemies. The consequence was that at no time while the two armies confronted each other, from January to June,[a] could Rosecrans have brought into the field to fight his foe a number of troops equal to that of his antagonist.

[a] 1863.

Rosecrans reorganized his army, and divided[b] it into three corps, known as the Fourteenth, Twentieth, and the Twenty-first, commanded respectively by Generals Thomas, McCook, and

[b] Jan. 9.

A. McDOWELL McCOOK.

---

[1] Bragg's army was in three divisions, one of which was cavalry, under the command of General J. H.

Crittenden, and a reserve and cavalry corps.[1]   The winter floods in the Cumberland favored him, and as rapidly as possible he collected large stores at
Nashville by the river steamers, and made Murfreesboro' a depot for ample
supplies.   Finally, he obtained a sufficient number of horses and mules to
warrant him in moving southward.   Before considering that important act,
which took place late in June,[a] let us take a brief survey of the
doings of the cavalry and mounted infantry of the two armies
during the suspension of operations in full force.

[1863.]

At the beginning of February, General Wheeler, Bragg's chief of cav-
alry, with four thousand five hundred mounted men, and having General
Wharton and Colonel N. B. Forrest as brigadiers, concentrated his forces at
Franklin, a little below Nashville, on the road between that city and
Decatur, for the purpose of attempting the recapture of Fort Donelson,
which, it was known, had not been repaired since it was taken by Grant.[2]
It had not even been occupied, for it was of little account, excepting as a
defense against gun-boats coming up the river.   The little village of Dover,
near by, had been partially fortified; and when Wheeler approached, the
garrison, under Colonel A. C. Harding, consisted of only about six hundred
effective men, mostly of the Eighty-third Illinois, with a section of Flood's
battery (four guns) and a 32-pound siege-gun mounted upon a turn-table,
and commanded by N. Grant Abbey, then a private in the Eighty-third
Illinois.[3]

The chief object of the Confederates at this time was to interrupt the
navigation of the Cumberland, and thus seriously interfere with the transportation of supplies for Rosecrans's army to Nashville, by way of the river.
Forrest had been at Palmyra for the same purpose; and now, at a little
past noon on the 3d of February,[a] he demanded the surrender of
Fort Donelson and the garrison.   Harding was weak in numbers, but strong in heart.   He defied his foe; and when the Confederates
moved up to attack, he sent out skirmishers to impede their progress as
much as possible, while a horseman was hastening to Fort Henry for aid,
and a little steamer was speeding down the river, to summon to his assistance some gun-boats then convoying a fleet of transports up the stream.
The skirmishers fell back, and when Wheeler and his men were within
cannon-range, Harding opened upon them his 32-pounder and four smaller
guns with great effect.   From that time until after dark, Harding maintained a gallant fight with his foe, losing forty-five of his sixty artillery

[b 1863.]

Wheeler. The First Corps was commanded by Lieutenant-General Leonidas Polk, with Generals B. F. Cheatham,
J. M. Withers, and S. B. Buckner as division commanders; and the Second by Lieutenant-General W. J. Hardee,
whose division commanders were Generals P. R. Cleburne and A. P. Stewart. The cavalry division commanders
were Generals J. A. Wharton and W. Martin.

[1] The division commanders were as follows:—*Fourteenth Army Corps*—First Division, General J. C.
Starkweather; Second Division, General J. S. Negley, Third Division, General J. M. Brannon; Fourth Divi-
sion, General J. J. Reynolds. *Twentieth Army Corps*—First Division, General J. C. Davis; Second Division,
General R. W. Johnson; Third Division, General P. H. Sheridan. *Twenty-first Army Corps*—First Division,
General T. J. Wood; Second Division, General C. Cruft; Third Division, General H. P. Van Cleve. There was
a reserve corps under General Gordon Granger, with General W. C. Whittaker commanding the First Division,
General G. W. Morgan the Second, and General R. S. Granger the Third. The cavalry corps was commanded
by General D. S. Stanley. The First Division was led by General R. B. Mitchell and the Second by General J.
B. Turchin.   [2] See page 220, volume II.

[3] This brave soldier was highly complimented by Colonel Harding for his skill and bravery on that occasion,
and he made him a present of a very fine revolver. He was promoted to sergeant. In May, 1865, he was mortally wounded in an encounter with guerrillas in Kentucky.

horses in the struggle. Finally, at eight o'clock in the evening, the gun-boat *Fair Play*, Lieutenant-commanding Fitch, came up, and gave the astonished Confederates a raking fire that dismayed them. They fled precipitately, and well for them they did, for other gun-boats were soon there. In this engagement Harding lost one hundred and twenty-six men, of whom fifty were made prisoners. Wheeler's loss was estimated at nearly six hundred. He left one hundred and fifty men dead on the field, and an equal number as prisoners. He withdrew to Franklin, and did not again attempt to capture Fort Donelson.

While Wheeler was upon the Cumberland, General J. C. Davis, with two brigades of cavalry under Colonel Minty, and a division of infantry, was operating in his rear. Davis went westward from Murfreesboro', [a] and in the course of thirteen days his force swept over a considerable space, in detachments, and returned to camp without having engaged in any serious encounter. The fruit of the expedition was the capture of one hundred and forty-one of Wheeler's men, including two colonels and several officers of lower rank.

[a] Jan. 31, 1863.

Both armies were now quiet for awhile. At length it was ascertained that General Van Dorn, with a considerable force of cavalry and mounted infantry, was hovering in the vicinity of Franklin; and Colonel John Colburn, of the Thirty-third Indiana, stationed at the latter place, and General Sheridan at Murfreesboro', were ordered to move in the direction of this menacing force. They marched simultaneously.[b] Colburn's command consisted of nearly twenty-seven hundred men, of whom six hundred were cavalry.[1] He was directed to move on Spring Hill, twelve miles south of Franklin. He had marched but a little way when he fell in with a party of Confederates, with whom he skirmished. They were repulsed, and he moved on; but toward evening they again appeared, with an additional force, and boldly confronted him. Colburn halted and encamped for the night, and soon after moving forward the next morning,[c] he was attacked by a greatly superior number of men, under Van Dorn and Forrest. After fighting until his ammunition was exhausted, Colburn was compelled to surrender about thirteen hundred of his infantry. The remainder of his infantry, and the cavalry and artillery not engaged in the fight, escaped. Van Dorn's force consisted of six brigades of mounted men. Sheridan, with his division, and about eighteen hundred cavalry, under Colonel Minty, first swept down toward Shelbyville, and then around toward Franklin, skirmishing in several places with detachments of Van Dorn's and Forrest's men. In a sharp fight at Thompson's Station, he captured some of the force which encountered Colburn. He finally drove Van Dorn beyond the Duck River, and then returned[d] to Murfreesboro', with a loss during his ten days' ride and skirmishing of only five men killed and five wounded. His gain was nearly one hundred prisoners.

[b] March 4.

[c] March 5.

[d] March 14.

On the 18th of March, Colonel A. S. Hall, with a little over fourteen

---

[1] A part of the Thirty-third and Eighty-fifth Indiana, Twenty-second Wisconsin, Nineteenth Michigan, and One Hundred and Twenty-fourth Ohio. The cavalry consisted of detachments from the Second Michigan, Ninth Pennsylvania, and Fourth Kentucky, under Colonel Jordan. A battery of six guns composed the artillery.

hundred men,[1] moved eastward from Murfreesboro' to surprise a Confederate camp at Gainesville. He was unexpectedly met by some of Morgan's cavalry, when he fell back to Milton, twelve miles northeast of Murfreesboro', and took a strong position on Vaught's Hill. There he was attacked by two thousand men, led by Morgan in person. With the aid of Harris's battery skillfully worked, Hall repulsed the foe after a struggle of about three hours. Morgan lost between three and four hundred men killed and wounded. Among the latter was himself. Hall's loss was fifty-five men, of whom only six were killed.

Early in April, General Gordon Granger, then in command at Franklin, with nearly five thousand troops, was satisfied that a heavy force under Van Dorn was about to attack him. He was then constructing a fort (which afterward bore his name), but only two siege-guns and two rifled cannon, belonging to an Ohio battery, were mounted upon it. The fort was on a commanding hill on the northern side of the Harpeth River, about fifty feet above that stream, and completely commanded the approaches to Franklin. Granger's infantry and artillery were under the immediate command of General's Baird and Gilbert, and his cavalry was led by Generals G. C. Smith and Stanley. Every precaution was taken to be ready for the foe, from whatever point he might approach. Baird was directed to oppose his crossing at the fords below Franklin, and Gilbert was placed so as to meet an attack in front, or to re-enforce either flank. Stanley's cavalry was pushed out four miles on the road toward Murfreesboro', and Smith's was held in reserve to assist him, if necessary.

Such was the disposition of Granger's troops when, on the 10th,[a] Van Dorn, with an estimated force of nine thousand mounted men and two regiments of foot, pressed rapidly forward along the Columbia and Lewisburg turnpikes, and fell upon Granger's front. The guns from the fort opened destructively upon the assailants, and their attack was manfully met by Granger's troops. Van Dorn soon found himself in a perilous situation, for Stanley came up and struck him a heavy blow on the flank. Smith was ordered forward to support Stanley, and Baird's troops were thrown across the river to engage in the fight. The Confederates were routed at all points on Granger's front, with a heavy loss in killed and wounded, and about five hundred prisoners. Van Dorn then turned his whole force upon Stanley before Smith reached him, and with his overwhelming numbers pushed him back and recovered most of the captured men. By this means Van Dorn extricated himself from his perilous position, and, abandoning his attempt to capture Franklin, he retired to Spring Hill, with a loss of about three hundred men in killed, wounded, and prisoners. The Union loss was about thirty-seven killed, wounded, and missing.[2]

[a] April, 1863.

---

[1] The One Hundred and Fifth Ohio, Eightieth, and One Hundred and Twenty-third Illinois, a section of Harris's Nineteenth Indiana Battery, and one company of Tennessee cavalry.

[2] Van Dorn's earthly career was closed soon after this event by a bullet sent by a husband (Doctor Peters) with whose wife the former had formed a criminal intimacy. When Peters was assured of the dishonor, he walked into Van Dorn's head-quarters and demanded satisfaction. Van Dorn was at his writing-table, surrounded by his staff. He refused to give the satisfaction demanded, and ordered the injured husband to leave the room. The latter drew a revolver, shot the criminal dead, sprang out of the room and on to his horse, and escaped immediate pursuit. Then he had his long hair and whiskers cropped short, changed his dress, and, thus disguised, made his way to the Union lines at Nashville. "Van Dorn was a brilliant, fascinating bad man. Wine and women had ruined him." The correspondent of the *Richmond Enquirer* wrote from Chattanooga, on

Ten days after the affair at Franklin, General J. J. Reynolds, with his division, Colonel Wilder's mounted brigade, and seventeen hundred cavalry under Colonel Minty, moved from Murfreesboro' [a] upon McMinnville, then occupied by about seven hundred of Morgan's men. ^{[a] April 20, 1863.} The guerrilla's troopers were driven out and dispersed, and a Confederate wagon-train, which had just left for Chattanooga, was pursued, and some of the wagons were destroyed. The Nationals burned a Confederate cotton factory and other public property at McMinnville, destroyed the railway, its buildings, trestle-work, and bridges, and returned to Murfreesboro' [b] without accident, their triumph graced by one hundred and thirty captives. Other smaller expeditions were sent ^{[b] April 26.} out at about this time, and the Confederate raiders were taught to be very circumspect.

Toward the middle of April, a more ambitious expedition than any yet sent out by Rosecrans, started from Nashville, upon the important service of sweeping around to the rear of Bragg's army, cutting all the railways in Northern Georgia, destroying depots of supplies, manufactories of arms and clothing, and in every possible way to cripple the Confederate army, upon which Rosecrans was exceedingly anxious to move. The expedition consisted of the Fifty-first Indiana, Eightieth Illinois, and a part of two Ohio regiments, numbering in all about eighteen hundred men, commanded by Colonel A. D. Streight, of the first-named regiment. His force was called, by General Garfield, Rosecrans's chief of staff, who gave the leader his instructions, " an independent provisional brigade," created for " temporary purposes." In accordance with his instructions, he left Nashville with his command on the 11th of April, in steamers, and, landing at Dover, marched across the country to Fort Henry, on the Tennessee River,[1] where he remained until the boats went around to the Ohio and came up to that point. Then he went up the Tennessee to Eastport, where he debarked, and, marching southward, joined the forces of General Dodge, then moving on Tuscumbia, on the Memphis and Charleston railway, in Northern Alabama. This was to mask the real intention of the expedition, Streight being instructed to march long enough with Dodge to give the impression that his was a part of that leader's force, and then to strike off from Tuscumbia southward to Russellville or Moulton.

Streight's troops were not mounted when they left Nashville. They were directed to gather up horses and mules on the way; so they scouted for them over the region they passed through, yet when they joined Dodge one half of the command was on foot. They marched with him to the capture of Tuscumbia, and then, after receiving a supply of horses and mules, they started [c] for Russellville, with only about three hundred men on ^{[c] April 27.} foot. There they turned eastward, their chief objective being the important cities of Rome and Atlanta, in Northern Georgia. The former was the seat of extensive Confederate iron-works, and the latter the focus of several railway lines. At the same time Dodge also struck off southward in Alabama, and sweeping around into Mississippi, striking Confederate detach-

the 12th of May: "He always sacrificed his business to his pleasure. He was either tied to a woman's apron strings or heated with wine."
[1] See page 203, volume II.

ments here and there, and destroying public property, returned to the railway at Corinth, from which he departed on his expedition against Tuscumbia.

When the Confederates were informed of Streight's independent move-ment, the cavalry of Forrest and Roddy, who had been watching the Union-ists, started in pursuit of them, and overtook them not far from Moulton, in Lawrence County, Alabama. After nearly a whole day's fight, at Driver's Gap of the Sand Mountain, they commenced a running fight, which con-tinued over a space of about one hundred miles, along a wide curve, through several counties in Alabama, across the head-waters of the Tombigbee and Great Warrior rivers, to the Coosa. On their way, Streight's men, marching in detachments, destroyed a large quantity of Confederate property, and were pushing on toward Rome, in Georgia, when a large part of their jaded animals gave out, and their supply of ammunition failed. A detachment, sent forward to seize and hold Rome, was compelled to fall back upon the main column. Then the whole body pressed on, and destroyed the Round Moun-tain iron-works between Gadsden and Rome, where cannon, shot, and shell were made for the Confederates. On they pressed toward Rome, and when within about fifteen miles of that town, the pursuers, four thousand strong, under Forrest, fell upon Streight's rear. He was so exhausted every way that he was compelled to surrender.[a] His loss during the raid was about one hundred men, including Colonel Hathaway. The num-ber surrendered was thirteen hundred and sixty-five. The captives were all sent to Richmond, and thrown into Libby Prison, from which the leader and over one hundred officers confined in that loathsome jail escaped early in February, 1864, by digging under the foundation walls of the build-ing. They were treated not as prisoners of war, but as common felons, in compliance with a demand of the Governor of Georgia, on the soil of whose State they were taken, and who charged them with the violation of a law of that State, which made the inciting of slaves to insurrection to be a high crime—a charge wholly unfounded. This unusual treatment of prisoners of war caused the Government to suspend the exchange of captives for awhile, and also the confinement of Morgan and his raiders in felon's cells in the Ohio Penitentiary, as already mentioned.[1]

[a] May 3, 1863.

May passed by without any important movements of the armies of Rose-crans and Bragg.[2] The former still lay at Murfreesboro' and vicinity, and

---

[1] See page 96.

[2] Forrest, with a large force, continued to menace Franklin, and early in June he invested it and cut off communication with Nashville. At that time, when an attack upon Franklin was hourly expected, two young men rode up to the quarters of Colonel J. P Baird, and represented themselves as Colonel Autun and Major Dunlap. They were well mounted, neatly attired in the National uniform of the rank of each, but had neither orderlies nor baggage with them. They represented themselves as officers of Rosecrans's army, detailed for special duty by the War Department, and said they had narrowly escaped capture by rebels, who seized their orderlies and baggage. They showed proper papers from the Adjutant-General (Thomas) and General Garfield, then Rosecrans's chief of staff, and asked Colonel Baird to loan them $50, to enable them to go to Nashville to refit. The money and a pass was handed them, and they started off on a full gallop. They were instantly sus-pected of being spies, and Colonel Watkins was sent after them. He overtook them before they passed the lines, and took them back to Baird, who telegraphed to Rosecrans, and ascertained that there were no such offi-cers in his department. They were closely examined, and on the sword of Autun the letters "C. S. A." were found. This confirmed the suspicions of Baird and Watkins, and the fact was communicated to Rose-crans by telegraph, he directed them to be tried by a court-martial as spies, and, if found guilty, to be instantly hung. They made a full confession. At past midnight the court found them guilty, and between nine and ten o'clock next morning they were hanged on a gallows attached to a wild cherry-tree, on the slope of the hill on which Fort Granger stood, three-fourths of a mile from Franklin.

The spies were young men, and were relations, by marriage, of General Lee, the chief of the Confederate

the latter stretched along the general line of the Duck River, as we have observed,[1] with the mountain passes well fortified. Bragg's position was a very strong one for defense, and few outside of the Army of the Cumberland could comprehend the necessity for the wise caution that governed its commander. As June wore away the public became impatient because of his delay, and the Government, considering the facts that Grant and Porter were then closely investing Vicksburg; Banks and Farragut were encircling Port Hudson with armed men; Lee was moving in force toward the Upper Potomac, and rumor declared that Bragg was sending re-enforcements to Johnston, in Grant's rear,[2] thought it a favorable time for Rosecrans to advance against his antagonist, push him across the Tennessee into Georgia, relieve East Tennessee, and drive a fatal wedge into the heart of the Confederacy. Orders were accordingly given. Rosecrans was ready, for his cavalry was then in fair condition, and his supplies were abundant. He issued orders on the 23d of June for a forward movement, his grand objective being the possession of Chattanooga, with its many advantages in a military point of view. It was begun the next day. General Burnside was ordered to co-operate with Rosecrans by moving from Kentucky, through the mountain passes, into East Tennessee, where General Buckner was in command of a

armies. "Autun" was Colonel Orton Williams, about twenty-three years of age, son of a gallant officer of the National army and graduate of West Point, who was killed in the war with Mexico. "Dunlap" was Lieutenant W. G. Peter. Young Williams was, at that time, on the staff of General Bragg, and Peter on that of General Wheeler. Williams resigned a lieutenancy of cavalry in 1861, and joined the rebels. He is represented as an excellent young man; but, influenced by the example of his kinsman, General Lee, he took sides with the enemies of his country, and lost his life in trying to serve them. He had lately married a young widow, formerly Miss Hamilton, of South Carolina. Over his act we may draw the veil of Christian charity,

CASTLE THUNDER.*

and forgive him, for young, ardent, and impressible, he was the victim of his more wicked elders, who taught him to sin against his country.

The execution of Williams and Peter made a deep impression because of their family and official connections. The Confederate authorities at Richmond were exasperated, and sought an opportunity for retaliation in kind. It was offered a few months later, when a young man from Northern New York, named Spencer Kellogg Brown, only twenty-one years of age, was brought to Richmond from the Mississippi. He had been in the naval service under Commodore Porter, as a common sailor, and had charge of a gun on the *Essex* when the ram *Arkansas* (see page 529, volume II.) was destroyed. He was sent in an armed boat to burn a Confederate ferry-boat near Port Hudson. He had accomplished the work, and was returning alone to his boat, along the shore, when he was seized by three guerrillas. He was taken to Jackson, and then to Castle Thunder, in Richmond, charged with being caught as a spy within the Confederate lines. He was subjected to a mock trial, under the direction of the notorious Winder, and on the 25th of September, 1863, was hung as a spy "in the presence of all Richmond." The circumstances of his capture had none of the conditions of a spy; and his execution, judged by the laws and ethics of civilized warfare, was simply a savage murder. Brown was a very promising young man. He was enthusiastic as a patriot, and was a sincere, manly, religious soldier. Congress made provision (June, 1864) for his young widow, in the form of a pension.

[1] See page 115.

[2] See page 620, volume II.

---

* This was one of the noted prisons of Richmond. It was a large brick building used as a tobacco warehouse by Mr. Grainer before the rebellion. It was on the corner of Carey and Nineteenth streets. It was used chiefly for the confinement of civilians, and was to the offenders against Confederate authority, by citizens under their rule, what Fort Lafayette or Fort Warren was to like offenders against the Government.

Confederate force, then holding the country between Knoxville and Chattanooga.   The latter was to be the rallying point of the Confederates in Tennessee, should Bragg not be able to withstand Rosecrans.

At that time Bragg's left wing, eighteen thousand strong, under General
(Bishop) Polk, lay at Shelbyville, the terminus of a short railway from the
main track at Wartrace.   His troops were behind formidable intrenchments,
about five miles in length, cast up by several thousand slaves drawn from
Georgia and Alabama.   General Hardee, with twelve thousand men, was at
Wartrace, covering the railway, and holding the front of rugged hills
admirably adapted for defense, behind which was a strongly intrenched
camp at Tullahoma.   Bragg now had about forty thousand men, and Rosecrans about sixty thousand.

It was known that Bragg's position was a very strong one, and Rosecrans determined to maneuver him out of it, if possible, before giving him
battle.   For this purpose he planned deceptive movements.   These were to
be a seeming advance from Murfreesboro' by the main army, directly on
Bragg's center, at the same time threatening his left, and giving the real
blow or chief attack on his right, and, if successful, march upon Tullahoma,
and compel him to fall back, in order to secure his lines of communication
with Georgia.   Accordingly, on the morning of the 23d of June,
the forward movement began, and on the 24th,[a] while rain was
falling copiously, the whole army moved forward, McCook on the right,
Thomas in the center, and Crittenden on the left.   McCook moved toward
Shelbyville, Thomas toward Manchester, and Crittenden in the direction of
McMinnville.   The latter was to march much later than the other two, with
Turchin's brigade of cavalry, while the remainder of Stanley's horsemen
were thrown out on the right.   General Gordon Granger's reserve corps,
which had advanced to Triune, now moved forward in support of the corps
of McCook and Thomas.

    a June, 1863.

Rosecrans's plans were quickly and successfully executed.   McCook moved
early in the morning[b] toward Shelbyville, with Sheridan's division
in advance, preceded by one half of the Thirtieth Indiana
mounted infantry, under Lieutenant-Colonel Jones.   The divisions of Johnson and Davis followed Sheridan a few miles, and then turned off to the left
toward Liberty Gap, eastward of the railway, which was fortified.   At the
same time Colonel Wilder's mounted infantry were moving toward Manchester, followed by General Reynolds and the remainder of his division, the
Fourth of Thomas's corps.   The latter was followed a few hours later by the
divisions of Negley and Rousseau, of the same corps.   Wilder was instructed
to halt at Hoover's Gap until the infantry should come up, but finding it
unoccupied he marched into it, captured a wagon-train and a drove of beeves
passing through, and was pushing to the other extremity of it, when he was
met by a heavy force of Confederates and pushed back.   He held the Gap,
however, until Reynolds came up and secured it.   Meanwhile, McCook's
troops, that turned toward Liberty Gap, with Willich's brigade in advance,
soon encountered the Confederates.   These were driven, their tents, baggage,
and supplies, were captured, and the Gap was seized and held, against
attempts to repossess it.

    b June 24.

While Rosecrans was securing these important mountain passes, other

operations in accordance with his plan were equally successful. General
Granger had started from Triune, on the extreme right, on the
afternoon of the 23d,[a] and sweeping rapidly on, encountering and   *a June, 1863.*
pushing back the Confederates in several places, reached Christiana, on the
road between Murfreesboro' and Shelbyville, without much trouble. There
he was joined by Stanley and his cavalry, and, pressing on to Guy's Gap,
secured it after a struggle of about two hours. The Confederates fled,
closely pursued for seven miles without stopping, the former making for
their rifle-pits, about three miles from Shelbyville. There the fugitives made
a stand, but a charge by Stanley's horsemen drove them back upon the near
defenses of the town—three guns and a considerable body of foot soldiers.
At six o'clock in the evening, Granger came up with his infantry, when
Stanley charged again, and before seven o'clock Shelbyville was in possession of the National troops. The spoils were three guns and a quantity of
corn, and the trophy, five hundred prisoners. Wheeler and his cavalry escaped
by swimming their horses across Duck River, but another troop of horsemen
were killed or captured.

Rosecrans pressed through the mountain passes he had seized, and on
the 27th[b] his head-quarters were at Manchester, which Wilder
had surprised and captured that morning; and two days after-   *b June.*
ward the whole of the corps of Thomas and McCook were there also. The
Nationals were now prepared to flank Tullahoma, to which Bragg had
fallen back, as they had done Shelbyville. Wilder was sent to strike the
railway in Bragg's rear, at Decherd, destroy the bridge over the Elk River,
and do whatever mischief he could to the foe. Decherd was reached and
the railway was injured by the bold riders, but the bridge defied them.
This raid, and the evidences that Rosecrans was about to move in force to
turn his right, so alarmed Bragg, that on the night of the 30th of June he
fled from Tullahoma, leaving, without giving a blow in their defense, the
extensive works he had cast up in the course of several months in the hill
country between Shelbyville, Wartrace, Tullahoma, and Decherd. "Thus,"
said Rosecrans, in his report, "ended a nine days' campaign, which drove
the enemy from two fortified positions, and gave us possession of Middle
Tennessee."[1] The detention of the Nationals at Hoover's Gap and in front
of Winchester, alone prevented their gaining possession of Bragg's communications, and forcing him to give battle or to surrender.

On the day after Bragg retreated, Thomas and McCook advanced to
Tullahoma and pressed hard upon the rear of the fugitives, hoping to strike
them a fatal blow before they could reach the Elk River. They failed to do
so. The roads, cut up by the retreating army and saturated with continual
rain—a rain almost without example in Tennessee—were impassable, and
Bragg escaped across the river with his trains, his rear gallantly covered by
Wheeler's cavalry. The Nationals did not cross it until the 3d,[c]
when Sheridan forced a passage at Rock Creek Ford, and other   *c July.*
troops crossed at different points. The Confederates, having the railway for
use in heavy transportation, were then swarming in comparatively light

---

[1] Rosecrans said the campaign was "conducted in one of the most extraordinary rains ever known in Tennessee at that period, over a soil that became almost a quicksand." In that campaign Rosecrans lost 560 men,
and captured from Bragg 1,624 men.

marching order on the lofty and rugged ranges of the Cumberland Mountains, by way of Tantallon and University, and were well on their way toward Chattanooga. Rosecrans advanced his army to near the foot of these mountains, when finding Bragg, who had destroyed all the bridges over the swollen streams in his rear, too far ahead to be easily overtaken, halted his entire force, chiefly on the high rolling table-land between Winchester, Decherd, Manchester, and McMinnville. On the 5th of July, Van Cleve, who had been left at Murfreesboro', arrived, and moved with his division to McMinnville. Bragg pushed on over the mountains,[1] crossed the Tennessee River at Bridgeport and its vicinity, where he destroyed the railway bridge behind him, and made his way to Chattanooga. His expulsion from Middle Tennessee, by which a greater portion of that State and Kentucky was left under the absolute control of the National authority, was a disheartening event for the Confederates; and now they felt that every thing depended upon their holding Chattanooga, the key of East Tennessee, and, indeed, of all Northern Georgia. Every effort was therefore made for that purpose; and the risk of fatally weakening Lee's army in Virginia, by withdrawing Longstreet's corps from it, was taken, and that efficient officer and his troops, as we have observed, were sent to re-enforce Bragg.[2]

Rosecrans now caused the railway to Stevenson, and thence to Bridgeport, to be put in order under the skillful direction of Colonel Innis and his Michigan engineers, and Sheridan's division was advanced to the latter section of the road, to hold it. At the same time Stanley swept down in a southwesterly direction, by way of Fayetteville and Athens, to cover the line of the Tennessee from Whitesburg up. As forage was scarce in the mountain region over which he was to pass, and Bragg had consumed the last blade of grass, Rosecrans delayed his advance until the Indian corn in cultivated spots was sufficiently grown to furnish a supply. Meanwhile, he gathered army supplies at Tracy City and Stevenson,[3] and thoroughly picketed the railway from Cowan to Bridgeport. Finally, at the middle of August, the army went forward to cross the Tennessee River at dif-

PICKET HUT NEAR STEVENSON.

ferent points, for the purpose of capturing Chattanooga. Thomas's corps

---

[1] The Cumberland range is lofty and rocky, and separate the waters which flow into the Tennessee River from those which are tributary to the Cumberland River. The range extends from near the Kentucky line almost to Athens, in Alabama. Its northwestern slopes are steep and rocky, with deep coves, out of which flow the streams that water East Tennessee. Its top is barren and undulating. Its southeastern slope, toward Chattanooga, is precipitous, and the undulating valley between its base and the Tennessee River averages about five miles in width. In the range, and parallel with its course is a deep clove, known as the Sequatchie Valley, three or four miles in width, and about fifty miles in length, which is traversed by a river of the same name. West of this valley the Nashville and Chattanooga railway crossed the Cumberland range through a low gap by a tunnel near Cowan, and down the gorge of Big Crow Creek to Stevenson, at the foot of the mountain. Walden's Ridge is on the eastern side of the Sequatchie, and its lofty rocky cliffs abut upon the Tennessee River, northward of Chattanooga.   [2] See page 99.

[3] At the latter place the Nashville and Chattanooga railway and the Memphis and Charleston railway conjoin, making it a very important point in a military point of view.

took the general direction of the railway; the divisions of Reynolds and Brannan moving from University on the mountain top, by way of Battle Creek, to its mouth, and those of Negley and Baird by Tantallon and Crow Creek. McCook's moved to the right of the railway, Johnson's division by way of Salem and Larkin's Ford, to Bellefonte; and Crittenden's, designed to feel the enemy and menace Chattanooga with a direct attack, moved well eastward in three columns, commanded respectively by Generals Wood, Van Cleve, and Palmer, with Minty's cavalry on the extreme left, marching by way of Sparta to drive Confederate horsemen from the vicinity of Kingston, strike Buckner's force in the rear, and to cover Van Cleve's column, as it passed at the head of the Sequatchie Valley. From that valley Crittenden sent two brigades of mounted men, under Minty and Wilder, and two of infantry, under Hazen and Wagner, over Walden's Ridge, to proceed to points on the Tennessee, near and above Chattanooga, and make the feigned attack. General Hazen[1] was in chief command of these four brigades in the Tennessee Valley, with instructions to watch all the crossings of the river for seventy miles above Chattanooga, and to give Bragg the impression that the whole of Rosecrans's army was about to cross near that town. Hazen's command had four batteries of artillery.

In the course of four or five days the mountain ranges were crossed, and the Army of the Cumberland, stretching along the line of the Tennessee River for more than a hundred miles of its course, was preparing to cross that stream at different points, for the purpose of closing around Chattanooga, to crush or starve the Confederate army there. Pontoon-boat, raft, and trestle bridges were constructed at Shellmound, the mouth of Battle Creek, Bridgeport, Caperton's Ferry, and Bellefonte. So early [a] as the 20th,[a] Hazen reconnoitered Harrison's, above Chattanooga, [a August, 1863.] and then took post at Poe's cross-roads, fifteen miles from the latter place; and on the following day, Wilder's cannon thundering from the eminences opposite Chattanooga, and the voice of his shells screaming over the Confederate camp, startled Bragg with a sense of imminent danger. At the same time Hazen was making " show marches," displaying camp-fires at different points, and causing the fifteen regiments of his command to appear like the advance of an immense army. This menace was soon followed by information that Thomas and McCook were preparing to cross below, and that the remainder of Crittenden's corps was swarming on the borders of the river, at the foot of Walden's Ridge, below Chattanooga.

Thomas passed over with his corps at different places, from Caperton's up to Shellmound, and crossed the mountain not far from the latter place, near which is the famous Nickajack Cave, where the Confederates had extensive saltpeter works. On the 8th of September he had concentrated his forces near Trenton, in the valley of the Lookout Creek, at the western foot of Lookout Mountain, and seized Frick's and Stevens's Gaps, the only practicable passes into the broad valley east of Lookout, and stretching toward Chattanooga, called McLemore's Clove. McCook also crossed, advanced to Valley Head, and took possession of Winston's Gap on the 6th, and a large portion of Crittenden's corps passed over and took post the same

---

[1] See page 546, volume II.

day at Wauhatchie, near the Point of Lookout Mountain, where it abuts upon the Tennessee River, well up toward Chattanooga, and threatening that post by the pass called the Nickajack Trace.

NICKAJACK CAVE.[1]

Having passed the first mountain ranges south of the Tennessee without opposition, and being informed of the movements of Confederates from East Tennessee to Chattanooga, Rosecrans determined to advance his right through the Lookout Mountain passes, and with his cavalry on his extreme right, threaten Bragg's railway communications between Dalton and Resaca Bridge, while his left and center should move through other passes upon the Confederate front. Anticipating this, when he discovered that the main army was below, Bragg abandoned Chattanooga,[a] passed through the gaps of the Missionaries' Ridge[2] to the West Chickamauga

Sept. 7, 8, 1863.

---

[1] This cave is at the base of Raccoon Mountain, and its wide mouth may be plainly seen from the Shellmound Station, about twenty miles from Chattanooga. The mountain there rises abruptly more than a thousand feet above the level of the Tennessee, and in the face of a perpendicular cliff is the entrance to the cave. It is not irregularly arched, as such caves generally are, but is in horizontal strata of rock that gives one an idea of the grand Egyptian architecture. The roof is so high above the floor, that a man may ride into it a considerable distance on horseback. Out of it flows a considerable stream of water of a light green color. The opening is about one hundred feet in width and forty feet in height. This cave was one of the chief sources from which the Confederates derived saltpeter, and its possession was of great importance to them. In earlier times it was the habitation of a band of robbers, who murdered and plundered emigrants and traders when descending the Tennessee River.

[2] The writer was informed by the late John Ross (see page 476, volume I.), the eminent Cherokee chief that this undulating ridge, which passes three miles east of Chattanooga and rises about three hundred feet above the Tennessee River, was named the Missionaries' Ridge because missionaries among the Cherokees had a station on the southeastern slope of it. The site of Chattanooga was known as Ross's Landing, the chief having a warehouse and trading port there. His dwelling was near a pass in the Missionaries' Ridge, about five miles from Chattanooga, and was yet standing and well preserved when the writer visited that region and sketched it in May, 1866. It was a long, low building, two stories in height, with heavy stone chimneys. It was called Rossville. A few rods in front of it was the dividing line between Tennessee and Georgia. In the picture, the

ROSS'S HOUSE.

wooded Missionaries' Ridge is seen just in the rear. Near it is a famous spring, known all over that region. Mr. Ross told the writer that the word Chattanooga was Cherokee, and meant "The Great Catch," the Tennessee

River, in Georgia, and posted his army along the highway from Lee and Gordon's Mill on that stream, south to the village of Lafayette, in a position facing Pigeon Mountain,[1] through the passes of which he expected the National army would approach from McLemore's Clove. The fact of this retreat was revealed to General Crittenden, when, on the 9th, with the main body of his corps, which had crossed the Tennessee at and above Bridgeport, he made a reconnoissance on Lookout Mountain,[2] and from its lofty summit, near Summertown, looked down upon Chattanooga, where no tent or banner of the enemy might be seen. He at once moved his corps around the point of Lookout Mountain, to enter and take possession

THOMAS L. CRITTENDEN.

of the deserted village, and on the evening of the following day[a] it encamped at Rossville, within five miles of Chattanooga. Thus, without a battle, the chief object of the grand movement of the Army of the Cumberland over the mountains was gained.

[a] Sept. 10, 1863.

General Burnside, who had been assigned to the command of the Army of the Ohio in March,[b] taking with him the Ninth Corps, with the expectation of speedily undertaking the liberation of East Tennessee, was now brought into active co-operation with the Army of the Cumberland. There had occurred, now and then, some stirring events in his department, the most important of which was the defeat of Pegram by Gillmore, at Somerset,[c] the raid of Colonel H. S. Sanders into East Tennessee,[d] and the extensive raid of Morgan into Indiana and Ohio,[e] already mentioned. Pegram was a Virginian, and crossed the Cumberland Mountains and river with a considerable force of mounted men, professedly the advance of a larger body, under Breckinridge, and commenced plundering Southeastern Kentucky, and expelling Unionists from the State. He was finally attacked in a strong position at Somerset, by General Quincy A. Gillmore,[3] with about twelve hundred men, the united commands of Gillmore and Colonel Wolford, and driven back into Tennessee with a loss of something over two hundred men. The Union loss was about thirty men. A little more than two months later, Colonel Sanders crossed the Cumberland Mountains from Kentucky, struck the East Tennessee and Georgia railway at Lenoir Station, destroyed the road a great

[b] 1863.

[c] March 30.

[d] June.

[e] July.

River at the bends there around Cameron's Hill and Mocassin Point being celebrated as a place for catching many fish.

[1] This is en offshoot of Lookout Mountain. Starting about forty miles south of Chattanooga, and running toward it, it loses itself in the general level near where the West Chickamauga River crosses the road between Chattanooga and Lafayette.

[2] The summit of Lookout, near Chattanooga, is about 1,500 feet above the Tennessee River, and 2,400 feet above the level of the sea.

[3] See page 318, volume II.

portion of the way tò Knoxville, passed round that city, and struck it again at Strawberry Plain, and burned a bridge over the Holston there, sixteen hundred feet in length, and another at Mossy Creek, above. With trifling loss, Sanders made his way back to Kentucky, after capturing three guns, ten thousand small-arms, and five hundred prisoners, and destroying a large quantity of Confederate munitions of war.

The Ninth Army Corps being detached from Burnside's command, to assist Grant before Vicksburg, the former was compelled to be comparatively idle, his chief business being to keep disloyal citizens in Kentucky and elsewhere in check, and to protect the Unionists of that State, for which purpose he found it necessary, in August,[a] to declare that commonwealth to be under martial law. Soon afterward he was called into East Tennessee, to co-operate with Rosecrans, in his struggle with Bragg for the possession of the Chattanooga region, by cutting off communication between the army of the latter, and Lee's, in Virginia, and preventing, as far as possible, re-enforcements being sent from the Rapid Anna to the Tennessee. When this call was made, the Ninth Corps had not yet returned. The exigency would not allow Burnside to wait for it. Fortunately, he had thoroughly organized and equipped his command, which was then about twenty thousand in number, at Camp Nelson, near Richmond, in Kentucky. He concentrated his forces at Crab Orchard, near the southern line of Lincoln County, and then prepared for a rapid movement to the new field of active operations, by a way to avoid the principal mountain gaps, where the Confederates might seriously oppose him. His infantry were mostly mounted. All of his cavalry and artillery were furnished with excel-

[a] August 3, 1863.

lent horses, and his supplies were placed on pack-mules, that more facile movements might be made than a wagon-train would allow. Thus prepared, they began the march on the day when Wilder opened his guns on Chattanooga,[b] with the cavalry brigade of General S. P. Carter, an East Tennessean, in advance. Just after crossing the boundary-line into Scott County, Tennessee, they were joined[c] by General Hartsuff and his corps ; and the combined forces pressed forward at the

[b] Aug. 21.

[c] Aug. 28.

PACK-MULES.[1]

rate of twenty miles a day over the great and rugged plateau of the Cumberland Mountains to Montgomery, in Morgan County, where they were joined by a column of infantry, under Colonel Julius White. After brief rest, Carter's force pushed rapidly onward in three columns, one under Colonel Bird (accompanied by Burnside), for Kingston, at the mouth of the Clinch River, where communication was had with Colonel Minty's cavalry, of Rosecrans's

---

[1] This shows the manner of carrying commissary stores on mules, in the mountain regions. A long string of mules were tethered together by rope or chain, in tandem, the leader guided by a soldier or servant.

extreme left; another, under General Shackelford, for Loudon Bridge, farther up the Tennessee; and a third, under Colonel Foster, for Knoxville, on the Holston River. Bird and Foster reached their respective destinations on the first of September, without opposition, but when Shackelford approached Loudon, he found the Confederates there in considerable force, and strongly posted. After a brisk skirmish, they were driven across the bridge—a magnificent structure, over two thousand feet in length—which they fired behind them, and so laid it in ruins. The main army moved steadily forward, and was soon posted on the line of the railway from Loudon, southwesterly, so as to connect with Rosecrans, then in possession of Chattanooga.

General Simon B. Buckner was in command of about twenty thousand troops, in East Tennessee, with his head-quarters at Knoxville, when Rosecrans moved upon Bragg, and Burnside began his march. To hold Chatta nooga, as we have observed, was of vital importance to the Confederacy, and, as its fall would involve the abandonment of East Tennessee, Bragg ordered Buckner to evacuate the valley, and hasten to his assistance at Chattanooga. Buckner accordingly fled from Knoxville on the approach of Burnside, and it was his rear-guard which Shackelford encountered at Loudon Bridge. At that time, the stronghold of Cumberland Gap, captured by General Morgan eighteen months before, was in possession of the Confederates, and held by one of Buckner's brigades, under General Frazer. That officer was ordered to join Buckner in his flight, but, on the recommendation of the latter, he was allowed to remain, with orders to hold the pass at all hazards. There he was hemmed in, by troops under Shackelford on one side, and on the other by a force under Colonel De Courcey, who came up from Kentucky. He held out for three or four days, when Burnside joined Shackelford, with cavalry and artillery, from Knoxville, and Frazer surrendered.[a] In the mean time a cavalry force had gone up the valley to Bristol, destroyed the bridges over the Watauga and Holston rivers, and driven the armed Confederates over the line into Virginia. Thus, again, the important pass of Cumberland Gap[1] was put into the possession of the National troops, and the great valley between the Alleghany and Cumberland Mountains, from Cleveland to Bristol, of which Knoxville may be considered the metropolis, seemed to be permanently rid of armed Confederates. The loyal inhabitants of that region received the National troops with open arms as their deliverers; and Union refugees, who had been hiding in the mountains, and Union prisoners from that region, who had escaped from the clutches of their captors, and had been sheltered in caves and rocks, all ragged and starved, now flocked to their homes, and joined in ovations offered to Burnside and his followers at Knoxville and elsewhere.[2]

[a] Sept. 9, 1863.

---

[1] See page 304, volume II.

[2] It is difficult to conceive the intensity of the feelings of the Union people along the line of Burnside's march. "Everywhere," wrote an eye-witness, "the people flocked to the roadsides, and, with cheers and wildest demonstrations of welcome, saluted the flag of the Republic and the men who had borne it in triumph to the very heart of the 'Confederacy.' Old men wept at the sight, which they had waited for through months of suffering; children, even, hailed with joy the sign of deliverance. Nobly have these persecuted people stood by their faith, and all loyal men will rejoice with them in their rescue at last from the clutch of the destroyer." "They were so glad to see Union soldiers," wrote another, "that they cooked every thing they had and gave it freely, not asking pay, and apparently not thinking of it. Women stood by the roadside with pails of water, and displayed Union flags. The wonder was, where all the 'Stars and Stripes' came from."

The authorities at Washington, at this time, were greatly perplexed by the military situation. No logic seemed sufficiently subtle to penetrate the real designs of the Confederates in the field. Spies and deserters from Lee's army, reported at the capital that he was receiving re-enforcements from Bragg, and from the Atlantic coast, to enable him to make another and more

UNION REFUGEES IN EAST TENNESSEE.[1]

successful invasion of Maryland and Pennsylvania. The slight resistance offered to Burnside, and the abandonment of Chattanooga without a struggle, made the rumor appear plausible. Halleck questioned the propriety of allowing Rosecrans to pursue Bragg, and telegraphed[a] to him to hold firmly the mountain-passes in the direction of Atlanta, to prevent the return of the Confederates until Burnside could connect with him, when it would be determined whether the Army of the Cumberland should penetrate farther into Georgia. He also mentioned the reports that Bragg was sending troops to Lee. On the same day, he ordered Burnside to hold the mountain-passes in East Tennessee, to prevent access to or from Virginia, and to connect, with his cavalry at least, with Rosecrans.

[a] Sept. 11, 1863.

In reply to Halleck, Rosecrans said he did not believe any troops had been sent to Lee by Bragg. On the contrary, there were indications that Bragg himself was being re-enforced from Mississippi, and was preparing to turn the flanks of the Army of the Cumberland and cut its communications; and he suggested the propriety of ordering some of Grant's troops to cover the line of the Tennessee River, westward, to prevent a raid on Nashville. This was followed by an electrograph from General Foster, at Fortress

---

[1] This is a careful copy of a photograph presented to the author, at Knoxville, in which is delineated a group of the returned refugees, at the time we are considering. They consisted, in a large degree, of young men belonging to the best families in East Tennessee. Their sufferings had been dreadful. Their clothing, as the picture shows, was in tatters, and at times they had been nearly starved. Yet they held fast to hope, and resolved to save their country if possible.

Monroe, saying trains of cars had been heard running night and day for thirty-six hours on the Petersburg and Richmond railway, indicating the movement of troops; and the General-in-Chief was inclined to believe that a movement against Norfolk, similar to that in the spring,[1] was about to be made in favor of Lee, the Confederates hoping thereby to draw off some of the troops from Meade.   But this suspicion was dispelled by another dispatch from General Foster the next day,[a] bearing a report ᵃ Sept. 14, 1863. that Longstreet's corps was passing southward into North Caro- lina.   Then Halleck directed Meade to ascertain the truth or falsity of the latter report, when it was found to be true, as we have observed.[2]   Mean- while Halleck had ordered Burnside to move down and connect with Rose- crans, and directed General Hurlbut, at Memphis, to send all of his available force to Corinth and Tuscumbia, to operate against Bragg, should he attempt the anticipated flank movement, and, if necessary, to ask Grant or Sherman, at Vicksburg, for re-enforcements.   He also telegraphed to the commander at Vicksburg to send all available forces to the line of the Tennessee River.[3] Similar orders were sent to Schofield, in Missouri, and Pope, in the North- western Department; and the commanders in Ohio and Kentucky were ordered to make every exertion to secure Rosecrans's communications.   It was determined that Bragg should not recross the Tennessee River, and that the redeemed commonwealths of Kentucky and Tennessee should not be again subjected to Confederate rule.

The Army of the Cumberland was now the center of absorbing interest to the Government and to the loyal people.   Bragg's was of like interest to the Conspirators and their friends, and they spared no effort, fair or foul, to give him strength sufficient to drive Rosecrans back toward the Cumberland or capture his army.   Buckner, as we have seen, was ordered to join him. Johnston sent him a strong brigade from Mississippi, under General Walker, and the thousands of prisoners paroled by Grant and Banks at Vicksburg[4] and Port Hudson,[5] who were falsely declared by the Confederate authorities to be exchanged, and were released from parole, were, in shameful violation of the terms of the surrender, and the usages of civilized nations, sent to Bragg to swell his ranks, while every man that it was possible to draw from Georgia and Alabama by a merciless conscription, was mustered into the service to guard bridges, depots, &c., so that every veteran might engage in battle.   In this way Bragg was rapidly gathering a large force in front of Pigeon Mountain, near Lafayette, while Longstreet was making his way up from Atlanta,[6] to swell the volume of the Confederate army to full eighty thousand men.

Deceived by Bragg's movements—uninformed of the fact that Lee had sent troops from Virginia to re-enforce him, impressed with the belief that he was retreating toward Rome, and ambitious of winning renown by cap- turing his foe, or driving him in confusion to the Gulf—Rosecrans, instead of concentrating his forces at Chattanooga, and achieving a great as well as

---

  [1] See page 41.   [2] See page 101.
  [3] At that time Grant was in New Orleans, and Sherman was in command in the vicinity of Vicksburg.
  [4] See note 2, page 630, volume II.
  [5] See page 637, volume II.
  [6] Finding Burnside in his way in East Tennessee, Longstreet had passed down through the Carolinas with his corps, to Augusta, in Georgia; thence to Atlanta, and then up the State Road (railway) toward Chattanooga.

an almost bloodless victory, scattered them over an immense space of rough country, to operate on the rear and flank of what he supposed to be a flying adversary. He ordered Crittenden to call his brigades from across the river, near Chattanooga, and leaving one of them there to garrison the town, push on to the East Chickamauga Valley and the railway to Ringgold or Dalton to intercept the march of Buckner from East Tennessee, or strike the Confederate rear, as circumstances might determine. Thomas, who had just passed through Stevens's and Cooper's gaps of Lookout Mountain, into McLemore's Cove, was directed to push through Dug Gap of Pigeon Mountain, and fall upon the supposed flank of the Confederates at Lafayette. At the same time McCook was to press on farther south, to Broomtown Valley, to turn Bragg's left. These movements were promptly made, and revealed the alarming truth to Rosecrans. His cavalry on the right, supported by McCook's corps, descended Lookout Mountain, reconnoitered Broomtown Valley as far as Alpine, and discovered that Bragg had not retreated on Rome. Crittenden moved rapidly to Ringgold, where, on pushing Wilder forward to Tunnel Hill, near Buzzard's Roost (where he skirmished heavily), it was discovered that the Confederates, in strong force, were on his front, and menacing his communications; and when Negley, with his division of Thomas's corps, approached Dug Gap, he found it securely guarded by a force so overwhelming, that when, on the following morning, Baird came to his aid, both together could make no impression, and they fell back to the main body.

Rosecrans was at last satisfied that Bragg, instead of fleeing before him, was gathering force at Lafayette, opposite his center, to strike a heavy blow at the scattered Army of the Cumberland. He saw, too, that its position was a perilous one. Its wings, one at Lee and Gordon's Mill, on the Chickamauga, and the other at Alpine, were full forty miles apart, and offered Bragg a rare opportunity to terribly cripple, if not destroy or capture his foe. But the golden opportunity too soon passed. Rosecrans, on perceiving the danger, issued orders for the concentration of his forces in the Chickamauga Valley, in the vicinity of Crawfish Spring, about half-way between Chattanooga and Lafayette. Crittenden, alarmed by threatened danger to his communications, had already made[a] a rapid flank movement in that direction, from Ringgold, covered by Wilder's brigade, which was

[a] Sept. 12, 1863.

compelled to skirmish heavily at Lett's tan-yard, with Confederate cavalry, under Pegram and Armstrong. Thomas crossed the upper end of the Missionaries' Ridge, and moved toward the Spring; and McCook, after much difficulty in moving up and down Lookout Mountain, joined Thomas on the 17th. Granger's reserves were called up from Bridgeport, and encamped at Rossville; a division under General Steedman was ordered up from the Nashville and Chattanooga railway, and a brigade, led by Colonel D. McCook, came from Columbia. On the night of Friday, the 18th,[b] when it was positively known to Rosecrans

[b] Sept.

that troops from Virginia were joining Bragg, the concentration of his army was completed, excepting the reserves at Rossville and cavalry at Blue Bird's Gap of Pigeon Mountain, and at Dougherty's Gap that separates the latter from Lookout Mountain. The divisions of Wood, Van Cleve, Palmer, Reynolds, Johnson, Baird, and Brannan, about thirty thousand in number, formed the first line, ranging from Lee and Gordon's Mill northward; and the remainder were posted on the right, in reserve. Minty and Wilder, with their mounted men, were on the extreme left, watching the crossings of the roads from Ringgold, and Napier Gap, at Reed and Alexander's bridges.

Meanwhile Bragg had been making dispositions for attacking Rosecrans's left. His scouts, looking down from Pigeon Mountain, had observed the exact position of the Army of the Cumberland, and the Confederate leader had the advantage of knowing the strong and weak points of his foe, while his own position was more than half concealed. Bragg concentrated his

CRAWFISH SPRING.[1]

army on the eastern side of the Chickamauga, and, early on the morning of the 18th, when the advance of Longstreet's corps, under Hood, was coming up, he massed his troops heavily on his right, attacked Minty and Wilder, who fought gallantly at the bridges, and pushed the National left back to the Lafayette and Rossville road. Early in the evening, Hood, with a division, took post on Bragg's extreme right. Bushrod Johnson's Virginians took a firm position on the west side of the creek, and, before mid-

---

[1] This is from a sketch made by the author, in May, 1866. The spring is really the outlet of a large subterranean brook, that here flows out at the foot of a rocky, wooded hill, whose summit is about fifty feet above. It was on the estate of the Widow Gordon, whose fine brick mansion stood near. There Lieutenant Murdoch, a gallant young officer, wounded in the Battle of Chickamauga, died. Near the spring was the house of Lowry, the second chief of the Cherokees. Here was the hospital of the Army of the Cumberland at the time of the Battle of Chickamauga.

night, nearly two-thirds of the Confederates had crossed over, and held all the fords of the Chickamauga, from Lee and Gordon's Mill, far toward the Missionaries' Ridge.

Bragg was now ready for battle, on the general plan pursued by him at Stone's River, namely, crushing, by superior weight, a flank of his foe, and

gaining his rear and his communications. Bragg formed his army into two corps, the right commanded by General Polk, and the left by General Longstreet, Hood taking the place of the latter until the arrival of his chief. Arrangements were made for crossing the Chickamauga at different points simul-

LEE AND GORDON'S MILL.[1]

taneously, from Lee and Gordon's Mill northward, in heavy force, so as to fall heavily on the National left, while the front should be hard pressed, and the passes of Pigeon Mountain well guarded by Wheeler's cavalry, to prevent a flank attack from that direction. But the wise movements of the Nationals during the night disconcerted Bragg's well-laid plans, and, instead of finding Rosecrans comparatively weak on his left, he found him positively strong. By a continuous night-march up the Dry Valley road, Thomas, with his heavy corps, followed by a part of McCook's corps,

THOMAS'S POSITION NEAR KELLEY'S FARM.[2]

had reached an assigned position on a southern spur of Missionaries' Ridge, near Kelley's Farm, on the Lafayette and Rossville road, facing Reed and Alexander's burnt bridges; and there, a mile or two to the left of Crittenden's corps, early on the morning of the 19th,[a] he proceeded to strike without waiting to be struck. He was informed by Colonel D. McCook, who, with his brigade of reserves, had been holding the front

[a] Sept., 1863.

---

[1] This is from a sketch made by the author in May, 1866. This mill is on the left bank of the Chickamauga Creek, and near the Lafayette and Rossville road, about twelve miles south of Chattanooga. In this view the mill-dam is seen. The banks of the stream are here precipitous and rocky.

[2] This sketch is given to show the general character of the battle-ground, which was mostly wooded; and much of the heaviest fighting was in the forest, along the line of the Rossville and Lafayette road.

at that point during the night, that a Confederate brigade was on that side of the Chickamauga, apparently alone, and that as he (McCook) had destroyed Reed's bridge behind them, he thought they might easily be captured. Thomas at once ordered General Brannan to advance with two brigades on the road to Reed's bridge, while Baird should throw forward the right of his division on the road to Alexander's bridge, and in that manner attempt to capture the isolated brigade. This brought on a battle.

While Thomas's troops were making the prescribed movements, a portion of Palmer's division of Crittenden's corps came up and took post on Baird's right; and at about ten o'clock in the morning Croxton's brigade of Brannan's division became sharply engaged with Forrest's cavalry, which was strongly supported by the infantry brigades of Ector and Wilson, from Walker's column. Back upon these Croxton had driven Forrest, when the latter was stoutly resisted. Then Thomas sent Baird's division to aid Croxton, and after a desperate struggle the Confederates were hurled back with much slaughter. Walker now threw Liddle's division into the fight, making the odds much against the Nationals, when the latter were in turn driven; and the pursuers, dashing through the lines of three regiments of regulars (Fourteenth, Sixteenth, and Eighteenth United States troops), captured two batteries and over five hundred prisoners. One of the batteries lost was Loomis's, of Michigan, which had done so much service from the beginning of the war, that the very metal and wood were objects of affection. In the charge of the Confederates all its horses and most of its men were killed or wounded. Its commander, Lieutenant Van Pelt, refused to leave it, and he died by the side of his guns, fighting a regiment of men with his single saber.

At the critical moment when this charge was made, Johnson's division of McCook's corps, and Reynolds's, of Thomas's, came rapidly up, and were immediately thrown into the fight. So also was Palmer's division of Crittenden's corps, which took position on Baird's right. The Nationals now outnumbered and outflanked the Confederates, attacked them furiously, and drove them back in great disorder for a mile and a half on their reserves near the creek, and killing General Preston Smith. By this charge, the lost battery was recovered, and Brannan and Baird were enabled to re-form their shattered columns. The position of the Confederates on the creek, between the two bridges already mentioned, was so strong, that it was not deemed prudent to assail it. Then there was a lull in the battle for an hour, during which Brannan and Baird took position on commanding ground between McDaniel's house and Reid's bridge, with orders to hold it to the last extremity. It was now about four o'clock in the afternoon.

At five o'clock the Confederates renewed the battle, by throwing the divisions of Liddle and Gist in heavy charges upon Reynolds's right, and while Thomas was trying to concentrate his forces, they fell with equal fury on Johnson, Baird, and Van Cleve, producing some confusion, and threatening the destruction of that part of the line. Fortunately, General Hazen had been sent back to the Rossville road, to take charge of a park of artillery, composed of four batteries, containing twenty guns, which had been left there without guards. These Hazen quickly put into position, on a ridge, with such infantry supports as he could hastily collect, and brought them to bear upon the Confederates, at short range, as they dashed into the road in pursuit of the flying Nationals. This caused them to recoil in disorder, and thereby the day was saved on the left. Just at sunset General Cleburne made a charge upon Johnson's front with a division of Hill's corps, and pressed up to the National lines, but secured no positive advantage.

There had been some lively artillery work on the National right during the day, and in an attack by three of Bragg's brigades in succession, one of the National batteries (three guns) was for a time in possession of the foe. But the assailants were soon driven back, and the guns were recovered. At three o'clock in the afternoon Hood threw two of his divisions, (his own and that of Bushrod Johnson) upon Davis's division of McCook's corps, pushing it back and capturing the Eighth Indiana Battery. Davis fought with great pertinacity until near sunset, when Bradley's brigade, of Sheridan's division, came to his aid. Then a successful counter-charge was made, the foe was driven back, the battery was retaken, and a number of prisoners were captured from the Confederates. When night fell the battle ceased, with apparent advantage to the Nationals. They had lost no ground; had repulsed the assailants at all points, and made a net gain of three guns. But they were clearly outnumbered. Nearly the whole army had been engaged in the struggles of the day, and no re-enforcements were near. The Confederates had not many fresh reserves; and that night Hindman came up with his division, and Longstreet arrived with two brigades of McLaws's veterans from Virginia. Longstreet took command of Bragg's left; and on the morning of the 20th,[a] the Confederates had full seventy thousand men opposed to fifty-five thousand Nationals.[1]

[a] Sept., 1863.

Preparations were now made for a renewal of the struggle in the morning, which Rosecrans knew must be severe. After hearing the reports of his corps commanders, he ordered General Negley, who had come down from the extreme right during the afternoon and fought his way to Van Cleve's side, to report to General Thomas early in the morning. McCook was ordered to replace Negley's troops by one of his own divisions, and to close up well on Thomas, so as to cover the position at the Widow Glenn's house, at which the latter now had his head-quarters. Crittenden was ordered to hold two of his divisions in reserve, ready to support McCook or Thomas, as circumstances might require. These orders were issued at an early hour, and the remainder of the night was spent in needed repose.

---

[1] The troops engaged in this struggle were commanded by the following officers:—NATIONAL TROOPS.—*Fourteenth Corps*—General Thomas, four divisions, commanded by Generals Baird, Negley, Brannan, and Reynolds. *Twentieth Corps*—General McCook, three divisions, commanded by Generals Davis, Johnson, and Sheridan. *Twenty-first Corps*—Three divisions, commanded by Generals Wood, Palmer, and Van Cleve. *Reserved Corps*—General Granger, two divisions, commanded by Generals Steedman and Morgan. The division of General R. S. Granger, of this corps, and two brigades of Morgan's division, were not present. *Cavalry Corps*—General Stanley, two divisions, commanded by Colonel E. M. McCook and General George Crooke. General Stanley being too sick to take the field, General R. B. Mitchell commanded the cavalry in the battle of Chickamauga.

Confederate Troops—General J. Longstreet's corps, three divisions, commanded by Generals J. B. Hood, E. M. McLaws, and B. R. Johnson. General L. Polk's corps, three divisions, commanded by Generals B. F. Cheatham, T. C. Hindman, and P. Anderson. General D. H. Hill's corps, two divisions, commanded by Generals Patrick Cleburne (called the "Stonewall Jackson of the Southwest") and J. C. Breckinridge. General S. B. Buckner's corps, two divisions, commanded by Generals A. P. Stewart and W. Preston. General W. H. T. Walker's corps, two divisions, commanded by Generals J. R. Liddell and S. R. Gist. General J. Wheeler's cavalry corps, two divisions, commanded by Generals S. A. Wharton and W. Martin. General N. B. Forrest's corps, two divisions, commanded by Generals F. Armstrong and J. Pegram.

Bragg had likewise made preparations for a vigorous attack at dawn. Longstreet arrived at eleven o'clock in the evening, and immediately received his instructions as commander of the left, where his own troops were stationed; and Polk was ordered to assail the Nationals at daylight, and "to take up the attack in succession rapidly to the left. The left wing was to await the attack by the right, and take it up promptly when made, and the whole line was then to be pushed vigorously and persistently against the enemy throughout its extent." [1]

The battle was to have been opened at dawn by Hill, whose corps was to fall upon the National left. Before that hour Bragg was in the saddle, and he waited with great impatience for the sound of battle when day dawned, for he had heard the noise of axes and the falling of trees during the night, indicating that his adversary was intrenching. But Polk was silent, and when Bragg rode to the right, he found that the reverend leader had not even prepared for the movement. He renewed his orders, but another golden opportunity for Bragg was passed.[2] At the hour appointed for the attack, Thomas was comparatively weak, for Negley had not yet joined him, and Rosecrans, riding along his lines at dawn, had found his troops on his left not so concentrated as he wished. The defect was speedily remedied. Under cover of a dense fog that shrouded the whole country, re-enforcements joined Thomas, until nearly one-half of the Army of the Cumberland present was under his command, behind breastworks of logs, rails, and earth, which his industrious troops had piled in the space of a few hours.

When the fog lifted, between eight and nine o'clock,[a] Breckinridge, of Hill's corps, with fresh divisions, was found facing and partly overlapping Thomas's extreme left, held by Baird, and flanking it. Breckinridge instantly advanced, and, fighting desperately, pushed across the Rossville road toward a prescribed position. Other divisions in succession toward Bragg's center followed this example, the intention being to carry out the original plan of interposing an overwhelming force between Rosecrans and Chattanooga, which Thomas had prevented the previous day. At this moment Beatty's brigade of Negley's division, moving from the National right center, went into action by the side of Baird, on the extreme left, and checked Breckinridge's advance; but both he and Baird were outnumbered, and the latter began to lose ground. Several regiments of Johnson's division were pushed forward to his support, and these, with Vandever's brigade of Brannan's division, and a part of Stanley's, of Wood's division, so strengthened the wavering line, that Breckinridge was thrown back in much disorder, with the loss of Generals Helm [3] and Deshler, killed, his chief of artillery (Major Graves) mortally wounded, and General D. Adams severely so. He rallied his troops on a commanding ridge, with his guns well posted, and then fought desperately, re-enforced from time to time by the divisions of Walker, Cheatham, Cleburne, and Stewart. Fearfully the battle raged at that point, with varying fortunes for the combatants. The carnage on both sides was frightful, and for awhile

a Sept. 20, 1863.

---

[1] Bragg's *Report of the Battle of Chickamauga*, "published by order of Congress," in 1864, page 13.

[2] Bragg said in his report: "The reasons assigned for this unfortunate delay by the wing commander appear in part in the reports of his subordinates. It is sufficient to say they are entirely unsatisfactory."

[3] The wife of General Helm was a half-sister of the wife of President Lincoln.

it was doubtful with·whom the palm of victory would be left.   Thomas had given an order for the massing of cannon on the Missionaries' Ridge, just west of the State Road, as strongly supported by infantry as possible, to command Breckinridge's artillery, and sweep the ground to the left and rear of Baird, but it seems to have been misunderstood, and the work was not done.   Yet the attempt to turn the National flank was not accomplished,

GEORGE H. THOMAS.

for Thomas and his veterans stood like a wall in the way, and the assailants had much to do to maintain the battle nearer the center, where the conflict was, for awhile, equally desperate, bloody, and decisive.

While the struggle was going on at the left and the left center, the right became involved in disaster. The divisions of Negley and Van Cleve moved successively, after the battle had commenced, to the support of Thomas, and Wood was directed to close up to Reynolds on the right center, and Davis to close on Wood.   McCook, commanding on that wing, was ordered to close down on the left with all possible speed.   These dangerous movements were now made disastrous by the blunder of an incompetent staff officer, who was sent with orders to Wood.   The latter understanding that he was directed to support Reynolds, then hard pressed, pulled out of the line and passed to the rear of Brannan, who was, *en echelon*, slightly in the rear of Reynolds's right.   This left a gap, which Longstreet quickly saw, and before Davis, by McCook's order, could fill it with three light brigades, he thrust Hood into it.   The latter, with Stewart, charged furiously, with Buckner supporting him by a simultaneous advance on the National right.   Hood's column struck Davis on the right and Brannan on the left, and Sheridan in the rear, severing the army by isolating five brigades which lost full forty per cent. of their numbers.   The whole right wing of the Nationals was so shattered by this charge, that it began crumbling, and was soon seen flying in disorder toward Rossville and Chattanooga, leaving thousands behind, killed, wounded, or prisoners.   This turbulent and resistless tide carried along with it Rosecrans, Crittenden, McCook, and other commanders, while Sheridan and Davis, who were driven over to the Dry Valley road, rallying their shattered divisions, re-formed them by the way, and, with McCook, halted and changed front at Rossville, with a determination to defend the pass at all hazards against the pursuers.   Rosecrans, unable to join Thomas, and believing the whole army would be speedily hurrying pell-mell toward Chattanooga, with exultant victors in their rear, pushed into that place, to make provision for holding it, if possible.

Thomas, meanwhile, ignorant of the disaster that had befallen the right, was maintaining his position most gallantly, little suspecting, however, that he must soon confront a greater portion of Bragg's army.   He had sent

Captain Kellogg, at a little past noon, to hasten the march of Sheridan, whose support had been promised, and he had returned with tidings that a large Confederate force was approaching cautiously, with skirmishers thrown out to the rear of Reynolds's position. Thomas sent General Harker, whose brigade was on a ridge in the direction of this reported advance, to resist them, which he did. In the mean time General Wood came up, and was directed to post his troops on the left of Brannan, then in the rear of Thomas's line of battle on a slope of the Missionaries' Ridge, a little west of the Rossville road, where Captain Gaw, by Thomas's order, had massed all the artillery he could find in reserve, and brought as many infantry to its support as possible. To that position Thomas now withdrew from his breastworks and concentrated his command.

Wood had barely time to dispose his troops on the left of Brannan, before they were furiously attacked, the Confederates keeping up the assault by throwing in fresh troops as fast as those in their front were repulsed. Meanwhile General Gordon Granger, who, at Rossville, had heard the roar of guns where Thomas was posted, had moved to his support, without orders, and appeared on his left flank at the head of Steedman's division of his corps.[1] He was directed to push on and take position on Brannan's right, when Steedman gallantly fought his way to the crest of the hill at the appointed place, and then turning his artillery upon the assailants, drove them down the southern slope of the ridge with great slaughter. They soon returned to the attack, with a determination to drive the Nationals from the ridge. They were in overwhelming force, and pressed Thomas in front and on both flanks. Finally, when they were moving along a ridge and in a gorge, to assail his right in flank and rear, Granger formed the brigades of Whittaker and Mitchell into a charging party, and hurled them against the Confederates, of whom General Hindman was the commander, in the gorge. They were led by Steedman, who, seizing a regimental flag, headed the charge. Victory followed. In the space of twenty minutes Hindman and his Confederates disappeared, and the Nationals held both ridge and gorge. The latter had lost heavily. Steedman's horse was killed, and he was badly bruised by a fall, and Whittaker was stunned by a bullet and fell from his horse.

There was now a lull of half an hour. It was the deep calm before the bursting of the tempest. A greater portion of the Confederate army was swarming around the foot of the ridge, on which stood Thomas with the remnant of seven divisions of the Army of the Cumberland. Longstreet was then in immediate command of his own veterans, for Hood had lost a leg during the morning; and to human vision there seemed no ray of hope for the Nationals. But Thomas stood like a rock, and assault after assault was repulsed, until the sun went down, when, by order of General Rosecrans, sent by General Garfield, his chief of staff (who reached the ridge at four o'clock), he commenced the withdrawal of his troops to Rossville. His ammunition was nearly exhausted. His men had not more than three rounds

---

[1] Granger, as we have observed, was posted with his troops at Rossville, as a reserve. From that point General Steedman, with six regiments, made a reconnoissance to within two miles of Ringgold on the 17th, and on the 18th he burned Reid's bridge over the Chickamauga. Granger also sent the brigades of General Whittaker and Colonel D. McCook to the Chickamauga, and held the roads in that direction on the extreme left, until the roar of Thomas's guns satisfied him that he could do better service by helping him.

apiece when Steedman arrived, and furnished them with a small supply, and this was consumed in the succeeding struggle. Garfield and a company officer gave Thomas the first reliable information concerning the disaster to the center and right of the army. They bore an order from Rosecrans for

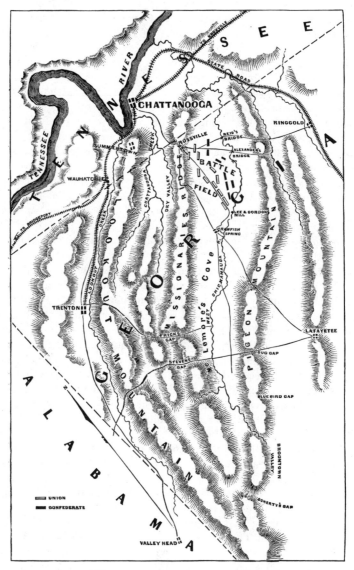

THE BATTLE-FIELD OF CHICKAMAUGA AND ITS VICINITY.

Thomas to take command of all the forces, and with McCook and Crittenden to secure a strong position at Rossville, and assume a threatening attitude. This was done by divisions in succession, Reynolds's leading, and the whole covered by Wood's division. On the way Turchin's brigade charged upon a heavy body of Confederates, who were seeking to obstruct the movement.

They were driven, with a loss of two hundred men, made prisoners. So ended the BATTLE OF CHICKAMAUGA. There was no pursuit.[1] The Nationals quietly took position in the Rossville and Dry Valley gaps of the Missionaries' Ridge.[2] On the following morning[a] a reconnoitering force of Confederates on the Ringgold road, drove in Minty's cavalry, but did little harm. That evening the whole army withdrew in perfect order to a position assigned it by Rosecrans, in front of Chattanooga, and, on the following day, Bragg advanced and took possession of Lookout Mountain and the whole of the Missionaries' Ridge. [a Sept. 21, 1863.]

The Confederates won a victory on the field in the Battle of Chickamauga, at a fearful cost to both armies,[3] and without any other decisive result. Rosecrans might have held Chattanooga, Lookout Mountain, and the Missionaries' Ridge, with his communications secure, without that fearful cost; while Bragg, although he had reaped "glory," as the phrase is, on the battle-field, secured none of the harvest of solid victory, such as the capture or dispersion of the army of his adversary. "Rosecrans," said a Confederate historian, "still held the prize of Chattanooga, and with it the possession of

---

[1] "The troops were halted by their respective commanders," said Bragg, in his report on the 23d of December, 1863, "when the darkness of the night and the density of the forest rendered further movements uncertain and dangerous, and the army bivouacked on the ground it had so gallantly won."

[2] Crittenden's corps held the left of the Ringgold road; McCook's was on the right of the Dry Valley road, with his right thrown forward nearly to the Chickamauga, and Negley's, Reynolds's, and Brannan's divisions were posted in the Rossville Gap and along the ridge on its right, back of Ross's house. See page 126. Minty's brigade of cavalry was over a mile in advance of Crittenden, on the Ringgold road.

Probably the youngest person who ever bore arms in battle was engaged in the strife near the Chickamauga River. His name was JOHN CLEM, and his home was at Newark, Ohio. He was a volunteer in the Twenty-second Michigan Infantry, and was only twelve years of age. He was serving as marker of a regiment in a review at Nashville, when he was brought to the notice of General Rosecrans, who made him welcome at head-quarters. He performed faithfully whatever duty was imposed upon him while the Army of the Cumberland was making its way to and across the Tennessee River; and in the Battle of Chickamauga he won for himself the rank of a sergeant by a deed of great valor. He had been in the thickest of the fight, and three bullets had passed through his hat, when, separated from his companions, he was seen running, with a musket in his hand, by a mounted Confederate colonel, who called out, "Stop! you little Yankee devil!" The boy halted, and brought his musket to an order, when the colonel rode up to make him a prisoner. With swift motion young Clem brought his gun up and fired, killing the colonel instantly. He escaped; and for this achievement on the battle-field he was made a sergeant, put on duty at the head-quarters of the Army of the Cumberland, and placed on the Roll of Honor by General Rosecrans. The engraving is from a photograph from life, taken in Cincinnati.

JOHN CLEM.

[3] The National loss was reported at 16,326, of whom 1,687 were killed, 9,384 were wounded, and 5,255 were missing. The total loss of officers was 974. It is probable the entire Union loss was full 19,000. Among the killed were General W. H. Lytle, of Ohio, Colonels Baldwin and Heg, commanding brigades, and Colonels E. A. King, Alexander, and Gilmer. The Confederate loss, according to a compilation made from the reports of Bragg's commanders, was 20,950, of whom 2,673 were killed, 16,274 were wounded, and 2,003 were missing. Rosecrans reported that he brought off the field 2,003 prisoners, 36 guns, 20 caissons, and 8,450 small-arms, and that he lost in prisoners, including 2,500 of his wounded left on the field, 7,500. Bragg claimed to have captured over 8,000 prisoners, including the wounded; 51 guns, and 15,000 small-arms. The Confederates left a large number of the Union dead unburied.

East Tennessee Two-thirds of our niter-beds were in that region, and a large proportion of the coal which supplied our founderies. It abounded in the necessaries of life. It was one of the strongest countries in the world, so full of lofty mountains, that it had been called not unaptly, the Switzerland of America. As the possession of Switzerland opened the door to the invasion of Italy, Germany, and France, so the possession of East Tennessee gave easy access to Virginia, North Carolina, Georgia, and Alabama."[1]

The incompetency of Bragg, who was the pliant servant of the will of Jefferson Davis, was universally felt, and when his operations in the vicinity of Chattanooga became known, there was wide-spread discontent. Yet few men were bold enough to oppose the will of the Arch-conspirator, and murmuring was scarcely audible. Pollard quotes a private letter from a " distinguished general officer in the West," who most severely and ably criticised the operations of the army under the leadership of Bragg during the year preceding the battle of Chickamauga, and evidently pointed directly to Jefferson Davis as the chief obstacle to the success of the Confederate arms. But the more Davis's chosen instruments were found fault with, the more determined was the Conspirator to keep them in places of the highest trust. When Bragg, a few weeks after the Battle of Chickamauga, was thoroughly beaten before Chattanooga, as we shall observe presently, and tried to hide his own incompetence under fault-finding with his officers—"a resource to which he showed, on all occasions, a characteristic and injurious tendency"[2] —and there was a general feeling that he ought to be relieved from all command, Davis showed his contempt for the opinion of others, by making him[a] General-in-Chief of the armies of the Confederacy.[3] "No

[a] February 24, 1864. doubt," said an officer in the "War Department" at Richmond, at the time, "Bragg can give the President valuable counsel— nor can there be any doubt that he [the President] enjoys a secret satisfaction in triumphing thus over popular sentiment, which just at this time is much averse to General Bragg. The President is naturally a little oppugnant."[4] When the appointment was made, the boldest opposers of Bragg dared not utter their disapprobation openly and manfully.[5]

---

[1] Pollard's *Third Year of the War*, page 128.   [2] Pollard's *Third Year of the War*, page 130.

[3] The following is a copy of the order creating Bragg General-in-Chief, which was dated, "War Department, Adjutant and Inspector-General's Office, Richmond, February 24, 1864," and designated as "General Order No. 23 :"—

"General Braxton Bragg is assigned to duty at the seat of government, and, under the direction of the President, is charged with the conduct of military operations in the armies of the Confederacy. By order of the Secretary of War. S. Cooper, *Adjutant and Inspector-General*."

[4] *A Rebel War Clerk's Diary*, ii. 157.

[5] On the day before Bragg's appointment, the *Richmond Enquirer* had a long editorial, denouncing in advance his assignment to any prominent position, and severely criticising his conduct in the West; but, on the day after his appointment, the same journal, inspired by a proper reverence for the power of "the President," said : "The judicious and opportune appointment of General Bragg to the post of Commander-in-Chief of the armies will be appreciated as an illustration of that strong common-sense which forms the basis of the President's character, that regard for the opinions and feelings of the country, that respect for the Senate, which are the keys to all that is mysterious in the conduct of our public affairs. The Confederate armies cannot fail to be well pleased. Every soldier's heart feels that merit is the true title to promotion, and that glorious service should insure a splendid reward. From Lookout Mountain, a step to the highest military honor and power is natural and inevitable. Johnston, Lee, and Beauregard learn with grateful emotions that the conqueror of Kentucky and Tennessee has been elevated to a position which his superiority deserves. Finally, this happy announcement should enliven the fires of confidence and enthusiasm reviving among the people, like a bucket of water on a newly-kindled grate." This was keen irony, but it was not denunciation, and the writer avoided Castle Thunder.

CHAPTER V.

THE CHATTANOOGA CAMPAIGN.—MOVEMENTS OF SHERMAN'S AND BURNSIDE'S FORCES.

N returning to Chattanooga, Rosecrans commenced the formidable line of fortifications around that town, under the skillful directions of General James St. Clair Morton, of the engineers, which excited the admiration of all; and within twenty-four hours after the army moved from Rossville, it was strongly intrenched—so strongly that Bragg could not, with safety, make a direct attack upon it. He did not attempt it, but took measures for starving it into a surrender, by cutting off its avenues of supplies.

Bragg found himself in a most unpleasant predicament. Regarding the failure of Polk and Hindman to bring on the battle at an earlier hour on the morning of the 20th[1] as the chief cause of his inability to secure a substantial victory, he had them placed under arrest, and thereby caused widespread murmuring, and a mutinous spirit in his army. He was severely censured for not securing that victory himself, by pursuing the fugitives when they moved from the Missionaries' Ridge, and striking them in the open, broken plain, in front of Chattanooga. More aggravating still was a requirement by the authorities at Richmond that he should attempt the impossible feat of moving by his left across the Tennessee River, and advancing on Nashville. So preposterous was this requirement, that he could scarcely conceal his contempt when saying to his superiors, "The suggestion requires notice only because it will find a place in the files of the War Department." He told them that such a movement was utterly impossible, for want of transportation; that half his army consisted of re-enforcements that had joined him just before the recent battle, without transportation or artillery horses; that a third of his own artillery horses were lost; that he had no means of crossing a wide river liable to be flooded any hour by a rain-storm in the mountains; and that by such movement he would have to abandon all the fruits of his victory on the Chickamauga, and leave exposed vast supplies for the use of the Confederate army.

Bragg did not entertain the proposition from the " War Department" for a moment, but proceeded at once to the more practicable business of starving the Army of the Cumberland. For this purpose he had now great advantages. By his advance to Lookout Mountain, and its vicinity, when Rosecrans retired to Chattanooga, he gained possession of the left bank of the Tennessee to Bridgeport, by which he commanded the navigation of that stream, and the road along its margin opposite, at the foot of the precipitous mountain ranges that skirt it. He thus cut off Rosecrans from direct com-

---

[1] See page 187.

munication with his bases of supply at Bridgeport and Stevenson, and compelled him to transport these in wagons from the former place, over the rugged mountains by way of the Saquatchie Valley, fifty or sixty miles, and then across the Tennessee, at Chattanooga, on pontoon bridges. This service was most severe, and its operations were perilous and precarious, for the autumn storms were beginning to howl among the mountains, and small streams were often converted into torrents in the space of an hour. The consequence was that for a time the Army of the Cumberland was on short allowance, and thousands of its horses and mules—not less than ten thousand, it is said—were starved or worked to death in the business of transportation.

While the Army of the Cumberland was thus imprisoned at Chattanooga, a salutary change was wrought in its organization. We have observed that when Halleck was satisfied that Longstreet had gone to Tennessee, he telegraphed to Grant and Sherman, and other commanders in the West, to give all possible aid to Rosecrans.[1] Grant was then in New Orleans, disabled by a fall from his horse,[2] and Sherman, who represented him at Vicksburg, did not receive the dispatch till several days after it was issued. Hearing nothing from either, and startled by the saddening news from the Chickamauga, Halleck at once, as we have observed,[3] detached the Eleventh (Howard's) and Twelfth (Slocum's) corps from the Army of the Potomac, and sent them, under the general command of Hooker, to Middle Tennessee, with orders, until further directed, to guard Rosecrans's communications between Nashville and Bridgeport. These troops were moved with marvelous celerity under the wise direction of General Meigs, the Quartermaster-General, and the skillful management of Colonel D. E. McCallum, the Government Superintendent of railways, and W. Prescott Smith, Master of Transportation on the Baltimore and Ohio road. In the space of eight days, the two corps, twenty thousand strong, marched from the Rapid Anna to Washington, and were thence conveyed through West Virginia, Ohio, Kentucky, and Tennessee, to the Tennessee River.

Halleck determined to hold Chattanooga and East Tennessee at all hazards. For that purpose he ordered the concentration of three armies there, under one commander, and on the 16th of October,[a] an

[a] 1863.

order went out from the War Department, saying: "By order of the President of the United States, the Departments of the Ohio [Burnside's], of the Cumberland [Rosecrans's], and of the Tennessee [Grant's], will constitute the Military Division of the Mississippi. Major-General U. S. Grant, United States Army, is placed in command of the Military Division of the Mississippi, with his head-quarters in the field." By the same order General Rosecrans was relieved of the command of the Army of the Cumberland, and General Thomas was assigned to it. General Sherman was promoted to the command of the Army of the Tennessee. On

[b] October.

the 18th,[b] Grant, then at Louisville, whither he had gone from

---

[1] See page 131.

[2] Grant arrived at New Orleans on the 2d of September, to visit General Banks, and confer concerning future operations in the Mississippi region. On the 4th he attended a grand review at Carrollton, and on his return to the city, his horse became frightened by the noise of a steam-whistle, and, springing against a vehicle with great violence, caused the fall of himself and rider to the pavement. Grant's hip was temporarily paralyzed by the concussion, and he was compelled to use crutches for several weeks.

[3] See page 99.

New Orleans, and was yet suffering from the effects of his accident, assumed the command, and issued his first order. His field of authority comprised three departments and nine States and parts of States, from the Mississippi, between the Gulf and the great Lakes eastward, into the heart of the Appalachian range of mountains. Rosecrans left for Cincinnati on the 19th, after issuing a touching farewell address to his army.

Let us here pause for a moment in the consideration of events in South-eastern Tennessee, to take a glance at military movements in the department commanded by Grant, from the fall of Vicksburg to his promotion just mentioned. We left him at Vicksburg, the winner of the then greatest and most important victory yet achieved by the National troops,[1] and the recipient of the highest encomiums from his superiors[2] and fellow-citizens, while his paroled prisoners were making their way back to Jackson, then reoccupied by Johnston, and thence into the ranks of the Confederate army, in violation, on the part of the Conspirators at Richmond, of all honor.[3]

Johnston, as we have observed,[4] was still hovering in Grant's rear when Vicksburg was surrendered. Sherman had been pushed out in that direction with a considerable force to keep him back, and had constructed a line of works from the Yazoo, at Haines's Bluff, to the Big Black River. This movement was effectual, and Johnston, as we have seen, was endeavoring to aid Pemberton by co-operative movements farther down the stream,[5] when Vicksburg was surrendered. Grant at once sent out to Sherman all that remained of that officer's and McPherson's corps, to drive Johnston from Jackson and the railway. In the afternoon of the 4th of July[a] the re-enforcements were in motion, and when, the next day, they joined Sherman, that leader had about fifty thousand effective men under his command. With these he crossed the Big Black,[b] his right, under Ord, passing at the site of the railway bridge;[6] his center, under Steele, at Messenger's Ford, above; and his left, under Parks, still farther up the river.

[a] 1863.

[b] July 6.

In sweltering heat and blinding dust—men and horses almost maddened by thirst, where little water might be found on account of a parching drought—the army pressed forward over a country which, by Grant's orders,[c] had been desolated by General Baird for scores of miles around Vicksburg, and pushed Johnston back to Jackson, where he took shelter[d] behind his breastworks and rifle-pits, and from which, with a ludicrous show of faith at such a moment and under such circumstances (which he evidently did not feel), he issued a florid order[e] to his troops, telling them that "an insolent foe, flushed with hope by his recent success at Vicksburg, then confronted them, threatening the homes of the people they were there to protect, with plunder and conquest." "The enemy," he said, "it is at once the duty and the mission of you, brave men, to chastise and expel from the soil

[c] May 26.

[d] July 7.

[e] July 9.

---

[1] See page 628, volume II.

[2] On the 13th of July, the generous President wrote a letter to Grant, in which, after saying that he did not remember that he and the general had ever met, and that he then wrote as a grateful acknowledgment for the almost inestimable service he had done the country, he referred to operations and proposed operations which the President thought would be best in the siege of Vicksburg, but which Grant did not, and said, "I now wish to make a personal acknowledgment that you were right and I was wrong."

[3] See page 131. [4] See page 631, volume II. [5] See page 625, volume II. [6] See page 612, volume II.

of Mississippi. The commanding general confidingly relies on you to sustain his pledge, which he makes in advance, and he will be with you in the good work, even unto the end."

A week later these defenders of threatened homes, and the chastisers of "an insolent foe," twenty-four thousand strong, were flying over the "soil of Mississippi," toward the heart of the State, in search of safety from the wrath of the "invaders." Sherman had invested Jackson on the 10th,[a] each flank of his army resting on the Pearl River, that runs hard by, with his cannon planted on the hills around. With a hundred of these he opened upon the doomed city on the 12th, but his scanty supply of ammunition, on account of the tardiness of his trains, would not allow him to continue the attack. In that assault General Lauman, by misapprehension of orders, pressed his troops too near the Confederate works, and in the course of a few minutes he lost five hundred men, by a galling fire from sharp-shooters and twelve cannon charged with grape and canister shot. Two hundred of his men were made prisoners, and with them went the colors of the Twenty-eighth, Forty-first, and Fifty-third Illinois.

a July, 1863.

Johnston was aware that Sherman's ammunition train was behind, and he hoped to remove a greater portion of his stores before it should come up, satisfied that he could not hold the place against the host then hemming it in. Under cover of a fog, on the morning of the 13th,[b] he made a sortie, but with no other result than the production of some confusion, and a considerable loss of life on his part. Finally, on the 16th, when he knew that Sherman's ammunition had arrived, he prepared for a speedy departure, and that night[c] he hurried across the Pearl River, burning the bridges behind him, and pushed on through Brandon to Morton.[1] Sherman did not pursue in force beyond the former place, his chief object being to drive off the Confederate army and make Vicksburg secure. For this purpose he broke up the railway at intervals for many miles in every direction, and destroyed every thing in Jackson that could be useful to the foe, and more. The place was shamefully sacked by the soldiers;[2] and the capital of Mississippi, one of the most beautiful towns, in its public buildings and elegant suburban residences, in all that region, was totally ruined. The business part of the city was laid in ashes, and many of the fine dwellings in the neighborhood, owned by known secessionists, shared the same fate. Among these was the residence of Bishop Green, of the Protestant Episcopal Church, that stood on a beautiful shaded eminence. House, furniture, and fine library of three thousand volumes, were committed to the flames. When the writer visited the spot, in the spring of 1866, nothing remained of it but broken walls, as delineated in the picture on the next page. It was a sad sight. Only the day before he had traveled

b July.

c July 16, 17.

---

[1] Sherman's loss in the recapture of Jackson, excepting Lauman's troops, was trifling. Johnston reported his loss in Jackson at about 600, and added that on his retreat desertions were frequent.

[2] "The first few hours," wrote an eye-witness, "were devoted by our soldiers to ransacking the town, and appropriating whatever of value or otherwise pleased their fancy, or to the destruction of such articles as they were unable to appreciate or remove. Pianos and articles of furniture were demolished, libraries were torn to pieces or trampled in the dust, pictures thrust through with bayonets, windows broken and doors torn from their hinges. Finally, after every other excess had been committed in the destruction of property, the torch was applied." Household furniture, beds, &c., costly and otherwise, were dragged into the streets and burned. It was one of the most shameful exhibitions of barbarism of which the Union soldiers were occasionally guilty, and soiled, with an indelible stain, the character of the Patriot Army.

with the venerable prelate from Vicksburg to Jackson. A hotel near the railway station, kept by a violent rebel known as Dick Edwards, called the "Confederate House," was a special object of the wrath of the Union sol-

diers, because, when General Prentiss and his fellow-prisoners were taken to Jackson by railway, after the battle of Shiloh,[1] the proprietor refused the famished soldiers food or drink, and the women, who crowded the galleries in front of his house, sent boys to the captives with insulting,

RUINS OF BISHOP GREEN'S HOUSE.

and, in some cases, indecent messages. The building was reduced to ashes, and when the writer was there, three years afterward, only a few scattered bricks lying among rank grass marked its site. Another object of their hatred was soon demolished. It was a portion of an old covered bridge

BRIDGE PRISON AT JACKSON.

over the Pearl River, which had been inclosed and converted into a prison for Union captives. There, over the often turbulent waters, in cold and storm, they had been crowded and most cruelly treated. Two or three were in it when Sherman's troops took possession of the town. It seems to have been selected by the Confederates as a place to torture and permanently disable their captives in, as was their practice elsewhere, for they had many other places in the city in which to confine prisoners.

When Sherman had completed his work of destruction, he fell back by way of Clinton, across the Big Black, toward Vicksburg, followed by a great multitude of negroes, of both sexes and all ages. Most of these were the infirm and children, the able-bodied having been sent farther south by their masters. On Sherman's departure, some Confederate troops in the vicinity re-entered Jackson, and burned Bowman's large hotel, because he had given shelter to wounded National soldiers. By Sherman's operations, Vicksburg was secured from all danger of an immediate attack. Grant proceeded to cast up a line of strong works for its defense,[2] and sent out expeditions to other places.

---

[1] See page 273, volume II.

[2] These works were completed at the beginning of 1864. They were three miles in length, extending around the city from river to river. The entire line, including eleven batteries, was called Fort Grant. The batteries were named and located as follows:—Battery Rawlins, on the Warrenton road, half a mile south of the town. Battery Castle (site of Mr. Burwell's house), near the railroad bridge, on the prolongation of Washington Street. Battery Comstock, in the southeastern portion of the town, on Crawford Street, near the residence of

We have observed, that, on the fall of Vicksburg, Grant was about to send General Herron to the aid of Banks, then besieging Port Hudson,[1] when he heard of the surrender of that post. Herron had already embarked with his troops, when the order was countermanded, and he was sent[a] in lighter draft vessels up the Yazoo, for the purpose of capturing a large fleet of steamboats, which had escaped Porter's fleet, and were then lying at Yazoo City. The transports were convoyed by the armored gun-boat, *De Kalb*, and two of lighter armor, called "tin-clad" vessels, under Captain Walker. When they approached Yazoo City, a small garrison there, of North Carolinians, fled, and the steamboats, twenty-two in number, moved rapidly up the river. The *De Kalb* pushed on, and, just as she was abreast the town, the explosion of a torpedo under her sunk her. Herron's cavalry were landed, and, pursuing the steamers up the shore, captured and destroyed a greater portion of them. The remainder were sunk or burned, when, soon afterward, Captain Walker went back after the guns of the *De Kalb.* Herron captured three hundred prisoners, six heavy guns, two hundred and fifty small-arms, eight hundred horses, and two thousand bales of Confederate cotton. After finishing his work at Yazoo City, he started[b] to cross the country to Benton and Canton, in aid of Sherman, when information reached him of Johnston's flight from Jackson. Then he returned to Vicksburg.[c]

a July 12, 1863.

b July 18.

c July 21.

On the day when Vicksburg was surrendered, there were stirring events at Helena, Arkansas, farther up the Mississippi, which the Confederates hoped would have a salutary bearing upon the fortunes of the garrison of the doomed city below. Helena had been held by National troops as a depot of recruits and supplies for about a year, since Washburne's cavalry of Curtis's army took possession of it;[2] and in the summer of 1863 the post was in command of General B. M. Prentiss, whose troops were so sorely smitten at Shiloh.[3] The Confederates in Arkansas, under such leaders as Sterling Price, Marmaduke, Parsons, Fagan, McRae, and Walker, were then under the control of General Holmes, who, at the middle of June, asked and received permission of General Kirby Smith, commander of the Trans-Mississippi Department, to attack Prentiss. He designated Clarendon, on the White River, as the rendezvous of all the available troops under his command, and left Little Rock for that point on the 26th of June. Some of his troops were promptly at the rendezvous, while others, under Price, owing to heavy rains and floods, did not reach there until the 30th.[d] This delay baffled his plans for surprise, for Prentiss had been apprised of his movement and was prepared for his reception.

d June.

The post of Helena was strongly fortified, and behind the earth-works and heavy guns and the *abatis* in front of them, was a garrison of three thousand eight hundred men. The gun-boat *Tyler*, Lieutenant-commanding

---

Mr. Willis. Battery Clark, in the eastern part of the city, between Grove and Jackson Streets. Battery Boomer, one half mile east of the city, on the Jackson road. Battery Sherman, one hundred yards in advance of Battery Wilson, between Jackson road and Win bayou. Battery Crocker, three-fourths of a mile north of Win bayou. Battery Ransom, one-fourth of a mile north of Fort Crocker. Battery Smith, one-fourth of a mile west of Ransom. Battery Hickenlooper, one mile north of the city, on the Valley road. I am indebted to Captain William J. White, aid-de-camp of General T. J. Hood. for the information contained in this note. See note 1, page 616, volume II,

Pritchett, was lying there, ready to give support. The main work, near the town, was called Fort Curtis. The exterior defenses, on bluffs a mile in rear of the town, were under the immediate command of General F. Salomons, at whose suggestion they had been constructed.[1]

Holmes's entire force—the remnants of armies decimated by the war—was less than eight thousand effective men. He was ignorant of Prentiss's real strength, and when, on the 3d of July,[a] he and his army were within four miles of Helena, they were marching to certain defeat and humiliation. They advanced at midnight, and took position within a mile of the outer works;[b] and at daylight moved to the assault in three columns: Price, with the brigades of Parsons and McRae, over three thousand strong, to attack a battery on Graveyard Hill; Fagan, with four regiments of infantry, to assail another on Hindman's Hill; and Marmaduke, with seventeen hundred and fifty men, to storm a work on Righton's Hill.

[a] 1863.

[b] July 4.

Price was accompanied by Harris Flanagan, the Confederate Governor of Arkansas, as volunteer aid-de-camp. His troops, under cover of artillery firing, moved up gallantly to the attack, in the face of a heavy storm of bullets, and grape and canister shot, captured some of the guns, and turned them upon the Nationals. But these were useless, owing to a lack of matches, or friction tubes. Then, with a wild shout, they charged down the hill upon Fort Curtis, six hundred yards distant, exposed to a terribly galling fire from the other batteries, and especially from the *Tyler*. So fearfully were they smitten, that one-third of them were lost.[2]

Fagan, meanwhile, under the immediate direction of Holmes, had attacked the battery on Hindman's Hill with his little force. He left his artillery at the first obstructions, and with his infantry rushed up ravines and steep acclivities and over *abatis*, driving the National sharp-shooters from their rifle-pits, and pushing on to carry the battery by assault. The assailants fought desperately but uselessly, and suffered fearful loss. Toward noon Holmes ordered a retreat, to save this little force from utter destruction. Marmaduke, at the same time, was attempting to take the battery on Righton's Hill, but failed on account of a heavy fire from artillery and musketry from behind the levee, and a lack of co-operation on the part of some cavalry. At three o'clock in the afternoon the assailants were repulsed at all points and withdrew, with a loss, reported by Holmes, of twenty per cent. of his entire force.[3] Holmes hastily retreated with his shattered army, and thenceforth Confederate soldiers never molested Helena. There was quiet for some time along the eastern borders of the Mississippi, likewise, for the attention and the material forces of both parties were drawn toward Chattanooga,

---

[1] Helena lies upon flat ground, on the western bank of the Mississippi River. Back of it are high ridges, running parallel with the river, and commanding the city and approaches. Fort Curtis was erected on the low ground, and being commanded by these bluffs, it was thought proper to place strong batteries upon them. The work was done under the immediate directions of Lieutenant J. G. Patton, of the Thirty-third Missouri. There were four batteries, mounting heavy guns. On the low ground above and below the town there were rifle-pits, with flanking batteries of 10-pounder Parrott guns and 6 and 12-pounder brass pieces.

[2] Price reported his loss at 1,111, of whom 106 were killed, 505 were wounded, and 500 were missing.

[3] He reported his entire loss at 1,636 men. Prentiss (whose loss was only 250 men) made that of Holmes appear much greater, by stating that he buried 300 Confederates left dead on the field, and took 1,100 of them prisoners.

where a decisive conflict was impending. Let us return to a consideration of events there.

It was evident that the Army of the Cumberland could not long exist a prisoner in Chattanooga, its supplies depending on such precarious avenues of reception as the mountain roads, and the transportation animals so rapidly diminishing. General Thomas had nobly responded to Grant's electrograph from Louisville,[a] " Hold Chattanooga at all hazards," saying, " I will hold the town until we starve ;" yet it was not prudent to risk such disaster by inaction, for already Bragg's cavalry had been raiding over the region north of the Tennessee River, destroying supplies, and threatening a total obstruction of all communications between Chattanooga and Middle Tennessee. On the 30th of September, a greater portion of Bragg's horsemen (the brigades of Wharton, Martin, Davidson, and Anderson), about four thousand strong, under Wheeler, his chief of cavalry, crossed the Tennessee, between Chattanooga and Bridgeport, pushed up the Sequatchie Valley, fell upon a National supply-train[b] of nearly one thousand wagons on its way to Chattanooga, near Anderson's cross-roads, and burned it before two regiments of cavalry, under Colonel Edward M. McCook, which had been sent from Bridgeport in pursuit, could overtake them. Wheeler's destructive work was just finished when McCook came up and attacked him. The struggle lasted until night, when Wheeler, who had been worsted in the fight, moved off in the darkness over the mountains, and fell upon another supply-train of wagons and railway cars at McMinnville. These were captured, together with six hundred men ; and then a large quantity of supplies were destroyed. There, after the mischief was done, he was overtaken by General George Crook,[c] with two thousand cavalry, and his rear-guard, as he fled toward Murfreesboro', was charged with great spirit by the Second Kentucky Regiment of Crook's cavalry, under Colonel Long. Wheeler's force greatly outnumbered Long. They dismounted, and fought till dark, when they sprang upon their horses and pushed for Murfreesboro', hoping to seize and hold that important point in Rosecrans's communications. It was too strongly guarded to be quickly taken, and as Wheeler had a relentless pursuer, he pushed on southward to Warren and Shelbyville, burning bridges behind him, damaging the railway, capturing trains and destroying stores, and crossing Duck River pressed on to Farmington. There Crook struck him again, cut his force in two, captured four of his guns and a thousand small-arms, took two hundred of his men, beside his wounded, prisoners, and drove him in confusion in the direction of Pulaski, on the railway running north from Decatur. Wheeler's shattered columns reached Pulaski that night, and made their way as speedily as possible into Northern Alabama. He crossed the Tennessee near the mouth of Elk River, losing two guns and seventy men in the passage, and made his way back to Bragg's lines, after a loss of about two thousand men. He had captured nearly as many as that, and destroyed National property to the amount of, probably, three million dollars in value. When Roddy, who had crossed the Tennessee at the mouth of Gunter's Creek, and moved menacingly toward Decherd, heard of Wheeler's troubles, and his flight back to the army, he retreated, also, without doing much mischief.

[a] October 19, 1863.

[b] Oct. 2.

[c] Oct. 4.

When Grant arrived at Chattanooga,[a] he found General Thomas alive to the importance of immediately securing a safe and speedy way to that post for supplies for the Army of the Cumberland. It [a] October 23, 1863. could not exist there ten days longer, unless food and forage could be more speedily and bountifully furnished. In concert with General

W. F. Smith, who had been appointed Chief Engineer of the army, he had been making prepa- rations for the im- mediate concentra- tion of Hooker's corps at Bridgeport, with the view of opening the river and main wagon road from that point

GRANT'S HEAD-QUARTERS AT CHATTANOOGA.[1]

to Brown's Ferry on the Tennessee, by which supplies might be taken to Chattanooga across the peninsula known as Moccasin Point,[2] and thus avoid the Confederate batteries and sharp-shooters at Lookout Mountain altogether. Grant approved Thomas's plan, and ordered its execution. It was that Hooker should cross the river at Bridgeport with all the force at his command, and, pushing on to Wauhatchie, in Lookout Valley, threaten Bragg with a flank attack. General Palmer was to march his division down the north side of the Tennessee to a point opposite Whitesides, where he was to cross the river and hold the road passed over by Hooker. General Smith was to go down the river from Chattanooga, under cover of darkness, with about four thousand troops, some in batteaux, and some on foot along the north side, and make a lodgment on the south bank of the stream, at Brown's Ferry, and seize the range of hills at the mouth of Lookout Valley, which commanded the Kelly's Ferry road.

The movements of Hooker and Palmer might be made openly, but Smith's could only be performed in secret. Hooker crossed at Bridgeport on pontoon bridges on the morning of the 26th[b] without oppo- sition,[3] and pushed on to Wauhatchie, which he reached on the [b] October. 28th; and on the nights of the 26th and 27th, Smith successfully performed his part of the plan. Eighteen hundred of his troops, under General Hazen, were embarked at Chattanooga on batteaux, intended to be used in the construction of a pontoon bridge, and at two o'clock in the morning they floated noiselessly, without oars, close under the banks past the point of Lookout Mountain, along a line of Confederate pickets seven miles in length, without being discovered, and arrived at Brown's Ferry just at

---

[1] This was the appearance of Grant's head-quarters on the high bank of the Tennessee, as it appeared when the writer sketched it in the spring of 1866. It was near the bridge which the Nationals constructed across the Tennessee, at the upper part of Chattanooga. The eminence in the distance is Cameron's Hill, between the town and the river, which was strongly fortified.

[2] This is so called because of its shape, which resembles an Indian moccasin, as Italy does that of a boot.

[3] His troops consisted of a greater portion of the Eleventh Corps, under General Howard; a part of the Second Division of the Twelfth Corps, under General Geary; one company of the Fifth Tennessee Cavalry, and a part of a company of the First Alabama Cavalry.

dawn.[1] They landed quickly on the south side, captured the pickets there, and seize'd a low range of hills, about half a mile in length, which commanded Lookout Valley. The remainder of Smith's force, twelve hundred strong, under General Turchin, had, meanwhile, moved down the north bank of the stream, across Moccasin Point, and reached the ferry before daylight. They were ferried across, and by ten o'clock in the morning a pontoon bridge was laid there. Before the bewildered Confederates could fairly comprehend what had happened, a hundred axes had laid an *abatis* in front of Hazen's troops; and the foe, after an ineffectual attempt to dislodge the intruders, withdrew up the valley toward Chattanooga. Before night the left of Hooker's line rested on Smith's at the pontoon bridge, and Palmer had crossed to Whitesides, in his rear. By these operations the railway from Bridgeport, well up toward Chattanooga, was put in possession of the Nationals, and the route for supplies for the troops at Chattanooga was reduced by land from sixty to twenty-eight miles, along a safe road, or by using the river to Kelly's Ferry, to eight miles. "This daring surprise in the Lookout Valley on the nights of the 26th and 27th," said a Confederate newspaper in Richmond, "has deprived us of the fruits of Chickamauga."

We have observed that Hooker reached Wauhatchie on the 28th. He left a regiment at the bridge-head where he crossed, and to hold the passes leading to it through Raccoon Mountain, along the base of which his route lay to Running Waters. He met no opposition the first day, excepting from retiring pickets. Leaving guards for the protection of the road over which he was passing, he followed the course of Running Waters, and on the morning of the 27th his main army descended through a gorge into Lookout Valley, between the Raccoon and Lookout mountains, which has an average width of about two miles, and is divided in its center by a series of five or six steep, wooded hills, from two hundred to three hundred feet in height. Between these and Lookout Mountain flows Lookout Creek. The Confederates had possession of these hills, and also of the lofty crest of Lookout Mountain, on which they had planted batteries. From these and the heights of Raccoon Mountain, Bragg could look down upon his foes and almost accurately number them. In that valley, and occupying three ridges near its mouth, toward Brown's Ferry, was a part of Longstreet's troops, and these were the ones we have just mentioned as having been encountered by Hazen.

As Hooker pushed on toward Brown's Ferry, Howard in advance, the latter was sharply assailed by musketeers on the wooded hills where the railway passes through them, near Wauhatchie. These were quickly dislodged. They fled across Lookout Creek, burning the railway bridge behind them. In this encounter Howard lost a few men, and others were killed by shells hurled upon Hooker's column from the batteries on Lookout Mountain. At six o'clock the advance halted for the night within a mile or so of Brown's Ferry, and, as we have observed, touched Smith's troops. Being

---

[1] In a letter to the author, August 23, 1866, General Hazen, speaking of his movement down the river, said: "Fifty-two batteaux had been constructed, that would carry twenty-five men each. At twelve o'clock that night I marched fifty-two squads, each under the command of a tried and trusty officer, to the river landing, and quietly embarked them. These boats were organized into three battalions, under officers who had been tried on many fields. They had been taken in the afternoon nine miles below, to Brown's Ferry, and shown where to land and what to do. Not until the boats were loaded did the leaders of squads know what was expected of them."

anxious to hold the road leading from the Lookout Valley to Kelly's Ferry, through a gorge of the Raccoon Mountain, General Geary, with his small force, was ordered to encamp at Wauhatchie, the junction of the Memphis and Charleston, and Trenton railways, three miles from Howard's position, with a very thin line of pickets connecting them.

From the hour when he entered the valley, Hooker's movements had been keenly watched by McLaws's division of Longstreet's corps, then holding Lookout Mountain, with a determination to fall upon and crush the Nationals at some favorable moment. McLaws did not feel strong enough to fight Hooker's full force in open daylight, so he descended stealthily and swiftly at

JOHN W. GEARY.

midnight[a] upon Geary's weak force, lying at Wauhatchie, not doubting his ability to capture and destroy it, and then to burn Hooker's train of supplies and seize the remainder of his army in that rough, wooded country, from which escape would be difficult.

[a] Oct. 28, 29, 1863.

With wild screams his troops swept down from the hills, drove in Geary's pickets, and charged furiously upon his camp on three sides, while the batteries upon Lookout Mountain sent down their shells in fearful lines upon the aroused camp. But McLaws had not surprised Geary. That vigilant officer, like all the others of Hooker's little army, knew that a strong and wary foe was hovering over their heads and lurking among the hills on every side, with a determination to prevent, at all hazards, the establishment by the Nationals of a short and safe route for supplies between Bridgeport and Chattanooga, for that result once accomplished, that post and its advantages would be lost to the Confederates. Geary's vigilance was therefore sleepless, and he was prepared for the assault, which came at about one o'clock in the morning.[b] He met the assailants with a steady, deadly fire, and made them recoil. The rattle of musketry and

[b] October 29.

the booming of cannon, borne on the midnight air, aroused Hooker, who sent General Schurz's division of Howard's corps to Geary's aid. General Tyndale's brigade first reached the battle-field, where Geary was fighting gallantly and keeping his assailants at bay.[1] He drove the Confederates from a hill to the left of Geary's camp, while a thin brigade of General Steinwehr's division, led by Colonel Orlan Smith, of the Seventy-third Ohio, charged up a steep and rugged acclivity behind Schurz's division, drove a force three times the number of the Nationals from its crest, took some of them prisoners, and scattered the remainder in every direction.[2] "No

---

[1] In his report of the battle on the 6th of November, General Hooker said: "At one time they had enveloped him [Geary] on three sides, under circumstances that would have dismayed any officer except one endowed with an iron will and the most exalted courage. Such is the character of General Geary."

[2] The troops engaged in this charge were the Seventy-third Ohio, Colonel Smith, and Thirty-third Massachusetts, Colonel Underwood, supported by the One Hundred and Thirty-sixth New York, Colonel Greenwood.

troops," said Hooker, in his report of the battle, "ever rendered more brilliant service."[1] For three hours the struggle continued, when the assailants fled, leaving one hundred and fifty of their number dead on Geary's front, also over one hundred prisoners and several hundred small-arms. Thus, at a little past four o'clock in the morning, ended THE BATTLE OF WAUHATCHIE.[2] Its most practical result was the security of a safe communication for the Nationals between Bridgeport and Chattanooga, already obtained by Smith forty-eight hours before, and the defeat of Bragg's plans for starving the Army of the Cumberland into surrender. A little steamboat, named

the *Chattanooga*, which had been built at Bridgeport by the soldiers,[3] was immediately loaded with two hundred thousand rations, and started up the river. It ran the blockade of Lookout Mountain, to Brown's Ferry, and thus the army at Chattanooga was saved from actual famine. Bragg was then in no condition for aggressive movements against the Nationals, for he had weakened his army by sending Longstreet, with a greater portion of his command, against Burnside, in East Tennessee, and was compelled to content himself with

THE CHATTANOOGA.

simply holding his very strong position on the northern acclivities of Lookout Mountain and across the narrow Chattanooga Valley, near the mouth of Chattanooga Creek, and so along the crests of the Missionaries'

Colonel Smith's regiment was commanded on the occasion by Captain Thomas Higgins, acting Major. These were very thin regiments. Those of Ohio and Massachusetts numbered only about two hundred effective men each.

[1] Among the gallant officers wounded in this engagement was Colonel Underwood, of the Thirty-third Massachusetts, who, on the recommendation of General Hooker, was promoted to Brigadier-General.

[2] The National loss in this engagement was 416. The entire loss since crossing the Tennessee, 437; of whom 76 were killed, 339 wounded, and 22 were missing. Among the killed was Captain Geary, son of the General. General Green and Colonel Underwood were severely wounded.

An amusing incident of this night's battle is related. When it began, about two hundred mules, frightened by the noise, dashed into the ranks of Wade Hampton's Legion, and produced a great panic. The Confederates supposed it to be a charge of Hooker's cavalry, and fell back at first in some confusion. The incident inspired a mock-heroic poem, of six stanzas, in imitation of Tennyson's "Charge of the Six Hundred" at Balaklava (see note on page 633, volume II.), two verses of which were as follows:—

"Forward, the mule brigade!	"Mules to the right of them—
Was there a mule dismayed?	Mules to the left of them—
Not when the long ears felt	Mules all behind them—
All their ropes sundered.	Pawed, neighed, and thundered;
Theirs not to make reply—	Breaking their own confines—
Theirs not to reason why—	Breaking through Longstreet's lines
Theirs but to make them fly—	Testing chivalric spines,
On! to the Georgia troops	Into the Georgia troops
Broke the two hundred.	Stormed the two hundred."

[3] When Rosecrans's troops reached Bridgeport, and it was known that there was no steamboat to be found on the river, mechanics of the army set about building one for the public service. In a very short time the *Chattanooga* was made ready; and when the operations of the National troops in the Lookout Valley secured the safe navigation of the river from Bridgeport to Brown's Ferry, she commenced regular trips between the two places, under the command of Captain Arthur Edwards. She was called the "Cracker line" by the Confederates, the word "Cracker" being a name applied to the "mean whites" of Georgia." The *Chattanooga* was the first vessel of the kind built by the soldiers for their use. Others were begun soon afterward. She was constructed chiefly by the Michigan engineer regiment already mentioned.

Ridge to the tunnel of the Knoxville and Chattanooga railway, not far from the Chickamauga River. While the two armies are thus confronting each other, with a space of only three or four miles between them at furthest, let us see what was going on between Burnside and Longstreet in the great Valley of East Tennessee.

We have observed how little difficulty Burnside encountered in throwing his army into the Valley of East Tennessee, and taking position at Knoxville. It was because the Confederates were then moving to re-enforce Bragg at Chattanooga. Halleck ordered Burnside to concentrate his forces in that direction, but circumstances prevented his strict obedience, so he set about the task of keeping the valley clear of armed and organized Confederates, who were threatening it at different points. In this business his forces were, for awhile, considerably diffused, and had many lively experiences. Colonel Foster encountered[a] a considerable force near Bristol, on the eastern border of the State ; and a little later there was a   [a] Sept. 21, 1863. smart but desultory engagement during two days at Blue Springs, not far from Bull's Gap. To that point the Confederates had pressed down. Burnside then had a cavalry brigade at Bull's Gap, supported by a small force of infantry at Morristown. He dispatched[b] a body of   [b] Oct. 10. horsemen, by way of Rogersville, to intercept the retreat of the Confederates, and advanced with infantry and artillery to Bull's Gap. Cavalry were then thrown forward to Blue Springs,[c] where the Con-   [c] Oct. 10. federates, under General Sam. Jones, were in considerable force. After a desultory fight for about twenty-four hours,[d] the Confed-   [d] Oct. 10, 11. erates broke and fled, leaving their dead on the field. They were pursued and struck from time to time by General Shackleford and his cavalry, and driven out of the State. The latter captured a fort at Zollicoffer, burned the long bridge at that place and five other bridges, destroyed a large amount of rolling stock on the railway, and did not halt until he had penetrated Virginia ten miles beyond Bristol. In THE BATTLE OF BLUE SPRINGS, and the pursuit, the Nationals lost about one hundred men in killed and wounded. The loss of the Confederates was a little greater.

When Shackleford returned from the chase, he took post at Jonesboro' with a part of his command, while another portion, under Wilcox, encamped at Greenville, and two regiments and a battery under Colonel Garrard of the Seventh Ohio Cavalry, were posted at Rogersville. There, at daybreak on the 6th of November, Garrard was attacked by a portion of Sam. Jones's troops, under General W. E. Jones, almost two thousand strong. It was a surprise. The Nationals were routed, with a loss of seven hundred and fifty men, four guns, and thirty-six wagons. This disaster created great alarm at Jonesboro' and Greenville, and Shackleford's troops at those places fled back in great haste to Bull's Gap. At the same time, Jones's troops, not doubting Shackleford's horsemen would be after them in heavy force, were flying as swiftly toward the Virginia line, in the opposite direction. In a short space of time there was a wide space of country between the belligerents.

While Burnside was thus engaged in spreading his army so as to cover many points southward of the Holston and Tennessee rivers, Longstreet was ordered to make his way up the line of the East Tennessee and Georgia railway, to seize Knoxville, and drive the Nationals out of East Tennessee.

He advanced swiftly and secretly, and on the 20th of October he struck a startling blow at the outpost of Philadelphia, on the railway southwest from Loudon, then in command of Colonel Wolford with about two thousand horsemen, consisting of the First, Eleventh, and Twelfth Kentucky Cavalry, and Forty-fifth Ohio Mounted Infantry.   Wolford had just weakened his force at that point, by sending two regiments to protect his trains moving to his right, which, it was reported, were in danger; and, while in that condition, he was assailed on front and flank by about seven thousand Confederates.   He fought this overwhelming force gallantly for several hours, hoping the sound of cannon would bring him aid from Loudon.   But none came, and he cut his way out with a desperate struggle, losing his battery and over thirty wagons.   He lost very few men, and took with him over fifty of the Confederates as prisoners.   The detachment he had sent out (First and Eleventh Kentucky), under Major Graham, to protect his trains four miles distant, found them in possession of Longstreet's vanguard. Graham instantly recaptured them, drove the Confederates some distance, and made a number of them prisoners.   He was, in turn, attacked by a greatly superior force, and, in a running fight toward Loudon, to which Wolford fled, lost heavily.[1]

When Burnside heard of the disaster southward of Loudon, he hastened to Lenoir Station, on the railway, where the Ninth Army Corps was encamped, and took command of the troops in person, having received from General Grant a notice of Longstreet's approach, and an order for him to fall back, lure the Confederates toward Knoxville, intrench there, and hold the place to the last extremity.   Grant saw with satisfaction the blunder of Bragg, in detaching Longstreet to fight Burnside, and he resolved to assail the Confederates on the Missionaries' Ridge immediately, and in the event of success, to send a sufficient force to assist the troops at Knoxville, and possibly to capture Longstreet and his command.   With this view he had bidden Burnside to hold on to Knoxville with a firm grasp, as long as possible, until he should receive succor in some form.

Longstreet, meanwhile, was pressing rapidly forward.   By a forced march he struck the Tennessee River at Hough's Ferry, a few miles below Loudon, crossed it on a pontoon bridge there, and pressed on toward the right flank of Burnside, at Lenoir Station.   At the same time Wheeler and Forrest were dispatched, with cavalry, by way of Marysville, across Little River, to seize the heights on the south side of the Holston, which commanded Knoxville, the grand objective of Longstreet—the key to East Tennessee.   Perceiving the danger threatened by this flank movement, and in obedience to his instructions, Burnside sent out a force on the Loudon road, under General Ferrero, to watch and check the foe, and secure the National trains, and, at the same time, ordered the whole force to fall back as rapidly as possible to Knoxville.   A portion of the Ninth Corps, under General Hartranft, was advanced to Campbellville Station, at the junction of the Lenoir and Kingston roads, about sixteen miles from Knoxville, and there the whole force was rapidly concentrated.   And there it was so closely pressed, that Burn-

---

[1] Wolford lost of his command that day 324 men, with six guns; and he took 111 prisoners. About 100 men were killed on each side. Longstreet captured in all, before he reached the Tennessee at Loudon, 650 Union troops.

side found it necessary to abandon his trains or fight. He chose the latter alternative, and taking a good position, with his batteries well posted, he turned upon his pursuer,[a] and gave him a stunning blow. A con-flict ensued, which lasted several hours, during which Burnside's trains moved rapidly forward. The battle ceased at twilight, ending in a repulse of Longstreet, and a loss to the Nationals of about three hundred men.[1] The Confederate loss was about three hundred and seventy.

[a] Nov. 6, 1863.

Taking advantage of this check, Burnside moved on to the shelter of his intrenchments at Knoxville, the chief of which was an unfinished work on a hill commanding the southwestern approaches to the town, and afterward called Fort Sanders. Longstreet followed as rapidly as possible. Wheeler and Forrest had failed to seize the height on which works had been thrown up on the south side of the Holston, owing to the gallant bearing of some of the troops of General W. P. Sanders, of Kentucky, who was in immediate command at Knoxville.[2] Equally gallant was the reception of the same force, which dashed up in advance of Longstreet, and attacked the out-posts there, on the 16th of November.[b] The main body of the Confederates were then near, and, on the morning of the 18th, Longstreet opened some guns on the National works, sharply at-tacked Sanders's advanced right, com-posed of four regiments,[3] who offered determined resistance, drove them from the ridge they occupied, and making his head-quarters at the fine mansion of R. H. Armstrong, near the bank of the Holston, less than a mile from Fort Sanders, planted batteries a little in advance of it. In the attack on Sanders's right, that leader was killed,[4] and the National loss,

[b] 1863.

LONGSTREET'S HEAD-QUARTERS.

---

[1] Among the slain was Lieutenant P. M. Holmes, son of Professor Oliver Wendell Holmes, of Charlestown, Massachusetts. On his breast he wore the badge of the *Bunker's Hill Club*, on which was engraved the line from Horace, quoted by General Warren, just before his death on Bunker's Hill—"*Dulce et decorum est, pro patriâ mori.*"—"It is sweet and glorious to die for one's country."

[2] Knoxville is on the northern bank of the Holston River, one of the main streams that form the Tennessee River, and a large portion of it stands on a table-land, 150 feet above the river, about a mile square in area. On the northeast is a small creek, running through a deep ravine, beyond which is Temperance Hill. Still farther to the east is Mayberry Hill. On the northwest the table-land slopes down to a broad valley, along which lies the railway. On the southwest boundary of the town is another creek, flowing through a ravine, beyond which is College Hill. Farther to the southwest is a high ridge, running nearly parallel with the road that enters Knoxville from below, on which, at the time we are considering, was an unfinished work, afterward known as Fort Sanders, so named in honor of General Sanders, who lost his life near. College Hill was fortified with a strong work carrying a piece of siege artillery. On the height near the Summit House was another work. There were two forts on Temperance Hill, and on each of two other eminences near was a battery. On the principal height, south of the Holston, was a fort, and in the town, near the street leading to the railway station, was a considerable work. Extending around the town, from river to river, was a line of rifle-pits and breastworks. The fortifications for the defense of Knoxville were constructed under the skillful direction of Captain Poe, of Burnside's engineers. "Under Poe's hands," said a participant, "rifle-pits appear as if by magic, and every hill-top of the vast semicircle around Knoxville, from Temperance Hill to College Hill, is frowning with cannon and bristling with bayonets."

[3] The One Hundred and Twelfth Illinois, Forty-fifth Ohio, Third Michigan, and Twelfth Kentucky.

[4] General Sanders was killed in a field, a short distance from the residence of Mr. Armstrong, on the left of the road leading to the town. The bullet that killed him was from a sharp-shooter (supposed to have been young

beside, was about one hundred.[1] Longstreet now nearly invested Knoxville, and began a close siege. Wheeler, Forrest, and Pegram were sent to cut off Burnside's supplies and line of retreat.

While Longstreet was pressing the siege of Knoxville, stirring events occurred in the vicinity of Chattanooga, which had an important bearing upon the Confederate cause in East Tennessee. Grant, as we have observed, intended to attack Bragg immediately after Longstreet left him, so as to relieve Burnside, but such was the condition of his army—not yet supplied with food and munitions of war, his artillery horses mostly broken down, and few others remaining fit for active cavalry service—that he was constrained to wait for the arrival of Sherman with the most of the Fifteenth Army Corps, then on the line of the Memphis and Charleston railway, eastward of Corinth, repairing the road as they moved toward Stevenson. They were there in obedience to an order of General Grant, on the 22d of September, then at Vicksburg, to proceed immediately to the help of Rosecrans at Chattanooga. Sherman's corps was then lying in camp along the line of the Big Black River.[2] He was first directed to send only one division ; and on the same afternoon Osterhaus was moving to Vicksburg, there to embark for Memphis. On the following day[a] Sherman was ordered by Grant to the same destination, with the remainder of his corps.

[a] Sept. 22, 1863.

Tuttle's division was left behind, with orders to report to General McPherson ; and a division of the corps of the latter, under General J. E. Smith, already on the way to Memphis, was placed under Sherman's command.

The water was low in the Mississippi, and the vessels bearing the last of Sherman's troops did not reach Memphis until the 3d of October. There he received instructions from Halleck to conduct his troops eastward, substantially along the line of the Memphis and Charleston railway, to Athens, in Alabama, and then report by letter to General Rosecrans, at Chattanooga.

[b] October.

The troops were moved forward, and on Sunday, the 11th,[b] Sherman left Memphis for Corinth, in the cars, with a battalion of the Thirteenth Regulars as an escort. When, at noon, he reached the Colliersville Station, he found a lively time there. About three thousand Confederate cavalry, with eight guns, under General Chalmers, had just attacked the Sixty-sixth Indiana (Colonel D. C. Anthony), stationed there. Osterhaus had already pushed on to the front of Corinth, and had aroused to activity the Confederates in that region. This attack was one of the first fruits. With his escort Sherman helped beat off the assailants, and then, moving on, reached Corinth that night.

Gist, mentioned in the next note), sent from a window in the tower of Armstrong's house. He was taken to the Lamar House, in Knoxville, and died the next day (Nov. 19), in the bridal chamber of that hotel. His body was buried at midnight, in the Presbyterian churchyard at Knoxville, after the celebration of the impressive funeral service of the Protestant Episcopal Church, by the Rev. Mr. Hume.

[1] In this engagement Mr. Armstrong's house was considerably injured, it being filled with sharp-shooters, upon whom volleys of bullets were poured. These passed through windows and doors. When the writer visited and sketched the house, in the spring of 1866, he saw a bullet lodged in the back of a piano, and the bloodstains upon the stairs leading down from the tower, made by the ebbing of the life-current of a young amateur sharp-shooter, a nephew of Judge Gist, of Charleston, South Carolina, who had been amusing himself by firing from a window in the tower. He was shot between the eyes, the ball passing through his head and into the wall behind him. He died while his comrades were carrying him to a bedroom below.

[2] The Fifteenth (Sherman's) Corps was composed of four divisions, commanded respectively by Generals B. J. Osterhaus, M. L. Smith, J. M. Tuttle, and Hugh Ewing.

Sherman's troops engaged in repairing the road were continually annoyed by Confederate cavalry under General S. D. Lee, whose force, about five thousand strong, was composed of the brigades of Roddy and Ferguson. With these, Osterhaus's division, supported by M. L. Smith's (J. E. Smith's covering the working parties), was constantly skirmishing. Finally, Lee attempted, near Tuscumbia, to dispute the further advance of the Nationals, when General Frank Blair took the advance divisions and soon swept away the opposing force.[a] On that day Sherman received a dispatch from Grant, then at Chattanooga, who, fearing the Confederates, reported to be gathering in force at Cleveland on his left, might break through [a] October 27, 1863. his lines and make a dash on Nashville, ordered Sherman to drop all work on the railway and move with his entire force to Stevenson. He assured Sherman that in the event of the Confederates moving on Nashville, his forces were "the only ones at command that could beat them there."[1]

Fortunately, Sherman's forethought had caused a supply of means, at this critical moment, for his army to cross the Tennessee River, a movement which the general had expected to be very difficult, with the Confederates in strong force hovering around him. He had requested Admiral Porter to send up gun-boats from Cairo, to assist him in that perilous task. He did so, and on the day when, in obedience to Grant's call, Sherman marched to Eastport, on the river, he found two gun-boats there. Three other vessels soon arrived, and on the 1st of November he crossed and pushed on eastward, Blair covering his rear. He went by way of Fayetteville, Winchester, and Decherd, in Tennessee, and then down to Stevenson and Bridgeport, arriving at the latter place on the 14th.[b] On the following [b] November. day he reported to Grant at Chattanooga, in person.

Grant had been somewhat anxious about Burnside's situation, for he could not send him aid when Longstreet advanced, though strongly importuned to do so, especially by Halleck, who deplored the danger of losing Knoxville, and with it East Tennessee. But Grant had plans for relief, which he could not communicate to the General-in-Chief, but which were perfectly satisfactory to Mr. Dana, the Assistant Secretary of War, then at head-quarters in Chattanooga. If, as Grant believed he could, Burnside should hold out at Knoxville until Sherman's approaching re-enforcements should arrive, he felt certain that a double victory might be obtained, for he could then scatter the forces of Bragg on the Missionaries' Ridge, and by such blow possibly so demoralize and weaken Longstreet's force as to compel him to raise the siege of Knoxville. He sent Colonel Wilson, of his staff, accompanied by Mr. Dana, to Knoxville, to communicate his plans to Burnside, and immediately after Sherman's arrival he proceeded to put them into execution. The two leaders proceeded, together with General Smith, in a personal reconnoissance of Bragg's position, and a plan of attack was speedily perfected.

Grant's first movement was to deceive Bragg into the belief that he was to be attacked in heavy force on his left. For this purpose Sherman's troops were put in motion at Bridgeport. Ewing's division moved to Shell-

---

[1] Grant's dispatch was dated the 24th of October. It had been conveyed by a messenger who floated down the Tennessee River in a boat to Florence, and made his way to Tuscumbia, when Blair sent the message to Sherman, at Iuka.

mound, and thence over the mountains toward Trenton, some distance up the Lookout Valley, to menace Bragg's left front, while the remainder of Sherman's force, excepting Osterhaus's division, moved up quickly and secretly to Brown's Ferry, crossed the river there on Smith's pontoon bridge, and marched round behind Chattanooga toward Grant's left, thereby giving Bragg the impression that they were more likely to be moving to the relief of Burnside than to attack his extreme right. The latter was the real movement intended. These troops, as we shall observe presently, crossed the Tennessee to Chattanooga, and at a proper time took position on Thomas's left.

Ewing's troops were stealthily withdrawn from near Trenton, and ordered to follow the others of the corps to the extreme left of the Union Army, leaving only Hooker, with the addition of Osterhaus's division, on Bragg's left. The latter had been prevented from crossing the river at Brown's Ferry, on account of the breaking of the pontoon bridge by drift-wood, and was ordered to join Hooker.

On account of bad roads, caused by heavy rains, Ewing's march was more tardy than was contemplated, and he did not reach his assigned position until the 23d, instead of on the 21st, when Grant expected to make his attack. The latter was impatient, for he knew that Burnside was in peril; and by a note from Bragg on the 20th,[1] and the report of a Confederate deserter on the 22d, he was impressed with a belief that his adversary was preparing to fly southward. Bragg was simply repeating the trick he so successfully played upon Rosecrans, to draw Grant into action prematurely, before his re-enforcements should arrive. It succeeded in a degree, for before Sherman's troops had crossed the river, he ordered[a] Thomas to move the center forward to find out what was going on behind the strong line of Confederate pickets in front of Chattanooga. The fact was, Bragg, instead of preparing to retreat, was making dispositions for a formidable resistance to the impending attack.

[a] Nov. 23, 1863.

In the arrangement for the attack on the 21st, Hooker was to assail Bragg's left on Lookout Mountain. This movement was suspended, and Howard's corps was called to Chattanooga and temporarily attached to Thomas's command. The Fifteenth Army Corps (Sherman's) was now under the command of General Blair, with orders to take position on the extreme left, near the mouth of the West Chickamauga River. They had with them on their march up the north side of the Tennessee, a concealed train of one hundred and sixteen pontoon boats, wherewith to construct a bridge for passing over; and on the afternoon of the 23d, when Thomas moved out, they were at the crossing point.

When Thomas moved, the heavy guns of Fort Wood, at Chattanooga, were playing upon the Missionaries' Ridge and Orchard Knob,[2] the latter a much lower hill considerably in front of the former. The column

---

[1] Bragg's note, dated "Head-quarters Army of the Tennessee, in the field, November 20, 1863," was as follows: "General—As there may still be some non-combatants in Chattanooga, I deem it proper to notify you that prudence would dictate their early withdrawal."

[2] In the picture, on the next page, of that portion of the Missionaries' Ridge that was the chief theater of war, Orchard Knob is the eminence on the left of the figures on Cemetery Hill, rising above the rolling plain to about half the height of the ridge. That ridge is made up of a series of connected knobs, with depressions, the most considerable of which is Rossville Gap.

moved in close and admirable order, the division of General T. J. Wood, of Granger's (Fourth) corps, leading, on the left, and advancing almost to Citico Creek, and Sheridan's on the right. Palmer, of the Fourteenth Corps, supported Granger's right, with Baird's division refused, while Johnston's division remained in the intrenchments, under arms, and Howard's corps was in reserve, both ready to move to any required point. Grant, Thomas, Granger, and Howard, stood upon the ramparts of Fort Wood, watching the advance, and were speedily gratified by hearing shouts of victory from the lips of the patriot soldiers, and seeing the foe flying in confusion. Steadily but swiftly the Nationals had moved toward Orchard Knob, like a

THE MISSIONARIES' RIDGE.

deep torrent, driving every thing before them, and by a vigorous charge carrying the rifle-pits on that eminence and taking two hundred prisoners.[1] The movement was so quick and vigorous, that Bragg had not time to throw forward supports before it was too late. Wood immediately intrenched. Howard moved up and took position on his left, and Bridges's (Illinois) battery was placed in position on the crest of Orchard Knob, which was thus secured. That evening Bragg was satisfied that he had been almost fatally out-generaled.

It was now important to get Sherman's army over the river without being discovered. To attract the chief attention of the Confederates to another quarter, Hooker was ordered to attack them on the northern face of Lookout Mountain.[2] He was under arms and ready for the movement at

---

[1] These were of the Twenty-eighth Alabama Regiment, whose colors were among the trophies of Hazen's brigade, which captured the prisoners.

[2] Hooker's force now consisted of Osterhaus's division of the Fifteenth Corps; Cruft's, of the Fourth; and Geary, of the Twelfth, excepting some regiments left to guard the roads in the rear and to Kelly's Ferry. His artillery was composed of Battery K of the First Ohio, and Battery K of the First New York. He had also a part of the Second Kentucky Cavalry and a company of the Fifteenth Illinois Cavalry, making his entire force only 9,681 men. "We were all strangers," he said in his report, "no one division ever having seen one of the others."

At that time the Confederate pickets formed a continuous line along the right bank of Lookout Creek, with reserves in the valley, while their main force was encamped in a hollow half way up the slope of the mountain. The summit was held by several brigades of Stevenson's division. The side of the mountain toward Hooker was steep, rugged, and wooded, with a palisaded crest, the rocks rising perpendicularly from fifty to eighty feet. On the northern slope, toward Chattanooga, was a belt of arable land, extending well up toward the palisades. This was traversed by a continuous line of earth-works, with redoubts, redans, and rifle-pits; also *abatis* and stone walls, to resist an attack from Lookout or Chattanooga Valley. There was no road to the summit in that region, excepting a zigzagging one on the Chattanooga side.

four o'clock the next morning, when he found that the recent heavy rains had damaged his pontoon bridge at the mouth of Lookout Creek, and the stream was not fordable. He at once ordered Geary to march to Wauhatchie, supported by Cruft, cross the creek there, and hold the right bank of the stream, while the rest of the troops should build temporary bridges nearly in front of the detachment. Fortunately for the Nationals, a heavy mist lay upon the country that morning, and while the vigilant eyes on Lookout Mountain above were watching the bridge-builders, as the mist drifted now and then in the breeze, they did not observe Geary's movement. He crossed the creek at eight o'clock, seized a whole picket guard there, of forty-two men, and extended his line to the right to the foot of the mountain, facing northward. Hooker now advanced Gross's brigade, which seized the bridge just below the railway crossing, and pushed over the stream. Oster-haus's division, which, as we have seen, had been left at Brown's Ferry, now came up, and Wood's brigade was pressed to a point half a mile above Gross, where it laid a temporary bridge and crossed. The two batteries, meanwhile, had been well planted on little hills near, and by eleven o'clock Hooker was at work, with a determination to assail the Confederates and drive them from Lookout Mountain—"an enterprise," he said, under the circumstances, "worthy the ambition and renown of the troops to whom it was in-trusted." [1] His adversary in immediate command before him, was General Walthall.

SLOPE OF LOOKOUT MOUNTAIN. [2]

Hooker's guns all opened at once on the breastworks and rifle-pits along the steep, wooded, and broken slopes of the mountain, with a destructive enfilading fire. Wood and Gross having com-pleted their bridges, dashed across the creek under cover of this fire, and joining Geary on his left, pushed swiftly and vigorously down the valley, sweeping every thing before them, capturing the men in the rifle-pits, and allowing very few to escape up the mountain. At the same time the troops scaling the rugged sides from the valley, pushed on over bowlders and ledges, rocky crests and tangled ravines,

---

[1] Hooker's Report, February 4, 1864.

[2] In this sketch is seen a portion of the slope of Lookout Mountain, with its felled trees, up which the National troops climbed and fought. In the distance is seen the Tennessee, where it winds around Cameron's Hill at Chattanooga and by Moccasin Point.

cutting their way through the felled trees with which the mountain-side had been covered, under the very muzzles of the Confederate cannon, driving the foe from his camp in the hollow or plateau well up toward the crest, and forcing him around the arable belt toward the Chattanooga Valley. In this work, Cobham's brigade, posted on high ground, did effective service, by pouring destructive volleys from above and behind the Confederates, while Freeland's brigade was rolling them up on the flank. Both were supported, closely and warmly, by the brigades of Whittaker and Creighton.

Not knowing to what extent the Confederates might be re-enforced, and fearing a fatal entanglement and disordering of his troops in the mountain, Hooker now directed them to halt. But they could not be restrained. Inspired by their success they pushed on, and notwithstanding their adversaries had been re-enforced, they continued to be irresistible. Two of Osterhaus's regiments, meanwhile, had been sent forward on the Chattanooga road, near the base of the mountain, and the remainder of his division joined Geary. After a little more struggle the plateau was cleared, and from near Craven's house, where the Confederates made their last stand, they were seen flying pell-mell, in utter confusion, down the precipices, ravines, and rugged slopes, toward the Chattanooga Valley. During all the struggle, a battery planted on a little wooded hill on Moccasin Point, under Captain Naylor, had been doing excellent service. It actually dismounted one of the guns in the Confederate battery on the top of Lookout Mountain, nearly fifteen hundred feet above it.

It was now about two o'clock in the afternoon. The mountain was completely enveloped in a dense cloud—so dense as to make further movements perilous, if not impossible. All the morning, while the struggle was going

VIEW OF LOOKOUT MOUNTAIN AND VALLEY FROM CHATTANOOGA.[1]

on, the mountain was hooded with vapor that went up from the valley, and it was only at intervals, when it broke away, that glimpses of the lines and banners of the Nationals might be caught by straining eyes at Chattanooga

---

[1] This is from a sketch from Cameron's hill, at Chattanooga, made by the writer in May, 1866, in which the ruins of Mr. Cameron's house is seen in the foreground. Below is seen the Tennessee River, winding around Moccasin Point. In the distance, at the center, rises Lookout Mountain, on the face of which the white spot indicates the place of Craven's house, on the plateau. In Lookout Valley, to the right, is the hill on which Hooker was stationed during the fight. Farther to the right are seen the northeastern slopes of Raccoon Mountain.

and Orchard Knob, where ears, filled with the thunders of battle high in air, were making all hearts anxious. Hooker had been literally fighting in the clouds, and gaining a substantial victory, while all below was doubt and painful suspense. He established his line firmly on the eastern face of the mountain, his right resting on the palisades at the summit, and his left near the mouth of Chattanooga Creek, completely commanding, by an enfilading fire, the line of the Confederate defenses, stretching across the Chattanooga Valley to the Missionaries' Ridge. Communication with Chattanooga was established toward evening, and at sunset General Carlin, with his brigade, joined Hooker, and was placed on his right, to relieve the troops of Geary, exhausted by hours of climbing and fighting. During the night the right was attacked, but the assailants were gallantly repulsed. The assault was to mask the retreat of the Confederates from the top of the mountain, to which they were impelled by the fear of being cut off in the morning from the only road leading down to the Chattanooga Valley. They left behind them, in their haste, twenty thousand rations, the camp and garrison equipage of three brigades, and other war material.[1] Before daylight, in anticipation of this retreat, parties from several regiments were detached to scale the palisades at some broken point. The Eighth Kentucky were the first to do so, climbing up a narrow, rocky passage, one at a time, for there was no one above to oppose them. At sunrise,[a] in the clear, crisp autumn air, they unfurled the National banner from Pulpit Rock, on the extreme point of the mountain overlooking Chatta-

[a] Nov. 25, 1863.

PULPIT ROCK.[2]

nooga, with cheers that were re-echoed by the troops below. From that "pulpit" Jefferson Davis had harangued his troops only a few days before, when he gave them assurances that all was well with the Confederacy. This brilliant victory made absolutely secure the navigation of the river from Bridgeport to Chattanooga, the needful highway for supplies for the National army.

While Hooker was fighting on Lookout Mountain, Sherman's troops were crossing the Tennessee above Chattanooga. At one o'clock in the morning,[b] three thousand men embarked on the pontoon boats already mentioned, at the mouth of the North Chickamauga Creek, behind the shelter of Friar's Island. They floated silently down the river, landed some troops above the mouth of the South Chickamauga, to capture Confederate pickets

[b] Nov. 24.

<hr/>

[1] Bragg, in his report, complained of the remissness of General Stevenson, in command on the summit of the mountain, for not rendering assistance to Walthall. He said Stevenson had "six brigades at his disposal." "Upon his urgent appeal," said Bragg, "another brigade was dispatched in the afternoon to his support, though it appears that his own forces had not been brought into action."

[2] This shows the character of a portion of the summit of Lookout Mountain, where it abuts upon the Tennessee River. There lie in picturesque confusion immense laminated bowlders, and occasionally columnar

there, and then moved in equal silence to a point just below the mouth of the last-named stream. Then the boats, with the assistance of a river steamer and two barges, ferried over troops, and at dawn eight thousand were on the south shore of the Tennessee. These, under the direction of General W. F. Smith, commenced the construction of a pontoon bridge there thirteen hundred and fifty feet long, and also one across the Chickamauga. By noon both bridges were finished, when the rest of Sherman's troops passed over, and in a slight drizzle of rain from the low, hanging clouds, which, as we have seen, hooded Lookout Mountain, proceeded in three columns, *en echelon*,[1] to attack the Confederates on the northern end of the Missionaries' Ridge, between the Chickamauga and the tunnel, where the railway passes through. Between three and four o'clock in the afternoon the desired point was gained, after some sharp fighting, and near the tunnel Sherman rested and fortified his position, making it a strong point of departure for the grander movements the next day. In the mean time Colonel Loring, with a brigade of Thomas's cavalry, had been raiding on Bragg's communications with East Tennessee, along the line of the railway between Chattanooga and Cleveland. He burned Tyner's Station, and, pushing on to Cleveland, captured two hundred Confederates, with one hundred wagons, and destroyed the railway station there, a gun-cap factory, and a large amount of stores, gathered for the supply of Longstreet.

The night of the 24th was spent in preparations for a great struggle on the morrow. The nearly full moon shone out resplendently in the unclouded sky. Camp-fires blazed along the heights from Lookout Mountain to the Chickamauga. On Bragg's flanks, in strong positions gained by hard struggling, hung two of the most determined fighters in the armies of the Republic. Hooker was on his left, holding the field of victory on Lookout Mountain, and Sherman was on his right, well intrenched, on the north end of the Missionaries' Ridge. There was now an uninterrupted communication between these extremes of Grant's army, Carlin, as we have seen, connecting Hooker with the center, and now Howard, with his (Eleventh) corps, connected that center with Sherman. The head-quarters of the chief were with Thomas, at Orchard Knob.

Bragg, in the mean time, had also been preparing for the inevitable encounter. He went to the summit of Lookout Mountain toward sunset, and found, to his dismay, that all the advantages of position at that point were irretrievably lost. He then gave orders for the ground to be disputed until he could withdraw all the troops of his left across Chattanooga Creek to the Missionaries' Ridge. That movement was accomplished during the night, and on Wednesday morning[a] his whole force was concentrated on the Ridge, and extended heavily to the right, to meet what seemed to be the point chosen for the most formidable assault on his lines, and to protect the railway between the Ridge and Dalton, to

[a] Nov. 25, 1863.

---

masses of rock. Not far from Summertown (a place of summer resort on the top of the mountain), on the road to Lula Falls, is a curious collection of these, called Rock City. Two columnar masses, called the Two Sisters, rising near each other, appear like the huge boundaries of an immense gateway.

[1] The left column was that of direction, under General M. L. Smith, and followed the general line of the Chickamauga River. The center, under General J. E. Smith, in columns doubled on the center at full brigade intervals, to the right and rear ; and the right was Ewing's column, prepared to deploy to the right, on the supposition that an attack might be made from that direction.

which his supplies were sent up from Atlanta. He had placed Lieutenant-General W. J. Hardee in command of his right wing, facing Sherman, and Major-General J. C. Breckinridge in command of his left, to confront Hooker. That night he evacuated all of his works at the foot of the Ridge, excepting the rifle-pits, and formed a new line on its top.

Hooker moved down from Lookout Mountain on the morning of the 25th, and proceeded to cross Chattanooga Valley in the direction of Rossville. There he was delayed until about two o'clock in the afternoon, in consequence of the destruction, by the Confederates, of the bridge over Chattanooga Creek, where the road that wound down from Summertown, on Lookout Mountain, crossed it.

As soon as possible Osterhaus's division was thrown across the creek on the timbers of a new bridge the troops were constructing. Pushing on toward Rossville, they drove the Confederates out of the Gap there by a flanking movement, capturing a large quantity of artillery, small-arms, ammunition, wagons, ambulances, and stores that filled Ross's house. In the mean time Hooker's whole force had passed the creek and pushed on toward Rossville. There he set about his prescribed duty of clearing the Ridge of Confederates, who, under the immediate command of General Stewart, were well posted behind intrenchments cast up there by Thomas at the time of the battle of Chickamauga. He sent Osterhaus through the Gap to move parallel with the Ridge on its eastern side. Cruft was ordered to move along its crest, and Geary, with the batteries, marched up the valley at its base on the western side.

Bragg's skirmishers were ordered to meet this dangerous movement, when the Ninth Indiana dashed forward, formed a line under a heavy fire, and, charging furiously upon the foe, drove them back to the main body. The remainder of Cruft's column, meanwhile, formed in battle-line and moved forward at a charging pace, Gross's brigade, with the Fifty-first Ohio and Thirty-fifth Indiana of Whittaker's brigade, in advance, closely supported by the remainder of the latter's command. Back, back, back, they steadily pushed the Confederates, their front line, under General Stewart retreating, while fighting, upon the second line, under General Bate, while Geary and Osterhaus were pouring murderous fires upon their flanks. So the half-running fight continued until near sunset, when the Confederates broke into hopeless confusion and fled. The few who ran down the western slope of the Ridge were captured by Geary, and the many who sought safety in flight down the eastern slope were made prisoners by Osterhaus, full two thousand in number; while those who skurried along the Ridge toward the stronger right, fell into the hands of Johnson's division, of the Fourteenth (Palmer's) Corps, which had been advanced from Chattanooga. Few escaped. Hooker's victory on that part of the field was complete at twilight, and his troops went into bivouac for the night " with cheers and rejoicing." [1]

While Hooker was thus clearing one portion of the Missionaries' Ridge, Sherman was busy at the other extremity of the battle-line. He had strongly intrenched his position during the night, and, in obedience to

---

[1] Hooker's Report.

orders, prepared to attack Hardee at daylight, leaving the brigades of General Lightburn and Colonels Cockrell and Alexander to hold his fortified position as his key-point. His order of battle was similar to that of Hooker, sweeping along the crest and flanks of the Ridge. All was in readiness at sunrise, when General Corse, with three of his own regiments and one of Lightburn's, moved forward, while General M. L. Smith and his command advanced along the eastern base of the Ridge, and Colonel Loomis, with his brigade, supported by two brigades under General J. E. Smith, moved along the western base.

Sherman found the ground to be traversed more difficult than he had supposed. Instead of a continuous ridge, there was a chain of hills,[1] each wooded and well fortified, so that, should one elevation be gained, another equally commanding would confront it. But no difficulties were formidable to men who had been taught by experience to disregard them; and Corse moved on, the Fortieth Illinois in advance, supported by the Twentieth and Forty-sixth Ohio. They swept rapidly down the hill held by Sherman and up the next eminence to within eighty yards of the Confederate works, where they found, seized, and held a secondary crest. Then Corse called up his reserves and asked for re-enforcements to attempt to carry the position before him, by assault. A severe hand-to-hand struggle ensued, which lasted for an hour, the tide of battle ebbing and flowing with equal success on both sides, and heavy loss on the part of the Nationals, who were subjected to an enfilading fire. Corse was unable to carry the works on his front, and the Confederates were equally unable to drive him from his position. Meanwhile, Smith and Loomis, on each side of the Ridge, were steadily advancing, fighting their way to the Confederate flanks without wavering. A heavy and unexpected artillery fire made the supporting brigades of General J. E. Smith recoil, and gave the impression to the anxious watchers at Chattanooga that Sherman was losing ground. It was not so. The real attacking forces under Corse (who was severely wounded at ten o'clock, and his place taken by Colonel Wolcott, of the Forty-sixth Ohio), M. L. Smith, and Loomis, made no retrograde movement, but held their ground, and struggled " all day persistently, stubbornly, and well."[2] When J. E. Smith's reserves recoiled, the Confederates made a show of pursuit, but were soon struck on their flank and compelled to seek safety in retiring to the shelter of their works on the wooded hills.

Up to three o'clock in the afternoon, Sherman had not been able to gain any thing of decisive importance. General Grant, meanwhile, from his position on Orchard Knob, had been watching the progress of the battle, and waiting impatiently for tidings from Hooker, intending, if he should be successful, to order Thomas to advance on the Confederate center. He was ignorant of Hooker's detention at Chattanooga Creek, and expected to hear from him by noon. No tidings came, but when, between one and two o'clock, Grant saw that Bragg was weakening his center to support his right, and believing Hooker to be at or near Rossville, he gave Thomas an order to advance. It was promptly obeyed at two o'clock. The divisions of Wood, Baird, Sheridan, and Johnson moved steadily forward, with a

---

[1] See picture on page 161.   [2] General Sherman's Report, December 19. 1863.

double line of skirmishers in front, followed at a short distance by the whole body. Pressing in a continuous line, they created such a panic among the occupants of the rifle-pits at the base of the Ridge, that they fled precipitately toward the crest, swarming up the hill-side, Grant said, " like bees from a hive." The Nationals stopped but for a moment to re-form, when, inspired by an irresistible impulse, they pushed vigorously forward up the steep and

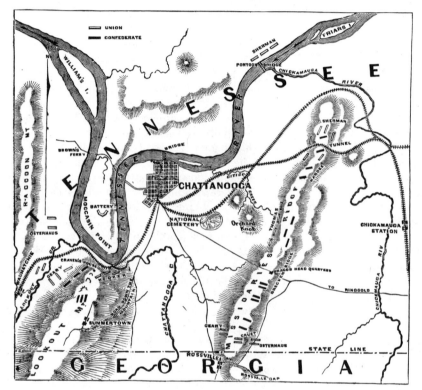

CHATTANOOGA AND VICINITY.

rugged declivities in pursuit, in the face of a terrible storm of grape and canister-shot from about thirty guns on the summit, and from murderous volleys of musketry in the well-filled rifle-pits at the crest.[1] But the

---

[1] In a letter to his father, written by a friend of the author (Isaac N. Merritt, of the Eighty-ninth Illinois, known as " the Railroad Regiment "), a few weeks after the battle on the Missionaries' Ridge, he said: " The storming of the ridge by our troops was one of the greatest marvels in military history. No one who climbs the ascent by any of the roads that wind along its front can believe that eighteen thousand men were moved simultaneously upon its broken and uneven surface, unless it was his fortune to witness that daring deed. It seemed as awful as the visible interposition of God. Neither Generals Grant nor Thomas intended it. Their orders were to carry the rifle-pits along the base of the Ridge and cut off their occupants ; but when this was accomplished, the unaccountable spirit of the troops bore them bodily up the impassable steeps over the bristling rifle-pits on the hill's crest, and cannon enfilading every gully. The orders to storm appear to have been quite simultaneous by Generals Sheridan and Wood, because the men could not be held back, hopeless as the attempt appeared to military prudence, with any prospect of success. The generals caught the inspiration of the men, and were ready themselves to undertake impossibilities and run fearful risks for the chances of glorious and undying gains."

General Hazen, in a letter to the author, says : " The men of Willich's and my brigades commenced running forward for security under the Ridge, but as they reached it they commenced its ascent. I then gave the order, ' Forward !' and sent my staff officers to carry everybody forward up the Ridge. The fire we passed through was

Nationals did not waver for a moment. They pressed on, and Lieutenant-Colonel Langdon, of the First Ohio, with a group of men of his own regiment and several others, who were foremost in the chase, sprang forward and made the first lodgment on the hill-top, within five hundred yards of Bragg's head-quarters, with shouts that were repeated by thousands of voices.[1] This gap in the Confederate line speedily widened as the assailants pressed up, and it was not long before the entire battle-line of the Missionaries' Ridge was in possession of the Union troops, with all the Confederate cannon and ammunition, and many of the soldiers in the trenches; and the captured artillery was soon playing fearfully upon the defeated columns with an enfilading fire. Sherman soon drove the Confederates from his front, when the battle ceased at that end of the line; but the divisions of Wood and Baird, on the right, were obstinately resisted until dark, for the Confederates in their front were re-enforced from Bragg's right. Yet these were steadily pressed back; and at the edge of the evening they fled in haste, Breckinridge barely escaping capture. Thus ended THE BATTLE OF CHATTANOOGA, in complete victory for the National arms. Grant modestly summed up the result, in a dispatch to Halleck, saying, "Although the battle lasted from early dawn till dark this evening, I believe I am not premature in announcing a complete victory over Bragg. Lookout Mountain top, all the rifle-pits in Chattanooga Valley, and Missionary Ridge entire, have been carried, and are now held by us."[2]

During the night succeeding the battle, the Missionaries' Ridge blazed with the Union camp-fires, while the discomfited Confederates were retreating in haste toward Ringgold, by way of Chickamauga Station. Early the next morning, Sherman, Palmer, and Hooker were sent in pursuit, the first directly in the track of the fugitives, the other two by the Rossville road, toward Ringgold. Bragg destroyed the bridges behind him, and Hooker was very much delayed at Chickamauga River by a failure to supply him promptly with bridge materials. Sherman found every thing in flames at Chickamauga Station, which he passed and pushed on toward Greysville, encountering on the way, just at night, a rear-guard of the fugitives, with which he had a sharp skirmish. There General Grant overtook him. On the following morning he marched on to Greysville, on the East Chickamauga, where he found Palmer and his command, who, on the previous evening, had struck a rear-guard under General Gist, and captured three of his guns and some prisoners. There Sherman halted, and sent Howard to destroy a large section of the railway which connected Dalton with Cleveland, and thus severed the communication between Bragg and Burnside.

Hooker, meanwhile, had pushed on to Ringgold,[a] Osterhaus in advance, Geary following, and Cruft in the rear, and finding at every step evidences of Bragg's precipitate flight. Stragglers were numerous, and were made prisoners. When the head of the pursuers

[a] Nov. 27, 1863.

---

dreadful, but the men, without preserving lines, formed into groups where accidents of the ground gave cover, and each group, led by a color, steadily made its way up. These colors were often shot down—those of the First Ohio six times—but they were at once seized and borne along."

[1] Lieutenant-Colonel Langdon received a shot through his face and neck at the moment when he reached the hill-top, which felled him to the ground. He at once rose, the blood streaming from his wounds, and shouting "Forward!" again fell. His hurt, though severe, was not mortal.

[2] Grant reported the Union loss, in the series of struggles which ended in victory at Missionaries'

reached Ringgold, the rear of the pursued had just left it.   A little beyond
is a narrow gap in Taylor's Ridge, sufficiently wide for the passage of the
East Chickamauga River and the railway, with margins rising several hundred feet.   There General Cleburne (called, as we have observed, the
"Stonewall Jackson of the West"), covering Bragg's retreat, had made a
stand, with guns well posted, determined to impede the pursuers as long as
possible.   Hooker's guns, detained at the crossing of the Chickamauga, were
not yet up.   His troops, flushed with success, could not be easily restrained,
and they were allowed to attack with small-arms only.   The Thirteenth
Illinois made a desperate attempt to dislodge the foe, but failed, with heavy
loss.   Yet the struggle went on, and finally, in the afternoon, when some of
Hooker's guns were brought into position and the post was flanked by his
infantry, Cleburne retreated, having inflicted a loss on the Nationals of four
hundred and thirty-two men, of whom sixty-five were killed.
Cleburne left one hundred and thirty killed and wounded on
the field.   So ended THE BATTLE OF RINGGOLD.[a]

[a] Nov. 27,
1863.

General J. C. Davis's division, which had been attached to Sherman's
command, reached Ringgold just after Cleburne fled, ready to press on in
pursuit; but there it ended.   Grant would gladly have continued it, and
would doubtless have captured or destroyed Bragg's army; but he was compelled to refrain, because Burnside needed immediate relief, so as to save
East Tennessee from the grasp of Longstreet.   He had informed Grant that
his supplies would not last longer than the 3d of December, a week later.
This statement was a powerful appeal.   Grant was in a condition to respond
with vigor, for his foe was utterly demoralized by defeat and almost mutinous discontent among his troops,[1] and Sherman's forces were interposed
between him and Longstreet, so as to prevent any possibility of their forming
a junction.   The victorious troops fell back toward Chattanooga,[2] and the
campaign against Bragg ended.[3]   The Confederate retreat was continued to
Dalton, where the army established a fortified camp.

Ridge, at 757 killed, 4,529 wounded, and 330 missing, making a total of 5,616.   Bragg's loss was about 3,100 in
killed and wounded, and a little over 6,000 prisoners.   Of the latter, 239 were commissioned officers.   Grant
also captured 40 pieces of artillery, with caissons and carriages, and 7,000 small-arms.

[1] Bragg, at this time, as at the battle of Chickamauga, tried to cover up his own incompetence under cen-
sures of others.   He attributed his failure to gain a victory in the former case to the tardiness of Polk and
Hindman; now he attributed his defeat to what he was pleased to call "the shameful conduct of the troops on
the left," commanded by Breckinridge.   And Jefferson Davis, in order to shield from censure this, his creature
and favorite, disparaged his troops, who fought as gallantly and successfully as the bad management of their
commander would allow.   "It is believed," Davis said, "that if the troops who yielded to the assault [Hooker's]
had fought with the valor which they had displayed on previous occasions, and which was manifested in this
battle in the other parts of the line, the enemy would have been repulsed with very great slaughter, and our
country would have escaped the misfortune, and the army the mortification, of the first defeat that has resulted
from misconduct by the troops."—Pollard's *Third Year of the War*, 159.

[2] Gross's brigade visited the battle-field of Chickamauga for the purpose of burying the Union dead, whom
Bragg had inhumanly left to decay on the surface.   The name of each soldier thus buried, whenever it could be
ascertained, was placed upon a board at the head of his grave, with the number of his regiment.

[3] "Considering the strength of the rebel position and the difficulty of storming his intrenchments," said
Halleck, "the Battle of Chattanooga must be regarded as the most remarkable in history.   Not only did the
officers and men exhibit great skill and daring in their operations in the field, but the highest praise is also due
to the commanding general for his admirable dispositions for dislodging the enemy from a position apparently
impregnable."

CHAPTER VI.

SIEGE OF KNOXVILLE.—OPERATIONS ON THE COASTS OF THE CAROLINAS AND GEORGIA.

E left Burnside in Knoxville, closely besieged by Longstreet.[1] His head-quarters were at the pleasant brick mansion of Mr. Crozier, on Gay Street, in the central part of the town. During the dark days of the siege his bearing toward the citizens and his soldiers—kind, generous, and humane—won for him the profound respect of all, even the most rebellious. He visited the families of Dr. Brownlow, Mr. Maynard, Colonel Baxter, Colonel Temple, and other prominent citizens who were then exiles from their homes, and gave them every comfort and encouragement in his power; and at the office of the *Knoxville Whig*, Brownlow's newspaper, through which that stanch Unionist had so long and effectively fulminated his scathing thunderbolts of wrath against secessionists and rebels, Burnside's orders, and other printing, was done by willing Union hands. In the lurid light of the Civil War, that long, low building, in an obscure alley, looms up into historical importance. Who shall estimate the value of the influence of that sheet, which went out daily from its walls, to the cause of the Union in East Tennessee?

BURNSIDE'S HEAD-QUARTERS.

Burnside's forces, as we have observed, were well intrenched, and he had little to fear, excepting a failure of his supplies. He was cheered with hope, because of his confidence in Grant, that aid would come before they were exhausted. Longstreet, doubting Bragg's ability to cope with his new adversary, anxiously pressed forward the siege, with the mistaken idea that starvation would compel a surrender in

KNOXVILLE WHIG OFFICE.

a few days. He was diligent in closing every avenue of supply, and in

---

[1] See page 158.

these efforts skirmishes frequently occurred, for sorties were made from the trenches.[1] Finally, on the 25th, the day when the Nationals were carrying the Missionaries' Ridge, he threw a considerable force across the Holston, near Armstrong's (his head-quarters),[2] to seize the heights, south of the river, that commanded Knoxville. Quite a severe struggle ensued, in which the Confederates were worsted. They succeeded, however, in seizing another

THE HOLSTON, NEAR ARMSTRONG'S.[3]

knob, lower down, which rises about one hundred and fifty feet above the river, and so planted a battery on it that it commanded Fort Sanders, five hundred yards north of it. This advantage had just been gained, and the besiegers were huzzaing with delight, when information reached Longstreet of Bragg's defeat at Chattanooga. He well knew that columns from Grant's victorious army would soon be upon his rear, so he determined to take Knoxville by storm before aid could reach Burnside. He was now strengthened by the arrival of troops under Generals Sam. Jones, Carter, "Mudwall" Jackson, and "Cerro Gordo" Williams, and he could expect no more. For thirteen days he had been wasting strength in pressing an unsuccessful siege, and from that moment he must grow weaker. Burnside was cheered by the same news that made Longstreet desponding, and he resolved to resist the besiegers to the last extremity.

Such was the situation of affairs, when, at eleven o'clock on Saturday night,[a] the air cold and raw, the sky black with clouds, and the darkness thick, Longstreet proceeded to attack Fort Sanders, then occupied by the Twenty-ninth Massachusetts, Seventy-ninth New York, two companies of the Second and one of the Twentieth Michigan. The fort was bastioned, and the northwest was the salient of the angle, the point seen in the engraving on the next page. In front of it the woods had been cleared over several acres, sloping gently to a ravine. From

Nov. 28.
1863.

---

[1] When the siege commenced there was in the commissary department little more than one day's rations, and supplies could then be received only from the south side of the Holston, across a pontoon bridge, the foe holding the avenues of approach to Knoxville on the north side of the river. Burnside's efforts were directed to keeping open the country between the Holston and the French Broad, and every attempt of Longstreet to seize it was promptly met. A considerable quantity of corn and wheat, and some pork, was soon collected in Knoxville, but almost from the beginning of the siege the soldiers were compelled to subsist on half and quarter rations, without coffee or sugar. Indeed, during the last few days of the siege, the bread of their half rations was made of clear bran.

Longstreet tried to break the pontoon bridge, by sending down the swift current from Boyd's Ferry, a heavy raft. Captain Poe, Burnside's able engineer, advised of this work, stretched an iron cable across the Holston above the bridge, a thousand feet in length, and farther up the river he constructed a boom of logs. These foiled the attempts of the Confederates to destroy the pontoon bridge.

[2] See page 157.

[3] This is from a sketch by the author, taken from the piazza of Mr. Armstrong's house. The knob seen over the low point of land around which the Holston sweeps, is the one on which the Confederates planted the battery that commanded Fort Sanders.

thirty to eighty rods in front were rifle-pits and *abatis* for the shelter and use of the advanced line, should it be driven back; and between these and the fort strong wires were stretched from stump to stump, a foot above the

VIEW FROM FORT SANDERS.[1]

ground, in an entangling net-work that would trip and confuse a storming party. The armament of the fort consisted of four 20-pounder Parrott guns, forming the battery of Lieutenant Benjamin, Burnside's chief of artillery; four light 12-pounders, forming Buckley's battery, and two three-inch guns.

All that was done by Longstreet on the night of the attack was to drive in the National advance, and seize and hold the rifle-pits. Just after six o'clock the next morning[a] he opened a furious cannonade from his batteries in advance of Armstrong's. This was answered   [a] Nov. 29, 1863. by Roemer's battery, on College Hill, and was soon followed by a tremendous yell from the Confederates, as they rushed forward at the double-quick to storm the fort.[2] These were picked men, the flower of Longstreet's army; and, in obedience to orders, one brigade pressed forward to the close assault, two brigades supporting it, while two others watched the National line, and kept up a continual fire. The tumult was awful for a few minutes, for it was composed of the yells of voices, the rattle of musketry, the thunder of cannon, and the screams of shells. The charging party moved swiftly forward to the *abatis*, which somewhat confused their line. The wire net-work was a worse obstacle, and whole companies were prostrated by it. While they were thus bewildered, the double-shotted guns of General Ferrero, the skillful commander of the fort, were playing fearfully on the Confederates, under the direction of Benjamin. Yet the assailants pressed on, gained the ditch, and attempted to scale the parapet. One officer (Colonel McElroy) actually gained the summit, and planted the flag of the Thirteenth Mississippi there, but a moment afterward his body, pierced by a

[1] This is from a sketch made by the author in the spring of 1866, looking in the direction of Longstreet's approach. Below the single bird is seen Longstreet's head-quarters—Armstrong's. Below the two birds, in the middle-ground, was the place of Longstreet's principal batteries, in advance of Armstrong's. The man and dog, in front, are on the bastion where the principal assault was made. The stumps to which the wires mentioned in the text were attached, and some of the net-work, was yet there when the sketch was made.

[2] The storming party consisted of three brigades of General McLaws's division—Wolford's, Cobb's, and Phillips's, all Georgians; General Humphreys's brigade of Mississippians, and a brigade composed of the remains of Anderson's and Bryant's, consisting of South Carolina and Georgia regiments. The leader of the Mississippi troops was the present (1868) Governor Humphreys, of Mississippi.

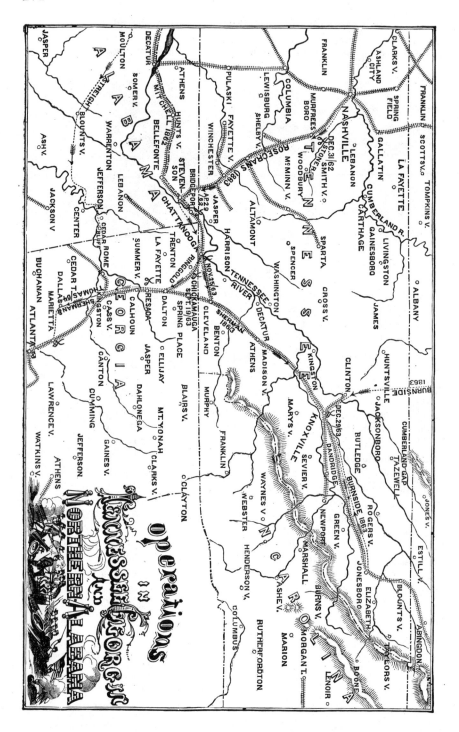

dozen bullets, rolled, with his flag, into the ditch, which Benjamin's guns in the salient swept with a murderous enfilading fire. That hero actually took shells in his hand, ignited the fuses, and threw them over into the ditch with terrible effect. The storm was too heavy for the assailants there, and about three hundred of them surrendered. Then the assault ceased. Fort Sanders was saved, and with it, without doubt, Knoxville, and possibly Burnside's army.[1] Longstreet had promised his soldiers that they should dine in Knoxville that day; but they were otherwise engaged, in burying their dead outside of its defenses, by permission of General Burnside, who lent them ambulances to remove the bodies of their comrades within the Confederate lines.

While Burnside was thus resisting Longstreet, heavy columns were, moving to assist him. So soon as he was assured of victory at Chattanooga, on the night of the 25th,[a] General Grant ordered General Granger, with his own (Fourth) corps, and detachments from others, twenty thousand strong, to re-enforce Burnside. Sherman was ordered in the same direction, so as to make the business of relief surely successful, and on the night of the 30th he was at Charleston, where the East Tennessee and Georgia railway crosses the Hiawassee River. There was also Howard, Davis, and Blair, who had concentrated at Cleveland the day before; and there Sherman received orders from Grant to take command of all the troops moving to the relief of Knoxville, and to press forward as rapidly as possible. This was done. The army crossed the Hiawassee the next morning, and pushed on toward Loudon, Howard in advance, to save the pontoon bridge there. The Confederates stationed at that point burned it when Howard approached, and fled,[b] and Sherman's entire force, including Granger's troops, was compelled to move along the south side of the river, with the expectation of crossing Burnside's bridge at Knoxville. Sherman sent forward his cavalry, which entered the Union lines on the 3d, when Longstreet, finding his flank turned and an overwhelming force of adversaries near, raised the siege and retreated toward Russellville, in the direction of Virginia, pursued by Burnside's forces. Thus ended the SIEGE OF KNOXVILLE, a day or two before the beginning of which occurred the memorable raid of General Averill upon the railway east of it, already mentioned.[2] Burnside issued[c] a congratulatory order to his troops after Longstreet's flight,[3] and a few days afterward[d] another was promulgated, which directed the naming of the forts and batteries at Knoxville, that constituted its defenses, in honor of officers who fell there.[4]

a Nov. 1863.

b Dec. 2.

c Dec. 5.

d Dec. 11.

---

[1] The ground in front of the fort was strewn with the dead and wounded. In the ditch, alone, were over two hundred dead and wounded, including two colonels—McElroy, of the Thirteenth Mississippi, and Thomas, of the Sixteenth Georgia—killed. "In this terrible ditch," says a Confederate historian, "the dead were piled eight or ten feet deep. In comparatively an instant of time we lost 700 men, in killed, wounded, and prisoners. Never, excepting at Gettysburg, was there in the history of the war a disaster adorned with the glory of such devoted courage, as Longstreet's repulse at Knoxville."—Pollard's *Third Year of the War*, 168. The National loss in the fort was only eight killed and seven wounded. Pollard says: "The Yankees lost not more than twenty men killed and wounded." The entire Union loss in the assault was about one hundred.

[2] See page 113.

[3] "The Army of the Ohio," he said, "has nobly guarded the loyal region it redeemed from its oppressors, and rendered the heroic defense of Knoxville memorable in the annals of the war."

[4] The following is a list of the forts and batteries, their position and their names, as mentioned in Burnside's order: *Battery Noble*, south of Kingston road, in memory of Lieutenant and Adjutant William Noble,

With the re-enforcements brought by Granger, Burnside felt able to cope with Longstreet, and advised the return of Sherman's troops to Knoxville, because Bragg, informed of the weakness of that post on account of their absence, might return in force and place it in great peril, at least. Sherman accordingly fell back, and before the close of December his troops were in winter quarters in the vicinity of Chattanooga. Bragg had already been relieved of command, at his own request, his forces turned over to the equally incompetent Hardee, and, as we have seen, a commission was given to the former, which charged him "with the conduct of the military operations of the Confederacy."[1] Already the hearts of the loyal people of the land were overflowing with joy and gratitude because of the victories at Chattanooga and Knoxville. The President recommended[a] them to meet in their respective places of worship, and render united thanks to God "for the great advancement of the National cause;" and in a brief letter to Grant,[b] he thanked that soldier and his men for their skill and bravery in securing a "lodgment at Chattanooga and Knoxville." Congress voted thanks and a gold medal for Grant,[c] and directed the President of the Republic to cause the latter to be struck "with suitable emblems, devices, and inscriptions." Grant was the recipient of other tokens of regard of various kinds; and the Legislatures of New York and Ohio voted him thanks in the name of the people of those great States.

[a] Dec. 7, 1863.

[b] Dec. 8.

[c] Dec. 17.

The writer visited the theater of events recorded in this and the two chapters immediately preceding it, in the spring of 1866. He left Murfreesboro' on the morning of the 10th of May,[2] with his traveling companions already mentioned (Messrs. Dreer and Greble), and went by railway to Chattanooga. It was a very interesting journey, for along the entire route, at brief intervals, we saw vestiges of the great war in the form of forts, intrenchments, rifle-pits, block-houses, chimneys of ruined dwellings, battered trees, and the marks of wide-spread desolation. The block-houses were conspicuous, and sometimes picturesque, features in the landscape, and each one had a stirring history of its own. One of these, at Normandy (of which the sketch on the next page is a representation), built by a detachment of the One Hundred and Fiftieth New York, under Captain Richard Titus, was a good specimen. We noticed it just at the opening of a deep cove in the hills at the southern verge of the Duck River Valley, and from that point to Chatta-

---

Second Michigan. *Fort Byington*, at the College, in memory of Major Cornelius Byington, Second Michigan. *Battery Galpin*, east of Second Creek, in memory of Lieutenant Galpin, Second Michigan. *Fort Comstock*, on Summit Hill, in memory of Lieutenant-Colonel Comstock, Seventeenth Michigan. *Battery Wiltsie*, west of Gay Street, in memory of Captain Wiltsie, Twentieth Michigan. *Fort Huntington Smith*, on Temperance Hill, in memory of Lieutenant Huntington Smith, Twentieth Michigan. *Battery Clifton Lee*, east of Fort H. Smith, in memory of Captain Clifton Lee, One Hundred and Twelfth Illinois Mounted Infantry. *Fort Hill*, at the extreme eastern point of the Union lines, in memory of Captain Hill, Twelfth Kentucky Cavalry. *Battery Fearns*, on Flint Hill, in memory of Lieutenant and Adjutant C. W. Fearns, Forty-fifth Ohio Mounted Infantry. *Battery Zoellner*, between Fort Sanders and Second Creek, in memory of Lieutenant Frank Zoellner, Second Michigan. *Battery Stearman*, in the gorge between Temperance Hill and Mabrey's Hill, in memory of Lieutenant William Stearman, Thirteenth Kentucky. *Fort Stanley*, comprising all the works on the central hill on the south side of the river, in memory of Captain C. B. Stanley, Forty-fifth Ohio Mounted Infantry. *Battery Billingsley*, between Gay Street and First Creek, in memory of Lieutenant J. Billingsley, Seventeenth Michigan. *Fort Higley*, comprising all the works on the hill west of the railway embankment, south side of the river, in memory of Captain Joel P. Higley. *Fort Dickerson*, comprising all the works between Fort Stanley and Fort Higley, in memory of Captain Jonathan Dickerson, One Hundred and Twelfth Illinois Mounted Infantry.

[1] See page 142.

[2] See page 558, volume II.

THE UNION GENERALS.

E. B. TYLER. B. G.

ALEXANDER HAYS. B. G.

PHILIP H. SHERIDAN. M. G.

JOHN G. FOSTER. M. G.

JOHN A. DIX. M. G.

MICHAEL CORCORAN. B. G.

DAN¹ BUTTERFIELD. M. G.

QUINCY A. GILMORE. B. G.

DAVID HUNTER. M. G.

JOHN A. LOGAN. M. G.

FRED⁴ STEELE. M. G.

A. J. SMITH. M. G.

GEORGE W. CHILDS PUBLISHER 628 & 630 CHESTNUT ST. PHILADELPHIA.
J.B. Neagle Sc.

nooga similar structures were frequently seen. We passed by the fortifications of Tullahoma, dined at Decherd, and in the afternoon descended the Big Crow Creek hollow, in the Cumberland mountains, to Stevenson, where we remained long enough to visit Battery Harker, in front of it. It was a strong work, that covered the village and its approaches, and had within its heavy earth-walls a very substantial citadel, octagonal in form, and made of logs, after the manner of the block-houses. Stevenson was then almost entirely a village of shanties, standing among the ruins of a once pleasant town, on a slope at the foot of a high rocky mountain.

BLOCK-HOUSE AT NORMANDY.[1]

Passing on from Stevenson, we observed many earth-works and block-houses; and at each end of the temporary railway bridge at Bridgeport, where we crossed the Tennessee River, we noticed heavy redoubts. At Shellmound we entered the mountain region south of the Tennessee. The road gradually ascended, and in some places skirted the margin of the river, high above its bed. We soon reached one of the deep mountain gorges through which Hooker passed,[2] and crossed it upon delicate trestle-work two hundred feet in air above the stream that passed through it, the whole trembling fearfully as our heavy train moved over it at a very slow pace. Then we were among the lofty hills of the Raccoon mountains, and in a little while descended by a gentle grade into Lookout Valley, crossed the Lookout Creek at Wauhatchie, swept along the margin of the Tennessee, at the foot of Lookout Mountain, and arrived at Chattanooga at sunset, where we took lodgings at the Crutchfield House.

A letter of introduction to the Rev. Thomas B. Van Horn, post-chaplain at Chattanooga, gave us a valuable friend, and a competent guide to historical places during the two or three days we were in that town and its vicinity. He was then in charge of the National Cemetery near Chattanooga, laid out under his directions, into which he was collecting the bodies of Union soldiers from the battle-fields of Southeastern Tennessee and Northern Georgia and Alabama, and from posts and stations within a circle from eighty to one hundred miles radius. Mr. Van Horn was residing, with his family, in the house not far from Grant's head-quarters,[3] which both Thomas and Sherman had occupied as such—a pleasant embowered dwelling, unscathed by the storm of war that swept over the town. He kindly offered to accompany us to all places of interest around Chattanooga; and on the morning after our arrival we were seated with him in his light covered wagon, drawn by his spirited horses, "Joseph Hooker" and "John Brown." We first rode to the summit of Cameron's Hill, an alluvial bluff between the town and the river, which rises to an altitude of about three hundred feet. From its top we had a comprehensive view of the country around, including almost the entire battle-field on Lookout Mountain and along the Mission-

---

[1] This shows the elevation of the block-house, with the entrance to its bomb-proof magazine in the mound beneath it. It was constructed of hewn logs from 16 to 20 inches in thickness, with which walls from three to four feet in thickness were constructed. The lower story was pierced for cannon, and the upper story, or tower, for musketry.

[2] See page 152.　　　　　　　　　　　　　　　　　　　　　[3] See page 151.

aries' Ridge. It received its name from its owner, Mr. Cameron, an artist from Philadelphia, who, in the pleasant wood that covered it, built a house,

HEAD-QUARTERS OF THOMAS AND SHERMAN.[1]

and there enjoyed the luxury of a delightful climate and picturesque scenery. When the war broke out he left his home. The hill was soon stripped of its trees, scarred by trenches, and crowned with a heavy battery, built by Bragg; and a week before our visit his house was burned by accident. The ruined walls of it may be seen in the foreground of the picture on page 163.

From Cameron's Hill we rode to the Cemetery, in the direction of the Missionaries' Ridge, where Chaplain Van Horn officiated at the funeral of the child of a captain at the post. When the solemn service was over we carefully examined the Cemetery grounds and the holy work going on there under the direction of the chaplain. The Cemetery was beautifully laid out in the form of a shield, on an irregular knoll, whose summit is forty or fifty feet above the surrounding plain. It was arranged in sections, the graves close by the side of each other in rows, with graveled walks between. In the center, on the top of the knoll, was a space reserved for a monument, in commemoration of the martyrs whose remains would be around it. The receiving-vault, as we have already observed,[2] was a natural cave, in which we saw the coffins containing the remains of the Union raiders hung at Atlanta. On the summit just above it, was made the sketch of Orchard Knob and the Missionaries' Ridge, on page

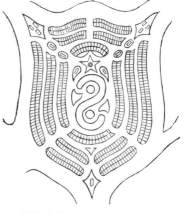

PLAN OF CEMETERY AT CHATTANOOGA.

161, at the time of this visit. Then several hundred bodies were already gathered into the Cemetery, and that number of the tenants has since increased to thousands.[3]

On Friday morning,[a] Mr. Van Horne took us to the battle-ground of Chickamauga, with which he was well acquainted, having been a participant in the action there, and since then an explorer of it

[a] May 11, 1866.

---

[1] This house was on Walnut Street, near Fort Sherman. It belonged to an Englishman named Richardson, who had espoused the cause of the Confederates.

[2] See page 302, volume II.

[3] According to the report of the Quartermaster-General, under the title of "Roll of Honor," No. XI. there were, a few months after our visit, 9,628 bodies buried in that cemetery, of whom 2,360 were unknown. Of the whole number, 778 were colored.

in search of the bodies of the dead.[1] We passed through Rossville Gap, and traveled the Lafayette road, visiting on the way the position of General Thomas, near Kelly's Farm,[2] and Lee and Gordon's Mill.[3] We rode on to

Crawfish Spring,[4] and there, in the cool shadow of the trees, by the side of that wonderful fountain of sweet water, we lunched and rested. Then we returned by another road a part of the way, but again passed through Ross's Gap, when the sketch of the eminent chief's house on page 126 was made. We returned to Chattanooga in time to make a drawing of the superb

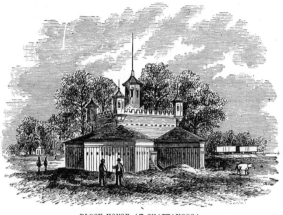

BLOCK-HOUSE AT CHATTANOOGA.

block-house there, near the railway station, the most extensive and beautiful of any built by the National troops.

On Saturday we ascended Lookout Mountain by the zigzag road from Chattanooga Valley, a part of the way on foot, and a part in an ambulance kindly furnished us, with horses and a boy-driver, by Captain Wainright, the

REDOUBT ON LOOKOUT MOUNTAINS.

post quartermaster. It was a slow, tedious, and wearisome journey, and it was late in the afternoon when we reached good quarters at the hotel in Summertown,[5] on the crest of the mountain, where we spent the night, and a greater portion of the next day. We had time before twilight to walk out

---

[1] The bodies were buried here and there, all over the battle-field, where they fell. The method pursued by Mr Van Horne in searching for them, was to have one hundred men move in a line abreast, about three feet apart, through the woods and over the cleared ground where the battle was fought, first marking the graves found, and then disinterring the remains. Having thus swept in one direction, they wheeled, making the man next the space just gone over, the pivot, and in the same manner moving in the other direction. In this way the entire battle-field was traversed.

[2] See page 134.   [3] See page 134.   [4] See page 133.   [5] See map on page 168.

to the extreme rocky point of the palisades overlooking Chattanooga, and sketch the remains of Stevenson's redoubt;[1] visit the photographic establishment on the verge of the cliff, where we procured many views of the region, and to go to the strong fort of pentagonal form, with a citadel of logs, which was constructed by National troops on the top of the mountain after the Confederates were driven away. On the highest point of the crest, near the fort, was the Confederate signal station, which commanded the Missionaries' Ridge in the range of vision; and the remains of the "signal tower," composed of a tree and a platform, were yet there.

On Sunday morning we rode out to the National barracks, on the top of the mountain, where an institution of learning for young men and women

SIGNAL TREE.

was about to be opened, through the liberality of Christopher R. Roberts, of New York, under the charge of the Rev. Edward F. Williams, who, with a corps of teachers, had arrived at Summertown the previous evening. Passing on, we visited the sites of the encampments of the Eighteenth and Nineteenth regular infantry, one of which occupied Rock City, already mentioned. Still farther on, at a distance of about five miles from Summertown, we came to Lula's Creek, and visited the famous Lula's Lake and Falls, and Lula's Bath, in the midst of the forest, and among scenery of the wildest grandeur. That stream, and its picturesque surroundings with Lula's Lake, and Falls, and Bath, were famous in the legends and romances of the Cherokees, which told of the strange events of the life of Lula, a charming Indian maiden. We cannot stop to rehearse them here, and will only record the prosaic fact that we returned to Summertown to dinner, and enjoyed for an hour or more the pleasure of the grand panorama from that point, embracing mountain-peaks, in North Carolina, more than a hundred miles distant; Buzzard's Roost, in the direction of Atlanta; the whole line of the Missionaries' Ridge; the Valley and town of Chattanooga; the winding Tennessee, and the near mountain ranges in every direction. We descended to the valley in time to reach Chattanooga before sunset. On the following morning we went southward by railway, in the track of Sherman's march from Chattanooga to Atlanta. That journey, and our visit to Knoxville and its vicinity, we will consider hereafter.

Let us now turn again to the Atlantic coast, and consider events there after the departure of Burnside from North Carolina to join McClellan on the Peninsula,[2] and the seizure of the coasts of South Carolina, Georgia, and Florida, from Edisto Island, a little below Charleston, to St. Augustine.[3]

---

[1] See page 179. This battery commanded Chattanooga; also Moccasin Point, upon which it might throw plunging shot. It was one of the guns of this battery which was dismounted by the one on Moccasin Point, 1,500 feet below, and a mile distant in a straight line, mentioned on page 163.

[2] See page 315, volume II.   [3] See page 323, volume II.

General Burnside left General Foster in command of the troops in North Carolina, and for awhile he had his head-quarters at Morehead City. He soon established them at New Berne, where the bulk of the army was held, and where, in the course of a few weeks, re-enforcements began to arrive. The sea-coast of that State was in possession of the National troops, but until near the close of the year[a] these were barely sufficient to hold the territory against attempts made by the Confed-

[a] 1862.

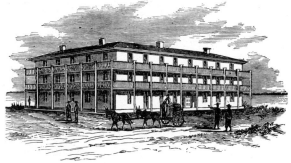

FOSTER'S HEAD-QUARTERS AT MOREHEAD CITY.[1]

erates, now and then, to repossess themselves of lost posts. One of these attempts was made at the village of Washington, on the Little Pamlico River, then held by a small land force under Colonel Potter,[2] and two gun-boats (*Pickett* and *Louisiana*) lying in the stream near. The post was surprised by Confederate cavalry at early dawn on a foggy September morning.[b] These swept through the village almost unopposed at first. But the garrison was soon under arms, and, with some troops which had marched out to go to another point, and now returned, sustained a vigorous street-fight with the assailants for nearly three hours, the gun-boats at the same time giving assistance, until the *Pickett* exploded.[3] The Confederates were finally repulsed, with a loss of thirty-three men killed and one hundred wounded. The Union loss was eight killed and thirty-six wounded.

[b] Sept. 6.

Foster was soon satisfied that preparations were making for a vigorous effort to drive him from the posts in his possession, and as re-enforcements were now strengthening his little army, he resolved to strike some aggressive blows that might intimidate his adversaries. Early in November,[c] he moved with the bulk of his army to Washington, and thence marched, by way of Williamson (near which he had a skirmish), for Hamilton, on the Roanoke River, where he expected to find some Confederate armored gun-boats a-building. He was disappointed; so he marched inland toward Tarboro', when, being informed that a force larger than his own was gathered there, he turned oceanward, and made his way to Plymouth, where his troops were embarked for New Berne. Little of importance was accomplished by this expedition, excepting the liberation of several hundred slaves.

[c] 1862.

A little later Foster undertook a more important expedition with a larger force.[4] He set out from New Berne[d] for the purpose of striking and breaking up at Goldsboro', the railway that connected

[d] Dec. 11.

---

[1] This is a view of the Macon House, where Foster had his head-quarters, on the corner of Arundell and Ninth Streets. Beyond it is seen Bogue Sound and Bogue Island. See page 311, volume II.

[2] These were composed of a company of the Third New York Artillery, with 6 guns; six companies of cavalry, two companies of the First North Carolina, and two of the Massachusetts Twenty-fourth.

[3] By this explosion nearly twenty persons lost their lives.

[4] His force consisted of the brigade of General Wessel, of Peck's division; the brigades of Colonels Amory,

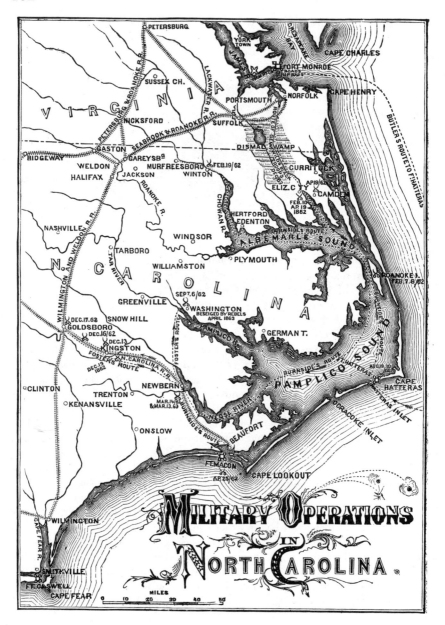

Richmond with the Carolinas, and then forming a junction with the National
forces at Suffolk and Norfolk. He moved on without much hinderance,
other than that of felled trees and broken bridges, until, after a
slight skirmish of his cavalry, under Captain Hall, he reached the ^a Dec. 13,
Southwest Creek.[a] There the bridge had been destroyed, and   1863.

Stevenson, and Lee; the Third New York and First Rhode Island Batteries, with sections of the Twenty-third
and Twenty-fourth New York Independent Batteries; and the Third New York Cavalry.

about two thousand Confederates, with three pieces of artillery, under General Evans, posted on the opposite bank, disputed his passage. These were soon routed by a charge of the Ninth New Jersey, assisted by a flank movement by the Eighty-fifth Pennsylvania. Foster then pressed on toward Kinston, skirmishing heavily on the way, and when within a mile of that village,[a] he encountered a larger force (about six thousand), under Evans, well posted between the Neuse River and an impassable [a] December 14, 1863. swamp. After a sharp fight the Confederates were driven across the river. They fired the bridge behind them, but the flames were put out, and about four hundred of the fugitives were made prisoners, with eleven guns and a large amount of commissary stores. Evans fled through the town, re-formed his forces two miles beyond it, and commenced a retreat toward Goldsboro', before Foster could bring up artillery to attack him. The latter pressed on toward Goldsboro', the objective of the expedition, driving the Confederates from Whitehall, and distracting them by feints, until, near his goal, he was checked[b] by a heavy force under General G. W. Smith. He succeeded, however, in destroying the [b] Dec. 17. bridge of the Weldon and Wilmington railway,[1] over the Neuse, at that place; also several other bridges, about six miles of the railway, and a half-finished iron-clad gun-boat. Then he retreated rapidly to New Berne, having lost during his eight days' absence with his troops, five hundred and seven men, of whom ninety were killed. The Confederate loss was near nine hundred, about five hundred of whom were prisoners.

The failure of Burnside at Fredericksburg prevented any further attempts of Foster to establish communication with the National forces at Norfolk and Suffolk, and he was compelled to content himself with sending out raiding expeditions to keep the Confederate troops in that region so well employed in watching the railway communications between Virginia and the Carolinas, that they could not well be spared to re-enforce Lee or others. At the middle of January,[c] he sent out Colonel Mix, [c] 1863. with his Third New York Cavalry, to raid through the counties of Onslow, Trent, and Jones. For five days those troops swept over that region, driving Confederate detachments before them, capturing prisoners, mules, and arms, and liberating many slaves.

At about this time Foster's forces were greatly diminished by the withdrawal of a large number of his troops to assist in a meditated siege of Charleston. Yet he was not inactive. During the first ten days of March he sent out four raiding expeditions, but they effected no other important result than the arousing of the Confederates of North Carolina, and the concentration of a considerable force under General D. H. Hill. That leader was directed to make a diversion in favor of Longstreet, before Suffolk,[2] when he marched in force upon New Berne, and with twenty guns attacked an unfinished earth-work on the north side of the Neuse, then held by the Ninety-second New York. Hill was repulsed, when he turned northward, and marched on Little Washington. Foster hastened to the threatened post

---

[1] This was destroyed by Lieutenant George W. Graham, of the Twenty-third New York, assisted by Lieutenant B. N. Mann, of the Seventeenth Massachusetts, after several persons who had attempted the work had been picked off by sharp-shooters.

[2] See page 48.

by water.　He left General Palmer in command at New Berne, and sent to General Peck, at Suffolk, for aid.　Hill soon invested the place, and on the 30th of March[a] demanded its surrender.　Foster refused, and a siege was begun.　Batteries were erected by Hill at commanding points, and in a day or two the little garrison of twelve hundred men was cut off from all communication outside by land or water, excepting through the precarious methods of small boats, with supplies, making their way in the night, or by some bold adventurer, like Captain McDermot, of the gun-boat *Ceres*, who, on the night of the 3d of April, volunteered to run the blockade of the Pamlico, with his vessel laden with ammunition.　This was accomplished at great risk, for the besiegers had removed all stakes and buoys from the river.　He felt his way cautiously, and restaked the channel as he went on. · His vessel was under fire nearly all night, and was somewhat bruised; but, at six o'clock in the morning,[b] she passed the obstructions within a short distance of the Confederate batteries, and reached Washington in safety.

a 1863.

b April 4.

On the 8th of April, General Spinola led an expedition for the relief of Little Washington, but failed, when the veteran Fifth Rhode Island (one of Spinola's fourteen regiments) asked permission of General Palmer to run the blockade, or land and capture Hill's batteries.　Consent was given, and in the transport steamer *Escort*, Captain Wall, they left New Berne at midnight, accompanied by General Palmer, Lieutenant Hoffman, of Foster's staff, and Colonel McChesney, of the First Loyal North Carolinians.　They reached the flotilla of National gun-boats, assembled below the Confederate batteries,[1] without difficulty, and on the night of the 13th of April—a still and beautiful night—the *Escort*, under cover of a heavy fire from the flotilla upon the land batteries, went boldly up the river with its load of supplies and troops.　Guided by the stakes planted by McDermot, she pushed on, and gallantly ran the gauntlet of sharp-shooters, who swarmed the banks, and several light field-batteries, for about six miles.　Before morning the little vessel, somewhat bruised, reached Washington[c] with its precious freight.　On her return the next night, with General Foster on board, she was more battered than in her upward trip, but passed the ordeal without very serious injury to the vessel.[2]　Foster, on his arrival at New Berne, set about organizing an expedition competent to raise the siege of Washington, but before he could put the troops in motion, Hill abandoned the siege and fled, pursued by General Palmer, who struck him severely within eight miles of Kinston, and drove him into the interior of the State, when he marched to re-enforce Longstreet in front of Suffolk.[3]

c April 14.

Foster continued to send out raiding parties, who made many captures, broke railways, seized or destroyed a large amount of Confederate property, and quantities of arms, munitions of war, and animals.　In May an expedition, under Colonel J. Richter Jones, of the Fifty-eighth Pennsylvania (act-

---

[1] These had carried about 3,000 troops, under General Prince, who was ordered by Foster to land and capture a battery on Hill's Point.　Believing it to be impracticable, Prince refused to undertake it.

[2] Eighteen solid shot and shells passed through the *Escort* on her return trip, completely riddling her upper works, and somewhat injuring her machinery, while the bullets of the sharp-shooters on shore scarred all her woodwork.　Mr. Pederick, the pilot, was killed, when a New York pilot, assisted by a negro, took his place.

[3] See page 41.

ing brigadier), attacked the Confederates in their works at Gum Swamp, eight miles from Kinston. A portion of the forces, commanded by Colonels Jones and Pierson, in person, drove away the foe, and captured their intrenchments. They took one hundred and sixty-five prisoners, and with these and a quantity of stores, returned to the outpost line at Bachelor's Creek. There the exasperated Confederates attacked them,[a] but were repulsed; yet they inflicted a heavy loss on the Nationals, May 23, 1863. by slaying Colonel Jones, one of the best and bravest soldiers in the Union army.[1] At the beginning of July another force destroyed an armory at Keenansville, with a large amount of small-arms and stores; and on the 4th of the same month General Heckman and his troopers destroyed an important bridge over the Trent River, at Comfort. Later in the month, General Edward E. Potter, Foster's chief of staff, led a cavalry expedition, which laid in ruins a bridge and trestle-work, seven hundred and fifty feet long, over the Tar River, at Rocky Mount, between Goldsboro' and Weldon, with cotton and flouring mills, machine shops and machinery, rolling stock, and other railway property, a wagon-train, and eight hundred bales of cotton. At Tarboro', the terminus of a branch railway running eastward from Rocky Mount, they also destroyed two steamboats and an iron-clad, nearly finished; also, mills, cars, cotton, and stores; captured a hundred prisoners, and many horses and mules, and liberated many slaves, who followed them back to camp. The country was aroused, and such efforts were made to cut the raiders off, that they were compelled to fight almost continually on their return. Yet their entire loss did not exceed twenty-five men. At about this time General Foster's command was enlarged, so as to include the Virginia Peninsula and Southeastern Virginia, which constituted General Dix's department. On account of the riots in New York and threatened resistance to the Draft there,[2] Dix had been sent to take command in that city, and Foster, leaving General Palmer in charge at New Berne, made his headquarters at Fortress Monroe.

Let us now consider events farther down the coast, particularly in the vicinity of Charleston.

We left General T. W. Sherman in quiet possession of Edisto Island, not far below Charleston, from which the white inhabitants had all fled; and also Admiral Dupont, who had just returned from conquests along the coasts of Georgia and Florida, prepared to co-operate with General Hunter, the new commander of the Department of the South,[3] in an attempt to capture Charleston.[4] Hunter worked with zeal toward that end. Martial law was declared[b] to exist throughout his Department. Giving a free interpretation to his instructions from the War Department, he [b] April 25. took measures for organizing regiments of negro troops; and to facilitate the business of recruiting, he issued[c] a general order, [c] May 9. which proclaimed the absolute freedom of all slaves within his Department;

---

[1] Colonel Jones was shot by a Confederate, who was concealed behind a chimney, several hundred yards distant. He died almost instantly, in the arms of his faithful orderly, Michael Webber. He was a distinguished member of the Philadelphia bar, which, in a series of resolutions passed at a meeting soon after his death, paid a warm tribute to his character. "By the death of Colonel Jones," General Foster said, "a most brave, zealous, and able officer has been lost to the service and to this Department."

[2] See page 89.

[3] This included the States of South Carolina, Georgia, and Florida.

[4] See page 323, volume II.

and declared "that slavery and martial law in a free country were altogether

ᵃ May 19, 1863.
incompatible." This was a step too far in advance of public sentiment and the Government policy at that time, so President Lincoln annulled the order,ᵃ and "President" Davis outlawed Hunter.[1]

At about that time measures were perfected for seizing Wadmelaw and John's Islands, that the National troops might gain a position within cannon-shot of Charleston. Careful reconnoissances had been made, soundings taken, and the channel of Stono River, which separates the islands of John's and James's, had been carefully marked by buoys. Every thing was in readiness for an advance toward the middle of May,ᵇ when that movement was hastened by information given respecting military affairs at Charleston by an intelligent slave, named Robert Small, the pilot of the Confederate gun-boat *Planter*, who, with eight dusky companions

ᵇ 1863.

THE PLANTER.

(composing, with himself, the pilot and crew of the steamer), escaped in that vessel from Charleston harbor, and on the evening of the 12thᶜ placed her alongside the *Wabash*, Dupont's flag-ship, not far from Hilton Head.[2] The information given by Small (who was taken

ᶜ May.

into the National service) was valuable, and on the 20th the gun-boats *Unadilla*, *Pembina*, and *Ottawa* crossed the bar at the mouth of the Stono and proceeded up that stream. The Confederates occupying the earth-works along the banks of that river, which were shelled by the boats, fled at their approach, and the vessels moved cautiously on without hinderance to the junction of the Stono and Wappoo Creek, a few miles from Charleston, from which points the spires of the city were easily seen. Unfortunately, the gun-boats were unsupported by land troops, and their presence served only to announce to the Confederates an evident preparation for attacking Charleston.

---

[1] On the 21st of August following, Davis issued an order at Richmond, directing that Generals Hunter and Phelps (see page 225, volume II.) should "no longer be held and treated as public enemies of the Confederate States, but as outlaws." Such fulminations of the chief Conspirator, who was always ready to raise the black flag when he thought it safe to do so, were quite common during the earlier years of the war.

[2] The *Planter* was a high-pressure, side-wheel steamer, and drew only about five feet of water. Small and his colored companions arranged for the escape, and when, on the evening of the 11th of May, the white officers of the vessel went on shore to spend the night, the negroes proceeded to put their plans into execution. The family of Small and that of the engineer were taken on board. The remainder of the company (consisting of John Small and Alfred Gourdine, engineers; Abraham Jackson, Gabriel Turno, William Morrison, Samuel Chisholm, Abraham Allston, and David Jones) were without families. In the darkness the vessel passed down the harbor, but did not reach Fort Sumter until daylight, when a proper signal was given, and she passed on unsuspected. When out of reach of Confederate batteries, Small raised a white flag and went out to the blockading squadron, where he gave up the vessel to the captain of the *Augusta*. That officer sent her with her pilot and crew to Dupont, who placed the families in safety at Beaufort, and took Small and his companions, with the vessel, into the service. In the autumn, when the white captain of that vessel refused to act as such when she was about to go under fire, he was removed, and Small was put in his place, with his titles and duties.

General Hunter had been for some time making preparations for throwing troops suddenly upon James's Island, and then advancing rapidly upon Charleston, where General Pemberton was then in chief command. He had called General Brannan with his force from Key West to Hilton Head, and began the concentration of troops on Edisto Island. It was expected to have the latter co-operate with the gun-boats when they entered the Stono, but for lack of transportation they were unable to do so. It was nearly a fortnight after the steamers reached Wappoo before a part of the troops were landed[a] on James's Island, under the immediate command of General Benham, accompanied by General Hunter; and it was nearly a week later before General Wright arrived with the remainder.   [a] June 2, 1863.   Meanwhile, General Stevens had been sent with a small force[1] to strike the Charleston and Savannah railway at Pocotaligo, with a view of cutting off communication between those cities. There he encountered a thousand Confederates well posted, but these were soon driven, and the railway was destroyed for several miles. Stevens then retired and joined the troops destined for the direct attack on Charleston.

While these movements were going on, the Confederates, who much outnumbered the Nationals then on James's Island, were strengthening their position at Secessionville, a pleasant little group of the summer residences of the James's Island planters, about two miles from the Stono, with salt water on three sides. It was upon a narrow ridge, with swamps bordering it, and accessible from the land only from the west. There, under the direction of Colonel J. G. Lamar, the Confederates constructed a formidable battery, which commanded the Union camp. Perceiving this, General Benham,[2] who had been left in command by General Hunter a few days before, determined to carry the battery by assault. The time fixed for the attempt was the dawn of the 11th.[b] He was anticipated by Lamar, who made offensive movements the evening before. Skirmishing ensued,   [b] June.   and the attack was postponed. A battery was constructed to silence the Confederate guns. It failed to do so, and Benham proceeded to execute his original plan of assault. He arranged about six thousand troops for the purpose, under Generals Wright and Stevens,[3] the forces of the latter forming the assaulting column, covered by the troops of the former. These were put in motion at four o'clock on the morning of the 16th. Stevens's command was about three thousand three hundred strong, composed of the brigades of Colonels W. M. Fenton and D. Leasure.[4] Swiftly and silently they moved over the uneven cotton-fields in the gloom, for the sky was covered with thick clouds, and it was scarcely dawn when they started. The Confederate pickets were mostly captured, and it was hoped that the garrison might be surprised. The Eighth Michigan (Fenton's own) led the way, closely supported by the New York Highlanders, a storming party of the

---

[1] These consisted of the Fifteenth Pennsylvania, two companies of the First Massachusetts Cavalry, and a section of the First Connecticut Battery.

[2] See page 95, volume II.

[3] Brigadier-General Isaac Stevens, who was killed near Chantilly, in Virginia, a few weeks afterward. See page 461, volume II.

[4] Fenton's brigade was formed of the Eighth Michigan, Seventeenth Connecticut, and Twenty-eighth Massachusetts. Leasure's brigade consisted of the Seventy-ninth (Highlanders) and Forty-sixth New York, and One-Hundredth Pennsylvania, with four detached companies of artillery.

Michigan regiment in the extreme advance.[1] While these were pressing along the narrow strip of land by which, only, the battery might be reached, Lamar, who had been watching the movement, opened upon the column a murderous storm of grape and canister-shot from six masked guns. At the same time heavy volleys of musketry were poured upon their right flank. A severe struggle ensued, in which General Wright's troops participated.[2] It was soon found that the battery, protected by a strong *abatis*, a ditch seven feet in depth, a parapet seven feet in height, and a full garrison well armed, could not be carried by assault, and the Nationals fell back, with a loss, in a short space of time, of about six hundred men.[3]

The BATTLE OF SECESSIONVILLE, in which Benham was in general command, in the field, was marked by great prowess on both sides. It was fatal to the plan of an immediate advance upon Charleston. The National troops withdrew from James's Island, and no further attempt to capture the capital of South Carolina was made for some time.

General O. M. Mitchel, who, as we have observed, was called to Washington City from Tennessee,[4] was appointed to succeed General Hunter in

command of the Department of the South. He reached Hilton Head on the 16th of September, made his head-quarters in the spacious one-storied building occupied by General Hunter, and began, with his usual vigor, to plan and execute measures for the public good. He found

HEAD-QUARTERS OF HUNTER AND MITCHEL.

Hilton Head Island swarming with refugee slaves, disorganized and idle, and he at once took measures for their relief, and to make them useful. On the plantation of the Confederate General Drayton, a short mile from Hilton Head, he laid out a village plot, and caused neat and comfortable huts to be built along regular and wide streets. They were constructed chiefly of pine saplings, uniform in size and style, and each had a garden plot attached. Into these he gathered the refugee families to the aggregate of full five thousand souls, and made the labor of the men regular and useful in some way. When the writer visited Mitchelville, as the little town was called, in the spring of 1866, it contained between three and four thousand inhabitants. The houses and

HOUSE AT MITCHELVILLE.

---

[1] Companies C and E, led by Lieutenant B. R. Lyons, of General Stevens's staff, and guided by a negro.

[2] His command consisted of the brigades of Acting Brigadier-General Williams, composed of New Hampshire, Rhode Island, and Pennsylvania troops, with a section of artillery; of Colonel Chatfield, composed of Connecticut and New York troops, and of Colonel Welsh, composed of Pennsylvania and New York troops, two sections of artillery, and a squadron of cavalry. To Williams's brigade were added the Ninety-seventh Pennsylvania Regiment and a section of Hamilton's battery, which did good service.

[3] The Confederate loss was a little over two hundred. Among the wounded were Colonel Lamar, their commander, and Lieutenant-Colonel Gaillard.   [4] See page 304, volume II.

lots had been sold to the occupants for ten dollars each, and they had created for themselves a regular municipal government. Their mayor was an intelligent negro, very black, who had once been a slave at Savannah. His name was Murchison, and he occupied a larger dwelling than did any of his fellow-citizens. They had a neat chapel, and a flourishing school, in charge of feminine teachers from the North, was an interesting feature of the village society. The men

DRAYTON'S MANSION.

were employed largely in cultivating the soil of Hilton Head Island, and were making the desolated plantation of Drayton (whose mansion-house, deserted and ruined, stood near) quite as productive as when its owner was master of scores of slaves upon it.[1]

When Mitchel had settled the policy of affairs near head-quarters, he prepared to use his military force with vigor. He planned an advance, not directly upon Charleston, but having that city as the final objective. He projected an expedition to the Coosawhatchie River, to destroy the Charleston and Savannah railway at Pocotaligo and vicinity. But before his arrangements were completed he was smitten by disease similar to yellow fever, when he was conveyed to the more healthful locality of Beaufort. There, in one of the fine mansions of that deserted town, he died on the 30th of October.[a] General Brannan, meanwhile, had perfected the arrangements and attempted to carry out Mitchel's plans. With an effective force of about four thousand five hundred men, he embarked on gun-boats and transports at Hilton Head,[b] went up the Broad River to the Coosawhatchie, landed, and pushed on four or five miles in the direction of Pocotaligo without hinderance. There he encountered and easily drove Confederate pickets, who burned the bridges behind them, and retarded Brannan's march. He pressed forward, skirmishing a little, and in front of Pocotaligo was met by a heavy fire of artillery from a swamp across a creek, supported by an infantry force under General W. S. Walker. Brannan's ammunition wagons were behind, and his powder soon ran low. His foe was in a position to be re-enforced quickly from Charleston and Savannah, so, taking counsel of prudence, he fell back to Mackay's Landing and re-embarked for Hilton Head. It was a fortunate movement, for Walker had telegraphed to both Charleston and Savannah for help, and it was nigh.

Colonel Barton, of Brannan's command, had, meanwhile, gone up the Coosawhatchie in gun-boats, with about four hundred men, toward a village of the same name. The boats grounded. Barton landed his men, and was pushing on, when he encountered a train of cars filled with troops from Savannah, hastening to the relief of Walker. He fired upon it while in

[a] 1862.

[b] Oct. 21, 22.

motion, killing the Confederate commander, Major Harrison. A greater portion of the Confederates escaped to the woods and joined a detachment stationed at the railroad bridge at Coosawhatchie, toward which Barton pushed. He found superior numbers strongly posted on his front, with three guns, when he, too, retreated to his boats, feebly pursued. The expedition returned to Hilton Head, with a loss of about three hundred men. The Confederate loss was about the same.

Very little was done in the Department of the South (over which Hunter resumed command after the death of Mitchel) during the succeeding winter,[a] toward attempting to capture Charleston, excepting preparations such, as it was believed, would surely lead to success. Other important movements were made in that Department, all tending to cripple the resisting power of the Confederates, who were now in a defensive attitude there. One of these occurred near Fort McAllister[1] a few miles up the Ogeechee River from Ossabaw Sound, where the Confederate war-steamer *Nashville*, a former blockade-runner,[2] was lying under the guns of the fort, watching an opportunity to slip out to sea. Late in February,[b] a squadron of "monitors" and mortar-vessels[3] were at the mouth of the Ogeechee, where Commander J. L. Worden had been for some time, with the monitor *Montauk*, watching the *Nashville*. He finally discovered[c] that she was aground, just above the fort, and on the following morning he proceeded with the *Montauk*, followed by the *Seneca, Wissahickon,* and *Dawn,* to destroy her. Unmindful of torpedoes and the heavy guns of the fort, Worden pushed by the latter unharmed by either, and when within twelve hundred yards of the *Nashville* he opened upon her with twelve and fifteen-inch shells. The gun-boats could not pass the fort, but fired upon the doomed ship at long range. Not more than twenty minutes had elapsed, after Worden opened his guns, before she was in flames. One of his shells had exploded within her, setting her on fire. One after the other of her heavy guns were exploded by the heat, and then her magazine blew up, and she was reduced to the total wreck delineated on page 327 of volume II. Shells from the fort struck the *Montauk* five times, but did no damage; and when she dropped down the river a torpedo exploded under her, but injured her a very little. The destruction of the *Nashville* was effected without the loss of a man.[4]

Worden's success determined Dupont to try the metal of the monitors and mortar-boats upon Fort McAllister. They went up the Ogeechee on the 3d of March, the *Passaic*, Commander Drayton, leading. The obstructions in the river would not allow her to approach nearer the fort than twelve hundred yards. The others were still farther off, and the mortar-boats were the most remote. The *Passaic, Patapsco,* and *Nahant* opened fire at a little past eight o'clock in the morning, and kept it up until four in

1862–63.

b 1863.

c Feb. 27.

---

[1] This was a strong earth-work built by the Confederates for the blockade of the Ogeechee, and to protect the railway bridge that spans it about ten miles south of Savannah.

[2] See note 8, page 310, volume II.

[3] These consisted of the *Passaic, Montauk, Ericsson, Patapsco,* and *Nahant,* all monitors; three mortar-vessels, and gun-boats *Seneca, Wissahickon,* and *Dawn.*

[4] A little earlier than this, the *Monitor,* the first of the turreted iron-clad vessels, which Worden commanded in her conflict with the *Merrimack,* was lost off Cape Hatteras. She was then in charge of Commander Bankhead, and was in tow of a side-wheel steamer, making her way to Port Royal. She foundered in a gale on the night of the 30th of December, and went to the bottom of the sea with some of her crew.

the afternoon, when the mortar-boats began throwing a shell every fifteen minutes, and kept it up until next morning.[a] Then Drayton went up as near the fort as possible with the *Passaic*, for observation, shielded from the guns by the turret of his vessel. He was satisfied that further efforts to drive out the Confederates would be useless, and the enterprise was abandoned.[1]

[a] March 4, 1863.

A little earlier than this the Nationals lost the steamer *Isaac Smith*, Acting Lieutenant Conover, while reconnoitering near Charleston. She went up the Stono River, some miles beyond Legareville, without molestation, but when she was within a mile of that place, on her return, three masked batteries opened a cross fire upon her at a bend in the stream, when she was captured and sent to Charleston. On the following morning another blow was given to National vessels. The Confederates at Charleston had been informed that the two larger ships of the blockading fleet lying off the bar (*Powhatan* and *Canandaigua*) had gone to Port Royal to coal, so two Confederate armored gun-boats, of the "ram" class (*Palmetto State*, Captain Ingraham,[2] and *Chicora*, Captain Tucker), went out before daylight[b] and in a shrouding haze, to strike the weaker National vessels then watching the harbor entrances. Softly they stole over the bar, when the *Palmetto State*, acting as a ram, struck the *Mercidita*, Captain Stellwagen, with full force, amidships, and at the same time fired a 7-inch rifled shell into her side, that went crashing through her machinery, releasing steam that scalded many men, and so completely disabling her that she could neither fight nor fly. The victor then attacked the *Keystone State*, Captain Le Roy, and sent a shell into her forehold, setting it on fire. As soon as the flames were put out, Le Roy attempted to run down his antagonist (the *Keystone State* having a full head of steam), but was foiled by a huge shot sent by the *Palmetto State*, which went through both steam-chests of his vessel, and so utterly disabled her that, like the *Mercidita*, she was surrendered. Ten rifled shells had struck her, and two of them had burst on her deck.[3]

[b] Jan. 31.

Day was now dawning, and the remainder of the blockading squadron, wide awake, dashed into the fight,[4] when the *Memphis* towed the *Keystone* out of danger. The assailants then retreated toward Charleston, where Beauregard, then in command there,[5] and Ingraham, "flag-officer commanding naval forces of South Carolina," proclaimed, without the shadow of truth, the blockade of Charleston "to be raised by a superior force of the Confederate States." Not a single vessel of the blockading squadron had been lost, for the Confederates did not make the *Mercidita* a prize by putting men on board of her, and the *Keystone State* was saved by her friends. In the face of these facts, the raising of the blockade was falsely announced, for effect abroad, and the British consul at Charleston and the commander of

---

1 The earth-works of the fort were very little damaged, and only one of its nine great guns was dismounted. This was effected by one of the 15-inch shells, which weighed 345 pounds. No man was killed on either side, and only one wounded. This engagement is sometimes called THE BATTLE OF GENESIS POINT.

2 Duncan N. Ingraham, formerly a useful officer of the National Navy, who had abandoned his flag and given his services to the Conspirators.

3 The *Mercidita* had three men killed and four wounded. The *Keystone State* had twenty men killed, chiefly by the steam, and twenty wounded.

4 The *Augusta*, *Quaker City*, *Memphis*, and *Housatonic*

5 Pemberton had been ordered to Mississippi.

the British ship *Petrel* there, hastened to attest the truth of the proclamation. Judah P. Benjamin, the Confederate "Secretary of State," issued a

circular to "the foreign consuls in the Confederacy," reiterating the misrepresentation,
saying to each, this is "for the information
of such vessels of your nation as may choose
to carry on commerce with the now open
port of Charleston." The mendacity of Benjamin and his fellow-conspirators was then
so well known, that no vessel was decoyed
into an open attempt to enter Charleston
harbor, which was continually watched by a
competent blockading squadron. As usual,
the venturesome blockade-runners crept in
under cover of fog and night.

This movement determined the Govern-

BEAUREGARD'S HEAD-QUARTERS IN
CHARLESTON.

ment to proceed at once to the task of capturing Charleston. A strong naval force had
been prepared under the direction of Admiral Dupont; and General Halleck
ordered Foster to leave North Carolina at once with a greater portion of his
corps (the Eighteenth) and go to the assistance of the naval commander.
Foster promptly obeyed, and sailed from Beaufort, North Carolina, on the
2d of February, with twelve thousand men, mostly veterans. On his arrival
at Hilton Head, he found that General Hunter, the commander of the
Department, had received no notice from Halleck of his order to Foster, and
regarded the movement as intrusive. Difficulty ensued. Foster, not finding Dupont at Port Royal, went to Fortress Monroe for siege-guns, when
Hunter took command of the newly-arrived troops, broke up their corps
organization, and incorporated them with his own. Foster, at his own
request, was allowed to retire to his Department, leaving his troops as re-enforcements for Hunter, who now had an apparently competent force to make
a speedy conquest of Charleston.

February and March were spent in the final preparations by Dupont.
The appointed place of rendezvous for his vessels was at the mouth of the North
Edisto River, well up toward Charleston; and as fast as they were prepared
at Hilton Head,[2] each was sent quietly to that point, where they were all
assembled, to the number of fourteen,[3] at the beginning of April. On the

---

[1] This is a view of the fine brick building, No. 40 Broad Street, occupied by Beauregard as his head-quarters at that time.

[2] For the purpose of saving to the service the time spent by vessels of the blockading squadron in going
North for repairs, Admiral Dupont established a floating machine-
shop in Station Creek, near Hilton Head, where such work was
done. He took two of the whale-ships which were sent down with
the "Stone fleet," (see page 128, volume I.), placed them side by
side, and on one of them had a sort of house built, in which a
steam-engine was put, with all the requisite machinery to be driven
by it. The building was properly divided for different operations,
as in ordinary machine-shops, such as pattern-room, boiler-makers'
room, with heavy forges, brass-founders' room, &c. On the other
vessel were furnaces, a store-house, and quarters for "contrabands."
This establishment, represented in the annexed engraving, was set
up by W. B. Coggswell, the master mechanic.

[3] The vessels consisted of nine "monitors" and five armored gun-

FLOATING MACHINE-SHOP.

night of Sunday, the 5th,[a] in the light of a full moon, the air calm and serene, Dupont anchored his fleet off Charleston bar, himself on board the *James Adger*, in which he had come up from [a] April, 1863. Port Royal. Already, during the afternoon, Commander Rhind, with the *Keokuk*,[1] assisted by Mr. Boutelle, of the Coast Survey, commanding the

Bibb, Ensign Platt, and pilots of the squadron, had buoyed the bar and arranged guides; and at dawn the next morning,[b] [b] April 6. the monitor squadron moved over it, leaving the gun-boats, under the

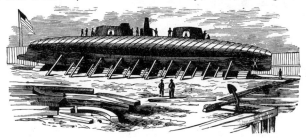

KEOKUK ON THE WAYS.

general command of Captain Green, outside the bar, as a "squadron of reserve," to assist in an attack on Morris Island, should one be made. Dupont had now transferred his flag from the *Adger* to the *New Ironsides*, from which he intended to direct the movements of his squadron, and in which he determined to share in the labors and dangers of the impending conflict.

The works around Charleston harbor to be attacked were numerous and formidable.[2] Along its northern margin, and commanding its channels, were five of them, the first being on the outward extremity of Sullivan's Island, guarding Maffit's Channel. The next, near the Moultrie House, on the same island, was a strong sand battery, called Fort Beauregard. Fort Moultrie, a little farther westward, had been greatly strengthened since the beginning of the war; and near it, on the western end of Sullivan's Island, was a strong earth-work called Battery Bee. On the main, at Mount Pleasant, near the mouth of Cooper River, was a heavy battery; and in front of the city, about a mile from it, was old Castle Pinckney, which had been strengthened by banking earth against its walls on the outside. In the channel, between Sullivan's and Morris Islands, stood Fort Sumter,[3] the most formidable of all the works to be assailed, grimly guarding the entrance to the inner harbor. On the southern side of the harbor, near the city, was the Wappoo Battery, on James's Island, which commanded the mouth of the Ashley River. Next to this was Fort Johnson; and between it and Castle Pinckney was Fort Ripley, constructed on a submerged sand-bank, called the "Middle Ground," of heavy timber, and armed with large guns. It was

---

boats. The names of the monitors and their respective commanders were as follows: *Weehawken*, Captain John Rodgers; *Passaic*, Captain Percival Drayton; *Montauk*, Commander John L. Worden; *Patapsco*, Commander Daniel Ammen; *New Ironsides*, Commander Thomas Turner; *Cattskill*, Commander George W. Rodgers; *Nantucket*, Commander Donald M. Fairfax; *Nahant*, Commander John Downes, and *Keokuk*, Lieutenant-Commander Alexander C. Rhind. The gun-boats were the *Canandaigua*, Captain Joseph H. Green; *Housatonic*, Captain Wm. R. Taylor; *Unadilla*, Lieutenant-Commander S. P. Quackenbush; *Wissahickon*, Lieutenant-Commander J. G. Davis; *Huron*, Lieutenant-Commander G. A. Stevens.

[1] The *Keokuk* was a double-turreted vessel, which had lately been built at New York. The turrets were immovable, the guns being arranged so as to be pivoted from one port-hole to the other. She was both a "monitor" and a "ram," of smaller dimensions than the "monitor" first constructed by Ericsson.

[2] See map of Charleston harbor on page 157, volume I.   [3] See page 128, volume I.

sometimes called the Middle-Ground Battery.   On Cummings's Point of Morris Island was Battery Gregg, and about a mile south of it, commanding the main channel, was a very strong and extensive work, called

MIDDLE GROUND BATTERY.

Fort Wagner. A little farther south, at Light-House inlet, which divides Folly and Morris Islands, was a battery that commanded the landing-place there. On these works several hundred guns were mounted, a large portion of them of English manufacture. Further to protect the city, the southerly channel of the inner harbor was obstructed by several rows of piles, one of them having an open space that might invite a vessel to enter, but to perish in the attempt, for under the water, at the threshold of that open door, was a mine containing five thousand pounds of gunpowder. Besides these, there were chains composed of linked railway-iron, to obstruct channels; and there lay, between Forts Sumter and Moultrie, a heavy rope buoyed up by empty casks, and bearing a perfect tangle of nets, cables, and other lines, below,

PIECE OF CHAIN.

attached to torpedoes, chiefly of the form shown in the engraving,[1] the whole kept in place by anchors of peculiar form, represented in the cut. These torpedoes were prepared for explosion, by means of electricity transmitted through wires from batteries at Forts Sumter and Moultrie. The harbor and its approaches were also sown with torpedoes,

TORPEDO.

one kind of which, represented in the engraving, was supplied with a head, filled with detonating powder, from which radiated tubes. When any of these were struck, an explosion was produced by means

TORPEDO ANCHOR.

of the percussion powder. Such were some of the contrivances for obstructing Charleston harbor—such were the fortifications which have been alluded to, against which the squadron of Dupont was arrayed on a bright and balmy day in early April, 1863.

Dupont intended to move up the main ship-channel, immediately after crossing the bar, to an attack on Fort Sumter, without returning any fire that might be opened on Morris Island. But a thick haze that spread over land and water, just after sunrise, obscured the more distant guides for the pilots, and the squadron lay quietly within the bar, in the main ship-channel, until little past noon the next day,[a] when it advanced in a prescribed manner of "line ahead," the *Weehawken*, Captain Rodgers,

TORPEDO.[2]   [a] April 7, 1863.

leading, the others following in the order named in note 3, page 192. "The ships will open fire on Sumter," ran Dupont's directions, "when within easy range, and will take up a position to the northward and westward of

---

[1] These were made of common barrels, with solid pointed ends of palmetto wood, and filled with gunpowder.
[2] The upper half of this torpedo was an empty hollow cone of tin, that acted as a buoy for the lower half, which was a mine containing about twenty pounds of gunpowder.

that fortification, engaging its left or northwest face [its weakest side,[1]] at a distance of from one thousand to eight hundred yards; firing low and aiming at the central embrasure."
The commander then knew nothing of the great hawser and its dreadful festoons, that hung in the prescribed path of his warriors. But it was soon discovered, and the silence of the lower Confederate batteries, and especially

FORT WAGNER, SEA FRONT.

of powerful Fort Wagner, as the squadron moved by them—a silence which created the most painful forebodings and suspense—was explained.

The *Weehawken*, its bow furnished with a contrivance for exploding torpedoes and removing obstructions, went forward, leading the procession of strange monsters of the deep, and at three o'clock came suddenly upon that fearful boom, and could go no farther. Her propeller became entangled in the horrid net-work, and she seemed subject only to the action of the tide. The other vessels were drawing nearer and nearer, their people wondering why the *Weehawken* hesitated, when suddenly the silence was broken, as the heavy *barbette* guns of Fort Sumter poured a stream of plunging shot and shell upon the thralled vessel. Rodgers saw that contest there would be fatal to his ship, and he managed to withdraw. Then, followed by the other vessels, he attempted to pass by Sumter, in the channel between it and Cummings's Point, but was there confronted by the rows of piles. It was well that he was stopped, for had he gone into the open way through one of the rows, the *Weehawken* would doubtless have been blown to atoms by the monster torpedo just mentioned.

Meanwhile Dupont was bringing the monitors into position for a simultaneous attack on Fort Sumter, when his ponderous flag-ship, the *New Ironsides*,[2] struck by the tide, became almost unmanageable, and confused the line. He signaled for the other vessels to disregard her, and take positions for the most effective work. Lieutenant-Commander Rhind then ran the little *Keokuk* within five hundred yards of the fort, and hurled upon it her immense projectiles, until she, herself, was riddled, began to sink, and was compelled to withdraw. The *Montauk* and *Catskill* were almost as near, and these, with the remainder of the monitors, poured a tremendous storm of heavy metal on the fort.[3] At the same time the guns of Forts Sumter,

---

[1] See notice of the character of Fort Sumter on page 118, volume I.

[2] This vessel was built at Philadelphia by Merrick & Sons, at a cost of $780,000. She was of 3,486 tons burden. She was launched in May, 1862. Her armament was of 200-pounder rifled Parrott guns, capable of throwing solid shot six miles, and her complement of men was 500. She did good service during the war, and was accidentally burnt near Philadelphia, in December, 1866.

[3] Mr. Swinton, author of *Campaigns of the Army of the Potomac*, who was on board the flag-ship during the action, and sent a graphic account of it to the *New York Times*, thus depicted the scene in the turret of a "monitor" in action: "Here are two huge guns which form the armanent of each monitor—the one 11, the other 15 inches in diameter of bore. The gunners, begrimed with powder and stripped to the waist, are loading the gun. The allowance of powder, 35 pounds to each charge, is passed up rapidly from below; the shot, weighing 420 pounds, is hoisted up by mechanical appliances to the muzzle of the gun, and rammed home; the gun is run out to the port and tightly compressed. The port is open for an instant; the captain of the gun stands behind, lanyard in hand—'Ready, fire!'—and the enormous projectile rushes through its huge parabola, with the weight of 10,000 tons, home to its mark."

Moultrie, Wagner, and the batteries within range, having an aggregate of nearly three hundred pieces,[1] were hurling heavy shot and shells upon the squadron then within the focus of their concentric fire, at the distance of from only five to eight hundred yards. These were thrown at the rate of one hundred and sixty a minute.[2] The greater portion of them glanced off the mailed ships as harmlessly as if they had been pistol-shot, while others made severe bruises. The weaker *Keokuk* suffered most, having been hit ninety times. Both her turrets were riddled, and nineteen holes were made in her hull, some of them eighteen inches in diameter.[3] She withdrew, went down the coast of Morris Island to Light-House inlet, and there sunk, at eight o'clock in the evening, after her people had safely abandoned her.

" The best resources of the descriptive art," wrote an eye-witness, " I care not in whose hand, are feeble to paint so terrific and awful a reality. Such a fire, or any thing even approaching it, was simply never seen before. The mailed ships are in the focus of a concentric fire of five powerful works, from which they are removed only from five to eight hundred yards, and which, in all, could not have mounted less than three hundred guns. And, understand, these not the lighter ordnance, such as thirty-two or forty-two pounders, which form the ordinary armament of forts, but of the very heaviest caliber—the finest and largest guns from the spoils of the Norfolk Navy Yard, the splendid ten and eleven-inch guns cast at the Tredegar Works, and the most approved English rifled-guns (Whitworth and others) of the largest caliber made. There was something almost pathetic in the spectacle of those little floating circular towers, exposed to the crushing weight of those tons of metal, hurled against them with the terrific force of modern projectiles, and with such charges of powder as were never before dreamed of in artillery firing. It was less the character of an ordinary artillery duel, and more of the proportions of the war of the Titans in the elder mythologies. There was but one conviction in the minds of all who were made acquainted with the facts, whether among the naval officers engaged or intelligent outside observers—the fight could not be renewed. And yet it was fully expected, on the night of the battle, that another trial would be made in the morning. I saw many of the captains of the iron-clads during that night. All were ready to resume the battle, though each man felt that he was going to an inevitable sacrifice. I confess I prayed that the fiery cup might pass from them, and that no impetuosity might prompt our leader to throw the fleet again into that frightful fire. . . . . No man could possibly feel with greater intensity all the instincts and motives that prompted the renewal of the battle, than the grand old sailor, the noble Dupont; and yet no man could possibly see with more clearness the blind madness of such an attempt. He dared to be wise."[4]

The terrible fight did not last more than forty minutes, during which time, it was estimated, the Confederates fired three thousand five hundred

---

[1] According to the report of General Ripley, who was in charge of the defenses of Charleston, only 76 of these guns were brought to bear on the squadron.

[2] Mr. Swinton said: "Some of the commanders of the iron-clads afterward told me that the shot struck their vessels as fast as the ticking of a watch."

[3] The turrets of the *Keokuk* were made of iron, nearly six inches in thickness, and yet they were penetrated, without much difficulty, by the steel-pointed shot hurled against them.

[4] Mr. Swinton in the *New York Times.*

shots. Dupont, seeing the *Keokuk* nearly destroyed, half his other vessels injured,[1] his flag-ship placed in peril, and Fort Sumter apparently but slightly injured, he was satisfied that further efforts to reduce that work by the navy alone would be futile, so at five o'clock he signaled the squadron to retire.

The attack on Sumter was a failure, but did not involve disaster. Dupont lost but few men,[2] and only one vessel (the *Keokuk*), the remainder of his squadron being in a condition to be easily repaired. He was blamed by the inexpert and zealous for not longer continuing the fight, or renewing it the next day, but subsequent events vindicated the soundness of his judgment. His withdrawal gave the Confederates great joy, and "the happy issue," Beauregard said in a general order, "inspired confidence in the country that the ultimate success of the Confederates would be complete."[3] Had a sufficient supporting land force been employed in vigorously attacking the Confederates on Morris Island, and keeping the garrisons of Battery Gregg and Fort Wagner engaged while the squadron was attacking Fort Sumter, the result might have been different. But only about four thousand of Hunter's troops had aught to do with the expedition directly. These, under General Truman Seymour, Hunter's chief of artillery, were posted behind a thicket of palm-trees, on Folly Island, at Light-House inlet, with pontoons and cannon, ready to dash across to Morris Island and attack the Confederates there when the squadron should reduce Fort Sumter and silence the guns of Fort Wagner and Battery Gregg; but they were not permitted to co-operate in that work. The squadron failed, and the land troops had nothing to do. "A mere spectator," General Hunter wrote to Admiral Dupont the next day[a] from the transport *Ben Deford*, "I could do nothing but pray for you, which, believe me, I did most heartily."

[a] April 8, 1863.

---

[1] The *Nahant* received thirty wounds, one of which was produced by a heavy rifled-shot which struck her pilot-house, and dislodged several bolts, by which Edward Cobb, quartermaster, was fatally hurt, and the captain and pilot were injured. The *Passaic* received as many wounds. One of the shot which struck the top of her turret broke all of the eleven one-inch plates of iron that composed it, and injured the pilot-house. The port of the *Nantucket* was firmly closed by a shot that damaged it. The *New Ironsides* had one of her port shutters carried away by a shot, and her wooden bows were penetrated by shells; and the deck-plating of the *Catskill* was torn up by a shell.

[2] Only one man died of injuries received, and about twenty-five were wounded, principally on board the *Keokuk* and *Nahant*.

[3] All the trophies of victory secured by the Confederates were "two 11-inch Dahlgren guns, two United States flags, two pennants, and three signal flags." The guns were immediately put into the Confederate service—"substantial trophies of the affair," Beauregard said.

CHAPTER VII.

THE SIEGE OF CHARLESTON TO THE CLOSE OF 1863.—OPERATIONS IN MISSOURI, ARKANSAS, AND TEXAS.

HERE was comparative quiet along the coasts of South Carolina and Georgia for some time after the attack of the iron-clad squadron on Fort Sumter. Dupont kept a careful watch over the movements of the Confederates, especially those on Morris Island. He had been instructed not to allow them to erect any more fortifications on that strip of land, for it had been determined to seize it, and begin a regular and systematic siege of Charleston by troops and ships.

General Hunter was relieved of the command of the Department of the South, and General Q. A. Gillmore, who captured Fort Pulaski the year before,[1] was assigned to it.[a] He arrived at Hilton Head on the 12th of June, and immediately assumed command. He found there not quite eighteen thousand land troops, mostly veterans. A greater portion of them were the men left there by General Foster. The lines of his Department did not extend far into the interior, but were of great length, parallel with the coast. He had to picket a line about two hundred and fifty miles in length, besides establishing posts at different points. This service left him not more than eleven thousand men that might be safely concentrated for operations directly against Charleston. He had at his disposal ninety-six heavy guns, but only eighty were effective, a dozen 13-inch mortars being too large. He was well supplied with materials of every kind to carry on a siege, and he worked diligently in preparations for it. The National forces were then in possession of most of the sea-coast islands west of the Stono River, and also of Folly Island, eastward of Stono inlet, where their pickets confronted those of the Confederates on Morris Island, at Light-House inlet.

At about the time of Gillmore's arrival, rumors reached Dupont that his blockading vessels were in danger from a very powerful iron-clad ram, which for fourteen months had been in preparation at Savannah, and was then completed. The rumor was true. A swift British blockade-runner, named *Fingal*, built in the Clyde, which had gone up the Savannah River full eighteen months before with a valuable cargo, and had not been able to get out to sea again, had been converted into a warrior which the Confederates believed would be a match for any two monitors then afloat. She was thoroughly armed with a coat of thick oak and pine, covered with heavy

a June 2, 1863.

---

bars of iron. She bore four great guns, and was provided with a powerful beak. She was named *Atlanta*, and her commander was Lieutenant W. A. Webb, formerly of the National Navy, who had a crew of one hundred and sixty men.[1]

Deserters from the *Atlanta* reported her ready for work, and Admiral Dupont sent the *Weehawken*, Captain Rodgers, and *Nahant*, Commander Downes, to Wassaw Sound, to watch her. She was considered by her commander a match for both, and on the morning of the 17th of June, she was seen moving rapidly down the Wilmington River to attack them, accompanied by two wooden gun-boats of Tattnall's Mosquito Fleet, which were intended to tow up to Savannah the captured monitors. After the battle, the *Atlanta* was to proceed to sea, and destroy or disperse the blockading squadrons off Charleston and Wilmington. She was provided with instruments, and with stores of every kind for a long cruise, especially of choice liquors. No one among the Confederates doubted her invincibility. The gun-boats that accompanied her were crowded with people from Savannah, many of them women, who went down to see the fight and enjoy the victory; and when the National vessels appeared in sight, Captain Webb assured the "audience" that the Yankee monitors would be in tow before breakfast.

Like many prophesies of the Confederates, Webb's was not fulfilled, and the spectators were grievously disappointed. As the ram pushed swiftly toward the *Weehawken*, the latter held back its fire until its antagonist was within short range, when a gun, sighted by Rodgers himself, sent a fifteen-inch solid shot, which carried away the top of the *Atlanta's* pilot-house, wounded two of her pilots, and sent her aground. Rodgers fired only four more shots. The last one struck the ram point blank, fearfully bent her iron armor, and shivered twelve inches of live-oak planking and five of Georgia pine back of it. One man was killed and seventeen were wounded by the blow, when Webb ran up a white flag. In the space of fifteen minutes after the first shot was fired, the *Atlanta* was prisoner to the *Weehawken*, and the astonished Webb said to his crew, "Providence, for some good reason, has interfered with our plans, and we have failed of success. I would advise you to submit quietly to the fate that has overtaken you."[2] In that brief space of fifteen minutes, the glowing visions of ruin to the National Navy, the raising of the blockade of Wilmington, Charleston, and Mobile, and the speedy recognition of the Confederacy as a nation by Great Britain and France, which the Conspirators and their friends had indulged when contemplating the *Atlanta*, faded away. Instead of raiding up the Atlantic coast, spreading terror among the inhabitants of seaport towns, she was taken

---

[1] The Atlanta was 190 feet in length, and 40 in width. Her main deck was only a few inches above the water. From this rose her gun-deck 8 feet, sloping at an angle of about 30 degrees, leaving a flat surface on the top. She was heavily plated with strips of iron two and a half inches in thickness, covering thick oak and pine planking. She was armed with four of Brooke's (English) rifled cannon, whose projectiles were steel-pointed, and at her bow was an iron beak six feet in length, to which was suspended a submarine torpedo, charged with 50 pounds of gunpowder, for blowing up any vessel she might attack.

[2] Captain Rodgers said his first shot took away from the *Atlanta* her desire to fight, and the last, her ability to get away. He captured 145 men, including officers, without losing a man himself. The Secretary of the Navy spoke of the affair as "the most marked and extraordinary in the service during the year." The *Atlanta* made another of the list of Confederate iron-clads which the Nationals had recently captured or destroyed.

quietly to Philadelphia, and there exhibited for awhile for the benefit of the fund of the Union Volunteer Refreshment Saloon.[1] It is said that the cost of the *Atlanta* was defrayed entirely by the proceeds of the voluntary sale of their jewelry by the misguided women of the Confederate States. The example was followed at Charleston, where the building of a gun-boat was begun, with the expectation of money from similar sources, to carry it on.

Although the attack on Sumter in April was a failure, the Government was determined to renew the attempt in connection with a land force. Dupont's views were so decidedly in opposition to the measure, because he could anticipate no other result than failure again, that soon after the capture of the *Atlanta*, when Gillmore was preparing to move vigorously in a siege of Charleston, Dupont was relieved, and Commodore Foote[2] was appointed his successor. The latter died in New York while on his way to his new post of duty, and Admiral Dahlgren was ordered to the command of the

JOHN A. DAHLGREN.

squadron. That officer reached Port Royal on the 6th of July, and heartily sympathizing with Gillmore in his plans, entered vigorously upon the duties assigned him.

Gillmore found Folly Island well occupied by National troops under General Vogdes, who had employed them in preparations for future work. Through its almost impenetrable jungles[3] he had cut roads, and it was thoroughly picketed in every part. He constructed a strong work on the southern end of it, to command the approaches down the Stono River. Another was erected on Folly River that commanded Secessionville; and at a narrow part of the island, a mile from its northern end, a line of intrenchments was cast up, with a redoubt at each end. Such was the situation on that island, soon to be made famous in history, when Gillmore arrived there, and, with the practiced eye of a skillful engineer, after traversing it, selected positions for batteries to bear upon the fortifications on Morris Island. His plan of campaign was quickly conceived. It was to approach Charleston by Folly and Morris Islands. To do this, he must overcome Fort Wagner, on the latter island, a very strong work, lying within twelve hundred yards of Fort Sumter, heavily

GILLMORE'S HEAD-QUARTERS ON FOLLY ISLAND.

---

[1] See page 578, volume I.   [2] See page 202, volume II.

[3] Folly Island is about seven miles in length, and not over one in width at its broadest part. On the west it is separated from James's Island by marshes traversed by Folly River, a narrow but deep stream. The eastern side borders on the ocean. Light-House inlet, which separates it from Morris Island, is five or six hundred yards wide. At the time we are considering, the island was covered with pine timber throughout nearly its whole extent, with an almost impenetrable tangled undergrowth. "I have never seen such a mass of briers and

armed and fully garrisoned by veterans, under Colonel Lawrence M. Keitt. This carried, Battery Gregg, on Cummings's Point, must fall as a consequence, when the National guns might be brought to bear heavily on Fort Sumter, and possibly hurl their shot and shell into the city of Charleston. To this work Gillmore now addressed himself.

The first movement of the new commander was to cause the erection of strong batteries on the northern end of Folly Island, to cover the passage of his troops over Light-House inlet. These were begun under the direction of General Vogdes, on the 15th of June,[a] and were prose-cuted with vigor under a heavy fire, frequently, from the Confed- [a] 1863. erate guns on Morris Island. The Nationals were completely masked by the thick pine forest, and their foe could only guess their position and what they were about, for they were as silent as mutes. Their works were completed at the beginning of July, and were superior of their kind. They were made of sand and marsh sod. The batteries were embrasured and revetted, with maga-zines and bomb and splinter-proofs; and at the end of twenty days after the works were begun, Gillmore had forty-eight heavy guns in position within range of the Confederate pick-ets, with two hundred rounds of ammunition for each.

BOMB AND SPLINTER-PROOF.[1]

When all was in readiness, Gillmore pro-ceeded to distract the attention of the Confederates, and mask his real design, by sending[b] General A. H. Terry, with nearly four [b] July 8. thousand troops, up the Stono River, to make a demonstra-tion against James's Island, while Colonel Higginson, with some negro troops, went up the Edisto to cut the Charleston and Savannah railway, so as to prevent troops from being sent from the latter to the former place. Higgins went in the gun-boat *John Adams*, with two transports, but in his attempt[c] to reach the railway he was repulsed, and returned with two hundred "contrabands,"[2] who gladly followed him. Terry's [c] July 10. movement was successful, for it drew the attention of the Confederates to James's Island, and caused them to send re-enforcements thither from Mor-ris Island.

Thirty hours after Terry's departure, General George C. Strong silently

---

thorns anywhere else," wrote a conspicuous actor in the military events there. "There was not a road of any description, and the only way to pass from one end of the island to the other, was along the beach, which was not always practicable at high tides."—*History of the One Hundred and Fourth Pennsylvania Regiment*, by its commander, Brevet Brigadier-General W. W. H. Davis, page 218.

[1] This was the appearance of one of the bomb and splinter-proofs of Gillmore's works on Folly Island, at the time of the writer's visit there, in the spring of 1866. This picture is from a photograph by Samuel A. Cooley, photographer of the Fourth Army Corps.

[2] See explanation of this word in this connection on page 501, volume I.

embarked[a] two thousand men[1] in small boats, on Folly River, and rowed softly, thoroughly masked by the tall marsh grass and the shadows of night, to the junction of that stream with Light-House inlet. The movement was unperceived by the Confederate sentinels, and the occupants of Morris Island were astounded when at dawn, the next morning,[b] Vogdes's unsuspected batteries opened a tremendous cannonade, and Dahlgren's monitors, *Weehawken, Catskill, Montauk,* and *Nahant,* at the same time opened a cross fire, and there stood revealed a strong force ready to pass over and give battle. After a two-hours' cannonade, during which Dahlgren's guns were directed toward Fort Wagner to keep its garrison quiet, General Strong threw his men rapidly ashore in the face of a heavy fire of artillery and musketry, and by nine o'clock in the morning, after a sharp but short struggle, he had full possession of all the Confederate works on the southern end of Morris Island, with eleven guns and much camp equipage. The Confed-

[a] July 9, 1863.

July 10.

BEACON HOUSE.

erates fled toward Fort Wagner, hotly pursued by Strong as far as a once-fine mansion, known as the Beacon House,[2] where they came in range of the guns of the fort, and halted. Three-fourths of the island was now in possession of the Nationals. Strong's skirmishers pushed up to within musket-range of Fort Wagner. But prudence required a suspension of operations for awhile, for the weather was intensely hot, and the victorious troops had been under arms all night. Strong's troops rested the remainder of the day and the night following, and at five o'clock the next morning[c] he led them to an assault on Fort Wagner. They pressed boldly up, and had reached the parapet, when they were met by a fire so withering that they recoiled, yet without very serious loss.[3] The Nationals were not disheartened by the repulse, while the attack created the greatest consternation at Charleston. Mayor Macbeth, after consultation with Beauregard, "advised and earnestly requested all women and children, and other non-combatants, to leave the city as soon as possible," in anticipation of an attack; and the Governor of the State made a requisition of three thousand negroes, to work on additional fortifications for the defense of the city. The Charleston press made frantic appeals to the people that revealed its fears,[4]

[c] July 11.

---

[1] These consisted of the Third New Hampshire, Sixth and Seventh Connecticut, Ninth Maine, Seventy-sixth Pennsylvania, four companies of the Forty-eighth New York, and a battalion of sharp-shooters.

[2] This was the appearance of the Beacon House after the struggle for the possession of Fort Wagner, on the 18th of July. It was the head-quarters, for awhile, of Acting Brigadier-General W. W. H. Davis, of the One Hundred and Fourth Pennsylvania, and was used by Gillmore as a signal station.

[3] The loss of the Nationals on Morris Island since the landing of Strong, the day before, was about 150 men. Beauregard reported the Confederate loss during the same time at 300 men. The troops engaged in this assault were the brigades of Generals Strong and Seymour, and consisted of the Seventy-sixth Pennsylvania, Forty-eighth and One Hundredth New York, Third New Hampshire, Ninth Maine, and Sixth and Seventh Connecticut.

[4] The *Charleston Courier* urged the exertion of every effort to retake the sea-coast islands. "Failing in this," it said, "and even should Sumter become untenable, then let us resolve on a Saragossa defense of the

and Beauregard, as usual, issued bombastic orders, and fulminated harmless thunder of words against the "Yankee abolitionists."[1]

It was now evident to General Gillmore that Fort Wagner was stronger than he supposed it to be, and that it could only be taken by regular approaches. He carefully calculated the chances of success, and concluded that while the Confederates might concentrate a greatly superior force on his front, the island was so narrow, with the sea on one side and a deep creek and marshes on the other, that he need not fear danger from flank movements. Besides, should the Confederates attempt an advance from Fort Wagner, Dahlgren's guns would fatally sweep them with an enfilading fire. Satisfied that he might proceed with safety, he did so, and at once cast up sheltering works in the vicinity of the Beacon House, preparatory to a bombardment and another assault on Fort Wagner.

In the mean time General Terry, who had made a lodgment on James's Island, had found lively work to do. Beauregard had received re-enforcements of Georgia troops from Virginia, and these he sent to co-operate with troops on James's Island in an attempt to surprise and capture Terry and his command. At the dawn of the 16th,[a] these advanced rapidly upon Terry, from near Secessionville, under General Hagood, driving in the Fifty-fourth Massachusetts, on picket duty. But Terry was never asleep in the presence of danger. His troops, with the gun-boats *Pawnee, John Adams, Huron, Mayflower,* and *Marblehead,* in Stono and Folly rivers, were ready to receive the assailants, who were very easily repulsed. This accomplished, Terry, whose whole movement had been a feint, withdrew from James's Island, according to arrangement, to join in the meditated attack on Fort Wagner. In this engagement Terry lost about one hundred men, and Hagood about two hundred.[2]

[a] July, 1863.

In his order congratulating his troops for their success on the 10th, Gillmore, after saying they had moved three miles nearer Sumter, frankly declared that their labors were but just begun. "While the spires of the rebel city still loom up in the distance," he said, "the hardships and privations must be endured before our hopes and expectations can find full fruition in victory." To this the troops gave full assent; and with a corresponding spirit he made preparations for another assault on Fort Wagner. Five batteries were erected across the island, from the sea to the marshes, by the New York Volunteer Engineers, in

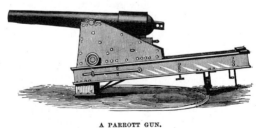

A PARROTT GUN.

---

city, manning and defending every wharf—fighting from street to street, and house to house—and, if failing to achieve success, yielding nothing but smoking ruins and mangled bodies as the spoil of the ruthless conquerer."

[1] After the Emancipation Proclamation went forth, the epithet of "Abolitionist" was applied to the National troops, on the recommendation of Beauregard, hoping thereby to keep alive the fire of hatred in the bosoms of the people of the Slave-labor States. We find the Confederate commanders, in their reports, taking special pains to make the idea very prominent that the war was only for the abolition of slavery.

[2] In his report to General Jordan, Beauregard's chief of staff, General Ripley, in command of the defenses of Charleston harbor, says: "Brigadier-General Hagood succeeded in driving the enemy, about two thousand in number, from James's Island." He suppressed the fact that Hagood was repulsed, and that Terry left the island at his leisure for a more important field of action.

which Parrott guns and heavy mortars were mounted. Besides these, he had three light batteries. Behind these works a storming party was formed, and when all was in readiness, at noon on the 18th,ᵃ he opened a bombardment on the doomed fort. Dahlgren at the same time moved his monitors near to it, regardless of the fire from both Fort Sumter and Fort Wagner, and poured upon the latter a continuous fire of heavy shells. This bombardment was to have been opened at dawn, but a storm prevented the perfecting of the arrangements for assault until noon. From that hour until sunset a hundred great guns were steadily assailing the fort, which replied with only two guns at long intervals. The Confederates knew how useless and destructive of men would be the fighting of their own guns in such a conflict. They also believed that the bombardment was only precedent to another assault by troops; so the garrison was kept safely in the bomb-proofs, in readiness for closer and more hopeful work.[1]

* July, 1863.

When, as darkness was coming on, the roar of cannon ceased, it was followed by the roar of thunder among the clouds, for a fearful storm swept over land and water at sunset. The Confederate flag still waved defiantly over Fort Wagner. The garrison might be decimated by the bombardment, or driven away, but the flag was still there. It must be humbled; and a storming party, composed of three brigades, was prepared to do it while the tempest was in full career; and just as the twilight was deepening, the first assaulting column, under General Strong, moved toward the fort. It was composed of the Fifty-fourth Massachusetts (colored), under Colonel Robert G. Shaw; Sixth Connecticut, Colonel Chatfield; Forty-eighth New York, Colonel Barton; Third New Hampshire, Colonel Jackson; Seventy-sixth Pennsylvania, Colonel Strawbridge; and the Ninth Maine, Colonel Emory. The Fifty-fourth Massachusetts was the first regiment of colored troops organized in a Free-labor State, and its young colonel, anxious to prove the efficiency of men of that race in battle, eagerly sought the post of danger in the front ranks of the assaulting column, notwithstanding his men had arrived only two hours before, after a most fatiguing march, without rest or food, to reach the front.[2]

Strong moved forward to within half a mile of Fort Wagner, when he advanced his whole column at the double-quick, in the face of a shower of shot and shell, not only from the work in his front, but from Fort Sumter and Battery Gregg. Not many men had been hurt when the column had almost reached the ditch within short musket-range of the fort, and many believed that few of the garrison were left to oppose them. They were instantly undeceived, when the parapet suddenly blazed with the flame of musketry, and the howitzers in the bastions swept the ditch as the assailants crossed it. At the same time hand-grenades sent over from within made sad work among the Unionists; yet some of them scaled the second parapet, near the sally-port, and planted the National standard there. The bearer and the flag disappeared almost instantly. At about the same time the gallant Shaw was

---

[1] Very few persons were injured during the tremendous bombardment that afternoon. In the fort four men were killed and fourteen were wounded. No one was hurt in the squadron, and only one man was killed and one wounded in Gillmore's trenches.

[2] This regiment had been assigned to Strong's brigade at the request of its colonel, and to be with it in the contemplated assault, it had been marching for about two days through heavy sand, across marshes and creeks, in pelting rain and sweltering heat.

shot dead, a short distance from the fort, and fell among the slain of his faithful dusky followers. Near him General Strong and Colonel Chatfield were mortally wounded; and Colonels Barton, Green, and Jackson were severely so, at the heads of their regiments, while many other officers of lower grades and scores of men were killed or maimed. The bereaved brigade, fearfully shattered and unable to continue the contest, fell back under Major Plympton, of the Third New Hampshire. Very few of the colored troops, whose bravery and fortitude had been well tested, remained unhurt, and these were led away by Lieutenant Higginson, a mere lad, into the sheltering gloom.

FORT WAGNER AT THE POINT OF ASSAULT.[1]

On the repulse of the first brigade of assailants, the second and smaller one, commanded by Colonel H. L. Putnam, of the Seventh New Hampshire, acting as brigadier-general, hurried forward and resumed the assault vigorously. This brigade was composed of Putnam's own regiment, the Sixty-second and Sixty-seventh Ohio, commanded respectively by Colonels Steele and Voorhees, and the One Hundredth New York, under Colonel Dandy. For half an hour these brave men continued the assault unflinchingly, though losing fearfully every moment. Many of them scaled the parapet, got into the fort, and there fought hand to hand with the garrison, not only in getting in, but in getting out again. Finally, when their brave leader, Colonel Putnam, was killed at the head of his troops, and nearly all of his subordinate commanders were slain or wounded, and no supports were at hand, the remains of the brigade, like the first, were led away into the gloom, and the assault ceased. The contest was too unequal. The Confederate garrison was in full force, and did not lose, in that fearful struggle, over one hundred men, while the Nationals, marching up uncovered toward the fort, lost a little more than fifteen hundred men. The Confederates said they buried six hundred bodies of the Unionists. Among them was that of Colonel Shaw, which was thrown into a deep trench that was filled above him with the slain of his colored troops, and so they were buried.[2]

---

[1] This shows the land-front of the fort, with the sally-port, near which Colonel Shaw was killed.

[2] The deaths of Colonels Shaw and Putnam caused the most profound sorrow, not only in the army, but throughout the country. Colonel Shaw was only twenty-seven years of age when he gave his life to the cause of Right and Justice. He was son of Francis G. Shaw, of Staten Island, New York, and when the war broke out was a member of the New York Seventh Regiment, so conspicuous in the movement for opening the way to Washington through Maryland. See chapter 18, volume I. He was with his regiment in those opening scenes of the war, and then received a commission in the Second Massachusetts, in which he did brave service, and had narrow escapes from death in the battles of Cedar Mountain and Antietam. He was appointed colonel of the first regiment of colored troops raised in Massachusetts, and at the head of these he fell just as he gave the word, "Onward, boys!" He is spoken of as one possessed of a most genial nature; of "manners as gentle as a woman's; of a native refinement that brooked nothing coarse; and of a clear moral insight that no evil association could tarnish." Because he commanded negro troops the Confederates hated him; and they foolishly thought they had dishonored him when, as it was savagely proclaimed, his body had been "buried in a pit under a heap of his niggers."

Colonel Haldimand S. Putnam, who was about the same age as Shaw, was a young man of most exemplary character and great promise. He was a graduate of West Point Military Academy, and had reached the rank of captain in the army when the war broke out. He shared the unlimited confidence and respect of General Scott, who, in the spring of 1861, made him his messenger to carry important military papers into the Southern States and to Fort Pickens. He was engaged in laying out the fortifications of Washington in the autumn of that

Gillmore now modified his plans for reducing Fort Wagner. Abandon-ing the idea of assaults, which had proven so disastrous, he prosecuted the work of regular approaches with great vigor. It was a difficult task, and required all of the rare engineering skill of the commander to accomplish it, for the dry part of the island, along which his approaches must be made, was narrower than that on which the fort stood, the whole width of which the latter covered. At the same time the besiegers were exposed to a cross-fire from Fort Sumter, Battery Gregg, and batteries on James's Island. Fort Wagner could be easily re-enforced from Charleston at any time, and a crushing force might be called by railway to that city, and sent to Morris Island. Gillmore weighed all these contingencies, and worked on hopefully and successfully. Five days after his repulse,[a] he had completed his first parallel, and had in position two 200-pounder Parrott guns and two 84-pounder Whitworth's, under the direction of Commander F. A. Parker, of Dahlgren's squadron, and ten siege-mortars. In addition to these were two 30-pounder Parrott field-guns, and three Requa batteries of rifle barrels for defensive service. The distance of these batteries from Fort Sumter was about four thousand yards. He had also opened his second parallel, six hundred yards in advance of his first, in which three heavy breaching-batteries named respectively Brown, Rosecrans, and Meade, were speedily made ready. These were composed of two 200-pounder and five 100-pounder Parrott guns, all trained upon Fort Wagner, Battery Gregg behind it, and Fort Sumter beyond. Besides these, there were four breaching-bat-teries established on the left, a little over four thousand yards from Fort Sumter, named Hayes, Reno, Stevens, and Strong. These mounted one 300-pounder, two 200-pounders, four 100-pounders, and four 20-pounder Parrott guns. Near the Beacon House were five 10-inch siege-mortars in position. These works were constructed with great difficulty, and chiefly under cover of night.[1] The heavy guns and mortars had to be dragged through deep sand and mounted under heavy fire from the Confederate works; yet with great patience and fortitude the National troops labored on and completed them.

[a] July 28, 1863.

For some time General Gillmore had contemplated the planting of a bat-tery in the marsh west of Morris Island, at a point whence, he believed, he might throw shells into the city of Charleston, or at least reach the wharves and shipping there. This was now attempted, under the direction of Colonel Serrell. At a point midway between Morris and James's island's, and a mile from the former, a battery was erected upon a platform of heavy tim-bers imbedded several feet in the black mud, there about sixteen feet in depth, overgrown with reeds and rank marsh grass, and traversed by winding and sluggish streams.[2] When the foundations were laid, the redoubt was

---

year, when he was appointed Colonel of the Seventh New Hampshire Volunteers. With these he went boldly to the assault of Fort Wagner, and there became a martyr to the cause of Justice and Civil Liberty. His countrymen will always delight to honor his memory.

[1] The Confederates had constructed a heavy work on James's Island, which they named Battery Simkins. This, with two or three smaller works in that direction, annoyed the flank of the besiegers very much, while the works in front continually galled them.

[2] Colonel Serrell assigned to a lieutenant the superintendence of the work. When the spot chosen for building the battery was shown to the latter, he said the thing was impossible. "There is no such word as 'impossible' in the matter," the colonel answered, and directed the lieutenant to build the battery, and to call for every thing required for the work. The next day the lieutenant, who was something of a wag, made a requisi-

piled upon it. It was composed wholly of bags of sand taken from Morris Island through the little creeks, in boats, during the nights. Under the gun platform heavy piles were driven entirely through the mud, into the solid earth, and on it was mounted a single 8-inch (200-pounder) rifled Parrott gun, which Sergeant Felter, of the New York Volunteer Engineers, named "The Swamp Angel."[1] It was thoroughly protected by the sand-bag parapet. In fifteen days from the time the battery was commenced[a]

THE SWAMP ANGEL BATTERY.

[a] August 4, 1863.

it was finished, and the "Angel" was ready to carry into the citadel where the rebellion was planned its messages of wrath.[2]

Gillmore's preparations for attack were all completed by the middle of August, and on the morning of the 17th,[b] the heavy guns of twelve batteries and from Dahlgren's entire naval force at hand, were opened on Forts Sumter and Wagner and Battery Gregg, the first in command of Colonel Alfred Rhett, the second under Colonel Lawrence M. Keitt, and the third under Captain Lesesene. Fort Sumter, lying at a distance of two miles and a half from Gillmore's batteries, was the chief object of attack, for it was necessary to make it powerless for offensive purposes before the siege of Fort Wagner might be prosecuted, without great loss of life. Upon it Gillmore's breaching-guns and the heavy ones of the *Passaic* and *Patapsco* (the monitors lying at a distance of two thousand yards) were brought to bear, and before night its walls had begun to crumble fearfully. The firing was renewed every morning until the 24th,[c] when Gillmore sent a dispatch to Halleck, saying, "I have the honor to report the practical demolition of Fort Sumter, as the result of our seven days' bombardment of that work, including two days of which a powerful northeasterly storm most seriously diminished the accuracy and effect of our fire. Fort Sumter is to-day a shapeless and harmless mass of ruins. My chief of artillery, Colonel J. N. Turner, reports its destruction so far complete that it is no longer of any avail in the defenses of Charleston."

[b] August.

[c] August.

In the mean time the "Swamp Angel" had been ready for business, and Gillmore sent a summons to Beauregard to evacuate Morris Island and Fort Sumter within four hours after the reception of his message, on penalty of a

tion on the quartermaster for one hundred men, eighteen feet in height, to wade through mud sixteen feet deep, and then went to the surgeon to inquire if he could splice the eighteen-feet men, if they were furnished him. This pleasantry caused the lieutenant's arrest, but he was soon released, and constructed the work with men of usual height.—Davis's *History of the One Hundred and Fourth Pennsylvania*, page 253.

[1] This gun was taken through the sand on a sling cart, or truck (see page 240, volume II.), and then floated on a raft of pine timber to its destination.

[2] Its distance from Charleston, in a direct line, was 8,800 yards, or about five miles; and to carry a shell that distance, it had to be fired at an elevation of thirty-five degrees.

bombardment of Charleston, from which, as we have seen, the non-combatants had been requested by Mayor Macbeth to retire.[1]   Gillmore knew this, and hence the short time given for a reply.   Hearing nothing from Beauregard, he ordered the "Angel" to take some messages to the deeply-offending city.   Several were sent in the form of shells weighing one hundred and fifty pounds each.   Some of these fell in Charleston, and greatly alarmed the few people, but injured nobody.   It gave Beauregard an opportunity to attempt to "fire the Southern heart," by a letter which he sent to Gillmore, and published in the newspapers, in which he denounced the course of his adversary as "atrocious and unworthy of any soldier,"[2] and said: "I now solemnly warn you that if you fire again on this city from your Morris Island batteries, without giving a somewhat more reasonable time to remove the non-combatants, I shall feel compelled to employ such stringent means of retaliation as may be available during the continuance of this attack."   Gillmore laughed at this foolish threat, and the "Angel" continued its ministrations from time to time, until just as its thirty-sixth message was about to leave, the great gun burst and its labor ceased.

Fort Sumter being disabled, Gillmore now turned his chief attention to the reduction of Fort Wagner.   While the walls of the former were crumbling, and its *barbette* guns were tumbling from their platforms under the fire of the batteries and the squadron, he had completed[a] his fourth parallel to about three hundred yards from the fort on his front, and only one hundred from a ridge of sand dunes from behind which Confederate sharp-shooters greatly annoyed the workers.   These were charged upon and driven away at the point of the bayonet by General Terry, when a fifth parallel was established close to the ridge.   But the space there was so narrow that the concentring fire of the fort at short range, and enfilading ones from James's Island, not only made a farther advance almost impossible, but the position nearly untenable.   Gillmore now saw that another assault upon the fort was an imperative necessity.   The first work to be done in that direction was to silence its guns and drive its garrison to the bomb-proof.   For that purpose the light mortars were taken to the front, and the rifled cannon of the left batteries were trained on the fort.   Powerful calcium lights were made to blaze upon it at night, exposing every thing on the parapet, blinding the garrison to all that was going on within the Union lines, and enabling the National sharp-shooters to prevent the Confederates repairing at night the damage done to the fort by bombardment during the day, which was kept up moderately without cessation.   Finally, when every thing was in readiness, the *New Ironsides*, Captain Rowan, moved up to within one thousand yards of the sea face[3] of the fort; and at the dawn of the 5th of September, his broadsides of eight guns, carrying

[a] August 21, 1863.

---

[1] See page 202.

[2] In his letter Beauregard said, that after an unsuccessful attack of more than forty days on the defenses of Charleston, and despairing of carrying them, Gillmore resorted "to the novel measure of turning his guns against the old men, the women and children, and the hospitals, of a sleeping city," which he denounced as an act of "inexecrable barbarity."   To this Gillmore replied that it was a well-established principle of civilized warfare, that the commander of a place attacked and not invested, had no right to a notice of an intimation of bombardment, other than which is given by the threatening attitude of his adversary; and that it was the duty of such commander to see to it that the non-combatants were removed.   In this instance, Beauregard, by his own admission, had had forty days in which to perform that act of humanity.

[3] See page 195.

11-inch shells, and the land batteries, opened simultaneously upon the parapet. The garrison soon abandoned their cannon, and took refuge in the bomb-proof, upon which, for nearly forty hours, the great guns thundered without any sensible effect.

When the guns of Fort Wagner were silenced, Gillmore's sappers pushed rapidly forward, under the direction of Captain Walker, until Battery Simkins and its fellows on James's Island could annoy them no more, without danger of hurting the garrison. The men now worked without danger, and early in the evening of the 6th,[a] the sap was carried by the south face of the fort, leaving it to the left; the counter-scarp of the [a] Sept., 1863. ditch was crowned near the flank of the east, or sea-front, by which all the guns in the work were masked, excepting in that flank; a line of palisades, which there protected it, were pulled up, and the trenches were widened and deepened so as to hold the assaulting troops.

The business of assault was intrusted to General Terry. He was directed to move upon the fort at nine o'clock (time of low tide), on the morning of

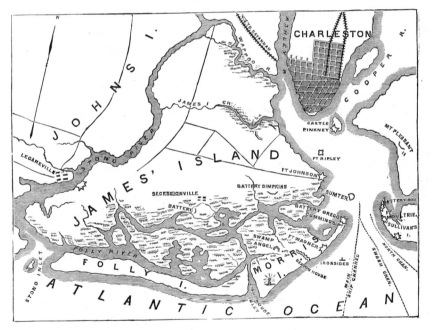

SIEGE OF CHARLESTON.

the 7th, with about three thousand men, in three columns, composed of the brigades of General Stevenson and Colonel Davis, and the Ninety-seventh Pennsylvania and Third New Hampshire. The last two regiments were to form the storming party, and a regiment of colored troops, under Colonel Montgomery, was to be held in reserve near the Beacon House. The One Hundred and Fourth Pennsylvania (Davis's own) was to carry intrenching tools. In accordance with this arrangement, these troops were in readiness at two o'clock in the morning, near the Beacon House, when General Terry announced to them that the fort was evacuated. The Confederates had begun to leave it and Battery Gregg before midnight, and had fled from Cummings's Point in boats so precipitately that all but seventy escaped. During forty hours no less than one hundred and twenty-two thousand pounds of iron, in the form of balls and shells, each weighing not less than one hundred pounds, had been rained upon the fort, and yet its bomb-proof, capable of sheltering eighteen hundred men,[1] was but little injured. The symmetry of the fort was destroyed, but it was soon put into proper shape. An apparatus for blowing up the magazine when the victors should enter the fort, was happily discovered and destroyed. The nineteen heavy guns left in Fort Wagner and Battery Gregg, with others, were speedily turned on the harbor defenses and the city of Charleston. The captured forts were strengthened and heavily armed, and other works were soon erected. These were all a mile nearer the city than the "Swamp Angel," and commanded its wharves and full one half of the town. Blockade running was effectually stopped, and Charleston, properly called "the Cradle of Secession," was made a desolation in the world of business.[2] "You now hold in undisputed possession the whole of Morris Island," said Gillmore, in a congratulatory address to his troops on the 15th, "and the city and harbor of Charleston lie at the mercy of your artillery from the very spot where the first shot was fired at your country's flag, and the rebellion itself was inaugurated.[3]

Gillmore expected the iron-clad squadron to force its way past Fort Sumter into the inner harbor and up to the city, as soon as that fortress was effectually silenced, but Dahlgren did not think it prudent to do so, chiefly because he believed the channels to be swarming with torpedoes. But immediately after the capture of Fort Wagner, a portion of the men of the squadron attempted the important enterprise of surprising and capturing Fort Sumter without Gillmore's knowledge. For this purpose about thirty row-boats, filled with armed men, were towed close to Fort Sumter on the night of the 8th,[a] where they were cast off, and made their way to the base of the shattered walls. The expedition was in charge of Commander Stephens, of the *Patapsco*, and when the boats reached the fort, the crews of three of them, led by Commander Williams, Lieutenant Renny, and Ensign Porter, scaled the steep ruin, with the belief that the garrison was sleeping. It was wide awake, for the vigilant Major S. Elliott[4] was in command; and at the moment when the bold adventurers were expecting to win victory and renown, they were greeted with musket-balls and hand grenades, and the fire of neighboring batteries, a gun-boat and a ram, which made havoc among the men and boats. Two hundred of the assailants were killed, wounded, or captured, with four boats and three colors, and the remainder escaped.

[a] Sept., 1862.

---

[1] Fort Wagner was garrisoned by about 1,400 effective men, and Battery Gregg by about 150 men.

[2] In his annual report to Congress, in December, 1863, the Secretary of the Navy, in summing up the operations of that arm of the service on the Southern coast, said: "Not a blockade runner has succeeded in reaching the city for months, and the traffic which has been to some extent, and with large profits, previously carried on, is extinguished. As a commercial mart, Charleston has no existence; her wealth, her trade, has departed. In a military or strategic view, the place is of little consequence; and whether the rebels are able, by great sacrifice and exhaustion, to hold out a few weeks, more or less, is of no importance."

[3] From Battery Gregg, on Cummings's Point, Edmund Ruffin, it will be remembered, fired the first shot on Fort Sumter, on the 12th of April, 1861. See page 320, volume I.

[4] See page 122, volume II.

For some time after this disastrous meddling with the slumbering but yet powerful monster guarding Charleston harbor, very few stirring events broke the monotony of camp life on Morris Island, or the tedious blockading service, excepting an occasional visit to the squadron of some prowler of the harbor on a deadly errand; the battering of Fort Sumter now and then by Gillmore's guns, to keep the garrison from doing mischief, or the sad destruction of the *Weehawken* in a heavy December gale.[1] Gillmore continually strengthened his new position, and the *Ironsides* lay not far off, watching the main ship channel. Finally, on a dark night in October,[a] a small vessel of cigar shape, having a heavy torpedo hanging from its bow, went silently down to blow the *Ironsides* into fragments. ^{a October 6, 1863.}

The sum of its exploit was the explosion of the mine by the side of the vessel, making her shiver a little, and casting up a huge column of water high in air. A little later, when Gillmore was told that the Confederates were mounting guns on the southeast face of Sumter, to command Fort Wagner, he opened[b] upon that face of the fort his heavy rifled cannon, and speedily reduced it to ruins, making a sloping heap of rubbish from the parapet to the water.[2] From that time until near the close of the year he kept up a slow and irregular fire upon the fort and Charleston, when, seeing no prospect of the passage of the squadron into the inner harbor, he kept silence. ^{b October 26.}

Let us now change our field of observation from the sea-coast to the region beyond the Mississippi, a thousand miles farther westward, and see what of importance, not already considered, occurred there down to the beginning of 1864. Our record of military events in that part of the Republic closed with the Battle of Prairie Grove, in Arkansas, early in December, 1862;[3] the recapture of Galveston[4] and the reoccupation of all Texas, by the Confederates, at the beginning of 1863;[5] Banks's triumphant march through the interior of Louisiana to the Red River, in April and May, 1863,[6] and the Battle of Helena, in July following.[7]

Turning to Missouri and Arkansas, in which the Unionists were the majority and the political power was held by loyal men, especially in the former State, we see those commonwealths, after brief repose, again convulsed in 1863 by the machinations of disloyal resident citizens, and the contests of hostile forces in arms. One of the worst enemies of Missouri (the rebel Governor Jackson[8]) had died in exile at Little Rock,[c] in Arkansas, but Sterling Price, Marmaduke, Cabell, Reynolds (the former lieutenant-governor), and other rebel chiefs, were yet active and mischievous. ^{c Dec. 6, 1862.}

Early in January, 1863, Marmaduke, with about four thousand men, mostly mounted, burst suddenly out of Northern Arkansas, and fell upon Springfield, in Missouri, then fairly fortified by five earth-works, and defended

---

[1] The *Weehawken* lay at anchor in the outer harbor off Morris Island when the gale came on, and, in consequence of her hatches being left open, she foundered on the 6th of December, carrying down with her thirty of her crew.

[2] See on page 331, volume I., a picture of Fort Sumter in ruins, as it appeared from Fort Wagner, at the close of 1863.

[3] See pages 535 and 536, volume II.   [4] See page 594, volume II.   [5] See page 595, volume II.

[6] See pages from 595 to 600 inclusive, volume II.   [7] See page 148.   [8] See page 201, volume I.

by a small force, under General E. B. Brown, of the Missouri militia.[1] The attack was sharp and heavy, but General Brown gallantly fought the assailants with his little band from ten o'clock in the morning until dark, when Marmaduke withdrew, with a loss of two hundred men, and a gain of one cannon, which he carried away.[2] Brown lost one hundred and sixty-four men, of whom fourteen were killed. The general himself was severely wounded, and lost the use of his right arm.

From Springfield Marmaduke marched eastward, and at dawn on the 10th,[a] his advance encountered, at Wood's Fork, near Hartsville, [a] Jan., 1863. in Wright County, the Twenty-first Iowa, Colonel Merrell, whom General Fitz-Henry Warren had ordered to Springfield. After a skirmish, the Unionists were flanked, and Marmaduke's whole force pushed on toward Hartsville. But Merrell was there before him, re-enforced by the Ninety-ninth Illinois, and portions of the Third Iowa and Third Missouri Cavalry, supported by a battery commanded by Lieutenant Wald Schmidt. A sharp engagement ensued, when Marmaduke was repulsed, with a loss of about three hundred men, including a brigadier-general (McDonald) and three colonels, killed. Merrell's loss was seventy-one men, seven of them killed. His ammunition was running low, so he fell back on Lebanon, while Marmaduke, having no spirit for further fighting in Missouri, fled swiftly southward that night, and escaped into Arkansas. With a part of his force he took post at Batesville, on the White River, where he was [b] Feb. 4. attacked[b] by the Fourth Missouri Cavalry, Colonel G. E. Waring, and driven across the stream, with the loss of a colonel and several men made prisoners. At about the same time a small force, under Major Reeder, broke up[c] a band of guerrillas at Mingo Swamp, and killed [c] Feb. 8. their leader, McGee; and, on the 28th of the same month, Lieutenant-Colonel Stewart, scouting from Fayetteville (the National outpost in Northwestern Arkansas), with one hundred and thirty cavalry, captured, near Van Buren, on the Arkansas River, a Confederate steamer, [d] March 28. with about three hundred prisoners. A month later,[d] the steamer Sam Gaty, on the Missouri River, was captured at Sibley's Landing by a gang of guerrillas, led by George Todd, who committed great atrocities. They robbed the boat and all persons on board, and then murdered several of the white passengers, and about twenty negroes, who, with sixty others (who escaped), were flying from bondage. An attempt to gain freedom was a heinous crime in the eyes of the ruffians, and the poor fugitives were placed in a row alongside of the boat, and one after another was shot through the head.

In the spring of 1863, Fayetteville was occupied by some Union cavalry and infantry, under Colonel M. L. Harrison, and, on the 18th of April, they were attacked by nearly two thousand mounted Confederates and two guns, led by General W. L. Cabell. He had marched rapidly over the Boston mountains from Ozark, with the intention of surprising Harrison at dawn,

---

[1] His force consisted of about 1,200 State militia, the One Hundred and Eighteenth and One Hundred and Fifty-sixth Iowa, under Lieutenant-Colonel Thomas Cook, and 300 convalescents, who re-enforced the garrison just as Marmaduke was approaching.

[2] In this engagement Springfield suffered much. Houses were riddled and set on fire by the shells. One exploded in a room occupied by four women and two children, who lay upon the floor under feather-beds, and thus escaped injury.

but he did not arrive until after sunrise. About five hundred of the Unionists kept up a spirited fight with the assailants until about noon, when the latter were repulsed, and returned over the mountains as swiftly as they came. Harrison, for lack of horses, could not pursue. His foe had inflicted on him a loss of seventy-one men (four killed), and he had received in exchange fifty-five prisoners, fifty horses, and a hundred shot-guns.

Meanwhile Marmaduke had gone to Little Rock, and there, with the chief Conspirators and military leaders in Arkansas, he planned a raid into Missouri, having for its chief objective the capture or destruction of a large depot of National stores at Cape Girardeau, on the Mississippi River. With a force of about eight thousand men, in four brigades, known as "Price's First Corps of the Trans-Mississippi Department," he pushed rapidly into Missouri, and following the general line of the St. Francis River, reached Fredericton, between Pilot Knob and Cape Girardeau, on the 22d of April.[a] There he turned quickly to the southeast, and marched on Cape Girardeau; but General John McNeil, who, at Bloomfield, in Stoddard County, had heard of the raid and divined its object, beat him in a race for that point, and, with his twelve hundred followers, reached Cape Girardeau two days before Marmaduke's arrival.[b] McNeil found there about five hundred men, mostly of the First Nebraska, under Lieutenant-Colonel Baumer, with four guns rudely mounted. The works were immediately strengthened, a greater portion of the stores were sent away in steamboats, and when Marmaduke appeared and demanded a surrender of the place, giving McNeil only thirty minutes to consider an answer, the latter was well prepared to fight, and told the Confederate leader so. Early the next morning Marmaduke shelled his adversary for awhile, and then again demanded a surrender. McNeil answered with his guns, when the assailant, seeing some armed vessels in the Mississippi coming to the aid of the besieged, beat a retreat[c] across the St. Francis River, and hurried on toward Arkansas, burning the bridges behind him. McNeil was now ranked by General Vandever, who was of a different temperament, and the pursuit was made so cautiously under his orders, that Marmaduke escaped, after his rear-guard had skirmished several times with McNeil's pursuing column.[1]

On the 20th of May,[d] Fort Blunt, not far from Fort Gibson, in the Cherokee country west of Arkansas, was menaced by about three thousand Confederates, under Colonel Coffey. The fort was commanded by Colonel William A. Phillips, and garrisoned by about eight hundred white men and a regiment of Creek Indians, some of the latter being employed as scouts. These were treacherous, and failed to give notice of the approach of the foe. Coffey found Phillips too strongly posted to warrant an attack, so he crossed the river (Arkansas), and seized cattle grazing there, belonging to the garrison. The Indian regiment refused to join in a charge for the recovery of the animals, and only a part were saved. Coffey encamped in a strong position, about five miles from the fort, where Phillips attacked him with energy. The Confederates fled across the river with their

[a] 1863.

[b] April 25.

[c] April 26.

[d] 1863.

---

[1] Marmaduke took with him his fourteen pieces of artillery, and full as many prisoners as had been taken from him. His loss in killed and wounded was much greater than that of the Nationals.

booty, and escaped with a loss of about sixty men. Phillips's loss was about the same.

Four weeks later, a train of three hundred wagons, on the way from Kansas with supplies for Fort Blunt, under a convoy of ten cavalry companies, the First Kansas (colored), Colonel J. M. Williams, eight hundred in number, and about\five hundred Indians led by Major Forman, was attacked [a] at the crossing of the Cabin Creek, in the Indian Territory, by seven hundred Texans and some Creeks, led by a Confederate Indian chief named Standwatie. The assailants were repulsed, and fled in haste, leaving forty of their dead and nine wounded on the field. The Union loss was twenty-three. The train pressed forward, and reached Fort Blunt in safety, followed immediately afterward by General Blunt, who arrived there from Fort Scott,[b] one hundred and seventy-five miles distant, by a forced march during five days, just in time to meet great peril that threatened the post. That peril consisted of a force of Confederates, estimated at six thousand strong, under General Cooper. They were then at Honey Springs, behind Elk Creek, about twenty-five miles south of Fort Blunt, where they were waiting for three regiments from Texas, under General Cabell, to join them in an attack on the post. Blunt had heard of this peril, and hence his rapid march. He was informed that the Texans would arrive on the 17th, so he marched at once upon Cooper's camp, with three thousand troops, infantry and cavalry, and twelve light cannon, to assail him before his re-enforcements should come up. He left the fort at midnight, and at ten o'clock the next day [c] he attacked Cooper in two columns, led respectively by Colonels Phillips and Judson, his cavalry, dismounted, acting as infantry on each flank, with carbines. At the end of two hours' hard fighting the Confederates gave way. They were pursued through the woods into an open prairie, and scattered in wild disorder, leaving one hundred and fifty of their number dead, and seventy-seven of them prisoners, with a disabled gun and two hundred small-arms. The number of their wounded was estimated at four hundred. Blunt lost seventy-seven men, of whom seventeen were killed. Within an hour after Cooper fled, Cabell came up with his Texans, nearly three thousand strong. He did not think it prudent to attack the victorious Nationals, so during that night he moved rapidly southward, and disappeared beyond the Canadian River, when the Union force returned to Fort Blunt.

In the mean time guerrilla bands were becoming exceedingly active in Blunt's rear. One of these, led by Colonel Coffey, went up from Northern Arkansas, and struck [d] the Sixth Missouri Cavalry, Colonel Catherwood, at Pineville, in Southwestern Missouri; but he was beaten, and driven away with great loss. His retreat was so precipitate, that he left behind him his wagons and supplies, and about two hundred men killed, wounded, and prisoners. At the same time a most savage raid was made into Kansas from Missouri, by a band of desperadoes collected in the western part of the latter State, and led by a human fiend under the assumed name of Quantrell. His followers numbered about three hundred. They gathered secretly, and then swept swiftly and stealthily over the border toward Lawrence, whose inhabitants were mostly Unionists. They entered that town just at daybreak,[e] and awakened the

[Marginal notes:]
[a] July 1, 1863.
[b] July 16.
[c] July 17.
[d] Aug. 13.
[e] Aug. 13.

sleeping and unsuspecting inhabitants by their horrid yells. The town was wholly without defenders, excepting the citizens, who were mostly unarmed. The guerrillas picketed every road leading out of Lawrence, so that no person should escape; and whenever a citizen emerged from his house with arms in his hands, he was shot dead. The place was speedily pillaged and burnt. Banks, stores, and private dwellings were robbed, and the courthouse and many of the finest houses were fired. A band of unarmed Union recruits were butchered. Such also was the fate of every German and negro, and many other unarmed citizens, who fell into the hands of the assassins. At ten o'clock in the morning, when the horrid work ceased, one hundred and forty men had been murdered, and one hundred and eighty-five buildings were in flames.

Among those who escaped from Lawrence at this time was General Lane, then a member of the National Senate. He, with some other citizens, organized a pursuing party, but Quantrell had the advantage of six miles the start in the race, with all the horses he could lay hands on. The pursuers killed or captured about one hundred of the murderers. The remainder escaped. Their special work, the sacking of the "Abolition town" of Lawrence, being finished, they were disbanded, and joined themselves to other organizations. Their crime produced the greatest horror and indignation, and for awhile there was no disposition to give quarter to guerrillas; and when, ten days after the sacking of Lawrence, Colonel Woodson, with six hundred Missourians, swept down from Pilot Knob into Northern Arkansas, and at Pocahontas, on the Big Black River, captured the famous guerrilla chief, General M. Jeff. Thompson, and about fifty of his men,[1] it was difficult to shield them from personal peril.

Soon after the attack on Helena,[2] the surrender of Vicksburg and Port Hudson, and the retreat of Johnston from Jackson,[3] by which Grant's army was relieved from pressure, General Frederick Steele was sent to Helena to organize an expedition to capture Little Rock, the capital of Arkansas. His forces gathered there at the beginning of August numbered about six thousand men (including five hundred Indiana and Kansas cavalry), with twenty-two guns. He was soon joined by General Davidson (then operating in Arkansas, under the command of General Hurlbut) with an equal number of men, mostly mounted, with eighteen guns, making his whole force, when he moved from Helena on the 10th of August, about twelve thousand men and forty guns. Davidson and his horsemen took the lead in the march. The White River was crossed at Clarendon,[a] when Davidson pushed forward, on its western side, on a reconnoissance toward Brownsville, the capital of Prairie County, then held by Marmaduke. Meanwhile Steele sent his extra supplies, and over a thousand sick men, in boats, to Duvall's Bluff,[4] on the White River, which was considered the most healthful place in all that region.

When Davidson, with a strong vanguard of skirmishers, approached

[a] August 17, 1863.

---

[1] Colonel Woodson sent forward Captain Gentry, of the Second Cavalry of the Missouri State Militia, to seize Thompson. He found that famous chief sitting quietly in his office, tracing a map of Southeastern Missouri, in perfect security as he supposed, for he did not think there was a National soldier within a hundred miles of him. Thompson was astonished, but not disconcerted. He declared it was too bad to interrupt him, for, if they had let him alone two weeks longer, he would have had three thousand men at his command.

[2] See page 148.   [3] See page 146.   [4] See page 582, volume II.

Brownsville, driving Confederate skirmishers before him, Marmaduke evacuated the place[a] and fell back to a line of intrenchments on the
Bayou Metoe, when he was driven across the stream, after some
fighting.[b] He checked pursuit by burning the bridges behind
him, and fled toward Little Rock. Four days afterward Steele
was joined by True's brigade, sent from Memphis, and then concentrated his
whole available force at Brownsville. A reconnoissance by Davidson showed
that great difficulties lay in the way of a direct march upon Little Rock,
across the Bayou Metoe and its fringe of swamps; so Steele took a more
southerly course, with Davidson in the advance, passed that stream at Shallow's Ford, and pushed on to the Arkansas River. He reached its banks at
Ashley's Mills on the 7th of September, after Davidson and his horsemen had
severely skirmished there. He left seven hundred more of his sick, with his
supply-trains, there, in charge of True's brigade and Ritter's cavalry, and
then pushed up the northern side of the Arkansas River, toward Little Rock,[1]
with Davidson in the advance, who skirmished much of the time.

  a August 26, 1863.

  b August 27.

When well up toward the Arkansas capital, Davidson, supported by
two infantry divisions, with two batteries, crossed the river on a pontoon
bridge,[c] under cover of darkness and his great guns, and by
eleven o'clock in the morning was ready for an advance. He
moved directly on the city without much impediment until he reached Bayou
Fourche, five miles from the town, where he was met by Marmaduke's
cavalry, dismounted, and two infantry brigades, with two batteries, strongly
posted. Price had undoubtedly intended to give battle in his trenches,
when the unexpected crossing of the river by the Nationals, endangering
his flank and his line of retreat, caused him to prepare for retiring.[2]
The stand made at the bayou was only a cover for the more important
movement. He was expecting Cabell from the Indian country, with about
four thousand men, but he was satisfied that these would not reach him
before the Nationals would be upon him.

  c Sept. 9, 10.

When Davidson was confronted at the Bayou Fourche, Steele was
moving in a parallel line on the north side of the river, and after the former
had been struggling nearly two hours with his foe, the latter opened upon
Marmaduke a heavy enfilading fire from across the stream. Hard pressed
in front and flank, the Confederates fell slowly back toward the city, where
columns of black smoke indicated the evacuation of the place. Seeing this,
Davidson ordered a vigorous advance by Glover's brigade, and then a charge
by Ritter's brigade (which had been held in reserve) and Strange's battery,
supported by a part of the First Iowa Cavalry. This was done with the
most abundant success. The Confederates broke, and fled through the city,
closely followed by the Union cavalry, sabers in hand. At seven o'clock
that evening,[d] when Steele and his immediate followers were
occupying the Confederate works on the north side of the river,

  d Sept. 10.

---

[1] Little Rock is on the right bank of the Arkansas River, about three hundred miles from its mouth, and
over a thousand miles, in a direct line, from the National capital. It is upon a high, rocky bluff, nearly two hundred feet above the river; and it contained, when the war broke out, nearly five thousand inhabitants. There
was a National Arsenal and the State Penitentiary there.

[2] Price's line of retreat was on the Arkadelphia road. On that highway he had six hundred wagons parked.
Price, with General Holmes and Governor Flanagan, left about four o'clock, after turning over the command
to Marmaduke. The entire force at Price's command was estimated at about fifteen thousand men.

opposite Little Rock, the city and its military appurtenances were formally surrendered to Davidson by the civil authorities. The troops had all fled in hot haste toward Arkadelphia, on the Washita River. A pursuing column was organized, but the National forces, men and horses, were too much exhausted to chase with vigor, and they followed the fugitives only about twenty miles. Steele's army, at the end of a campaign of forty days from the time he reached Helena, quietly took possession of the capital of Arkansas. It saved three pontoon bridges which Price had fired, and found the National Arsenal, which he intended to blow up, unharmed,[1] but eight steamers (one of them a powerful gun-boat, just receiving her iron plating) were in flames and beyond recovery when the National troops entered the city.

While Steele was engaged in his short campaign, Blunt was in the Indian country, trying to bring the forces of Cabell and the Creek chief, Standwatie,[2] to battle. He pressed them closely at Perryville, in the Choctaw Reservation, late in August, and then driving them past Fort Smith, he took peaceable possession of that post,[a] and appointed Colonel J. M. Johnson, of the First Arkansas, its commander. Cabell had avoided Blunt, in order to join and help Price in his defense of Little Rock. He failed to do so, but joined the fugitives in their retreat to Arkadelphia, whence, with Price, he fell back to the Red River. About a month after Blunt took possession of Fort Smith, he was on his way to that post from Kansas, with a small escort of cavalry (about one hundred Wisconsin and Kansas men), when he was attacked[b] near Baxter's Spring's, in the Cherokee Reservation, by six hundred guerrillas, under the notorious Quantrell. Nearly the whole of Blunt's escort who remained to fight[3] were killed or disabled in the battle. The wounded were murdered, and an accompanying train of wagons was plundered and burned. Blunt rallied a little more than a dozen of his guard, and, by skillful movements and great personal courage, they managed to escape.[4] Quantrell then attacked a weak post close by, called Fort Blair, commanded by a few men, under Lieutenant Pond, of the Third Wisconsin Cavalry. The guerrillas were beaten off, with a loss of about thirty men, and that night Blunt and his companions, who had been concealed several hours in the prairie, made their way to the little fort.

The Confederates in the Indian country and on its borders found their supplies of food running low as the autumn advanced, and so, at about the time we have just been considering, a part of Cabell's command, under Colonel Shelby, undertook a raid into Missouri, in quest of supplies. They crossed the Arkansas River a little eastward of Fort Smith, and swept rapidly northward into Southwestern Missouri, where, at a place called

a Sept. 1, 1863.

b October 4.

---

[1] Steele reported his own losses in action during this short campaign at about one hundred men, killed, wounded, and prisoners, while he captured about one thousand prisoners. But the National loss by sickness was very heavy—not less, probably, than two thousand men.

[2] See page 214.

[3] Blunt reported that some of his escort behaved most shamefully—flying without firing a shot; and declared that if they had acted like soldiers, the assailants could have been driven in ten minutes.

[4] Among the killed was Major Curtis, son of General S. R. Curtis; also Mr. O'Neil, an artist employed by Frank Leslie, the publisher of an illustrated weekly paper in New York. The band wagon was captured, and all of the musicians were murdered after they were made prisoners. General Blunt estimated the number of his killed at about seventy-five.

Crooked Prairie, they were joined[a] by a considerable force under Colonel Coffey, when Shelby, the ranking officer, found himself at the head of about twenty-five hundred men. They marched rapidly through Western Missouri to Boonville,[1] on the Missouri River, expecting to be joined in large numbers and gladly assisted by the disloyal inhabitants of that region. But they were disappointed. Under the menace of the lash of the loyal militia of the commonwealth, the resident rebels were very quiet, and Shelby beat a hasty retreat, but not in time to avoid a severe blow from a militia force hastily gathered by General E. B. Brown. By these Shelby was severely struck on the evening of the 12th of October, near Arrow Rock. Darkness put an end to the contest that night, but it was renewed at eight o'clock in the morning, and lasted about five hours, when Shelby was driven in great disorder, with a loss of about three hundred men, killed, wounded, and prisoners, with all his artillery but one gun, and baggage.

[a] October 1, 1863.

General McNeil, whose head-quarters were at Lebanon, was in St. Louis, when he heard of Shelby's raid. He hastened back to camp, gathered what men he could, and hurried in a direction to intercept the fugitives. He reached Humansville, in Polk County, just as they had passed through it, closely pursued by others. There the guerrillas lost their remaining gun. McNeil joined in the chase, which led into Arkansas, the Confederates flying through Huntsville, in Madison County, and over the Buffalo mountains to Clarksville, in Johnson County. There McNeil halted, for the more nimble-footed guerrillas had crossed the Arkansas River, and disappeared. McNeil then marched leisurely up the river to Fort Smith, and, in obedience to authority, assumed the command of the Army of the Frontier, in place of General Blunt, who had been relieved.

There was now general quiet throughout Missouri and Arkansas. One or two guerrilla bands showed some vitality, and late in October Marmaduke made an effort to capture Pine Bluff, the capital of Jefferson County, a post on the south side of the Arkansas River, fifty miles below Little Rock, then in command of Colonel Powell Clayton, of the Fifth Kansas, with three hundred and fifty men and four guns. Marmaduke marched from Princeton, forty-five miles south of Pine Bluff, with over two thousand men and twelve guns. He advanced[b] upon the post in three columns, and opened upon the little town with shells and canister-shot. He met unexpected resistance. Clayton had been re-enforced by the First Indiana Cavalry, which made his effective fighting force about six hundred men and nine light guns. He had also employed two hundred negroes in building barricades of cotton-bales in the streets, so that he was well protected from Marmaduke's fire. The conflict was kept up for about five hours. The court-house and many dwellings were burned by the shells, and a greater portion of the remaining buildings were sadly shattered by them. At two o'clock in the afternoon Marmaduke gave up the attack and retired, with a loss of one hundred and fifty men killed and wounded and thirty-three prisoners. Clayton's loss was fifty-seven, of whom seventeen were killed.

[b] October 25.

---

[1] See page 540, volume I.

Later in the year, a motley horde of white and red marauders, composed of the united forces of Quantrell and Standwatie, the Creek chief, attacked one of Colonel Phillips's outposts, near Fort Gibson,[a] in the Indian Territory. A contest of over four hours ensued, when the assailants were repulsed and driven across the Arkansas River. After that there was no fighting of importance in all the region between the Red and Missouri rivers for some time.

[a] Dec. 18, 1863.

Let us now observe what occurred farther southward in the region west of the Mississippi, over which General N. P. Banks held control, as commander of the Gulf Department.

When Banks suddenly withdrew from Alexandria, on the Red River, and marched to invest Port Hudson—a service which required nearly all of his available troops—General Dick Taylor, whom he had driven into the wilds of Western Louisiana,[1] took heart, and soon reappeared with about four thousand followers, including a large number of Texas cavalry. He reoccupied Alexandria and Opelousas, and garrisoned Fort de Russy, early in June. He then swept rapidly through the State, over the

FORT DE RUSSY.

route he had been driven a few weeks before, and pushed toward New Orleans, hoping to find it sufficiently weak in defenders to allow him to capture it, or at least by his menace to draw Banks from Port Hudson, to defend it.

Banks's outposts were drawn into Brashear City, where there seems to have been very little preparation made for a defense of that important interior post, and the vast amount of National property collected there. Even its only railway communication with New Orleans appears to have been strangely undefended, and it was not until word suddenly reached Lieutenant-Colonel Stickney, in command at Brashear, that the Confederates had struck the road at La Fourche Crossing, near Thibodeaux, that a suspicion of danger in that quarter was entertained. Stickney at once hastened with the greater portion of his command to oppose that dangerous movement, and in so doing he left Brashear exposed. Taylor's troops found little difficulty in raiding all over the country between Brashear and the Mississippi at New Orleans. They captured little posts here and there; and some Texans, dashing into Plaquemine,[b] on the Mississippi, captured some convales-cent prisoners, and burnt four steamers, seventy-five bales of cotton, and a barge. At the same time a co-operating force, under the

[b] June 18.

Confederate Generals Green and Mouton, appeared on the site of Berwick, a small village opposite Brashear, which Lieutenant Ryder, in command of a gun-boat, had bombarded and burnt a little while before. The weak garrison in Fort Buchanan, at Brashear, was then in command of a sick colonel, and illy prepared for an attack. Major Hunter, with three hundred and twenty-five Texans, crossed the bayou below it, and assailed and carried the fort[a] in a few minutes. Ryder had fled with his gun-boat on the approach of danger, and before ten o'clock on the day of the capture, Taylor and Green, Mouton and Hunter, were in conference in Brashear as victors, with one thousand prisoners, a strong fort mounting ten guns, and a large amount of small-arms, munitions, stores, and other National property, the whole valued at full $2,000,000. By this calamity about five thousand refugee negroes were seized and remanded into slavery worse than they had endured before.

June 24, 1863.

Meanwhile the Confederates had struggled with the Forty-seventh Massachusetts, under Stickney, for the possession of La Fourche Crossing. They attacked[b] the little force with great vigor, and were repulsed. They renewed the assault the next day, and were again repulsed, with a loss, in both actions, of nearly three hundred men, killed, wounded, and made prisoners. Finding the Confederates in heavy force in his rear, Stickney evacuated the post and withdrew to New Orleans, leaving the way open for the foe to Algiers, opposite that city.

[b] June 20.

Four days after the capture of Brashear City, General Green attempted to seize Fort Butler, at Donaldsonville,[1] by a midnight assault. The fort was garrisoned by two hundred and twenty-five men of the Twenty-eighth Maine, under Major Bullen, who were assisted in the fight by the gun-boats *Winona*, *Kineo*, and *Princess Royal*, the latter a captured British blockade runner. The assailants were repulsed with a loss of over three hundred men, of whom one hundred and twenty-four were prisoners. Three weeks later,[c] General Green, with a superior force, attacked the advanced brigade of General Grover, commanded by General Dudley, about six miles in the rear of Donaldsonville, and drove them back with some loss at first, but the Nationals, in turn, with the assistance of reserves, drove the Confederates, and on the following day the latter commenced their retreat from La Fourche District.[2] This was almost the last struggle of Taylor's troops in the vicinity of the Mississippi at that time, for Banks's forces, released by the fall of Port Hudson, quickly expelled the Confederates from the region eastward of the Atchafalaya. Although New Orleans was garrisoned by only about seven hundred men when the way was opened for Taylor to Algiers, he dared not attempt the capture of that city, because of the war vessels of Farragut that were watching the broad bosom of the stream over which he would be compelled to pass, and the facility with which troops might be brought down from Port Hudson. Before the close of July, Taylor had evacuated Brashear City[d] (but not until he had secured every thing valuable, and burned every thing else combustible), and retired to Opelousas and Alexandria.

[c] July 12.

[d] July 22.

---

[1] See page 528, volume II.

[2] *History of the One Hundred and Fourteenth Regiment New York State Volunteers*, by Brevet-Major E. P. Pellet, page 135.

General Banks now turned his thoughts to aggressive movements. He was visited early in September by General Grant, and the two commanders united in an earnest expression of a desire to make a movement, with their combined forces, on Mobile, the only place of importance then held by the Confederates on the Gulf eastward of the Mississippi. Influential loyalists from Texas, then in Washington, had the ear of the Government, and were strongly urging an attempt to "repossess" that State by force of arms. The Government yielded to their desires, and Banks was ordered to move for the conquest of Texas, in a way according to the dictates of his own judgment, but with the suggestion that the most feasible route would be by the Red River to Natchitoches and Shreveport. Banks believed that route to be impracticable at that season of the year, so, in the exercise of his discretionary powers, he fitted out an expedition to make a lodgment on Texas soil at Sabine City, at the Sabine Pass.[1] There was the terminus of a railway leading into the heart of Eastern Texas, and which was crossed by another leading to Houston, the capital of that State.[2] For the purpose of making such lodgment, four thousand disciplined troops were placed under the command of General Franklin as leader, who was instructed to land them a few miles below Sabine Pass, and then move directly upon Confederate works, if any were found there and occupied. Admiral Farragut detailed a naval force of four gun-boats to form a part of the expedition. These were commanded by Lieutenant Frederick Crocker, who made the *Clifton* his flag-ship.[3] The expedition sailed on the 5th of September.

Instead of following his instructions, to land his troops below Sabine Pass, Franklin arranged with Crocker to have the gun-boats make a direct attack upon the Confederate works, without landing the troops until the garrison should be expelled, and two gun-boats, which it was understood were there, should be captured or driven up the river, when the business of the soldiers would be to go ashore and take possession. For this operation about one hundred and fifty sharp-shooters were taken from the army and distributed among the vessels.

Early in the forenoon of the 8th of September, the gun-boats and transports crossed the bar at Sabine Pass, and in the afternoon the *Clifton*, *Sachem*, and *Arizona*, went up two separate channels to attack the fort (which mounted eight heavy guns, three of them rifled), leaving the *Granite City* to cover the landing of a division of troops, under General Weitzel, at a proper time. The Confederate garrison was ready for them, the expedition having been in sight for twenty-eight hours, and when the three gun-boats were abreast the fort they received a fire from the whole eight guns on shore. The boilers of the *Clifton* and *Arizona* were penetrated by shells, and the vessels, instantly enveloped in scalding steam, displayed white flags

---

[1] This is the name of the outlet from Sabine Lake into the Gulf of Mexico. Sabine Lake is an expansion of the Sabine River, about five miles from its entrance into the Gulf of Mexico at the southwest extremity of Louisiana, between which State and that of Texas the Sabine River, for a long distance, forms the boundary line.

[2] Banks felt certain that by a successful movement at this point he might speedily concentrate full 15,000 men at Houston, which would place in his hands the control of all the railway communications of Texas, and the most populous part of the State, and enable him to move into the interior in any direction, or fall back upon Galveston, thus leaving the army free to move upon Mobile.

[3] The flotilla consisted of the *Clifton*, Lieutenant Crocker; *Sachem*, Lieutenant Amos Johnson; *Arizona*, Acting-Master H. Tibbetts; and *Granite City*, Acting-Master C. W. Samson—all light-draft vessels.

and surrendered. Twenty minutes after the attack, the two vessels were in tow of Confederate steamers—small bay craft that had been converted into rams. The *Arizona* ran aground, and Franklin, seeing the naval force suddenly disabled, made no serious attempt to land, but, with the transports and the grounded vessel, which floated at midnight, hastened over the bar and returned to New Orleans. He left behind him, as trophies for the Confederates, two hundred men as prisoners, fifty killed and wounded,[1] and two gun-boats, with fifteen heavy rifled guns. Loudly the Texans shouted because of this victory, and with good reason, for the garrison of the fort which repulsed four gun-boats and four thousand land troops consisted of

JEFF. DAVIS MEDAL.

only about two hundred men. Of these, only forty-two were present and participated in the action. These were mostly Irishmen, whose little company was called the "Davis Guards." For their achievement on that occasion, Jefferson Davis presented each soldier with a little silver medal, the only honor of the kind known to have been bestowed by the Conspirators upon their servants during the war.[2] Had Franklin landed a major's command for action, the squad in the fort might have been easily driven away by them, and Houston, only forty miles distant, and flanking Galveston, might have been captured, for General Washburne, with a force equal to Franklin's, was ready at Brashear City to co-operate with the latter.

After the failure of Franklin's expedition, and the notification given by it to the Confederates of the intention of the Nationals, it was impracticable to renew the effort there. Banks, therefore, concentrated his forces on the Atchafalaya, with the intention of marching directly on Shreveport. He soon perceived that it would be almost impossible to do so. The country to be traversed, after leaving the railway, was exhausted, having been overrun by both armies. A great drouth was drying up the springs; and over the bad roads through that flat region, liable at that season to being drowned by sudden rains, he could not carry in wagons, full four hundred miles, sufficient supplies of food and forage. So he abandoned the attempt, and determined to grasp Texas by the throat, as it were, by seizing and holding the harbors on its coast.

---

[1] Among the killed, by the steam, was Lieutenant Robert Rhodes, of the navy. Of the killed, wounded, and captured, were ninety of the sharp-shooters of the army.

[2] This medal, the appearance of which is given in the above engraving, the exact size of the original, was made of a thin plate of silver, with the initials of "Davis Guards" and a Maltese cross rudely engraved on one side, and the place and date of the achievement on the other. The original, from which the drawing was made, is in the possession of Thomas L. Thornell, of New York City, to whom it was presented by an officer who received it from one of the Guards. The writer is indebted for its use to the courtesy of his friend, Henry T. Drowne, of New York.

In the mean time, Taylor, still westward of the Atchafalaya, became quite active. His most efficient leader, General Green, was particularly so, and made occasional raids toward the Mississippi. "Bushwhackers," as armed residents of the country were called, were continually annoying vessels at sharp turns in the river, in the vicinity of Port Hudson, and General Herron was sent to Morgansia to suppress these gangs of annoyers. An out-post was established several miles in the interior, held by the Nineteenth Iowa and Twenty-sixth Indiana, with two guns, under Colonel Lake, supported by one hundred and fifty cavalry under Colonel Montgomery. The whole number of men at the post was less than one thousand. These were surprised on a dark night by General Green, who stealthily crossed a bayou,[a] surrounded the camp, and captured the guns and a large portion of the infantry. Lake and about four hundred of his men became prisoners. Fifty-four were killed and wounded. The cavalry escaped with a loss of five men. _{a Sept. 30, 1863.}

A month later the Unionists of that region suffered another disaster. In order to mask his expedition against Texas by sea, Banks ordered General C. C. Washburne to advance from Brashear upon Opelousas, to give the impression that a march upon Alexandria or Shreveport was begun. Washburne reached Opelousas without resistance, but when, in obedience to orders, he commenced falling back, Taylor and Green pursued him closely. Finally, they swept[b] stealthily, swiftly, and unexpectedly, out of a thick wood, and fell upon Washburne's right, held by General Burbridge. So little was an attack suspected, that the Twenty-third Wisconsin were engaged in voting for State officers.[1] Before the men could seize their arms and form for battle they were terribly smitten. The regiment was quickly reduced from two hundred and twenty-six men to ninety-eight, most of them made prisoners. The right, on which the weight of the attack fell, was broken, and the utter ruin of the whole force seemed at one time certain. General McGinnis brought up some troops, and these, and a few others, with Nims's battery, saved the day. The Confederates were driven to the shelter of the woods, and Washburne pursued his way to Brashear with his shattered force.[2] _{b Nov. 3.}

In the mean time Banks's expedition, consisting of six thousand troops and some war-vessels, had sailed[c] from New Orleans, directly for the Rio Grande. It was accompanied by that officer in person, but was immediately commanded by General Napoleon J. T. Dana. On the 2d of November the troops debarked at Brazos Santiago, drove a small cavalry force stationed there, and followed them to Brownsville, thirty miles up the river, which Banks's advance entered on the 6th.[d] Point Isabel was taken possession of on the 8th; and as soon as possible Banks, who made his head-quarters at Brownsville, sent as many troops as he could spare, up the coast, to seize and occupy the water passes between the Rio Grande and Galveston. By the aid of steamers obtained on the Rio Grande, troops were transported to Mustang Island, off Corpus _{c October 26.} _{d November.}

---

[1] Several of the States provided for the voting of the troops in the field, so that citizens, fighting for their country away from home, should not be deprived of the sacred right of choosing their rulers.

[2] The Union loss was 716 men, of whom 26 were killed and over 500 were made prisoners. The Confederates lost over 400, of whom 60 were killed.

Christi Bay, from which a force, under General T. E. G. Ransom, went to
the Aranzas Pass, farther up the coast, and by a gallant assault [a]
carried the Confederate works there, and captured one hundred
prisoners.   Corpus Christi was occupied by National troops the
same day.   Then a force, under General Washburne (then commanding the
Thirteenth Army Corps), moved upon Pass Cavallo, at the entrance to Matagorda Bay, where the Confederates had a strong fort, called Esperanza, garrisoned by two thousand men of all arms.   It was invested, and, after a
sharp action, the Confederates blew up their magazine and fled, [b]
most of the garrison escaping.

> [a] Nov. 18, 1863.

> [b] Nov. 30.

These important conquests, achieved in the space of a month, promised a
speedy closing of the coast of Texas to blockade-runners, and great advantage to the Union cause in that region.   No place of importance on that
coast was now left to the Confederates, excepting at the mouth of the
Brazos and on Galveston Island, at each of which they had formidable works;
and a greater portion of their troops in Texas, commanded by General
Magruder, were concentrated on the coast, between Houston, Galveston, and
Indianola.   Banks was anxious to follow up his successes by moving on
Indianola, on the west side of Matagorda Bay, or upon Matagorda, at the
mouth of the Colorado.   This would have brought him into collision with a
greater portion of Magruder's troops.   He did not feel strong enough to
undertake a task so perilous.   He asked for re-enforcements, but they could
not be furnished, and at about the close of the year he returned to New
Orleans, leaving General Dana on the Rio Grande.   That officer sent a force
more than a hundred miles up that river, and another toward Corpus Christi,
but they found no armed Confederates; and when, by order of General
Banks, he left the Rio Grande and took post at Pass Cavallo, [c] he
found some National troops in quiet possession of Indianola and
of the Matagorda Peninsula, on the opposite side of the bay.

> [c] Jan. 12, 1864.

The Confederates had withdrawn to Galveston; and all Texas, west of the
Colorado, was abandoned by them.   With a small additional force Banks
might have driven them from Galveston, and secured a permanent military
occupation of the State.

It remains for us now, in considering the military events west of the Mississippi, to the close of 1863, only to take a glance at the trouble with the
Indians, toward the head-waters of that stream, in the State of Minnesota.   As
these troubles had no immediate connection with the war, further than in
drawing some troops from the grand theaters of strife, we must be content
with only a brief passing note of the events.

At midsummer, 1862, bands of the warlike Sioux Indians, in the State of
Minnesota, made open war upon the white people in that region.   It is not
positively known by what special motive, or under what particular influence
they were impelled; and the suspicion that they were incited to hostilities
by emissaries of the Conspirators, with the hope of thereby causing a large
number of troops fighting the rebellion to be drawn away to a distant point,
rests only upon conjecture.   The fact is, that a Sioux chief, named Little
Crow, a most saintly-looking savage in civilized costume, was the most conspicuous of the leaders in the inauguration of the war, by the butchery of
the white inhabitants at Yellow Medicine, New Ulm, and Cedar City, in

Minnesota, in August and September,[a] and at outposts beyond the boundaries of that State. For nine days in October the Indians besieged Fort Ridgeley. Fort Abercrombie was also besieged, [a] 1862.
and twice assaulted by the savages; and in that region they butchered about five hundred white inhabitants, consisting mostly of defenseless women and children.

General H. H. Sibley, with a body of militia, was sent to crush the Indians, but the latter were too numerous to suffer more than partial disasters here and there. Sibley attacked a large force of Indians, under Little Crow, at Wood Lake, and drove them into Dakota, with a loss of five hundred of their number made prisoners. These were tried by court-martial, and three hundred of them were found guilty and sentenced to be hanged. Their execution was stayed by the President. Finally, thirty-seven of the worst offenders were hanged at Markato,[b] and the [b] Feb. 28, 1863.
remainder were released. But the "Sioux War" was not ended until the following summer,[c] when General Pope took command [c] 1863.
of the Department, picketed the line of settlements in the far Northwest with two thousand soldiers, and took vigorous measures to disperse the hostile bands. In June, Sibley moved westward from Fort Snelling, and General Sully went up the Missouri River to co-operate with him. Both fought and drove the savages at different places, and finally scattered them among the wilds of the eastern slopes of the spurs of the Rocky Mountains.[1]

Our horror and indignation because of the atrocities committed from time to time by the savage tribes on the borders of civilization, should be somewhat tempered by the reflection, that these may be logical and righteous retributions for wrongs committed by the Government in its dealings with the Indians, which, unfortunately, fall upon individuals. It is believed that the origin of nine-tenths of the troubles with the Indians may be traced directly to the agents of the Government in their dealings with these ignorant and confiding children of the forest. Such being the acknowledged fact, the important question arises, whether it would not be wiser and more humane to incorporate all the nations and tribes of Indians into the body politic of each State and Territory in which they exist, and hold each individual amenable to the laws, as a citizen. An army of officials might thus be dispensed with, the chief causes of irritation be removed, and the work of civilizing and Christianizing of the savages be greatly facilitated.

---

[1] Little Crow, the "foremost hunter and orator" of the Sioux, was shot near Hutchinson, in Minnesota, by Mr. Lamson, while the chief was picking blackberries. His skeleton is preserved in the collections of the Minnesota Historical Society. It is said that Little Crow (whose Indian name was Tah-o-ah-ta-doo-tah, "his scarlet people") was urged into making war against his better judgment. For a full account of this "Indian trouble," see *History of the Sioux War*, by Isaac V. D. Heard.

CHAPTER VIII.

CIVIL AFFAIRS IN 1863.—MILITARY OPERATIONS BETWEEN THE MOUNTAINS AND THE
MISSISSIPPI RIVER.

EFORE proceeding to a consideration of military affairs in 1864, let us take a brief glance at the aspect of civil affairs at the beginning of that year.

The management of the finances of the nation was yet in the able hands of Secretary Chase; and so fully did the people and Congress confide in his judgment and patriotism, that his suggestions were generally accepted as eminently wise, and the measures he proposed were usually carried into execution. From the day when he assumed the duties of Minister of Finance, and his plans began to develop, the public credit became stronger every hour; and at the time we are considering, when the public debt had reached the appalling sum of over a thousand million dollars, the great war in full career, and that debt increasing enormously every day, the public credit, especially among the people of this country, had never stood higher. "The history of the world," said the Secretary, a year later, when he had been fully sustained by the people, " may be searched in vain for a parallel case of popular financial support to a National Government."[1]

When Congress met in December, 1862, Secretary Chase laid before them a statement and estimate which would have appalled the representatives of a less hopeful people. He reported, that, on account of greatly increased expenditures, there remained a balance of disbursements to the amount of nearly two hundred and seventy-seven million dollars, for which provision must be made; and he asked for an additional sum to meet the estimated expenditures of the Government to the close of the fiscal year, at the end of June, 1864, which would make the whole sum to be provided for, for the next eighteen months, more than nine hundred million dollars.[2] The important question, How is this vast sum to be provided? had to be met. The able Minister of Finance was ready with an answer. Keeping in mind the four objects in view which had controlled his action up to that time, namely, " moderate interest, general distribution, future controllability, and incidental utility," he now renewed propositions which he had already made, and recommended two immediate measures of safety, in connection with a

---

[1] Annual Report, December, 1863.
[2] The National debt on the first of July, 1863, was $1,098,793,181. It was estimated that at the same period in 1864 it would be $1,686,956,190. The average rate of interest on the whole debt, without regard to the varying margin between coin and notes, had been reduced from 4·36 per cent., on the first of July, 1862, to 3·77 per cent. on the first of July, 1863.

scheme for establishing a system of National bank paper. One of these was to drive home, by a tax, the State bank paper circulation, and the other was the funding of Government notes.

The Secretary proposed a moderate tax on the State bank circulation; that no issue of Government notes beyond the limits authorized should be made, unless a clear public exigency should demand it; the organization of banking associations for the improvement of the public credit, and to supply the public with a safe and uniform currency; and the repeal of restrictions concerning the conversion of certain Government bonds. To these proposi- tions Congress responded, first by authorizing[a] an additional issue of $100,000,000 of Government notes; then by an act, ap- [a] January 17, 1864. proved on the 25th of February, to provide a National currency through a National banking system; then by another, approved on the last day of the session,[b] authorizing the Secretary to issue $300,000,000 [b] March 3. for the current fiscal year, and $600,000,000 for the next fiscal year, ending June 30, 1864. These amounts were to be issued in " 10-40" bonds, at six per cent. interest, both principal and interest to be paid in coin. The Secretary was authorized to exchange the same for certificates of indebt- edness or deposit, any Treasury notes or lawful money of the United States. He was also authorized to issue $400,000,000 of six per cent. Treasury notes, payable within three years, to be a legal tender for their face value, exclud- ing interest, and exchangeable for and redeemable by Government notes, for which purpose alone $150,000,000 of the latter was authorized. He was given authority, also, to issue $150,000,000 Government notes, including the $100,000,000 authorized in January; also to issue $50,000,000 of fractional notes, in lieu of the postage and revenue stamps, for fractional currency. He was also authorized to receive deposits of gold coin and bullion, and to issue certificates therefor; and to issue certificates representing coin in the Treas- ury, in payment of interest, which, with the certificates of deposits issued, should not exceed twenty per cent. beyond the amount of coin and bullion in the Treasury. A tax of one per cent. half-yearly was imposed on the cir- culation of the State banks.

Such was one of the provisions of Congress, made early in 1864, for carrying on the war vigorously. These acts concerning the finances were followed by an immediate revival of the public credit,[1] and within two months after the adjournment of Congress,[c] the whole mass [c] March 4. of suspended requisitions had been satisfied, all current demands promptly met, and full provision made for the pay of the army and navy.

The Confederates, at the beginning of 1864, were sadly straitened, financially. The fiscal agent of the Conspirators (Memminger) reported their public debt, in round numbers, at $1,000,000,000, of which $800,000,000 were treasury notes, with a prospective increase, at the end of 1864, to about $2,510,000,000. The currency in circulation amounted to $600,000,000, and was so depreciated that the Conspirators could see nothing ahead but ruin,

---

[1] So confident were the loyal people in their ability to put down the rebellion, and the consequent assurance of the stability of their Government, that on the first of May, or only two months after Congress adjourned, they had loaned to the Government $169,000,000; and at the end of the fiscal year, the Secretary of the Treasury had the gratification to see that the disbursements did not greatly exceed his estimates, and that the increase of the public debt did not equal his estimates.

unless a change in their system of finance might be adopted. Davis declared that there was no other remedy than a "compulsory reduction of the currency to the amount required by the business of the country." To do this, it was proposed to substitute for the outstanding notes, interest-bearing bonds, which the holders of the currency would be obliged to take in exchange, to render their property of any possible value. Memminger, at the same time, told the victims of his financial mismanagement, that the "Government" found itself "unable to comply with the letter of its engagement," and with this assurance he offered his bonds to the people.

These bonds, as well as all other "Government" securities issued by the Conspirators, never had a really substantial basis, and were now avoided by every sensible person in the Confederacy, as far as possible. Through the grossest misrepresentations by the Confederate agents abroad, European capitalists were induced to take their bonds to the amount of $15,000,000, their payment professedly secured by the sales of cotton, to be sent to England. These bonds were eagerly sought after by confiding and hopeful Englishmen, who sympathized with the Conspirators, and a large number of the members of the "Southern Independence Association"[1] became heavy holders of the worthless paper.

The Confederate currency, at the close of 1863, had become so nearly worthless, that it was sold at four and six cents on the dollar, and the prices of every necessary of life to be purchased with it, ruled correspondingly. Producers, such as agriculturists, were unwilling to exchange their products for the detested stuff, and starvation for the army was threatened. In consequence of this state of things, the "Congress" at Richmond proceeded with a high hand, and, as we have seen, authorized the seizure of supplies for the troops.[2] Had not the despotic heel of the Conspirators been firmly planted on the necks of the people, a revolution would have followed. As it was, no man dared to murmur audibly. At the same time the railways in the Confederacy were rapidly decaying, and means for transportation were hourly decreasing, while the blockade, rendered more and more stringent by the repossession of sea-ports by the Government, diminished supplies of every kind from abroad. The country in the vicinity of the great armies was stripped, and poverty and want stalked over the land. The distress of the people was very great and almost universal, while favored officers of the "Government," having large ownership in blockade-runners, were living on luxuries brought from Europe and the islands of the sea, and growing rich at the expense of the suffering people.[3]

---

[1] See page 46.   [2] See page 97.

[3] Among the members of "Congress" at Richmond, who were not favorites of Jefferson Davis, and consequently not allowed to share in the good things of the "court," was Henry S. Foote, formerly United States Senator, and then misrepresenting Tennessee at the Confederate capital. His wife, in a letter to a friend, on the 6th of February, 1863, gives us a glimpse of the hardships endured by the "common folk" of the "ruling classes" in Richmond. After saying that her little boy had been named "Malvern," by his papa, "after the Battle-ground of Malvern Hills," and that "he spits at Yankee pictures and makes wry faces at old Abe's picture," she said: "We are boarding at Mrs. Johnson's, in Governor Street, just opposite Governor Letcher's mansion. It is a large boarding-house, high prices and starvation within. Such living was never known before on earth. We have to cook almost every thing we eat, in our own room. In *our* 'larder' the stock on hand is a boiled bacon ham, which we gave only $11 for; three pounds of pure Rio coffee, we gave $4 a pound for, and one pound of green tea, $17 per pound; two pounds of brown sugar, at $2.75 per pound; one bushel of fine apples, about the size of a good common marble, which were presented to me by a member from Missouri; one pound of butter, about six months old, at $2 per pound, and six sweet potatoes, at 50 cents. We have to give a dollar for a very small slice of pound-cake at the confectioner's. . . . . . Yesterday, for dinner, we had nothing on the table

Notwithstanding these disabilities, and the fading away of every hope of recognition by foreign governments, or the moral support of any civilized people, the Conspirators at Richmond, holding the reins of despotic power with firm grasp, resolved to carry on the war regardless of consequences to their deluded and abused victims.[1] The Emancipation Proclamation "fired the Southern heart" somewhat, and, for a time, strengthened the power of the Conspirators. It produced great exasperation, and led to the authorization of cruel retaliatory measures by the Confederate "Congress," on the recommendation of Jefferson Davis.[2] The most flagrant misrepresentations were put forth as solemn truths, in order to inflame the passions of the people at home and excite the sympathies of those abroad. In this work Confederate clergymen were not ashamed to appear conspicuous. Ninety-six persons of that class signed an "Address to Christians throughout the World," which was sent out from Richmond in April, 1863, in which, after asserting that the Union could not be restored, said they considered the President's proclamation of freedom to the slaves a "suitable occasion for a solemn protest on the part of the people of God, throughout the world." Then, without a shadow of truth, they, like the chief Conspirator, charged Mr. Lincoln with intending to produce a general insurrection of the slaves,[3] and solemnly declared that such insurrection "would make it *absolutely necessary for the public safety that the slaves be slaughtered.*"

The advice of more sagacious men in Confederate councils was heeded, through fear of consequences; and threats of vengeance and retaliation were seldom executed. The most serious result, in this regard, of the President's Proclamation, was the suspension, for a time, of the exchange of captives, in consequence of the Confederate authorities refusing to recognize Negro soldiers as legitimate and exchangeable prisoners of war.[4] The Government took the just ground, that it would give equal protection to *all* its soldiers, and, at the close of July,[a] the President issued an order to that effect, in which he declared, in allusion to a threat to reduce negro captives to bondage, that if the Confederates should sell or enslave any Union captive, in consequence of his color, the offense should be punished by retaliation upon the prisoners of the enemy.[5] The sad consequences of

[a] 1863.

---

but two eggs and a slice of cold baker's bread, and a glass of water." She added, in a postscript, that Jefferson Davis looked "care-worn and troubled." ' He is very thin," she said, "and looks feeble and bent. *He prays aloud in church,* and is a devout Episcopalian."

[1] See page 97.

[2] The portion of Davis's "Message" relating to retaliation was referred to the "Committee on Ways and Means." That committee reported to the "House" joint resolutions, which were adopted, by which full power was given to Davis to use retaliatory measures "in such manner and to such an extent as he might think proper." It was resolved that every commissioned white officer, who should be engaged in disciplining and leading freedmen as soldiers in fighting the Confederates, or in inciting slaves to rebel, should, if captured, "be put to death, or otherwise punished;" and that all negroes engaged in war or taken in arms, or known to give "aid and comfort to the enemy, should be delivered to State authorities," and dealt with in accordance with the sanguinary slave codes "of the State in which the offender should be caught." There were propositions to sell into slavery all free negroes who should be caught with arms in their hands, and to butcher all slaves guilty of such offense; but the more sensible members of the "Congress," plainly perceiving that such measures would be a two-edged sword that would cut both ways, took ground against them, and prevented the passage of many mischievous laws on that subject.

[3] See note 1, page 82.

[4] The *Richmond Examiner* revealed the secret reasons for refusing to treat negro soldiers as regular prisoners of war, when it said: "If we were insane enough to yield this point, to treat black men as the equals of white, and insurgent slaves as equivalent to our brave soldiers, *the very foundations of Slavery would be fatally wounded.*"

[5] "It is therefore ordered," said the President, "that for every soldier of the United States killed in viola-

the suspension of exchange fell heavily upon the Union captives, who suffered terribly in Confederate prisons. The story of their wrongs in that respect forms one of the darkest chapters in the history of crime.

In regard to the fiat of emancipation, the President stood firm. He did not recede a line from the original stand-point of his proclamation. It was the exponent of the future policy of the Government. Congress passed laws in consequence of it, and authorized the enlistment into the military service of the Republic of one hundred and fifty thousand negroes. The slave-holding Oligarchy raved. The voices of their organs, especially of those at Richmond, sounded like wails from Bedlam. The Peace Faction protested. They denounced every thing calculated to crush the rebellion to be "unconstitutional."[1] Yet the President and Congress went steadily forward in the path of duty prescribed by the necessities of the hour.[2] The successes of the National arms at Gettysburg and on the Mississippi gave the most strengthening encouragement. In the campaigns in the West, fifty thousand square miles of the National domain had been recovered from the Confederates before the middle of August, when the President said: "The signs look better. The Father of Waters again goes unvexed to the sea, thanks to the great Northwest for it. Nor yet wholly to them. Three hundred miles up, they met New England, Empire, Keystone, and Jersey, hewing their way right and left. The sunny South, too, in more colors than one, also lent a hand. On the spot their part of the history is jotted down in black and white. The job was a great National one, and let none be banned who bore an honorable part in it. And while those who have cleared the great river may well be proud, even that is not all. It is hard to say that any thing has been more bravely and better done than at Antietam, Murfreesboro', Gettysburg, and on many fields of lesser note. Nor must Uncle Sam's web-feet be forgotten. At all the waters' margins they have been present, not only on the deep sea, the broad bay, and the rapid river, but also up the narrow, muddy bayou, and wherever the ground was a little damp, they have been and made their tracks. Thanks to all! For the great Republic— for the principles by which it lives and keeps alive—for man's vast future, thanks to all! Peace does not appear so distant as it did. I hope it will come soon, and come to stay; and so come as to be worth the keeping in all future time. It will then have been proved that, among freemen, there can be no successful appeal from the ballot to the bullet, and that they who take such appeal are sure to lose their cause and pay the cost. And then there

---

tion of the laws of war, a rebel soldier shall be executed, and for every one enslaved by the enemy or sold into slavery, a rebel soldier shall be placed at hard labor on the public works, and continued at such labor until the other shall be released and receive the treatment due to a prisoner of war."

[1] To these he said: "You desire peace, and you blame me that we do not have it. But how can we obtain it? There are but three conceivable ways. First, to suppress the rebellion by force of arms. This I am trying to do. Are you for it? If you are, so we are agreed. If you are not for it, a second way is to give up the Union. I am against this. If you are, you should say so plainly. If you are not for force, nor yet for dissolution, there only remains some imaginary compromise. I do not believe that any compromise, embracing the maintenance of the Union, is now possible."

[2] William Whiting, the able Solicitor of the War Department (see page 558, volume II.), in a letter to a convention of colored citizens at Poughkeepsie, New York, at the close of July, said: "The policy of the Government is *fixed* and immovable. Abraham Lincoln takes no backward step. A man once made free by law cannot be again made a slave. The Government has no power, if it had the will, to do it. Omnipotence alone can re-enslave a freeman. Fear not the Administration will ever take the back track. The President wishes the aid of all Americans, of whatever descent or color, to defend the country. He wishes every citizen to share the perils of the contest and to reap the fruits of victory."

will be some black men who will remember that, with silent tongue, and clinched teeth, and steady eye, and well-poised bayonet, they have helped mankind on to this great consummation; while I fear there will be some white men unable to forget that, with malignant heart and deceitful speech, they have striven to hinder it. Still, let us not be over-sanguine of a speedy final triumph. Let us be quite sober. Let us diligently apply the means, never doubting that a just God, in his own good time, will give us the rightful result." [1]

Other encouraging " signs " soon appeared, and gave evidence of a determination of the loyal people to stand by the Government in its struggle with the assassin. That struggle had assumed, to the view of most thinking men, the grander features of a war for free institutions, rather than those of a strife for party supremacy, and thousands of the Opposition, impelled by patriotic emotions, refused longer to follow the leadings of the disloyal Peace Faction. When the autumn elections [c] had passed, it was found that the friends of the Government, who had spoken at the ballot-box, were in overwhelming majorities everywhere. The majorities of the Opposition the previous year [2] were wiped out, and the weight of their numbers appeared largely on the Republican or Union side. Ohio, as we have observed, gave over a hundred thousand majority against Vallandigham; and in New York, Governor Seymour's majority, of ten thousand in 1862, was annihilated, and a majority of nearly thirty thousand appeared on the opposite side of the political balance-sheet. Even in Maryland, where the emancipation of the slaves was made a distinct issue in the canvass, there was given a very large Union majority.

[c] 1863.

This political reaction, and the progress of the National armies in " repossessing " territory, emboldened the Government to take measures for prosecuting the war with great vigor in 1864. The reports of the Cabinet officers accompanying the President's first message to the new Congress [b] (XXXVIIIth), [3] were very encouraging. With the hope of weakening the moral as well as the material strength of the Confederates,

[b] Dec. 8.

---

[1] Letter of President Lincoln, dated August 26, 1863, and addressed to James M. Conkling, in answer to an invitation to attend a mass meeting of unconditional Union men, to be held at Springfield, Illinois.

[2] See page 18.

[3] There was a good working majority of Republicans and unconditional Unionists in the XXXVIIIth Congress. In the Senate there were 36 Unionists to 14 of the Opposition. In the House of Representatives there were 102 Unionists against 75 of the Opposition.

The following is a list of the members of the XXXVIIIth Congress, with the names of the States they severally represented :—

SENATE.

California.—John Conness, James A. McDougall. *Connecticut.*—James Dixon, Lafayette S. Foster. *Delaware.*—George Read Riddle, Willard Saulsbury. *Illinois.*—W. A. Richardson, Lyman Trumbull. *Indiana.*—Thomas A. Hendricks, Henry S. Lane. *Iowa.*—James W. Grimes, James Harlan. *Kansas.*—James H. Lane, Samuel C. Pomeroy. *Kentucky.*—Lazarus W. Powell, Garrett Davis. *Maine.*—Lot M. Morrill, William P. Fessenden. *Maryland.*—Reverdy Johnson, Thomas H. Hicks. *Massachusetts.*—Charles Sumner, Henry Wilson. *Michigan.*—Zachary Chandler, Jacob M. Howard. *Minnesota.*—Alexander Ramsay, M. S. Wilkinson. *Missouri.*—B. Gratz Brown, J. B. Henderson. *New Hampshire.*—John P. Hale, Daniel Clarke. *New Jersey.*—William Wright, John C. Ten Eyck. *New York.*—Edwin D. Morgan, Ira Harris. *Ohio.*—Benjamin F. Wade, John Sherman. *Oregon.*—Benjamin F. Harding, G. W. Nesmith. *Pennsylvania.*—Charles R. Buckalew, Edward Cowan. *Rhode Island.*—William Sprague, Henry B. Anthony. *Vermont.*—Solomon Foot, Jacob Collamer. *Virginia.*—John S. Carlile. *West Virginia.*—Waitman T. Willey, P. G. Van Winkle. *Wisconsin.*—James R. Doolittle, Timothy O. Howe. HANNIBAL HAMLIN, Vice-President of the Republic and President of the Senate.

HOUSE OF REPRESENTATIVES.

California.—Thomas B. Shannon, William Higbee, Cornelius Cole. *Connecticut.*—Henry C. Deming, James E. English, Augustus Brandegee, John H. Hubbard. *Delaware.*—Nathaniel B. Smithers. *Illinois.*—

the President appended to that message a proclamation, in which he offered full pardon and restoration of all rights of property, excepting as to slaves, to all persons (with specified exceptions)[1] who had participated in the rebellion, who should take a prescribed oath of allegiance to the Government.[2] In it he also offered a prescription for reorganizing civil governments in States in which rebellion existed, by which the people might be restored to all the political privileges guaranteed by the National Constitution; at the same time pointing to the fact that the vital action necessary to consummate the reorganization by the admission of representatives of those States to seats in Congress, rested "exclusively with the respective Houses, and not to any extent with the Executive."[3]

Isaac N. Arnold, John F. Farnsworth, Elihu B. Washburne, Charles M. Harris, Owen Lovejoy, Jesse O. Norton, John R. Eden, John T. Stuart, Lewis W. Ross, A. L. Knapp, J. C. Robinson, William R. Morrison, William J. Allen, James C. Allen. *Indiana.*—John Law, James A. Cravens, H. W. Harrington, William S. Holman, George W. Julian, Ebenezer Dumont, Daniel W. Voorhees, Godlove S. Orth, Schuyler Colfax, J. K. Edgerton, James F. McDowell. *Iowa.*—James F. Wilson, Hiram Price, William B. Allison, J. B. Grinnell, John A. Kasson, A. W. Hubbard. *Kansas.*—A. Carter Wilder. *Kentucky.*—Lucien Anderson, George H. Yeaman, Henry Grider, Aaron Harding, Robert Mallory, Green Clay Smith, Brutus J. Clay, William H. Randall, William H. Wadsworth. *Maine.*—L. D. M. Sweat, Sidney Perham, James G. Blane, John H. Rice, Frederick A. Pike. *Maryland.*—John A. G. Cresswell, Edwin G. Webster, Henry Winter Davis, Francis Thomas, Benjamin G. Harris. *Massachusetts.*—Thomas D. Elliot, Oakes Ames, Alexander H. Rice, Samuel Hooper, John B. Alley, Daniel W. Gooche, George S. Boutwell, John D. Baldwin, William B. Washburn, Henry L. Dawes. *Michigan.* —Fernando C. Beaman, Charles Upson, J. W. Longyear, Francis W. Kellogg, Augustus C. Baldwin, John F. Driggs. *Minnesota.*—William Windom, Ignatius Donnelly. *Missouri.*—Francis P. Blair, Jr., Henry T. Blow, John G. Scott, J. W. McClurg, S. H. Boyd, Austin A. King, Benjamin Loan, William A. Hall, James S. Rollins. *New Hampshire.*—Daniel Marcy, Edward H. Rollins, James W. Patterson. *New Jersey.*—John F. Starr, George Middleton, William G. Steele, Andrew J. Rodgers, Nehemiah Perry. *New York.*—Henry G. Stebbens, Martin Kalbfleisch, Moses F. Odell, Ben. Wood, Fernando Wood, Elijah Ward, J. W. Chanler, James Brooks, Anson Herrick, William Radford, Charles H. Winfield, Homer A. Nelson, John B. Steele, John V. L. Pruyn, John A. Griswold, Orlando Kellogg, Calvin T. Hulburd, James M. Marvin, Samuel F. Miller, Ambrose W. Clark, Francis Kernan, De Witt C. Littlejohn, Thomas T. Davis, Theodore M. Pomeroy, Daniel Morris, Giles W. Hotchkiss, R. B. Van Valkenburg, Freeman Clarke, Augustus Frank, John B. Ganson, Reuben E. Fenton. *Ohio.*—George H. Pendleton, Alexander Long, Robert C. Schenck, J. F. McKinney, Frank C. Le Blond, Chilton A. White, Samuel S. Cox, William Johnson, Warren P. Noble, James M. Ashley, Wells A. Hutchins, William E. Finck, John O'Neill, George Bliss, James R. Morris, Joseph W. White, Ephraim R. Eckley, Rufus P Spaulding, J. A. Garfield. *Oregon.*—John R. McBride. *Pennsylvania.*—Samuel J. Randall, Charles O'Neill, Leonard Myers, William D. Kelley, M. Russell Thayer, John D. Stiles, John M. Broomall, S. E. Ancona, Thaddeus Stevens, Myer Strouse, Philip Johnson, Charles Denison, W. H. Tracy, William H. Miller, Joseph Bailey, A. H. Coffroth, Archibald McAllister, James T. Hale, Glenni W. Scofield, Amos Myers, John L. Dawson, J. K. Moorhead, Thomas Williams, Jesse Lazear. *Rhode Island.*—Thomas A. Jenckes, Nathan F. Dixon. *Vermont.*—Frederick E. Woodbridge, Justin S. Morrill, Portus Baxter. *Virginia.*—Joseph Segar, L. H. Chandler, B. M. Kitchen. *West Virginia.*—Jacob B. Blair, William G. Brown, Killian V. Whaley. *Wisconsin.*—James S. Brown, Ithamar C. Sloan, Amasa Cobb, Charles A. Eldridge, Ezra Wheeler, Walter D. McIndoe. SCHUYLER COLFAX, Speaker of the House of Representatives.

DELEGATES FROM TERRITORIES.

New Mexico.—Francisco Perea. *Utah.*—John F. Kinney. *Washington.*—George E. Cole. *Nebraska.*— S. G. Daily. *Colorado.*—Hiram P. Bennett. *Nevada.*—Gordon N. Mott. *Dakota.*—Contested seat. *Idaho.* —W. H. Wallace. *Arizona.*—No Delegate.

[1] The persons excepted were all who were or had been civil or diplomatic agents of the so-called Confederate Government; all who had left judicial stations under the United States to aid the rebellion; all who were or had been military or naval officers of the so-called Confederate Government above the rank of colonel in the army and lieutenant in the navy; all who left seats in the National Congress to aid the rebellion; all who resigned commissions in the National army or navy, and afterward aided the rebellion; and all who had engaged in any way in treating colored persons, or white persons in charge of such, otherwise than lawfully as prisoners of war.

[2] The following was the form of the oath: "I, ————, do solemnly swear, in the presence of Almighty God, that I will henceforth faithfully support, protect, and defend the Constitution of the United States, and the Union of the States thereunder; and that I will, in like manner, abide by and faithfully support all acts of Congress passed during the existing rebellion with reference to slaves, so long and so far as not repealed, modified, or held void by Congress or by decision of the Supreme Court; and that I will, in like manner, abide by and faithfully support all proclamations of the President made during the existence of the rebellion having reference to slaves, so long and so far as not modified or declared void by decisions of the Supreme Court. So help me God."

[3] The President proclaimed "that whenever, in any of the States of Arkansas, Texas, Louisiana, Mississippi,

Let us now consider military events in the year 1864.

Standing at the opening of the year, and taking a general survey of military affairs as we left them in the preceding record, we find the Army of the Potomac, under Meade, and the Army of Northern Virginia, under Lee, confronting each other in the vicinity of the Rapid Anna. Looking farther southward, we observe almost absolute quiet in North Carolina. Gillmore and Dahlgren are seen besieging Charleston very quietly. Mobile is held by the Confederates, and Banks, at New Orleans, anxious to attempt its capture, is restrained by superior authority. His hold on Texas is by a feeble tenure, and the confining of Taylor westward of the Atchafalaya may be of very short duration. Steele has a considerable army at Little Rock, threatening Taylor's flank, and Rosecrans, who was succeeded by Thomas in the command of the Army of the Cumberland, is at the head of the Department of the Missouri. Between the Mississippi River and the Appalachian chain of mountains little more than guer-rilla operations are seen; while near the southern extremity of that chain of hills, at and near Chattanooga, Grant lies with a strong force, watching the army he has lately conquered, under Bragg, which is now in the vicinity of Dalton, in Georgia, commanded by General Joseph E. Johnston. It is about fifty thousand strong, including troops sent to Mobile.[1] Burnside and Longstreet are confronting each other in East Tennessee.

CONFEDERATE HEAD-QUARTERS AT MOBILE.[2]

The National forces in the field now numbered about eight hundred thousand. Those of the Confederates numbered about four hundred thousand. The former were ready and disposed to act on the offensive; the latter, generally, stood on the defensive. Both parties were resolved to make the campaign about to be opened a decisive one, if possible, and made preparations accordingly. The Government and the people were tired of delays, and the almost undecisive warfare of posts, as the struggle had been, in a great degree, up to that time. It was evident to both that proper vigor to secure quick success in efforts to crush the rebellion, could only be obtained by committing the supreme control of the armies in the field to some person more competent than General Halleck, and all eyes were turned to General Grant, whose ability as a leader appeared pre-

Tennessee, Alabama, Georgia, Florida, South Carolina, and North Carolina, a number of persons, not less than one-tenth in number of the votes cast in such States at the Presidential election of the year of our Lord 1860 each having taken the oath aforesaid, and not having since violated it, and being a qualified voter by the election law of the State existing immediately before the so-called act of secession, and excluding all others, shall re-establish a State Government, which shall be republican in form."

[1] The Confederates reported the Army of the Tennessee at 54,000 men of all arms. This included four divisions sent to re-enforce General Polk in the heart of Alabama, and two divisions sent to Mobile, with the entire body of cavalry, under Wheeler, Wharton, and Morgan. Johnston's command embraced all the Confederate troops in Georgia, Alabama, and Mississippi, excepting those at Mobile, and others in Tennessee, under Forrest, who had a sort of roving commission.

[2] This is a view of the Custom-House at Mobile, which was used as the head-quarters of the Confederates in that Department. It is a very fine building, of Quincy granite. The picture shows its fronts on Royal and St. Francis Streets.

eminent. There was a general willingness, when the question presented itself in action at Washington, to intrust him with almost unlimited powers as a general-in-chief. To effect this seemingly desirable object, Congress created the office of lieutenant-general, which had expired with Washington; and when the President approved the measure, he nominated General Grant for the high position. This was confirmed by the Senate,[a] and Grant was made General-in-Chief of all the armies of the Republic.[1] He was then not quite forty-three years of age, or a few months younger than Washington was when the latter took the chief command of the Continental armies.

[a] March 2, 1864.

Grant had shown a proper appreciation of the demands of the crisis. He had no sympathy with a system of warfare, under the circumstances, which carried the lash of coercion in one hand and the sugar-plums of persuasion in the other. That had been tried too long for the National good. He believed the Government to be right and the rebellion against its authority wrong. He knew that compromise, with safety and honor for the Republic, was impossible, and his plan was to make war with all the terrible intentions of war, as the most speedy and effectual way to crush the rebellion. He knew that such war would be more merciful and humane than its opposite—that sharp, decisive battles, waged not exclusively for any post, but for the destruction of his adversary's armies, would require fewer lives and less treasure than feeble blows, which would wound, but not destroy. Knowing these to be the views of the new General-in-Chief, expressed by his actions, his appointment gave general satisfaction and hope to the loyal people.

The President immediately summoned the Lieutenant-General to Washington. He arrived there on the afternoon of the 8th of March, and on the following day[b] he and Mr. Lincoln met, for the first time, in the Cabinet chamber of the White House. There, in the presence of the entire Cabinet, General Halleck, General Rawlins (Grant's chief of staff), and Colonel Comstock, his chief engineer, Owen Lovejoy, a member of Congress, and Mr. Nicolay, the President's private secretary, the Lieutenant-General received his commission from the Chief Magistrate, when the two principal actors in the august scene exchanged a few words appropriate to the occasion.[2] On the following day,[c] the President issued an order investing the Lieutenant-General with the chief command of all the armies of the Republic. It was also announced that General Hal-

[b] March 9.

[c] March 10.

---

[1] On the 14th of December, 1863, E. B. Washburne proposed in the House of Representatives the revival of the grade of lieutenant-general of our armies. Mr. Ross, of Illinois, offered an amendment, [d] Feb. 1. recommending General Grant for the office. In this shape the proposition was carried[d] in the House by a vote of 111 to 44, and it was concurred in by the Senate[e] by a vote of 31 to 6, after it was amended by making the office perpetual, and prescribing that the Lieutenant-General should be, under the President, the General-in-Chief of the Armies of the Republic. A Committee [e] Feb. 24. of Conference was appointed, and a bill substantially in accord with the views of the Senate was passed. The President signed it on the 1st of March, and on that day nominated General Grant for the post, which the Senate confirmed the next day.

[2] The President said: "General Grant, as an evidence of the nation's appreciation of what you have already done, and its reliance upon you for what still remains to be done in the existing great struggle, you are now presented with this commission, constituting you Lieutenant-General of the Armies of the United States. With this high honor devolves upon you, also, a corresponding responsibility. As the country herein trusts you, so, under God, it will sustain you. I scarcely need to add that, with what I here speak for the nation, goes my own hearty personal concurrence."

To this Lieutenant-General Grant replied: "Mr. President, I accept the commission with gratitude for the

leck had been relieved of that command " at his own request," and assigned to duty as "chief of staff of the army."[1]

General Grant made a flying visit to the head-quarters of the Army of the Potomac, and then started for the West, to make arrangements for inaugurating the grand campaign of the spring of 1864. At Nashville he issued the following modest order on the 17th of March, dated " Head-quarters of the Armies of the United States ":—

" In pursuance of the following order of the President :—

'EXECUTIVE MANSION, WASHINGTON, *November* 10, 1864.

' Under the authority of the Act of Congress to appoint to the grade of Lieutenant-General in the Army, of March 1, 1864, Lieutenant-General Ulysses S. Grant, United States Army, is appointed to the command of the armies of the United States.

ABRAHAM LINCOLN.'

I assume command of the Armies of the United States. Head-quarters will be in the field, and, until further orders, will be with the Army of the Potomac. There will be an office head-quarters in Washington, to which all official communications will be sent, except those from the army where the head-quarters are at the date of their address."

General Grant spent the remainder of March and a greater portion of April in making arrangements for the decisive campaigns which followed, the grand geographical objectives being Richmond and Atlanta, and the prime object the destruction or capture of the two principal armies of the Conspirators, one under Lee and the other under Johnston. To General Meade, as commander of the Army of the Potomac, Grant assigned the task of conquering Lee and taking Richmond, and to Sherman was intrusted the duty of conquering Johnston and taking Atlanta. In these two generals Grant reposed the most perfect confidence, and was not disappointed. He made his head-quarters thenceforth with the Army of the Potomac, and gave to Meade the help of his counsel and the prestige of his name; while Sherman, who was appointed to succeed Grant in the command of the Military Division of the Mississippi, with Major-General J. B. McPherson as commander of the

JAMES B. McPHERSON.

Department and Army of the Tennessee,[2] was left to his own resources, under general but explicit orders from the Lieutenant-General.

high honor conferred. With the aid of the noble armies that have fought on so many battle-fields for our common country, it will be my earnest endeavor not to disappoint your expectations. I feel the full weight of the responsibilities now devolving on me, and I know that, if they are properly met, it will be due to those armies, and, above all, to the favor of that Providence which leads both nations and men."

[1] *General Order of the War Department*, March 12, 1864. In that order occurred the following sentence: " In relieving Major-General Halleck from duty as General-in-Chief, the President desires to express his approbation and thanks for the zealous manner in which the arduous and responsible duties of that position have been performed." [2] *Order of the War Department*, March 12, 1864.

Meanwhile the Conspirators at Richmond made the most frantic efforts to avert their impending doom. They heard with dismay of the gigantic preparations making by the Government against them. They keenly realized the fact that in the wide world they had no sympathizing friend among the rulers, to speak a word of substantial comfort, excepting the Pope of Rome,[1] whose power to help was less than nothing. They knew that the sentiment of the civilized world, unbiassed by self-interest, was against their cause. They saw England, from which they had hoped most, virtually laughing at their calamity, and its people offering no other aid than such as the greed of traffic might supply for a full equivalent of profit;[2] and they beheld with the greatest concern the despondency of their own dupes and victims within the bounds of the Confederacy. It was vitally important to speak to the latter words of encouragement. Truth could furnish none. So Jefferson Davis, equal to the occasion, as usual, issued an address to the troops in the field early in February, and the members of "Congress" at Richmond put forth a long epistle "to the People of the Confederate States," both of which, undeniable facts warrant us in saying were deceptive and untruthful in the highest degree. They were filled with the most artful misrepresentations of events in the past and current history of the war.

Davis assured his poor conscripts that they were patriotic volunteers, and that "the pulse of the people beat in unison with theirs;" and he compared their "*spontaneous and unanimous offer of their lives for the defense of their country*[3] with the halting and reluctant service of the mercenaries," who were "purchased by the enemy at the price of higher bounties than have hitherto been known in war." He assured them that "debt, taxation, repetition of heavy drafts, dissensions occasioned by the strife for power, by the pursuit of the spoils of office, by the thirst for the plunder of the public treasury, and, above all, the consciousness of a bad cause, must tell with fearful force upon the overstrained energies of the enemy. His campaign of 1864," he said, "must, from the exhaustion of his resources of men and

---

[1] See page 47.

[2] On the 1st of April, 1864, Lord Lyons, the British minister at Washington, forwarded to Jefferson Davis, by permission of our Government, a letter from Earl Russell, the British Foreign Secretary, in which, in the name of "her Majesty's Government," he protested against the further procuring of pirate vessels within the British dominions by the Confederates. After courteously reciting facts connected with the matter, Russell said: "Under these circumstances, her Majesty's Government protests and remonstrates against any further efforts being made on the part of the so-called Confederate States, or the authorities or agents thereof, to build, or cause to be built, or to purchase, or cause to be purchased, any such vessels as those styled 'rams,' or any other vessels to be used for war purposes against the United States, or against any country with which the United Kingdom is at peace and on terms of amity; and her Majesty's Government further protest and remonstrate against all acts in violation of the neutrality laws of the realm."

These words, from one who personally and as the representative of the British Government, had given the insurgents all the "aid and comfort" a wise business prudence would allow, kindled the hottest indignation of the Conspirators, and Jefferson Davis instructed one of his assistants (Burton N. Harrison) to reply that it "would be inconsistent with the dignity of the position he [J. Davis] fills as Chief Magistrate of a nation comprising a population of more than twelve millions, occupying a territory many times larger than the United Kingdom, and possessing resources unsurpassed by those of any other country on the face of the globe, to allow the attempt of Earl Russell to ignore the actual existence of the Confederate States, and to contemptuously style them "so-called," to pass without a protest and a remonstrance. The President, therefore, does protest and remonstrate against this studied insult; and he instructs me to say that in future any document in which it may be repeated will be returned unanswered and unnoticed." The scribe of the irate "President" added: "Were, indeed, her Majesty's Government sincere in a desire and a determination to maintain neutrality, the President would not but feel that they would neither be just nor gallant to allow the subjugation of a nation like the Confederate States, by such a barbarous, despotic race as are now attempting it."

[3] Compare this with the fact mentioned on page 97, that by a late act of the Confederate "Congress," every able-bodied white man, of prescribed age, in the Confederacy, was to be considered "*in the military service*," and liable to be punished as a deserter if not found there.

money, be far less formidable than those of the last two years." The address of the "Congress" was a most notable example of a few men "clothed with a little brief authority" by usurpation, and, conscious of their wickedness and weakness, trying to shield themselves from popular wrath for carrying on a useless struggle, and sacrificing all other interests for one—the aggrandizement of the slave-holding Oligarchy—by a shameful perversion of the plainest truth. In that address they sought to make the enemies of the Government the innocent party, and, with an amazing affront to the common sense of their people and mankind, after saying, "the red glare of battle kindled at Sumter dissipated all hopes of peace, and the two Governments were arrayed in hostility against each other"—an act originating wholly with the Conspirators—they said, "*We charge the responsibility of this war on the United States.* . . . The war in which we are engaged was wickedly, and against all our protests, and the most earnest efforts to the contrary, forced upon us."

Before considering the great campaigns of the principal armies, let us notice other important movements in the country between the mountains and the Mississippi River, and beyond that stream.

When General Sherman was ordered to the assistance of Rosecrans, he left General McPherson in command at Vicksburg.[1] That officer soon found the Confederates swarming again upon the railway running north and south in the rear of Vicksburg, and so, at the middle of October, he took the divisions of Tuttle and Logan, about eight thousand strong, and pushed out in the direction of Canton, where the heaviest force was concentrating.[2] He was soon met, after crossing the Big Black, by a heavy body of cavalry, under General Wirt Adams, with ample infantry supports. After pushing these back some distance, he found himself suddenly confronted by a superior force, some of which had hastened down from Grenada, and some had come even from distant Mobile. Deeming it imprudent to give battle, McPherson retreated[a] to Vicksburg by way of Clinton.   [a] October 21, 1863.

Forrest, meanwhile, with about four thousand men, had been watching an opportunity to break through the line of National troops then holding the Memphis and Charleston railway, for the purpose of a raid in Tennessee in search of supplies. The repulse of McPherson emboldened him, and early in December, under cover of demonstrations at Colliersville, and other places between Corinth and Memphis, by other detachments, he dashed through the line near Salisbury, east of Grand Junction, and pushed on to Jackson, in Tennessee, without molestation. There he found himself in the midst of friends, from whose plantations he drew supplies, and from whose households he gained many recruits. He made Jackson his head-quarters, and sent out raiding parties in various directions to gather up cattle and other supplies. But his career in that region was short. General Hurlbut sent out troops

---

[1] Page 158.

[2] Soon after Sherman left, General Hurlbut, then in command in West Tennessee, sent out raiding parties of cavalry, or mounted infantry. Some of the latter were under Lieutenant-Colonel J. J. Phillips, of the Ninth Illinois Infantry, and detachments of the former were led by Lieutenant-Colonel W. R. M. Wallace, Fourth Illinois, and Major D. E. Coon, Second Iowa Cavalry. They swept through Northern Mississippi to Grenada, an important railway junction, where, on the 16th of August, they captured and destroyed fifty locomotives and about five hundred cars of all kinds collected there. McPherson had sent word not to destroy this rolling stock, but the messenger arrived too late to save it.

from Columbus, on the north, and from Corinth, on the south, to oppose him, the former under the command of General A. J. Smith, and the latter composed of General Mower's brigade of infantry and Colonel Mizner's cavalry. At the same time, the Seventh Illinois Cavalry, under Colonel Prince, moved out from Memphis to Bolivar. Owing to the state of the roads, these several columns could not co-operate, and Prince, surrounded by a *Dec. 25, 1863. superior force near Somerville *—a thousand to his five hundred— barely escaped capture, with a considerable loss. Forrest was satisfied that a web of danger was gathering around him (for Hurlbut had an ample supply of troops for the emergency), and started to make his escape into Mississippi. His progress was slow, for the streams were brimful. Hurlbut's troops burned the bridges in his track, and he had but few pontoons with him. One bridge—an important one, near Lafayette—was left standing, and over that he passed with a large drove of cattle and other plunder, and nearly all fresh horses, and escaped under cover of an attack on Colliersville, by General Richardson. This attack misled Grierson, who was waiting and watching for Forrest at La Grange; and the wily guerrilla had too much the start when Grierson, properly informed, pressed on in pursuit, to be easily caught. Grierson gave up the chase at Holly Springs, and Forrest found safety farther south.

Sherman now reappeared in Mississippi. After the return of his troops to Chattanooga from Knoxville, his command was stationed along the line of the Memphis and Charleston railway, in Northern Alabama, from Scottsboro' to Huntsville. There he remained with them until toward the close of January, when he was ordered to Vicksburg, to command an expedition that was to be impelled eastward from that city to perform such service for the National cause as circumstances might allow. Its first object was to strike Meridian at the intersection of the railway from Vicksburg, in the direction of Montgomery, Alabama, and another from Mobile to Corinth. A further object was contemplated in the destruction of the great Confederate iron-founderies in Selma, Alabama; also in a march upon Mobile.

Sherman left Vicksburg on the 3d of February with four divisions, two each from the corps of McPherson and Hurlbut, and accompanied by those leaders at the head of their respective troops, together with other cavalry and infantry, in all less than twenty-three thousand effective men.[1] His whole force was in light marching order, and prepared for quick movements. He marched in the advance with McPherson's corps. He crossed the Big Black at the old railway bridge, skirmished some, and reached Jackson on the 6th.* There he crossed the Pearl River, on pontoons left by the *Feb., 1864. Confederates in their hasty flight, and advanced rapidly through Brandon, Morton, and other towns on the line of the railway, and reached Meridian, on the eastern borders of the State of Mississippi, at the middle of the month, driving General Polk across the Tombigbee, some distance eastward of that town. Notwithstanding the Bishop had nine thousand infantry, under Generals French and Loring, and half that number of cav-

---

[1] These were composed of the divisions of Generals Veatch and A. J. Smith, of Hurlbut's (Sixteenth) corps, and of Generals Leggett and Crocker, of McPherson's (Seventeenth) corps; a brigade of cavalry, under Colonel Winslow; a brigade of infantry, under Colonel Chambers; a battalion of cavalry, under Captain Foster (Fourth Ohio, of McPherson's body-guard); two pioneer corps, and seven batteries of light artillery.

alry, under S. D. Lee, Wirt Adams, and Ferguson, he did not make a serious stand anywhere.

Sherman's object being the infliction of as much injury upon the Confederate cause as possible, the line of his march from Jackson eastward, presented a black pathway of desolation. No public property of the Confederates was spared. The station-houses and the rolling stock of the railway were burned; and the track was torn up, and the rails, heated by the burning ties cast into heaps, were twisted and ruined, and were often, by bending them when red-hot around a sapling, converted into what the men called "Jeff. Davis's neck-ties."[1]

JEFF. DAVIS'S NECK-TIE.

General Sherman had made arrangements for a junction of his forces at Meridian with a division, chiefly of horsemen, that was to be sent from Memphis, under General W. S. Smith, then chief of cavalry in the Division of the Mississippi. His troops consisted of about seven thousand cavalry,[2] a brigade of infantry, and a respectable artillery force. Brigadier-General Grierson was placed under his command. These troops were called in from Middle Tennessee and Northern Mississippi, and concentrated at Colliersville, twenty-four miles east of Memphis. Smith was ordered to be at Meridian on the 10th of February, but for some reason he did not leave Colliersville until the 11th, when he pushed across the country as rapidly as possible, crossed the Tallahatchie River at New Albany without opposition, and moved on to Okolona, on the Mobile and Ohio railway. Then they pressed southward, along the line of that road, toward Meridian. Colonel Grierson was sent to threaten Columbus, while Smith, with the main body, moved on toward West Point, tearing up the railway track, and burning nearly a million bushels of corn, and about two thousand bales of cotton. Negroes flocked to his lines by hundreds, mounted on the horses and mules of their masters, welcoming him as their deliverer, and becoming, necessarily, great incumbrances.

On the 20th of February,[a] Smith was met by what he supposed to be the combined forces of Forrest, Lee, and Chalmers, not far from West Point, and nearly a hundred miles north of Meridian. Their number he supposed to be greatly superior to his own, and comparatively fresh. Feeling himself unable, with his inferior force and the living incumbrances with which he was burdened, to cope with his adversaries, he ordered a retreat. The Confederates (who were really only about three thousand in number, under Forrest) followed him closely, and struck him heavily at Okolona, where, after a gallant struggle, he lost five guns. He pushed

[a] 1864.

---

[1] In regard to the treatment of the people, General Sherman thus discoursed in a long letter to his Adjutant-General[b] just before setting out on his expedition: "To those who submit to rightful law and authority, all gentleness and forbearance; but to the petulant and persistent secessionists, why, death is mercy, and the quicker he or she is disposed of, the better. Satan, and the rebellious saints of heaven, were allowed a continuous existence in hell, merely to swell their just punishment. To such as would rebel against a government so mild and just as ours was in peace, a punishment equal would not be unjust."   [b] Jan. 31.

[2] The cavalry consisted of three brigades. The First was commanded by Colonel G. E. Waring, Jr., of the Fourth Missouri Cavalry; the Second was under Lieutenant-Colonel Hepburn, of the Second Iowa Cavalry; and the Third was led by Colonel McCrellis, of the Third Illinois Cavalry.

steadily on toward Memphis as rapidly as possible, skirmishing frequently, but found no formidable assailants after crossing the Tallahatchie. He reached Memphis late in the evening of the 25th,[a] after marching that day about fifty miles. Although the chief object of the expedition was not accomplished, Smith had inflicted heavy injuries upon the Confederates; and during the thirteen days of marching and skirmishing—a march of three hundred and fifty miles—he lost only about two hundred men. But the remainder were worn down and dispirited, and one-third of them were dismounted.

Feb., 1864.

Expecting Smith at Meridian every hour, Sherman remained there several days, during which time he laid that town in ashes, with the arsenal, several buildings containing commissary stores, and all the railway property there. "We staid at Meridian a week," said Sherman in a dispatch to General Grant,[b] "and made the most complete destruction of the railroads ever beheld—south below Quitman, east to Cuba Station, twenty miles north to Lauderdale Springs, and west, all the way back to Jackson." By this work one of the prime objects of the expedition was accomplished; but Smith's failure to reach Meridian, and so give Sherman ample cavalry, prevented the infliction of tenfold more injury. Without that cavalry, Sherman did not think it prudent to go farther, nor remain at Meridian, so he retraced his steps leisurely back to Canton, where he arrived on the 26th, with four hundred prisoners, a thousand white Unionist refugees, and about five thousand negroes of all ages. He reported his own loss during the whole expedition at only one hundred and seventy-one men.

b March 10.

During that raid, Sherman destroyed a vast amount of property, and spread dismay throughout the Confederacy from the Mississippi to the Savannah. When he first started, Watts, the Governor of Alabama, issued an appeal[c] to the people of that State, and called upon them to turn out to resist the threatened invasion. General Polk telegraphed[d] to General D. Maury, commander at Mobile, that Sherman was marching from Morton on that city, when the non-combatants were requested to leave it; and it was believed, when he was at Meridian, that both Selma and Mobile would be visited by him. Great relief was felt when he turned his face westward, leaving Meridian a heap of smoldering embers. When the writer, in April, 1866, passed over the line of Sherman's raid from Jackson to Meridian, two years before, the marks of his desolating hand were seen everywhere. Meridian was then only a little village, mostly of rude cabins. When a fellow-passenger in the cars, who was the mayor of that "city," and also county judge, was asked by the writer, whether Sherman injured the place much, he replied, with emphasis: "Injured! Why he took it with him!" It was almost literally so, for when he turned back a strong east wind was blowing, and smoke and ashes—almost all that remained of the ruined town—were wafted in the direction of the march of the army toward Vicksburg.[1]

c Feb. 6.

d Feb. 10.

---

[1] The sum of injury done to the Confederates during Sherman's raid, including that of Smith, and an expedition which Porter sent simultaneously to attack Yazoo City and distract the Confederates, may be stated in general terms as follows: The destruction of 150 miles of railway, 67 bridges, 700 trestles, 20 locomotives, 28 cars, several thousand bales of cotton, several steam mills, and over 2,000,000 bushels of corn. About 500 prisoners were taken, and over 8,000 negroes and refugees followed the various columns back to Vicksburg.

The expedition sent to Yazoo City consisted of some gun-boats, under Lieutenant Owen, and a detachment

When General Johnston, then at Dalton, in Northern Georgia (where the railway up from Atlanta forks, the left to Chattanooga and the right to Cleveland), in command of Bragg's army, heard of Sherman's advance on Meridian, and perceived that General Polk and his fifteen thousand men were not likely to impede his march to Rome, Selma, Mobile, or wheresoever he liked, he sent two divisions of Hardee's corps, under Generals Stewart and Anderson, to assist the prelate. The watchful Grant, then in command at Chattanooga, quickly discovered the movement and perceived its aim, and at once put the Fourteenth Army Corps, under General Palmer, in motion[a] to counteract it. These troops moved directly upon Dalton. The divisions of Jefferson C. Davis, Johnson, and Baird marched along the direct road to that place, passing to the left of the Chickamauga battle-ground and over Taylor's Ridge; and Stanley's division, under General Crufts, which had been in camp at Cleveland, moved down from the latter place farther to the left, and joined the other three between Ringgold and Tunnel Hill. Then the whole column pressed forward, driving the Confederate cavalry, under Wheeler, before them, who made a stand at Tunnel Hill Ridge, a short distance from the village. There a line of log breastworks stretched along the crest of the ridge, and a battery of four pieces was planted in a commanding position. These were opened upon the advancing column, but were soon silenced by the Second Minnesota and Nineteenth Indiana Batteries, when Wheeler, finding his position flanked by troops under General Morgan and Colonel Hambright, fell back.

[a] Feb. 22, 1864.

It was now between two and three o'clock in the afternoon. The Nationals passed on, Morgan and Colonel D. McCook in advance, keeping up a close pursuit of Wheeler, and at five o'clock[b] approached the range of hills called Rocky Face Ridge, one of which, near Dalton, rises into a lofty peak, called Buzzard's Roost. Through a deep gorge in that ridge the railway and turnpike passed. It was a strong defensive position, and there the Confederates made another stand. They kept up a furious cross-fire from six guns until dark, when Morgan and McCook advanced, took position in the mouth of the gorge, and held it until morning, when it was found that the Confederates were still retreating toward Dalton.

[b] Feb. 24.

The Nationals moved on into Rocky Face Valley, skirmishing heavily, but continually pushing their adversaries, until they reached a point which, if held by the Unionists, would make a descent into the Dalton Valley comparatively easy. There the Confederates made a stand, with the evident determination to resist to the last. A hill in the center of the valley, on which they were posted, was the key-point of the position. General Palmer determined to carry it. To General Turchin the task was committed. With a portion of his brigade (Eleventh, Eighty-ninth, and Ninety-second Ohio, and Eighty-second Indiana) he advanced through a wood, and forming his battle-line on the slope of the hill to be carried, pressed rapidly forward. A heavy battle instantly opened. The Unionists swept steadily up the hill,

of troops, under Colonel Osband. They did not then capture the place, but inflicted considerable damage, and returned with a loss of not more than 50 men. Yazoo City was soon afterward occupied by a Union force, composed of the Eighth Louisiana and 200 of the Seventh Mississippi colored troops, and the Eleventh Illinois. They were attacked by a superior force on the 5th of March. A desperate fight ensued. The assailants were finally driven away by some re-enforcements from below, and soon afterward the town was evacuated. The Union loss in this struggle was 130. That of the Confederates was about the same.

drove the Confederates from it, and planted the National standard on its crest. The triumph was momentary. The Confederates rallied half way down the other side of the hill, and, supported by re-enforcements, returned to the attack with overwhelming numbers, and drove Turchin from his prize. The Nationals fell back, and Palmer, finding his adversaries gathering in much larger force than his own in his front, and hovering on his flanks, and informed that Johnston, on hearing of Sherman's retreat from Meridian, had

BUZZARD'S ROOST AND ROCKY FACE.[1]

ordered back the divisions of Hardee sent to re-enforce Polk, he thought it prudent to retreat to Tunnel Hill. This was done at once, and on the 10th of March his command took post at Ringgold. In this short campaign the Nationals lost three hundred and fifty killed and wounded, and the Confederates about two hundred.

The sphere of General Forrest's duties were at this time enlarged, and their importance increased. He was acknowledged to be one of the most daring and skillful of the Confederate leaders in the West, notwithstanding he was subordinate to S. D. Lee, Commander-in-Chief of the mounted men in that region. He seems to have had a sort of roving commission, and the service in which he was engaged partook more of the character of guerrilla than of regular warfare. It being evident that there would be a great struggle between the opposing troops in Northern Georgia, below Chattanooga, Forrest was charged with the special duty of keeping the National forces then on the line of the Mississippi, from Vicksburg to Cairo, employed, and prevent their re-enforcing the army opposed to Johnston. In the performance of this duty, Forrest, taking advantage of the withdrawal

---

[1] This is from a sketch made by the author from the railway, in May, 1866. The view is from a point a little south of Dalton.

of troops from Vicksburg, to assist General Banks in another expedition against Texas, started[a] on another raid into Tennessee a few days after Palmer fell back from before Dalton. He extended it into Kentucky, and, under the inspiration of the tone of feeling and action among the chief Conspirators at Richmond, he marked it, on his part, with a most inhuman spirit toward the negro soldiers in the Union army, and the white troops associated with them. The ferocity of the Conspirators had been bridled, as we have seen, by their fears and the suggestions of expediency;[1] but men in the field, like Forrest, ready and willing to carry the black flag[2] at any time, and especially so against negro troops, found occasions to exercise it whenever the shadow of an excuse might be found. [a March 14, 1864.]

Forrest led about five thousand troops on his great raid. He swept rapidly up from Northern Mississippi into West Tennessee, rested a little at Jackson, and then pushed on[b] toward Kentucky. He sent Colonel Faulkner to capture Union City, a fortified town at the junction of railways in the northwestern part of Tennessee, then garrisoned by four hundred and fifty of the Eleventh Tennessee Cavalry, under Colonel Hawkins. Faulkner appeared before the town on the 24th,[c] and demanded its surrender. Hawkins refused. Faulkner attacked, and was repulsed, when, on renewing his demand for surrender, Hawkins made no further resistance, but gave up the post, contrary to the earnest desires of his men. He surrendered the garrison, about two hundred horses, and five hundred small-arms. At that moment General Brayman, who had come down from Cairo, was within six miles of Union City, with an ample force for Hawkins's relief. [b March 23.] [c March.]

This conquest opened an easy way for the possession of Hickman, on the Mississippi. A small Confederate force occupied that town. Meanwhile, Forrest moved with Buford's division directly from Jackson to Paducah, on the Ohio River, in Kentucky, accompanied by Buford and General A. P. Thompson. Paducah was then occupied by a force not exceeding seven hundred men,[3] under the command of Colonel S. G. Hicks; and when word came that Forrest was approaching in heavy force, that officer threw his troops into Fort Anderson, in the lower suburbs of the town. Before this, Forrest appeared[d] with three thousand men and four guns, and, after making a furious assault and meeting with unexpected resistance, he made a formal demand for its surrender, and with it a threat of a massacre of the whole garrison in the event of a refusal and the carrying of the works by storm.[4] To this savage demand Hicks gave a [d March 25.]

---

[1] See page 229.

[2] The shallow Beauregard was continually anxious to make the war as ferocious as possible. We have already noticed (note 1, page 295, volume II.) his coincidence of opinions with "Stonewall" Jackson, that "the time had come for raising the black flag." In a letter to William Porcher Miles, one of the most bitter of the South Carolina Conspirators (see chapter IV., volume I.), dated at "Charleston, October 13, 1862," Beauregard said: "Has the bill for the execution of Abolition prisoners, after January next, been passed? Do it; and England will be stirred into action. *It is high time to proclaim the black flag after that period. Let the execution be with the garrote.*—G. T. BEAUREGARD."

[3] They consisted of portions of the Sixteenth Kentucky Cavalry, under Major Barnes; of the One Hundred and Twenty-second Illinois, Major Chapman, and nearly three hundred colored artillerists (First Kentucky), under Colonel Cunningham.

[4] The following is a copy of the ferocious summons: "Having a force amply sufficient to carry your works and reduce the place, in order to avoid the unnecessary effusion of blood, I demand the surrender of the fort and

flat refusal, when the assault was renewed with increased vigor, while other portions of Forrest's command were plundering and burning in the town. Fighting was kept up all the afternoon, and the crack of musketry was heard until midnight. The garrison were materially aided by the gun-boats *Peosta* and *Paw Paw*, which shelled the buildings within musket range of the

fort, in which the Confederate sharp-shooters swarmed.[1] Satisfied that he could not carry the fort by storm, Forrest lingered about the place until the 27th,[a] hoping

[a] March, 1864.

something would turn up to his advantage,[2] when, hearing of the approach from Cairo of re-enforcements for the garrison, he decamped, having lost, it was estimated, over three hundred men, killed and wounded. General Thompson was torn in pieces by a shell that passed through him. Other officers were killed or maimed. The Union loss was fourteen killed and forty-six wounded.

N. B. FORREST.

Forrest was greatly chagrined by the failure of his arms and his trickery at Paducah, and, hastening back to Tennessee, he sought more successful employment for both in an attack upon Fort Pillow, on the Mississippi, above Memphis.[3] That post was then garrisoned by about five hundred and fifty men, including officers, under the command of Major L. F. Booth. Two hundred and sixty-two of the soldiers were colored, under the immediate command of Major Booth, and the remainder were white, commanded by Major W. F. Bradford.[4] Booth ranked Bradford, and held chief command. The regular garrison stationed at Fort Pillow had been withdrawn toward the close of January, to accompany General Sherman in his expedi-

---

troops, with all the public stores. *If you surrender, you shall be treated as prisoners of war; but if I have to storm your works, you may expect no quarter.*—N. B. FORREST."

[1] Paducah suffered terribly from the bombardment and conflagration. Besides the ravages by fire made by the Confederates, all the buildings near the fort, in which the sharp-shooters were concealed, were burned by order of Colonel Hicks, on the night after the assault. The Confederates burned a steamboat on the marine ways; also sixty bales of cotton.

[2] At Paducah, as elsewhere, Forrest's conduct was marked by bad faith. He took advantage of his flag of truce to gain positions for his men not otherwise attainable; and when the women and children went to the river-side to cross over and escape danger before the bombardment of the place, his sharp-shooters mingled with them, and so protected from assault in return, fired upon the gun-boats. The Confederates also placed women in front of their lines as they moved on the fort, or were proceeding to take positions, while the flag of truce was at the fort, so as to compel the garrison to withhold their fire upon the faithless assailants. In this cowardly manner Forrest tried to win what real valor could not accomplish.—Report of a Committee of Congress on the Massacre at Fort Pillow.

On the morning after Forrest's repulse he tried twice to gain some advantage of position by the means of a flag of truce, to renew his attack, but failed. He proposed to open negotiations for an exchange of prisoners. Hicks told him he had no authority to do so. Then he proposed a private interview with Hicks, to which the latter replied he would meet Forrest, each accompanied by two officers of designated rank. To this Forrest made no reply; and, having failed in force and trickery, he sullenly withdrew.

[3] See page 296, volume II.

[4] These troops comprised one battalion of the Sixth United States Heavy Artillery of Colored Troops, under Major Booth; and one section of the Second United States Light Artillery, Colored; and one battalion of the Thirteenth Tennessee Cavalry (white), under Major Bradford.

tion to Meridian, and these had been sent by General Hurlbut to occupy it, so that the Confederates might not obstruct the navigation of the river. The fort was upon a high bluff, with a deep ravine on each side; and its armament, at the time we are considering, consisted of two 6-pounders, two 12-pounder howitzers, and two 10-pounder Parrott guns.

Forrest approached Fort Pillow on the morning of the 13th of April, and before sunrise he drove in the pickets and began an assault. A sharp battle ensued, and continued until about nine o'clock, when Major Booth was killed. Up to that time some of the garrison had been gallantly defending outworks some distance from the fort. Major Bradford, on whom the command devolved, now called the whole force within the fort, and gallantly maintained the fight until past noon, when the fire of both parties slackened, to allow the guns to cool. Meanwhile, the gun-boat *New Era*, Captain Marshall,

of the Mississippi squadron, lying near, had taken part in the defense, her guns directed by the indications of signals at the fort, by which they were made more effective. But the height of the bank was such that her efficiency was impaired, for the Confederates, when shelled by her up one ravine, would move to the other.

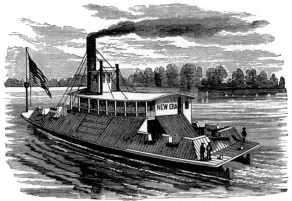

NEW ERA.

Failing to make any impression on the fort, Forrest now resorted to the trick of a flag of truce, to gain some advantage secretly. He sent one to demand an unconditional surrender of the post within twenty minutes. Bradford asked for an hour, that he might consult with his officers and Captain Marshall, of the *New Era*. Forrest waited awhile, and then sent word that if the fort was not surrendered within twenty minutes from that time he should order an assault. Bradford refused, and prepared for another struggle. Meanwhile, Forrest had carried out a part of his treacherous and cowardly plan. While the negotiations were going on, he had sent large numbers of the troops down the ravines to sheltered positions behind bushes, fallen timbers, and some buildings, from which they might more safely and effectually fall upon the fort. Captain Marshall saw this movement, but did not fire upon the foe for fear, should they succeed in taking the fort, they would plead his act in seeming violation of the flag, as an excuse for any atrocities they might be pleased to commit.

When Forrest received Bradford's refusal, he gave a signal, and his concealed men sprang from the hiding-places they had so treacherously gained, and, with the cry of "No quarter!" pounced upon the fort at different points, and in a few minutes were in possession of it. The surprised and overwhelmed garrison threw down their arms, and many of them attempted to escape down the steep bank to the river, or to find concealment and refuge from the wrath of the assailants in the bushes, or among the fallen timber. The conquerors followed, butchering the defenseless fugitives at every step. In the fort and out of it the most fiendish atrocities were exhibited—atrocities which find no parallel in the history of war between civilized men. Soldiers and civilians—men, women, and children, white and black—were indiscriminately slaughtered by methods most cruel. The massacre continued until night, and was renewed the next morning, when " at least three hundred were murdered in cold blood," and the ferocity of Forrest, under the inspiration of the chief Conspirators at Richmond, exhibited in his summons to Hicks at Paducah, was fully gratified. Major Bradford, being a native of a Slave-labor State, and therefore considered a " traitor to the South," was reserved for a special act of barbarity. While on his way toward Jackson, Tennessee, the day after the Confederates retreated from Fort Pillow, he was led about fifty yards from the line of march, and then deliberately murdered. He fell dead, pierced with three musket-balls.[1] " Forrest's motto," said Major Charles W. Gibson, of his command, to the writer, was : " War means fight, and fight means kill—*we want but few prisoners.*"[2] By his foul deed at Fort Pillow, Forrest won for himself an imperishable record of infamy in the annals of his country, as dark as that gained by Butler, the leader of the Tories and Indians in the massacre in the Wyoming Valley during the Old War for Independence.[3]

---

[1] Testimony of one of Forrest's men before a Congressional committee. See the Report on the *Massacre at Fort Pillow.*

[2] See page 638, volume II.

[3] " The officers and men seemed to vie with each other in the devilish work. Men, women, and even children, wherever found, were deliberately shot down, beaten, and hacked with sabers. Some of the children, not more than ten years old, were forced to stand up and face their murderers while being shot; the sick and the wounded were butchered without mercy the rebels even entering the hospital building, and dragging them out to be shot, or killing them as they lay there, unable to offer the least resistance. All over the hill-side the work of murder was going on; numbers of our men were collected in lines or groups, and deliberately shot." The most fiendish cruelty was shown toward the colored people. " All around were heard cries of 'No quarter! Kill the damned niggers! Shoot 'em down!' and all who asked for mercy were answered by the most cruel taunts and sneers. Some were spared for a time, to be murdered under circumstances of the greatest cruelty. . . . . One negro, who had been ordered by a rebel officer to hold his horse, was killed by him when he remounted; another, a mere child, whom an officer had taken up behind him, was seen by Chalmers [General Chalmers one of Forrest's leaders], who at once ordered the officer to put him down and shoot him, which was done." They burned huts and tents in which the wounded had sought shelter, and were still in them. " One man was deliberately fastened down to the floor of a tent, face upward, by means of nails driven through his clothing and into the boards under him, so that he could not possibly escape, and then the tent set on fire. Another was nailed to the side of a building outside of the fort, and then the building set on fire and burned. . . . . These deeds of murder and cruelty ceased when night came on, only to be renewed the next morning, when the demons carefully sought among the dead, lying about in all directions, for any of the wounded yet alive, and those they found were deliberately shot. . . . . Many other instances of equally atrocious cruelty might be enumerated, but your committee feel compelled to refrain from giving here more of the heart-sickening details, and refer to the statements contained in the voluminous testimony herewith submitted."—Report of Messrs. Wade and Gooch, a sub-committee of the *Joint Committee of Congress on the Conduct and Expenditures of the War.* This committee visited Fort Pillow two weeks after the massacre, and made a thorough investigation. They took the testimony of a large number of eye-witnesses and sufferers, all of which was submitted to Congress.

General S. D. Lee, Forrest's chief, after denying the truth of the report of the committee, undertook to show, by the most feeble special pleading, that the massacre was justifiable, especially on the ground that some of the soldiers were of " a servile race ;" and said, without pretending to cite an instance of such atrocity among civilized nations, " I respectfully refer you to history for numerous instances of indiscriminate slaughter after successful assault, even under less aggravated circumstances."—Letter of S. D. Lee, June 28, 1864. The friends of Forrest afterward attempted to avert from him the scorn of mankind, by alleging that he was not in immediate command, and therefore not responsible for the massacre. Confederate reports silenced the falsehood by saying: " Generals Forrest and Chalmers both entered the fort from opposite sides, *simultaneously*, and an indiscriminate slaughter followed. *One hundred prisoners were taken, and the balance slain.* The fort ran with blood."—Cited by W. J. Tenney, in his *Military and Naval History of the Rebellion,* page 519.

On the day after the capture of Fort Pillow, Buford appeared[a] before Columbus, and, in imitation of his chief, demanded an unconditional surrender, saying : " Should you surrender, the negroes now in arms will be returned to their masters.   Should I be compelled to take the place by force, *no quarter will be shown negro troops whatever.*" The demand was refused.   Buford did not attack, but, with Forrest, retreated rapidly out of Tennessee, on hearing that General S. D. Sturgis (who had come down from East Tennessee), with a heavy force, was about to march from Memphis to intercept him.   It was soon found that the practice of the indiscriminate slaughter of prisoners, which Forrest inaugurated for the purpose of intimidating the negroes and preventing their enlistment in the National armies, had an opposite effect, and was likely to react with fearful power ; so it was abandoned.

[a] April 13, 1864.

Sturgis did not move from Memphis in time to intercept Forrest.   He marched[b] out to Bolivar with about twelve thousand men, but his intended prey had already escaped across the Wolf River, and was safe in Northern Mississippi with his plunder.   Several weeks later, when it was known that Forrest was gathering a larger force than he had ever before commanded, for the purpose, it was supposed, of either making another raid into Tennessee and Kentucky, or re-enforcing Johnston, then contending hotly with Sherman in Northern Georgia, Sturgis started from Memphis with a force of nine thousand infantry and artillery, and three thousand cavalry under General Grierson (including a greater portion of General A. J. Smith's corps, lately returned from the Red River region), with instructions to hunt up and beat the bold cavalry leader.   Sturgis pushed in a southeasterly direction, and struck the Mobile and Ohio railway near Gun Town.   Grierson, in advance with the cavalry, there met[c] a large force of Forrest's horsemen, and pushed them back to their infantry supports, when they took a strong position for battle on a commanding ridge.   Grierson had sent back word to Sturgis, six miles in the rear, of the situation of matters at the front, when that commander pushed forward the infantry at double-quick, under a blazing sun, and with them a train of about two hundred wagons.   Finding Grierson hotly engaged, the exhausted infantry, without being allowed time to rest, or be properly formed in battle order, were thrown into the fight directly in front, no attempt being made to turn the flank of the Confederates.   The result was most disastrous. The whole National force were speedily routed, and their wagon-train, which had been parked within range of Forrest's guns, was captured and lost. The vanquished troops were driven in wild confusion over a narrow and ugly road, without supplies, and with no re-enforcements near, covered, as well as possible, by the Second Brigade, under Colonel Winslow, which formed the rear-guard.   The pursuit was close and galling, until the fugitives crossed a stream at Ripley, where they turned[d] upon the pursuers, and gave battle.   The struggle was fierce for awhile, and was favorable to the Nationals ; and thereafter the retreat was less fatiguing, because the chase was less vigorous and more cautious.   When Sturgis returned to Memphis he found his army full three thousand five hundred less in number than when he left, and stripped of almost every thing but their arms.

[b] April 30.

[c] June 10.

[d] June 10.

This disastrous failure produced alarm and indignation, and another expedition was speedily fitted out for the purpose of wiping out the disgrace and accomplishing the object sought for. It was estimated that Forrest had about fourteen thousand troops under him, with his head-quarters in the neighborhood of Tupelo, and in that direction, from Salisbury, fifty miles east of Memphis, General A. J. Smith marched with about twelve thousand men, early in July. He met Forrest's cavalry at the outset, and skirmished with them nearly all the way to Tupelo, on the Mobile and Ohio railway, where the Confederate leader had made up his mind to give battle.

The expedition arrived at Pontotoc, west of Tupelo, on the 12th,[a] and when moving forward the next morning, General Mower's train was attacked by a large body of cavalry. These were repulsed, and the expedition moved on, and when, the next day, it approached Tupelo, Forrest's infantry, in heavy numbers, attacked the line. They were repulsed, after a sharp battle. The assault was repeated on the same day,[b] with a similar result, when the Confederates were driven, leaving on the field a large number of their dead and badly wounded comrades. Smith pushed no farther southward at that time, but, after a pretty severe cavalry fight the next day at Old Town Creek, he retraced his steps, and encamped his troops not far from Memphis. There he allowed them to rest about three weeks, when, with ten thousand men, he again moved[c] for Mississippi. He penetrated that State as far as the Talla-hatchie, which he reached on the 17th, but found only a few Confederate cavalry to oppose him. Forrest's men were not there. Where could they be? was a perplexing question. The bold leader himself answered it, by dashing into Memphis at dawn on the morning of the 21st of August, and making directly for the Gayoso House, where, according to information fur-nished by spies, he might expect to find Generals Hurlbut, Washburne, and Buckland, it being their quarters. He failed to secure his hoped-for prizes, but seized and carried away several of their staff-officers, and about three hundred soldiers as prisoners. He hoped to open the doors of the prison there, in which Confederate captives were confined, but pressing necessity made his stay too short to perform that achievement, and within an hour after entering the city he was driven out of it, carrying away his prisoners and some plunder, but losing there, and in a sharp skirmish a short distance from the town, about two hundred men. His exploit was a bold and bril-liant one. Informed that Smith was in Mississippi looking for him, and believing that Memphis was nearly bare of troops, he flanked the National force with three thousand of his best horsemen, performed the feat here recorded, and then retreated to his starting-place, notwithstanding there were about six thousand troops in and around Memphis. And so it was that For-rest performed his prescribed duty in keeping re-enforcements from the National army in Northern Georgia, in the spring and summer of 1864.

As we have from time to time, in these pages, noticed the employment of negro troops, and in this chapter have observed how the Confederates were disposed to treat them, it seems to be an appropriate place here to give, in a few sentences, a history of the measure.

During the white-heat of patriotic zeal that immediately succeeded the attack on Fort Sumter, and the massacre of troops in Baltimore, a few col-ored men in New York City, catching inspiration from the military move-

[a] July, 1864.

[b] July 14.

[c] August 4.

ments around them, hired a room and began to drill, thinking their services might be wanted. The Superintendent of Police found it necessary, because of threats made by sympathizers with the insurgents, to order the colored people to desist, lest their patriotism should cause a breach of the public peace. So they waited until called for. More than a year later, General Hunter, as we have seen,[1] directed the organization of negro regiments in his Department of the South. It raised a storm of indignation in Congress, and Wickliffe, of Kentucky, asked the Secretary of War, through a resolution of the House of Representatives, several questions touching such a measure, and, among others, whether Hunter had organized a regiment composed of fugitive slaves, and whether he was authorized to do so by the Government. The Secretary answered that he was not authorized to do so, and allowed General Hunter to make explicit answers.[2] Yet a few weeks later Secretary Stanton, by special order, directed[a] General Rufus Saxton, Military Governor of the sea-coast islands, to "arm, uniform, equip, and receive into the service of the United States, such number of volunteers of African descent, not exceeding five thousand," as he might deem expedient to guard that region and the inhabitants from injury by the public enemy.

[a] Aug. 25, 1862.

Then followed a proposition from General G. W. Phelps to General Butler, his chief, to organize negro regiments in Louisiana, to be composed of the fugitive slaves who were flocking to his camp at Carrollton, near New Orleans. Receiving no reply, he made a requisition[b] for arms and clothing for "three regiments of Africans," to be employed in defending his post. Butler had no authority to comply, and told Phelps to employ them in cutting trees and constructing *abatis*. "I am not willing to become the mere slave-driver you propose, having no qualifications that way," Phelps replied, and, throwing up his commission, returned to Vermont. Not long afterward, General Butler, impressed with the perils of his isolated situation, called for volunteers from the free colored men in New Orleans, and within a fortnight a full regiment was organized. A second was soon in arms, and very speedily a third; and these were the colored troops whom Butler turned over to his successor, General Banks, as we have observed on page 352, volume II.

[b] July 30.

Another year passed by, and yet few of the thousands of negroes freed by the President's Proclamation were found in arms. There was a universal prejudice against them. Yet, as the war was assuming vaster proportions, and a draft was found to be inevitable, that prejudice, which had been growing weaker for a long time, gave way entirely, and, when Lee invaded Pennsylvania, the Government authorized the enlistment of colored troops in the Free-labor States, as we have observed.[3] Congress speedily authorized[c] the President to accept them as volunteers, and prescribed that "the enrollment of the militia shall in all cases include all able-bodied male citizens," &c., without distinction of color. Yet

[c] July 16, 1863.

---

[1] Page 185.

[2] General Hunter said: "To the first question, I reply, that no regiment of 'fugitive slaves' has been or is being organized in this Department. There is, however, a fine regiment of persons whose late masters are *fugitive rebels*—men who everywhere fly before the appearance of the National flag, leaving their servants behind them to shift as best they can for themselves."

[3] See note 1, page 91.

opposition to the enlistment of negro soldiers was very strong. It was illustrated by the fact that, when, in May, 1863, the Fifty-fourth (colored)
Massachusetts, which performed such gallant acts at Fort Wagner under
Colonel Shaw,[1] was ready to start for South Carolina, the Superintendent of
the Police of New York declared, in answer to a question, that they could
not be protected from insult in that city, if they should attempt to pass
through it. So they sailed directly from Boston for Port Royal. But there
was soon a change of public sentiment on the subject there, a few months
later, as we have observed,[2] when a regiment of colored troops, bearing a
flag presented by the women of the city and cheered by thousands, marched
through its streets for the battle-field. From that time such troops were
freely enlisted everywhere, and as freely used; and the universal testimony
of experts is, that as soldiers they were equal to the white men. Nearly
two hundred thousand of them fought for the preservation of our free
institutions, in which their own race was deeply involved. Their brethren
in bondage had been freely used by the Confederates from the beginning of
the war, not as soldiers, but as laborers, as we have observed. We frequently saw notices of their enrollment into the military service of the Conspirators, but arms were never put into their hands. It would have been a
fatal experiment, and the Oligarchy knew it. They were organized into
companies, under white leaders, but were always "armed and equipped with
shovels, axes, spades, pickaxes, and blankets." Such employment of the
colored race by the Confederates, in carrying on the war, was well known,
yet the Opposition in Congress and elsewhere most strenuously opposed
their enlistment as soldiers; but the Government went steadily forward in
the path of prescribed duty, and in March, 1863, Adjutant-General Thomas
was sent to the Mississippi Valley for the express purpose of promoting the
enlistment of colored troops. In that work he labored zealously. He visited
Memphis, Helena, Vicksburg, and other places where large numbers of
colored people were gathered, and he addressed them on the subject of
emancipation, their duties as citizens, and the importance of their doing all
in their power to assist the Government in its struggle for life against the
common enemy of both. He also addressed the National officers and soldiers in favor of the employment of colored troops, reminding them that the
strength of the Confederate cause lay, in a large measure, in the employment of negroes in the cultivation of the soil while the white people were
in the army, and showing that it was policy in every way, either by enlisting
the negroes in our armies, or otherwise employing them, to deprive the
enemies of the Government of the labor of these men. "All of you," he
said, "will some day be on picket-duty, and I charge you all, if any of this
unfortunate race come within your lines, that you do not turn them away,
but receive them kindly and cordially. They are to be encouraged to come
to us; they are to be received with open arms; they are to be fed and
clothed; they are to be armed."

---

[1] See page 204.   [2] See page 91.

CHAPTER IX.

THE RED RIVER EXPEDITION.

ET us now look across the Mississippi River and see what was occurring there in 1864.

We left General Banks at New Orleans, after his failure to "repossess" Texas in the autumn and early winter of 1863, engaged in planning another expedition to that State, the first important work to be the capture of Galveston. While so engaged he received[a] a dispatch from General Halleck, dated the 4th of ⌐ᵃ Jan. 23, 1864. January, informing him that it was proposed to operate against Texas by the line of the Red River, that route having "the favor of the best military opinions of the generals of the West." Halleck proposed to have the expedition to consist of the forces of Banks and Steele, and such troops as Grant might spare for the winter, to act in combination or in co-operation, together with gun-boats. He informed Banks that both Grant and Steele had been written to, and instructed him to communicate with them upon the subject. The grand object was the capture of Shreveport, on the Red River, near the boundary between Louisiana and Texas; the capture or dispersion of the Confederates in that region, then under General E. Kirby Smith,[1] as commander of the Trans-Mississippi Department, and then the recovery of Texas and the opening of the way for trade in the immense supplies of cotton in the latter State.

The objections to this route, which Banks had hitherto urged, still existed, and he had apprehensions of disastrous results in a campaign without a unity of command and purpose. But so often had this inland route been urged upon him by Halleck, as the most feasible way for winning a conquest of Texas, that he did not feel at liberty to offer serious opposition again; so he promptly replied, on the day when he received Halleck's dispatch, that with the forces proposed the expedition might be successful and important, and that he should cordially co-operate in the movement. He thought it proper, however, to send to the General-in-Chief a memorial prepared by his chief engineer (Major D. C. Houston), on the proposed expedition, in which was explicitly stated the obstructions to be encountered and the measures necessary to accomplish the objects in view. It recommended as indispensable to success: (1.) Such complete preliminary organization as would avoid the least delay in movements after the campaign had opened; (2.) That a line of supply be established from the Mississippi, independent of water-courses, because these would become unmanageable at certain seasons of the year;

---

[1] See page 501, volume II.

(3.) The concentration of the forces west of the Mississippi, and such other force as should be assigned to this duty from General Sherman's command, in such a manner as to expel the enemy from Northern Louisiana and Arkansas; (4.) Such preparation and concert of action among the different corps engaged as to prevent the enemy, by keeping him constantly employed, from operating against our positions or forces elsewhere; and (5.) That the entire force should be placed under the command of a single general. Preparations for a long campaign was also advised, and the month of May was indicated as the point of time when the occupation of Shreveport might be anticipated.[1] "Not one of these suggestions," said General Banks, in his report, " so necessary in conquering the inherent difficulties of the expedition, was carried into execution, nor was it in my power to establish them."

The general plan laid out was for Admiral Porter to move from Vicksburg with a powerful fleet of armored gun-boats and transports, carrying ten thousand men of Sherman's old army, under General A. J. Smith, and, passing up the Red River, capture Fort de Russy, and join Banks at Alexandria. The latter was to march overland from the Atchafalaya to Alexandria with his disposable force, say sixteen thousand men, while General Steele, with about fifteen thousand men, operating independently, should

FREDERICK STEELE.

move directly on Shreveport from Little Rock. The Confederates in that region, according to the most reliable reports, were disposed as follows: Magruder, with about fifteen thousand effective men, was in Texas, his main body covering Galveston and Houston; Walker's division, about seven thousand strong, was on the Atchafalaya and Red River, from Opelousas to Fort de Russy; Mouton's division, numbering about six thousand men, was between the Black and Washita rivers, from Red River to Monroe; and Price, with a force of infantry estimated at five thousand, and of cavalry from seven to ten thousand, held the road from Monroe to Camden and Arkadelphia, in front of Steele. Magruder could spare ten thousand of his force to resist an attack from the east, leaving his fortifications on the coast well garrisoned, while Price could furnish at least an additional five thousand from the north, making, with those in the vicinity of the Red River, an army of from twenty-five to thirty thousand men—a force equal to any that could be brought against them, even with the most perfect unity and co-operation of commands.[2] Considering this disposition of the Confederate forces, we perceive that the problem was presented by authority for solution,—How shall the National forces achieve a victory in the campaign by threatening Shreveport with forty thousand men, so disposed in parts

---

[1] General Banks's Report to the Secretary of War.   [2] General Banks's Report to the Secretary of War.

that a solid and easily movable body of twenty-five thousand men may quickly strike each separate portion of the divided forty thousand in turn, with superior numbers? To the practical solution of this problem the Nationals now addressed themselves.

Being charged with other important duties at this time which required his presence in New Orleans, General Banks intrusted the arrangement of his portion of the expedition to General Franklin, who was to move on the 7th of March, and reach Alexandria on the 17th. Meanwhile, Admiral Porter, who had agreed to meet Banks there on that day, was promptly at the mouth of the Red River on the 7th, with his powerful fleet of fifteen iron-clads and four light steamers,[1] and there he was joined on the 11th by the transports, with four divisions[2] of Sherman's army, under General A. J. Smith, and the Marine Brigade, under General Alfred Ellet, three thousand strong. There was just water enough for the larger gun-boats to pass; and on the morning of the 12th they moved up the river, led by the *Eastport*. That vessel, with others that might follow, was charged with the duty of removing obstructions in the river, and to amuse Fort de Russy by a feigned attack until the army should land at Simms' Port, on the Atchafalaya, and get in the rear of that post, to attack it.

To cover the landing of the troops on the site of Simms' Port (the town had been destroyed), nine of the gun-boats turned into the Atchafalaya, followed by the transports. The crew of the *Benton* landed, and drove back Confederate pickets upon their main body, three miles in the rear; and when the divisions of Generals Mower and T. Kilby Smith landed,[a] the entire opposing force fell back toward Fort de Russy. Mower, with a brigade, then reconnoitered toward Yellow Bayou, when he found that the Confederates had fled from a post there, burning the bridge behind them.

[a] March 13, 1864.

It was now decided to land the whole column, and march it overland to Fort de Russy, a distance of about thirty miles; and at daybreak on the morning of the 14th it moved, in light marching order, Mower in the advance. Very soon the Nationals began to feel their foe, and they were compelled to skirmish with the Confederate cavalry, in front and rear, nearly all the way, until they approached the fort in the afternoon. They had marched, fought, and built a bridge over the Yellow Bayou (which consumed two hours), since dawn, and now, without rest, attacked the fort, which was armed with eight siege-guns and two field-pieces, two of the former in position to command the river.

In the mean time the gun-boats had removed the obstructions in the

---

[1] Porter's fleet consisted of the following vessels: *Essex*, Commander Robert Townsend; *Benton*, Lieutenant-Commander James A. Green; *Lafayette*, Lieutenant-Commander J. P. Foster; *Choctaw*, Lieutenant-Commander F. M. Ramsey; *Chillicothe*, Acting Volunteer Lieutenant S. P. Couthony; *Ozark*, Acting Volunteer Lieutenant George W. Browne; *Louisville*, Lieutenant-Commander E. K. Owen; *Carondelet*, Lieutenant-Commander J. G. Mitchell; *Eastport*, Lieutenant-Commander S. L. Phelps; *Pittsburg*, Acting Volunteer Lieutenant W. R. Hoel; *Mound City*, Acting Volunteer Lieutenant A. R. Langthorne; *Osage*, Lieutenant-Commander T. O. Selfridge; *Neosho*, Acting Volunteer Lieutenant Samuel Howard; *Ouachita*, Lieutenant-Commander Byron Wilson; and *Fort Hindman*, Acting Volunteer Lieutenant John Pearce. These were the armored vessels. The lighter boats consisted of the *Lexington*, Lieutenant George M. Bache; *Cricket*, Acting Master H. H. Gorringe; *Gazelle*, Acting Master Charles Thatcher; *Black Hawk*, Lieutenant-Commander K. R. Breese.

[2] The First and Third Divisions of the Sixteenth Army Corps, and First and Fourth Divisions of the Seventeenth Army Corps.

river, and the *Eastport* and *Neosho* moved up within range of the fort, just as a heavy artillery duel between the fort and the land troops, which lasted about two hours, was closing. The *Eastport* fired a few shots, when the troops charged, and at half-past four o'clock the works were carried, and the Confederates, about five thousand strong, under General Walker, retreated up the river.[1] Before sunset the Nationals had full possession of the fort, when Porter sent two of his swiftest gun-boats (*Ouachita* and *Lexington*) followed by the *Eastport* and *Neosho*, to reach Alexandria before the arrival of the fugitives. This was accomplished, and that place soon fell into the hands of the Nationals without a struggle. The Confederates burned two steamboats and a considerable quantity of cotton, and then fled up the river, their rear-guard just beyond danger from pursuit, when, on the evening of the 16th,[a] the transports arrived, on which Smith's troops had re-embarked at Fort de Russy. These landed and occupied the town. General Smith had left a small force behind to assist the *Essex* and *Benton* in destroying the fort, so that it could not be reoccupied by the Confederates.

^a *March, 1864.*

General Franklin was not ready to move with Banks's column from the Teche region until the 13th.[b] He met with very little opposition. His cavalry division, under General A. L. Lee, with General Charles P. Stone (Banks's chief of staff), and others of that officer's military family, reached Alexandria on the 19th. Banks followed, and made his head-quarters there on the 24th, but his whole column, composed of the Nineteenth and detachments of the Thirteenth Army Corps, did not reach there until the 26th. Meanwhile, four brigades of Smith's forces, led by General Mower, went out[c] from Alexandria to attack a Confederate force at Henderson's Hill, twenty-five miles westward. The expedition, prosecuted in the midst of a cold rain and hail-storm, was eminently successful. The Confederates were surprised, and lost two hundred and fifty of their men captured, with two hundred horses, and four guns, with their caissons. A few days later[d] General Smith's force moved to Bayou Rapide, twenty-one miles above Alexandria, in the direction of Shreveport.

^b *March.*

^c *March 21.*

^d *March 27.*

Formidable difficulties in the way of the expedition now appeared. Near Alexandria are rapids in the Red River, and at this time the water immediately below them was of barely sufficient depth to float Porter's heavier iron-clads. The gun-boats were essential to the success of the expedition, but none of them could easily pass above the rapids. Finally, after the heaviest labor for more than a week,[e] about one half of them were forced up, but with the loss of the hospital-vessel, *Woodford*, of the marine brigade, wrecked in the rapids. Many of that corps were then suffering from the small-pox, and were in a very discontented state. As the transports could not pass the rapids, and as they had no available land or water transportation for advancing farther, they were permitted to return to the Mississippi, in compliance with an earnest call for them to do so by General McPherson, at Vicksburg, who desired them for the special duty of guarding the great river from raids. This

^e *April 2.*

---

[1] With the works, 10 guns, and 1,000 muskets, the Nationals captured 283 prisoners. Their own loss was only 34, of whom 4 were killed. The Confederates lost 9 killed and wounded.

reduced the force of the expedition three thousand, and General Banks was compelled to make an equal deduction from his force by an unforeseen necessity. It had been intended to carry supplies the whole distance, in the advance on Shreveport, by water, but the river was now so low that but few transports could pass the rapids, and it was found necessary to establish a depot of supplies at Alexandria, and a wagon-train to take them from vessels below to vessels above the rapids. To protect this depot and train required a considerable force, and to that duty General Grover was assigned, with three thousand men. General Banks then found his available force with which to move forward from Alexandria reduced to about twenty thousand men, without any expectation of co-operation with General Steele. There was no unity of command, and experts prophesied, at the beginning of April, a probable failure of the expedition.[1]

Before the gun-boats had passed up the rapids, General Banks's column, under General Franklin, advanced[a] to Natchitoches, near the river, eighty miles above Alexandria by land,[2] where he arrived on the 3d of April. The Confederates had continually retreated before him, frequently stopping to skirmish with his vanguard, but offering no serious resistance, and now they continued their flight toward Shreveport. At about the same time, General Smith's command was embarked at Bayou Rapide, and moved up the river with the fleet. The difficulties and dangers of the expedition increased every hour, for the water in the river, instead of rising, as it was expected it would, was slowly falling, making the navigation more and more difficult. And now, the advance of Banks and Smith had placed a strong Confederate force between their columns, and that of General Steele, which was expected to co-operate with them.[3]

> [a] March 28, 1864.

Now, too, another most serious danger to the expedition appeared, in the possibility of its numbers being reduced full one-third more, before its object could be accomplished, by the withdrawal of General Smith's command. Expecting no delay on account of low water in the Red River, General Banks had told General Sherman, at New Orleans, that the troops under Smith might be spared from the expedition within thirty days after their arrival at Alexandria. Acting upon this assurance Lieutenant-General Grant, on assuming supreme command, sent word[b] to General Banks,[4] that if he should find that the taking of Shreveport would occupy ten or fifteen days more time than General Sherman gave his troops to be

> [b] March 15.

---

[1] While the forces under the four commanders, Banks, Smith, Steele, and Porter, were operating together, "neither one of them," says the first named, in his report, "had a right to give any order to the other. General Smith never made any report to me, but considered his as a substantially independent force." He could get no information readily from General Steele. "It took us twenty days," Banks said, "to communicate with him," and then the sum of advantage was a simple statement of position, and a few words of advice. Halleck himself said, as late as the 5th of March, that he had no information of General Steele's plans, other than that he was to facilitate Banks's march on Shreveport; and on the day after Banks's arrival at Alexandria, he received a dispatch from Halleck, dated ten days earlier, saying he had directed General Steele to make a real move on Shreveport, instead of a demonstration only, as that officer had thought advisable. From time to time Banks was told that Steele would co-operate with him, but, at the close of April, the latter sent him word to the effect that co-operation with him was out of the question, for reasons that we shall observe presently.

[2] Natchitoches is on the margin of the old Red River, four miles southward of Grand Ecore, which is on the bank of the new channel of that stream.

[3] A scout was sent from Natchitoches across the country to Steele, and an aid-de-camp (Captain R. T. Dunham) was sent to the same destination by way of the White River, and both succeeded in delivering dispatches. But the operation was of no practical use.

[4] General Banks received this dispatch at Alexandria, on the eve of his departure for Natchitoches.

absent from their command, he must send them back at the time specified, even if it should lead to an abandonment of the main object of the expedition. General Grant was anxious to have all the armies acting in concert with each other in the contemplated grand and simultaneous movement upon Richmond and Atlanta, and for that purpose he directed Banks, in the event of the success of his expedition, to hold Shreveport and Red River with such force as he might deem necessary, and return the remainder of his troops to New Orleans as quickly as possible, with a view to a movement on Mobile, if it should be thought prudent. So anxious was the new General-in-Chief for the co-operation of Banks's force, that, in another dispatch, he said : " I had much rather that the Red River expedition had never been begun, than that you should be detained one day beyond the first of May in commencing the movement east of the Mississippi."

It was under circumstances such as these that the expedition advanced from Natchitoches upon Shreveport, a hundred miles distant, by land, over a barren and almost uninhabited country. The heavier gun-boats could ascend the river no farther than Grand Ecore, and from that point all supplies had to be taken in wagons, and on few transports inadequately guarded by armed vessels. Under these circumstances, and others just mentioned, Banks would have been justified in going no farther, for he had ascertained that the Confederates from Texas and Arkansas, under Taylor, Price, Green, and others, were gathering on his front, to the number of about twenty-five thousand, with over seventy guns. But his own troops and those of General Smith were anxious to secure the main object of the expedition,[1] and so, on the morning of the 6th of April,[a] Franklin moved forward, with General Lee's cavalry in the van, followed by two thin divisions of the Thirteenth Corps, under General Ransom. General Emory followed Ransom with the First Division[2] of the Nineteenth Corps, and a brigade of colored troops, which had just come up from Port Hudson. On the following morning,[b] General Smith followed with a part of the Sixteenth Corps, while a division of the Seventeenth, under T. Kilby Smith, twenty-five hundred strong, went up the river as a guard to the transports, which moved very slowly. General Smith was directed to conduct them to Loggy Bayou, opposite Springfield, about half way between Natchitoches and Shreveport, and there to halt and communicate with the army, at Sabine Cross Roads, fifty-four miles from Grand Ecore.

General Lee had already encountered the Confederates. In a reconnoissance westward from Natchitoches on the 2d, with the First, Third, and Fourth Brigades of his division, and, at a distance of about twelve miles from that town, he found the pickets of the foe. These were driven upon the main body, and the whole force was chased to and beyond Crump's Hill, twenty miles from Natchitoches, before the pursuit ended. There, where the route of the army would be more to the northwest, General Lee waited for the head of it to come up.

[a] 1864.
[b] April 7.

---

[1] They were stimulated by a successful encounter on the 4th, near Compte, on the north side of the Red River, by fifteen hundred cavalry, under Colonel O. P. Gooding, with an equal number of Marmaduke's cavalry. Gooding drove them from their camp and captured their equipage.

[2] This was a division of picked men, composed of the Third Iowa, Forty-first, Eighty-first, and Ninety-fifth Illinois, Fourteenth and Thirty-third Wisconsin, and the Fifty-eighth Ohio, all infantry.

Franklin ordered Lee to attack the enemy whenever he could find him, but not to bring on a general engagement. On the 7th, he skirmished almost continually with an ever-increasing cavalry force, driving them before him, until he had passed Pleasant Hill two or three miles, when he found the main body of the Confederate horsemen, under General Green, at Wilson's farm, strongly posted. There a sharp struggle for two hours occurred, when the Confederates were driven to St. Patrick's Bayou, near Carroll's farm, nine miles from Pleasant Hill, and there Lee halted. His loss in the engagement was ninety-two men. That of the Confederates was greater, including many prisoners. Franklin, at Lee's request, had sent forward a brigade of infantry to his support, but these were withdrawn before reaching the ground, on perceiving that the firing had ceased. Franklin advanced to Pleasant Hill and encamped, and there General Banks, who had remained at Grand Ecore until all the troops had left, reached the front, after a ride of thirty-five miles.

It was now evident that the farther advance of the Nationals would be obstinately contested, and General Lee, who had been ordered to push forward, asked Franklin to allow his heavy wagon-train to remain behind, so as to be safe in the event of a sudden and formidable attack, and also requested a supporting infantry force. By order of General Banks, Colonel Landrum's brigade of the Thirteenth Corps was sent to him, and, at daybreak,[a] Lee moved forward, drove the Confederates from [a] April 8, 1864. St. Patrick's Bayou, and slowly, by the free use of his artillery, pushed them back to the woods beyond the clearing at Sabine Cross Roads, three or four miles below Mansfield, where he found the Trans-Mississippi army, full twenty thousand strong, under Generals Kirby Smith, Taylor, Mouton, and Green.

Finding the position and strength of his foes much superior to his own, they being behind the crest of a hill covered with pine woods, over which passed the only road to Shreveport, Lee concluded to wait until the main body of the Nationals should come up. But the Confederates would not allow him to wait, and so, at noon, when General Ransom came up with the Second Brigade of the Thirteenth, to relieve Landrum's, the two commanders formed a line of battle, and prepared to resist the foe as long as possible. At this juncture, at a little past noon, General Banks arrived at the front, and found the skirmishers hotly engaged. He had passed Franklin at ten o'clock, giving him directions to close up his column as speedily as possible. Perceiving the situation, Banks sent back orders to Franklin to hurry forward the infantry, at the same time directing Lee to hold his ground steadily, but not to advance until re-enforcements should arrive.

Every moment the situation of the van of Banks's army was becoming more critical, for the Confederates were concentrating to crush it. Officer after officer was sent to hurry Franklin up, but the head of his column having halted at St. Patrick's Bayou in the morning, and waited, for the remainder to come up, he was too far in the rear to reach the scene of action in time to give assistance. Skirmishing became hotter and hotter, and was incessant; and at half-past four o'clock the whole Confederate force, eight thousand footmen and twelve thousand horsemen, fell upon the Nationals along their whole line, striking with special weight and vigor on their right flank. The resistance was gallant and desperate for about an hour and a half, but the force of the assailants was so overwhelming in numbers, and their charges were so heavy in front and flank, that the Union troops were compelled to fall back to the woods in the rear of the open space at the Cross Roads, with heavy loss, but in good order. In this retreat, three pieces of Nims's battery were lost. The Confederates strove hard to get in the rear of the Nationals, but Lee's cavalry repulsed them at every attempt.

At about five o'clock General Franklin came up with the Third Division of the Thirteenth Corps, under General Cameron, and a new and stronger line was formed, but this was speedily broken up by the Confederates, who, inspirited by success, fell upon it with great fury, turning its flanks, and striking its center heavily. This assault, like the first, was stubbornly resisted, but finding the Confederates gaining their rear, the Nationals fell as steadily back as they could along the narrow, winding forest road, filled with the wagons and mules of the cavalry supply-train. These so blocked the way that it was difficult for men and artillery to retreat. There General Ransom lost ten guns and about a thousand men captured, and Lee lost nearly the whole of his wagons (one hundred and fifty-six), filled with supplies. The confusion was terrible, and efforts to re-form the line were unavailing.[1] Generals Franklin and Ransom, and Colonel Robinson of the Third Cavalry, were wounded, and Colonel Vance, of the Ninety-sixth Ohio, Lieutenant-Colonel Webb, of the Seventy-seventh Ohio, and Captain Dickey, of General Ransom's staff, were killed. So ended, in disaster to the Union arms, THE BATTLE OF SABINE CROSS ROADS.

Fortunately for the shattered columns of Franklin's advance, General W. H. Emory was then approaching rapidly with his fine division. He had been advised of the condition of affairs at the front, and was directed to form a line of battle in the strongest position he could select, to support the troops in retreat, and check the advance of the pursuers. At Pleasant Grove, three miles behind Sabine Cross Roads, he halted for the purpose at about six o'clock in the evening, and formed a line in the edge of a wood, with an open field before him sloping to the front. The One Hundred and Sixty-second New York, Colonel Kinsey, were deployed as skirmishers, and ordered to the foot of the hill on the crest of which the line was formed, so as to cover the rear of the retreating forces. Across the road along which the fugitives and pursuers were advancing, General Dwight formed his (First) brigade, and to the left of him was placed the Third Brigade, from which the skirmishers were taken, commanded by Colonel Lewis Benedict. The Second Brigade, under General McMillan, was held in reserve. But

---

[1] An eye-witness wrote: "Suddenly there was a rush, a shout, the crashing of trees, the breaking down of rails, the rush and scamper of men. It was as sudden as though a thunderbolt had fallen among us, and set the pines on fire. What caused it, or when it commenced, no one knew. I turned to my companion to inquire the reason of this extraordinary proceeding, but before he had a chance to reply, we found ourselves swallowed up, as it were, in a hissing, seething, bubbling, whirlpool of agitated men. We could not avoid the current; we could not stem it; and if we hoped to live in that mad company, we must ride with the rest of them. Our line of battle had given away. General Banks took off his hat and implored his men to remain; his staff-officers did the same; but it was of no avail. Then the general drew his saber, and endeavored to rally his men, but they would not listen. Behind him the rebels were shouting and advancing. Their musket-balls filled the air with that strange, file-rasping sound that war has made familiar to our fighting men. The teams were abandoned by the drivers, the traces cut, and the animals ridden off by the frightened men. Bareheaded riders rode with agony pictured in their faces, and for at least ten minutes it seemed as if we were going to destruction together."—Correspondent of the Philadelphia *Press*.

before the line was fairly formed, the flying columns came dashing on in wild confusion, and passed through the opened ranks to the rear. The Confederates, close upon their heels, and flushed with the inspiration of victory, fell heavily upon the skirmish line, and pressed it back to the main body. In strong force they now assailed Emory, first threatening his right most seriously, which he strengthened by placing McMillan's reserves on the right of Dwight. Meanwhile the fire of the Unionists had been reserved, but when the foe was at close quarters they opened upon them such murderous volleys of musketry that they recoiled. A severe battle ensued, which lasted an hour and a half, during which the Confederates made the most vigorous efforts to turn the National left, held by Colonel Benedict. With great skill and gallantry that noble officer sustained the attack, and finally the assailants were so thoroughly repulsed, chiefly by his One Hundred and Sixty-second (his own regiment), and the One Hundred and Seventy-third New York, of his brigade, that the battle ceased in that part of the field. Everywhere else the Confederates were speedily thrown back with great slaughter. Among their slain was General Mouton, who fell dead at the first charge.

Thus ended in victory for the Nationals, just as darkness covered the scene, the sanguinary BATTLE OF PLEASANT GROVE, where, no doubt, the Confederates expected to end the campaign by the capture or dispersion of the Union forces. They knew the water in the Red River was steadily falling, to the great peril of the gun-boats and transports above the rapids at Alexandria, and they were elated with the prospect of capturing or destroying them. With these hopes and desires, they fought desperately at Sabine Cross Roads and at Pleasant Grove. "Nothing," said Banks in his report, "could surpass in impetuosity the assault of the enemy but the inflexible steadiness and valor of our troops. The First Division of the Nineteenth Corps, by its great bravery in this action, saved the army and navy." It should be remembered that it went into action under fire and under the demoralizing effect of stemming a torrent of fugitives.

Although Banks was victorious at Pleasant Grove, he thought it prudent to fall back to Pleasant Hill, fifteen miles in the rear, for the Confederates were within reach of re-enforcements, while he was not certain that General Smith could get up in time to aid him should he be attacked in the morning. So he moved to that position during the night, with General Emory covering his retreat, and bringing away the army material, after burying his dead and caring for his wounded. Banks's whole force reached their destination between eight and nine o'clock the next morning.[a]

[a] April 9, 1864.

It was soon discovered that the Confederates were following closely in strong force, and a line of battle was at once formed at Pleasant Hill to receive them. General Smith had arrived the evening before with a portion of his troops. The brigade of colored troops, under Colonel Dickey, was also there, so that Banks was ready to meet an attack with about fifteen thousand men. He formed a line of battle with Emory's division in front, his First Brigade, under Dwight, taking the right, and resting on a ravine which ran north of the little village of Pleasant Hill; his Second, General Millan, in the center; and his Third, Colonel Benedict, in a ditch on the left, his left resting in an open field. The Twenty-fifth New York Battery was placed on a hill between the First and Second Brigades. This battle-line

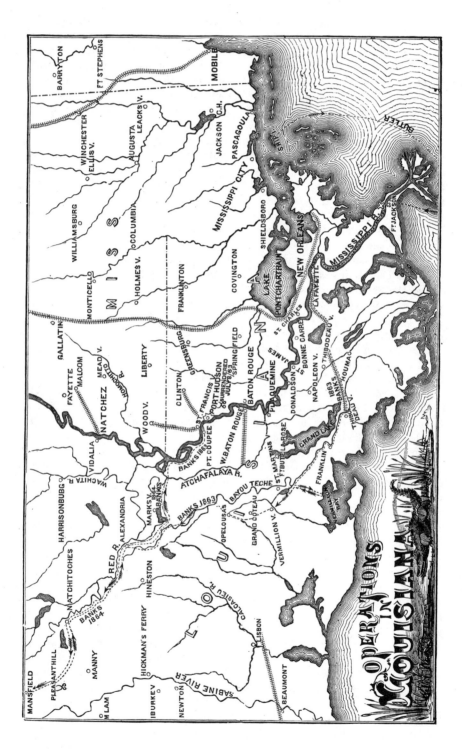

OPERATIONS IN LOUISIANA

was along a thickly-wooded acclivity half a mile west of Pleasant Hill, upon and around which the main body of the Unionists were posted. A second line was formed of two brigades; and the Thirteenth Corps, with a large portion of General Smith's command, were held as a reserve. The army trains, heavily guarded by most of Lee's cavalry division, the brigade of colored troops, and Ransom's shattered columns, were sent some distance on the road toward Grand Ecore, so as to be out of the way of danger in the impending battle, and not be liable to obstruct retreat should it become necessary.

Toward noon the Confederate advance appeared, skirmishing very cautiously, for Emory had taught them circumspection the previous evening; and so slight were these demonstrations until the middle of the afternoon, that the general belief was that there would be no attack in force before morning. That the Confederates were near in force was well known, for Colonel Gooding, who went out with his cavalry a mile or two on the Shreveport road to reconnoiter, was roughly handled by a large body of Texas horsemen, under Colonel Sweitzer.

Between three and four o'clock the Confederates opened a battery, the skirmishing increased in intensity, and there was an evident intention of attempting to turn Emory's right, whereupon the Second Brigade, which occupied the center, and lay across the Shreveport road, along which the foe was advancing, was posted on the right and rear, and its place was supplied by one of Smith's brigades.[1] Then the sounds of the skirmish-firing died away, but the lull was brief, and at a few minutes past five o'clock the Confederates burst out of the woods in heavy lines in all directions,[2] driving in the National skirmishers by two charging columns, and outflanking, by a quick oblique movement, Emory's left, held by Benedict's brigade,[3] fell upon it with crushing force. Outnumbered as well as outflanked, and being without any near support, the brigade fell steadily back, fighting gallantly as they were pushed up the acclivity of Pleasant Hill, suffering heavily until they filed behind Shaw's brigade. Sweitzer undertook to break the line of this covering force by a charge with his Texas cavalry, when he was met by one of the most destructive fires known in the annals of war. Of his regiment, not more than ten escaped death or wounds.[4] In the conflict down the slope at the first shock of the onset, and while trying to rally his men to a charge, the gallant Benedict was first wounded by a bullet in the arm, and a few moments afterward was killed by another, which passed through his head. No braver or more beloved soldier and citizen than he gave his life for his country during the war.[5]

---

[1] This was the Second Brigade, Third Division, of the Sixteenth Army Corps, commanded by Colonel W. T. Shaw, of the Fourteenth Iowa. The brigade consisted of the Fourteenth, Twenty-seventh, and Thirty-second Iowa, and Twenty-fourth Missouri.

[2] The Confederate line of battle was as follows: General Green's division, on the extreme left; that of the slain Mouton, under General Polignac, a French officer, on Green's right; next to him General Walker, and a division of Arkansas and Missouri troops, under General Churchill, on the extreme right.

[3] This was composed of the One Hundred and Sixty-second (Benedict's own), One Hundred and Sixty-fifth, and One Hundred and Seventy-third New York, and Thirtieth Maine.

[4] "Reserve your fire, boys, until he gets within thirty yards, and then give it to him!" said Colonel Shaw. As the cavalry came dashing up, "each infantry man," said an eye-witness, "had selected his victim, and, waiting till the three or four hundred were within about forty yards, the Fourteenth Iowa emptied nearly every saddle as quickly as though the order had been given to dismount."

[5] Colonel Benedict, then in the prime of life, was a ripe scholar, an able lawyer, and a greatly esteemed

While the left was overpowered and pushed back, and the Confederates succeeded in getting temporary possession of four guns on that flank, Emory's right stood firm, until, enveloped on three sides by superior force, it was crowded back a little, and allowed the assailants to pass on toward General Smith's position in reserve. A few volleys were exchanged, when the tide of battle was quickly turned by a heavy counter-charge of some of Smith's veterans, under General Mower, and Emory's troops, which had been skillfully formed on the right of these. The right of the Confederates was driven more than a mile by this charge. The whole of the reserves were ordered up, and the foe was completely routed, and pursued until dark. So ended,[a] in complete victory for the Nationals, THE BATTLE OF PLEASANT HILL. It "was desperate and sanguinary," said General Banks in his report. "The defeat of the enemy was complete, and his loss in officers and men more than double that sustained by our force.[1] We fought the battle at Pleasant Hill with about fifteen thousand against twenty-two thousand men."

[a] April 9, 1864.

Banks gave orders for a forward movement toward Shreveport the next morning, and communicated the fact to General Smith that evening. He sent word for his trains to re-form and advance at daybreak, and active preparations were commenced for following up the victory, when representations concerning the condition and circumstances of his command by Franklin and the general officers of the Nineteenth Corps, caused a suspension of the order. A conference of general officers was held that evening, when, upon the urgent recommendation of them all, and with the acquiescence of General Smith, it was determined to retire upon Grand Ecore the following day, "to the great disappointment of the troops," Banks said, "who, flushed with success, were eager for another fight."

In the mean time the command of T. Kilby Smith and the transports had reached Springfield Landing, at Loggy Bayou, where the river was obstructed by a sunken steamboat. Farther advance was not required, for word soon came of the disaster at Sabine Cross Roads, followed by an order from Pleasant Hill for the troops and flotilla to fall back to Grand Ecore as quickly as possible. Obedience was a difficult task, for the troops so sorely smitten by Banks were turning their attention to the capture or destruction

citizen of Albany, New York. He entered the service of the Republic at the beginning of the rebellion, and served it faithfully until his death ; and in whatever position he was placed, he was found ever equal to all demands upon him. While in McClellan's army, under Hooker, and fighting gallantly in front of Williamsburg, he was made a captive, and was confined in Libby Prison many weeks. On his return he was appointed commander of the One Hundred and Sixty-second New York, just organized, and which was assigned to duty in the expedition under General Banks. In the Department of the Gulf, under that commander, the regiment, in the hands of Colonel Benedict, became distinguished. He was soon placed in the position of acting-brigadier, and in that capacity performed gallant service before Port Hudson during Banks's siege of that post. He was then in General Dwight's division, which occupied the left of the attacking line. He was ever ready for perilous duty, and often performed it. When, on the 15th of June, Banks called for one thousand volunteers to storm the works at Port Hudson, Colonel Benedict offered to lead a battalion in the perilous duty, which circumstances made unnecessary. His death produced most profound sorrow in the army, and in his native State, where he was widely known and appreciated. The newspapers teemed with eulogies of him, and he was honored with a public funeral in the city of Albany.

[1] General Banks reported his losses in "the severe battles of the 7th, 8th, and 9th of April," at 3,969, of whom 289 were killed, 1,541 wounded, and 2,150 missing. Most of the latter were prisoners. In addition to these, the Nationals had lost in the campaign, thus far, 20 pieces of artillery, 160 wagons, and 1,200 horses and mules, including many that died of disease. The gains were the capture of Fort De Russy, Alexandria, Grand Ecore, and Natchitoches, the opening of the Red River, and the capture of 2,300 prisoners, 25 pieces of artillery (chiefly by the fleet), and 3,000 bales of cotton. The Confederate losses in the engagements just mentioned were never reported.

of the vessels and troops above Grand Ecore. The banks of the river, at its turns, were now swarming with sharp-shooters. The water was very low, and continually falling, and great labor was necessary in getting the vessels over the numerous bars and shoals. The men employed in this service were exposed to murderous musket-firing, and the flotilla did not move over thirty miles a day.

The first regular attack upon the vessels, in force, was at Coushattee, by nearly two thousand cavalry, with four guns, under Colonel Harrison, who, after that, continually annoyed the Nationals, the slow progress of the boats, which were tied up at night, enabling him to keep up with them. General Smith fitted the transports under his command for defense as well as his means would allow, by barricading them with boxes, barrels, bales of hay, and the mattresses of the steamers. He felt that the salvation of both the gun-boats and the transports depended much upon the valor and fortitude of his troops, for the water was so low that the cannon on the war-vessels could do but little execution upon the high banks, at short range. He succeeded in mounting two thirteen-inch Rodman guns on a platform upon the hurricane deck of the *Emerald*, and these performed excellent service, not only in action, but in keeping the Confederates at a respectful distance.

On the evening of the 12th the most determined attack was made on a part of the flotilla, near Pleasant Hill landing, where a heavy transport lay aground. A large majority of the gun-boats and transports, including Porter's flag-ship, with the Admiral on board, had gone down the river, leaving two or three gun-boats and transports with General Smith's command behind. Doubtless aware of this weakening of the forces on the river, caused the Confederates to attempt the capture of the remainder, and accordingly about two thousand infantry and dismounted cavalry, under General Thomas Green, appeared on the right bank of the river, charged up to its edge, and demanded the surrender of the transports, at the same time opening fire on the monitor *Osage*. It was answered by a sharp fire from the two Rodman guns and from other vessels—gun-boats and transports, — with fearful effect. The first discharge of a Rodman blew off the head of the Confederate commander.[1] He was one of the most useful officers in Kirby Smith's depart-

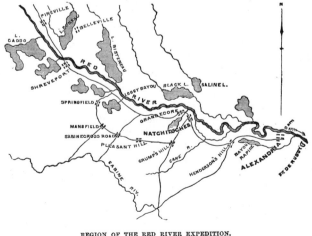

REGION OF THE RED RIVER EXPEDITION.

---

[1] In his report to the Secretary of the Navy on the 14th of April, Admiral Porter claimed the entire credit of the repulse of the Confederates for himself and his command, and did not even mention the presence of General T. Kilby Smith and his troops.

ment, and his loss was greatly deplored. The Confederates rallied, and again charged most recklessly, receiving the fire of Smith's soldiers and of the gun-boats, especially of the *Lexington*, Lieutenant Bache, which gave them a raking fire of canister-shot, that strewed the bank with their dead bodies for a mile. At the same time Harrison appeared on the opposite side of the river, and received such rough treatment, that he kept at a distance, and the whole flotilla passed down toward Grand Ecore without much further trouble. So terrible was the lesson given to the Confederates in this engagement, that a force of five thousand, which was hastening to intercept the flotilla at a point below, turned back. In the mean time Banks and all the land troops had returned to Grand Ecore, when a part of them were sent six miles up the river, to protect a large portion of the descending gun-boats and transports there aground. These were speedily brought down without further annoyance.

The army was again upon the Red River, but the troubles of the expedition were not at an end. Porter found most of his larger vessels aground at Grand Ecore, some of them drawing a foot more water than there was on the bar there, and the river was still falling. The momentous question arose, If it shall be found expedient or necessary to continue the retreat to Alexandria, and so on to the Mississippi, how shall the vessels of the expedition be taken over the rapids below? This question had come up before the battle at Pleasant Hill. Lieutenant-Colonel Joseph Bailey, Engineer of the Nineteenth Corps, had foreseen this difficulty, and conceived a way of overcoming it, by damming the river at the foot of the rapids, so as to deepen the waters above, and then, by opening a sluice, have a sufficient depth, as the pent-up volume flowed down, to float the vessels safely through. He mentioned this project to General Franklin in the morning before the battle at Pleasant Hill, who approved it, and after that struggle Franklin named it to General Banks, who also approved it. The latter officer, in a personal interview with Admiral Porter, six days later,[a] suggested it, in

[a] April 15, 1864.

case it was thought best for the expedition to return to the Mississippi; but the latter evinced no faith in it. He expressed his belief that the Red River would rise in time to give sufficient water at the rapids, notwithstanding army officers, from long experience in that region, held a contrary opinion. In a dispatch to the Secretary of the Navy the day before, he had said: "If nature does not change her laws, there will, no doubt, be a rise of water," and to this opinion he adhered until satisfied that nature would not accommodate the fleet, and that the scientific skill of an army officer was necessary to save it from destruction, as we shall observe presently.

Porter succeeded in getting all his vessels over the bar at Grand Ecore, and then went down the river[b] toward Alexandria, leaving the fleet in charge of Lieutenant-Commander Selfridge. The whole naval

[b] April 17.

force at once started down the river. When about eight miles below, the *Eastport* was sunk by a torpedo, and several days were consumed in getting her afloat. Meanwhile, General Banks had received the letter from General Grant, already alluded to, concerning General Sherman's troops,[1] and he determined

---

[1] See page 255.

to go on to Alexandria so soon as the *Eastport* should be raised and the fleet
be enabled to proceed. The *Eastport* floated on the 21st,[a] and on
that day orders were issued for the army to move; and before _{a April, 1864.}
dawn the next morning, two divisions, the cavalry under General Arnold,
and the artillery under Captain Classon, the whole commanded by General
Emory, were on their way toward Cane River, in rapid march, for it had
been ascertained that the Confederates were gathering on that stream, at
the only ferry, to dispute the passage of the Nationals. They marched
forty miles that day, so as to strike the Confederates early in the morning
and force a passage for the army.

About eight thousand Confederates, with sixteen guns, under General
Bee, had taken a strong position on Monet's Bluff, on the east side of Cane
River, at the ferry, which was securely flanked by the unfordable stream on
one side and an impassable swamp on the other. The plan was for Bee to
oppose the passage of the Nationals, and draw them into a sharp engagement, while the remainder of the Confederate army, lying not far distant,
should fall upon their flank and rear. Banks's quick movement deranged
the plan. The Confederates were not ready for its execution. Emory was
there too soon. His van drove the Confederate pickets on the west side of
the river, across the stream, early on the morning of the 23d,[b]   b April.
but the main position was found to be too strong to be carried
by direct attack.

It was extremely important to open the way there for the army to cross
the river. A failure to do so implied the necessity of throwing it across the
Red River, in the presence of the enemy on both sides of that stream. A
flanking movement was determined upon. General H. W. Birge was
ordered to take his own brigade, that of Colonel Fessenden (Third of the
First Division of the Nineteenth Corps), and General Cameron's division of
the Thirteenth Corps, and, crossing the river three miles above the ferry,
turn the left of the Confederates and carry their position in reverse. The
march was made wearily across bayous and swamps, and through tangled
woods, and it was late in the afternoon before they reached the desired
position, after carrying two strong ones occupied by pickets and skirmishers.
To Fessenden's brigade was assigned the duty of assault. It was gallantly
performed. After sharp resistance, until dark, the Confederates fled in disorder along the Fort Jessup road, toward Texas, taking their artillery with
them. In this brilliant achievement the National loss was about two hundred men killed and wounded. Among the latter was Colonel Fessenden.

Meanwhile the main body of the National army had moved toward Cane
River, and when its advance arrived within range of the cannon on the bluff,
the Confederates opened fire upon them. A spirited artillery duel ensued,
and was kept up at intervals a greater part of the day, while the troops were
held in reserve for the purpose of forcing the passage of the river when
Birge should attack. This was done, and the action lasted until dark,
when, as we have observed, the Confederates fled, and the bluff was occupied
by the Nationals.

In the mean time, that portion of the Confederates which were expected
to fall on the flank and rear of the Nationals, were active, and greatly
annoyed the rear of General A. J. Smith's column, which was covered by

the command of General T. Kilby Smith. The latter was charged with the arduous duty of covering the retreat to Alexandria. He was hotly pressed, and compelled to skirmish with the foe hovering on flank and rear, almost from the beginning of the march; and, on the morning of the 23d,[a] he had a severe engagement near Clouterville, on the Cane River, where he formed a battle-line, with General Mower on his right. Smith gallantly and skillfully conducted the engagement for about three hours, when the Confederates, repulsed at every point, withdrew. The National loss was about fifty men; that of the Confederates was estimated at one hundred, at least. On the afternoon of the following day, the whole army moved on without encountering serious resistance, and, on the 27th, entered Alexandria, after an absence of twenty-four days.

[a April, 1864.]

While the army was making its way toward Alexandria, the navy was having a difficult passage in the same direction. The *Eastport*, as we have seen, was floated, but she was found difficult to manage. She grounded several times, and finally, at a point about sixty miles below Grand Ecore, she became so fast on a bed of logs that she could not be moved. Lieutenant-Colonel Bailey had offered to help her over the numerous bars, by means of wing dams; but his assistance was declined, for "no counsel of army officers was regarded in nautical affairs."[1] Satisfied that she could not be floated before a rise in the river, and finding delay to be very dangerous, on account of the gathering of the Confederates on the shores of the stream, Porter ordered her to be blown up. The explosion and ensuing fire made her destruction complete.[b] At the same time, more than a thousand Confederates had gathered near, and taking advantage of the situation, rushed to the right bank of the river to board the *Cricket*, Master H. H. Goninge, lying there. She moved out, and gave them such a storm of grape and canister-shot, while the *Fort Hindman* poured a heavy cross-fire upon them, that, in the space of five minutes, not a guerrilla was to be seen. Then the vessels which had been convoying the *Eastport* went on down the river without molestation, until they reached the mouth of Cane River, twenty miles below, when the *Cricket*, which was ahead, with Admiral Porter on board, received eighteen shots from as many cannon planted on the shore at a bend in the stream. Nearly every shot went through her; one of her guns was disabled, and every gunner was killed or wounded. This first fire was followed by a shell, which exploded near her forward gun, killing or wounding every man attached to it, and in the fire-room close by. Her decks were now deserted, when Porter ordered her to be run by the battery. It was done, under a heavy fire. Then, having made gunners of some negroes on board, and placed the navigation of the boat, whose engineer and pilot had been disabled, in other hands, he attempted to assist the other boats still above the battery. He found he could not do much, so he ran the *Cricket* a few miles down the river, to a point where he had directed the *Osage* and *Lexington* to meet him, to summon them to the assistance of the *Fort Hindman* and two or three other vessels. He found these fighting a Confederate field-battery. Darkness fell before the struggle ended, and the *Cricket* could not return. But during the gloom the other

[b April 26.]

---

[1] General Banks's Report.

vessels above, ran by the battery at Cane Creek, and escaped, with the exception of the pump-boat, *Champion*, which was disabled and burned.[1] After that, the vessels were not impeded on their way to Alexandria.

The land and naval forces of the Red River expedition were now all at Alexandria. What next? Banks found General Hunter there,[a] with orders from General Grant to close up the campaign against [a] April 25, 1864. Shreveport as speedily as possible, for Sherman's troops were wanted eastward of the Mississippi. Hunter was sent back with a letter to Grant, telling him that the fleet was above the rapids, and would be in danger of capture or destruction if abandoned by the army, and informing him that it would require some time to get them below, if it could be effected at all. Any attempt to renew the Shreveport campaign of course was now out of the question, and all eyes were turned toward the Mississippi, as the next point of destination for the expedition. To get the fleet below the rapids was the first work to be accomplished. Porter did not believe in damming the river, except by words. Banks did, and ordered Colonel Bailey to do it. He went to work on Sunday, the first of May, with liberty to employ as many men as he might desire. Nearly the whole of the army were engaged in the business, in some way, at different times; and on Sun-

BAILEY'S RED RIVER DAM.

day, the 8th of May, a main dam of stone and timber, and sunken coal-boats, was finished.[2] It stretched across the river, there nearly eight hundred feet in width, and then from four to six feet in depth, and running at the rate of ten miles an hour.

The work was successful. The water was raised seven feet on the rapids, and that afternoon the gun-boats *Osage*, *Fort Hindman*, and *Neosho*, with

[1] In this affair, the *Cricket* was hulled thirty-eight times, and lost half her crew of fifty men, killed and wounded. The *Juliet* was badly damaged, and lost fifteen men; and the gun-boat, *Fort Hindman*, was also badly maimed. As she ran by the battery, her wheel-ropes were cut by the shot, and she drifted helplessly down the stream.

[2] Admiral Porter, in his dispatch to the Secretary of the Navy, says: "The work was commenced by running out from the left bank of the river a tree-dam, made of the bodies of very large trees, brush, brick, and stone, cross-tied with other heavy timber, and strengthened in every way ingenuity could devise. This was run about three hundred feet into the river. Four large coal-barges were then filled with brick, and sunk at the end of it. From the right bank of the river cribs filled with stone were built out to meet the barges." Speaking of the break in the dam, he said it was a fortunate occurrence, for it was caused by the swinging around of two barges at the center, which formed a cushion for the vessels passing through, and prevented their striking the rocks.

two other vessels, passed the rapids, and lay just above the dam. But the greater portion of the fleet was still, and evinced no disposition to move. Banks inspected the work, and perceiving an immense pressure upon it, feared it might give way before the fleet could pass. He rode up the shore to a point opposite the fleet, at midnight, and sent a note to Porter, telling him of his fears, and urging him to put his vessels in condition, by lightening them, to pass over the rapids. This was not done. At five o'clock the next morning, a portion of the dam gave way. The three vessels went safely down through the sluice thus made, and the *Lexington*, the only one ready, followed with equal safety. Had all been ready, the whole fleet might have passed over in the course of a few hours, before the water became too shallow.[1] The damage to the dam was partially repaired. It was also strengthened by wing dams, and, on the 12th of May, when it was completed, and the vessels above had been lightened, they all passed into the deeper water below with safety, before eight o'clock the next morning. Then Admiral Porter wrote[a] to the Secretary of the Navy, saying: "There seems to have been an especial Providence looking out for us, in providing a man [Colonel Bailey] equal to the emergency. . . . This proposition looked like madness, and the best engineers ridiculed it, but Colonel Bailey was so sanguine of success, that I requested General Banks to have it done."

[a] May 16, 1864.

While the army was detained at Alexandria on account of the fleet, it was re-enforced[b] by a large portion of the troops that had been garrisoning ports in the vicinity of Matagorda Bay, on the Texan coast.[2] They were led by General John A. McClernand, who left General Fitz-Henry Warren in command of the remainder at Matagorda. These posts had been evacuated by order of General Grant; and McClernand was soon followed by Warren, who likewise ascended the Red River, until stopped by Confederate batteries, when he fell back to the remains of Fort de Russy, and took post there. Banks had also received a dispatch from Halleck, in the name of General Grant, which directed the modification of previous orders, so that no troops should "be withdrawn from operations against Shreveport and on the Red River." But it was too late, and when the fleet was all below the rapids, and found the back-water of the then brimful Mississippi, one hundred and fifty miles distant, flowing up to Alexandria, and thus insuring a safe passage over all bars below, orders were given[c] for the army to move. The fleet moved likewise, with the transports laden with cotton, which had been captured as prize for the navy.[3] Caution marked the advance, for the Confederates were hovering near, and swarming on the banks below. A week before the expedition moved, the gun-boats *Signal* and *Covington*, convoying the transport *Warren* down the river, the three bearing about four hundred soldiers, were fired upon[d] at Dunn's Bayou, thirty miles

[b] April 29.

[c] May 13.

[d] May 5.

---

[1] General Banks's Report. [2] See page 224.

[3] When the fleet moved up the river, Admiral Porter proclaimed that all cotton seized within a league of that river should be lawful prize for the naval force under his command. There was but little opportunity for such seizures while the fleet was above Alexandria; but while lying there, and the army was hard at work constructing the dam for the benefit of the fleet, the Government wagons were kept very busy bringing in the staple from the neighboring plantations. In this profitable part of the public service the officers and soldiers of the army had no share. It is said that the transports were so laden with cotton, that there was no room for the Union inhabitants of Alexandria to flee, with their effects, from the vengeance of the Confederates.

below Alexandria, by a large Confederate force, at the morning twilight, and were so badly injured that the *Covington* was abandoned and burnt, and the other two vessels were surrendered. Of the soldiers, about one hundred and fifty were captured, and about one hundred were killed. The remainder took to the shore and escaped. Soon afterward, the *City Belle*, with a little more than four hundred Ohio troops, was captured by another guerrilla party, when about one-half of them escaped.

But the army in its march for Simms' Port met with very little opposition, excepting by a considerable force of Confederate cavalry, who, at daybreak on the 16th, confronted its advance at Mansura, near Marksville, where the National skirmishers and artillery, after pushing the foe back across an open prairie to a wood, kept up a fire for about three hours, until the main body came up. A battle-line was then formed, with General Emory and his forces on the right, and General A. J. Smith and his command on the left. After a sharp but brief struggle, the Confederates were dispersed, losing a number of men by capture. Among these were some of the prisoners they had taken on the *Signal* and *Warren* some days before. That evening the army reached the Atchafalaya at Simms' Port, where, under the direction of Colonel Bailey, a bridge, more than six hundred yards long, was constructed of steamboats. Over it the wagon-train passed on the afternoon of the 19th, at which time the rear of the army, composed of the command of A. J. Smith, was attacked at Yellow Bayou by a Confederate force under Polignac. He was beaten back with a heavy loss in killed, wounded, and prisoners, while the Nationals lost one hundred and fifty in killed and wounded. On the following day[a] the army crossed the Atchafalaya, when General E. R. S. Canby, who had arrived the day before, assumed the command of Banks's troops   [a] May 20, 1864. as a part of the forces of the Military Division of West Mississippi, to the charge of which he had been assigned. General Banks then hastened to New Orleans.

General Smith returned to Memphis, stopping on his way up the Mississippi at Sunnyside, in the extreme southeastern part of Arkansas, to seek a reported force of Confederates, under Marmaduke, who had gathered there with mischievous intent. He found them, three thousand strong, near Columbia, the capital of Chicot County, posted across a bayou that empties into Lake Chicot. He attacked and drove them away, with a loss of about one hundred men. They retreated westward, and were

EDWARD R. S. CANBY.

no more seen in that region. Smith's loss was about ninety men. Admiral Porter, meanwhile, had passed quietly down the Red River, nearly parallel with the march of the army, and resumed the duty of keeping open and safe the navigation of the Mississippi.

Let us now see what the Seventh Army Corps, under General Steele, was doing in the way of co-operation with the Red River expedition while it was in progress. General Steele was at his head-quarters at Little Rock when that expedition moved. On the 23d of March^a he started ^{a 1864.} southward, on the military road, with about eight thousand troops, horse and foot, the former commanded by General Carr. On the previous day General Thayer, commanding the Army of the Frontier, left Fort Smith with about five thousand men, for the purpose of joining Steele at Arkadelphia; and Colonel Clayton marched from Pine Bluff with a small force to the left of Steele, in the direction of Camden, a place held and well fortified by the Confederates. That was Steele's first objective, for Sterling Price, with a considerable force, was holding a line from that place westward to Washington, the capital of Hempstead County. It was necessary to dispose of this force before marching toward Shreveport.

The roads were so wretched that the junction of forces could not be relied upon, and Thayer failed to join Steele at Arkadelphia. The latter had been compelled to skirmish at the crossings of streams all the way from Benton, and his troops were somewhat worn by fatigue, but, after waiting two days for Thayer, he pushed on in the direction of Washington, for the purpose of flanking Camden, and drawing Price out of his fortifications there. He encountered the cavalry of Marmaduke and Cabell at almost every step, and day after day skirmished, sometimes lightly and sometimes heavily, with them, until the 10th of April, when he found Price in strong force across his path at Prairie d'Anne, not far from Washington, prepared to make a decided stand. Steele had been joined by Thayer, and he readily accepted battle. An artillery fight ensued, which lasted until dark. The Confederates made a desperate attempt in the darkness to capture Steele's guns, but failed. He pushed nearer their position the next day, and at the dawn of the 12th attempted to turn their flank, when they retreated to Washington, pursued for several miles by cavalry.

Steele now heard of the disaster to the Union troops at Sabine Cross Roads,[1] and, instead of pursuing Price toward Washington, turned sharply toward Camden. The Confederates quickly perceived his purpose, and, stimulated to stronger action by the news from Western Louisiana, they made vigorous efforts to save Camden from Steele's grasp. While his army was corduroying Bogue bottom, one of the worst in the State, his rear, under Thayer, was strongly attacked by General Dockery. The Confederates were repulsed, and the army moved on, but to find itself confronted by Cabell and Shelby. These were driven from position to posi- ^{b April.} tion, and on the evening of the 15th^b the National troops entered Camden.

Although Steele was in a strong place, and supplies could be easily obtained by way of the Washita, he found Camden to be an uncomfortable and dangerous post. The Confederates were swarming thickly around him, for there was no occasion for their employment in the direction of the Red River. Three days after his arrival they attacked and captured^c ^{c April 18.} a forage train, little more than a dozen miles from the Union

---

¹ See page 258.

OPERATIONS IN MISSOURI AND ARKANSAS

lines, by which Steele lost two hundred and fifty men and four guns. This was followed by another disaster, five days later, when the escort of a supply-train, which had come down from Little Rock, and was return-

* April 23, 1864. ing empty, was attacked * twelve miles from Camden by Shelby's cavalry. The escort consisted of a brigade of infantry, four guns, and a small cavalry force, commanded by Lieutenant-Colonel Drake, of the Seventy-seventh Ohio. The assailants were beaten off, and the train and escort pressed on, until again attacked, as it emerged from a swamp at Marks's Mill, by an overwhelming force under General Fagan. A desperate fight ensued between his force and the Forty-third Indiana and Thirty-sixth Ohio, until Drake was mortally wounded, and the Confederates had wedged in between the troops in conflict and the Seventy-seventh Ohio, guarding the rear of the train, when all were compelled to surrender. The National loss was two hundred and fifty men. The negro servants of the officers were butchered after the surrender. The Confederate loss was estimated at full six hundred.

Steele now felt it necessary to retreat to Little Rock, for he was informed that Fagan was marching on that place, and that E. Kirby Smith had heavily re-enforced Price. He accordingly threw his army across the Washita on the night of the 26th of April, and at daylight the next morning began a retreat by way of Princeton and Jenkinson's Ferry, on the

b April 30. Sabine River. At the latter place he was attacked b by an over-whelming force, led by Kirby Smith in person. Steele's troops were nearly famished, having eaten but little since they left Camden, and were exceedingly weary. A part of them had already crossed the river, when the foe struck the Thirty-third Iowa, Colonel Mackey, covering the rear, a very heavy blow. The Fiftieth Indiana pressed forward to its aid, when both were pushed back behind the Ninth Wisconsin and Twenty-ninth Iowa. These were then furiously assailed, when all the troops yet on the south side of the river were ordered up, and a most sanguinary battle ensued, in which General S. A. Rice was in immediate command of the Nationals.

Three times the Confederates charged heavily, and were repulsed each time. Then they threatened the National right flank, when the Forty-third Illinois and a part of the Fortieth Iowa dashed across a swollen, miry stream, and drove the enemy back. The latter then made a desperate attempt to crush the left and center. They turned the extreme left, held by the Thirty-third Iowa, whose ammunition had given out, when four companies of the Fortieth Iowa, led by Colonel Garrett, hastened to its support, formed under a tremendous fire, and restored the line, when it pressed forward, and for a full hour drove the Confederates steadily back. It was a fight by infantry alone, and at noon the Nationals had gained a complete victory. Then they crossed the river leisurely, and moved on toward Little Rock, leaving only a burial party behind. These the Confederates captured, and then claimed a victory in THE BATTLE OF JENKINSON'S FERRY. In that struggle the Confederates lost over three thousand men, including three general officers. The loss of the Nationals was seven hundred killed and wounded.

Steele pressed on toward Little Rock as rapidly as possible, to prevent its capture by Fagan, and succeeded. It was a terrible march from Jenkins's Ferry over the swampy country, the half-famished men dragging cannon and caissons over corduroy roads they had made for the purpose, for the animals were so exhausted that they could not draw even the wagons, which had to be destroyed. A supply-train met them, and on the 2d of May the broken and dispirited troops entered Little Rock.

So ended, in all its parts, the disastrous campaign against Shreveport. Its result caused much disappointment and dissatisfaction; and General Banks was specially blamed for not pressing forward after his victory at Pleasant Hill. The narrative here given, drawn from authentic sources,[1] and the reasons offered by General Banks in his report, seem to the writer to be his sufficient justification in the judgment of candid observers.[2] He was nowise responsible for the radically defective plan of the campaign, and his troops evidently did all that it was possible for them to do under the circumstances.

---

[1] The authorities from which the facts of this narrative have been chiefly derived, are the Reports of General Banks and his subordinates; of Admiral Porter and his subordinates; of the Confederate General E. Kirby Smith and his subordinates; the narratives of newspaper correspondents, and the manuscript diaries of General T. Kilby Smith and Brevet Brigadier-General George Bernard Drake. The latter was the Adjutant-General of Banks's forces engaged in the Red River expedition, and, at the request of the writer, kindly furnished him with a copy of his diary.

[2] The chief reasons offered were : (1.) The difficulty in bringing his trains on the road toward Grand Ecore in time to move quickly after the flying Confederates; (2.) A lack of water for man or beast in that region, excepting such as the wells afforded; (3.) The fact that all surplus ammunition and supplies of the army were on board the transports sent up to Loggy Bayou, and the impossibility of knowing whether these had reached their destination; (4.) The falling of the river, which imperiled the naval part of the expedition; and (5.) The report of a scouting party, on the day of the battle, that no tidings could be heard of the fleet. "These considerations," said Banks, "the absolute deprivation of water for man or beast, the exhaustion of rations, and the failure to effect a connection with the fleet on the river, made it necessary for the army, although victorious in the struggle through which it had just passed, to retreat to a point where it would be certain of communicating with the fleet, and where it would have an opportunity for reorganization. The shattered condition of the Thirteenth Army Corps and the cavalry made this indispensable."

CHAPTER X.

THE LAST INVASION OF MISSOURI.—EVENTS IN EAST TENNESSEE.—PREPARATIONS FOR
THE ADVANCE OF THE ARMY OF THE POTOMAC.

HE failure of the Red River expedition, and the expulsion of Steele from the country below the Arkansas River, by which two-thirds of the State of Arkansas was given up to the Confederates, had a disastrous effect upon the Union cause and people in that State, where the restoration of civil power in loyal hands, amply sustained by the military, had been, it was believed, made permanent.[1] The dream of security was now dispelled. Steele was placed on the defensive at the State capital, and the Confederates everywhere showed, by their boldness and activity, a determination to repossess the State, if possible. Their cavalry roamed at will over all the region below the Arkansas, after Steele retreated to Little Rock, plundering and overawing the Unionists. Nor did

[a] 1864.   they confine themselves to that region. Late in June [a] Shelby, with a considerable body of Confederate cavalry, dashed across the Arkansas eastward of Little Rock, and pushed on to the White River, on the eastern border of Arkansas County, where they were attacked and thrown back, in the vicinity of St. Charles, by four regiments under General Carr, with a loss of about four hundred men, of whom two hundred were made prisoners. Carr's loss was about two hundred. Shelby was speedily re-enforced by Marmaduke, when Carr was pushed northward to Clarendon, when he, in turn, was re-enforced, and the Confederates retreated southward.

This bold movement was followed by others in that section of the State. In July about four hundred colored troops, led by Colonel W. S. Brooks,

[b] July 26.   went up the country a short distance from Helena, when they were attacked [b] by a heavier force under General Dobbins. Fortunately, Major Carmichael was then passing down the Mississippi on a steamer, with one hundred and fifty of the Fifteenth Illinois Cavalry, and

---

[1] The occupation of Little Rock by General Steele in the autumn of 1863, and the seeming acquiescence of the Confederates in the necessity of giving up the State to National rule, emboldened the Unionists, who finally
[c] Jan. 8.   met, by delegates, in a State Constitutional Convention,[c] at Little Rock, in which forty-two of the fifty-four counties in the State were represented. A State Constitution was framed, whereby slavery was forever prohibited. Isaac G. Murphy, the only stanch Unionist in the Secession Convention of that State [see page 474, volume I.], was chosen Provisional Governor,
[d] Jan. 22.   and duly inaugurated,[d] with C. C. Bliss Lieutenant-Governor, and R. J. T. White Secretary of State. The Constitution was ratified [e] by a vote of the people of the State, there being 12,177
[e] March 14.   in favor of it, and only 226 against it. Representatives in Congress and State officers were chosen under it, and the Legislature elected [f] United States Senators. By every usual form the
[f] April 25.   State was restored to its proper situation in the Union, in partial accordance with the terms of the President's Proclamation. See page 232. Such was its position when the military power of the Government began to wane, at the close of May.

hearing the firing, he landed and hastened in the direction of its sounds. He found Brooks and his men gallantly fighting double their number, so, with his followers, he dashed through the Confederate lines, joined the colored troops, and assisted them in repulsing their assailants. Colonel Brooks was killed, and fifty of his men were slain or wounded. The foe had lost more. The Union troops fell back to Helena, followed some distance by Dobbins. At about the same time fifteen hundred Confederates surprised[a] an outpost of Fort Smith, on the border of the Indian country, which was held by two hundred of the Fifth Kansas, under Captain Mefford. After a sharp fight, in which he lost twenty-five men, Captain Mefford was compelled to surrender. The Confederates lost thirty-two killed and wounded. Less than a month later, Shelby, with about two thousand men, struck[b] the line of the railway between Duvall's Bluff and Little Rock, and captured nearly the whole of the Fifty-fourth Illinois, who were guarding it at three points. Guerrillas hovered in large numbers around Little Rock and other places, making communications between the military posts dangerous, and requiring heavy escort duty, which wore down men and horses. Gradually several of these posts were abandoned, and at the close of 1864 only Helena, Pine, and Duvall's Bluffs, Little Rock, Van Buren, Fort Smith, and one or two other posts in that region, were held by the National troops. These being insufficient to protect the Unionists of the Commonwealth, they became disheartened, silent, and inactive, for the guerrillas, who roamed over the State, dealt vengeance upon these "traitors" and "renegades," as they called them.

[a] July 27, 1864.

[b] August 23.

General Steele, like other old officers of the regular army, was opposed to the emancipation policy of the Government, and his alleged sympathy with the slave-holding Oligarchy of Arkansas made the army under his command a feeble instrument in upholding the National cause in that State. The consequence was, that, at the close of 1864, that Commonwealth was practically surrendered to the Confederates. The disloyal Governor called a session of the Legislature, which met at Washington,[c] and chose a Senator (A. P. Garland) to represent the State in the "Congress" at Richmond.

[c] Sept. 22.

The condition of affairs in Arkansas was favorable to a long-contemplated scheme of invasion of Missouri, by her recreant son, General Sterling Price, which had both a military and political object in view, and, when undertaken, might have been most disastrous to the National cause but for the sleepless vigilance of General Rosecrans, who, late in January, had arrived[d] at St. Louis as commander of the Department of Missouri. He soon discovered that the State was seriously menaced by openly armed foes on one side, and by hidden and malignant ones on the other, and within its bosom, in the form of secret associations, known as "Knights of the Golden Circle," and "American Knights," or "Sons of Liberty."[1] He employed competent and trustworthy spies, who reported that these secret organizations were numerous and powerful; that they were preparing to join Price, when he should invade Missouri, in numbers not less than twenty-three thousand strong, each man of whom was sworn to perform

[d] Jan. 28.

---

[1] See page 83.

his part of the drama, which contemplated also an invasion of the Northwest, and a formidable uprising there of the sympathizers with the Confederate cause. They reported that General Price was the "Grand Commander" of the Missouri and Southern members of these secret leagues, and that C. L. Vallandigham was the Grand Commander of the Northern members, composed of the general and local leaders of the Peace Faction, and their dupes. It was also reported that Vallandigham was to enter Ohio boldly from Canada, to take part in the Democratic Convention for nominating a candidate for President, which was to meet at Chicago. It was also discovered that arms were extensively coming into the State, and distributed secretly among the sympathizers with the rebellion; and it was evident to the general that over the Union cause in that region great peril was impending.

Rosecrans promptly laid before the Government the information he had gathered, and asked for re-enforcements. Instead of complying with his request, an officer (General Hunt) was sent to Missouri, who made a tour of observation in the State, and reported that Rosecrans was unduly alarmed. The latter continued his investigations, and obtained positive information that danger was great and near. One of his spies visited the lodges of the secret associations, and ascertained that measures had been taken for commencing the revolution in St. Louis by murdering the Provost Marshal, and seizing the Department head-quarters. On the strength of testimony thus obtained, he arrested the Belgian consul at St. Louis, who was the "State commander" of these disloyal citizens, together with his deputy, secretary, "lecturer," and about forty members. The still incredulous Government ordered their release. Rosecrans, satisfied of danger, did not comply, but sent such information to Washington that the Government, convinced that he was right, approved his course, and countermanded the order. No doubt the vigilance and firmness of Rosecrans at that time was of incalculable service to the National cause.

In the mean time Price and his friends, in and out of his army, were preparing to carry out their part of the drama of invasion and revolution. The circumstances were favorable. Missouri had been stripped of troops for service elsewhere. The secessionists and guerrillas were bold, especially in the western and the river counties of Missouri. These had been watched with keen eyes, and the movements of the Confederates in Arkansas were under the vigilant scrutiny of General Washburne, at Memphis, who gave[a] Rosecrans the first clear note of warning concerning a coming invasion. He informed him that General Shelby was at Batesville, in Northern Arkansas, waiting for Price to join him, when the invasion would begin. Rosecrans sent the information to Washington, and Halleck telegraphed to Cairo, directing A. J. Smith, then ascending the Mississippi with about six thousand troops, infantry and cavalry, destined to re-enforce Sherman in Northern Georgia, to be halted there, and, with his command, be sent to St. Louis to re-enforce Rosecrans. This strengthening of the troops in Missouri was timely, for Price soon crossed the Arkansas River,[b] joined Shelby, and, with nearly twenty thousand men, entered Southeastern Missouri between the Big Black and St. Francis rivers, and pushed on to Pilot Knob, more than half way to St. Louis from the Arkansas border, almost without a show of opposition.

[a] Sept. 3, 1864.

[b] Sept. 21

Rosecrans had only about six thousand five hundred mounted men in his Department when this formidable invasion began, and these were scattered over a country four hundred miles in length and three hundred in breadth, with only a partially organized infantry force and dismounted men, guarding from the swarming guerrillas the greater depots, such as Springfield, Pilot Knob, Jefferson City, Rolla, and St. Louis, and the railway bridges. These were concentrated as quickly as possible after ascertaining the route and destination of Price, yet so swiftly did that leader move, that when it was seen that St. Louis was probably his first and chief objective, only a single brigade was at Pilot Knob (which is connected with the former place by a railway) to confront him. This was commanded by General Hugh S. Ewing,[1] who had for defenses only a little fort and some rude earth-works. But he made a bold stand, fought Price and his ten thousand men gallantly, with his little force of twelve hundred, repulsed two assaults, and inflicted on the Confederates a loss of about one thousand men. His own loss was about two hundred. His foe, with his superior force, soon took positions to command his entire post, so Ewing spiked his guns, blew up his magazine, and, finding his chosen line of retreat northward, by way of Potosi, blocked, fled westward during the night toward Rolla, where General McNeil was in command, and had just been re-enforced by cavalry under General Sandborn. At Webster he turned sharply to the north, and, pushing on, struck the Southwestern railway at Harrison, after a march of sixty miles in thirty-nine hours, with an accumulating encumbrance of refugees, white and black. There his exhausted troops were struck by a heavy force, under Shelby, which had been chasing him. Ewing's ammunition was short, but he held his ground for thirty hours, when the Seventeenth Illinois Cavalry, under Colonel Beveridge, sent by General McNeil from Rolla, came to his relief. Shelby was driven off, and Ewing and Beveridge marched leisurely to Rolla.

Ewing's bold stand astonished Price, and he was greatly disappointed by the lack of the promised re-enforcements pledged by the "Knights of the Golden Circle," and the "Sons of Liberty." The hearts of most of these had failed at the critical moment. They were satisfied, by the arrest of their "State Commander," that Rosecrans and the Government were fully informed of their meditated treason, and they were made exceedingly timid. Instead of seeing an uprising of "at least twenty-three thousand Sons of Liberty,"· as he was promised, Price received but few recruits, in the stealthiest manner, and, conscious of peril in his farther pathway northward, he moved with great caution. That tardiness, and the check given him by Ewing, gave Rosecrans time to concentrate a considerable force at St. Louis. For a week the Confederate element seemed to have the upper hand, and guerrillas and incendiaries were active everywhere. But these soon showed circumspection, as troops poured into St. Louis. General A. J. Smith's infantry, between four and five thousand strong, were there. Soon eight regiments of the enrolled militia of the State[2] arrived, and these were associated with

---

[1] The brigade was composed of the Forty-seventh Missouri Volunteer Infantry, detachments of the First, Second, and Third State Militia, and the Fourteenth Iowa.

[2] These were the First, Second, Third, Fourth, Tenth, Eleventh, Thirteenth, and Eightieth Regiments.

six regiments of Illinois one hundred days' men,[1] whose term of service had expired, but who patriotically went to the assistance of Rosecrans.

Meanwhile, the troops in the central portion of the State were concentrated at the capital, Jefferson City, by General Brown, who was re-enforced by General Fisk with all available troops north of the Missouri River. The Union citizens in that region cordially co-operated with the military, and before Price turned his face in that direction, the capital was well fortified. The invader advanced by way of Potosi to the Meramec River, crossed it, and took post at Richwood's, within forty miles of St. Louis, when, after remaining a day or two, and evidently satisfied that an attempt to take that city would be very hazardous, he burned the bridge at Moselle, and then marched rapidly in the direction of Jefferson City, followed by General A. J. Smith and his entire command.

Price burned bridges behind him, to impede his pursuers, and appeared before the Missouri capital on the 7th of October, just after Generals McNeil and Sandborn, with all the mounted men they could muster, had reached there by a forced march from Rolla. The united forces made a garrison of a little more than four thousand cavalry and less than three thousand infantry. A slight resistance was offered to Price at the crossing of the Little Moreau River, four or five miles east of the city, when the opposers fell back, and the Confederates enveloped the town in a line semicircular in form and nearly four miles in length, the wings resting on the Missouri. Taking counsel of prudence, after looking at the defenses which the troops of Brown and Fisk and the strong hands of the citizens had thrown up in the space of a few days, the invader sent his trains westward, and followed with his whole army, leaving the capital untouched by his guns.

General Pleasanton arrived at Jefferson City on the day after Price left it, assumed chief command, and sent General Sandborn with his cavalry in pursuit of the fugitive, with instructions to delay his march, so that General Smith might overtake him. Sandborn struck his rear-guard at Versailles, and ascertained that Price was marching directly on Booneville. Shelby's cavalry quickly enveloped Sandborn, who made a timely retreat, and, falling back a short distance to California, was overtaken there by Smith's cavalry, under Colonel Catherwood, with needed supplies. In the mean time re-enforcements from the Nationals were coming from St. Louis. General Mower had followed Price out of Arkansas, and struck the Mississippi at Cape Girardeau, after a fatiguing march of three hundred miles in the space of eighteen days. His army was so worn, man and beast, that Rosecrans sent steamboats to Cape Girardeau for them, and they were taken to St. Louis, whence the infantry were conveyed up the Missouri on steamers, while the cavalry, fifteen hundred strong, under General Winslow, marched to Jefferson City by land.

Price was now moving toward Kansas, with a heavy force, in pursuit. The National cavalry, with Pleasanton in immediate command, led in the chase. As the Confederates marched westward they found more sympathizers, and became bolder. Price sent Shelby across the Missouri River at

---

[1] These were the One Hundred and Thirty-second, One Hundred and Thirty-fourth, One Hundred and Thirty-sixth, One Hundred and Thirty-ninth, One Hundred and Fortieth, and One Hundred and Forty-second Regiments.

Arrow Rock, to strike a Union force at Glasgow, in Howard County.   After a sharp fight for several hours, he captured the place, with its defenders, under Colonel Harding, composed of a part of his Forty-third Missouri, and small detachments of the Ninth Missouri militia and Seventeenth Illinois Cavalry.   This temerity would have been punished by a serious, if not fatal, blow upon Price's main body, had not the pursuing General Smith been detained at the Lamine River, on account of the destruction of the railway bridge at the crossing on his route.   There he was overtaken by General Mower, when, with a few days' provisions, and in light marching order, he pushed on directly westward, toward Warrensburg, while Pleasanton, with his cavalry, including those under Winslow, was sweeping over the country northward to the Missouri River, in the direction of Lexington, which Price's advance reached on the 20th of October.   Blunt, who had come out of Kansas, had been driven back to Independence, near the western border of Missouri, by Price, and the ranks of the latter were being increased by recruits.

And now a single false step of the pursuers deprived them of the solid advantages they had been gaining.   Rosecrans, at St. Louis, not fully comprehending the importance of cutting off Price's retreat into Arkansas, ordered Pleasanton (by telegraph) to move directly on Lexington, and directed Smith to abandon his westward line of march and follow Pleasanton in the direct pursuit of Price.   The orders were obeyed, and the game was lost.   The pursued, burning bridges behind him, outstripped his pursuers. He had left Lexington when Pleasanton's advance, under McNeil and Sandborn, reached that place on the evening of the 20th,[a] and was moving rapidly westward.   At Little Blue Creek he struck [a Oct., 1864.] Blunt's Kansas troops, then under General Curtis, who had just assumed command of them.   After a sharp contest of a few hours, Curtis, hard pressed on front and flank by a superior force, fell back to the Big Blue Creek, where he took a strong position and awaited an attack.   Meanwhile, Pleasanton, with all his cavalry, had pushed on after Price with great vigor. When he reached the Little Blue[b] he found the bridge destroyed, [b October 23.] and the Confederate rear-guard prepared to resist his passage with strong force.   They were soon driven, and Pleasanton pressed on to Independence, then held by the enemy.   He captured that place at seven o'clock in the evening by a brilliant charge, by which he drove the Confederates and seized two of their guns.

From Independence Pleasanton sent McNeil with his cavalry toward Little Santa Fé, to intercept Price's retreat, and at the same time asked Rosecrans, by telegraph, to order Smith to the former place.   Rosecrans did so.   Meanwhile, Pleasanton pushed vigorously on after the fugitives, and on the following morning approached the Big Blue, where he found the main body of the Confederates, who had striven in vain, the day before, to drive Curtis from his position.   Pleasanton fell upon them at seven o'clock in the morning.[c]   A sharp struggle ensued, which lasted until past noon, when the Confederates gave way and fled toward [c October 23.] Little Santa Fé, closely pursued by Pleasanton and Curtis.   On the same afternoon Smith reached Independence, with nine thousand infantry and five batteries.   His men were very weary, yet they were moved at once southward, with a hope that they might strike Price's flank. They were too late. The false movement in departing from the direct westward line of march was now painfully evident. The delay occasioned by it left Price a way of escape, and he eagerly accepted it. Instead of twenty-three thousand recruits, which had been promised him, the Confederate leader had not received over six thousand; and he felt the necessity of getting out of Missouri, and beyond the grasp of his pursuers, as quickly as possible. He fled rapidly southward, and passed into Arkansas, not, however, without receiving some parting blows. One of these was given by Pleasanton at the Marais des Cygnes, where, at four o'clock on the morning of the 25th,[a] he opened his cannon upon the camp of the astonished *[a] Oct., 1864.* fugitives. Price instantly arose and fled, and was followed by Pleasanton to the Little Osage River, where he made a stand, with eight guns in position. The brigades of Benteen and Phillips, of Pleasanton's command, gallantly charged upon the Confederate lines, captured the eight guns and a thousand men, including Generals Marmaduke and Cabell, and five colonels; also many small-arms, wagons, mules, and other materials of war. Sandborn now came up, and then Pleasanton took his jaded men and horses to Fort Scott for rest, while Smith marched his wearied troops to Harrisonville, the capital of Cass County, for the same purpose.

The Kansas troops, with Benteen's brigade, continued the pursuit, followed by Sandborn's cavalry. They drove the fugitives whenever they attempted to make a stand, until they reached Newtonia, in the southwest corner of Missouri. Price was then moving at a panic pace, strewing the line of his march with the wrecks of wagons and other materials of war, broken and burnt. He turned at Newtonia and offered battle.[b] *[b] October 28.* He was gaining decided advantages, when Sandborn, who had marched one hundred and two miles in thirty-six hours, came up and assisted in defeating him. Price again fled, and made his way into Western Arkansas, followed by Curtis, who found[c] Colonel La Rue, who was occupying Fayetteville, with the First Arkansas (Union) Cavalry, *[c] Nov. 14.* closely besieged by an overwhelming force. Colonel Brooks had surrounded the post with two thousand Confederates, whom La Rue easily kept at bay until Fagan's division of Price's flying army came to his assailant's assistance. The united forces were carrying on the siege vigorously, when Curtis came up and drove off the Confederates, with heavy loss to them of men and materials. This was the end of the last invasion of Missouri. Price went out of the State much weaker than when he went in, while the total loss of the Nationals, in officers and private soldiers, during his invasion, was only three hundred and forty-six. And his exit was made under very discouraging circumstances. The autumnal elections in the Free-labor States had gone heavily against the Opposition, and consequently the last hope of the Confederates of securing peace and independence by the aid of the Peace Faction, and such of the Opposition party as were willing to follow them, faded away. Grant was then closely besieging Petersburg and Richmond; Atlanta had been captured by the Nationals, and Sherman, the conqueror, was on his march toward the sea; and everywhere eastward of the Mississippi the strength of the Confederate armies and the moral supports of the cause of the Conspirators were rapidly diminishing.

Let us now turn our eyes for a moment eastward, and see what events of importance were occurring in the hilly country of Central and Eastern Kentucky and in East Tennessee, before we proceed to a consideration of the great campaigns against Richmond and Atlanta which Lieutenant-General Grant organized after his appointment to the chief command of the Armies of the Republic.

On the retirement of Longstreet from Knoxville[1] and his withdrawal toward Virginia, he was pursued by cavalry under Shackleford, Wolford, Graham, and Foster, into Jefferson County, where, near Bean's Station, on the Morristown and Cumberland Gap road, he turned[a] sharply upon his pursuers. A brisk conflict was kept up until night, [a] Dec. 14, 1863. when the Nationals had been pushed back nearly a mile. The contest was indecisive, but somewhat sanguinary, Shackleford, who was in chief command of the pursuers, losing about two hundred men. Longstreet's loss, it was computed, was much greater. He sought, during the struggle, to strike Shackleford in the rear, by sending a force down the left bank of the Holston, to cross at Kelly's Ford, and come up from the west. The vigilant General Ferrero prevented this movement, by sending General Humphrey to hold that ford. Longstreet, being unable to follow up his advantage acquired at Bean's Station, on account of the snow and cold, a large number of his men being barefooted, now fell back toward Bull's Gap, at the junction of the Rogersville branch with the main railway.

General Burnside had now retired from the command of the Army of the Ohio, which was assumed[b] by General John G. Foster, his [b] Dec. 11. successor in North Carolina. The first event of much importance that occurred after Foster's accession and the affair at Bean's Station, was a fight,[c] between Mossy Creek and New Market, by the [c] Dec. 29. National advance at Knoxville, under General S. D. Sturgis, with an estimated force of nearly six thousand Confederates, under the notorious guerrilla chief, J. H. Morgan, and Martin Armstrong. The Confederates were vanquished, with a loss never reported, but estimated at full three hundred men. Sturgis's loss was about one hundred. At the same time, Wheeler, with about twelve hundred mounted men, had come up from Georgia, and was boldly operating between Knoxville and Chattanooga, his most notable achievement being an attack[d] upon a National sup- [d] Dec. 28. ply-train, near Charlestown, on the Hiawassee, which was guarded by only one hundred men, under Colonel Siebert. Of course, Wheeler easily captured the train, but it was not so easy to hold it, for, immediately after the seizure, Colonel Long came up to Siebert's assistance, with one hundred and fifty of the Fourth Ohio Cavalry and Colonel Laibold's Second Missouri Infantry. These, with Siebert's men, retook the train, and drove Wheeler back, with a loss of forty-one killed and wounded and one hundred and twenty-three made prisoners. The Union loss was only sixteen.

A little later, when Sturgis was occupying Dandridge, the capital of Jefferson County, he was attacked[e] by the troops of Morgan and Armstrong, and after fighting them until night, and breaking [e] Jan. 16, 1864. their force by a charge led by Colonel D. M. McCook, fell back

---

[1] See page 175.

to Strawberry Plain, on the railway, with a loss of about one hundred and fifty men.[1] At about the same time General Robert Vance went over the Smoky Mountain from North Carolina, into East Tennessee, with about four hundred cavalry and two pieces of artillery. It was a most perilous march, over icy roads. Vance left the bulk of his force at the foot of the mountain, and led one hundred and seventy-five men on a reconnoissance toward Sevierville, south of Dandridge. On the way he heard of a National wagon-train moving not far off. On this he pounced[a] in a fierce charge, and captured seventeen wagons and twenty-six men. With his plunder he attempted to return by way of the head of Cosby Creek, where, on the following morning, he was surrounded by the Fourth Illinois Cavalry, under Major Davidson, who thoroughly dispersed the Confederates and captured General Vance, with a part of his staff and about a hundred men, and recaptured the prisoners and wagons. From that time until the close of January, Sturgis was continually menaced by Longstreet, who appeared to be determined to repossess himself of Knoxville; but his movement was only a mask, behind which his army soon retired into Virginia.[2]

a Jan. 14, 1864.

Morgan and his men lingered in East Tennessee about four months after Longstreet withdrew into Virginia. His numbers were comparatively few, but he managed to so magnify them as to command the respect of the National forces in that region. Finally, late in May, when Union troops were co-operating with the Grand Army of the Potomac in its movement on Richmond, and were making their way into Southwestern Virginia for the purpose of seizing the great railway communications between Lee and Johnston, Morgan, who, even with some disjointed cavalry forces co-operating, was too feeble to oppose them, was sent over the mountains into Kentucky to raid through that State, and, if possible, divert some of the National forces from Southwestern Virginia and East Tennessee. As this was the last important raid in which that dashing leader was engaged, and as his career was brought to a close a few months later, when he disappeared from the scenes of the great drama, we will here anticipate the depending order of events a little, and trace in outline a record of Morgan's most notable experiences during the summer of 1864.

---

[1] The cold at that time was intense, and the soldiers suffered much for want of food for awhile. The men had nothing but shelter tents, and their clothing was nearly worn out; and yet, in this condition, with patriotism undiminished by suffering, these half-naked, half-starved soldiers, whose terms of service there expired, cheerfully re-enlisted. It was the history of Valley Forge repeated at Strawberry Plain.

[2] At the beginning of January, 1864, some spicy but courteous correspondence occurred between Generals Foster and Longstreet, concerning the circulation of handbills among the soldiers of the latter, containing a copy of President Lincoln's Amnesty Proclamation. See page 232. It was having a powerful effect, and Longstreet found the number of desertions from his army rapidly increasing. Whereupon he wrote to Foster, saying he supposed the immediate object of such circulation was to induce desertions and win his men to the taking of an oath of allegiance to the National Government. He suggested that it would be more proper to make any communications to his soldiers on the subject of peace and reconciliation through the commanding general, rather than by handbills. Foster replied that he was right in supposing that the object of the handbills was to induce men in rebellion against their Government to lay down their arms and become good citizens, and he sent twenty copies of the Amnesty Proclamation to Longstreet, that he might himself, in accordance with his own suggestion, show his desire for peace, by circulating them among his officers and men. Longstreet regarded this as "trifling over the great events of the war," when Foster replied by communicating through him to his army the terms upon which there might "be a speedy restoration of peace throughout the land," which was, in substance, absolute submission to the National authority. He also inclosed a copy of an order, which he had felt compelled to issue, on account of the frequent capture of Confederates in the National uniform, by which corps commanders were directed to shoot dead "all rebel officers and soldiers wearing the uniform of the United States Army, captured in future within our lines."

At the close of May, Morgan entered Kentucky by way of Pound Gap,[a] with about twenty-five hundred men, indifferently mounted. He managed to evade General Burbridge, who was in that region [a] May 29, 1864. with a strong force, contemplating an advance into Southwestern Virginia in co-operation with Crook and Averill, who were to march up the Kanawha, in the direction of the Blue Ridge. Morgan always managed to live off the country he was in; so now he sent men ahead to seize fresh horses from friends or foes, and by that means his followers were soon so well mounted that they were enabled to sweep rapidly through the eastern counties of Kentucky, from Johnson to Harrison, by way of Paintville on the west fork of the Big Sandy, through Hazel Green, Owensville, and Mount Sterling, to Paris and Cynthiana, in the richest part of the commonwealth, and to give to that region a new claim to the title of "the dark and bloody ground." He captured Mount Sterling, Paris, Cynthiana, and Williamstown, almost without resistance; and burnt railway trains, stations, and bridges, tore up tracks, and plundered without fear, for the troops in the path of his desolation were too few or feeble to check him. His men were divided into raiding parties, and one of these, three hundred strong, led by Colonel Giltner, actually pushed General Hobson, with twelve hundred well-armed men, into a bend of the Licking River, in Nicholas County, and captured him and his troops.

When General Burbridge was told of Morgan's passage of the mountains, he started promptly in pursuit, and, by a forced march of ninety miles, surprised him by a stout blow[b] at Mount Sterling, which sent him [b] June 9. bounding forward. With a part of his force the guerrilla pushed into Lexington, and entering it just past midnight, burned the railway station there and other property, and then hurried toward Frankfort. At the same time another portion of his followers set fire to Cynthiana, but near there Burbridge struck them an awfully shattering blow while they were breakfasting. That blow killed or wounded three hundred of them, while four hundred men were made prisoners, and a thousand horses were spoils for the victors. It also liberated some of Hobson's men. Burbridge's loss was about one hundred and fifty men.

Morgan was amazed and bewildered by this staggering blow, and, with the wreck of his command, he reeled back into Southwestern Virginia, and made his way into the valley of East Tennessee. There, with a small band, he did what he might to harass the Union troops in that region and distress the loyal inhabitants. Finally, early in September, when he was at Greenville, with his thin brigade lying near, his force was assailed by troops under General Gillem. These made a forced night march from Bull's Gap, sixteen miles distant. The Confederates were surprised and driven with a loss of about one hundred killed and seventy-five wounded. Morgan and a portion of his staff were then at the house of Mrs. Catherine D. Williams, in Greenville, which was surrounded by the Union troops, and the guerrilla leader was shot dead while trying to escape.

The writer, with his traveling companions already mentioned (Messrs. Dreer and Greble), visited Greenville and other places in the great Valley of East Tennessee, while on our journey, in May, 1866, from the scenes of Sherman's Atlantic campaigns, into Virginia, to visit the theater of the simultaneous campaign against Richmond.   Having visited the principal places of conflict between Sherman and Johnston on our way to Atlanta from Chattanooga, we now journeyed back without halting until we reached Cleveland, the place of junction of the railways leading into the valley from Chattanooga and Dalton.   There, at a little cottage-like inn, embowered in trees, and then sweetly perfumed by its garden of roses, we spent a night and part of a day, a portion of the time with Dr. Hunt, one of the stanch Unionists and patient sufferers of East Tennessee.   Cleveland was a pleasant little village before the war, situated in the midst of a beautiful region, but now it was scarred and disfigured by the ravages of the demon of Discord. Troops of both parties had trampled upon all its pleasant places.   Nearly seventy thousand were there at one time.   On eminences around it were earth-works for cannon and the shelter of troops; and upon a ridge over-

HOWARD'S HEAD-QUARTERS.

looking the railway station was the fine brick mansion of Mr. Raht, which General Howard used as head-quarters when he was there with his corps.

From Cleveland we journeyed to Knoxville by railway, seeing the evidences of the recent strife everywhere along the line of its track.   At Charleston, where the railway crosses the Hiawassee, we saw strong earth-works, and a block-house on the margin of that little river, so beautiful in name and appearance.   At Loudon these were still more numerous and strong; and some, cast up by the soldiers of both parties, were seen at Lenoir and other places, between the Tennessee crossing and Knoxville.   That region is extremely fertile, and was then fast recovering its former beauty and fruitfulness under the hand of intelligent and industrious cultivators.   It presented a great contrast to the region in Georgia between Dalton and Atlanta, which was yet in the desolate state in which Sherman and Johnston had left it.

At Knoxville we were the guests of Governor Brownlow, whose name and deeds are so conspicuous in the annals of the Civil War in Tennessee. His house was the abode of intellectual culture and social refinement, and the open-handed hospitality which we found there will ever form one of the pleasantest recollections of our traveling experience.   And there was something more precious than intellectual culture and social refinement under that roof.   It was abounding patriotism and highest moral courage, exhibited not only by the master of the house, but by all, even the weakest members of it.   In all the fiery trials of the Civil War to which that household was subjected—when the father, because of his devotion to the old flag of his country, was hunted like a wild beast in the mountains—the wife, and sons and daughters kept the altar fire of patriotism burning brightly within that dwelling.   The National flag was kept waving over its roof in defiance of the scorn and threatenings of traitors; and when a company was sent from a Texan regiment encamped near the city, to haul down that flag, a young widowed daughter of Governor Brownlow (Mrs. Sawyer, afterward Mrs. Dr. Boyington), appeared on the street porch with a revolver in her hand, and threatened to shoot the first man who should attempt the sacrilege. The rude rebels

quailed, parleyed, and then retreated; and over that dwelling was seen floating the last Union flag kept aloft in East Tennessee before the advent of General Burnside.

While in Knoxville we visited the various localities of interest in and around that city, accompanied by Colo-

GOVERNOR BROWNLOW'S HOUSE.[1]

nel John Bell Brownlow, then editing his father's newspaper, the *Knoxville Whig*, and also by several young Union officers, whose courtesy we can never forget. On the morning of the 23d[a] we rode to the railway station, behind the large, stout, black family horse of Governor Brownlow, which bore General McClellan through his campaigns in Western Virginia; and in company with Colonel Brownlow and Captain A. W. Walker, one of the most noted of the Union scouts in East Tennessee, we journeyed by railway to Greenville, near which occurred many events illustrative of the patriotism of the East Tennesseans. We arrived there toward evening, and took lodgings at the hotel of Mr. Malony, who told us that he was a fellow-craftsman, and rival in the tailoring business in that village, of Andrew Johnson, then acting President of the United States.[2] We remained there until the next evening, gathering up information concerning military events in the vicinity, and in visiting the place where Union men were hung,[3] and the spot where the notorious Morgan was killed in the vineyard of Mrs. Williams.[4]

a May, 1866.

---

[1] This is from a sketch made by the author in May, 1866. The street porch alluded to in the text is seen at the front of the house. The nearer building to the right of it, partly covered by a high fence, was used by Governor Brownlow for his library and study. For awhile, when the Confederates held Knoxville, the family were absent, having joined the head of it, then in exile. In the gratification of a petty spite toward the stanch patriot, General E. Kirby Smith, when in Knoxville, stabled a pair of mules in Dr. Brownlow's library. When Buckner was holding East Tennessee, at the time Burnside entered it from Kentucky, he had his head-quarters at the pleasant house of the unflinching Unionist, and Member of the National Congress, Horace Maynard, on Main Street.

[2] This was for many years the home of Andrew Johnson, and the place of his useful business as the maker of garments, in which, it is said, he excelled, and was consequently prosperous. While in Greenville we were shown his family Bible, in which, in the beautiful handwriting of Valentine Sevier, Clerk of the Circuit Court, were the following records:—

"Andrew Johnson, born 29th December, 1807.

"Eliza, his wife, born 4th September, 1810.

"Married, at Greenville, by Mordecai Lincoln, Esq., on the 17th day of May, 1827, Andrew Johnson to Eliza McCardal."

That excellent young woman, then only seventeen years of age, taught her husband, aged twenty years, to read and write. From that humble social position he rose to the highest public one in the gift of his country-men. When the writer was at Greenville, Mr. Johnson's place of business was pointed out to him. It had lately been repaired, and the sign, A. JOHNSON, TAILOR, which for long years was seen over the door, had been removed. The career of its occupant, from the time of the beginning of his useful pursuit in that shop at Greenville, and his official life and its termination in the Presidential mansion at the National capital, affords a most striking illustration of the admirable workings of our free system of government.

[3] See page 39, volume II.

[4] It was charged by the Confederates that Morgan was killed after he had surrendered. This was a most

The whole region of the great Valley of East Tennessee, eastward as well as westward of Knoxville, is clustered with the most stirring associations of the Civil War. We passed on our journey from Knoxville, Strawberry Plain, Bull's Gap, Blue Springs, and other places already mentioned as scenes of conflict; and from Greenville to Bristol, on the borders of Virginia, such notable places were many. Over that region and beyond we passed on the night of the 24th and 25th,[a] and at six o'clock in the morning were at Mount Airy, twenty-eight hundred feet above the Richmond basin, and said to be the most lofty point of railway travel in the United States. We descended into the rugged valleys eastward of this Appalachian range, and then ascended the western gentle slope of the Blue Ridge, one of the most beautiful and thoroughly cultivated regions in the world. The ravages of war had not been felt just there. We descended the more precipitous side of that lofty range into the fine high valleys around the upper waters of the James River, and arrived at Lynchburg in the evening, whence we traveled the next day, by way of Charlottesville and Gordonsville, to Richmond,[1] the track of the more direct route of railway being yet in ruins.

[a] May, 1866.

Morgan's raid into Kentucky, though disastrous to his immediate command, accomplished its object in a degree, for it drew Burbridge, as we have

---

serious accusation, and required an authoritative denial, for the sake of the fair fame of the Union officers and soldiers. While at Greenville, a greater portion of the writer's time was occupied in the investigation of the matter, by the use of competent witnesses, and the following is the result:—

Morgan, as we have observed, was at Greenville, and General Gillem, then his direct opponent, was at Bull's Gap. See page 283. Morgan made his head-quarters at the fine house of Mrs. Williams, with his staff. On the night of the 8d of September, on his return from a visit to his wife at Abingdon, in Virginia, he made arrangements for surprising and attacking Gillem at Bull's Gap the next morning. On account of rain at midnight he countermanded the order, and retired without any suspicion of danger. During that stormy night parts of two companies of the Third Tennessee Cavalry, under Colonel Columbus Wilcox, made their way to Greenville, while Morgan's brigade was lying a short distance from the town. While a greater portion of these troops were attacking the Confederates, a party surrounded Mrs. Williams's house at seven o'clock in the morning (September 4), and the cry of one of the guards, "Take care, General Morgan!" was the first intimation given the guerrilla chief that danger was near. Morgan seized his pistols, declaring he would die before he would surrender, and fled out of the house into the garden without his coat. He first ran under the Episcopal church, back of the garden, and then, breaking the paling of the fence, passed through a lot and sought shelter under the old tavern of Colonel Fry, a Unionist, then in prison by order of Morgan. In his flight thus far he was accompanied by Major Gassett, of his staff. Now, fearing Mrs. Fry might report his whereabouts, he left the tavern and leaped over a fence into the vineyard of Mrs. Williams, adjoining her garden. He was called upon to halt, but refused, and at the junction of two paths in the vineyard, while crouching for concealment behind a grape-vine, he was shot by Andrew Campbell, a Union soldier, who was stationed in Market Street, near by. His dead body was carried into the street by two white soldiers and two colored men, and was finally left with his friends at Mrs. Williams's. General Gillem thought it best to retire his small number of troops on account of the strength of Morgan's brigade, but, on the approach of a larger body of Unionists, the Confederates fled eastward, pursued five or six miles by Lieutenant-Colonel John B. Brownlow, of the Ninth Tennessee Cavalry, with a part of two brigades.

The persons from whom the writer received the substance of the above brief account of Morgan's death, were Mrs. Williams, who pointed out the place where he was killed, and who said he was in the act of firing his pistol when he was shot through the heart; Mary Hunter, formerly a slave of Mrs. Williams, and living in a house at the corner of the vineyard, and saw the whole transaction; and Mrs. Lucy Williams, daughter-in-law of Mrs. Williams, whose sister was at the house when Morgan left it, and heard him say he would never be taken alive. Mrs. Lucy Williams was a spirited young woman from Virginia, and thoroughly patriotic. She gave the Unionists much information concerning the movements of Morgan's brigade; and under the erroneous impression that she had betrayed him at this time, when his command entered Greenville on the withdrawal of Gillem, they brought a halter wherewith to hang her on a pear-tree near the place of their chief's death. She was then safe from harm, in Knoxville.

Coincident with the testimony of the above cited witness, was a letter written the next day to Morgan's wife by C. A. Withers, of the staff of the guerrilla chief, in which he says: "General Morgan was killed in the garden of Mrs. Williams, in Greenfield, *while endeavoring to escape.* He was struck in the center of his breast, the ball passing through his heart." It is stated that Morgan, when killed, was dressed in the National uniform. See *Knoxville Whig,* September 14, 1864.

[1] See page 435, volume II.

seen, away from the combined movement upon Southwestern Virginia, and gave the Confederates time to strengthen their forces in that direction, especially along the line of the great railway. Burbridge remained several weeks in Kentucky after his expulsion of Morgan, reorganizing and remounting his worn army, and then, late in September, he started with a fresh column directly for the salt works of the Confederates, near Abingdon, in Washington County, Virginia, to destroy them. He was met by a heavy force under Breckinridge, and after a sharp conflict[a] was [a] Oct. 2, 1864. thrown back, with a loss of about three hundred and fifty men. His ammunition was running low, so he retreated that night, leaving his wounded to the care of his foe.

Encouraged by this success, Breckinridge soon moved into East Tennessee, and threatened Knoxville. Meanwhile General Gillem discovered a Confederate force in his rear, at Morristown, when he attacked them suddenly,[b] routed them, and inflicted upon them a loss of [b] Oct. 28. four hundred men and four guns. Soon after this Breckinridge moved cautiously forward, and on a very dark night[c] fell suddenly upon Gillem, at Bull's Gap, charged gallantly up a steep, half-wooded [c] Nov. 12, 13. hill in the gloom, drove the Nationals from their intrenchments, and utterly routed them. Gillem fell back to Russellville, where he was again attacked and routed, and after a loss of his battery, train, nearly all of his small-arms, thrown away by his soldiers in their flight, and two hundred and twenty men, he fled to the shelter of the intrenchments at Knoxville. Breckinridge pursued him as far as Strawberry Plain, and for awhile held the country eastward of that point in subjection to the Confederates.

Other military movements in that mountain region were so intimately connected with, and auxiliary to, those of the Army of the Potomac against Richmond, that we will now turn to a consideration of the general events of that campaign from the Rapid Anna to the James, after noticing earlier movements of some detachments of National troops on the flanks and rear of the Army of Northern Virginia.

The first of these movements which attracted much attention occurred early in February, when General B. F. Butler, then in command of the Department of Virginia and North Carolina, lately vacated by General Foster, planned and attempted the capture of Richmond, and the release of the Union prisoners there, by a sudden descent upon it. Arrangements were made for a diversion in favor of this movement by the Army of the Potomac, and when, on the 5th of February,[d] a column of cavalry and infantry, under General Wistar, about fifteen hundred strong, [d] 1864. pushed rapidly northward from New Kent Court-House to the Chickahominy, at Bottom's Bridge, intending to cross it there, General Sedgwick, then in temporary command of the Army of the Potomac, in the absence of General Meade, made the diversion, in obedience to orders from Washington. He sent Kilpatrick's cavalry across the Rapid Anna at Elly's Ford, and Merritt's at Barnett's Ford, while two divisions of Hancock's infantry waded the stream at Germania Ford. These skirmished sharply with the Confederates, who stood unmoved in their position, and when the prescribed time for the execution of the raid had expired, these troops recrossed the Rapid Anna, with a loss of about two hundred men. Wistar's raid was fruitless, owing to the escape, by bribery, of a culprit from prison, who gave the Confederates information of the approaching danger. Wistar found Bottom's Bridge and the line of the Chickahominy too strongly guarded, and there appeared too many evidences of strength beyond it to warrant him in attempting to cross the stream, so he returned to New Kent, without loss, his infantry having marched eighty miles within fifty-six hours, and his cavalry one hundred and fifty miles in fifty hours.

This raid was followed a little later by a more formidable one from the Army of the Potomac, led by General Kilpatrick. Its object was to effect the release of the Union captives at Richmond, then suffering terribly by cruelty and starvation in the filthy Libby Prison, and more horribly on bleak Belle Isle, in the James River, in front of Richmond—circumstances which we shall consider hereafter. Kilpatrick left camp at three o'clock on Sunday morning,[a] with five thousand cavalry, picked from his own and the divisions of Merritt and Gregg, and crossing the Rapid Anna at Elly's Ford, swept around the right flank of Lee's army, by way of Spottsylvania Court-House, and pushing rapidly toward Richmond, struck the Virginia Central railway, at Beaver Dam Station, on the

[a] Feb. 28, 1864.

BELLE ISLE.[1]

evening of the 29th, where he had his first serious encounter with the Confederates. While small parties were out, tearing up the road and destroying public property, he was attacked by some troops that came up from Richmond, under the Maryland traitor, Bradley T. Johnson. These he defeated, in a sharp skirmish, when he struck across the South Anna, and cut the Fredericksburg and Richmond railway at Kilby Station. This accomplished, he pushed on by Ashland, and along the Brooks turnpike, and, early on the first day of March,[b] halted within three miles and a half of Richmond, and within its outer line of fortifications, at which the Confederates had thrown down their arms and then fled into the city.

[b] 1864.

At Spottsylvania Court-House, about five hundred of Kilpatrick's best men, led by Colonel Ulric Dahlgren, a dashing young officer, and son of Admiral Dahlgren, then before Charleston, diverged from the main column, for the purpose of sweeping through the country more to the right, by way of Frederickshall, and through Louisa and Goochland Counties, to the James River, above Richmond, where they intended to destroy as much of the James River canal as possible, cross the stream, and, attacking the Confederate capital from the south simultaneously with Kilpatrick's assault

---

[1] This is from a sketch made by the author immediately after the evacuation of Richmond, in April, 1865, from the high bank of the James River, near the Tredegar Works. looking across that stream southward.

from the north, release the prisoners on Belle Isle. Kilpatrick listened eagerly for the sound of Dahlgren's guns, but hearing nothing from his force, and being stoutly opposed when attempting to push through the

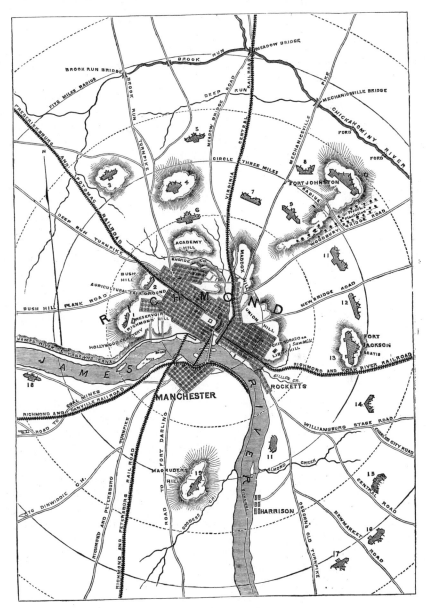

FORTIFICATIONS AROUND RICHMOND.

second line of the Richmond fortifications, he thought it prudent to withdraw. He did so, after a severe fight, and moving along the road toward Mechanicsville, bivouacked within six miles of Richmond. Late in the evening, and just as the wearied troopers were falling into needed slumber, they were called to action by the summons of a two-gun battery that opened upon them, followed by a sharp charge. The assailants were quickly repulsed, but it being evident that little repose could be obtained there, Kilpatrick's column moved on, crossed the Chickahominy, and pushed for the Pamunkey. There were no means at hand for passing over that stream, so the raiders moved across the Richmond and York River railway, not far from White House, where they met a force coming up from New Kent Court-House, which General Butler had sent to the aid of Kilpatrick.[1] Thus far Kilpatrick had been pretty hotly pursued by the Confederates, with whom he skirmished frequently, but now the chase was at an end. He had lost about one hundred and fifty men during the raid, and gained five hundred prisoners and many horses. Although he failed to accomplish his main object, he had inflicted a serious blow upon the Confederates in the destruction of railway property and stores.

Let us note the fortunes of the less-favored Dahlgren and his men meanwhile. After destroying the railway station at Frederickshall, about an hour after General Lee had passed over the road, he moved southward, led by a negro guide, who, ignorantly or treacherously, took the column to the James River, near Goochland Court-House, instead of to a fording place nearer Richmond. The exasperated men, believing the negro to have betrayed them, hung him on a tree, and then passed on down the north side of the James, somewhat injuring the canal on the way, and destroying the outbuildings of the farm of James A. Seddon, then Confederate "Secretary of War." They reached the outer line of fortifications around Richmond, on the northwest side of the city, at dark on the 2d of March, while rain was falling copiously, and carried them, but were met by such an overwhelming force when they approached the second line, that they were speedily repulsed, with loss. With the remnant of his force Dahlgren retreated toward the Chickahominy, annoyed at every step, for Kilpatrick's swoop had aroused the Confederates into intense action, and they swarmed around the pathway of the weaker invader. Dahlgren and about a hundred of his horsemen became separated from the rest, and on the evening of the 3d,[a]
March, 1864. just as they had crossed the Mattapony at Dabney's Ferry, into King-and-Queen County, they were attacked by a body of local Confederate militia, when the gallant young leader of the troopers was shot dead, five bullets having entered his body. Several others were killed, and nearly all of the remainder of the one hundred were made prisoners. The rest of Dahlgren's command were scattered, and made their way to the Union lines as best they might.

The slayers of Dahlgren acted like savages in the treatment of his dead body, and the alarmed, mortified, and exasperated Conspirators, whose haughty pride had been deeply wounded by this invasion of their Capital by a handful of "cowardly Yankees," were disposed to make the ninety unfortunate prisoners captured when Dahlgren was killed, to feel the weight of their hatred and vengeance, by executing the whole of them. It was con-

---

[1] These consisted of a brigade of colored infantry, 2,000 strong, under Colonel Dunkin, 800 cavalry, under Colonel Spear, and Belger's Rhode Island Battery.

sidered in "cabinet" meeting, and Seddon, the Confederate "Secretary of War," wrote a letter to General Lee, asking his views concerning the matter, in which he said the contemplated murder had "*the sanction of the President* [Davis], *the Cabinet, and General Bragg.*"[1]   General Lee had a good reason for not sanctioning such a proceeding then, for his own son was a captive, and held for retaliation whenever any Union prisoner should be put to death, and the plea that prevailed against it was, "It is cruelty to General Lee."

The Conspirators were also ready to commit a still more diabolical act, by directing Libby Prison to be blown up with gunpowder, with its crowd of captives, in the event of the latter attempting to escape.[2]   For the twofold purpose of "firing the Southern heart" and offering to mankind some justification for a deed so revolting, on the plea of retaliation, the Conspirators caused to be published what purported to be copies of papers found on the person of Dahlgren, comprising an address to his men, a special order and memoranda, in which it was avowed that the object of the expedition was to release the Union prisoners, and, with their aid, destroy the bridges at Richmond with torpedoes and fire, murder "Jeff. Davis and his cabinet," and burn the city.   It must be remembered that Dahlgren was not killed until two days after Winder had "placed in readiness," according to the written testimony of one of Seddon's men, just cited, the powder for the massacre of the Union prisoners; so the plea of retaliation fails.   It was afterward clearly proven that the papers were forgeries, based upon instructions and orders found in Dahlgren's pocket, which in letter and spirit were in perfect accordance with the rules and usages of honorable warfare.   This invention of the Conspirators availed them nothing.   It only added another stain to the black character of the rebellion, and with the relative preparations for murder at Libby Prison, presents another evidence of the wickedness of its leaders.

In Dahlgren's special order, found in his pocket, he said: "As General Custer may follow me, be careful not to give a false alarm."   This referred to an expedition on which Custer set out,[a] for the purpose, chiefly, of diverting the attention of the Confederates from that of Kilpatrick.   Custer crossed the Rapid Anna at Banks's Mills Ford, with fifteen hundred cavalry,[3] in light marching order, flanked Lee's army on the west, and pushed rapidly on by way of Madison Court-House to the Rivanna River at Berner's Bridge, within four miles of Charlottesville,

[a] Feb. 27, 1864.

---

[1] *A Rebel War Clerk's* [J. B. Jones] *Diary,* March 5, 1864. The Richmond press, in the interest of the Conspirators, strongly recommended the measure. "Let them die," said the *Richmond Whig,* not by court-martial, not as prisoners, but as *hostes humani generis* by general order from the President, Commander-in-Chief."

[2] *A Rebel War Clerk's Diary,* March 2, 1864. "Last night," says the Diary, "when it was supposed probable that the prisoners of war at the Libby might attempt to break out, General Winder ordered that a large amount of powder be placed under the building, with instructions to blow them up if the attempt were made." Seddon would not give a written order for the diabolical work to be done, but he said, significantly, "the prisoners must not be allowed to escape, *under any circumstances;*" "which," says the diarist, "was considered sanction enough. Captain —— obtained an order for and procured several hundred pounds of gunpowder which was placed in readiness. Whether the prisoners were advised of this I know not; but I told Captain —— it would not be justifiable to spring such a mine in the absence of their knowledge of the fate awaiting them in the event of their attempting to break out, because such prisoners are not to be condemned for striving to regain their liberty. Indeed it is the *duty* of a prisoner of war to escape if he can."

[3] These consisted of detachments from the First, Second, and Fifth Regulars, Sixth Ohio, Sixth Pennsylvania, First New York, and First New Jersey.

where he was checked by a superior force, with a battery. Then he turned northward, in the direction of Stannardsville, skirmishing at times with Confederate cavalry, and then returned to camp, followed by a large number of refugees from slavery. This menace of the railway communication with the Shenandoah Valley, and the attacks on Richmond, produced the greatest alarm. When the danger disappeared, General Elzy,[1] in command at the Confederate capital,[a] issued a congratulatory order, that produced a pleasant quietude in the public mind, which was but little disturbed again until Lieutenant-General Grant made his appearance, at the beginning of May, like a baleful meteor in the firmament.

[a] March 8, 1864.

We have seen that Lieutenant-General Grant, in his first order after assuming chief command, declared his head-quarters to be with the Army of the Potomac "until further orders." A week afterward he arrived[b] in Washington City from the West, with a portion of his domestic and military families, and went immediately to the head-quarters of General Meade at Culpepper Court-House, where, on the following day, the Army of the Potomac was reorganized by consolidating and reducing the five army corps to three, named the Second, Fifth, and Sixth. These were respectively, in the order named, placed under the commands of Generals Hancock, Warren, and Sedgwick.[2] Generals Sykes, Newton, French, Kenly, Spinola, and Meredith, were relieved and sent to Washington for orders. General Burnside, who, since his retirement from the command of the Army of the Ohio, at Knoxville, in December, had been at Annapolis, in Maryland, reorganizing and recruiting his old Ninth Corps, was ready for the field at the middle of April. His corps (composed partly of colored troops) was reviewed by the President on the 23d of that month, when it passed into Virginia and joined the Army of the Potomac. With this accession of force, that army, at the close of April, numbered over one hundred thousand men. Re-enforcements had been pouring in during that month, and before its close Grant and Meade had perfected their arrangements for a grand advance of the Army of the Potomac and its auxiliaries.[3]

[b] March 23.

---

[1] See page 396, volume II.

[2] Hancock's (Second) corps consisted of four divisions, commanded respectively by Generals F. C. Barlow, J. Gibbon, D. B. Birney. and J. B. Carr. His brigade commanders were Generals A. S. Webb, J. P. Owen, J. H. Ward, A. Hayes, and G. Mott; and Colonels N. A. Miles, T. A. Smythe, R. Frank, J. R. Brooke, S. S. Carroll, and W. R. Brewster. Colonel J. C. Tidball was chief of artillery, and Lieutenant-Colonel C. H. Morgan was chief of staff.

Warren's (Fifth) corps consisted of four divisions, commanded respectively by Generals C. Griffin, J. C. Robinson, S. W. Crawford, and J. S. Wadsworth. The brigade commanders were Generals J. Barnes, J. J. Bartlett, R. B. Ayres. H. Baxter, L. Cutler, and J. C. Rice; and Colonels Leonard, Dennison, W. McCandless, J. W. Fisher, and Roy Stone. Lieutenant-Colonel H. C. Bankhead, chief of staff; Colonel C. S. Wainwright, chief of artillery.

Sedgwick's (Sixth) corps comprised three divisions, commanded respectively by Generals H. G. Wright, G. W. Getty, and H. Prince. The brigade commanders were Generals A. T. A. Torbert, A. Shaler, F. Wheaton, T. H. Neill, A. L. Eustis, and D. A. Russell; and Colonels E. Upton, H. Burnham, and L. A. Grant. Chief of staff, Lieutenant-Colonel M. T. McMahon; chief of artillery, Colonel C. H. Tompkins.

The reserve park of artillery was under the chief direction of General H. J. Hunt, chief of artillery of the Army of the Potomac, and under the immediate command of Colonel H. S. Burton. A brigade of engineers and the pontoon trains were placed in charge of Major J. C. Duane; and the vast park of supply-wagons were under the direction of General Rufus Ingalls, Chief Quartermaster.

The cavalry of the entire army was consolidated, and General Philip H. Sheridan, of the Regular Infantry, was placed in command of it; and General Kilpatrick was assigned to the command of the cavalry of Sherman's army in Northern Georgia. General Pleasanton was ordered to report to General Rosecrans, in Missouri, where we have just observed him engaged in chasing Price out of that State.

[3] The staff of General Grant was nearly thirty less in number than that of General McClellan, and was composed of fourteen officers, as follows: Brigadier-General John A. Rawlins, chief of staff; Lieutenant-Colonel

The general plan for the advance was for the main army to make an overland march from the Rapid Anna to the James, with co-operating or auxiliary forces menacing communications with Richmond from different points. For the latter purpose General Butler was to advance from Fortress Monroe with about thirty thousand troops, establish himself in an intrenched position in the vicinity of City Point, at the junction of the Appomattox River with the James, whence he might operate, either against Richmond directly, or its communications, or effect a junction with the Army of the Potomac marching down from the North, as circumstances might require. Another force was organized for the purpose of menacing the westward communications with Richmond. This force was to be composed of the army of General Franz Sigel, then engaged in protecting Western Virginia and the frontiers of Maryland and Pennsylvania. He was to form his army into two columns, one of them, about ten thousand strong, under General Crook, to march up from the Kanawha region and operate against the Virginia and East Tennessee railway, and the other, about seven thousand strong, under Sigel, in person, to go up the Shenandoah Valley as far as possible, and, by thus menacing Lee's westward lines of supply, compel him to send detachments for their protection, and thereby weaken his forces opposed to the Army of the Potomac. Lee's army was then occupying a line nearly twenty miles on each side of Orange Court-House, its left covered by the Rapid Anna and mountains near, and its right by a strong line of works on Mine Run, which he had strengthened since Meade's threat in November.[1] The corps of Ewell and Hill composed the bulk of Lee's army near the Rapid Anna, while Longstreet's corps, lately returned from East Tennessee, was in the vicinity of Gordonsville, within easy supporting distance of Lee.

Such was the general position of the opposing forces in Virginia on the first of May, when Lieutenant-General Grant gave orders for an advance of the great armies of Meade[2] and Sherman, to operate against the rebellion, in

---

T. S. Bowers and Captain E. S. Parker, assistant adjutants-general; Lieutenant-Colonel C. B. Comstock, senior aid-de-camp; Lieutenant-Colonels Orville E. Babcock, F. T. Dent, Horace Porter, and Captain P. T. Hudson, aids-de-camp; Lieutenant-Colonel W. L. Dupp, assistant inspector-general; Lieutenant-Colonels W. R. Rowley and Adam Badeau, secretaries; Captain George K. Leet, assistant adjutant-general, in office at Washington; Captain H. W. Janes, assistant quartermaster, on duty at head-quarters, and First-Lieutenant William Dunn, acting aid-de-camp. General Meade's chief of staff was Major-General A. A. Humphreys, and Brigadier-General Seth Williams was his adjutant-general.

[1] See page 111.

[2] On the 3d of May, General Meade issued the following order to the Army of the Potomac, which was read to every regiment:—

"SOLDIERS:—Again you are called upon to advance on the enemies of your country. The time and the occasion are deemed opportune by your commanding general to address you a few words of confidence and caution. You have been reorganized, strengthened, and fully equipped in every respect. You form a part of the several armies of your country—the whole under an able and distinguished general, who enjoys the confidence of the Government, the people, and the army. Your movement being in co-operation with others, it is of the utmost importance that no effort should be spared to make it successful.

"*Soldiers!* The eyes of the whole country are looking with anxious hope to the blow you are about to strike in the most sacred cause that ever called men to arms. Remember your homes, your wives, and children; and bear in mind that the sooner your enemies are overcome, the sooner you will be returned to enjoy the benefits and blessings of peace. Bear with patience the hardships and sacrifices you will be called upon to endure. Have confidence in your officers and in each other.

"Keep your ranks on the march and on the battle-field, and let each man earnestly implore God's blessing, and endeavor, by his thoughts and actions, to render himself worthy of the favor he seeks. With clear conscience and strong arms, actuated by a high sense of duty, fighting to preserve the Government and the institutions handed down to us by our forefathers, if true to ourselves, victory, under God's blessing, must and will attend our efforts."

accordance with a plan which his view of the necessity of the case suggested, and which he so clearly set forth in his final general report, saying:—

"From an early period in the rebellion I had been impressed with the idea that active and continuous operations of all the troops that could be brought into the field, regardless of season and weather, were necessary to a speedy termination of the war. The resources of the enemy, and his numerical strength, were far inferior to ours; but, as an offset to this, we had a vast territory, with a population hostile to the Government, to garrison, and long lines of river and railroad communication to protect, to enable us to supply the operating armies.

"The armies in the East and West acted independently and without concert, like a balky team, no two ever pulling together, enabling the enemy to use to great advantage his interior line of communication, for transporting troops from east to west, re-enforcing the army most vigorously pressed, and to furlough large numbers, during seasons of inactivity on our part, to go to their homes and do the work of producing, for the support of their armies. It was a question whether our numerical strength and resources were not more than balanced by these disadvantages and the enemy's superior position.

"From the first I was firm in the conviction that no peace could be had that would be stable and conducive to the happiness of the people, both North and South, until the military power of the rebellion was entirely broken. I therefore determined, first, to use the greatest number of troops practicable against the armed force of the enemy, preventing him from using the same force at different seasons against, first one and then another of our armies, and the possibility of repose for refitting and producing necessary supplies for carrying on resistance. Second, to hammer continuously against the armed force of the enemy and his resources, until by mere attrition, if in no other way, there should be nothing left to him but an equal submission with the loyal section of our common country to the Constitution and laws of the land."

Grant felt encouraged to work in accordance with these views, for the loyal people everywhere evinced entire confidence in him, and a disposition to furnish him with all necessary materials for making a vigorous and decisive campaign. Volunteering was rapidly increasing; and on the 21st of April[a] the Governors of the younger States of Ohio, Indiana, Illinois, Iowa, and Wisconsin, tendered to the President the services of one hundred thousand men, for one hundred days, without requiring any bounty to be paid or the service charged or credited on any draft. This patriotic offer was accepted, and the Secretary of War was directed[b] to carry the proposition of the Governors into effect.

[a] 1864.

[b] April 23.

CHAPTER XI.

ADVANCE OF THE ARMY OF THE POTOMAC ON RICHMOND.

N the evening of the 3d of May, 1864, the Army of the Potomac was ready to advance, and at midnight it moved toward the Rapid Anna in two columns, the right from near Culpepper Court-House, and the left from Stevensburg. The right was composed of the corps of Warren (Fifth) and Sedgwick (Sixth); and the left, of the Second, under Hancock. The right was led by Warren, preceded by Wilson's cavalry division, and, on the morning of the 4th, crossed the Rapid Anna at Germania Ford, followed, during the forenoon, by Sedgwick's corps. The left, preceded by Gregg's cavalry, and followed by the entire army-train of wagons, four thousand in number, crossed at Elly's Ford at the same time.

The right column pushed directly into The Wilderness, and Warren, with Wilson's cavalry thrown out in the direction of Robertson's Tavern,[1] bivouacked that night at the Old Wilderness Tavern, while Sedgwick encamped near the river. The left column pushed on to Chancellorsville, and bivouacked the same night on the battle-field around it,[2] with Gregg's cavalry thrown out toward Todd's Tavern.[3] Burnside's (Ninth) corps, which had been lying on the Rappahannock, intended, it was supposed, as a reserve for the defense of Washington City, had now moved rapidly for- ward, and, on the morning of the 5th,[a] crossed the Rapid Anna at Germania Ford, and joined the Army of the Potomac, into which it was afterward incorporated.

[a] May, 1864.

Full one hundred thousand men, fresh and hopeful, with the immense army-train, were now across the Rapid Anna, and well on the flank of the Confederate army lying behind the strong intrenchments on Mine Run. In this advance the Nationals had met no opposition, and it was an achievement, Grant said, which removed from his mind the most serious apprehensions which he had entertained concerning the crossing of the river "in the face of an active, large, well-appointed, and ably commanded army."[4] He now felt confident that by another day's march the Army of the Potomac

---

[1] See map on page 111.   [2] See map on page 37.   [3] See page 24.
[4] *Report of Lieutenant-General Grant of the Armies of the United States*, 1864-5, page 6. General Grant took occasion at the outset of the report to refer to the anomalous position of General Meade, who was the commander of the Army of the Potomac. He says he tried to leave General Meade in independent command of the army. His instructions were all given through Meade. They were general in their nature, leaving all the details to him. "The campaigns that followed," Grant said, "proved him to be the right man in the right place." His commanding in the presence of an officer of superior rank drew from him much of the public attention.

might pass The Wilderness, using it for a mask, and, by advancing rapidly on Gordonsville, take a position in the rear of the Army of Northern Virginia. For this purpose Sheridan was directed to move with the cavalry divisions of Gregg and Torbert against the Confederate cavalry, in the direction of Hamilton's Crossing, near Fredericksburg, and, at the same time, Wilson's division was ordered to move to Craig's Meeting-House, on the Catharpin road, and to send out from that point detachments upon other highways to watch the foe. Hancock was directed to move to Shady Grove Church, and extend his right toward the Fifth Corps, at Parker's store, while Warren, marching to the latter place, should extend his right toward the Sixth Corps, at the Old Wilderness Tavern, to which Sedgwick was ordered.

JOHN SEDGWICK.[1]

So the advance was begun early in the morning of the 5th.[a] Preparations for it had not been unobserved by the Confederates, who were standing on the defensive, with heavy forces at points, *en echelon*, between the Rapid Anna and Gordonsville, and were exceedingly vigilant. Lee's scouts, in the thickets of The Wilderness, and his signal officers on the lofty summit of Clark's Mountain, had carefully watched the movements of the Nationals, and when these had fairly developed Grant's intentions, the Confederate commander, with singular boldness and skill, changed his front, and proceeded to foil his antagonist. From Lee's center, near Orange Court-House, about twenty miles from the prescribed line of march of the Nationals, two roads running eastwardly, almost parallel to each other, penetrated and passed through The Wilderness. One (the more northerly) was an old turnpike, the other a plank road. Along these, when, on the 4th, the Army of the Potomac was passing the Rapid Anna and moving southward, a large portion of the Army of Northern Virginia was moving, leaving behind them the strong defenses on Mine Run as a place of refuge in the event of disaster. In two columns the Confederates were pressing along these roads, to confront the Nationals before they should reach the intersection of these highways with that from Germania Ford, and compel them to fight while in that wooded, tangled, and, to the latter, unknown region, so familiar to the former, where cavalry and artillery would be almost useless, and where the clouds of sharp-shooters belonging to Lee's army might ply their deadly vocation almost with impunity. General R. S. Ewell was leading the more northerly column along the turnpike, and A. P. Hill the other along the plank road; and that night Ewell's advance division, under Edward Johnson, bivouacked within three miles of the Old Wilderness Tavern, at the junction of the Orange turnpike with the Germania Ford road, near which Warren's corps was reposing. Neither party suspected the close proximity of the other.

[a] May, 1864.

---

[1] This is from a fine photograph, from life, by Rockwood, of New York City.

Warren was nearest the foe in the prescribed order of advance, and, early on the morning of the 5th,[a] he had thrown out the division of Griffin on the turnpike, to watch in that direction, and prevent [a] May, 1864. any interference with the march of Sedgwick's corps following the Fifth from the ford; while Crawford's division, forming Warren's advance, was set in motion along a wood-road toward Parker's store, near which Johnson had bivouacked. These movements were scarcely begun, when the foe was felt. Griffin's skirmishers on the turnpike were driven in, and some of Crawford's horsemen out on the plank road now came galloping back, with word that the Confederates were in front in strong force. Crawford sent forward a reconnoitering party of cavalry, which soon became warmly engaged, and asked for help, when he sent to their aid the Pennsylvania Bucktails, who reached the front in time to meet an attack of a Confederate infantry force which had arrived. The force in front of Crawford composed Hill's column, and that which attacked Griffin's skirmishers was the van of Ewell's column.

Such was the condition of affairs when, at near eight o'clock in the morning,[b] Grant and Meade came up from the ford, and took a position beneath the shadow of pine trees by the road-side, not [b] May 5. far from The Wilderness Tavern. They could not at first believe that Lee had been guilty of the rashness of sending the bulk of his army five or six miles in front of his intrenchments to attack his foe, already in strong force on his flank, and it was supposed that the assailing columns were only parts of a strong rear-guard covering Lee's retreat. They were soon undeceived; but not fully, until after a battle was begun, and developed the fact that the bulk of Lee's army was there with the intention of fighting. With the impression that it was only his rear-guard, dispositions to sweep it away and seize the intrenchments on Mine Run were made. Perceiving that the heavier portion of the Confederates

GRANT'S HEAD-QUARTERS IN THE WILDERNESS.[1]

seemed to be on the turnpike, Crawford was directed to suspend operations on the plank road, while Griffin, with General Wadsworth's division on his left, and Robinson's division as a support, should attack the foe on their front. Crawford sent McCandless, with his brigade, to act on the left of Wadsworth, and then, with the remainder of his division, he withdrew, sharply followed.

---

[1] From a sketch made by the author, in June, 1866.

Preparations were now made for the attack. The ground on which the struggle was to occur—a struggle not anticipated by the National leaders— exhibited a little oasis in The Wilderness. Looking from Warren's quarters, near The Wilderness Tavern, was seen a little brook (Wilderness Run), and beyond it a gentle ridge, over which lay the turnpike. On the southern slope of that ridge was the house of Major Lacey, whose fine residence opposite Fredericksburg is delineated on page 19. Around it was a green lawn and meadows, and these were bounded by wooded hills, and thickets of pines and cedars—that peculiar covering of the earth which abounded in The Wilderness. On the right of the turnpike this thicket was very dense; and farther to the right was a ravine, which formed the dividing line of the forces of Griffin and Ewell on that eventful morning. The whole region, excepting the little opening around Lacey's house, was an irregular and broken surface, covered with small, thickly-set trees, and an almost impassable undergrowth, in the midst of which full two hundred thousand fighting men were now summoned to combat.

At noon, the Nationals, in force sufficient, it was thought, to set Lee's rear-guard flying, moved to the attack, on the turnpike, when the brigades of Ayres and Bartlett, of Griffin's division, the former on the right and the latter on the left of the highway, pressed rapidly forward, and bore the brunt of the first impetuous onset. The Confederates were easily driven, for only Johnson's division was in battle-line, with General Sam. Jones's brigade stretched across the turnpike. With the aid of a larger force then at hand, Ewell's corps might have been crushed. But its presence was unsuspected, and that force was not brought to bear. Ewell's column was saved by Stewart's brigade instantly coming up and taking the place of Johnson's shattered column, and the timely arrival of Rodes's division at the scene of strife. These fresh forces at once took the offensive. It had been arranged for the right of Warren's line to be assisted by the left of Sedgwick's, under General Wright; but so difficult was the passage through the thick wood, that the latter could not get up in time. Warren's right was thus left exposed, and against it the Confederates struck a quick and vigorous blow, by which Ayres and his regulars were hurled back, and so also was Bartlett's brigade. The fighting was desperate and sanguinary, during which the Confederates captured two guns and a number of prisoners, and gained a decided advantage. Meanwhile General Wadsworth, who had moved his division at the same time with that of Griffin, unable to co-operate with the latter on account of the tangled woods between them, had been somewhat misled, and found his flank exposed to a murderous fire, which caused his command to recoil in some confusion. At the same time the brigade of McCandless, sent by Crawford, found itself in an isolated position on the left of Wadsworth, where it was nearly surrounded, and escaped with great difficulty, after losing two full regiments. And so it was, that every rood of ground gained by the Nationals when they advanced was recovered by the Confederates, and Warren, with his corps bereaved of about three thousand men by this encounter, formed a new line a little in the rear, but still in front of The Wilderness Tavern.

At a little after one o'clock the head of the Sixth Corps was attacked by Ewell, while it was working its way into a position to support the Fifth, when the Confederates, after a severe struggle, were repulsed, and gave way between three and four o'clock with a loss of Generals Jones and Stafford killed. Then Rodes's division, led by General Gordon, made a furious charge that caused the advance of the Sixth to recoil with loss, when, in a counter-charge, the Confederates were driven with the loss of General Pegram, who was severely wounded. A general advance of the Nationals was now ordered, but night came on before preparations for the movement were completed, and it was postponed.

Before this repulse of the Fifth Corps, and at least two hours before Griffin advanced, Grant was satisfied that Lee was disposed to give battle in considerable force in The Wilderness, and he and Meade made dispositions accordingly. Hancock, with the Second Corps, was marching on his prescribed line, ten miles distant, when, at a point two or three miles from Todd's Tavern, he received orders first to halt, and then to hasten to the main body by the Brock road. At the same time Meade ordered General Getty, of the Sixth Corps, to seize and hold with his division, until Hancock should come up, the junction of the Brock with the plank road, along which Hill was advancing, and had passed Parker's store. Getty did so, and found himself at once pressed more and more by Hill, who had evidently been aiming to secure the same strategic point before Hancock should reach it. Getty held it firmly until about three o'clock, when Hancock's advance, under Birney, came up and secured the position absolutely. The whole of the Second Corps were soon there, in double line of battle in front of the Brock road, facing Hill's line stretched across the plank road.[1] Hancock at once began to throw up breastworks on his front, but before they were completed, he was ordered to advance on Hill and drive him beyond Parker's store. Getty, moving on each side of the plank road, had already made a vigorous attack on Heth, driving in his pickets, and becoming hotly engaged. Then Hancock ordered to his support the divisions of Mott and Birney, with Ricketts's Battery and a company of the First Pennsylvania Artillery, when a most sanguinary battle ensued, at close distance, the musket-firing being deadly and continuous along the whole line. The brigades of Carroll and Owen, of Gibbon's division, and the Irish brigade under Colonel Smythe, of the Second Delaware, and others of Barlow's division, were soon involved in the fight. The battle-lines swayed to and fro. Mott's division gave way, and as General Alexander Hays was heading his command to fill the gap, he was shot dead while at the head of his troops in the thickest of the fight.

Grant and Meade were satisfied by sounds that reached their ears that there was heavier or more pressing work to be done in front of Hill than in a contest with Ewell, and so Wadsworth was ordered to lead his division, and Baxter's brigade of Robinson's, through the thickets, and fall upon Hill's flank and rear. So difficult was the march in the tangled way, and in the face of skirmishers, that it was dark, and the conflict had nearly ceased, before Wadsworth was in position for attack, so his men rested on their arms that night, close by Hill's reposing skirmishers, ready for assault in the morning. Hancock had continued unavailing efforts to drive Hill, until after dark,

---

[1] Hill's corps consisted of the divisions of Generals Anderson, Heth, and Wilcox.

when his wearied troops also laid down upon their arms, the combatants so near each other that both drew water from the same brook. At midnight all was silent in The Wilderness, where the roar of battle had been sounding for many hours, during which time the opposing forces exhibited the curious spectacle of each being divided almost as effectually as if a high wall was between them. Hancock was entirely separated from Warren and Sedgwick by a thicket that forbade co-operation, and for the same reason Hill and Ewell were unable to assist each other.

Notwithstanding their heavy losses, the opposing commanders determined to renew the struggle in the morning on that strange battle-field—an arena more fitted for the system of savage warfare than for that of civilized men. Preparations were made accordingly. Burnside was summoned to the front by Grant, and Longstreet was called up from Gordonsville by Lee.

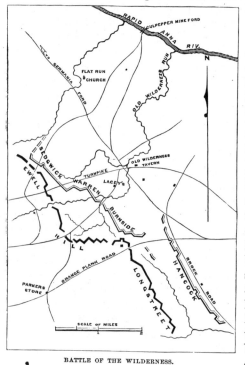

BATTLE OF THE WILDERNESS.

Burnside arrived before daybreak on the morning of the 6th;[a] and Longstreet, arriving before midnight of the 5th, had bivouacked not far from the intrenchments on Mine Run. Burnside took position in the interval between Warren, on the turnpike, and Hancock, on the plank road, and Longstreet was directed to take position on Hill's right. Meade's line of battle, fully formed at dawn, was five miles in length, facing westward, with Sedgwick on the right of Warren, and Burnside and Hancock on the left. Lee's army remained the same as on the evening of the 5th, Ewell's corps, forming his left, being on the turnpike, and Hill's on the right, lying upon the plank road. Each line had been extended so as to form a connection, and Longstreet was ready to take his prescribed position on Hill's left.

[a] May, 1864.

So stood the two great and veteran armies in the morning twilight on the 6th of May, 1864, ready for a struggle that must be necessarily almost hand to hand, in a country in which maneuvering, in the military sense, was almost impossible, and where, by the compass alone, like mariners at murky midnight, the movements of troops were directed. The three hundred guns of the combatants had no avocation there, and the few horsemen not away on outward duty were compelled to be almost idle spectators. Of the two hundred thousand men there ready to fall upon and slay each other, probably no man's eyes saw more than a thousand at one time, so absolute was the concealments of the thickets. Never in the history of war was such a spectacle exhibited. Military skill was of little account, ana Grant knew it, and so he gave but the single general order, Attack along the whole line at five o'clock.

Lee was not quite ready at Grant's appointed hour, for he had made arrangements to strike the left of his antagonist a terrible and fatal blow, by which he hoped to drive him back to the Rapid Anna. It was for this purpose that Longstreet was ordered to the right of Hill. That general's force was not in position so early as Lee had hoped it would be, and therefore, to distract attention until Longstreet should be in position, and possibly to penetrate the National line at some weak point, he made a demonstration against Meade's right. This was done, at a little before five o'clock, by a fierce musketry attack upon Seymour's brigade, on the extreme right, which involved first Ricketts's division, and then Wright's. The assailants made desperate attempts to break through the lines, but were easily thrown back, when Sedgwick advanced his corps a little. At the same time Warren and Hancock made a simultaneous attack upon the foe on their front. The latter opened the battle on the left by advancing two divisions under Birney, with Getty's command, supported by the brigades of Owen and Carroll, of Gibbon's division. At the same time Wadsworth moved from his bivouack, and, gallantly fighting his way entirely across the portion of the Second Corps posted on the north of the plank road, wheeled up that highway, and commenced driving the Confederates, for Longstreet had not yet come into position, and Anderson's division was absent. Heth and Wilcox were driven a mile and a half back upon their trains and artillery, and nearly to Lee's head-quarters. The Confederate rifle-pits were captured, with many prisoners, and five battle-flags. A speedy and substantial triumph seemed to be promised for the Nationals, when, for some unexplained reason, the victors paused. It was a halt fatal to their hopes of success. During that interval Anderson came up and checked Hill's confused retreat, and at the same time the van of Longstreet's column, which had been marching to flank Hancock, appeared in front.

It was now about nine o'clock in the morning.[a] Hancock re-formed his somewhat broken line, which had been re-enforced by Stevenson's division of Burnside's corps in addition to that of Wadsworth, and resumed his advance, when he found his way blocked by an unexpectedly large and determined force. Lee had recalled Longstreet from his flanking march to the assistance of Hill, and it was a greater portion of the Confederate army which Hancock had before him. He had been informed of Longstreet's flanking march, and was expecting him from another quarter. For awhile the noise of guns where Sheridan, at eight o'clock, encountered Stuart's cavalry far on Hancock's left, was supposed to be the sounds of Longstreet's contest with National skirmishers, but while Hancock was looking for him on his flank, his van, as we have seen, had taken position on his front. Ignorant of this, the latter resumed the attack most vigorously, but could make no headway. Finally, after losing heavily, he found himself compelled, at about 11 o'clock, to fall back before an overwhelming force, sent, according to Lee's original plan, to double up the National left, and drive the whole army back to the Rapid Anna. Wadsworth was then fighting gallantly, and pushing into a weak part of the Confederate line, when his own gave way. While trying to rally his flying

[a] May 6, 1864.

troops, who were hard pressed, he had two horses shot under him, and soon afterward a bullet pierced his brain, and he fell to the earth. The Confederates seized the dying man and sent him to their rear, where he expired the next day; but it was several days before his fate was known to his friends.[1]

This was a critical moment for the Army of the Potomac, for the superior mind of Longstreet was then evidently the chief director of the move-

ment for executing Lee's plan for giving a deadly blow to the National left. He had sent a heavy force to seize the Brock road, on Hancock's left, while pushing him back on the front, when one of those incidents which some call "Providence," and others "accident," occurred, which doubtless saved the Army of the Potomac from great disaster. Longstreet, with his staff, was riding in front of his pursuing column, when he came suddenly upon the van of his flanking force. The latter, mistaking him and his attendants for National cavalry, fired upon them.

JAMES S. WADSWORTH.

Longstreet was severely wounded and disabled, when Lee took the immediate direction of the important movement. With less executive skill than his able lieutenant possessed, he occupied four hours in getting ready to carry it out. This caused a lull in the battle on that portion of the field, and enabled Hancock, who had been pressed back to his *abatis* and intrenchments on the Brock road, to make dispositions for meeting another attack, then evidently impending.

Meanwhile Sedgwick's corps, on the right, had lost heavily in unsuccessful attempts to carry Ewell's intrenched positions. Warren's had remained mostly on the defensive, but at almost every part of the line there was more or less skirmishing throughout the day. Finally, at four o'clock, when Lee had the troops of Hill and Longstreet well in hand, he hurled them heavily, in four columns, upon Hancock's intrenched position. They pushed up to within a hundred yards of the first line, when a sharp musketry battle ensued, without decisive results, until a fire in the woods was communicated to the logs of the breastworks, and soon enveloped them in flames. The smoke and ashes of the conflagration were driven by the wind directly in

---

[1] The death of General Wadsworth produced the most profound sorrow. He was a man of large wealth, of the first social position in the State of New York, and universally known as a model of a Christian gentleman. At the breaking out of the rebellion he at once offered his person, and his wealth and influence, in defense of the Republic. He was a patriot in the highest sense of the term. He had been brought prominently before the public as a candidate for Governor of his State. Such was his high character, and his rank in the army, that the Governor of New York (Horatio Seymour) felt constrained, in deference to public feeling, to take notice of his death. Being opposed to the war, Mr. Seymour could not consistently commend him as a patriot; so, after speaking of him highly as a man and citizen, he said: "From the outset an ardent supporter of the war, to him belongs the merit of freely periling his own person in upholding the opinions he advocated." It is proper to say that this low view of General Wadsworth's motives in taking up arms was entirely unjust. He was actuated by aims higher than the vulgar aspirations of the mere politician, who cannot easily comprehend unselfishness. He was fighting *for his country and the rights of man*, not for the "opinions" of himself or a party.

the face of the Nationals. Taking advantage of this, the Confederates swept forward, driving back a body of the troops at the first line, and then striking Stevenson's division of Burnside's corps, which had taken position between Warren and Hancock. These, too, were thrown back toward Chancellorsville in great disorder, and the assailants, pressing through the gap they had formed, planted their flag on the breastworks. At that critical moment Colonel J. W. Hoffman, with parts of nine broken regiments (less than five hundred men), struck the assailants a blow that made them recoil, and thus saved the day on the left, as Hancock then declared.

Thus ended the struggle on the National left, where the heaviest of the fight had been carried on, and it was supposed that the battle was over for the day. But Lee made another desperate effort to achieve a victory, by swiftly massing his troops on the National right, and directing Ewell to attempt to turn it. At sunset a heavy column, led by General Gordon, moved swiftly from Ewell's extreme left, and in the twilight fell suddenly upon the brigades of Seymour and Shaler, of Ricketts's division, driving them back in much confusion, and capturing both commanders and nearly four thousand of their officers and men. It was a complete surprise for those wearied troops, who had cast themselves on the ground for rest; and for a little while the entire right wing of the army seemed to be in great peril. General Sedgwick prevented further confusion by promptly checking the advance of the Confederates, and the darkness made it impossible for them to do any thing more. Both armies rested that night, the Nationals holding precisely the ground they had occupied in the morning. So ended THE BATTLE OF THE WILDERNESS, with heavy losses on both sides.[1]

Lee was evidently satisfied that he could not maintain a further contest with his antagonist on the ground he (Lee) had chosen for the struggle, so he retired behind intrenchments, where he was found standing on the defensive by the skirmish line of the Nationals sent out at daybreak on Saturday morning, the 7th.[a] Grant had no desire to renew the conflict there, and at an early hour he determined to resume his march southward, and get out of The Wilderness and its entanglements as soon as possible. He chose for his immediate destination the village of Spottsylvania Court-House, about thirteen miles southeast of the battle-ground in The Wilderness, and proceeded to plant his army, according to his original plan, between that of Lee and Richmond. Warren was directed to lead in the movement, which was to be along the Brock road, by way of Todd's Tavern.[2] Hancock was to follow him, and Sedgwick and Burnside were to take a little more indirect route, by way of Chancellorsville. The army trains were to be parked at Chancellorsville toward evening, ready to follow the troops.

Warren moved at nine o'clock in the evening,[b] his column preceded by cavalry. He pushed vigorously on, with the hope and expectation of reaching Spottsylvania Court-House before Lee should

[a] May, 1864.

[b] May 7.

---

[1] According to the most careful estimates, the National loss in this sanguinary battle of two days' duration was nearly, if not quite, 18,000 men, of whom 6,000 were made prisoners. The Confederate loss was probably about 11,000. Among the wounded of the Nationals were Generals Getty, Gregg, Owen, Bartlett, and Webb, and Colonel Carroll. The Confederates lost in killed, Generals Sam. Jones and A. G. Jenkins; and the wounded were Generals Longstreet, Stafford (mortally), Pickett, Pegram, and Hunter. Longstreet was disabled for several months.   [2] See page 24.

be apprised of the movement. He was foiled by delays. First, at Todd's Tavern (where Gregg had fought and defeated Fitz Hugh Lee that day),

SPOTTSYLVANIA COURT-HOUSE.[1]

General Meade's cavalry escort blocked his way for nearly two hours. Two miles farther on, in the midst of a magnificent woods, and near a little tributary of the River Po, he was again impeded by the cavalry division of Merritt, which the day before had been fighting Stuart's cavalry, whom Lee had sent to hold the Brock road. There he was detained almost three hours, and when he was ready to advance it was daylight. The road was barricaded by heavy trees, which had been cut and felled across it, and it was about eight o'clock on Sunday morning [a] before the head of Warren's column, composed of two brigades under General Robinson, emerged from the woods in battle order at Alsop's farm, upon the high open plain two or three miles from Spottsylvania Court-House. There the road from Todd's Tavern forks, one branch leading toward the court-house, and the other to Laurel Hill. Beyond this plain was a slight depression, and where the road ascended to Spottsylvania Ridge the slope was covered with woods.

[a] May 8, 1864.

Up to this time Warren had met with no resistance, excepting from Stuart's dismounted cavalry, but now, as Robinson advanced over the plain toward the wood, he was met by a cannonade from the ridge and a murderous musket-fire from the forest. Robinson returned the cannonade promptly, but was soon severely wounded, when his troops, wearied by the night's hard march and toil, and depressed by their terrible experience in The Wilderness, were made to recoil. They would have fled in wild confusion back upon the main body, had not Warren appeared at their head at a timely moment. He rallied and re-formed them in the open wood on the edge of the plain, and so prevented a sad disaster. Later in the day Griffin's division, which advanced on the road to the right of Robinson's march, had a similar experience, and, after gallantly fighting, fell back of the second line, when the divisions of Crawford and Wadsworth (the latter now commanded by General Cutler) came up and drove the Confederates from the woods on the right. Warren's entire corps then formed a battle-line, and the troops, without waiting for orders to do so, fell to intrenching.

The foe thus encountered by Meade's advance was the head of Longstreet's corps (then commanded by General Anderson), and was there by seeming accident. The withdrawal of the trains of the Army of the Poto-

---

[1] This is a view of the county building of the shire of Spottsylvania, around which grew up a village that derived its name from the edifice. This county received its name from Alexander Spottswood, Governor of Virginia, who owned and worked iron mines in that region, and at what is now known as Germania Ford, he founded a town, the inhabitants of which being chiefly German miners, it was called Germania. The last syllable of Spottswood's name, *wood*, was Latinized, and hence the name of Spott*sylvania*.

mac from the battle-field of The Wilderness apprised Lee of the fact that the army was about to move,[1] but whither he knew not. It might be to Spott-sylvania, or it might be back to Fredericksburg. So he ordered Anderson to take his corps from the breastworks and encamp that night in a position to move on Spottsylvania in the morning. Finding no suitable place for bivouacking, on account of the burning woods, Anderson marched that night, simultaneously with Warren, each ignorant of the other's movement. The former arrived in time to throw the head of his column across the latter's path, to confront him with cannon and intrenchments, and to foil his attempt to seize Spottsylvania Court-House. Such were the events which produced the situation we have just considered.

Warren did not feel strong enough to encounter the troops on his front, who were continually increasing in numbers and industriously intrenching on Spottsylvania Ridge, so he awaited the arrival of Sedgwick. He reached the front in the afternoon, and took command of the field in the absence of Meade, who, with all of Hancock's corps but Gibbon's division, had remained at Todd's Tavern, in anticipation of an attack by Lee on the rear of the Army of the Potomac. Sedgwick felt strong enough with the two corps to attempt to drive the Confederates from their advantageous position, but it was nearly sunset before his dispositions for attack were finished. Then a fruitless assault was made by a New Jersey brigade of Neill's division. General Crawford again advanced, when he was unexpectedly struck upon his flank by a part of Ewell's corps that was coming up, and was driven a full mile, with a loss of about one hundred men made prisoners. When night closed in, nearly the whole of Lee's army was in the vicinity of Spottsylvania Court-House, and holding the ridge in front of it, with strong intrenchments, growing more formidable every hour. During the day Wilson had pene-trated to the village with his cavalry, but, being unsupported, was compelled to retire. On the same day the brigade of General Miles was thrown out by Hancock on the Catharpin road, with a brigade of Gregg's cavalry and a battery of artillery, to meet any hostile approach from that direction. Near Corbyn's Bridge they were attacked, when the assailants were repulsed and driven. On Sunday night, the 8th of May,[a] Lee stood squarely and firmly across the path of the southward march of the Army of the Potomac, and he held that army in check there for twelve days.   [a] 1864.

On the morning of the 9th, Meade's army was formed in battle order before the Confederate lines. Hancock came up from Todd's Tavern at an early hour, and two divisions of Burnside's corps, on the left, pushed to the Fredericksburg road, driving the Confederates across the little River Ny. In the arrangement of the line, Hancock occupied the right, Warren the center, and Sedgwick the left, with Burnside on his left. General Sheridan

---

[1] Speaking of this event, a late writer (Professor Henry Coppée) observes: "Spies and traitors were all around our head-quarters. Our signals were discovered and repeated; and with a rapidity which savored of magic and diabolic arts, no sooner had an order been issued by Grant than it was known at Lee's head-quarters. On the other hand, we had no such information. There were not in the rebel ranks, wicked as they were, men as vile as Northern traitors, who, while wearing the uniform of the Republic, living on its bounty, and sworn to protect its glorious banner, were in secret league with the enemy, and doing more to defeat Grant's plans than did the men who were arrayed in battle against him."—*Grant and his Campaigns*, by Henry Coppée, page 302. It is well understood that emissaries of the Peace Faction, professing loyalty, were at this time in Gov-ernment employment in the Department at Washington and in the armies in the field, secretly giving aid, in every possible way, to the enemies of the Republic

was sent that morning, with a heavy cavalry force, to break up Lee's communications with Richmond, and the greater part of the day was spent
chiefly in intrenching, and making other preparations for battle. There was
skirmishing now and then, when troops moved to take new positions; and
the Confederate sharp-shooters, having convenient places for concealment,
were particularly active. One of these inflicted irreparable injury upon the
Union army, by sending a bullet through the brain of the gallant Sedgwick,

THE PLACE WHERE SEDGWICK WAS KILLED.[1]

while he was giving directions for strengthening the intrenchments on his
front. He fell dead; and then there was sincere mourning throughout the
army, for the soldiers loved him; and the loyal people of the land felt
bereaved, for a true patriot had fallen. He was succeeded in the command
of the Sixth Corps, on the following day, by General H. G. Wright. On
the same day Brigadier-General W. H. Morris, son of the lyric poet, the late
George P. Morris, was severely wounded.

Every thing was in readiness for battle on the morning of the 10th.[a] By
a movement the previous evening, having for its chief object the
capture of a part of a Confederate wagon-train moving into
Spottsylvania Court-House, Hancock had made a lodgment, with three of
his divisions, on the south side of the Ny, and he was proceeding to develop
the strength of the enemy on the National right, when General Meade suspended the movement. It had been determined to make an attack upon an
eminence in front of the Fifth and Sixth Corps, known as Laurel Hill, whose
crest was thickly wooded, and crowned with earth-works, which had been
previously constructed as a remote defense of Richmond, and Hancock was
ordered to recall two of his divisions from the south side of the Ny, to assist
in the assault. The divisions of Gibbon and Birney at once retired, when
that of the latter was sharply assailed in the rear. The remaining division
(Barlow's) was left in a perilous condition, for his skirmishers had just been
driven in. With great skill and valor their commander managed his troops,
when a new peril appeared. The woods, between his column and the river,

[a] May, 1864.

---

[1] This is from a sketch made by the author in June, 1866, taken from the breastworks in front of the Union line.
Toward the right is seen the logs of the battery, the construction of which Sedgwick was superintending, and
near which he fell. The bullet came from the clump of trees on the knoll seen more to the right, on rising ground.

had burst into flames, and the brigades of Brooke and Brown were compelled to fight Confederates and fire at the same time. They succeeded in repelling the assailants, and recrossed the stream, but with a heavy loss of men and one gun.

Arrangements were now made for assailing Laurel Hill across the Ny, the most formidable position of the Confederate line. It had been attacked, at eleven o'clock in the morning, by the brigades of Webb and Carroll, and, at three o'clock, the divisions of Crawford and Cutler had assailed it, in order to prepare the way for the grand assault, in aid of which Hancock's troops had been recalled. In both attacks the Nationals were repulsed with heavy loss.

Now came the more desperate struggle. At five o'clock in the evening, when the Second Corps had joined the Fifth, both moved to the attack. The conflict that ensued was fearful. The Nationals struggled up the slopes in the face of a terrible storm of deadly missiles, and penetrated the breastworks at one or two points. But they were soon repulsed, with dreadful loss. The assault was repeated an hour later, with a similar result. In the two encounters nearly six thousand Union troops had fallen, while not more than six hundred of the Confederates had been disabled. Among the Union killed were Generals J. C. Rice and T. G. Stevenson. The enterprise was abandoned, but fighting was not over. Still later, two brigades of the Sixth Corps, commanded respectively by General Russell and Colonel Upton, attacked and carried the first line of Confederate works on their front, and captured over nine hundred prisoners and several guns. They were too far in advance to receive immediate support, expected from General Mott, and were compelled to fall back, taking with them their prisoners, but leaving the guns behind. So ended, at dark, the first day of the Battle of Spottsylvania Court-House. It had been a day of awful strife and slaughter. Not less than nine thousand Unionists and eight thousand Confederates were lost to the service by death, wounds, or captivity. Yet the respective commanders, each comprehending the value of victory in the strife upon which they had entered, determined to renew it on the morrow, and made preparations accordingly. Although a vast number of Unionists had fallen or had been captured within the space of five days, the Lieutenant-General was hopeful, and, on the morning of the 11th, he sent a cheering dispatch to the Secretary of War, closing with words characteristic of the man,—"*I propose to fight it out on this line, if it takes all summer.*"[1]

The 11th was mostly spent in preparations for another battle. There were reconnoiterings and skirmishes, but no serious engagements. The afternoon was rainy, and the night that followed was dark and dismal, for the moon was in its first quarter, the clouds were thick, and the rain still fell. Grant had determined to strike Lee's line at its right center, not far from Mr. Landrum's house, which seemed to be its most vulnerable point, and Hancock was chosen to give the blow. At midnight he left the front of

---

[1] The dispatch was as follows, dated at eight o'clock on the morning of the 11th: " We have now ended the sixth day of very heavy fighting. The result, to this time, is much in our favor. Our losses have been heavy, as well as those of the enemy. I think the loss of the enemy must be greater. We have taken over 5,000 prisoners by battle, while he has taken from us but few, except stragglers. I propose to fight it out on this line, if it takes all summer."

Hill's corps, and moving silently to the left, guided only by the compass, he took post between Wright and Burnside, near the house of Mr. Brown, to be in readiness for work in the morning. Then in two lines, the first composed of the divisions of Barlow and Birney, and the second of those of Gibbon and Mott, he moved, under cover of a dense fog, swiftly and noiselessly over the broken and thickly-wooded ground, toward the salient of an earth-work occupied by the division of Edward Johnson, of Ewell's corps. At a proper moment the silence was broken by loud cheers, as the brigades of Barlow and Birney dashed upon the works in a fierce charge, fought hand to hand with bayonets and clubbed muskets, and captured Johnson, with almost his entire division, who were breakfasting. With these, General George H. Stewart[1] and his two brigades were made prisoners, and nearly thirty guns and many colors were the trophies. Hancock sent over three thousand prisoners back to Grant, with a note, written in pencil, saying : " I have captured from thirty to forty guns. I have finished up Johnson, and am going into Early." It afterward appeared that he had almost captured Lee, and cut the Confederate army in two.

Hancock failed to " go into Early " in the way he anticipated. The enthusiasm of his troops after their success, was unbounded, and seemed equal to any demand. Indeed, they could not be restrained. They pushed forward after flying Confederates through the woods toward Spottsylvania Court-House, for a mile, when they were checked by a second and unfinished line of breastworks, behind which the fugitives rallied and turned upon their pursuers. The entire Confederate line had been aroused by the surprise, to a sense of great peril, and the most desperate efforts were made to prevent further disaster, and to recover what had been lost. Ewell was immediately re-enforced by troops from the corps of Hill and Longstreet, and Hancock's victors were thrown back to the line they had captured, and upon them these heavy masses of the foe were thrown.

Grant had anticipated this, and provided for it. Wright was ordered up with the Sixth Corps to the assistance of Hancock. He arrived at six o'clock, and, at eight, Warren and Burnside gallantly attacked the whole Confederate line on their front. Charge followed charge in quick succession, and with great slaughter on both sides, but without avail to the assailants ; and, at length, the attack was intermitted, and the divisions of Griffin and Cutler, of Warren's corps, were sent to the assistance of Hancock, who was firmly holding the prize he had won, against great odds. The position of the Confederates in front of Warren and Burnside was so strong, that they not only held it firmly, but sent aid to their friends in front of Hancock, where the battle was raging furiously, for Lee was determined to retake the works Johnson and Stewart had lost. Five times he hurled a tremendous weight of men and weapons upon Hancock, in order to dislodge him. The combatants fought hand to hand most desperately, and the flags of both

---

[1] Stewart was a Maryland rebel, who was conspicuous in Baltimore at the time of the massacre of Massachusetts troops there in the spring of 1861. See page 415, volume I. His fine house and grounds in Baltimore, at this time, were used as an asylum for the sick and wounded, known as the Jarvis Hospital. He was an old army friend of Hancock, and it is related that the latter, on the occasion we are considering, cordially offered his hand to the prisoner, saying: " How are you, Stewart." The absurd rebel haughtily refused it, saying : " I am General Stewart, of the Confederate army, and under the circumstances I decline to take your hand." Hancock instantly replied: " And under any other circumstances, General, I should not have offered it."

were several times seen planted on each side of the breastworks, simultaneously, and within a few feet of each other.

Lee's assaults were repulsed with dreadful carnage on both sides, and yet he persisted, notwithstanding rain fell heavily all the afternoon. It was midnight before he ceased to fight, when he sullenly withdrew with his terribly-shattered and worn columns, after a combat of twenty hours, leaving Hancock in possession of the works he had captured in the morning, and twenty guns. So ended the BATTLE OF SPOTTSYLVANIA COURT-HOUSE, one of the bloodiest of the war. It had been fought chiefly by infantry, and at short range, although artillery was freely used. Probably there never was a battle in which so many bullets flew in a given space of time and distance. When the writer visited the scene of

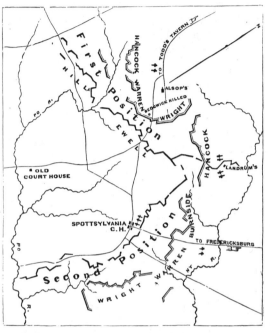

BATTLE OF SPOTTSYLVANIA COURT-HOUSE.

strife, two years afterward,[a] full one-half of the trees of the wood, at a point

where the fiercest struggle ensued, within the salient of the Confederate works, were dead, and nearly all the others were scarred from the effect of musket-balls. At the War Department, in the National Capital, may now[b] be seen a portion of the trunk of a large oak-tree, which was cut in two by bullets alone. Its appearance is given in the annexed engraving.[1]

[a] June 7, 1866.

[b] 1868.

On the morning of the 13th,[a] the Confederates were behind an inner and shorter line of intrenchments, immediately in front of Hancock. Their

[a] May, 1864.

BULLET-SEVERED OAK.

position seemed as invulnerable as ever, yet they had lost much ground since the struggle began. Notwithstanding the Army of the Potomac had lost nearly thirty thousand men in the space of eight days,[2] the commander saw much encouragement in the situation, and on that morning

---

[1] This oak stood inside of the Confederate intrenchments, near Spottsylvania Court-House. It was presented to the Secretary of War by the gallant General N. A. Miles, who commanded a brigade of Barlow's division of the Second Corps, in the battle on the 12th of May. This section of the tree is five feet six inches in height, and twenty-one inches in diameter at the place where it was cut in two.

[2] The official report of the National losses, since the passage of the Rapid Anna to the close of the battle on the 12th of May, was as follows: Killed, 269 officers and 3,019 enlisted men; wounded, 1,017 officers and 18,261 men; missing, 177 officers and 6,667 men, mostly made prisoners, making a total of 29,410 men.

he addressed a stirring congratulatory epistle to his troops, in which he recapitulated their achievements since the campaign began, during "eight days and nights almost without intermission, in rain and sunshine," against a foe "in positions naturally strong, and rendered doubly so by intrenchments." He told them that the work was not yet over, but that every thing was encouraging. "We shall soon receive re-enforcements," he said, "which the foe cannot expect. Let us determine to continue vigorously the work so well begun, and, under God's blessing, in a short time, the object of our labors will be accomplished." [1]

In the mean time the whole country was deeply stirred by the events of the campaign thus far, as reported by the electric and electrifying tongue of the telegraph. Upon Grant and Lee the thoughts of the whole nation were directed. From the office of Edwin M. Stanton, the successful rival in fame of L. M. N. Carnot, as a War Minister, went out bulletins, day after
May, 1864. day, which produced the most intense anxiety and cheering hope; and on the 9th,[a] when the Army of the Potomac had passed The Wilderness, and confronted its foe near Spottsylvania Court-House, the President issued an address "To the friends of Union and Liberty," telling them that enough was then known of the operations of the army to claim a feeling "of special gratitude to God;" and he recommended "that all patriots, at their homes, in their places of public worship, and wherever they may be, unite in common thanksgiving and prayer to Almighty God." At the National Capital the excitement on that day was intense, and the loyal people went by thousands in a procession, with music and banners, to the
b May 11. White House, to congratulate the President. Then came Grant's dispatch,[b] declaring that he proposed to fight it out on that line if it took all summer, to which were added Meade's congratulatory address on the 13th, and cheering dispatches from Grant and Mr. Dana, the Assistant Secretary of War, sent on the same morning.[2]

From the 13th to the 18th of May, the two armies confronted each other with sleepless vigilance, engaged in maneuvers and counter-maneuvers, and watching for the appearance of some weak point in the position or disposition of each other that might warrant an attack. During these movements several sharp skirmishes occurred, and a vast amount of fatiguing labor was endured by the troops. Finally, Grant was satisfied that it would be almost impossible for him to carry Lee's position, so he prepared to turn it, and thereby bring him out of his intrenchments. This was resolved upon after
c May. an abortive attempt to carry a portion of the Confederate works, early on the morning of the 18th,[c] by the divisions of Gibbon and Barlow, supported by the division of Birney, and another of foot artillerists, under General R. O. Tyler, which had just come down from the defenses of Washington. The movement was arrested at the *abatis* in front of the works by a heavy fire, which repulsed the assailants, and at ten o'clock Meade withdrew the assaulting force.
d May 19. On the following day [d] preparations were made for the turning movement. Knowing or suspecting it, Lee made dispositions for

[1] General Meade's address to his soldiers, May 13, 1864.
[2] Grant spoke of the success of Hancock and the capture of prisoners, and said: "The enemy are obstinate, and seem to have found the 'last ditch.' We have lost no organization, not even a company, while we have destroyed and captured one division (Johnson's), one brigade (Dobbs's), and one regiment entire, of the enemy."

foiling it. He took the aggressive, by sending nearly the whole of Ewell's corps to strike Meade's weakened right, held by Tyler's artillerists, who lay across the road from Spottsylvania Court-House to Fredericksburg, which was the main line of communication with the base of the army supplies, at the latter place. Ewell swept across the Ny, seized that important road, and attempted to capture a wagon-train upon it, when he was stoutly resisted by Tyler and his artillerists. These had never been under fire before, but they fought with the coolness and steadiness of the veterans of the Second and Fifth Corps, who came to their assistance, but not until after Ewell had been repulsed. They did not fight with the caution of the veterans, and lost heavily. They and their gallant leader have the honor of repulsing Ewell; and they share with others in the credit of scattering the foe in the woods up the Valley of the Ny, and capturing several hundred of them.

By this attack Grant's flanking movement was disturbed and temporarily checked, but it was resumed on the following night,[a] after he had buried his dead and sent his wounded to Fredericksburg. His fearful losses up to the 13th had been greatly increased,[1] yet with full hope and an inflexible will he kept his face toward Richmond. When the army abandoned its base north of the Rapid Anna, it established another at Fredericksburg (from which was a route for supplies from Washington by a short railway, and by steamboat from Belle Plain and Acquia Creek), to which point the sick and wounded were sent. There they were met and ministered to by the angelic company sent by the loyal people with the comforts and consolations of the Sanitary and Christian commissions. As the army moved on toward Richmond, new bases were opened, first at Port Royal, and then at White House, under the direction of that most efficient Chief Quartermaster, General Rufus Ingalls.

[a] May 20, 21, 1864.

The writer visited the region where the battles of Chancellorsville, The Wilderness, and of Spottsylvania Court-House, were fought, early in June, 1866, with his traveling companions (Messrs. Dreer and Greble), accompanied by quite a cavalcade of young army officers, some of them in charge of the military post at Fredericksburg, and others connected with a burial party, then in the vicinity, busied in gathering up the remains of the patriot soldiers for interment in the National Cemetery there. We had just come up from the battle-fields around Richmond, and had visited places of interest around Fredericksburg, mentioned in chapter XVIII., volume II.; and at the morning twilight of the 7th of June, we left the latter city for the neighboring fields of strife.

We went out on the plank road, by way of Salem Church, to Chancellorsville, and so on to The Wilderness, visiting in that gloomy region the place where Wadsworth fell; the spot where Hancock and his companions struggled with Hill, and Warren and others fought with Ewell. Everywhere we saw mementoes of the terrible strife. The roads were yet strewn with pieces of clothing, shoes, hats, and military accouterments; the trees were scarred and broken; lines of earth-works ran like serpents in many directions, half concealed by the rank undergrowth, made ranker in places by the

---

[1] The official returns show that from the 12th until the 21st of May, when the Army of the Potomac moved from Spottsylvania Court-House, its losses were 10,381, making an aggregate of loss, since it crossed the Rapid Anna, of 39,791. The Confederate losses were never reported, but careful estimates make them over 30,000.

horrid nourishment of blood; and near where Wadsworth was smitten was a little clearing, inclosed with palings, and used as "God's acre" for the bodies of the slain heroes of the war.

Returning to Chancellorsville, we took the road for Spottsylvania Court-House, over which Warren and his troops passed and Hancock followed, lunching at Aldrich's,[1] passing the now famous old wooden building of Todd's Tavern,[2] then a school-house, early in the afternoon, and not long afterward emerging from The Wilderness at the point where Warren's troops did. As we rode over the high plain where Robinson fought, we began to see the scars of the Battle of Spottsylvania Court-House. After visiting and sketching the place where Sedgwick was killed, we rode over the ground where Hancock and the Confederates struggled so fearfully for the salient of the intrenchments, everywhere seeing the terrible effects of the battle. At sunset we rode into the battered village of Spottsylvania Court-House, sketched the old building depicted on page 304, crossed the Ny at twilight, arrived at Fredericksburg at near midnight after a ride of nearly fifty miles, with a dozen sketches made during the day, and left the next morning for Washington City, by way of Acquia Creek and the Potomac River.

We have observed that when the Army of the Potomac emerged from The Wilderness, Sheridan was sent to cut Lee's communications. This was the first of the remarkable raids of that remarkable leader, in Virginia, and, though short, was a destructive one. He took with him a greater portion of the cavalry led by Merritt, Gregg, and Wilson,[3] and cutting loose from the army, he swept over the Po and the Ta,[4] crossed the North Anna on the 9th,[a] and struck the Virginia Central railway at Beaver Dam Station, which he captured. He destroyed ten miles of the railway; also its rolling stock, with a million and a half of rations, and released four hundred Union prisoners on their way to Richmond from The Wilderness. There he was attacked in flank and rear by General J. E. B. Stuart and his cavalry, who had pursued him from the Rapid Anna, but was not much impeded thereby. He pushed on, crossed the South Anna at Ground-squirrel Bridge, and at daylight on the morning of the 11th, captured Ashland Station, on the Fredericksburg road, where he destroyed the railway property, a large quantity of stores, and the road itself for six miles.

Being charged with the duty of not only destroying these roads, but of menacing Richmond and communicating with the Army of the James, under General Butler, Sheridan pressed on in the direction of the Confederate capital, when he was confronted by Stuart at Yellow Tavern, a few miles north of Richmond, where that able leader, having made a swift, circuitous march, had concentrated all of his available cavalry. Sheridan attacked him at once, and, after a sharp engagement, drove the Confederates toward Ashland, on the north fork of the Chickahominy, with a loss of their gallant leader, who, with General Gordon, was mortally wounded. Inspirited by this success, Sheridan pushed along the now open turnpike toward Richmond, and

[a] May, 1864.

See page 27.   [2] See page 24.

[3] The dismounted men of the divisions of these leaders, and those whose horses were jaded, were left with the army to guard the trains.

[4] In this region there are four small streams, named respectively Mat, Ta, Po, and Ny. These, combined, form the volume and the name of a larger stream, one of the chief affluents of the York River, called the Matta-po-ny.

made a spirited dash upon the outer works. Custer's brigade carried them at that point, and made one hundred prisoners. As in the case of Kilpatrick's raid, so now, the second line of works were too strong to be carried by cavalry. The troops in and around the city had rallied for their defense, and in an attack the Nationals were repulsed. Then Sheridan led his command across the Chickahominy, at Meadow Bridge, where he beat off a considerable force of infantry sent out from Richmond, and who attacked him in the rear, while another force assailed his front. He also drove the foe on his front, when he destroyed the railway bridge there, and then pushed on southward to Haxhall's Landing,[a] on the James River, where [a] May 14, 1864. he rested three days and procured supplies. Then, by way

PHILIP H. SHERIDAN.

of White House and Hanover Court-House, he leisurely returned to the Army of the Potomac, which he rejoined on the 25th of May.

Before proceeding to follow the Army of the Potomac further in its advance toward Richmond, let us see what had been doing for awhile on its right by forces which, as we have observed, had been arranged in Western Virginia for co-operating movements. For some time that region had been the theater of some stirring minor events of the war. Confederate cavalry, guerrilla bands, and resident "bushwhackers" had been active and mischievous; while Moseby, the marauding chief, was busy in the region east

JUBAL EARLY.

of the Blue Ridge, between Leesburg and the Rappahannock, which his followers called his "Confederacy." So early as the beginning of January,[b] Fitz-Hugh [b] 1864. Lee, with his cavalry, made a fruitless raid on the Baltimore and Ohio railway, west of Cumberland. A little later, General Jubal Early, in command of the Confederates in the Shenandoah Valley, sent General Rosser on a foraging excursion in the same direction. He was more successful, for in Hardy County [c] Jan. 30. he captured[c] ninety-three six-mule wagons heavily laden with supplies, twelve hundred cattle, and five hundred sheep, with two [d] Feb. 2. hundred and seventy men of the guard, who made only slight resistance. Four days later, he suddenly appeared[d] at Patterson's Creek Station, west of Cumberland, and captured a company of Union soldiers, but on his return he was struck a severe blow by General Averill, not far from Romney, and driven entirely out of the new Commonwealth, with a loss of his prisoners and a large proportion of his own men and horses. Ten days afterward, Champe Ferguson, one of the most notorious of the lower order of guerrilla leaders, was surprised while at the Rock House, in Wayne County, of West Virginia, by Colonel Gallup, who was in command on the eastern border of Kentucky. Ferguson and fifty of his men were made prisoners, and fifteen others were killed. A few days before that, Lieutenant Verdigan, one of Ferguson's followers, with ten men, surprised and captured a steamboat on the Kanawha River, on board of which was General Scammon (then commanding at Charleston, in the Kanawha Valley), four officers and twenty-five private soldiers. All but Scammon and his two aids were paroled by the guerrillas. These officers were sent to Richmond and confined in the loathsome Libby prison.

These events were followed by others of greater magnitude and importance in that region, after Grant assumed the general command. General Sigel, as we have observed, was placed with a large force in the Shenandoah Valley, to co-operate with the Army of the Potomac. He gave the immediate command of his forces in the Kanawha Valley to General George Crook, and with the remainder, about eight thousand strong, under his own personal command, he moved up the Shenandoah Valley, along its fine turnpike, on the first of May.[a] His first destination was Staunton, at the head of the valley, whence he was to move over the Blue Ridge to Charlottesville, and then to march right or left, to Lynchburg or Gordonsville, as circumstances might determine. When near New Market, almost fifty miles from Winchester, he was met by an equal force under General Breckinridge, whom Lee had sent to oppose his advance, with such troops as he might hastily gather. Breckinridge found it necessary to oppose Crook also, and for that purpose he sent General McCausland westward with as many troops as could be spared from the Valley.

[a] 1864.

After much maneuvering and skirmishing near New Market, Breckinridge made an impetuous charge[b] upon Sigel, and ended a sharp fight by driving him more than thirty miles down the valley, to the shelter of Cedar Creek, near Strasburg, with a loss of seven hundred men, six guns, a thousand small-arms, a portion of his train, and his hospitals. Grant immediately relieved General Sigel, and General Hunter took command of his troops, with instructions to push swiftly on to Staunton, destroy the railway between that place and Charlottesville, and then, if possible, move on Lynchburg.

[b] May 15.

Meanwhile, General Crook, whose cavalry was led by General Averill, had moved[c] up the Kanawha Valley from Charleston, for the purpose of operating against the Virginia and Tennessee railway, between Dublin Station, in Pulaski County, and Wytheville, on New River, in Wythe County, in Southwestern Virginia. Unfortunately, Crook divided and weakened his command by sending Averill, with his two thousand horsemen, to destroy the lead mines near Wytheville, while he advanced with his six thousand infantry toward Dublin Station, farther east. Averill's descent upon Wytheville and its vicinity was no more fruitful of benefit

[c] May 1.

than was his raid to Salem the previous year,[1] for he was there met by Morgan and his men,[a] sent from Saltville by General W. E. Jones, and, after a sharp fight, was compelled to retire without accomplishing [a May 10, 1864.] his object. Meanwhile, Crook had approached Dublin Station, and when within four miles of it, was met by McCausland with an inferior force. A battle ensued, and was fought gallantly by both parties. It resulted in the defeat of the Confederates, but with a loss on the part of the Nationals of over seven hundred men, of whom one hundred and twenty-five were killed. Crook destroyed the railroad a few miles, when, on the appearance of a strong force sent by Morgan from Wytheville, before Averill reached there, he withdrew and retreated to Meadow Bridge, in the direction of the Kanawha. When Averill retired from Wytheville and marched to meet Crook at Dublin Station, the latter had departed, and the former had no safe alternative but to follow.

General Hunter, on assuming command of Sigel's troops, immediately advanced on Staunton with about nine thousand men, some re-enforcements having arrived. At Piedmont, near Middle River, a tributary of the Shenandoah, in Augusta County, not far from Staunton, he encountered[b] an equal force of Confederates, under Generals W. E. [b June 5.] Jones and McCausland. These were all of the concentrated forces in that region, Breckinridge having been called, with a greater portion of his command, to assist in the defense of Richmond. An obstinate and hard-fought battle ensued, which ended with the daylight, and resulted in the complete defeat and route of the Confederates. "A worse whipped or more utterly demoralized crowd of beaten men never fled from a field," wrote one of General Hunter's staff. Their leader, General Jones, was killed by a shot through his head, and with him many others were slain or wounded. Fifteen hundred Confederates were made prisoners, and the spoils of victory were several battle-flags, three guns, and three thousand small-arms.

Three days after THE BATTLE OF PIEDMONT, Hunter was joined, at Staunton, by the forces of Crook and Averill, when the whole body, about twenty thousand strong, moved toward Lynchburg by way of Lexington. That city was the largest in the western part of Old Virginia, in the center of a fertile and populous region around the upper waters of the James River, with extensive manufactures, and in direct communication with Richmond by railroad and canal, and also with Petersburg and all the South by railway. It was the focal point of a vast region from whence Richmond and Lee's army must draw supplies, and on that account, and its relations as a strategic point with the struggle then going on for the possession of Richmond, made it almost as important as the Confederate capital itself. This Lee well knew, and, notwithstanding he was then most sorely pressed by the armies of the Potomac and the James, he sent a considerable force to assist in holding Lynchburg. Hence it was, that when Hunter arrived before it, and made an attack[c] upon the southern side of the city, its [c June 18.] garrison and the strong works around it were able to defy him. Hunter soon perceived its strength, and the fact that an overwhelming force was gathering to crush him. Considering these things, and the alarming cir-

---

[1] See page 113.

cumstance of his ammunition being nearly exhausted, he thought it prudent not to prosecute an attack on the city, but to retire. Neither was it
prudent to go back by the way he had advanced, for a heavy Confederate
force might easily be thrown upon his rear by means of the Virginia Central
railway; so he retired westward to Salem, hotly pursued as far as that
place, and then made his way, with a very scanty supply of food for man
and beast, over the mountains, by the village of New Castle, to Meadow
Bridge, in the direction of the Kanawha. There, only a few days before,
Crook and Averill had left a million and a half of rations in charge of two
regiments of Ohio one hundred days' men, and expected to find a supply for
the famishing army. They were disappointed. A band of guerrillas had
swept away rations and men, and it was not until the 27th[a] that
a supply was obtained. The army had suffered dreadfully in
that exhausted mountain region, and was much weaker in numbers and
moral strength than when it left Staunton. It had inflicted vast injury
upon the Confederates in the destruction of founderies, mills, factories, and
other property of value to the Confederates, but had achieved little that had
any important bearing on the campaign. Its now far distance from the
grand theater of operations against Richmond, caused it to be lost to that
campaign for several weeks.

[a] June, 1864.

The ravages of the war upon the head waters of the streams between the
Potomac and James Rivers, at that time, were dreadful. It was a region

wherein lay the estates of
some of the older and most
distinguished families of
Virginia, and the sudden
change wrought in the condition of the residents was
lamentable. It was saddening to see the wealthy and
refined, the noble and gentle
—men and women who had
never experienced poverty
nor the necessity for toiling,
—instantly reduced from
abundance and ease, to want
and hardship. Elegant man-

AN ANCIENT COACH IN RUINS.

sions filled with rare and costly furniture, valuable books and works of art,
were laid waste; and the broad lands were stripped of laborers, utensils, and
almost every living creature. Family coaches, which had descended from
generation to generation since colonial times, were converted into ambulances
for the sick and wounded, and reduced to ruin by the rough usages of war;
and other precious heir-looms, with valuable records, public and private,
were sacrificed to the appetite of the demons of Discord and Desolation.

CHAPTER XII.

OPERATIONS AGAINST RICHMOND.

HILE Meade and Lee were struggling in the vicinity of the Rapid Anna, General Butler, then in command of the Army of the James, was co-operating with the Army of the Potomac in accordance with a plan which he had proposed to the General-in-Chief, and which that officer had approved. That plan contemplated a vigorous movement against Richmond on the south side of the James River, the first objective being City Point, at the mouth of the Appomattox River. Grant issued[a] orders accordingly, and directed General Butler to move simultaneously with Meade.

[a] April 2, 1864.

Butler was well prepared for the execution of his part of the plan, when, at the beginning of May, he received orders to advance. His effective force was about forty thousand men, and was composed chiefly of the Eighteenth Army Corps, commanded by General W. F. Smith, and the Tenth Army Corps,

which had lately been ordered from South Carolina, led by General Gillmore, who arrived at Fortress Monroe on the 3d of May.

Butler's first care was to mislead the Confederates concerning his intentions. For that purpose he first sent[b] Henry's brigade of New York troops to West Point, at the head of York River, to begin the construction of wharves,

[b] May 1.

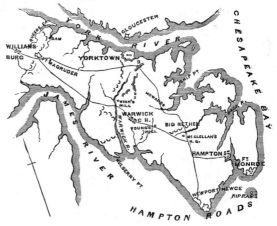

CONFEDERATE DEFENSES BETWEEN HAMPTON AND WILLIAMSBURG.

while cavalry made a demonstration in the direction of Richmond. He also sent the bulk of his army in that direction as far as the old lines of McClellan[1] at Yorktown and Gloucester Point; and so successful was the

---

[1] For an account of the operations of McClellan between Fortress Monroe and Williamsburg, see Chapters XIV. and XV., volume II. The route from Hampton; the fortifications at Big Bethel, and in the vicinity of Yorktown and Williamsburg, are indicated in the little map on this page.

stratagem, that the Confederates were satisfied that Butler was about to move on Richmond in the pathway trodden by McClellan two years before,[1] and they made preparations accordingly. They were quickly undeceived, but not until it was too late to prevent the mischief wrought by the decep-

^a May, 1864. tion. On the night of the 4th,^a transports, sent up from Hampton Roads, conveyed Butler's army around to the James River, and by dawn the next morning, artillery and infantry, to the number of thirty-five thousand men, accompanied by a squadron of war vessels, under Admiral Lee, were rapidly ascending that stream for the purpose of seizing City Point.[2] At the same time General A. V. Kautz, with three thousand cavalry, moved out from Suffolk, forced a passage over the Blackwater River, and, pushing rapidly westward, struck the Weldon railway at Stony Creek, some distance south of Petersburg, and burned the bridge there; while Colonel Robert M. West, with about eighteen hundred cavalry (mostly colored men), advanced from Williamsburg up the north bank of the James River, keeping parallel with the great flotilla of war vessels and transports on its bosom. This expedition, and the advance of the Army of the Potomac from the north, were grand movements preliminary to another dreadful struggle for the possession of Richmond in the vicinity of the Chickahominy River—a region made forever memorable by the seven days' battles there, in the summer of 1862.

The expedition moved so unexpectedly and rapidly up the river, that the Confederates could make no effective dispositions for opposing it. Portions of Wilde's brigade of negro troops were landed at Wilson's wharf, on the north side of the river, and at Fort Powhatan, on the south side, thus securing and holding, for the protection of its navigation, important points at bends in the stream. On the afternoon of the same day, Hink's division landed at City Point, and took possession without any opposition. That night General Graham captured the Confederate signal-station near, and the war vessels moved up to a position above the mouth of the Appomattox. At the same time a heavy force landed upon an irregular triangle of land at the mouth of the Appomattox, lying between it and the James River, called Bermuda Hundred, and proceeded to cast up a line of intrenchments across the western side of the camp from river to river, while gun-boats in both streams completely covered each flank of the position. Thus, in the space of twenty-four hours, Butler gained a commanding and important foothold within fifteen miles of Richmond, in a straight line, and only about eight from Petersburg.[3] The movement was a complete surprise to the Confed-

[1] See chapters XIV., XV., and XVI., volume II. The map on the opposite page, omitted by accident when that record was printed, will not only give the reader an idea of the entire region of stirring operations in Southeastern Virginia at that time, but may be usefully consulted when studying the great and decisive campaign we are now considering.

[2] The transports were preceded by three army gun-boats, under the command of General Charles R. Graham, formerly of the navy. The remainder of the naval force consisted of four "monitors," the iron-clad *Atlanta*, and ten gun-boats, commanded by Rear-Admiral S. P. Lee, whose flag-ship was the *Malvern*, formerly a blockade-runner.

[3] "At sunset on the 4th, you were threatening the enemy's capital from West Point and White House, within thirty miles on its eastern side. Within twenty-four hours, at sunset on the 5th of May, by a march of 130 miles, you transported 35,000 men—their luggage, supplies, horses, wagons and artillery—within fifteen miles of the south side of Richmond, with such celerity and secresy, that the enemy were wholly unprepared for your coming, and allowed you, without opposition, to seize the strongest natural position on the continent. A victory all the more valuable because bloodless!"—*General Butler's Address to the Soldiers of the Army of the James,* October 11, 1864.

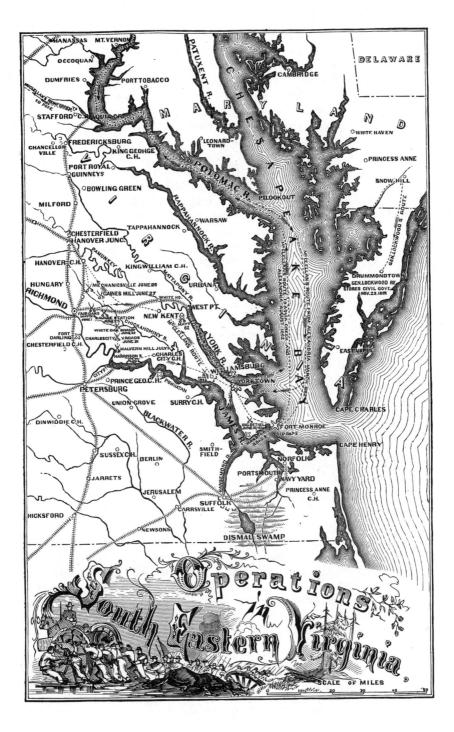

Operations in South Eastern Virginia

SCALE OF MILES

erates, and produced great consternation at Richmond. In the mean time the armed vessels had been busy in keeping the river open, and they now engaged in the perilous work of fishing up torpedoes, with which, in places, its channel had been sown. Notwithstanding the great precautions observed, one of the smaller gun-boats, named *Commodore Jones*, was totally destroyed by the explosion of one of these mines under it,[1] by which twenty of its officers and crew were killed, and forty-eight were wounded. In the mean time Colonel West, with his cavalry, had made his way across the Chicka-hominy to the shore of the James at Harrison's Landing, and been taken thence, on transports, to Bermuda Hundred.

A quick and vigorous movement upon Petersburg and Richmond at that time might have resulted in the capture of both cities, for very few Confed-erate troops appear to have then been in either place. That fact was unknown by the Nationals, and a wise caution, rightfully exercised, caused a delay fatal to the speedy achievement of such victories, for strength was quickly imparted to both posts. When the movement of Butler and the arrival of Gillmore with troops from Charleston harbor was first known to the Confederates at Richmond, Beauregard was ordered to hasten from Charleston to the latter place, with all possible dispatch, with the troops under his command there, others drawn from Georgia and Florida, and such as he might gather in his passage through North Carolina. He instantly obeyed, and when General Kautz struck the Weldon road, as we have seen, he found these re-enforcements for Lee passing over it. A large portion of them were left south of that cutting,[2] but as Kautz could not hold the road nor advance toward Petersburg, he returned to City Point,[a] leav-ing the Confederates to make their way without further molesta-tion. Before Petersburg was seriously threatened by Butler, Beauregard's troops were there in strong force.

[a] May 8, 1864.

It was expected that General Butler's movements, after he should gain a position on the south side of the James River, and intrench it, should be governed much by those of the Army of the Potomac, with which he was acting as an auxiliary. It was believed that the latter would march quickly from the Rapid Anna to the lines before Richmond, defeating Lee, or driv-ing him within the intrenchments at the Confederate capital. So soon as Butler should hear the sounds of battle on the north side of the James, in front of the beleaguered city, he was to move against it on the south side, and in perfect co-operation, and even junction, the two armies were thus to work together. But the unexpected detention of the Army of the Potomac at The Wilderness, and at Spottsylvania Court-House, compelled Butler to stand much on the defensive; and in the absence of orders to march on either Richmond or Petersburg immediately after seizing City Point and Bermuda Hundred, he was forced to be governed by circumstances, and assume grave responsibilities. He therefore resolved to do what he might

---

[1] These torpedoes were simply cases of tin, containing about seventy-five pounds of gunpowder, and were exploded by means of a string extending to the shore, which, when pulled, caused an apparatus like that of a gun to explode a percussion cap.

[2] D. H. Hill, with 3,000 troops, had passed northward, and Beauregard, with 5,000, was south of Stony Creek Station. Besides the bridge and track, a large quantity of provisions and forage was destroyed at that place.

THE UNION GENERALS.

George W. Childs Publisher 628 & 630 Chestnut St. Philadelphia.

to keep re-enforcements from reaching Lee from the south; and his first effort for that purpose was to destroy the railway between Richmond and Petersburg, lying at an average of about three miles from his line of intrenchments. So early as the 6th,[a] he sent out General Heckman to reconnoiter that road, and on the 7th five brigades, under General Brooks, advanced upon the Port Walthall branch of the railway, not far from the junction,[1] and began its destruction. They soon found a strong Confederate force, under D. H. Hill, on their front, for, on the previous night, nearly all of Beauregard's troops had reached Petersburg. Heavy skirmishing ensued, and the Nationals, after gaining some advantages, were compelled to withdraw, with a loss of about two hundred and fifty men.

[a] May, 1864.

Another advance upon the railway was made early on the morning of the 9th, by a force composed of the divisions of Generals Terry, Ames, and Turner, of the Tenth Corps, and of Weitzel and Wistar, of the Eighteenth. General Gillmore commanded the right of the column, and General Smith the left. They struck the railway at different points, and destroyed it without molestation, and then, with Weitzel in the advance, they moved on Petersburg. They were confronted by a heavy Confederate force at Swift Creek, within three miles of that city, where a sharp action ensued. The Confederates were driven across the stream; and that evening Butler sent a dispatch to the Secretary of War, saying, "Lieutenant-General Grant will not be troubled with any further re-enforcements to Lee from Beauregard's forces." And, encouraged by the success that day, Butler determined to improve the advantages gained by driving the Confederates across the Appomattox into Petersburg, and, if possible, capture that place. But that evening news came from Washington that Lee, vanquished by Meade, was in full retreat on Richmond. If so, he might quickly and heavily fall, with crushing force, on the Army of the James, so Butler recalled his troops from Swift Creek, strengthened his lines, and prepared for active co-operation in an attack on Richmond. The story was not true.

On the 12th, Butler pushed a heavy column northward, the right, under General Smith, moving up the turnpike in the direction of Fort Darling, on Drewry's Bluff,[2] and the left, under General Gillmore (who left General Ames to watch the Confederates at Petersburg), following the line of the railway further westward. The Confederates fell back to, and across Proctor's Creek, and took position upon a fortified line (outworks of Fort Darling) behind it on the following morning.[b] Gillmore turned the right of that line and held it. The other column had pressed well up toward the Confederate left, and Generals Butler and Smith made their quarters at the fine mansion of Dr. Friend, less than nine miles from Richmond.[3] Orders were given for a general attack the next morning,[c] but the National line was then so thin that the movement was thought too hazardous, and it was postponed until the morning of the 16th. The Confederates, meanwhile, had prepared for a similar

[b] May 13.

[c] May 14,

---

[1] Port Walthall is on the left bank of the Appomattox River, between Petersburg and City Point, and at the head of navigation for the large steamers on the James River. A branch of the Richmond and Petersburg railway extends to that point.

[2] See page 402, volume II.

[3] This was a fine brick mansion at the head of a shaded lane leading from the turnpike. The house and its surroundings were in a dilapidated state when the writer visited it at the close of May, 1866. See the next page.

movement at the same time.   Beauregard was in command of them in person.   The evening of the 15th was still and clear, but after midnight, a

DR. FRIEND'S HOUSE.

heavy fog arose from the bosom of
the James River, and enveloped both
armies.   Under cover of this and the
darkness, before the dawn, Beauregard advanced and aroused the slumbering Nationals by a sudden and
heavy fire of musketry and artillery.
The assailed were illy prepared for the
unexpected attack, and presented on
their right a weak point, which Beauregard had discovered the evening before, and now quickly took advantage
of.   Between that right and the river
was a space of open country, for a mile, picketed by only about one hundred and fifty negro cavalry.   To turn that flank was Beauregard's first
care.   At the same time a division under General Whiting was to move
from the Richmond road, strike Gillmore heavily, and cut off the Union line
of retreat.   The plan, if fully carried out, would, it seemed, insure the capture or dispersion of Butler's army.

General Heckman's brigade, of Weitzel's division, held Smith's right.
After a gallant fight it was overwhelmed by the sudden and heavy blow,
and the general was captured.   The Confederates gained the rear of that
flank, and were pressing on to seize the road leading to Bermuda Hundred,
when the One Hundred and Twelfth New York, of Ames's division, of
Gillmore's corps, which had been sent to Smith, came up.   Being at that
instant joined by the Ninth Maine, the two regiments checked the assailants
by such stubborn resistance, that the astonished Confederates, ignorant of
the numbers on their front (for the fog was yet dense), first halted and then
withdrew.   Meanwhile the front of Smith's column and the right of Gillmore's (the former held by the divisions of Brooks and Weitzel) were
fiercely attacked, but a repetition of the performance in front of Fort
Sanders, at Knoxville,[1] made their repulse an easy task.   General Smith
had caused the stretching of telegraph wire from stump to stump, a short
distance above the ground, in front of his line, which tripped the assailants
when they charged, in the dense fog, and they were shot or bayoneted before
they could rise.   They recoiled; and Whiting, failing to obey Beauregard's
orders to seize the Union way of retreat on the left, the plans of the Confederate general entirely miscarried.   Seeing this, Beauregard renewed his
effort to turn Smith's right, and so far succeeded, with a heavier force, as
to cause that commander to fall back and form a new line, extending from
the Half-Way House,[2] on the turnpike, nine miles from Richmond, almost to
the river.   Gillmore was compelled by this movement to fall back, and
Beauregard pressed the whole National line closely and heavily, with increasing numbers.   Perceiving the danger to his communications, Butler withdrew his whole force within his lines at Bermuda Hundred, when his antag-

---

[1] See page 173.   [2] See picture on the next page.

onist proceeded to cast up a line of intrenchments in front of and parallel to those of the Army of the James, at that place.

In the operations of the 16th, the Nationals lost about four thousand men, and the Confederates a little over three thousand. Butler was now in an almost impregnable position, with the rivers on each flank at his command, and was about to strike a determined blow for the capture of Petersburg, when he received orders to send nearly two-thirds of his effective men to the north side of the James, to assist the army contending with Lee in the vicinity of the Chickahominy. Butler complied with the requisition

THE HALF-WAY HOUSE. [1]

which deprived him of all power to make further offensive movements, saying "the necessities of the Army of the Potomac have bottled me up at Bermuda Hundred." [2]

While Butler's main army was making movements toward Richmond, Kautz was out upon another raid on the railways leading to that city from the South and Southwest. He left Bermuda Hundred on the 12th of May, with two brigades,[3] and passing near Fort Darling, swept on the arc of a circle by Chesterfield Court-House and struck the Richmond and Danville railway, at Coalfield Station, eleven miles west of the Confederate capital. He struck it again at Powhatan; menaced the railway bridge over the Appomattox, which was strongly guarded; swept around eastward, and struck the road again at Chula Station; and then, with a part of his command he crossed to the Southside railway at White and Black Station, while the remainder went on to the junction of the Danville and Southside roads. All now turned eastward, moving down far toward the North Carolina line, crossing the Weldon road and destroying it at Jarratt's Station, south of the scene of their devastations a few days before, and passing by Prince George's Court-House, returned to City Point on the 17th. Kautz had seriously damaged the railways that lay in his track, skirmished sharply at many places, and took to City Point one hundred and fifty prisoners, of whom thirteen were officers.

When Beauregard had perfected his batteries in front of Butler's lines at Bermuda Hundred, he opened their fire upon the Nationals,[a] and pressed their picket line heavily. This was repeated the next morning, and under cover of these guns the Confederates assailed the advance of the divisions of Generals Ames and Terry. The pickets of the former were driven from their rifle-pits, and the line of the latter was

[a] May 19, 1864.

---

[1] This was the appearance of the old tavern, on the stage route between Richmond and Petersburg, known as the Half-Way House, as it appeared when the writer sketched it in May, 1866.

[2] See Report of Lieutenant-General U. S. Grant, of the Armies of the United States—1864–'65, July 22, 1865.

[3] Composed of the Third New York, First District of Columbia, and Fifth and Eleventh Pennsylvania. The brigades were commanded respectively by Colonel Spear and Major Jacobs.

forced back; but the rifle-pits were soon recovered by a brigade under Colonel Howell, after heavy fighting and much loss on both sides. The attack was renewed on the following day, with no better success, when Beauregard ceased all attempts to dislodge Butler. Two or three days later, Fitzhugh Lee, with a considerable body of Confederate cavalry,[a] attacked the post at Wilson's Wharf, then held by two regiments of negro troops, under General Wilde. After being three times repulsed, Lee withdrew.[1]

RIFLE-PITS.[2]

[a] May 24, 1864.

Operations of greater magnitude and importance nearer Richmond, now absorbed attention. Let us consider them.

We left the Army of the Potomac at Spottsylvania Court-House, about to resume its march toward Richmond.[3] It was then disencumbered of its twenty thousand sick and wounded men, who were taken to the hospitals at Washington and elsewhere, and of about eight thousand prisoners who had been sent to the rear. At the same time twenty-five thousand veteran recruits, with ample supplies, were on their way to join the army, and full thirty thousand volunteers, recruited for one hundred days' service, had been mustered in. It was under these favorable auspices that the Army of the Potomac began another flank and forward movement on the night of the 20th and 21st of May.[b] It was begun by Hancock's corps, which, at midnight, moved eastward to Mattaponax Church, and then turned southward, with Torbert's cavalry in advance. Lee, anticipating the movement, was very vigilant, and Longstreet's corps was put in motion southward immediately after Hancock's started. Warren followed the latter on the morning of the 21st, when Ewell marched in the track of Longstreet. Then began another exciting race of the two great armies, the immediate goal being the North Anna River. The Confederates had the more direct

[b] 1864.

---

[1] At about this time a forgery, in the form of a proclamation by the President, calculated to inspirit the Confederates, alarm and distract the loyal people, depress the public securities, and embarrass the Government at a most critical moment, appeared in two Opposition newspapers in the city of New York. The pretended proclamation was dated the 17th of May, at the moment when Grant's march toward Richmond was temporarily checked at Spottsylvania Court-House, and the news of the failure of the Red River expedition was creating much disappointment. It declared that the campaign of the Army of the Potomac was "virtually closed," and, in view of the gloomy aspect of affairs, it recommended the setting apart of an early day throughout the United States as one for "fasting, humiliation, and prayer." It also called for 400,000 more troops, and threatened an "immediate and peremptory draft" for that number if they were not forthcoming within thirty days. The Secretary of State immediately pronounced the paper a forgery, and the publication offices of the offending newspapers were taken possession of by the military. Their proprietors at once declared themselves the innocent victims of an adroit forgery, and offered rewards for the apprehension of the perpetrator. He was discovered to be one of the editors of an Opposition newspaper in Brooklyn, and declared that his purpose was simply to make a profitable speculation in stocks, and that no political designs had been considered.

[2] This picture gives the appearance of a rifle-pit in summer, when the men in them have little canvas shelters from the sun. Rifle-pits are of two kinds, namely, a hole for the shelter of one man, or a short trench for the use of several men. They are shallow, with a parapet formed of the earth thrown out, in which is often a loop-hole or embrasure formed of bags of sand. These pits are used by pickets, and by infantry placed in advance of fortifications or fortified camps.

[3] See page 311.

and better way, for the Nationals, in order to flank the former, were compelled to make a more circuitous march over indifferent roads.

The departure of the corps of Hancock and Warren (Second and Fifth), left those of Wright and Burnside (Sixth and Ninth) at Spottsylvania Court-House, where they were confronted by A. P. Hill's. Burnside's left on the afternoon of the 21st, after a sortie, as a covering movement, by General Ledlie's brigade of Crittenden's division, and Wright's was preparing to follow, when it was attacked by Hill's. The assailants were easily repulsed, and that night the works at Spottsylvania Court-House were abandoned by both parties, and the entire army of each was moving as rapidly as possible toward the North Anna. Torbert had captured Guiney's Station, on the Richmond and Fredericksburg railway, on the night of the 20th and 21st, without very serious opposition, and opened the way for the army, which reached the North Anna on the morning of the 23d, at three fords, known respectively as Island, Jericho, and Chesterfield, or Taylor's Bridge—the latter near where the Richmond and Fredericksburg railway crosses that river.

Lee, marching by the shorter route, had outstripped his antagonist in the race, and was found strongly posted and intrenched on the opposite side of the North Anna, in close communication with the Virginia Central railway, over which Breckinridge, who had beaten Sigel in the Shenandoah Valley,[1] was hastening with re-enforcements. There Lee had evidently determined to make a stand. Grant took immediate measures to dislodge him. His left, under Hancock, was at the Chesterfield bridge, a mile above the railway crossing. Warren was at Jericho Ford, four miles above, where no formidable opposition appeared, for Lee was engaged in holding the more important passage in front of Hancock. So Warren prepared to cross and take the Confederates in reverse. Bartlett's brigade waded the stream, armpit deep, and formed a battle-line to cover the construction of a pontoon bridge. This was quickly done, and early that afternoon the whole of Warren's corps passed over to the south side of the river, and formed a line of battle. Cutler's division was on the right, Griffin's in the center, and Crawford's on the left. They took position at a piece of woods, where, at five o'clock, the divisions of Heth and Wilcox, of Hill's corps, fell upon Griffin's division. They were repulsed, when three Confederate brigades, under General Brown, struck Cutler's division a sudden blow, which threw it into confusion and uncovered Griffin's right. The Confederates pushed quickly forward to attack it, but the danger was avoided by a refusal of that flank. Bartlett was hurried to its support, and in that movement a volley of musketry, given at close quarters by the Eighty-third Pennsylvania,[2] Lieutenant-Colonel McCoy, on the flank and rear of the Confederates, threw them into utter disorder, and caused their rout, with a loss of their leader and almost a thousand men made prisoners. In this encounter Warren lost three hundred and fifty men. He then proceeded to establish a line and intrench it, without further resistance.

---

[1] See page 314.

[2] The Eighty-third Pennsylvania swept close by the Confederate flank in its advance to the support of Griffin, when McCoy suddenly wheeled his forward companies into line, and delivered the fatal volley. One of the men caught General Brown by the collar, and dragged him into Warren's lines.

Hancock, in the mean time, had been preparing to force a passage of the stream at Chesterfield bridge, where he was confronted by McLaws's division of Longstreet's corps. These troops were mostly on the south side of the river, but held a *tête-du-pont*, or bridge-head battery of redan form, on a tongue of land on the north side. This, after a brief cannonade by three sections of field-pieces, planted by Colonel Tidball, the chief of artillery, was stormed and carried at six o'clock in the evening by the brigades of Pierce and Eagan, of Birney's division. They lost one hundred and fifty men, and captured thirty of the garrison. That night the Confederates tried in vain to burn the bridge; and before morning they abandoned their advanced works on the south side of the stream, and withdrew to a stronger position a little in the rear. Hancock passed over the bridge in the morning[a] which his troops had preserved, without feeling the enemy, and at the same time Wright's corps crossed the river at Jericho Ford, and joined Warren's.

May 24, 1864.

The Army of the Potomac was now in peril. Its two powerful wings were on one side of a stream, difficult at all times to cross, and liable to a

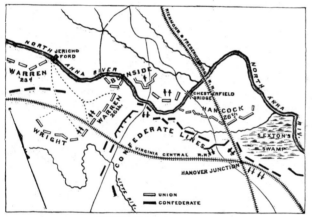

POSITION ON THE NORTH ANNA.

sudden increase of volume, by rains, while the weaker center was on the other side. Its antagonist was disposed in a blunt wedge-form, with its chief strength at the point, for the purpose of severing the National force. Lee had thrown back the two wings of his army, the left resting on Little River; and the right, covering Sexton's junction of the two railways running into Richmond, rested on the marshes of Hanover. The powerful center, at the point of the wedge, was near the river, and menaced Grant's center. And so it was, that when Burnside's (Ninth) corps, of that center, attempted to cross between the two wings of the Army of the Potomac, his advance division (Crittenden's) was quickly met, and repulsed with heavy loss. And when Warren, on the right, attempted to connect with Burnside, by sending Crawford's division in that direction, an overwhelming force fell upon him with almost fatal weight.

Grant paused, and for more than two days he studied the position of his adversary, and came to the conclusion that Lee could be dislodged only by a flanking movement, which he proceeded to make. He secretly recrossed the river on the night of the 26th,[b] and going well eastward, so as to avoid a blow on his flank, resumed his march toward Richmond, his objective being the passage of the Pamunkey, one of the affluents of the York, formed by the junction of the North and South

[b] May.

Anna rivers, which would force Lee to abandon the line of those streams, and give to the Army of the Potomac an admirable water base of supplies, at White House.[1]

Sheridan, who, as we have seen,[2] had just returned[a] to the army after his great raid toward Richmond and across the head of the Peninsula, now led the flanking column with two divisions of cavalry, immediately followed by Wright's corps, leading Warren's and Burnside's. Hancock's remained on the North Anna until morning,[b] to cover the rear, at which time the head of the column, after a march of more than twenty miles, was approaching the Pamunkey at Hanovertown, about fifteen miles from Richmond. Wright's corps crossed that stream at once, and early on Saturday, the 28th,[c] the whole army was south of the Pamunkey, and in communication with its new base at White House.

[a] May 25, 1864.

[b] May 27.

[c] May.

Grant's movement summoned Lee to another compulsory abandonment of a strong position, and he again fell back toward Richmond. Having, as usual, the shorter and better way, he was already in a good position to confront the Army of the Potomac before it had reached the Pamunkey. He had taken a stand to cover both railways and the chief highways leading into Richmond, and to dispute the passage of the Chickahominy.

The only direct pathway to the Confederate capital, for the Army of the Potomac, was across the Chickahominy. Before its passage could be effected, Lee must be dislodged, and to that task Grant and Meade now addressed themselves. Reconnoissances to ascertain the strength and exact position of the Confederate army, were put in motion. Sheridan was sent out southward on the afternoon of the 28th, with the brigades of Davis, Gregg, and Custer. At Hawes's store, not far from the Tolopatomoy Creek, they encountered and vanquished cavalry under Hampton and Fitzhugh Lee. Both parties were dismounted and fought desperately. The Confederates lost nearly eight hundred men, and the Nationals about one half that number. This success inspirited the army, and it was followed by a reconnoissance in force,[d] in which Wright moved on Hanover Court-House; Hancock marched from Hawes's store in the same direction; Warren pushed out toward Bethesda Church, and Burnside held a position to assist either Hancock or Warren. The right and rear were covered by Wilson's cavalry. This movement quickly developed Lee's position, which was in front of the Chickahominy, and covering the railway from well up toward Hanover Court-House, southward to Shady Grove and the Mechanicsville pike, with pickets toward Bethesda Church.

[d] May 29.

Wright reached Hanover Court-House without much opposition, but the march of both Hancock and Warren was arrested[e] by strong forces in advance of Lee's line. The former was checked at Tolopatomoy Creek, after a sharp encounter, by intrenched troops; and the latter encountered Rodes's division of Ewell's corps, with cavalry, reconnoitering near Bethesda Church. These struck the flank of Colonel

[e] May 30.

---

[1] The chief base of the army, while it was at Spottsylvania Court-House, was at Fredericksburg; while it was on the North Anna that base was Port Royal, on the Rappahannock.

[2] See page 313.

Hardin's brigade, of the Pennsylvania Reserves, and compelled it to fall back to the Shady Grove road, when General Crawford brought up the remainder of the Reserves, and Kitching's brigade, and effectively repulsed an impetuous assault by Rodes, who attempted to turn Warren's left. This repulse enabled the Nationals to establish the left of their line on the Mechanicsville pike, not much more than seven miles from Richmond. To relieve General Warren, when first assailed by Rodes, Meade had ordered an attack along the whole line. Only Hancock received the order in time to act before dark. He moved forward, drove the Confederate pickets, and captured and held their rifle-pits. Meanwhile, Wright had formed on the left of Hancock and Burnside on his right; while Lee strengthened his own right, now menaced by Warren.

Grant was now satisfied that he would be compelled to force the passage of the Chickahominy River, and he was equally satisfied that it would be folly to make a direct attack upon Lee's front. So he planned a flank movement, and prepared to cross the Chickahominy on Lee's right, not far from Cool Arbor,[1] where roads leading to Richmond, White House, and other points diverged. That important point was seized by Sheridan on the afternoon of the 31st, after a sharp contest with Fitzhugh Lee's cavalry and Clingman's infantry; and toward it Wright's corps, moving from the right of the army, in its rear, marched that night, unobserved by the enemy, and reached it the next day.[a] At the same time, and toward the same place, a large body of troops under General W. F. Smith, which had been called from the Army of the James at Bermuda Hundred, were moving, and arrived at Cool Arbor just after Wright's corps reached that place, and took position on the right of the latter. General Smith had left Bermuda Hundred on the 29th, with four divisions of the Tenth and Eighteenth Corps, sixteen thousand in number, which had been taken in transports around to White House. The two armies were now upon the old battle-field of Lee and McClellan two years before. The Confederate line, which had just been re-enforced by troops under Breckinridge, extended, with its cavalry on its flanks, a short distance from Hanover Court-House, down nearly to Bottom's Bridge. A. P. Hill's corps occupied its right, Longstreet's its center, and Ewell's its left.

On the morning of the first of June, an attempt was made by Hoke's division to retake Cool Arbor. Sheridan had been ordered to hold it at all hazards, and he did so. His men dismounted, and fought desperately with their carbines. The assailants were repulsed, but were quickly re-enforced by McLaws's division. Wright's corps arrived in time to meet this new danger; and when, at three o'clock in the afternoon, General Smith came up, after a march of twenty-five miles,[2] he was met by an order to form on the right of the Sixth Corps,[3] then in front of Cool Arbor, on the road leading to Gaines's Mill, and co-operate in an immediate attack upon the Con-

a June 1, 1864.

---

[1] See note 2, page 386, volume II.

[2] He had been erroneously directed to march to New Castle, instead of New Cool Arbor, and he had, by that means, made the journey from White House, more than ten miles further than was necessary.

[3] General Martindale commanded Smith's right; General W. H. Brooks his center, and General Devens, his left. General Ricketts commanded the right of the Sixths Corps, General Russell the center, and General Neill the left.

federates.   These were now in heavy force and in battle order, in that vicinity, for when Lee discovered the withdrawal of the Sixth Corps from Grant's
right, he suspected its destination, and had sent the whole of Longstreet's
corps to strengthen his own right, which was then partially concealed by
thick woods.

Between the two armies was a broad, open, gently undulating field, and
a thin line of woods, beyond which, and in front of the thicker forest, the
Confederates had lines of rifle trenches.   Over this open field the
Nationals advanced[a] at four o'clock, with great spirit, the veter-   [a] June 1,
ans of Smith seemingly unmindful of their fatigue, and in the face   1864.
of a murderous fire, quickly captured nearly the whole of the first line of
rifle trenches and about six hundred men.   They pushed on and assailed the
second and much stronger line, but the Confederates gallantly held it until
night fell and the struggle ceased.   In these desperate encounters, the
Nationals lost full two thousand men,
but they held the ground they had
gained, and bivouacked upon it that
night, partly in the shelter of the thin
wood, where some of the troops constructed rude bullet-proofs, that they
might repose in safety.   But they
found little opportunity even for rest,
for during the night the Confederates
made desperate efforts to retake the
lost rifle trenches, and greatly annoyed the troops by an enfilading
fire.   The assailants were repulsed;
and the result of the day's work on
the part of the Nationals was the

A BULLET-PROOF IN THE WOODS.

firm occupation of Cool Arbor, which commanded the road to White
House, and was the chosen place from which to force a passage of the
Chickahominy.

That night Grant ordered important but dangerous movements.   Hancock was directed to move from the right, and take position on the left of
the Sixth Corps, at Cool Arbor.   Warren was ordered to extend his line to
the left, from Bethesda Church, so as to connect with Smith; and Burnside
was withdrawn entirely from the front to the right and rear of Warren.
These movements were nearly all accomplished, but not without some
trouble and loss.   The Confederates observed that of Burnside, which took
place on the afternoon of the 2d, and following up his covering skirmishers,
captured some of them.   Then striking Warren's flank they took four hundred of his men prisoners.   But so satisfactory were all arrange-   [b] June 2.
ments that night,[b] that Grant and Meade, then at Cool Arbor,
determined to attempt to force the passage of the Chickahominy the next
day, and compel Lee to seek shelter within the fortifications around Richmond.
Grant was now holding almost the position of Lee in the battle of Gaines's
Mill,[1] two years before, and Lee had the place of McClellan on that occasion.

---

[1] See page 423, volume II.

At dawn on the morning of the 3d, the National army was in battle order, Hancock's corps on the Dispatch Station road on the left, the Sixth next, Smith's command adjoining these, and Warren and Burnside on the right, extending to the Tolopatomoy Creek. Wilson's cavalry were on the right flank, and Sheridan's were holding the lower crossings of the Chickahominy, and covering the roads to White House. Orders had been given for a general assault along the whole lines, at half-past four.[a] A few minutes later the signal for advance was given, and then opened one of the most sanguinary battles of the war. The Confederates were equally ready, equally brave, and equally determined to gain a victory.

[a] June 3, 1864.

Swiftly the Nationals advanced to the attack. On the right it was made by the divisions of Barlow and Gibbon, of Hancock's corps, that of Birney

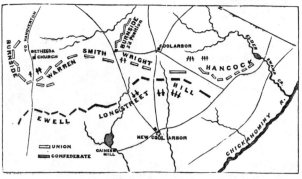

BATTLE OF COOL ARBOR.

supporting. Barlow drove the Confederates from a strong position in a sunken road, in front of their works, captured several hundred prisoners, a battle-flag, and three guns, and turning the latter upon his foes, sent them back in confusion. But, before Barlow's second line reached the front, the Confederates rallied in stronger force, and retook the position from which they had been pushed. Barlow was driven back about fifty yards, when he so speedily covered his front, that he could not be dislodged. Gibbon, who charged at the same time, at the right of Barlow, was checked by a marsh of the Chickahominy, which partly separated and weakened his command. A part of them gained the Confederate works. Colonel McKeen planted the National flag on their intrenchments; but a moment afterward he fell, mortally wounded. Gibbon's troops did not hold any part of the Confederate works; yet some of them intrenched themselves so close to them, that they could not well be reached, nor could they get away, excepting under the cover of fog or thick darkness. In these assaults Hancock lost about three thousand men.

Smith's command and the Sixth Corps were heavily engaged at the same time; and on the extreme right, Wilson's cavalry had a sharp fight with Hampton's, without any decisive results. But Warren's corps was too extended to allow him to do more than to hold his line intact, while Burnside brought two divisions of the Ninth to bear upon the left of Lee's line. These were hotly engaged, and would doubtless have vanquished their adversaries on that part of the field, had not the assault quickly ceased along the front. The battle had been "quick, sharp, and decisive." The Nationals had been repulsed, at nearly every point, with great slaughter. It was estimated that within twenty minutes after the struggle began, ten thousand Union men lay dead or wounded on the field, while the Confederates, sheltered by their works, had not lost more than one thousand.

A consciousness now pervaded the mind of every soldier that further attempts to force the Confederate lines would be useless; and upon this impression they acted with marvelous unanimity, when, some hours later, General Meade sent orders to each corps commander to again attack, without regard to the doings of other corps. The whole army, as if controlled by a single will, *refused to stir!* And so, at one o'clock in the afternoon, the BATTLE OF COOL ARBOR was ended in a dreadful loss of life to the Nationals, but of nothing else, for they held their position firmly, with all their munitions of war.[1]

Grant now resolved to transfer his army to the south side of the James River, and by this grand flank movement, to cut off the chief sources of supplies of men

VIEW ON COOL ARBOR BATTLE-GROUND.[2]

and provisions for Lee's army from the south and southwest, and compel its surrender. His prime object, as we have observed, had been the destruction of that army, by capture or dispersion. He had hoped to accomplish that

[1] The National loss in this engagement, and in the immediate vicinity of Cool Arbor, was reported at 13,153, of whom 1,705 were killed, 9,042 wounded, and 2,406 were missing. Among the killed were Acting Brigadier-Generals Peter A. Porter, Lewis O. Morris, and F. F. Weed, of the New York troops. Other prominent officers were severely wounded, among them General O. P. Tyler. The Confederates lost General Doles. Lawrence M. Keit, one of the most active of the South Carolina conspirators in Congress in 1861, had been killed the day before.

[2] This view is from the ground occupied by the troops from the Army of the James, under General W. F. Smith, at the ruins of a mansion destroyed at the time of the battle, about a quarter of a mile northeast of the road from Gaines's Mill. See map on page 423, and narrative on pages 436 and 437, volume II. The woods seen in the distance were those in which the Confederates were partially concealed, and along the edge of which they had cast up a line of intrenchments. Their rifle trenches were in the open field, between the chimney and the woods. When the writer visited the spot, in May, 1866, the thin strip of woods mentioned in the text had disappeared.

object north of Richmond, but had failed to do so. He was disappointed, but not disheartened, by his failure and his enormous losses, which were to Lee's as three to one;[1] and he proceeded to carry out, as far as possible, the remainder of his original design.[2] He had seriously crippled his adversary, who lacked means for recuperation, and he now determined to starve him into submission. Having considered all the contingencies incident to the bold movement of throwing his army to the south side of the James, he feared no mischief from it, but anticipated much benefit.

On the day after the battle, Grant caused slight intrenchments to be thrown up in front of his line, and that night the Confederates made a furious assault on that front, but were quickly repulsed at every point. On the following day an assault was made on the National left (Smyth's brigade of Hancock's corps), with the same result. Meanwhile the army, preparatory to its march to the James, was gradually moved toward the left by the withdrawal of corps in that direction; and on the night of the 6th,[*] a sharp but unsuccessful assault was made upon the right, then held by Burnside. On the following morning there was a brief armistice, for the purpose of gathering up the dead between the two lines, which had lain there four days; and before night Grant's line was extended to the Chickahominy, and Sheridan was dispatched, with two divisions of cavalry, to more effectually destroy the railways in Lee's rear, and render Washington more secure.[3] He struck and broke the Richmond and Fredericksburg road at Chesterfield Station, and then, pushing across the upper branches of the North Anna, smote the Virginia Central railway at Trevilian's Station, where he expected the co-operation of General Hunter. That leader, as we have seen,[4] was at Staunton, and Sheridan was left to deal, alone, with the gathering Confederates on the railway. At Trevilian's he encountered and routed some horsemen under Hampton, and then destroyed the road almost to Louisa Court-House, where he was attacked by a much larger force. After a contest, he was compelled to retrace his steps to Trevilian's, where he fought a sanguinary battle, and then withdrew. He swept around, by Spottsylvania Court-House and Guiney's Station, to White House, and rejoined Grant's army, having lost during his raid over seven hundred men, and captured nearly four

* June, 1864.

---

[1] The entire loss of men in this campaign, from the 4th of May to the 12th of June, when the troops proceeded to cross the James River, was about 60,000, while that of the Confederates was not more than 20,000. A tabular statement by Mr. Swinton, in his *Campaigns of the Army of the Potomac*, page 491, tells the losses in the battles and attendant movements, as follows: Battles of the Wilderness, 29,410; of Spottsylvania Court-House, 10,831; of the North Anna, 1,607; and of Cool Arbor, 13,153. Total, 54,551. To this number must be added the losses in the Ninth Corps (Burnside's, which, until the Battle of Cool Arbor, was independent of Meade's command), estimated at 5,000, makes the grand total about 60,000. The loss in officers was about 3,000.

[2] "My idea, from the start, had been to beat Lee's army north of Richmond, if possible. Then, after destroying his lines of communication north of the James River, to transfer the army to the south side, and besiege Lee in Richmond, or follow him south, if he should retreat. After the battle of The Wilderness, it was evident that the enemy deemed it of the first importance to run no risks with the army he then had. He acted purely on the defensive, behind breastworks, or feebly on the offensive immediately in front of them, and where in case of repulse, he could easily retire behind them. Without a greater sacrifice of life, then, than I was willing to make, all could not be accomplished that I had designed north of Richmond."—*Report of Lieutenant-General U. S. Grant, of the Armies of the United States*—1864-'65, July 22, 1865.

[3] Grant's determination to transfer his army to the south side of the James River startled the authorities at Washington with fears that Lee might suddenly turn back and seize that city. Grant had no fears on that account. He knew that the country between Lee's shattered army and Washington was thoroughly exhausted by the troops that had just passed over it; and had Lee attempted such a movement, Grant could have sent troops from the James, by way of the Potomac, for the protection of the Capital, much sooner than Lee could have marched upon it.

[4] See page 315.

hundred. He inflicted a loss of men upon the Confederates quite equal to his own. Among their killed was the active General Rosser.

Grant continued moving slowly to the left, and keeping up the appearance of an intention to cross the Chickahominy and march on Richmond, until the evening of the 12th,[a] when every thing was in readiness for the army to move to the James. White House was [a] June, 1864. abandoned as a base of supplies; the rails and ties of the York River railway leading from it to Richmond were taken up and sent in barges to City Point, and the command of General Smith was re-embarked at the head of the York, and sent back by water to Bermuda Hundred. Then the Army of the Potomac moved. Warren's corps, preceded by Wilson's cavalry, forced the passage of the Chickahominy at Long Bridge with very little trouble, and made demonstrations in the direction of Richmond, to mask the real movements of the army. Hancock followed Warren across the stream, and marched directly to Wilcox's Wharf, on the James, below Harrison's Landing, between Charles City Court-House and Westover,[1] where he was ferried across. Wright and Burnside crossed the Chickahominy at Jones's bridge, lower down; while the trains, for greater safety, took a route still further east, and crossed at Coles's Ferry.

Lee discovered the withdrawal of his antagonist from his front on the morning of the 13th; but finding Warren across the Chickahominy, and on the road leading through White Oak Swamp to Richmond, he concluded that Grant was about to march by that route upon the Confederate capital. With this impression, he retired to the fortifications of that city, while Grant's army was making a rapid journey in another direction. Warren quickly followed the Nationals, and on the night of the 14th,[b] a pontoon bridge, more than two thousand feet in length, [b] June. was thrown across the James River, at Douthard's,[2] a little below Wilcox's,

over which the entire remainder of the army had passed before noon of the 16th, with very little molestation by the enemy, and was moving in the direction of Petersburg. Grant, meanwhile, had gone up to City Point, and there, upon the beautiful elevated grounds of

GRANT'S HEAD-QUARTERS, CITY POINT.[3]

Dr. Eppes, near the junction of the Appomatox and the James, he established his head-quarters.

---

[1] See page 435, volume II.

[2] This bridge was laid in the space of about fifteen hours, under the immediate supervision of General Benham Its site was selected and the general directions for its construction were given by General Weitzel, chief engineer of Butler's Department of Virginia and North Carolina.

[3] This was the appearance of Grant's head-quarters when the writer visited City Point, at the close of 1864. The building seen in the center was the General's quarters. It was very neatly built of small hewn logs, excepting the front, which was of planed pine timber, the bark left on the edges, and the whole well "chinked" with cement. It had two wings, making the whole quite spacious. A building at the left of it, was occupied by

• When Grant determined to throw Meade's army to the south side of the James, he hastened to Butler's head-quarters for the purpose of arranging a plan of co-operation from Bermuda Hundred, against Petersburg,[1] the possession of which would be of vast importance as a *point d'appui*, or fixed place for the forming of troops for chief operations against Richmond. Butler's line of works, erected under the direction of General Weitzel, were then perfected, and were not surpassed, in complete-

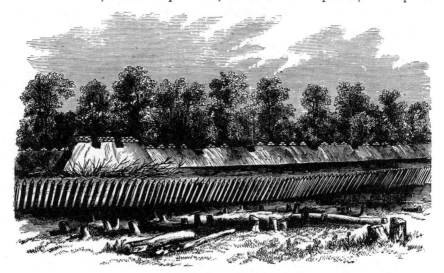

LINE OF DEFENSE AT BERMUDA HUNDRED.[2]

ness for defensive operations by any made during the war. His position was almost impregnable; yet, while Smith was absent with a greater portion of the Army of the James, he was too weak to attempt formidable offensive movements. It was for this reason that Smith was so quickly sent back to Bermuda Hundred, as we have observed.[3]

General Rawlins, Grant's chief of staff; and one on the right was the quarters of General Barnard, the engineer-in-chief. Grant's house was presented by the Lieutenant-General, at the close of the war, to George H. Stuart, President of the U. S. Christian Commission, who caused it to be taken to Philadelphia. By permission of the city authorities he re-erected it in Fairmount Park, where it yet (1868) remains.

[1] Petersburg is situated on the south bank of the Appomattox River, about ten miles from its mouth at City Point. That river is navigable to Petersburg for vessels of one hundred tons burden; but larger ones ascend only to Port Walthall, six miles below it, near the high eminence on the north side, known as Point of Rocks. Through Petersburg passed the railway that connected Richmond with the Carolinas. Another, called the Southside road, extended westward to Lynchburg; another, running in a southeasterly direction, connected Petersburg and Norfolk, and a short one also connected Petersburg with City Point.

[2] This shows a portion of the line of works constructed by General Weitzel. First, there was a strong line of earthworks, consisting of redoubts and intrenchments, with embrasures made more efficient by bags of sand.

CHEVAUX-DE-FRISE.

Outside of this was a ditch, with *abatis* in front, and outside of all a row of pointed palisades of timber, inclining toward the approaches of assailants. The Confederate engineers also constructed admirable defensive works around Petersburg, in which they extensively employed a species- of movable *chevaux-de-frise*, delineated in the annexed engraving. These were made of saplings, through which passed strong spikes of wood, sharpened at each end, and presenting four or six radiating arms. The sapling forming the center of each was connected by wires or chains with another and so continuous lines of *chevaux-de-frise* were formed to any required extent.

[3] See page 333.

In the mean time, Butler endeavored to do what he might in furtherance of Grant's plans, and on the 10th of June he sent three thousand five hundred infantry, under Gillmore, and fifteen hundred cavalry, under Kautz, against Petersburg. At the same time two gun-boats were sent up the Appomattox, to co-operate with a battery in bombarding an earthwork a little below Petersburg, called Fort Clinton. These combinations were well arranged. The troops crossed the Appomattox at Point of Rocks, four miles above City Point. Gillmore marched up the turnpike, while Kautz made a little circuit, so as to strike the city from the south. The former found no resistance until he was within two or three miles of Petersburg. He had easily driven in the Confederate skirmish line; but at the outer works of the defenses of Petersburg, already thrown up, he first halted, and then fell back to his camp, with the impression that his force was inadequate for the task assigned him. Kautz, meanwhile, had performed his part of the drama. While a greater portion of the defenders of Petersburg were watching Gillmore, he dashed into the city at about the time when the latter fell back, when the Confederates, relieved of danger from the infantry column, fell upon Kautz in force, and drove him from the town and its defenses.

Five days later, the attempt to capture Petersburg was renewed. When the Army of the Potomac began its passage of the James, Grant went to Bermuda Hundred, and finding the van of Lee's army, under A. P. Hill, already on the south side of the river, near Fort Darling, and ready to act in co-operation with Beauregard, he directed Butler to send General Smith and his command immediately across the Appomattox, and in conjunction with Gillmore and Kautz, make another attempt upon Petersburg. He was so well satisfied that such attempt, if vigorously made, would be successful, that he looked for the possession of that city by the Army of the Potomac, within the space of three days, as a certainty.

Smith arrived at Bermuda Hundred on the night of the 14th. His troops, having rested on the transports, were fresh; and early the next morning,[a] they crossed the Appomattox on a pontoon bridge, and before noon were in front of the defenses of Petersburg, northeastward of the city. The troops had marched in three columns. Kautz had kept well to the left, and threatened the defenses of the Petersburg and Norfolk railway. Brooks led the center, and Martindale the right. On the way General Hinks, with his negro brigade, had carried advanced rifle-pits and captured two guns; and the whole column was inspirited with the expectation of a quick and easy victory. But this exultation was diminished when a reconnoissance revealed the fact that there was a strong line of works on their front, the guns of which swept the ditches and ravines, which cut a broad valley in various directions, over which the Nationals must pass to the assault.

[a] June 15, 1864.

General Smith paused. He did not then know how few and inferior were the soldiers behind the works he was facing, and it was nearly sunset before his cautious preparations for assault were completed. Then a part of his troops, under Martindale, Brooks, and Hinks, forming a heavy skirmish line, pressed forward, and at seven o'clock in the evening drove the Confederates from their formidable line of rifle-pits. Pushing on, they soon captured a powerful salient, four redoubts, and a connecting line of intrenchments along distance of two and a half miles. With these they took fifteen guns, and made three hundred men prisoners. Meanwhile, two divisions of Hancock's corps had come up and joined Smith's command,[1] when the united forces were ordered to rest upon their arms within the works just captured. Smith thought it more prudent to hold what he had obtained, than to risk all by attempting to gain more.[2] So, during the calm hours that succeeded, the nearly full moon shining brightly until past midnight, the assailants reposed, while nearly the whole of Lee's army was crossing the James to the south front of Richmond, and troops were streaming down toward Petersburg and into the lines around it. There, in a few hours, these worked wonders, and on the following morning[a] there was a startling apparition of a new line of works around the city, with a cloud of veterans deployed in battle order behind them. The prize so much coveted by Grant was lost. Twenty-four hours before, Petersburg might have been easily taken;[3] now it defied its foes, and continued to do so during a most distressing siege of about ten months from that time. That delay of twelve hours—whether wise or unwise let the reader judge—was the turning-point in the campaign.

a June 16, 1864.

And now, at the middle of June, a large portion of the Army of Northern Virginia were in Petersburg, and within the lines in front of it, or were on their way and near by; and that evening[b] the greater part of the Army of the Potomac, with the command of Smith on its right, resting on the Appomattox, confronted the Confederates. Grant had gone to the front at an early hour that day, and ascertaining the state of affairs, was returning to City Point, when he met General Meade on the road, and directed him to post his army as quickly as possible, and at six o'clock that evening open fire on the Confederate lines. It was expected that Burnside would join Smith and Hancock by that time. He did so. The bombardment was opened at the appointed hour, and was kept up, with varying intensity, until six o'clock in the morning. The result of the fearful combat on that warm June night was a general advance of the National lines, but at a serious cost to the corps of Hancock and Burnside. Birney, of the former, stormed and carried the ridge on its front. Burnside could make no impression during the night, and was kept at bay by a murderous fire; but at dawn General Potter's division made a desperate charge upon the works in front of the Ninth Corps, carried them, and captured four guns and four hundred prisoners. His division was at once relieved by General Ledlie's,

b June 16.

---

[1] Between five and six o'clock in the afternoon, Hancock, then pressing forward with his column from Windmill Point toward a designated spot in front of Petersburg, received orders from Grant to hasten to the assistance of Smith. The divisions of Birney and Gibbon were then in advance, and these were pushed forward to Smith's position. Hancock, who was blamed by some for being yet on his march so late in the day, pleaded the fact that he had been misled by an incorrect map, and stated that the order from General Grant, to assist Smith, was the first intimation he had received of an intended attack on Petersburg that day.

[2] General Smith, in his *Report of Operations before Petersburg*, says that he was aware of the crossing of the James by Lee's army that night. He deemed it, he said, "wiser to hold what we had, than, by attempting to reach the bridges [that spanned the Appomattox at the city], to lose what we had gained, and have the troops meet with a disaster." "Heavy darkness was upon us," he said, "and the troops were placed so as to occupy the commanding positions and wait for daylight."

[3] In his report, written more than a year afterward, General Grant said, in speaking of these operations of General Smith: "Between the lines thus captured and Petersburg, there were no other works, and there was no evidence that the enemy had re-enforced Petersburg with a single brigade from any source. The night was clear, the moon shining brightly, and favorable to further operations."

which advanced to within a mile and a half of the city, and held a position from which shells could be thrown into the town. This menacing projection of Burnside's line was furiously attacked that night, and the National troops were driven back with great loss. At other points they were repulsed. Their loss much exceeded that of the Confederates.

The danger threatening the Petersburg lines having drawn a large portion of the troops from Butler's front, that officer sent out General Terry on the same day,[a] to force Beauregard's lines, and destroy and hold, if possible, the railway in that vicinity. Terry easily *a June 16, 1864.* passed through those lines, and reached the road without much opposition, and was proceeding to destroy the track, when he was attacked by Pickett's division of Longstreet's corps, then on its way from the Virginia capital to the beleaguered city.[1] Smith's corps (Eighteenth) having been relieved by the Sixth, was sent by Grant to aid Butler, in the event of an exigency such as had now occurred; but it arrived too late to assist Terry, and the latter, after a sharp engagement, was driven back to the defenses of Bermuda Hundred, when the Confederate works in front of them were at once heavily garrisoned.

On the morning of the 17th, the Second and Ninth Corps renewed the attack upon the works before Petersburg, when the hill upon which Fort Steadman was afterward built, was carried and held by the former corps. Another attack was made by the Ninth in the afternoon, when the battle that ensued continued until night, with great slaughter, in which Barlow's division suffered most severely. Crawford was sent to Burnside's support. He became entangled in the ravines, and could do but little. He penetrated the Confederate lines, however, and brought away a number of prisoners. Several times during the day, desperate but unsuccessful attempts were made to recapture what the Nationals had seized, and that night a heavy force drove back the Ninth Corps.

Impressed with the belief that much of Lee's army yet remained near Richmond, and hoping to capture Petersburg before that army should all be upon his front, Grant ordered a general assault along the entire chain of works before him, on the morning of the 18th.[2] At dawn it was discovered that the Confederates had abandoned their broken and imperiled line at their front, and had taken a new and stronger position on an inner line, which had been constructed with the best engineering skill (and none was better) that Lee could command. This change compelled Grant to readjust his own lines for attack, which delayed an advance until afternoon. The attack which followed resulted in disaster to the Nationals, who were repulsed at every point. Only Martindale's division gained any success. That carried the Confederate skirmish line on its front, and made a few prisoners.

---

[1] In co-operation with Pickett's movement was a naval demonstration by the Confederates, who sent three iron-clad steamers down the James River from Drewry's Bluff, to Dutch Gap, hoping to divert the attention of Admiral Lee from the attack that might be made upon Butler if he should attempt to interfere with the passage of the troops to Petersburg; also with a hope of damaging the National squadron. But they effected nothing, and were easily driven back.

[2] The National line was then formed as follows: The division of General Martindale, of the Eighteenth Corps, which had been left before Petersburg when Smith withdrew to the Peninsula, occupied the right, and the line was extended to the left by the Sixth, Second, Ninth, and Fifth Corps, in the order named.

And now, after a loss of nearly ten thousand men, further attempts to take the Confederate lines by storm were abandoned for awhile. It was evident to the Lieutenant-General that the bulk of Lee's army was behind them, and he prepared for a regular siege of them. He at once began intrenching, and to extend his left in the direction of the Petersburg and Weldon railway, which he desired to seize, and thus envelop Petersburg with his army. The corps of Hancock[1] and Wright were moved[a] stealthily to the left, for the purpose of turning the Confederate right; but when the former, moving in the advance, reached the Jerusalem plank road, between the Norfolk and Weldon railways, it was met by a Confederate force, and pushed back to a position where it connected with the Fifth Corps. On the following morning[b] both corps (Second and Sixth) advanced together, and were maneuvering to turn the works, when a division of the command of A. P. Hill, who had been keenly watching the movements of the Nationals, suddenly projected itself between Wright and Birney's commands, and in rapid succession struck the flanks of the divisions of Barlow, Mott, and Gibbon, rolling them up and driving them back with heavy loss. Wright's corps was considerably shocked by a blow, at the same time, by another of Hill's divisions. Both corps soon recovered and re-formed, and a fierce attack on the brigade of the ever-gallant General Miles, of the Second, was repulsed. Meade came up at about that time, and just at sunset he ordered both corps to advance and retake what they had lost. Hill, unsupported, suddenly withdrew, carrying with him twenty-five hundred prisoners. Nearly all the lost ground was recovered.

[a June 21, 1864.]

[b June 22.]

On the following morning the Second and Sixth Corps again advanced, and reached the Weldon road without much opposition; but three regiments in the van had scarcely begun the destruction of the track, when they were suddenly attacked by a part of Hill's corps, and were driven back upon the main line with the loss of many of their number made prisoners. The Weldon road had now been reached; but the result of the movements thus far was little more than an extension of the Union line to the left, at a cost of about four thousand men, chiefly made captives.

Meanwhile, a cavalry expedition, eight thousand strong, under Generals Kautz and Wilson, had been sent out to operate upon the railways leading southward from Petersburg. The latter was in chief command. They destroyed the railway buildings at Reams's Station, ten miles south of Petersburg, and the track for a long distance, and then pushed on to the Southside railway at Ford's Station, fifteen miles from Petersburg, and destroyed it to Nottaway Station, over a space of twenty-two miles. There they fought and defeated a brigade of Virginia and North Carolina cavalry, under Fitzhugh Lee. Kautz then pushed on to Burke's Station, at the junction of the Southside and Danville railways, tore up both roads, and, pushing southward along the latter, was joined by Wilson at Meherrin Station.[c] The united forces then destroyed the road to the Staunton River, when the rapid gathering of the armed and mounted men in that region caused them to turn back. They were com-

[June 24.]

---

[1] Hancock was now disabled by the breaking out afresh of his wound received at Gettysburg, and General Birney was in temporary command of the Second Corps.

pelled to fight their way to Reams's Station, on the Weldon road, which they expected to find in the possession of the Nationals. On the contrary, the cavalry of Hampton, and infantry under Mahone and Finnegan were there in great strength. In attempting to force their lines, Wilson and Kautz were defeated with heavy loss, and with difficulty they made their way back to the army before Petersburg, with the men and horses of their terribly shattered columns nearly exhausted.[1] No other raid in the rear of the Confederates was undertaken for several months after the return of this one. It was too dangerous and expensive a service, under the circumstances, to be made profitable.

And now, after a sanguinary struggle for two months, both armies were willing to have a little repose, and there was a lull in the active operations of the campaign, excepting what pertained to intrenching. The Union army thus investing Petersburg, at which point Richmond, twenty miles distant, was best defended, had lost, within eight or nine weeks, nearly seventy thousand men. Re-enforcements had kept up its numbers, but not the

PONTOON BRIDGE AT DEEP BOTTOM.[2]

quality of its materials. Many veterans remained; but a vast portion of the army was composed, if not of entirely raw troops, of those who had been little disciplined, and in a great degree lacked the buoyant spirit of the early

[1] In the fight at Reams's Station, they lost their guns, a small train, and many men and horses. The Confederates claimed to have captured 1,000 effective men, besides the wounded, 13 guns, and 30 wagons. Wilson estimated his entire loss during the raid at between 750 and 1,000 men. Grant said, in his report, that the damage done to the enemy "more than compensated for the losses we sustained." The raiders destroyed about sixty miles of railway, with mills, factories, and blacksmith shops. At Reams's Station, about 1,000 negroes, most of them mounted on horses "borrowed for the occasion," and following the Union cavalry, were captured by the Confederates. Many of these, Wilson reported, were slaughtered without mercy, and the remainder were remanded to slavery.

[2] This shows the appearance of the pontoon bridge at Deep Bottom, with Butler's little dispatch-steamer, *Grey Hound*, lying just above it.

Army of the Potomac, when led by McClellan and Hooker. It was now in front of a formidable line of redans, redoubts, and infantry parapets, with the outer defenses of abatis, stakes, and chevaux-de-frise, constructed by skillfully-directed labor. This line was nearly forty miles in length, extending from the left bank of the Appomattox, around the western side of Petersburg, and so on to and across the James, to the northeastern side of Richmond. To menace that line, and to keep the defenders within it, required an equally extended and strong line, and this was speedily provided. Re-enforcements swelled the weakened ranks of the Nationals, and strong works were cast up along the front of the whole Confederate line, from the Weldon road to the region of the Chickahominy.

On the night of the 20th of June, Butler, by one of his prompt movements, had thrown the brigade of General Foster across the James River at Deep Bottom, where he formed an intrenched camp; and this post, within ten miles of Richmond, was immediately connected with the army at Bermuda Hundred by a pontoon bridge, represented in the engraving on the preceding page. There Smith's (Eighteenth) corps was transferred to Bermuda Hundred, and thenceforth served with the Army of the James a greater part of the time during the siege. The lodgment of Foster, and the laying of the pontoon bridge at Deep Bottom, provided a way for Grant to move heavy masses quickly to the north side of the James, if desired. This advantage was perceived by Lee, who met it by laying a similar bridge across the river at Drewry's Bluff, by which he could make countervailing movements. By the close of July, a greater portion of that wonderful network of fortifications in front of Petersburg, which commanded the admiration of visitors, was nearly completed, and the Lieutenant-General was in a position to choose his method of warfare, whether by a direct assault, the slower process of a regular siege, or by heavy operations on the flanks of the Confederates.

CHAPTER XIII.

INVASION OF MARYLAND AND PENNSYLVANIA—OPERATIONS BEFORE PETERSBURG AND
IN THE SHENANDOAH VALLEY.

T has been observed that the authorities at Washington feared a visit from Lee's troops when the Army of the Potomac should be placed on the south side of the James River.[1] At about the time we are considering—the midsummer of 1864— these fears were realized. Finding the pressure of his antagonist very severe, and the dangers to his army at and around Richmond hourly increasing, Lee sought to avert impending calamity by diverting so much of the Union army to some distant point, as to practically relieve Petersburg and Richmond of siege. That contemplated point of diversion was the National Capital, the most feasible way to which, by Confederate troops, seemed to be by the Shenandoah Valley and across the Potomac into Maryland, taking it in reverse. Lee eagerly watched an opportunity for the movement. It was offered when Hunter fled from before Lynchburg into Western Virginia, with an exhausted and broken army,[2] and left the Shenandoah Valley, and its door opening into Maryland at Harper's Ferry, guarded only by a moderate force under General Sigel, posted at Martinsburg.

General Early, in command of troops in the upper part of the Valley, was directed by Lee to gather to his own all the troops in that region, and move rapidly to and across the Potomac into Maryland, with the threefold object, it appears, of drawing National troops from before Petersburg, procuring supplies, and attempting the capture of Washington City. Early quickly obeyed. With from 15,000 to 20,000 troops of all arms,[3] he swept rapidly down the Valley toward Williamsport. Sigel, too weak to resist the avalanche, fled[a] into Maryland, with a heavy loss of stores, and General Weber, in command at Harper's Ferry, retired to Maryland Heights. Grant, meanwhile, had directed Hunter, who was then on the Kanawha, to hasten to Harper's Ferry with all possible dispatch; but insuperable obstacles kept him back until it was too late to be of essential service, and Early found no troops at hand to oppose his invasion, except a few in the Middle Department, commanded by General Lewis Wallace, whose head-quarters were at Baltimore.

[a] July 3, 1864.

Early crossed the river at Williamsport, accompanied by Bradley T. Johnson[4] as commander of a brigade, and a notorious guerrilla leader named

---

[1] See note 3, page 332. [2] See page 316.
[3] Composed of two infantry corps, under Breckinridge and Rodes, a division of cavalry under Ransom, and three batteries of artillery. [4] See page 416, volume I.

Harry Gilmor,[1] both bitter Maryland rebels, who now, as the chosen guides
and assistants of the chief of the invaders, brought war with all its horrors
to the doors of their neighbors and
friends. Early pushed on
to Hagerstown,[a] where he
levied a contribution on
the inhabitants of $20,000, and then
swept over the country toward the
Pennsylvania line, plundering friend
and foe alike of horses, cattle, provisions and money.[2]

[a] July 6,
1864.

WEBER'S HEAD-QUARTERS, HARPER'S FERRY.[3]

Vague rumors had reached General Wallace, at Baltimore, concerning
the perils of Sigel. Then came positive information of the passage of the
Potomac by the Confederates, and
their raiding within the borders of General Couch's Department; and finally,
on the 5th of July, he was informed that their movements indicated an
intention to march upon Baltimore or Washington in heavy column. Finding his Department thus threatened, Wallace took measures for checking the
invaders at the Monocacy River, with the few available troops under his
command.[4] General E. B. Tyler, was then at the railway bridge over the
Monocacy, with about one thousand men, and thither Wallace hastened,
to ascertain, in person, the true state of affairs in that direction.[5] Wild
rumors were afloat, but no reliable information concerning the number or
the whereabouts of the invaders could be obtained. He prepared for any
emergency, and chose a commanding position on the east side of the Mo-

---

[1] This young man was a member of a respectable Maryland family. He entered the Confederate service as
one of Turner Ashby's cavalry in the Shenandoah Valley, in the summer of 1861, and the field of his operations,
as follower and leader, was chiefly in that and the mountain region around. After the war he, with an obtuse-
ness of moral perceptions hardly to be conceived, published a confession of his crimes against his country, in a
book with the title of *Four Years in the Saddle.* His excessive egotism is the most prominent feature of the book,
and continually inspires the reader with just doubts concerning the truthfulness of his narratives of exploits of
which he says he was the hero. In the raid into Maryland which we are now considering, this man was one of
the chief instruments in distressing the inhabitants of his native State. He appears to have taken special delight,
according to contemporary writers, in plundering and devastating expeditions; and, according to his own confession (see page 210), he was chosen by General M'Causland as the proper person for burning the city of Chambersburg, in Pennsylvania. For a full account of the conduct of this man and his followers, at Chambersburg,
see the narrative of the burning of that place, by the Reverend B. S. Schenck, D. D., who was an eye-witness.
[2] This invasion produced great alarm, and caused the Government to issue an urgent call upon Pennsylvania,
New York, and Massachusetts, for troops to meet it. The President called for 12,000 from Pennsylvania, and
5,000 each from New York and Massachusetts.
[3] This spacious building, on the corner of Shenandoah and High Streets, in the village of Harper's Ferry, and
belonging to the Government, was used as head-quarters by all of the commanding officers there, of both parties,
during the war.
[4] General Wallace assumed command of the Middle Department, consisting of Delaware and a portion of
Maryland, on the 22d of March, 1864. That Department was then seemingly remote from danger, external and
internal, and the entire number of available troops in it, and composed chiefly of Home Guards and One Hundred days' men, did not much exceed 2,500. These were chiefly employed in garrisoning the forts and prisons
in Maryland, and in co-operating with the troops in the Department of Washington, under General Augur,
in guarding the fords of the Potomac as far up as Point of Rocks.
[5] General Wallace left the direction of the affairs of the Department, at head-quarters, with Lieutenant-Colonel
Samuel B. Lawrence, Assistant Adjutant-General and Chief-of-Staff. Fortunately, Wallace had assisted the Union
League of Baltimore to organize for military service, and they reported promptly for duty. To General W. W.
Morris was assigned the command of the garrison of Baltimore, and General H. H. Lockwood, then in that city
awaiting orders, was invited to take command of the civil forces. These two officers performed efficient service
at that crisis.

nocacy for the concentration of his forces, so as to cover the Baltimore and Ohio railway crossing, and the chief highways leading to the menaced cities.[1] On the evening of the 6th, all of his effective men that could be spared from watching the railways leading into Baltimore from the north, which the Confederates were evidently trying to seize, were gathered at the appointed rendezvous, under Tyler.[2] That night,[a]   [a] July 6, 1864. Wallace ordered Colonel Clendennin to go out toward Middletown with four hundred men, in search of positive information concerning the Confederates. He marched at daylight,[b] with a section of Alexanders' artillery, and at that village he encountered a thou-   [b] July 7. sand horseman, under Bradley Johnson, who pushed him steadily back toward Frederick by threatening his flanks. Gilpin's regiment, with one gun, and the mounted infantry, were sent to help Clendennin; and late in the afternoon there was a sharp fight in front of Frederick with artillery and small-arms. At six o'clock Gilpin charged the Confederates, and drove them back to the mountains.

Meanwhile, General Grant, aware of the peril that threatened the Capital, ordered the Sixth Corps to Washington. The advance division,   [c] July. under General Ricketts, arrived there late on the 6th,[c] and were sent to Baltimore that night, with orders to push on to the Monocacy River as quickly as possible. Informed of the fact that veterans were coming, Wallace ordered Tyler to Frederick; and when, at dawn on the 8th, a portion of Ricketts's (First) brigade, under Colonel Henry, reached the Monocacy, they, too, were sent to join Tyler. At that time the wildest rumors filled the air of the force and position of the Confederates. Wallace was soon satisfied that the defense of Frederick was a secondary consideration, for news reached him that the invaders were pressing toward the Washington turnpike in heavy column, and were threatening his line of retreat. Impressed with the belief that Washington City was their chief objective, and knowing it to be without sufficient troops to defend it against the reported strength of the invaders, Wallace determined to throw his little army across their path, and, if possible, keep them at bay until succor should reach the Capital. So he withdrew his troops from Frederick to his chosen position on the Monocacy, where he found a greater portion of Ricketts's division.

Early on the morning of the 9th, Wallace made dispositions for battle. His right, under Tyler, covered the railway and the Baltimore pike, and Ricketts held the Washington pike, on the left, where the main attack was expected. Each had three guns. Colonel Brown, with his command and the mounted infantry, held a stone bridge of the Baltimore pike, on Tyler's

---

[1] There, within the space of two miles and a half, converged the turnpikes to Baltimore and Washington, and the Ohio and Baltimore railroad; and there was the iron bridge of the railway upon which depended railroad communication with Harper's Ferry. The river covered the entire front of the position, making it very strong. That position was on commanding heights, while the ground on the other side of the river was low.

[2] These were composed of the Third (Maryland) Potomac Home Brigade, Colonel Charles Gilpin; Eleventh Maryland Infantry, Colonel Landstreet; seven companies of the One Hundred and Forty-ninth, and three companies of the One Hundred and Fifty-ninth Ohio National Guard, under Colonel A. L. Brown; Captain Alexander's (Maryland) battery; and one hundred men of the One Hundred and Fifty-ninth Ohio, serving as mounted infantry, under Captains S. H. Lieb and N. S. Allen. In addition to these, Wallace had the services of Lieutenant-Colonel Clendennin's squadron of cavalry, two hundred and fifty strong, and four companies of the First (Maryland) Potomac Home Brigade, about two hundred in number, under Captain Brown. The Eleventh Maryland and all the Ohio troops were "hundred days' men."

right, and was Wallace's chief dependence in the protection of that flank. Clendennin and his cavalry watched the lower fords, and skirmishers were sent out some distance in advance of the Monocacy bridges. At a block-house near the railway was a rude earthwork, bearing a 24-pounder howitzer. Such was the disposition of Wallace's little force to resist the attack of what proved to be an army full twenty thousand strong, with a large park of artillery,[1] that advanced from Frederick at eight o'clock in the morning.[a] Three of Ricketts's regiments were yet behind, but were expected by railway at one o'clock in the afternoon.

^{a July 9 1864.}

Planting his Napoleon guns, sixteen in number, behind his skirmish line as he advanced, Early opened the battle at about nine o'clock. The contest rapidly grew warmer and more general as he drew near, and Brown soon found it difficult to maintain his position at the stone bridge. At the same time a large body of Confederates, moving by their right out of range of Ricketts's guns, forced a passage of the Monocacy at a ford on his left, and at half-past ten moved upon him in battle order. Ricketts changed front to meet the attack, his right resting on the river; but in so doing he exposed himself to an enfilading fire from Early's guns across the stream; and so over-matched was he in numbers, that he was likely to be soon enveloped. Perceiving this, the watchful Wallace sent, first, two of Tyler's guns to Ricketts, and then every man that could be spared from other points.

The invader's first line made a furious charge, and was quickly thrown back. The second then charged, and after a more protracted struggle, was also repulsed, and fled to the woods in confusion. So great was the disparity in numbers, that Wallace would have been justified in retreating at that time, and could easily have done so; but his desire was to develop the strength of the invaders, and to keep them at bay as long as possible. Expecting Ricketts's three fresh regiments at one o'clock, and believing that with them he might maintain his position, he stood firm and fought desperately until that time and an hour beyond. Then, having no tidings of the approaching troops,[2] and seeing the Confederates issuing from the woods in two strong columns to make another charge, he reluctantly ordered Ricketts to retreat by the Baltimore pike. That retreat began at four o'clock in the afternoon.

In the mean time, Tyler had been as gallantly fighting the foe on the right of the National line, and Brown yet possessed the stone bridge which Wallace had said must be held at all hazards until Ricketts could cross over to the Baltimore pike. This position was now of vital importance. Tyler sent Brown all of his reserves, and held his own position firmly, though pressed by an eager and vastly superior foe. He fought on with the greatest gallantry until Ricketts's column was safe, when at five o'clock Brown was compelled to abandon the bridge, and retreated down the Baltimore pike.

---

[1] In a memorandum of events connected with these operations, given to the author by Colonel Lawrence, Wallace's chief-of-staff, he avers that an officer of Early's staff, after the battle, said that the Confederate army (nearly all of which was in the engagement) consisted of about 16,000 infantry, 52 pieces of artillery, and nearly 6,000 of the best cavalry.

[2] "At one o'clock," says Wallace, in his report, "the three re-enforcing regiments of veterans would be on the ground; and then the splendid behavior of Ricketts and his men inspired me with confidence. One o'clock came, but not the re-enforcements; and it was impossible to get an order to them, for my telegraph operator, and the railroad agent with both his trains, had run away."

Tyler's remaining force, half enveloped by the swarming foe, was compelled to follow; and the general and his staff, separated from them, dashed into the woods, and barely escaped capture. "His gallantry and self-sacrificing devotion," said Wallace, "are above all commendation of words." Pursuit was feeble, for the bulk of Early's cavalry, under Johnson, was then marching on Baltimore by the Liberty road, and the remainder, under M'Causland, were too badly cut up in the fight, for any vigorous action after it.[1] The fugitive army was joined by Ricketts's three absent regiments at Newmarket, and covered the retreat of the wearied troops; and at the distance of twelve miles from the field of strife, the whole army bivouacked.

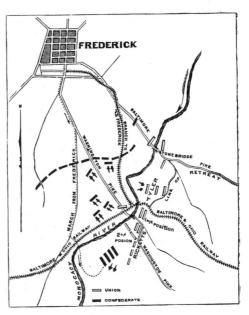

BATTLE OF THE MONOCACY.

So ended THE BATTLE OF THE MONOCACY, in the ultimate defeat of the few National troops there engaged, but in triumph for the National cause; for the check given to the flushed invaders, by Wallace, in that gallant fight of eight hours, which gave time for re-enforcements to reach Washington, saved the Capital.[2] So declared the Secretary of War and the Lieutenant-General.[3] But for that check of full thirty hours (for Early was so smitten that he could not move until noon the next day), the Capital would doubtless have been his prize, and a heap of black ruins its possible fate. In view of all the circumstances, the battle of the Monocacy appears as one of the most important and brilliant of the war.

On the evening after the battle, the inhabitants of Baltimore were in-

[1] Wallace warmly commended the gallantry of Colonel Clendenin, who, he said, was "as true a cavalry soldier as ever mounted a horse." He was cut off from the main body at the time of Ricketts's retreat. Throwing his followers into the village of Urbana, he there repeatedly repulsed the pursuing cavalry, and in one bold charge, saber in hand, he captured the battle-flag of the Seventeenth Virginia.

[2] The number of National troops engaged in the battle, including Ricketts's command, was about 5,500, while about 20,000 of the Confederates were in the fight, or near enough to furnish assistance. The character of the battle may be inferred from the fact that the loss of the Nationals was more than thirty per cent. of their number, being 1,959, of whom 98 were killed, 579 were wounded, and 1,282 were missing, many of the latter having straggled in the retreat. The Confederates took only 700 of them prisoners. The estimated loss of the Confederates was equal to that of the Nationals.

On account of the urgency of the retreat, the want of ambulances, and especially because of the desertion of the railway agent with his trains, Wallace was compelled to leave his dead and wounded on the field. In his report he said that orders had been given to collect the bodies of the slain "in one burial-ground on the battlefield, suitable for a monument, upon which I propose to write: *These men died to save the National Capital, and they did save it.*"

[3] General Grant, in his final report, said: "His (Wallace's) force was not sufficient to insure success; but he fought the enemy, nevertheless, and although it resulted in a defeat to our arms, yet it detained the enemy, and thereby served to enable General Wright to reach Washington with two divisions of the Sixth, and the advance of the Nineteenth Corps, before him."

tensely excited by the report that Wallace's little army was annihilated, and that the victorious Confederates were marching in triumph on that city. The Unionists were alarmed and distressed;[1] the Secessionists were exultant with the belief that they might speedily greet a "liberating army." These feelings were intensified when it was known that Johnson, with his cavalry, were approaching Baltimore next day,[a] which he expected to capture instantly and with ease. He was mistaken. Generals Lockwood and Morris were there, and were ably assisted by Lieutenant-Colonels Lawrence and Woolley.[2] These had rallied thousands of the loyal citizens, who garrisoned all the earthworks thrown up around the city, and guarded every avenue of approach. Johnson saw that the prize could not be won by a dash, as he had expected, and he dared not attempt to do more; so he contented himself with burning bridges and destroying some of the track of the Northern Central railway, and in sending the notorious Gilmor to cut the railroad connection between Baltimore and Philadelphia. This Gilmor did by burning the trestle-work over Gunpowder Inlet; and near Magnolia he stopped the morning trains going north, plundered the passengers and mails, and burned the cars.[3]

[a] "July 10, 1864.

Early, meanwhile, taking counsel of prudence, after his bitter experience at the Monocacy, moved cautiously toward Washington, along the great highway from Frederick to Georgetown, while the remnant of the National troops, under Wallace, took position at Ellicott's Mills. The latter passed into the temporary command of General Ord, and Wallace resumed the special and most difficult and delicate duties of the Middle Department at that time.[4] Had Early pushed rapidly forward after the battle, he might have

---

[1] The following extract of a letter from the wife of the commander of the Department, then in Baltimore, to the wife of the author, written a few days after the battle of Monocacy, will give an idea of the mental sufferings of many of the Union people of that city, at the crisis we are considering: "The papers have told you of the occupation and evacuation of Frederick. Meanwhile, I was at the Eutaw House. Sunday morning the bells rang at daylight for the arming of the militia. Cavalry dashed through the streets, drums beat, men collected in crowds, and terrified women looked from windows on the crowded streets. At about noon it was supposed the rebels were advancing on the city, in which case it would have to be surrendered. Colonel Woolley (Provost-Marshal) came and told me L—— had been defeated, and he expected to surrender the city, and advised me to make every thing ready for flight. I sat a moment and deliberated. I was a thousand miles from home and child—among strangers—my husband in battle against fearful odds. Whatever might come, *I must not break down.* This done, I calmly packed every thing—had bonnet, gloves, all at hand, for instant flight on the boat. The excitement in the city grew more intense. The very air seemed full of rumors, and all knew the place was defenseless, as L—— had taken all the reliable troops with him. I sat a long time waiting, and expecting to hear the rattle of musketry every moment. A message was handed me from L——; I had hardly strength to read— 'I will see you to-night.' A load was off my heart. There was no need of further fortitude; so I gave way, and cried heartily, which was a great relief."

[2] General Wallace says in his report: "On the evening of the 10th (Sunday) I returned to Baltimore, and found the city, very naturally, in a state of alarm, occasioned by the approach of Johnson's cavalry. Thanks, however, to the energy of Lieutenant-Colonel S. B. Lawrence, A. A. General, and Lieutenant-Colonel John Woolley, Provost-Marshal, every measure of safety had been taken that intelligence could suggest. The railroad communications north had been the subject of the former's special care."

[3] Major-General Franklin was one of the passengers, and was in citizen's dress. There were feminine secessionists of Baltimore on the train, who found opportunity to inform Gilmor of the fact. The latter discovered him, and made him his prisoner. He was sent in a light wagon toward Towsontown, with a guard. These, while resting in a wheat-field near the road, fell asleep, Franklin having disarmed their vigilance by pretending to be asleep himself. He arose, walked leisurely by the sleeping sentinels to the road when he ran to a woods, and in an opening beyond concealed himself until night. The Confederates sought for him in vain. Venturing to a house for food on the following day, he found Union people. They sent word to Baltimore, when a squadron of cavalry went out and escorted him back to that city. Gilmor said that when he found that Franklin had escaped, he "swore with unusual energy."

[4] Slavery in Maryland was abolished on the 13th of October, 1864, when the people of Maryland, by a majority of 379, ratified a new Constitution for that State, making provision for the freedom of all. Evil-disposed slave-holders tried to evade the law, and General Wallace found it necessary to issue a general order on the 9th

captured Washington and inflicted serious damage, but he could not have held the city. But, as we have observed, he was so crippled by the fight, that he did not move until noon the next day, and then he marched so carefully, that it was not until two days after the battle that he appeared in formidable force in front of the northeastern fortifications of Washington,[1] in the vicinity of Fort Stevens. By that time the safety of the city was assured, for during that day[a] the remainder of the Sixth [a] July 11, 1864. Corps arrived there, and was speedily followed by the divisions of Dwight and Grover, of Emory's (Nineteenth) corps, which had just arrived at Fortress Monroe by sea, from New Orleans, and had been sent immediately up the Potomac to the Capital by Grant.

On the following day Early menaced Washington, when Augur sent out a strong reconnoitering party from Fort Stevens, to develop the strength of the Confederates. A sharp skirmish ensued, in which each party lost almost three hundred men. Satisfied that the opportunity for seizing Washington was passed, and alarmed by information of the concentration of troops there, the Confederate leader began a retreat with his entire force, now reduced to fifteen thousand men. He crossed the Potomac at Edwards's Ferry [b] July 12. that night[b] with a large amount of booty,[2] and moved through Leesburgh and Snicker's Gap to the Shenandoah Valley. General Wright, of the Sixth Corps, to whom Grant had now assigned the command of all the troops at Washington available for operations in the field, pursued in the track of the fugitives. His advance overtook them[c] at Snick- [c] July 18. er's Ferry, on the Shenandoah River. General Crook, with his cavalry, had struck them at Snicker's Gap the previous day. At the ferry

---

of November, establishing a freedman's bureau—the first ever organized—and placing "all persons within the limits of the Middle Department, heretofore slaves, but now free by the operation of the new Constituttion,"

under "special military protection." The chain of the last slave in Maryland was literally removed by Wallace. That slave was a bright girl, nineteen years of age, named Margaret Toogood. She left her former master in Anne Arundel County, on gaining her freedom, and went to Baltimore. That master procured her arrest on a charge of theft. She was taken back, when he withdrew the charge, his object of getting possession of her being accomplished. Then, to prevent her going away again, he put an iron

. LAST SLAVE-CHAIN IN MARYLAND.

chain about her neck, and fast-ened it with a rude clasp which a blacksmith had prepared. Hearing of this outrage, Wallace ordered the girl to be brought to Baltimore, where, in the office of the Provost-Marshal, the chain was removed, and *the last bond-slave in Maryland* was set free. That chain—that relic of a barbarous social system—is before me while I write. It was made of rough iron; its links were two inches in length, and its entire weight, with the clasp, was between three and four pounds, and its length 17 inches. The girl wore this horrible necklace seven weeks.

[1] See map on page 24, volume II.

[2] While the invaders were in Maryland, the cavalry, under Johnson, especially those under Gilmor, destroyed a vast amount of public and private property, and carried a great deal away with them. The railways, the telegraph lines, and the Chesapeake and Ohio canal were injured to the estimated aggregate value of over $600,000. The Baltimore and Ohio railway suffered to the amount of $400,000, and the other two, running north, to the amount of $100,000 each. The damages to fences and small farms was estimated at $250,000. The invasion cost Maryland, according to the report of the committee of the Legislature, $2,030,000. Among the private property wantonly destroyed were the dwellings of the then Governor of Maryland (Bradford) and Montgomery Blair, who had lately left the position of Postmaster-General.

there was a sharp skirmish, when the passage was cleared, and Crook and his horsemen crossed the stream. Then Breckinridge turned upon them,

and drove them back with considerable loss. Another portion of the National cavalry had a fight, at about the same time, at Ashby's Gap, and in the two encounters the Union loss was about five hundred men. Early then moved forward as if continuing his retreat, when Wright, handing the command over to Crook, returned to Washington, and the former, with the troops, went to Harper's Ferry. General Averill, in the mean time, had moved toward Winchester from Martinsburg, and near the former place encountered a body of Confederates, with whom he fought[a] about three

[a] July 20, 1864.

HORATIO G. WRIGHT.

hours, and vanquished them. They lost nearly four hundred men (two hundred of them made prisoners), with four guns. Averill's loss was about two hundred. He was compelled to fall back, for he was menaced by Early, who approached from Snicker's Ferry.

Grant found it difficult to understand exactly the situation in the Shenandoah Valley. There was confusion in dispatches; but there seemed to be a general agreement in saying that Early was retreating up the Valley toward Lynchburg or Richmond, whereupon the Lieutenant-General ordered the Sixth and Nineteenth Corps to hasten to Petersburg by water, to assist in an assault upon the Confederate lines there, before the invaders of Maryland should rejoin Lee. But events soon caused that order to be countermanded. Supposing Early was moving up the Valley, Crook marched from Harper's Ferry on Winchester. When at Kernstown, a little beyond that city, he suddenly felt the heavy pressure of his foe on front and flank. His cavalry were pushed back[b] on the main body, and on the following day Crook's entire force was driven, in some confusion, to Martinsburg, with a loss of twelve hundred men, including General Mulligan,[1] who was killed. Early pursued as far as that town, and on the following day[c] there was a sharp cannon fight there, which enabled Crook to get his trains safely across the Potomac. He followed with his troops, and Early was left sole master of the southern side of the river, from Shepherdstown to Williamsport.

[b] July 23.

[c] July 25.

Emboldened by his success, and animated by the knowledge that he had many sympathizers in Maryland and Western Pennsylvania, Early sent about three thousand cavalry, under M'Causland, Johnson, and others, upon a plundering and devastating raid in the direction of the Susquehanna. They swept in excentric lines over the country, thereby distracting the armed defenders of it, and on the 30th of July entered the defenseless and partially

---

[1] See an account of Mulligan's defense of Lexington, in Missouri, volume II., page 69.

deserted village of Chambersburg,[1] in Pennsylvania, and demanded of the inhabitants two hundred thousand dollars in gold, or five hundred thousand dollars in "greenbacks"[2] or currency, as a tribute to insure the town from destruction. The tribute was not offered, and two-thirds of the town was laid in ruins by fire.[3] No time was given for the removal of the infirm or sick, or the women and children; but in ten minutes after M'Causland ordered Gilmor, his torch-bearer on the occasion, to apply fire, the village was in flames.[4] The Confederate leader offered as an excuse for the act, the fact that Hunter a few weeks before had burned the house of Governor Letcher, at Lexington, in Virginia.[5]

The incendiaries did not remain long, for General Averill, who, with twenty-six hundred cavalry, was at Greencastle, ten miles distant, when Chambersburg was fired, charged by General Couch to watch the raiders, was moving against them. He pursued them to Hancock, on the Potomac (where they crossed), smiting them on the way with sufficient effect to save McConnellstown from the fate of Chambersburg. All Western Pennsylvania and Upper Maryland were filled with a panic. It was the general belief that Early was again north of the Potomac in full force. The alarm was intensified by a dash across the river by Moseby the marauder,[6] who carried back with his plunder a few horsemen as prisoners. The order of Grant for the two corps to hasten to Petersburg was countermanded. They had been halted at Georgetown when news of the defeat of Crook at Winchester was received, and were turned back. They had reached Harper's Ferry on the day when Chambersburg was burnt, and were there joined by some of Hunter's long-expected troops, coming from West Virginia; and then the entire force, with an immense train, went on a fruitless search for Early, who was supposed to be laying waste Western Pennsylvania. But the Confederate troopers were getting back to Virginia as fast as possible. General Kelley,[7] in command at Cumberland, struck Johnson when he was passing; and Johnson, in turn, had routed five hundred Nationals in that region, and captured their leader and ninety of his men. As the invaders retreated up the south branch of the Potomac, Averill closely pursued them, and at Moorfield he attacked[a] and vanquished them,

[a] August 4, 1864.

---

[1] Capital of Franklin County, and then containing about 5,000 inhabitants.

[2] The National currency had devices and lettering printed on the back of each bill, in green ink, as a protection against counterfeiting. Hence, these bills were called "greenbacks."

[3] This act was in accordance with the instructions of General Early, if the Marylander who was commissioned to fire the town tells the truth. Gilmor says, in his *Four Years in the Saddle*, page 210: "He (M'Causland) ordered me to fire the town, and showed me General Early's order to that effect."

[4] Letters of Rev. B. S. Schenck, D. D., an eye-witness. "They would beat in the door of each house with iron bars or heavy plank," says Dr. Schenck, "smash up furniture with an ax, throw fluid or oil upon it, and apply the match. They almost invariably entered every room of each house, rifled the drawers of every bureau, appropriated money, jewelry, watches, and any other valuables, and often would present pistols to the heads of inmates, men and women, and demand money or their lives." Twenty-five hundred persons were rendered houseless in the space of two hours, and the value of property destroyed was estimated at $1,000,000.

[5] This act had already been twice avenged, by the burning of the houses of Governor Bradford and Montgomery Blair, in Maryland, as we have observed. "Circumstances alter cases." The destruction of Letcher's house was held, by publicists, to have been justified by the ethics of war. Letcher was a traitor to his Government and a public enemy, and the destruction of his house was incited wholly by the finding, in a newspaper office at Lexington, a handbill, issued and signed by him, calling on the people of that region to "bushwack" Hunter's men, that is to say, murder them by bullets from concealed places. The citizens of Chambersburg were non-combatants, and innocent of all crime in relation to the Confederates.

[6] See page 22.

[7] See page 496, volume I.

and captured their guns, trains, and five hundred men, with a loss to himself of only about fifty men.[1]

Grant was now satisfied that an efficient force was needed in the Shenandoah Valley, for the protection of Washington from seizure, and Maryland and Pennsylvania from invasion, and he proceeded to consolidate the Washington, Middle, Susquehanna, and Southwest Virginia Departments into one, called the Middle Military Division, under the command of General Hunter. The latter expressed a willingness to be relieved, and Grant assigned[a] General Philip H. Sheridan to the command of the new organization. He entered at once upon his duties, and found himself at the head of over thirty thousand troops, with which to confront Early with about twenty thousand.[2]

August 7, 1864.

Let us here leave Sheridan, and return to the army before Petersburg. We have observed that the Nationals had secured a footing at Deep Bottom, on the north side of the James, and a quick communication between it and the main army by means of a pontoon bridge.[3] This movement was a part of a plan of assault on the Confederate lines at Petersburg, in connection with the blowing up of one of the most powerful of the enemy's forts, situated within about a thousand yards of the city. This was to be done by the explosion of a mine under the fort, which had been for nearly a month in preparation, under the immediate supervision of Lieutenant-Colonel Henry Pleasants, of the Forty-eighth Pennsylvania, of Burnside's corps. He was a practical miner; and a greater portion of the men of his regiment had been recruited in the mining district. He suggested the enterprise to General Potter, and when that officer proposed it to General Burnside, their corps commander, he heartily approved it. With indifferent tools and a great lack of proper materials, Pleasants began the task on the 25th of June, and on the 23d of July the mine was ready for use.[4]

---

[1] So wild were rumors, that on the day when Averill defeated the Confederates at Moorfield, the impression was so strong that Early was across the Potomac with his army, heading toward the Susquehanna, that Governor Curtin issued[a] a proclamation calling out 30,000 militia, and the inhabitants of the Cumberland Valley commenced another exodus from their homes, with cattle and other property.

August 4.

[2] Sheridan's column for active operations consisted of the Sixth and Nineteenth Corps, and the infantry and cavalry of West Virginia, under Generals Crook and Averill. To these were added the cavalry divisions of Torbert and Wilson, sent to him from the army before Petersburg. His cavalry force was about ten thousand strong, and in fine condition.

[3] See page 339.

[4] The advance of the Ninth (Burnside's) Corps was within 200 yards of one of the strongest of the Confederate forts on the Petersburg lines, under which a mine was constructed. It was commenced in a hollow within Burnside's lines, just in the rear of a deep cut of the City Point railway, entirely concealed from the Confederates. The work was performed by the enlisted men of the Forty-eighth Regiment, nearly 400 in number, under the special direction of Lieutenant-Colonel Pleasants. The excavation was made through soft earth for some distance, when a stratum of marl, of the consistence of putty, was encountered, to avoid which the direction of the gallery was made to assume that of an inclined plane for about 100 feet. The earth (18,000 cubic feet in bulk) was taken out in barrows constructed of cracker-boxes, and concealed under brushwood, for it was important that no knowledge of the work should reach the Confederates. On the 17th of July the main gallery was completed, 510 feet in length, when lateral galleries were made under the doomed fort, for the magazines of gunpowder. These extended about 37 feet on each side of the termination of the main gallery. The powder, consisting of 320 kegs in bulk, or about 8,000 pounds, was placed in eight magazines, connected by wooden tubes half filled with powder. These were connected with three lines of fuses in the main gallery. These excavations were made secure from accident by lining the sides and tops of the galleries with timber and plank, in the manner shown by a section of the main gallery here represented. The gallery was 4½ feet in height, and a little less in width at the bottom.

SECTION OF MAIN GALLERY

It was at about this time that the lodgment at Deep Bottom was made. Lee sent troops to expel Foster, but their attempts to do so were unsuccess-

ful. Finally, when the mine was ready, Grant ordered Hancock to join Foster, and with his Second Corps and two divisions of Sheridan's cavalry, to flank the Confederates at Deep Bottom, and push on toward Chapin's Bluff, a little below opposite Fort Darling, on Drewry's Bluff, by which Lee's line of communi-

CHAPIN'S BLUFF FROM FORT DARLING.[1]

cation across the river would be seriously menaced. These troops crossed the James on the night of the 26th,[a] and on the following morning, while Foster amused the Confederates on their front, Miles's

[a] July, 1864.

brigade of Barlow's division flanked them, and captured four of their guns. They fell back to a strong position behind Baylis's creek, where they blocked the way to the heavy works on Chapin's Bluff, which Sheridan attempted to flank. He gained an advantageous position on high ground, and was preparing to make an attempt to get in the rear of the Confederate stronghold, when night compelled him to suspend his movement.

These menacing operations had the desired effect. To meet the seemingly impending danger to Richmond, Lee withdrew five of his eight remaining divisions from the south side of the James, between the 27th and 29th,[b] and the opportunity for the assault which Grant had been

[b] July.

waiting for was now offered. The lines before him were weakened, and Early was yet in the Shenandoah Valley; so he arranged for an explosion of the mine on the morning of the 30th, and a co-operating assault upon the Confederate works in front of Burnside's corps, where, within one hundred and fifty yards of his lines, a strong six gun fort projected beyond the average of the front of his adversary. This was the doomed fortification. About four hundred yards behind it was Cemetery Hill, crowned by a battery, which commanded Petersburg and the most important of the Confederate works. It was believed that if that crest could be seized and held by the Nationals, the city must quickly fall, with heavy loss to its defenders. This crest was, therefore, the chief objective in the impending assault.

Every thing was in readiness on the night of the 29th of July. The explosion was to be followed by an immediate opening of the great guns all along the front, and by an assault at the breach to be made by the active mine. This was to be done by a division of Burnside's corps, one of which was composed of negro troops. The Lieutenant-General refused to have the

[1] In this little picture Chapin's Bluff is denoted in the extreme distance by a series of white spots along the edge of the water. The spectator is standing in an embrasure of Fort Darling, on Drewry's Bluff, looking directly down the James River. The single bird in the distance is over the place of the fortifications at Chapin's Bluff. The three birds nearer are hovering over the remains of obstructions in the river, just below Fort Darling.

latter-named division employed for the purpose, and Ledlie's, composed of white men, was chosen by lot for the perilous duty.[1] It stood ready for action at half-past three o'clock in the morning, the hour appointed for the explosion. An accident postponed that event until almost five o'clock,[2] when the fort, its guns, caissons, and other munitions of war, and its garrison of three hundred men, were thrown high in air and annihilated. In the place of the fortification was left a crater of loose earth two hundred feet in length, full fifty in width, and twenty-five to thirty feet in depth. The National guns then opened a heavy cannonade and bombardment, with precision and effect,[4] all along the line. To this only a feeble response was given by the astounded Confederates,[5] and the way seemed open for the easy capture of the coveted Cemetery Hill beyond the crater, by the assaulting column.

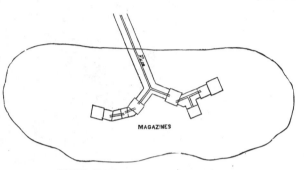

OUTLINE OF THE CRATER AND THE MAGAZINES.[3]

But that column moved slowly and feebly, first in clearing away most dangerous obstructions,[6] and then in halting in the crater, as if seeking shelter from a storm of shot and shell. No such storm occurred until long after the explosion;[7] yet Ledlie's division went no further than the site of the ruined fort. Portions of the divisions of Potter and Wilcox followed, but their way toward the crest was blocked by Ledlie's halted column. Then the division of colored soldiers, under General Ferrero, was sent forward to storm the hill. For a moment it seemed as if those troops would be successful. They pushed well up toward the crest, and captured some men; but they,

---

[1] This division was composed of two brigades, the first led by General J. J. Bartlett, and the second by Colonel Marshall, and consisted of the Ninth, Twenty-first, Thirty-fifth, Fifty-sixth, Fifty-seventh, and Fifty-ninth Massachusetts, under Bartlett, and the One Hundredth Pennsylvania, One Hundred and Seventy-ninth New York, Third Maryland, Second Pennsylvania Heavy Artillery, and the Fourteenth New York Heavy Artillery, under Marshall.

[2] Pleasants lighted the fuse at a quarter past three o'clock, and waited an hour for the explosion, when Lieutenant Jacob Douty and Sergeant Henry Reese, of Pleasants's regiment, volunteered to go in and examine into the cause of the delay. The fire had stopped where the fuses had been spliced. They were relighted by these daring men, and at sixteen minutes before five o'clock the mine exploded. See Pleasants's Report.

[3] This shows the outline of the crater and the position of the magazines which composed the mine. It is copied from Pleasants's Report.

[4] General Hunt, the Chief of Artillery, in his report, speaks of the manner of firing on that occasion, as "partaking of the nature of target practice," and which "was very effective."

[5] The Confederates had received intimation of the construction of this mine, and had begun a counter-mine in search of it; but they had no positive knowledge concerning its progress or destination.

[6] In front of their works the Confederates had strong *abatis*, and also tripping wires, such as the Nationals used at Knoxville and elsewhere. Among these were sharp stakes, which might impale those who were thrown down by the wires.

[7] Lieutenant-Colonel Pleasants, in his report, made on the 2d of August, says:—"I stood on the top of our breastworks, and witnessed the effect of the explosion on the enemy. It so completely paralyzed them, that the breadth of the breach, instead of being two hundred feet, was practically four or five hundred yards. The rebels in the forts both on the right and left of the explosion ran away, and for over an hour, as well as I could judge, not a shot was fired by their artillery. There was no fire from the infantry from the front for at least half an hour, none from the left for twenty minutes, and but few shots from the right."

too, were soon hurled back by a heavy fire. They rallied and again advanced, when they were repulsed a second time. Then they fled in confusion to the vicinity of the crater, where the whole body of disordered troops, huddled in small space, were confused and mingled, and subjected to a concentrated fire from the Confederates, who had rallied and were bringing to bear upon the swarm of assailants their musketry and heavy guns with terrible effect. Shot and shell and minie bullets were poured upon the confused mass like hail, and the slaughter was dreadful. To remain was to court death; to retreat was to invite destruction; for the ground between the lines was swept by the Confederate artillery. At length a column of the foe charged upon the Nationals at the crater, and were repulsed. A second charge scattered the dismayed fragments of the Ninth Corps, which had made attempts to retreat in squads, when it was found that their comrades in the trenches could not aid them. Each man was now attentive only to his own safety in flight. In this wretched affair the Nationals lost about four thousand four hundred men, and the Confederates less than one thousand, including those who were blown up with the fort. It was a most conspicuous and disastrous failure, and the Confederates were greatly encouraged and comforted by it.

Grant was disappointed, but not discouraged, by the failure of the 30th. He paused about twelve days, and then ordered Hancock to attack the Confederates in front of Deep Bottom. Hancock was joined, for the purpose, by the remainder of the Tenth Corps (to which Foster's division belonged), under Birney,[1] and Gregg's cavalry division; and for the purpose of misleading the foe, the whole expeditionary force was placed on transports at City Point, and its destination was reported to be Washington City. That night[a] it went up the James River to Deep Bottom; but so tardy was the debarkation, that an intended surprise of the Confederates was prevented. ^a *a August 12, 1864.*

It was nine o'clock in the morning[b] before the troops were ready to move, when Hancock pushed out the Second Corps by the Malvern Hills and New Market road, to flank the Confederate defenses behind Baylis's Creek. He sent Barlow with about ten thousand men to assault the flank and rear of the foe, while Mott's division threatened their intrenched front, and Birney's corps attacked them nearer the river. But the delay had allowed Lee to send re-enforcements, and the operations of the day were of little account to the Nationals, excepting advantages gained by Birney, who captured four guns. *b August 13.*

Considering Richmond in danger, Lee rapidly sent re-enforcements, and the Nationals were compelled to adopt new plans and make other dispositions. On the morning of the 16th,[c] General Birney made a direct attack on the Confederate lines with General Terry's division. That gallant officer carried the lines, and captured nearly three hundred men, with three battle-flags; but the foe soon rallied in heavier force, and drove him back. In the mean time, Gregg, supported by Miles's "fighting brigade," of Barlow's division, had been operating on the Charles *c August.*

---

[1] Several changes had been made. General Gillmore was succeeded in the command of the Tenth Corps by General Birney, and General W. F. Smith, of the Eighteenth Corps, was succeeded by General Ord.

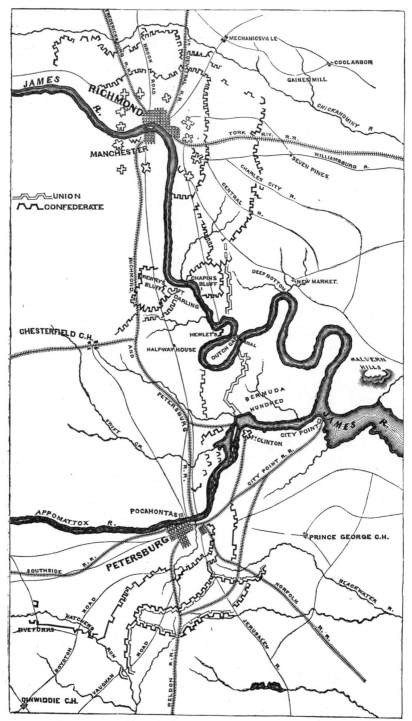

DEFENSES OF RICHMOND AND PETERSBURG.

City road, with the view of drawing the Confederates out of their intrenchments. He drove their van some distance, and killed their General Cham-
bliss; but he was soon driven back, and no special advantage to the Union
cause was obtained.

Other efforts to draw the Confederates from their intrenchments were made,
one of which was the sending of a fleet of vessels up to Deep Bottom on the
night of the 16th, to give the impression that the Union troops were about
to be withdrawn. The deception did not succeed; and after spending two
or three days, chiefly in reconnoitering, Hancock and Gregg were ordered to
return to the lines before Petersburg. This they did, by way of
Bermuda Hundred, on the 20th. Meanwhile, Birney was at- ª August 18
tacked ª by a heavy force; but after a fight of twenty minutes, in   1864.
which Miles, with two brigades, participated, the Confederates were repulsed.
In this demonstration against Richmond the Nationals lost about five thousand men, and the Confederates a somewhat less number.

Taking advantage of the absence of many of Lee's troops from Petersburg, Grant made a vigorous movement for securing possession of the Weldon road, not more than three miles from the left flank of his lines on the
Jerusalem plank road. This movement was made by Warren, with the
Fifth Corps, on the morning of the 18th of August, and at noon he reached
the coveted railway without opposition, where he left Griffin to hold the
point seized, while with the divisions of Ayres and Crawford he moved
toward Petersburg. He had marched but a short distance, when a division
of Confederates suddenly and heavily fell upon his flank, and plucked from
a Maryland brigade two hundred prisoners. That brigade immediately received shelter and aid from the Fifteenth New York Heavy Artillery, acting
as infantry, who soon repulsed the assailants. Warren held the ground he
had gained at a cost of one thousand men killed, wounded and prisoners,
and from that moment the use of the important Weldon railroad was lost to
the Confederates.

Lee now sent a heavy force, under Hill, to drive Warren from the road,
and on the following day [b] that leader flanked the Nationals, and
fell furiously upon Crawford's division in flank and rear, compel-   b August 19.
ling the whole of his force and the right of Ayres to fall back. In this struggle Hill captured twenty-five hundred Nationals, including General J. Hays.
Yet the troops clung to the railway; and when, shortly afterward, the brigades of Wilcox and White, of Burnside's corps, came up,[1] Hill hastily withdrew. Then Warren recovered the ground he had lost, re-established his
lines, intrenched his position, and prepared for desperate attacks, for he was
satisfied that the Confederates would make every possible effort to repossess
the road.

Warren's expectations were soon realized. Three days later [c]
he was suddenly assailed by a cross-fire of thirty guns, and then   c August 21.
by two columns of infantry, one moving against his front, and the other
making an effort to turn his flank. He was so well prepared, that the force
on his front was easily repulsed; and flanking the turning column, he broke

---

[1] General Wilcox was now in command of the Ninth Corps, General Burnside having been relieved a few
days before.

it into wild confusion, and captured five hundred prisoners. The Confederate loss in this affair was full twelve hundred men. In his entire movement for the possession of the road, Warren lost in killed, wounded, and missing, four thousand four hundred and fifty men. He now rendered his position almost impregnable, and General Lee was compelled to see one of his most important lines of communication wrested from him.

On the day of Warren's victory,[a] Hancock, who, as we have seen, had been called from the north bank of the James, and who had moved with a part of his corps rapidly toward the Weldon road, in the rear of Warren, struck that highway north of Reams's Station, and destroyed the track to that point and some miles south of it. He formed an intrenched camp at Reams's, and his cavalry kept up a vigilant scout in the direction of the Confederate army. These on the 25th reported the approach of foes, when to the divisions of Gibbon and Barlow (the latter then in command of General Miles) was assigned the duty of defending the intrenched position. The blow, given as usual by Hill, fell first on Miles, who promptly repelled the assailants. In a second attack they were again repulsed, with heavy loss. But Hill was determined to capture the works, and he ordered Heth's division to do so at all hazards. That commander then concentrated a powerful artillery fire on the Nationals, and this was followed by a storming force, which, by desperate charges, succeeded in breaking Miles's line, and in capturing the batteries of McKnight, Perrin, and Sleeper. Hancock then ordered Gibbon to retake the works and guns; but his efforts to do so failed. Miles rallied a part of his broken column (Sixty-first New York), and by desperate fighting recovered some of the lost ground and McKnight's guns. At the same time Gibbon was assailed by some dismounted cavalry and driven, when the pursuit was checked by a flank fire. The Nationals retreated to a rear line, where the troops had been rallied, and when night fell Hancock withdrew from Reams's Station. He had lost in the fight twenty-four hundred of his eight thousand men, and five guns. Seventeen hundred of the men were made prisoners. Hill's loss was but little less, and he, too, withdrew from Reams's. But this disaster did not loosen Warren's hold upon the Weldon road, and the Confederates gained nothing by their victory.

For about a month after THE BATTLE OF REAMS'S STATION, there was comparative quiet along the lines of the opposing armies.[1] It was broken by General Grant, who, believing that only a few troops were then occupying the Confederate works on the north side of the James, ordered General Butler to cross over the river from Bermuda Hundred, with the Tenth and Eighteenth Corps (commanded respectively by Generals Birney and Ord), and Kautz's cavalry, and attempt, by a sudden and rapid movement, to capture Richmond before Lee could send troops to prevent it. If Lee should do so, and successfully resist the movement, his withdrawal of forces from the

[a] August 21, 1864.

---

[1] During this time the Confederates made a bold and successful dash for food. General Hampton, with a heavy cavalry force, made a wide circuit around the National left from Reams's Station,[a] and [a] Sept. 16. swept down to Sycamore Church, near Coggins's Point, opposite Harrison's Landing, where he seized, and then drove back to the Confederate lines, 2,500 beef cattle, and carried with him about 300 men and their horses, of the Thirteenth Pennsylvania, who were guarding the herd; also 200 mules and 32 wagons. Hampton lost about 50 men.

south side for the purpose, would favor the contemplated movement of Meade's army against the right flank of the Confederates at Petersburg. And so the enterprise promised success for the Nationals, at one end of the line at least. Birney was to cross the river at Deep Bottom, and Ord at Aiken's Landing, eight miles above. Both were to be on the north side of the river, and ready to advance rapidly at daybreak on the morning of the 29th of September. Birney was to capture the Confederate works in front of Deep Bottom, and gain the New Market road; and Ord was to capture the works near Chapin's Bluff, and destroy Lee's pontoon bridge across the river there. Then the two corps were to press on rapidly toward Richmond.

Already a strong party of colored soldiers had been set to work[a] by General Butler, on the north side of the James, under cover of a battery on that side mounting 100-pounder Parrott guns, in dig-   [a] Aug. 15, 1864. ging a canal across the narrow isthmus of a peninsula, formed by a sharp bend in the river, called Farrar's Island. By this canal it was intended to secure a nearer base of oper-ations against Rich-mond, and afford a passage for the Na-tional war vessels, by which they might flank several import-ant works of the Confederates, and avoid formidable ob-structions in the river around that bend of six or seven miles. One of the most im-

BATTERY NEAR DUTCH GAP.[1]

portant of these works was on a hill on the right bank of the James, near the dwelling of Dr. Howlett, and known as the Howlett House Battery. During the period of about one hundred and forty days, while troops were engaged in the excavation of the canal, this battery annoyed the workmen by throwing a shell in that direction once in every hour or two, by which quite a number were killed or wounded. To avoid this danger as much as possible, they excavated the high alluvial bank of the James, and there built their huts to dwell in, and to use as a shelter from the missiles of the foe.[2] The work on the canal was considerably advanced when the enterprise we are now considering was undertaken.

---

[1] This shows the interior of the battery, as it appeared when the writer visited it, at the close of December, 1864. It was a powerful work, called Fort Brady. The picture shows one of the embrasures, with a 100-pounder Parrott gun.

[2] This canal was finished at the close of December, 1864, with the exception of blowing out the bulkhead of earth, which had been left on the upper side, to keep out the water. It was five hundred yards in length, 60 feet in width at the top, and 60 feet below the surface of the bluff. It was excavated 15 feet below high water mark. On New Year's day (1865) a mine of 12,000 pounds of gunpowder was exploded under the bulkhead, and the water rushed through, but not in sufficient depth for practical purposes, for the mass of the bulkhead, a part of it blue clay, fell back into the opening after the explosion. That opening being now swept by Con-federate cannon, the channel could not be dredged. As an engineering operation for the improvement of the river navigation, it was a success; as a military operation it was a failure. The work was done under the direction of Major Peter S. Michie, Acting Chief-Engineer of the Army of the James.

According to arrangement, Ord and Birney crossed the river on pontoon bridges muffled with hay on the night of the 28th, the former at

HUTS AT DUTCH GAP.[1]

Aiken's and the latter at Deep Bottom. Ord pushed along the Varina road at dawn. His chief commanders were Generals Burnham, Weitzel, Heckman, Roberts and Stannard, and Colonel Stevens. His van soon encountered the Confederate pickets, and after a march of about three miles, they came upon the intrenchments below Chapin's farm, the strongest point of which was Battery Harrison, on a hill overlooking a great extent of country. It was a very important work—the strongest around Richmond—but had not then its full complement of men, though re-enforcements were hurrying toward it. This fort Ord stormed and carried, together with a long line of breastworks, capturing twenty-two pieces of heavy ordnance, and about three hundred men. But the victory was gained at fearful cost. General Burnham was killed; Stannard lost an arm; Ord was severely wounded; and about seven hundred men were lost by death or maiming, chiefly of Stannard's command, which bore the brunt of the assault. Weitzel assumed the direction of the Eighteenth Corps when Ord was disabled; and Battery Harrison was named Fort Burnham, in honor of the slain general. An attempt was made to capture Fort Gilmer, a little further on, but the assailants were repulsed with a loss of about three hundred men.

In the mean time Birney had moved out from Deep Bottom to assail the works on Spring Hill of New Market Heights. Three thousand colored troops of the Eighteenth Corps, under General Charles Paine, were put in column of division by General Butler, and sent in the advance. They pushed rapidly forward, drove in the Confederate pickets, and proceeded to assail a redoubt on Spring Hill. This was a strong work, with a tangled marsh, and a brook fringed with trees, that traversed it on the front; and it was further defended by *abatis*. These obstacles were little hinderance to the eager troops. They swept across the marsh and the stream, scaled the height, carried the work at the point of the bayonet, and thus secured[a] the key-point to the Confederate defenses in that quarter. Because of its importance it was desperately defended; and it was won by the black warriors at a fearful cost. Two hundred of that storming party fell dead before reaching the works, and not less than one thousand, or one-third their number, were lost to the army by death, wounds, or captivity. For their gallantry on that occasion, General Butler,

[a] Sept. 29, 1864.

---

[1] This was the appearance of the north bank of the James River, at Dutch Gap, when the writer sketched it, at the close of 1864. The bank was there almost perpendicular, and rose about thirty feet above the water. These huts and excavations were near the top.

at the close of the war, presented a silver medal to the most meritorious actors.[1]

Battery Harrison was so important to the Confederates, that a desperate attempt was made[a] to retake it under the immediate direction of General Lee, who massed some of his best troops against it, under Generals Hoke and Field.   They were driven back with a loss of seven battle-flags, and the almost annihilation of Clingman's (North Carolina) brigade.[2]   Meanwhile General Kautz had pushed up the Charles City road to the inner lines of the Confederates, within three or four miles of Richmond, where he was attacked[b] and driven back with a loss of nine guns and about four hundred men made prisoners, by General Anderson, who tried to turn the National right.   The assailants speedily encountered the Tenth Corps, and in a severe battle that ensued, they were driven back toward Richmond, with a loss of three commanders of brigades, and about seven hundred men.

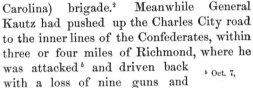

Oct. 1, 1864.

b Oct. 7,

THE BUTLER MEDAL.

Taking advantage of the absence of a part of Lee's force from his right, General Meade sent Warren with two divisions of his corps, Parke with two divisions of the Ninth, and Gregg, with his cavalry division, to attempt the extension of the National left beyond the Weldon road, in the direction of the Southside railway.   In this movement, during the first and second days of October, there was much, and, at times, severe fighting, with varying fortunes for both parties.   The Confederates determined to protect the Southside road at all hazards, and fought desperately to maintain advanced and intrenched positions.   But they were gradually pushed back toward the Boydton road, where the Nationals seized, held, and intrenched

---

[1] The engraving represents the medal, in form, device, and size. The design on each side is simple, and explains itself. The medal was suspended by a strong red, white, and blue ribbon. In reply to a question concerning the history of the medal, made by the author, General Butler wrote on the 8th of March, 1868 :— "Never was a charge more gallantly made, or works more splendidly carried, although with very considerable loss, but the troops never faltered. Some of the companies, by the loss of their officers, were under the command of their colored sergeants only, and yet were carried forward in good order. As I could not promote these men to officers for their gallantry, and as Congress had made no provision for a medal to colored troops, I determined to have one struck, and designed the one you have, some two hundred of which were afterward distributed to these brave men—the only silver medals given to private soldiers during the war."

[2] General Butler's Address to the Soldiers of the Army of the James, October 11, 1864.

a position about three miles westward of the Weldon road, at a cost of about twenty-five hundred men. In one of these encounters, the Confederate General Dunnovan was killed.

Now, again, there was a pause, but not a settled rest,[1] for Grant had determined not to put his troops into winter quarters until another effort should be made to turn the flanks of the Confederate army, capture or disperse it, and seize Petersburg and Richmond. He proceeded to find the right of Lee's line, for the purpose of turning it and seizing upon the Southside railroad, now become the principal channel of supplies for the Confederate troops.[2] The expedition for the purpose was composed of the Second, Fifth, and Ninth Corps of the Army of the Potomac. Of these, a sufficient number of men was left to hold the Union intrenchments in front of Petersburg. At the same time General Butler was to make a demonstration in force against Lee's left, on the north side of the river, with the Army of the James.

A few miles west of the Weldon road was the Boydton plank road, which was now Lee's chief channel of communication in that quarter; and for its protection he had extended his intrenchments some distance along its line, in the vicinity of its passage of a stream called Hatcher's Run. These works also constituted defenses for the Southside railroad, which there ran parallel with the plank road. The task of attacking the extreme right of that intrenched line was assigned to the Ninth (Parke's) Corps, supported by the Fifth (Warren's) Corps, while the Second (Hancock's), accompanied by Gregg's cavalry division well to its left, should swing round to the west side of Hatcher's Run, sweep across the Boydton road, and seize the Southside railway.

These movements began before daybreak on the morning of the 27th of October.[a] The Ninth and Fifth Corps, the former on the right and the latter on the left, struck the right of the Confederate line at nine o'clock in the morning. Parke failed to break the line, and was repulsed; whereupon Warren, according to arrangement, proceeded to cross Hatcher's Run in an attempt to turn the Confederate flank and gain its rear. In the mean time, Hancock, who was passing round further to the left, had gained the Boydton road near Burgess's mill, without much opposition, and with Gregg's cavalry was about to push on and strike the Southside road, when he was halted by an order from General Meade, who informed him that a division of Warren's corps was making its way to the west of Hatcher's Run, with instructions to form a connection with the Second Corps, and open the way for the rest of the troops in that direction.

Warren had attempted his turning movement by sending Crawford's division, supported by one of Ayres's brigades, across Hatcher's Run, at Armstrong's mill, with instructions to move up that stream in the direction of the Boydton road. Crawford soon found himself in an almost impenetrable swamp, in which his forces were broken and confused. In the course

---

[1] While no great movements were in progress during this pause, there was almost daily cannonading and picket-firing along the intrenched front of the two armies, and sometimes sanguinary encounters, yet none of these events had any special bearing upon the final result.

[2] This was the direct railway communication with Lynchburg, then the principal depot of supplies for the Confederate army.

of more than two hours of exhausting efforts, he reached a position directly on the flank of the Confederate line, with the run between his forces and Warren's main body. The latter, finding the nature of the country very different from what he supposed it to be, ordered Crawford to halt until Meade could be consulted. At the same time Gibbon's division, under General Eagan, was pushing out from Hancock's column, to form a connection with Crawford's; but so dense was the tangled wood of the swamp, that each commander was ignorant of the proximity of the other, though the distance between them was scarcely a mile.

These movements had been eagerly watched by the Confederates, and Hill's leading division, under Heth, was sent to attack Hancock's isolated force before the remainder of the Army of the Potomac should cross Hatcher's Run. Heth moved so stealthily, that the first intimation of his presence was given at four o'clock in the afternoon by volleys of musketry and a furious charge upon Pierce's brigade of Mott's division. That startled brigade gave way, and left two guns as spoil for the assailants. The latter eagerly pursued the fugitives over an open space along the Boydton road, when they were struck heavily by Eagan, who, on hearing the sounds of battle in his rear, had changed front and hastened to the rescue. He swept down the plank road with the brigades of Smythe and Willett of his own division, and McAllister's brigade of Mott's division, while the brigade of De Trobriand and Kirwin's dismounted cavalry advanced at the same time. The Confederates were driven back, the guns were recaptured, and a thousand of their men were made prisoners. Others, in their flight, to the number of two hundred, rushed into Crawford's lines, and were captured. Had that officer been ordered to advance at that moment, the capture or dispersion of Heth's whole force might have been the result. Ayres was on the way, but night fell, and he halted before reaching Hancock, who, meanwhile, had been sorely pressed on his left and rear by five brigades of cavalry under Wade Hampton. Gregg fought them gallantly, and Hancock sent him all the infantry supports he could spare. The conflict continued until after dark, and the Confederates had gained no ground, when the struggle known as THE BATTLE OF THE BOYDTON ROAD ended. In these encounters Hancock lost about fifteen hundred men, and his antagonist at least an equal number. Uncertain whether the forces of Ayres and Crawford would join him in time to meet or make an attack the next morning, and

ARMY CABIN.[1]

his ammunition being short, Hancock withdrew at midnight, and the whole army was behind the intrenchments at Petersburg, and those of Warren on the Weldon road, the following morning.[a]

[a] October 28, 1864.

---

[1] This shows the form of some of the better class of army cabins. They were generally made of rough logs. in the common style of cabins on the frontier. Some of the chimneys were built of bricks procured by the destruction of houses, and others were made of wood and mud, and surmounted by a barrel.

With these movements Grant's campaign was practically closed for the year 1864, and his army prepared themselves huts for comfortable winter quarters. The movement of General Butler, on the north side of the James, at the same time in co-operation with that on the extreme left, was made with vigor and success, and being intended chiefly as a feint, ceased with the other. The Tenth and Eighteenth Corps had pushed well out to the right, the latter as far as the battle-ground of the Seven Pines, within a few miles of Richmond. These fell back to their lines, extending from New Market Heights to the James at Dutch Gap, and went into winter quarters.

GENERAL BUTLER'S HEAD-QUARTERS.[1]

General Butler established his head-quarters at the mansion of a farm about two miles from Aiken's Landing, and one from Dutch Gap.[2]

---

[1] This was the appearance of General Butler's head-quarters when the writer made the sketch at the close of 1864. The general occupied the two log-houses seen in the front, and his staff some of the smaller ones near. The mansion is seen in the rear of head-quarters.

[2] Professor Coppée, author of *Grant and his Campaigns*, was furnished, by an officer of the Lieutenant-General's staff, with the following tabular statement of casualties in the Army of the Potomac, from May 5 to November 1, 1864.

BATTLES.	DATES.	KILLED.		WOUNDED.		MISSING.		AGGREGATE.
		Officers.	Enl'ed men.	Officers.	Enl'ed men.	Officers.	Enl'ed men.	
Wilderness.......	May 5 to 12......	269	3,019	1,017	18,261	177	6,667	29,410
Spottsylvania....	May 12 to 21.....	114	2,032	259	7,699	31	248	10,381
North Anna......	May 21 to 31.....	12	138	67	1,063	3	324	1,607
Cool Arbor......	June 1 to 10.....	144	1,561	421	8,621	51	2,355	13,153
Petersburg.......	June 10 to 20....	85	1,113	361	6,492	46	1,568	9,665
Ditto	June 20 to July 30	29	576	120	2,374	108	2,109	5,316
Ditto	July 30..........	47	372	124	1,555	91	1,819	4,008
Trenches.........	Aug. 1 to 18......	10	128	58	626	1	45	868
Weldon Railroad..	Aug. 18 to 21.....	21	191	100	1,055	104	3,072	4,543
Reams's Station...	Aug. 25..........	24	93	62	484	95	1,674	2,432
Peeble's Farm....	Sept. 30 to Oct. 1.	12	129	50	738	56	1,700	2,685
Trenches.........	Aug. 18 to Oct. 30	13	284	91	1,214	4	800	2,417
Boydton Road....	October 27 to 28..	16	140	66	981	8	619	1,902
		796	9,776	2,796	51,161	775	23,083	88,387

During the period above named, according to the same statement, the number of prisoners captured by the Army of the Potomac was 15,373; the number of colors captured, 67; the number of guns captured by the Army of the Potomac, 32; the number lost by it, 25.

The above statement does not include the losses of the Army of the James, which, if added, would make the aggregate loss of the forces operating against Lee and the post of Richmond, during six months, the appalling number of 100,000 men. General Hancock said, in a letter to General Burns, that from the crossing of the Rapid Anna to the crossing of the James, he had lost his entire corps (25,000 in number). Its ranks had been kept full by re-enforcements. It is estimated that of the whole number captured, wounded, and missing (mostly prison-

Let us now turn for a moment to the consideration of the movements of the detachments of the two contending armies in Virginia, under Generals Sheridan and Early, whom we left in the region west of the Blue Ridge, between the Potomac and Winchester.[1]

Sheridan assumed the command, with his head-quarters at Harper's Ferry, on the 7th of August. He spent a month in getting his forces well in hand for an aggressive campaign, and in maneuvers to prevent the Confederates from getting the bountiful crops in the Lower Shenandoah Valley. During that time there were some stirring events there. Early tried to lure Sheridan far enough up the Valley to allow him to swoop down to the Potomac and beyond, by the National flank and rear. Sheridan was too wily for his antagonist, and contented himself with driving him toward Strasburg, and keeping the way into Maryland and Pennsylvania closely guarded against another raid, until he was ready to move in force offensively. He had been anxious to begin such movements; but Grant, made extremely cautious by late experiences, withheld consent, for, in the event of defeat, Maryland and Pennsylvania would be laid open for another invasion. In order to understand the situation in that region, Grant visited Sheridan at the middle of September.[a] "I met him," says the Lieutenant-General, "at Charlestown, and he pointed out so distinctly how each army lay; what he could do the moment he was authorized, and expressed such confidence of success, that I saw there were but two words of instruction necessary—'Go in!'" In those two words and no more, Grant showed his unreserved confidence in Sheridan's ability; and the events of a few weeks satisfied him and the country that he had judged and trusted wisely.

[a] Sept. 16, 1864.

Sheridan's troops, at that time, lay in front of Berryville, on the turnpike leading from that town across the Opequan Creek to Winchester. Early was on the same road, west of the ford of the Opequan, which is about four miles east of Winchester, and thus covered that city. Contemplating an offensive movement, he had extended the bulk of his army, by his left, to Bunker's Hill, leaving his right on the Berryville road, weak and isolated. Sheridan, who was about to make a bold movement to Early's rear, had watched him with keenest scrutiny; and when, on the 18th, the Confederate leader sent half his army from Bunker's Hill, on a reconnoissance to Martinsburg (which Averill repulsed), he determined to "Go in!" at once, and crush that weak right, and cut up the remainder in detail.[2] He put his forces under arms that evening, and at three o'clock in the morning[b] they were all in motion toward Winchester, Wilson's cavalry leading. The Sixth Corps, under General Wright, followed in double columns, flanking the Berryville turnpike, with its artillery and wagon-train moving along that highway. The Nineteenth Corps, under General Emory, followed in the same order, it being the intention of Sheridan to have his whole force across the Opequan before Early could bring back his troops

[b] Sept. 19.

---

ers), 30,000 afterward rejoined the army, making the total loss of effective force 70,000. The estimated loss of the Confederates, during the same period, including over 15,000 prisoners, was 40,000.

[1] See page 350.

[2] The Union army was then inspirited by the success of Wilson and his cavalry, a few days before, who struck the flank of Kershaw's division, and captured 171 of the Eighth South Carolina, with their colonel.

from Bunker's Hill to his endangered right.   Crook's (Eighth) corps, then in the vicinity of Summit Point, was ordered to join the main forces at the Opequan ford, while Averill and Torbett were to make demonstrations on the Confederate left.

Wilson crossed the Opequan at daybreak, and moved swiftly along the pike, which passed through a narrow mountain gorge, charging upon and

THE OPEQUAN FORD OF THE BERRYVILLE TURNPIKE.

sweeping away all opposers, and securing a space within two miles of Winchester, for the deployment of the army.   He was closely followed by the Sixth Corps; but the Nineteenth was so delayed by the wagon-train of the former, that the battle-line was not formed until nine o'clock in the morning. Then it stood with the Sixth Corps on the left, flanked by Wilson's cavalry, the Nineteenth Corps in the center, and Crook's Kanawha infantry in the rear, in reserve.   In the mean time, Early had hurried the bulk of his troops up from Bunker's Hill to Winchester, and before Sheridan was ready for attack, these were strongly posted in a fortified position on a series of detached hills northwestward of the town.   They had a powerful line thrown forward for the purpose of breaking that of the Nationals by a vigorous charge, and seizing the gorge already mentioned, through which, alone, the Unionists, if beaten, might retreat.   Averill had followed the Confederates closely from Bunker's Hill, and now formed a junction with Merritt's horsemen.   These two powerful cavalry divisions enveloped Winchester on the east and north.   Early's position compensated him, in a degree, for his inferiority in numbers, while Sheridan's superior cavalry gave the Nationals a very great advantage.

Between the two armies lay a broken, wooded country, over which it was difficult for troops to move; and to reach the left and center of Early's

---

[1] This is from a sketch, from the eastern bank of the stream, looking toward Winchester, made by the author in October, 1866. It shows the place where the whole of Sheridan's army crossed the stream on the morning of the 19th of September, 1864.

line (which seemed to be the only vulnerable points, for the right was too
strongly posted to be moved by assault), the Nationals had to go through the
narrow pass among wooded hills already mentioned.   This was undertaken at
ten o'clock, first by Ricketts's division of the Sixth Corps, followed by Grover's
of the Nineteenth.   These pressed forward vigorously over the rough country,
in the face of a terrible storm of shells, and charging Early's center furiously,
carried his first line, and inflicted upon him the loss of the gallant General
Rodes, who was killed.   Early quickly hurled upon the assailing columns two
of his most powerful divisions, hoping to succeed in his plan of breaking the
line and seizing the pass.   The Nationals were thrown back in great disorder, and with heavy loss, the confusion and the bereavement being greatly
increased by a heavy fire on their flank, as they reeled toward the pass from
which they had emerged, and which the victors were striving to reach first. It
seemed, for a moment, as if the day was lost to the Nationals, when Captain
Rigby, with a sergeant and twelve men of the Twenty-fourth Iowa, on
reaching a designated rallying point, turned and faced the pursuers.   In the

BATTLE OF WINCHESTER.

space of a few minutes, scores of brave men were added to their number.
At the same time, Grover ordered two guns of the First Maine Battery,
Captain Bradbury, to a position in a gap.   These opened upon the Confederates, who were pressing forward to seize them, and at the same moment the
enemy received a volley in their rear from the One Hundred and Thirty-first
New York, which Emory had rallied and placed in a projecting wood.   This
caused the Confederates to recoil, when the new-forming line poured upon
them a shower of musketry that sent them flying back to their lines.   This
was followed by a rapid rallying of the broken columns, and re-forming of

the National line, with Crook on the right, flanked by the cavalry of Merritt and Averill. This second line speedily advanced. Desperate fighting ensued, and continued until about four o'clock in the afternoon, when a loud shout was heard from beyond the woods on the Union right. It was from Crook's (Eighth) corps—the Army of Western Virginia—who, with Torbert's cavalry, pressed forward in the face of a murderous fire, and charged heavily upon Early's left. At the same time there was a general charge upon the Confederate center by the infantry, and by Wilson's cavalry on Early's right, driving the Confederates back from the open space in front of Winchester to the fortified heights. Before five o'clock the latter were carried, and Early's broken and confused columns were "whirling through

SHERIDAN'S HEAD-QUARTERS IN WINCHESTER.

Winchester" in full retreat, their faces turned toward Strasburg. They left behind them two thousand five hundred of their comrades as prisoners, with nine battle-flags and five pieces of artillery. The fugitives were followed until dark, when the pursuit ceased, and thus ended THE BATTLE OF WINCHESTER. Sheridan made his head-quarters that night at the spacious brick house of Lloyd Logan, in Winchester,[1] where he wrote a hasty dispatch to the Secretary of War, saying: "We have just sent the enemy whirling through Winchester, and are after them to-morrow. We captured two thousand five hundred prisoners, five pieces of artillery, nine battle-flags, and all the rebel dead and wounded.[2] Their wounded in Winchester amount to some three thousand." Early did not halt until he reached the very strong position of Fisher's Hill, beyond Strasburg, about twenty miles south of Winchester.

Sheridan kept his promise to be after the retreating Confederates, and he appeared in front of Fisher's Hill on the 22d[a] in full force.[3]
There Early was intrenched, with his left resting on the adjacent North Mountain. Sheridan made immediate preparation for a direct attack, and sent Torbert with two divisions of cavalry by way of the Luray Valley to seize New Market, thirty miles in Early's rear. He sent the Eighth Corps around to gain the left and rear of the position, and then advanced the Sixth and Nineteenth Corps against the left and front. There was much maneuvering in efforts to force the position, and it was four o'clock in the afternoon before a general attack was made. Then, under cover of a cavalry

^a Sept., 1864.

---

[1] This fine mansion stood on the corner of Braddock and Piccadilly Streets, in Winchester.

[2] It was estimated that Early lost about 1,000 men, besides the prisoners. Among his killed were Generals Rodes and Godwin. Sheridan's loss was about 3,000.

[3] This was considered the strongest defensive position in the valley. Fisher's Hill is a high eminence between the Massanutten and North Mountain ranges. The former rises abruptly from the general level near Strasburg, and extends almost to Harrisonburg, a distance of full forty miles, where the range as abruptly terminates. This mountain divides the Shenandoah Valley, one fork being called the Luray Valley, between the Massanutten and the Blue 'Ridge, and the other the Strasburg Valley, between the Massanutten and the North Mountain. At the mouth of this valley lies Fisher's Hill, its base washed by one branch of the Shenandoah River.

attack, an impetuous assault was made on Early's left, which drove that part of his line from the North Mountain. At the same time his whole front was broken by a general attack, when his entire force retreated in much disorder, and fled swiftly up the valley, leaving behind them sixteen guns and over a thousand prisoners. So ended, in a complete victory for Sheridan, THE BATTLE OF FISHER'S HILL. Meanwhile Torbert and his horsemen had been held in check at Milford, in the Luray Valley, by a cavalry force under General Wickham, who had fought Wilson at Front Royal the *Sept. 21, 1864.* previous day.*a* This check doubtless saved Early's army from total destruction by capture or dispersion.

SHERIDAN'S HEAD-QUARTERS NEAR CEDAR CREEK.

Sheridan followed the Confederates sharply, chasing them with horse and foot to Port Republic,[1] where he destroyed Early's train of seventy-five wagons. Thence he sent his cavalry in pursuit as far as Staunton, where the remnant of Early's army sought and found shelter in the passes of the Blue Ridge. At Staunton the Nationals destroyed a large amount of army supplies, and passing on to Waynesborough, they laid waste the Virginia Central railway, and burned a large Confederate tannery. The cavalry was then recalled, and Sheridan with his whole army went down the Shenandoah Valley, executing on the way an order given by Grant to Hunter, to see to it that "nothing should be left to invite the enemy to return."[2] He soon placed his forces behind

---

[1] See page 399, Volume II.

[2] Grant directed Hunter, whom Sheridan succeeded, to "take all provisions, forage, and stock," wanted for the use of his command, when he should move up the valley, and to destroy what he could not consume; "for," he said, "it is desirable that nothing should be left to invite the enemy to return." He enjoined him not to burn, but rather to protect the buildings. He was to inform the people that so long as an army could subsist among them, raids like Early's must be expected, and that the Government was determined to put a stop to them. This order Sheridan executed to the fullest extent, and he reported from Woodstock,[b] thirty miles south of Winchester, saying: "In moving back to this point, the whole country, [b October 7, from the Blue Ridge to the North Mountain, has been made untenable for a rebel army. I have destroyed over 2,000 barns, filled with wheat, hay, and farming implements, and over 70 mills filled with flour and wheat; have driven in front of this army over 4,000 head of stock, and have killed and issued to the troops not less than 3,000 sheep." He also reported that since he entered the valley from Harper's Ferry, "every train, every small party, and every straggler, had been bushwhacked by the people, many of whom have protection papers." Lieutenant Meigs, his engineer officer, was thus murdered near Dayton. "For this atrocious act," says Sheridan, "all the houses within an area of five miles were burned."

Because of these devastations, a Richmond paper, echoing the sentiments of the chief Conspirators at that capital, proposed an atrocious scheme of retaliation. It was nothing less than the destruction of Northern cities by secret hired incendiaries. It was proposed to pay liberally for the service. "A million of dollars," said the *Richmond Whig*, "would lay in ashes New York, Boston, Philadelphia, Chicago, Pittsburg, Washington, and all their chief cities, and the men to do the business may be picked up by the hundred in the streets of those very cities. If it should be thought unsafe to use them, there are daring men in Canada, of Morgan's and other commands, who have escaped from Yankee dungeons, and would rejoice at an opportunity of doing something that would make all Yankeedom howl with anguish and consternation." The enterprise was actually undertaken, and on the night of the 25th of November, 1864, an attempt was made to destroy New York City. Barnum's Museum, several hotels, and one or two theaters, were fired in the evening, by a combustible compound left by secret emissaries of the public enemies. Jacob Thompson, one of the conspirators, then in Canada (see page 45, volume I.), appears to have had the incendiary business in charge, and to have been engaged, in connection with those at Richmond, in the iniquitous scheme long before Sheridan's operations. So early as the beginning of August, he wrote to the Confederate "Secretary of War," saying the *work* would not probably begin before the middle of August.—[See *A Rebel War Clerk's Diary*, ii., 260.] The Richmond journals, impatient because the work had not been begun sooner, and stirred by Sheridan's operations, spoke out without reserve, as we have seen in the above extract.

Cedar Creek, about half way between Middletown and Strasburg, and made his head-quarters near, at the fine mansion of Benjamin B. Cooley.

Early rallied his troops, and his cavalry, under Rosser, hung upon Sheridan's rear as he moved down the valley. At length the latter ordered Torbert with his cavalry to turn upon Rosser. It was done.[a] At the first charge the Confederates broke and fled, leaving behind them over three hundred prisoners, a dozen guns, and nearly fifty wagons.

[a] Oct. 9, 1864.

They were chased twenty-six miles. Three days later Early attempted to surprise Sheridan, who had halted near Fisher's Hill, when the Confederates were so severely chastised that it was supposed they would remain quiet for some time. With that impression Sheridan went to Washington on official business, leaving General Wright in temporary command of the army.

The Nationals were so strongly posted on the east side of Cedar Creek, that they had no expectation of being attacked by any force known to be in the valley. They were upon three ridges. Crook's division was in front; Emory's was half a mile behind it; and Wright's, then under the temporary command of Ricketts, with Torbert's cavalry on its right flank, was to the

VIEW AT CEDAR CREEK.[1]

right and rear of Emory. Kitching's division lay behind Crook's left. The cavalry divisions of Merritt and Custer were thrown out to guard the right, and Averill's (then under Powell) picketed the north fork of the Shenandoah from Cedar Creek to Front Royal.

Strong as was this line and its position, it was soon broken and imperiled by Early, who felt keenly the humiliation to which Sheridan had subjected him. Having been re-enforced by Kershaw's division and six hundred

---

[1] This is a view of Cedar Creek, within the lines of Sheridan's army, near the house and mill of Mr. Stickley, on the right side of the stream. The high hill in the distance was called the Shenandoah Peak, at the northern extremity of the Massanutten Mountain. On the hills between the creek and that mountain, the earth-works of the Nationals were plainly seen, when the writer made the sketch, in October, 1866.

cavalry from Lee's army before Petersburg, he determined to make a bold movement, swiftly and stealthily, against the authors of his misfortunes, to retrieve the loss of his reputation. For this purpose he gathered his forces at Fisher's Hill, and in secresy, behind a mask of woods, he formed them in two columns, for the purpose of making a simultaneous attack upon both flanks of the Nationals. He moved soon after midnight, in October,[a] almost noiselessly along rugged paths that stretched over steep wooded hills, with horse, foot, and artillery, not daring to take the highway for fear of discovery. The divisions of Gordon, Ramseur, and Pegram, forming his right column, thus crept softly toward the National left along the line of the Manassas Gap railway. They twice forded the north fork of the Shenandoah, the last time at a point a little east of the mouth of Cedar Creek, when they turned in the direction of Sheridan's army. Early's left, composed of the divisions of Kershaw and Wharton, moved with equal caution toward the National right.

[a] Oct. 19, 1864.

At two o'clock in the morning,[b] General Crook was made vigilant by reports of mysterious sounds like the dull heavy tramp of a multitude of men moving cautiously, but he could obtain no positive information of the near proximity of an enemy. The rest of the army slumbered on in fancied security, while the Confederates, concealed by a dense fog that arose before dawn, reached their appointed places without being discovered. At the early morning twilight the order for attack was given, when the rattle of musketry on right, left, and rear, and the ringing battle-shout, summoned the Nationals from repose and to arms. But before they could take position in the trenches, the assailants, who had captured the pickets, were there. So furious and successful was their assault, that in the space of fifteen minutes Crook's corps was broken into fragments, and sent flying in wild disorder back upon the other corps, leaving seven hundred men as prisoners in the hands of the Confederates, with many cannon, small-arms, and munitions of war as spoils. Emory vainly tried to stop the fugitives, and keep his own line intact. Assailed in front, flank, and rear, and having one-third of the brigade of McMillen (which he had thrown forward to check the fierce torrent of the victors until the Sixth Corps could come up) killed or wounded, he, too, was compelled to give way, and leave several guns behind. These, with Crook's lost pieces, eighteen in all, were turned upon the fugitives with fearful effect, while Early's right column, led by Gordon, continued their flanking advance with vigor, turning the Nationals out of every position where they attempted to make a stand, and trying to wedge in between the corps so as to split the Union army. At the same time Kershaw and Wharton were fearfully pressing the National right. Perceiving the peril that threatened the whole army, Wright ordered a general retreat, which the Sixth Corps, yet in good order, covered with great skill. So ended THE BATTLE OF CEDAR CREEK.

[b] Oct. 19.

The whole army fell back to Middletown, a little village five miles north of Strasburg, the forces all tending in their route toward a concentration on the turnpike from which they had been pushed. At that town Wright rallied the broken columns, but there was yet too much disorder to give hope of the formation of a strong line, so he fell back a mile or so further, and left Early in possession of Middletown. There the Confederates stopped to plunder, eat, and rest after sixteen hours of hard service, and during that lull in the pursuit Wright re-formed his lines, and took a position for the purpose of changing front and advancing upon the foe, or making an orderly retreat toward Winchester.[1] It was now about ten o'clock. The Nationals had lost, since daybreak that morning, twelve hundred men made prisoners, besides a large number killed and wounded ; also, camps and equipage, lines of defenses, and twenty-four pieces of artillery.

At that critical moment Sheridan appeared upon the field. He had returned from Washington, and slept at Winchester the night before. He had heard the booming of cannon up the valley early in the morning, but supposed it to be the noise of a reconnoissance only. After breakfast he mounted his horse, and moved leisurely out of the city southward. Before he reached Kernstown he met the van of the fugitives from the army, who told him a piteous tale of disaster. He immediately gave orders for parking the retreating train on each side of the turnpike. Then directing his escort to follow, he put his horse upon a swinging gallop, and at that pace rode nearly twelve miles, to the front. The fugitives became thicker and thicker every moment. He did not stop to chide or coax, but as his power-ful horse thundered on over that splendid stone road, he waved his hat, and shouted to the cheering crowds: "Face the other way, boys ! Face the other way ! We are going back to our camp. We are going to lick them out of their boots !" The man and the act were marvelously magnetic in their effects. The tide of disordered troops was instantly turned and drawn after the young general by a wonderful and irresistible influence, akin to the faith of the Christian believer. His presence was an inspiration. As he

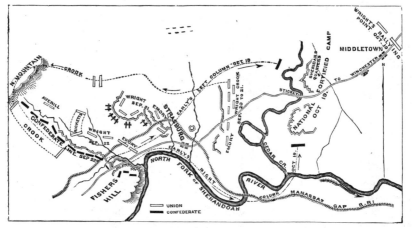

OPERATIONS AT FISHER'S HILL AND CEDAR CREEK.

dashed into the lines, and rode along the front of forming regiments, he gave to each stirring words of cheer and encouragement, and declared, in substance, to all, "We'll have all those camps and cannon back again." The men believed him, and showing their faith by their works, secured a speedy fulfillment of the prophecy.

---

[1] This line was formed on the lands of David Dingee and Abraham Stickley, about a mile from the toll-gate, at the northern end of the village.

General Wright, as we have seen, had already brought order out of confusion, and had made disposition for an advance upon the foe. Sheridan approved his arrangements, and at about three o'clock gave the order, "The entire line will advance. The Nineteenth Corps will move in connection with the Sixth. The right of the Nineteenth will swing toward the left, so as to drive the enemy upon the pike." It was followed by an immediate forward movement. Already, at one o'clock, Emory had quickly repulsed an attack, which inspirited the whole army. Now a general and severe struggle ensued. The first line of the Confederates was soon driven. Then Early opened his cannon upon the new position of the Nationals. They were checked for a moment, when two most gallant charges by Emory's corps, and by the cavalry coming down upon both flanks, sent the Confederates in hot haste up the valley pike. It was a perfect rout. In great disorder,

BRIDGE NEAR STRASBURG.[1]

pressing close upon each other's heels, the fugitives fled through Middletown and Strasburg to Fisher's Hill, leaving the highway strewn with abandoned hinderances to speedy flight. As they pressed along the narrower dirt road beyond Strasburg, the way became clogged by masses of men, wagons, cannon, and caissons; and at a little bridge over a small stream in a deep channel, Early, hard pressed, felt compelled to abandon his guns and train. With the remnant of his ruined army he escaped to Fisher's Hill. That army was virtually destroyed; and, with the exception of two or three skirmishes between cavalry, there was no more fighting in the Shenandoah Valley. That night

SHERIDAN'S HEAD-QUARTERS AT KERNSTOWN.[2]

---

[1] This is a view of the bridge, half a mile from Strasburg, where Early lost his artillery. Sheridan's sharpshooters killed the artillery horses, which fell on the bridge and clogged the way. The little clear stream comes out of the base of a hill near by. A little beyond it is seen Fisher's Hill, and in the far distance a peak of the Massanutten range.

[2] This house was also the head-quarters of General Shields, and to it he was taken when he was wounded on the 22d of March, 1862. See page 369, volume II. Shields was wounded on a ridge a little to the northwest of the house.

the National troops occupied their old position at Cedar Creek. Sheridan's promise, "We will have all the camps and cannon back again," had been kept. The conqueror returned to Kernstown, near Winchester, and there, in the house of Mrs. Francis Mahaney, he established his head-quarters for awhile. Government and people united in praise of the young leader, and there was joy in every loyal heart because of his achievements. Art and song celebrated "Sheridan's Ride" from Winchester to the front; and when, less than three weeks afterward, General McClellan resigned,[a] and thereby created a vacant major-generalship in the regular army, the victor in the Shenandoah Valley was substantially rewarded by a commission to fill his place.

[a] Nov. 4, 1864.

The writer, with friends already mentioned (Messrs. Buckingham and Young), visited the theater of Sheridan's exploits in the Shenandoah Valley, from the Opequan and Winchester to Fisher's Hill, early in October, 1866.[1] We left Gettysburg in a carriage, for Harper's Ferry, on the morning of the first, and followed the line of march of the corps of Howard and Sickles, when moving northward from Frederick, in the summer of 1863.[2] We passed through the picturesque region into which the road to Emmettsburg led us, with the South Mountain range on our right, dined at Creagerstown, twenty miles from Gettysburg, and rode through Frederick toward evening, stopping only long enough to make the sketch of Barbara Freitchie's house.[3] Then we passed along the magnificent Cumberland road over the lofty mountain range west of Frederick, into the delightful Middletown Valley. From the road, on the summit of that range, we had some of the most charming views to be found anywhere in our broad land. The valley was smiling with plenty, for the most bountiful crops, gathered and a-gathering, were filling barns and barracks on every side. We passed through the valley, and following the line of march of a portion of McClellan's army,[4] reached the summit of South Mountain after dark, where we lodged. We visited the battle-ground there—the place where the gallant Reno was killed[5]—early the next morning, and rode on to Sharpsburg. There we remained long enough to visit the Antietam battle-ground, the National Cemetery, McClellan's head-quarters, and other localities of special interest,[6] and after a late dinner, went down the Antietam Valley to the Potomac, at the mouth of the Antietam Creek. Then we passed over the rugged hills west of Maryland Heights, and descending through gorges, passed along the margin of the river at the base of that historical eminence at twilight, and at dark reached Harper's Ferry.

Having visited places of interest at and around Harper's Ferry, we left that picturesque place in the afternoon of the 3d, for Winchester, where we arrived in time to ramble over the hills and among the fortifications on the northern side of the town, before nightfall. We spent the following morning in visiting Kernstown, and places of interest in the city of Winchester;[7] and in

---

[1] See page 400, volume II.   [2] See page 59.   [3] See page 466, volume II.   [4] See page 468, volume II.
[5] See page 470, volume II.   [6] See page 475, volume II.

· Among these were the quarters of different commanders during the war. Sheridan and Milroy occupied Mr. Logan's house (see page 366). Banks's was at the house of George Seavers, on Water Street. "Stonewall Jackson" occupied the house of Colonel Moore. We visited the site of old Fort Frederick, on Loudon Street, at the northern end of the city, and drank from the fort well, which is one hundred and three feet deep, where, during the French and Indian war, Washington often appeased thirst. We also visited the grave of General Daniel Morgan, the Hero of the Cowpens: it is in the Presbyterian church-yard, covered by a broken marble slab.

the afternoon, Colonel Russell, the post commander, kindly took us in his carriage to the Opequan Ford, where Sheridan's army crossed,[1] and on the following morning he sent us on our way up the valley, in an ambulance, as far as Middletown. There we dined, and hiring a light carriage, went on to Strasburg, stopping at Cedar Creek on the way. After making arrangements for

taking the stage for Harrisonburg, that evening, we rode to Fisher's Hill, along an excellent road, making the sketch of the bridge seen on page 371. That road crosses a little stream at Fisher's Hill, over a picturesque stone bridge, and turning at a right angle, passes along a shelf in the almost perpendicular acclivity, in a gradually rising course, to the summit. There we found the lines thrown up

STONE BRIDGE AT FISHER'S HILL.[2]

by Early well preserved. And from that eminence we had a very extended view of the rolling valley in the direction of Winchester, overlooking Strasburg at our feet, and Middletown a little beyond, with the lofty range of the Blue Ridge on our right, and the Massanutten Mountains nearer. We supped at Strasburg that evening, and at nine o'clock took passage in a crowded stage-coach for Harrisonburg, fifty miles up the valley.[3]

Let us here leave, in winter quarters, the troops destined to capture Richmond and Lee's army, and consider the events of the important campaign of General Sherman in Georgia.

---

[1] See page 364.

[2] At this bridge, where the road turns at an acute angle and is very narrow, a large number of prisoners were taken from Early. This bridge was choked by the fugitives, and there was no other way for them to reach the shelter of the works on the summit of the hill. The sycamore tree seen at the left was an Anak of the primitive forest, twenty feet in circumference.

[3] See page 400, volume II.

CHAPTER XIV.

SHERMAN'S CAMPAIGN IN GEORGIA.

T the same time when the Army of the Potomac moved from the Rapid Anna toward Richmond, at the beginning of May,[a] General William T. Sherman, who had succeeded General Grant in the command of the Military Division of the Mississippi, marched southward from the vicinity of Chattanooga,[b] with nearly one hundred thousand men,[1] having for his chief objectives, the destruction of the Confederate army under General Joseph E. Johnston, then at Dalton, in Northern Georgia,[2] and the capture of the city of Atlanta.

[a] 1864.

[b] May 6.

General Sherman received his orders from Lieutenant-General Grant to advance, on the 30th of April, and he moved on the 6th of May. On that morning the Army of the Cumberland lay at and near Ringgold; that of the Tennessee at Lee and Gordon's Mill,[3] on the Chickamauga, and that of the Ohio near Red Clay, on the Georgia line north of Dalton. The Confederate army then lay in and about Dalton. To strike that position in front was impracticable, for between the armies lay a rugged mountain barrier known as the Rocky Face Ridge. Through it, at an opening called Buzzard's Roost Gap,[4] a

WILLIAM T. SHERMAN.

---

[1] His forces were composed as follows: *Army of the Cumberland*, Major-General GEORGE H. THOMAS, commanding; Infantry, 54,568; Artillery, 2,377; Cavalry, 3,828. Total, 60,773. Number of guns, 130. *Army of the Tennessee*, Major-General J. B. McPHERSON, commanding; Infantry, 22,437; Artillery, 1,404; Cavalry, 624. Total, 24,465. Number of guns, 96. *Army of the Ohio*, Major-General J. M. SCHOFIELD, commanding; Infantry, 11,183; Artillery, 679; Cavalry, 1,697. Total, 13,559. Number of guns, 28. Grand aggregate number of troops, 98,797, and of guns, 254.

About this number of troops were kept up during the campaign, the number of men joining from furlough and hospitals about compensating for the loss in battle and from sickness. "My aim and purpose was," says Sherman in his report, "to make the Army of the Cumberland 50,000 men, that of the Tennessee 35,000, and that of the Ohio 15,000."

[2] Johnston's army was composed of about 55,000 men—45,000 (according to Sherman's estimate) heavy infantry and artillery, and 10,000 cavalry under Wheeler. It was arranged in three corps, commanded respectively by Generals W. J. Hardee, J. B. Hood, and Leonidas Polk.

[3] See page 134.   [4] See page 242.

small stream flowed and the railway and wagon road passed; but it was so thoroughly fortified that no army could safely attempt the passage. Sherman therefore determined to turn the Confederate position at Dalton, and for that purpose he sought a passage of the great hills at Snake Creek Gap, farther south. To mask that movement, General Thomas menaced [a] Johnston's front; but in so doing, he had quite a severe engagement with the Confederates at Buzzard's Roost Gap. He pushed their cavalry well through the pass, and two divisions (Newton's of Howard's [Fourth] corps, and Geary's, of Hooker's [Twentieth] corps) gained portions of the Ridge. But they were soon driven off with considerable loss. Meanwhile, Schofield, with the Army of the Ohio, came down from the north and pressed heavily on Johnston's right; and McPherson, marching rapidly from the Chickamauga, by way of Ship's Gap and Villanow, passed through Snake Creek Gap, at the southern end of the Chattanooga Mountain, and appeared suddenly before the Confederate works at and near Resaca, on the railway south of Dalton. These works were too formidable to warrant an attack with his force alone, and so McPherson fell back to a strong position in Snake Creek Gap, to await the arrival of the main army.

[a] May 7, 1864.

Sherman was somewhat disappointed by the result of McPherson's movement, but felt that an advantage was gained. On the 10th [b] he ordered Thomas to send Hooker's corps to the support of McPherson, and to follow with Palmer's (Fourteenth) corps. Schofield was ordered to follow on the same day with his entire force; and on the 11th the whole army, excepting Howard's corps and some cavalry left to menace Johnston's front at Dalton, was marching in the grand turning movement, westward of Rocky Face Ridge, for Snake Creek Gap and Resaca. This compelled Johnston to abandon Dalton, and fall back, closely pursued by Howard, to the menaced position. That position, by good and direct roads, he reached, and took post behind a line of intrenchments, before Sherman could get to Resaca over the rough country from Snake Creek Gap. McPherson was pushed forward from that gap, preceded by Kilpatrick's cavalry, which drove the Confederates from a cross-road near Resaca. Kilpatrick was wounded, and his command was turned over to Col. Murray. McPherson pressed on, drove the Confederate pickets within their intrenchments, and took post on a ridge of bald hills, with his right on the Oostenaula River, and his left abreast the village. Thomas came up on his left, facing Camp Creek, and Schofield forced his way through the dense woods to the left of Thomas, and confronted the Confederate intrenchments on a group of hills covered with chestnut-trees, at the north of the village.

[b] May.

Such was the position of the opposing forces at Resaca, on the 14th of May, when Sherman ordered a pontoon bridge to be laid across the Oostenaula at Lay's Ferry, and directed Sweeny's division, of the Sixteenth Corps, to cross and threaten Calhoun, farther south. At the same time the cavalry division of General Garrard moved from Villanow in the direction of Rome, with orders to destroy the railway between Calhoun and Kingston. Sherman, meanwhile, was severely pressing Johnston at Resaca, at all points, and a general engagement ensued in the afternoon and evening of the 15th. [c] McPherson had secured a lodgment across Camp Creek, near the town, and held a hill which commanded the bridges across

[c] May.

the Oostenaula, while Thomas, pressing along Camp Creek Valley, threw Hooker's corps across the head of that stream to the main Dalton road, close to Resaca. Schofield came up on Thomas's left, and at that point the heaviest of the severe battle occurred. Hooker drove his foe from several strong

BATTLE-FIELD OF RESACA.[1]

hills, and captured a four-gun battery and many prisoners. That night Johnston abandoned Resaca, fled across the Oostenaula, firing the bridges behind him, and leaving as spoils a four-gun battery and a considerable quantity of stores.

On the following morning,[a] the Nationals took possession of Resaca, when Sherman's whole force started in pursuit. Thomas followed directly in the track of Hardee, who covered the retreat. McPherson crossed on the right, at Lay's Ferry, and Schofield made a wide circuit to the left, across the considerable streams which form the Oostenaula. General J. C. Davis's division, of Thomas's army, moved down the Oostenaula, to Rome, where they gave the Confederates a severe blow by destroying important mills and founderies there, and capturing nearly a dozen of their heavy guns. Davis left a garrison to hold the place. In the mean time, Sherman pressed on. He met slight opposition near Adairsville, the location of the Georgia State Arsenal, which he destroyed. But Johnston made only a brief stand; he quickly moved on, closely followed by his implacable pursuers, and was found at Cassville, on the 19th, holding a strong position and apparently determined to fight. Prudence told him to move on, and he did so that night, under the friendly cover of darkness, and crossing the Etowah River, burned the bridges, and placed that stream between his army and the hosts of Sherman. He halted near the Allatoona Pass, in a very strong position among rugged hills, where he was not molested for two or three days, because Sherman gave his army rest on the right bank of the Etowah, while supplies were brought forward to that point for the next stage of the campaign.

Sherman determined to flank Johnston out of his new position, by mov-

[a] May 16, 1864.

---

[1] This is a view of the battle-ground, eastward of Camp Creek, about two miles northwest of Resaca, as it appeared when the writer sketched it, on the anniversary of the battle, 1866. In the middle, on the hill, is seen the residence of Mrs. Margaret Wright, which was perforated with the bullets. The trees on the hill to the right, where General Judah made a charge on the Confederates, were nearly all dead, from the effects of bullet wounds.

ing far to the right, and concentrating his troops at Dallas. Thomas advanced along the road from Kingston, while McPherson moved farther to the right by way of Van Wert. Schofield went eastward of both, so as to come in on Thomas's left. The Confederate leader quickly perceived his peril, and prepared to avert it. As the latter was moving toward Dallas from Burnt Hickory, Hooker's corps in the advance, Geary's division of that corps was met[a] near Pumpkinvine Creek, by Confederate cavalry. These he pushed over that stream, and saved a bridge they had fired. Following them eastward two miles, he came [a] May 25, 1864. upon the foe in strong battle order. A sharp conflict ensued ; and when, at four o'clock, Hooker had his whole corps well in hand, he made a bold push, by Sherman's order, to secure possession of a point at the New Hope Church, where the roads from Ackworth, Marietta, and Dallas meet. But a stormy night coming on, Hooker, though he gained some ground, could not drive the Confederates from that position. Meanwhile, Johnston's troops had been very busy with their pickaxes and spades, and on the following morning[b] Sherman found his antagonist strongly intrenched, with lines extending from Dallas to Marietta. [b] May 26.

Sherman now found formidable difficulties in his way. The approach to Johnston's intrenchments must be made over a rough, broken, and wooded country, and he was engaged several days, constantly skirmishing, in making disposition for pushing through them to the railway east of Allatoona Pass. For this purpose McPherson was moved up to Dallas, and Thomas's troops were deployed against New Hope Church, in the vicinity of which there were many severe encounters, while Schofield was directed to turn and strike Johnston's right. Garrard's horsemen were operating with McPherson, and Stoneman's with Schofield. Just as General McPherson was on the point of closing to the left on General Thomas, in front of New Hope Church, that Sherman might more easily and safely envelop Johnston's right, the Confederates struck[c] him a severe blow at Dallas. They were repulsed with heavy loss; and at about the same time Howard, nearer the center, was repulsed. [c] May 28

Sherman now moved his army to the left, seized the roads leading to Allatoona Pass and Ackworth, and, enveloping the former stronghold, compelled Johnston to evacuate it. The cavalry of Garrard and Stoneman were pushed on to occupy it, and a garrison to hold it was placed there. The bridge over the Etowah was rebuilt, the railway was repaired, and Allatoona was made a secondary base of supplies for Sherman's army.

On the 4th of June Johnston abandoned his works covering New Hope Church and Ackworth, when Sherman advanced[d] to the latter place and took possession of the railway. There, on the 8th, he [d] June 6. was joined by General Frank Blair, with two divisions of the Seventeenth Corps, and the cavalry brigade of Colonel Long, of Garrard's division. These re-enforcements raised the number of Sherman's effective force nearly to what it was when he moved from the Chattanooga region.[1] His communications in his rear being now secure, he moved on to Big Shanty[e] where before him arose the Twin Mountain of Kene- [e] June 9.

---

[1] By losses in battle and in hospitals, and the detention of detachments at Resaca, Rome, Kingston, and Allatoona, his army was considerably diminished when he reached Ackworth.

saw (Big and Little), with Lost and Pine mountains forming with it a triangle, on each of which the Confederates had signal-stations.   Batteries covered
their summits, and thousands of men were busy in the dark forest, casting up
intrenchments from base to base, in a connected chain, in preparation for a
great struggle.   Cannon on the summit of Great Kenesaw completely commanded the beautiful town of Marietta.   There Johnston, with the Chattahoochee River at his back, determined to make a vigorous stand.   "The scene
was enchanting," said Sherman, in his report; "too beautiful to be disturbed
by the harsh clamors of war, but the Chattahoochee lay beyond, and I had to
reach it."

After much planning and maneuvering, and drawing his lines close to
those of the Confederates, Sherman made disposition for breaking through
those of Johnston between Kenesaw and Pine mountains.   Hooker was on
the right and, front of his line, Howard on its left and front, and Palmer
between it and the railway.   Under cover of a heavy cannonade, the advance
began on the 14th.[a]   The troops pressed over the rugged ground
June, 1864.   with difficulty, fighting at almost every step, and on the morning
of the 15th they found that the Confederates had abandoned Pine Mountain,
and taken position on their line of intrenchments between Kenesaw and
Lost mountains.[1]   Upon these Thomas, Schofield, and McPherson advanced,
while rain was falling copiously, and on the 17th the Confederates abandoned

SUMMIT OF GREAT KENESAW MOUNTAIN.[2]

Lost Mountain, and the long line of works connecting it with Kenesaw.
Sherman continued to press them heavily at all points, skirmishing in dense
forests that were furrowed by ravines and tangled with vines, and compelling

---

[1] At the time of this advance, General Polk, formerly Protestant Episcopal Bishop of the diocese of
Louisiana, was killed instantly, by a piece of shell which passed through his body. Polk, Johnston, and Hardee,
were upon the summit of Pine Mountain when the cannonade commenced, reconnoitering. Seeing the group,
General Thomas, it is said, ordered a shot to be fired at them from Knapp's battery. This caused them to
retreat to a place of safety. Polk soon reappeared, when another shell was fired, which exploded near him, and
killed him instantly. The two shells were fired by a young man named William Atwell, of Alleghany City,
Pennsylvania, attached to Knapp's battery.

[2] This was the appearance of the summit of Great Kenesaw, when the writer sketched it, in May, 1866. In
the foreground is seen the remains of a Confederate battery and signal-station. To the left is seen the top of
Little Kenesaw. In the distance, at the center of the picture, rises Lost Mountain; and on the extreme right,
the higher elevation, seen beyond the two large stones in the foreground, is Pine Mountain or Knob, on which
General Polk was killed. A little to the left of Lost Mountain was New Hope Church.

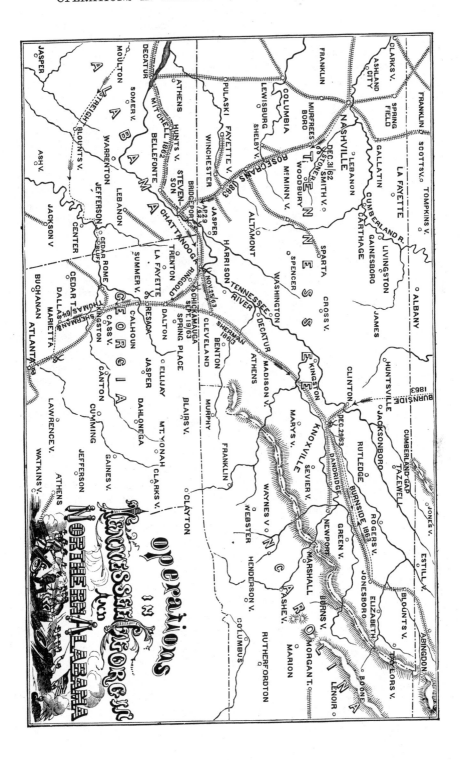

Johnston to contract his lines and take a position of great strength, with Kenesaw as his salient. From this lofty height he could look down upon the entire host of his antagonist, and his batteries could hurl terrible plunging shot and shell. His right was bent back so as to cover Marietta, and his left was behind Nose Creek, in a position to cover the railway leading from Marietta to the Chattahoochee.

For three weeks, at the period we are considering, rain fell copiously, almost without intermission, drenching the contending armies, and flooding the whole country. "During our operations about Kenesaw," said Sherman, "the weather was villainously bad," the rain "rendering our narrow, wooded roads, mere mud gullies, so that a general movement would be impossible." Yet he did not cease his labors, and every hour his army worked closer to the lines of his antagonist. McPherson watched Kenesaw, and worked his left forward. Thomas, in a sort of grand left wheel, swung round, with his left on Kenesaw, touching McPherson, while Schofield moved to the south and east along the old Sandtown road. Finally, when Hooker had considerably advanced his line, with Schofield on his right, General J. B. Hood, leading his own corps and detachments from others, sallied out and attacked the Nationals,[a] with the intention of forcing a passage through Sherman's line, between Thomas and Schofield.

[a] June 22, 1864.

Although his movement was sudden and unexpected, he was received with a terrible return blow, which made him recoil in great confusion, leaving, in his retreat, his killed, wounded, and many prisoners, in the hands of the Nationals. He had aimed his blow chiefly at the division of Williams, of Hooker's corps, and Hascall's brigade of Schofield's, in comparatively open ground. Those gallant troops so punished his audacity, that Sherman said he could not expect Hood to repeat his mistake "after the examples of Dallas and the Kulp House." The struggle was brief and sanguinary, and is known as THE BATTLE OF THE KULP HOUSE.

The repulse of Hood inspirited the Nationals. Taking advantage of that feeling, Sherman prepared to assault the Confederates. Both armies believed it was not his policy to assail fortified lines, as Grant was doing north of Richmond. They were soon undeceived. He regarded Johnston's left center as the most vulnerable point in his line, and on the 24th of June he ordered an assault to be made upon it there, on the 27th,[b] with the hope of breaking through it and seizing the railway below Marietta, cut off the Confederate left and center from its line of retreat, and then, by turning upon either part, overwhelmn and destroy the army of his antagonist. The assault was made at two points south of Kenesaw, and was sadly disastrous. The Nationals were repulsed, with an aggregate loss of about three thousand men, among them General C. G. Harker and D. McCook killed, and many valuable officers of lower grade wounded. This loss was without compensation, for the injury inflicted upon the Confederates, who were behind their breastworks, was very slight.[1]

[b] June.

---

[1] General Sherman avowed, in his report of his campaign from Chattanooga to Atlanta, dated September 15, 1864, that his object in making this assault was to produce a salutary moral effect on his troops; for, he said, "an army, to be efficient, must not settle down to one single mode of offense. . . . . Failure as it was, and for which I assume the entire responsibility, I yet claim it produced good fruits, as it demonstrated to General Johnston that I would assault, and that boldly; and we also gained and held ground so close to the enemy's parapets, that he could not show a head above them."

Sherman knew that it would not do for his troops to rest long under the influence of a mistake or failure, so he at once began a vigorous turning movement, after he had buried his dead and cared for his wounded. Schofield was working strongly on the Confederate left, and McPherson, having been relieved by Garrard's cavalry in front of Kenesaw, was ordered to rapidly throw his whole force by his right down to and threaten Nickajack Creek and Turner's Ferry, across the Chattahoochee River. Stoneman was directed to push on, at the same time, with his cavalry, to the river below Turner's, and thus seriously threaten Johnston's rear. The movement was begun at near the evening of the 2d of July, and the intended effect was instantaneous. Johnston abandoned Kenesaw and all his works that night, and when, at dawn,[a] Sherman's skirmishers stood on the top of that mountain, they saw the Confederate hosts flying through and beyond Marietta, in hot haste, toward the Chattahoochee, in the direction of Atlanta. Thomas's corps pressed closely upon the heels of the

[a] July 3, 1864.

MORRIS HOUSE, MARIETTA.[1]

fugitives; and between eight and nine o'clock in the morning, Sherman rode into Marietta just as the cavalry of Johnston's rear guard left it, and made his head-quarters at the pleasant embowered mansion known as the "Morris House."

Sherman expected to strike Johnston a destructive if not fatal blow, while the latter should be crossing the Chattahoochee. For that purpose he directed McPherson and Schofield to press on, cross the Nickajack, and attack the Confederates on flank and rear. But the skillful and vigilant Johnston had too quickly provided for the safety of his army to invite such attack. He had made a forced march to the right bank of the Chattahootchee where the railway crossed it, and there, in the course of a few hours, he caused to be constructed earth-works of sufficient strength to enable a detachment to keep the pursuers at bay until a greater portion of his army should make the passage of the river. He had also an intrenched line at Smyrna camp-meeting ground, five miles from Marietta. There the pursuing Thomas halted, and there Sherman overtook that army, paused, and considered. On the following day[b] he pushed a heavy skirmish line forward, captured the entire line of Confederate rifle-pits, with some prisoners, and made strong demonstrations toward Turner's Ferry. That night Johnston abandoned his advanced works, and the next morning his whole army was across the Chattahoochee, excepting heavy garrisons for the works covering the bridges. Sherman promptly advanced to the river at several uncovered points, but did not deem it prudent to attack the works of his adversary.

[b] July 4

Before the patriot army now flowed a deep and rapid stream, and on its

[1] This was one of the few places in Marietta spared by the ravages of war. When the writer sketched it, in May, 1866, it was occupied as a boarding-house, and was the head-quarters of the post-commander. It was then known as the "Hunt House," its occupant being E. J. Hunt.

opposite side a host of men were piling fortifications, with a determination to dispute the passage of their foe.   General Thomas's force lay at Paice's Ferry, McPherson's right rested on the river at the mouth of the Nickajack, and Schofield was in reserve on the Sandtown road.   Heavy skirmishing on the 5th satisfied Sherman that he could gain no advantage by attacking Johnston in his works, so he proceeded to turn him out of them in the usual way.   Schofield was sent, in rapid march, to the National left, and quickly crossed the Chattahoochee [a] at Powell's Ferry, where he surprised the guard, captured a gun, intrenched himself on commanding hills on the left bank of the river, and constructed a pontoon and a trestle bridge across it.   At the same time General Garrard moved on Roswell, and destroyed factories there in which cloth was manufactured for the insurgents.

a July 7, 1864.

Schofield's position commanded good roads running eastward, and he soon found himself supported by Howard, who laid a pontoon bridge at Power's Ferry, two miles below, crossed over, and took a commanding position on the right of the Army of the Ohio.   At the same time there was a general movement [b] of Sherman's forces from right to left, and thereby Johnston was compelled to abandon his position on each side of the river.   He drew his entire army to the left bank of the stream, and took position on a new line that covered Atlanta, its left resting on the Chattahoochee, and its right on Peachtree Creek.   On the 10th of July, or sixty-five days from the time he put his army in motion southward, Sherman was master of the country north and west of the river upon which he was resting—of nearly one-half of Georgia—and had accomplished one of the major objects of the campaign, namely, the advancement of the National lines from the Tennessee to the Chattahoochee.

b July 9.

The possession of Atlanta, the key-point of military advantage in the campaign in that region, was to be the next prize for which the contending armies were to struggle.   It had been, previously, well fortified; and now Johnston's forces were employing their utmost skill and strength to make that post absolutely impregnable against Sherman's army.   In that labor Johnston was assiduously engaged, when he was suddenly deprived of command.   The Conspirators at Richmond had become exceedingly nervous because of Sherman's steady advance southward, and were dissatisfied with Johnston's policy, which regarded the salvation of his army·as of more importance than the possession of posts.   He well knew that if his army should be destroyed, there could be no hope indulged that another could be raised, for the country was nearly exhausted of able-bodied men, and therefore it was of vital importance to spare the troops.   Johnston had certainly done nobly in the campaign with his inferior force; and the energy with which he had used it, whenever prudence would counsel vigorous action, may be inferred from the fact that when he reached the defenses of Atlanta, he had lost about one-fourth of the army with which he left Dalton.[1]   Experts say that he had managed the campaign with the greatest skill, and for the best interests of the Confederacy; but this fact the reckless and conceited Davis, and his

---

[1] Pollard, the Confederate Historian, says that he lost about 10,000 in killed and wounded, and 4,700 from all other causes.

incompetent lieutenant, Bragg, could not comprehend or would not acknowledge, and Johnston was ordered to surrender the command of the army to the more dashing, but less skillful soldier, General Hood. This was done at the time we are considering, while Sherman was giving his worn and wearied soldiers some rest on the borders of the Chattahoochee. When Hood took command, his army numbered about fifty-one thousand effective men, of whom ten thousand were cavalry.

J. B. HOOD.

The main armies remained quiet in their camps until the middle of July. Meanwhile, Sherman was busy in collecting stores at Allatoona, Marietta, and Vining's Station, between the latter place and the Chattahoochee, and in taking measures for making and keeping his communications perfect. When this was accomplished, he was impelled forward by considerations which could not be unheeded. "Atlanta lay before us," he said, "only eight miles distant, and was too important a place, in the hands of an enemy, to be left undisturbed, with its magazines, stores, arsenals, workshops, founderies, &c., and more especially its railroads, which converge there from the four great cardinal points." Accordingly, on the 17th of July, he resumed active operations, by throwing Thomas's army across the Chattahoochee, close upon Schofield's right, with directions to move forward by Buckland. Schofield was ordered to move by Cross Keys, at the same time, and with McPherson, who was on the extreme left, at Roswell, to march rapidly against the Augusta railway, at some point east of Decatur, and near Stone Mountain.

In obedience to these orders, the whole army made a right-wheel movement, and closed in upon Atlanta from the northeast. McPherson struck the railway seven miles east of Decatur, on the 18th,[a] and with Garrard's cavalry and the infantry division of General M. L. Smith, broke up about four miles of the track. At about the same time, Schofield seized Decatur. McPherson entered it on the 19th, when the former marched in the direction of Atlanta. On the same day Thomas crossed Peachtree Creek, at several points, in the face of the Confederate intrenchments, skirmishing heavily at every step. Indeed, in all of these forward movements there were severe and almost incessant struggles.

[a] July, 1864.

At about this time Sherman was strengthened by the arrival of General Rousseau, with two thousand cavalry. He was in command of the District of Tennessee, and when Sherman planned a raid against the railway between Atlanta and Montgomery, one of Johnston's chief channels of supplies for his army, he asked permission to lead the expedition. It was granted, and when Johnston crossed the Chattahoochee and Sherman began maneuvering against Atlanta, the latter telegraphed orders to Rousseau to move. That active officer instantly obeyed. He left Decatur, Alabama, at the head of

well-appointed cavalry, on the 10th,[b] pushed rapidly southward   [b] July.
crossed the Coosa at the Ten Islands, fought and defeated General Clanton, and passing through Talladega, reached the railway twenty-five
miles west of Opelika on the 16th, and broke it up to the latter place. He
also destroyed several miles of the track of branch railways. Then, turning
northward, he reached Marietta on the 22d, with a loss, during the raid, of
only about thirty men.

On the 20th, the armies had all closed in, converging toward Atlanta.
At about four o'clock that day, the Confederates, under Hood, sallied swiftly
from their works in heavy force, and struck Hooker's corps, Newton's division of Howard's corps, and Johnson's division of Palmer's corps. The
blow was so gallantly received, and vigorously returned, that the assailants
were repulsed and driven back to their intrenchments. Hooker's corps
being uncovered, and on mostly open ground, suffered most severely. The
entire National loss in the combat was fifteen hundred men. Sherman estimated Hood's entire loss at not less than five thousand men. He left five
hundred dead on the field, one thousand severely wounded, many prisoners,
and several battle-flags.

The 21st was spent by Sherman in reconnoitering the Confederate intrenched position on the south side of Peachtree Creek, during which Brigadier-General L. Greathouse (formerly Colonel of the Forty-Eighth Illinois)

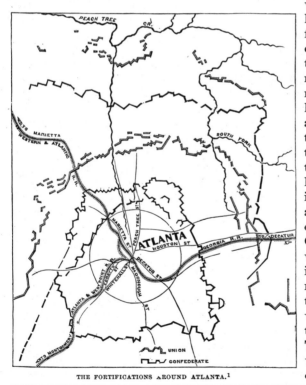

THE FORTIFICATIONS AROUND ATLANTA.[1]

was killed. On the fol-
lowing morning it was
found that the Confed-
erates had abandoned
those heights, and Sher-
man supposed that
movement to be pre-
liminary to the evacu-
ation of Atlanta. With
that impression, the
troops pressed eagerly
toward the town in
lines forming a narrow-
ing semicircle, when,
at an average distance
of two miles from the
Court-House, they
were confronted by an
inner line of intrench-
ments, much stronger
than the first, behind
which were swarming
the Confederate hosts.
This line consisted of
well-armed redoubts,
connecting intrench-

---

[1] This shows the general outlines of the fortifications around Atlanta, cast up by both parties, as they
existed when Sherman departed from that city on his grand march toward the sea.

ments, rifle trenches, *abatis* and *chevaux-de-frise* covering every road connected with Atlanta.

Hood's policy was to fight for positions, not to abandon them, as Sherman discovered, when, on the 22d,[a] the Army of the Tennessee, [a] July, 1864. with McPherson at its head, was preparing to move against the Confederate works. That army, describing in its line of march the arc of a circle, rapidly diminishing in radius, moved from Decatur on the direct road to Atlanta. Logan's corps formed the center, Dodge's the right, and Blair's the left. On the previous night, the latter, after a severe struggle, had driven the Confederates from a hill that overlooked the heart of the city, and McPherson now made preparations for planting heavy batteries upon it, to be supported by Dodge's corps, which was ordered from the right to the left, to make that point a strong general left flank.

While, at near noon, Dodge's troops were making their way along an obscure road in the rear of Logan, Sherman, who was at Howard's house, with General Schofield, some distance off, heard the sound of battle on the left and rear of McPherson's troops, first as a mere sputter of musketry, then as volleys, and then as the thunder of artillery. McPherson had left Sherman only a little while before, for that part of his line, and the latter, who quickly comprehended the situation, felt sure that the commander of the Army of the Tennessee would do all that man could to avert calamity. Hood had made a bold movement, and this was the first revelation of it. He had left a sufficient number of troops within his intrenchments on the front of Sherman, to hold them, and with his main body, led by Hardee, had made a long night march to the left and rear of the Nationals, and struck them there a severe and unexpected blow. It fell with heaviest force upon Giles A. Smith's division of Blair's corps, and it was received with gallantry and fortitude. Alas! McPherson was not there to order the further movements of the troops. He had ridden from Sherman to Dodge's moving column, when he sent nearly the whole of his staff and orderlies on various errands, and moved forward into a wood, for observations, in the rear of Smith's troops. At that moment Hardee made his first charge. His troops were pouring into a gap between Dodge and Blair; and just as McPherson had given an order for a brigade to move up and fill that gap, a Confederate sharp-shooter, of the same name, shot the brave leader dead.[1] His riderless and wounded horse made his way back to the Union lines, and the body of the hero was recovered during the heat of battle, and was sent in charge of his personal staff back to Marietta.

"The suddenness of this calamity," General Sherman afterward said, "would have overwhelmed me with grief, but the living demanded my whole thoughts."[2] He ordered General John A. Logan to take command of the Army of the Tennessee, and hold the ground McPherson had chosen, and especially a hill which General Leggett had secured the night before. At the gap, into which the charging Confederates poured, Murray's battery of six guns was

---

[1] General McPherson had thrown himself flat on his horse, and attempted to fly, when Major McPherson, of the Fifth Regiment of the Confederate army, drew up his carbine, took deliberate aim, and shot the General.— *Oral Statement to the author by Major Charles W. Gibson, of Forrest's cavalry.*

[2] Speaking of General McPherson, Sherman said: "He was a noble youth, of striking personal appearance [see page 235], of the highest professional capacity and with a heart abounding in kindness, that drew to him the affections of all men."

captured by them, but Wangelin's brigade, obeying McPherson's last order, came up in time to check the assailants there. One wing of Smith's divi-

sion was forced back, and two more guns were lost. Fortunately for the Nationals, General Stewart, who was to attack Blair in front simultaneously with Hardee's assault on flank and rear, was not up in time to effect much.

When Logan assumed command, the battle had been general along the whole line, and it raged fiercely for several hours. The Nationals had the advantage of position, and inflicted very heavy loss on the Confederates, who had been unable to drive Blair and Dodge. The latter gave their assail-

JOHN A. LOGAN.

ants very severe blows on their right, killing and wounding many, and capturing a considerable number of prisoners. Finally, at four o'clock in the afternoon, there was a lull in the contest. Meanwhile, Wheeler, with his cavalry, finding no opposition on the left of Sherman's army, in consequence of the absence of Garrard and his horsemen at Covington, between Decatur and

VIEW ON THE ATLANTA BATTLE-GROUND.[1]

Augusta, engaged in destroying the railway there, attempted to capture McPherson's wagon-train at the former town. But Colonel (afterward General) Sprague, in command there, so skillfully guarded the wagons that he succeeded in sending all but three of them out of the reach of danger.

The lull in the battle was brief. The Confederates soon charged up the railway and main Decatur road, scattering an advanced regiment acting as pickets, and capturing its two guns in battery at the foot of a tall pine-tree,

---

[1] This is a view of the remains of a National battery, by the side of one of the roads leading from Atlanta to Decatur, which did great execution on the 22d of July, as it appeared when the writer sketched it, in May, 1866. It was in the woods seen in front of it, and not more than eighty rods distant from it, that McPherson was killed. Here was the place of some of the heaviest fighting in the battle of Atlanta.

used as a signal station.[1] Then advancing rapidly, they broke through the Union line between the divisions of Wood and Harrow, of Logan's corps, posted on each side the roads, and pushed back, in much disorder, Lightburn's brigade, about four hundred yards, to a point held by it the night before. The Confederates took possession of two important batteries, and held them, at the point of separation which they had made between the divisions of Wood and Harrow. Sherman, who was near, fully comprehending the importance of the unity of the army at that point, and of checking the farther advance of the Confederates, ordered up several of Schofield's batteries, and directed Logan to regain the ground just lost, at any cost, while Wood was directed to press forward, supported by Schofield, and recover the captured guns. The orders were all promptly executed, Sherman said, "in superb style, at times our men and the enemy fighting across the narrow parapet." At length the Confederates gave way, and fell back to their defenses; and so ended, in advantage to the Nationals, THE BATTLE OF ATLANTA, on the 22d of July. It was a sanguinary one, and was much more disastrous in the loss of men to the Confederates than to the Patriots.[2]

SIGNAL TREE.

On the day after the battle[a] just recorded, General Garrard returned from Covington, where he had sufficiently injured the Augusta railway to make it useless to the Confederates.[3] At the same time Generals Thomas and Schofield had well closed up, and Hood was firmly held behind his inner line of intrenchments. Considering the situation in all its bearings, Sherman concluded to make a flank movement by his right, and in the mean time to send out the bulk of his cavalry to raid on the railways in Hood's rear. He accordingly ordered Stoneman to take his own and Garrard's cavalry, about five thousand in all, and move by the left around Atlanta to Macdonough, while McCook, with his own, and the fresh cavalry brought by Rousseau (now commanded by Colonel Harrison, of the Eighth Indiana), was to move by the right to Fayetteville, and, sweeping round, join Stoneman on the railway south of Atlanta leading to Macon, at Lovejoy's Station, on the night of the 28th.

These bodies of mounted men moved simultaneously. McCook went

[a] July 23, 1864.

---

[1] This station was for the purpose of directing the fire of the Nationals on the Confederate army, the country being so broken and wooded that the artillerists could not certainly know the position of their foes. Lieutenant Reynolds was at the platform near the top of this tree, acting as signal officer when the Confederates made the charge mentioned in the text, and was shot dead at his post. This tree was between the railway and the Decatur road, and the writer sketched it, in May, 1866.

[2] The total loss of the Nationals was 3,722, of whom about 1,000 were well prisoners. General Logan computed the Confederate dead, alone, at 3,240. He delivered to Hood, under a flag of truce, 800 dead bodies and reported that 2,200, by actual count, were found on the field. Sherman estimated Hood's entire loss on the 22d of July, "at full 8,000 men." Among the Confederate killed was General W. H. T. Walker, of Georgia.

[3] Garrard destroyed the railway bridges over the Ulcofauhatchee and Yellow rivers, burned a train of cars and 2,000 bales of Confederate cotton, the depots of stores at Covington and Conyer's Station, and captured 200 men and some good horses. His loss was only two men.

down the west side of the Chattahoochee to Rivertown, where he crossed the stream on a pontoon bridge, tore up the track of the railway between Atlanta and West Point, near Palmetto Station, and pushed on to Fayette-ville. There he captured five hundred of Hood's wagons and two hundred and fifty men, and killed and carried away about a thousand mules. Press-ing on, he struck and destroyed the Macon railway at the appointed time and place, but Stoneman was not there. McCook had no tidings of him; so, being hard pressed by Wheeler's cavalry, he turned to the southwest and struck the West Point road again at Newman's Station. There he was met by a heavy body of infantry from Mississippi, on its way to assist Hood at Atlanta. At the same time his rear was closely pressed by Confederate cavalry, and he was compelled to fight great odds. He did so gallantly, and fought his way out, but with the loss of his prisoners, and five hundred of his own men, including Colonel Harrison, who was made a captive.

Stoneman, in the mean time, attempting to do too much, failed in nearly all things. At the last moment before leaving, he obtained General Sher-man's consent to go farther after striking the railway at Lovejoy's, and sweeping southward, capture Macon, the capital of Georgia, and pushing on to Andersonville, release the thousands of Union prisoners then suffering horribly there. He had gone but a short distance, when he cut loose from Garrard's cavalry, and, in disobedience of Sherman's orders, omitted to co-operate with McCook in his movement upon the railway at Lovejoy's. With his own command, about three thousand in number, he pressed directly upon Macon. There he was met so stoutly by Confederate cavalry, under General Iverson, that he not only abandoned all thoughts of capturing Macon, or becoming the liberator of the prisoners at Andersonville, but he turned hastily back, impelled by the urgent business of trying to escape. In so doing, he weakened his force by dividing it, and instructing the three brigades of which it was composed, to seek safety by separate paths. Iver-son pressed closely upon the fugitives. One of the brigades, commanded by Colonel Adams, reached Atlanta without much loss. Another, under Colo-nel Capron, was dispersed by a charge of Confederate cavalry; and the remainder, about one thousand strong, commanded by Stoneman himself, and who had been employed in checking Iverson while the others should escape, were surrounded by the active Georgian, and seven hundred of them were made prisoners. The remainder escaped. Iverson had only about five hundred men, but deceived his antagonist with a show of superior force. Stoneman's unfortunate expedition cost Sherman about one-third of his cav-alry, without any compensating advantage. Garrard, meanwhile, had been compelled to skirmish heavily with Wheeler's cavalry, near Flat Rock, where Stoneman had left him. Hearing nothing from his superior, he returned to the army before Atlanta.

Simultaneously with the raids just mentioned, Sherman began a movement for flanking Hood out of Atlanta. Some important changes in the commands of his army had just been made.[a] By order of the Presi-dent, O. O. Howard[1] was made the successor of McPherson in the command of the Army of the Tennessee. This preference was regarded by Gen-

July 27, 1864.

---

[1] See page 61.

'eral Hooker as a disparagement of himself, and he resigned the command of the Twentieth·Corps, which was assigned to General H. W. Slocum. The latter was then at Vicksburg, and the corps was ably handled by General A. S. Williams, until the arrival of his superior. General Palmer resigned the command of the Fourteenth Army Corps,[a] and was succeeded[b] by that true soldier and most useful officer, General Jefferson C. Davis. The latter at once announced as his chief-of-staff, Colonel A. C. McClurg, an active young officer of the West, who had been the adjutant-general of the Fourteenth Corps since soon after the battle of Missionaries' Ridge, in which he was distinguished. General D. S. Stanley succeeded[c] General Howard as commander of the Fourth Corps.

[a] August 6, 1864.

[b] August 22.

[c] July 27.

H. W. SLOCUM.

Sherman began his new flanking movement by shifting[d] the Army of the Tennessee

[d] July 27.

from his extreme left on the Decatur road, to his extreme right on Proctor's Creek. General Howard had the chief supervision of the movement, which was made *en echelon*. Dodge's corps was on the left nearest the Confederates. Blair's was to come up on its right, and Logan's on Blair's right, refused as a flank. By ten o'clock on the morning of the 28th, the army was in position. The vigilant Hood had penetrated Sherman's design, but not until the change of the position of the Army of the Tennessee was substantially effected, and the men were casting up rude breastworks along their new front.

Hood acted promptly on his discovery. Under cover of an artillery fire, he moved out from his works,[e] on the Bell's Ferry road, west of Atlanta, with a larger portion of his army, led by

[e] July 28.

JEFFERSON C. DAVIS.

Hardee and S. D. Lee,[1] with the expectation of finding Howard's forces in some confusion, on account of their shifting movements. He was mistaken, and disastrous consequences followed his misapprehension. His heavy masses were thrown swiftly against Logan's corps, on Howard's right,

[1] When Hood took command of the army, his corps was placed in charge of General S. D. Lee, an experienced officer, who had performed much service in Tennessee.

which was posted on a wooded ridge, with open fields sloping from its front. That gallant leader was well prepared for battle, and the assailants were met by a fire that made fearful havoc in their ranks. They recoiled; but with amazing gallantry and fortitude they returned to the attack again and again, and the battle raged furiously from noon until nearly four o'clock in the afternoon, when the smitten columns refused to fight longer. They suddenly retired to their intrenchments, leaving several hundred of their comrades dead on the field. Hood's entire loss in this desperate conflict was about five thousand men. That of the Nationals did not exceed six hundred.[1] So ended the second BATTLE OF ATLANTA.[2] The conflict was so disastrous to the persons, and so demoralizing to the spirit, of the Confederate army, that Hood thereafter was constrained to imitate, in a degree, the caution of Johnston.

Sherman was near the scene of the conflict on the 28th,[a] and was busy in extending his right. For this purpose he brought down Schofield's Army of the Ohio and the Fourteenth Corps to Howard's right, and stretched an intrenched line nearly to East Point, the junction of two railways, over which came the chief supplies for Atlanta and Hood's army. The latter extended a parallel line of works; and with great impatience of spirit, Hood acted on the defensive for more than a fortnight, while obvious dangers were gathering thick around him. Sherman's long range guns shelled Atlanta, and kindled destructive fires in the city; yet its defenders kept quiet within the intrenchments. At length, taking counsel of his impulses rather than of his judgment, and seemingly unmindful of the fact that he had wasted nearly one-half of his infantry in rash acts, Hood sent out Wheeler, with the greater part of his cavalry, to capture supplies, burn bridges, and break up railways in the rear of Sherman's army, with a hope of depriving him of subsistence.

[a] July, 1864.

Wheeler moved swiftly with about eight thousand horsemen. He struck and broke the railway at Calhoun, captured nine hundred beeves in that vicinity, and seriously menaced the depot at Allatoona. This was just at the time when Sherman had issued an order[b] for a grand movement of his army upon the West Point and Macon railway, for the purpose of flanking Hood out of Atlanta. The first named road was to be struck at Fairborn Station, and the other at near Jonesboro', some twenty miles south of Atlanta. When he heard of Wheeler's raid he was rejoiced. "I could have asked nothing better," he said, "for I had provided well against such a contingency, and this detachment left me supe-

[b] Aug. 16,

---

[1] Logan estimated Hood's loss at a much greater number. The Confederate leader said it was only 1,500. But he left 642 dead on the field, which were counted by the Union burial parties, and these were not all. Making allowance for the usual proportion of the wounded and missing to the killed, would make Hood's loss about 5,000. Logan reported that he captured nearly 2,000 muskets, and took 233 prisoners, of whom 73 were wounded.

[2] Sherman ordered General Davis's division, of the Fourteenth Army Corps, to move round toward East Point, and, in the event of a battle, to fall upon Hood's flank and rear. These troops were delayed in consequence of misinformation given by defective maps concerning roads, and did not participate in the action. Sherman said in his report: "Had General Davis's division come up on the Bell's Ferry road, as I calculated, at any time before four o'clock, what was simply a complete repulse would have been a disastrous rout to the enemy. But I cannot attribute the failure to want of energy or intelligence, and must charge it, like many other things in this campaign, to the peculiar tangled nature of the forests, and the absence of roads that would admit the rapid movement of troops." Only those persons who have traveled in that region can fully understand the significance of this statement.

rior to the enemy in cavalry. I suspended the execution of my orders for the time being, and directed General Kilpatrick to make up a well appointed force of five thousand cavalry, and to move from his camp about Sandtown, during the night of the 18th, to the West Point road, and break it good near Fairborn; then to proceed across to the Macon road and tear it up thoroughly; to avoid, as far as possible, the enemy's infantry, but to attack any cavalry he could find."[1] Sherman hoped this expedition would obviate the necessity of the contemplated grand movement of the army, and leave him in better position to take advantage of the result.

Kilpatrick made the prescribed movement with strict fidelity to orders. When he reached the Macon road, a little above Jonesboro', he was confronted by Ross's cavalry. These he routed, and drove through Jonesboro', when he began tearing up the track and destroying other of the railway property. He had done but little mischief, when a brigade of infantry and some cavalry came up from the south, and compelled him to desist and fly. Making a circuit eastward, he again struck the road at Lovejoy's, below Jonesboro', where he was met by a large force. Through the opposing cavalry line he dashed, capturing and destroying a four-gun battery, excepting a single piece that he took with him, and securing and carrying [a Aug., 1864.] away seventy prisoners. Sweeping around eastward again, he reached Decatur on the 22d,[a] and on the same day proceeded to Sherman's head-quarters.

Kilpatrick declared that he had so much damaged the Macon railway, that it would be useless to the Confederates for ten days. But Sherman was not satisfied that the expedition would produce the desired result, so he renewed his order for a movement of the whole army. The siege of Atlanta was raised on the night of the 25th, and all munitions of war, supplies, and the sick and wounded men, were sent to Sherman's intrenched position on the Chattahoochee, whither the Twentieth Corps (General Slocum's) marched for their protection. In the grand movement that followed, the Fourth Corps (Stanley's) was on the extreme left, nearest the enemy. The Army of the Tennessee (Howard's) drew out and moved rapidly in a circuit to the West Point road at Fairborn, where the Army of the Cumberland (Thomas's) came into position just above Howard's at Red Oak, and the Army of the Ohio (Schofield's) closed in upon Thomas's left, only a short distance from the strong Confederate works covering the junction of the roads at East Point. So quietly, secretly, and quickly, were these movements performed, that Hood was not informed of them until Sherman was thoroughly at work[a] destroying the West Point railway over a distance of [a Aug. 28.] twelve miles.[2] To that business the Union commander devoted

<hr/>

[1] General Sherman's official report, September 15, 1864.

[2] "Twelve and one-half miles were destroyed, the ties burned, and the iron rails heated and tortured by the utmost ingenuity of old hands at the work. Several cuts were filled up with the trunks of trees, with logs, rock and earth, intermingled with loaded shells, prepared as torpedoes, to explode in the case of an attempt to clear them out."—Sherman's Report.

In an interesting narrative of the services of the First District of Columbia Cavalry, while it was in the division of General Kautz, kindly furnished me by Colonel D. S. Curtiss, a member of that regiment, and the most conspicuous leader of charges upon railways in the business of destroying them, a vivid account is given of the methods employed in effectually ruining the roads. In his account of Kautz's raid from Bermuda Hundred, by way of Chesterfield Court-House [see page 323], Colonel Curtiss says, speaking of the destruction of a railway track: "It was done by detailing the men, dismounted, along the track, with levers, who lifted it up.

only one day; and on the 29th he threw his army forward to the Macon road. Schofield moved cautiously, because he was nearest Atlanta, and reached the road at Rough and Ready Station, ten miles from that city. Thomas struck it at Couch's, and Howard, crossing the Flint River half a mile from Jonesboro', approached it at that point. He encountered strong and entirely unexpected opposition, while Schofield felt none. The reason was that Hood, on account of Kilpatrick's raid, had divided his army, and sent one half of it to Jonesboro', under Hardee, and with the remainder he held the defenses of Atlanta, and was too weak to attempt to strike Schofield under the vigilant eye of Slocum.

Howard fought gallantly at the passage of the Flint, and on the following morning[a] found himself in the presence of a very formidable antagonist. Placing his army in battle order, with the Fifteenth (Blair's) Corps in the center, and the Sixteenth and Seventeenth on its flanks, while the men, as usual, cast up rude breastworks in front, he awaited an expected attack. It came very soon, for Hardee, hoping to crush Howard before he could receive re-enforcements, threw upon him, as quickly as possible, the weight of his own and Lee's column. He failed to effect his purpose. The Nationals thus attacked were veterans, and had faced equal danger on many a field. For two hours there was a desperate strife for victory. It was won by Howard. Hardee recoiled, and in his haste to escape destruction, left four hundred of his dead on the field, and three hundred of his badly wounded in Jonesboro'. Hardee's entire loss was estimated at twenty-five hundred men. Howard's was about five hundred.

a Aug. 31, 1864.

At the time of this encounter, Sherman was at Couch's, where Thomas was destroying the railway. The noise of battle, in the voices of great guns, caused the chief to order both Thomas and Schofield to the assistance of Howard. At the same time Kilpatrick was sent down the west bank of the Flint to strike the railway below Jonesboro', and Garrard was left at Couch's to scout the country in the direction of Atlanta. Davis's corps, of Thomas's army, very soon touched the left of Howard's forces, and relieved Blair's (Fifteenth) corps, which was disposed so as to connect with Kilpatrick's horsemen. By four o'clock in the afternoon,[b] all was in readiness for an advance, when Davis charged, and almost instantly carried the Confederate line of works covering Jonesboro' on the north, and captured General Govan and a greater portion of his brigade, and a four-gun battery. Stanley and Schofield, who had been ordered forward, did not arrive until it was too late to make another charge that evening, owing to the peculiar character of the country. In the morning there was no foe on their front. Hardee had fled, and so ended THE BATTLE OF JONESBORO'.

b August 31.

At two o'clock in the morning[c] sounds like the low bellowing of distant thunder reached the ears of Sherman from the north. He was a little puzzled. Surely Slocum had not ventured to

c Sept. 1.

All moved uniformly at the word of command, turning over long spaces, like sward or land-furrows. Then knocking the ties loose from the rails, the former were piled up, the latter laid upon them, and a fire kindled under, which, burning away, soon caused the rails to bend so badly as to be unfit for use. In this way many miles were quickly destroyed, at various places, on our march." When there was time, the heated rails were bent around trees, and some were twisted into what the raiders called "Jeff Davis's neck-ties," as seen on page 239.

attack the strong defenses of Atlanta with only the Twentieth Corps. Hood must be blowing up his magazines preparatory to his flight from that city. With this impression, Sherman ordered a vigorous pursuit of Hardee. He

BATTLE-GROUND NEAR JONESBORO'.[1]

was found at Lovejoy's, not far distant, strongly intrenched, with the Walnut Creek and Flint River on his flanks. While Sherman was preparing with deliberation' to dislodge him, rumors reached that leader that Hood was, indeed, evacuating Atlanta. The truth was given him on the 4th by a courier from Slocum, and revealed the fact that his adversary, outgeneraled, and overwhelmed with perplexity, had blown up his magazines and seven trains of cars, destroyed the founderies and workshops in Atlanta, and fled; Stewart's corps hastening in the direction of Macdonough, while the demoralized militia were marched to Covington. Slocum had entered the city unopposed, on the morning after Hood left[a] it, and was holding it as a conqueror. Hardee's forces now became an object of secondary consideration to Sherman, and he turned the faces of his troops northward. On the 8th they were all encamped around Atlanta, Howard in the direction of West Point, and Schofield near Decatur. The commander-in-chief made his head-quarters at the fine brick mansion of Judge Lyon, not far from the Court-house, and prepared to give his army needed rest. Atlanta, one of the chief objectives of the campaign, was won, and by the victory an irreparable injury had been inflicted on the Confederates, in the loss of an immense amount of materials of war, as well as of prestige.[2] Yet the Confederate army, shattered, it is true, but still for-

[a] Sept. 2, 1864.

---

[1] This is a view of the portion of the battle-ground near Jonesboro', where the Confederate works crossed the railway and the common highway, about a mile and a half from the village, and gives the appearance of the place when the writer sketched it, late in May, 1866.

[2] The losses of the Confederates during this campaign, down to the capture of Atlanta, was estimated as follows:—In skirmishing from Chattanooga to Atlanta, 6,000; Battle of Resaca, 2,500; battles around Dallas,

midable, was in the field, and Sherman saw clearly that a difficult prob-lem lay before him, all unsolved.

SHERMAN'S HEAD-QUARTERS IN ATLANTA.

When General Slocum was satisfied that Hood had abandoned Atlanta, he sent out, at dawn,[a] a strong recon-noitering column in that direction. It encountered no opposition, and en-tered the city—much of which was reduced to a smoking ruin by Hood's incendiary fires—at 9 o'clock, when it was met by Mayor Calhoun, who formally surrendered the place. Gen-eral Ward's division then marched in, with drums beating and colors flying, and the National flag was un-furled over the Court-house.[1] Two days afterward, General Sherman, satis-fied that the demands of the service required that the city should, for awhile, be appropriated exclusively for military purposes, issued an order[b] for the removal of all citizens, excepting those in the employment of the Government.[2] He proposed to General Hood, then encamped at Lovejoy's, a truce of ten days, for the purpose of executing the order. The latter acceded to the proposition, and offered to give all the assistance in his power for expediting the business, at the same time protest-ing against the measure "in the name of God and of humanity."[3] The civil

* Sept. 2, 1864.

b Sept. 4.

3,500; Battle of Kenesaw Mountain, 1,000; battles of July 20, 22, and 28, near Atlanta, 22,500; other contests around Atlanta, 1,500; and battles near Jonesboro', 5,000; total, 42,000. They lost more than twenty general officers, and nearly fifty pieces of cannon (of which 8 were 64-pounders), and full 25,000 small-arms.

The losses of the Nationals during the campaign were estimated as follows:—In skirmishing from Chatta-nooga to Resaca, 1,200; Battle of Resaca, 4,500; skirmishing from Resaca to Allatoona, 500; battles around Dallas, 3,000; Battle of Kenesaw Mountain, July 27, 3,000; other contests around Kenesaw, 4,500; skirmishing between the Kenesaw and the Chattahoochee, 1,000; battles of July 20, 22, and 28, near Atlanta, 6,200; skir-mishing afterward, 3,000; battles near Jonesboro', 1,500; in cavalry raids, 2,000; total, 30,400. The Nationals also lost fifteen cannon, ten of them in the severe battle of the 22d of July. Notwithstanding Sherman lost nearly one-third of his army, re-enforcements had been so judiciously given, that on his arrival at Atlanta he maintained his original strength in men.

[1] On the day of the evacuation of Atlanta [September 2], the telegraph gave information of the fact to the Government, whereupon the President, on the same day, publicly tendered the thanks of the nation to General Sherman, "and the gallant officers and soldiers under his command." Orders were issued for the firing of National salutes at the principal arsenals, and the 11th day of September was designated as one for offering solemn national thanksgiving "for the signal success of General Sherman in Georgia, and of Admiral Farragut at Mobile." The services of the latter will be narrated presently. On the 8th General Sherman issued a stirring congratulatory address to his army, telling them of the thanks they had received from the nation, recounting their exploits, and assuring them that if they continued faithful, it required "no prophet to foretell that our country will, in time, emerge from this war, purified by the fires of war, and worthy its great founder, Washington."

[2] This order directed the families, whose representatives were in the Confederate service, or who had gone south, to leave the city within five days. The citizens from the North, not having permission to remain, were ordered to leave within the same period, under penalty of imprisonment. And all masculine residents of the city were required to register their names with the Provost-Marshal within five days, and receive authority to remain, under penalty of imprisonment.

[3] "And now, sir," said Hood, "permit me to say that the unprecedented measure you propose transcends, in studied and ingenious cruelty, all acts ever before brought to my attention in the dark history of war. In the name of God and humanity I protest, believing that you will find you are expelling from their homes and firesides the wives and children of a brave people."

To this Sherman replied. He mentioned the fact that General Johnston had removed families all the way from Dalton down. "You, yourself," he said, "burned dwelling-houses along your parapet; and I have seen to-day fifty houses that you have rendered uninhabitable because they stood in the way of your forts and men." After declaring that it was a kindness to remove women and children from a vortex of war, and that a "brave

authorities of Atlanta made an appeal to Sherman to revoke or modify his order.[1] He refused to do so, but caused it to be executed with all the tenderness and consideration it was possible for him to exercise.[2]

While Sherman was resting his army at Atlanta, Hood, who was joined by Hardee, near Jonesboro', and was otherwise re-enforced, flanked Sherman's right, crossed the Chattahoochee, and made a formidable raid upon his communications.[3] In the mean time, Wheeler, who, as we have seen, had struck the railway at Calhoun,[4] had swept around so as to avoid the National forces

---

people " should have scorned to leave them there to the mercy of such "rude barbarians" as Hood represented the Patriot army to be, Sherman said :—

"In the name of common sense I ask you not to appeal to a just God in such a sacrilegious manner—you, who, in the midst of peace and prosperity, have plunged a nation into civil war—'dark and cruel war ;' who dared us to battle ; who insulted our flag; seized our arsenals and forts that were left in the honorable custody of a peaceful ordnance sergeant; seized and made prisoners of war the very garrisons sent to protect your people against negroes and Indians, long before any overt act by the (to you) 'hateful Lincoln Government ;' tried to force Kentucky and Missouri into rebellion in spite of themselves; falsified the vote of Louisiana ; turned loose your privateers to plunder unarmed ships; expelled Union families by the thousand ; burned their houses, and declared by act of 'Congress' the confiscation of all debts due Northern men for goods had and received. Do not talk thus to one who has seen these things, and will this day make as much sacrifice for the peace and honor of the South, as the best born Southerner among you. If we must be enemies, let us be men, and fight it out as we propose to-day, and not deal in such hypocritical appeals to God and humanity. God will judge me in good time, and he will pronounce whether it be more humane to fight with a town full of women, and the families of a 'brave people' at our backs, or to remove them in time to places of safety among their own friends and people." Hood received this terrible rebuke in silence.

[1] They drew a dreadful picture of war, and the sufferings that must be endured in the removal of the citizens from Atlanta. Sherman replied, assuring them that they could not qualify war in harsher terms than he would, and that it was in the power of those who made the war to have peace, by submission to the rightful authority of the Government they had wickedly assailed. The Government, he said, was resolved to put down the rebellion by force of arms. To secure peace, rebels must stop war. "Once admit the Union," he said, "once more acknowledge the authority of the National Government, and instead of devoting your houses, and streets, and roads, to the dread uses of war, I, and this army, become at once your protectors and supporters, shielding you from danger, let it come from what quarter it may." The civil authorities of Atlanta made no further appeals.

[2] No distinction was made between the families of the friends or foes of the Government, in furnishing means for transportation. Those who preferred to go south numbered 446 families, with an aggregate of 2,035 souls. These were transported in wagons, at the National expense, with furniture and clothes averaging 1,651 pounds for each family, to Rough and Ready, ten miles from Atlanta, while those who preferred to go North were taken at the Government cost by railway to Chattanooga. So humanely was the righteous act performed, that General Hood, through Major Clan, of his staff, tendered to General Sher- " Sept. 21. man," through Colonel Warner, of his staff, his acknowledgments in writing of the uniform courtesy which the Confederate General and his people had received on all occasions, in connection with the removal.

[3] It was at about this time that Jefferson Davis hastened from Richmond to Georgia to view the situation, and in a speech at Macon, on the 23d of September, he talked to them with the air of a Dictator, as he tried to be, using the personal pronoun as freely as an autocrat. He was much disturbed by the condition of affairs in that region, and the evident distrust of himself by the people ; and, while admitting that great disasters had befallen the cause of the Conspirators—that he met them as "friends drawn together in adversity," he endeavored to feed their hopes upon the husks of promises of great disasters that were to befall Sherman. He spoke of the disgrace because of Johnston's falling back from Dalton to Atlanta, and said, with the fact before him that Hood's rashness had ruined the army, "I then put a man in command who I knew would strike a manly blow for the defense of Atlanta, and many a Yankee's blood was made to nourish the soil before the prize was won." He advised the young women to marry an empty sleeve rather than a young man who had "remained home and grown rich ;" and, to give them an idea that he, like King Louis, was "the State," told them that if they knew of any young man who kept away from the service, who could not be made to go in any other way, to write to him. "I read all letters," he said, "sent to me." He admitted that not many men between eighteen and forty-five years of age were left. Then, with low cunning, he tried to give an excuse for the detention of their friends as captives, and the horrors of Andersonville, the wailings from which might almost have reached his ears, by pretending that it was the fault of the United States Government that prisoners were not exchanged. Imitating the vulgarity of Beauregard, he said: "Butler, the beast, with whom no commissioner of exchange would hold intercourse, had published in his newspapers that if we would consent to the exchange of negroes, all difficulties might be removed. This is reported as an effort of his to get himself whitewashed, by holding intercourse with gentlemen." The whole speech was full of the evidences of the desperation of a charlatan, satisfied that his tricks were discovered. He felt the chill of the silence and contempt of the thinking men and women who listened to him; and he went on to the head-quarters of Hood, at Palmetto, on the Atlanta and Lagrange railway, with the most gloomy forebodings of the future.

[4] See page 391.

at Allatoona, and appeared before Dalton and demanded its surrender. The little garrison there, under Colonel Liebold, held the post firmly until General Steedman came down from Chattanooga and drove Wheeler off. The latter then pushed up into East Tennessee, made a circuit around Knoxville by way of Strawberry Plains, crossed the Clinch River near Clinton, went over the Cumberland Mountains by way of the Sequatchie, and appeared at McMinnville, Murfreesboro', and Lebanon. Rousseau, Steedman, and Granger, in Tennessee, were on the alert, and they soon drove the raider into Northern Alabama by way of Florence. Although he had destroyed much property, his damage to Sherman's communications was so slight, that the latter said, in writing from Atlanta on the 15th of September:[a] "Our roads and telegraphs are all repaired, and the cars run with regularity and speed."[1]

1864.

Sherman and Hood took advantage of the lull in the campaign, in September, to reorganize their respective armies for vigorous work, and it was at nearly the close of the month when active operations were resumed.[2] Then, convinced that Hood intended to assume the offensive, and, in all probability, attempt to seize Tennessee, Sherman sent[b] General Thomas, his second in command, to Nashville, to organize the new troops expected to assemble there, and to make preliminary preparations to meet such an event. Thomas arrived at Nashville on the 3d of October.

b Sept. 28.

Meanwhile, the Confederates had crossed the Chattahoochee, and by a rapid movement had struck the railway in the vicinity of Big Shanty, not far from Kenesaw, and destroyed it for several miles. At the same time a division of infantry, under General French, pushed northward, and appeared before Allatoona,[c] where Colonel Tourtellotte, of the Fourth Minnesota, was guarding one million rations with only three thin regiments. Sherman was startled, and moved at once for the defense of his communications and stores. Leaving Slocum, with the Twentieth Corps, to hold Atlanta and the railroad bridge across the Chattahoochee, he commenced[d] a swift pursuit of Hood with the Fourth, Fourteenth, Fifteenth, Seventeenth, and Twenty-third Corps, and two divisions of cavalry.

c Oct. 5.

d Oct. 4.

On the morning of the 5th, Sherman was at the strong position around Kenesaw, and his signal officers were soon at work upon its summit. Expecting an attack on Allatoona, and knowing the weakness of the garrison there, he had telegraphed (and now signaled) to General Corse, at Rome, to hasten thither with re-enforcements. The order was promptly obeyed, and Corse was there and in command when French appeared at dawn[e] with an overwhelming force, and invested the place. After a cannonade of two hours the Confederate leader demanded

e Oct. 5.

---

[1] Sherman's Report.

[2] At that time the Army of the Cumberland, General Thomas commanding, occupied Atlanta; the Army of the Tennessee, General Howard commanding, was grouped about East Point; and the Army of the Ohio, commanded by General Schofield, was at Decatur. Sherman's cavalry consisted of two divisions; one, under General Garrard, was at Decatur, and the other, led by General Kilpatrick, was stationed near Sandtown, where he could watch the Confederates on the west. Sherman strengthened the garrisons to the rear; and to make his communications more secure, he sent Wagner's division, of the Fourth Corps, and Morgan's division, of the Fourteenth Corps, back to Chattanooga, and Corse's division, of the Fifteenth Corps, to Rome. Hood's army was arranged in three corps, commanded respectively by Generals Cheatham, Lee, and Stewart. His cavalry under Wheeler, had been re-enforced.

the surrender of the post. It was refused. Then he assailed it furiously, but was met with fires so murderous from two forts on the ridge that his columns were continually driven back.

The battle raged fiercely. From the top of Kenesaw, Sherman could see the smoke of conflict and hear the thunder of the cannon, though eighteen

ALLATOONA PASS.[1]

miles distant. He had sent General J. D. Cox, with the Twenty-third Corps, to assist the garrison by menacing French's rear in the direction of Dallas; and he was enabled to say to the commander at Allatoona, by signal flags from Kenesaw, "Hold out, for relief is approaching."[2] And when Sherman was assured that Corse was there, he exclaimed: "He will hold out! I know the man!" And so he did. He repelled assault after assault, until more than one-third of his men were disabled. Then the assailants, apprised of the approach of Cox, hastily withdrew and fled toward Dalton, leaving behind them two hundred and thirty of their dead, and four hundred made prisoners, with about eight hundred muskets. Corse lost seven hundred and seven men, and was severely wounded in the face. Among the many badly hurt were Colonels Tourtellotte and Howell.

When Davis visited Hood at Palmetto,[3] he instructed him to draw Sherman out of Georgia, for his presence there was causing alarming disaffection to the cause of the conspirators.[4] In obedience to these instructions, Hood now moved

---

[1] This shows the appearance of Allatoona Pass when the writer sketched it in May, 1866. The railway there passes through a cut in a ridge, on the summit of which, to the left of the picture, looking up from between the two houses, is seen Fort Hammond, so called because of a house standing there then, belonging to Mr. Hammond, a proprietor of the Allatoona Iron Works. The house on the ridge, at the right of the railway, belonged to Mr. Moore, and a fort on the extreme right was called Fort Moore.

[2] The value and the perfection of the signal system employed in the army, under the general superintendence of Major Albert J. Myer, was fully illustrated in the event recorded in the text, when from hill to hill, at a distance of eighteen miles, intelligent communication was kept up by the mere motion of flags, discerned by telescopes. An account of the method of signaling, perfected by Major Myer, may be found in the Supplement to this work.

[3] See note 3, page 396.

[4] At this time there was great disaffection to the Confederate cause in Georgia. Governor Brown, Alexander H. Stephens, and others, seemed to have been impressed with the utter selfishness and evident incompetency of Davis, and were disposed to assert, in all its strength, the doctrine of State supremacy. Davis's speech at Macon, already noticed, did not help his cause. The people were tired of war—tired of furnishing men and means to carry out the ambitious schemes of a demagogue—and three days after that speech, a long letter from Governor Brown was received [a] at the Confederate "War Department," in which he absolutely refused to respond to Davis's call for militia from that State. He said he would not encourage Davis's ambitious projects "by placing in his hands, and under his unconditional control, all that remains to preserve the reserved rights of the State." He bitterly and offensively criticised Davis's management of mili-

[a] Sept. 26, 1864.

rapidly northwestward, and threatened Kingston and other important points on the railway. Sherman followed as rapidly. He pressed through the Allatoona Pass and across the Etowah, and by a forced march reached Kingston[a] and saved it. There he found that Hood had turned westward, threatened Rome, and was crossing the Coosa over a pontoon bridge, eleven miles below that town. Sherman then hurried on to Rome,[b] and pushed Garrard's cavalry and Cox's (Twenty-third) corps across the Oostenaula, to threaten Hood's flank should he turn northward. That vigorous leader had moved so rapidly that he avoided the intended blow, excepting a slight one by Garrard, which drove a brigade of Confederate cavalry, and secured two of their guns; and he suddenly appeared before Resaca, and demanded its surrender. Sherman had re-enforced that post with two regiments of the Army of the Tennessee, and Colonel Weaver, the commander, gallantly repulsed a vigorous attack. The assailants then moved on, closely followed by Sherman. They destroyed the railway from Tilton to the tunnel at Buzzard's Roost, and captured the Union garrison at Dalton.

> [a] Oct. 10, 1864.

> [b] Oct. 11.

On his arrival at Resaca,[c] Sherman determined to strike Hood in flank, or force him to fight. He was now puzzled by Hood's movements, and knew no better way to force him to develop his designs. General Howard moved to Snake Creek Gap, and skirmished with the Confederates there, for the purpose of holding them while General Stanley, with the Fourth and Fourteenth Corps, should move round to Hood's rear, from Tilton to the vicinity of Villanow. But the Confederates gave way and withdrew to Ship's Gap, and on the following day[d] Sherman's forces moved directly toward Lafayette, with a view of cutting off Hood's retreat. That leader was watchful, and being in lighter marching order than his pursuer, outstripped and evaded him. Sherman still pressed on and entered the Chattanooga Valley, and on the 19th, his forces were all grouped about Gaylesville, a fertile region in Northern Alabama.

> [c] Oct. 14.

> [d] Oct. 16.

Sherman was now satisfied that Hood was simply luring him out of Georgia, and did not intend to fight. He had an army strong enough to endanger the National communications between Atlanta and Chattanooga, but not of sufficient power to engage in battle. So the patriot leader determined to execute a plan, which he had already submitted to the consideration of General Grant, namely, to destroy Atlanta and its railway communications with Chattanooga, and, moving through the heart of Georgia, capture one or more of the important seaport towns—Savannah or Charleston, or both. So he remained at Gaylesville a week, watching the movements of Hood,

---

tary affairs, in not re-enforcing Johnston and Hood. Georgia, he said, had then fifty regiments in Virginia; and he demanded their return to their own State, for its defense, if re-enforcements were not sent to Hood for that purpose.—[See *Rebel War Clerk's Diary*, ii., 392. It was this practical application of the principles of State sovereignty, so destructive of National unity in Georgia, that caused Davis to visit that State.

In recording the fact of Davis's absence at that time, *A Rebel War Clerk* said, in his diary: "'When the cat's away, the mice will play.' I saw a note of invitation to-day, from Secretary Mallory to Secretary Seddon, inviting him to his house, at 5 P. M., to partake of 'pea-soup' with Secretary Trenholm. His 'pea-soup' will be oysters and champagne, and every other delicacy relished by epicures. Mr. Mallory's red face and his plethoric body indicate the highest living; and his party will enjoy the dinner, while so many of our brave men are languishing with wounds, or pining in cruel captivity. Nay, they may feast, possibly, while the very pillars of the Government are crumbling under the blows of the enemy."

when, satisfied that he had marched westward over the Sand Mountains, he
proceeded[a] in preparations to put into execution his important
plan, with a full understanding with Generals Grant and Thomas,   [a] Oct. 26,
and the approval of the General-in-chief.   Stanley was ordered to   1864.
proceed to Chattanooga with the Fourth Corps, and report to General
Thomas, and Schofield was directed to do the same.

   To General Thomas, Sherman now delegated full power over all the
troops under his command, excepting four corps, with which he intended to
march from Atlanta to the sea.   He also gave him the two divisions of General A. J. Smith, then returning from the business of driving Price out of
Missouri;[1] also all the garrisons in Tennessee, and all the cavalry of the
Military Division, excepting a single division under Kilpatrick, which he
reserved for operations in Georgia.   General Wilson had just arrived from
the front of Petersburg and Richmond, to assume the command of the cavalry of the army, and he was sent back to Nashville, with various dismounted
detachments, with orders to collect and put in fighting order all the mounted
men serving in Kentucky and Tennessee, and report to General Thomas.
Thus the latter officer was furnished with strength believed to be sufficient
to keep Hood out of Tennessee; and he was invested with unlimited discretionary powers in the use of his material.   Sherman estimated Hood's force
at thirty-five thousand infantry and ten thousand cavalry.

   By the first of November, Hood made his appearance near the Tennessee
River, in the vicinity of Decatur, and passing on to Tuscumbia, laid a pontoon bridge across that stream at Florence.   Then Sherman turned his force
toward Atlanta, preparatory to taking up his march for the sea.   The Army
of the Tennessee moved back to the south side of the Coosa, to the vicinity
of Smyrna Camp-ground.   The Fourteenth Corps moved to Kingston,
from which point all the sick and wounded, and all surplus baggage and
artillery, were sent to Chattanooga.   The garrisons north of Kingston withdrew to the same place, with the public property and rolling stock of the
railway.   Then the mills and founderies at Rome were destroyed, and the
railway was thoroughly dismantled from the Etowah to the Chattahoochee.
The army crossed that stream, destroyed the railroads in and   [b] 1864.
around Atlanta, and, on the 14th of November,[b] the entire
force destined for the great march to the sea was concentrated around that
doomed city.

   The writer, accompanied by his traveling companions already mentioned
(Messrs. Dreer and Greble), visited the theater of the Georgia campaign in
1864, from Dalton to Atlanta, in the delightful month of May, 1866.   We
left Chattanooga early on the morning of the 15th,[c] by railway.   [c] May, 1866.
After passing through the tunnel at the Missionaries' Ridge, we
crossed the Chickamauga River several times before reaching Tunnel Hill,
in Rocky Face Ridge.   The country in that region was quite picturesque,
but utterly desolate in appearance.   Over it the great armies had marched,
and left the horrid foot-prints of war.   At Dalton, a once flourishing Georgia
town, where Bragg and Johnston had their quarters for several months, we
saw the first terrible effects of the campaign upon the works of man.   Ruin

---

[1] See page 280.

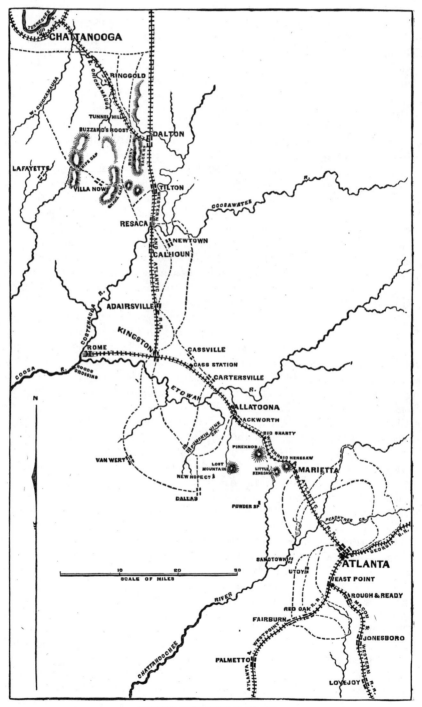

CAMPAIGN FROM DALTON TO ATLANTA.

was seen on every side; but on an eminence on the east of the railway, were heavy earth-works, cast up by the Confederates, in perfect order for battle, excepting armament and men. From that point all the way to Atlanta, block-houses, afterward built by the National troops for the protection of the railway, such as were erected between Murfreesboro' and Chattanooga,[1] were frequently seen.

We arrived at Resaca at about noon on the second anniversary [a] of the battle there.[2] It was then a ruined hamlet, with the earth-works left by the Confederates clustered around it. On the east side of the railway, between the station and the bridge over the Oostenaula River, were two considerable forts, built of earth, upon a low ridge; and at

[a] May 15, 1866.

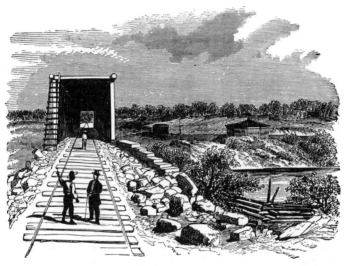

BRIDGE AT RESACA.[3]

about the same distance, on the west side, on gentle eminences, were three forts. Across the Oostenaula, at the bridge, was a block-house (seen in the picture), erected by the Nationals after the Confederates left, and another earth-fort near by.

The heaviest of the battle was fought near Camp Creek, about two miles from the station, in the direction of Snake Gap. The day was very. warm, and we desired to ride, rather than walk, to the battle-ground. It was difficult to find an animal or a vehicle for the purpose. At length, through the kind offices of Dr. Johnston, who had been a surgeon in the Confederate army, and was in the Battle of Resaca, we were furnished with a rickety wagon and a most forlorn-looking little white mule, arrayed in rope harness. The doctor was our driver and guide. Three almost bottomless splint-bottomed chairs were the furniture of the wagon. They were sufficient, for Mr. Dreer was too ill to go far in the sun, and he remained at the station.

---

[1] See pages 177 and 179.   [2] See page 375.
[3] This was a new bridge, not quite complete, erected on the site of the old one destroyed by Johnston when he fled from Resaca. The block-house is seen to the right. The Oostenaula is here a considerable stream, flowing between high banks.

We soon left the highway, and took a direct line across the fields for the battle-ground, opening fences for a passage, receiving curses from a planter because we crossed his cornfield, and laboring a little harder, on the whole, than if we had walked the entire distance. Our frowsy little mule was faithful to the instincts of his race, and varied our experience by running away down a hill, deep-gullied, and giving the writer an opportunity to display his agility by leaping from the bouncing wagon to a gravel bank full fifteen feet "from the place of beginning."

After visiting places of interest connected with the struggle near the head of Camp Creek, and sketching the theater of the hottest of the fight, delineated on page 376, we went over the hills, along which lay the Confederate trenches, to the main Dallas road, and returned by it to Resaca, where we lodged that night. Our friend was better in the morning,^a and we left at seven o'clock in a freight car for Allatoona, forty-four miles farther South. At Calhoun, Adairsville, Kingston, and other places, we stopped long enough to observe the sad effects of war. At Adairsville, the Georgia State Arsenal was in ruins; and from that point all the way to the Etowah River, solitary chimneys, small redoubts, and lines of intrenchments, with marks of desolation and stagnation everywhere, proclaimed the operations of an active and destructive campaign.

* May 16, 1866.

We crossed the Etowah River and its rich valley not far from Cartersville, in the heart of the beautiful and picturesque land of the ancient Cherokees— the mountaineers of the Southern tribes—where the few fields planted with cotton-seed were becoming delicately green with the springing germs; and at noon we arrived at Allatoona Pass, just as a thunder-storm was approaching. We found time to visit Fort Hammond and make the sketch on page 397 before much rain fell, and observed the relative position of the assailants and the assailed on the day when Corse and French fought so desperately there.[1] Only the chimneys of Hammond's house were standing. The rough ridge was denuded of its covering of forest trees, and dreariness brooded over the whole scene. From the fort, looking southward, we saw the blue summits of Big and Little Kenesaw, about eighteen miles distant, and in that direction we proceeded, in another freight car, at three o'clock on the same afternoon.

And now the doings of the Demon of War became more and more manifest and manifold in features. After passing Ackworth and approaching Big Shanty, in the vicinity of Kenesaw, the country seemed to be overspread with a net-work of intrenchments. These stretched away from the railway to Lost Mountain (which, with Pine Knob, on which Polk was killed, arose on our right), around to New Hope and Dallas, and became lodes of lead, placed there by the muskets of the belligerents in the terrible fights in which they were engaged in that region. These, for a long time after the armies disappeared, were sources of supply to the inhabitants of that region of means for purchasing subsistence. At the time of our visit, they had sold, in Marietta alone, over two hundred thousand pounds of lead in the form of bullets, which they had dug from these works or picked up over the intervening country.

---

[1] See page 397.

We arrived at Marietta—once beautiful and delightsome Marietta—about three miles from Kenesaw, toward evening, where we lodged in one of the houses which had escaped the ravages of war. That town, having about five thousand inhabitants when the war broke out, was noted for the beauty of its situation among the wooded hills, the salubrity of its climate, and the wealth, taste, and refinement of its people. It was a favorite summer resort in the hill-country of Georgia, for the residents of the coast. When we visited it, it was a ghastly ruin. Much of the natural beauty of its surroundings was preserved; and we can never forget the delight experienced by us

in an early morning walk along the broad and winding Powder Springs road, shaded with magnificent old forest trees, that led up to the eminence on which stood the Georgia Military Institute, until, by the torch of National soldiers, it was all reduced to ashes, excepting the broken ruins delineated

RUINS OF GEORGIA MILITARY INSTITUTE, MARIETTA.

in the engraving. In that sketch, made during the morning ramble, Kenesaw is seen in the distance, on the right. A few hours later we were on the summit of that great hill, whither we rode on spirited horses, in company with W. H. Tucker, of Marietta, as cicerone, who was the guide of General Johnston in that region during his campaign. At the foot of the mountain we struck the Confederate intrenchments, and found them winding up its northeastern slopes, so as to cover and command the railroad. They were in a continuous line of rifle-pits, redans, and redoubts, all the way to the summit, on which were the remains of a battery, and the signal station for both armies.[1]

From that lofty eminence we had a broad view of the surrounding country, and overlooked a theater of some of the most wonderful military events which history has recorded. It was within a circle of vision with an average of thirty miles radius, and every point was familiar to our guide. To the westward we looked off over the wooded country to Dallas and New Hope Church. Farther to the north and northwest were Lost and Pine mountains, and the Allatoona hills; and eastward, away beyond Atlanta, at a distance of thirty-six miles, arose, seemingly from a level country covered with forest, the magnificent dome of Stone Mountain. The air was full of little showers in all directions, which sometimes veiled what we desired to see; and just as we had finished our sketches and observations, one passed over Kenesaw, and drenched us gently while we descended to the rolling plain, and galloped back to Marietta. There we lodged again *May 18, that night, and on the following morning* went on to Atlanta, 1866.

---

[1] See page 378.

passing through heavy fortifications on the right bank of the Chattahoochee River, near the railway bridge, and then among others more thickly strewn around the ruined city.

We spent a greater portion of two days in and about Atlanta, visiting places of chief interest connected with the siege, accompanied by Lieutenant Holsenpiller, the post commander, and two other officers. Then we went down to Jonesboro', twenty-one miles south of Atlanta, on the Macon road. It was a little village of seven hundred inhabitants when the war began. It, like others in the track of the armies, was nearly ruined. The Court-house, and almost twenty other buildings, were destroyed. An intelligent young man, who was a Confederate soldier in the battle there between Howard and Hardee,[1] accompanied us to places of interest connected with that struggle, and at about noon we returned to the village and took the cars for Atlanta. We went out to Marietta that night and lodged, and on the following morning we journeyed by railway from that town to Cleveland, in East Tennessee, on our way to Richmond, in Virginia, by way of Knox-ville.[2]

---

[1] See page 393.   [2] See page 284.

CHAPTER XV.

SHERMAN'S MARCH TO THE SEA.—THOMAS'S CAMPAIGN IN MIDDLE TENNESSEE.—EVENTS IN EAST TENNESSEE.

 HERMAN'S force, with which he proposed to march to the sea, was composed of four army corps in two grand divisions, the right wing commanded by Major-General O. O. Howard, and the left wing by Major-General H. W. Slocum. The right was composed of the Fifteenth Corps, led by General P. J. Osterhaus, and the Seventeenth, commanded by General F. P. Blair. The left consisted of the Fourteenth Corps, commanded by General J. C. Davis, and the Twentieth, led by General A. S. Williams.[1] General Kilpatrick commanded the cavalry, consisting of one division. Sherman's entire force numbered sixty thousand infantry and artillery, and five thousand five hundred cavalry.

On the 14th of November, as we have observed, Sherman's troops, destined for the great march, were grouped around Atlanta. Their last channel of communication with the Government and the loyal people of the North was closed, when, on the 11th, the commander-in-chief cut the telegraph wire that connected Atlanta with Washington City. Then that army became an isolated moving column, in the heart of the enemy's country. It moved on the morning of the 14th, Howard's wing marching by way of Macdonough for Gordon, on the railway east of Macon, and Slocum's by the town of Decatur, for Madison and Milledgeville. Then, by Sherman's order, and under the direction of Captain O. M. Poe, chief engineer, the entire city of Atlanta (which, next to Richmond, had furnished more war materials for the Confederates than any in the South), excepting its Court-house, churches, and dwellings, was committed to the flames. In a short space of time, the buildings in the heart of the city, covering full two hundred acres of ground, were on fire; and when the conflagration was at its height, on the night of the 15th,[a] the band of the Twenty-third Massachusetts played, and the soldiers chanted, the air and words of the stirring song, "John Brown's soul goes marching on." Sherman left desolated Atlanta the following morning, and accompanied Slocum's wing in its march, at the beginning.

[a] November 1864.

---

[1] The Fifteenth Corps, General Osterhaus commanding, was composed of four divisions, commanded respectively, by Generals C. R. Woods, W. B. Hazen, J. M. Corse, and J. E. Smith. The Seventeenth Corps, General Blair, consisted of three divisions, commanded by Generals J. Mower, M. D. Leggett, and Giles A. Smith. The Fourteenth Corps, General Davis, consisted of three divisions, commanded by Generals W. P. Carlin, J. D. Morgan, and A. Baird. The Twentieth Corps, General Williams, was composed of three divisions, commanded by Generals N. J. Jackson, J. W. Geary, and W. T. Ward.

Sherman's first object was to place his army in the heart of Georgia, between Macon and Augusta, and so compel his foe to divide his forces, to defend not only these two important places,[1] but also Millen (where a large number of Union prisoners were confined), and Savannah and Charleston. For that purpose his troops marched rapidly. Kilpatrick swept around to, and strongly menaced Macon,[a] while Howard moved steadily forward and occupied Gordon, on the Georgia Central railroad, east of Macon, on the 23d. Meanwhile, Slocum moved along the Augusta railway to Madison, and after destroying the railroad bridge over the Oconee River, east of that place, turned southward and occupied Milledgeville, the capital of Georgia, on the same day[b] when Howard reached Gordon.[2] In these marches the National troops found no military resistance of any consequence,[3] excepting near Macon, and no serious obstacle, excepting such as wretched roads presented. Each wing had its separate pontoon train; and during the march to the sea, Sherman accompanied first one wing, and then the other, with his personal staff of only five officers, none of them above the rank of major.[4]

[a] Nov. 22, 1864.

[b] Nov. 23.

---

[1] At Augusta were some of the most important works in the Confederacy for the manufacture of cannon, shot and shell. A report of Colonel Rains, superintendent of those works, made in May previous to the time we are considering, gives the following list of war materials supplied to the Confederate army, by the works at Augusta, in the space of two months: "1,400,000 small-arm cartridges; 6,000 fixed ammunition (shot and shell attached to cartridges for field batteries); 2,500 Colonel Rains's percussion hand-grenades; 1,500 rifle shells for field artillery; 54 tons eight and ten-inch shot and shell for columbiads; 100 tons of gunpowder; 3 complete batteries of brass twelve-pounder Napoleon guns, with carriages, limbers, caissons, harness, equipments, ammunition, traveling forges, &c.; one battery of three-inch rifle and banded iron guns, and twelve-pounder bronze howitzers; 1 battery of four twelve-pounder bronze howitzers. The above two batteries were complete at all points, with carriages, limbers, caissons, harness, ammunition, equipments, &c.

"All of these guns, except the rifle battery (for General Morgan), were sent to General Johnston's army, which has altogether sixteen complete batteries of brass guns, which were mainly manufactured in every part at the government foundery and machine works and gun-carriage department in this place.

"The most of these batteries are composed of the new twelve-pounder Napoleon guns, introduced in the service of the war by the present Emperor of the French; of these, over 85, weighing in the aggregate more than 50 tons, have been cast at the government foundery in this city, mainly within the past year. In the same period, over 500 tons of the first quality of gunpowder have been made at the powder works and distributed throughout the Confederacy.

"In addition to the foregoing, there has been an immense number of small-arm cartridges, cartridge bags, fixed ammunition, canteens, haversacks, horse-shoes, time-fuses, and percussion-caps made at the arsenal, as well as large amounts of signal rockets, portfires, sets of artillery harness, infantry accouterments, &c., manufactured within the past twelve months."

[2] The legislature of Georgia was in session when Slocum approached. The members fled, without the formality of adjournment. The Governor followed their example, and a large number of the white citizens did likewise. Many of the young officers of Sherman's army took the places of the fugitive legislators at the Capitol, and immediately rescinded the Georgia Ordinance of Secession and other obnoxious acts, and declared that State to be back again in the Union. They elected General Sherman governor of the commonwealth, and made an immense appropriation for the pay of the new legislature. The currency in which they were paid was Confederate. About a million dollars were disbursed by the treasurer for that purpose, Colonel Coggswell, of New York. Some of the members received $50,000 for their few hours of service.

[3] The Conspirator, Howell Cobb, who plotted treason while in Buchanan's cabinet as Secretary of the Treasury (see page 44, volume I.), was in command of the Georgia militia in that section of the State, and was very careful to keep out of the way of peril. Like Toombs, he seems to have been brave in boasting, but otherwise in acting. Sherman encamped on one of his plantations, not far from Milledgeville, and there received a Macon newspaper containing a proclamation by Cobb, in which he called upon his fellow white citizens to "rise and defend their liberties and homes" from the invader, and "to burn and destroy every thing in his front, and assail him on all sides." Cobb had left the defense of his own home to his slaves, and had omitted the patriotic duty he enjoined upon others, of burning his own buildings and crops. This fact reminds us of the manifesto put forth by this man and his fellow-conspirator, Toombs, the year before. (See note 2, page 471, volume II.) These self-constituted leaders were willing to sacrifice others while sparing themselves.

Major Nichols, who was with Sherman, thus wrote concerning Cobb: "Becoming alarmed, Cobb sent for and removed all the able-bodied mules, horses, cows, and slaves. He left here some fifty old men—cripples—and women and children, with nothing scarcely covering their nakedness, with little or no food, and without means of procuring it. A more forlorn, neglected set of human beings I never saw."—*Story of the Great March*, page 58.

[4] These were Major M'Coy, aid-de-camp; Captain Audenried, aid-de-camp; Major Hitchcock, assistant-adjutant-general; Captain Dayton, aid-de-camp, and Captain Nichols, aid-de-camp. "Attached to his head-

The army had moved, with twenty days' provision of bread, forty days' of beef, coffee, and sugar, and three of forage in their wagons, with instructions to each subordinate commander to live off the country, and save the supplies of the train for an expected time of need, when the army should reach the less productive region near the sea-coast. This they were enabled to do, for the hill country through which they were moving was very fertile, and had not been exhausted by the presence of great armies. Sherman's audacity, and the uncertainty concerning his real destination, because of the widely separated lines of march of the two wings of his army, astounded, bewildered and paralyzed the inhabitants and the armed militia, and very little resistance was offered to foragers, who swept over the country in all directions. Kilpatrick's march from Atlanta to Gordon had appeared to them, like a meteor-flash to the supersitious, mysterious and evil-boding. At East Point he met some of Wheeler's cavalry, which Hood had left behind to operate against Sherman. These were attacked and driven across the Flint River. Kilpatrick crossed that stream at Jonesboro', and pursued them to Lovejoy, where Murray's brigade, dismounted, expelled them from intrenchments, captured the works, took fifty prisoners, and, in the pursuit, Atkins's brigade seized and held two of their guns. Pressing forward, Kilpatrick went through Macdonough and Monticello to Clinton, and then made a dash upon Macon, driving in some of Wheeler's cavalry there, threatening the strongly-manned works, burning a train of cars, tearing up the railway, and spreading the greatest consternation over that region.

By this time the Confederates began to comprehend the grand object of Sherman's movement, but could not determine his final destination. The evident danger to Georgia and the Carolinas caused the most frantic appeals to be made to the people of the former State. "Arise for the defense of your native soil," shouted Beauregard in a manifesto, as he was hastening from the Appomattox to the Savannah. He told them to destroy "all the roads in Sherman's front, flank and rear," and to be confident, and resolute, and trustful in an overruling Providence. He dismayed the thinking men of the State by saying, "I hasten to join you in defense of your homes and firesides," for they knew his incompetency and dreaded his folly. From Richmond, B. H. Hill, a Georgia "Senator," cried to the people of his State: "Every citizen with his gun, and every negro with his spade and ax, can do the work of a soldier. You can destroy the enemy by retarding his march. Be firm!" Seddon, the "Secretary of War," indorsed the message; and the representatives of Georgia in the Confederate "Congress" sent an earnest appeal to the people to fly to arms, assuring them that "President Davis and the Secretary of War" would do every thing in their power to help them in "the pressing emergency." "Let every man fly to arms," they said. "Remove your negroes, horses, cattle, and provisions from Sherman's army, and burn what you cannot carry. Burn all bridges, and block up the roads in his route. Assail the invader in front, flank and rear, by night and by day.

---

quarters," says Brevet-Major G. W. Nichols, in his *Story of the Great March,* "but not technically members of his staff, were the chiefs of the separate departments for the Military Division of the Mississippi." These were General Barry, chief of artillery; Lieutenant-Colonel Ewing, inspector-general; Captain Poe, chief of engineers; Captain Baylor, chief of ordnance; Dr. Moore, chief medical director; Colonel Beckwith, chief of the commissary department; and Captain Bachtal, chief of the signal corps.

Let him have no rest." And Governor Brown, just before he fled from Milledgeville, issued a proclamation ordering a levy, *en masse*, of the whole white population of the State between the ages of sixteen and forty-five years; and offered a pardon to the prisoners in the penitentiary at Milledgeville, if they would volunteer and prove themselves good soldiers. But the people neither flew to arms nor burned property, nor set the negroes at work making obstructions; and only about one hundred of the convicts seemed to think that fighting Sherman was to be preferred to imprisonment, for only that number accepted the Governor's offer. All confidence in "President Davis" and the "Confederate Government" had vanished. The great mass of the people were satisfied that it was "the rich man's war and the poor man's fight," as they expressed it, and would no longer lend themselves to the wicked work of the corrupt Conspirators at Richmond.

When Howard struck the Georgia Central railway at Gordon, his troops began the work of destroying the road eastward from that point to Griswoldsville, and while thus engaged, the most serious contest of the Georgia campaign occurred. While the right wing of the Fifteenth Corps, under General Walcott, was operating at Griswoldsville, about five thousand Confederates came upon them from the direction of Macon.[a] These consisted of several brigades of militia, under General Phillips, and a part of Hardee's command, which had been sent up from Savannah. Walcott's troops quickly intrenched themselves, and, with small loss, repulsed six desperate assaults made upon them, while the assailants, who finally fled toward Macon, left three hundred dead upon the field. The entire loss of the Confederates was estimated at twenty-five hundred men, including General Anderson severely wounded. Howard could easily have taken Macon, after **this blow upon** its defenders, but such was not a part of Sherman's plan, and **the former was** content to cover the roads diverging from that city toward the Oconee River.

Howard and Slocum now moved eastward simultaneously, the former from Gordon to Sandersville, destroying the railway to Tennille Station. He was confronted at the Oconee River, when laying a pontoon bridge for the passage of his army, by a force under General Wayne, of Georgia, composed of some of Wheeler's cavalry, a body of militia, and convicts from the Milledgeville penitentiary, already mentioned. Most of the latter, dressed in their prison garb, were captured in a skirmish that ensued, and Howard crossed the river without much difficulty. Slocum also moved to Sandersville from Milledgeville, and had some skirmishing near the former, with the main body of Wheeler's cavalry. At the same time Kilpatrick moved from Gordon to Milledgeville, and thence by Sparta and Gibson to Waynesboro', on the Augusta and Millen railway, for the threefold purpose of making a feint toward Augusta, covering the passage of the main army over the Ogeechee River, and making an effort to liberate the prisoners at Millen.[1]

Kilpatrick had several skirmishes with Wheeler on the way, but no severe battle; and on the 27th[b] a portion of his troopers, under

Nov. 22, 1864.

November.

---

[1] It was intended to deceive the Confederates with the impression that Augusta, and not the sea-coast, was Sherman's destination, and so possibly prevent the removal of the captives from Millen. The value of Augusta to the Confederates, as a manufactory of cannon, *et cetera*, caused a general belief that it was Sherman's chief objective, until after he had passed Millen.

Colonels Hayes and Estes, dashed in to Waynesboro' and burned the railroad bridge over Brier Creek, near by. Then, being assured that the prisoners had been removed from Millen, he fell back with his whole force to the vicinity of Louisville, to which point Slocum had advanced. In this rétrograde movement, Kilpatrick was closely pressed by Wheeler, and at one time, the former, with his staff, and the Eighth Indiana and Ninth Michigan, was, through a misunderstanding of orders, cut off from the main body and nearly surrounded by the foe. They fought their way out with very little loss, and rejoined their companions. Wheeler still pressing, Kilpatrick chose a good position, dismounted his men, cast up a breastwork, and received a desperate charge from his antagonist. It was repulsed at all points. Soon after this, Kilpatrick was met by Hunter's brigade of Baird's division of the Fourteenth Corps, which Davis had sent out to his relief. The peril was over. Wheeler was keeping at a respectful distance, and Kilpatrick joined the left wing of the army near the Ogeechee River. Meanwhile the right wing, under Howard, had been moving toward the Ogeechee, southward of the railway, and on the 30th,[a] Sherman's ^a November, 1864. entire army, with the exception of the Fifteenth Corps, which covered the right wing, had passed that stream, and was ready to march on Millen.

Sherman's admirable stratagem in securing the passage of the Ogeechee—a most formidable barrier—without serious difficulty or loss, was highly applauded by experts. Thus far his march had been a wonderful success. His orders had been faithfully executed, and no plan, as to time or circumstance, had miscarried. He had destroyed, over long distances, the great railways of Georgia. That leading from Atlanta to Augusta was utterly ruined from the former place to the Oconee; and the Georgia Central road was destroyed from Gordon to the Ogeechee. The Conspirators at Richmond, and the local

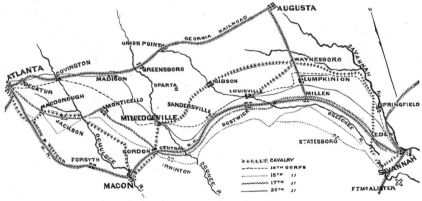

THE MARCH FROM ATLANTA TO THE SEA.

politicians and military leaders, who had been trying to deceive the people into a belief that Sherman was making a most disastrous retreat from Atlanta, were now compelled to own that he was making a thorough conquest of Georgia. It cannot be denied that Sherman's march to the sea, was a necessity imposed by the perils of his situation at Atlanta, with a powerful enemy commanding, in a large degree, his communications, yet it was in no sense a retreat, but a new campaign, offensive in all its plans and their execution.

Sherman was with Blair's corps when it crossed the Ogeechee[a] and moved down the left bank of that stream towards Millen. In order to distract his foe, he directed Kilpatrick to leave his wagons and all obstructions with the left wing, make demonstrations in the direction of Augusta, and give Wheeler all the fighting he desired. At the same time Howard, with the divisions of Woods and Corse, was moving south of the Ogeechee, along the dirt road leading to Savannah, while the divisions of Hazen and J. E. Smith were still further to the right. At Statesborough the former had a severe skirmish[b] with some Confederate cavalry, which he dispersed.

[a] Nov. 30, 1864.

[b] Dec. 4.

Slocum marched from Louisville with the left wing, on the 1st of December, the Twentieth Corps in advance. It moved down the left bank of the Ogeechee, everywhere met by fallen trees or other obstructions in the swamps. The Fourteenth Corps moved farther to the left, and Kilpatrick, supported by Baird's infantry division of that corps, pushed on toward Waynesboro'. At Thomas's Station, on the railway connecting Millen and Augusta, he fought Wheeler,[c] and drove him from his barricades through Waynesboro' and across Brier Creek, full eight miles, while Baird was breaking up the iron road and destroying bridges. Then cavalry and infantry rejoined the Fourteenth Corps, which was concentrated in the vicinity of Lumpkin's Station, on the Augusta railway.

[c] Dec. 4.

THE PRISON-PEN AT MILLEN.[1]

Sherman reached Millen, with the Seventeenth Corps, on the 3d of December. It had destroyed the railway from the Ogeechee to that town, where, so lately, thousands of Union prisoners had been confined. The sight of the horrid prison-pen, in which they had been crowded, and tortured with hun-

---

[1] This pen was built of large logs driven in the ground, with sentry posts on the top, at short intervals. No shelter whatever was afforded the prisoners, and they were compelled to burrow in the earth, to avoid the scorching sun or the biting frost, for their captors robbed them of most of their clothing, with all their money, watches, *et cetera*. The ground inclosed within the stockade was about three hundred feet square, and at times it was crowded with the suffering captives. Just inside of the palisades was a light rail fence, which marked the "dead line," or a boundary beyond which no prisoner was allowed to pass, under penalty of death from the bullet of a guardsman.

ger, cold, and cruel treatment, in the midst of plenty, and in which seven hundred and fifty had died, made the blood of their living companions-in-arms course more quickly in their veins, because of indignation, and nerved them to the performance of every service required to crush the wicked rebellion. These captives had all been removed, no one then knew whither, and were suffering in other prisons with equal severity.

The army now pushed vigorously on among swamps and sands, with the city of Savannah, where General Hardee was in command, as the chief objective. Howard, with the Fifteenth Corps (Osterhaus), moved down the southern side of the Ogeechee, with instructions to cross it near Eden Station, in Bryan County, while the Seventeenth (Blair) moved along the railway. Slocum, with the Twentieth (Williams), marched in the middle road, by way of Springfield, and the Fourteenth (Davis), along the Savannah River road. The latter was closely followed by Wheeler, but Kilpatrick and Baird gallantly covered the rear of the moving columns between the Ogeechee and Savannah rivers. While there was frequent skirmishing, and fallen trees and other obstructions were met everywhere, no enemy in force was seen anywhere, until the heads of columns were within fifteen miles of the city of Savannah. All the roads leading into that town were obstructed by felled trees, earth-works, and artillery. These were easily turned and the foe expelled, and by the 10th of December the Confederates were driven within their lines,[1] and Savannah was completely beleagured. Sherman forbore making an immediate attack, for the only approaches to the city were by five narrow causeways,[2] all of which were commanded by heavy guns that were too much for the light field-pieces of the Nationals. The military force in the city was unknown, and so Sherman gave orders to closely invest the place, while he should open communication with the Government fleet, which he knew was waiting for him in the waters not far from Savannah.

On approaching Savannah, General Slocum had seized the Charleston railway, at the bridge, and General Howard had broken up and occupied the Gulf railroad for some distance to the Little Ogeechee, so that no supplies could reach the city by the accustomed channels of communication. Sherman's army was well supplied, and had the open country behind it, yet he deemed communication with the fleet of vital importance, and desired the possession of the Ogeechee as a proper avenue of future supply for his troops, from the sea. He therefore ordered Kilpatrick to cross the Ogeechee on a pontoon bridge, reconnoiter Fort McAllister, that commanded it below the railway, and proceeding to Sunbury, open communication with the fleet. Howard had already sent a scout (Captain Duncan) in a canoe down the Ogeechee for the same purpose. Finally, on the 13th,[a] Sherman ordered General Hazen to carry Fort McAllister by assault with his second division of the Fifteenth Corps. That active officer at once crossed the Ogeechee at King's Bridge, and by one o'clock on that day his force was deployed in front of Fort McAllister, a strong inclosed redoubt,

[a] December, 1864.

---

[1] These lines followed substantially a swampy creek, which emptied into the Savannah River three miles above the city, and across to the bend of a corresponding stream which emptied into the Little Ogeechee River. These streams, bordered by swamps and rice-fields flooded at high water, formed excellent flanks for the Confederates.

[2] These were for two railways, and the Augusta, Louisville, and Ogeechee dirt roads.

garrisoned by two hundred men, under Major Anderson, artillery and infantry, and having one mortar and twenty-three guns *en barbette*.

At about this time Sherman and Howard reached Cheves's rice-mill, used as a signal station, where, for two days the officer in charge had been looking anxiously in the direction of Ossabaw Sound, for a Government steamer. Hazen and Fort McAllister were then exchanging shots, the former with the hope of thereby attracting the attention of the fleet. With their glasses the two commanders could see Hazen's skirmishers approach the fort, and very soon that leader signaled that he had invested it. Then Sherman signaled back that it was important to capture it at once. Meanwhile the smoke-stack of a steamer had been seen in the dim distance, at the mouth of the Ogeechee. The vessel soon appeared, and signaled that she had been sent by General Foster and Admiral Dahlgren to communicate with the National army, but was in doubt whether Fort McAllister was in the hands of friends or foe.[1]

That doubt was soon removed. Hazen had signaled back to Sherman, "I am ready and will assault at once." He did so. It was toward evening of a beautiful day. His bugles sounded a charge, and over *abatis* and every other obstruction his troops swept impetuously, in the face of a heavy storm of grape and canister shot, up to the parapets and over them,[2] fighting hand to hand, and after a brief but desperate struggle won a victory. Before sunset Fort McAllister, its garrison and armament, were in the hands of the Nationals, the Union flag was planted upon it, and the way was opened to the sea. The triumph was gained at the cost of ninety patriots killed and wounded. The Confederates lost nearly fifty men.

Sherman saw the entire conflict from the rice-mill; and when the smoke floated away, and the National flag was seen waving over the redoubt, and the shouts and *feu de joie* of the victors were heard, he entered a boat, and with Howard, was rowed quickly down to Fort McAllister, unmindful of the danger of torpedo explosions in the river. He tarried there a moment to offer congratulations to Hazen, and then pushed on to meet the tug, from which he had received a message by signal. She was the *Dandelion*, whose commander, Captain Williamson, told Howard that his scout, Captain Duncan, had passed the fort and communicated with Foster and Dahlgren, whom he then hourly expected in Ossabaw Sound.

The capture of Fort McAllister was a brilliant ending of the Great

---

[1] General Foster was in command of the coast islands of South Carolina when Sherman was engaged in his Georgia campaign, and he was directed to make a demonstration in his favor, when, as it was expected, he would approach Pocotaligo, on the Charleston and Savannah railway, between the two cities, at the close of November. He could spare only 5,000 men from his various garrisons, for this purpose, and at the head of these he ascended the Broad River on steamers, and landed at Boyd's Neck on the 30th of November. From that point he sent General J. P. Hatch to seize the railway near Grahamsville. Having missed his way, Hatch did not reach his destination till the next morning, when he was met by a strong Confederate force intrenched on a hill covering Grahamsville and the road. This position he assailed, when an obstinate fight ensued, which resulted in his defeat, and retreat at evening, with a loss of 746 men. Foster then sent General E. E. Potter, with two brigades, across the Coosawhatchie, to Devaux Neck, when he advanced and seized a position *a* Dec. 6, within cannon range of the railway, which he fortified and firmly held until the remainder of 1864. Foster's column came up to his help. It was here that the commanding general first heard, on the 12th of December, of Sherman being before Savannah, when he hastened to meet him, as recorded in the text. By direction of Sherman, he held on to the position near the Charleston and Savannah railway, and after Hardee fled to Charleston he took possession of and occupied the Confederate works at Pocotaligo, and at the railway crossings of the Tullifinny and Coosawhatchie rivers.

[2] A novel way for scaling the parapets was exhibited in this assault. The front line of soldiers rushed forward and leaped into the ditch, and their shoulders formed a bridge for those who followed.

March from the Chattahoochee to the sea, and crowned General Hazen with an unfading chaplet of honor. It opened to Sherman's army a new base of supplies; and it was a chief cause of the speedy fall of Savannah, for the soldiers in that city, amazed by the seeming rashness and yet perfect success of the assault, felt that it would be a useless waste of life to attempt to defend it against such assailants. The citizens shared in this feeling, and many of them, accompanied by the mayor and aldermen of the city, waited upon General Hardee, at his head-quarters in Oglethorpe Barracks, and insisted upon his surrender of the post.

HARDEE'S HEAD-QUARTERS.[1]

After putting into Captain Williamson's hands communications for Foster, Dahlgren, and the War Department, Sherman returned to Fort McAllister, and lodged that night; and early the next morning[a] he met General Foster, who had come up the Ogeechee

[a] Dec. 14, 1864.

in the steamer *Nemaha*, during the night.[2] He accompanied that officer to Ossabaw Sound, where, at noon, they had an interview with Admiral Dahlgren, on board the *Harvest Moon*. Sherman made arrangements for Foster to send him some heavy siege-guns from Hilton Head, wherewith to bombard Savannah, and with Dahlgren, for engaging the forts below the city during the assault. On the following day[b] he returned to his lines.

[b] Dec. 15.

Several 30-pounder Parrott guns reached Sherman on the 17th, when he summoned Hardee to surrender. He refused. Three days afterward, Sherman left for Hilton Head, to make arrangements with Foster for preventing a retreat of Hardee toward Charleston, if he should attempt it, leaving Slocum to get the siege-guns into proper position. Unfavorable winds and tides detained him, and on the 21st, while in one of the inland passages with which that coast abounds, he was met by Captain Dayton in a tug, bearing the news that during the previous dark and windy night,[c] Hardee had fled from Savannah with fifteen thousand men, crossed the river on a pontoon bridge, and was in full march on Charleston;

[c] Dec. 20.

also, that the National troops were in possession of the Confederate lines, and advancing into Savannah without opposition. The story was true. Hardee's movement had been unsuspected by the National pickets. Under cover of a heavy cannonade during the day and evening of the 20th, he had destroyed two iron-clads, several smaller vessels, the navy yard, and a large quantity of ammunition, ordnance stores, and supplies of all kinds. Then

---

[1] This was the appearance of the large brick building on the corner of Bull and Harris streets, Savannah, known as Oglethorpe Barracks, as it appeared when the writer sketched it in April, 1866. This was the military head-quarters of the Confederates in Savannah, from the beginning of the war.

[2] The first vessel that passed Fort McAllister from the sea, was the mail-steamer bearing Colonel Markland and twenty tons of letters and papers for the officers and men of Sherman's army.—See page 225, volume II.

he fled in such haste that he did not spike his guns, nor destroy a vast amount of cotton belonging to the Confederacy, stored in the city. He was beyond pursuit when his flight was discovered. Our troops immediately took possession, the Twentieth Corps marching first into the city, and on

SHERMAN'S HEAD-QUARTERS.

the morning of the 22d,[a] General Sherman, who had hastened back, rode into the town, and made his head-quarters at the fine residence of Charles Green, on Macon Street, opposite St. John's Church.[1] On the 26th he sent a dispatch to President Lincoln, saying: "I beg to present to you, as a Christmas gift, the city of Savannah, with one hundred and fifty heavy guns and plenty of ammunition, and also about twenty-five thousand bales of cotton." The President replied, thanking Sherman for his gift, and giving to him all the honor. The

[a] Dec., 1864.

Government, he said, was "anxious, if not fearful," when he was about to leave Atlanta for the coast. "I believe none of us," said Mr. Lincoln, "went further than to acquiesce."

So ended in perfect success, and vast advantage to the National cause, Sherman's autumn campaign in Georgia—his marvelous march to the sea. In that march, of two hundred and fifty-five miles in the space of six weeks, during which he made a substantial conquest of Georgia, he lost only five hundred and sixty-seven men.[2] His entire army, of over sixty-five thousand men and ten thousand horses, had lived generously off the country, having appropriated to their use thirteen thousand beeves, one hundred and sixty thousand bushels of corn, more than five thousand tons of fodder, besides a large number of sheep, swine, fowls, potatoes and rice. He forced into the service five thousand horses and four thousand mules. He captured thirteen hundred and twenty-eight prisoners, and one hundred and sixty-seven guns; burned twenty thousand bales of cotton, and captured and secured to the Government twenty-five thousand bales. Full ten thousand negroes followed the flag to Savannah, and many thousand others, mostly women and children, had been driven back at the crossings of rivers, and denied the privilege. The pathway of Sherman's march averaged about forty miles in width, and by his admirable strategy in bewildering his foe, he made that march with ease and with abundant success.[3]

Let us leave the victorious army in repose at Savannah, while we con-

---

[1] General Howard's quarters were at the house of Mr. Molyneaux, late British consul at Savannah. Slocum's were at the residence of John E. Ward; and General Geary, who was appointed commander of the post, had his office in the bank building next door to the Custom House.

[2] Of these, 63 were killed, 245 wounded, and 159 missing.

[3] In his report, Sherman said: "I estimate the damage done to the State of Georgia and its military resources, at $100,000,000 at least—$20,000,000 of which has inured to our advantage, and the remainder is simple waste and destruction. This may seem a hard species of warfare, but it brings the sad realities of war home to those who have been directly or indirectly instrumental in involving us in its attendant calamities." In Sherman's estimate of destruction above given, must be included over two hundred miles of railroads destroyed.

sider the fortunes of the strong and co-operating force assigned to General Thomas for the defense of Tennessee against Hood. Before doing so, let us take a brief glance at some operations by National troops, sent out from the Lower Mississippi, to prevent the concentration of forces west of Georgia against Sherman during his march to the sea.

One of these expeditions, composed of mounted men, was led by General Dana, who went out[a] from Vicksburg, fought and vanquished Confederates on the Big Black River, and destroyed several [a] Nov. 25, 1864. miles of the railway connecting New Orleans with Tennessee, with its bridges and rolling stock, much cotton and valuable stores. Another cavalry expedition, led by General Davidson, was sent out from Baton Rouge, and struck the same railway at Tangipaha,[b] laying waste [b] Nov. 30. its track and other property. Then Davidson pushed on eastward, in the direction of Mobile, almost to the Pascagoula River, causing much alarm for the safety of that city.

Still another expedition, and more important than the two just mentioned, went out from the Mississippi three weeks later.[c] It was sent [c] Dec. 21. from Memphis, and was led by General Grierson. His force consisted of thirty-five hundred well-mounted men, and their destination was the Mobile and Ohio railway. Taking a nearly straight course through Northern Mississippi, they struck that road at Tupelo, and destroyed it to Okolona. On the way, Colonel Karge surprised[d] and dis- [d] Dec. 25. persed, at Verona, a guard over ordnance and supplies destined for Hood's army. These were a-loading in two hundred wagons, which Forrest took from Sturgis in June.[1] Thirty-two cars, eight warehouses filled with supplies, and the wagons, were destroyed.

When he arrived at Okolona, Grierson discovered that the Confederates were in considerable force and well intrenched at Egypt Station, a few miles below; and intercepted dispatches from General Dick Taylor, at Mobile, informed him that re-enforcements were to be given to the garrison immediately. He resolved to attack before they should arrive. He did so at daybreak the next morning,[e] and while the struggle was going on, [e] Dec. 27. two trains of cars came up with fresh troops. Grierson quickly repulsed these, and routed the body he at first assailed, numbering about sixteen hundred men. Grierson captured a train, and made about five hundred prisoners. Among the Confederates killed in this engagement was General Gholson, of Mississippi.

Grierson now moved southwestward, distracting his foe by feints. He finally struck the Mississippi Central railroad at Winona Station, and tore up the track several miles each way, while the Fourth Iowa destroyed cloth and shoe factories at Bankston. This was followed by the defeat of Confederate cavalry under Colonel Wood, at Benton, by Colonel Osband, and the speedy march of the expedition to Vicksburg, with its trophies of five hundred prisoners, eight hundred beeves, and a thousand liberated slaves. It had been a destructive and alarming raid,[2] and effectually held back Confederate troops from Sherman, in Georgia.

---

[1] See page 247.

[2] During the raid, Grierson's men destroyed 95 railway cars, 300 wagons, 30 full warehouses, and liberated, by taking them prisoners, 100 Union soldiers who had been famishing in Confederate prisons, and had joined the army with a hope of thus effecting their escape.

Let us now see what was occurring in Tennessee and on its southern borders, from the time when Sherman captured Atlanta until his arrival at Savannah.

We have observed that Hood, late in September, crossed the Chattahoo-chee, and began operations against Sherman's communications.[1] Meanwhile, and in co-operation with Hood (whose chief objective was evidently Nash-ville), Forrest, the bold and active cavalry leader, who had been in Northern Alabama for several weeks keeping re-enforcements from joining Sherman from the Mississippi, proceeded to prepare the way for an invasion of Ten-nessee. He crossed the Tennessee River near Waterloo, and on the 25th,[a] appeared before Athens, in Northern Alabama, with a force of light cavalry, about seven thousand strong, and invested it. He opened a 12-pounder battery on the town, and twice demanded its surrender. It was refused, but finally, at a personal interview between Forrest and Colonel Campbell, the commander of the little garrison of six hundred negro troops, the latter was persuaded to surrender the post. Re-enforce-ments sufficient to hold the place (the Eighth Michigan and One Hundred and Second Ohio), came up half an hour afterward, and, with the garrison, became prisoners of war, after a sharp contest.

a Sept. 1864.

Flushed with his victory, Forrest pushed on northward to Pulaski, in Tennessee, destroying the railway as he moved, and capturing a fortified post, at Sulphur Branch Trestle, on the way. He found Pulaski too strong for him. General Rousseau was there, and made the assailants cautious. After sharp skirmishing the greater part of a day,[b] Forrest withdrew, and marched eastward, toward the Chattanooga railway, with his whole force. He struck it between Tullahoma and Decherd, but had scarcely begun its destruction, when he was confronted by Rousseau, who had hastened by railway, around by Nashville, and reached Tullahoma, while General Steedman, who had crossed the Tennessee from Northern Georgia, was coming up rapidly from the southwest with five thousand troops. At the same time, General Morgan's division of the Fourteenth Corps was hastening into Tennessee for the same purpose. These combined forces drove Forrest from the railway before he had damaged it much, when he retraced his steps to Fayetteville, the termination of a railroad from Decherd. There he divided his forces, giving Buford, his second in command, four thousand of them, and reserving three thousand for himself. Buford went directly south, threatened Huntsville, and again attacked Athens, which General Granger, in command at Franklin, had re-garrisoned with the Seventy-third Indiana, Lieutenant-Colonel Slade. For a part of two days,[c] Buford tried to carry the place, when he was effectu-ally repulsed, and sought safety by flight across the Tennessee, at Brown's Ferry.

b Sept. 29.

c Oct. 2-3.

Forrest, in the mean time, had pushed on to Columbia, on the Duck River, with his three thousand horsemen, but did not attack that place, for Rousseau was coming down from Nashville with four thousand mounted men. At the same time, General C. C. Washburne, with four thousand five hundred men (three thousand of them cavalry), was moving up the Tennes-

---

[1] See page 396.

see on steamers to assist in capturing the invaders, while Lieutenant-Commander Forrest was patroling that stream in Northern Alabama, with several gun-boats, to intercept them should they fly southward. Generals Rousseau, Steedman, Morgan, Washburne and Croxton, were now (under the direction of General Thomas, who had arrived at Nashville on the 3d of October) joined in the grand hunt for Forrest. The latter, looking out from Columbia, saw his peril, and met it as usual. Paroling the thousand prisoners he had captured, he destroyed five miles of the railroad southward from the Duck River, and then pushing across the country by way of Mount Pleasant and Lawrenceburg, he escaped over the Tennessee[a] at Bainbridge, with very little loss.

THOMAS'S HEAD-QUARTERS,[1]

[a] Oct. 6, 1864.

While these operations were going on in Tennessee and Northern Alabama, the movements of Hood against Sherman's communications northward of the Chattahoochee, already considered,[2] were begun. To watch and meet Hood's troops, as his plans might be developed, Thomas ordered Croxton's cavalry brigade to patrol the line of the Tennessee River, from Decatur to Eastport. Morgan's division was moved from Athens to Chattanooga, and Rousseau's troops were concentrated at the latter place. Steedman's division was moved from Decatur to Bridgeport.

We have already considered the movements of Sherman and Hood, until late in October, when the latter went over the Sand Mountains, westward, and threatened Decatur, and the former gave up the pursuit of his antagonist in the beautiful Chatooga Valley.[3] At that point of time and circumstance, we will resume the narrative of the movements of Hood.

Decatur was an important place in connection with military movements at that time. The railway from Nashville on the north there crossed the Tennessee River, and met the one extending westward to Memphis, and eastward to Chattanooga. There General Granger was stationed with a considerable force, when Hood approached on the 26th of October, sat down before it, established a line of rifle-pits within five hundred yards of the National lines, cast up intrenchments, and threatened an assault. Two days afterward, some of Granger's troops made a sortie, gained the rear of the left of Hood's rifle-pits, drove out the occupants and captured two hundred men. On the same day a regiment of negro troops, led by Colonel Morgan, captured one of Hood's batteries and spiked the guns; and on the following day,[b] the third of the siege (which was only a feint to cover preparations for a more important movement), it was abandoned, and Hood went westward to Tuscumbia. That important move-

[b] Oct. 29.

---

[1] This is a view of the fine mansion of Mr. Cunningham, 15 High Street, Nashville, occupied by Generals Buell and Thomas, and other commanders, in that city.

[2] See page 397.   [3] See page 399.

ment was the passage of the Tennessee River by Hood's army, a part of
which crossed it at the mouth of Cyprus Creek,[a] not far from
Florence, in the face of strong opposition from Croxton's brigade,
which was pressed back to the east bank of Shoal Creek.

[a] Oct. 31,
1864.

It was now evident that Hood intended to advance into Middle Tennessee. General Hatch was ordered to move, with his cavalry division, from
Clifton, to the support of Croxton;
and, as we have seen, the Twenty-
third Corps, under General Schofield, was directed to report to General Thomas, to whom was given full
control of all the troops in the Military Division of the Mississippi, excepting those which were to accompany Sherman.[1] General Thomas
J. Wood's division of the Fourth
Corps reached Athens on the 31st,
closely followed by the other divisions, when Stanley, the commander
of the corps, concentrated his whole
force at Pulaski.

THOMAS J. WOOD.

In the mean time, Forrest had
turned his face northward again, and
was busy in aiding Hood. Leaving Corinth, he pushed up through Tennessee
with a heavy mounted force and nine guns, and struck the Tennessee River
opposite Johnsonville, in Stewart County, which was connected with Nashville by railway. This was an important depot of supplies for Nashville,
and these Forrest came to destroy. They were guarded by one thousand
negro troops under Colonel C. R. Thompson, and three gun-boats, commanded by Lieutenant E. M. King. Forrest opened his guns upon the
post,[b] and after several days' sharp contest, he withdrew[c] on
hearing of the approach of Schofield, with his corps, from Nashville, by railway. Forrest's work was accomplished, but by other
hands. In a conflict with the gun-boats, he had so far won a
victory, that it was feared they would fall into his hands. So, just before
the appearance of Schofield, they and the transports were set on fire. The
flames communicated to the storehouses on the shore, and commissaries'
and quartermasters' stores, valued at a million and a half of dollars, were
destroyed. Finding no enemy at Johnsonville, Schofield left Ruger's division as a garrison at that post, and, with the rest of his troops, marched to
Pulaski and assumed command of all the forces there.

[b] Oct. 28.

[c] Nov. 5.

At this time, Thomas's effective force, under Schofield, confronting Hood,
was only about thirty thousand men,[2] while his antagonist, just re-enforced

---

[1] See page 400.

[2] These consisted of the Fourth Corps, under Stanley, 12,000, and the Twenty-third Corps, 10,000, which
made the total of infantry and artillery, 22,000. The division commanders were Generals N. Kimball, G. A.
Wagner, T. J. Wood, of the Fourth Corps, and T. H. Ruger and J. D. Cox, of the Twenty-third Corps. The
cavalry, 7,700 in number, was commanded by General J. H. Wilson, assisted by Brigadier-Generals Edward
Hatch, R. W. Johnson, and J. H. Hammond. Co-operating with these troops, then concentrated at Pulaski,
were the cavalry brigades of Generals Croxton and Capron, the former numbering about 2,500 men, and the
latter about 1,200.

by a part of General Taylor's army at Mobile, had about fifty-five thousand men.[1] Thomas had twenty-five or thirty thousand other men under his command, holding widely separated but important posts, which prudence forbade him to concentrate. So he resolved to keep as strong as possible in front of Hood, if he should advance, and falling slowly back toward Nashville, avoid battle until sufficiently strengthened to promise success in a conflict. Fortunately, Hood lingered on the bank of the Tennessee until past the middle of November; for, while Sherman remained north of the Chattahoochee, he was not sure that active leader might not suddenly appear upon his rear. But when, at length, intelligence came that he had severed all communications with the North and turned his face toward the sea, Hood threw the remainder of his army over the Tennessee[a] on a pontoon bridge at Florence, and two days afterward, moved on parallel roads in the direction of Nashville, through Waynesboro' and Lawrenceburg, driving General Hatch from the latter place.[b]

[a] Nov. 17, 1864.
[b] Nov. 22.

Thomas had hoped to meet Hood in battle south of Duck River, but the two divisions under General A. J. Smith, coming from Missouri,[2] had not arrived, and he did not feel well prepared to do so, when his adversary moved; so he ordered Schofield to fall back to Columbia. He did so in good order, while Capron's brigade at Mount Pleasant covered all flank approaches from that direction. Schofield withdrew Ruger's division from Johnsonville, and on the 24th of November his forces were concentrated at Columbia. In the mean time General Granger had withdrawn the garrisons at Athens, Decatur, and Huntsville, and returned to Stevenson, from which he sent five fresh regiments to Murfreesboro'. The officer left in command at Johnsonville was ordered to remove the property there across to the Cumberland at Fort Donelson, and, with it and the garrison, take post at Clarksville.

Hood moved promptly to Pulaski, and pushed on toward Columbia, but showed no disposition to attack Schofield in front of that town. But he made movements so indicative of an intention to cross Duck River on one or both of Schofield's flanks, that the latter withdrew[c] to the north side of the stream, and sent his trains toward Nashville. Then, informed that Hood had crossed the river six miles above Columbia, he ordered Stanley to follow his trains to Spring Hill. The command was promptly executed just in time to save them from Forrest's cavalry, hovering near, and which Stanley drove off just as they were about to pounce upon the wagons and their guard. Stanley was speedily attacked by a very strong force of horse and foot, which he fought until night fell, and, though with great difficulty, he firmly held the road over which the retreating army was to pass.

[c] Nov. 27-28.

On that day[d] Schofield had been continually employed in keeping the Confederates from crossing the Duck River at

[d] Nov. 28.

---

[1] Hood's army was composed of about 42,000 infantry and artillery, and 13,000 cavalry, many of whom were Kentuckians and Tennesseeans, jubilant with the idea that they were about to expel the invader from their native soil. They had great confidence in their dashing leader, and were in high spirits. Hood's army was arranged in three divisions, commanded respectively by Generals B. F. Cheatham, A. P. Stewart, and S. D. Lee. The division commanders were as follows: Cheatham's corps—Generals P. R. Cleburne, Jas. C. Brown, and W. B. Bate. Stewart's—W. W. Loring, S. G. French, E. C. Walthall. Lee's—C. L. Stevenson, E. Johnson, and Clayton. Forrest commanded the cavalry. His division commanders were Generals W. Jackson, A. Buford, and J. R. Chalmers.

[2] See page 280.

Columbia, driving them back, with great loss on their side, whenever they advanced. When, late in the afternoon, he heard of Stanley's peril, he took Ruger's division, and hastened to his support, leaving orders for the remainder of his force to follow. He encountered some detachments of cavalry on the way, and when he arrived at Spring Hill, he found the main body of the Confederates bivouacked within half a mile of the road over which his army must pass. He left them undisturbed. His troops passed by at midnight, and pushed on northward, closely pursued, and sometimes severely pressed after the day dawned. Hour after hour skirmishing went on, while the patriots gradually moved northward during that day [a] Nov. 30, 1864. and night, and early the following morning[a] they were in a strong position at Franklin, on the Harpeth River, where some stirring events had occurred the previous year.[1] There Schofield halted

SCHOFIELD'S HEAD-QUARTERS.[2]

on the southern edge of the village, in order that his trains, then choking the road for miles, might be taken across the Harpeth and put well on their way toward Nashville, eighteen miles distant. It was better to give battle there, with this encumbrance out of the way, than to be compelled to fight, as he doubtless would that day or the next, with his trains close at hand.

Schofield was satisfied that his foes were concentrated directly in his rear; for his cavalry, following the Lewisburg pike several miles eastward of his line of march, had encountered no enemy. He disposed his troops accordingly in a curved line south and west of the town, the flanks resting on the Harpeth; and then cast up a line of slight intrenchments along their entire front. The cavalry, with the Third Division of the Fourth Corps (Wood's), were posted on the north bank of the river, and Fort Granger, on a bluff,[3] commanded the gently rolling plain over which Hood must advance in a direct attack. Within the entire lines around Franklin, Schofield had not to exceed eighteen thousand men, when Hood, at four o'clock in the afternoon,[b] came up with all his force, and assailed [b] Nov. 30. the Nationals, with the intention and expectation of crushing them with one heavy blow. He had assured his soldiers that, if they should break through Schofield's line, they would disperse or destroy his army, capture his trains, drive Thomas out of Tennessee and might march on, without opposition, to the Ohio River.

Hood had formed his columns for attack behind a line of dense woods; Stewart on his right, next the Harpeth, Cheatham on his left, and Lee in the rear, in reserve. A greater part of his cavalry, led by Forrest, was on his right, and the remainder were on his left. Thus prepared, the Confederates

---

[1] See page 118.

[2] Schofield's head-quarters were at the house of Dr. D. B. Cliffe, on Main Street, in the village of Franklin. That village was the capital of Williamson County, Tennessee, and was situated in a bend of the Harpeth River, which formed two sides of a square, with a sharp curve at the angle, as seen in the map on page 421.

[3] See page 118.

rushed forward upon Schofield's center (composed of the divisions of Ruger and Cox, of the Twenty-third Corps, about ten thousand strong),

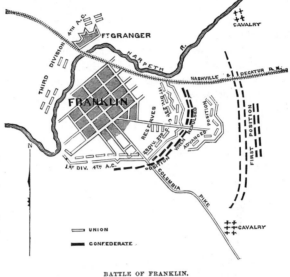

BATTLE OF FRANKLIN.

with the greatest impetuosity, in columns four deep, with a cloud of skirmishers in their front. Their appearance, so soon, was unexpected to Schofield, and it amounted to almost a surprise. He was at Fort Granger, across the river, when the attack commenced, and could not return to his lines, so the command in the battle devolved on General Stanley, and Schofield could only watch the struggle from the ramparts, which he did with great anxiety.

Two brigades of Wagner's division of the Fourth Corps, were thrown forward, and held some slight breastworks a few hundred yards in front of the main line, whose key-point was Carter's Hill, a gentle eminence crossed by the Columbia and Nashville pike, leading through Franklin. Behind the main line at this point was Opdyke's brigade of Wood's division. Toward that hill, the National center, the heaviest blow was directed. The charge of Hood's columns was so impetuous and weighty, notwithstanding it was met by a fearful fire of musketry and artillery, that it was irresistible. The Union advance was hurled back in utter confusion upon the main line, and all but those who were killed or made prisoners, were driven through it. It not only opened to receive the fugitives, but it kept crumbling into a wider breach after they had passed by. The outworks held by Wagner, were gained, and his division was driven back on the stronger lines still held by Cox and Ruger. The hill was lost, and, with it, eight guns. The victors pressed on, and after a most desperate contest, forced their way within the second line and planted the Confederate flag upon the intrenchments.

All now seemed to be lost, and as the Confederates re-formed to follow up their victory, large numbers of the Nationals, inspired with a sense of defeat, were seen thronging toward the bridges over the Harpeth. At that critical moment Stanley rode forward to the head of Opdyke's brigade, in reserve, and ordered it, with Conrad's in support, to endeavor to stem the tumultuous torrent of pursued and pursuers. Opdyke's voice was instantly heard ringing out clearly above the tumult in an order for an advance. That order was instantly obeyed. Swiftly, steadily, and irresistibly, his men charged the exultant columns and drove them back with fearful slaughter. Conrad was close by to give assistance. The works and the guns were recovered, and three hundred prisoners and ten battle-flags were captured. The Union line was restored, and was not again broken.[1] Again and again, Hood hurled his men against it, but it did not even bend. The struggle continued until long after dark, the Confederates working their way around to the National right, where Stanley's first division (Kimball's) gallantly repulsed them. It was almost midnight before the last shot was fired, and the Confederates, sorely disappointed and chagrined, gave up the contest. The advantage was with Schofield. Hood was checked, and had lost heavily. He was bereaved of thirteen general officers and over six thousand men. Schofield had lost a little more than twenty-three hundred.[2] Thomas thought it not prudent for him to risk another battle in the morning, and ordered him to retreat to Nashville. A little after midnight he left Franklin, and, notwithstanding they were sharply followed by Forrest after daybreak, the troops, with all their trains were safely within the lines at Nashville by noon on the day after the battle. The result of the contest, known as THE BATTLE OF FRANKLIN, was quite as disastrous to Hood in the breaking of the spirit of his followers as in the loss of men. They were discouraged, and began to reflect again upon Hood's reckless waste of life at Atlanta, and the probabilities of defeat in all the future.

The writer visited the battle-field of Franklin early in May, 1866. He went down from Nashville by railway, at evening, with General James Brownlow, then adjutant-general of Tennessee, who was severely wounded in that battle while fighting for the Union. He was carried to the house of Dr. R. B. Cliffe (Schofield's head-quarters), where he was skillfully treated and tenderly nursed, until his recovery; soon after which he married the beautiful young daughter of his surgeon, who had been his attentive companion during his tedious weeks of suffering and convalescence. On the following morning I rode over the battle-field on horseback, with Captain James R. Cliffe, of the Twelfth Tennessee Cavalry. The battle was fought chiefly on the farm of General Carter, who was wounded in sight of his own house, seen toward the left in the picture on the next page. After making that sketch, taken from the National line of breastworks, at the point where the Confederates broke through,[3] we rode back to the village, crossed the Harpeth over a long bridge, and visited Fort Granger and the place near it where young Williams and Peter, the spies, were hung.[4] We then returned to the village, where I dined with the family of Dr. Cliffe, who was absent.

---

[1] In an official communication, recommending Opdyke for promotion, General Thomas said he "displayed the very highest qualities as a commander. It is not saying too much," he continued, "to declare that but for the skillful dispositions made by General Opdyke (all of which was done entirely on his own judgment), the promptness and readiness with which he brought his command into action at the critical and decisive moment, and the signal personal gallantry he displayed in a counter assault on the enemy, when he had broken our lines, disaster instead of victory would have fallen on us at Franklin."

[2] The Nationals lost 189 killed, 1,033 wounded, and 1,104 missing, making a total of 2,326. General Stanley had a horse shot under him, and was severely wounded. General Bradly was also wounded, but less severely. Hood reported his entire loss, in round numbers, at 4,500. General Thomas officially reported it at 1,75 killed, 3,800 wounded, and 702 prisoners, making a total of 6,252. Hood lost the following general officers: Cleburne, Williams, Adams, Gist, Strahl, and Granberry, killed; Brown, Carter, Manigault, Quarles, Cockerell, and Scott wounded, and Gordon captured. Cleburne was called "the Stonewall Jackson of the West," and his loss was severely felt.

[3] The building with machinery, seen in the foreground of the picture, was a cotton-press, from the frame of which we took several bullets. It stood upon the site of the severe struggle between the Confederates and Opdyke's brigade. Between it and the house in the distance, the fight was hottest.

[4] See page 120.

His accomplished wife was a most active patriot during the war. Dr. Cliffe's was almost the only Union family in Franklin. He was compelled to flee

for his life, at one time, but his patriotic wife remained and served the country and its cause nobly, in various ways. She kept up a continual communication with the Union commanders at Nashville, often going thither in person with important information. On such occasions she rode an old blind mare, and traveled along unfrequented ways. She was several times arrested on suspicion of being an "enemy to the Confederacy," but proof was always wanting. She was once in Forrest's custody; and at one time she was confined a week at Bragg's head-quarters in Murfreesboro', where she was paroled to report when called for, to be sent to Atlanta. Rosecrans sent Bragg in that direction so suddenly that he seems to have forgotten Mrs. Cliffe. Under every circumstance of peril, disdain and weariness, that noble woman stood firm in her allegiance to the Government and to Christian duty; and by her manifold public services, and labors and sacrifices for the comfort of the sick, and wounded, and dying Union soldiers, she won an unfading chaplet of honor and gratitude from her countrymen, which ought not to be unnoticed by the chronicler. That Christian matron, Mrs. V. C. Cliffe, belongs to the glorious army of patriotic women who gave their services to their imperiled country, and should never be forgotten.

When General Schofield reached Nashville,[a] General A. J. Smith had arrived, with his two divisions, from Missouri, and by   [a] Dec. 1, 1864. noon that day, the forces in the vicinity were put in battle array in an irregular semicircular line upon the hills around the city, on the southern side of the Cumberland River. General A. J. Smith's troops (detachment of the Army of the Tennessee) were on the right, resting on the river; the Fourth Corps—commanded by General T. J. Wood, in the absence of the wounded Stanley—in the center; and the Twenty-third Corps, under General J. M. Schofield, on the left, also resting on the Cumberland. General Steedman had been called up from Chattanooga, with detachments of Sherman's army, and a brigade of negro troops under Colonel Thompson, in all five thousand men; and these were posted on the left of Schofield, to supply the place of the cavalry under Wilson, which was stationed at Edgefield, on the north side of the Cumberland. To these were added the troops composing the garrison of Nashville. Wood's line was in advance of all others, crossing the Granny White and Hillsboro' pikes; and his head-quarters were at the elegant residence of Mrs. Ackling, between those highways, a short distance from the city.[1]

Thomas was now superior to Hood in the number and character of his infantry, but was yet so deficient in cavalry, that he withheld his intended

WOOD'S HEAD-QUARTERS.[2]

blow against his adversary for about a fortnight, that he might strengthen that arm of the service, and be well provided with means for transportation. He expected to drive Hood, and he desired ample means for following and destroying his fugitive army. His delay was misunderstood and misinterpreted at Washington, and even at the head-quarters of the army. At each there was amazement and perplexity, because of Hood's audacious penetration of Tennessee to its very heart, while the fate, and even the position, of Sherman in Georgia was a hidden fact and problem. Grant finally started from City Point for Nashville, to seek a solution of the riddle that puzzled him; but at Washington City he was met by electrographs from the West that convinced him that Thomas was "the right man in the right place," and he returned to his quarters satisfied that all was well in Tennessee.

Hood pressed up in full strength to invest Nashville, and on the morning of the 4th of December had formed his line, with his salient on Montgomery Hill, not more than six hundred yards from Wood's, at Thomas's center. His main line occupied the high ground on the southeast side of Brown's Creek, with his right resting on the Nolensville pike, and his left behind Richland Creek, retiring on the Hillsboro' pike, with cavalry on both flanks, extending to the river.

---

[1] General Thomas's army, before Nashville, was composed of the Fourth Corps, commanded by General T. J. Wood, with Generals N. Kimball, W. L. Elliott, and S. Beatty as division commanders; the Twenty-third Corps, General J. M. Schofield, with Generals D. M. Couch and J. D. Cox as division commanders; detachment of the Army of the Tennessee, under General A. J. Smith, with Generals J. McArthur, K. Garrard, and J. B. Moore as division commanders; a provisional detachment under General J. B. Steedman, with Generals C. Cruft and J. F. Miller as assistants. The negro brigade was commanded by Colonel Thompson, the garrison of Nashville by General J. F. Miller, and the quartermaster's division by General J. L. Donaldson. The cavalry corps was under the command of General J. H. Wilson, assisted by Generals J. T. Croxton, Edward Hatch, R. W. Johnson, and J. T. Knipe.

[2] This is from a sketch made by the writer, at sunset, early in May, 1866, when the beautiful grounds around the mansion, which had been disfigured during the war, were restored, in a great degree, to their former appearance.

On the same day, there was a smart contest at the railway crossing of Overall's Creek, five miles north of Murfreesboro', where there was a block-house well-manned and armed. General Thomas was unwilling to relax his hold upon Chattanooga, and endeavored to keep open the railway communication between himself and Granger, at Stevenson. For that purpose, he placed General Rousseau, with eight thousand troops, in Fort Rosecrans,[1] at Murfreesboro'. When the block-house at Overall's Creek was attacked[a] by Bate's division of Cheatham's corps, General Milroy was sent out from Fort Rosecrans with a small force to its assistance. The little garrison held it firmly until Milroy came, when the assailants were quickly driven away.

[a] Dec. 4, 1864.

During the next three days, Bate was re-enforced by two divisions of infantry and about twenty-five hundred cavalry, and then menaced Fort Rosecrans, but did not actually assail it. Buford's cavalry, after its batteries had opened briskly upon Murfreesboro', dashed into the town,[b] but they were quickly expelled by a regiment of infantry, when they swept around by way of Lebanon, to the Cumberland, with the intention of getting upon Thomas's communications with Louisville by rail. The gun-boats patrolling the river foiled their designs. On the same day, Milroy went out again with a stronger force, and fought the Confederates on the Wilkeson pike, routing them, with a loss on his part of two hundred and five men killed and wounded, and capturing from his antagonist over two hundred men and two guns.

[b] Dec. 8.

For a week after this the cold was intense, and little of importance was done. The soldiers of both armies felt its severity much; but the Confederates, more thinly clad and more exposed than the Nationals, suffered most. The torpor of that week was advantageous to Thomas, and when, on the 14th, the cold abated, he was ready to take the offensive, and gave orders accordingly. Hood was then behind strong intrenchments, extending from the Hillsboro' pike around to the Murfreesboro' railroad.

Thomas ordered a general advance upon Hood from his right, early on the morning of the 15th,[c] while Steedman should make a vigorous demonstration from his left upon Hood's right, to distract him. The country that morning was covered with a dense fog, and it did not rise until near noon. This, with the hilly character of the ground, gave Thomas a great advantage, and Steedman's attack, east of the Nolensville pike, caused Hood to strengthen his right at the expense of his left and center, where the main blow was to be struck. When Steedman had completed his prescribed movement, with some loss, General Smith pressed forward, *en echelon*, along the line of the Hardin pike, while Wilson's cavalry made a wide circuit to gain the flank of Hood's infantry on his left. Johnson's division moved along the Charlotte pike, on the extreme right, and attacked and routed Chalmer's cavalry; and late in the afternoon they assaulted a battery at Bell's Landing, eight miles below Nashville, in conjunction with gun-boats under Lieutenant-commander Fitch. The battery was not captured, but it was abandoned that night.

[c] December.

Meanwhile, Hatch's division, moving on Smith's flank, with General

---

[1] See note, page 549, volume II.

Knipe's in reserve, struck Hood's left on Richland Creek, near Hardin's house. These troops were dismounted, and, in conjunction with a part of McArthur's infantry, struck vigorous blows, drove the foe from his position, and captured many prisoners and wagons. Pushing on, they captured a four-gun redoubt, and turned the artillery upon the Confederates; and a little farther on they carried a stronger redoubt, and captured four more guns and three hundred prisoners.

While these successful movements were occurring on the right, General Wood, commanding the center, had moved forward parallel with Smith's advancing column, and at one o'clock in the afternoon, the Third Brigade of Wagner's division, led by Colonel S. P. Post, of the Fifty-ninth Illinois, gallantly charged and carried Hood's works on Montgomery Hill, and took some prisoners. Then Thomas sent Schofield, who was held in reserve, rapidly to the right of Smith, by which the National cavalry was allowed to operate more freely in the Confederate rear. The whole line then moved forward. Wood carried the entire body of Confederate works on his front, captured several guns, and took five hundred prisoners, while Smith and Schofield, and the dismounted cavalry, pressed back the left flank of the Confederates several miles, to the foot of the Harpeth hills. But they still held their line of retreat along the Granny White and Franklin pikes. Steedman, meanwhile, had gained some advantage on Thomas's extreme left. Darkness closed the conflict, which resulted in the capture, by the Nationals, of twelve hundred prisoners and sixteen guns, forty wagons and many small-arms, and in forcing their enemy's strong defensive line from left to right.

Thomas now re-adjusted his lines. Wilson, with his cavalry, was placed on the extreme right, with Schofield at his left; Smith in the center, and Wood on the left. Steedman was on the extreme left, but less advanced. Such was the general disposition of the National forces on the morning of the 16th,[a] when, at six o clock, Wood advanced, forced back Hood's skirmishers on the Franklin pike, and then inclining a little to the right, pressed on due south until confronted by Hood's new line of defenses on Overton's Hill, five miles from the city. Then Steedman moved out of Nashville by the Nolensville pike, and forming on the left of Wood, gave full security to his flank. Smith came in on Wood's right, when the new-formed line faced southward, while Schofield, holding the position he had taken the previous evening, faced eastward, and threatened the Confederate left. Wilson's cavalry, dismounted, formed on his right.

It was now determined to continue the movement against Hood's left, so successfully begun the day before. The whole National line moved to within six hundred yards of that of the Confederates, at all points. Wilson was soon upon the rear of their left flank; and at three o'clock in the afternoon, Thomas ordered two of Wood's brigades to assault the foe on Overton's Hill, in front, while Thompson's negro brigade, of Steedman's command, should assault them further to the National left. The attack was made, but with fearful loss to the assailants. The movement had been discovered in time for Hood to send re-enforcements to the point of attack, and a heavy storm of grape, canister, and musket-shot was opened upon the troops as they pressed over the *abatis*, and up the hill. They had nearly

[a] Dec., 1864.

gained the crest, when reserves opened murderous volleys upon them, and they recoiled in confusion. Wood immediately restored order as they fell back, and re-formed his line, while Smith and Schofield, charging with impetuosity on the works on their respective fronts, carried all before them with very little loss. Wilson's dismounted horsemen charged farther to the

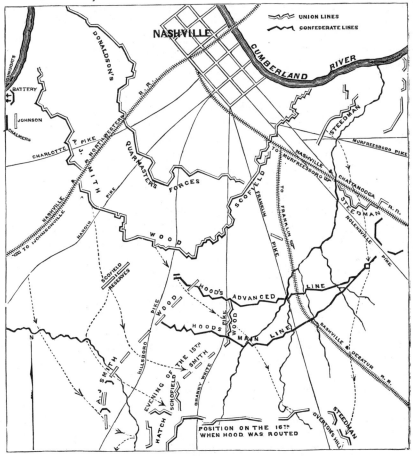

THE NASHVILLE BATTLE-FIELD.

right, and closed the way of retreat along the Granny White pike. These advantages were announced by shouts of victory. Wood and Steedman heard them, and again assailed the Confederates on Overton's Hill. They were met by a heavy fire; but they pressed forward, carried all before them, and drove the foe in such haste through the Brentwood Pass, where the Franklin pike goes through the hills, that they left behind them their dead, wounded, prisoners, and guns. It was a complete rout. During the two days in which THE BATTLE OF NASHVILLE was fought, Thomas captured from Hood four thousand four hundred and sixty-two prisoners, of whom two hundred and eighty-seven were officers. He had also captured fifty-three guns, and many small-arms. More important than these, he had broken the spirit of Hood's army beyond hope of recovery.

Wilson instantly remounted the divisions of Knipe and Hatch, and sent them toward Franklin, down the Granny White pike, with the hope that they might reach that place ahead of the fugitives. A mile on their way, they came to a barricade across the road, and behind it were Chalmer's cavalry. The position was immediately charged and carried by Colonel Spaulding and his Twelfth Tennessee Cavalry, who scattered the Confederates and took some prisoners, among whom was General E. W. Rucker. This detention allowed the fugitives to escape. It was too late for the pursuers to reach Franklin that night: they lay down upon the field of their victory, and slept on their arms.

The chase was renewed the next morning.[a] Knipe overtook
_{a Dec. 17, 1864.} the rear-guard of the Confederates at Hollow Tree Gap, four miles north of Franklin, and captured four hundred and thirteen of them. Meanwhile, Wilson had pushed on toward Franklin, and there he found Hood confronting him at the passage of the Harpeth. Johnson had gone rapidly down the Hillsboro' pike, and now coming suddenly upon Hood's rear, caused him to resume his flight in great haste, leaving behind him in Franklin eighteen hundred of his own wounded, and two hundred of the maimed Nationals, whom he had taken prisoners. Four miles south of Franklin his rear-guard made another stand, when Wilson's body-guard (Fourth Regular Cavalry) dashed through its center, while Knipe and Hatch pressed its flanks. It was scattered in confusion and lost more guns. Night came on, and the Confederates escaped.

The pursuit continued several days, while rain fell copiously. The country was flooded, and the streams were filled to the brim. The fugitives destroyed the bridges behind them, and rendered a successful pursuit impossible, for Thomas's pontoons were with Sherman. Then the weather became bitter cold, and the frozen, cut-up roads were almost impassable. Finally, at Columbia, Forrest, who was away on a raid when Thomas sallied out upon Hood, joined the latter, and, with his cavalry and four thousand infantry as a rear-guard, covered the broken Confederate army most effectually. This guard struck back occasionally, but the pursuit was continued
_{b December.} to Lexington, in Alabama, where, on the 28th,[b] it was suspended, when it was known that Hood had escaped across the Tennessee at Bainbridge, evading the gun-boats which Admiral S. P. Lee had sent up the river, at Thomas's request, to intercept him.[1]

_{c Dec. 18.} In the mean time Thomas had sent[c] Steedman with his forces across from Franklin to Murfreesboro', with directions to proceed around by railway to Decatur, in Alabama, and thus to threaten Hood's railroad communications west of Florence. He was instructed to send back

---

[1] While Hood was investing Nashville, he sent a cavalry force, under General Lyon, into Kentucky, to operate on the Louisville railroad. General Thomas detached General McCook's cavalry division, and sent it in pursuit of Lyon. McCook attacked and routed a part of Lyon's forces at Hopkinsville, when the latter commenced a hasty retreat. Colonel Lagrange's brigade came up with the fugitive near Greenburg, and attacked and routed him, when Lyon succeeded, making a circuit by the way of Elizabethtown and Glasgow, in crossing the Cumberland River at Burkesville, from whence he moved by way of McMinnville and Winchester, Tennessee, to Larkinsville, Alabama. On the 10th of January he attacked a little garrison at Scottsboro', and was repulsed, but succeeded in crossing the Tennessee River with a remnant of his command, only about 200 in number. He was still pursued, and at a place known as Red Hill, he was surprised by Colonel Palmer, and half his men were made prisoners, on the 14th of January. After surrendering, he escaped, by seizing a pistol, shooting a sentinel, and disappearing in the gloom of night.

the garrisons which General Granger had called to Stevenson,[1] to their former posts. ' He was joined by Granger at the latter place, and they reoccupied Decatur on the 27th, but too late to impede Hood's flight, for he had already crossed the Tennessee. But a cavalry force of six hundred men, under Colonel W. J. Palmer, was sent from Decatur in pursuit of Hood's train. Pressing back Roddy's cavalry near Leighton, Alabama, Palmer moved toward Columbus, Mississippi, and captured and destroyed Hood's pontoon train, ten miles from Russellville. Another force being reported in pursuit, under cover of darkness Palmer pushed for Moulton. Meeting the Confederates near Thorn Hill, he attacked and defeated them, and arrived safely at Decatur on the 6th of January. [a] 1865.

On the 30th of December, General Thomas announced to the army the termination of the campaign,[2] and gave orders for the proper distribution of his troops in winter cantonments at Eastport, in Northern Mississippi, at Athens and Huntsville, in Alabama, and at Dalton, in Georgia. But General Grant and the War Department had decided that there should be no rest until the Rebellion should be crushed. Sherman had reached the sea,[3] and was prepared for a march northward through the Carolinas into Virginia, and the siege of Petersburg and Richmond was to be prosecuted with vigor. Accordingly, orders were issued[b] for Thomas to send Wood with the Fourth Corps to Huntsville, and to concentrate the troops of [b] Dec. 31, 1864. Smith, Schofield and Wilson, at Eastport, to await a renewal of the winter campaign in Mississippi and Alabama. Hood's army, as an organization, had almost disappeared, when, on the 23d of January,[c] he was "relieved," as he said, "at his own request," at [c] 1865. Tupelo, in Mississippi.

It was during the active campaign in Middle Tennessee, just considered, that the stirring events in which Generals Gillem and Breckinridge were chief actors, occurred, as recorded on page 287. General Stoneman then took command in that region, and concentrated the forces of Gillem and Burbridge at Bean's Station. Thence he moved toward Bristol,[d] when his advance struck a force under Basil Duke, one of Morgan's officers, opposite Kingsport, dispersed them, captured their [d] Dec. 12, 1864. train, and took eighty-four of them prisoners. Burbridge pushed on to Bristol and Abingdon, capturing both places, with nearly three hundred prisoners, and destroying five loaded railway trains, and large quantities of stores and munitions of war. At Abingdon, Gillem joined Burbridge,[e] when Stoneman menaced the important salt-works at [e] Dec. 15. Saltville, in that vicinity.

By this rapid advance into Virginia, Vaughan, in command of the Confederate frontier cavalry, had been flanked, but he moved on a parallel line to Marion, where Gillem fell upon and routed him,[f] and chased him thirty miles into Wytheville. That place Gillem captured [f] Dec. 16.

---

[1] See page 419.

[2] Thomas estimated his entire loss during the campaign, in all the operations under his command, from the 7th of September, 1864, to the 20th of January, 1865, at about 10,000 men, or less than one-half the loss of his adversary. During that time he had captured 11,857 men, officers and privates, besides 1,332 who had been exchanged, making a total of about 13,000. He had administered the oath of amnesty and submission to 2,207 deserters from the Confederate service, and had captured 72 serviceable guns and 8,079 small-arms.

[3] See page 414.

at dusk the same evening, with two hundred men, eight guns, and a valuable wagon-train. After destroying Wytheville, and stores there, and the railway for some distance, Gillem returned to Mount Airy, from which place Stoneman had sent out a brigade under Colonel Buckley, to destroy lead mines in that region, which that officer accomplished, after driving off Vaughan, who was there. Stoneman now started [a] to destroy the great salt-works already mentioned. On the way, Burbridge, in the advance, met and fought Breckinridge near Marion, nearly all one day. Gillem approached from another point to cut the foe off from the salt-works, when Breckinridge, taking counsel of prudence, withdrew and retired over the mountains into North Carolina. Saltville, where the works were situated, was thus abandoned to its fate, after being guarded with the greatest care. These important works were now utterly destroyed, while spoils, in the shape of cannon, ammunition, and railway rolling stock, fell into Stoneman's hands. The object of the expedition having been accomplished, General Burbridge returned to Kentucky, and General Stoneman, with Gillem's command, went back to Knoxville.

[a] Dec. 17, 1864.

The writer visited Nashville, and the battle-field in its vicinity, at the beginning of May, 1866, after a voyage on the Cumberland to Fort Donelson and back,[1] and he was placed under many obligations to General Thomas, and members of his staff, and especially to Major Willard, for kind attentions, and for facilities for obtaining all necessary topographical and historical information concerning the battle of the 15th and 16th of December,[b] of which a description, in outline, is given in this chapter.

[b] 1864.

General Thomas took the writer, in his light carriage drawn by a span of beautiful dappled gray horses, to various points of interest, the most important of which, for the author's purpose, was the lofty hill between the Hardin and Granny White turnpikes, on which the commanding general stood, with the whole field of operations in view, and directed the battle on the 15th. With a large topographical map in his hand,[2] he pointed out every important locality and explained every movement, making the text of his official report perfectly luminous. Around us lay, upon bare hills once crowned with groves and forest, and across desolated vales once beautiful with the richest products of cultivation, the long lines of intrenchments, with forts and redoubts, cast up by both parties in the strife, and scarcely altered in feature since the day of battle. With these, and the ruins of houses battered by missiles or laid in ashes by fire, in full view, and with the clear and vivid descriptions of General Thomas, the chief actor in the events of that day, which consecrated every hill and valley, ravine and streamlet within the range of vision, it required but a small effort of the imagination, then and there, to reproduce the battle in all its awful grandeur and hideousness.

General Thomas kindly offered his carriage and a driver for the writer's use in revisiting for further study, and for sketching important points connected with the battle. In this way, accompanied by his traveling companions (Messrs. Dreer and Greble), who joined him at Nashville on the day

---

[1] See page 226, volume II.　　　　　[2] See reduced copy on page 427.

after his visit to the field with General Thomas, the writer went to and sketched several places of interest. Among these was Fort Negley,[1] and the spacious mansion of Mrs. Ackling, the head-quarters of General Wood,[2] from whose gallery the young wife of that gallant officer looked out and saw

RUINS ON MONTGOMERY HILL.

the dreadful storm of war in which her husband was conspicuous, when the attack was made upon Hood's salient on Montgomery Hill. It was just after sunset when that sketch was made. Then we rode to Montgomery Hill, passing up a lane among many evidences of the existence there of a once beautiful estate, then in utter ruin; and from the remains of Hood's strong intrenchments, north of the Montgomery mansion, the above sketch of its ruins was made, in the edge of the evening. They were partly inclosed in Hood's breastworks, and one of his redoubts, and presented a most melancholy picture of the ravages of war. The high grounds seen in the distance, toward the right of the sketch, are portions of the range of the Harpeth hills, to which Hood was driven when expelled from Montgomery Hill.

We spent a few days pleasantly and profitably in and around Nashville, the recipients of the kindest courtesies, and then went southward to visit Murfreesboro', and the extended theater of conflict between there and Chattanooga and Atlanta, already mentioned in other pages of this work.

---

[1] See page 265, volume II.　　　　　[2] See page 424.

CHAPTER XVI.

CAREER OF THE ANGLO-CONFEDERATE PIRATES.—CLOSING OF THE PORT OF MOBILE.—
POLITICAL AFFAIRS.

 ET us now turn a moment, from the consideration of the struggle on the land, to that of some events of the war on the ocean, carried on by pirate ships, and also some important naval events near Mobile.

We have noticed the organization of a so-called "Navy Department" by the Conspirators, at Montgomery, early in 1861, the measures taken for providing a naval force, and the commissioning of pirates to prey upon the National property on the ocean.[1] Also the doings of some of these cruisers in the earlier part of the war,[2] and the aid given to the Conspirators by British ship-builders, with the tacit consent of their Government, in constructing powerful sea-going pirate ships for the Confederate service.[3] The latter, as we have observed, were fitted out by British hands, and their commanders bore commissions from the Confederate "Government" so-called.[4]

These ships were provided with the best armament known to the British marine—Armstrong, Whitworth, Blakely, and other rifled cannon of heaviest

ARMSTRONG GUN.[5]

weight—which were also liberally furnished to the Confederates for land service, from British arsenals by the swift blockade-runners. By men of the same nation, every other material for destructive use by the pirate ships, was supplied, even to the most approved fire-balls for burning merchant vessels. These outrages

---

[1] See pages 372 to 374, inclusive, volume I.   [2] See pages 555 to 558, inclusive, volume I.
           [3] See pages 567 to 571, inclusive, volume II.
     [4] See page 570, volume II.   The Confederate "Navy Department" was organized with S. R. Mallory, formerly a National Senator, at its head, and he continued in office until the close of the war.   His department according to "A Register of the Commissioned and Warrant Officers of the Navy of the Confederate States, to January 1, 1864," printed at Richmond, was composed as follows: S. R. Mallory, Secretary of the Navy, with a chief clerk, three inferior clerks, and messenger; an Office of Orders and Details; Office of Ordnance and Hydrography; Office of Provisions and Clothing, and Office of Medicine and Surgery. The Register contains severa hundred names of officers, including all ranks known in our navy, from admiral down.   There was but one admiral (Franklin Buchanan), twelve captains, three provisional captains, and forty-one commanders.   A large number of these were formerly in the National service.
     [5] So called from its inventor, Sir William Armstrong.

against a people with whom the British Government was at peace and entertaining the most amicable commercial relations, were for a long time. as we have observed,[1] practically countenanced by that Government, which failed to act upon the earnest remonstrances of the American minister in London.

The most formidable of these piratical vessels fitted out in Great Britain and afloat in 1864, were the *Alabama* and *Florida*, already noticed, commanded respectively by Captains Semmes and Maffit.[2] The former was in command of the *Sumter*, whose career suddenly ended early in 1862.[3] The latter, as we have observed, went out from Mobile in the *Oreto*, afterward named *Florida*, to play the pirate by plundering on the high seas, without authority. Four other vessels were added by British shipmasters in 1864, named, respectively, *Georgia, Tallahassee, Olustee*, and *Chickamauga*, whose ravages greatly swelled the sum total of damages already inflicted upon American commerce by Anglo-Confederate marauders.[5] They sailed under British colors until a prize was secured, when they hoisted the Confederate flag. They were everywhere greeted with the greatest enthusiasm in British ports, and their officers were honored with receptions and dinners by British officials and British subjects; and wherever these corsairs appeared, whether in "proper person" on the water, or in discussions in the British Parliament, or among the ruling classes of Great Britain, they were ever the occasion for an exhibition of the practical hollowness of that neutrality proclaimed in good faith by the Queen at the beginning of the Rebellion.

The *Florida* hovered most of the time off the American coast, while the *Alabama* was seen in European and more distant waters. The former was closely watched by Government vessels, especially when the pirate was cruising among the West India Islands,[6] but she managed to elude them.

FIRE-BALL.[4]

---

[1] See page 568, volume II.   [2] See page 569, volume II.   [3] See page 568, volume II.

[4] This is a representation of a fire-ball taken from on board one of the Anglo-Confederate pirate ships. It was made of stout canvas, inclosed in netting, and filled with combustible material. It was egg-shaped, a little more than a foot in length, and at the larger end had a solid piece of wood, which was used for the same purpose as the *sabot* on projectiles. These fire-balls were thrown into vessels, as well as forts, from cannon. On board of the same vessel were found shells filled with a substance called Greek fire, terrible in its character, because inextinguishable. Also other shells, for hurling melted iron upon ships. All of these destructive materials were furnished to the pirate ships in Great Britain. They were seen and sketched by the author, at the Navy Yard in Washington City, with many other relics of the war, in 1866.

HOT METAL SHELL.

GREEK FIRE SHELL.

[5] At the beginning of 1864 the pirates then on the ocean had captured 193 American merchant ships, whereof all but 17 were burnt. The value of their cargoes, in the aggregate, was estimated at $13,445,000. So dangerous became the navigation of the ocean for American vessels, that about 1,000 American ships were sold to foreign merchants, chiefly British. Full two-thirds of the carrying trade between the United States and Europe was driven to British bottoms.

[6] While cruising in that region in May, 1863, the *Florida* captured the brig *Clarence*, and fitted her up as a pirate ship, with a crew under Lieutenant C. W. Read, formerly of the National Navy. She went up the coast of the United States, capturing valuable prizes, and near Cape Henry she seized the bark *Tacony*. To this vessel Read transferred his men and armament, and spread destruction and consternation among merchant and fishing vessels, from the coast of Virginia to that of Maine. Swift cruisers were sent after the *Tacony*. When informed of this, Read transferred his crew and armament to the prize schooner *Archer*, and destroyed the *Tacony*. Then he went boldly to the entrance of the harbor of Portland, Maine,[a] and at midnight sent two armed boats to seize the revenue cutter *Cushing*, lying there. It was done, when chase after the pirates was successfully made by two merchant steamers, hastily armed and manned for the purpose. The *Cushing* and *Archer*, with the pirates, were soon taken back to Portland, where the marauders were lodged in prison.

[a] June 24, 1863.

She would sometimes skim swiftly along the coast of the United States, leaving a track of desolation in her course, and then shoot off to some distant waters.[1] On one of these occasions, while in command of Captain Morris, she went down the Brazilian coast, destroyed the barque *Mondamon*, off the port of Bahia, and then ran into that harbor. There Morris saw with alarm the United States Steamer *Wachusett*, Captain Collins. As a precaution, he anchored the *Florida* in the midst of the Brazilian fleet, and under the guns of the most powerful fort guarding the town. The American Consul, T. F. Wilson, protested against the hospitality thus given to the pirate by the Brazilian authorities, to which no attention was paid.

Captain Collins determined that the *Florida* should never put to sea again. He tried to draw her into battle outside of the harbor, but did not succeed; and then, in disregard of the rights of the Brazilians in their own waters, he ran down[a] upon the *Florida* with a full head of steam, with the intention of crushing and sinking her. He failed. She was damaged, but not crippled. There was a little musket firing on both sides, without injury, when Collins demanded the surrender of the *Florida*. Her commander and half his crew were ashore, and the lieutenant in charge, having no choice, complied. The pirate ship was instantly boarded, and lashed to the *Wachusett*, when the latter put to sea under a full head of steam, towing her prize, unmindful of a challenge by the Brazilian fleet, and unharmed by shots from the Bahian fort. Captor and prize soon appeared in Hampton Roads; and not long afterward the *Florida* was sunk while lying off Newport-Newce.

[a] Oct. 7, 1864.

The capture of the *Florida* produced much excitement. It was brought to the notice of the Government of the United States by the Brazilian minister at Washington in the form of a protest, with the assumption that the rebels were lawful belligerents, and that the *Florida* was one of their vessels of war. The Government disavowed the act of its agents in the port of Bahia as a violation of neutrality laws and the rights of Brazil, and Consul Wilson, known to have been implicated in the capture, was recalled, and Captain Collins was suspended and ordered before a court-martial. At the same time, the assumption of the Brazilian Government was disallowed, and

---

Later in the year another daring act of piracy was committed. The merchant steamer *Chesapeake*, plying between New York and Portland, was seized on the 6th of December, by sixteen of her passengers, who proved to be pirates in disguise. They overpowered the officers, killed and threw overboard one of the engineers, and took possession of the vessel. She was soon afterward seized in one of the harbors of Nova Scotia, by a National gun-boat, and the pirates were taken to Halifax and handed over to the civil authorities, from whom they were snatched by a sympathizing mob.

[1] Maffit, the commander of the *Florida*, was represented by all who knew him as a man lacking all real sense of honor. His conduct in the capture of the *Jacob Bell*, a merchant ship on her way to New York from China, sufficiently proves the assertion. Among the passengers was Mrs. H. Dwight Williams, wife of the American Commissioner of Customs at Swartow, in China. She had in her trunk many valuable presents for friends at home, besides a large amount of clothing and silver plate. She gave Maffit a list of her personal effects, and begged him to spare them for her. He politely told her he could not, and then went to the *Jacob Bell*. She obtained permission to return to that ship, where she found Maffit and his fellow-officers engaged in appropriating her property to their own use. They broke open packages; and laces, letters, photographs of friends, which they could not use, they trampled under foot on the deck, in her presence. Mrs. Williams was soon taken back to the *Florida*, when the *Jacob Bell* was burned. One of Maffit's school-fellows, a recent writer asserts, remembers the following lines, written by another about twelve years of age, on an "exhibition day" of the school:—

> "And here's Johnny Maffit, as straight as a gun—
> If you face him square up, he'll turn round and run!
> The *first boy* in school, sir, if thieving and lies,
> Instead of good scholarship, bore off the prize."

the hospitality it had afforded to the *Florida* at Bahia, was denounced as an " act of intervention in derogation of the law of nations, and unfriendly and wrongful, as it was manifestly in-jurious to the United States." [1]

Long before the *Florida* was seized, the career of the *Georgia* was ended,[2] and the *Alabama*[3] had made her last cruise. It had been a long and prosperous one in the South Atlantic and Indian oceans, during which she had captured sixty-seven vessels, of which forty-five were de-stroyed. She returned to European waters early in the summer of 1864, and took refuge in the French harbor of Cherbourg. At that time the United States steamer *Kearsarge*,[4] commanded by Captain John A. Winslow, was lying in the Dutch port of Flushing. The American consul at Cherbourg immediately informed Winslow, by telegraph, of the presence of the *Alabama*, when he left Flushing and proceeded, with the *Kearsarge*, to look after the pirate ship.

The *Kearsarge* appeared off *Cherbourg* on the 14th of June,[a] and on the following day, Semmes, having made arrangements for all needful assistance, sent a note to Winslow, desiring him not to leave, as he (the pirate) intended to fight him. Winslow was glad to oblige the writer, and remained. Semmes then made ample preparations. He de-posited valuable property on the shore with his friends,[5] and at his own chosen time, which was Sunday, the 19th of June, he went out of the harbor with the *Alabama*, followed by the yacht *Deerhound*, belonging to one of the English gentry named Lambert. It was a sort of tender, to see that the pirate

a 1864.

---

[1] Exceptions have been taken to the use of the title of *pirate* applied to the vessels and men like the *Flor-ida*, *Alabama*, and others, and their officers and crews. The Secretary of State (W. H. Seward), with all the light that international arrangements and the laws of nations, as well as the letter and spirit of definition on these points, could give, not only considered these vessels and their crews in that light, but said so in his diplo-matic correspondence. In his letter to the Brazilian minister, on the occasion we are considering, he said, that the Government maintained that the *Florida* "like the *Alabama*, was *a pirate, belonging to no nation or lawful belligerent*, and, therefore, the harboring and supplying of these piratical ships and their crews, in bel-ligerent ports, were wrongs and injuries for which Brazil justly owes reparation to the United States, as ample as the reparation she now receives from them." Consult, also, page 570, of volume II., and note 1, page 556, volume I. of this work.

[2] The *Georgia* was an iron ship, built in Glasgow. She went to sea with the name of *Japan*, in April, 1863. Off the coast of France she received her armament, changed her name to *Georgia*, and began the career of a pirate. After committing many depredations, and destroying large and valuable merchant ships, she put into French ports, and then went to England where a pretended sale of her was made to a Liverpool merchant, who dispatched her to Lisbon, under the pretense that she had been chartered by the Portuguese Government. When twenty miles from Lisbon, she was captured by the United States steam-frigate *Niagara*, Captain Craven, who took her to England, and landed her crew at Dover. No one seemed willing to question the cor-rectness of the transaction, and that was the last of the *Georgia* as a pirate ship.

[3] See picture of the *Alabama*, on page 571.

[4] This name was given to the vessel by the wife of G. V. Fox, then the efficient Assistant Secretary of the Navy, who was the daughter of the late Levi Woodbury, of New Hampshire. It was the Indian name of a mountain in her native State.

[5] This consisted chiefly of a chest of coin, and 62 chronometers, which he had taken from the vessels he had captured. The Confederate agent at Cherbourg, M. Bonfils, took charge of this property, which was valued at about $25,000.

chief, if worsted in the fight, should not fall into Captain Winslow's hands.

Fearing the question of jurisdiction, Winslow steamed to sea about seven miles from the breakwater at *Cherbourg*, followed by *Semmes* at a distance of about a mile. The *Alabama* was accompanied by the French iron-clad frigate *Couronne* to a point beyond the territorial waters, and then went back. Then the *Kearsarge* rounded to, and made for the *Alabama*. When within twelve hundred yards of her, the latter opened fire. The *Kearsarge* received two or three broadsides without returning a shot, when she suddenly retorted with telling effect.[1] Winslow attempted to close and board his antagonist, but Semmes fought shy. His ship sheered off and steamed ahead, firing rapidly and wildly, while the *Kearsarge* delivered her fire slowly and with deliberate aim. For an hour they fought, the steamers moving in a circle, and thus each kept its starboard side from which it was firing, bearing upon the starboard side of the other. In the course of the conflict they described seven circles, as denoted in the annexed diagram, and were drifted by the tide about four miles from the place of the beginning of the fight, before it was ended.

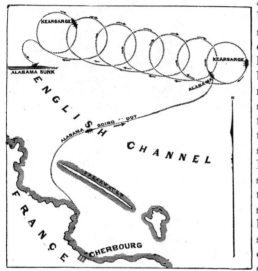

NAVAL BATTLE OFF CHERBOURG.

At a little past twelve o'clock, at noon, when the combat had continued an hour, the *Alabama* was at the mercy of her adversary. She had received several 11-inch shells, one of which disabled a gun and eighteen men. Another had entered her coal-bunker, and by the effects of its explosion had so blocked up the engine room as to compel a resort to sails; and her sides were shattered and pierced with holes. The *Kearsarge* was then in a position to fire grape-shot effectually. A few more guns brought down the *Alabama's* flag, but Winslow could not tell whether it had been shot away or hauled down. A white flag was then displayed over her stern; so, respecting it, the firing of the *Kearsarge* ceased. In the space of two minutes the *Alabama* treacherously opened two guns upon her adversary, and attempted to run to the protection of neutral waters, not more than three miles distant. This

---

[1] The two vessels were fairly matched in dimensions, equipment, and men. The extreme length of the *Alabama* was 220 feet; length on water line, 210; beam, 32; depth, 17; two engines of 300 horse power each, and tonnage 1,150. The extreme length of the *Kearsarge* was 214¼ feet; length on water line, 198¼ feet; beam, 33; depth, 16 feet; two engines 400 horse power each, and tonnage 1,030. The *Alabama* carried one 7-inch Blakely rifled cannon; one 8-inch smooth-bore 58-pounder, and six 32-pounders. The *Kearsarge* had two 11-inch smooth-bore guns; one 30-pounder rifled cannon, and four 32-pounders. The *Kearsarge* used 5 guns, the *Alabama* 7. The *Kearsarge* had 162 officers and men; the *Alabama* about 150. The gunners of the latter were trained artillerists from the British ship-of-war *Excellent*.

drew the fire of the *Kearsarge* again, and then she steamed ahead, and laid across the *Alabama's* bows, for raking. The white flag was still flying, and Winslow's fire was again reserved.[1] Very soon afterward the boats of the *Alabama* were seen to be lowering, and in one of them an officer came alongside the *Kearsarge* with information that her antagonist had surrendered, and was fast sinking.[2] At that moment, the *Deerhound*, with Lancaster and his family on board, having come out professedly to see the fight, but really for another purpose, passed by the *Kearsarge*, and Winslow humanely requested her owner to assist in saving the people of the *Alabama*. Twenty minutes afterward the pirate ship went down in the deep waters of the British Channel. Sixty-five of the unfortunate men were rescued by the *Kearsarge*. The *Deerhound* picked up Semmes, his officers, and some men, and carried them out of harm's way, to England, where the pirate commander was received with all the attentions due to a hero in honorable warfare.[3] It was an exhibition of which the honest heart of England was greatly ashamed.

Thus ended the great naval duel, seen by thousands from the French shore, with very little loss of life.[4] It resulted in closing the career of a vessel whose existence and doings were a perpetual outrage of the British Government against the citizens of our Republic. And the organs of British opinion, favorable to that Government, bewailed her loss as a British disaster; while thinking, honest Englishmen, representing the great heart of the British nation, blushed with shame, for they regarded her existence and career as a stigma upon the crown and the people. They insisted, also, what the Government of the United States has never ceased to claim, that the

---

[1] Semmes, in a letter to J. M. Mason, the Confederate "Envoy" in London, omitting to mention his own perfidious conduct in opening fire after he had displayed a white flag, said:—"Although we were but 400 yards from each other, the enemy fired upon me five times after my colors had been struck. It is charitable to suppose that a ship-of-war of a Christian nation could not have done this intentionally." The statement of Captain Winslow, given substantially in the text, which was corroborated by that of Semmes's friend Lancaster, shows the untruthfulness of the pirate's account. Semmes declared that the midship section of the *Kearsarge* was "on both sides thoroughly iron-coated, this having been done with chains constructed for the purpose, the whole covered with a thin outer coating of plank which gave no indication of the armor beneath." Winslow says that the *Alabama* had greatly the advantage in a much larger quantity of coal "which brought her down in the water," and added, "but as an offset to this, her sheet-chains were stowed outside, stopped up and down as an additional preventive, and protection to her more empty bunkers." The *Kearsarge* was very little damaged. Her stern-post was struck and shattered by an elliptical shell, as represented in the engraving. That part of her stern-post in which the shell lodged is preserved in the Museum of the Navy Yard, at Washington City, where the writer sketched it.

STERN-POST.

[2] Before going into action, Semmes made a speech to his crew, in which he declared that the *Kearsarge* must be conquered, or the *Alabama*, with her officers and crew, should go to the bottom. As that crew were nearly all Englishmen, he repeated to them the words of Lord Nelson on a more noble occasion:—"England expects every man to do his duty." But when the *Alabama* was found to be actually sinking, and Semmes saw his friend Lancaster near, he changed his mind, and with the spirit of his fellow-confederates on land, who were always talking of "dying in the last ditch," he determined to risk being hanged as a pirate rather than drown as a voluntary and foolish martyr.

[3] Lancaster carried the pirates to Southampton, and Winslow's claim that they were lawful prisoners of war, having formally surrendered, was denied. At Southampton a public dinner was given to Semmes and his officers; and Admiral Anson, of the British navy, headed a list of subscribers to a fund raised for the purpose of purchasing an elegant sword to be presented to the Corsair as a token of sympathy and esteem.

[4] The *Kearsarge* had three men badly wounded, one of them mortally. The latter was William Gowin, of Michigan, a genuine hero, whose leg was badly shattered at the beginning of the action, but who concealed the extent of his injuries and gave every encouragement to his comrades. The *Alabama* had nine men killed and twenty-one wounded. Of the latter, two were drowned before they could be saved.

British Government was bound to make full indemnity for all losses caused
by the destructive acts of the *Alabama*.[1]

It seems proper to record here, in anticipation of other transactions of
the war, the prominent events in the career of the last of the Confederate
pirate ships, and which performed the last acts of hostility against the Republic. She was the *Shenandoah*, a Clyde (Scotland) built vessel, long and
rakish, of seven hundred and ninety tons burden, with an auxiliary engine
of two hundred and twenty nominal horse power, and capable of an average
speed of ten knots an hour.

The *Shenandoah* was originally the *Sea-King*. She left London with that
name early in October, 1864, as an East Indiaman, armed with two guns, as
usual, and cleared for Bombay. A steamer, named *Laurel*, took from Liverpool a lot of "Southern gentlemen" (as the historian of the *Shenandoah's*
cruise called them), who had been in the *Sumter*, *Alabama*, and *Georgia*,
with an armament and a crew of Englishmen, all of which were transferred
to the *Sea-King* at Madeira, when she was named *Shenandoah*. Her captain was James I. Waddell, who was regularly commissioned by Mallory.
He addressed the crew, who were ignorant of their destination until then,
and informed them of the character and purpose of the *Shenandoah*, whereupon only twenty-three of the eighty men were found willing to become
pirates and take the risks of the perilous profession. The remainder returned
to Liverpool in the *Laurel*.

The *Shenandoah* sailed from Madeira to the Southern Ocean, plundering
and destroying American vessels whenever opportunity to do so was offered.
At Melbourne, Australia, her officers were received with great enthusiasm,
and were entertained with receptions, dinners, and balls; and free tickets
were given them for travel on the Hobson Bay railroad. Just before they
left, these "gentlemen" indulged in a drunken frolic, and a disgraceful
fight with some of the citizens. Then the *Shenandoah* cruised in the India
seas and up the Eastern coast of Asia to the Ochosk Sea and
a June, 1865. Behring's Straits,*a* to plunder and destroy the New England
whaling fleet on the borders of the frozen Arctic Ocean. There she made
havoc among the whalers, and lighted up the ice-floes of the Polar Sea with
incendiary fires. On the 28th of June, she appeared at a convention of
whaling ships in that region,[2] bearing the American flag, and exciting no
suspicions of her character, when she suddenly revealed her mission, and,
before five o'clock that evening, she had made prizes of ten whale ships, of
which eight were set on fire and burned in a group before midnight. "It
was an ill-omened day for them and the insurance offices in New Bedford,"
said the historian of her cruise. This was the last act in the horrid drama
of the Civil War.

On the 2d of August the commander of the *Shenandoah* was satisfac-

---

[1] The Manchester *Examiner*, in noticing her destruction, said:—"Thus ends the career of one of the most
notorious ships of modern times. Costly as has been her career to Federal commerce, she has been hardly less
costly to this country. She has sown a legacy of distrust and of future apprehension on both sides of the Atlantic; and happy will it be both for England and America, if with her, beneath the waters of the channel, may
be buried the memory of her career and of the mischief she has done."

[2] It was the custom of whalers, when a ship had been badly injured, to collect all the vessels within signaling distance, and if the craft was found so hurt that it was impossible to repair her, she was sold at auction to
the highest bidder. On the occasion under consideration, the ship *Brunswick*, from New Bedford, had been
stove, and blew signals of distress. This caused the gathering of the whaling fleet.

torily informed of the end of the Rebellion,[1] by an English bark, when, contrary to the wishes of the ship's company, Waddell proceeded with his vessel to England, and delivered her as a prize to the British national vessel *Donegal*, in the harbor of Liverpool.[2] According to the historian of the cruise, the object of Waddell was sordid and dishonorable, and he enriched himself at the expense of his companions. By a ruling of the British authorities, all of the men of the *Shenandoah*, not British subjects, were released, and this covered nearly the whole, for almost every man, however much his speech betrayed him, eagerly, on that occasion, claimed to be a native born or adopted citizen of the United States.[3]

Soon after the destruction of the *Alabama*, measures were taken for further diminishing the aid continually given to the Confederates through British vessels, by closing against the blockade-runners the ports of Mobile and Wilmington, the only ones now remaining open to them. These, having double entrances, made it difficult for blockading squadrons to prevent the swift, light-draft vessels used for running the blockade,[4] from slipping in with valuable cargoes of needful supplies, and slipping out again with equally valuable cargoes of cotton for the use of England's mills.

It was resolved to seal up the port of Mobile first, and for that purpose, Admiral Farragut appeared[a] off the entrance of Mobile Bay, full thirty miles below the city, with a fleet of eighteen vessels, four of them iron-clad,[5] while a land force, about five thousand strong, sent by General Canby from New Orleans, under General Gordon Granger, was planted upon Dauphin Island for the purpose of co-operating.

[a] Aug. 5, 1864.

The entrance to Mobile Bay is divided by Dauphin Island, making two passages; the easterly one four miles wide and twenty-five feet deep in the channel. The other, known as Grant's Pass, was a very narrow passage, between two little islands, and not more than five or six feet deep at low

---

[1] Before the raid on the whaling fleet, a San Francisco newspaper had reached the *Shenandoah*, with news of the surrender of Lee and Johnston, and the end of the war, but he did not choose to consider it authentic, "coming from the enemy."

[2] One of the pirates, an officer of the *Shenandoah*, named Cornelius E. Hunt, wrote a history of the cruise of the Shenandoah, from which this brief sketch has been chiefly compiled. He says when they were informed of the close of the war, each man felt himself a proper subject for the wrath of his outraged Government. "It had been three months," he says, "since hostilities ceased, leaving us without a flag or a country; and during that time we had been actively engaged in preying upon the commerce of a Government that not only claimed our allegiance, but had made good her claim by the wager of battle." Under these circumstances, Captain Waddell was solicited by a written petition of the ship's company, to proceed to Sydney, Australia, there abandon the ship to the British authorities, and let each man look out for his personal safety. He deceived them with professions of acquiescence, but steered for England.

The same writer complains of the coldness with which these corsairs were received in England. "The journals," he said, "once most clamorous for our cause, were the first to bestow upon us the epithet of 'pirates.' So much for the disinterested friendship of Great Britain. As long as their workshops were busy turning out arms and munitions of war for our armies in the field, and blockade-runners from Southern ports were arriving at Liverpool and London, laden with the coveted cotton, they were loud in their protestations of sympathy and friendship; but when the hour of adversity came—when there was nothing more to be made out of us, these fair-weather friends wholly ignored our existence."

[3] During her cruise, in which she circumnavigated the globe, the Shenandoah captured thirty vessels, whose aggregate value was $1,354,958.

[4] See page 312, volume II.

[5] The wooden vessels were the *Hartford* (flag-ship), Captain P. Drayton; *Brooklyn*, Captain James Alden; *Metacomet*, Lieutenant-commander J. E. Jonett; *Octorara*, Lieutenant-commander C. H. Green; *Richmond*, Captain T. A. Jenkins; *Lackawanna*, Captain J. B. Marchand; *Monongahela*, Commander J. H. Strong; *Ossipee*, Commander W. E. LeRoy; *Oneida*, Commander J. R. M. Mullaney; *Port Royal*, Lieutenant-commander B. Gherarde; *Seminole*, Commander E. Donaldson; *Kennebeck*, Lieutenant-commander W. P. McCann; *Itasca*, Lieutenant-commander George Brown, and *Galena*, Lieutenant-commander C. H. Wells. The ironclad vessels were the *Tecumseh*, Commander T. A. M. Craven; *Manhattan*, Commander T. W. A. Nicholson; *Winnebago*, Commander T. H. Stevens, and *Chickasaw*, Lieutenant-commander T. H. Perkins.

water.   On one of the little islands, and commanding the Pass, was a small earth-work, called Fort Powell, and across the channel, only a few yards distant, was a small light-house, as seen in the sketch made by the writer on an April evening, 1866.[1]   On the easterly point of Dauphin Island was a

VIEW AT GRANT'S PASS.

stronger work, called Fort Gaines, commanding the main entrance; and southeasterly from it, on Mobile Point, was the still stronger work, Fort Morgan, formerly Fort Bowyer, with a heavy light-house near it.   The ship channel passed close under the guns of Fort Morgan, and in it the Confederates had driven piles to obstruct it, and sown torpedoes in profusion. These forts were well armed and manned, and within the bay, and not far distant, lay a small Confederate squadron, commanded by Admiral Buchanan.[2]   His flag-ship was a powerful ram, called *Tennessee*,[3] one of the most formidable of that class of war-vessels; and she was accompanied by three ordinary gun-boats, named, respectively, *Selma, Morgan,* and *Gaines.*

Such were the defenses of the harbor of Mobile, at its entrance, thirty miles south of the city.   Considering all things, they were very formidable, but not sufficiently so to cause the gallant Farragut to hesitate for a moment. He had fixed upon the 4th of August as the day for the attack, but as the *Tecumseh* had not then arrived, operations were deferred until the next day, when they began before six o'clock in the morning.

Farragut had arranged his wooden ships in couples, lashed together, for the passage of the forts.   His flag-ship was tethered to the *Metacomet.*   In order to have a general oversight and direction of all movements, he took the perilous position of the main-top of the *Hartford*, his flag-ship, where he was lashed, that he might not be dislodged by the shock of battle.   By means of a tube, extending from his lofty position to the deck, he was able to give orders clearly, in defiance of the uproar of the strife.   In that exposed situation he remained during the perilous passage of the forts and the conflict with the gun-boats, that ensued.   It was a marvelous and sublime exhibition of faith and courage.   He illustrated his own remark that " exposure is one of the penalties of rank in the navy."   The exploit has been celebrated by the pencil and song.

At the hour above-named, Farragut's fleet steamed up toward Fort Morgan.   The four armored vessels passed the bar in advance, and at a little before seven o'clock, the *Tecumseh* opened fire upon the fort, then a mile off. The latter soon replied, when a general engagement ensued.   Because of

---

[1] This is from a sketch made from a steamer, looking east.   On the left are seen the mounds of Fort Powell; on the right the light-house, and in the channel, the remains of the obstructions placed there by the Confederates.   In the far distance is seen a part of Mobile Point.

[2] See page 360, volume II.

[3] The *Tennessee* was 209 feet in length, 48 feet beam, with timber sides 8 feet in thickness, and double-plated with two-inch iron.   She was fitted with a tower and turret; also, with a formidable beak.   She carried two 7-inch, and four 6-inch rifled guns, which cast projectiles respectively weighing 110 and 95 pounds. She was propelled by two powerful engines.

her having four chase-guns, peculiarly adapted for the work in hand, Farragut had allowed the *Brooklyn* and her tethered companion, the *Octorara*, to
lead the wooden ships. When
that vessel was within range of
the fort, whose guns were trained
upon the *Hartford* (which, with
the *Metacomet*, was close following), she opened a heavy fire of
grape-shot, that almost instantly
drove the gunners from the more
exposed batteries. Just then
the *Tecumseh*, about three hundred yards ahead of the *Brooklyn*, was seen to be suddenly
uplifted, and then to disappear
almost instantly beneath the
waters. She had struck a sensitive torpedo,[1] which exploded

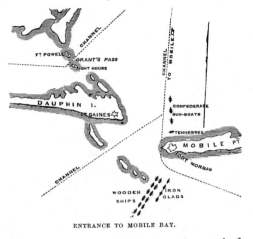

ENTRANCE TO MOBILE BAY.

directly under her turret, making a great chasm, into which the water rushed
in such volume that she sunk in a few seconds, carrying down with her commander Craven and nearly all of his officers and crew. Only seventeen, of
one hundred and thirty, were saved.

The *Brooklyn* recoiled at the appalling apparition before her, when Farragut ordered Captain Drayton to push on the *Hartford*, unmindful of torpedoes and every thing else, and directed the rest of the vessels to follow.
But no more mines were met. The storm of grape-shot which the ships
poured upon the fort, imposed almost absolute silence upon its guns; but,
as the National fleet passed in, the Confederate vessels opened upon them.
The ram *Tennessee*, rushed at the *Hartford*, but missed her, when the latter
returned the fire given by her adversary, and calmly passed on. Then the
fire of the three gun-boats was concentrated upon the flag-ship. The *Selma*
raked her at a disadvantage, when Farragut directed the *Metacomet* to cast
off, and close upon the annoying vessel. This was done, and, at the end of an
hour's contest, the *Selma*, armed with four heavy pivot guns, and with a force
of ninety-seven men, was a prize to the *Metacomet*. She had lost, in the
fray, fourteen men, killed and wounded. Among the latter was her commander, P. N. Murphy. The other two gun-boats sought safety under the
cannon of the fort; and that night, shielded by darkness, the *Morgan*
escaped and hastened to Mobile. The *Gaines*, badly injured, was run
ashore and burned.

Believing the contest to be over, Farragut now ordered most of his vessels to anchor; when, at a quarter before nine o'clock, the *Tennessee*, which
had run some distance up the bay, came down under a full head of steam,
and made directly for the *Hartford*. A signal was at once given for the
National vessels, armored and unarmored, to close in upon and destroy the
monster. It seemed invulnerable, even to the heaviest shot and shell, at
closest range. The *Monongahela* first struck it a blow square .in the side,

---

[1] See page 194.

and poured 11-inch shot upon it with very little effect. Giving the *Tennessee* another blow, the *Monongahela* lost her own beak and cut-water. The *Lancaster* then, running at full speed, struck the ram heavily, but crushed her own stem without much injuring her adversary.

The *Hartford* now tried her power upon the sea-giant. She gave the *Tennessee* a glancing blow and a broadside of 10-inch shells at ten feet distance. Then the armored *Chickasaw* ran under its stern, and at about the same time the *Manhattan*, approaching the same point, sent a solid 15-inch bolt that demolished its stearing-gear, and broke square through the iron plating of its hull, and the thick wood-work behind it. Meanwhile, Farragut ordered Drayton to strike the ram another blow with the *Hartford*, and he was about to do so, when the crippled *Lackawanna*, in making another attempt to bruise the foe, came in collision with the flag-ship, and damaged her severely. Both vessels then drew off, and started at full speed to give the *Tennessee* a deadly stroke by each. At the same time the *Chickasaw* was pounding away at its stern, and the *Ossipee* was running at full speed to strike. Thus beset, and now badly wounded, the *Tennessee* hauled down its flag, and flung out a white one in token of surrender. The *Ossipee*, then near, tried to avoid the victim, and gave it only a harmless glancing blow, in passing.

So ended the desperate struggle, at about 10 o'clock in the morning, in which the Confederate squadron was virtually destroyed. In that fight the *Tennessee* had depended more upon its invulnerability and its power as a ram, than upon its guns—not one of which was fired after the *Hartford* gave her first blow. It became so crippled, that it could no longer work. Its smoke-stack was shot away; its steering apparatus was gone, and several of its port-shutters were so battered by shot, that they could not be opened. Admiral Buchanan was found with his leg so badly injured, that he lost it, and six of his crew were dead or wounded.[1] So the *Tennessee*, perhaps one of the most powerful vessels ever built, and its officers and men, became captives to Admiral Farragut.[a]

August 5, 1864.

The Confederate squadron was destroyed, but Farragut's work was not done. There stood the forts guarding the entrance to Mobile Bay, almost unharmed, with full armaments and garrisons. These must be captured before the object of the expedition would be accomplished. To that business the admiral now addressed himself, after sending the wounded of both parties to Pensacola, on the *Metacomet*.

General Granger was on Dauphin Island, and had begun the siege of Fort Gaines. Farragut sent[b] the *Chickasaw* to help him. She shelled the fort with such effect that, on the following morning,[c] Col. Anderson, its commander, asked for conditions on which he might surrender. The frightened garrison at Fort Powell, at Grant's Pass, had

[b] August 6.
[c] August 7.

---

[1] In this engagement, Farragut took 280 prisoners, 190 of them from the *Tennessee*, and 90 from the *Selma*. His total loss in the battle was 165 killed, and 170 wounded; total 335. The number of killed included 113 that went down in the *Tecumseh*, and others slain by the explosion of a steam boiler on the *Oneida* that was penetrated by a shell from Fort Morgan. The greatest coolness was exhibited on that vessel. By that explosion, nearly all the firemen and coal-heavers on duty were killed or disabled, and a shell, exploding in her cabin, cut her wheel-ropes. Notwithstanding this, and even while the steam was escaping, her guns were loaded and fired as regularly as if no danger were near. A fire on the top of her magazine, caused by a shell, was quietly extinguished, while the powder was regularly served to the guns.

abandoned that fort, and blew up the works, as far as possible, on the night after the capture of the *Tennessee*. They fled in such haste, that they left the guns behind them. Aware of this, and seeing the National fleet in full possession of the bay, Anderson knew that further resistance would be useless. At nearly 10 o'clock in the morning of the 7th, the fort and its garrison of six hundred men were surrendered, and the National flag was unfurled over the works. It was greeted by cheers from the fleet.

Stronger Fort Morgan, on Mobile Point, still held out. It was in charge of General Richard L. Page, a Virginian. Being on the main land, he had hopes of receiving re-enforcements. He had signaled to Anderson to " Hold on," and when that officer surrendered Fort Gaines, Page cried out " Coward !" and the entire Confederacy echoed the slander. Page's turn for a similar trial came, and he met it with less honor than did Anderson. Granger's troops were transferred[a] from Dauphin Island to the rear of Fort Morgan, and there lines of investment were constructed across the narrow sand-spit. When every thing was in readiness, the fleet and these batteries[1] opened fire upon the fort at daylight,[b] and bombarded it furiously about twenty-four hours. The main work was not much injured; but the sturdy light-house, standing near, and

[a] August 9, 1864.

[b] August 22.

LIGHT-HOUSE AT FORT MORGAN.

in range of Farragut's guns, was reduced to the condition delineated in the engraving. Page made no resistance after the bombardment was fairly begun, but simply endured it until the next morning, when he displayed a white flag, and surrendered the post and garrison to Farragut, unconditionally, after damaging the guns and other materials of war to the extent of his ability.[2] With the three forts, the Government came into possession of

---

[1] Farragut had landed four 9-inch guns, and placed them in battery, under the command of Lieutenant H. B. Tyson, of the *Hartford*.

[2] When the Confederate officers were assembled on the outside of the fort, it was discovered that most of the guns within were spiked, many of the gun-carriages wantonly injured, and arms, ammunition, provisions, &c., destroyed. "There was every reason," said Farragut, " to believe that this had been done after the white flag had been raised. It was also discovered that General Page and several of his officers had no swords to deliver up, and further, that some of those which were surrendered, had been broken." Farragut added, that " the whole conduct of the officers of Forts Gaines and Morgan presented such a striking contrast in moral principle" that he could not fail to remark it. He mentioned the absolute necessity for a surrender imposed upon Colonel Anderson, and said, " From the moment he hoisted the white flag, he scrupulously kept every thing intact, and in that condition delivered it over; whilst General Page and his officers, with a childish spitefulness, destroyed the guns which they had said they would defend to the last, but which they never defended

one hundred and four guns, and fourteen hundred and sixty-four men. By this victory the port of Mobile was effectually closed to blockade-runners, and the land operations against the city which occurred some months later, thereby became easier, and were more speedily successful.

The victories at Mobile and Atlanta,[1] following close upon each other, with minor successes elsewhere, and the noble response given to the call of the President a few weeks before,[a] for three hundred thousand men, to re-enforce the two great armies in the field, in Virginia and Georgia, gave assurance that the end of the Civil War and the return of peace were nigh. Because of these triumphs, the President issued[b] the proclamation, and also the order for salutes of artillery,[2] mentioned in note 1, on page 395.

[a July 18, 1864.]

[b Sept. 3.]

Let us now turn for a moment to the consideration of the political affairs of the Republic.

While the National armies were struggling desperately, but almost everywhere successfully, during the summer and autumn of 1864, the people in the free-labor States were violently agitated by a political campaign carried on with intense vigor, the object being the election of a President of the Republic, in place of Mr. Lincoln, whose term of office would expire the ensuing spring.

The lines between the Administration and the Opposition parties which the Peace Faction of the latter had distinctly drawn the year before,[3] were now as prominent as then, and more clearly defined. The grand topic for consideration remained, and the questions to be answered at the Presidential election were, Shall the war be prosecuted with vigor until the Rebellion shall be suppressed and the life of the Nation secured? Shall the policy of emancipation and universal freedom and justice be sustained? The Administration was prepared to say *Yes*, by the ballot; the Opposition party was prepared to say *No*, by the same potential, but "still, small voice."

There were some in the Administration party, who were impatient because of the considerate and cautious policy of the President, and a few of these men, deprecating Mr. Lincoln's re-election on that account, called a National Convention of "The radical men of the nation." It was held at Cleveland, Ohio,[c] and was composed of about three hundred and fifty persons, very few of them regularly chosen delegates. They adopted a "platform of principles," consisting of thirteen resolutions, in which the duty of the Government to suppress the Rebellion by force of arms; the right of free speech and the enjoyment of the privilege of the writ of *habeas corpus;* an amendment of the Constitution so as to prevent the re-establishment of slavery; the wisdom of the "Monroe Doctrine;" gratitude to the soldiers and sailors; the policy of restricting the incumbency of the Presidential office to one term; the election of the President and Vice-President directly by the people; the commission of the business of "recon-

[c May 31.]

---

at all, and threw away or broke those weapons which they had not the manliness to use against their enemies; for Fort Morgan never fired a gun after the commencement of the bombardment, and the advanced pickets of our army were actually on its glacis."—Farragut's *Additional Report*, August 25, 1864.

[1] See page 394.

[2] At Washington, New York, Boston, Philadelphia, Pittsburg, Baltimore, Newport (Kentucky), St. Louis, New Orleans, Mobile Bay, Pensacola, Hilton Head, and New Berne.

[3] See chapter III.

struction" to the people, and not to the President; and the confiscation of the lands of rebels and their division among soldiers and actual settlers were enjoined. General John C. Fremont was nominated for the Presidency, and General John Cochrane for the Vice-Presidency. When, at a little later period, these candidates were satisfied that their nomination might create divisions in the Union ranks, and saw that another Union Convention had taken equally advanced ground, withdrew.

The other Convention alluded to, assembled at Baltimore, Maryland, on the 7th of June.[a] It was composed of supporters of the Administration, and was termed the Union National Convention. All the States and Territories were represented by chosen delegates, excepting those in which rebellion existed. A "platform of principles" embraced in eleven resolutions was adopted, in which was given a pledge to sustain the Government in its efforts to suppress the Rebellion; an approval of the determination of the Government not to compromise with the rebels; an approval of the acts of Government in relation to slavery, and of an amendment to the Constitution for the prohibition of slavery; a proffer of thanks to the soldiers and sailors who had helped to save their country; an expression of perfect confidence in Abraham Lincoln, the President of the United States, and an indorsement of his acts; a declaration that it was the duty of the Government to give equal protection to all persons in its service without regard to color; that foreign emigration should be encouraged; that a speedy completion of a railway to the Pacific Ocean was desirable; that the National faith in relation to the public debt must be kept inviolate; and that the Monroe Doctrine was wise and just. The Convention then nominated Abraham Lincoln for President, and Andrew Johnson, then Military Governor of Tennessee, for Vice-President.

[a] 1864.

At about that time, the Democratic or Opposition party had postponed the assembling of a National Convention to nominate a candidate for the Presidency, which had been appointed for the 4th of July, until the 29th of August, when it was to assemble in the city of Chicago. Meanwhile, there was a notable gathering of emissaries and friends of the Conspirators at the "Clifton House," on the Canada side of Niagara Falls,[1] partly for the purpose of co-operating with the leaders of the Peace Faction, in shaping the future policy of the Opposition which was to be announced at that Convention. Also, for carrying out a scheme for exciting hostile feelings between the United States and Great Britain through operations in Canada;[2] for burning Northern Cities;[3] rescuing Confederate prisoners on and near the borders of Canada;[4] spreading contagious diseases in the National mili-

---

[1] The chief agents of the Conspirators in Canada, were George N. Sanders, (see page 340, volume I.), Jacob Thompson (see page 45, volume I.), Clement C. Clay (see page 229, volume I.), J. P. Holcombe, and Beverly Tucker.

[2] They proceeded to organize plundering raids into the border States. One of these, composed of nearly thirty well-armed Confederates, crossed the border into Vermont,[b] penetrated to the village of St. Albans, robbed the bank of $50,000, stole horses enough to mount the whole party, fired [b] Oct. 19. upon unarmed citizens, wounding three (one mortally), and setting fire to one of the hotels. Thirteen of them were arrested on their return to Canada, but were released by a sympathizing judge at Montreal. The British minister (Lord Lyons) did all in his power to bring the offenders to justice, but the Canadian authorities threw over them their sheltering arms.

[3] See note 2, page 367.

[4] Johnson's Island, in Lake Erie, not far from Sandusky, Ohio, was made a prison-camp, chiefly for Confederate officers. Several thousand captives were there in the summer of 1864. The agents and friends of the

tary camps;[1] and ultimately, as circumstantial evidence seems to show, for the assassination of the President and his Cabinet, and other leading men near the head of the Government. These agents were visited by members of the Peace Faction; and when the Opposition Convention met at Chicago, that city swarmed with the enemies of the Republic, who dared to openly express sympathy with the Confederates.

Meanwhile, the Confederate agents, at the suggestion, it is said, of a conspicuous leader of the Peace Faction, arranged a scheme for making the great majority of the loyal people, who were earnestly yearning for an end of war, dissatisfied with the Administration, by placing the President and his friends in an attitude of hostility to measures calculated to insure peace. If that could be done, the election of the Chicago nominee might be secured, and the way would be thus opened for the independence of the "Confederate States," and the permanent dissolution of the Union. To do this, a letter was addressed[a] to Horace Greeley, of New York, from the "Clifton House," Canada, by George N. Sanders, a politician of the baser sort,[2] and then high in the confidence of the Conspirators, who said that himself and C. C. Clay, of Alabama, and J. P. Holcombe, of Virginia, were authorized to go to Washington City, in the interest of peace, if full protection should be guarantied to them.

[a] July 5, 1864.

This letter was sent by Mr. Greeley to the President, together with a "Plan of Adjustment"[3] drawn up by the former, and he urged Mr. Lincoln to respond to it. The sagacious President was satisfied that not only was there no hope for any adjustment with the Conspirators on terms compatible with the dignity of the Government and the integrity of the Union, but that there was a covered trick in the matter. Yet he was unwilling to seem heedless of any proposition for peace, and he deputed Mr. Greeley to bring to him any person or persons " professing to have any proposition of Jefferson Davis, in writing, for peace, embracing the restoration of the Union and abandonment of slavery," with an assurance of safe conduct for him or them, each way. Considerable correspondence ensued. Mr. Greeley went to Niagara Falls. Then there was, on the part of Davis's agents, real or pretended misunderstanding. The matter became vexatious, and the President put an end to the unofficial negotiations by sending instructions to Mr. Greeley, explicitly prescribing what kind of a proposition he would receive

---

Conspirators, in Canada, attempted their release in September. When the passenger steamer *Philo Parsons* was on her way from Detroit to Sandusky,[b] she stopped at Malden, where twenty passengers went on board of her. At six o'clock that evening they declared themselves to be Confederate soldiers, and seized the boat. They then captured and destroyed another steamer, the *Island Queen*, and stood in for Sandusky, where they expected to be joined by secret and armed allies in capturing the National gun-boat *Michigan*, lying there, and with her effect the release of the prisoners. Their signals were not answered, and the expected re-enforcements were not seen, so they hastened to the Detroit River, and running the boat ashore near Sandwich, escaped.

[b] Sept. 19.

[1] A physician, named Blackburn, was employed in gathering up clothing taken from the victims of small-pox and yellow fever, and sending them to National camps. Some of these were sent to New Berne, North Carolina, and produced great mortality among the soldiers and citizens. Jacob Thompson (see page 367, volume I.), seems to have been more directly concerned in this part of the business of the Confederate agents, than any of the others.

[2] See page 340, volume I.

[3] This plan contemplated a restoration of the Union; the abolition of slavery; a complete amnesty for all political offenses, and a restoration of all the inhabitants in States wherein rebellion existed, to all privileges, as if rebellion had never occurred; the payment by the Government of $400,000,000 to the owners of the emancipated slaves; a change in representation of the slave-labor States; and a National Convention to ratify and settle in detail, such adjustment.

and consider.[1] This was precisely what the Conspirators and their emissaries wanted. They knew Mr. Lincoln would not consider any other proposition than an unconditional surrender, which they were firmly resolved never to accept voluntarily;[2] so they used his declaration to "fire the Southern heart," and to sow the seeds of discontent among the loyal people of the land.

But on this, as on other occasions, the purposes of the enemies of the Government were frustrated by their own machinations. The peace errand to Niagara Falls thereby evoked, and made in good faith by a patriotic citizen, in connection with another peace errand to Richmond, at the same time, brought before the excited public mind the clear enunciation by the President and the chief Conspirator, the terms, in sharp-cut language, on which peace might be made. No room was left for doubt as to duty, on the part of a lover of the Union and his country; and the question of loyalty and disloyalty to the Republic was fairly before the people in the ensuing canvass. It was clearly perceived that, if the life of the Nation was to be preserved, the Administration must be sustained, and the war prosecuted with vigor. These services were nobly performed by the people.

The Opposition, or Democratic National Convention, assembled at Chicago, on the 29th of August, and Horatio Seymour, of New York, was chosen its president. His address, on taking the chair, gave the key-note to the proceedings of the Convention. It was extremely hostile to the Government and condemnatory of the war for the Union,[3] and gave encouragement to the open and secret foes of the Republic. The latter were then crowding Chicago, and represented, in large numbers, according to a report of the Judge-Advocate of the United States, the membership of a conspiracy in the form of a military organization, west of the Alleghanies. It was composed, at the time of this Convention, of about half a million men, with a commander-in-chief, and general and subordinate officers, all bound to a blind obedience to the orders of their superiors, and pledged "to take up arms

---

[1] The instructions, dated the 18th of July, were as follows:—" *To whom it may concern :*—Any proposition which embraces the restoration of peace, the integrity of the whole Union, and the abandonment of slavery, and which comes by and with an authority that can control the armies now at war against the United States, will be received and considered by the Executive Government of the United States, and will be met by liberal terms on substantial and collateral points; and the bearer or bearers thereof shall have safe conduct both ways."

[2] At about the time of Mr. Greeley's unofficial mission to Niagara, two other citizens were on a secret peace mission, at Richmond, whither they went clandestinely, without the President's permission, but with his knowledge. The men engaged in the errand were Colonel J. F. Jaques, of the Seventy-third Illinois, and J. R. Gilmore, a civilian, of New York. They were allowed to pass through the Union lines, and at Richmond they obtained an interview, first with Benjamin, "Secretary of State," and then with Jefferson Davis. They held a free talk with the latter, who said, after declaring that he had tried to avert the war, "Now it must go on till the last man of this generation falls in his tracks, and his children seize his musket and fight our battle, unless you acknowledge our right to self-government. We are not fighting for slavery. *We are fighting for Independence; and that, or extermination, we will have !* "

[3] The bitterness of that hostility was everywhere conspicuous, and seemed to increase with the manifest gains of the National forces over those in rebellion. In no way was that hostility more offensively and inappropriately manifested than by the Mayor of the City of New York, C. Godfrey Gunther, who took the occasion of officially announcing the proclamation of the President, setting apart the 4th of August as a day of fasting, humiliation, and prayer to Almighty God, to make an unseemly attack on the great body of the clergy of that city. The following sentence, excepting a few lines setting forth that it had become his duty to "call attention " to the President's proclamation, was the whole of the mayor's communication on the subject:—" To the ministers of the various churches on whom will devolve the duty of offering prayer in the presence of their congregations, and especially those ministers who have inculcated the doctrine of war and blood, so much at variance with the teachings of their Divine Master, I would humbly recommend that they will, on that solemn occasion, invoke the mercy of Heaven to hasten the relief of our suffering people, by turning the hearts of those in authority to the blessed ways of peace."

against any government found waging war against a people endeavoring to establish a government of their own choice,"—in other words, to assist the insurgents then in arms against their country. The method, as we have observed,[1] was a general rising of the members of this organization in Missouri, Illinois, Indiana, Ohio, and Kentucky, in co-operation with a force under Price, who was to invade Missouri. As we have already observed,[2] Price performed his part with the open enemies of the Republic; but the cowardly secret enemies failed to meet their engagements. The plot, it is said, originated with the Conspirators at Richmond, and was chiefly directed by Jacob. Thompson, in Canada, assisted by the agents of the Confederacy there, with whom leaders of the Peace Faction were in continual council.[3]

The first blow—the signal for the uprising—was to be struck at Chicago, during the sittings of the Democratic Convention, when eight thousand Confederate prisoners, confined in Camp Douglas, near that city, were to be liberated and armed by the rebel refugees from Canada there assembled, and five thousand sympathizers with the Conspirators, and members of the treasonable league, resident in Chicago. Then the Confederate prisoners at Indianapolis were to be released and armed, and the hosts of the Knights of the Golden Circle were to gather at appointed rendezvous, to the number of full one hundred thousand men. This force, springing out of the earth, as it were, in.the rear of Grant and Sherman, would, it was believed, compel the raising of the siege of Richmond and Atlanta, and secure peace on the basis of the independence of the "Confederate States." Vallandigham, as we have observed, was to go boldly from exile in Canada to Chicago, to act as circumstances should require. When the Convention met, he was there.[4] The rebel refugees in Canada were there; and a vast concourse of sympathizers with the cause of the Conspirators, and members of the traitorous league, were there, and were harangued from balconies of hotels and other places in the most incendiary and revolutionary language.[5]

Fortunately for the country, there was a young officer in command at Camp Douglas, possessed of courage, rare sagacity, and a cool brain; and

---

[1] See pages 275, 276. [2] See page 277. [3] See page 445.

[4] It will be remembered that the kind President modified the severe sentence of Vallandigham, who was condemned for treasonable practices, with the provision that if he should return from exile without permission, he should suffer the penalty prescribed by the court. (See page 84.) He did so return, at the time we are considering, and was unmolested. The Government was charged with weakness in not arresting and punishing him. It deserved praise for patriotism. The Speaker of the House of Representatives (Schuyler Colfax), in a speech at Peru, Indiana, explained the matter. He said :—" When Mr. Vallandigham returned, it was very natural that the first place he went to, should be a democratic convention. He thought Mr. Lincoln would arrest him. Mr. Lincoln knew the fact that, at that time, there was a secret organization in the Northwest, the details of which he may not have been familiar with; but he knew the intention was to make Vallandigham's arrest a pretext for lighting the torch of civil war all over the Northwest. Anxious to preserve the peace at your own homes, Mr. Lincoln passed over the return of Vallandigham."

[5] Mr. Greeley, in his *American Conflict*, ii. 667, gives specimens of speeches by two clergymen, belonging to the Peace Faction, at outside meetings in Chicago. One of them, named Chauncey C. Burr, said that Mr. Lincoln " had stolen a good many thousand negroes; but for every negro he had thus stolen, he had stolen ten thousand spoons. It had been said that, if the South would lay down their arms, they would be received back into the Union. The South could not honorably lay down their arms, for she was fighting for her honor. Two millions of men had been sent down to the slaughter-pens of the South, and the army of Lincoln could not again be filled, either by enlistments nor conscription." The other clergyman alluded to, named Henry Clay Dean, exclaimed :—" Such a failure has never been known. Such destruction of human life had never been seen since the destruction of Sennacherib by the breath of the Almighty. And still the monster usurper wants more men for his slaughter-pens. . . . Ever since the usurper, traitor, and tyrant had occupied the Presidential chair, the republican party had shouted ' War to the knife, and the knife to the hilt!' Blood has flowed in torrents, and yet the thirst of the old monster was not quenched."

exercised sleepless vigilance.   Disabled in the field, he had been sent there
for lighter duty, as successor to General Orme,[a] and he was there
made the instrument, under God's good providence, in saving his   [a] May 2,
country from a calamity with which it was threatened by one of   1864.
the most hellish conspiracies recorded in the history of the race.   This
young officer became acquainted with the secret of the Conspirators, and
took measures accordingly.[1]   The managers of the League were informed of
this, and prudently postponed action to a more propitious season;[2] and
Price and his ten thousand armed followers in Missouri found no adequate
support, as we have observed.[3]   That young officer was Colonel B. J. Sweet,
whose right elbow had been crushed by a bullet, in the battle of Perryville,
in Kentucky.

In the Democratic Convention, a committee composed of one delegate
from each State represented, was appointed to prepare a " platform of principles." James Guthrie, of Kentucky, was chosen its chairman.   Vallandigham was the ruling spirit in the committee.   The platform was soon constructed, in the form of six resolutions, which the Convention adopted.   By
these, that body, representing the Opposition party, declared its " fidelity to
the Union under the Constitution;" that the war was a failure, and that
" humanity, liberty, and the public welfare " demanded its immediate cessation;[4] that the Government, through its military power, had interfered with
elections in four of the late slave-labor States, and was, consequently, guilty
of revolutionary action, which should be resisted; that the Government
had been guilty of unwarrantable usurpations, which were specified, and
had also been guilty of a shameful disregard of duty respecting the
exchange of prisoners, and the release of its suffering captives.   The resolutions closed with an assurance that the Democratic party extended their sympathy to the Union soldiers, and that, " in the event," they said, " of our
attaining power," those soldiers " shall receive all the care and protection,

---

[1] We have observed that the Democratic Convention was to have been held on the 4th of July. In June,
the commandant at Camp Douglas observed that a large number of letters, written by the prisoners (which
were not sealed until they passed inspection at head-quarters), were only brief notes, written on large paper.
Suspecting all was not right, he submitted these letters to the action of heat, when it was found that longer
epistles were on the paper, written in invisible or " sympathetic " ink, and in which the friends of the writers
were informed that the captives at Camp Douglas expected to keep the 4th of July in a peculiar way. The Convention, as we have seen, was postponed to the 29th of August. The vigilance of the commandant never relaxed,
and more than a fortnight before that Convention assembled, he informed his commanding general of the impending danger. He had positive knowledge of the preparations in Canada for striking the blow at Chicago, at the time
of the Convention. " We outnumbered you two to one," said a leader in the conspiracy to a writer in the *Atlantic
Monthly*,[a] " but our force was badly disciplined. Success in such circumstances was impossible,   [a] July, 1865.
and on the third day of the Convention we announced from head-quarters that an attack at that
time was impossible."

[2] It was arranged for the blow for the release of the prisoners at Camp Douglas, and the subsequent action
dependent thereon, to be given on the night of the Presidential election. At that time a large number of rebel
officers were in Chicago. Their plans were all matured, but when they were about to put them into execution,
Colonel Sweet interfered by the arrest of about one hundred of these men and Illinois traitors. With them
hundreds of fire-arms were seized. Again that young officer had saved his country from great calamity.

[3] See page 277.

[4] The following is a copy of the resolution :—*Resolved*, That this Convention does explicitly declare, as the
sense of the American people, that, after four years of failure to restore the Union by the experiment of war,
during which, under the pretense of a military necessity, of a war-power higher than the Constitution, the
Constitution itself has been disregarded in every part, and public liberty and private right alike trodden down,
and the material prosperity of the country essentially impaired. Justice, humanity, liberty, and the public
welfare demand that immediate efforts be made for a cessation of hostilities, with a view to an ultimate convention of all the States, or other peaceable means, to the end that, at the earliest practicable moment, peace
may be restored on the basis of the Federal Union of the States."

regard and kindness," that they deserved.   Then General George B. McClellan, who had been relieved of military command about twenty-one months
before,[a] was nominated for the office of President, and George
H. Pendleton, of Ohio, for Vice-President.   The latter, in Congress and out of it, had been, next to Vallandigham, one of
the most outspoken of the opponents of the war.   The Convention soon
afterward adjourned, but did not dissolve.[1]

[a] Nov. 5, 1862.

The Platform adopted by the Convention was read by the people with
amazement.   The thinking men of the Democratic party were amazed by
the perpetration of such a political blunder.   The loyal people were amazed
at the spectacle of a large body of influential citizens, professing " fidelity to
the Union under the Constitution," censuring, without stint, the defenders
of that Union and Constitution, and refraining from uttering a word of
reproof to those who were attempting to destroy them; also their evident
willingness to abandon further attempts to save their country from ruin.
The soldiers were amazed by this outspoken impeachment of their valor, by
a declaration that their efforts in the field were failures, and that those who
had refused to support them in those efforts, and had opposed their exercise
of the privileges of citizens in the use of the ballot, while in the field, should
have the effrontery to offer them " sympathy " and " protection."   The open
enemies of the country—the Conspirators and their friends—were amazed
and delighted by this ominous breaking of the dark clouds of war, through
which gleamed a bright ray of hope of speedy peace and independence.[2]

The proposition at Chicago for the Government to abandon further
efforts to suppress the Rebellion by force of arms, because the war, had
proved a failure, had scarcely flashed over the telegraph wires, when the
glorious announcements followed that Sherman had taken Atlanta; that
Farragut had seized the defenses and shut up the harbor of Mobile, and
thereby laid the city at the mercy of the Union armies; and that the President of the Republic had, by proclamation,[b] asked the people to
give common thanks in their respective places of public worship on
the ensuing Sabbath, and directed salutes of one hundred guns
to be fired at all military and naval arsenals of the land.[3]

[b] Sept. 31, 1864.

---

[1] Mr. Wickliffe, of Kentucky, after saying, that circumstances might make it necessary, between that time
and the inauguration of a new President, for " the Democracy of the country to meet in Convention again," offered a resolution that the Convention should not dissolve, but retain its organization, and be subject to a call by
the proper committee.   This resolution was adopted.

[2] "The action of the Chicago Convention," Alexander H. Stephens wrote, on the 22d of September, "so far
as its platform of principles goes, presents a ray of light, which, under Providence, may prove the dawn of the
day to this long and cheerless night—the first ray of light I have seen from the North since the war began.   This
cheers the heart, and toward it I could almost exclaim, ' Hail, holy light, offspring of heaven, first born of the
eternal co-eternal beam, may I express thee, unblamed, since God is light !' "   The general sentiment of leading
men in the Confederacy was that the election of the Chicago nominees would secure the independence of that
Confederacy, and it stimulated them to fight our soldiers more desperately, feeling that success on the part of the
Confederate armies would assist the election of McClellan.   " All of us perceive," said the Charleston Courier,
"the *intimate connection* existing between the armies of the Confederacy and the peace men in the United
States.   These constitute two immense forces, that are *working together* for the procurement of peace.   *The
party whose nomination and platform we are considering are altogether dependent for success on the
courage and resolution of our fighting men.* If their generalship, sagacity, valor, and vigilance are unable
to obtain victories, and to arrest the progress of the invading hordes, the existing administration will laugh
to scorn all the efforts of the opposition, and, in spite of the most powerful combinations, will continue to
hold the places they occupy.   OUR SUCCESS IN BATTLE INSURES THE SUCCESS OF McCLELLAN.   OUR FAILURE
WILL INEVITABLY LEAD TO HIS DEFEAT.   It is the victories that have crowned our arms since this year began,
that have given existence, strength, and harmony to that organization which has arrayed itself with firm, defiant
front against the despot and his minions."   [3] See page 444.

The opposing parties carried on the canvass with great vigor during the autumn. The real practical question at issue was expressed in the two words, *Union* or *Disunion*.[1] Although the Opposition did not distinctly avow a willingness to give up the Union, that was a fair inference from the utterance of the resolutions of the Convention. The earlier autumn State elections gave very little indication of what the Presidential vote would be. When the latter was given, Mr. Lincoln's re-election in the Electoral College by an unprecedented majority was secured. General McClellan received the vote of only the two late slave-labor States, Delaware and Kentucky, and the State of New Jersey. The offer of sympathy and protection to the soldiers in the field, by the Chicago Convention, had been answered by the votes of those soldiers in overwhelming numbers against the nominees of that Convention. They gave one hundred and twenty-one thousand votes for Mr. Lincoln, and thirty-five thousand and fifty for General McClellan, or three to one in favor of the former.[2] They did not regard the war they had so nobly waged, as a " failure," and they required no "sympathy" or " protection" from any political party.

The result of the Presidential election gave great joy to all the true friends of the Union, at home and abroad. That election was waited for with the greatest anxiety by millions of men. A thousand hopes and fears were excited. Vast interests hung upon the verdict; and for awhile in our country every thing connected with trade and manufactures seemed to be stupefied by suspense. Gold, the delicate barometer of commercial thought, fluttered amazingly, as the hour of decision drew nigh.[3] At length, the result was announced. Principle had triumphed over Expediency. The nation had decided by its calmly expressed voice, after years of distressing war, and with the burden upon its shoulders of a public debt amounting to two thousand million dollars, to fight on, and put down the Rebellion at any cost. A load was lifted from the great loyal heart of the Republic. Congratulations came over the sea like sweet perfumes; and out of the mouths of the dusky toilers on the plantations of the South, went up simple, fervid songs of praise to God for this seal of their deliverance, for the election had surely proclaimed "liberty throughout all the land to all the inhabitants thereof." By it the hopes of the Conspirators were blasted. They well knew the power that slumbered behind that vote, and which would now be awakened in majestic energy. They well knew that all was lost, and that further resistance would be vain and wicked; and had Jefferson Davis and Robert E.

---

1 The Secretary of State (W. H. Seward), in a speech at Washington City, on the 14th of September, said: "The Democracy at Chicago, after waiting six weeks to see whether this war for the Union is to succeed or fail, finally concluded that it would fail; and therefore went in for a nomination and platform to make it the sure thing by a cessation of hostilities and an abandonment of the contest. At Baltimore, on the contrary, we determined that there should be no such thing as failure; and therefore we went in to save the Union by battle to the last. Sherman and Farragut have knocked the bottom out of the Chicago nominations; and the elections in Vermont and Maine prove the Baltimore nominations stanch and sound. The issue is thus fairly made up —McClellan and Disunion, or Lincoln and Union."

2 Fourteen of the States allowed their soldiers to vote. Those of some of the States voted in camp. Those of New York sent their ballots home to friends to deposit in the ballot-box for them in a prescribed way.

3 The following notice of the fluctuations in the price of gold during the space of a few hours, in one day (November 1, 1864), was given in an evening newspaper of that date:—

"The fluctuations in gold, as bulletined at Gilpin's Merchants' Exchange to-day, have been as follows: 10 A. M., 230; 10.20, 233; 10.25, 240; 10.35, 236; 10.40, 235¼; 11.15, 237⅜; 11.35, 238; 12, 237¼; 12.15, P.M., 237¼; 12.40, 236¼; 12.50, 234⅝; 1.10, 235¼; 1.25, 236; 1.35, 238½; 1.45, 238; 1.55, 239¼; 2.10, 238½; 2.20, 239¼; 2.45, 240¼; 2.55, 240¼; 3.00, 241; 3.25, 239¾; 4, 239¼; 4.15, 241."

Lee been less selfish and cold, and more humane, they might, by the simple fiat of their will, have closed the war six months before the time of its ending, saved thousands of precious lives, and hastened the return of peace and prosperity upon the land upon which they and their fellows had brought the terrible ravages of civil war. Upon these two men, more than upon all others, will the judgment of history and the verdict of posterity leave the stain of the guilt of prosecuting a hopeless war.

When Congress assembled, on the 6th of December, a month after the election, the President, in his annual message, spoke of "the purpose of the people within the loyal States to maintain the integrity of the Union," as having never been more firm, as evinced by the late vote; and he alluded with gratification to "the extraordinary calmness and good order with which the millions of voters met and mingled at the polls." He also noticed the pleasant fact that "on the distinct issue of Union, or no Union, the politicians had shown their instinctive knowledge that there is no diversity among the people." From this fact he derived the most precious hopes for the National cause. He deprecated any further attempts at "negotiation with the insurgent leaders," for the positive terms of fixed disagreement had been given by both parties, in the preceding summer.[1] He said, "I retract nothing heretofore said as to slavery. I repeat the declaration made a year ago, that 'while I remain in my present position, I shall not attempt to retract or modify the Emancipation Proclamation, nor shall I return to slavery any person who is free by the terms of that Proclamation, or by any of the acts of Congress. If the people should, by whatever mode or means, make it an executive duty to re-enslave such persons, another, and not I, must be their instrument to perform it. In stating a single condition of peace, I mean simply to say that the war will cease on the part of the Government whenever it shall have ceased on the part of those who began it." These declarations found a cordial response in the hearts of the loyal millions.

In that message the President urged the House of Representatives to concur with the Senate in adopting a Thirteenth Amendment of the National Constitution, for prohibiting slavery in the Republic forever. The Senate had adopted it[a] at the preceding session by the strong vote of thirty-eight to six.[2] The President's recommendation was acted upon, and the subject was taken up for consideration in the House on the 6th of January, 1865. On the 31st of the same month, it was adopted by a vote of one hundred and nineteen against fifty-six.[3] Thus the nation,

[a] April 8, 1864.

---

[1] See page 447.

[2] The following was the vote: YEAS.—*Maine*—Fessenden, Morrill; *New Hampshire*, Clark, Hall; *Massachusetts*—Sumner, Wilson; *Rhode Island*—Anthony, Sprague; *Connecticut*—Dixon, Foster; *Vermont*—Collamer, Foot; *New York*, Harris, Morgan; *New Jersey*, Tenyck; *Pennsylvania*—Cowan; *Maryland*, Reverdy Johnson; *West Virginia*—Van Winkle, Willey; *Ohio*—Sherman, Wade; *Indiana*—Lane; *Illinois*—Trumbull; *Missouri*—Brown, Henderson; *Michigan*—Chandler, Howard; *Iowa*—Grimes, Harlan; *Wisconsin*—Doolittle, Howe; *Minnesota*—Ramsay, Wilkinson; *Kansas*—Lane, Pomeroy; *Oregon*—Harding, Nesmith; *California*—Conness.—38.

Only two of these affirmative votes were Democrats, namely, Johnson and Nesmith. The NAYS were all Democrats, namely: *Delaware*—Riddle, Saulsbury; *Kentucky*—Davis, Powell; *Indiana*—Hendricks; *California*—McDougall.—6. Six Democrats did not vote, namely, Buckalew of *Pennsylvania*; Wright of *New Jersey*; Hicks of *Maryland*; Bowden and Carlisle, of *West Virginia*; Richardson of *Illinois*.

This measure was first submitted to the Senate by Mr. Henderson, of Missouri, on the 11th of January, 1864, and, as we have observed, was adopted on the 8th of April following.

[3] The following was the vote: YEAS.—*Maine*—Blair, Perham, Pike, Rice; *New Hampshire*—Patterson, Rollins; *Massachusetts*—Alley, Ames, Baldwin, Boutwell, Dawes, Elliott, Gooch, Hooper, Rice, W. D. Wash-

for the first time in its life, speaking through its representatives, declared its practical recognition of the great truth of the Declaration of Independence, that " *all* men are created equal." This act was the full complement of the Proclamation of Emancipation.[1] The work thus begun was in this way, and at this time, completed. In the school of a fiery experience the people had been educated in the lessons of goodness, and taught the truth that " righteousness exalteth a nation." When the nation, acting upon this lesson, declared by the act we are considering, its determination to be *just*, the seal of God's approval was instantly seen in the manifestations of the National power. From the hour when that righteous Amendment was adopted, the National arms were everywhere victorious. The Rebellion, still so rampant and defiant at the opening of the fourth year of its career, rapidly declined, and within the space of four months it disappeared, and the authority of the National Government was supreme in every part of the Republic. At last, when " there was not a house where there was not one dead," as it were, and the American Pharoah let the bondmen go, the plagun of war ceased.

The adoption of that Amendment by the House of Representatives, produced the most lively sensation of satisfaction in that body and among the spectators. Senator Henry Wilson, one of the most earnest and able men of the country in labors for this consummation, has put on record a vivid picture of the scene. " Notice had been previously given," he says, " by Mr. Ashley, that the vote would be taken on that day. The nation, realizing the transcendant magnitude of the issue, awaited the result with the most profound anxiety. The galleries, and the avenues leading to them, were early thronged by a dense mass intensely anxious to witness the scene. Senators, Cabinet officers, Judges of the Supreme Court, and even strangers, crowding on to the floor of the House, watched its proceedings with absorbing interest. During the roll-call, the vote of Speaker Colfax, and the votes of Mr. English, Mr. Ganson and Mr. Baldwin, which assured success, were warmly applauded by the Republican side. And when the Speaker declared that the constitutional majority of two-thirds having voted in the affirmative, the Joint Resolu-

---

burn; *Rhode Island*—Dixon, Jenckes; *Connecticut*—Brandegee, Deming, English, Hubbard; *Vermont*—Baxter, Morrill, Woodbridge; *New York*—A. W. Clark, Freeman Clark, Davis, Frank, Ganson, Griswold, Herrick, Hotchkiss, Hulburd, Kellogg, Littlejohn, Marvin, Miller, Morris, Nelson, Odell, Pomeroy, Radford, Steele, Van Valkenburg; *New Jersey* –Starr; *Pennsylvania*—Bailey, Broomall, Coffroth, Hale, Kelly, McAllister, Moorhead, A. Myers, L. Myers, O'Neill, Scofield, Stevens, Thayer, Tracy, Williams; *Delaware*—Smithers; *Maryland*—Cresswell, Davis, Thomas, Webster; *West Virginia*—Blair, Brown, Whaley; *Kentucky*—Anderson, Kendall, Smith, Yeaman; *Ohio*—Ashley, Eckley, Garfield, Hutchins, Schenck, Spaulding; *Indiana*—Colfax, Derwent, Julian, Orth; *Illinois*—Arnold, Farnsworth, Ingersoll, Norton, E. B. Washburne; *Missouri*—Blow, Boyd, King, Knox, Loan, McClurg, Rollins; *Michigan*—Baldwin, Beaman, Driggs, Kellogg, Longyear, Upson; *Iowa*—Allison, Grinnell, Hubbard, Kasson, Price, Wilson; *Wisconsin*—Cobb, McIndoe, Sloan, Wheeler; *Minnesota*—Donnelly, Windom; *Kansas*—Wilder; *Oregon*—McBride; *Nevada*—Worthington; *California*—Cole, Higby, Shannon.—119.

Fifteen of the above were Democrats. The NAYS were all Democrats, as follows: *Maine*—Sweat; *New York*—Brooks, Chanler, Kalbfleisch, Keirnan, Pruyn, Townsend, Ward, Winfield, B. Wood, F. Wood; *New Jersey*—Perry, Steele; *Pennsylvania*—Ancona, Dawson, Denison, Johnson, Miller, Randall, Styles, Strause; *Maryland*—Harris; *Kentucky*—Clay, Grider, Harding, Malloy, Wadsworth; *Ohio*—Bliss, Cox, Finck, Johnson, Long, Morris, Noble, O'Neill, Pendleton, C. A. White, J. W. White; *Indiana*—Cravens, Edgerton, Harrington, Holman, Law; *Illinois*—J. C. Allen, W. T. Allen; Edw. Harris; *Wisconsin*—Brown, Eldridge; *Missouri*—Hall, Scott.—56. Eight Democrats did not vote, namely, Lazear, *Pennsylvania;* Marcy, *New Hampshire;* McDowell and Voorhees, *Indiana ;* Le Blond and McKinney, *Ohio ;* Middleton and Rogers, *New Jersey.*

[1] The following is a copy of the Thirteenth Amendment of the Constitution:—

"SECTION 1. Neither slavery nor involuntary servitude, except as a punishment for crime, whereof the party shall have been duly convicted, shall exist within the United States, or any place subject to their jurisdiction.

"SECTION 2. Congress shall have power to enforce this Article by appropriate legislation,"

tion was passed, the announcement was received by the House, and the spectators on the floor, with a wild outburst of enthusiastic applause. The Republican members instantly sprang to their feet, and applauded with cheers and clapping of hands. The spectators in the crowded galleries waved their hats, and made the chamber ring with enthusiastic plaudits. Hundreds of ladies, gracing the galleries with their presence, rose in their seats; and, by waving their handkerchiefs, and participating in the general demonstrations of enthusiasm, added to the intense excitement and interest of a scene that will long be remembered by those who were fortunate enough to witness it. For several minutes, the friends of this crowning act of Emancipation gave themselves up to congratulations, and demonstrations of public joy."[1]

When the excitement had subsided, Mr. Ingersoll, of Illinois, arose and said : "In honor of this immortal and sublime event, I move that the House adjourn." It was carried by a vote of one hundred and twenty-one against twenty-four. The Amendment was subsequently submitted to the action of the several State Legislatures; and on the 18th of December following,[a] the Secretary of State officially announced its ratification by the requisite three-fourths of the Legislatures of the States. It then became a part of the Constitution, and the supreme law of the land. Thenceforth, slavery was made impossible within the borders of the Republic.

a 1865.

We have just observed that the Rebellion was yet defiant at the close of 1864. Such was the attitude of the Conspirators who originated and controlled it. In his annual "Message" to the "Congress" at Richmond,[b] Davis took a general survey of the situation, and treated the matter with his usual foolish bravado. He spoke of the fall of Atlanta, but said the result would have been the same had Richmond fallen. "The Confederacy," he said, "would have remained as erect and defiant as ever." "The purpose of the Government," he said, "and the valor of the troops would have remained unchanged. The baffled foe would in vain have scanned the reports of your proceedings, at some new legislative seat, for any indication that progress had been made in his gigantic task of conquering a free people." Then he tried to assure the "Congress" with the old story, which nobody believed, that the Government would soon be exhausted of men and money. "Not the fall of Richmond," he said, "nor Wilmington, nor Charleston, nor Savannah, nor Mobile, nor all combined, can save the enemy from the constant and exhaustive drain of blood and treasure which must continue until he shall discover that no peace is attainable unless based on the recognition of our indefeasible rights."

b Nov. 7, 1864.

In the same message Davis made an appalling exhibit of the desperate condition of the Confederate finances—a public debt of nearly $1,200,000,000, without a real basis of credit, and a paper currency depreciated several hundred per cent. He also showed the hollowness of his boastings of the inherent strength of the Confederacy by fairly admitting the fact, by implication, that the capacity of the white population to furnish men for the army was exhausted, and that the slaves must be looked to for strength in the future. It had been proposed to arm them; but this was considered dangerous, for

---

[1] *History of the Anti-Slavery Measures of the Thirty-Seventh and Thirty-Eighth United States Congresses*, 1861-1365; by Henry Wilson, page 393.

they would be more likely to fight the Confederates than the Nationals. Davis was averse to a general arming of the negroes, but recommended the employment of forty thousand of them as pioneer and engineer laborers in the army, and not as soldiers, excepting in the last extremity. "But," he said, "should the alternative ever be presented of a subjugation, or of the employment of the slave as a soldier, there seems to be no reason to doubt what should then be our decision." But they never ventured upon the arming of the negroes. And it was a significant indication of Davis's consciousness of the weakness of the hold of the Confederates upon them, either legally as slaves, or morally as men, that he suggested the propriety of holding out to the negro, as an inducement for him to give faithful service, even as a laborer in the army, a promise of his emancipation at the end of the war.[1] It was tried in Richmond, and failed, for the negroes would not trust the Confederates.

Davis's proposition disturbed the slave-holders, and made all but Unionists uneasy, for it indicated an opinion on the part of the "Government" that the cause was reduced to the alternative of liberating the slaves, and relying upon them to secure the independence of the Confederacy, or of absolute subjugation. The people had also observed, for some time, with gloomy forebodings, the usurpation of power on the part of Davis, and a tendency to the absolutism which precedes positive despotism. At about the time we are considering, that feeling was intensified by a decision of George Davis, the Confederate "Attorney-General," in a certain case, that the "Cabinet Ministers" must "see that all laws be faithfully executed," even should they be clearly and expressly unconstitutional.[2] This decision struck down the Constitution, the supposed bulwark of the liberties of the people. There was wide-spread discontent; and when the news came that Mr. Lincoln was re-elected by an unprecedented majority, they lost hope and yearned for *peace*, rather than for an *independence* that proved to be less desirable than that which they had enjoyed under the Government they had rebelled against. But Jefferson Davis and Robert E. Lee would not permit it, and the desolating war went on.

---

[1] "This," says a *Rebel War Clerk's Diary* (ii. 326), "is supposed to be an idea of Mr. Benjamin, for foreign effect." It is added, "the press is mostly opposed to the President's project of employing 40,000 slaves in the army, under promise of emancipation."

[2] See *A Rebel War Clerk's Diary*, ii. 322. "It makes the President absolute," wrote the Diarist. "I fear this Government, in future times, will be denounced as a cabal of bandits and outlaws, making and executing the most despotic decrees. This decision will look bad in history, and will do no good at present." At page 334, the Diarist says: "Both Houses of Congress sit most of the time in secret session, no doubt concocting strong measures under the influence of the existing crisis. Good news, only, can throw open the doors, and restore the hilarity of the members. When not in session, they usually denounce the President; in session, they are wholly subservient to him."

The Diarist further recorded, as follows, under date of January 7, 1865:—"How insignificant a legislative body becomes when it is not independent. The Confederate States Congress will not live in history, for it never really existed at all, but has always been merely a body of subservient men, registering the decrees of the Executive. Even Mr. Miles, of South Carolina, before introducing a bill, sends it to this department for approval or rejection."—Volume II., page 379.

CHAPTER XVII.

SHERMAN'S MARCH THROUGH THE CAROLINAS.—THE CAPTURE OF FORT FISHER.

 AVING made the necessary orders for the disposition of his troops at Savannah, General Sherman directed his chief engineer (Captain Poe) to examine the works around the city and its vicinity, with a view to their future use. He directed portions of them, including Forts McAllister, Thunderbolt, and Pulaski, to be put in perfect order. The remainder were to be dismantled and destroyed, and their heavy armament sent to Hilton Head. Savannah was made a base of supplies. The formidable obstructions in the river were sufficiently removed to allow the passage of vessels, and the torpedoes which abounded were gathered up under the direction of Admiral Dahlgren. These arrangements were completed by the first of January, when General Sherman was ready for a march northward through the Carolinas.

Sherman appointed the 15th of January [a] as the day when he would commence his march. The Seventeenth Corps, of Howard's troops,

• 1865.

was sent by water, around by Hilton Head, to Pocotaligo, on **the Charleston** and Savannah railway, where it had made a lodgment by the day above named, and from that point seriously menaced Charleston. The left wing, under Slocum, accompanied by Kilpatrick's cavalry, was to have crossed the Savannah River on a pontoon bridge laid at the city; but incessant rains, which flooded the country, swelled the streams and overflowed the swamps on their margins, had caused the submergence of a causeway which Slocum had constructed opposite Savannah, and broken up his pontoon bridge. He was compelled to look higher up the river for a passage, and marched his troops to Sister's Ferry, or Purysburg. The delay caused by the flood prevented Slocum getting his entire wing of the army across the Savannah River until the first week in February.

In the mean time, General Grant had sent to Savannah Grover's division of the Nineteenth Corps, to garrison that city, and had drawn the Twenty-third Corps, under General Schofield, from General Thomas's command in Tennessee, and sent it to re-enforce Generals Terry and Palmer, operating on

[b] January 18.

the coast of North Carolina, to prepare the way for Sherman's advance. Sherman transferred [b] Savannah and its dependencies to General Foster, then commanding the Department of the South, with instructions to follow Sherman's inland movements by occupying, in succession, Charleston and other places. Hardee, with the troops with which he fled from Savannah, was then in Charleston, preparing to defend it to the best of his ability.

Sherman had advised General Grant that it was his intention "to undertake, at one stride," after leaving Savannah, "to make Goldsboro', and open communications with the sea, by the New Berne railroad," and for that purpose, he sent Colonel W. W. Wright, superintendent of military roads, to New Berne to prepare for extending the railway from that place to Goldsboro'. Meanwhile, during the delay caused by the floods, some feints were made from Pocotaligo of an advance on Charleston,

HARDEE'S HEAD-QUARTERS IN CHARLESTON.[1]

and thereby Hardee was kept from interfering with Sherman's preparations for his proposed "stride." Finally, when the waters had somewhat subsided, and every thing was in readiness for an advance, the posts at the Tullifinny and Coosawhatchie rivers were abandoned as useless, and the troops along the Charleston and Savannah railway were concentrated at Pocotaligo.

Sherman's whole army moved forward on the first of February, nearly in a due north course, toward Columbia, the capital of South Carolina. All the roads in that direction had, for weeks, been held by Wheeler's cavalry, who had employed a large force of negroes in felling trees and burning bridges in the expected pathway of Sherman's march. In the face of these obstacles, and with a well-organized pioneer force to remove them, the Nationals moved forward. Slocum, with Kilpatrick's cavalry comprising the left wing, pressed through the wet swamps from Sister's Ferry toward Barnwell, threatening Augusta; while the right wing, keeping westward of the Salkhatchie River, made for the crossings of that stream at River's and Beaufort bridges, for the purpose of pushing on to the Edisto River, and thus flanking Charleston. These movements, at the outset, so distracted the foe with doubt whether Augusta or Charleston was Sherman's chief objective, that his forces were divided and weakened in the service of watching.

This formidable invasion, produced wide-spread alarm. When Sherman was lying at Savannah, the speculative opinion that he would attempt it, was met by the assurance and general belief that the march of a great army, with all its trains, across the swampy regions of South Carolina in midwinter, was a physical impossibility. Yet the fact that the National forces had so often overthrown all such speculations by actual achievements, had taught leaders wisdom; and, to prepare for any emergency, Governor Magrath[2] had, by proclamation, summoned [a] to   [a] Dec. 29, 1864.

---

[1] Hardee's head-quarters were at the house of Mr. Wickenberg, on Ashley Street, opposite the front of the United States Arsenal. General Saxton also had his head-quarters there, after the Confederates evacuated Charleston.

[2] See page 49, volume I.

the field, as militia, every white man in the State between the ages of sixteen and sixty years, not already in the service. So urgent seemed the need, that he threatened conscription for all who should not volunteer. But very few of that militia force confronted the National troops anywhere in South Carolina.

The Confederates occupied the line of the Salkhatchie with infantry and artillery, at important points, while Wheeler's cavalry hovered around the advance of the National army; and when the Seventeenth Corps, with which Sherman was moving, approached River's Bridge, over that stream, and the Fifteenth moved on Beaufort Bridge, they found a force ready to dispute the passage of each. Those at River's Bridge were soon dispersed by the divisions of Generals Mower and G. A. Smith, of the Seventeenth Corps, who made a flank movement under extraordinary difficulties. They waded through a swamp three miles in width, with the water from one to four feet in depth, the generals wading at the head of the columns. The weather was bitter cold, and the water was almost icy in temperature. But the work was accomplished. The foe was quickly scattered in a disorderly retreat to Branchville, behind the Edisto, burning bridges behind them, and inflicting a loss on the Nationals of nearly one hundred men. The latter pressed rapidly on to the South Carolina railroad, at Midway, Bamberg, and Graham's stations, and destroyed the track for many miles. Kilpatrick, meanwhile, was skirmishing briskly, and sometimes heavily, with Wheeler, as the former moved, by Barnwell and Blackville, toward Aiken and threat-

ᵃ Feb., 1865.   ened Augusta; and by noon, on the 11th,ᵃ the Nationals had possession of the railway from Midway to Johnson's Station, thereby dividing the Confederate forces which remained at Branchville and Charleston on one side, and Aiken and Augusta on the other.

Sherman now moved his right wing rapidly northward, on Orangeburg. The Seventeenth Corps crossed the south fork of the Edisto at Binnaker's Bridge, and the Fifteenth Corps passed over it at Holman's Bridge. These converged at Poplar Spring, where the Seventeenth, moving swiftly on Orangeburg, dashed upon the Confederates intrenched in front of the bridge near there, and drove them across the stream. The latter tried to burn the bridge, but failed. They had a battery in position behind the bridge, covered by a parapet of cotton and earth, with extended wings. This Blair confronted, with General G. A. Smith's division posted close to the Edisto, while two others were moved to a point two miles below. There Force's division, supported by Mower's, crossed on a pontoon bridge. When Force approached the Confederates, they retreated, and Smith crossed over and occupied their works. The bridge was soon repaired, and, by four o'clock

ᵇ Feb. 12.   that afternoon,ᵇ the whole of the Seventeenth Corps was in Orangeburg, and had begun the work of destruction on the railway connecting that place with Columbia.

Without wasting time or labor on Branchville or Charleston, which Sherman knew the Confederates would no longer hold, he now turned all his columns straight on Columbia. The Seventeenth Corps pushed the foe across

ᶜ Feb. 14.   the Congaree,ᶜ forcing him to burn the bridges, and then followed the State road directly for the capital of South Carolina, while the Fifteenth crossed the South Edisto from Poplar Spring at Schilling's

Bridge, and reached the State road at Zeigler's. They found the Confederates in strong force at a bridge over the Congaree Creek, which was defended by a heavy battery on the north side, that swept it, and a weaker one at the head of the bridge, on the south side. This *tete-du-pont* was turned by the division of General C. R. Woods, by sending Stone's brigade through a cypress swamp on the left. The Confederates fled after trying in vain to burn the bridge. Over it the main column of the Fifteenth passed, and bivouacked that night near the great bridge that spans the Congaree, in front of Columbia, where the Confederates, in and around that city, shelled them. That bridge was burned the next morning[a] by the occu- ^{[a] Feb. 16, 1865} pants of Columbia, when the National vanguard approached it.

In the mean time the left wing of the army, under Slocum, had pushed steadily forward some distance to the westward of the right, but with the same destination, Columbia. For awhile Augusta trembled with fear as his host passed by; and the troops for its defense were kept on the alert day and night. But Slocum was very little troubled excepting by Wheeler's cavalry; and those troopers were kept too busy by Kilpatrick to be very mischievous. Through the swamps and across the streams he trudged on, by Barnwell, Windom and Lexington, for the Saluda (which, with the Broad River, forms the Congaree at Columbia), hearing now and then of the approach of troops from the westward. Beauregard and Bragg had, in turn and in conjunction, tried in vain to thwart Sherman's plans, and the Conspirators, in their despair, had turned to General Johnston as their only hope for the maintenance of their cause below the Roanoke. That able officer was now again in command in that region, and at the time we are considering, Cheatham was moving from Northern Mississippi with the remnant of Hood's army, with orders to get in front of Sherman, and, in co-operation with Hardee at Charleston, arrest his progress through South Carolina.

But Sherman's movements were too rapid to allow Cheatham to execute his order, and the National army was at Columbia before any of Hood's men appeared. Slocum had not been molested by them, and he arrived upon the banks of the Saluda, a few miles from Columbia, at almost the same hour when Howard reached it, after the burning of the bridge over the Congaree. The Nationals had tried to save that fine structure, but failed. They could see the inhabitants hastening about the streets,[1] and occasional squads of cavalry. Upon the latter a single gun of De Grass's battery fired. But this Sherman checked, and limited him to a few shots at the unfinished State House.[2]

---

[1] "Terrible, meanwhile, was the press, the shock, the rush, the hurry, the universal confusion—such as might naturally be looked for in the circumstances of a city from which thousands were preparing to fly without previous preparations for flight—burdened with pale and trembling women, their children, and portable chattels, trunks and jewels, family bibles, and the *lares familières*. The railroad depot for Charlotte was crowded with anxious waiters upon the train, with a wilderness of luggage—millions, perhaps, in value—much of which was finally lost. The citizens fared badly. The Governments of the State and of the Confederacy absorbed all the modes of conveyance."—*Sack and Destruction of the City of Columbia*, page 10.

[2] The author of the little pamphlet above quoted, speaks of this firing as if a regular bombardment of the city had occurred. He says the shells "fell thick and fast about the town;" and he complains that "no summons to surrender had been made; no warning of any kind was given." I have recorded in the text substantially what Sherman says on the subject, in his report. The author above quoted says: "The damage was comparatively slight. The new capitol was struck five times, but suffered little or no injury." That building was commenced sometime before the war, and was designed to be the finest structure of the kind in the Union, and the most costly. It is of light-colored granite, with the surface smooth from base to roof. Its order of architecture is pure Corinthian throughout. It was not more than half completed when the war broke out, and labor upon it ceased. The picture on the next page shows it as it will appear when finished.

Howard had marched up from the burning bridge to the Saluda, by Sherman's orders, with directions to cross that stream and the Broad River, and

march upon Columbia, from the north. Slocum was also ordered to cross both rivers, and to march directly upon Winnsboro', destroying the Greenville and Columbia railroad around the village of Alston, where it crosses the Broad River. Both orders were executed. Howard crossed the Saluda,[a] on a pontoon bridge, near Granby, and made a flying bridge that night over the Broad River, three miles above

^a Feb. 16, 1865.

NEW STATE HOUSE AT COLUMBIA.

Columbia. Over that the brigade of Colonel Stone (Twenty-fifth Iowa Infantry), of Woods's division of the Fifteenth (Logan's) Corps, passed, and under its cover a pontoon bridge was laid on the morning of the 17th. General Sherman was there, and at eleven o'clock information reached him that Mr. Goodwyn, mayor of the city, with a deputation of the common council, had come out in a carriage, and made a formal surrender of Columbia to Colonel Stone.

There seemed to have been no adequate military force for its protection. Wheeler's cavalry had done all in its power, in front of the National army, but the advance of the latter was irresistible. The shallow Beauregard was in command at Columbia. As usual, he had promised much, but did little. He made a slight show of resistance and withdrew, leaving Hampton's cavalry as a rear-guard for covering the flight of the Creole's army. Governor Magrath and suite, and a large train of officials had fled, and nothing could save the town from destruction but a peaceable surrender. This was done at the time when a small party of the Seventeenth Corps had crossed the Congaree in a skiff, and entered the city from the west, unopposed. Before noon, on the 17th of February, the National flag, so dishonored at the chief seaport of South Carolina four years before, was waving in triumph over the old and new Capitols of the State at the seat of Government.

In anticipation of the occupation of the city, Sherman had made written orders to General Howard, touching the conduct of the troops. They were to destroy absolutely all arsenals and public property not needed for the use of the army, as well as all railroads, depots and machinery, useful in war to an enemy, "but to spare all dwellings, colleges, schools, asylums, and harmless private property."[1] The commanding general was the first to cross the pontoon bridge, and, in company with General Howard, rode into the city. It was already in possession of General Stone, who had posted men about it

---

[1] General Sherman's Report, dated April 4, 1865,

for the protection of persons and property. The wind was then blowing a gale. Citizens and soldiers were upon the streets, and general good order prevailed. Sherman had ratified the promise of protection given by Stone. "It will become my duty," he observed, substantially, "to destroy some of the Government or public buildings, but I will reserve this performance to another day. It shall be done to-morrow, provided the day be calm."[1]

That promise was faithfully kept, and had Wade Hampton, the commander of the rear-guard of the Confederates, who lingered in the town until ten o'clock that morning, been as careful of the interests of the citizens. as the Union troops, all would have been well. But he ordered all the cotton in the city, public and private, to be taken into the streets and burned, to prevent its falling into the hands of the Nationals. When Sherman entered the town, the cotton was in the streets. The cords and bagging of the bales had been cut, and the white wool in tufts was flying about the city in the gale, like snow, lodging in the trees and on the sides and roofs of houses. Notwithstanding the high wind, some of the bales, especially a pile of them in the heart of the city, near the court-house, were already on fire when Sherman entered.[2] His troops, by great exertions, partially subdued the flames.[3] They broke out again, with greater intensity, that night; and the beautiful capital of South Carolina—the destined seat of Government of the prospective independent "Confederate States of America"—was laid in ruins in the course of a few hours. Among the public buildings then destroyed, was the old State House, delineated on page 46 of volume I. Hampton, the real author of the conflagration, afterward charged it upon Sherman—a charge which Beauregard, ever ready to "fire the Southern heart" with the relation of "Yankee atrocities," did not make at the time, and which Pollard, the Confederate historian of the war, did not make afterward, except by implication, when he wrote that Sherman, "After having completed, as far as possible, the destruction of Columbia, continued his march northward."[4]

---

[1] *Sack and Destruction of the City of Columbia*, page 13.

[2] The Fifteenth Corps passed through the city in the course of the day, and went out on the Camden road. The Seventeenth did not enter the town; and the left wing was not within two miles of it at any time.

[3] See General Sherman's Report, April 4, 1865.

[4] General Sherman, in his Report, dated April 4, 1865, says: "Before one single building had been fired by order, the smoldering fires, set by Hampton's order, were rekindled by the wind and communicated to the buildings around. At dark they began to spread, and got beyond the control of the brigade on duty within the city. The whole of Woods's division was brought in, but it was found impossible to check the flames, which, by midnight, had become unmanageable, and raged until about 4 A. M., when, the wind subsiding, they were got under control. I was up nearly all night, and saw Generals Howard, Logan and Woods, and others, laboring to save houses and protect families thus suddenly deprived of shelter, and of bedding and wearing apparel. I disclaim, on the part of my army, any agency in this fire, but, on the contrary, claim that we saved what of Columbia remains unconsumed. And, without hesitation, I charge General Wade Hampton with having burned his own city of Columbia, not with a malicious intent, or as a manifestation of a silly 'Roman stoicism,' but from folly and want of sense, in filling it with lint, cotton, and tinder. Our officers and men on duty worked well to extinguish the flames; but others not on duty, including the officers, who had long been imprisoned there, rescued by us, may have assisted in spreading the fire after it had once begun, and may have indulged in unconcealed joy to see the ruin of the capital of South Carolina."*

The conduct of the Confederate troops, and especially of Wade Hampton, the commander, after the mayor

---

* Major Nichols, in his *Story of the Great March*, under date of Feb. 17, 1865 (page 166), says: "Various causes are assigned to explain the origin of the fire. I am quite sure that it originated in sparks, flying from the hundreds of bales of cotton which the Rebels had placed along the middle of the main street, and fired as they left the city. Fire from a tightly compressed bale of cotton is unlike that of a more open material, which burns itself out. The fire lies smoldering in a bale of cotton after it appears to be extinguished, and in this instance, when our soldiers supposed they had extinguished the fire, it suddenly broke out again with the most disastrous effect. There were fires, however, which must have been started independent of the above-named cause. The source of these is ascribed to the desire for revenge from some 200 of our prisoners, who had escaped from the cars as they were being conveyed from this city to Charlotte, and, with the memories of long suffering in the miserable pens I visited yesterday, on the other side of the river, sought this means of retaliation."

The fall of Columbia was the signal for Hardee to evacuate Charleston, for it was then flanked, and he was threatened with isolation. He was in command of about fourteen thousand troops. It was supposed, until the last moment, that Sherman's march on Columbia, was only a feint, and that Charleston was his chief objective. With this impression, Hardee had concentrated the troops under his command in and around that city. To cherish that belief, General Gillmore, then in command on the coast in that vicinity, had caused feints to be made in the direction of Charleston. One of these was composed of a considerable body of troops, under General Schimmel-fennig, who, on the 10th of February,[a] made a lodgment on James's Island, within three miles of Charleston. At the same time, gun-boats and a mortar schooner moved up the Stono River, and flanked the troops. An attack was made upon the Confederate works on the island, and their rifle-pits were carried, with a loss to the Nationals of about eighty men. Co-operative movements were made at the same time, by General Hatch, who led a column across the Combahee toward the South Edisto River, while General Potter, with another column from Bull's Bay, northward of Charleston, menaced the Northwestern railway.

[a] 1865.

These movements, with Columbia at the mercy of Sherman, warned Hardee that he must instantly leave Charleston by the only railway now left open for his use, and endeavor to join Beauregard and Cheatham, who were then, with the remnant of Hood's army, making their way into North Carolina, where Johnston intended to concentrate all his available forces, in Sherman's path. Having determined upon a speedy evacuation, Hardee employed a short time in destroying as much property in Charleston, that might be useful to the Nationals, as possible. At an early hour,[b] every building, warehouse, or shed, stored with cotton, was fired by a guard detailed for the purpose. The few inhabitants were filled with consternation, as they saw the hands of their professed friends, applying the torch to the already sorely smitten city. The fire engines were brought out to endeavor to save buildings adjoining the cotton stores, but in vain; and on the western side of the city, the flames raged furiously. The horrors of the scene were heightened by a catastrophe which destroyed many lives. Some boys had discovered powder at the depot of the Northwestern railway, and amused themselves by throwing some of it on burning cotton in the street. The powder dropping from their hands, soon formed a train, along which fire ran to the large quantity stored at the depot.

[b] Feb. 17,

---

and some of the council had gone out to surrender the city, had exasperated the National soldiers, and according to the laws and usages of war, subjected the city to lawful destruction. According to the author of *The Sack and Destruction of the City of Columbia*, the mayor and councilmen went out at *nine o'clock*, when "it was proposed," he says, "that the white flag should be displayed from the tower of the City Hall. But General Hampton, whose command had not yet left the city, and who was still eager to do battle in its defense, indignantly declared that, if displayed, he should have it torn down." The author adds: "Hampton's cavalry, as we have already mentioned, lingered till *near ten o'clock*, and scattered groups of Wheeler's command hovered about the Federal army at their entrance into the town." It appears by the testimony of this eager witness against the Nationals, who professes to have been an eye-witness of the destruction of Columbia, that the *Confederate soldiery, under the direction of Wade Hampton, continued to fight the Nationals in the streets of the city after it had been surrendered by competent authority.* That writer gives a terrible picture of the robberies committed by the Union soldiers not on duty. They seem to have followed the example of the Confederates themselves. He tells us of a building, in which valuable property of almost every kind had been stored, that was "broken open by a band of plunderers," early in the morning, before the arrival of the National troops, and says, "Wheeler's cavalry also shared largely in the plunder, and several of them might be seen bearing off huge bales upon their saddles."—Page 12.

A terrible explosion followed, by which the city was shaken to its foundations. The building was converted, in an instant, into an immense volume of fire, smoke, and fragments, shooting high in air. Full two hundred persons were destroyed. At least one hundred and fifty dead bodies were

RUINS OF CHARLESTON.[1]

taken from the ruins of the depot, from which point the fire spread rapidly through the adjoining buildings; and, before the flames were subdued, four squares, embracing an area bounded by Chapel, Alexander, and Washington Streets, were consumed.

That night, the last of Hardee's troops left ruined Charleston. They had made the destruction of property as complete as possible. Cotton warehouses, arsenals, quartermaster's stores, railroad bridges, two iron-clad steamers, and some vessels in the ship-yard, were destroyed. Many of the cannon about the city were temporarily disabled; and a 600-pounder Blakely gun, stationed at a huge mound which had been thrown up at

BREECH OF THE BLAKELY GUN.

the angle of East Bay and South Battery, for the purposes of a magazine and battery, was exploded that it might not fall into the hands of the Nationals. The shock of that explosion nearly ruined a fine mansion opposite. The remains of the great gun were at Adger's wharf when the writer sketched them,

---

[1] This was the appearance of a portion of the burnt district of Charleston, mentioned in the text, as it appeared when the writer visited that city, in April, 1866. The ruins of the Roman Catholic Cathedral are seen, in the distance, toward the left of the picture.

at the close of March, 1866. The dimensions of the breech (four feet three
inches in diameter) are indicated by the figure of a man, standing by the side
of it. The projectile of this monster rifled cannon, weighing six hundred

GRAINS OF POWDER.

pounds, is also here delineated, together with three grains of
the powder employed in projecting the bolt, drawn the exact
size of the original.

BLAKELY BOLT.

The evacuation of Charleston was not known to the Nationals until the
next morning, when Lieutenant-Colonel A. G. Bennett, commanding on
Morris Island, having hints to that effect, dispatched a boat toward Fort
Moultrie for information. When near Fort Sumter, it was met by another,
containing some musicians, which Hardee had left behind. They attested
the truth of the rumor. Major J. A. Hennessy was immediately sent to Fort
Sumter to raise the National flag over the ruins of that notable fortress,
where it had been so dishonored nearly four years before. It was done at
nine o'clock in the morning.[a] Flags were also raised over Forts
Ripley and Pinckney; and at 10 o'clock, Lieutenant-Colonel
Bennett arrived at Charleston. He found some of the Confederates still lingering, and engaged in incendiary work, while a portion of the
city was a glowing furnace of flame.

[a] Feb 18, 1865.

Mayor Macbeth gladly surrendered the city, that the remainder of it
might be saved. The act was promptly done, when a small force was hurried up from Morris Island, and set to work, with the negroes of the city,
who were impressed for the purpose, in extinguishing the flames. By their
exertions the arsenal was saved, and a large quantity of rice, which was distributed among the poor. On that day, the city of Charleston, and all its
defenses and dependencies, were "repossessed" by the Government, with
over four hundred and fifty pieces of artillery, mostly in fair condition, and
consisting chiefly of 8 and 10-inch columbiads; a large amount of powder,
and eight locomotives and other rolling stock of railways. Georgetown, on
Winyaw Bay, was evacuated on the same day; and when Gillmore took
possession of Charleston, Hardee was making his way, with his troops, as
speedily as possible, across the Santee and Pedee rivers, to avoid a crushing blow from Sherman, who pushed on rapidly from Columbia, in a northeasterly course, into North Carolina, with Goldsboro' as his destination.

The gallant Colonel Stewart L. Woodford, of the One Hundred and
Twenty-seventh New York (afterward Lieutenant-Governor of the State of
New York), was appointed military governor of Charleston, and by kind,

THE UNION GENERALS.

GEORGE W. CHILDS, PUBLISHER, 628 & 630 CHESTNUT ST. PHILADELPHIA.
118 Goffin St. Philad.

firm, and judicious management, he soon established friendly relations between the citizens and soldiers. His orders were marked by conciliation, justice, firmness, and forbearance, and commanded universal respect;[1] and, at the end of a month after the evacuation of the city by the Confederate troops, when Woodford resigned his command into the hands of Colonel Gurney, that which, it was supposed, would remain the most rebellious of all cities, was really the most docile and orderly. The inhabitants "accepted the situation," and society, in a large degree, resumed its normal condition.[2]

A few weeks after the fall of Charleston, and on the anniversary of the evacuation of Fort Sumter, four years before,[a] the identical flag which was then taken down, folded up and borne away by Major Anderson, the brave defender of the post,[3] was, by the same hand, again flung to the breeze over that fortress, which had been reduced

[a] April 14, 1861.

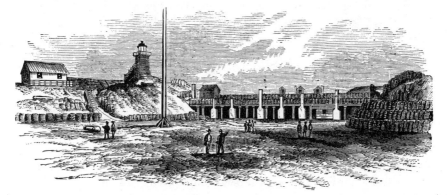

INTERIOR OF FORT SUMTER.[4]

to an almost shapeless mass of rubbish. Major Anderson had borne away the tattered flag, with a resolution to raise it again over the fortress, or be wrapped in it as his winding sheet, at the last. He was permitted to raise it there again, before the war had ended, and then to bear it away a second time, for the next office to which he had dedicated it.[5]

---

[1] There was a general expectation in Charleston, that a spirit of vengeance would be manifested by the conquerors, and they were astonished to find that about the only kind of "tyranny" to which they were to be subjected, was foreshadowed in the following paragraph in Colonel Woodford's first order:—

"The people are invited to open their schools and churches, and resume, as far as possible, the avocations of peace. They are required to behave in an orderly manner. *No disloyal act or utterance will be tolerated.* The National flag must be honored and the National laws obeyed."

James Redpath was appointed Superintendent of Education, for the post.

[2] The following extract, from Woodford's General Order No. 19, will indicate what had been accomplished in Charleston, in the space of a single month:—"The churches and stores have been generally opened. Three thousand children attend public school. Four thousand citizens have voluntarily taken the oath of allegiance, and the six offices established for that purpose, have been constantly thronged."

[3] See page 331, volume I.

[4] This was the general appearance of the interior of Fort Sumter, when the writer sketched it, at the beginning of April, 1866.

[5] When intelligence reached Washington of the evacuation of Charleston, the President of the United States appointed the anniversary of the fall of Fort Sumter,[b] as the day when the old flag should be raised again over that fortress, by Major (now General) Anderson. Preparations were made accordingly. A large number of citizens went from the harbor of New York in the steamer *Oceanus*, to assist in the ceremonies. Colonel Stewart L. Woodford had charge of the exercises of the day, at the fort. When the multitude were assembled around the flag-staff, William B. Bradbury led them in singing his song of *Victory at Last*, followed by *Rally Round the Flag*. The Rev. Mathew Harris, Chaplain of the United States Army, who made the prayer at the raising of the flag over Sumter on December 27, 1860 (see page

[b] April 14.

Before following General Sherman in the remainder of his march north-ward, let us consider events on the sea-board, in 1864, and the beginning of 1865, which had direct and indirect connection with his campaign.

First, let us turn back to the early part of 1864. We have seen how Fort Sumter and the city of Charleston seemed to be at the mercy of Gen-eral Gillmore, at the close of 1863, and yet how the award of their capture was withheld by the unwillingness of Admiral Dahlgren to expose his fleet to destruction, by running into the harbor among torpedoes.[1] Seeing no prospect of active operations against Charleston, for some time, Gillmore determined to send a part of his force on an expedition into Florida. He had been informed, by refugees, that Union sentiments predominated there, and that the people, generally, tired of the war, were ready for amnesty and restoration to the Union. This alleged fact was communicated to the Presi-dent, who commissioned John Hay, one of his private secreta-ries, as major, and sent him[a] to Hilton Head, to join the proposed expedition, as the representative of the Executive, to act in a civil capacity should circumstances require.

[a] Jan. 13, 1864.

Gillmore placed[b] the expedition under the command of Gen-eral Truman Seymour. It was embarked[c] at Hilton Head, on twenty steamers and eight schooners, and went down the coast under convoy of the gun-boat *Norwich*. It entered the St. John's River the next day, and arrived at Jacksonville at 5 o'clock that afternoon.[d] The troops were landed without other resistance than a few shots from a Confederate force there, which turned and fled before a company of colored troops sent in pursuit of them. Jack-sonville was in ruins, and only a few families, composed mostly of women and children, remained.

[b] Feb. 5.
[c] Feb. 6.
[d] Feb. 7.

Seymour, pursuant to instructions, immediately marched[e] from Jackson-ville to Baldwin, in the interior, at the junction of the railway leading from the former place with one from Fernandina. The army moved in three columns, under the respective commands of Colonels C. C. Barton of the Forty-eighth New York, J. R. Hawley of the Seventh Connecticut, and Guy V. Henry of the Fortieth Massachusetts. The latter led the cavalry, and was in the advance. It was known that General Joseph Finnegan[2] was in command of the Confederates in that region, but their num-ber and strength were not exactly computed; so the army moved cautiously. It was soon ascertained that Finnegan was encamped a dozen miles from Jacksonville, and it was determined to surprise him. That duty was assigned to Henry, who moved on with his horsemen, a horse battery, and the Fortieth

[e] Feb. 8.

130, volume I.), now offered an introductory prayer, and pronounced a blessing on the old flag. Dr. R. S. Storrs, of Brooklyn, read selections from the Psalms. Then General Townsend, Assistant Adjutant-General of the United States, read Major Anderson's dispatch of April 18, 1861, announcing the fall of Sumter. This was followed by the appearance of the faithful Sergeant Hart (see page 133, volume I.), with a new mail-bag, containing the precious old flag. It was attached to the halliards, when General Anderson, after a brief and touching address, hoisted it to the peak of the flag-staff, amid loud huzzas, which were followed by singing *The Star-Spangled Banner*. Then six guns on the fort opened their loud voices, and were responded to by the guns from all the batteries around, which took part in the bombardment of the fort in 1861. When all became silent, the Rev. Henry Ward Beecher, the chosen orator for the occasion, pronounced an eloquent address. A benediction closed the ceremonies; and thus it was that Fort Sumter was formally "repossessed" by the Government.

[1] See page 194.

[2] Joseph Finnegan was a resident of Jackson, and was President of the Florida Secession Convention, in 1861.—See notice of Yulee's letter to him, on page 166, volume I.

Massachusetts, while the infantry bivouacked.   He passed along a road, through a dark pine forest, in the direction of Baldwin, and soon encountered pickets.   He evaded a cavalry force, and at midnight dashed unexpectedly into "Camp Finnegan," guarded by only one hundred and fifty men.   He captured four cannon and a large amount of commissary stores, and at four o'clock in the morning[a] pushed on toward Baldwin.   [a] Feb. 9. 1864.
He reached that hamlet at seven, and there captured another gun, three cars, much cotton, rice and provisions, and munitions of war, valued at half a million dollars.   That evening General Gillmore, who had followed the expedition, accompanied by Seymour, arrived at Baldwin.

Henry had pushed on beyond Baldwin, and at the south fork of the St. Mary's River, five miles from the railway junction, he had a sharp skirmish, and drove the Confederates, but with a loss to himself of seventeen men. He reached Sanderson, forty miles from Jacksonville, at six o'clock in the evening, where he captured and destroyed much property; and, pushing on, he was almost to Alligator or Lake City, nearly half way to Tallahassee, from the coast, at two o'clock in the morning.   Then he rested until the middle of the forenoon,[b] when he found Finnegan so strongly   [b] Feb. 10.
posted across his path, that he thought it prudent to fall back about five miles.   There he halted in a drenching rain, and telegraphed to Seymour, then at Sanderson, for food and orders.   He was afterward informed that Finnegan, with three thousand men, fell back to Lake City and beyond, that night.

Gillmore did not tarry at Baldwin, but returned to Hilton Head, where he arrived on the 15th,[c] with the understanding that Seymour   [c] February
was not to attempt a further penetration of Florida.   And such was the latter's intention when Gillmore left; and on the 12th he telegraphed to his superior that he had ordered Henry to fall back to Sanderson.   To this Gillmore replied, "I want your command at and beyond Baldwin concentrated at Baldwin without delay."   Seymour demurred, alleging that to leave the south fork of the St. Mary's would make it impossible for him to advance again.

Deceived by the assertion that Finnegan had fallen back from Lake City, and acting upon his strong impulse to accomplish the work for which he had been sent, Seymour took the responsibility of advancing, and put his troops in motion toward the Suwanee River.   At the same time he telegraphed[d] the fact to Gillmore, and asked him to have an iron-clad vessel   [d] Feb. 17.
make a demonstration against Savannah, to prevent the Confederates in Georgia from re-enforcing Finnegan.   Gillmore was astonished; and he was not a little alarmed, because of the seeming danger to which Seymour would expose his six thousand troops to attack from an overwhelming force that might be quickly concentrated upon him, by railway, from Georgia and Alabama.   He sent a letter of remonstrance, but it was too late, for Seymour, on the day of its arrival,[e] had advanced, and fallen into most   [e] Feb. 20.
serious trouble near Olustee Station.

Seymour had pressed forward, that morning, from Barber's Station, at the south fork of the St. Mary's, with his whole force, moving along the dirt road that ran generally parallel with the railway.   He marched in three columns, Hawley's brigade forming the left, Colonel Barton's the center, and Colonel Scamman's regiment the extreme right.   Colonel Montgomery's

negro brigade was in the rear. The army numbered about five thousand
men, and had eight days' rations. Nothing of interest occurred until about
two o'clock in the afternoon, when the head of the column, after a weary
march of sixteen miles, reached a point on the railway, two or three miles
east of Olustee Station, where that road passed through a broad cypress
swamp, and the dirt road, turning at a right-angle, made a circuit to avoid
it. There Finnegan had disposed his men in ambush, under cover of the
swamp and a heavy pine forest, one flank resting on the latter, and the other
on Ocean Pond. Into this net Seymour's wearied van marched at the hour
above named, and were at close quarters with the enemy before they had
any suspicions of his presence.

That critical situation demanded prompt and skillful action. Colonel
Henry's cavalry, with Stevens's battalion and Hawley's Seventh Connecticut,
were in the advance, and drew the first fire. It was an eccentric one, and
very destructive. Finding his men falling rapidly, Hawley ordered up the
Seventh New Hampshire, Colonel Abbott, to its support, and the batteries
of Hamilton, Elder, and Langdon moved into action. The Nationals had
sixteen guns; the Confederates had only four left. Unfortunately, the former were placed so close up to the concealed foe, that the sharp-shooters of
the latter easily shot the artillerists and artillery horses. Hamilton's battery
went into the fight within one hundred and fifty yards of the Confederate
front, and, in the space of twenty minutes, forty of its fifty horses were
slain, and forty-five of its eighty-two men were disabled. Then the remainder fell back, leaving two of their four guns behind them.

The fight raged furiously, and Seymour was seen everywhere, at points
of greatest peril, directing it on the part of the Nationals. The Seventh
New Hampshire was soon losing so heavily, that Hawley ordered up the
Eighth United States negro regiment, Colonel Fribley, to its support. That
regiment had never been under fire. Its fortitude was remarkable. For
nearly two hours it held its position in front, and lost three hundred and
fifty men, with its commander mortally wounded. Then Colonel Barton led
his brigade (Forty-eighth, Forty-ninth, and One Hundred and Fifteenth
New York) into the hottest of the fight. It suffered dreadfully, but fought
on gallantly. Finally, Colonel Montgomery went into the battle with his
negro brigade (Fifty-fourth Massachusetts and First North Carolina), just
in time to check a Confederate charge. But they were soon overpowered
and driven back, the North Carolina regiment leaving its colonel, lieutenant-
colonel, major, and adjutant, dead on the field. This interference with the
Confederate charge, saved the Nationals from total rout, for Seymour took
advantage of it, to readjust his forces. Then, giving his foe four volleys of
grape-shot from his batteries, he ordered a retreat at about four o'clock. It
was performed in good order, covered by the Seventh Connecticut. There
was no effective pursuit. Seymour carried away about a thousand of his
wounded, and left about two hundred and fifty on the field, besides many
dead and dying. The estimated loss to the Nationals, in this expedition,
was about two thousand men, and provisions and stores burnt, to prevent
them falling into the hands of the Confederates, valued at one million dollars at least. The Confederate loss was about one thousand men, and several
guns. The National troops retreated to Jacksonville, and then returned to

Hilton Head, with the impression that active loyalty in Florida was a myth. Nothing of importance, bearing upon the great conflict, occurred in that State from THE BATTLE OF OLUSTEE, until the end of the war.[1]

Very little occurred in South Carolina during the year 1864 that affected the final result of the struggle. All through the year, there was occasional shelling of Charleston, at long range, from Morris Island, with very little effect. In May and June, as we have observed, Gillmore was on the James River, and all was quiet around Charleston. At the beginning of July, the four brigades of Birney, Saxton, Hatch, and Schimmelfennig, were concentrated on John's Island, and, with a gun-boat on the North Edisto, made some demonstrations against Confederate works there, but with no advantageous result. The Twenty-sixth United States negro troops, Colonel Silliman, were sent to take a Confederate battery, three miles northwest of Legaréville. They had no cannon, and were only six hundred strong. They made five desperate charges, and lost ninety-seven men killed and wounded. They were driven off, with the loss of their commander, prostrated by sun-stroke. This was called the BATTLE OF BLOODY BRIDGE. The object of the expedition does not clearly appear. After that, all was quiet until Foster moved, in anticipation of the approach of Sherman to the borders of the sea.[2]

In North Carolina there were some stirring and important events in 1864, particularly at the close of the year. After the twelve thousand veteran troops were taken from Foster and sent to the Department of the South,[3] the National force in that State was light; and, in February, General Pickett, commanding the Confederate troops in that section, made an effort to capture New Berne. On the 17th,[a] he attacked an outpost at Bachelor's Creek, eight miles above New Berne, held by the One [a] Feb., 1864. Hundred and Thirty-second New York. It was captured, with one hundred men, when Pickett advanced on New Berne. Then, a part of his force, under Colonel Wood, went in small boats and boarded the gun-boat *Underwriter*, lying near the wharf, and not more than one hundred yards from three batteries. Before the captors could get up her steam and move off, these batteries opened upon her, when the Confederates, seeing no chance to secure her, set her on fire and abandoned her. Pickett soon afterward withdrew, without attacking the defenses of New Berne, and claimed a victory, inasmuch, he said, as he had killed and wounded one hundred of the Nationals, made two hundred and eighty of them prisoners, captured two guns and three hundred small-arms, and destroyed a fine gun-boat of eight hundred horse-power, mounting four heavy guns. His own loss, he said, was only thirty-five killed and wounded.

A little later in the year, Plymouth, near the mouth of the Roanoke River, in North Carolina, was attacked by about seven thousand Confed-

---

[1] During the winter, extensive salt works belonging to the Confederates, on West Bay and Lake Ocola, valued at $3,000,000, were destroyed by orders of Admiral Bailey. In May, there was a gathering at Jackson, called the "State Convention of Unionists of Florida," and these appointed six delegates to the Republican Convention in Baltimore; but the affair amounted to nothing effective. At midsummer, General Birney moved out from Jacksonville, by order of General Foster, to Callahan Station, on the Fernandina railway,[b] burning bridges and other property. Other raids occurred, here and there, in the direc-   [b] July 20. tion of the St. Mary's; and, for a time, Baldwin, and two or three other places, were held by National troops. There were skirmishes without decisive results; and, at the end of the year, neither party had gained or lost much.

[2] See note 1, page 412.   [3] See page 192.

erates under General R. F. Hoke. These consisted of three infantry brigades, a regiment of cavalry, and seven batteries. The post was fairly fortified, and was held by General H. W. Wessells, with the Eighty-fifth New

PLYMOUTH IN 1864.

York, One Hundred and First, and One Hundred and Third Pennsylvania,
Sixteenth Connecticut, and six companies from other regiments; numbering,
in all, about twenty-four hundred men. In the river, in front of the town,
were the gun-boats *Southfield, Miami,* and *Bombshell.* A short distance
up the river was an out-post called Fort Warren.

Hoke approached Plymouth so secretly, that he was within two miles of
Fort Warren before Wessells was apprised of his proximity. That out-post
was first assailed,[a] and in the attack, the Confederates were assisted by the ram *Albemarle,* Captain Cooke, a formidable armored
vessel, which came down from the Roanoke River. The gun-
boat *Bombshell* went to the assistance of the post, but was soon disabled
and captured. The garrison continued the struggle vigorously, and, in the
mean time, Hoke opened fire on Fort Wessells, a mile nearer the town. His
troops, in heavy force, made charge after charge, but were continually hurled
back with severe loss. The superior numbers of the Confederates gave them
great advantages, and they soon invested the fort so closely with swarming
infantry, that it was compelled to surrender.

* April 17, 1864.

Plymouth was now closely besieged. Hoke pressed it heavily for a day
or two, when the *Albemarle* ran by Fort Warren, and fell upon the unarmored
gun-boats, *Southfield* (Lieutenant French) and *Miami* (Lieutenant-commanding Flusser), with great fury. Each carried eight guns, but they could
do little against the formidable ram in such close quarters. It first struck
and sunk the *Southfield,* and then turning upon the *Miami,* drove her down
the river, after killing her commander and disabling many of her crew.
Then the *Albemarle* turned her 32-pounder rifled guns upon the town, and
shelled it with serious effect.

On the following day[b] Hoke pushed his batteries to within an average
distance of eleven hundred yards of the town, and with these
he made a general assault. General Ransom led a brigade to
the attack on the right, and Hoke conducted, in person, two brigades in
the assault on the left. The defense was obstinate. The assault was equally

* April 20.

so. The Confederates, with the greatest bravery, pressed up in the face of a murderous fire, and, by desperate work, carried the two outer redoubts, which mounted eight guns, and made prisoners of their garrisons. Then the victors dashed forward to the town, and soon carried it. Meanwhile, Fort Williams was making terrible lanes in the ranks of the assailants with grape and canister shot. It, too, was soon so closely enveloped and enfiladed, that it was compelled to surrender. Thus ended THE BATTLE OF PLYMOUTH, when the post, about sixteen hundred effective men, twenty-five cannon, two thousand small-arms, and valuable stores passed into the possession of the Confederates. The Union loss in the siege was about one hundred men. The Confederate loss was about six hundred. The fall of Plymouth was a signal for the evacuation of Little Washington, at the head of Pamlico Sound, then held by General Palmer, for it was untenable. This [a] was done on the 28th,[a] when some of the lawless soldiery dishonored themselves and their flag by plundering and burning some buildings.

[a] Feb., 1864.

From Plymouth, Hoke went to New Berne and demanded its surrender; and, on being refused, he began its siege. The Captain of the *Albemarle*, elated by his exploits at Plymouth, felt confident that his vessel could navigate the broader waters, and he was preparing to go to the assistance of Hoke, when he was drawn into a severe and disastrous fight with the *Sassacus*. This was one of Captain Melancthon Smith's blockading squadron in Albemarle Sound, of which the principal vessels were the *Mattahessett*, *Miami*, *Sassacus*, *Wyalusing*, and *Whitehead*. The *Commodore Hull* and *Ceres* were picket-boats.

The squadron lay off the mouth of the Roanoke River, and early in May, the picket-boats were directed to decoy the ram from under the batteries at Plymouth. They did so, and on the 5th[b] the *Albemarle* came bearing down upon the squadron with the captive *Bombshell*, just [b] May. put into the Confederate service, and the river steamer *Cotton Plant*, with two hundred sharp-shooters. The latter soon put back. The ram and its tender pushed on, and first encountered the *Sassacus*. The latter, with the other steamers, more agile than the ram, played around it in search of its most vulnerable point, and in doing so the *Sassacus* gave the *Bombshell* a broadside which caused her to surrender and keep quiet.

The *Albemarle* was heavily armed with Brooks and Whitworth guns. After a brief cannonade, the *Sassacus*, Lieutenant-Commander F. A. Roe, moving with full force, struck the monster a blow which pushed it partly under water, and nearly sunk it. When it recovered from the shock, the two vessels exchanged 100-pound shots at a distance of a few paces. Most of the bolts of the *Sassacus* glanced from the mailed sides of her antagonist like hail from granite, but three of them entered one of its ports with destructive effect, at the moment that the *Albemarle* sent a 100-pound Brooks bolt through one of the boilers of the *Sassacus*. In its passage it killed three men and wounded six. The vessel was filled with scalding steam, and for a few minutes was unmanageable. When the smoke and vapor passed away, the crippled *Albemarle* was seen moving off in the direction of Plymouth, firing as she fled. The *Sassacus* slowly followed, and finally stopped for want of steam. The *Mattahessett* and *Wyalusing* engaged in the struggle, but the ram escaped. The victory was won by the Nationals, and their chief trophy was the recaptured *Bombshell*, with her valuable guns.   Hoke waited in vain for the *Albemarle* to help him in the siege of New Berne.   He soon afterward abandoned that siege in response to a call to hasten to the defense of Richmond, then seriously threatened by the armies of the Potomac and the James.[1]

For several months after this there was quiet in Albemarle Sound, and all along the coast of North Carolina.[2]   The conquests made by Burnside, in 1862, had been in some degree recovered by the Confederates, and very little remained to the Nationals excepting Roanoke Island and New Berne.

The *Albemarle* was a bugbear to the blockading vessels; and finally, late in October, Lieutenant William B. Cushing, one of the most daring of the young officers of the navy, undertook to destroy it.   It was then lying at a wharf at Plymouth, behind a barricade of logs thirty feet in width.   A small steam launch, equipped as a torpedo boat, was placed in Cushing's charge, and on a dark night[a] he moved,

WILLIAM B. CUSHING.

[a] October 27, 1864.

in her, toward Plymouth, with a crew of thirteen, officers and men, part of whom had volunteered for the service.   The launch had a cutter of the *Sham-rock* in tow.   They passed the *South-field*, and were within twenty yards of the ram, before the pickets of the latter discovered the danger, when they sprang their rattles, rang the bell, hailed, and commenced firing at the same instant.   Cushing cast off the cutter, and ordered its commander to board the *Southfield*, while he proceeded in his torpedo boat, in the face of a severe fire of musketry, to attack the *Albemarle*.   He drove his launch far into the barricade of logs, its bow resting on them.   Then the torpedo boom was lowered, and driven directly under the overhang of the *Albemarle*, and the mine was exploded at the moment when one of the guns of the ram hurled a heavy bolt that went crashing through and destroying the launch. The Confederates kept up a fire at fifteen feet range, and called upon Cushing to surrender.   He refused, and ordered his men to save themselves as they might.   The hero, with the others, leaped into the water, in the gloom, and swam to the middle of the stream without being hit by the Confederate shot.   But the most of the party were captured or drowned.   Only one, besides Cushing, escaped.   The latter managed to reach the shore, and just at daylight, almost exhausted, he crept into a swamp, where he was found and kindly cared for by negroes.   He sent one of these to ascertain the fate

---

[1] See chapter XIII.

[2] There were some raids that disturbed the peace of the Confederates in that region during the summer. One of the most formidable of these was made by General Wild, from Roanoke Island, with some colored troops. They penetrated into Camden County well up toward the Dismal Swamp, and after destroying much grain and other property, returned with many horses and cattle, and about twenty-five hundred slaves.   Wild lost thirteen men.

of the *Albemarle*, and learned, with joy, that she was a hopeless ruin, and had settled down upon the mud at the wharf. On the following night Cushing captured a skiff belonging to a Confederate picket, and at eleven o'clock was on board the *Valley City*, a gunboat in the offing. Plymouth was retaken a few days afterward,[a]

[a] October 31, 1864.

by a squadron under Commodore

THE RAM ALBEMARLE.[1]

Macomb, with some prisoners and valuable stores, and the National flag was unfurled over the sunken *Albemarle*. The Confederate soldiers of that region were then mostly in Virginia, for the defense of Petersburg against the Army of the Potomac.

Events of far greater importance occurred on the coast of North Carolina soon after this, which had a direct connection with and bearing upon Sherman's march through the Carolinas. These were the finally successful efforts of the Government to close the port of Wilmington, on the Cape Fear River, against blockade-runners, and to possess that port and town. We have observed that the Government had determined to close the harbors of Wilmington and Mobile, against those foreign violators of law.[2] When Farragut had effectually sealed the latter,[3] the attention of the Government, and especially of the Navy Department, was turned toward Wilmington, where blockade-runners continually evaded the vigilance and defied the power of the watchers off the entrances of the Cape Fear River. For their protection, and to prevent National vessels entering that stream, forts and batteries were erected at its mouth, on the borders of the sea, almost thirty miles below the city of Wilmington.[4]

Foiled in its efforts to absolutely close that port, the Government considered plans for capturing and holding the city. Among others was one submitted by Frederic Kidder, a citizen of Boston, who had for many years held intimate commercial and social relations with Wilmington, and was well acquainted with the country and the coast far around it. He had found means of communication with Wilmington during the war; and so early as the beginning of 1864, he laid his plan before General Burnside, then recruiting men in New York and New England to fill up his (Ninth) corps. Burn-

---

[1] This is from a photograph taken when the flag was raised over the vessel.   [2] See page 439.

[3] See page 444.

[4] These defenses consisted of Fort Fisher, on Federal Point, a formidable work, described elsewhere. It mounted twenty-six guns, twenty of which were in position to sweep the narrow sandy cape on which it stood. Nearer the end of Federal Point was Mound Battery, an artificial hill of sand, about fifty feet in height, on which two heavy columbiads were mounted. Between Fort Fisher and Mound Battery, and connecting them, was a line of intrenchments, on which were mounted sixteen guns. These ran parallel with the beach. Back of these, and running across to the Cape Fear River, was a line of rifle-pits. On the shore of the Cape Fear, across from Mound Battery, was another sand-hill, thirty feet in height, with four cannon upon it, named Battery Buchanan. These constituted the defenses on Federal Point, and commanded the entrance to the Cape Fear, by New Inlet. About seven miles southwest from Fort Fisher, at Smithville, on the old entrance to the Cape Fear, was Fort Johnson; and about a mile south of that work was Fort Caswell. The latter and Fort Fisher were the principal works. On Smith's Island, at Baldhead Point, was Battery Holmes.

side was so pleased with and interested in the plan, that he went with it to Washington, and he received from the War Department full permission to carry it out.[1] He collected a large force at Annapolis for the purpose, and was nearly ready to go forward, when General Grant arranged for the campaigns in Virginia and Georgia, and Burnside and the Ninth Corps were

THE NEW IRONSIDES [2] AND MONITORS.

ordered to join the Army of the Potomac.[3] This put an end to the expedition, and postponed the capture of Wilmington.

In the succeeding summer, when preparations were begun for Farragut's attack on the forts at the entrance to Mobile Bay,[4] similar arrangements were made for reducing the forts at the entrance to the Cape Fear River.

---

[1] Mr. Kidder's plan was as follows: Wilmington is thirty miles from the sea, by the Cape Fear River, but only about twelve miles from a navigable Sound east of it, into which, from the ocean, was Masonboro' Inlet, with seven feet of water at high tide. It was proposed to have a fleet of flat steamers rendezvous at Beaufort, fifty or sixty miles up the coast, on which to put 12,000 armed men, under an energetic commander. These were to be suddenly landed on the main, at Masonboro' Inlet, and marched directly on Wilmington. It was known that there were no defenses beyond two miles from the heart of Wilmington (and they not very strong), to oppose the force coming in from the sea. It was proposed to have a strong cavalry force move simultaneously from New Berne, to tear up the railway between Wilmington and Goldsboro', and, if possible, go down and destroy the bridge within ten miles of Wilmington. This force was to co-operate fully with that marching from Masonboro' Inlet.—Written statement to the author, by Mr. Kidder.

In the summer of 1864 General Graham submitted a plan for capturing Wilmington. It proposed to have a force, consisting of 500 cavalry, 500 infantry, and a section of artillery, go out from New Berne, or from Newport Barracks, and strike the railway between Wilmington and Goldsboro', while two picked squadrons of cavalry, and 2,000 infantry and a good battery, should land at Snead's Ferry, at the mouth of New River, forty-one miles from Wilmington. This force should march on Wilmington, while another, composed of 2,500 infantry, with ten pieces of artillery, should land at Masonboro' Inlet, and push on toward the city. These several bodies would so distract and divide the Confederates, that the capture of the city might be an easy matter.—Written statement to the author, by General Graham.

[2] The New Ironsides was a very powerful vessel, built in Philadelphia. It had a wooden hull covered with iron plates four inches in thickness. She had eight ports on each side, and carried sixteen 11-inch Dahlgren guns, two 200-pounder Parrott guns, and four 24-pounder boat howitzers. Her aggregate weight of guns was 284,800 pounds. She had two horizontal engines, and was propelled by a screw. She was furnished with sails, and was bark-rigged. At her bow was a formidable wrought-iron ram or beak. She first went to sea in August, 1862. We have already met her in Charleston harbor (see page 193). She fought Fort Fisher gallantly and unharmed, and at the close of the war she returned to the Delaware, whence she first set forth. There she was dismantled, and left to repose near League Island, a short distance below Philadelphia, where she was accidentally set on fire, and was destroyed, on Sunday, the 16th of December, 1866.

[3] See page 292.   [4] See page 439.

So early as August, armored and unarmored gun-boats began to gather in Hampton Roads; and in October full fifty war-vessels were there, under the command of Admiral Porter, including the *New Ironsides* and several monitors. Meanwhile, Governor Andrew had been to Washington, and laid before the Government[a] Mr. Kidder's plan, which was [a] September, 1864. again approved. That gentleman was sent for, and went from the National Capital to Fortress Monroe, with Admiral Porter, where he remained about a week. He had an interview with Lieutenant-General Grant, who approved the plan, and agreed to send, for the purpose, the bulk of Sheridan's army, then in the Shenandoah Valley. The movements of the Confederates in that region prevented the execution of that part of the plan; and, as no cavalry could be had to make the co-operating movement from New Berne with forces at Masonboro' Inlet, the plan was again abandoned, and arrangements were made for a direct attack upon Fort Fisher and its dependencies at the entrances to the Cape Fear.[1]

W. H. C. WHITING.

Already a reconnoissance of Fort Fisher, on Federal Point, the main defense of the seaward approach to Wilmington, had been made,[b] [b] September. by means of the blockading squadron, by Generals Godfrey Weitzel and Charles K. Graham, to determine the strength of that work, and the means necessary to carry it. Rumors of this reached the Confederates. Then, the gathering of a naval force in Hampton Roads attracted their attention, and the discussion of its meaning, in the public prints, pointed so certainly to an expedition against Wilmington, that the Confederates strengthened Fort Fisher, erected new works in its support, and increased the garrison. The skillful engineer and commander, General W. H. C. Whiting, was then in charge of the Confederates in that region, in the absence of Bragg. This caused a

---

[1] Fort Fisher was an earth-work of an irregular quadrilateral trace. The exterior sides would average about 250 yards. Its northeastern salient, which was nearest the sea (indicated in the accompanying sketch, where

THE LAND AND SEA FRONTS OF FORT FISHER.

the white and the shaded part of the picture of the fort divide), approached high-water mark within about 100 yards. From that salient, across the beach to the water, was a strong stockade or wooden palisade, indicated in the sketch, which was taken from near the water. The land face of the fort occupied the whole width of the cape known as Federal Point, and, exposed to an enfilading fire from the ocean, was heavily traversed, by which the twenty guns that commanded that strip of land were well guarded. The tops of these traverses were full six feet above the general line of the interior crests, and afforded bomb-proof shelters for the garrison. At a distance, as seen in the sketch, they had the appearance of a series of mounds. The slopes of the parapet were well secured by marsh sods. The quarters of the men were wooden shanties. They were just outside of the work, and to the north of it. All along the land front of the fort, across to the Cape Fear River, was a stockade, and on the beach, along its sea-front, were the wrecks of several blockade-runners. Many torpedoes were planted in front of the fort.

postponement of the expedition until the latter part of November, when General Grant provided six thousand five hundred troops from the forces under General Butler, to co-operate with the fleet under Admiral Porter. The immediate command of the troops was given to General Weitzel.

When the arrangements were all agreed upon, after Grant and Porter had a consultation in Hampton Roads, the commanding general was informed[a] that General Bragg had gone to Georgia, taking with him a greater portion of the troops at and around Wilmington, to operate against Sherman. Grant considered it important to strike the blow at Fort Fisher during Bragg's absence, and he gave immediate orders for the troops and transports to be put in readiness at Bermuda Hundred, as soon as possible. In the instructions given to General Butler,[b] it was stated that the first object of the expedition was to close the port of Wilmington, and the second the capture of that city. Butler was instructed to debark the troops on the main land between the Cape Fear River and the sea, north of the north entrance (or New Inlet) to the river. Should the landing be effected whilst the enemy still held Fort Fisher, and the batteries guarding the entrance to the river, the troops were to intrench themselves, and, by co-operating with the navy, effect the reduction and capture of those places, when the navy could enter the river, and the port of Wilmington would be sealed. General Butler was further instructed that "should the troops under General Weitzel fail to effect a landing at or near Fort Fisher, they will be returned to the armies operating against Richmond, without delay."[1]

Nov. 30, 1864.

December 6.

General Butler had read of the destructive effects, at a considerable distance, of the explosion of a large quantity of gunpowder, in England, and he suggested that a similar explosion, on board of a vessel run close under Fort Fisher, might demolish that work, or at least so paralyze the garrison, that troops, on hand, might make an easy conquest of the place. This suggestion was made just before he was ordered to New York, to keep the peace there during the Presidential election. When he returned, he found that the suggestion had been considered, that the powder experiment was to be tried, and that preparations for it were a-making.[2] These caused some delay in the movements of the navy, and the expedition was not ready to sail before the 13th of December.

The troops destined for the expedition consisted of General Ames's division of the Twenty-fourth Corps, and General Paine's division of the Twenty-

---

[1] General Grant's instructions to General Butler, December 6, 1864.

[2] It was proposed to explode a floating mine containing between two and three hundred tons of gunpowder. The proposition was submitted to experts, and, among others, to Chief-Engineer General Richard Delafield, who made an elaborate report, showing that experience taught the impossibility of very serious or extensive injury being done in a lateral direction, by an open-air explosion of powder (which the proposed operation would be, substantially), excepting to vertical objects. He gave a description of the form and position of Fort Fisher, and also of Fort Caswell, at the more southern or old entrance to the Cape Fear River, which it was proposed to treat in the same way, and cited several instances of explosions in this country and in Europe, the effects of which supported his opinion, that success would not attend the experiment there proposed to be tried. This report was submitted to the War Department on the 18th of November, 1864. Reports were also submitted by other experts, among them Captain Henry A. Wise, chief of the Bureau of Ordnance, who gave it as his opinion that no serious damage would be done beyond 500 yards from the point of explosion. A consultation of several experts was held,[c] by direction of Mr. Fox, the Assistant Secretary of the Navy, at the residence of Captain Wise. The subject was then fully discussed, and it was concluded that it was worth while to try the experiment, with the hope that the explosion might so paralyze the garrison for a few hours, that the troops might land and take possession, and so close the harbor of Wilmington.

Nov. 23.

fifth (negro) Corps. They left Bermuda Hundred on transports, on the 8th of December, and arrived at Fortress Monroe the next morning,[a] when General Butler reported to Admiral Porter that his troops were ready, and that his transports were coaled and watered for only ten days. Owing to the incompleteness of the great torpedo vessel, the armed fleet was not ready to move. Three days afterward, the admiral said he would sail on the 13th, but would be compelled to go into Beaufort harbor, on the North Carolina coast, for ammunition for his monitors. During the three days that the army waited for the navy, in Hampton Roads, the weather was cold and blustering, but on the 13th it was serene.

[a] Dec. 9, 1864.

Fearing that a knowledge, or at least a well-grounded suspicion, of the destination of the armada should reach the enemy, Butler sent the transport fleet up the Potomac, to Matthias Point, at three o'clock on the morning of the 13th, and during the day they were in full view of the Confederate pickets and scouts. That night they returned, and rendezvoused under the lee of Cape Charles. At noon on Wednesday, the 14th, Butler joined them in his flag-ship, the *Ben Deford*, off Cape Henry, and the whole fleet put to sea. The naval fleet had then been gone about thirty-six hours.[1]

On the evening of the 15th, the transports, with the troops, arrived at the prescribed rendezvous, about twenty-five miles at sea, east of Fort Fisher. The ocean was perfectly calm, and remained so for three days, while the army was anxiously waiting for the navy; for the landing of troops could have been easily effected in that smooth water. Eagerly all eyes were turned northward, day after day, but it was not until the evening of Sunday, the 18th, when a strong wind was coming up from the southeast, and the sea was covered with white caps, that it made its appearance. It was evident that the water was too rough for troops to land, and the attack was postponed. The wind increased in violence the next day. The transports had been coaled and watered for only ten days. That time had now been consumed in waiting for the fleet and voyaging; and, by the advice of Admiral Porter, the transports went to Beaufort, seventy miles up the coast, for coal and water. They made that harbor just in time to avoid the severest portion of one of the heaviest gales experienced on that coast in thirty years. It lasted three days.

On Friday, the 23d,[b] Butler sent Captain Clark, one of his aids, in the armed tug *Chamberlain*, to inform Admiral Porter that the troops would be at the rendezvous at sunset the next evening. Clark turned at sunrise on Saturday morning, and reported that Admiral Porter had determined to explode the powder-ship at one o'clock that morning, and begin the attack without waiting for the troops. Butler could not credit the report, because the presence of the troops would be essential to the success of the experiment with the powder-ship. But it was true. Soon after

[b] December.

---

[1] This was the most formidable naval armament ever put afloat. It consisted of the following vessels: *Malvern* (a river or bay steamer), the flag-ship; *New Ironsides, Brooklyn, Mohican, Tacony, Kansas, Unadilla, Huron, Pequot, Yantic, Maumee, Pawtuxet, Pontoosuc, Nyack, Ticonderoga, Shenandoah, Juniata, Powhatan, Susquehanna, Wabash, Colorado, Minnesota, Vanderbilt, Mackinaw, Tuscarora, Vicksburg, St. Jago de Cuba, Fort Jackson, Osceola, Sassacus, Chippewa, Maratanza, R. R. Cuyler, Rhode Island, Monticello, Alabama, Montgomery, Keystone State, Queen City, Iosco, Aries, Howquah, Wilderness, Cherokee, A. D. Vance, Moccasin, Eolus, Gettysburg, Emma, Lillian, Nansemond, Tristram Shandy, Britannia, Governor Buckingham, Saugus, Monadnock, Canonicus, Mahopac.* Total, 58. The last four were monitors.

Captain Clark left, on the night of the 23d, the *Louisiana* (the name of the powder-vessel) was run in, under the direction of Commander A. C. Rhind, of the navy, in the wake of a blockade-runner, and anchored within three hundred yards of the northeastern salient of Fort Fisher.[1]   There, at two o'clock in the morning,[a] the powder, two hundred and fifteen tons

[a] Dec. 24, 1864.

in amount, was exploded, but without any sensible effect upon the fort.[2]   A little more than ten hours afterward, Porter opened his guns upon the defenses at that entrance (New Inlet) to the Cape Fear River, consisting of Fort Fisher and Mound Battery.[3]   Brief and feeble

MOUND BATTERY. [4]

responses were made by the garrisons, which deceived Porter with the belief that he had disabled them all, and that nothing was needed to make the

---

[1] See sketch in note 1, page 475.

[2] The *Louisiana* was a propeller of 295 tons, having an iron hull. She was disguised as a blockade-runner, having two raking smoke-stacks, one of which was real, the other was a sham. It being desirable to have the powder above the water-line, a light deck was built for the purpose. On this was first placed a row of barrels of powder, standing on end, the upper one open. The remainder of the powder was in canvas bags, holding about 60 pounds each, the whole being stowed as represented in the accompanying sketch, in which the form of

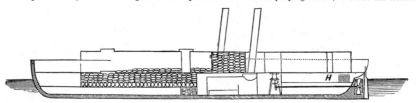

THE POWDER-SHIP.

the vessel is also delineated. The whole weight of the powder was 215 tons, or 430,000 pounds. To communicate fire to the whole mass simultaneously, four separate threads of the Gomez fuse were woven through it, passing through each separate barrel and bag. At the stern, and under the cabin, was a heap of pine wood (H) and other combustibles, which were to be fired by the crew, when they should leave the vessel. Three devices were used for communicating fire to the fuses, namely, clock-work, by which a percussion-cap was exploded; short spermaceti candles, which burned down and ignited the fuses at the same time; and a slow-match that worked in time with the candles and the clock-work. The powder-vessel followed a blockade-runner, and was anchored within 300 yards of the fort, according to the report of Commander Rhind. When the combustibles were fired, and the apparatus for igniting the fuses were put in motion, the crew escaped in a swift little steamer employed for the purpose. The explosion took place in one hour and fifty-two minutes after the crew left. Notwithstanding the concussion of the explosion broke window-glasses in a vessel twelve miles distant, and the whole fleet, at that distance, felt it, and it was also felt on land at Beaufort and New Berne, from 60 to 80 miles distant, there was no perceptible effect upon the fort and garrison. The edges of the parapets were as sharply defined as ever, and even the grass was not disturbed.

[3] See note 4, page 473.

[4] This is from a sketch taken from the line of intrenchments that connected this battery with Fort Fisher. On the left is seen the ocean. The vessel on the right indicates the position of the Cape Fear River.

victory, and the possession of them, complete, but a few troops to occupy them.[1] It was a great mistake. The works were almost entirely uninjured, and, according to a statement of General Whiting, only one man of the garrison of Fort Fisher was mortally hurt, three severely and nineteen slightly wounded, and five gun-carriages disabled. This was the sum of injury received.

The transports arrived off Fort Fisher just as Porter was closing the bombardment. An arrangement was made for a renewal of the attack and the co-operation of the troops, the next morning at eight o'clock. It was ten before the work commenced, when the lighter draught gun-boats were employed in shelling the Flag Pond Hill and Half-Moon batteries, two or three miles up the coast above Fort Fisher, preparatory to the landing of the troops. The bombardment continued seven hours without intermission. At a little past noon the transports moved within eight hundred yards of the shore, and soon afterward, when the batteries in front were silenced, the launches were prepared, and a part of Ames's division, or about one-third of the troops were landed. General Curtis was the first to reach the shore, and plant the flag on a deserted battery, when loud cheers went up from the transports, and the bands struck up *Yankee Doodle*. It was then about three o'clock. The *Malvern* passed by the *Ben Deford*, and Admiral Porter, standing on the wheel-house of his flag-ship, called out to General Butler, saying: "There is not a rebel within five miles of the fort. You have nothing to do but to march in and take it." This was a grave mistake, and led the Admiral to make most unkind reflections upon the military commander in his report two days afterward.[2] The fact was that the garrison, at that moment, was two hundred and fifty men stronger than it was the day before; and behind those sand walls were nine hundred effective men, in good spirits, according to a statement made by General Whiting, on his dying bed. Responses from the fort had been kept up all day. "The garrison was at no time," General Whiting said, "driven from its guns, and fired in return, according to orders, slowly and deliberately, six hundred and sixty-two shot and shell."[3]

---

[1] At about the middle of the afternoon, Admiral Porter sent off a dispatch to the Secretary of the Navy, in which he said that in half an hour after getting the ships in position, he silenced Fort Fisher, but there were no troops to take possession, and he was "merely firing at it to keep up practice." "The forts," he said, "are nearly demolished, and as soon as troops come, we can take possession." He added, "All that is wanted now is troops to land to go into them." This real complaining of the absence of troops was unfair, under the circumstances, and unjust to the army, which, as we have seen, had waited for the motion of the fleet already six days; and had the Admiral waited a few hours for the troops, which, he had been informed, would be there that day, he would have had them in full co-operation with him. As it was, he had defeated the intentions of both branches of the service concerning the powder-vessel, by exploding it when the army, in consequence of waiting for the navy, was seventy miles from the scene of action.

[2] In his dispatch to the Secretary of the Navy, December 27th, he spoke of his "disappointment at the conduct of the army authorities, in not attempting to take possession of the forts which had been so completely silenced by our guns. They were all blown up, burst up, and torn up," he said, "that the people inside had no intention of fighting any longer. Had the army made a show of surrounding it, it would have been ours; but nothing of the kind was done." He then repeated rumors, afterward shown to be untrue, which reflected on the commander. "There never was a fort," he said, "that invited soldiers to walk in and take possession more plainly than Fort Fisher. . . . . . . We silenced the guns in one hour's time." Observe what is said in the text, as to the strength and feelings of the garrison. The writer stood on the deck of the *Ben Deford*, during the entire bombardment, and avers that he saw and heard guns fire from the fort, at brief intervals, during the whole time, until twilight. The verity of history requires this notice of the Admiral's mistake. As to the guns being "blown up, burst up," &c., the statement of General Whiting shows that the "damage was very slight," and that only one gun and four gun-carriages were disabled; also, that every thing was thoroughly repaired that night.

[3] General Whiting was wounded in a second attack on Fort Fisher, and died a prisoner in the hospital, at Fort Columbus, Governor's Island, in the harbor of New York. General Butler addressed to him a series of pertinent questions, touching the first attack on Fort Fisher, which Whiting promptly answered. A certified copy of these questions and answers is before the writer.

General Weitzel, the immediate commander of the troops, accompanied by General Graham, and by Colonel Comstock of General Grant's staff, pushed a reconnoitering force to within five hundred yards of Fort Fisher, accepting the surrender, on the way, of Flag Pond Hill battery, with over sixty men, who were sent on board the fleet. The skirmishers went within seventy-five yards of the fort, when nearly a dozen were wounded by the bursting of shells from the fleet. One man ran forward to the ditch, and captured a flag the shells had cut down from the parapet; and another shot a courier near a sally-port, toward the Cape Fear, took his pistols from his holsters, and a paper from his pocket, and, mounting the dead Confederate's mule, rode back to the lines.[1] General Butler did not go on shore, but, in the tug *Chamberlain*, he moved toward Fort Fisher, abreast the troops, and kept up continual correspondence with Weitzel, by means of signals.

In the mean time the remainder of Ames's troops had captured over two hundred of the North Carolina Reserves, with ten commissioned officers. From them Butler learned that Hoke's division had been detached from the army at Petersburg and sent for the defense of Wilmington, and that two brigades were then within two miles of Fort Fisher, and others were pressing on. Knowing the strength of Hoke's division, Butler was satisfied that a force, outside of the fort, larger than his own, was at hand. In the mean time the weather had become murky, and a heavy surf was beginning to roll in, making it impossible to land more troops. Weitzel, who had thoroughly reconnoitered the fort, reported that, in his judgment, and that of officers of his command, a successful assault upon it, with the troops at hand, would be impossible, for the moment the fleet should cease firing, the parapets would be fully manned, and its nineteen heavy guns would sweep the land. Considering all these things, General Butler ordered the troops to withdraw and re-embark. While doing so, at twilight, the guns of the navy ceased work, when those of Fort Fisher sent a storm of grape and cannister shot after the retiring troops. It was impossible to get them on board that night; and it was thirty hours before they were rescued from their perilous situation. On the following day the transports departed for Hampton Roads, leaving the fleet lying off Fort Fisher, with its ammunition nearly exhausted.[2]

The failure to capture Fort Fisher at that time produced the keenest disappointment. Viewing the conditions dispassionately, after the lapse of years, experts say that the army officers unquestionably acted wisely and humanely in not attacking, under the circumstances. General Weitzel said to the writer at the time: "It would have been murder."[3] The chief cause

---

[1] Lieutenant Walling, of the One Hundred and Forty-second New York, was the brave soldier who performed the last-mentioned exploit. The dispatch taken from the pocket of the courier (now in possession of the writer) was an order from Colonel Lamb, the commandant of the fort, for some powder to be sent in.

[2] The loss of the Nationals, in this attack, was about fifty men killed and wounded, nearly all by the bursting of six heavy Parrott guns, of the fleet. The Confederate loss was three killed, fifty-five wounded, and three hundred made prisoners.

[3] Colonel Lamb, the commander of Fort Fisher, afterward said: "If I were a friend of General Butler, I could tell him facts which would prove that he did perfectly right in not attacking Fort Fisher when he was before the place. My battery, of nineteen heavy guns, so commanded the land approach that not a man could have lived to reach my works. It was only after the navy had, with beautiful precision, dismounted gun after gun, in regular order (at the second attempt), leaving only one in place, that the attacking party had any chance of success." General Whiting's replies to General Butler's questions on that point, were substantially the same.

of the failure may be found in the lack of co-operation on the part of the fleet with the land forces, at the beginning. During the delay caused by the first three days' waiting for the fleet, at the rendezvous, and the succeeding gale, the Confederates were apprised of the expedition, and took sufficient measures to meet and frustrate it. Wilmington was denuded of troops and the army was waiting off Fort Fisher, at the middle of December, when the garrison of that work consisted of only six hundred and sixty-seven men. It was nine hundred strong when Weitzel stood before it, and at least seven thousand men were within forty-eight hours' march of it. General Bragg had been called back from Georgia, and was in command there, which some Confederate officers say was the reason the whole of the National troops landed on the beach above Fort Fisher were not captured.

The writer was an eye and ear witness to much that is here recorded (and a great deal more) concerning the first attack on Fort Fisher and its dependencies, having been invited by both General Butler and Admiral Porter to accompany the expedition.[1] He visited Fort Fisher and its vicinity, from the land, after the war, when on his way southward, to the battle-fields and other places of interest in the late Slave-labor States. It was in March, 1866, that the author left Washington City, and journeyed by steamer, on the Potomac, to Aquia Creek, and thence by railway through Fredericksburg, Richmond, Petersburg, Weldon, and Goldsboro', to Wilmington, on the Cape Fear River, where, in the family of his excellent friend, Edward Kidder, he found a pleasant and hospitable home for two or three days.

Major Mann, the post commander at Wilmington, kindly offered to take the author, in a government tug, to Fort Fisher, and on Monday morning,[a] in company with that officer and a small party, we made an interesting voyage down the Cape Fear. At almost every mile of the way, we saw the remains of war, in the form of obstructions to navigation,[2] and forts and batteries on the shore. We landed at Fort Anderson, fifteen miles below Wilmington, and visited the ruins of Brunswick Church, within its embankments, which was built before the old War for Independence.

                          a March 27, 1866.

It was well toward noon when we landed on Federal Point (called "Confederate Point," during the war), near Battery Buchanan, and traveled across the moor-like peninsula to Mound Battery and Fort Fisher. There we spent a few hours, examining the fortifications and sketching. It was on our return voyage that we met the colonel of the National Secret Service, mentioned in note 1, page 35, volume II. Early the following morning I left Wilmington, and journeyed into the interior by railway, as far as Florence, where I turned southward and sea-ward, and, by the Northeastern railroad, reached Charleston that evening, at twilight. The latter portion of our journey was a very interesting one. We swept for more than two miles through a blazing pine-forest, and traversed the great swamps along the margins of the Santee River, which we crossed late in the afternoon. Ten days before, I had left Philadelphia in a snow-storm; now I was among

---

[1] See pages 511 and 514, volume I.

[2] Among other obstructions were sunken hulks. One of these was the famous *Arctic*, one of the vessels of the Grinnell Expedition to the Polar Seas, conducted by Dr. Kane, in search of Sir John Franklin, in 1850.

spring blossoms, and the dark swamps were glowing, as with sunlight, with the flowers of the trailing yellow jasmine.

At Charleston the writer was the guest of a friend who had endured the fiery furnace of war through which that city had passed. His elegant residence was in what was lately the suburbs of the city, and beyond the reach of shells from Morris Island. In company with one of his sons, who was in the Confederate army, at Charleston, I visited every place of interest in and around that city and harbor. General Devens, then in command there, kindly gave us the use of the government barge, fully equipped and manned, and in it we visited Castle Pinckney, and Forts Ripley, Johnson, Gregg, Wagner, Sumter, and Moultrie. We lunched at Fort Wagner, and picked delicate violets from the marsh sod among the sand dunes over the grave

SALLY-PORT IN 1866.

of the gallant Colonel Shaw and his dusky fellow-martyrs.[1] We rambled over the heaps of Fort Sumter, and made the sketch of the interior seen on page 465; and then we passed over to Fort Moultrie, which I had visited eighteen years before, when it was in perfect order. Now it was sadly changed. Its form and dimensions had been altered; and missiles from the National fleet had broken its tasteful sally-port and plowed its parapets and parade with deep furrows.

The writer spent a week in Charleston, making notes and sketches, during which time Easter Sunday occurred, and he worshiped in the venerable St. Michael's Church,[2] then decorated with wreaths and festoons of evergreens and the beautiful white flowers of the laurel. Its ceiling, torn by a message carried by Gillmore's "Swamp Angel,"[3] was yet unrepaired, and the Tables of the Law in the chancel recess, demolished by the same agency,[4] had not been replaced. The various buildings in which the Secession conventions were held, were all in ruins. These, and the tomb of Calhoun, within a few yards of the spot where the South Carolina Ordinance of Secession was signed;[5] the statue of William Pitt, in front of the Orphan House; the head-quarters of officers in the city, and the National Arsenal, fronting on Ashley Street, were all objects of great historic interest. At the latter place was the little six-pounder iron cannon, made rough as oak-bark by rust,

---

[1] See page 205.   [2] See page 105, volume I.   [3] See page 207.   [4] See page 105, volume I.

[5] The grave of Calhoun is in St. Philip's church-yard (see page 104, volume I.), just back of the ruins of the South Carolina Institute (see page 19, volume I.), and the Circular church. When the writer was in Charleston, at the time we are considering, he was informed by a general officer that once on returning to the Mills House, after a social party, at about midnight, he heard a screech-owl in the ruined tower of the Circular church, making its unpleasant noise, within the distance of the sound of a man's voice from the remains of the grave of Calhoun, the great apostle of Disunion. In the heart of the city which he and his disciples fondly hoped would be the commercial emporium of a great empire founded on human slavery, "the bats and owls" made "night hideous." See note 2, page 158, volume I. It may be mentioned, in this connection, as a curious fact, given to the writer by an old resident of Charleston, that not one of the *Palmetto Guard*, of which Edmund Ruffin (see page 48, volume I.) was a volunteer, who fired on Fort Sumter, and first entered and took possession of it in the name of the Conspirators (see page 330, volume I.), was living at the close of 1865, or six months after the war ceased.

which was fired back of the old post-office, in honor of the passage of the
South Carolina Ordinance of Secession.   It was also fired when news reached
Charleston that similar action of the Conspir-
ators in other States had taken place.   For
this reason it was known as the Secession
Gun.

SECESSION GUN.

   The writer voyaged from Charleston to
Beaufort, on a beautiful April day, in the
steamer *Emilie*—the same that conveyed
Jefferson Davis as a prisoner from Savannah
to Fortress Monroe.   We arrived at the latter place toward evening, but in time
for the author to visit and sketch objects of interest in that "Deserted Village."
Among these was the house of Edmund Rhett, the reputed gathering-place
of plotters against the
Republic, mentioned in
note 2, page 565, vol-
ume II.   Thence, on the
following day, the au-
thor sailed in a small
yacht to Hilton Head,
stopping on the way
at Spanish Fort and
Smith's Plantation, as
mentioned in the note
just cited.   At Hilton
Head he enjoyed the
hospitalities of General
Burns [1] and his interesting family.   That offi-

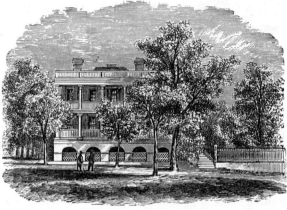

EDMUND RHETT'S HOUSE.

cer kindly furnished him with a conveyance to Savannah, in the Government
steamer *Resolute*, accompanied by the teachers of the Freedman's School at
Mitchelville, and the chaplain of the post, the Rev. Mr. Woart.   We had a
delightful voyage.   We stopped at Fort Pulaski, and arrived at Savannah
at sunset.   From that city the author journeyed by railway to Augusta and
Atlanta, in Georgia, and Montgomery, in Alabama, and thence by steamer
to Mobile and New Orleans.

---

[1] See page 412, volume II.

CHAPTER XVIII.

CAPTURE OF FORT FISHER, WILMINGTON, AND GOLDSBORO'. — SHERMAN'S MARCH
THROUGH THE CAROLINAS.—STONEMAN'S LAST RAID.

ENERAL GRANT was greatly disappointed by the result of the expedition against Fort Fisher, and in his
General Report of the Operations of the Army,[a]
he severely censured General Butler, and
charged him with " direct violation of the instructions given," by the " re-embarkation of the troops
and return of the expedition." In those instructions
General Grant had said: "Should such landing [on the beach
above the entrance to the Cape Fear] be effected whilst the
enemy still holds Fort Fisher and the batteries guarding the
entrance to the river, then the troops should intrench themselves, and, by
co-operating with the navy, effect the reduction and capture of those places."
Instead of doing so, Butler re-embarked his troops, after the reconnoissance
to the front of Fort Fisher. He claimed, in justification, that the conditions precedent to intrenching were lacking, in that he had not effected a
landing, as only twenty-two hundred of his six thousand five hundred men
had reached the shore, and without a single gun, when the sea ran so
high that no more guns or men could be landed, and that provisions could
reach the shore only by being headed up in casks, and sent on rafts. He
also said that the navy had nearly exhausted its ammunition, and could
not be expected to co-operate with the troops in further assault until supplied; and that he had positive information that Confederate troops, larger
in number than the whole military force of the expedition, were nigh at
hand. At the request of General Grant, General Butler was relieved, and
General E. O. C. Ord was assigned to the command of the Department of
Virginia and North Carolina.

On being informed that the fleet had not left the vicinity of Fort Fisher,
General Grant wrote to Admiral Porter,[c] asking him to remain,
and promising to send a force immediately, to make another
attempt to capture the Confederate defenses at the mouth of the Cape Fear.
He selected for the enterprise the same troops led by Weitzel, with the
addition of a thin brigade of fourteen hundred men, and two batteries.[1]
This force, numbering about eight thousand men, was placed under the com-

[a] July 22, 1865.

[b] Dec. 6, 1864.

[c] Dec. 30.

---

[1] The troops consisted of 3,300 picked men from the Second Division of the Twenty-fourth Army Corps,
under General Adelbert Ames; the same number from the Third Division of the Twenty-fifth Army Corps,
under General Charles J. Paine; 1,400 men from the First Division of the Twenty-fourth Army Corps, under
Colonel J. C. Abbott, Seventh New Hampshire; Sixteenth New York Independent Battery, with four 3-inch
guns, and a light battery of the Third Regular Artillery, with six light 12-pounders.

mand of General Alfred H. Terry, with instructions to proceed in transports from Fortress Monroe, as speedily as possible, to the Cape Fear River, and report the arrival to Admiral Porter. To Lieutenant-Colonel Comstock, who accompanied the former expedition, was assigned the position of chief engineer of this. The general instructions did not differ essentially from those given to General Butler. In them, Terry was informed that a siege train would be at his disposal at Fortress Monroe, if he should require it, to consist, as he was told by the Lieutenant-General, of twenty 30-pounder Parrott guns, four 100-pounder Parrotts, and twenty Cohorn mortars, with a sufficient number of artillerists and engineers. General Sheridan was directed to send a division to Fortress Monroe, to follow, in case of need.

The new expedition left Hampton Roads on the 6th of January,[a] and on the 8th rendezvoused off Beaufort, North Carolina, where Porter was supplying his vessels with coal and ammunition. Rough weather kept all the vessels there until the 12th, when they went down the coast, the war-vessels in three lines, accompanied by the transports, and appeared off Fort Fisher that evening. In the same order the navy took position the next morning,[b] and at eight o'clock nearly two hundred boats, besides steam tugs, began the landing of the troops, under cover of the fire of the fleet, a part of which had already attacked Fort Fisher. At three o'clock in the afternoon eight thousand troops were on the shore, their pickets exchanging shots with an outpost of Hoke's division, which was still there.

[a] 1865.

[b] Jan. 13.

Terry first wisely provided against an attack in the rear, from the direction of Wilmington, by casting up intrenchments across the peninsula, and thus also securing its free use to Masonboro' Inlet, where, if necessary, troops and supplies might be landed in still water. This was done a short distance above the head of Myrtle Sound, and about four miles from Fort Fisher. The first line was completed at nine o'clock that evening; another was made a mile nearer the fort, and still another within about two miles of the works. At the latter, on the morning of the 14th,[c] the troops were in a defensible position, behind strong breastworks, extending from the Cape Fear River to the sea, and partially covered by *abatis*. This being accomplished without serious difficulty, the landing of the lighter guns was commenced, and was completed that evening. Before morning they were all in battery, mostly near the Cape Fear, where the Confederates, if they should attack, would be the least exposed to the fire of the fleet. Thus a firm footing was gained on Federal Point, near Fort Fisher; and it was made more secure by the seizure of a small, unfinished outwork in front of the west end of the land face of that fortification, by Curtis's brigade of Ames's division, which was thrown forward for the purpose. Whilst making that movement, the brigade captured a small steamer coming down the river with shells and forage for the garrison.

[c] January.

The successful movement, thus far, against the fort, planned by General Terry, partook of all the elements of a siege, without some of its important operations on his part. He landed far up the beach, and made approaches without the necessity of zigzag intrenchments to protect his heavy guns, for none were needed, the batteries for that work being afloat in Porter's fleet.

A careful reconnoissance determined Terry to make a grand assault the
next morning,[a] and arrangements were accordingly made with
Porter, whose fleet had already been preparing the way . for
success.   On the morning of the 13th, it had taken its station in
three lines, as we have observed.   The *New Ironsides*, Commodore Radford,

[a] Jan. 15, 1865.

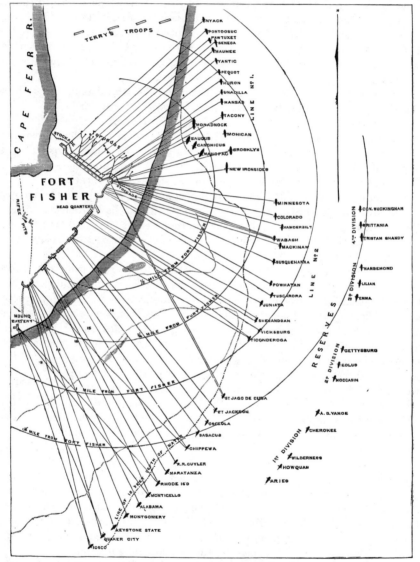

BOMBARDMENT OF FORT FISHER.[1]

leading the monitors *Saugus, Canonicus, Monadnoc,* and *Mahopac,* moved
toward the fort and received its fire unnoticed until they reached a position

---

[1] In this plan, the general form of Fort Fisher, described in note 4, page 473, is indicated.   Fort Buchanan,
on the extreme end of Federal Point, was almost due west from Mound Battery, and about once and a half the
distance from the latter, that Mound Battery was from the northeast salient of Fort Fisher.

within a thousand yards of it, when they opened their batteries, and a sharp fight ensued. Then Porter ordered his wooden vessels to engage in the conflict. Line No. 1, in the plan on page 486, was led by the *Brooklyn*, Captain Alden, and line No. 2 was led by the *Colorado*, Commodore Thatcher. The bombardment was continuous, but not rapid, until dark, to the severe hurt of the armament of the fort, when the wooden vessels fell back to their anchorage. But the iron-clads fired slowly throughout the night, by which the garrison was worried and fatigued. During the landing of the army ordnance on the 14th,[1] and the successful movements of Terry on the peninsula, all the vessels carrying 11-inch guns, led by the *Brooklyn*, joined the monitors in bombarding Fort Fisher, damaging it severely. "By sunset," says Porter, in his report, "the fort was reduced to a pulp; every gun was silenced by being injured or covered up with earth, so that they could not work."[2]

In the arrangement for the general attack by land and water, the fleet was to first concentrate its fire on the land face of Fort Fisher, for the purpose of disabling its guns and destroying the palisades upon its wings and front, when the army should make the assault at three o'clock in the afternoon. All night the monitors pounded the fort, and allowed the garrison no rest, nor opportunity to repair damages; and at eight o'clock in the morning,[a] the entire naval force, excepting a division left to aid in the defense of Terry's line across the peninsula, moved up to the attack, "and a fire, magnificent alike for its power and accuracy, was opened."[3]

[a] Jan. 15, 1865.

Meanwhile, fourteen hundred marines and six hundred sailors, armed with revolvers, cutlasses and carbines, were detached from the fleet to assist the land troops in the work of assault; and, digging rifle-trenches in the sand under cover of the fire of the ships, they reached a point within two hundred yards of the sea-front of the fort, where they lay awaiting the order for attack.

Ames's division had been selected for the assault. Paine was placed in command of the defensive line, having with him Abbott's brigade in addition to his own division. Ames's first brigade (N. M. Curtis's) was already at the outwork captured the day before, and in trenches close around it. His other two brigades (G. A. Pennybacker's and L. Bell's) were moved, at noon, to within supporting distance of him. At two o'clock, preparations for the assault were commenced. Sixty sharp-shooters from the Thirteenth Indiana, armed with the Spencer repeating carbine, and forty others, volunteers from Curtis's brigade, the whole under the command of Lieutenant Lent, of the Thirteenth Indiana, were thrown forward, at a run, to within less than two hundred yards of the work. They were provided with shovels, and soon dug pits for shelter, and commenced firing at the parapet, which, as the firing of the fleet at this point had ceased, was instantly manned, and a severe storm opened upon the assailants from musketry and cannon.[4]

---

[1] The siege train was there, but was not landed.

[2] "There was great difference in the position of the ships in the two attacks, and in the nature and effects of the fire. The first was a general bombardment, not calculated to effect particular damage; the second firing had for its definite object the destruction of the land defenses, and the ships were placed accordingly to destroy them by enfilade, and by direct fire. On that front, and the northeast salient, the whole enormous fire was poured without intermission, until the slope of the northeast salient was practicable for assault. Not a gun remained in position on the approaches; the whole palisade swept away; the mines [or torpedoes] cut off, rendering them useless, and the men unable to stand to the parapets during the fire."—*General Whiting's Answer to General Butler's 22d Question.*

[3] General Terry's Report, January 25, 1865.

[4] Terry's Report.

As soon as the sharp-shooters were in position, the fleet changed the direction of its fire from the land face and the palisades of the fort, to its center and right, and Curtis's brigade moved forward at the double-quick into line less than five hundred yards from the works, and there laid down. The other two brigades were moved forward, Pennybacker's to the outwork left by Curtis, and Bell's to a point two hundred yards in the rear of it. Perceiving a good cover on the reverse of a slope, fifty yards in the rear of the sharp-shooters, Curtis moved his men to it, where they instantly covered themselves in trenches. At the same time, Pennybacker followed Curtis and occupied the ground he had just left, and Bell advanced to the outwork.

It was now about half-past three o'clock in the afternoon. Every thing was in readiness for the assault. The signal was given, when Curtis's brigade sprang from its cover and dashed forward in line, its left exposed to a severe enfilading fire. It obliqued to the right, so as to envelop the left of the land-face of the fort. Preparations had been made for destroying the palisades with powder[1] and axes. But the fleet had done the work effectually. The axmen, however, accompanied Curtis's men. The palisades were soon passed, and a lodgment was made on the parapet, not far from the river. At the same time the sailors and marines, led by Fleet-Captain K. R. Breese, eager to be the first to enter the fort, advanced with great gallantry up the beach, and attacked the northeast bastion. There they were exposed to a murderous fire, and were unable to scale the parapet. After heavy loss of

INTERIOR OF FORT FISHER.[2]

officers and men, they were withdrawn. But they had done valuable work, for they had occupied a greater portion of the garrison, who thought theirs the main attack, and so helped Curtis to gain his advantage.

With this assault commenced the terrible struggle. Up to this time the National loss had been trifling, for the navy had kept the garrison quiet. Now it was compelled to cease firing at that part of the fort, for its shells would be as hurtful to friends as foes. Instantly the garrison sprang to its guns, and musketeers swarmed upon the parapet. But Curtis held his ground until Pennybacker, sent by Ames, came to his support. The latter advanced rapidly to Curtis's right, drove the Confederates from the strong and almost unharmed palisades, extending from the west end of the land-

---

[1] The powder was carried in bags, with fuses attached.

[2] This is a view of the interior of Fort Fisher at the point where Curtis's brigade made a lodgment on the parapet, as it appeared when the writer sketched it late in March, 1866. The timber-work shows the general line of the top of the fort, above which the immense traverses of sand, for the protection of the cannon, were made. The Cape Fear River, with a part of the palisades is seen on the left.

face of the fort to the river (see sketch on page 488), and captured a number of prisoners. The brigade broke through the palisades and joined Curtis. At the same time Bell's brigade had been sent forward to occupy the space between that end of the fort and the river; and Terry sent for Abbott's brigade to move down from the north line, while Reese led the sailors and marines up to occupy that position. He also ordered General Paine to send down one of his best regiments, when the Twenty-seventh, negro troops, Brevet Brigadier-General A. M. Blackman, was forwarded. These arrived when the heaviest of the work was done. It had been performed by the troops already there, who fought hand to hand with the garrison, while the fleet kept up its fire further to the southward, to prevent re-enforcements reaching the fort from Mound Battery, or Battery Buchanan.

The Confederates used the huge traverses of the land front for breastworks, and over the tops of these the combatants fired in each other's faces. The struggle was desperate. The Confederates were steadily pushed back, until, at dusk, they had lost nine of these traverses. At that time Blackman reported to Ames. His troops were kept under fire for awhile, when they were withdrawn. At six o'clock Abbott entered the fort with his little brigade, and at nine o'clock, when two more traverses had been carried by the Nationals, the contest ceased. Abbott's brigade drove the garrison from its last stronghold, and the occupation of the work was complete. The Confederates fled toward Battery Buchanan, hotly pursued by Abbott, accompanied by Blackman's regiment; and then the whole of the garrison not already in the hands of Terry, were captured, including Colonel Lamb, the commander of the fort, and General Whiting, who was mortally wounded.

The fall of Fort Fisher rendered all the other works at the mouth of the Cape Fear River untenable, and during the nights of the 16th and 17th,[a] the Confederates blew up Fort Caswell, on the right bank of the river. They also abandoned Battery Holmes, on Smith's Island, and their extensive works at Smithville and Reeves's Point, and fled toward Wilmington. The triumph of the army and navy was now complete.[1]

[a] Jan., 1865.

---

[1] The National loss in the attack was 681 men, of whom 88 were killed, 501 wounded, and 92 missing. Among the wounded was acting Brigadier-General Bell, mortally, and Generals Curtis and Pennybacker, severely. On the morning after the victory, while the exultant soldiers and sailors were swarming into the fort, its principal magazine, deep in the earth, at the center of the parade, was (it is supposed) accidentally exploded. Two hundred men were killed, and one hundred more wounded. The fleet lost about 300 men during the action and by the explosion in the fort. It expended in the bombardment about 50,000 shells. During the seven hours' bombardment on the 25th of December, about 18,000 shells were used. The loss of the Confederates was never reported. General Terry captured 2,083 prisoners, and in all the works he found 169 pieces of artillery, nearly all of which were heavy, over 2,000 stand of small-arms, and considerable quantities of ammunition and commissary stores. In all the forts at the mouth of the Cape Fear, were found Armstrong guns (see page 432), bearing the broad arrow of the British Government, and the name of Sir William Armstrong, the patentee, in full. As the British Government claimed the exclusive use of the Armstrong gun, and none could be sold without its consent, these seemed to form *prima facie* evidence of aid being furnished to the insurgents directly from that Government.

The capture of Fort Fisher, accomplished by the combined operations of the army and navy, gave the liveliest satisfaction to the loyal people, for it seemed like a sure prophecy of peace nigh at hand. Admiral Porter said an electrograph was picked up there from General Lee to Colonel Lamb, in which he said, "that if Forts Fisher and Caswell were not held he would have to evacuate Richmond." All the participants in the conquest were regarded with gratitude, and honored everywhere. When the *Ticonderoga*, Captain C. Steedman, and the *Shenandoah*, Captain D. B. Ridgley, of Porter's fleet, arrived at Philadelphia, a pleasing incident, illustrative of the public feeling, occurred. Some patriotic men and women of the city had established a *Soldiers' Reading Room*, for the benefit of the sick and wounded defenders of the Union who might be detained there. It was opened in October, 1862, with a dining-room attached, where a comfortable meal was furnished for the small sum of *five cents* to those who could pay, and gratuitously to those who could not. It was supported entirely by the contributions of the citizens of Philadelphia, and at the end of the first year it had a library of nearly 2,000 bound volumes. The establishment was under the general supervision of a Board

Bragg was in chief command of the Confederates in that region, but seemed to have been paralyzed by the prompt establishment, by Terry, of an intrenched line across the peninsula and the rapid assault by land and water.[1] Hoke, who was near, made some show on the afternoon of the assault, by Bragg's orders, but a peremptory command of the latter for the former to attack, was withdrawn, after the commander-in-chief had reconnoitered for himself.

Although a greater part of the guns of Fort Fisher were dismounted, or otherwise disabled, the work itself was so slightly damaged that it could be readily repaired. But the Nationals had no use for it. The port of Wilmington was closed to blockade-runners; and the town itself was to be the next object of visitation by Terry and Porter. The latter immediately ordered Lieutenant-Commander R. Chandler, commanding the *Maumee*, to buoy out the channel of New Inlet, when several of the lighter draught vessels went into the Cape Fear River. He also dispatched the gallant Cushing,[2] who was then in command of the *Monticello*, to ascertain the state of affairs on the right bank of the river. Cushing soon reported success, by raising the National flag over Fort Caswell and Smithville,[3] when preparations were made for taking up the torpedoes, and ascending the river in the lighter vessels, the heavier being excluded by the shallowness of the water. General Terry posted his troops at his intrenched line across the peninsula, two or three miles above Fort Fisher. But it was considered imprudent to attempt an advance until the army should be re-enforced, for Hoke was holding Fort Anderson, on the river, about half-way between Fort Fisher and Wilmington, and had cast up a line of intrenchments across the peninsula, from Sugar Loaf Battery, nearly opposite that fort, on the east bank of the Cape Fear, to the ocean, thus strongly confronting Terry. Behind these Hoke had about six thousand men. Fort Anderson was an extensive earth-work, with a large number of guns, which commanded the approaches by land and water. Immediately under cover of its guns was a large wharf; also various obstructions in the channel.

Re-enforcements were not long delayed. General Grant, as we have seen, had ordered General Schofield from Tennessee to the coast of North Carolina, with the Twenty-third Corps. Schofield received the command [a] while preparing to obey General Thomas's order to go into winter-quarters at Eastport, Mississippi.[4] He started the following day, in steamers, down the Tennessee River, and up the Ohio to

[a] January 14, 1865.

---

of Managers, of which Dr. F. W. Lewis was President, and William P. Cresson was Secretary, but its immediate management was intrusted to the care of Miss McHenry, a lady made well and widely known by her acts of benevolence and patriotism.

When the vessels above named arrived, the officers and crews of both were invited to dine at the Soldiers' Reading Room. They accepted the invitation. An elegantly arranged and sumptuous dinner was prepared, and a military band was in attendance. Charles J. Stillé welcomed the guests. After dinner, one of the seamen of the *Shenandoah* presented to the ladies two flags, one of which was shot from the mast-head of his ship during the bombardment of Fort Fisher. The eloquent Daniel Dougherty addressed the company. Altogether it was a memorable affair. *This was the only public entertainment given to the men of the navy during the war.*

[1] General Whiting said, "It was due to the supineness of the Confederate General that it [the attacking force] was not destroyed in the act of assault."—*Answer to Butler's 24th question.*

[2] See page 472.

[3] Lieutenant Cushing displayed blockade-runner signal-lights, and decoyed two of them under the guns of Fort Caswell, where they were captured. They were laden with arms and other supplies for the Conspirators.

[4] See page 429.

Cincinnati, with his whole corps, artillery and horses, leaving his wagons behind, and thence by railroad to Washington City[a] and Alexandria. There he was detained awhile by the frozen Potomac, [a January 23, 1865.] but finally went in steamers to the coast of North Carolina, where he landed near Fort Fisher, with Cox's (Third) division, on the 9th of February.

J. M. SCHOFIELD.

The remainder of the troops speedily followed (some going to New Berne), and swelled Terry's little army of eight thousand men to full twenty thousand. Terry was then also occupying Fort Caswell and Smithville, on the opposite side of the Cape Fear River. The Department of North Carolina had just been created, and Schofield was assigned to its command; so, on his arrival, he assumed the charge of all the troops in that Department.

The main object of the movement now to be undertaken was, as we have observed,[1] the occupation of Goldsboro', in aid of Sherman's march to that place. Grant had communicated[b] to that leader that Schofield had been ordered to the sea, where he would have under his command [b Jan. 21.] over thirty thousand troops. The grand object of all the movements now was the dispersion of Johnston's army gathering in North Carolina, and the capture of Lee's at Richmond and Petersburg. Grant went down to Fort Fisher with Schofield, and conferred with General Terry and Admiral Porter, and on his return to City Point he issued[c] instructions to Schofield to move on Goldsboro' either from Wilmington (if he should capture it), or from New Berne. "Sherman," he said, [c Jan. 31.] "may be looked for in the neighborhood of Goldsboro' any time from the 22d to the 28th of February."

Two days after Schofield's arrival at Fort Fisher with General J. D. Cox's division, Terry was pushed forward.[d] He drove the Confederate pickets, and established an intrenched line so close to Hoke's, [d Feb. 11.] that the latter was compelled to defend his in force. Then, by the aid of navy boats and pontoons, Terry attempted to turn Hoke's left flank, but was foiled by the high winds and waves of a storm. The turning of Hoke's right was then attempted, and crowned with success. For that purpose Schofield sent the divisions of Ames and Cox across the river to Smithville, where they were joined by Moore's brigade, of Couch's division, just debarked. Marching northward, they enveloped Fort Anderson.[e] At the same time the gun-boats opened a heavy fire on that work, the monitor *Montauk* lying close to the fort, and [e Feb. 18.] others enfilading it. Perceiving the peril, the garrison fled that night, taking with them six guns and many valuable things, and leaving behind

---

[1] See page 456.

ten heavy guns and much ammunition. On the following morning troops marched into the fort, and raised the National flag over it.

The garrison of Fort Anderson fled to intrenchments behind Old Town Creek, closely followed by General Cox, who crossed the little stream on a flat-boat, attacked[a] them on flank and rear, and routed them, with a loss to the defeated of three hundred and seventy-five men and two guns.

[a] Feb. 20, 1865.

The evacuation of Fort Anderson, and the defeat of the Confederates near Old Town Creek, caused the abandonment of all the defenses along the Cape Fear. Ames's division was sent to the east side to assist Terry, when Hoke, perceiving his peril, left his intrenchments and fell back toward Wilmington. The National troops pressed up both sides of the river, and the gun-boats, removing torpedoes, moved up the stream, silencing batteries on both banks. The most formidable of these were Fort Strong, on the east side, and Fort St. Philip, at the mouth of the Brunswick River.[1] These made very slight resistance, and on the morning of the 21st,[b] General Cox, who had crossed the Brunswick River to Eagle Island, opposite Wilmington, on Confederate pontoons, near the site of the railroad bridge which they had destroyed, was within rifle-shot of the wharves of the city. Terry, meanwhile, was pushing up in pursuit of Hoke, who, when Cox threw some shells into the town, ordered the destruction of all the steamers, and such military and naval stores as they could not carry away.[2] Among the vessels destroyed were the *Chickamagua* and *Tallahassee*, two of the Confederate pirate ships.[3] Having accomplished the work of destruction as nearly as their haste to depart would permit, the Confederates abandoned Wilmington, and on the following morning[c] Scofield's victorious troops marched in unopposed. That officer made his quarters at the house of P. K. Dickinson, and Terry made his at the dwelling of Mrs. Anderson, both on Front Street. So fell Wilmington, then, considering its relations to the commercial world by its operations in connection with blockade-running, the most important port in the control of the Confederates.[4]

[b] February.

[c] Feb. 22.

Schofield's next objective and final destination, in co-operation with Sherman, was Goldsboro',' on the railway, eighty-four miles north of Wilmington, toward which Hoke had fled. Having left his wagons in Tennessee, he lacked these and draft animals, and could not pursue Hoke directly. But he proceeded to put in motion five thousand troops at New Berne, whom General J. N. Palmer was directed to move on Kinston (a small town north of and near the Neuse River), as quickly as possible, to protect the work-

---

[1] Admiral Porter said that after the reduction of Fort Fisher, to the capture of Wilmington, the navy took possession of works bearing, in the aggregate, 83 guns.

[2] They burned about 1,000 bales of cotton, and 15,000 barrels of rosin. The Confederates had lost in the defense of Wilmington, after Schofield began his march upon it, about 1,000 men. Schofield's loss was about 200. He had captured 65 cannon and a large amount of ammunition.

[3] See page 433.

[4] The coast of North Carolina, and the peculiar character of the entrances to Cape Fear River, made intercourse with Wilmington, by means of blockade-runners, almost absolutely safe. When the wind blew off the coast, the blockading fleet was driven to sea. When it blew landward, it was compelled to haul off to a great distance to escape the dangers of a rocky coast, without a harbor within nearly a day's sail. The shoals were from five to twenty miles wide. The light-draft, swift-sailing, and fog-colored blockade-runners, could easily evade the watchers, especially in foul weather, for they could run close to the shore where the ships of war dared not approach.

men there repairing the railway between New Berne and Goldsboro,' and to establish a depot of supplies at Kinston. Ruger's division of the Twenty-third Corps was sent from Fort Fisher to re-enforce him. Palmer was not ready to advance so soon as desired, and General Cox was sent from Wilmington to take the command, leaving his own division in charge of Brigadier-General Reilly. He arrived at New Berne on the 6th of ⁱ March,[a] and immediately moved the troops, reaching Wise's Forks, a mile and a half below Southwest Creek, on the 8th, where he was joined by General Schofield the same day.[1] Meanwhile, Couch's division had arrived at Wilmington, and, with Cox's, was ordered to march across the country from that city to Kinston. Lack of transportation delayed their departure until the 6th,[b] when they proceeded parallel with the coast to avoid Holly Shelter Swamp, and then by way of Onslow and Richlands.

[a] 1865.

[b] March.

Behind Southwest Creek lay Hoke's division, with a small body of reserves, ready to dispute the passage of Schofield's troops. The march in that direction, through swamps made miry by recent rains, had been very fatiguing, but the troops were in good spirits; and when the Fifteenth Connecticut and Twenty-seventh Massachusetts were ordered forward, under Colonel Upham, to seize the crossing of the creek on the Dover road, they marched with alacrity. Hoke watched the movement keenly. He had just been re-enforced by a remnant of Hood's army, under Cheatham, and feeling strong, he sent a force, under cover of the tangled swamp, around Upham's flank, to fall upon his rear and surprise him. This was done, and the Nationals were routed, with a loss of seven hundred men made prisoners. Elated by this success, Hoke advanced a larger force, and attempted to wedge it in between, and separate, the divisions of Generals Palmer and Carter, respectively, holding the railway and the Dover road. The Nationals were pressed back, but the timely arrival of Ruger's division interfered with Hoke's operations. The result was a moderate battle, with slight loss—a conflict not much more severe than Savage's Twelfth New York Cavalry had engaged in on their march out from New Berne on the Trent road.

Schofield perceived that Hoke's force was fully equal to his own, and he ordered Cox to form an intrenched line, stand on the defensive, and wait for the arrival of Couch with his own and Cox's division, then moving on from Richlands.

Cox's line was heavily pressed by Hoke, and on the 10th,[c] being advised of the approach of Couch, and having been further re-enforced, he struck its left and center a severe blow, the chief weight of it falling upon Ruger's division. The assailed struck back with such force, that the Confederates were repulsed with severe loss. Schofield reported his own loss at three hundred men, and that of Hoke at fifteen hundred.

[c] March.

---

[1] Before leaving Wilmington, Schofield prepared a dispatch, in cipher, for Sherman, and placed it in the hands of Acting-Master H. W. Grinnell, on the 4th, to be carried to that commander. He left Wilmington in a dug-out, with Acting-Ensign H. B. Colby, Thomas Gillespie, seaman, and Joseph Williams, ship painter, all armed with Sharp's rifles, and revolvers, and carrying two days' rations. They went up the Cape Fear River about 12 miles, when, in consequence of meeting Confederate pickets, they abandoned their boat, and struck across the country for the Pedee River. After many stirring adventures, and experiencing the kindness and aid of the negroes in affording food and guidance, they reached Sherman's head-quarters at Fayetteville, North Carolina, on the 12th, at one o'clock in the afternoon.

The latter then retreated across the Neuse River, burning the railway bridge behind him. During that night Couch arrived, and Schofield pressed on to the Neuse; but, for lack of pontoons, he was delayed there until the 14th, when, having rebuilt the bridge, his whole force passed over without opposition, and entered Kinston. Sherman was then approaching that region, so the Confederates hastened to join General Johnston, who was concentrating his forces at Smithfield, on the road to Raleigh, to confront the conqueror coming up from Fayetteville. Schofield moved forward on the 20th,[a] and entered Goldsboro' on the evening of the next day, *a March, 1865.* with very little opposition. In the mean time, Terry had moved[b] *b March 15.* from Wilmington with a portion of the troops that had been left there, and pushing along the line of the railway northward, crossed the Neuse at Cox's Bridge on the 22d, and joined Schofield at Goldsboro'. And so it was that the co-operative movements with Sherman, on the coast, were promptly and successfully executed.

Let us now resume the consideration of Sherman's march through the Carolinas.

We left Sherman and his army at the smoldering capital of South Carolina, on the 18th of February,[1] and Charleston in possession of the National troops.[2] There was no unnecessary tarrying at Columbia, for Sherman had fixed the time for reaching Goldsboro'. He spent the 18th and 19th[c] in destroying the arsenal, machine shops, founderies, and *c February.* other structures at Columbia, devoted to the uses of the Confederates; also the railway tracks, one southeasterly as far as Kingsville and Wateree junction on the Wilmington road; and northward, in the direction of Charlotte, as far as Winnsboro'. Meanwhile, Kilpatrick, who had been out on quite an extensive raid, was working round toward the last point. He had first gone out toward Aiken, to make the Confederates believe that Augusta was Sherman's destination. Spencer's brigade had a severe skirmish[d] *d Feb. 8.* with some of Wheeler's cavalry, near Williston Station, and routed them. The track was torn up in that vicinity, and Atkins's brigade was sent to Aiken. Wheeler was there in force,[e] and drove him back, *e Feb. 11.* and marching out, charged Kilpatrick's entire command. Wheeler was repulsed with a loss of two hundred and fifty-one men. Kilpatrick then threatened Wheeler at Aiken until the night of the 12th, when he drew off, and, moving rapidly on the left of the Fourteenth Corps, struck the highway nine miles northwest of Lexington, when only about fifteen hundred of Wheeler's cavalry were between him and Columbia. But when Kilpatrick crossed the Saluda, on the day[f] when the main army reached Co- *f Feb. 17.* lumbia, he found Wheeler ahead of him. At that time the remnant of Hood's army, under Cheatham, was moving northeastward in that region, and for a day the Union cavalry marched parallel with it, a stream dividing the hostile columns. On the 18th, Kilpatrick struck the Greenville and Columbia railroad, and tore up the track to Alston, where he *f Feb. 19.* crossed[g] the Broad River, and pushed northerly almost to Chesterville. There he found that Wheeler had united with Hampton, and the combined forces were before him, on the road leading to Charlotte, in which

[1] See page 461.   [2] See page 464.

direction the troops of Beauregard and Cheatham had marched, not doubting Sherman's next objective to be Charlotte, judging from the course he had taken from Columbia.

In the mean time, Sherman's army had marched due north, in the direction of Charlotte, leaving behind it a most desolate track. Sherman had determined to make the war so felt as a dreadful calamity, that those who had begun it might be induced to abandon it speedily. He issued precise instructions for the conduct of the troops in their passage through South Carolina. "The army," he said, "will forage liberally on the country during the march;" and each brigade commander was directed to "organize a good and sufficient foraging party, under the command of one or more discreet officers," whose business it was to gather food for man and beast, "aiming at all times to keep in the wagon trains at least ten days' provisions for the command, and three days' forage." Soldiers were forbidden to enter private houses or commit trespasses, but were permitted to forage for food, in the vicinity of a camp, or at a halt. He gave the corps commanders power to "destroy mills, houses, cotton-gins," &c. Such destruction was not to be made in districts or neighborhoods where the army was not molested; but in those regions where guerrillas and bushwackers should infest the march, or the "inhabitants should burn bridges, or otherwise manifest local hostility, the corps commanders should order and enforce a devastation more or less relentless, according to the measure of such hostility." He permitted the cavalry to "appropriate, freely and without limit," horses, mules, wagons, &c., belonging to the inhabitants, "discriminating, however, between the rich, who are usually hostile, and the poor and industrious, usually neutral or friendly." Foragers were also permitted to exchange their jaded animals for fresh ones. They were also directed to "leave with each family a reasonable portion for their maintenance."

The simple execution of the orders for the army to live off the country, must have produced an almost absolute peeling of the inhabitants in the track of that host, which devoured every thing in its way over a path of more than forty miles in width. And so universal was the hostility of the inhabitants, incited by Wade Hampton and his fellow-traitors of South Carolina, that the restrictive conditions concerning devastation were nowhere applicable.[1] The feeling that South Carolina was the chief offender—the author of all the woes inflicted by the war, its politicians being the chief originators of treasonable designs, and the first to strike the intended deadly blow at the heart of the Republic—made many a soldier more relentless. The system of foraging allowed wide latitude, and afforded license for many outrages and cruelties on the part of unscrupulous soldiers, who always form a part of an army. Large numbers of these, called "bummers," went in

---

[1] Dr. J. F. G. Mittag, of Lancasterville, South Carolina, relates the following circumstance. When Sherman was approaching that place, it was expected that the cavalry, as usual, would burn the public buildings. Dr. Mittag's dwelling was close to the court-house, and would be consumed with it. How should he save it? He recollected that he had in his possession a number of letters from the late eminent Dr. John W. Francis, of New York City, in which that gentleman had expressed great kindness and respect for this South Carolina physician. These he determined to show to General Kilpatrick, as an evidence of his character as a man and physician. He did so. "After reading a part of a letter," says Dr. Mittag, in relating the circumstance, "Kilpatrick said twice to his aids, 'Tell them not to burn the court-house.'" And when he was about to leave the village, he issued an order to the same effect, and Lancasterville was saved from destruction. "I have no doubt," says the doctor, "that it was the letter of this great and good man that saved the village from conflagration."

advance of the columns, gathering up food according to instructions, and plundering for their private gain, in violation of instructions. Many of these were better marauders than fighters, and their conduct disgraced the army and the service. But the effect of Sherman's march through South Carolina was precisely what that leader desired and expected. War was made so terrible, that the offenders were glad to cry for mercy. A leading citizen of South Carolina said to the writer:—"Sherman's march was terrible, but it was merciful. It tended to a speedy ending of the war. We lost our *property*, but saved our *sons*. Had the war continued, we should have lost both."

Sherman moved his whole army from Columbia to Winnsboro', in the direction of Charlotte, and from that point, Slocum, who arrived there on the 21st of February with the Twentieth Corps, and the cavalry, caused the railway to be broken up as far as Blackstock's Station, well toward Chesterville. Then he turned suddenly eastward, toward Rocky Mount, on the Catawba, leaving to the left the Confederate forces which were concentrating for the purpose of disputing the expected march of the Nationals on Charlotte. The whole movement in that direction was a feint to deceive the foe, and was successful. The Confederate troops then in front of the Union army were the forces of Beauregard, and the cavalry of Hampton and Wheeler, which had fled from Columbia. Cheatham was near, earnestly striving to form a junction with Beauregard, at Charlotte.

Slocum crossed the Catawba on a pontoon bridge, at Rocky Mount, on the 23d, just as a heavy rain-storm set in, which flooded the country and swelled the streams. He pushed on to Hanging Rock,[a] over a region made memorable by the exploits of Sumter in the old war for Independence. There he waited for Davis's (Fourteenth) corps to come up, it having been detained at the Catawba, in consequence of the breaking of the pontoon bridge by the flood. When Davis arrived, the left wing was all put in motion for Cheraw, on the Great Pedee River. The right wing, meanwhile, had broken up the railway from Columbia to Winnsboro',[1] then turned eastward and crossed the Catawba at Peay's Ferry, before the storm began. It also pushed on to the Pedee at Cheraw. This wing passed a little north of Camden, and thus swept over the region made famous by the contests of Rawdon and Cornwallis, with Greene and Gates, eighty-five years before. It was a most fatiguing march for the whole army, for much of the country presented flooded swamps, especially in the region of Lynch's Creek, at which the left wing was detained. The right wing crossed it at Young's, Tiller's, and Kelly's bridges. On the 2d of March the leading division of the Twentieth Corps reached Chesterfield, skirmishing there with Butler's cavalry division; and at about noon the next day the Seventeenth Corps (Blair's) entered Cheraw, where it was expected Hardee, who was holding the post with his fugitives from Charleston, would make a stand. But he did not. He retreated across the Pedee, burning the railway bridge behind him, and fled to Fayetteville, leaving as spoils for his pursuers, twenty-five cannon, which he had brought from

[a] Feb. 26. 1865.

---

[1] Major Nichols says that at Winnsboro' they found many refugees from Nashville, Vicksburg, Atlanta, Savannah, Charleston, and, later, Columbia, who "never expected a Yankee army would come there." No place was secure.

Charleston, and considerable ammunition. Sherman caused the bridges and trestle-work of the road to be destroyed down as far as Darlington, and menaced Florence.

Sherman now pushed on toward Fayetteville, in North Carolina. The right wing of the army crossed the Pedee at Cheraw, and the left, with the cavalry, at Sneedsboro', on the State line. They marched in parallel lines, within easy supporting distance, Kilpatrick well on the left of all, and skirmishing some with Wade Hampton's cavalry, which was covering the rear of Hardee's retreating army, burning the bridges behind them. The weather was inclement, but the Nationals made good time, and on the 11th of March Sherman's whole force was concentrated at Fayetteville, from which Hardee had also retreated. There, on the following day, Sherman received the cipher dispatch from Schofield, at Wilmington, already mentioned.[1] On that morning the army-tug *Davidson*, commanded by the stalwart and fearless Captain Ainsworth, after much peril in ascending the Cape Fear River, arrived from Wilmington, with intelligence of what had occurred there and at the mouth of the stream. Just before reaching Fayetteville, Sherman had sent two of his best scouts to Wilmington, with intelligence of his position and plans. By Captain Ainsworth, who returned the same day, he sent dispatches to Terry and Schofield, informing them that he should move on Goldsboro' on the 15th, feigning Raleigh to deceive the foe.

Sherman had met with very little opposition in his march from the Catawba to the Cape Fear. The most serious encounter was by Kilpatrick with Hampton's cavalry. As the former was advancing on the extreme left, by way of Rockingham, he struck the rear of Hardee's column,[a] in its retreat on Fayetteville. Learning from prisoners that Hampton was behind, he resolved to intercept him. Posting a brigade, under Atkins, on the road he was traveling, he made a rapid night-march with Spencer's brigade, across to another road, and in doing so, passed through a division of Hampton's cavalry. It was a perilous feat. Kilpatrick lost his escort of sixteen men, but escaped with his staff. Hampton then moved stealthily around, and at daylight fell upon Spencer's brigade, and the house at which that officer and Kilpatrick had their quarters. It was a complete surprise. Spencer and most of Kilpatrick's staff were made prisoners, and they lost all their guns. The brigade was routed, and Kilpatrick barely escaped on foot to a swamp, where he rallied the men. Hampton's troopers, considering the rout complete, began to plunder the captured camp, when Kilpatrick and his rallied men fell upon and routed them, retaking head-quarters and guns, just as the foe was harnessing the horses to drag the latter away. The Confederates were driven in confusion. Hampton rallied them, and tried to recover what he had so suddenly won and lost, but his adversary kept him at bay until a brigade of infantry of the Twentieth Corps, under General Mitchell, came to his support. Then Hampton withdrew. He had inflicted a loss on the Unionists of one hundred and eighty-three men, of whom one hundred and three were made prisoners. Kilpatrick reached Fayetteville on the day[b] when the army was concentrated there.

^a March 8, 1865.

^b Feb. 11.

------

[1] See note i, page 493.

The National army rested three days at Fayetteville, during which time the United States Arsenal there,[1] with all the costly machinery which the Confederates brought to that place from Harper's Ferry, in the Spring of 1861,[2] was utterly destroyed by the First Michigan Engineers, under the direction of Colonel Poe.

Sherman was satisfied that, thereafter, on his march toward Goldsboro', he would have heavy and somewhat perilous work to do, for before him was now an army of about forty thousand veteran soldiers, under the able General Joseph E. Johnston. It was composed of the combined forces of Hardee, from Charleston; Beauregard, from Columbia; Cheatham, with Hood's men, and the garrison at Augusta; Hoke, with the forces which had been defending the seaboard of North Carolina, and the cavalry of Wheeler and Hampton. These, Sherman said, "made up an army superior to me in cavalry, and formidable enough in artillery and infantry to justify me in extreme caution in making the last step necessary to complete the march I had undertaken." He made disposition of his army accordingly, and on the 15th of March crossed the Cape Fear on pontoon bridges, and pressed forward.

In accordance with his usual plan of distracting the attention of his antagonist, General Sherman sent Slocum, with four divisions of the left wing, preceded by the cavalry, toward Averasboro', on the main road to Raleigh, feigning an advance upon the capital of the State, while the two remaining divisions of that wing, and the train, took the direct road to Goldsboro'. General Howard moved on roads to the right, holding four divisions light, ready to march to the assistance of the left wing, and sending his trains toward Faison's Station, on the Wilmington and Goldsboro' railway. Sherman was with Slocum, on the left. Incessant rains had made quagmires of the roads, and the army was compelled to corduroy them continually.

Near Taylor's Hole Creek, a little beyond Kyle's Landing, to which Slocum had advanced, Kilpatrick skirmished heavily with Hardee's rearguard, that evening, and captured some of them.[3] On the following morning,[a] Slocum advanced his infantry, and in the vicinity of Averasboro', near the road that ran eastwardly toward Bentonsville, he

[a] March 16, 1865.

found Hardee intrenched, with a force, of all arms, estimated at twenty thousand men, on a narrow, swampy neck of land between the Cape Fear and South rivers. Hardee's object was to hold Sherman there, while Johnston should concentrate his forces at Raleigh, Smithfield or Goldsboro'. It was necessary to dislodge him to prevent that consummation, and also to keep up the feint on Raleigh as long as possible, and hold possession of the road to Goldsboro', through Bentonsville. Slocum was, therefore, ordered to advance and carry the position.

The ground was so soft that horses sunk deep at every step, and men traveled over the pine-barren only with difficulty. But obstacles were not to be thought of. General Williams, with the Twentieth Corps, took the lead. Ward's division was deployed in the advance, and very soon his skirmishers developed Rhett's brigade of heavy artillery, armed as infantry, holding a slightly intrenched line across the road, on the brow of a hill, skirted by a

---

[1] See page 386, volume I.   [2] See page 390, volume I.
[3] Among the prisoners was Colonel Rhett, of the Charleston heavy artillery; a son of R. Barnwell Rhett, one of the most unworthy of the Conspirators of South Carolina. See page 96, volume I.

ravine and creek, with a battery that enfiladed an open field over which the Nationals must advance. To avoid the perils of a direct attack under such circumstances, Williams sent Case's brigade to turn the left of the Confederate line. This was promptly done, and, by a quick charge upon their flank, he broke that wing into fragments, and drove it back upon a second and stronger line, under fire of Winnegar's battery, directed by Major Reynolds.

Ward's division was now rapidly advanced upon the retreating force, and captured three guns and two hundred and seventeen men. The Confederates, in their haste, left one hundred and eight of their dead on the field. Jackson's division was quickly brought upon Ward's right, and two divisions of the Fourteenth (Davis's) Corps were placed on his left, well toward the Cape Fear, while Kilpatrick, acting in concert farther to the right, was directed to secure a footing on the road leading to Bentonsville. He reached it with one brigade, when he was furiously attacked by McLaws's division, and, after a hard fight, was pushed back. Then the whole of Slocum's line advanced, drove Hardee within his intrenchments, and there pressed him so heavily, that during the dark and stormy night that succeeded, he retreated to Smithfield (where Johnston was concentrating his forces), over the most wretched roads. So ended the conflict [a] known as THE BATTLE OF AVERASBORO', in which Slocum lost seventy-seven killed, and four hundred and seventy-seven wounded, but no prisoners. Hardee's loss was estimated at about the same. Ward, on the following morning,[b] pursued the fugitives through Averasboro',' but soon gave up the chase and rejoined the main army, which had now turned toward Goldsboro'.

[a] March 16, 1865.

[b] March 17.

General Sherman felt satisfied that he should have no more serious strife with the Confederates, on his march to Goldsboro'. "All signs," he said in his report, "induced me to believe that the enemy would make no further opposition to our progress, and would not attempt to strike us in flank, while in motion." In accordance with this impression he issued an order to the effect that further opposition being now past, corps commanders would march their troops in the easiest manner and by the nearest roads to Goldsboro'. That sense of security was almost fatal to Sherman's army, for at that moment, Johnston, who had come down from Smithfield in rapid but stealthy march, under cover of night, was hovering near in full force, ready to pounce upon his unsuspecting adversary at the earliest and most promising opportunity. He found the Union forces, under the assuring order of the commander-in-chief, in a favorable position for the execution of his designs. The Fourteenth (J. C. Davis's) Corps were encamped on the night of the 18th[c] on the Goldsboro' road, at the point where it was crossed by one from Clinton to Smithfield. Two divisions of the Twentieth (Williams's) Corps were camped ten or twelve miles in their rear, on the same road, near the Mingo Creek, in charge of Slocum's wagon train. The remaining two divisions of these two corps were on other roads some distance to the south. The Fifteenth (Logan's) and Seventeenth (Blair's) were scattered to the south and east.

[c] March.

Early on the morning of the 19th, Sherman was so assured of security, that he left Slocum's wing of the army, which was most exposed to the foe, and joined Howard's, farther to the right, which was scattered, and moving as rapidly as the wretched state of the roads would admit. When only six miles on his journey, to overtake Howard, he heard cannonading at the northwest, but was assured that it was only a slight encounter between Carlin's division and Dibbrell's cavalry, and that the former was easily driving the latter. It was true that Carlin and Dibbrell had met, but the matter soon assumed a most serious aspect. The divisions of Carlin and Morgan, of the Fourteenth Corps, had moved that morning *March 19, 1865.* at six o'clock, the former in advance. As usual, they soon encountered Confederate cavalry, but these made much stouter resistance than common. Each moment they revealed increased strength. Measures were taken to counteract it, and by ten o'clock the brigades of Hobart and Buell, of Carlin's division, were both deployed, and the former had made a vigorous assault on the Confederates and driven them back some distance. Meanwhile Buell's brigade, by order of General Slocum, had been sent around to the left to find the rear of the assailants.

By 12 o'clock the fighting had become stubborn; artillery was at work vigorously on both sides; and yet, up to this time, only cavalry and a battery of artillery, on the part of the assailants, had been developed. But an hour or two later, Morgan's division, deploying on Carlin's right, felt infantry in their front in the woods. By that time Buell, on the extreme left, had also struck infantry behind intrenchments. He outflanked them, but met with a most deplorable repulse. By this time the character and meaning of the severe pressure on Sherman's left was developed. A deserter, a "galvanized Yankee,"[1] had been brought to Generals Slocum and Davis, while they were in consultation, and in an excited manner he declared to them, what proved to be true, that the whole of Johnston's army, augmented by the commands of Hardee and Hoke, were in a fortified position immediately in front of the left wing, intending an immediate attack, and that Johnston had ridden along the column of his army, and assured them that victory over Sherman's entire force was now certain. It was a surprise.

It was now half-past two o'clock. Intelligence confirmatory of the deserter's declarations had come in from the right and left flanks of the Union forces engaged, and measures were immediately taken for the employment of all possible power to resist the expected overwhelming attack. A line of barricades was hastily thrown up. Orders had already been dispatched by Slocum to hurry up the two divisions of the Twentieth Corps, while Robinson's brigade, of that corps, which was much in advance of the rest of the troops, was put in to fill a gap between the divisions of Morgan and Carlin. Just then the Confederates dashed out of the woods, and fell with great fury mainly upon Carlin's division, already wearied and weakened by continual and severe fighting for hours. They were driven back at all points in much confusion. But Morgan's division on the right stood firm. The brigades of Mitchell and Vandevere were in line, and Fearing's was in reserve. It was now the crisis of battle. General Davis, who had thus far conducted his troops with great skill and coolness, seeing the mortal peril, and only one way to escape from it, extricated himself from the broken column of Carlin's

---

[1] Union prisoners of war were sometimes induced, by a hope of escaping the horrors of captivity, and perhaps, finally, an opportunity to desert, to go into the Confederate ranks. These were called by the Confederates, "galvanized Yankees."

division, rode rapidly to the right, faced Fearing's brigade to the left, and hurled them upon the flank of the Confederates, who were heavily pressing the broken center. The scene of conflict was in a densely wooded swamp, dark, and wet, and dismal. "Push right in the direction of that heaviest firing," shouted Davis to Fearing, as he gave him the order to move, "and attack whatever is in that swamp! Fight them for the best that is in your brigade! You'll stop that advance, sir, and we'll whip them yet!" The men caught up the words "we'll whip them yet," and dashed forward in an impetuous charge, under the immediate directions of Davis. That charge was a magnificent display of courage, discipline, and enthusiasm. The Confederates were staggered and paralyzed by this unexpected and stunning blow from a force hitherto unseen by them. They reeled and fell back in amazement, fearing they knew not what, and the attack was not renewed on that part of the field for more than an hour afterward. *The army was saved!* In that charge the gallant young General Fearing, the commander of the brigade, was disabled by a bullet, and hundreds of its dead and wounded strewed the field of conflict.

The check thus given to the Confederates was of infinite value to Sherman's army, for it gave an opportunity for re-forming the disordered left and center of Davis's line. It was drawn back and formed in open fields, half a mile in the rear of the old line. The artillery was massed on a commanding knoll, so as to sweep the whole space between the woods wherein the Confederates were stationed and the new line; and Kilpatrick massed his cavalry on the left. Meanwhile, the attack upon Morgan was terrible and unceasing. "Seldom have I heard such continuous and remorseless roar of musketry," said an actor in the scene.[1] "It seemed more than men could bear. Twice General Davis turned to me and said, 'If Morgan's troops can stand this, all is right; if not, the day is lost. There is no reserve—not a regiment to move—they must fight it out.' And fight it out they did. They were entirely surrounded. I, myself, trying to get to them from the rear, three times ran into heavy bodies of the enemy's troops. Two or three different times, after resisting attacks from the front, they were compelled to jump over their own works and fight to the rear. Soldiers in that command who have passed through their score of battles, will tell you they never saw any thing like the fighting at Bentonsville. In the midst of the hottest of it, at perhaps five o'clock, Coggswell's brigade of the Twentieth Corps, arrived to fill the gap between the new formation of Carlin's line and that of Morgan. They moved forward, and the roar of musketry resounded along that line as it did along Morgan's. They seized the position, and gallantly held it. Meanwhile, the enemy on the left moved to the attack several times, but the repulse they had already received seemed to have dispirited them, and the terrible havoc of our massed artillery drove them back almost before they reached the fire of the infantry, who were burning to avenge the morning's disaster." The National forces received, Sherman said, "six distinct assaults by the combined forces of Hoke, Hardee, and Cheatham, under the immediate command of General Johnston himself, without giving an inch of ground,

<hr />

[1] Brevet Brigadier-General (then Colonel) A. C. McClurg, in a letter to the author, dated "Chicago, February 18, 1868." See page 390.

and doing good execution on the enemy's ranks, especially with our artillery, the enemy having little or none."[1]

With the coming of darkness ended the conflict known as THE BATTLE OF BENTONSVILLE,[2] which, in brilliancy of personal achievements, and in lasting advantage to the cause of the Republic, must ever be ranked among the most memorable and important contests of the war. Indeed, it seems

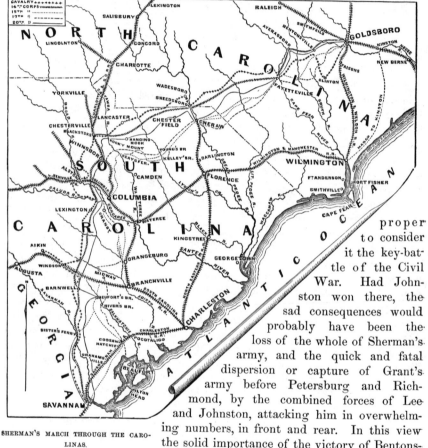

proper to consider it the key-battle of the Civil War. Had Johnston won there, the sad consequences would probably have been the loss of the whole of Sherman's army, and the quick and fatal dispersion or capture of Grant's army before Petersburg and Richmond, by the combined forces of Lee and Johnston, attacking him in overwhelming numbers, in front and rear. In this view the solid importance of the victory of Bentonsville can not be over-estimated. In that, his last battle, as in all others during the war, General Jefferson C. Davis exhibited in full relief those qualities which always distinguished him as a cool, discreet, and vigorous fighting commander.

SHERMAN'S MARCH THROUGH THE CAROLINAS.

[a] March 19-20.   During the night after the battle[a] Slocum's wagon-train and its guard of two divisions of the Twentieth Corps, also Hazen's

---

[1] General Sherman's Report, April 4, 1865.

[2] The aggregate loss of the National army near Bentonsville was reported by Sherman at 1,643, of which nearly 1,200 were from the divisions of Carlin and Morgan, of the Fourteenth Corps, which numbered between 10,000 and 12,000 men. The loss of the Confederates was never reported. It must have been heavy. The Nationals captured 1,625 of their men, and buried 267 of their dead. Johnston's force numbered between 30,000 and 40,000 men.

division, of the Fifteenth Corps, came up and made the position of the left wing almost impregnable. The right wing moving to the relief of the left, found its approach opposed by a considerable body of Confederate cavalry behind a barricade at the forks of the road near Bentonsville. Johnston's cavalry were soon dislodged, and Howard moved forward and joined his left to Slocum's right. The Confederates had thrown back their left flank, and had constructed a line of parapet connected with that in front of Slocum, in the form of a bastion, its salient on the main Goldsboro' road, interposing between Slocum on the west and Howard on the east, while the flanks rested on Mill Creek, covering the road back to Smithfield. By four o'clock in the afternoon,[a] after more or less skirmishing all day, the Nationals had a strong line of battle confronting this position, and putting Johnston on the defensive. The skirmish line pressed him steadily, and on the following day this pressure became so vigorous, that it almost amounted to a general engagement. There was skirmishing and hard fighting all day long.

[a] March 20, 1865.

Meanwhile, Schofield and Terry, as we have seen,[1] had been approaching Goldsboro', and at the very time[b] when Sherman was pressing Johnston at Bentonsville, the former entered that place, and Terry laid a pontoon bridge over the Neuse River, ten miles above, at Cox's Bridge. So the three armies were now in actual connection. Johnston, informed of this, perceived that all chance of success against Sherman had vanished; and that night, after having his only line of retreat seriously menaced by a flank movement by General Mower, covered by an attack along the Confederate front, he withdrew, and fled toward Smithfield in such haste that he left his pickets, many dead, and his wounded in hospitals, to fall into Sherman's hands. Pursuit was made at dawn,[c] but continued for only a short distance.

[b] March 21.

[c] March 22.

On the 23d of March all the armies, in the aggregate about sixty thousand strong, were disposed in camps around Goldsboro', there to rest and receive needed clothing. On the 25th, the railroad between Goldsboro' and New Berne was completed and in perfect order, by which a rapid channel of supply from the sea was opened. So ended, in complete triumph, and with small loss, Sherman's second great march through the interior of the enemy's country; and he was then in a desirable position of easy supply, to take an efficient part in the spring and summer campaign of 1865, if the war should continue. Considering it important to have a personal interview with the General-in-chief, Sherman placed Schofield temporarily in chief command of the army, and hastened by railway to Morehead City, and thence by water to head-quarters at City Point, where he arrived on the evening of the 27th of March. There he met Generals Grant, Meade, Ord, and other leading army commanders, and President Lincoln. He "learned," he said, "the general state of the military world," and then returned to New Berne in a navy steamer, and reached Goldsboro' on the night of the 30th.[d]

[d] March.

After his winter campaign in Southwestern Virginia, already noticed,[1] General Stoneman returned to Knoxville, and was ordered[e] to make a cavalry raid into South Carolina, in aid of Sherman's

[e] Feb. 7

movements. Before Stoneman was ready to move, Sherman had marched so far and so triumphantly that the aid of the former was not needed, and he was ordered to march eastward and destroy the Virginia and Tennessee railroad, as far toward Lynchburg as possible. He concentrated the cavalry brigades of Colonels Palmer, Miller, and Brown, of Gillem's division, about six thousand strong, at Mossy Creek, on the 20th of March. He moved eastward to Bull's Gap, where he divided his forces, sending Miller toward Bristol, to make a feint, and moving with the rest of his command to Jonesboro', when he crossed over Stone Mountain into North Carolina, to Boone. There, after a sharp skirmish,[a] he captured two hundred Home Guards. Thence he moved through mountain gaps to Wilkesboro', where the advance skirmished[b] and captured prisoners and stores. Continuing his march, he crossed the Yadkin River[c] at Jonesville, and, turning northward, went on to Cranberry Plain, in Carroll County, Virginia. From that point he sent Colonel Miller to Wytheville, to destroy the railway in that vicinity, and with the main force he moved eastward to Jacksonville, skirmishing with Confederates at the crossing of Big Red Island Creek. From Jacksonville, Major Wagner advanced on Salem, and sweeping along the railway eastward, destroyed it from New River Bridge to within four miles of Lynchburg. At the same time Stoneman, with the main body, advanced on Christiansburg, and, sending troops east and west, destroyed the railway for about ninety miles,[1] and then returned to Jacksonville.

[a March 28, 1865.]
[b March 29.]
[c April 2.]

Having performed his prescribed duty, General Stoneman turned his face southward, and, on the 9th of April, struck the North Carolina railroad between Danville and Greensboro'. At Germantown several hundred negroes, who had joined the column, were sent back into East Tennessee. At the same time Colonel Palmer was sent to destroy the railroad between Salisbury and Greensboro', and the factories at Salem, in North Carolina; while the main column moved on Salisbury, forcing the Yadkin at Huntsville,[d] and skirmishing near there. Palmer performed his duty well, and near Deep River Bridge, he captured a South Carolina regiment of four hundred men.

[d April 11.]

Salisbury was a prisoner-depot, and a considerable Confederate force was stationed there, under General W. M. Gardiner. They were about three thousand strong. They were found at Grant's Creek, ten miles east of Salisbury, early on the 12th,[e] with eighteen guns, under the direction of Pemberton, Grant's opponent at Vicksburg, now reduced from a lieutenant-general to a colonel. This force was gallantly charged by the brigades of General A. C. Gillem and Colonel Brown, of the Eleventh Michigan Cavalry, and instantly routed. Its guns were all captured, and over twelve hundred of its men were made prisoners. The spoils, besides the cannon, were three thousand small-arms, and a vast quantity of stores of every kind. Those of the Confederates who fled were chased several miles. In Salisbury were found a vast collection of ammunition, provision, clothing,

[e April.]

---

[1] Major E. C. Moderwell, of Palmer's brigade (from whom the author received a very interesting account of this raid), after describing the manner of destroying railroad tracks, similar to that mentioned in note 2, page 392, says, "A regiment of men could destroy from three to five miles an hour."

and medicine, with ten thousand small-arms, four cotton factories, and seven thousand bales of cotton. These were all destroyed, with the railway tracks in each direction from Salisbury. The Union prisoners had been removed. The prison-pens where they had suffered were destroyed.

On the 17th of April, Stoneman started, with a part of his command, for East Tennessee, taking with him the prisoners, captured artillery, and thousands of negroes. On the following day, General Palmer, whose command was at Lincolnton, sent Major E. C. Moderwell, with two hundred and fifty men of the Twelfth Ohio Cavalry, to destroy the bridge of the Charlotte and South Carolina railroad, over the Catawba River. At that time, Jefferson Davis, having fled from Richmond, was at Charlotte with a very considerable force; and the mounted men of Vaughn and Duke, who had come down from the borders of Virginia, were on the Catawba. On that account it was necessary to move with great

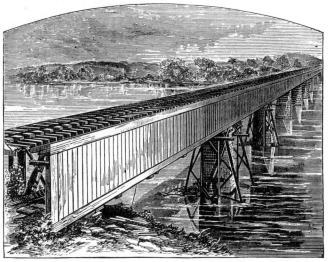

RAILWAY BRIDGE OVER THE CATAWBA RIVER.[1]

caution. At Dallas, Moderwell had a skirmish with these cavalry leaders, but evaded a battle with them; and at daybreak on the 19th,[a] the Union force arrived at the doomed bridge, where they cap-

[a] April, 1865.

tured the picket and surprised the guard. The bridge, delineated in the engraving, was a splendid structure, eleven hundred and fifty feet in length, and fifty feet above the water. Moderwell's men set it on fire at one end, and in thirty minutes it was completely destroyed. After skirmishing with Ferguson's Confederate cavalry (which came up on the north side of the bridge) for two hours, the raiders turned back, and, by marching all night, rejoined the brigade at Dallas, with three hundred and twenty-five prisoners, two hundred horses, and two pieces of artillery. This was one of the most gallant little exploits of the war.

During the raid just recorded, the National cavalry captured six thousand prisoners, twenty-five pieces of artillery taken in action, and twenty-one abandoned by the foe, and a large number of small-arms; and they destroyed an immense amount of public property.

---

[1] The writer is indebted to Major Moderwell for the above picture of the bridge.

CHAPTER XIX.

THE REPOSSESSION OF ALABAMA BY THE GOVERNMENT.

HE repossession of Alabama was an important part of General Grant's comprehensive plan of campaign for the winter and spring of 1865. The capture of the forts at the entrance to Mobile Bay[a] was a necessary preliminary movement. Had Farragut then known how weakly Mobile was defended, he and Granger might easily have captured it.[1] They closed the port, and its value to the Confederates as a commercial depot, or as a gate of communication with the outer world, was thereby effectually destroyed.

[a] Aug., 1864.

For several months after the harbor of Mobile was sealed, there was comparative quiet in that region. The grand movements in Georgia and in Middle Tennessee occupied the attention of all. At length, when Sherman had finished his triumphal march through Georgia, to the sea-board, and Thomas had decimated Hood's army in Middle Tennessee, Grant and the Government determined to take active measures for the repossession of Alabama, by a movement against Mobile, aided by other operations in the interior. The conduct of the expedition against Mobile was assigned to General E. R. S. Canby, then commanding the West Mississippi Army, with headquarters at New Orleans; and the co-operating movement was intrusted to General J. H. Wilson, the eminent cavalry leader, under the direction of General Thomas.

Mobile, at the beginning of 1865, was thoroughly fortified by three continuous lines of earth-works around the entire city. The first was constructed by Captain C. T. Lieurner, in 1862, at an average distance of three miles out from the business streets, and comprised fifteen redoubts. In 1863, after the fall of Vicksburg, when an attack upon Mobile was expected, General D. Leadbetter[2] constructed a second line of works, which passed through the suburbs of the city, comprising sixteen inclosed and strong redoubts. It was then estimated that a garrison of ten thousand effective men might, with these fortifications, defend Mobile against a besieging army of forty thousand men. In 1864, a third line of earth-works was constructed by Lieutenant-

---

[1] At that time there were no troops in or immediately about the city. The artillery, also, had been called away to oppose A. J. Smith's troops, then approaching from Memphis (see page 248), and then they were sent to West Point, in Georgia, for the support of General Hood, where they erected a strong work, commanding the railway and the Chattahochee River. But a large re-enforcement of Granger's command would have been necessary to have enabled the National forces to hold the post.

[2] See page 174, volume I., and page 38, volume II.

Colonel V. Sheliha, about half-way between the other two, and included nineteen heavy bastioned forts and eight redoubts, making, in all the fortifications around the city, fifty-eight forts and redoubts, with connecting breastworks. The parapets of the forts were from fifteen to twenty feet in thickness, and the ditches, through which the tide-water of the harbor flowed, were about twenty feet in depth and thirty in width. Besides these land defenses of Mobile, there were several well-armed batteries along the shore below the city, and in the harbor commanding the channels of approach to the town, besides several which

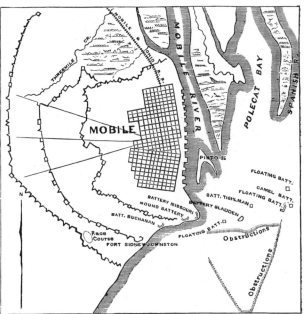

FORTIFICATIONS AROUND MOBILE.[1]

guarded the entrances to the rivers that flow into the head of Mobile Bay.[2] General J. E. Johnston said Mobile was the best fortified place in the Confederacy. It was garrisoned by about fifteen thousand men, including the troops on the east side of the bay, and a thousand negro laborers, subject to the command of the engineers. These were under the direct command of General D. H. Maury. General Dick Taylor was then in charge of the Department

REDOUBT AND DITCH AT MOBILE.[3]

---

[1] This shows the position of the defenses near the city, on land and in the harbor. The position of the more remote defenses, on the east side of the bay, are indicated on a subsequent page.

[2] Along the shore, below the city, were Batteries Missouri, Mound and Buchanan. Just below the latter, and terminating the middle line of fortifications, was Fort Sidney Johnston. In the harbor were two floating batteries and four stationary ones, named, respectively, Tighlman, Gladden, Canal, and McIntosh. The channels were obstructed by piles in many rows.

[3] This was the appearance of a portion of the inner line of works, in the suburbs of the city, near Dauphin Street, as it appeared when the writer sketched it in April, 1866. The picket fence indicates the line of Dauphin Street.

The movable forces under Canby's command, had been organized into brigades, called the "Reserve Corps of the Military Division of the West Mississippi," and numbered about ten thousand effective men. Early in January,[a] these were concentrated at Kenner, ten miles above New Orleans, and General F. Steele[1] was assigned to take command of them. A part of this force was soon afterward sent to Fort Barrancas, in Pensacola Bay, and the remainder followed directly. These, with the addition of seven regiments, and several light batteries, were organized as the Thirteenth Army Corps, comprising three divisions, and General Gordon Granger was assigned to its command. Meanwhile, the Sixteenth Army Corps (General A. J. Smith), which had assisted in driving Hood out of Tennessee, was ordered to join Canby. It was then cantoned at Eastport. Early in February, it went in transports, accompanied by Knipe's division of cavalry, five thousand strong, by the waters of the Tennessee, Ohio, and Mississippi rivers, to New Orleans, where it arrived on the 21st,[b] after a travel of over thirteen hundred miles in the space of eleven days. There the corps remained awhile, waiting for the perfection of the arrangements for the expedition under Wilson,[2] which was to sweep down from the north, through Alabama, simultaneously with Canby's attack on Mobile. The corps finally moved again, and arrived at Fort Gaines, on Dauphin Island, on the 7th of March, where a siege train was organized, consisting of seven batteries of the First Indiana Artillery, two of the Sixth Michigan, and one of Mack's Eighteenth New York. The cavalry marched overland from New Orleans. At the middle of March, every thing was in readiness for an attack on Mobile, with from twenty-five thousand to thirty thousand troops, composed of the Thirteenth and Sixteenth Corps, Knipe's cavalry division, and a brigade of cavalry, a division of infantry, and another of negro troops, under General Steele, at Barrancas. The West Gulf Squadron, commanded by Rear-Admiral Thatcher, was there, to co-operate.

Mobile was so strongly fortified, that a direct attack upon it on the western side of the bay, was deemed too hazardous, and involved a protracted siege; it was therefore determined to flank the post by a movement of the main army up the eastern shore, and in concert with the navy, seize the fortifications on the islands and main land at the head of the bay, and then approach Mobile by way of Tensas River, or one of the channels above the city. For this purpose, a point on Fish River, that empties into Bon Secour Bay, north of Mobile Point, was chosen as the place of rendezvous for the troops, and a base of operations, at a distance of not more than twenty miles from Spanish Fort, the heaviest of the fortifications to be attacked.[3] That movement was begun on the 17th,[c] when the Thirteenth Corps marched from Fort Morgan, on Mobile Point, and made its way slowly over a swampy region in heavy rains, consuming

[a] 1865.

[b] February.

[c] March.

---

[1] See page 252.

[2] The Twenty-ninth and Thirty-third Iowa, Fiftieth Indiana, Twenty-seventh, Twenty-eighth and Thirty-fifth Wisconsin, and Seventy-seventh Ohio.

[3] The old Spanish Fort, erected when the Spaniards had possession of Mobile, was a rectangular bastioned work on a bluff commanding Blakely River and its vicinity. The works known as Spanish Fort, erected by the Confederates, extended along the bluff nearly two miles, and included two other works, known, respectively, as Red Fort and Fort Alexis, or Dermett. These works were calculated for 36 guns, and a garrison of 2,500 men.

five or six days in the tedious and perilous journey. The Sixteenth Corps was already at the appointed rendezvous; having crossed the bay in transports from Fort Gaines to Danley's Ferry. Meanwhile, a feint on Mobile was made to attract attention while the main body was concentrating at Fish River. This was done by Moore's brigade of the Sixteenth Corps, which landed, with artillery, on Cedar Point, on the west side of the bay, under fire of the squadron. They drove away the Confederate occupants of the Point, and followed them to Fowle River, where the pursuers were ordered to cross the bay and rejoin the corps, which they did on the 23d.[a] The movement had created much uneasiness in Mo- *a March, 1865.* bile, for Moore's force was reported there to be from four thousand to six thousand strong.

While these movements were in progress on the borders of the bay, General Steele, with Hawkins's division of negro troops, and Lucas's cavalry, had been marching from Pensacola to Blakely, ten miles north of Mobile, destroying, on the way, the railroad at Pollard, and inducing the belief that Canby's real objective was Montgomery, and not Mobile. He encountered very little opposition, excepting from squads of Confederate cavalry. These fell back before him, until he reached Pringle's Creek, where he had a sharp fight[b] with about eight hundred Alabama cavalry, under General *b March 25.* Clanton. These were routed by a charge, with a loss of about two hundred of their number killed and wounded, and two hundred and seventy-five made prisoners. Among the latter was their leader. Steele found very little opposition after that until he reached the front of Blakely,[c] where he received supplies from General Canby, sent in seventy- *c April 1.* five wagons in charge of General J. C. Veatch.

On the 25th of March, the Thirteenth and Sixteenth Corps advanced from Fish River, on Mobile, up the east side of the bay, along the Belle Rose and Blakely roads, which were made perilous by torpedoes, that killed several men and horses. They met with skirmishers only, and on the next day were in the neighborhood of Spanish Fort, seven miles due east from Mobile. Canby perceived the necessity of reducing this work before passing on to Blakely; and, on the following morning,[d] before *d March 27.* ten o'clock, it was completely invested, on the land side. The divisions of Carr and McArthur, of the Sixteenth Corps, were, at first, on the right, the extreme of the former resting on Bayou Minette, and Benton's division of the Thirteenth Corps, was on the left, its extreme touching at Belle Rose. The remainder of the Sixteenth Corps seriously threatened Blakeley. Steele came up a few days afterward and joined that corps, and his troops then formed the extreme right in front of Blakely. Thatcher's squadron had moved up the bay parallel with the army, as far as the shallow water would allow, to assist in reducing the fort and cutting it off from communication with Mobile. Spanish Fort was garrisoned by nearly three thousand men of Hood's late army, under General R. L. Gibson.

It was soon found that Spanish Fort proper, with its near neighbors and dependents, Red Fort and Fort Alexis, were stout adversaries to contend with, and were ready and willing to give blow for blow. As the day advanced, collisions became warmer and warmer; and, before sunset, there

was a tremendous cannonade from besiegers and besieged, and the gun-boats of both parties, which was kept up all night, and afforded a magnifi-
_{• March 28, 1865.} cent spectacle for the citizens of Mobile. Then ^a a siege was for-mally begun. Canby had established his lines at distances of three hundred and four hundred yards from the fort, and at that short range, pounded it unmercifully. The siege continued a fortnight, during which time the greatest gallantry and fortitude were displayed on both sides.

Every day the Nationals mounted new pieces of heavy caliber, until, at length, no less than sixteen mortars, twenty heavy guns, and six field-pieces were brought to bear upon the fort. The gun-boat Cherokee got within range of the works at the beginning, and, at intervals throughout the siege, hurled a 100-pound shell into the fort. The squadron did good service, not only in shelling the works, but in driving the Confederate vessels so far to-ward the city, that their fire failed to reach the besiegers. The National vessels kept up a steady fire all day, and retired at night to anchorage at Great Point Clear. In these operations of the squadron, two of the gun-boats (*Milwaukee* and *Osage*) were destroyed by torpedoes.

When, on the 3d of April, the Nationals had built an earth-work and mounted large guns upon it within two hundred yards of the fort, the latter was completely and closely invested, and its doom was sealed. Yet the garrison fought bravely on, and the besiegers suffered greatly from the shells, for the lines were at short range from the fort. At length Canby determin-ed to make a grand assault by a concentric fire from all his heavy guns, his field-pieces, and the gun-boats, and, if necessary, by the troops. This was begun toward sunset on the 8th of April, and soon afterward, two companies of the Eighth Iowa, Colonel Bell, of Gedde's brigade of Carr's division, were sent as pickets and sharp-shooters, to gain a crest near the fort, intrench, and pick off the Confederate artillerists. This was done gallantly, in the face of a brisk fire, for General Gibson had doubled his line of sharp-shooters. They were Texans, brave and skillful, and stoutly disputed the advance of the Iowa men. But the latter pressed on, gained the prescribed point, but had to fight instead of digging. Bell saw this, and first sent one company to their aid. Then, seeing his brave men in great peril, he led the remainder of his regiment to their assistance. He found the place they were holding too hot to be comfortable. To retreat would be fatal; so he gallantly charged over their works, fought the Texans desperately, and finally, after a severe struggle in the dark, overpowered them. Then the victors swept along the rear, capturing men and portions of the works, until about three hundred yards of the intrenchments was in their possession, with three stands of colors and three hundred and fifty prisoners.

This gallant exploit determined Gibson to evacuate the fort, for it was evidently no longer tenable. Its fire, in response to the continued bombard-ment, became more and more feeble, and, before midnight, ceased altogether. Other troops pressed into the works, and by a little past two o'clock in the
_{• April 9.} morning,^b Bertram's brigade entered it without opposition, and was ordered to garrison it. So ended THE SIEGE OF SPANISH FORT. A greater portion of the garrison had escaped. About six hun-dred of them were made prisoners; and the spoils of victory were Spanish

Fort proper and its inclosing works, with thirty heavy guns and a large quantity of munitions of war. These guns were now turned upon Forts Huger and Tracy, at the mouth of the Appalachee or Blakely River, which held out gallantly until the night of • April, 1865. the 11th,[a] when the garrison spiked the twelve guns that armed the two forts, and fled.[1]

The key to Mobile was now in the hands of the Nationals.   Prisoners told the men of the navy where torpedoes were planted, when thirty-five of them were fished up, and the squadron moved in safety almost within shelling distance of the city. The army turned its face toward Blakely, on the east bank of the Appalachee, an insignificant village, at an important point in the operations against Mobile. Around this, on the arc of a circle, the Confederates had constructed a line of works, from a bluff on the river at the left, to high ground on the same stream at the right. These works comprised nine redoubts or lunettes, and were nearly three miles in extent. They were thoroughly built, and were armed with forty guns. The garrison consisted of the militia brigade of General Thomas, known as the Alabama reserves, and a brigade of veterans from Missouri and Mississippi, of Hood's army, under General Cockerell. The two brigades numbered about three thousand men, commanded by General St. John Lidell.

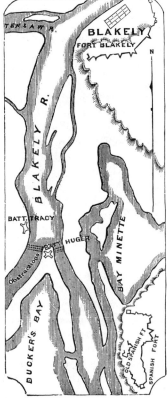

THE DEFENSES OF MOBILE ON THE EASTERN SHORE.

Ever since Steele's arrival from Pensacola, his troops, and particularly Hawkins's negro division, had held Fort Blakely, as the works there were called, in a state of siege ; and, for the first four days of the siege of Spanish Fort, it had been closely invested. It was now determined to carry it by assault, and then push on to Mobile. By the fall of Spanish Fort, the water communications of Blakely, with the city, had been cut off, and its reduction had been made sure. Yet it was capable of stout resistance. In front of its line of works was a deep and broad ditch ; also *abatis*, *chevaux-de-frise* and terra-torpedoes; and its forty cannon swept every avenue of approach. In front of these Canby formed a strong line of battle, with additional cannon brought up from before Spanish Fort. Hawkins's dusky

---

[1] The defense of Spanish Fort was skillfully and gallantly conducted, under General Gibson. From the beginning of the siege, the garrison had looked for assistance from General Forrest, then between Mobile and Montgomery, but Wilson was keeping him too thoroughly occupied in the interior to allow him to leave. The garrison displayed great courage and resolution. It made at least a dozen sorties during the siege. One of them, made on the 30th of March, was a brilliant success. At sunset the bombardment had ceased, when a party of the garrison, under Captain Watson, concealed by the smoke, rushed out over their works and captured Captain Stearns, of the Seventh Vermont, with twenty men, who were on the front skirmish line.

followers were on its right, the divisions of Generals J. C. Veatch and C. C. Andrews, of the Thirteenth Corps, formed the center, and Garrard's division of the Sixteenth Corps composed its left. Other divisions of the Sixteenth Corps were near, ready to afford aid to the battle-line, if necessary.

It was Sunday, the 9th of April. Half-past five o'clock in the afternoon was appointed as the time for the assault. At that hour dark clouds were rolling up from the west, and the low bellowing of distant thunder was heard. That "artillery of heaven" was soon made inaudible to the armies, by the roar of cannon. Hawkins's division first skirmished heavily toward the works, when Garrard sent one-third of his command,[1] under a heavy fire of the Seventeenth Ohio Battery, and in the face of a storm of shells, to discover the safest avenues for an attack in force. These gained a point within fifty yards of the works, and found that every way was equally perilous, and all extremely so. But the work must be done. So Garrard gave the magnetic word, "Forward!" when his whole division bounded toward the enemy with a loud shout, meeting the galling fire of a score of guns. For more than half an hour they struggled with the obstacles in front of the works, sometimes recoiling as the dreadful storm of shells and canister-shot became more dreadful, yet continually making headway, inspirited by the voice of Garrard, who was in the thickest of the fight. At length, the obstructions were cleared, and while Harris's brigade was passing the ditch and climbing the face of the works, those of Gilbert and Rinaker turned the right of the fort and entered it, capturing General Thomas and a thousand men. In an instant, a loud cheer arose, and several National flags were unfurled over the parapets.

While the struggle was going on upon the left, the whole line was participating in the assault. The center was feeling the storm from the works more seriously than the left. Dennison's brigade, of Veatch's division, and those of Spicely and Moore, of Andrews's division, were nobly braving the hail as they pushed onward in a charge, so soon as Garrard was fairly at work. Steadily they pressed forward, men falling at almost every step; and when Andrews's column was within forty yards of the works, it was terribly smitten by the fire of eight guns, that made lanes through its ranks. At the same time, the Eighty-third Ohio and Ninety-seventh Illinois, pushing forward as skirmishers, were just on the borders of a ditch, when more than a dozen torpedoes exploded under their feet, which threw them into confusion for a few minutes. This was followed by a tempest of grape and canister-shot, but the assault was pressed with vigor and steadiness, not only by the center, but by the right, where the brigades of Pile, Schofield, and Drew, of Hawkins's negro division, were at work, at twilight, fighting Mississippians, as their dusky brethren did at Overton's Hill, in the battle of Nashville.[2] At length, when ordered to carry the works at all hazards, their fearful cry of "Remember Fort Pillow!" ran from rank to rank, and they dashed forward over the Confederate embankments, scattering every thing before them. But these black men were more humane than Forrest and his fellow-butchers at Fort Pillow, for, unlike those ferocious men, they did not murder their captives.

---

[1] This division, composed of the brigades of General Gilbert and Colonels Rinaker and Harris. was the strongest in Canby's army.   [2] See page 426.

So ended, in triumph to the Nationals, THE BATTLE OF BLAKELY. By seven o'clock, or within the space of an hour and a half from the time the assault began, they had possession of all the works, with Generals Lidell, Cockerell, and Thomas, and other officers of high rank, and three thousand men, as prisoners of war. The spoils were nearly forty pieces of artillery, four thousand small-arms, sixteen battle-flags, and a vast quantity of ammunition. The Confederates lost, in killed and wounded, about five hundred men. The National loss was about one thousand.

The Nationals were now in undisputed possession of the whole eastern shore of the bay. The army and navy spent all the next day[a] in careful reconnoitering, preparing for an advance on Mobile. [a] April 10, 1865. Some of the gun-boats attempted to go up to Blakely, but were checked by a heavy fire from Forts Huger and Tracy. From these island batteries full two hundred shells were thrown at the navy during that and the next day, when, as we have seen, the garrisons of both spiked their guns, and fled in the shadows of night.[b] Meanwhile [b] April 11. the Thirteenth Army Corps had been taken across the bay, for an attack on Mobile, in connection with the gun-boats, which went from place to place, taking possession of abandoned batteries here and there. But the army found no enemy to fight. On the day after the fall of Blakely, Maury ordered the evacuation of Mobile; and on the 11th, after sinking the powerful rams *Huntsville* and *Tuscaloosa*,[1] he fled up the Alabama River, with nine thousand men, on gun-boats and transports. General Veatch took

BATTERY GLADDEN.

possession of Batteries Gladden and McIntosh, in the harbor, and Battery Missouri, below the city; and on the evening of the 12th, after a summons to surrender, made by General Granger and Rear-Admiral Thatcher, the authorities formally gave the place into their hands at Battery Missouri, below the town. On the following day Veatch's division entered the city, and the National flag was hoisted on the public buildings, thereby disgusting the rebellious inhabitants, who closed their stores, shut up their dwellings, and kept from the streets; and the publication of four of the newspapers was suspended. General Granger followed the army into the city, and General Canby and his staff entered soon afterward.[2] So Mobile was "repossessed" a little more

---

[1] It is a curious fact that a very large proportion of the most powerful iron-clad vessels constructed by the Confederates, were destroyed by their own hands. Only a few days after the evacuation of Mobile the Confederate ram *Webb*, from the Red River, freighted with cotton, rosin, and other merchandise, went down the Mississippi, passing New Orleans on the 20th of April, so unexpectedly that she received but two shots as she went by, from batteries there, the vessels of war being yet in Mobile Bay. The *Webb* was pursued by gun-boats from above, and was hurrying toward the Gulf, when she encountered the corvette *Richmond*, coming up the river. The commander of the ram, seeing no chance for escape, ran her ashore and blew her up. He and the crew took refuge in the swamps, but nearly all of them were captured.'

[2] A very full, faithful, and well-written account of the capture of Mobile and its dependencies, may be found in a volume of nearly three hundred pages, by General C. C. Andrews, one of the most active of the officers of the West. It is entitled, *History of the Campaign of Mobile, including the co-operative Operations of General Wilson's Cavalry, in Alabama.* It is illustrated by maps and delineations of scenes.

than four years after the politicians of Alabama raised the standard of revolt, and the foolish city authorities sought to blot out the memory of the old Union, by changing the names of its streets.[1] To accomplish that re-possession, in the manner here recorded, cost the Government two thousand men and much treasure. Four gun-boats (two iron-clad and two " tin-clad," as the lighter armored vessels were called) and five other vessels were de-stroyed by torpedoes. During that campaign, of about three weeks,[2] the army and navy captured about five thousand men, nearly four hundred cannon, and a vast amount of public property. The value of ammunition and commissary stores found in Mobile, alone, was estimated at $2,000,000. In that city Veatch found a thousand men, left behind, who became prison-ers, and upon the works for its immediate defense were one hundred and fifty cannon.[3]

Let us now consider the operations of General Wilson, in the field, while Canby was effecting the reduction of Mobile.

After the close of Thomas's active campaign in Middle Tennessee, the cavalry of the Military Division of the Mississippi, numbering about twenty-two thousand men and horses, were encamped on the north side of the Ten-nessee River, at Gravelly Springs and Waterloo, in Lauderdale County, Ala-bama. These had been thoroughly disciplined, when, in March,[*] they were prepared for an expedition into Alabama, having for its object co-operation with Canby in the reduction of Mobile, and the capture of important places, particularly Selma, on the Alabama River, where the Confederates had extensive iron founderies. The march of Cheat-ham toward the Carolinas, with a part of Hood's broken army, and the em-ployment of the remainder at Mobile, made nearly the whole of Thomas's force in Tennessee, disposable, and Wilson left Chickasaw Landing, on the Tennessee River, on the 22d of March, with about thirteen thousand men, composing the divisions of Long, Upton· and McCook.[4] He had six bat-teries. His men were all mounted excepting fifteen hundred, who were detailed as an escort to the supply and baggage trains of two hundred and fifty wagons. There was also a light pontoon train of thirty boats, carried by fifty six-mule wagons. Each man was well provided on the basis of a

* 1865.

---

[1] See page 175, volume I.

[2] During the siege of Spanish Fort and Blakely, General Lucas went out with all of his command excepting some Massachusetts mounted infantry, taking with him ten days' half-rations, and as much forage as the men could carry, for the purpose of occupying Claiborne, on the Alabama River, to prevent troops coming down to the relief of Mobile. He left on the 5th of April, and on the 7th he met a negro with dispatches from General Wilson to General Canby, carefully sewed up in the collar of his vest. Lucas furnished him with a guard and mule, and sent him on. From this courier he learned that a Confederate force was at Claiborne, and Lucas determined to capture it. On the way, the First Louisiana Cavalry encountered a mounted force at Mount Pleasant, charged and routed them, and in a pursuit of two miles, by Lucas in full force, he captured two battle-flags, three commissioned officers, and sixty men, with a loss of only five men. Pushing on to Claiborne, he went into camp there, and thither his scouts brought prisoners nearly every day On the 18th, when he received an order from Canby to return to Blakely, he had one hundred and fifty captives.

[3] Immediately after the surrender of the city, the navy was engaged in gathering up torpedoes in the channels, and blowing up and removing the obstructions in them. In this dangerous business three small vessels were destroyed by the explosion of torpedoes. On the 4th of May, Ebenezer Farrand, one of the traitors who placed the navy-yard near Pensacola in the hands of the Conspirators (see pages 168 and 169, volume I) in 1861, now in command of the few vessels belonging to the Confederates in the waters of Alabama, formally surrendered the whole, and the forces under his command, to Admiral Thatcher, at Sidney, on the terms which Grant had given to Lee a month before.

[4] Knipe's division, we have seen, went with the Sixteenth Army Corps to New Orleans. Hatch's division was left at Eastport.

sixty days' campaign, it being ordered that men and animals should subsist, as far as possible, on the country.[1]

To deceive the Confederates, and accommodate itself to the condition of the country, Wilson's command moved on diverging routes, the distances between the divisions expanding and contracting, according to circumstances. The general course was a little east of south, until they reached the waters of the Black Warrior River. Upton marched for Sanders's Ferry on the west fork of the Black Warrior, by way of Russellville and Mount Hope, to Jackson, in Walker County. Long went by devious ways to the same point, and McCook, taking the Tuscaloosa road as far as Eldridge, turned eastward to Jasper, from which point the whole force crossed the Black Warrior River. There, in the fertile region watered by the main affluents of the Tombigbee River, the columns simultaneously menaced Columbus, in Mississippi, and Tuscaloosa and Selma, in Alabama.

At that time General Forrest, in command of the Confederate cavalry, was on the Mobile and Ohio railway, west of Columbus, in Mississippi, and so rapid was Wilson's march through Alabama, that the watchful and expert enemy could not reach him until he was far down toward Selma. Forrest put his men in instant motion, to meet the danger. He sent Chalmers by way of Bridgeville toward Tuscaloosa. Hearing of this,[a] Wilson put his forces in rapid motion, with ample supplies, for Montevallo, beyond the Cahawba River. Arriving at Elyton,[b] he directed McCook to send Croxton's brigade to Tuscaloosa for the purpose of burning the public property and destroying founderies and factories there. The adventures of that brigade, which did not rejoin the main body until the expedition had ended, we shall consider presently. Upton's division was impelled forward. The small Confederate force found at Elyton, was driven across the Cahawba to Montevallo, as sharply pursued as felled trees, which the fugitives left behind them, would allow. Upton passed the Cahawba with his whole division, pushed on to Montevallo, and in that region destroyed the large Red Mountain, Central, Bibb, and Columbiana Iron-works, the Cahawba Rolling-mills, and five important collieries. These were all in operation, and were a serious loss to the Confederates.

> [a] March 27, 1865.

> [b] March 30.

Wilson arrived at Montevallo on the afternoon of the 31st of March. Upton was just ready to move forward. Just then the Confederates made their appearance on the Selma road, driving in Upton's pickets. These consisted of the commands of Roddy and Crossland. After a sharp fight with Alexander's brigade, they were routed by a charge of the Fifth Iowa Cavalry, and driven in confusion toward Randolph. They attempted to make a stand at Six-mile Creek, south of Montevallo, but were again routed with a loss of fifty men made prisoners. Upton bivouacked fourteen miles south of Montevallo that night, and early the next morning[c] rode into Randolph unmolested. There he captured a courier, whose

> [c] April 1.

---

[1] Each man was provided with five days' light rations in haversacks, 24 pounds of grain, 100 rounds of ammunition, and one pair of extra shoes for his horse. The pack animals were loaded with five days' rations of hard bread, and ten of sugar, coffee, and salt; and the wagons with 45 days' rations of coffee, 20 of sugar, 15 of salt, and 8 rounds of ammunition. Only enough hard bread was taken to last through the sterile regions of North Alabama. A greater portion of the men were furnished with the Spencer carbine.

dispatches informed him that Forrest was now on his front in heavy force; that one of that leader's divisions, under General Jackson, was moving easterly from Tuscaloosa, with all the wagons and artillery of the Confederate cavalry; and that General Croxton, on his way from Elyton, had struck Jackson's rear-guard at Trion, and interposed himself between it and Forrest's train. Informed, also, by the intercepted dispatch, that Jackson was about to fight Croxton, and from a subsequent dispatch from the latter to himself, that, instead of going on to Tuscaloosa, he should endeavor to fight Jackson and prevent his joining Forrest, Wilson ordered McCook to move rapidly, with La Grange's brigade, to Centreville, cross the Cahawba there, and push on by way of Scottsville to assist Croxton in breaking up Jackson's column. McCook found Jackson at Scottsville, well posted, with intrenchments covering his column. Croxton had not come up, and he could hear nothing of him. Feeling too weak to attack the Confederates, he skirmished with them a little, burned a factory at Scottsville, and then fell back. He destroyed ^a April 5, 1865, the bridge over the Cahawba, at Centreville, and rejoined ^a Wilson at Selma.

Wilson pushed southward from Randolph with the brigades of Long and Upton, and at Ebenezer Church, near Boyle's Creek, six miles north of Plantersville, he was confronted by Forrest who had five thousand men behind a strong barricade and *abatis*. Forrest was straining every nerve to reach and defend Selma, which was one of the most important places in the Confederacy, on account of its immense founderies of cannon and projectiles. Wilson advanced to the attack at once. Long's division, on the right, struck the first blow. Dismounting most of his men, he made a charge so heavy and irresistible, that it

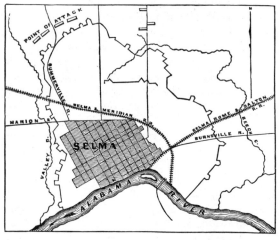

broke Forrest's line. Four mounted companies of the Seventeenth Indiana, under Lieutenant White, being ordered forward, dashed over the guns of the foe, into their midst, and cut their way out with a loss of seventeen men. General Alexander, then leading Upton's division, on hearing the sounds of battle, pressed forward, came up in fine order, dismounted and deployed his own brigade, and dashed into the fight with such vigor, that

SELMA AND ITS DEFENSES.

the Confederates were routed, and fled in confusion toward Selma, leaving behind them two guns and two hundred prisoners in the hands of Alexander, and ^a April 1, one gun as a trophy for Long. Winslow's brigade followed them as far as Plantersville, nineteen miles from Selma, where the chase ceased, and the victors bivouacked. Forrest had been driven on that day ^a twenty-four miles.

Selma was now the grand objective of pursued and pursuers. Because of its importance, it had been strongly fortified on its land side.[1] It lay upon a gently rolling plain, about one hundred feet above the Alabama River, and was flanked by two streams; one (Beech Creek) with high and precipitous banks, and the other (Valley Creek) an almost impassable mire. Toward this the troopers pressed on the morning of the 2d of April, Long's division leading in the pursuit of Forrest, Upton's following. At four o'clock in the afternoon, Wilson's whole force in pursuit, came in sight of Selma, and prepared for an immediate assault. Forrest was already there, and found himself in command of about seven thousand troops, a part of them Alabama militia, gathered for the occasion, composed of raw conscripts, mostly old men and boys. For the defense of Selma, the Confederates had, as Grant said on another occasion, "robbed the cradle and the grave." So inadequate was the force that Forrest was not disposed to attempt a defense, but General Taylor, the commander of the department, who was there, ordered him to hold it at all hazards. Then Taylor left in a train of cars going southward toward Cahawba, and was no more seen. Forrest resolved to do his best, and did so.

After a reconnoissance, Wilson directed Long to attack the Confederate works northwestward of the city, by a diagonal movement across the Summerville road, on which he was posted, while Upton, with three hundred picked men, should turn the right of the intrenchments eastward of the town. Before preparations for this movement could be made, Long was startled by information that Chalmers's Confederate cavalry, from Marion, was seriously threatening his rear-guard, in charge of his train and horses. He resolved to attack immediately. Sending six companies to re-enforce the train-guard, he charged the works furiously with about fifteen hundred of his men, dismounted.[2] In so doing he was compelled to cross an open space, six hundred yards, in the face of a murderous fire of artillery. It was bravely done; and in the course of fifteen minutes after the word "Forward!" was given, his troops had swept over the intrenchments, and driven their defenders in confusion toward the city. The fugitives at that point composed Armstrong's brigade, which was considered the best of Forrest's troops. They were sharply pursued, and at the beginning of the chase, Long was severely wounded, and Colonel Minty took temporary command. Wilson came up to the scene of action at that time, and made disposition for Upton to immediately participate in the work begun by the other division. At an inner but unfinished line, on the edge of the city, the pursued garrison made a stand. There, just at dark, they repulsed a charge of the Fourth United States Cavalry. This was quickly followed by the advance of Upton's division, and another charge by the Fourth Regulars, while the Chicago Board of Trade Battery was doing noble service in a duel with the cannon of the enemy, two of which it dismounted. The Confederates were dispersed. The elated victors swept on in an irresistible current, and Selma soon became a conquered city. Generals Forrest, Roddy, and Armstrong, with about one-

---

[1] The fortifications consisted of a bastioned line of an irregular semicircular form, and nearly three miles in extent. The portion on the western side of the city rested on Miry Valley Creek, and on the eastern side, on Beech Creek and a swamp, the respective ends touching the river. See plan on preceding page.

[2] The Seventeenth Indiana Mounted Infantry, the One Hundred and Twenty-third and Ninety-eighth Illinois Mounted Infantry, the Fourth Ohio Cavalry, and the Fourth Michigan Cavalry.

half of their followers, fled eastward on the Burnsville or river road, by the light of twenty-five thousand bales of blazing cotton, which they had set on fire. They were pursued until after midnight, and in that chase the Confederates lost four guns and many men made prisoners.[1]

General Winslow was assigned to the command of the city, with orders to destroy every thing that might benefit the Confederate cause. Selma soon presented the spectacle of a ghastly ruin. Ten thousand bales of cotton, not consumed, were fired and burnt; and all the founderies, arsenals, machine-shops, warehouses, and other property used by the Confederates, were destroyed; and some of the soldiery, breaking through all restraints, ravaged the town for awhile.

Wilson now prepared to move eastward into Georgia, by way of Montgomery. He directed Major Hubbard to construct a pontoon bridge over the Alabama River, at Selma, which had been made brimful by recent rains, and then he

RUINS OF CONFEDERATE FOUNDERY.[2]

hastened[a] to Cahawba, the ancient capital of Alabama,[3] a few miles down the stream, to meet General Forrest, under a flag of truce, by appointment, for the purpose of making arrangements for an exchange of prisoners. They met at the fine mansion of Mr. Mathews,[4] near the landing, in sight of a large cotton warehouse, on the high bank of the river, from which Wilson, on his march toward Selma, had liberated many Union captives, and which he had set on fire.[5] Forrest was indisposed to act fairly in the matter. He evidently expected to recapture the prisoners Wilson had taken at Selma, and was arrogant in manner and speech. The latter returned; but in consequence of the flood, which had three times swept away the pontoon bridge, 870 feet in length, which Hubbard had

[a] April 6, 1865.

---

[1] Wilson's loss in the capture of Selma was about 500 men. His gains were the important post, 32 guns (all field-pieces, except a 30-pounder Parrott), 2,700 prisoners, including 150 officers, several flags, and a large amount of stores of every kind.

[2] This was the appearance of a portion of the city of Selma, when the writer sketched it, in April, 1866. It was the site of the great Confederate iron-foundery there.

[3] This was the place where De Soto crossed the Alabama River, on his march toward the Mississippi River, which he discovered in the year 1541.

[4] This gentleman informed the writer that the two officers dined at his house; and after Forrest had eaten his food and drunk his wine, he plundered his plantation on leaving.

[5] See next page.

thrown across the river, Wilson's army did not make the passage of the stream until the 10th.ª McCook had rejoined him on the 5th, and now the whole army, excepting Croxton's brigade, on detached   ª April, 1865. service, moved upon Montgomery, where General Wirt Adams was in command. Adams did not

wait for Wilson's arri-
val; but, setting fire to
ninety thousand bales
of cotton in that city,
he fled. Wilson enter-
ed it, unopposed, on
the morning of the
12th, when Major Wes-
ton, marching rapidly
northward toward We-
tumpka, on the Coosa,
captured and destroy-
ed five heavily laden

UNION PRISON AT CAHAWBA.[1]

steamboats, which had fled up that stream for safety. Montgomery was formally surrendered to Wilson, by the city authorities, with five guns, and a large quantity of small-arms, which were destroyed. So it was that the original "Capital" of the Confederacy of Rebels was "repossessed" by the Government without hinderance, and the flag of the Republic was unfurled in triumph over the State House, where, on the 4th of March, 1861, the first Confederate flag was given to the breeze, when it was adopted as the ensign of the Confederacy by the "Provisional Government," at Montgomery.[2]

Wilson paused two days at Montgomery, and then pushed on eastward toward the Chattahoochee River, the boundary between Alabama and Georgia,—Columbus, in the latter State, ninety miles distant, being his chief objective. At Tuskegee, Colonel La Grange was detached and sent to West Point, at the crossing of the Chattahoochee River by the railway connecting Montgomery and Atlanta, while the main column passed on toward Columbus. That city was on the east side of the Chattahoochee, and when Wilson came in sight of it, in front of the Confederate works, on the evening of the 16th, he found one of the bridges on fire. Upton's division was at once arranged for an assault, and in the darkness of the evening a charge of three hundred of the Third Iowa Cavalry, supported by the Fourth Iowa and Tenth Missouri Cavalry, and covered by a heavy fire of grape, canister, and musketry, was made. They pushed through *abatis* that covered the works, and pressed back the Confederates. Two companies of the Tenth Missouri then seized another and perfect bridge, leading into Columbus, when Upton made another charge, sweeping every thing before him, and captured the city, twelve hundred men, fifty-two field guns in position, and large quantities of small-arms and stores. He lost only twenty-four men in achieving this conquest.[3] There Wilson destroyed the Confederate ram *Jackson*,

---

[1] Sketched from a steamboat, in April, 1866.   [3] See page 256, volume I.
[2] Among the killed was C. L. Lamar, of Howell Cobb's staff, formerly captain and owner of the *Wanderer*, a vessel engaged in the unlawful slave-trade, which was seized a few years before by a Government cruiser, but being taken into a southern port, evaded the penalties of the law.

which mounted six 7-inch guns, and burned one hundred and fifteen thousand bales of cotton, fifteen locomotives, and two hundred and fifty cars; also a large quantity of other property used by the enemy, such as an arsenal, manufactory of small-arms, four cotton factories, three paper-mills, military and naval founderies, a rolling-mill, machine-shops, one hundred thousand rounds of artillery ammunition, and a vast amount of stores. The Confederates burned the *Chattahoochee*, another of their iron-clad gun-boats, then lying twelve miles below Columbus.

In the mean time, La Grange had pushed on to West Point,[a] where he found a strong bastioned earth-work, mounting four guns, on a commanding hill, named Fort Tyler, in honor of its then commander, who built it, and had in it a garrison of two hundred and thirty-

[a April 16, 1865.]

five men, including officers. It was surrounded by a dry ditch, twelve feet wide and ten deep, and commanded the approaches to the bridge which crossed the Chattahoochee River, and the little village of West Point. This work La Grange assaulted on three sides, with his men dismounted, at a little past one

FORT TYLER.[1]

o'clock of the day of his arrival; but he was held in check, on the border of the ditch, by a galling fire of grape and musketry from the garrison. This was soon silenced by his sharp-shooters bringing their skill to bear upon the Confederate gunners, which kept them from duty while his men cast bridges across the ditch. Over these they rushed at the sound of the bugle, swarmed over the parapets, and captured the entire garrison, with the guns, and about five hundred small-arms. General Tyler and eighteen of his men were killed, and twenty-seven were wounded. At the same time the Fourth Indiana Cavalry dashed through the village, drove the Confederates from their works at the bridges, and took possession of those structures. After destroying nineteen locomotives and three hundred and forty-five loaded cars at West Point, La Grange crossed the river, burned the bridges behind him, and moved on[b] due east toward Macon, in Georgia. On the same day, Minty's (late Long's) division moved from Columbus for the same destination, and Upton's marched the next day. Minty, accompanied by Wilson, arrived at Macon on the 20th, when the Confederate forces there surrendered without resistance; and Wilson was informed by Howell Cobb, of the surrender of Lee to Grant, and the virtual ending of the war. Hostile operations were then suspended, in accordance with an arrangement between Sherman and Johnston, which we shall consider presently.

[b April 17.]

---

[1] This is from a sketch made by the author, from near the railway, in April, 1866. The fort was upon a hill overlooking the little village that rambled along the railway track.

La Grange rejoined the main column soon after its arrival at Macon, but Croxton's brigade was still absent, and Wilson felt some uneasiness concerning its safety. All apprehensions were ended by its arrival on the 31st,[a] after many adventures.   [a] April, 1865.

We left Croxton not far from Tuscaloosa, in Alabama, on the 2d of April, outnumbered by Jackson, of Forrest's command.[1] From that point he moved rapidly to Johnson's Ferry, on the Black Warrior, fourteen miles above Tuscaloosa, where he crossed that stream, and sweeping down its western bank, surprised and captured[b] the place he had been   [b] April 5. sent against from Elyton, together with three guns and about fifty prisoners. Then he destroyed the military school and other public property there, and leaving Tuscaloosa, burned the bridges over the Black Warrior, and pushed on southwesterly, to Eutaw, in Greene County. There he was told that Wirt Adams was after him, with two thousand cavalry. He was not strong enough to fight them, so he turned back nearly to Tuscaloosa, and pushing northeastward, captured Talladega. Near there he encountered and dispersed a small Confederate force. He kept on his course to Carrollton, in Georgia, destroying iron-works and factories in the region over which he raided, and then turned southeastward, and made his way to Macon. With his little force he had marched, skirmished, and destroyed, over a line six hundred and fifty miles in extent, in the space of thirty days, not once hearing of Wilson and the main body during that time. He found no powerful opposition in soldiery or citizens, anywhere, excepting at a place called Pleasant Ridge, when on his way toward Eutaw, where he had a sharp skirmish with some of Adams's men, then on their way to join Forrest. The attack was made by Adams, first upon the Sixth Kentucky Cavalry. The Second Michigan gave assistance, and finally bore the brunt of the attack, and repulsed the assailants with considerable loss to the Confederates.

Wilson's expedition through Alabama and into Georgia, was not only useful in keeping Forrest from assisting the defenders of Mobile, but was destructive to the Confederates, and advantageous to the Nationals in its actual performances. During that raid he captured five fortified cities, two hundred and eighty-eight pieces of artillery, twenty-three stand of colors, and six thousand eight hundred and twenty prisoners; and he destroyed a vast amount of property of every kind. He lost seven hundred and twenty-five men, of whom ninety-nine were killed.

The writer visited the theater of events described in this chapter in the spring of 1866. He arrived at Savannah from Hilton Head[2] the first week in April, and after visiting places of historic interest there, left that city on an evening train[c] for Augusta and farther west.   [c] April 5. Travel had not yet been resumed, to a great extent. The roads were in a rough condition, the cars were wretched in accommodations, and the passengers were few. The latter were chiefly Northern business men. We arrived at Augusta early in the morning, and after breakfast took seats in a very comfortable car for Atlanta. It was a warm, pleasant day, and the passengers were many. Among them the writer had the pleasure of

---

[1] See page 516.   [2] See page 483.

discovering two highly-esteemed friends,[1] traveling for the purpose of seeing the country; and he enjoyed their most agreeable companionship many days, until parting at New Orleans. We had just reached the beginning of the more picturesque hill-country of Georgia, which seemed to be peculiarly charming in the region of Crawfordsville, the home of Stephens, the "Vice-President" of the Confederacy, whose house we saw on an eminence to the right. As we approached Atlanta, we noticed many evidences of the devastating hand of Sherman, when he began his march to the sea, in the ruins of railway stations, twisted iron rails, and charred ties, along the roadside. Toward evening the grand dome of Stone Mountain, a heap of granite fifteen hundred feet in height, loomed up a mile or so north of us. From Decatur onward, the earth-works of both parties were seen in thickening lines, and at twilight we were in the midst of the ruined city of Atlanta, then showing some hopeful signs of resurrection from its ashes.

We passed a rainy day in Atlanta, the writer leaving the examination of the intrenchments and the battle-fields around it until a second visit,[2] which he intended to make a few weeks later, and on the morning of the 8th,[a] in chilling, cheerless air, we departed on a journey by railway, to Montgomery, on the Alabama River. We passed through the lines of heavy works in that direction, a great portion of the way to East Point, and from there onward, nearly every mile of the road was marked by the ravages of camping armies, or active and destructive raiders. The country between Fairborn and La Grange was a special sufferer by raids. In the vicinity of Newham the gallant Colonel James Brownlow was particularly active with his Tennessee troopers, and swam the Chattahoochee, near Moore's Bridge, when hard pressed. We crossed the Chattahoochee at West Point, where we dined, and had time to visit and sketch Fort Tyler, the scene of Colonel La Grange's achievements a year before.[3] That gallant Michigan officer was kindly spoken of by the inhabitants of West Point, who remembered his courtesy toward all non-combatants.

[a April, 1866.]

Between West Point and Montgomery we saw several fortifications, covering the passage of streams by the railway; and ruins of station-houses everywhere attested the work of raiders. At Chiett's Station, near a great bend of the Tallapoosa River, whose water flowed full thirty feet below us, we saw many solitary chimneys, monuments of Wilson's destructive marches. His sweep through that region was almost as desolating as were the marches of Sherman, but in a narrower track. But among all these scathings of the hand of man, the beneficent powers of Nature were at work, covering them from human view. Already rank vines were creeping over heaps of brick and stone, or climbing blackened chimneys; and all around were the white blossoms of the dogwood, the crimson blooms of the buckeye, the modest, blushing honeysuckle, and the delicate pink of the the red-bud and peach blossom.

It was eight o'clock in the evening before we arrived at Montgomery, and found lodgings at the Exchange Hotel, from whose balcony, the reader may remember, Jefferson Davis harangued the populace early in 1861, after

---

[1] Mr. and Mrs. I. B. Hart, of Troy, New York, who were then members of General Wool's family.
[2] See page 404.   [3] See page 521.

a speech at the railway station, in which he said, concerning himself and fellow-conspirators: — " We are determined to maintain our position, and *make all who oppose us smell Southern powder and feel Southern steel.*" [1] In the harangue from that balcony in the evening, with a negro slave standing each side of him, each holding a candle that the people might distinctly see his face, the arch-conspirator addressed them as " Brethren of the Confederate States of America," and assured them that all was well, and they had nothing to fear at home or abroad. [2]

On the following morning we visited the State capitol,[3] on the second bluff from the river,[4] that fronted a fine broad avenue extending to the water's edge.[5] There we were taken to the Senate Chamber, or " Legislative Hall " in which the Conspirators organized the hideous Confederacy that so long warred against the Government.[6] It remained unchanged in feature and furniture, excepting in the absence of the portraits mentioned on page 249, volume I., which our negro attendant, who had been seven years about the building, said the soldiers of Wilson's command carried away. " De Yankees," he said, " bust in and smash up ebery ting, when dey come, and tear 'um out and carry away a mighty heap. Dey terrible fellers !" But Adams had been more terrible, for he destroyed ninety thousand bales of cotton belonging to his friends, and nothing was left where they lay, but the broken walls of the warehouses along the brow of the river bluff.

From the cupola of that Capitol, we had a very extensive view of the country around, the winding Alabama River, and the city at our feet; and from the portico, where Jefferson Davis was inaugurated " Provisional President of the Confederate States of America," we could look over nearly the whole of the town. Montgomery must have been a very beautiful city, and desirable place of residence, before the war.

We spent a greater part of the day in visiting places of interest about Montgomery, and toward evening, we embarked in the steamer *John Briggs*, for Mobile. The passengers were few. Among them were three or four young women, who, at the beginning of the voyage, uttered many bitter words, in a high key, about the " Yankees " (as all inhabitants of the free-labor States were called), intended for our special hearing. Their ill-breeding was rebuked by kindness and courtesy, and we found them to be far from disagreeable fellow-travelers after an acquaintance of a few hours, which changed the estimate each had set upon the other. The voyage was, otherwise, a most delightful one, on that soft April evening, while the sun was shining. The Alabama is a very crooked stream, everywhere fringed with trees. Bluffs were frequent, with corresponding lowlands and swamps, opposite. It is a classic region to the student of American history, for its banks and its bosom, from Montgomery to Mobile, are clustered with the most stirring associations of the Creek War, in which General Jackson and his Tennesseeans, and Claiborne, Flournoy, and others, appear conspicuous, with Weatherford as the central figure in the group of Creek chieftains.

We were moored at Selma, on the right bank of the stream, at about

---

[1] See page 257, volume I.   [2] See page 257, volume I.   [3] See page 248, volume I.
[4] Montgomery stood upon a bluff on the river, which rises 50 or 60 feet from the water. A short distance back was another bluff, on which was the Capitol and the finer residences of the city.
[5] See page 340, volume I.   [6] See picture of this hall, on page 32, volume II.

midnight, at the foot of the bluff on which the town stands, and whchi
was then crowned with the ruins of the cotton warehouses and other buildings, fired by Forrest.[1] We spent a greater part of the next day there. It,
too, must have been a beautiful city in its best estate before the war. It
was growing rapidly, being the great coal and cotton depot of that region.
Its streets were broad, and many of them shaded ; and, in all parts of the
town, we noticed ever and full-flowing fountains of water, rising from arte-
sian wells, one of which forms the tail-piece of this chapter. It received its
title from Senator King of Alabama, the Vice-President elected with President Pierce. The name may be found in the poems of Ossian.

We left Selma toward evening, and at sunset our vessel was moored a

few minutes at Cahaw-
ba, to land a passenger
whose name has been
mentioned, as the en-
tertainer of Wilson and
Forrest.[2] Our voyage
to Mobile did not end
until the morning of
the third day, when
we had traveled, from
Montgomery, nearly
four hundred miles. In
that fine City of the
Gulf we spent sufficient
time to make brief vis-
its to places of most

RUINS AT THE LANDING PLACE, SELMA.

historic interest, within and around it. Its suburbs were very beautiful before
they were scarred by the implements of war ; but the hand of nature was rapidly covering up the foot-prints of the destroyer. Although it had been only
a year since the lines of fortifications were occupied by troops, the embankments were covered with verdure, and the fort or redoubt, delineated on
page 507, was white with the blossoms of the blackberry shrub, when the
writer sketched it.

It was at a little past noon, on a warm April day, when we left Mobile
for New Orleans, in the fine new steamer, *Frances.* We passed the various

batteries indicated on the map on page 507, as we
went out of the harbor into the open waters of the
bay. A little below Choctaw Point, and between it
and Battery Gladden,[3] lay a half-sunken iron-clad floating battery, with a cannon on its top. The voyage
down the bay was very delightful. We saw the

FLOATING BATTERY.

battered light-house at Fort Morgan,[4] in the far distance, to the left,
as we turned into Grant's Pass,[5] and took the inner passage. The
waters of the Gulf were smooth ; and at dawn the next morning, we were
moored at the railway wharf on the western side of Lake Pontchartrain.
We were at the St. Charles Hotel, in New Orleans, in time for an early break-

fast; and in that city, during his stay, the writer experienced the kindest courtesy and valuable assistance in the prosecution of his researches, from Generals Sheridan and Hartsuff.[1] Having accomplished the object of his errand in that great metropolis of the Gulf region, he reluctantly bade adieu to his traveling companions for ten days (Mr. and Mrs. Hart), and embarked on the Mississippi River for Port Hudson and Vicksburg, in the steamer *Indiana*. That voyage has already been considered.[2]

---

[1] Two works of art, then in New Orleans, were objects of special interest, when considering the inscriptions upon each, in their relation to the rebellion. One was the equestrian statue of Andrew Jackson, in Jackson Square, the principal place of public resort on fine days and evenings, where the citizens may enjoy the fresh air and perfumes of flowers. On the pedestal of that statue, in letters of almost imperishable granite, might have been read, while the friends of the Conspirators had possession of the city, and were trying to destroy the Republic, the memorable words of Jackson's toast at a gathering in Washington City, at the instance of Calhoun, to inaugurate a secession movement:—" THE UNION—IT MUST, AND SHALL BE PRESERVED." The other was a statue of Henry Clay, in the middle of Canal Street, on which, during all the period of the preparation of the slaveholders for actual rebellion, and whilst it was rampant in New Orleans, might have been read these words of that great statesman:—" IF I COULD BE INSTRUMENTAL IN ERADICATING THIS DEEP STAIN, SLAVERY, FROM THE CHARACTER OF MY COUNTRY, I WOULD NOT EXCHANGE THE PROUD SATISFACTION I SHOULD ENJOY, FOR THE HONOR OF ALL THE TRIUMPHS EVER DECREED TO THE MOST SUCCESSFUL CONQUEROR." While no living lips dared, for many months, to utter a word of reproof to those who, in New Orleans, were trying to destroy the Union and establish an empire founded upon slavery, these mute but terrible accusers, rebuked the criminals unmolested.

[2] See page 638, volume II.

CHAPTER XX.

PEACE CONFERENCE AT HAMPTON ROADS.—THE CAMPAIGN AGAINST RICHMOND.

T THE opening of the spring of 1865, the Rebellion was so shorn of its inherent strength and props that it was ready to fall. The last effort to win peace by other means than by conquering it, had been tried in vain. That effort was a notable one, as the outline here given will show.

We have seen how futile were the missions of Mr. Greeley to Niagara, and of Messrs. Jaques and Gillmore to Richmond, the previous summer, in the interest of peace.[1] A few months later, Francis P.

ROBERT OULD.

Blair, senior, a venerable politician of Maryland, who had given his support to the administration, and who was personally acquainted with the principal actors in the rebellion, then in Richmond, conceived the idea that he might bring about reconciliation and peace by means of his private influence. So he asked the President for a pass through Grant's lines, and on the 26th of December,[a]

 * 1864.

Mr. Lincoln handed him a card on which was written—" Allow the bearer, F. P. Blair, Sr., to pass our lines to go south, and return," and signed his name to it. " I was informed," said Mr. Lincoln, in response to a resolution of the House of Representatives,[b] "that Mr. Blair sought the card as a means of getting to Richmond, Virginia, but he was given no authority to speak or act for the Government, nor was I informed of any thing he would say or do, on his own account, or otherwise."

[b] February 8, 1865.

With this the self-constituted peace commissioner went to Richmond, where, for several days, he was the guest of Robert Ould, the Confederate Commissioner for the exchange of prisoners, and had several interviews with Davis. Finally, at the middle of January, he made his way back to Washington, with a letter written to himself by Jefferson Davis, in which the

---

[1] See page 446, and note 2, page 447.

Chief Conspirator expressed a willingness to appoint a commission "to renew the effort to enter into a conference with a view to secure peace to the
two countries." This letter Blair placed in Mr. Lincoln's hands. Ready to
show his willingness for peace on proper terms, the President wrote a note
to Blair, that might be shown to Davis, in which he said, "You may say to
him that I have constantly been, am now, and shall continue ready to receive any agent whom he or any other influential person, now resisting the
National authority may informally send me, with a view of securing peace
to the people of our common country." With this letter Blair returned to
Richmond, and his reappearance there excited high hopes of peace, for he
was regarded as a commissioner authorized by the Government. The expression "our common country," in Mr. Lincoln's letter, as opposed to
Davis's words, "the two countries," deprived the latter of all hope of a
negotiation on the terms of independence for the "Confederate States." But
he was compelled to yield to the popular desire for an end of the war, and
appointed commissioners to proceed to Washington to confer on the subject.
These were Alexander H. Stephens, John A. Campbell, and R. M. T. Hunter.
The latter was one of the most active members of the Confederate "Senate."
They were permitted to go on a steamer only as far as Hampton Roads,
without the privilege of landing, and there, on board of the vessel
that conveyed them, they held a conference of several hours [a] with   [a] Feb. 3,
the President and Secretary of State.[1]   1865.

Davis's commissioners were very cautious, yet, during the conference,
what they desired and what the Government expected, were clearly defined.
An amicable spirit prevailed, and question after question was deliberately
discussed and disposed of. What they seemed most to desire was a postponement of the settlement of the real question at issue, and upon which
the war was waged, namely, the separation of the "Confederate States" from
the Union. They desired to bring about a sort of armistice, by which an
immediate peace might be secured, and the trade and commerce of the different sections of the Union might be resumed. To this the President
firmly replied, that the Government would agree to no cessation or suspension of hostilities, except on the basis of disbandment of the insurgent forces,
and the recognition of the National authority throughout the Republic;
also, that the complete restoration of the National authority, everywhere,
was an indispensable condition of any assent, on the part of the Government,
to whatever form of peace might be proposed. He declared that he should
not recede from the position he had taken on the subject of slavery. The
commissioners were then informed that Congress had, three days   [b] January 31.
before,[b] adopted an amendment to the Constitution, which would

---

[1] The President first sent Mr. Seward, the Secretary of State, to meet the commissioners. He arrived at
Fortress Monroe on the night of the first of February. He was instructed to insist upon (1.) the restoration of the
National authority throughout the Republic; (2.) no receding on the part of the Executive from his position on
the subject of slavery; and (3.) no cessation of hostilities until the Confederates should lay down their arms
and disband. On this basis alone, he might hear what they had to say, and report to the President, but not
definitely consummate any thing. Meanwhile a note, sent to General Grant by the commissioners, requesting
permission for them to go to Washington, had reached the President, in which he found that they desired a
conference "without any personal compromise on any question in the letter" of the President to Mr. Blair, meaning his expression of "our common country." On account of this proviso, Mr. Lincoln was about to recall the
Secretary of State, when he was assured by an electrograph from Grant that the commissioners doubtless had a
real desire for peace. With a desire that something might be done that should lead to a cessation of hostilities,
he went immediately to Fortress Monroe, to join in the conference.

doubtless be ratified by the requisite number of States,[1] for the prohibition of slavery throughout the Republic.

The conference had no other result than that of the efforts made in July, which was to more clearly define the views of the Government and the Conspirators.[2] The commissioners returned to Richmond, when Davis laid[a] their report, submitted to him, before the "Congress."

*Feb. 5, 1865.

On the following day a great meeting was held in Richmond, which was addressed by Davis and the Governor of Virginia. The former said, in reference to Mr. Lincoln's expression "our common country": "Sooner than we should ever be united again, I would be willing to yield up every thing I have on earth, and, if it were possible, would sacrifice my life a thousand times before I would succumb." Then, with his usual pretense of confidence in final victory, he called upon the people to unite with those already in arms, "in repelling the foe, believing," he said, "that thereby we will compel the Yankees, in less than twelve months, to petition us for peace upon our own terms."[3] The meeting passed resolutions spurning with indignation the terms offered by the President, as "a gross insult" and "premeditated indignity" to the people of the "Confederate States." And at a great war-meeting held on thé 9th, at which R. M. T. Hunter presided, it was resolved they would never lay down their arms until their independence was won. They expressed a belief that their resources were sufficient for the purpose, and they invoked the people, "in the name of the holiest of all causes, to spare neither their blood nor their treasure in its support."

It has transpired that at that time, Davis and his fellow-Conspirators had strong hopes of the support of foreign armies.[4] But the speech of Benjamin

---

[1] See page 454.

[2] At that conference, it is related that Mr. Lincoln insisted that the States had never separated from the Union, and consequently he could not recognize another Government inside the one of which he alone was President, nor admit the separate independence of States that were a part of the Union. "That," he said to Mr. Hunter, who had urged him to treat with Davis as the head of a Government de facto, "would be doing what you so long asked Europe to do, in vain, and be resigning the only thing the armies of the Union are fighting for." Hunter made a long reply, insisting that the recognition of Davis's power to make a treaty was the first and indispensable step to peace, and cited, as a precedent, the correspondence of Charles the First with the Parliament—a constitutional ruler treating with rebels. "Mr. Lincoln's face," says the narrator (said to be Alexander H. Stephens), "then wore that indescribable expression which generally preceded his hardest hits, and he remarked: 'Upon questions of history I must refer you to Mr. Seward, for he is posted in such things, and I don't profess to be. But my only distinct recollection of the matter is, that Charles lost his head.' That settled Mr. Hunter for awhile." From the Augusta (Georgia) Chronicle, cited in Raymond's Life, Public Services, and State Papers of Abraham Lincoln, page 663.

[3] Davis appears to have spoken with much folly and arrogance. He denounced the President as "His Majesty, Abraham the First," and said that "before the campaign was over, he and Seward might find they had been speaking to their masters, when demanding unconditional submission."—A Rebel War Clerk's Diary, Feb. 7, 1865.

[4] Jones, in his Rebel War Clerk's Diary, under date of January 24th, 1865, in recording the presence of Blair, in Richmond, says:—"The Northern papers say he is authorized to offer an amnesty, including all persons, with the 'Union as it was—the Constitution as it is," my old motto in the Southern Monitor in 1857); but gradual emancipation. No doubt some of the people here would be glad to accept this; but the President will fight more, and desperately yet, still hoping for foreign assistance."

Henry S. Foote, a member of the Confederate Congress (once United States Senator), says:—"The fact was well known to me that Mr. Davis and his friends were confidently looking for foreign aid, and from several quarters. It was stated, in my hearing, by several special friends of the Confederate President, that one hundred thousand French soldiers were expected to arrive within the limits of the Confederate States, by way of Mexico; and it was more than rumored that a secret compact, wholly unauthorized by the Confederate Constitution, with certain Polish commissioners, who had lately been on a visit to Richmond, had been effected, by means of which Mr. Davis would soon be supplied with some twenty or thirty thousand additional troops, then refugees from Poland, and sojourning in several European States, which would be completely at the command of the President for any purpose whatever." He adds, in that connection, that he was satisfied that Mr. Davis would, in sending peace commissioners, "so manacle their hands by instructions as to render impossible all attempts at successful negotiation."—War of the Rebellion, &c., by Henry S. Foote.

THE UNION GENERALS.

George W. Childs Publisher 628 & 630 Chestnut St. Philadelphia.
J. M. Goffin St. Philad.

on that occasion was calculated to prevent the feeling of confidence which Davis and his friends tried to inspire. It produced indignation and alarm, and the press did not report it literally as it was spoken. He declared that the white fighting men of the Confederacy were exhausted, and that black men must recruit the army. He told the slaveholders, that they must either fight themselves, or let their slaves fight; and that Lee had told him that " negroes would answer," and that he must abandon Richmond if not soon re-enforced. " Let the negroes volunteer and be emancipated," said Benjamin, " it is the only way to save the slave-women and children."[1] These words, from a member of the " cabinet," produced great commotion. There was a general aversion to putting the slaves into the army, and it was not done. A bill was introduced in the Confederate "Congress," authorizing the enlistment of two hundred thousand slaves, with the consent of their owners. It passed the lower House, but was lost in the Senate, notwithstanding General Lee wrote[a] a public letter, advocating the measure, in which he admitted that the white people could not well meet the de-   [a] Feb. 18, 1865. mands of the army for more men. It was afterward passed.

The Peace conference in Hampton Roads did not affect the armies in the field. The National forces were quite sufficient for all practical purposes,[2] and Mr. Lincoln entered[b] upon the second term of his Presidency   [b] March 4. of the Republic with the most abundant hopes of a speedy return of peace. His address on the occasion of his second inauguration, commanded the most profound attention among thinking men, loyal and disloyal, throughout the entire Union. It was marked by the greatest solemnity and tenderness, and was imbued with the deepest religious spirit. Its chief burden was the emancipation of the slaves, and the triumph of justice and mercy;[3] and it closed with the following remarkable sentence: " With malice toward none, with charity for all, with firmness in the right as God gives us to see the right, let us strive to finish the work we are in, to

---

[1] See *A Rebel War Clerk's Diary*, ii., 415. Speaking of Benjamin, the Diarist says:—" No doubt he is for a desperate stroke for independence, being out of the pale of mercy; but his moral integrity is impugned by the representatives from Louisiana, who believe he has taken bribes for passports, &c., to the injury of the cause."

[2] In July, as we have observed, the President called for 500,000 men. This produced a goodly number of recruits, and none of the armies suffered for lack of re-enforcements, yet the requisition was largely filled by credits given for men already in the army or navy. In view of this, and with a determination to crush the rebellion in the spring campaign, if possible, the President issued another call, on the 19th of December, for 200,000 more.

[3] After speaking of slavery as the cause of the war, Mr. Lincoln remarked: "To strengthen, perpetuate and extend this interest, was the object for which the insurgents would rend the Union, even by war; while the Government claimed no right to do more than to restrict the territorial enlargement of it. Neither party expected for the war the magnitude nor the duration which it has already attained. Neither anticipated that the cause of the conflict might cease with, or even before, the conflict itself should cease. Each looked for an easier triumph, and a result less fundamental and astounding. Both read the same Bible, and pray to the same God, and each invokes his aid against the other. It may seem strange that any men should dare to ask a just God's assistance in wringing their bread from the sweat of other men's faces. But let us judge not, that we be not judged. The prayer of both could not be answered; that of neither has been answered fully. The Almighty has His own purposes. ' Woe unto the world because of offenses; for it must needs be that offenses come; but woe to that man by whom the offense cometh.' If we shall suppose that American slavery is one of those offenses which, in the providence of God, must needs come, but which, having continued through His appointed time, He now wills to remove, and that He gives to both North and South this terrible war as the woe due to them by whom the offense came, shall we discern therein any departure from those divine attributes which the believers in a loving God always ascribe to Him? Fondly do we hope, fervently do we pray, that this mighty scourge of war may speedily pass away. Yet if God wills that it continue until all the wealth piled by the bondman's two hundred and fifty years of unrequited toil shall be sunk, and until every drop of blood drawn with the lash shall be paid by another drawn with the sword, as was said three thousand years ago, so still it must be said. ' The judgments of the Lord are true and righteous altogether.' "

bind up the Nation's wounds, to care for him who shall have borne the battle and for his widow and his orphan, to do all which may achieve and cherish a just and lasting peace among ourselves and with all nations." [1]

Let us now return to a consideration of the operations of the armies of Grant and Lee, on the borders of the James and Appomattox' rivers. We have seen nearly all of the other armies of the Conspirators discomfited, and these, with those of Sherman and Johnston not far off, now demand our exclusive attention, for they, at the period we are considering, were about to decide the great question whether the Republic should live or die. Let us see in what manner that question was decided.

We left the armies of the Potomac and the James in winter quarters in front of Lee's army of Northern Virginia, with which he was defending the Confederate capital. The left of the Army of the Potomac was maintaining its firm grasp on the Weldon road ;[2] and the Army of the James on the north side of that river, and forming the right of the besiegers, had its pickets within a few miles of Richmond.[3] Sheridan was in good quarters at Kerns-town, near Winchester, full master of the Shenandoah Valley, from Harper's Ferry to Staunton, and bearing the honors of a major-general in the regular army.[4]

Grant held the besieging forces in comparative quiet during the winter of 1864–'65, their chief business being to keep Lee from moving, while Sherman, Thomas, and Canby were making their important conquests in accordance with the comprehensive plan of campaign of the General-in-chief. To this business those forces were specially directed, when the operations against Wilmington, and Sherman's approach to the coast and his march through the Carolinas, were going on, for it was well known that the Conspirators were contemplating a transfer of both the Confederate " Government" and Lee's army to the Cotton States, where that of Johnston and all the other forces might be concentrated. No doubt this would have been ordered by Davis before it was evidently too late, had not the politicians of Virginia clamored loudly against the abandonment of that State, and the almost certainty that the Army of Northern Virginia would not have been permitted to go.[5]

[a] 1865.   It was at about the close of March [a] before Grant was ready for a general movement against Lee. Meanwhile, there had been some events that broke the monotony of his army in winter quarters ; and Sheridan had been performing gallant and useful services north and west of Richmond. To prevent Lee from receiving any supplies by the Weldon road, Meade sent Warren, early in December, with his own (Fifth) corps, Mott's division of the Third Corps, and Gregg's mounted men, to destroy that

---

[1] On entering upon his second term, Mr. Lincoln retained the members of his cabinet then in office. There had been some changes. For the public good he had requested Montgomery Blair to resign the office of Post-master-General. He did so, and William Dennison, of Ohio, was put in his place. On the death of Chief-Justice Taney, a few months before, he had appointed Salmon P. Chase, the Secretary of the Treasury, to that exalted station, and Hugh McCulloch was placed at the head of the Treasury Department.

[2] See page 361.   [3] See page 362.   [4] See page 372.

[5] Alluding to this contemplated abandonment of Richmond, Mr. Jones, in his *Diary*, says, after mentioning the gayety with which Davis and his aids had ridden past his house: "No one who beheld them would have seen any thing to suppose that the capital itself was in almost immediate danger of falling into the hands of the enemy; much less that the President himself meditated its abandonment at an early day, and the concentration of all the armies in the Cotton States."

railway farther south than had yet been done. This service was promptly performed. Warren moved[a] with his whole command along the road, without much opposition, and destroyed it all the way to Meherrin River, driving the few Confederates in his path across that stream to a fortified position at Hicksford.

[a] Dec. 7, 1864.

A few weeks later, while a greater portion of the naval force on the James River was engaged in a second expedition against Fort Fisher,[1] the Confederates sent down from under the shelter of strong Fort Darling,[2] on

FORT DARLING.

Drewry's Bluff, a squadron of vessels,[3] for the purpose of breaking the obstructions at the lower end of Dutch Gap Canal, and destroying the pontoon bridges below, thereby separating the National troops on both sides of the river, precedent to an attack in overwhelming force on the wing on the north bank of the James. The squadron moved silently, under cover of darkness, but was observed and fired upon when passing Fort Brady. To this attack the vessels responded, and in so doing they dismounted a 100-pounder Par-

---

[1] See page 484.

[2] This fort, which has been frequently mentioned in this work, was one of the most substantially and skillfully built fortifications constructed by the Confederates, and with the obstructions in the river just below it and covered by it, it defied the entire naval force of the Nationals, on the James River, during the war. See page 402, volume II. It was situated, as we have observed, on a bluff rising nearly two hundred feet above the level of the river, at a curve, and commanded the stream to Chapin's Bluff, below. On the lower side of the bluff was a deep ravine, with almost inaccessible sides, which formed an admirable flank to the fort. The picture above given, is from a sketch made by the author in June, 1866, from the side of the ravine opposite the fort, in which is shown some of the river in the direction of Richmond. The fort was inclosed by a dry ditch, swept by rifle batteries, one of which is delineated in the engraving on the next page. Within the outworks of the fort was a neat chapel, a burial-ground, and quite a little village of cabins.

[3] The squadron consisted of the *Virginia* (the Flag-ship), *Fredericksburg*, and *Richmond*, all armored and carrying four guns each; the wooden steamers *Drewry*, *Nansemond* and *Hampton*, two guns each; the *Buford* one gun; and the steamer *Torpedo*, with three torpedo boats.

rott in the fort, and soon afterward passed out of reach of its guns. Then the *Fredericksburg* broke the obstructions at Dutch Gap, and passed through,

but the other two iron-clads, and the *Drewry*, in attempting to follow, grounded. The *Drewry* could not be floated, so she was abandoned, and at daybreak a shell from a National battery fired its magazine, and the vessel was blown to a wreck. A monitor hurled a 300-pound bolt upon the *Vir-*

RIFLE BATTERIES IN FORT DARLING.

ginia, and killed five of her crew; and so stout was the opposition that the Confederate squadron could not go farther down the river. A fire was kept up all day, and at night all of the assailants, excepting the ruined *Drewry*, fled up the river.

A little later, another movement was made on the extreme left of the besieging army, the object being the seizure of the South Side railroad and a development of the strength of Lee's right, by throwing a strong flanking column far beyond the right of the Confederate works along Hatcher's Run, in a manner to take them in reverse, and then, if possible, turn north and seize the coveted railway. To be prepared for whatever the movement might develop, the entire army in front of Petersburg received marching orders;[a] and on Sunday morning,[b] four days afterward, the flanking movement began. It was led by Warren, who marched with his own corps, the Second, under General Humphreys, and Gregg's cavalry, from the left of the line. The cavalry moved down the Jerusalem plank road at an early hour, and reached Reams's Station before sunrise. The Fifth Corps moved along the Halifax road at a little later hour, with Ayres's division in the advance, Griffin's following, and Crawford's in the rear. The Second and Third Divisions of the Second Corps (Mott's and Smyth's) were on the Vaughan road, with instructions to fall upon the right of the Confederate works on Hatcher's Run, while the Fifth should move around the flank and strike the rear of the enemy. The cavalry, meanwhile, had pushed on from Reams's Station toward Dinwiddie Court-House, and on Rowanty Creek encountered a portion of Wade Hampton's cavalry, dismounted and intrenched. After a spirited skirmish, the bridge over the creek, and the works, were carried, and twenty-two of the garrison were made prisoners. Some of the cavalry pressed on to the Court-House and scouted in various directions; and that night the whole cavalry force bivouacked on Rowanty Creek.

a Jan. 31, 1865.

b February 5.

While Gregg was making these movements, the Second and Fifth Corps were executing their part of the plan. The Confederates were not in very heavy force, and the Third Division of the Second Corps soon carried the works, and uncovered the ford of Hatcher's Run to the safe passage of the troops. In this achievement, the Ninety-ninth Pennsylvania, of De Trobriand's brigade, was most conspicuous. That brigade pressed forward, drove the Confederates rapidly to the woods, and took position and intrenched on a commanding hill. The Second Division, under General Smyth, had turned off to the right, toward Armstrong's Mill, and very soon found the Confederates in a strong position. Their pickets were driven in after a sharp fight, when Smyth formed a line that connected the left of his division with the right of the Third, commanded by General Mott. Temporary earth-works were thrown up, and these, at two o'clock in the afternoon, were assailed. Under fire of artillery the Confederates pressed through the tangled swamp, and furiously assaulted the rifle-pits covering Smyth's right. They were repulsed with considerable loss. Twice afterward they attempted to turn his flanks and were repulsed, and at twilight they gave up the attempt. Smyth lost about three hundred men, and his antagonist a few more.

During that night the Fifth Corps was brought into connection with the Second, on the left of the latter. Gregg's cavalry had been recalled, and now covered the Fifth; and the Sixth and Ninth Corps were disposed so as to assist the Second and Fifth, if necessary. Toward noon[a] Crawford was sent toward Dabney's Mills, in order to reach the Boydton plank road, when he met a division of Confederates under General Pegram. After a sharp fight, about two miles from the Vaughan road, the latter were pushed back, but the advance of Crawford was checked by the division of Evans, who came to Pegram's assistance. Ayres was now sent to Crawford's assistance; and a brigade of Griffin's division was ordered to the support of Gregg, on the left, who had been heavily assailed by Confederate cavalry, which had been sent around to strike his flanks and rear. Gregg was, finally, toward evening, pressed back to Hatcher's Run. Ayres was struck on the flank soon after Gregg was assailed, and also driven back; and then a severe blow fell upon Crawford, which also made him recoil, with heavy loss. Eagerly following up these successes, the Confederates attacked Humphrey's corps, but were repulsed in much disorder. Behind the intrenchments on the Vaughan road and Hatcher's Run, thrown up the previous day, the Nationals were rallied, and stood firm. In the course of the conflict, General Pegram had been killed, and about one thousand of the Confederates were slain or wounded. The National loss was nearly two thousand men. Their gain was the permanent extension of their line to Hatcher's Run. There was some skirmishing the next day,[b] but no serious attempt was afterward made to recover the lost ground. The City Point railroad, which had been extended as fast as the left seized new ground, was now built to Hatcher's Run. All was quiet now, for some time, excepting along the Petersburg lines, where there were occasional artillery duels.

Grant considered it of the utmost importance, before a general movement of the armies operating against Richmond, that all communications with that city, north of the James River, should be cut off. At the middle of February circumstances favored an effort to that end. Lee had drawn the greater portion of the forces from the Shenandoah Valley[1] for service

[a] February 6, 1865.

[b] February 7.

---

[1] The few Confederates in Northern Virginia, under Rosser, Moseby, and others, had been quite active during the winter. The former, with a mounted force, went over the mountains into Western Virginia, and at Beverly surprised a guard of horses and stores, 700 strong, and captured 400 of the men and all the property, on the 11th of January. On the 21st of February a squad of Confederate cavalry, under Lieutenant McNeil, dashed into Cumberland. between midnight and dawn, and with the assistance of disloyal residents, seized Generals Kelley and Crook, in their beds, placed them on horses, and carried them off to Richmond.

at Richmond, or with Johnston, below the Roanoke. Knowing this, and desiring to move upon Lee in force, as quickly as possible, Grant instructed Sheridan[a] to make a grand cavalry raid upon his adversary's communications generally, and specially to seize Lynchburg, if possible; and he gave him liberty, if it should seem advisable, to move southward, to the assistance of Sherman, whose cavalry was weak in numbers.[1]

[a] Feb. 20 1865.

Sheridan left Winchester on the 27th of February, on a damp and cheerless morning, with about ten thousand men, composed of the First Cavalry Division, under General W. Merritt, and the Third Cavalry Division, under General George A. Custer. To the latter division was added a brigade of the cavalry of the old Army of West Virginia, under Colonel Capeheart. Sheridan's men were all mounted. They moved rapidly up the Shenandoah Valley, passing the little villages along the quiet pike without halting, their destination being Charlottesville, by way of Staunton and the Rockfish Gap of the Blue Ridge. At Mount Crawford, on the Middle Fork of the Shenandoah River, they met Rosser, with four hundred men, disposed to dispute their passage of the stream. Colonel Capeheart dashed upon him, drove him across the river, and secured the bridge, which Rosser tried to burn behind him.

The whole column now moved on to Staunton, and thence marched for Rockfish Gap, Custer in the advance. At Waynesboro' he found Early, behind strong intrenchments, with twenty-five hundred men, ready to support his boastful declaration, that he would never permit Sheridan to pass through Rockfish Gap. Custer fell upon him[b] vigorously, and before the rest of the command had come up, he had routed Early, and almost annihilated the effectiveness of his force. He captured sixteen hundred of the twenty-five hundred of Early's troops, with eleven guns, seventeen battle-flags, and two hundred loaded wagons. Custer lost less than a dozen men. This finished Early as a military leader in the Rebellion. His troops not captured, attempted to escape over the Blue Ridge, by the railway. They were pursued about eleven miles. It was estimated that at least a million dollars' worth of Confederate property was destroyed at Waynesboro', and between it and the eastern side of Rockfish Gap.

[b] March 2.

Sheridan pushed across the Blue Ridge, in a drenching rain, during the night after the defeat of Early, and entered Charlottesville at two o'clock in the afternoon of the next day, when the authorities surrendered that place to him. There he remained two days, waiting for his ammunition and pontoon trains to come over the mountains. That time was employed by his troops in destroying bridges, factories, depots, and the railway in the direction of Lynchburg, for about eight miles.

---

[1] Sheridan had sent out two raids since he sent Early "whirling up the Valley" from Fisher's Hill. One, under General W. Merritt, started from Winchester on the 28th of November, 1864, passed through Ashby's Gap, by Middleburg, to Fairfax Court-House, Centreville, and other points in Loudon Valley, and returned on the 3d of December by way of Grove Creek, Snicker's Gap, and Berryville. Another left Winchester under General A. T. A. Torbert, on the 19th of December, 1864, and went by way of Stony Point to Front Royal, and through Chester Gap, by Sperryville and Madison Court-House, to Gordonsville, which they reached on the 23d. Thence, on their return, they went by Culpeper Court-House, to Warrenton. There the column divided, a part going by Salem, and the other by White Plains and Middleburg, to Paris, and thence to Winchester, where they arrived on the 28th.

Satisfied that Lynchburg was too strong for him, Sheridan now divided his command, and pushed for the James River. One column, under General Devin, pressed rapidly to it at Scottsville, in Albemarle County, and the other by way of Lovingston, to the same stream at New Market, in Nelson county. The right column then proceeded along the canal to Duguidsville, hoping to cross the James there, over a bridge, but the vigilant Confederates had burned it ; also one at Hardwicksville. The rains had made the river so full that Sheridan's pontoons could not span it, and he was compelled to choose whether to return to Winchester, or to pass behind Lee's army to White House, and thence to the Army of the James, on Grant's right. He chose the latter course, and proceeding eastward, destroyed the James River canal, then the chief channel of supplies for Richmond, to Columbia, and making a general destruction of bridges over all that region.

"Everybody is bewildered by our movements," Sheridan said in a dispatch from Columbia.ᵃ He might have added, had he known the fact, that he had produced the greatest consternation in Richmond. The "Government" prepared to fly. The families of officials "packed" for a journey. Lee hastened up to Richmond, from his lines ᵃ March 10, 1865.

at Petersburg, and held earnest consultations with Davis and his "cabinet;" and his family, living in a pleasant house on Franklin Street, not far from the Capitol, made preparations, it was said, for an early departure. Boxes were sent to the "Departments" for packing up the archives, and directions were given to do the business as secretly as possible, so as "not to alarm the people."[1] The "Congress" were very nervous, and wanted to adjourn and fly, but Davis persuaded them that the public necessity required them to remain as long as possible.

LEE'S RESIDENCE.

Sheridan halted in Columbia only a day, during which a brigade destroyed the canal as far as Goochland, in the direction of Richmond. Then the whole command dashed off in a northeasterly direction, for the Virginia Central railroad, which they struck at Tolersville, and destroyed it from there to Beaver Dam Station, a distance of fifteen miles. Then Custer, in one direction, and Devin in another, made complete destruction of the railways and bridges, as well as supplies, in the rear of Lee's army, inflicting a more fatal blow upon the Confederate cause than any victories on the sea-board, or in the interior, during the last campaign. Having done the work thoroughly, which he was appointed to do, he swept around by the Pamun-

[1] Jones, in noting this fact in his *Diary*, under date of March 7, says: " A large per cent. of the population would benold the exodus with pleasure!" On the day before, he wrote : " Four days hence we have a day of fasting, &c., appointed by the President ; and I understand there are but *three* days' rations for the army—a nice calculation." On the night after Sheridan's arrival at Columbia, the " Government" was so frightened by a rumor that that bold rider was at the outer fortifications of the capital, that " Secretary Mallory and Postmaster-General Reagan," Jones recorded. " were in the saddle ; and rumor says," he added, " that the President, and the remainder of his Cabinet, had their horses saddled in readiness for flight."

key River and White House, and joined the besieging army on the 26th of March. He had swept out of existence the Confederate power northward of Richmond. He had disabled full two hundred miles of railway, destroyed a vast number of bridges, and great quantities of stores, and inflicted a loss of several million dollars. His campaign was most potential in demoralizing the Confederate soldiers, and disheartening the people.

Sheridan's raid; the successful march of Sherman, through the Carolinas; the augmentation of the Union forces on the sea-board by the transfer thither of a part of Thomas's army from Tennessee, and the operations in Alabama, satisfied Lee that he could no longer hope. to maintain his position, unless, by some means, his army might be vastly increased, and new and ample resources for its supply opened. For these means of salvation he could not indulge a hope. He had strongly recommended the emancipation and enlistment of the negroes, expressing a belief that they would make good soldiers; but the selfishness and the fear of the slaveholders opposed him. The wretched management of the Commissary Department, under Northrup, who was unlawfully kept at the head of it by Davis, because he was a willing instrument in his hands for every cruel work that was to be done, had not only caused immense numbers of desertions from the army,[1] because of inadequate and unwholesome subsistence, but the villainous way in which, by imprisonment and otherwise, the producers were robbed by the agents of that man, had caused wide-spread discontent and bitter feeling.[2] The effect was a great decrease in production, for the producer was not certain that the fruits of his labor would not be taken from him without reward. Viewing the situation calmly, Lee saw no hope for the preservation of his army from starvation and capture, nor for the existence of the Confederacy, except in his breaking through Grant's lines and forming a junction with Johnston, in North Carolina. He knew that the attempt to do so, would be perilous, but the least of two evils. He chose it, and prepared for a retreat from the Appomattox to the Roanoke.

On the 24th of March, Grant issued instructions to Meade, Ord, and Sheridan,[3] for a general movement on the 29th. Lee had been, for several days, evidently preparing for some important movement, and, on the day after Grant issued his instructions, his army made a bold stroke for existence in an attempt to break the National line at the strong point of Fort Steadman, situated in front of the Ninth Corps of the Army of the Potomac, and forming a salient not more than one hundred yards distant from the Confederate intrenchments. It was toward the extreme right of Grant's army,

---

[1] It was officially reported at about the first of March, 1865, that the number of deserters from the Confederate armies was about 100,000. The author of *The Campaigns of the Army of the Potomac* (Mr. Swinton), says, on the authority of General Johnston, that "two main armies of the Confederacy showed four men on their rolls to one in their ranks."

[2] Henry S. Foote, a member of the Confederate Congress, in his book on the Rebellion, speaks of Northrup as "servile and fawning to his Executive Chief," and of the "heartless tyranny practiced by this monster of iniquity in all the States of the South, in connection with the system of forcible impressment of produce, established," as having never been equaled. "His brutal indifference to the sufferings of the Confederate soldiery," Foote said, was notorious, yet Davis retained him in office for four years, against remonstrances. and direct charges of delinquency, and "proceedings of both Houses of Congress;" and he "never deigned to present his name to the Senate for the sanction of that body, up to the latest moment of his own official existence."

[3] These were commanders of three distinct and independent armies,—the Potomac, under Meade—the James, under Ord (who had succeeded Butler after the failure to capture Fort Fisher), and the cavalry, under Sheridan; but all acted as a unit under the general command of Grant.

south of the Appomattox. If that fort should be carried, and possession obtained of the high ground in its rear, the National army would thereby be cut in two, and Lee would have control of the military railway from City Point to Hatcher's Run. This would doubtless open a gate through which the Confederate army might pass, and, by forced marches, escape across the Roanoke, join Johnston, and crush Sherman by a single overwhelming blow. The risk was great, but the value of the advantage sought justified the attempt.

Lee assigned to the duty of assaulting Fort Steadman, the two divisions of Gordon's command, with a larger portion of Bushrod Johnson's in support. He massed behind them all of his disposable force, to the number of twenty thousand men, ready, in the event of a successful assault, to pounce through the open door. They were well supplied with ammunition and provisions for a long struggle.

At four o'clock on the morning of the 25th,[a] Gordon advanced to the assault. Fort Steadman was garrisoned by the Fourteenth New York Artillery. They had no suspicion of danger near. The Confederates advanced cautiously, but rapidly, over the narrow space between the works, and seized about half a mile of the picket line. Then two brigades (Crook's and Ransom's) dashed forward, and before the garrison were fairly awake to danger, they were pouring over the parapets into the fort. It was a complete surprise, and the assailants met no resistance. A

[a] March, 1865.

INTERIOR OF FORT STEADMAN.[1]

part of the garrison fled, and the remainder were made prisoners. The Third Brigade of the First Division of the Ninth Corps, met a similar fate. The guns, abandoned without a struggle, were immediately turned upon redoubts near, known as batteries Nine, Ten, and Eleven, and the connecting line of intrenchments, compelling their instant evacuation. That was the moment when Lee's army might have passed through and crowned the hill in the rear with their guns and men. It did not, and the golden moment was lost forever. The troops were not ordered forward, or failed to promptly respond.

The victors attempted to extend their conquest. On the left of Fort Steadman was a large work called Fort Haskell, commanded by Major Woermer. This they assailed, but were repulsed, when the guns of Fort Steadman poured a rapid storm of shot and shell upon it. Woermer responded

---

[1] This was the appearance of a portion of the interior of Fort Steadman, when the writer sketched it, about a month after the attack. It shows the form of the quarters and the bomb-proofs proper. Both the former and the latter were made of timbers, and covered with from four to six feet of earth. The fort was in a grove of fine large trees.

in kind, and the assailants were held at bay. Other Confederate columns, pressing through the gap at Fort Steadman, were subjected to a murderous fire of artillery; and to this was soon added the presence of General Hartranft's division of the Ninth Corps, which came upon them in a counter assault. The Confederates were too few to withstand the attack, while the ground between them and their own lines was so swept by an enfilading fire of the National artillery, that it would be almost sure death to those who should attempt to make the passage. The consequence was, that about nineteen hundred men surrendered rather than to attempt it.[1] Others, who tried to reach their lines, were cut down in great numbers. Fort Steadman and the other works were recovered, and more, for General Meade, satisfied that Lee must have weakened his whole line, for this movement, ordered an advance along the front of the Second and Sixth Corps, to the left of Fort Steadman. The result was, that the strongly intrenched picket line of the Confederates was seized and permanently held by the Nationals.[2] The failure at Fort Steadman, and the losses, greatly disheartened Lee and his troops. It was evident that there was hardly the shadow of a hope for escape.[3]

Grant's instructions for a general advance on the 29th, prescribed a movement of nearly the whole army, by its left, for the purpose of turning Lee's right with overwhelming force, and compelling him to evacuate Petersburg; also, to insure the success of the cavalry of Sheridan in efforts to reach and destroy the South Side and Danville railroads, now Lee's only avenues of supply. The right of Lee's intrenched line, which ran southwestward from Petersburg, crossed Hatcher's Run at the Boydton plank road,[4] and thence extended westward parallel with the run, and along the White Oak road. This line covered Lee's communications by the South Side railway, directly. About four miles west of the termination of this line, was a detached one, also stretching along the White Oak road, and covering a strategic point at the junction of several highways from the north and south with the White Oak road, which formed what was called the Five Forks. It was against these intrenchments, and the men who held them, that the grand turning column was to march, and did march, on the morning of the 29th.[a] Three divisions of the Army of the James, under Ord, had already[b] been withdrawn from the northern side of the river, and transferred to the left of the lines before Petersburg, leaving the remainder of Ord's command in charge of General Weitzel. The troops thus transferred, consisted of two divisions of the Twenty-fourth Corps, under General Gibbon; one division of the Twenty-fifth, led by General Birney, and a small division of cavalry, under General McKenzie. They took position on the left of the National intrenched line, lately occupied by the Second and Fifth Corps. The Ninth Corps, under General Parke, and the force under General Weitzel, were left to hold the

[a] March, 1865.

[b] March 27.

---

[1] The Confederates lost, in this operation, besides the men captured, about 800 killed and wounded. The National loss was a little over 900, of whom only 68 were killed, 337 wounded, and 506 missing.

[2] In this operation, the Nationals lost a little more than 1,100 men, of whom only 52 were killed. The Confederates lost 834 prisoners, and a number in killed and wounded fully equal to that of the Nationals.

[3] At the time of this attempt of Lee to break through the National line, General Meade was on a temporary visit to City Point. President Lincoln was there also, and he and General Grant saw a part of the engagement. Two days afterward, as we have observed, General Sherman came up from North Carolina by water, and held a conference at Grant's head-quarters, with the President and leading army officers.

[4] See map on page 354.

extended line of the National intrenchments, full thirty-five miles in length. Wide discretion was given to these commanders concerning attacks on the Confederate lines during the grand movement by the left. "I would have it particularly enjoined upon corps commanders," the General-in-chief said, "that in case of an attack from the enemy, those not attacked are not to wait for orders from the commanding officers of the army to which they may belong, but that they will move promptly, and notify the commander of their action." All dismounted men were ordered to report to General Benham, at City Point, who was left in charge of the immense depository of supplies at that place.

Sheridan crossed the Appomattox from Bermuda Hundred, passed to the rear of the army before Petersburg, and early on the morning of the 29th,[a] marched down the Jerusalem plank road,[1] and turning westward, pushed on by way of Reams's Station, to Dinwiddie Court-House, where, at five o'clock in the afternoon, he halted for the night.

[a] March, 1865.

Meanwhile, the corps of Warren and Humphreys (Fifth and Second) had moved at a very early hour. The former started at three o'clock in the morning,[b] and marching well to the left, crossed Rowanty Creek (which is formed by the junction of Hatcher's Run and Gravelly Creek), and soon turning to the right, marched northward along the Quaker road. Humphreys passed Hatcher's Run by the Vaughan road, four miles above Warren's crossing-place, and also turning northward, followed the line of that stream. On nearly parallel roads the two corps moved against the flank of the Confederate intrenchments, over a very tedious way, with great toil, in consequence of heavy rain. Very little opposition was experienced until Warren, when within two miles of the Confederate works, encountered a line of battle. A sharp contest ensued, the brunt of which fell upon Chamberlain's brigade of Gibbon's division, which was in front. The Confederates were repulsed, with a loss of many killed and wounded, and one hundred made prisoners. Warren lost three hundred and seventy men. He bivouacked that night in front of the Confederate works covering the White Oak road, after drawing fire from them. Humphreys had a more difficult march, but meeting skirmishers only; and he had not reached the works when night compelled him to halt. Dinwiddie Court-House, where Sheridan was resting, was only six miles distant from Warren and Humphreys. The Union line was practically unbroken from that point to the Appomattox.

[b] March 29.

It had been arranged for Sheridan to cut loose from the rest of the army on the morning of the 30th, for the purpose of making the contemplated raid on the South Side and Danville railways; but Grant changed his plan. He said in substance, in a note to Sheridan, "I want to end the matter, if it is possible to do so, before going back. Leave the railways at present; push around the enemy in the morning and get to his rear, and we will act all together, as one army, until we shall see what can be done with the forces before us." Dispositions were made accordingly.

Lee now fully comprehended the immediate perils that menaced him, for he saw that his only lines of communication with the rest of the Confederacy

---

[1] See map on page 354.

might be cut at any hour. He also perceived the necessity of strengthening his right, to avert the impending shock of battle. He also felt the necessity of maintaining his extended line of works covering Petersburg and Richmond. Ignorant of the fact that Grant had withdrawn a greater portion of the Army of the James from the north side of the river, he left Longstreet's corps, eight thousand strong, to guard the defenses of Richmond, until it was too late. Mahon's division, of Hill's corps, was kept in front of the National lines at Bermuda Hundred, while the divisions of Wilcox, Pickett, Bushrod Johnson, and the remnant of Ewell's corps, commanded by Gordon, held the lines before Petersburg. Drawing from these as many as prudence would allow, Lee concentrated a force about fifteen thousand strong, and with these and Fitzhugh Lee's cavalry, he hastened, during the stormy night of the 29th and 30th, to place them in position in front of the Fifth and Second Corps. All night long they toiled in the drenching rain, and were not ready for battle when the day dawned. Fortunately for them, the rain made the roads so almost impassable, that Grant's infantry, though ready to strike, did little more that day[a] than to perfect their formation and connection. Sheridan sent a part of his cavalry, under Devin, supported by General Davies, to the Five Forks; but the works there were too strongly armed and manned to be ridden over, and his troops, drenched by rain and soiled by mud, were driven back to Dinwiddie Court-House, where they encamped that night.

[a] March 30, 1865.

The storm had ceased on the morning of the 30th,[b] but the ground was so wet and soft, that Grant proposed to remain quiet a little longer. Lee had determined otherwise. He was in a desperate strait, and it was important for him to act without unnecessary delay. He had resolved to make another effort to break through the National line at the point where he had massed the great body of his troops. His cavalry, which had been posted far to his right, on Stony Creek, and had become isolated by Sheridan's sudden advance to Dinwiddie Court-House, had made a wide circuit westward, and were coming in, so that, on the morning after the storm, he was prepared to strike. Warren's corps was then westward of the Boydton road, and pressed on the extreme right of the Confederate works on the White Oak road.

[b] March.

The divisions of Ayres, Crawford, and Griffin were *en echelon*, Ayres in front, and Griffin in the rear. Sheridan was too far distant to form a covering for Warren's flank. In this delicate and exposed position, the Fifth Corps, with skirmishers out in the direction of the White Oak road, and with Winthrop's brigade, of Ayres's division, well advanced in support of them, received an unexpected and stunning blow. It fell upon Ayres's rear, causing his division to go back in great confusion upon Crawford's, which was broken in consequence of the recoil. There was, for a brief space, promise of perfect success for Lee, but his hopes soon faded. Griffin's division stood firm. It stemmed the torrent of assailants, while Ayres and Crawford rallied their columns behind it, and very soon Warren was enabled to assume the offensive. He made a counter-charge, and in so doing was nobly supported by Miles's division, sent by Humphreys from the Second Corps, who marched in on Warren's right, and struck the Confederates on their left flank. They were driven back behind their intrenchments on the White Oak road, after a heavy loss, especially in men made prisoners. In this charge, Chamberlain's brigade of the Fifth Corps was specially distinguished. Humphreys tried to carry the Confederate works covering the intersection of the Boydton and White Oak roads, and also those on Hatcher's Run, but failed.

Lee now sought to strike another blow, quickly, at a supposed weaker point, which was the extreme left of Grant's line, held by Sheridan, who, while Warren and the Confederates were battling farther to the right, had boldly pushed forward the troops of Devin and Davies to the Five Forks. They captured the works there, and so held the key to the whole region that Lee was striving to protect. Lee sent the divisions of Pickett and Bushrod Johnson to regain this key-point. They struck the Union cavalry holding it, so severely, that they were driven out, and hurled back in confusion toward Dinwiddie Court-House. By a vigorous pursuit, with cavalry and infantry, but with much difficulty, the Confederates interposed between the troops of Devin and Davies and Sheridan's main body, at Dinwiddie Court-House. This compelled Devin to make a long, circuitous march, by the Boydton road, to rejoin his chief. The movement was mistaken by the Confederates for a forced retreat, and they attempted pursuit, when Sheridan, with the brigades of Gregg and Gibbs, charged upon their flank, and compelled them to give up the chase. Devin soon rejoined the main body, upon which the Confederates fell with vigor, expecting to drive them. They were foiled by Sheridan, who dismounted his men and placed them behind light breastworks, from which they gave their antagonists such a deadly musket fire that the latter recoiled. Before the Confederates could rally for another attack, darkness came and fighting ceased.

Before midnight, Sheridan was satisfied that Lee was withdrawing his troops[1] from the front of the Union cavalry, and felt quite at ease. The feeling at head-quarters was quite otherwise. It was an anxious night there. Only the fact, that the cavalry had been driven back from the Five Forks, and had been attacked at Dinwiddie in force, was known. It was supposed that Sheridan could not maintain his position, and Warren was directed to hasten to his relief, with the Fifth Corps. Ayres's division was first started, but in consequence of the destruction of a bridge over Gravelly Run, it did not reach Dinwiddie Court-House until dawn,[a] just [a] April 1, 1865. as the rear guard of the retreating Confederates was leaving.

On the arrival of Ayres, Sheridan started in pursuit, directing the former to follow in support. At seven o'clock he was joined by Warren, with the other two divisions of the Fifth Corps. Ranking Warren, Sheridan became commander of the whole. Leaving the Fifth Corps at the point where he had joined the cavalry, about half way between Dinwiddie Court-House and the Five Forks, Sheridan pressed boldly on toward that point, with cavalry alone, and by two o'clock had driven the Confederates into their works there, where they were enveloped by the overwhelming number of horsemen. While thus holding them, he ordered Warren forward to the White Oak road, on his right, so as to be fully on the Confederate left, and directed

---

[1] These were Pickett's division, Wise's independent brigade of infantry, and Fitzhugh Lee's, Rosser's, and W. H. Lee's commands.

Merritt to make a strong demonstration, as if about to turn the right of the adversary. At the same time M'Kenzie was sent with a small body of cavalry to a position on the White Oak road, to cover the National right flank from any force moving from that direction. There he drove a body of Confederates toward Petersburg, and, returning, was in the neighborhood of the Five Forks before Warren was prepared to charge.

Pursuant to Sheridan's orders, Warren formed his whole corps in battle order before resuming his march. This consumed time, and he informed Sheridan that he could not be ready for an assault before four o'clock. He placed Ayres's division on the left, Crawford's on the right, and Griffin's behind, in reserve. At the hour named he was ready for the attack, and advanced in perfect order. Crawford's division, in crossing an open field, received a severe fire on its left, causing it to oblique a little, so as to gain the shelter of woods and a ridge. This produced a gap between it and Ayres's right, upon which the same fire was directed. Some of the troops of that flank wavered and recoiled in disorder, but the misfortune was soon remedied by Griffin, whose division was thrown into the gap, while Ayres's, in an impetuous charge upon the Confederate right, carried a portion of the line, and captured more than a thousand men and several battle-flags. Merritt, meanwhile, charged the front, and Griffin fell upon the left with such force that he carried the intrenchments, and seized fifteen hundred men. Crawford, meanwhile, had pressed rapidly forward to the Ford road, northward of the post, cut off their retreat in the direction of Lee's main force, and turning southward on that highway, struck them in the rear, and captured four guns. In this perilous position, with Warren upon their flank and rear, and the cavalry assailing them front and right, the Confederates fought on with the most determined gallantry and fortitude. At length the cavalry charged over the works simultaneously with the turning of their flanks by Ayres and Griffin, and, bearing down upon the Confederates with wild fury, caused a large portion to throw down their arms, while the remainder sought safety in a most disorderly flight westward, pursued many miles, long after dark, by the cavalry of Merritt and M'Kenzie.[1] So ended THE BATTLE OF FIVE FORKS, in complete victory for the Nationals, whose loss was about one thousand men.[2] The loss to the Confederates was a large number of men killed and wounded, and over five thousand made prisoners. The trophies for the victors were several guns and colors.

---

[1] Mr. Swinton, in his *Campaigns of the Army of the Potomac*, page 600, says of Warren, who was in the van of the charging column, "his horse was fatally shot within a few feet of the breastworks, and he, himself, was in imminent peril, when a gallant officer (Colonel Richardson of the Seventh Wisconsin) sprang between him and the enemy, receiving a severe wound, but shielding from hurt the person of his loved commander."

During this grandly fought battle, General Sheridan, who was watching and directing the movements, became impatient at the seeming tardiness of Warren, and when he saw Crawford's division oblique, and Ayres's give way, he conceived the idea that the troops were not managed with proper skill and decision. He at once issued an order depriving Warren of his command, and giving it to Griffin. It did not reach Warren until after the action. In his report, made more than a month afterward,[a] Sheridan spoke disparagingly of Warren's conduct on this occasion, but the General-in-chief seemed so well satisfied that Sheridan had acted upon erroneous impressions, that he showed his confidence in Warren in appointing him, immediately after the battle of The Five Forks, commander of the Department of the Mississippi then the theater of war. Warren afterward published a full vindication. The misunderstanding between such noble men and true soldiers, as Generals Sheridan and Warren, produced an unpleasant feeling in the public mind.

[a] May 16, 1865.

[2] Of these, the infantry lost 634 killed and wounded. Among the former was General Winthrop, cousin of Major Winthrop (see page 501, volume I.), killed at Big Bethel, at the beginning of the war.

The shout of victory at the Five Forks had scarcely died away on the evening of the day of battle, when, by Grant's orders, the National guns in position before Petersburg were all opened on the Confederate lines, from right to left, from the Appomattox to Hatcher's Run. Sheridan, at the close of the battle, had ordered Griffin, then in command of the Fifth Corps, to impel two divisions in the direction of Petersburg, to reopen communication with the rest of the army, while Griffin's own division, now commanded by General Bartlett, was directed to push northward up the Ford road to Hatcher's Run, supported by McKenzie's cavalry. Wright, Parke, and Ord, holding the intrenchments in front of Petersburg, were ordered to follow up the bombardment by an assault the next morning. Apprehensive that Lee might withdraw his troops from the intrenchments during the night, and fall upon Sheridan in heavy force, in his isolated position, Grant ordered Miles's division of the Second Corps to his support.

The cannonade at Petersburg was kept up until four o'clock in the morning.[a] The assault began at daybreak. Parke, with the Ninth Corps, carried the outer line of the Confederate works on his front, but was checked at an inner line. Wright, with the Sixth Corps, [a April 2, 1865.] supported by two divisions of Ord's command, assaulted the works on their front at about the same hour, and speedily drove every thing before him to the Boydton plank road, where he turned to the left toward Hatcher's Run, and, pressing vigorously along the rear of the Confederate intrenchments, captured several thousand men and many guns. In the mean time, Ord's other division had broken the Confederate line on Hatcher's Run, when the combined forces swung round to the right, and pushed up the Boydton road, toward Petersburg, from the southwest.

When the triumphs were known, Humphreys, holding the Union left to the westward of Hatcher's Run, advanced with the divisions of Hays and Mott, and stormed and captured a redoubt on his front. The Confederates retired, and the two divisions moved up the Boydton road, and took position on the left of the Sixth Corps. Miles, in the mean time, had joined Sheridan, by whom he was directed to push toward Petersburg by the White Oak road, and attack the remains of the Confederate army west of Hatcher's Run, gathered at the intersection of the Claiborne road. Sheridan followed with the divisions of Bartlett and Crawford, of the Fifth. Miles carried the point designated, drove the Confederates across Hatcher's Run, and pursued them sharply to Sutherland's Station on the South Side railroad, well up toward Petersburg. When about to attack them there, Humphreys reclaimed Miles's division, when Sheridan returned to the Five Forks, and then, with the Fifth Corps, took a route across the South Side railway at Ford's and Wilson's stations, to strike the Confederates at Sutherland's, in the rear. Miles, by Humphreys's order, had, meanwhile, attacked and routed the foe, capturing two guns and six hundred men. And so it was, that on the 2d of April,[b] the South Side railway was first struck at three points [b 1865.] and the long coveted triumph in cutting that very important line of Lee's communications, was achieved. At about the same time the Confederate lines at the south of Petersburg were assaulted by Gibbon's division of Ord's command, and Forts Gregg and Alexander—two strong redoubts—were carried, by which the defenses of the city were much weakened, and the besieging lines shortened. In this assault Gibbon lost about five hundred men. Fort Gregg was manned by two hundred and fifty Mississippians, who fought so gallantly that, when it was surrendered, only thirty effective men were left.

The Confederates were now confined to the inner line, close around Petersburg. There they were strong, because more concentrated; and Longstreet, who had crossed the James from the defenses of Richmond on the north side, with some brigades, had pushed forward with Benning's, of Field's division, and joined Lee at ten o'clock that morning. So strong did Lee feel, that he ordered a charge on the besiegers, to regain some of the works on his left, carried by the Ninth Corps. Heth commanded the charging party, which consisted of his own division of A. P. Hill's corps. So heavily did the Confederates press, that the troops holding City Point, were ordered up to the support of the Ninth Corps. Heth was repulsed, and so ended the really last blow struck for the defense of Richmond by Lee's army. In that movement, General A. P. Hill, one of Lee's best officers, and who had been conspicuous throughout the war, was shot dead while reconnoitering.

Lee now perceived that he could no longer hold Petersburg or the capital, with safety to his army, then reduced, by enormous losses in the space of a few days, to about thirty-five thousand men, and he resolved to maintain his position, if possible, until night, and then retreat with the hope of making his way to Johnston by the Danville railroad. Immediately after the repulse of Heth, or at half-past ten o'clock in the morning, he telegraphed to Davis, at Richmond, saying, in substance, "My lines are broken in three places; Richmond must be evacuated this evening." It was the Sabbath. The Arch-conspirator was in St. Paul's (Episcopal) church, when the message reached him by the hand of Colonel Taylorwood. With evidences in his face of a crushing weight upon his feelings, he immediately but quietly left the church, when, for a moment, the deepest and most painful silence prevailed.[1] The religious services were closed; and before Dr. Minnegerode, the rector, dismissed the congregation, he gave notice that General Ewell, the commander in Richmond, desired the local forces to assemble at three o'clock in the afternoon.

For hours after the churches were closed, the inhabitants of Richmond were kept in the most painful suspense. Rumor said the city was to be immediately evacuated. The "Government" was as silent as the Sphynx. Panic gradually took the place of judgment; and when, toward evening, wagons were seen a-loading with trunks and boxes, at the "Departments," and were driven to the station of the Danville railway, and the inhabitants were satisfied that the capital was about to be abandoned, the wildest confusion and alarm prevailed among the open and conspicuous enemies of the Republic, who felt constrained to follow the Conspirators in their flight, to avoid the expected wrath of their outraged Government.[2] Gathering up the

---

[1] A Confederate staff officer, who accompanied the "Government" in its flight that night, says that, at that time, Benjamin, "Secretary of State," being a Jew, was not at church, but was "enjoying his pipe and solitude." Mallory, "Secretary of the Navy," a Roman Catholic, was at mass in St. Peter's Cathedral. Trenholm, "Secretary of the Treasury," was sick. Reagan, "Postmaster-General," was at Dr. Petre's Baptist church, and Breckinridge, "Secretary of War," was at Dr. Duncan's church.

[2] An eye-witness wrote: "At all the private houses that I passed—houses of regular Richmond families—the balconies were filled with ladies, evidently resolved to brave the dangers consequent on being left alone. They were mute. They looked terror-stricken, and, in many cases, powerless and mute. The crisis had come with fearful suddenness upon them, although for years it impended. "Wolf" was cried so often, when, at last it came, they could not credit the fact, or, crediting it, they were palsied. It was not resignation; it was nearer akin to desperation. It was woeful to witness their sturdy, stolid sadness."

most valuable and portable articles within reach, they packed for a journey they knew not whither. So great was the demand for vehicles beyond the supply, because of their having been pressed into the "Government" service, that as much as one hundred dollars in gold were given for a conveyance from a dwelling to the railway station.[1] The open disloyalists literally "ran to and fro, and were at their wits' end;" and, at eight o'clock in the evening, President Davis left the city by railway, taking with him horses and carriages, in case the road should be interrupted, declaring that he was determined not to give up the struggle, but to make other efforts to sustain the hopeless cause. At nine o'clock, the Virginia Legislature fled from the city to Columbia, in canal boats. The "Congress" had already departed, and all that remained of the "Confederate Government," at midnight, was the "War Department," represented by Major Melton. The gold of the Louisiana banks, that had been sent to Richmond for safety, and that of the Richmond banks, was sent away by the Danville road early in the day.

With the darkness came greater confusion, alarm, and dread; and then, when it was too late, the city authorities, and others, remembered the warnings given them by General Ewell, of the great dangers to which the city would be exposed in the event of evacuation, and the execution of an order of Congress for the destruction of cotton, tobacco, and other property which the owners could not carry away, stored in four great warehouses in Richmond,[2] to prevent its falling into the hands of the Government.[3] The City Council were assembled in the evening, and the only thing that they could do for the public safety, was to order the destruction of all liquors that might be accessible to lawless men, that so they might be kept from the outgoing or incoming soldiers. This was done, and, by midnight, hundreds of barrels of spirituous liquors were flowing in the gutters, where it was gathered up in vessels by some stragglers of the retreating army, and rough citizens, and produced the very calamity the authorities were trying to avert. Meanwhile, Ewell had been directed, in spite of his own remonstrances, and that of private and public citizens, to issue an order for the firing of the warehouses, at three o'clock in the morning. There was a fresh breeze from the south, and such fires might produce the destruction of the whole city. A committee of the common council went to the war office to remonstrate with whomsoever might represent the "Department," against the execution of the order. Major Melton rudely replied, in the cruel spirit evinced by

---

[1] Mrs. Davis, the wife of the chief Conspirator, had already sold every thing which she could not conveniently carry with her, excepting the furniture of the house, and had gone, five days before, to Danville, in North Carolina, to await the coming of her husband.

[2] Public warehouse at the head of the basin situated near the Petersburg railway station; Shockoe warehouse, near the center of the city, by the Gallego Flouring Mills; and the warehouses of Mayo & Dibbrell, in Cary Street, a square below Libby prison.

[3] So early as the first of February, General Lee called General Ewell's attention to that order of "Congress," when the latter conferred with the Mayor and Councilmen and leading citizens, warning them of the danger of mob violence between the time of the exit of the Confederate troops and the entrance of the National troops. He urged them to obtain the passage of a law by the Virginia Legislature, for enrolling, as a local guard for defense, all men whose age exempted them from military duty, but nothing was done. "My efforts were useless," says General Ewell, in a letter to the author, in November, 1866, giving an account of the evacuation. "The Legislature thought it inhuman to make old men perform any military service (I thought some were afraid of their popularity), and they would do nothing more than authorize any persons to volunteer into an organization for city guards that chose, while the citizens were only active in trying to get others to volunteer. The result was that only three men volunteered." The Legislature of Virginia, at that time, "was far from being a Roman body of men, and many would not risk losing their seats," said an eminent Confederate officer, to the writer.

Davis earlier in the evening, just before he left, when a similar remonstrance was offered to him, that their statement that the burning of the warehouses would endanger the city, was " a cowardly pretext on the part of the citizens, trumped up to endeavor to save their property for the Yankees." Ewell had no alternative, as a soldier, but to obey; for the law, and the order from the "War Department," were imperative. The torch was applied by somebody. At daybreak the warehouses were in flames. The city was already on fire in several places. The intoxicated Confederate soldiers, joined with many of the dangerous class of both sexes, had formed a marauding mob of fearful proportions, who broke open and pillaged stores, and committed excesses of every kind. From midnight until dawn, the city was a pandemonium. Here and there stores were set on fire. The roaring mob released the prisoners from the jail and burned it. They set fire to the arsenal, and tried to destroy the Tredegar Iron Works.[1] Early in the morning, one of the large mills on the borders of the river was set on fire; and at about the same time, the doomed warehouses burst into flames.[2] From these the conflagration spread rapidly, for the fire department was powerless, and by the middle of the forenoon, a greater portion of the principal business part of the town was a blazing furnace.

While the terrible drama was in action, between midnight and dawn, the Confederate troops were making their way across the bridges, to the south side of the James River. At about three o'clock, the magazine near the the almshouse was fired and blown up, with a concussion that shook the city to its foundations, and was heard and felt for many miles around. This was soon followed by another explosion. It was the blowing up of the Confederate ram, *Virginia*, below the city. At seven o'clock in the morning,[a] the retreating troops were all across the stream, when the torch was applied to Mayo's Bridge and the railway bridges, and they were burned behind the fugitives. At about the same time, two more Confederate iron-clads (*Fredericksburg* and *Richmond*[3]) were blown up. The receiving-ship, *Patrick Henry*, was scuttled and sunk, and a number of small vessels, lying at Rocketts, were burned. The bursting of shells in the arsenal, when the fire reached them, added to the horrors of the scene. At noon, about seven hundred buildings in the business part of the city, including a Presbyterian church, were in ruins.

[a] April 3, 1865.

---

[1] See page 36, volume II. "Many buildings," said General Ewell, "were fired by the mob, which I had carefully directed should be spared. Thus the arsenal was destroyed against my orders. A party of men who proceeded to burn the Tredegar Iron Works, were only deterred by General Anderson's arming his employees and threatening resistance. The small bridge on Fourteenth Street, over the canal, was burnt by incendiaries, who fired a barge above and pushed it against the bridge.— *Ewell's Letter to the Author.*

[2] General Ewell said: " I left the city about seven in the morning, and, as yet, nothing had been fired by my orders, yet the buildings and depot near the bridge were on fire, and the flames were so close as to be disagreeable as I rode by them."—[*Letter of General Ewell to the Author.*] He also mentions seeing from the hills above Manchester, the flames burst through the roof of a fire-proof mill, " on the side farthest from the large warehouses;" and he was informed that Mr. Crenshaw found his mill full of plunderers, who were about to burn it, and he saved it by giving them all the flour. Ewell was offered, by the " Ordnance Department," turpentine to mix with the tobacco, to make it burn more fiercely, but he refused to use it because it would endanger the city. After considering all the facts and circumstances, the writer is impressed with the belief, that the humane Ewell never issued the prescribed order for firing the warehouses, but that the work was done by a less scrupulous hand, connected with the " War Department." Ewell had specially advised care in keeping the fire-engines in order, in the event of a conflagration. " These," he said, " were found to be disabled: and Jones, who was connected with the " War Department," says, in his *Diary*, under date of April 3, "shells were placed in all the warehouses where the tobacco was stored, to prevent the saving of any."

[3] See note 3, page 531.

It was while Richmond was in flames, on Monday morning, that National troops entered that city. General Godfrey Weitzel, as we have observed, was left on the north side of the James River, with a part of Ord's command, to hold the works there. He had with him Kautz's division of the Twenty-fourth Corps, and Ashborne's and Thomas's divisions of the Twenty-fifth Corps. He had been instructed by Grant, to make all possible show of numbers and strength. This had been done, and Longstreet was deceived by his antagonist's noisy demonstrations, for four or five days. On Sunday evening, while the Confederates were preparing to steal away from Richmond, and their "Government" had actually taken wing, his bands gave out a great amount of music. It ceased at midnight, and the occupants of camps were all in repose, excepting the sentinels and the commanding general and some of his staff. He was watching, for he suspected what was actually occurring; and when the sound of the magazine explosion reached his alert ear, he was quick to seek knowledge of its meaning. Lieutenant Johnston Livingston De Peyster, one of his aids, ascended a signal tower, near head-quarters, seventy feet in height, and reported that he saw a great light in the direction of Richmond, but could not determine its meaning. Soon afterward, a Confederate picket was

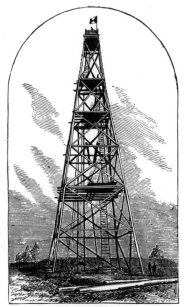

SIGNAL TOWER.[1]

---

[1] This is a picture of the Signal Tower at Point of Rocks, on the Appomattox River, from a drawing by the author, made in December, 1864. The one alluded to in the text, was similar in construction but not so high. That at Point of Rocks was 125 feet in height. It was built of pine timber, under the direction of General Weitzel. From its summit the writer saw the church-spires in both Petersburg and Richmond, and the sentinels along the Confederate lines, in front of Bermuda Hundred.

Signals and the signal corps have often been mentioned in this work, and illustrations of signal stations of various kinds have been given, the most common being trees used for the purpose. The value of the signal corps to the service during the civil war, has been hinted at; it can not be estimated. That value was most conspicuously illustrated during M'Clellan's campaign on the peninsula of Virginia; at Antietam and Fredericksburg; at Vicksburg, Port Hudson, Fort Macon, and Mobile; during Sherman's march from Chattanooga to Atlanta, and his approach to the coast, and especially in connection with the attack at Allatoona Pass, mentioned on page 398. The system of signaling by night and by day, on land and on the water, in use during the Civil War, was the invention of Colonel Albert J. Myer, of the National Army, who was the chief of the signal corps throughout the conflict.

PLATE I.

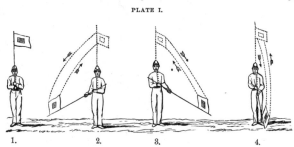

1.   2.   3.   4.

He has written, fully illustrated, and published a volume on the subject, entitled, *A Manual of Signals*, in which may be found a full description of the character and practical workings of the system. We may here consider only a few facts in relation to the system, by which the reader may have a general idea of its workings. It may properly be remarked, that it is so simple and flexible, that it may be used through the medium of sounds, forms, colors, and motions, all of which are regulated and understood by a *Code*.

captured, who could give no account of his regiment, excepting its number (Thirty-seventh Virginia Artillery), and the fact that it had disappeared.

The most common method of signaling during the war, was by the use of a waving flag by day, and a waving torch by night, which the figures in this note, copied from Colonel Myer's *Manual*, illustrate.

Plate I. illustrates the manner of using the flag-signal. The operator has a flag of any color or colors that may make it conspicuous at a distance. He places himself in position of *Ready*, or figure 1. The flag is held directly over the head of the flagman, the staff vertical. Suppose he is to make words or sentences, by a combination of Arabic numerals. To make the numeral "1," the flag is waved from the vertical position to the ground, to the *right*, and instantly brought to the first position, as indicated in figure 2, the arrows showing the direction of the motion. To make numeral "2," the flag is waved to the ground to the *left*, and instantly brought to the first position, as seen in figure 3. To make numeral "3," the flag is waved to the ground in *front*, and instantly brought to the first position, as seen in figure 4. We now have, by a combination of the three figures, in this simple operation by three elements, the number "123." There is a *signal-code*, which every operator carries with him, if he has not committed it all to memory, in which is given several hundred combinations of numerals, with the significance of each. As, for example, "123" may mean, a "mile to the right;" "321" may mean, "the brigade has moved;" "1123" may mean, "cavalry approaching by the turnpike;" and so on, in hundreds of combinations. Now, suppose a flagman is directed to signal to an officer, who is looking at the former from a

SIGNALING.

distance, through a telescope resting on the hilt of his sword, as seen in the above picture, or in any other position, the direction of certain troops, or of the range of a gun, "a mile to the right." The flagman will make the motions already described, and indicated in Plate I. If the officer to whom the message has been sent, is not very familiar with the *Code*, he will consult it and he will find that the numbers given by the flagman, "123," signify, "a mile to the right." The officer wishes to reply to the one with the distant flagman, "the brigade has moved;" he will direct his own flagman, seen standing near him, to make the numerals "321," by first making the motion of figure 1, for "ready," then of figure 4 for "3," of figure 3 for "2," and of figure 2 for "1," making the number, "321."

PLATE II.

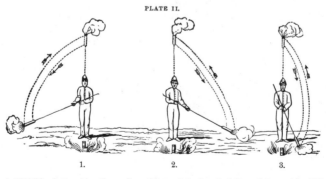

1.　　　　　　　2.　　　　　　　3.

The same principle is carried out in night-signaling, in the motions of a torch, instead of a flag, as seen in Plate II. The operator lights a stationary foot-torch, at which he stands firmly, it being the indication or "point

It was evident to General Shepley, who had prosecuted the inquiry, that the Confederates were leaving their capital.[1] Then a deserter came in, and said they were; and his story was confirmed by a negro, who drove into the Union lines, in a buggy, at four o'clock.

Weitzel would have advanced upon Richmond at once, but for the known fact, that the ground in front of the intricate Confederate works was thickly strewn with terra-torpedoes. He waited until broad daylight, when Draper's negro brigade was put in motion. They found the road as they approached Richmond, thickly strewn with abandoned munitions of war. Cannons were left unharmed on the deserted works; and the place of every torpedo was marked by a little red flag. These indicators of their position had been placed there for the safety of the Confederates, and, in their hasty flight, they had forgotten to remove them.

General Weitzel's whole force moved toward Richmond, and at six o'clock, he and his staff, at the head of the Second Brigade of the Third Division of the Twenty-fourth Army Corps, commanded by General Ripley, were in the near suburbs of the town. At that time the shells in the burning arsenal were exploding, and these, with the roar and light of the flames,

and the crashing of falling walls, presented a scene grand and impressive beyond description. Major A. H. Stevens, of the Fourth Massachusetts, and Major E. Graves, of General Weitzel's staff, were sent, with a small squadron of cavalry, to demand of the mayor, Joseph Mayo, the surrender of the city. They were courteously received, and the keys

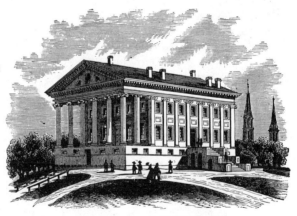

THE VIRGINIA CAPITOL OR STATE-HOUSE.

of the public buildings were handed to them, at the City Hall, at seven o'clock.[a] Then they placed two small cavalry guidons on the top of the State Capitol. At eight o'clock, General Weitzel and staff rode in, at the head of Ripley's brigade of negro troops, who had

[a] April 3, 1865.

---

of reference," to the other operator, of the position of his correspondent. Then the torch is moved in the same way, *right, left,* and *front.* The waving torch is a large lamp, filled with turpentine, and wick'd. This is attached to a staff, the same length as that of the flag-staff, which is usually 12 feet. The foot-torch is made of a copper lamp, similarly equipped. Each torch has an extinguisher. At the end of each message, the waving torch is extinguished. With both the flag and the torch-signal, there are motions which indicate spaces between the combination of numbers. For example: When the flagman has made the motions for "123," he makes a space motion, and then goes on to "321," and so on.

A party in the field for signaling, need consist of only an officer, seeking or imparting information, a flag and torch man, and an orderly to hold their horses, as seen in the group on page 548. The orderly has charge of the supplies for the torches, the turpentine or camphene being carried in a large canteen, seen back of the saddle of the white horse, in the picture. The flagman's horse (the black one) is furnished with a case for carrying his staff in. The signal service was always a most perilous one. and required much courage and fortitude, for those engaged in it were obliged, frequently, to be in front of the army, and in the most exposed situations.

[1] General George F. Shepley was now General Weitzel's chief of staff. Lieutenant De Peyster had been on his staff, and, when his chief was transferred to the military family of General Weitzel, that young officer became an aid of the commanding general.

the honor of first entering the late Confederate capital,[1] when Lieutenant De Peyster, ascended to the roof of the Virginia State-House, in which the Confederate "Congress" had so lately held its sessions, and, assisted by Captain Langdon, Weitzel's chief of artillery, hoisted over it the grand old flag of the Republic.[2] In the senate chamber of that building, the office of head-quarters was established; and General Weitzel made the late and sumptuously-furnished residence of Jefferson Davis[3] his own dwelling-place, during his stay in Richmond. The city was placed under military rule. General Shepley[4] was appointed Governor, and Lieutenant-Colonel Manning was made Provost-Marshal. The troops, meanwhile, had been set at work to extinguish the flames then devouring the city, and by the greatest exertions they succeeded in doing so, but not until nearly one-third of the town was destroyed, and property valued at many million dollars had been annihilated.[5]

Such was the way in which Richmond, which had been the head-quarters of the Conspirators for nearly four years, was "repossessed" by the Government. Among the spoils were full five hundred heavy guns, with which the works around Richmond and its vicinity had been armed. These, with five thousand small-arms, thirty locomotive engines, three hundred cars, and other property, were the spoils found there. Five thousand sick and wounded men, and one thousand effective ones, were made prisoners of war, and Libby prison was filled with Confederate captives, where lately Union men were languishing.[6] Among these was the infamous Turner, the keeper of that jail, whose cruelty to Union prisoners, under the direction of General Winder, was unmerciful, as we shall hereafter observe.

Tidings of the fall of Richmond vent, with lightning-speed, over the land, and produced intense joy among the loyal people. Before the setting of the sun on that memorable third day of April, public demonstrations of delight and satisfaction were visible everywhere. In the National Capital,

---

[1] These troops were received with demonstrations of great joy by the negro population.

[2] The flag used on that occasion was a storm-flag, which General Shepley had brought from Norfolk. It had formerly belonged to the Twelfth Maine Volunteers, of which he had originally been colonel. It had floated over the St. Charles Hotel, in New Orleans, when General Butler made that house his head-quarters. Shepley had made the remark, one day, in the hearing of young De Peyster, that it would do to float over Richmond, and that he hoped to see it there. His listening aid said: "May I be allowed to raise it for you?" "Yes," Shepley replied, "if you take it with you, and take care of it, you shall raise it in Richmond." When the troops were about to move for the city, De Peyster reminded the General of his promise. "Go to my tent," he said, "and get the flag, and carry it on your saddle; I will send you to raise it, if we get in." In this way young De Peyster won the distinguished honor of raising the first flag over the ruins of the fallen Confederacy. For this act, and his usual good conduct, the Governor of his native State of New York (Fenton) gave him the commission of lieutenant-colonel, by brevet. He was the son of Major-General J. Watts De Peyster, of Dutchess County, New York. He was only sixteen years of age, when, in 1862, he was active in raising a company for service in the One Hundred and Twenty-eighth Regiment New York Volunteers, and at the date of the raising of the flag over the Virginia Capitol, he was between nineteen and twenty years of age.

[3] See page 549, volume I.

[4] General Weitzel issued an order announcing the occupation of the city by the National troops, and saying to the inhabitants of Richmond, "We come to restore to you the blessings of peace, prosperity and freedom, under the flag of the Union," and requesting them to "remain for the present quietly within their houses, and to avoid all public assemblages or meetings in the streets." Kindness and conciliation was freely offered, but it was met, on the part of the disloyal portion of the inhabitants, with foolish sullenness and impotent scorn.

[5] There were but two fire-engines in the city fit for use. The conflagration was checked by the soldiers, who pulled down buildings in the pathway of the fire, and so left it nothing to feed upon. "As I stood near the Capitol," said President Ewell, of William and Mary College, to the writer, "and saw the exertions of those troops, put forth as eagerly in subduing the flames, as if they were trying to save their own property—troops, who, only a few hours before, had a right, by the usages of war, to bombard and destroy the city—the scene impressed me as one of great moral sublimity. But for these efforts all Richmond would doubtless have become a heap of ruins."

[6] The Union prisoners had been removed and exchanged.

all the public offices were closed, and all business, among those who were in sympathy with the Government, was suspended.[1] In New York, the commercial metropolis of the nation, there was an immense spontaneous gathering of men in Wall Street, who listened to the thick-coming electrographs from the War Department, the voices of orators, and the sweet chimes of the bells of Trinity Church which looks down that great mart of money-changers. The multitude lingered long. A deep religious feeling, born of joy and gratitude, because of the deliverance of the Republic from great peril, prevailed in that almost innumerous throng, and was remarkably manifested when thousands of voices broke out spontaneously in singing the Christian's Doxology, to the grand air of "Old Hundred." The emotion of the hour, in every loyal heart throughout the land, was expressed by Charles J. Lukens, of Philadelphia, who wrote, on the same day—

> Uphoist the Union pennon—uplift the Union jack—
> Upraise the Union standard—keep not a banner back!
> Fling out in silk or bunting, the ensign of the stars!
> God grant it never more may know accurs'd intestine jars!
>
> Hurrah for skill! Hurrah for will! Hurrah for dauntless hearts!
> Mourn those who bled, praise those who led, against insidious arts!
> A cheer for those who lived it out; a tear for those who died:
> Richmond is ours! we thank the Lord, with heartfelt chastening pride!

[1] The loyal people of Washington City gathered in a great throng and called upon Mr. Seward, the Secretary of State, for a speech. He addressed them, saying: "I am now about writing my foreign dispatches. What shall I tell the Emperor of China? I shall thank him, in your name, for never having permitted a piratical flag to enter the harbors of the empire. What shall I say to the Sultan of Turkey? I shall thank him for always having surrendered rebel insurgents who have taken refuge in his kingdom. What shall I say to the Emperor of the French? I shall say to him that he can go to Richmond to-morrow and get his tobacco, so long held under blockade there, provided the rebels have not used it up. To Lord John Russell I will say that British merchants will find the cotton exported from our ports, under treaty with the United States, cheaper than cotton obtained by running the blockade. As for Earl Russell himself, I need not tell him that this is a war for freedom and national independence, and the rights of human nature, and not a war for empire; and if Great Britain should only be just to the United States, Canada will remain undisturbed by us, so long as she prefers the authority of the noble Queen to voluntary incorporation in the United States. What shall I tell the King of Prussia? I will tell him that the Germans have been faithful to the standard of the Union, as his excellent Minister, Baron Gerolt, has been constant in his friendship to the United States, during his long residence in this country. To the Emperor of Austria, I shall say that he has proved himself a very wise man, for he told us in the beginning that he had no sympathy with rebellion anywhere."

In this pleasant way the Secretary showed the relations of foreign governments to our own, during the war, and presented the fact, in bold relief, that while Great Britain and France—Christian nations—were doing all they dare to assist the Conspirators in destroying the Republic, Pagan China and Mohammedan Turkey, led by principles of right and justice, were its abiding friends. Andrew Johnson, the Vice-President, was also called upon for a speech. With great vehemence, he said: "At the time that the traitors in the Senate of the United States plotted treason against the Government, and entered into a conspiracy more foul, more execrable, and more odious than that of Cataline against the Romans, I happened to be a member of that body, and, as to loyalty, stood solitary and alone among the Senators from the Southern States. I was then and there called upon to know what I would do with such traitors, and I want to report my reply here. I said, if we had Andrew Jackson, he would hang them as high as Haman. But as he is no more, and sleeps in his grave in his own beloved State, where traitors and treason have even insulted his tomb and the very earth that covers his remains, humble as I am, when you ask what I would do, my reply is, I would arrest them; I would try them; I would convict them, and I would hang them. . . . . Since the world began there has never been a rebellion of such gigantic proportions, so infamous in character, so diabolical in motive, so entirely disregardful of the laws of civilized warfare. . . . . I am in favor of leniency; but, in my opinion, evil-doers should be punished. *Treason is the highest crime known in the catalogue of crimes, and for him that is guilty of it—for him that is willing to lift his impious hand against the authority of the nation, I would say death is too easy a punishment. My notion is, that treason must be made odious; that traitors must be punished and impoverished; their social power must be broken; they must be made to feel the penalty of their crimes. . . . . Let us commence the work. We have put down these traitors in arms; let us put them down in law, in public judgment, and in the morals of the world."*.

So soon as Mr. Johnson was invested, by the death of Mr. Lincoln, with power to punish the offenders, he pardoned scores of the most conspicuous of them; and during his administration of the affairs of the nation, as President, he used his official and personal power to the utmost in efforts to place the Government under the control of those who had sought to destroy it.

CHAPTER XXI.

CLOSING EVENTS OF THE WAR.—ASSASSINATION OF THE PRESIDENT.

 HILE the Confederates were leaving Richmond with great noise, those holding the lines before Petersburg were stealing away so silently, that they did not awaken even the suspicions of the Union pickets only a few yards distant from the works; and when, at dawn, the abandonment of the Confederate intrenchments was discovered, their late occupants were miles away to the westward, seeking to join the column hurrying from Richmond, in a flight for safety. The fugitive "Government" had then reached Danville with its archives and gold, whither Lee hoped to conduct his army, and was now straining every nerve to do so. When Grant was informed of the evacuation of Richmond and Petersburg, and the direction of Lee's retreat, he pushed forward his columns with all possible energy to intercept the march of his adversary.

The appointed place of concentration of Lee's troops, in their retreat, was Amelia Court-House, on the south side of the Appomattox River, where the forces would reach the Danville railway, and thereafter use it in their flight. Lee, therefore, simultaneously with the sending of his dispatch to Richmond, saying it must be evacuated that night, ordered commissary and quartermasters' stores to be forwarded from Danville to Amelia Court-House. They were promptly sent; but when, on Sunday afternoon, the loaded trains reached their destination, the officer in charge received orders from the Confederate authorities at Richmond to push on to that city, the object being to use the trains for the transportation of the "Government" and its effects. The stupid officer obeyed, but took with him all the supplies that were to be left at Amelia Court-House for the use of Lee's army on its re-treat, and these were among the things destroyed by the confla-
^a April 4, 1865. gration. When Lee arrived at the Court-House ^a and discovered the calamity, hope forsook him. He knew that Grant, for the sake of celerity in pursuit, would break up his army in detachments; and Lee intended, with a bountifully supplied force kept well in hand, to fall upon these fragments, and cut up the Union army in detail. Now, instead of being able to have all his forces in hand for such a purpose, he was compelled to detach nearly one-half of it for foraging for supplies; and instead of pushing on toward Danville, and eluding the Union army pressing on to intercept him, he was compelled to remain at Amelia Court-House all of the 4th, and the next day, waiting for supplies.

Meanwhile, Grant had taken possession of Petersburg, and his army was moving in vigorous pursuit. Sheridan, with his cavalry and the Fifth Corps, were far in advance, and on the afternoon of the 4th[a] he struck the Danville road at Jetersville, seven miles southwest of Amelia [a April, 1865.] Court-House, when some of his cavalry swept along its course almost to Burkesville Station, at the junction of that road with the South Side railway. Sheridan was now squarely across Lee's pathway of retreat, with his infantry intrenched, and ample cavalry to support them. Lee's only important avenue of supply from Lynchburg and Danville was now cut off, and he was compelled to choose between the perilous business of falling with his whole force upon Sheridan's isolated troops, before support could arrive, or attempting to escape to Lynchburg and the mountains beyond, by taking a westerly course at the left of Jetersville, and recrossing the Appomattox at Farmville, thirty-five miles from Amelia Court-House, where the South Side railway touched that stream. Lee hesitated; and on the evening of the 5th[b] an attack on Sheridan was out of the question, for [b April.] General Meade had joined the latter at Jetersville, with the Second and Sixth Corps of the Army of the Potomac, late that afternoon. Then it was too late for Lee to indulge much hope of escape by way of Farmville, for Sheridan was operating in the direction of the Appomattox, yet he attempted it. Sheridan sent out General Davies, toward evening, with his cavalry, on a reconnoissance to the left and front of Jetersville. He found a part of Lee's army moving westward from Amelia Court-House, his cavalry escorting a train of one hundred and eighty wagons in front of his infantry. Upon them Davies fell, at Fame's Cross-Roads, destroyed the wagons and captured many men and five guns. Lee's foot-soldiers tried to envelop and crush Davies's isolated cavalry force, but by the timely arrival of re-enforcements, under Generals Gregg and Smith, he extricated himself after some heavy fighting, and fell back to Jetersville.

On the morning of the 6th[c] nearly the whole of the Army of the Potomac was at Jetersville, and was moved upon Amelia [c April.] Court-House to attack Lee. Sheridan had returned the Fifth Corps to Meade, and now operated with the cavalry alone. He soon discovered that Lee, during the night, had left Amelia Court-House, had passed the left flank of of the Union army, and was moving rapidly westward towards Deatonsville. The latter made as rapid a pursuit, in three columns; one directly in Lee's rear on the Deatonsville road, another parallel with it on the north, and another parallel with it on the south. In the mean time, the main body of the Army of the James, under Ord, which had been pressing along the line of the South Side railway, toward Burkesville Station, had reached that point; and on the morning of the 6th, Ord was directed to move quickly on Farmville. He sent forward a light column of infantry and cavalry, under General Theodore Read, to destroy the bridges near Farmville. These troops met the van of Lee's army there, and attacked it, so as to arrest its march until the main body might come up. The odds was too great. Read was repulsed with heavy loss, in a sharp conflict that ensued, in which he was killed. The Confederates saved the bridges, but Read's attack had caused them the loss of precious time, during which Ord arrived with his main body.

Sheridan, meanwhile, had been pushing on at the head of the column moving on the left parallel line in pursuit of Lee, with the most strenuous endeavors to head off the Confederates. Near Deatonsville, he ordered Crook, who was on his left, to strike another of Lee's wagon trains, which was escorted by a formidable cavalry force. Crook did so, but with the expectation of only checking the Confederates, while Custer, with his division, should pass on and attack a point farther in advance. Such was the result. Crook was repulsed, and Custer gained the road at Sailor's Creek, a small tributary of the Appomattox. The divisions of Crook and Devin pressed up to his support, when the Confederate line was pierced, and four hundred wagons, sixteen guns, and many men were captured. By this blow, Ewell's corps, which was following the train, was cut off from Lee's main body. Sheridan resolved to detain them until the Sixth (Wright's) Corps, should come up, and for that purpose, Colonel Stagg's mounted brigade charged upon them. This enabled Seymour's division, which was leading the Sixth, to come up, when Ewell recoiled, and was driven to Sailor's Creek, but striking back such vigorous blows, that there was a halt until Wheaton's division should come up. Ewell's gallant veterans stoutly resisted, until enveloped by cavalry and infantry, and charged on flank and rear by horse and foot, when they threw down their arms and surrendered. Among the six thousand men then made prisoners, were Ewell and four other generals.

Lee succeeded in crossing the Appomattox over the bridges at Farmville that night,* with his dreadfully shattered army. He tried to make that stream an impassable barrier between his force and its pursuers, by destroying the bridges behind him. Only the railway bridge was consumed, that of the wagon road being saved by the van of Humphreys's corps. The flames were smothered, and Barlow's brigade crossed over in expectation of a fight, but he found there only a feeble rearguard, which retired after a slight skirmish, abandoning eighteen guns in

* April 6 and 7, 1865.

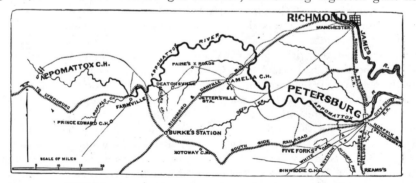

RETREAT OF THE CONFEDERATE FORCES FROM RICHMOND AND PETERSBURG.[1]

two redoubts, one at the bridge-head on the south bank of the Appomattox, which they blew up when they left it, and the other on the heights on the north side. Their starving draught-animals had been too weak, in consequence of fatigue and lack of food, to draw the cannon farther. Hundreds of Lee's

---

[1] The course of the retreat from Richmond and Petersburg, to Appomattox Court-House, is indicated in the above map by dotted lines.

men, from the same causes, had dropped by the way, and thousands had let their muskets fall and left them because they could not bear them and walk. They had begun their retreat with only one ration; and so poor and exhausted was the country through which they moved, that there was a famine after the first day's march. The horrors of that retreat, after leaving Amelia Court-House—the troops without supplies, without sleep, harassed in front, rear and flank, and compelled to fight when hardly able to walk—were among the most terrible on record; and the fortitude of the soldiers that endured it was truly sublime.

On the night of the sixth, after Lee's army was across the Appomattox, a council of his general officers was held. Lee was not present. They agreed that all was lost, and that a capitulation was inevitable. Famine had caused nearly one-half of their soldiers to drop their arms, because they could not carry them. Their cannon must all be lost if they should attempt a rapid flight, because they had no draught-animals sufficient to drag them. They came to the conclusion that a surrender, on the best obtainable terms, would be the wisest course, and that decision they communicated to their General-in-chief[1] by the hand of General Pendleton. Lee refused to listen favorably to the opinions of his officers, and professed not to then see the necessity for a surrender. Davis, his colleague, was then at Danville, trying to reorganize the " Government ;" and they seem to have agreed to continue the contest "so long as there was a man left in the Confederacy."

The remains of Lee's army were now in a compact mass on the stage and plank roads to Lynchburg, a few miles north of Farmville, with strong intrenchments covering these roads, and batteries commanding, over a considerable distance, the way of approach by the Nationals from the Appomattox. He resolved to make further efforts to escape, and success in battle on the 7th[a] encouraged him. Humphreys had crossed the Appomattox with the Second Corps, and resumed pursuit with the divisions of Miles and De Trobriand. He soon found himself confronted by Lee's intrenched army. He thought a flanking of the position would be the most effectual way of dislodging his antagonist, but he perceived that it could not be done with his single corps. He therefore resolved to assault, and ordered Barlow up to attack the front, while Miles should assail the Confederate left. The latter did so before Barlow came up, and was repulsed with a loss of about six hundred men.[2] When Barlow got into position it was too late to attack that night, and the assault was postponed until morning. On the same day Sheridan had dispatched two divisions of cavalry, under Merritt, to Prince Edward Court-House, to oppose the retreat of Lee on Danville, and a third division, under Crook, was sent to Farmville, where it crossed with difficulty, the horsemen being compelled to ford the Appomattox. Pushing on toward the left of Humphreys, Crook fell

a April, 1865.

---

[1] The continued interference of Davis in military affairs, and his keeping in place inefficient favorites to the exclusion of able men, had produced wide-spread discontent, and there was bold talk in and out of the " Congress," of making General Lee dictator, thereby stripping the Arch-Conspirator of power. To avoid this humiliation, Davis consented to allow the " Congress " to appoint Lee General-in-chief of all the armies of the Confederacy. This was done on the first of February, 1865. The same influence caused the reappointment of General Johnston to the command of the troops opposing Sherman.

[2] Among the killed were General Smyth and Major Mills. Generals Mott, Madill, and McDougall were severely wounded; so also was Colonel Starbird of the Nineteenth Maine.

upon a body of Confederate infantry guarding a train and was repulsed with the loss of General Gregg, commanding a brigade, who was captured.

Just after the repulse of General Miles, Lee received a note from Grant, dated at Farmville, that morning, in which he said : " The result of the last week must convince you of the hopelessness of further resistance on the part of the Army of Northern Virginia in this struggle. I feel that it is so ; and regard it as my duty to shift from myself the responsibility of any further effusion of blood by asking of you the surrender of that portion of the Confederate States army known as the Army of Northern Virginia." To this Lee replied : " Though not entertaining the opinion you express on the hopelessness of further resistance on the part of the Army of Northern Virginia, I reciprocate your desire to avoid useless effusion of blood, and, therefore, before considering your proposition, ask the terms you will offer on condition of its surrender." After dispatching this note to Grant, Lee resumed his retreat so silently, under cover of darkness, that his departure was not known to the Nationals until morning, when the Confederates had put many miles between themselves and their pursuers.

Grant did not receive Lee's reply until the morning of the 8th,[a] when he instantly dispatched a response, saying, " Peace being my great desire, there is but one condition I would insist upon, namely, that the men and officers surrendered shall be disqualified for taking up arms again against the Government of the United States, until properly exchanged." He then proposed to meet Lee in person, or to delegate officers to meet such as Lee might appoint, for the purpose of definitely arranging the terms of surrender.

[a] April, 1865.

Almost simultaneously with the forwarding of this dispatch, Grant set his whole army in motion, in pursuit of the flying Confederates. The Second and Sixth Corps, under Meade (who was accompanied by the General-in-chief), moved directly on their track, north of the Appomattox, skirmished with the rear-guard of Lee's forces, and unsuccessfully tried to bring on a general engagement. Sheridan, meanwhile, had pushed on with all his cavalry (Crook having recrossed the river), on the south side of the Appomattox, to gain some point in front of Lee, and oppose his march on Lynchburg. In that direction Lee was hurrying, along the narrowing neck of land between the head-waters of the Appomattox and small tributaries of the James. If Sheridan should reach his front, and close this only outlet to Lynchburg, all would be lost. To pass that perilous point, Lee was now putting forth all his energies, and while in that desperate situation, hoping against hope that he might find refuge among the ranges of the Blue Ridge, beyond Lynchburg, the Confederate generalissimo sent back to Grant a reply to the Lieutenant-General's note of that morning, saying : " In mine of yesterday, I did not intend to propose the surrender of the Army of Northern Virginia, but to ask the terms of your proposition. To be frank, *I do not think the emergency has arisen to call for the surrender of this army ;* but as the restoration of peace should be the sole object of all, I desired to know whether your proposals would lead to that end. I can not, therefore, meet you with a view to surrender the Army of Northern Virginia ; but as far as your proposal may affect the Confederate States forces under my command, and tend to the restoration of peace, I should be pleased to meet you at 10 A. M. to-morrow, on the old stage road to Richmond, between the picket lines of the two armies."

General Grant received Lee's note at near midnight,[a] and the next morning replied that he had "no authority to treat on the subject of peace," and that the proposed meeting could lead to no good. He said that he and the whole North were equally as anxious for peace as Lee, and added: "The terms upon which peace can be had are well understood. By the South laying down their arms, they will hasten that most desirable event, save thousands of human lives, and hundreds of millions of property not yet destroyed." He closed by the expression of a hope that all difficulties might be settled without the loss of a single life. Sheridan, in the mean time, had settled the question, and rendered further parley unnecessary, by utterly extinguishing Lee's hopes. By a forced march of about thirty miles, his advance, under General Custer, had reached Appomattox Station, on the Lynchburg railroad, and captured four trains of cars, laden with supplies for Lee's starving army, whose vanguard was just then approaching. These Custer, supported by Devin, pushed back to Appomattox Court-House, five miles northward, near which was Lee's main body, capturing twenty-five guns, a hospital train, a large number of wagons, and many prisoners. Sheridan hurried forward the remainder of his command to the support of Custer, and on the evening of the 8th he stood directly across the pathway of the flying Confederates, with a determination to hold Lee in check there until morning, when the detachment of the Army of the James also, with the corps under Griffin, would be upon his front, and most of the Army of the Potomac on his rear. He had closed Lee's last avenue for escape.

> [a] April 8, 1865.

Lee now saw that his only hope was in cutting his way successfully through Sheridan's line. This he attempted at daybreak.[a] Of all the grand Army of Northern Virginia, which menaced the National Capital a year before, not quite ten thousand effective men were now in arms. These composed two thin battle lines, consisting of the remains of Gordon' (Hill's) command and the wreck of Longstreet's corps. Lee directed the former to cut through at all hazards. The charge was made with such impetuosity, that Sheridan's men, who had dismounted to meet the attack, were forced back. Sheridan had just reached Appomattox Station, whither he had gone to hasten forward the Army of the James. He at once sent orders for his troops to gradually fall back, but to continually offer resistance, until the wearied and foot-sore infantry could come up and form in battle-line under their cover. The whole maneuver was well performed, when the cavalry, moving swiftly to the right, revealed to the dismayed Confederates a solid phalanx of men armed with muskets and glittering bayonets. Appalled, the Confederates staggered back in a recoil. Sheridan's bugles had sounded the order to remount, and in a few minutes his horsemen were on the left of the stunned and confused remnant of Lee's army, ready to charge, when a white flag appeared, in token of surrender, before the van of the troopers held by Custer. Sheridan rode to Appomattox Court-House, where he was met by Gordon with the information that Grant and Lee were then making arrangements for a surrender of the Army of Northern Virginia.

> [a] April 9.

Grant, after sending Lee his note, written that morning,[a] had left Meade, crossed the Appomattox, and was hurrying on to join Sheridan and Griffin, when he was handed a letter from the Confederate leader, in which he said: "I received your note of this morning on the picket line, whither I had come to meet you, and ascertain definitely what terms were embraced in your proposal of yesterday, with reference to the surrender of this army. I now ask an interview, in accordance with an offer contained in your letter of yesterday, for that purpose." Grant sent Lee word that he assented to his request, and arrangements were made for the interview in the parlor of the neat brick dwelling of Wilmer McLean,[1]

[a] April 9, 1865.

M'LEAN'S HOUSE.

at Appomattox Court-House. There the two commanders met, with courteous recognition, at two o'clock on Palm Sunday, the 9th of April. Grant was accompanied only by his chief aid, Colonel Parker. Lee was attended by Colonel Marshall, his adjutant-general. The terms of surrender were discussed and settled. They were put in the form of a written proposition by Grant, and a written acceptance by Lee. They were engrossed, and at about half-past three o'clock were signed on a neat mahogany center-table, with a marble top, delineated in the annexed engraving.

CAPITULATION TABLE.

The terms prescribed by Grant were most extraordinary, under the circumstances, for their leniency and magnanimity. They simply required Lee and his men to give their parole of honor that they would not take up arms against their Government, until regularly exchanged; gave to the officers their side-arms, baggage, and private horses, and pledged the faith of the Government that they should not be punished for their treason and rebel-

---

[1] It is a curious fact that Mr. McLean, whose residence, at the beginning of the war, was on a portion of the battle-field of Bull Run, and who had left that region for another that promised more quiet, was again disturbed by the clash of arms at the close of the war. See note 1, page 589, volume I.

lion, so long as they should respect that parole and be obedient to law.[1] Grant even went so far, in his generosity, at Lee's suggestion, that he gave instructions to the proper officers to allow such cavalrymen of Lee's army as owned their horses, to retain them, as they would, he said, need them for tilling their farms.

Lee professed to be touched by this leniency and magnanimity of his conqueror, who represented his deeply injured country ; yet, on the following day, in disregard of that generosity, and with a feeling of perfect security under the protection of a promise made in the name of his Government, which had ever been kind and just to himself and his kindred, he issued a farewell address to his army, which no right-minded and right-hearted man would care to imitate under like circumstances. Under the disguise of very guarded language, he told his soldiers, in effect, that in taking up arms against their country, and trying to destroy the Republic, in whose government they had always shared, they had done a patriotic act, and for which they would take with them " the satisfaction that proceeds from consciousness of duty faithfully performed ;" therefore, he invoked God's blessing upon their acts. He gave them to understand that they had no " country "— no Government to which their allegiance was due, excepting the territory and rule, over which, for four years, the Conspirators had held sway ; and he spoke of his " unceasing admiration " of their " constancy and devotion " to that " country," which had " endeared them to their countrymen." They were instructed, in that address, to consider themselves unfortunate patriots who had " been compelled to yield to the overwhelming numbers and resources" of a tyrannical and unjust Government. His words were treasured, in memory and feeling. That farewell address was afterward beautifully lithographed, in Baltimore, with a portrait of Lee at its head, surrounded by Confederate flags, and a fac-simile of his signature at its foot ; and it became a cherished document and ornament in the houses of the enemies of the Re-

---

[1] The following is the text of the Capitulation :—

" APPOMATTOX COURT-HOUSE, VA., *April* 9, 1865.

" GENERAL—In accordance with the substance of my letter to you of the 8th instant, I propose to receive the surrender of the Army of Northern Virginia on the following terms, to wit : Rolls of all the officers and men to be made in duplicate ; one copy to be given to an officer to be designated by me, the other to be retained by such other officer or officers as you may designate. The officers to give their individual paroles not to take up arms against the Government of the United States until properly exchanged ; and each company or regimental commander to sign a like parole for the men of their commands. The arms, artillery, and public property, to be parked and stacked, and turned over to the officers appointed by me to receive them. This will not embrace the side-arms of the officers, nor their private horses or baggage. This done, each officer and man will be allowed to return to his home, not to be disturbed by United States authority so long as they observe their paroles and the laws in force where they reside.

" U. S. GRANT, *Lieutenant General.*

SIGNATURES OF GRANT AND LEE. " General R. E. LEE."

" HEAD-QUARTERS, ARMY OF NORTHERN VIRGINIA, *April* 9, 1865.

" GENERAL—I received your letter of this date, containing the terms of the surrender of the Army of Northern Virginia, as proposed by you. As they are substantially the same as those expressed in your letter of the 8th instant, they are accepted. I will proceed to designate the proper officers to carry the stipulations into effect. R. E. LEE, *General.*

" Lt.-General U. S. GRANT."

public. "By that warrant," these people said, substantially, to the writer, "we will attempt to regain the 'Lost Cause.'"[1]

When terms of surrender were agreed upon, the starving Confederate soldiers were fed from the National stores; and on Wednesday, the 12th,[a] they were marched by divisions to an appointed place, near Appomattox Court-House, where they stacked their arms and accouterments, and the private soldiers and warrant officers received their paroles. So the Army of Northern Virginia disappeared. The kindness of the Government followed the offending ones, even to their homes, transportation and food for their journey being afforded to large numbers of them. The victorious army all returned to Burkesville Station (excepting the infantry of Gibbon and Griffin, and McKenzie's cavalry, who were left at Appomattox Court-House until the business of the surrender was finished), and thence, a few days later, they moved on to Petersburg and Richmond. General Grant and his staff left for City Point on the 11th, leaving General Meade to attend to the details of the surrender.[2] It was exactly a fortnight from the time when Grant broke up head-quarters at City Point, to enter upon the spring campaign, until his return there, with the campaign ended, and the war substantially closed. Lee had started on that campaign with about sixty-five thousand men. He went back to Richmond alone; and for a month, he and his family were kindly supplied with daily rations from the National commissariat there. The announcement of the great victory had been sent over the land by the Secretary of War, together with thanks to Grant and his soldiers;[3]

[a] April, 1865.

[1] The following is a copy of Lee's Farewell Address:—

"HEAD-QUARTERS ARMY NORTHERN VIRGINIA, APPOMATTOX C. H., *April* 10, 1865.

"GENERAL ORDERS,
No. 9.

" After four years of arduous service, marked by unsurpassed courage and fortitude, the Army of Northern Virginia has been compelled to yield to overwhelming numbers and resources. I need not tell the brave survivors of so many hard fought battles, who have remained steadfast to the last, that I have consented to this result from no distrust of them; but feeling that valor and devotion could accomplish nothing to compensate for the loss that must have attended a continuation of the contest, I determined to avoid the useless sacrifice of those whose past services have endeared them to their countrymen. By the terms of agreement, officers and men can return to their homes and remain until exchanged. You will take with you the satisfaction that proceeds from the consciousness of duty faithfully performed, and I earnestly pray that a merciful God will extend to you his blessing and protection. With an unceasing admiration of your constancy and devotion to your country, and a grateful remembrance of your kind and generous consideration for myself, I bid you all an affectionate farewell."

[2] Lee lost, during the movements of his army, from the 26th of March to the 9th of April, about 14,000 killed and wounded, and 25,000 made prisoners. The remainder, who were not present at the surrender, had deserted on the retreat. The number of men paroled, was about 26,000, of whom not more than 9,000 had arms in their hands. About 16,000 small-arms were surrendered; 150 cannon; 71 colors; about 1,100 wagons and caissons, and 4,000 horses and mules.

[3] The Secretary wrote: " Thanks be to Almighty God for the great victory with which He has this day crowned you and the gallant armies under your command! The thanks of this Department and of the Government, and of the people of the United States—their reverence and honor have been deserved—will be rendered to you and the brave and gallant officers and soldiers of your army, for all time."

Those of the grateful people who could know and appreciate the marvelous and patriotic services of the Secretary of War, during the struggle, were then, and ever will be ready to make him an equal sharer with the generals of the army, in their honor and reverence. General Hancock paid a just tribute to the worth of that able Minister, when he said, in a speech at the New England Dinner, in New York, in December, 1865: "Much credit has been given to the army; praise without stint has been given by a grateful people to its generals. We have had many generals, among whom the honors have been divided, and whose fame will live in more enduring form than in wreaths of laurel, but during the period of our greatest perils, we have had but one Minister of War, and during his administration, substantial victories crowned our arms. One who has been unequaled in furnishing the means of war, and placing them in the hands of our generals; one who has rivaled Carnot in all that is accorded to him for preparation; one who never faltered, however dark the hour. And shall we not honor him? I know him to be generous and mindful of faithful service. Among the people I predict an increasing tide of popularity in his favor, and that he will be one of those whom the country will delight to honor—Edwin M. Stanton, Secretary of War. A model for a War Minister, in momentous times: wise, firm, fruitful of resources, patriotic, incorruptible. To him a nation's gratitude is due."

also, an order for a salute of two hundred guns at the head-quarters of every army and department, and at the Military Academy at West Point, on the Hudson. There was joy throughout the entire Republic, because of the evident swift coming of Peace. The loyal people felt that a score of golden medals, such as Congress had awarded to General Grant,[1] would be too few

THE GRANT MEDAL.

to attest their appreciation of him as one of the chief instruments of the Almighty in working out the salvation of the Republic.

President Lincoln had been at City Point and vicinity, for several days before the fall of Richmond, in constant communication with the General-in-chief, at the front, receiving dispatches from him and transmitting them instantly to the Secretary of War, whence they were diffused over the country, by the telegraph. On the day after Richmond was evacuated, he went up to that city [a] in Admiral Porter's flag-ship, the *Malvern*. Captain Ralph Chandler, with the *Sangamon*, several tugs, and thirty small boats, with about three hundred men, had already cleared the channel of the river of torpedoes, and made the navigation comparatively safe.[2] When near Rocketts, the President and the Admiral left

[a] April 4, 1865.

[1] See page 172. The engraving of that medal, here given, is about one-third less, in size, than the original. On one side is a profile of General Grant, with his name on a segment of a circle, above; and below, the words, "JOINT RESOLUTION OF CONGRESS, DECEMBER 17, 1863." The whole is encircled in a wreath, the upper portion detached, composed of branches of the oak and olive, indicative of strength and peace, and the lower of the products of the country—Indian corn, sugar, cotton, tobacco, and wheat. On the obverse is the city of Vicksburg, at the left, and a mountain region, indicating Chattanooga, on the right. Over these, and embracing them and the space between, is a rainbow, on which sits the figure of a beautiful young girl, in a loose, white dress—the impersonation of *Peace*—holding the horn of plenty in one hand, and the shield of the Republic in the other. Across the face of the latter, on a ribbon, is the name, "FORT DONELSON." Beneath is a group of military trophies. Around all, and forming a broad circle, is the Mississippi River, on which are gun-boats of different forms; and outside of the whole, at the edge of the medal, are thirteen stars.

[2] When news reached the fleet in the James River, at nine o'clock in the morning, that Weitzel had entered Richmond, Captain Chandler left Dutch Gap with his fleet of torpedo hunters, on his perilous expedition, and worked so skillfully and rapidly, that he was at Richmond at five o'clock the same afternoon. The *Sangamon* and the tugs were protected by torpedo-nets, formed of ropes, weighted with pieces of iron or lead, and provided with hooks to catch the little mines, as delineated in the engraving. These were hung from spars placed athwart the bowsprit. The *Sangamon*, on

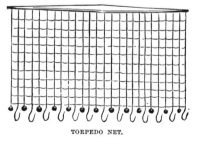

TORPEDO NET.

the *Malvern,* and proceeded to the city in the commander's gig. With its crew, armed with carbines, they landed and walked to Weitzel's quarters, in the late residence of Davis, cheered on the way by the huzzas and grateful ejaculations of a vast concourse of emancipated slaves, who had been told that the tall man was their Liberator. They crowded around him so thickly, in their eagerness to see him, and to grasp his hand, that a file of soldiers were needed to clear the way. After a brief rest at Weitzel's, the President rode rapidly through the principal streets of Richmond, in an open carriage, and, at near sunset, departed for City Point.

Two days afterward,[a] the President went to Richmond again, accompanied by his wife, the Vice-President, and several Senators, when he was called upon by leading Confederates, several of them members of the rebel Virginia Legislature, whose chief business was to endeavor to arrange a compromise whereby the equivalent for submission should be the security to the Virginia insurgents, as far as possible, of their political power and worldly possessions. The President was assured by Judge Campbell,[1] a member of the Confederate "Government" (who, for two years, had been satisfied, he said, that success was impossible), that the so-called Virginia Legislature, if allowed to reassemble, with the Governor, would work for the reconstruction of the Union, their first step being the withdrawal of the Virginia troops from the field, on condition that the confiscation of property in Virginia should not be allowed.[2] Anxious to end the war without further bloodshed, if possible, and satisfied that the withdrawal of the Virginia troops—in other words, nearly all of Lee's army—would accomplish it, he

[a] April 6, 1865.

---

the occasion under consideration, had similar protections along its sides, the nets being suspended from spars fastened to and projecting from the deck.

The torpedoes used by the Confederates were various in form and construction, as several illustrations in this work show. The most efficient ones were the *galvanic* and *percussion.* The former were provided with a wire connected with a galvanic battery on the shore, by which the mine might be exploded at any moment. The percussion or "sensitive" ones exploded by the act of forcible contact. Some of these were made in the form of a double cone, with percussion tubes arranged around the cylinder thus formed, at the point of contact of the bases of the cones, as seen in the illustration here given. Others were arranged as delineated on page 194. In the James River, at the time we are considering, the torpedoes were chiefly galvanic. Some were cylindrical, with one end conical; but a greater portion were pear-shaped. These were anchored in the channels or in shallow water, by means of a segment of a hollow iron sphere, called a "mushroom," which was attached to the buoyant mine by a chain. These were generally sunken opposite batteries, where the wires connected with bomb-proofs on shore. One of these, containing nearly a ton of powder, was planted in the center of the deep channel at Drewry's Bluff. On account of the depth of water, it was attached to a long rod, and that to the "mushroom" anchor, by a chain, as it was desirable to have the torpedo only the depth of a vessel below the surface.

PERCUSSION TORPEDO.

In fishing for torpedoes, a net with hooks, like that which depended from the bows of vessels, was dragged as a fisherman's net is dragged; also, common grapnels—four-pronged anchors without a stock, fastened to long lines—were dragged after the boats, like trolling; and when a torpedo was caught, it was carefully hauled up to the surface, and towed ashore. When a nest of torpedoes were found, a little float was anchored above them, with a small National flag upon it, by which pilots of vessels might be warned of the presence of danger.

"The torpedo," says Captain Chandler, in a letter to the author, descriptive of these "infernal machines," "is destined to be the least expensive but most terrible engine of defense yet invented. No vessel can be so constructed as to resist its power; and the uncertainty of its locality would prevent the hostile fleet from approaching the supposed position. In all collisions between hostile powers, whether army against army, ship against ship, or ship against fort, more or less bravery has been, and is destined to be, displayed; but the uncertainty of the locality of the foe—the knowledge that a simple touch will lay your ship a helpless, sinking wreck upon the water, without even the satisfaction of firing one shot in return, calls for more courage than can be expressed; and a short cruise among torpedoes will sober the most intrepid disposition."

[1] See page 302, volume I.

[2] This selfish proposition of the Virginians, in which they showed a willingness to sacrifice "the cause" in order to save themselves from harm, was bitterly commented upon in other parts of the Confederacy.

left with General Weitzel, on his departure from Richmond,[a] authority to allow "the gentlemen who have acted as the Legislature of Virginia, in support' of the rebellion, to assemble at Richmond and take measures to withdraw the Virginia troops and other support from resistance to the General Government." A safeguard was given. The fugitives returned, with the Governor, but instead of performing in good faith what had been promised in their name, they began legislating generally, as if they were the legal representatives of the people of Virginia. So soon as notice of this perfidy was given to the President after his return to Washington, he directed Weitzel to revoke the safeguard, and allow "the gentlemen who had acted as the Legislature of Virginia" to return to private life. The surrender of Lee had, meanwhile, made the contemplated action unnecessary. The President was blamed by the loyal people for allowing these men to assemble with acknowledged powers; and the Confederates abused him for dissolving the assembly.[1]

The President returned to Washington City on the day of Lee's surrender, where he was the recipient of a multitude of congratulations because of the dawn of peace. On the 11th he issued proclamations, one declaring the closing, until further notice, of certain ports in the Southern States, whereof the blockade had been raised by their capture, respectively; and the other, demanding, henceforth, for our vessels in foreign ports, on penalty of retaliation, those privileges and immunities which had hitherto been denied them on the plea of according equal belligerent rights to the Republic and its internal enemies. On the same evening, Washington City was brilliant with bonfires and illuminations because of the surrender of Lee. The Executive Mansion was filled with light; and there, to a vast assemblage of citizens, the President spoke earnest words concerning the past and the future—the last words with which he ever publicly addressed the people orally. He took that occasion to set forth his views concerning the reorganization of society in the States wherein rebellion had existed, in which he evinced an entire absence of bitterness of feeling toward those who had conspired and rebelled; and he remitted to Congress all questions connected with the political reorganization of States, and their representation in the National Legislature. On the following day an order was issued from the War Department, which had been approved by General Grant, putting an end to all drafting and recruiting for the National army, and the purchase of munitions of war and supplies; and declaring that the number of general and staff officers would be speedily reduced, and all military restrictions on trade and commerce be removed forthwith.

This virtual proclamation of the end of the war went over the land on the anniversary of the evacuation of Fort Sumter,[b] while General Anderson was replacing the old flag over the ruins of that fortress.[2] Preparations for a National thanksgiving were a-making, and the atmosphere of the Republic, so to speak, was radiant with sunlight, when a

[a] April 6, 1865.

[b] April 14.

---

[1] In his note to General Weitzel, giving him authority to allow the so-called Virginia Legislature to assemble, the President, having no confidence in their truth and integrity, made a provision for treachery, by saying: "If they attempt it [action for restoration], give them permission and protection until, if at all, they attempt some act hostile to the United States; in which case you will notify them, giving them a reasonable time to leave, and at the end of which time, arrest any who remain."

[2] See page 465.

dark cloud appeared, and suddenly overspread the firmament as with a pall. Before midnight the electric messengers went over the land with the tidings that the President had been murdered ! The sad story may be briefly told as follows :—

On the morning of the 14th, General Grant arrived in Washington.[1] Captain Robert Lincoln, the President's son, was one of his staff officers. They had arrived in time for the latter to breakfast with his father, and give him the narrative of an eye-witness, as he was, of the scenes of Lee's surrender. At 11 o'clock the President attended a Cabinet meeting, at which Grant was present. When the meeting adjourned, he made an arrangement with the General to attend Ford's Theater in the evening, and sent a messenger to engage a box. When, awhile afterward, Schuyler Colfax, the Speaker of the House of Representatives, visited him, he invited that gentleman to accompany Mrs. Lincoln and himself to the theater, but previous engagements caused Mr. Colfax to decline. General Grant was called to New York that evening.

It was publicly announced in the afternoon, that the President and General Grant would be at the theater. The house was crowded. Mr. Lincoln and a little party[2] arrived just after eight o'clock. The President was seated in a high-backed rocking-chair, with Mrs. Lincoln and Miss Harris on his left. The box had been draped with an American flag in honor of the President. The play, " Our American Cousin," was drawing to a close, when, at a little past ten o'clock, John Wilkes Booth, an actor by profession, passed near the box where the President and his party were seated, and after presenting a card to Mr. Lincoln's messenger, in the passage way,[3] he stood and looked down upon the orchestra and the audience for a few minutes. He then entered the vestibule of the President's box, closed the door and fastened it from the inside with a piece of plank previously provided, so that it might not be opened from the outside. He then drew a Derringer pistol, and with this in his right hand, and a long two-edged dagger in his left, he entered the inner door of the box directly behind the President, who was leaning a little forward, absorbed in the interest of the drama. Holding the pistol over the back of the chair, he shot Mr. Lincoln in the head. The ball entered back of the ear, and passing through the brain, lodged just behind the right eye. The President's head fell slightly forward, and his eyes closed; he lived nine hours afterward, but was not conscious.

Major Rathbone was startled by the report of the pistol, and seeing Booth, who was half hidden by the powder-smoke that filled the box, seized him. The murderer tore away from his grasp, dropped his pistol, and striking with his dagger, made a serious wound on the Major's left arm. The assassin then rushed to the front of the box, with the gleaming weapon in his hand, and shouted, " *Sic Semper Tyrannis !*"—so may it be always with Tyrants—the motto of the seal of Virginia, and then leaped upon the stage.

---

[1] Unlike most conquerors, Grant did not enter the capital of the conquered, and enjoy the sensations that await visitors on such occasions, but following simply in the path of duty, when his work was done, he went directly to his own capital to report its results to his Government.

[2] Composed of Mrs. Lincoln, Major H. R. Rathbone, and Miss Clara W. Harris, daughter of Senator Ira Harris.

[3] At nine o'clock a man appeared at the same place, with a large package, and inquired for General Grant. No doubt the intention was to murder the General at the same time Mr. Lincoln was assassinated.

He was booted and spurred for a night ride. One of his spurs caught in the flag, and he fell. Rising, he turned to the audience and exclaimed, "*The South is avenged!*" and then escaped by a back door, where he mounted a horse a boy was holding for him, fled across the Anacosta, and found temporary refuge with some sympathizing friends, among the Maryland slave-holders. The President was carried from the theater to the house of Mr. Peterson, on the opposite side of the street, where he died the next morning[a] at twenty-two minutes past seven o'clock.[1]

[a] April 15, 1865.

So fell, by the hands of an assassin—an embodiment of the dark spirit of the Conspirators against the Republic—ABRAHAM LINCOLN,[2] the best rep-

---

[1] Mrs. Lincoln, half dead with fright and grief, was taken to the house where her husband lay. He was soon surrounded by the prominent officers of the Government, and other distinguished gentlemen, who remained with him until the last.

[2] There is evidence on record, that during the whole war, as well as before Mr. Lincoln's inauguration, plots were formed, from time to time, for his assassination, not only in this country, but among the friends of the Conspirators in Europe. But, having in his heart, "Charity toward all, and malice toward none," he could not believe that anybody would be so wicked as to deliberately murder him; and he never took a precaution against assassination, voluntarily.

In the first and second volumes of this work may be found extended narratives of events connected with a plot to assassinate Mr. Lincoln while on his way to Washington City, in February, 1861. The following interesting account, not only of those circumstances, but of early movements in the preparations for overturning the Government, have been kindly communicated to the author by S. M. Felton, the Superintendent of the Philadelphia, Wilmington and Baltimore railway. Mr. Pinkerton, mentioned in this narrative, has, in an interesting pamphlet, given a history similar in the tenor of many facts. Mr. Felton's communication, dated Nov. 15, 1867, is as follows, after speaking of the determination of the Southern politicians to rebel, after the election of Mr. Lincoln:—

"My own business relations for the last ten years, as manager of a railroad connecting the North with the South, had brought me into relations somewhat intimate with Southern men. I saw trouble, and tried to avert it as far as I could by my personal influence. I advised on both sides a conservative policy, and endeavored, so far as I could, to bring both parties together by adjusting differences. The plot was, however, more deeply laid than appeared on the surface, and soon broke out in open rebellion. From this moment I did not hesitate to decide what course I was to pursue, and this was to support the Government with all the means at my disposal. I was importuned to remain neutral, and also to decline to place the road at the disposal of the Government for the transportation of troops and supplies; but I regarded such a course as no less treasonable than open rebellion. It soon came to my knowledge, first from rumors, and then from evidence which I could not doubt, that there was a deep-laid conspiracy to capture Washington, destroy all the avenues to it, from the north, east and west, and thus prevent the inauguration of Mr. Lincoln in the Capitol of the country; and if this plot did not succeed, then to murder him on his way to the Capital, and thus inaugurate a revolution which, they hoped, would end in establishing a Southern Confederacy, uniting all the slave States, while the North was to be divided into separate cliques, each striving for the destruction of the other. Early in the year 1861, Miss Dix, the philanthropist, came into my office on a Saturday afternoon. I had known her for some years, as one engaged in alleviating the sufferings of the afflicted. Her occupation in Southern hospitals had brought her in contact with the prominent men South. She had become familiar with the structure of Southern society, and also with the working of its political machinery. She stated to me that she had an important communication to make to me personally. I listened attentively to what she had to say for more than an hour. She put in a tangible and reliable shape, by the facts she related, what before I had heard, in numerous and detached parcels. The sum of it all was, that there was then an extensive and organized conspiracy throughout the South, to seize upon Washington, with its archives and records, and then declare the Southern Conspirators, *de facto*, the Government of the United States; at the same time they were to cut off all modes of communication between Washington and the North, East, and West, and thus prevent the transportation of troops, to wrest the Capital from the hands of the insurgents. Mr. Lincoln's inauguration was thus to be prevented, or his life was to fall a sacrifice. In fact, she said troops were then drilling on the line of our own road, the Washington and Annapolis line, and other lines of railroad. The men drilled were to obey the commands of their leaders, and the leaders were banded together to capture Washington. As soon as the interview was ended, I called Mr. N. P. Trist, who was then, and is now, in confidential relations with the railroad, into my office, and told him I wanted him to go to Washington that night and communicate these facts to General Scott. I also furnished him with some data for General Scott, as to the other routes to Washington, that might be adopted in case the direct route was cut off. One was the Delaware railroad to Seaford, and then up the Chesapeake and the Potomac to Washington, or to Annapolis, and thence to Washington; another to Perryville, and thence by water to Annapolis, and thence to Washington. Mr. Trist left that night, and arrived in Washington at six the next morning. He immediately had an interview with General Scott, who, after listening to him, told him he had foreseen the trouble that was coming, and in October previous, had made a communication to President Buchanan predicting trouble at the South, and urging strongly the garrisoning of all the Southern forts and arsenals with forces sufficient to hold them, but that his advice had been unheeded and nothing had been done, and he feared nothing would be done; that he was powerless, and that he feared it would be necessary to inaugurate Mr. Lincoln at Philadelphia. He should, however, do all he could to bring troops to Washington, sufficient to make it secure; but he had no influence with the administration, and feared

resentative of true Democracy in America, known in this generation. His
death occasioned the most profound grief throughout the Republic, and sor-

the worst consequences. Thus matters stood on Mr. Trist's visit to Washington, and thus they stood for some
time afterward. A few days subsequently, a gentleman from Baltimore came out to Back River Bridge, on
the railroad, about five miles east of the city, and told the bridge-keeper that he had come to give information,
which had come to his knowledge, of vital importance to the road, which he wished communicated to me. The
nature of this communication was, that a party was then organized in Baltimore for burning our bridges in case
Mr. Lincoln came over the road, or in case we attempted to carry troops for the defense of Washington. This party
had combustible materials then prepared to take out and pour over the bridges; that they were to disguise themselves as negroes, and be at the bridge just before the train, bringing Mr. Lincoln, arrived. The bridge was then to
be burned, and the train attacked, and Mr. Lincoln to be put out of the way. This man appeared to be·a gentleman, and in earnest, and honest in what he said; but he would not give his name, nor allow any inquiries to be
made as to his name or exact abode, as he said his life would be in peril were it known that he had given this
information. He said if we would not attempt to find him out, he would continue to come and give us information. He came, subsequently, several times, and gave items of information as to the movements of the Conspirators, but I have never been able to ascertain who he was. Immediately after the development of these
facts, I went to Washington, and there met a prominent and reliable man from Baltimore, who was well
acquainted with Marshal Kane, then the chief of police. I was anxious to ascertain whether he was loyal and
reliable, and made particular inquiries upon both these points. I was assured that he was perfectly reliable,
whereupon I made known some few of the reports that had come to my knowledge in reference to the designs
to burn the bridges, and requested that they should be laid before Marshal Kane, with a request that he should
detail a police force to make the necessary investigation. Marshal Kane was seen, and it was suggested to him
that there were reports of a conspiracy to burn the bridges and cut off Washington, and his advice was asked, as
to the best way of ferreting out the Conspirators. He scouted the idea that there was any such thing on foot,
said he had thoroughly investigated the whole matter, and there was not the slightest foundation for such
rumors. Kane's manner of treating the subject, satisfied me that he was not reliable. I then determined to
have nothing more to do with him, but to investigate the matter in my own way, and at once sent for a celebrated
detective, Allan Pinkerton, who resided in the West, and whom I had before employed in an important matter.
He was a man of great skill and resources. I furnished him with a few hints only, and at once set him on the
track, with eight assistants. There were then drilling on the line of the railroad, some three military organizations, professedly for home defense, pretending to be Union, and, in one or two instances, tendering their
services to the railroad in case of trouble. Their propositions were duly considered, but the defense of the
road was never intrusted to them. The first thing done by Pinkerton was to enlist a volunteer in each of these
military companies. They pretended to come from New Orleans and Mobile, and did not appear to be wanting
in sympathy for the South. They were furnished with uniforms at the expense of the road, and drilled as often
as their associates in arms; became initiated into all the secrets of the organization, and reported every day or
two to their chief, who immediately reported to me the designs and plans of the companies. One of these
organizations was loyal, but the other two were disloyal and fully in the plot to destroy the bridges and march
to Washington, to help wrest it from the hands of the legally constituted authorities. Every nook and corner on
the road and its vicinity was explored by the chief and his detectives, and the secret working of secession and
treason made bare, and brought to light. Societies were formed in Baltimore, and various modes, known to and
practiced only by detectives, were resorted to to win the confidence of the Conspirators and get into their secrets.
The plan worked to a charm, and the midnight plottings and the daily consultations of the Conspirators were
treasured up as a guide to our future plans for thwarting them. It turned out that all that had been communicated by Miss Dix and the gentleman from Baltimore, rested upon a foundation of fact, and that the half had not
been told. It was made as certain by these investigations, as strong circumstantial, and positive evidence could
make it, that there was a plot to burn the bridges and destroy the road, and murder Mr. Lincoln on his way to
Washington, if it turned out that he went there before troops were called. If troops were first called, then the
bridges were to be burned, and Washington cut off and taken possession of by the South. I at once organized
and armed a force of about two hundred men, whom I distributed along the line, between the Susquehanna and
Baltimore, principally at the bridges. These men were drilled regularly by drill-masters, and were apparently
employed in whitewashing the bridges, putting on some six or seven coats of wash, saturated with salt and
alum, to make the outside of the bridges as nearly fire-proof as possible. This whitewashing, so extensive in
its application, became the nine days' wonder of the neighborhood. Thus the bridges were strongly guarded
and a train was arranged so as to concentrate all the forces at one point in case of trouble. The programme of
Mr. Lincoln was changed, and it was decided that he should go to Harrisburg from Philadelphia, and thence
over the Northern Central road by way of Baltimore, and thence to Washington. We were then informed by
our detective, that the attention of the Conspirators was turned from our road to the Northern Central, and that
they would there await the coming of Mr. Lincoln. This statement was confirmed by our Baltimore gentleman,
who came out again, and said that their designs upon our road were postponed for the present, and until we carried troops, would not be renewed. Mr. Lincoln was to be waylaid on the line of the Northern Central road,
and prevented from reaching Washington, or his life was to fall a sacrifice to the attempt. Thus matters stood
on the afternoon of his arrival in Philadelphia. I felt it my duty to communicate to him the facts that had come
to my knowledge, and urge his going to Washington privately that night in our sleeping-car, instead of publicly
two days after, as was proposed. I went to a hotel in Philadelphia, where I met the detective, Pinkerton, who
was registered under an assumed name, and arranged with him to bring Mr. Judd, Mr. Lincoln's intimate friend,
to his room, in season to arrange for the journey to Washington that night. One of our sub-detectives made
three efforts to communicate with Mr. Judd while passing through the streets in the procession, and was three
times arrested and carried out of the crowd by the police. The fourth time he succeeded, and brought
Mr. Judd to the room at the hotel, where he met the detective-in-chief and myself. We lost no time

row wherever civilization prevailed.   The manner of his death sent a thrill of horror everywhere; the rebound of feeling decreed his earthly apotheosis. By the consent of the common conscience and judgment, the honored and beloved Emancipator became an adored Martyr; and Democrats in all lands instantly placed him by the side of Washington, in the calendar of their saints and sages.   The solemn words of his last inaugural address were recalled in nearly all civilized languages;[1] and forty thousand French Demo-

in making known to him the facts which had come to our knowledge in reference to the conspiracy, and I most earnestly advised that Mr. Lincoln should go to Washington privately that night in our sleeping-car. Mr. Judd fully entered into the plan, and said he would urge Mr. Lincoln to adopt it. On his and Pinkerton's communicating with Mr. Lincoln after the services of the evening were over, he answered that he had engaged to go to Harrisburg and speak the next day, and he would not break his engagement, even in the face of such peril, but that after he had fulfilled the engagement he would follow such advice as we might give him in reference to his journey to Washington. It was then arranged by myself and Pinkerton that Mr. Lincoln should go to Harrisburg the next day, and make his address, after which he was apparently to retire to Governor Curtin's house for the night, but in reality to go to a point about two miles out of Harrisburg, on the Pennsylvania railroad, where an extra car and engine awaited to take him to Philadelphia. At the time of his retiring, the telegraph lines east, west, north and south from Harrisburg were cut, so that no message as to his movements could be sent off in any direction. Mr. Lincoln could not probably arrive in season for our regular train that left at 11 P. M., and I did not dare to send him by an extra, for fear of its being found out or suspected that he was on the road, and it became necessary for me to devise some excuse for the detention of the train. But three persons on the road besides myself knew the plan. One of these, Mr. Wm. Stearns, I sent by an earlier train to say to the people of the Washington branch road that I had an important package which I was getting ready for the 11 P. M. train; that it was necessary I should have this package delivered in Washington early the next morning, without fail; that I was straining every nerve to get it ready by 11 o'clock, but in case I did not succeed, I should delay the train until it was ready, probably not more than half an hour, and I wished, as a personal favor, that the Washington train should await the coming of ours from Philadelphia, before leaving. This request was willingly complied with by the managers of the Washington branch, and Mr. Stearns, whom I had sent to Baltimore, so informed me by telegraph in cipher. The second person in the secret, Mr. H. F. Kenney, I sent to West Philadelphia, in company with Pinkerton, in a carriage, to await the coming of Mr. Lincoln. I gave him a package of old railroad reports, done up with great care, with a great seal attached to it, and directed, in a fair round hand, to a person at Willard's 'E. J. Allen' (the assumed name of Pinkerton). I marked it 'very important, to be delivered without fail by 11 o'clock train,' indorsing my own name upon the package. Mr. Lincoln arrived in West Philadelphia, and was immediately taken into the carriage with Mr. Kenney and Pinkerton, and driven to within a square of our station, where Mr. Kenney jumped off with the package and waited till he saw the carriage drive up to the door and Mr. Lincoln and the detective get out and go in. He then came up and gave the package to the conductor, who was waiting at the door to receive it, in company with a police officer. Tickets had been bought beforehand for Mr. Lincoln and party to Washington, including a tier of berths in the sleeping-car. He passed between the conductor and the police officer at the door, and neither suspected who he was. The conductor remarked as he passed, 'Well, old fellow, it is lucky for you that our President detained the train to send a package by it, or you would have been left.' Mr. Lincoln and the detective being safely ensconced in the sleeping-car, and my package safely in the hands of the conductor, the train started for Baltimore, about fifteen minutes behind time. Our man number three, George Stearns, started on the train to go to Baltimore, and hand it over, with its contents, to man number one, William Stearns, who awaited its arrival in Baltimore. Before the train reached Gray's Ferry bridge, and before Mr. Lincoln had resigned himself to slumber, the conductor came to George Stearns, and accosting him, said: 'George, I thought you and I were friends. Why did you not tell me Old Abe was on board?' George, thinking the conductor had, in some way, become possessed of the secret, answered: 'John, we are friends, and, as you have found it out, Old Abe is on board, and we will still be friends, and see him safely through.' John answered, 'Yes, if it costs me my life, he shall have a safe passage,' and so George stuck to one end of the car, and the conductor to the other every moment that his duties to the other passengers would admit of it. And Mr. Lincoln did arrive safely. It turned out, however, that the conductor was mistaken in his man. A man strongly resembling Mr. Lincoln had come down to the train about half an hour before it left, and bought a ticket to Washington, with a ticket for the sleeping-car. The conductor had seen him, and concluded he was the veritable 'Old Abe.' George delivered the sleeping-car and train over to William, in Baltimore, and William, as had been previously arranged, took his place at the back and rode to Washington, where he arrived on the rear of the sleeping-car, at about six A. M. on time, and saw Mr. Lincoln in the hands of a friend, safely delivered at Willard's, when he secretly ejaculated, 'God be praised!' He also saw my package of railroad reports marked 'highly important,' safely delivered into the hands for which it was intended. This being done, he performed his morning ablutions in peace and quiet, and enjoyed with unusual zest a breakfast at Willard's. At eight o'clock, the time agreed upon, the telegraph wires were joined, and the first message flashed across the line was, 'Your package has arrived safely, and been delivered.—WILLIAM.' Then there went up from the writer of this a shout of joy, and a devout thanksgiving to Him from whom all blessings flow, and the few in the secret joined in a heartfelt amen. Thus began and ended a chapter in the history of the Rebellion that has never been before written, but about which there have been many hints entitled a Scotch cap and riding cloak, &c., neither of which had any foundation in truth. Mr. Lincoln was safely inaugurated, after which I discharged our detective force, and also the semi-military whitewashers, and all was quiet and serene again on the railroad."

[1] The *British Standard*, a leading English journal, said of it: "It is the most remarkable thing of the sort ever pronounced by any President of the United States, from the first day until now. Its Alpha and its Omega

crats testified their appreciation of his character and services, and "their desire to express their sympathy for the American Union, in the person of

MEDAL FROM THE FRENCH DEMOCRATS.

one of its most illustrious and purest representatives," by causing a magnificent gold medal to be struck and presented to the President's widow.[1]

---

is *Almighty God*, the God of Justice and the Father of Mercies, who is working out the purpose of his love. It is invested with a dignity and pathos which lift it high above every thing of the kind, whether in the Old World or the New. The whole thing puts us in mind of the best men of the English Commonwealth; there is, in fact, much of the old prophet in it."

[1] The writer is indebted to the kindness of Robert Lincoln, son of the President, for a photograph of the medal, of which the engraving here given is a copy, in outline, about one-third less in size than the original, which is about four inches in diameter. On one side, in relief, is a profile of Mr. Lincoln, surrounded by the words, in French: "DEDICATED BY THE FRENCH DEMOCRACY. TWICE ELECTED PRESIDENT OF THE UNITED STATES." On the reverse is an altar, bearing the following inscription, also in French: "LINCOLN, HONEST MAN, ABOLISHED SLAVERY, RE-ESTABLISHED THE UNION, AND SAVED THE REPUBLIC, WITHOUT VEILING THE STATUE OF LIBERTY. HE WAS ASSASSINATED THE 14TH OF APRIL, 1865." Below all are the words, "LIBERTY, EQUALITY, FRATERNITY." On one side of the altar stands winged Victory, with her right hand resting upon a sword, and her left holding a civic wreath. On the other side stand two emancipated slaves—the younger, a lad, offering a palm-branch, and the elder pointing him to the American eagle, bearing the shield, the olive-branch, and the lightning, with the motto of the Union. The elder freedman holds the musket of the militia-man, to which their citizenship entitles them. Near them are emblems of industry and progress. Back of Victory are seen an anchor, merchandize, and ships, emblematical of commerce. Over the altar is a triangle, emblematical of trinity—the trinity of man's inalienable rights—LIBERTY, EQUALITY, AND FRATERNITY.

The funds for the medal were obtained by very small subscriptions, to which forty thousand French citizens subscribed. The French Government tried to prevent this, but failed. The medal was struck, and sent to Mrs. Lincoln, with the following letter, signed by the committee having the matter in charge:—

"PARIS, *ce* 13 *Octobre*, 1866.

MADAME:—

"Nous sommes chargés de vous offrir la médaille qu'ont fait frapper, en l'honneur du grand honnête homme dont vous portez le nom, plus de 40,000 citoyens Français, désireux de manifester leurs sympathies pour l'Union Américaine, dans la personne de l'un de ses plus illustres et de ses plus purs représentants.

"Si la France possédait les libertés dont jouit l'Amérique républicaine, ce n'est pas par milliers, mais par millions, que se seraient comptés avec nous les admirateurs de Lincoln, et les partisans des opinions auxquelles il vouà sa vie, et que sa mort a consacrées.

"Veuillez agréer, Madame, l'hommage de notre profond respect.

"Les membres du Comité: Etienne Arago, Ch. L. Chassin. L. Greppo, Laurent Pichat, Eng. Despois, L. Kneip, C. Thomas Albert, J. Michelet, Jules Barni, T. Delord, V. Chauffour, E. Littré, V. Schœlcher, V. Joigneaux, Vᵒʳ Mangin, Edgar Quinet, Louis Blanc, Eugène Pelletan, Victor Hugo."

TRANSLATION.

"PARIS, *October* 13, 1866.

"MADAM:—

"We have been charged with the duty of presenting to you the medal in honor of the great and honest man whose name you bear, and which 40,000 French citizens have caused to be struck, with a desire to express their sympathy for the American Union, in the person of one of its most illustrious and purest representatives.

The night of the assassination of Mr. Lincoln was one of horrors in the National Capital. According to a proclamation by his successor (Andrew Johnson), there was "evidence in the Bureau of Military Justice," that there had been a conspiracy formed by "Jefferson Davis, Jacob Thompson, Clement C. Clay, Beverly Tucker, George N. Saunders, William C. Cleary, and other rebels and traitors against the Government of the United States, harbored in Canada," to assassinate the President, and the Secretary of State, Mr. Seward;[1] and circumstances seemed to warrant the charge that they had intended the same fate for other members of the Cabinet, General Grant, and several leading Republicans, their object evidently being to put out of the way men in high places, opposed to the Conspirators, who, on the death of the President, might administer the Government, hoping thereby to produce anarchy, which, in some way, might lead to the accession to power of the leaders of the rebellion. Accordingly, on the night, and at the same hour, when Mr. Lincoln was murdered, a man named Lewis Payne Powell, of Florida, who had been a Confederate soldier, attempted to slay Mr. Seward, the Secretary of State, who was seriously ill at his house, in consequence of having been thrown from his carriage a few days before. Powell, or "Payne," as his associates called him, went to the Secretary's house with the pretense that he was a messenger of the Minister's physician. When the porter refused him admittance, he rushed by him and up two flights of stairs to Mr. Seward's chamber, at the door of which he was met and resisted by the Secretary's son, Frederick William. Payne struck the younger Seward to the floor with the handle of his pistol, fracturing his skull and making him insensible. The Secretary's daughter was attracted to the room-door by the noise, when Payne rushed by her, sprang like a furious tiger upon the bed, and inflicted three severe wounds upon the neck and face of Mr. Seward, with a dagger, when an invalid soldier, named Robinson, who was in attendance as nurse, seized the assassin from behind. The feeble resistance offered by the Secretary barely saved his life. While Payne was struggling with Robinson, Miss Seward shouted "Murder!" from the open window, and the porter ran into the street, crying for help. Payne, perceiving his peril, did not stop to finish his murderous work; but, with a great effort, he escaped from Robinson, rushed down the stairs to the street, mounted a horse that he had in readiness, and fled into the open country beyond the Anacosta, in search of Booth, the principal executor of the assassination plot.

At the time of the murder, the Secretary of War (Mr. Stanton) was absent from his own house. He had left Mr. Seward half an hour before the attack upon him. He was now called to action. Measures were immediately adopted for the discovery and arrest of the assassin, then unknown.

"If France possessed the liberty enjoyed by republican America, we would number with us not merely thousands, but millions of the admirers of Lincoln, and of the partisans of those opinions to which he devoted his life, and which are consecrated by his death.

"Please to accept, Madam, the homage of our profound respect.

"The members of the Committee."

[1] See President Johnson's Proclamation, May 2, 1865. In that proclamation, signed by him and by W. Hunter, Acting Secretary of State, a reward of one hundred thousand dollars was offered for the arrest of Jefferson Davis; twenty-five thousand dollars apiece for the arrest of Jacob Thompson, C. C. Clay, George N. Saunders, and Beverly Tucker; and ten thousand dollars for the arrest of William C. Cleary, late clerk of C. C. Clay.

Suspicion pointed toward Booth as the murderer of the President.   Cavalry and a heavy police force speedily shot out from the capital in radiating lines, in search of the offenders, but without success, when, at the end of three days, Colonel Lafayette C. Baker, the Chief Detective of the War Department, who had been at the head of the secret service from the beginning of the struggle, returned to Washington, and skillfully formed a plan for the service of justice in the matter.   Men were designated as the accomplices of Booth, now known to have been the assassin of the President, and cavalry and police were sent in pursuit of them.   Booth was overtaken in Virginia, below Fredericksburg, concealed in a barn.[a]   He refused to surrender.   The barn was fired, and the assassin was shot by a sergeant named Boston Corbett.   Payne, who had attempted to kill Mr. Seward, was soon arrested, with other accomplices of Booth, and some of them, with a woman named Surratt, whose house, in Washington City, appears to have been a place of rendezvous for Booth and his accomplices, were tried, by a military commission, for murder, and hung.[b]   Others were imprisoned.[1]

[a] April 21, 1865.

[b] July 7.

The President's body was taken to the Executive Mansion, and embalmed; and in the "East Room"[2] of that mansion, funeral services were held on Wednesday, the 19th of April.   Then the body was taken, in solemn procession, by way of Baltimore, Philadelphia, New York City, and Albany, and thence westward, to his private home, in Springfield, Illinois, and buried. It everywhere received tokens of the people's love and grief.   Funeral honors were displayed in many cities of the land, and the nation was really in mourning and tears.   But the Republic survived the shock which might have toppled down, in other lands, an empire or a dynasty.   By a seeming oversight in the managers of the assassin scheme, Andrew Johnson, the Vice-President, was not included in their list of victims.   He, who must legally succeed the dead President, seems not to have been put in jeopardy by the Conspirators; and six hours after Mr. Lincoln expired, Chief-Justice Chase administered to him the oath of office as President of the Republic.   Thoughtful people, who regarded private virtue as the basis of public integrity, and who sadly remembered the conduct of the Vice-President only a few weeks before, which shocked the moral sense of right-minded citizens, were filled with gloomy forebodings concerning the future of the Republic—for the most profound wisdom and exalted virtue in the Chief Magistrate were needed at that critical time.   He took the chair of Washington, assumed the reins of Government as Chief Magistrate, and invited the members of Mr. Lincoln's cabinet to retain their offices under his administration.[3]

With the surrender of Lee, the war was virtually ended.   Although he

---

[1] The persons hung were David E. Herrold, George A. Atzerott, Lewis Payne Powell, and Mary E. Surratt. Michael O'Laughlin, Samuel A. Mudd, and Samuel Arnold were sentenced to imprisonment at hard labor, for life.   Edward Spangler was sentenced to imprisonment at hard labor for six years.

[2] See page 425, volume I.

[3] At that time they consisted of William H. Seward, Secretary of State; Hugh McCulloch, Secretary of the Treasury; Edwin M. Stanton, Secretary of War; Gideon Welles, Secretary of the Navy; John P. Usher, Secretary of the Interior; James Speed, Attorney-General; and William Dennison, Postmaster-General.   Mr. Chase, the former Secretary of the Treasury, had been elevated to the seat of Chief-Justice of the United States, on the death of Judge Taney.   Mr. Stanton had succeeded Mr. Cameron in the War Department, early in 1862; and President Lincoln, satisfied that the public good required the removal of Montgomery Blair, the Postmaster-General, asked him to resign.   The request was granted, and Mr. Dennison was put in his place. Caleb Smith had died, and Mr. Usher had taken his place.

was general-in-chief, he included in the capitulation only the Army of Northern Virginia. That of Johnston, in North Carolina, and smaller bodies elsewhere, were yet in arms; but in the space of about a month after Lee's surrender, the last gun of the Rebellion was fired.

Let us see what these hostile forces were about.

We left Sherman's army around Goldsboro', resting and refitting for a further prosecution of the campaign.[1] Sherman intended to push northward, feign an attack on Raleigh, and make a lodgment at Burkesville, at the junction of the South Side and Danville railways, between the armies of Lee and Johnston. The auspicious events in the vicinity of the Appomattox, recorded in this chapter, made that movement unnecessary; and when, on the 6th of April, Sherman was informed of the victory at the Five Forks, and the evacuation of Petersburg and Richmond, he put his whole army in motion as quickly as possible, and moved on Johnston, who was yet at Smithfield, on the Neuse, with full thirty thousand men.

It was on the 10th of April[a] that Sherman's army moved, starting at daybreak. Slocum's column marched along the two most direct roads to Smithfield. Howard's moved more to the right, feigning the Weldon road; and Terry and Kilpatrick pushed up the west side [a] 1865. of the Neuse, for the purpose of striking the rear of Johnston's army between Smithfield and Raleigh, if he should retreat. Johnston knew that resistance would be in vain, and did retreat through Raleigh, and along the lines of the railway westward, toward Greensboro'. Jefferson Davis and his "cabinet" were then at Danville, where they had been playing "Government" for four or five days, making that village the new "capital of the Confederacy."[2] But on that day, they heard of the surrender of Lee, and fled, by railway to Greensboro', with anxious thoughts for the safety of themselves and the treasures which they had carried off from Richmond. They had proposed to Johnston a plan for that salvation, which that leader spurned. They proposed that he should disperse his army, excepting two or three batteries of artillery, the cavalry, and as many infantry as he could mount, with which he should form a guard for the "Government," and strike for the Mississippi and beyond, with Mexico as their final objective.

Johnston, deprecating the bad example of Lee, in continuing what he knew to be a hopeless war, and governed by the nicest sense of honor,

---

[1] See page 503.

[2] At Danville, on the 5th of April, Davis issued a Proclamation. After mentioning the causes which compelled the abandonment of Richmond, he said: "We have now entered upon a new phase of the struggle. Relieved from the necessity of guarding particular points, our army will be free to move from point to point, to strike the enemy in detail, far from his base. Let us but will it, and we are free. Animated by that confidence in spirit and fortitude, which never yet failed me, I announce to you, fellow-countrymen, that it is my purpose to maintain your cause with my whole heart and soul; that I will never consent to abandon to the enemy one foot of the soil of any one of the States of the Confederacy." He declared his purpose to defend Virginia, and that no peace should "ever be made with the infamous invaders of her territory." He added: "If, by the stress of numbers, we should ever be compelled to a temporary withdrawal from her limits, or those of any other border State, again and again will we return, until the baffled and exhausted enemy shall abandon, in despair, his endless and impossible task, of making slaves of a people resolved to be free."

It is worthy of note, that, while the Chief of the Confederacy was thus indulging in boastful language to deceive the people, he was ready to desert the cause, when necessity should compel him to do so, for the preservation of himself. One of Davis's staff officers, who went with the "Government" in its flight, speaking of Davis's proclamation, said, it was "to reassure the public, and to persuade them that it was for the special accommodation of Lee's new tactics—field tactics as opposed to intrenched positions—that Richmond was abandoned. The proclamation was very spirited, and breathed defiance to the last."—*History of the Last Days and Final Fall of the Rebellion*, by a Rebel Staff Officer (Lieutenant C. E. L. Stuart).

justice, and humanity, had the moral courage to do his duty according to the dictates of conscience. He not only refused to fight any more in a hopeless cause, but indignantly spurned the base proposition to desert his army, leave the soldiers far away from their homes, and unprovided for, and subject the people in the region where the army would be dispersed, to the sore evils of plunder which lawless bands of starving men would engage in. He did more. He stated frankly to the people of North and South Carolina, Georgia, and Florida, included within his military department, that "war could not be longer continued by them, except as robbers," and that he should take measures to stop it, save both the army and the people from further evil, as far as possible, and "to avoid the crime of waging a hopeless war." [1]

When Sherman arrived [a] at Smithfield, he found the bridges that had spanned the Neuse destroyed, and his antagonist in full retreat through Raleigh, toward Hillsboro'. There he heard of the surrender of Lee. He at once dropped his trains, and pushed on after Johnston as rapidly as possible, in heavy rain, taking formal possession of deserted Raleigh on his way. [2] His right wing was directed to follow the line of retreat, while his left should take a more southerly route by Pittsboro' and Asheboro', with the expectation that Johnston would follow the line of the railroad southwestward, from Greensboro' to Salisbury.

[a] April 11, 1865.

The Nationals were pressing on in pursuit with great vigor, when Sherman received a note [b] from Johnston, inquiring whether, "in order to stop the further effusion of blood, and devastation of property," he was "willing to make a temporary suspension of active operations, and to communicate to General Grant the request that he would take like action in regard to other armies, the object being to permit the civil authorities to enter into the needful arrangements to terminate the existing war." [3] Sherman made a prompt response to this communication, in which

[b] April 14.

---

[1] The "Rebel Staff Officer," just mentioned, speaking of a personal interview between Davis, Johnston, and other leaders, on a hill near Greensboro', said: "Mr. Davis felt much concerned, and rather showed it. *He distrusted Johnston*, but relied on Breckinridge to foil him in an untimely move. Johnston was instructed to fight. He did not approve the order, and *disputed, not only its wisdom, but its power over his actions.*"

[2] When the Commissioners, appointed by Governor Vance (see note 3, below) to carry a message to General Sherman, returned, as they approached Raleigh, they saw the railway station in flames. The city was deserted by the Governor and State officers, and by nearly all of the inhabitants, who had been scared away by Sherman's approach. The Confederate cavalry, under Wheeler, were in possession of the city. These had plundered and fired the station house. The Commissioners found a single servant in the Governor's room at the State-House, who had been intrusted by Vance with the keys, to deliver them. Vance had also left with the Mayor, W. B. Harrison, authority to surrender the city to Sherman, in the form of a letter to the General, begging him to extend the favor of his protection to the citizens, the charitable institutions, and the precious documents and other property in the State Capitol. President Swain alone was at the State-House when the National officers arrived to hoist the Union flag over it. They took quiet possession, after Mayor Harrison had formally surrendered the place. No doubt, the arrival of Swain and Graham saved the city of Raleigh and the State archives from destruction, for some of Wheeler's cavalry were there, breaking open and plundering stores on Fayetteville Street. Swain, joined by a leading citizen, begged them to desist, the former telling them that he was just from Sherman, who had promised that, if no resistance should be offered, the town should be protected. "Damn Sherman, and the town, too; we care for neither!" was their reply. The appearance of the head of Kilpatrick's column was an efficient argument. They then left in haste, excepting a single trooper, who waited until Kilpatrick's advance was within a hundred yards of him, when he discharged his revolver at them, six times in rapid succession. He then turned and fled, was pursued, caught, and hung in a grove, in the suburbs of the city.

[3] The incipient steps in the direction of a conference to bring about a suspension of hostilities, had been taken by ex-Governor David L. Swain, one of the best and most distinguished men of the State, who had been for thirty years President of the University of North Carolina, at Chapel Hill. So early as the 8th of April, when news of the evacuation of Richmond and Petersburg had caused universal gloom, President Swain addressed a note to ex-Governor William A. Graham who was a member of the Confederate "Congress," proposing action

he declared that he was fully empowered to arrange with Johnston any terms for the suspension of further hostilities, as between the armies they respectively commanded, and that he was willing to hold a conference. He said he would limit the advance of his main column, the next day, to Morrisville, a little west of Raleigh, and the cavalry to the University at Chapel Hill, with the expectation that Johnston would also maintain the position of his forces then held, until each had notice of a failure to agree. He further said that, as a basis of action, he would undertake to abide by the terms and conditions made by Grant and Lee at Appomattox Court-House, and would obtain from the General-in-chief an order to suspend the movements of any troops, from the direction of Virginia; also that he would direct General Stoneman to "suspend any devastation or destruction contemplated by him."

Sherman halted his army, but did not receive any communication from Johnston until the 16th,[a] when a message reached Kilpatrick, from Hampton, saying it was the desire of his chief to meet the Union commander at ten o'clock the next day, at Durham's Station, about half way between Raleigh and Hillsboro'. They met there at twelve o'clock, when Johnston gave Sherman to understand that he regarded the Confederate "cause" as lost, and that further war on the part of the Confederate troops was folly. He admitted that Grant's terms conceded to Lee were magnanimous, and all that he could ask, but he wanted some general concessions, he said, concerning the safety of his followers, from harm from the outraged Government; and he insisted upon conditions of general pacification, involving political guarantees, which Sherman had no authority to agree to. They separated without agreeing, but at a second conference the next day,[b] Sherman consented to a Memorandum of agreement, as a basis for the consideration of the Government. If it had been carried out, it would, in effect, have instantly restored to all persons who had been engaged in the rebellion, every right and privilege, political and social, which they had enjoyed before they rebelled, without any liability to punishment. It proposed, practically, an utter forgetfulness of the events of the war, and made it a hideous farce, with the features of a

[a] April, 1865.

[b] April 18.

on the part of the people of North Carolina, independent of the Confederate "Government," looking to a termination of the war. Graham agreed with Swain, and said, in a letter to him in reply:—"I left Richmond thoroughly convinced that (1) Independence for the Southern Confederacy was perfectly hopeless; (2) that through the administration of Mr. Davis, we could expect no peace, so long as he shall be supplied with the resources of war; and that (3) it was the duty of the State Government immediately to move for the purpose of effecting an adjustment of the quarrel with the United States."

These two gentlemen held a consultation with Governor Vance, at Raleigh.[c] The result was their appointment as commissioners, to carry to General Sherman a communication from the Governor, proposing a conference, or to treat directly for a suspension of hostilities, until the further action of the State (its legislature was about to meet) should be ascertained in regard to the termination of the war. With a flag of truce, and a safeguard from General Hardee, at Raleigh, Messrs. Swain and Graham proceeded in a special train, on the 12th, for Sherman's head-quarters. Wade Hampton, through whose lines they must pass, did all in his power to thwart the movement, but failed. The commissioners reached Sherman's quarters, where they passed the night, and returned with a friendly letter to the Governor. This led the way to the proposition made by Johnston. For full particulars of this mission, and of events in North Carolina at that period, the reader is referred to an interesting volume, entitled *The Last Ninety Days of the War in North Carolina*, by Cornelia Phillips Spencer.

Speaking of the interview of the commissioners with General Sherman, Mrs. Spencer says, without comment:—" Reference was made to the burning of Columbia. The General remarked, with great emphasis:—' I have been grossly misrepresented. I changed my head-quarters eight times, during that night, and with every general officer under my command, strained every nerve to stop the fire. I declare, in the presence of my God, that Hampton burned Columbia, and that he alone is responsible for it.' "

[c] April 9.

dreadful tragedy.[1]   That memorandum, drawn up, it is said, by Breckinridge, in a very adroit manner, was signed by the commanding generals, in duplicate, and Sherman immediately sent a copy of it to his Government, by the hands of Major Hitchcock.

In his anxiety to end the war and restore the Union, Sherman, with the purest motives, and most earnest desire to do right, made a grave mistake. It occurred at a time when such a mistake could hardly be excused by the loyal people. The "Memorandum" arrived at Washington when the excitement, occasioned by the murder of the President, was at its height, and the friends of the Government felt little disposed to be lenient, or even merciful, much less unnecessarily magnanimous toward the Conspirators and their abettors, for, with Cicero, they felt that "mercy toward traitors is cruelty to the State." The "Memorandum" was published, and created universal indignation and alarm. The effect, at that critical moment, might have produced calamitous acts, had not information that the "Memorandum" had been rejected by the new President and his Cabinet, with the approval of General Grant, went out with it, with such explicit reasons for its rejection, given by Mr. Stanton, the Secretary of War, that the people were assured that the Government was not disposed to yield an iota of the fruits of its victory over Rebellion.[1]

---

[1] The following is a copy of the Memorandum or Basis of Agreement:—

"1st. The contending armies now in the field to maintain the *status quo* until notice is given by the commanding general of any one to his opponent, and reasonable time, say forty-eight hours, allowed.

"2d. The Confederate armies now in existence to be disbanded and conducted to their several State capitals, there to deposit their arms and public property in the State Arsenal, and each officer and man to execute and file an agreement to cease from acts of war, and to abide the action of both State and Federal authorities. The number of arms and munitions of war to be reported to the Chief of Ordnance at Washington City, subject to the future action of the Congress of the United States, and in the mean time to be used solely to maintain peace and order within the borders of the States respectively.

"3d. The recognition, by the Executive of the United States, of the several State Governments, on their officers and legislators taking the oath prescribed by the Constitution of the United States; and where conflicting State Governments have resulted from the war, the legitimacy of all shall be submitted to the Supreme Court of the United States.

"4th. The re-establishment of all Federal Courts in the several States, with powers, as defined by the Constitution and the laws of Congress.

"5th. The people and the inhabitants of all States to be guaranteed, so far as the Executive can, their political rights and franchises, as well as their rights of person and property, as defined by the Constitution of the United States, and of the States respectively.

"6th. The Executive authority or Government of the United States not to disturb any of the people by reason of the late war, so long as they live in peace and quiet, and abstain from acts of armed hostility, and obey the laws in existence at the place of their residence.

"7th. In general terms it is announced that the war is to cease; a general amnesty, so far as the Executive of the United States can command, on condition of the disbandment of the Confederate Armies, the distribution of arms, and the resumption of peaceful pursuits by officers and men hitherto composing said armies."

Not being fully empowered by our respective principals to fulfill these terms, we, individually and officially, pledge ourselves to promptly obtain authority, and will endeavor to carry out the above programme.

[2] The following were the reasons:—

"1st. It was an exercise of authority not vested in General Sherman, and, on its face, shows that both he and Johnston knew that General Sherman had no authority to enter into any such arrangements.

"2d. It was a practical acknowledgment of the rebel Government.

"3d. It undertook to re-establish rebel State Governments that had been overthrown at the sacrifice of many thousand loyal lives, and immense treasure; and placed arms and munitions of war in the hands of rebels at their respective capitals, which might be used so soon as the armies of the United States were disbanded, and used to conquer and subdue loyal States.

"4th. By the restoration of rebel authority, in their respective States, they would be enabled to re-establish Slavery.

"5th. It might furnish a ground of responsibility on the part of the Federal Government, to pay the rebel debt, and certainly subjects loyal citizens of rebel States to debts contracted by rebels in the name of the State.

"6th. It puts in dispute the existence of loyal State Governments, and the new State of West Virginia, which had been recognized by every department of the United States Government.

General Grant was immediately sent to Raleigh to declare the rejection of the "Memorandum," to relieve General Sherman of command if he should think it best to do so, and to direct an immediate and general resumption of hostilities. When Grant reached Morehead City, he telegraphed to Sherman the decision of the Government. Pressing forward he reached Sherman's head-quarters, at Raleigh, on the morning of the 24th,[a] [a April, 1865.] and directed that officer to communicate the decision of the Government to Johnston, immediately, and notify him that the truce would close within forty-eight hours after the message should reach the Confederate lines. The notification was accompanied by a demand for the immediate surrender of Johnston's army, on the terms grant-ed to Lee. Then Sher-man directed his corps commanders to re-sume the pursuit of Johnston at noon, on the 26th.

PLACE OF JOHNSTON'S SURRENDER TO SHERMAN.

Well satisfied that Sherman's mistake was the result of zeal for peace, acting un-der misapprehen-sions,[1] Grant left him in command; and, from the hour when he directed him to end the truce, and demand the surrender of Johnston's army, he was untrameled by any order from his superior. Johnston did not even know that Grant was at the head-quarters of the Union army, when, on the 25th, he replied to Sherman's note, and asked for another confer-ence at the place where they met before. Johnston's request was granted. The two commanders met at the house of James Bennett, near Durham's Station, in Orange County, North Carolina, on the 26th of April, 1865, and then agreed upon terms of capitulation precisely the same as those at Appo-mattox Court-House, it being stipulated that all arms and public property of the Confederates should be deposited at Greensboro'. Grant, who was waiting at Raleigh, approved of the terms, when Johnston's army, excepting a body of cavalry, led by Wade Hampton, was surrendered, in number about twenty-five thousand.[2] The capitulation included all the troops in

<hr />

"7th. It practically abolished confiscation laws, and relieved rebels of every degree, who had slaughtered our people, from all pains and penalties for their crimes.

"8th. It gave terms that had been deliberately, repeatedly, and solemnly rejected by President Lincoln, and better terms than the rebels had ever asked in their most prosperous condition.

"9th. It formed no basis of true and lasting peace, but relieved rebels from the presence of our victorious armies, and left them in a condition to renew their efforts to overthrow the United States Government and subdue the loyal States whenever their strength was recruited and any opportunity should offer."

[1] For a vindication of his acts in the matter of the truce and "Memorandum," see General Sherman's Report, dated City Point, May 4, 1865.

[2] This was, in round numbers, the sum of men surrendered and paroled. There were also 108 pieces of artillery surrendered, with equipments complete; also about 15,000 small-arms. A large number had strayed away with arms, horses, mules and wagons. General Johnston, in an "Address to the People of the Southern States,"

Johnston's Military Department, which comprised the sea-board States south of Virginia. On the 4th of May, General Taylor surrendered, at Citronelle, the Confederate forces in Alabama, to General Canby, on terms substantially like those accorded to Lee and Johnston. At the same time and place, Commander Farrand, as we have observed,[1] surrendered, to Rear-Admiral Thatcher, the Confederate navy in the Tombigbee River.[2]

The capitulation was followed, the next day,[a] by special Field Orders, issued by General Sherman, in which the surrender of the Confederate army was announced; directions given for the cessation of hostilities and relief of the distressed inhabitants near the army, and orders for the return of a greater portion of the soldiers to their homes. General Schofield, commanding the Department of North Carolina, was left there with the Tenth and Twenty-third Corps and Kilpatrick's cavalry. Stoneman was ordered to take his command to East Tennessee, and Wilson was directed to march his from Macon to the neighborhood of Decatur, on the Tennessee River. Generals Howard and Slocum were directed to conduct the remainder of the army to Richmond, Virginia, in time to resume their march to Washington City by the middle of May.

[a] April 27, 1865.

We have observed that all of Johnston's army was surrendered excepting some cavalry under Wade Hampton.[3] That leader refused to abide by the terms of the capitulation, and dashed off with a considerable body of troopers, toward Charlotte, to follow the fortunes of Jefferson Davis. He had returned from the presence of Davis (who had resolved to gather all the fragments of armies possible, and find or force his way to Mexico), after the capitulation was signed, but he cared not for faith or honor, for he was, as one of his partisans declared, "the most uncompromising cavalier in all the South."

Davis, as we have observed, with the "Government," fled from Danville on hearing of the surrender of Lee. They journeyed to Greensboro', where they found very few sympathizers, and were compelled to make their resi-

---

on the 6th of May, said that on the day of the capitulation the forces under his command, present and absent, were 70,510, including cavalry, reported on the 7th of April at 5,440. The total present with him, was 18,578, but the total effective or fighting force was only 14,179.

[1] See note 3, page 514.

[2] In the brief account of the Confederate pirate ships, given in Chap. XVI., in which the cruise of the Shenandoah, the last of these vessels afloat, was mentioned [see page 438], a notice of the powerful ram *Stonewall* was omitted. She was a British built, armed and manned steamer. She depredated upon American commerce for awhile, and was finally blockaded in the port of Ferrol, on the coast of Spain, by the National vessels *Niagara* and *Sacramento*. She slipped out, and ran across the Atlantic to Havana, where she arrived after the end of the war. The Spanish authorities there took possession of her, and handed her over to Rear-Admiral Godon, who was then cruising among the West India Islands, with a powerful squadron, in search of her. Godon took her to Hampton Roads,[b] and handed her over to the Government.

[b] June 12,

[3] In a communication to General Kilpatrick, this leader signed his name "Ned Wade Hampton." Major Nichols, in his *Story of the Great March*, speaking of this notorious rebel, at the first conference between Sherman and Johnston, says: "It should be said of Hampton's face—that is, what could be seen of it behind a beard which was unnaturally black for a man of fifty years of age—that it seemed bold, even beyond arrogance, and this expression was, if possible, intensified by the boastful fanfaronade which he continued during the whole period of the conference."

Of General Johnston, Major Nichols says: "He was a man of medium height and striking appearance. He was dressed in a neat gray uniform, which harmonized gracefully with a full beard and mustache of silvery whiteness, partly concealing a genial and generous mouth, that must have become habituated to a kindly smile. His eyes, dark brown in color, varied in expression—now intense and sparkling, and then soft with tenderness, or twinkling with humor. The nose was Roman, the forehead full and prominent. The general cast of the features gave an expression of goodness and manliness, mingling a fine nature with the decision and energy of the capable soldier."

dence in a railway carriage. There they remained until the 15th,[a] when, it being seen that the surrender of Johnston was inevitable, they [a] April, 1865. again took flight, on horseback and in ambulances (for Stoneman had crippled the railway), for Charlotte, in Mecklenburg County, which Davis proposed to make the future capital of the Confederacy. There the fugitives first heard of the surrender of Johnston, through an electrograph to his wife, then abiding in Charlotte, telling her he would be with her in a few days. This was the final blow to the insurgent armies; and now the Confederate "Government" vanished into nothingness. The ring of Stoneman's sabers was heard, and startled the Conspirators, and away they fled on horseback, escorted by two thousand cavalry, across the Catawba, with their faces toward the Gulf of Mexico, for the way to the Mississippi and beyond, was barred. George Davis, the "Attorney-General," resigned his office at Charlotte; Trenholm gave up the place of "Secretary of the Treasury" on the banks of the Catawba, when Davis appointed his now useless "Postmaster-General," Reagan, to take Trenholm's place, temporarily. On they went, the escort continually dwindling. "Delays," said one of the party, "were not now thought of, and on toward Abbeville, by way of Yorkville, in South Carolina, the party struck, taking full soldiers' allowance of turmoil and camping on the journey, only intent on pushing to certain points on the Florida coast. Rumors of Stoneman, rumors of Wilson, rumors of even the ubiquitous Sheridan, occasionally sharpened the excitement. The escort, for the sake of expedition, was shorn of its bulky proportions, and by the time we reached Washington,[b] in Georgia, there was only [b] May 4. enough to make a respectable raiding party." [1]

At Washington, after there had been a scramble for the gold which the "Government" was running away with,[2] the remainder of the "Cabinet," excepting Reagan, deserted the "President." Mallory, the "Secretary of the Navy," doubting whether his official services would be needed on the Gulf, fled, with the notorious Wigfall, by railway, to La Grange, where he found his family, and was subsequently arrested. Benjamin, the "Secretary of State," mysteriously disappeared, after making ample provision for his own comfort. He afterward solved the enigma by showing his person in England. Of all the "ministers," only Reagan remained faithful to the person of the chief.

Up to this time, Davis's wife and children, and Mrs. Davis's sister, Miss Howell, had accompanied the fugitive "Government" from Danville. Now, for prudential reasons, this family took another, but nearly parallel route, in the flight toward the Gulf, traveling in wagons. Information soon reached Davis that some Confederate soldiers, believing that the treasure was with Mrs. Davis, had formed a plot to seize all her trunks, in search of it. He instantly hastened to the rescue of his family and property, and to provide for the protection of all. For this purpose he rode rapidly eighteen

---

[1] *History of the Last Days and Final Fall of the Rebellion*, by Lieutenant C. E. L. Stuart, of Jefferson Davis's staff.

[2] "At Washington there was a scramble for specie. It was determined to give the cavalry some few dollars each. They were impatient, and helped themselves as soon as they discovered where to get it. The result was an inequitable distribution—many got too much, many got nothing; and 'dust-hunters' picked up a good deal the following day—a good deal that was trampled under foot during the contemptible scramble."—*History, &c.*, by C. E. L. Stuart.

miles.　When he reached them, they were approaching Irwinsville, the capital of Irwin County, Georgia, nearly due south from Macon.　They had pitched tents for the night, and in one of these the wearied husband and father lay down to rest, intending to retrace his steps before the dawn.

Vigilant eyes were now looking for the notable fugitive.　General Wilson, at Macon, had been informed of Davis's flight toward the Gulf, and sent out two bodies of horsemen to attempt his capture.　One was led by Lieutenant-Colonel Pritchard, of the Fourth Michigan Cavalry, and the other by Lieutenant-Colonel Hardin, of the First Wisconsin Cavalry.　A reward of one hundred thousand dollars for the proclaimed criminal, made vision keener and muscle more untiring.　The seekers pushed on, by different roads, down the western side of the Ocmulgee River, and soon came upon the desired trail.　The two parties approached the camp of the sleeping fugitives, simultaneously, from opposite directions, just at dawn.ᵃ　Mistaking each other for enemies, they exchanged shots with such precision, that two men were killed and several wounded before the mistake was discovered.　The sleepers were aroused.

ᵃ May 11, 1865.

DAVIS'S PRISON, FORTRESS MONROE.

The camp was surrounded, and Davis, while attempting to escape, disguised in woman's clothing, was captured by Pritchard and his men, and with the rest of the fugitive party, was conveyed to General Wilson's head-quarters, at Macon.[1]　Thence they were sent to Savannah, and forwarded by sea to Fortress Monroe.　Judge Reagan, who was captured with Davis, and Alexander H. Stephens, the "Vice-President" of the Confederacy, who was arrested at about the same time, were sent to Fort Warren, in Boston Harbor, from which they were released on parole, a few months afterward.　Davis was confined at Fortress Monroe, in a casemate—a comfortable prison—on a charge of being concerned in the mur-

---

[1] The method of Davis's capture, and the account of his disguise, are related by two persons as follows:—

"When the musketry firing was heard in the morning at 'dim, gray dawn,' it was supposed to be between the apprehended Confederate marauders and Mrs. Davis's few camp defenders.　Under this impression, Mr. Davis hurriedly put on his boots, and prepared to go out for the purpose of interposing, saying, 'They will at least, as yet, respect me.'　As he got to the tent door, thus hastily equipped, he saw a few cavalry ride up the road and deploy in front.　'Ha! Federals!' was his exclamation.　'Then you are captured!' cried Mrs. Davis, with emotion.　In a moment she caught an idea—a woman's idea—and, as quickly as women, in an emergency, execute their designs, it was done.　He slept in a wrapper—a loose one.　It was yet around him.　This she fastened, ere he was aware of it, and then, bidding him adieu, urged him to go to the spring, a short distance off, where his horses and arms were.　Strange as it may seem, there was not even a pistol in the tent.　Davis felt that his only course was to reach his horses and arms, and complied.　As he was leaving the door, followed by a servant with a water-bucket, Miss Howell *flung a shawl over his head.*　There was no time to remove it without exposure and embarrassment, and, as he had not far to go, he ran the chance exactly as it was devised for him.　In these two articles consisted the woman's attire of which so much nonsense has been spoken and written, and under these circumstances and in this way, was Jefferson Davis going forth to perfect his escape.　No bonnet, no gown, no petticoats, no crinoline, no nothing of all these.　And what there was happened to be excusable under ordinary circumstances, and perfectly natural as things were.　But it was too late for any effort to reach his horses, and the Confederate President was at last a prisoner in the hands of the United States."—*Narrative* of Lieutenant C. E. L. Stuart, of Davis's staff.

After receiving the report of the capture, from Lieutenant-Colonel Pritchard, General Wilson said in his dispatch: "The story of Davis's ignoble attempt at flight, is even more ignoble than I told it.　Mrs. Davis, and her sister, Miss Howell, after having clothed him in the dress of the former, and put on his head a woman's

der of the President, and of treason, where he remained a long time, treated with the greatest kindness and consideration, and was finally admitted to bail, and went to Europe with his family and has [*] never been brought to trial.   ^{* September 1868.}

Notwithstanding the downfall of the civil and military power of the Confederates eastward of the Mississippi, the Rebels west of it, under the command and the influence of General E. Kirby Smith, were disposed to continue the contest longer. That leader issued a general order, containing an address to his soldiers, on the 21st of April, in which, after saying, "Great disasters have overtaken us; the Army of Northern Virginia and our commander-in-chief, are prisoners of war," he told them that upon their action depended the hopes of the Confederacy—"the hopes of the nation"—and he exhorted them to fight on in the defense of all that was dear. "You possess the means of long resistance," he said; "you have hopes of succor from abroad. Protract the struggle, and you will surely receive the aid of nations who already deeply sympathize with you." He entreated them to stand by their colors, and assured them of final success. Public meetings were held in Texas, and resolutions to continue the contest were adopted. To meet this danger, General Sheridan was sent to New Orleans with a large force, and made vigorous preparations for a campaign in Texas.

In the mean time, there had been collisions between the hostile forces on the borders of the Rio Grande. Colonel Theodore H. Barrett, of the Sixty-second United States Colored Infantry, was in command of the National forces at Brazos Santiago, in Texas, and on the evening of the 11th of May,^b he sent about three hundred men, composed of two hundred and fifty of his own regiment and fifty of the Second Texas   ^{b 1865.} Cavalry, not mounted, to the main-land, under Lieutenant-Colonel Branson, to attack some Confederates on the Rio Grande. The principal object of the Nationals was to procure horses for mounting the cavalry. They marched all night, and early the next morning attacked and drove the foe at Palmetto Ranche, and seized their camp and its contents, with some horses and cattle, and a number of men made prisoners. Bronson fell back, and on the morning of the 13th,^c he was joined by Lieutenant-Colonel Mor   ^{c May.} rison, with about two hundred men of the Thirty-fourth Indiana, veterans, when Colonel Barrett assumed command, in person, and ordered an advance in the direction of Palmetto Ranche, where the Confederates were again in considerable force. These were again driven off, and stores not destroyed before, were now consumed, and the buildings burned. Nearly all the forenoon was spent in skirmishing, and early in the afternoon a slight engagement took place, but without much effect. By a vigorous charge, the Confederates were driven several miles.

Colonel Barrett relinquished the pursuit for the purpose of resting his men, on a hill about a mile from Palmetto Ranche. There, at about four o'clock, he was assailed in front by a large body of Confederates, infantry

---

head-dress, started out, one holding each arm, and besought Colonel Pritchard's men, in most piteous terms, to let them take their poor old mother out of the way of the firing. Mrs. Davis said, 'Oh, do let us pass with our poor old mother, who's so frightened, and fears to be killed.' One of Pritchard's men, catching sight of the 'President's' boots below the skirts of the dress, suspected at once who the poor old mother was, and replied, 'Oh, no, you don't play that game on us; those boots don't look much like they belong to a woman. Come down, old fellow!' "—General J. H. Wilson's Report.

and artillery, and at the same time a heavy body of cavalry and a section of a battery, under cover of a chaparral, succeeded in flanking his little force, with the intention of getting in his rear. The attacking force was under the command of General J. E. Slaughter. The Rio Grande was on Barrett's left. He had no artillery; his situation was extremely critical; and he had no alternative but to fall back, fighting. This was done with skill and bravery. Forty-eight men of the Thirty-fourth Indiana, thrown out as skirmishers to protect the flank of that regiment, were cut off and captured by Slaughter's cavalry.

One half of the Sixty-second United States (colored) troops, covering the recoiling force, were deployed as skirmishers, and formed a line a mile in length, protecting both front and right flank. It resisted every attempt of the Confederate cavalry to penetrate it. Such attempts were repulsed with loss to the assailants. The entire regiment moved back with great precision. The running fight continued about three hours, when the Confederates desisted. So ended THE BATTLE OF PALMETTO RANCHE. It was the last one in the great struggle. At about sunset, on the 13th of May, 1865, between White's Ranche and the Boca Chico Strait, in Texas, the Sixty-second United States Colored Infantry, *fired the last volley of the war.*[1] The conflict was near the old battle-ground of General Taylor, at Palo Alto, in 1846, about two thousand miles from the first considerable battle-ground at Bull Run. The extent of the field of conflict occupied in the Civil War may be comprehended by considering the fact, that the region between Bull Run and the Rio Grande, had been fought over, lightly or heavily, at almost every league.

Sheridan's appearance at New Orleans sent dismay to the hearts of the Confederates in the Trans-Mississippi region, and the men in arms refused longer to follow their leaders in a hopeless struggle. Kirby Smith formally surrendered[a] his entire command to General Canby, and thereby rendered an advance of Sheridan into Western Louisiana and Texas unnecessary. Before the surrender was actually effected, Kirby Smith exhibited "the bad faith of first disbanding most of his army, and permitting an indiscriminate plunder of the public property."[2] The soldiers helped themselves to whatever Confederate property they could lay their hands on—subsistence and transportation—and departed for their homes. General Smith and a few of his followers fled into Texas.

* May 26, 1865.

---

[1] Written communication to the author, by Colonel Barrett, dated June 16, 1868. His reported loss in this expedition, in killed, wounded and prisoners, was 4 officers and 111 men. His force was 450 strong; Slaughter's 675, with a battery of six 12-pounder field-pieces. *The last man wounded in the war by a rebel bullet* was Sergeant Crockett, of the Sixty-second United States Colored Infantry, who received it in his leg in this engagement. He bound up the wound with his handkerchief, and kept on fighting to the end.

[2] General Grant's Report, July 22, 1865. In closing that report, General Grant said: " It has been my fortune to see the armies of both the West and the East fight battles, and from what I have seen, I know there is no difference in their fighting qualities. All that it was possible for men to do in battle, they have done. The Western armies commenced their battles in the Mississippi Valley, and received the final surrender of the remnant of the principal army opposed to them, in North Carolina. The armies of the East commenced their battles on the river from which the Army of the Potomac derived its name, and received the final surrender of their old antagonist, at Appomattox Court-House, Virginia. The splendid achievements of each have nationalized our victories, removed all sectional jealousies (of which we have unfortunately experienced too much), and the cause of crimination and recrimination, that might have followed, had either section failed in its duty. All have a proud record, and all sections can well congratulate themselves and each other, for having done their full share in restoring the supremacy of law over every foot of territory belonging to the United States. Let them hope for perpetual peace and harmony with that enemy whose manhood, however mistaken the cause, drew forth such 'herculean deeds of valor.' "

So ended THE CIVIL WAR, in the field; and on the anniversary of the Declaration of the nation's Independence, a few weeks later,[a] and just four years from the time when the National Congress met in the Capitol at Washington, and proceeded to make provision for suppressing the rebellion and saving the Republic, the Loyal League, of

[a] July 4, 1865.

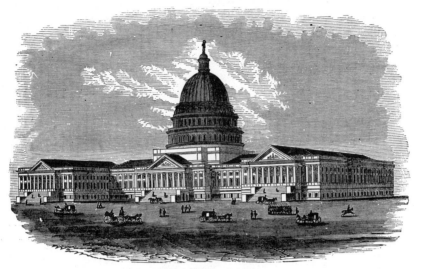

THE NATIONAL CAPITOL.

Philadelphia, chanted the following hymn,[1] to the air of "Old Hundred";

Thank God! the bloody days are past;
Our patient hopes are crowned at last;
And sounds of bugle, drum, and fife,
But lead our heroes home from strife!

Thank God! there beams o'er land and sea,
Our blazing Star of Victory;
And everywhere, from main to main,
The old flag flies and rules again!

Thank God! Oh dark and trodden race,
Your Lord no longer veils his face;
But through the clouds and woes of fight,
Shines on your souls a better light!

Thank God! we see on every hand,
Breast-high the ripening grain-crops stand;
The orchards bend, the herds increase;
But Oh, thank God! thank God for PEACE!

Before that National Anniversary, the soldiers of the Grand Armies of the Republic, whose skill, valor, and fortitude had saved its life, and, as an incident, had achieved the holy work of emancipation for an enslaved race, were making their way homeward, everywhere received with the warmest demonstrations of gratitude and affection.[2] With the exception of a few left in

---

[1] Written for the occasion by George H. Boker, of Philadelphia.
[2] In almost every village and city there were public receptions of the returning regiments. As these demonstrations had all features in common, the writer will endeavor to convey to the reader an idea of the manner in which the citizen-soldiers were received, by giving an outline sketch of the reception of the rem-

Virginia and North Carolina, the soldiers of the great armies that confronted Lee and Johnston, and achieved a victory over them, were marched to the vicinity of the National Capital, and there, during two ᵃ May 22 and 23, 1865. memorable days,ᵃ they moved through that city, with tens of thousands of moistened eyes gazing upon them, and passed in review before the Chief Magistrate of the nation and his Ministers. It was a spectacle such as human vision had never seen. Then began the work of disbanding the armies, by mustering out of service officers and men; and on the 2d of June, the General-in-Chief issued an address to them, saying:—

"*Soldiers of the Armies of the United States:* By your patriotic devotion to your country in the hour of danger and alarm, your magnificent fighting, bravery and endurance, you have maintained the supremacy of the Union, and the Constitution, overthrown all armed opposition to the enforcement of the laws and of the proclamation forever abolishing slavery—the cause and pretext of the Rebellion—and opened the way to the rightful authorities to restore order, and inaugurate peace on a permanent and enduring basis on every foot of American soil. Your marches, sieges, and battles, in distance, duration, resolution, and brilliancy of results, dims the luster of the world's past military achievements, and will be the patriot's precedent in defense of liberty and right, in all time to come. In obedience to your

---

nant of the One Hundred and Fiftieth Regiment of New York Volunteers, at Poughkeepsie, on the Hudson River, his place of residence.

The One Hundred and Fiftieth Regiment left Poughkeepsie in October, 1862, under Colonel John H. Ketcham, and returned, in a Government transport, from New York, late on a Saturday night, in June, 1865, under Colonel A. B. Smith, who went out as major. Ketcham had been wounded at Savannah, and promoted to brigadier-general. The regiment was expected; and as soon as the transport appeared, the street in the vicinity of the landing was made brilliant by blazing bonfires. Hundreds of citizens quickly assembled and escorted the soldiers to quarters, many of them walking hand in hand with loving wives, mothers, and sisters, who came out at almost midnight to embrace them. At their quarters the soldiers were paroled for the Sabbath.

The public reception was on Monday, the 12th of June. A finer day for the occasion could not have been chosen. The people of Dutchess County and its neighborhood flocked in by thousands, for almost every family had a personal interest in the soldiers. It was estimated that forty thousand persons participated in the ceremonies of the day. A grand procession was formed near the river, in charge of a Marshal and Aids. It was composed of the returned regiment, the city authorities in carriages, the local military, the Fire Department, various civic associations, and a vast concourse of citizens, on horseback and on foot. As it moved from its rendezvous into Main Street, it was greeted by a multitude of the pupils of the public schools of the city, arrayed in order, on a grassy bank in front of the residence of the Mayor, George Innis. They sang a song of welcome, and then presented to each soldier a bouquet of flowers. These were placed in the muzzles of their guns, and when they moved it seemed as if a garden in bloom was floating along the street. The buildings along the line of march were radiant with flags and banners. The streets were spanned with arches, covered with evergreens and flowers, and having patriotic and affectionate inscriptions; and songs of welcome were sung at two seminaries of learning for young women, as the procession passed. Colonel Smith and his horse were covered with bouquets, wreaths, and festoons of flowers, showered upon the gallant soldier, from the sidewalks, windows, and balconies. His lieutenant, Cogswell, and General Ketcham were recipients of like tokens of regard.

The regiment, bearing its tattered flags, was the center of attraction, and received a thousand tokens of gratitude, as it moved along the streets and into Mansion Square, where it was greeted by a multitude of the fairer sex. Among these were thirty-six young girls, representing the number of States, all dressed in colors of red, white and blue, excepting one, who personified Illinois, the home of the dead President. She was clad in deep mourning. They all wore diadems that glittered with golden stars. They came in a wagon prepared for the occasion, from one of the towns of the county. From a platform in the Park, the regiment was welcomed in a speech, by Judge Emott, of the Circuit Court of New York, to which Colonel Smith replied. The soldiers then partook of a collation, when the war-worn flags which had first been rent by bullets at Gettysburg, had followed Sherman in his great march from Chattanooga to Atlanta, thence to the sea and through the Carolinas, and had been enveloped in the smoke of battle at Bentonsville, were returned to the ladies of Dutchess County (represented by a committee of their number present), from whom the regiment received them on the day before its departure.

Such was the reception given at Poughkeepsie, to the returned defenders of the Republic. Such was the greeting given to them everywhere, by the loyal people of the land. In those receptions, they who, in the hour of their country's peril, refused a helping hand, and even cast obstacles in the way of its earnest defenders, had no part nor lot. That exclusion from a privilege so glorious for an American, left a sad picture in memory for them to contemplate, and an unpleasant record for their children to look upon.

. ountry's call, you left your homes and families, and volunteered in her defense. Victory has crowned your valor, and secured the purpose of your patriotic hearts; and, with the gratitude of your countrymen, and the highest honors a great and free nation can accord, you will soon be permitted to return to your homes and families, conscious of having discharged the highest duty of American citizens. To achieve these glorious triumphs, and secure to yourselves, your fellow-countrymen, and posterity, the blessings of free institutions, tens of thousands of your gallant comrades have fallen, and sealed the priceless legacy with their blood. The graves of these, a grateful nation bedews with tears, honors their memories, and will ever cherish and support their stricken families."[1]

The records of the War Department show that on the first of March, 1865, the muster-rolls of the army exhibited an aggregate force of 965,591 men, of whom 602,593 were present for duty, and 132,538 were on detached service. The aggregate force was increased, by the first of May, by enlistments, to the number of 1,000,516, of all arms, officers and men. The whole number of men called into the service during the war, was 2,656,553.[2] Of these, about 1,490,000 were in actual service. Of this number, nearly 60,000 were killed on the field, and about 35,000 were mortally wounded. Disease in camps and hospitals slew 184,000.[1] It is estimated that at least 300,000 Union soldiers perished during the war. Full that number of the Confederate soldiers lost their lives; and the aggregate number of men, including both armies, who were crippled, or permanently disabled by disease, was estimated at 400,000. The actual loss to the country, of able-bodied men, in consequence of the Slave-holders' Rebellion, was full 1,000,000.

The disbanding of the army went steadily on from the first of June,[a] and by the middle of the autumn nearly 786,000 officers and men were mustered out of the service. The wonderful spectacle was

[a] 1865.

---

[1] It has been said that there was a great disparity in numbers between the forces of Grant and Lee, during the campaign from the passage of the Rapid Anna to the surrender at Appomattox Court-House. According to official records, this does not appear. Grant began the campaign with 98,019 effective men, and Lee with 72,278 effective men. The latter had such advantages of position, breastworks, and a friendly country, with shortening lines of supplies, that his real force was greater than Grant's. According to Lee's field-returns on the 28th of February, 1865, he had 73,349 men present, of whom 59,094 were "present for duty," exclusive of the local militia of Richmond. When Lee reached Petersburg, owing to recruits from the South and elsewhere, he had more men with him than at the beginning of the campaign.

[2] The Provost-Marshal-General, James B. Fry, reported that the aggregate quotas charged against the several States, under all calls of the President for troops, from the 15th of April, 1861, up to the 14th of April, 1865, when a cessation of drafting and recruiting was ordered, were 2,759,049. The aggregate number of men credited on the several calls, and put into the service of the Republic (in the army, navy, and marine corps) during that period, was, as stated in the text, 2,656,553, leaving a deficiency of 102,496, when the war closed, "which," says the Provost-Marshal-General, "would have been obtained in full, in fact in excess, if recruiting and drafting had been continued."

We have observed that in enforcing the draft, those thus chosen for service were allowed to pay a commutation fee. The Provost-Marshal gives the following table of the amounts paid in this way, by the people of the several States:—

Maine	$610,200	Connecticut	$457,200	Maryland	$1,131,900	Indiana	$235,500
New Hampshire	286,500	New York	5,485,799	Dis't of Columbia	96,900	Michigan	614,700
Vermont	593,400	New Jersey	1,265,700	Kentucky	997,530	Wisconsin	1,533,600
Massachusetts	1,610,400	Pennsylvania	8,634,300	Ohio	1,978,887	Iowa	22,500
Rhode Island	141,300	Delaware	446,100	Illinois	15,900	Minnesota	316,800

Total $26,366,316

This sum was collected by the Provost-Marshal's Bureau, at an expense of less than seven-tenths of one per cent., and without the loss of a dollar through neglect, accident, fraud, or otherwise. The whole number of negro troops recruited and enlisted during the war, was 186,017.

[3] See Report of the Secretary of War, November 22, 1865.

exhibited for the contemplation of the civilized world, of vast armies of men, surrounded by all the paraphernalia of war, transformed, in the space of one hundred and fifty days, into a vast army of citizens, engaged in the blessed pursuits of peace. No argument in favor of free institutions and a republican form of government, so conclusive and potential as this, was ever before presented to the feelings and judgment of the nations of the earth. The important political problem of the nineteenth century was solved by our Civil War. Our Republic no longer appeared as an *experiment*, but as a *demonstration*.

The services of the National Navy during the war, on account of their peculiarity, attracted less attention than those of the army, and were not appreciated by the people. They have an equal claim to the gratitude of the nation, so freely accorded to the other branch of the service. The Confederates having no navy, in a proper sense, and only flotillas here and there, with some powerful "rams" on rivers and in harbors, and not a ship on the ocean, excepting roving pirate-vessels—built, armed, furnished and manned chiefly by the British, and cruising alone—there were few occasions for purely naval battles. The whole force of the Navy Department was employed in the services of blockade, in assisting the attacks of the armies on fortifications along the rivers, and on the borders of the Gulf and the Ocean, or in chasing the pirates. In these fields of great usefulness, the National vessels performed labors of incalculable value, and officers and men exhibited skill, valor, and fortitude unsurpassed.

Never, in the history of the world, were there occasions for such exhausting labors, and highest courage in service afloat, as the American Navy was subjected to in its operations among the rivers and bayous of the southwestern regions of the Republic. This the records of these volumes attest; records which, after all, give but a delicate outline—a mere shadowy picture—of the most wonderful exploits of brain and muscle. Many a victory over which the people have shouted themselves hoarse in giving plaudits to the gallant army, might never have been achieved but for the co-operation of the navy. To the common observer it, in many instances, seemed to be only an auxiliary, or wholly a secondary force, when, in truth, it was an equal, if not the chief power in gaining a victory. Without it, what might have been the result of military operations at Forts Henry and Donelson, Shiloh and all along the Mississippi River, especially at Vicksburg, Port· Hudson, and New Orleans; what at Mobile, Pensacola, Key West, along the Florida sea-board, the sea-coast Islands, Charleston, and the borders of North Carolina, and even in holding Fortress Monroe and Norfolk?

The energy displayed by the Navy Department, under the chief management of Gustavus Vasa Fox,[1] the Assistant Secretary of the Navy, was most remarkable. The weakness and the position of the navy in the spring of 1861 have already been noticed.[2] It was a navy reduced to smallest proportions during fifty years of peace, and kept in existence only by the necessity of protection for the continually expanding commercial interests of the nation. Its men numbered only 7,600 when the Civil War was kindled; and of its officers, 322 traitorously abandoned the service to which

---

[1] See page 308, volume I.   [2] See page 299, volume I.

they had dedicated their lives, proved false to their flag which they had sworn to protect, and to the Government which had confided in their honor, and relied on their fidelity, to sustain it in conflict and peril. [1]

Notwithstanding this condition of the naval service, the decree went forth, in the spring of 1861, that all the ports of the States wherein rebellion existed, must be closed against commerce, by a strict blockade. Foreign nations protested and menaced, but the work was done. There were no dockyards or workmen adequate to construct the vessels needed for the service, yet, such was the energy of the Department, in the hands of Mr. Fox, that an unrelaxing blockade was maintained for four years, from the capes of the Chesapeake to the Rio Grande, while a flotilla of gun-boats, protecting and aiding the army in its movements, penetrated and patroled our rivers, through an internal navigation almost continental, from the Potomac to the Mississippi. Ingenuity and mechanical skill developed amazing inventions. That marine monster, the *Monitor*, was created, and began a new era in naval warfare; and the world was suddenly enriched by new discoveries in naval service. Vessels of the merchant service were purchased and changed into strong warriors; and men from that service were invited to officer and man them. Schools were established for nautical instruction; dock-yards were enlarged and filled with workmen; and very soon a large number of vessels were afloat, watching the harbors under the ban. The places of the traitors were quickly filled by better men from the merchant marine, educated, and vastly more efficient, who promptly volunteered their services, in many instances at great pecuniary sacrifice, to fight the battles of the Union. About 7,500 of these gallant spirits, after examination, received appointments, and were employed in the navy; and the rank and file in the service, numbering 7,600, when the war broke out, numbered 51,500 when it closed. The aggregate of artisans and laborers in the navy-yards was 3,844 at the beginning; at the end the number was 16,880, exclusive of almost an equal number then employed in private ship-yards and establishments, under contracts. No less than 208 war vessels were constructed, and most of them fitted out during the four years; and 418 vessels were purchased and converted into war-ships. Of these, 313 were steamers, the whole costing nearly $19,000,000. [2]

The blockading service was performed with great vigor and efficiency under the triple stimulus of patriotism, duty, and personal emolument. The British Government professed to be neutral, but British merchants and adventurers were allowed to send swarms of swift-winged steamers, laden with arms, ammunition, clothing, and every thing needed by the insurgents, to run the blockade. The profits of such operations were enormous, but the risks were equally so; and it is believed that a true balance-sheet would show no profits left, in the aggregate, with the foreign violators of law. The number of such vessels captured or destroyed during the Rebellion, by the National Navy, was 1,504. The gross proceeds of property captured and condemned as lawful prize before the first of November following the close of

---

[1] Report of Gideon Welles, Secretary of the Navy, December 4, 1865.

[2] At the close of the war, the monitors and iron-clads were laid up in ordinary, at League Island, near Philadelphia, and, within six months after hostilities had ceased, 340 of these vessels had been sold, for the aggregate sum of nearly $6,000,000.

of the war, amounted to nearly \$22,000,000, which sum was subsequently enlarged by new decisions. The value of the vessels captured and destroyed, (1,149 captured and 355 destroyed), was not less than \$7,000,000, making a total loss, chiefly to British owners, of at least \$30,000,000.

The writer, accompanied by his friends already mentioned in these pages, (Messrs. Dreer and Greble), visited the theater of some of the events recorded in this chapter, immediately after the evacuation of Richmond. We had been to the front of the Army of the Potomac, and the Army of the James, a few months before, after the return to Hampton Roads of the first expedition against Fort Fisher on the evening of the 28th of December.[a] On the following day we went up the James River, with General Butler, on his elegant little dispatch steamer, *Ocean Queen*, to City Point, where, after a brief interview with General Grant, we proceeded to Aiken's Landing, the neutral ground for the exchange of prisoners. It was dark when we arrived there. We made our way in an ambulance, over a most wretched road, to Butler's head-quarters,[1] within seven miles of Richmond, where we passed the night. On the following day we rode through the camp of the Army of the James, on horses kindly furnished us by the general, first visiting the head-quarters of General Weitzel's Twenty-fifth

* 1864.

INTERIOR OF A CHAPEL OF THE CHRISTIAN COMMISSION.[2]

(colored) corps, whose huts were decorated with evergreens, it being the Christmas holidays. We rode to the head-quarters of General Ord, on New Market Heights, where we were joined by Major Seward, of his staff, who accompanied us along the lines for several miles, to the Dutch Gap Canal.[3] On the way we visited a chapel of the United States Christian Commission; also, Battery Harrison, captured by the colored troops not long before,[4] and Fort Brady.

Near the Dutch Gap Canal, just then completed, we dismounted, and took a pathway like a shelf along the steep bank of the James, where the excavators had made their subterranean huts,[5] when we found ourselves in much peril. The battery at Howlett's, which, as we have observed, cast a shell among the workmen about once an hour, now hurled one at the end of every five minutes, compelling us to seek shelter in the caves. We succeeded in peeping into the canal, and then made our way back, finding warm fragments of a shell in the path. We found the orderly in in charge of the horses much disturbed by the explosion of one of them

---

[1] See picture on page 362.

[2] This was substantially built of logs, with a double row of benches of timber, leaving a broad aisle between. It was lighted with a few candles; and two tables composed its entire furniture.

[3] See page 357.   [4] See page 358.   [5] See page 358.

near him. We all remounted as quickly as possible, each obeying the injunction, "Stand not upon the order of your going, but go at once," and were soon out of range of the battery, when the firing ceased. The Confederates had doubtless heard of the return of Butler from Fort Fisher, and, mistaking our little party of five for the General and his staff, gave this salute with shotted guns.

We returned to General Butler's head-quarters at twilight, where we found George D. Prentice, editor of the *Louisville Journal*, who had just come through the lines from Richmond. With him and Captain Clarke, of Butler's staff, we journeyed the next day on horseback to Aiken's Landing, crossed the James on a pontoon bridge, rode to Bermuda Hundred, and then went up the Appomattox to Point of Rocks in the *Ocean Queen*, which the general placed at our disposal. There we mounted to the summit of the signal-tower delineated on page 547, and viewed the marvelous lines of intrenchments in that vicinity; and saw plainly the church-spires at Richmond and Petersburg. We passed that night on the barge of the United States Sanitary Commission, at City Point, and the next morning went down to Fortress Monroe, bearing an order from General Butler for a tug to take us to Norfolk. We spent New Year's day in that city, and then went homeward by way of Chesapeake Bay, Baltimore and Philadelphia.

Soon after the news of the evacuation of Richmond reached us, early in April,[a] we started for that city, and were in Baltimore on the night when the President was murdered. There we were detained until Sunday afternoon,[b] in consequence of an order from the Government, prohibiting all public conveyances entering into or departing from Baltimore, because search was a-making for the assassin. Admiral Porter was among the blockaded there. We should not have been permitted then to pass southward, had not the writer possessed special passes and letters from the heads of the War and Navy departments, and a note from the late President, requesting commanders of each service to give him facility for observation,[1] for no passes were issued from the War Department for many days after the assassination. We went down the Chesapeake to Fortress Monroe on Sunday night, where we met the gallant Captain Ainsworth,[2] who took us in his tug to the double-turreted monitor *Monadnoc*, to

[a] 1865.

[b] April. 16.

---

[1] The following are copies of the letters alluded to:—

"WAR DEPARTMENT, WASHINGTON CITY, *December* 6, 1864.

"Permission is given to Mr. Benson J. Lossing to visit the various battle-fields of the present war, so far as they are within our lines, and to make all drawings that he may require, of the same, for historical purposes. He will be allowed to take with him, as assistants, F. J. Dreer and Edwin Greble. This permission is subject to the approval of the generals commanding in the various Departments, where the battle-fields, which he desires to examine, may be situated.

"By order of the Secretary of War.

"C. A. DANA, *Assistant Secretary of War*."

To this the following was subjoined:—

"I shall be obliged for Mr. Lossing to have every facility consistent with the public service.

"A. LINCOLN."

"NAVY DEPARTMENT, *December* 6, 1864.

"To the Commanding Officers of the Navy:—

"Benson J. Lossing, Esq., who is engaged upon a history of the present Rebellion, is about to visit the various places connected with the different battles, accompanied by F. J. Dreer, Esq., and Edwin Greble, Esq., and has requested a general letter of introduction to naval commanders, which is hereby given, to facilitate him in any investigations which Mr. Lossing may consider essential in preparing his work. The usual courtesies, not interfering with the public service, may be extended to them.

"GIDEON WELLES, *Secretary of the Navy*."

[2] See page 497.

visit Rear-Admiral Radford. We found him in another vessel, when he gave
an order for a tug to take us to City Point, but finding better accommodations on a transport, we went up the river in that ship. We arrived at head-
quarters at evening, and the next morning[b] went up to Richmond
in the mail steamer *Trumpet*, thridding our way among nests of
torpedoes, indicated by the floats and flags placed there by Captain Chandler.[1]

a April 18,
1865.

We found the ruins of Richmond yet smoking. In that city we remained
several days, gathering up materials for history, the recipient of kind attentions from General Ord (who was in command there), and other officers.
We visited and sketched the Capitol, Libby Prison, Castle Thunder, Belle
Isle, and other places of interest connected with the Civil War, delineated on
preceding pages of this work; also the fortifications in the immediate vicinity
of the city. Then we went to Petersburg, by railway, where General Hartsuff
was in command, with his head-quarters in the elegant Bolling mansion, which
had been sadly shattered by the passage of a shell from the Union batteries.
There we enjoyed the kind hospitalities of the general and his wife. He furnished us with horses, and an intelligent orderly as guide, and with these we
rode over the marvelous net-work of fortifications, fresh from the hands of the
builders, which enveloped Petersburg on the southern side of the Appomattox. From that shattered city we went, by railway, to City Point, and
thence to Washington in a Government steamer, by way of the James and
Potomac rivers.

---

[1] See page 561.

CHAPTER XXII.

PRISONERS.—BENEVOLENT OPERATIONS DURING THE WAR.—READJUSTMENT OF NA-
TIONAL AFFAIRS.—CONCLUSION.

N THE downfall of the Confederacy, the prisoners were all set free, and the captive insurgents, who had been gener- ously treated, comfortably housed, and abundantly fed, at all times and in all places, while in the custody of the Na- tional authorities, were sent to their homes at the expense of their ever kind Government. Gladly would the writer testify to like generous treatment, comfortable shelter, and wholesome and abundant food, accorded to the Union pris- prisoners by the Confederate authorities. Alas! the truth revealed by thou- sands of sufferers, and the admissions of the Confederates themselves, compel a widely different record—a record which presents one of the darkest chapters in the history of human iniquity. Gladly would he omit the record, for it relates to the wickedness of some of his countrymen, but duty and honor require him, in making a chronicle of the Rebellion and Civil War, to tell the whole truth, and conceal nothing, so that posterity may be able to form a correct judgment of that Rebellion and Civil War.

Soon after actual hostilities began, and prisoners were taken by both parties in the conflict, the important question arose, Can the Government exchange prisoners with rebels against its authority, without thereby tacitly conced- ing belligerent rights to the insurgents, and, as a consequence, practically acknowledging the Confederate Government, so called, at Richmond, as a Government in fact? Humanity took precedence of policy in the Cabinet councils, and an arrangement was made for the exchange of prisoners. A commissioner was appointed by each party for the purpose. Colonel W. H. Ludlow was chosen for the service by the Government, and the Conspirators appointed Robert Ould to perform like duties. The former had his head- quarters at Fortress Monroe, and the latter had his at Richmond. Prisoners were sent in boats to and from each place. Aiken's Landing and its vicinity, on the James River, finally became a sort of neutral ground, where the ex- changes took place. The operations of exchange were facilitated by the Government, as much as possible, because of accounts which came, from the beginning of the war, like a flood, concerning the cruel treatment accorded to the Union prisoners in the hands of the insurgents, at Richmond and elsewhere.

The business of exchange went regularly on until it was vio- lently interrupted by Jefferson Davis, at near the close of 1862, when he issued[a] an extraordinary proclamation, glowing with the fiery anger with which he was moved. That anger was kindled chiefly

[a] Dec. 23, 1862.

because the Government had chosen to use the loyal negroes for military purposes, as the Conspirators had done, but ostensibly because the National Commander at New Orleans had punished a low gambler for overt acts of treason, and accepted the highly immoral conduct of certain women "of the better sort," in that city, as fair evidence that they belonged to an immoral class of the community.[1] In that proclamation there was a tone of savagism, which made the rulers of other lands pause in their willingness to admit, by recognition as such, the "Confederacy" into the family of civilized nations. In it, Davis outlawed a major-general of the National army, and commander of a military department, speaking of him as "a felon, deserving of capital punishment," and ordered that he should not be "treated simply as a public enemy of the Confederate States of America, but as an outlaw, and common enemy of mankind; and that in the event of his capture, the officer in command of the capturing force do cause him to be immediately executed by hanging."[2] He also ordered the same treatment for commanding officers serving under the outlawed general, and further directed that all negro soldiers who might be taken prisoners, and all commissioned officers serving in company with them, who should be captured, should be handed over to State governments for execution, the negroes as insurgent slaves, the white officers as inciters of servile insurrection.[3]

This savage position of the insurgent Chief made the Government pause and consider. It was morally bound to afford equal protection to *all* its citizen soldiers, irrespective of color. The proclamation produced wide-spread indignation throughout the country, and when, in January,[a] Davis, in a "message" to the Confederate "Congress," announced his determination to deliver all officers of the National army commanding negro troops, captured after that date, to the respective State authorities to be hung, and to treat those troops as rebels against their masters, Congress took up the matter, and a joint resolution was offered providing for retaliation for any cruel treatment of Union prisoners, of whatever grade or hue. But in this, as in the matter of exchange, Humanity took precedence of Policy, and the National Executive and legislature were governed by the ethics involved in the following words of Charles Sumner, who opposed the measure, in the Senate: "I believe that this body will not undertake, in this age of Christian light, under any inducement, under any provocation, to counsel the Executive Government to enter into any such competition with barbarism. The thing is impossible; it cannot be entertained; we cannot be cruel, or barbarous, or savage, because the rebels, whom we are now meetign in warfare, are cruel, barbarous, and savage! We cannot imitate that detested example."

It was the proclamation and the "message" of Davis that first seriously interrupted the exchange of prisoners, these being followed by the refusal of Ould, the Confederate Commissioner, under the instructions of his Chief, to con-

[a] Jan. 12, 1863.

---

[1] See pages 350 and 351, volume II.

[2] General Butler, the officer alluded to, was a political friend of Davis's, until the latter became an open enemy of the Government. In the winter of 1860–61, Butler was in Washington, and told Davis and his traitorous companions, that if they attempted to break up the Union, they would find him (Butler) fighting to preserve the Union. They rebelled, and he fought them as rebels. Former political friendship intensified Davis's hatred of Butler. The animus of his proclamation was the low spirit of partisan malignity.

See note 4, page 351, volume II.

sider captive negro soldiers as prisoners of war. In many instances no quarter was given them in battle or afterward; and the black flag was carried against the white officers commanding them, of whom several were hung without even the form of a trial. With such a high hand did the Conspirators exercise their horrid rule at that time, and so utterly perfidious was their conduct in the matter of paroled prisoners, as in the case of Grant's captives at Vicksburg and Banks's at Port Hudson, already mentioned,[1] that justice interposed between humanity and policy, and demanded a cessation of all exchanges until the Conspirators should act in accordance with the common usages of civilized nations. When in August, 1863, General Merideth, who had succeeded Colonel Ludlow as Commissioner, demanded that negro troops and their officers should be treated as other prisoners of war and exchanged, Robert Ould replied, "We will die in the last ditch before giving up the right to send slaves back to slavery."[2] And the *Richmond Enquirer*, speaking the sentiments of the Conspirators, said, on the 24th of August, 1863: "This day Mr. Commissioner Ould meets for the first time the new Federal Commissioner, a certain General Merideth, to confer upon the terms of the cartel, and endeavor to settle the principles of exchange for the future. It is scarcely possible to hope that any conclusion satisfactory to both sides can be arrived at in this conference. The Federal Government has planted itself insolently upon the demand that our runaway negroes, when taken in arms against their masters, shall be treated as prisoners of war, and shall be exchanged against white men. Confederates have borne and forborne much to mitigate the atrocities of war; but this is a thing which the temper of the country cannot endure. Our Government has issued an order as to the treatment of revolted negroes when captured. Certain captured negroes, under that order, have been imprisoned at Charleston to await the disposition of the State Government."

---

[1] See page 131.

[2] Letter of General S. A. Merideth, Ludlow's successor as Commissioner, to the editor of the *Buffalo Commercial Advertiser*, August 25, 1868. General Merideth in his official communication to Robert Ould, the Confederate Commissioner, on the 29th of October, 1863, said, in relation to the interruption of the exchange of prisoners: "The history of this matter, as I understand it, is briefly this: While my predecessor, on duty at this place, was here, in discharge of the duties now committed to me, you at one time made a declaration of exchange embracing no great number of prisoners of war, not in accordance with the requirements of the cartel and you invited Colonel Ludlow, my predecessor, to make a corresponding declaration of equivalents. Such a declaration was made by Colonel Ludlow, doubtless without anticipating the magnitude of the evil which appears now as the result of that departure from the cartel first inaugurated by yourself. Subsequently to my coming on duty here, the events of the war threw upon your hands a large body of paroled officers and men (over 30,000) captured by General Grant at Vicksburg, and not long afterward some 6,000 or more captured by General Banks at Port Hudson. Suddenly, and without any proper conference or understanding with me, and but a few days prior to the important events at Chickamauga, as if for the express purpose of increasing the force of General Bragg against General Rosecrans, you gave me notice that, on the next day after the date of that notice, you would declare exchanged a large portion of the troops which had been captured by General Grant."

Further, in relation to the conduct of the Confederates, in this matter, General Merideth says, in his letter of the 25th of August, 1868: "Another cause of the suspension of the cartel was its constant violation by the rebels, in making illegal declarations of exchange, for the purpose of putting men into the field, and there is no doubt, whatever, that all prisoners paroled by the United States authorities were immediately returned to active duty in the rebel army. Many officers and men captured at Vicksburg were in the battle of Chickamauga. [See page 131.] Thus the rebels were making use of our well-conducted prisons as recruiting depots for their army. Another insuperable obstacle to returning exchanges, was in the matter of paroles. Mr. Ould had some 18,000 or 20,000 which he claimed as valid. Most, if not all of these paroles were taken by guerrillas, bushwhackers, and detached commands in the West. No possession was ever had, no delivery was ever made, and no rolls were ever furnished. On the capture of a town by a rebel cavalry raid, the command remained long enough to take the parole of unarmed citizens there, and then decamped, leaving the paroled men behind, and forwarding the paroles to Richmond. And the rebels had the assurance to require the United States Government to exchange prisoners legitimately captured in battle for such paroles as these."

The practical application of Davis's inhuman order, here referred to, was met by a letter from the Secretary of War to the Secretary of the Navy, which made the Conspirators pause, for it showed a determination on the part of the Government to use the law of retaliation, when necessary.[1] Yet the Confederates refused to treat the negro as a subject for exchange, and that humane arrangement in war entirely ceased in March, 1864, because justice required it. Then the Government referred the matter of exchange to General Grant, when that officer first instructed General Butler, in charge of the business at Fortress Monroe, with the active Colonel Mulford (who afterward became the chief Commissioner of exchange of prisoners) as his assistant, to decline, until further ordered, all negotiations for exchange, and afterward instructed him to consider the determination of the Confederate authorities to make a distinction between white and colored prisoners, as a refusal on their part to agree to further exchange. Thus the Conspirators, by their perfidy and barbarity, shut the door of exchange, increased the number of Union prisoners, and fearfully augmented their sufferings.

Unimpeached and unimpeachable testimony shows, that in refusing to acknowledge the captive negro soldiers, and the officers who led them, to be proper subjects for exchange, and other acts which they well knew that, through the high sense of honor and justice which always guided the Government, would lead to a cessation of exchange, was only a part of a plan of the Conspirators, deliberately formed, *for murdering, or permanently disabling by the slow process of physical exhaustion, the Union captives in their hands.* This is a grave charge, and should not be made against any man or body of men, without a firm conviction of its truth, and the most conclusive proof. With such conviction, and satisfied that such proof is not only conclusive, but abundant, the charge is here made, and put on record, that the world may know somewhat of the character of the men who conceived, planned, and carried on a rebellion against a beneficent Government, without any other excuse than that of the sorely tempted sinner—the overpowering influence of that depravity which the slave system generated by allowing an unbridled exercise of the baser passions of human nature[2]—a depravity which culminated after a career of two hundred years or more, in what Blackstone declares to be the sum of all wickedness denounced in the Decalogue, namely, TREASON. Proofs from ten thousand tongues certify and justify the con-

---

[1] That letter, given below, explains itself:—

"WAR DEPARTMENT, WASHINGTON CITY, *Aug.* 3, 1863.

"SIR:—Your letter of the 3d instant, calling the attention of this Department to the cases of Orrin H. Brown, William H. Johnston, and William Wilson, three colored men, captured on the gun-boat *Isaac Smith,* has received consideration. This Department has directed that three rebel prisoners of South Carolina, if there be any such in our possession, and if not, three others, be confined in close custody and held as hostages for Brown, Johnston, and Wilson, and that the fact be communicated to the rebel authorities at Richmond.

"Very respectfully, your obedient servant,

"EDWIN M. STANTON, *Secretary of War.*"

[2] John G. Whittier wrote, during the war:—

"The poison plant the fathers spared　　　　　What points the rebel cannon?
　　All else is overtopping.　　　　　　　　　What sets the roaring rabble's heel
　　East, West, South, North,　　　　　　　　On the old star-spangled pennon?
　　It curses the earth;　　　　　　　　　　　What breaks the oath
　　All justice dies,　　　　　　　　　　　　　Of the men of the South?
　　And fraud and lies　　　　　　　　　　　What whets the knife
　　Live only in its shadow.　　　　　　　　For the Union's life?
What gives the wheat-field blades of steel?　Hark to the answer: Slavery!"

clusions of a National Senator (Howard), who, while holding in his hand the report of a Committee appointed by the United States Sanitary Commission in May, 1864,[1] said, after speaking of the barbarities at Andersonville: "*The testimony is as clear as the noonday sun, that their barbarities were deliberately practiced upon our men for the double purpose of crippling and reducing our armed force, and of striking terror into the Northern population in order to prevent enlistments. There does not remain ground for a doubt that the rebel Government designedly resorted to the slow process of torture and death by starvation, and to freezing and starving united, operating minute by minute, hour by hour, day by day, week by week, and month by month, until the man became a living skeleton and idiot, no longer able to recognize his wife, his children, or his friends ; no longer of any value either to himself or to his country ; and this for the purpose of weakening our military arm, and deterring our people from prosecuting the war.*" It was this horrid fact, that General Merideth, well informed in the matter, alluded to in the letter[a] we have cited, when he said : "On the 25th of November, 1863, I offered to send immediately to City Point, twelve thousand or more Confederate prisoners, to be exchanged for Union soldiers confined in the South. This proposition was distinctly and unequivocally refused by Mr. Ould. And why ? *Because the damnable plans of the rebel*

[a] Aug. 25, 1868.

In the Convention that framed the National Constitution, George Mason, grandfather to the author of the Fugitive Slave Law (see page 384, volume I.), and a slave-holder, said of slavery : " It produces the most pernicious effects in manners. Every master of a slave is born a tyrant. They [slaves] bring the judgment of Heaven on a country. As nations cannot be rewarded or punished in the next world, they must be in this. *By an inevitable chain of causes and effects, Providence punishes national sins by national calamities.*"

[1] This Committee was composed of Doctors Valentine Mott and Edward Delafield, and Gouverneur Morris Wilkins, of New York, and Doctor Ellerslie Wallace, Hon. John J. Clark Hare, and Rev. Treadwell Walden of Philadelphia. They were appointed by the Commission for " ascertaining, by inquiry and investigation, the true physical condition of prisoners recently discharged, by exchange, from confinement at Richmond and elsewhere within the rebel lines; whether they did, in fact, during such confinement, suffer materially for want of food, or from its defective quality, or from other privations or sources of disease ; and whether their privations and sufferings were designedly inflicted on them by military or other authority of the rebel Government, or were due to causes which such authorities could not control." The Committee visited camps of paroled prisoners at Annapolis and elsewhere, took large numbers of depositions in writing, and otherwise collected information which justified the conclusion of Senator Howard, mentioned in the text. The Committee said : " It is the same story everywhere ; prisoners of war treated worse than convicts, shut up either in suffocating buildings, or in outdoor inclosures, without even the shelter that is provided for the beasts of the field ; unsupplied with sufficient food ; supplied with food and water injurious and even poisonous; compelled to live on floors, often covered with human filth, or on ground saturated with it; compelled to breathe an air oppressed with an intolerable stench; hemmed in by a fatal dead-line, and in hourly danger of being shot by unrestrained and brutal guards; despondent even to madness, idiocy, and suicide; sick, of diseases (so congruous in character as to appear and spread like the plague) caused by the torrid sun, by decaying food, by filth, by vermin, by malaria, and by cold; removed at the last moment, and by hundreds at a time, to hospitals corrupt as a sepulcher, there, with few remedies, little care, and no sympathy, to die in wretchedness and despair, not only among strangers, but among enemies too resentful either to have pity or to show mercy. These are positive facts. Tens of thousands of helpless men have been, and are now[b] being, disabled and destroyed by a process as certain as poison, and as cruel as the torture or burning at the stake, because nearly as agonizing and [b] September, more prolonged. This spectacle, is daily beheld and allowed by the rebel Government. No sup- 1864. position of negligence, or indifference, or accident, or inefficiency, or destitution, or necessity, can account for all this. So many, and such positive forms of abuse and wrong cannot come from negative causes. *The conclusion is unavoidable, therefore, that these privations and sufferings have been designedly inflicted by the military and other authority of the rebel Government, and cannot have been due to causes which such authorities could not control.*"

Such was the verdict of a committee of men whose ability, honor, integrity and fidelity, to the duties demanded by truth and justice, no man can rightfully question. It is the testimony of eye and ear-witnesses which no one, competent to speak, has ever dared to deny. We read with feelings of horror of the cruelty of the British in India, in blowing their Sepoy prisoners to atoms from the muzzles of cannon. That act was merciful compared to the fiendishness exhibited toward Union prisoners in the late Civil War. We read with feelings of horror of the tortures formerly inflicted upon prisoners by the savages of our wilderness. These were mild sufferings compared with those to which the Conspirators and their instruments subjected the soldiers of the Republic when they fell into their hands.

Government, in relation to our poor captured soldiers, had not been fully carried out."

For obvious reasons, the revolting details of the cruelties practiced upon the Union prisoners at Richmond, Andersonville, Danville, Salisbury, Millen, Charleston, and other places, and the results of those cruelties, are not put upon record here. General statements are considered quite sufficient for the purpose already avowed; and the reader may consult, for a knowledge of those details, the report of the Commission alluded to; the published statements of scores of victims; the testimony elicited by the Committee on the Conduct of the War; the testimony on the trial of Captain Wirz, and the painfully interesting book written by Ambrose Spencer (who lived near Andersonville, and was personally acquainted with the method of proceeding there), entitled *A Narrative of Andersonville.*

From the beginning of the war, the charge and disposition of the Union prisoners were committed to John H. Winder, formerly of the National army, whose acquaintance we have already made.[1] He appears to have been, according to the testimony of friend and foe, an exceedingly bad man; cruel in his nature; repulsive in features; rude in manners; and foul and profane in speech. While a cadet at West Point, he engaged in a conspiracy, and was saved from punishment by an adroit construction of law by John C. Calhoun, then Secretary of War. He was an inciter of the mob at Baltimore, who attempted to prevent Massachusetts troops passing through that city to Washington, in April, 1861. Then he went to Richmond, and was appointed a brigadier-general in the insurgent army, but never had command in the field. The Arch-Conspirator, Davis, who knew his character well, made him Chief Commissary of Prisoners, and kept him in that office until his death in Georgia,[2] in spite of the remonstrances of officials above and below him, and the frequent exposure of the infamy of his deeds. "He was supplied with rank," says Mr. Spencer, "without a command, from his peculiar fitness for the work to be required of him." It is well known that he did not disappoint his master in the execution of the duties assigned to him; and it is doubtful if, within the limits of the so-called Confederacy, another man could be found so well fitted for the performance of the mission to which he was destined.

Winder's chief executive officer in the exercise of cruelty toward the captives in Richmond, and especially in Libby Prison, was Major Turner; and Captain Henry Wirz, who was hanged[a] for his crimes, at the National Capital, was his most trusted and efficient lieutenant at Andersonville. His coadjutor in the work of destroying prisoners, seems to have been "Commissary-General" L. B. Northrup, that special favorite of Jefferson Davis, already mentioned, whom one of the Confederate Congressmen (Henry S. Foote) published as a "monster of iniquity."[3] The writer was told by an officer of the Confederate Commissary Department,

a Nov. 10, 1865.

---

[1] See page 26, volume II.

[2] Jones, in his " *Rebel War Clerk's Diary*," under date of February 8, 1865, says: " Intelligence was received to-day of the sudden death of Brigadier-General Winder, in Georgia; from apoplexy, it is supposed. He was in command of the prisons, with his staff, or 'plug uglies' around him."

[3] This man was in the regular army of the United States at one time. He was dismissed from the service for misdemeanor, but when Jefferson Davis became President Pierce's Secretary of War, he reinstated Northrup. The grateful delinquent became his benefactor's willing instrument, and did his bidding throughout the rebellion.

who knew Northrup well, long before the war, that he invented a method, after many experiments, that would surely effect the utter prostration of prisoners, while there should not seem to be actual starvation. It was the giving to each prisoner, for a day's sustenance, *six ounces of flour, two ounces of bacon, one gill of molasses, and a pint of cow-peas:* a composition calculated to disorder the bowels, and produce marasmus and death ! " Print this," said the indignant officer, when he gave the writer an account of it, " and give my name as authority, if you like." Such were the instruments employed by Jefferson Davis, in the case of Union prisoners. Jones, in his *Rebel War Clerk's Diary*, frequently shows his detestation of Winder ; and even the *Richmond Examiner* exclaimed, when, at the age of seventy years, Davis's commissary of prisoners went to Andersonville because there was a wider field for his awful vocation :—" *Thank God that Richmond is at last rid of old Winder ! God have mercy upon those to whom he has been sent !* "[1]

Everywhere the Union prisoners were closely crowded in ill-ventilated and unwholesome places. Libby Prison[2] contained six rooms, each one hundred feet in length and forty in breadth. At one time, these held twelve hundred Union officers of every grade, from a lieutenant to a brigadier-general. They were allowed no other place in which to cook, eat, wash and dry their clothes and their persons, sleep, and take exercise. Ten feet by two was all that might be claimed for each man. They were usually despoiled of their money, watches, and sometimes portions of their clothing, before entering, with promises, rarely fulfilled, of a return of them, when exchanged. At one time, they were not allowed a seat of any kind to sit upon. The floors of rough boards were always washed in the afternoon, so that at night they were damp. On these, some without any thing under them, the prisoners were compelled to sleep, and many thereby took cold, which ended in consumption and death. The windows were numerous, and most of the glasses were broken, in consequence of which they suffered intensely from cold.[3] The captives were subjected to the caprices of Turner, who, among other cruelties, ordered that no one should go within three feet of the windows, a rule that seems to have been adopted in other prisons in the South. A violation of the rule gave license to the guard to shoot the offending prisoner. It was enforced with the greatest cruelty. Sometimes by accident, or unconsciously in his sufferings, an officer would go by a window, and be instantly shot at, without warning. The brutal guards took pleasure in the sport of " shooting Yankees," and eagerly watched for opportunities to indulge in it.[4]

---

[1] Quoted by Spencer, page 43.   [2] See page 46.

[3] The captives had only one blanket each. These, in time, became ragged and filthy, and, in spite of all precautions, filled with vermin.

[4] They did not always wait for an infraction of the rule. Lieutenant Hammond was shot at while in a boarded inclosure, where there was no window, only an aperture between the boards. The guard caught sight of his hat through this opening, and aiming lower, so as to reach his heart, fired. A nail turned the bullet upward, and it passed through his ear and hat-brim. The officer reported the outrage to Turner, who merely replied :—" The boys are in want of practice." The culprit guard said he " had made a bet that he would kill a damned Yankee, before he came off duty." No official notice was taken of the occurrence, and the fellow tried to murder another officer (Lieutenant Huggins) in the same way, but failed. At Danville, a prisoner was standing at a window, but in such a position that only his shadow could have given the guard knowledge of the fact. The sentinel went many feet from the line of his beat, and shot at and killed the captive, the bullet entering his brain. Similar cruelties were practiced at all other Confederate prisons. It appeared in evidence that, at Atlanta, a sick soldier, who was near what was called "the dead-line," beyond which prisoners were not allowed to go, put his hand

"But there were cruelties worse than these," said the report of the Committee, "because less the result of impulse and recklessness, and because deliberately done." It was the starvation of the prisoners, by a systematic diminution in the quantity, and deterioration of the quality of their daily allowance with which they were supplied, the character of which may be understood by the remark of a young officer, "I would gladly have preferred the horse-feed in my father's stable." The process of the slow starvation of the captives began in the autumn of 1863, and was so general and uniform in all the prisons and prisoner-pens, that there can be no doubt of its having been done by direct orders from the Conspirators at Richmond. "The corn bread," says the report, "began to be of the roughest and coarsest description. Portions of the cob and husk were often found ground in with the meal. The crust was so thick and hard that the prisoners called it iron-clad. To render the bread eatable they grated it, and made mush of it; but the crust they could not grate. Now and then, after long intervals, often of many weeks, a little meat was given them, perhaps two or three mouthfuls. At a later period, they received a pint of black peas, with some vinegar, every week. The peas were often full of worms, or maggots in a chrysalis state, which, when they made soup, floated on the surface." And this was done when there was abundance of food at the command of their jailors.[1]

For awhile, the prisoners were allowed to receive boxes of food and clothing, sent by their friends in the North, and by the Sanitary Commission, but it was found that this privilege would defeat the starvation scheme of the Conspirators, and in January, 1864, it was denied, without any reason being given. "Three hundred boxes," says the report, "arrived every week, and were received by Colonel Ould, Commissioner of Exchange, but instead of being distributed, were retained, and piled up in a warehouse near by.[2] The contents of many of these boxes were used by the Confederates. "The officers," says the Report, "were permitted to send out and buy articles at extravagant prices, and would find the clothes, stationery, hams, and butter, which they had purchased, bearing the marks of the Sanitary Commission.

---

over to pluck a bunch of leaves, that were not a foot from the boundary. The instant he did so, the guard caught sight of him, fired, and killed him.—*Report of the Committee of the United States Sanitary Commission,* September, 1864.

The conduct of the National authorities toward the Confederate captives in Libby Prison, after the former entered Richmond, in April, 1865, was in marked contrast to that of the agents of the Conspirators. There were not more than twenty-five prisoners on each floor. The rooms were kept clean and well-ventilated, and supplied with an abundance of pure water; and sympathizing friends were allowed to furnish the prisoners with whatever they pleased. The writer, who was in Richmond a few days after its evacuation by Lee, visited Libby Prison. He saw dozens of knapsacks let down by ropes from the windows, filled by a crowd of friends outside, and drawn up, while the Union guard, instead of having license either from authority or desire to harm the prisoners, looked on with seeming pleasure, because the wants of the poor captives were relieved. The writer saw two women, each dressed in silk, filling a knapsack with food which he had seen the same women receive from the Union Commissary Department, or its place of distribution, not far from the Capitol, half an hour before. These women, at the place of distribution, pretended to be entirely destitute of food for themselves and little ones, and so they received from their kind Government relief for their wants. The food thus obtained by false pretenses, was carried to prisoners who were already supplied with abundant and wholesome rations.

[1] One day by pulling up a plank in the floor of Libby Prison, they gained access to the cellar, and found there an abundance of provisions—barrels of wheat flour, potatoes, and turnips. Of these they ate ravenously, until the theft was discovered.—*Report of the Committee.*

[2] There was some show of delivery, however, but in a manner especially heartless. Five or six boxes were given during the week. The eager prisoner, expecting, perhaps, a wife's or mother's thoughtful provision for him, was called to the door and ordered to spread his blanket, when the opened cans, whether containing preserved fruits, condensed milk, tobacco, vegetables, or meats, were thrown promiscuously together, and often ruined by the mingling.—*Report of the Committee.*

Over three thousand boxes, sent to the captives in Libby Prison, and on Belle Isle in the James River, near, were stored close by the former building, where the writer saw a large portion of them, immediately after the evacuation of Richmond.

In the few indications here given of the condition of the Union captives in Libby Prison, we have a glimpse, only, of the horrors of the "starving time," in the history of such captives, in all parts of the country under the rule of the Conspirators.   The finishing touch in the ghastly picture of the iniquity of those Conspirators, is given in the fact, that they prepared to blow up Libby Prison, with its starving inmates, with gunpowder, rather than allow them to regain their liberty.   To the testimony concerning that premeditated act, already given in this work,[1] may be added that of Turner, the commandant of the prison, who said, in answer to the question of a captive officer, " Was the prison mined ?"   " Yes, and I would have blown you all to Hades before I would have suffered you to be rescued." A remark of Bishop Johns was corroborative as well as curious, in reply to the ques-

tion, " Whether it was a Christian mode of warfare to blow up defenseless prisoners ?"   The Bishop replied, " I suppose the authorities are satisfied on that point, though I do not mean to justify it."[2]

The sufferings of the captives on Belle Isle, during the "starving time" were much greater than of those in Libby Prison, for the latter were under shelter.

THE RICHMOND "BRIDGE OF SIGHS."

Belle Isle was a small island of a few acres, in the James River, in front of Richmond,[3] near the Tredegar Iron Works.   A part of it was a grassy bluff, covered with trees, and a part was a low sandy barren, a few feet above the surface of the river, which there flows swiftly.   There was a bridge across the James, over which the captives passed on their way to Belle Isle, which became truly a " Bridge of Sighs."[4]   Over the Richmond entrance to it might have been appropriately placed, the inscription which Dante saw over the gate of Hell—" He who enters here, leaves hope behind."

For the captives, the cool green grass that carpeted the hill on Belle Isle, and the shade of the trees that adorned it, had no blessings, for the prisoners were confined to the low and treeless sand-barren, and were never allowed,

See page 291.   [2] Report of the Committee.   [3] See engraving on page 288.
[4] This was the bridge of the Richmond and Petersburg railroad.

in the hottest weather, to leave it and go to the cooler spot a few rods off, that appeared so much like heaven, in comparison with the hell in which they were compelled to suffer. That barren spot, not to exceed five acres in extent, was surrounded by earth-works about three feet in height, with a ditch on both sides. Along the outer ditch guards were stationed about forty feet apart, and kept watch night and day. The prisoners were without shelter. At first there were a few ragged Sibley tents, but these soon disappeared. Notwithstanding this, an established station for prisoners, was in a country of forests, with lumber plentiful, not a movement was made, from the beginning, to erect barracks, or to make any humane provision for the comfort of those confined there. Quickly would the hundreds of mechanics sent there have constructed comfortable shelter for all, from the scorching sun and biting frost, but they were not allowed to have the raw material for the purpose.

At one time there were no less than eleven thousand captives on that bleak space of five acres—" so crowded, according to the estimated area given them," says the Report, " there could not have been but the space of two feet by seven given them, and, at the most, three feet by nine, per man..... Stripped of blankets and overcoats, hatless often, shoeless often, in ragged coats and rotting shirts, they were obliged to take the weather as it came.....

The winter came—and one of the hardest winters[a] ever experienced in the South—but still no shelter was provided. The

a 1863-'64.

mercury was down to zero, at Memphis, which is further south than Richmond. The snow lay deep on the ground around Richmond. The ice formed in the James, and flowed in masses upon the rapids, on either side of the island. Water, left in buckets on the island, froze two or three inches deep in a single night. The men resorted to every expedient to keep from perishing. They lay in the ditch, as the most protected place, heaped upon one another, and lying close together, as one of them expressed it, 'like hogs in winter,' taking turns as to who should have the outside of the row. In the morning, the row of the previous night was marked by the motionless forms of those who were sleeping on in their last sleep—*frozen to death!*"

And while thus exposed to the frost, the prisoners were *starving*, and the only defender of exposed men from the severity of the cold, namely, wholesome and abundant food, was denied them. " The cold froze them," says the Report, " because they were hungry,—the hunger consumed them because they were cold. These two vultures fed upon their vitals, and no one in the Southern Confederacy had the mercy or the pity to drive them away." And while hundreds of women were administering comforts to the sick and wounded insurgents in Northern prisons and hospitals, *not one woman was ever seen upon Belle Isle while the Union captives were there.* Many methods of cruelty to aggravate the sufferings of the prisoners on Belle Isle were resorted to. Unnecessary restrictions; brutal treatment of slight and oftentimes unconscious offenders; deprivation of the use of the running water, for bathing, in the summer, and scores of other operations calculated to crush the life out of the poor men. The sick were tardily taken to hospitals, there neglected and prematurely returned;[1] and every precaution seems to have

---

[1] The Confederate Surgeon-General's Report showed that in the months of January, February and March, 1864, out of nearly 2,800 patients, about 1,400, or one-half the number, died. There was only a single hospital tent on Belle Isle. The sick were laid on dirty straw, on the ground, with logs for pillows.

been taken to secure a daily diminution of the strength of the victims. As at Libby, so on Belle Isle, food and clothing sent to the captives, by friends, were withheld, and often appropriated by the Confederates.[1] "As the weary months drew on, hunger told its inevitable tale on them all. They grew weak and emaciated. Many found that they could not walk; when they attempted it, a dizziness and a blindness came, and they fell to the ground. Diarrhea, scurvy, congestion of the lungs, and low fevers set in. . . . . And what was done in prison and hospital to our private soldiers on Belle Isle, and to our officers in Libby, was done nearly all over the South. . . . The very railroads can speak of inhuman transportations from one point to another of the sick, the wounded, and the unwounded together, crowded into cattle and baggage cars, lying and dying in the filth of sickness, and the blood of undressed wounds."[2]

But we will consider the revolting picture of atrocities at Libby Prison and Belle Isle no longer. It remains for us only to briefly notice Andersonville Prison, the most extensive, as it was the most infamous, of all the prisoner-pens into which Union captives were gathered. It was in an unhealthy locality,[3] on the side of a red-clay hill, near Anderson Station, on the Southwestern railroad, in Georgia, about sixty miles south from Macon, and surrounded by the richest of the cotton and corn-growing regions of that State. The site was selected, at the suggestion it is said of Howell Cobb, the commander of the District, by Captain W. S. Winder, son of the Confederate Commissary of prisoners. It comprised twenty-seven acres of land, with a swamp in its center. A choked and sluggish stream flowing out of another swamp, crawled through it, while within rifle-shot distance from it flowed a large brook fifteen feet wide and three feet deep, of pure, delicious water. Had this been inclosed within the pen, the prisoners might have drank and bathed as much as they pleased.[4] As that would have endangered the success of the murderous scheme of the Conspirators, it was not included. Another comfort was denied.[5] The spot selected for the pen was covered with pine trees, which would have made a grateful shade for the captives. Winder gave orders for them to be cut down. When a spectator ventured to suggest that the shade would alleviate the sufferings of the captives, that officer, acting under higher authority, replied: "That is just what I am not

---

[1] Colonel Ely, of the Eighteenth Connecticut, saw one of his men, a school-mate, and highly respectable citizen of Norwich, starving, and was permitted to throw him a ham. When the poor fellow crawled to get it, the rebel guard charged bayonets upon him, called him a "damned Yankee," and took the ham themselves. This is only a single item of like testimony of a cloud of witnesses examined by the Committee of the Sanitary Commission.

[2] Report of the Committee, &c.

[3] "It is said to be the most unhealthy part of Georgia, and was probably selected as a depot for prisoners, on account of this fact."—*Report of Captain James M. Moore to the Quartermaster-General.*

[4] Report of an *Expedition to Andersonville*, by Miss Clara Barton, for the purpose of identifying and marking the graves of the dead prisoners there. The labors of that remarkable young woman, during the war, in acts of benevolence and humanity, in hospitals and on the field, can scarcely be appreciated.

[5] A most curious circumstance, attested by many eye-witnesses, occurred in that prisoner-pen during its occupation. The stream that moved sluggishly through the pen, and which was made a noisome cess-pool by the guards outside, was the only water the prisoners were allowed to drink. They dug some shallow wells, and thus obtained a little water that, for awhile, was somewhat purer than the surface pools. At length, one night the captives had a prayer-meeting around a large stump of a tree. A thunder-storm soon followed. On the following morning a spring of delicious water was found flowing out of the ground from near the stump, and continued to do so during the remainder of the confinement of the prisoners there It was a fountain of unspeakable blessings from the hand of God. Miss Barton, in her *Narrative*, says, it "broke out from the solid ground. near the foot of the northern slope, just under the western dead-line. It is still there—cool and clear—the only pleasing object in this horrid place."

going to do! I will make a pen here for the damned Yankees, where they
will rot faster than they can be sent." [1]

Howell Cobb issued orders for six hundred negroes to be impressed for
the purpose of constructing a stockade around the designated inclosure. It
received its first prisoners (soldiers of the New Hampshire, Connecticut,
New Jersey and Michigan infantry), eight hundred in number, on the 15th
of February, 1864, when batteries were planted at four points, bearing upon
the inclosure, and a heavy guard was established, numbering at one time,
three thousand six hundred men. The pen was a quadrangle, with two
rows of stockades, from twelve to eighteen feet in height; and seventeen
feet from the inner stockade was the " dead-line," over which no man could
pass and live. Raised above the stockade, were fifty-two sentry boxes, in
each of which was a guardsman perpetually, ready and eager to " kill a Yankee" whenever the infraction of a rule would permit. The perpetrators of
such murders were generally rewarded by the Winders with a furlough.

The fiendish intentions of these men were carried out as far as possible,
and the atrocities committed in the great prisoner-pen there established were
awful in the extreme. It is difficult to write with calmness, with the terrible testimony in full volume before us. The details are too shocking even
to make it proper to present an abstract here. Suffice it to say, that Winder,
with his son, nephew, Wirz, and others, performed their horrid task, with
full license to do as they pleased, with alacrity and awful effect. [2] At one
time more than thirty thousand human beings—the fathers, husbands,
brothers, sons, of anxious, waiting, watching women in desolate homes hundreds of miles away, were confined on that twenty-seven acres of land, reek-
ing with generators of disease and death; sometimes parched with the sun, at

---

[1] Spencer's *Narrative of Andersonville.*

[2] It is with extreme reluctance that the writer puts on record in this work, the coarse and profane language
of one of the agents of the Conspirators, in the business of the starving of prisoners. It is only given to show
the manner in which efforts to relieve the sufferings of the Union captives were met. It is but one of many
instances, at Andersonville and elsewhere, and may account for the fact that no woman was ever seen in the
prison camp at Belle Isle. The incident here given is related by Mr. Spencer, in his *Narrative of Andersonville.* He says a humane physician of Americus, in Georgia (Dr. B. J. Head), and his wife, moved to pity by a
knowledge of the sufferings of the prisoners, attempted to furnish them with some food and clothing. Mrs.
Head interested other women, and in the face of insults and discouragements, they collected a quantity sufficient
to be of real service. A clergyman (Mr. Davies) told General Winder what the women were about, and the
latter promised to allow them to give the relief. A little party soon afterward proceeded to Andersonville with
supplies, and a permit was asked of the provost-marshal, Lieutenant Reed, for them to be passed in. Reed, with
an oath, refused, and when told by Dr. Head that General Winder had authorized it, said that he did not believe
it—that he "was not such a damned fool as that." Some rebel officer sitting there, said the doctor ought to be
hung for his Yankee sympathies, and that he was ready to put the rope around his neck. Driven from the
office, the doctor went to General Winder, when the following conversation, reported by Mr. Spencer, occurred,
in the presence of the benevolent women who accompanied him :—

The doctor requested a pass to take the things to the hospital. "I'll see you in hell first," returned the
general. "You're a damned Yankeee sympathizer, and all those connected with you." "You are mistaken,
general," said the doctor. "You know that *I* am no Yankee sympathizer, sir. I do sympathize with suffering
humanity, and this is a mission of mercy." "God damn your mission of mercy!" cried the general. "I wish that
you, and every other damned Yankee sympathizer, and every God damned Yankee, too, were all in hell together!"
"But, general," rejoined the doctor, "we are here by your express permission, given to Mr. Davies." "It's a
damned lie!" he replied. "I never gave him or any one else permission to keep the damned ———— from
starving, and rotting, too, if they choose." "Well, general, will you allow the provisions to go in this time, now
that they are up here?" "No, by God, not the first damned morsel shall go in," returned the general. At this
moment the little provost-marshal, Reed, entered the office hastily, and said, "Give me an order to have these
goods confiscated." "I don't think I've got the power to do that, Reed," replied he, "but I've got the power to
prevent the damned Yankees from having them, and, by God, they sha'n't!" Fearing the women and himself
might be subjected to personal violence, if he pressed the matter further, Dr. Head advised the relinquishment
of the attempt to do an act of mercy. The load of necessaries which they brought, filled a four-mule wagon, and
were seized and used by the Confederates.

others flooded with filthy water; exposed to frost and heat; to the bullets of brutal guards used in wanton sport; beaten, bruised and cursed; driven to madness and idiocy; starved into skeletons; and, worse than all, tortured by the false declaration, made only to lacerate, that their Government had forsaken them, thus leaving them no other hope for relief from misery, than death. To nearly fourteen thousand sufferers, that everlasting relief came. The graves of twelve thousand nine hundred and twenty of the victims tell the dreadful tale. Of these only about four hundred and fifty are unknown.[1]

It was pleaded, in extenuation, that the Confederates had not the means for feeding the Union prisoners, and that the lack of food for them was caused by its great scarcity. The Committee of the Sanitary Commission say that, after collecting all testimony possible to be obtained, "it appears that the Southern army has been, ever since its organization, completely equipped in all necessary respects, and that the men have been supplied with every thing which would keep them in the best condition of mind and body, for the hard and desperate service in which they were engaged. They knew nothing of famine or freezing. Their wounded and sick were never neglected. So do the few details of fact that could be extracted, without suspicion of their object, from the soldiers of the Southern army, confirm the reasoning which accounts for its efficiency.

"The conclusion is inevitable. It was in their power to feed sufficiently, and to clothe, whenever necessary, their prisoners of war. They were perfectly able to include them in the military establishments, but they chose to exclude them from the position always assigned to such, and in no respect to treat them like men taken in honorable warfare. Their commonest soldier was never compelled, by hunger, to eat the disgusting rations furnished at the Libby to United States officers. Their most exposed encampment, however temporary, never beheld the scenes of suffering which occurred daily and nightly among United States soldiers in the encampment on Belle Isle. The excuse and explanation are swept away. There is nothing now between the Northern people and the dreadful reality."

To this conclusion of the Committee may be added the fact, mentioned on page 414, that throughout Georgia, the State in which the Andersonville prisoner-pen was situated, and where starvation was most rife, General Sherman found a superabundance of food.

It was pleaded that the Conspirators and military officers nearest to them, were ignorant of the cruelties inflicted by these subordinates. And General Robert E. Lee,—"a greatly over-rated military leader—a man of routine—cold, undemonstrative, ambitious, the pet of the Virginians because he was a member of one of their 'first families'—without the moral courage to take the responsibility—so popular with the army that he might have ended the war any time after the capture of Atlanta," as one of the most success-

---

[1] Dorrance Atwater, of Connecticut, was a prisoner at Andersonville, and, in June, 1864, was detailed as clerk in the Confederate Surgeon's office, to keep the daily record of deaths. While there, he secretly copied the entire list of the dead, which he furnished to the Government after his release. In the cemetery, not far from the prisoner-pen, and which contained fifteen acres, a stick was placed at the head of each grave, on which was inscribed the name of the occupant, his rank, regiment, and company, and the date and cause of his death. By this means Miss Barton, and Government officers sent for the purpose, were enabled to identify the graves of nearly every dead soldier there. Mr. Atwater accompanied Miss Barton on her visit to the Andersonville prisoner-pen.

ful of the Confederate military leaders said to the writer,—Robert E. Lee, the commander of the Army of Northern Virginia, never a hundred miles from Richmond after the autumn of 1863, and in constant personal communication with that city, the place of his family residence, actually declared,[a] before the Joint Committee on Reconstruction, that he was not aware of any bad treatment suffered by Union prisoners—was not aware that any of them died of cold and starvation—that no report was ever made to him of the sad condition of Union prisoners anywhere—that he never knew who was in command at Andersonville, Salisbury, and other prisoner-pens, until after the war; and that he "knew nothing in the world" of the alleged cruelties about which complaints had been made.[1]

[a] Feb. 17, 1866.

If General Lee spoke truly, he exhibited one of the most remarkable cases on record of ignorance of facts which it was his business to know as commander of a Department in which it was charged that these atrocities had been committed. He might have known, what the public records of the Confederate "Government," now in Washington City, show, that so early as September, 1862, the fact of cruelties toward Union prisoners was so well known to all the world, that the Conspirators felt the necessity of official action, and that Augustus R. Wright, chairman of a committee of the "House of Representatives" made a report[b] on the prisons at Richmond confining Union captives, to George W. Randolph, then "Secretary of War," in which report it was said that the state of things was "terrible beyond description;" that "the committee could not stay in the room over a few seconds;" that a change must be made, and that "*the committee makes the report to the Secretary of War, and not to the House, because in the latter case, it would be printed, and, for the honor of the nation, such things must be kept secret.*" He might have known that, on the ninth of December, 1863, Henry S. Foote offered a resolution in the Confederate "House of Representatives," for the appointment of a committee of inquiry concerning the alleged ill-treatment of Union prisoners, and that in the course of his remarks, he admitted the charges to be true, by saying, alluding to Commissary-General Northrup: "This man has placed our Government in the attitude charged by the enemy, *and has attempted to starve the prisoners in our hands!*" Foote then read testimony which, he said, was on record in Ould's office, to prove that the charge was true; and he declared that Northrup had actually said, in an elaborate report to the Secretary of War, that "for the subsistence of a human Yankee carcass a vegetable diet was the most proper that could be adopted."[2]   Lee might

[b] Sept. 22, 1862.

---

[1] See the Report of the Joint Committee on Reconstruction, page 135.

[2] Foote's humane resolution was voted down, and no investigation was allowed, at that time. In the spring of 1865, a committee published a report, in which they admitted the mining of Libby Prison, and, by implication, the charges of cruelty and starvation, but tried to give excuses for the deeds. Foote, in a letter written from Montreal, after the appearance of that report, commented upon it severely, and declared that a "Government officer of respectability" told him "*that a systematic scheme was on foot for subjecting these unfortunate men to starvation.*" He further declared that Northrup's fiendish proposition was "indorsed by Seddon, the Secretary of War," who said, substantially, in that indorsement, that "the time had arrived for *retaliation upon the prisoners of war of the enemy.*" In that letter Foote proved, (1) That the starving of Union prisoners was known to the Confederate authorities; (2) That the rebel Commissary-General proposed it; (3) That the rebel Secretary of War approved and indorsed it; (4) That Robert Ould, rebel Commissioner of Exchange, knew it; and (5) That the rebel House of Representatives knew of it, and endeavored to prevent an investigation. Foote said the proofs were in the War Department, which was afterward burned.

have remembered that a committee of the Christian Commission,[1] in 1864, appeared before his lines, and sought access to the prisoners in Richmond and on Belle Isle, to afford them relief, with the understanding that a similar commission would be allowed to go to the prisons of Confederate captives, and that they were not allowed to pass, because the authorities at Richmond dared not let the outside world know, from competent witnesses, the horrible truths such a visit would have discovered.[2] He might have read, all through the year 1864, in the Northern papers, which he received almost daily, the grave charges concerning the treatment of prisoners at Richmond, and also the report of the Committee of the United States Sanitary Commission, published seven months before the end of the war. And any day, while visiting his family in his elegant brick mansion on Franklin Street,[3] he might have stepped out upon its upper gallery on the south, and with his field-glass, looked into the ghastly faces of the starved, blistered, freezing captives on Belle Isle;[4] or he might have walked down Cary Street, for the space of eight minutes, and looked into Libby Prison to satisfy himself whether a committee of the "Confederate Congress," had told the truth or not. He seems not to have considered such inquiries proper to be imposed upon him as a department commander, as general-in-chief, as a man, or as a Christian.[5] His remarkable ignorance concerning the matter, was equaled only by the treachery of his memory, which did not allow him to recollect whether he ever took an oath of allegiance to the "Southern Confederacy."[6]

What General Lee was so ignorant of, the Confederate authorities, and everybody else were familiar with, as ample testimony shows. When the starvation plan had accomplished its work, and in all the Confederate prisons, the Union captives were generally no better for service than dead men—an army of forty thousand skeletons—Ould, the rebel Commissioner, proposed to General Butler,[a] a resumption of an exchange, man for man. The Conspirators knew how well their men had been fed in Northern prisons, and how strong and effective they were for service,[7] and they

[a] Aug. 10, 1864.

---

[1] This committee consisted of George H. Stuart, Chairman of the Christian Commission, Bishops McIlvaine, Janes, and Lee; William Adams, D.D., and Norman White, of New York, and Horatio Gates Jones, of Philadelphia.

[2] The reply to the application, that came from Richmond, was, "It is not expedient at present."

[3] See page 535.

[4] See page 423, volume I.

[5] "As regards myself, I never had any control over the prisoners, except those that were captured on the field of battle. These, it was my business to send to Richmond, to the proper officer, who was then the provost-marshal-general. In regard to their disposition afterward, I had no control. I never gave an order about it. It was entirely in the hands of the War Department."—*Lee's testimony before the Joint Committee on Reconstruction.* See Report, page 135.

[6] "Question. You say that you do not recollect having sworn allegiance and fidelity to the Confederate Government?"

"Answer. I do not recollect it, nor do I know that it was ever required. I was regularly commissioned in the army of the Confederate States, but I really do not recollect that that oath was required. If it was required, I have no doubt I took it; or if it had been required, I would have taken it."—*Lee's testimony before the Joint Committee on Reconstruction.* See Report, page 134.

[7] It was within the province of the Committee of the United States Sanitary Commission to ascertain the condition of the Confederate prisoners in the hands of the Government. This they did, and reported uniform good treatment, ample shelter, and abundant and wholesome food everywhere. The Conspirators, to parry the terrible charge against them, made a counter-charge of great cruelties which their prisoners experienced, and this brought from Lord Wharncliffe, the President of the British "Southern Independence Association" (see page 45), a proposition to send to the "suffering prisoners in the North, £17,000 in gold," which had been collected for the purpose, from British sympathizers with the rebels. These meddlers were informed by Secretary Seward, that there were no prisoners in the hands of the Government suffering for any thing but the privileges of liberty to fight the Government.

Another member of the British aristocracy, Sir Henry de Hoghton, who, it is said, invested more than $1,700,000

were now willing and anxious, in order to secure the advantages which their cruelty for a year had given them, to have their hale soldiers back. That such was the relative condition of the respective prisoners—Union skeletons and Confederate men in full vigor—Ould exultingly declared, in a letter to General Winder, from City Point, where exchange had been resumed, in which he said: "The arrangement I have made, works largely in our favor. *We get rid of a set of miserable wretches, and receive some of the best material I ever saw.*"

On account of this state of things, General Grant hesitated to resume exchange.[1] Finally, at the middle of autumn, arrangements for special exchanges were made, and Lieutenant-Colonel Mulford went with vessels to Savannah, after about 12,000 Union prisoners from Andersonville and elsewhere. They were brought to Annapolis, in Maryland, and in them the writer saw the horrible workings of the barbarity of the Conspirators.[2]

The records of the War Department show that, during the struggle, 220,000 Confederate soldiers were captured, of whom 26,436 died of wounds or diseases, during their captivity, while of 126,940 Union soldiers captured, nearly 22,576 died while prisoners. This shows that of the Union prisoners, 17.6 per cent. died in the hands of the Confederates, while only a little more than 11 per cent. of the Confederate prisoners died in the hands of the Government.[3]

The arrangements of the Government for the care of its sick and wounded soldiers, were extensive and complete. When the war closed there were no less than two hundred and four General Hospitals, fully equipped, with a

---

in Confederate bonds, sent to Secretary Seward, what purported to be a petition from the people of the United Kingdom, to the people of the United States, entreating the latter, "in the name of humanity," to end the war by acknowledging the independence of the Confederacy. Sir Henry's "humanity" seems to have been inspired by his desire to save his money. He was one of the most active of the members of the "Southern Independence Association."

[1] General Grant said[a] in a letter to General Butler: "It is hard on our men held in Southern prisons not to exchange them, but it is humanity to those left in the ranks to fight our battles. Every man released, on parole or otherwise, becomes an active soldier against us at once, either directly or indirectly. *If we commence a system of exchange* which liberates *all prisoners* taken, we will have to fight on until the whole South is exterminated. If we hold those caught, they amount to no more than dead men. At this particular time, to release all rebel prisoners North would insure Sherman's defeat, and would compromise our safety here."

[a] Aug. 18, 1864.

In his letter to Commissioner Ould, in reply to the proposition to resume exchange, General Butler, alluding to the fact that the Conspirators, after delaying eight months to consider a proposition (which, by thus accepting, they acknowledged to be right), and thereby produced great suffering, said, significantly—"One cannot help thinking, even at the risk of being deemed uncharitable, that the benevolent sympathies of the Confederate authorities have been lately stirred by the depleted condition of their armies, and a desire to get into the field, to effect the present campaign, the hale, hearty, and well-fed prisoners held by the United States, in exchange for the half-starved, sick, emaciated, and unserviceable soldiers of the United States, now languishing in your prisons."

[2] The writer, under the kind direction of Dr. Vanderkieft, the Post Surgeon, visited the tents and hospital wards at Annapolis, containing some of these prisoners, soon after their arrival. They were then somewhat recruited by wholesome food, and a sea voyage, but exhibited a sight most shocking. The testimony of all with whom the author conversed, was corroborative of the statements made in this chapter. Many died at Annapolis. In the little chapel, there were from two to fifteen coffins each day, with the remains of the dead who received the honors of religious funeral rites. We followed a procession from that little chapel out to the soldiers' cemetery, where the graves already numbered thousands. That cemetery was in sight of the old State-House, wherein Washington resigned his commission as commander-in-chief of the Continental armies, when the independence of his country was achieved. These soldiers died in defense of the great Republic, the offspring of that independence.

[3] Facts found here and there, bearing upon this subject, seem to show that these figures concerning Union prisoners are too low, and that their number during the war was about 185,000, and the number of deaths, in captivity, about 37,000. The mortality among negro soldiers, under every circumstance, was greater than among the white soldiers. The records show, that of 180,000 negro soldiers, 29,298 died, or nearly one in six. Under the title of "Roll of Honor," the Quartermaster-General has published a series of little volumes, containing the names, as far as they could be ascertained, of all the soldiers buried in the National and other cemeteries in all parts of the Republic.

capacity of one hundred and thirty-six thousand eight hundred and ninety-four beds. Besides these, there were numerous temporary and flying hospitals, the former in camps and on vessels, and the latter on battle-fields. Of these general sanitary establishments, one of the most perfect in all its arrange-

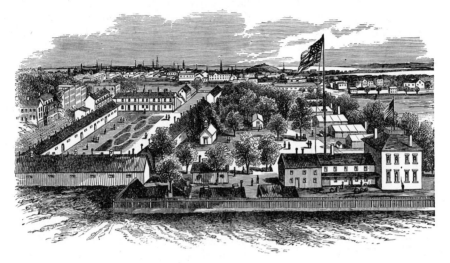

JARVIS HOSPITAL. [1]

ments and management, visited by the writer, was the Jarvis Hospital, on the verge of the city of Baltimore, situated upon high ground, overlooking the town and harbor, and blessed with salubrious air. It occupied the mansion, and about four acres of ground attached to it, which belonged to George Stuart, an enemy of the Republic, who was a general officer in the Confederate army. The Government took possession of the property, and used it until the close of the war. The hospital was arranged upon the general plan of all others, but had some advantages which to others were denied. It had a capacity for fifteen hundred beds, and was never lacking in force, for the Union women of Baltimore made it their special charge.[2]

---

[1] In this picture, Stuart's mansion is seen at the right hand corner, in the foreground. In the distance beyond, a portion of the city, and to the left of the point of the flag is seen Federal Hill, which General Butler took possession of at the beginning of the war; and to the right is Fell's Point, projecting toward Chesapeake Bay, on the extremity of which is Fort McHenry. See page 308.

[2] The following notes, made by the writer on the occasion of a visit to the Jarvis Hospital, early in December, 1864, will give the reader a general idea of the workings of those vast sanitary establishments during the war.—

"The Medical Director is Doctor De Witt C. Peters, and has under his control 8 medical assistants; 1 cadet; 1 chaplain; a lieutenant of the guard, or military assistant; 5 stewards; 1 chief ward-master, with 3 or 4 assistants, who has the charge of all the masculine nurses, who average in number 1 to every 20 men; a chief matron, who has charge of all the feminine nurses; 1 chief laundress, who has charge of all the laundry women, about 30 in number; and 3 chief feminine cooks, in charge of all the cooks (colored), who number about 40. There are about 130 nurses of both sexes in the establishment, and now there are 1,300 patients.

"With this number of patients and employees, there is consumed monthly, in the hospital, over 3,000 pounds of butter; 1,400 gallons of milk; 2,500 dozen eggs; 22,000 pounds of beef; 4,200 pounds of bread; 9,000 pounds of potatoes; 2,500 pounds of beets; 2,500 pounds of turnips; and about 120 gallons of sirup. Of pork, beans, rice, coffee, sugar, &c., they have full rations. In the laundry about 20,000 pieces are washed each week. Last month (November, 1864), there were issued at the hospital, 1,150 suits of military clothing for the destitute.

"There is a safe kept, in which money and other valuables belonging to the patients are held. Their clothing, arms, and accouterments are received and taken care of by the check system, the same as on railways or at hotels. These are kept in a dry and well ventilated room.

The report of the Surgeon-General, Joseph K. Barnes, at the close of the war, showed that, from the beginning, in 1861, to July 1, 1865, there had been treated, in the general hospitals alone, 1,057,423 cases, among whom the rate of mortality was only eight per cent. That rate varied in different portions of our widely extended country; the central, or the region of the Mississippi basin, being much the larger. The rate was much smaller than had ever been known before. The annual mortality of the United States army, in the Mexican war, from diseases, was over ten per cent. That of the British army, in the Crimean war, was nearly twenty-four per cent., and that of their French allies was still greater.

The low rate of mortality in the Union army was due to several causes, the chief of which was the employment, by the Government, of a sufficient number of competent surgeons;[1] a bountiful provision in all hospitals of every necessary; the beneficent labors of two powerful popular organizations, known as the *United States Sanitary Commission,* and the *United States Christian Commission,* and the untiring labors of women, everywhere. The latter worked with tenderness and devotion, day and night, in hospitals, in camps, and in the field, as efficient nurses. They had healing words of cheer and consolation for the languishing, threatened with that despair which defies the medicine of the apothecary; and by their presence, they continually brought images of home to the yearning soul of the sick and wounded son or husband, whose best ideal of earthly happiness was in the fashion of a loving woman.

To this catalogue of chief causes for the low rate of mortality, must be added, as most important sanitary helps, the potent influences of the Chaplains, who numbered at least one hundred thousand. As a class, they were faithful servants of their Divine Master, and full of love toward their fellowmen, their country, and their God. Their work as spiritual guides, was amazingly potential, for they administered "medicine to a mind diseased," by which the physician's prescriptions were often made doubly curative. They formed a trusted link between the sick soldier and his home—a ladder for the angels of thought and affection, between his Bethel and heaven on earth—and to many a bereaved heart did their written words, telling of the joy and hope of a loved one at the gate that leads to immortality, convey messages that sweetened tears. Without hope of reward in the plaudits of the people for deeds of valor in battle, and with their names only faintly written in the records of Patriotism, they nevertheless braved danger and death in every form, for the sake of the souls and bodies of those in their spiritual keeping. The value of their services in the field of moral agencies, during the war, can not be overestimated. The most profound respect and gratitude of the nation is due to the Chaplains of the hospitals of the army and the navy.

"Since the establishment of this hospital, in June, 1862, until this time, or two years and a half, about 16,000 patients have been treated here, of whom, only two hundred have died. The Ladies' Union Relief Association of Baltimore are assiduous in their attentions to the patients in this hospital. Four or five of their members are here every day to assist, especially in the cooking department."

[1] During the war, there were appointed five hundred and forty-seven surgeons and assistant-surgeons of volunteers; mustered into service, two thousand one hundred and nine volunteer regimental surgeons, and three thousand eight hundred and eighty-three volunteer assistant regimental surgeons; seventy-five as acting staff-surgeons, and five thousand five hundred and thirty-two acting assistant-surgeons; making a grand total of twelve thousand one hundred and forty-five. Of these nearly three hundred perished, some in battle, but most of them from disease.

We have alluded to the labors of the *United States Sanitary Commission*, and the *United States Christian Commission*. These were mighty agencies for good, evolved by the kindling fires of Civil War from the noblest impulses of a patriotic people.

The *Sanitary Commission* appeared first, in tangible form. Its origin and organization have been mentioned in a few words, in this work.[1] It was the product of divine seed, that took root in the heart of woman, and by her it was chiefly nourished. It is well to take a note of the germs, while contemplating the majestic plant.

On the day[a] when the President called for seventy-five thousand men to suppress the Slave-holders' insurrection, women of Bridge-port, Connecticut, organized a society for the purpose of affording relief and comfort to the volunteers. This was the first in all the land. In Charlestown, Massachusetts, on the same day, a woman took steps for the formation of a society, for the same purpose;[2] and a few days later, the women of Lowell did the same.[3] Their numbers were few. Their zeal was unbounded, but their power was inadequate to carry out their plan, which was to supply nurses for the sick and wounded, and provisions, clothing, and other comforts not furnished by the Government; also to send books and newspapers to the camps, and to keep up a constant communication with their friends in the field. The women of Cleveland, Ohio, formed an association[b] for the more immediately practical purpose of taking care of the families of volunteers.

a April 15, 1861.

b April 19.

These were the first outcroppings of the tenderest feelings of women, everywhere, when the men were summoned to the field. They were suggestions which speedily developed the most powerful associated effort. Earnest women in New York, at the suggestion of the Reverend H. W. Bellows, D. D., and Doctor Elisha Harris, met,[c] with a few earnest men, as we have observed,[4] and formed the *Women's Central Asso-*

c April 29,

---

[1] See pages 574 and 575, volume I.

[2] On the afternoon of that day, Miss Almena Bates, of Charlestown, Massachusetts, read the President's call for men, and the idea at once occurred to her that some of the men must go from Charlestown, and that they would need aid and comfort from home. She suggested the formation of a society for the purpose of affording such aid, and it was done.— *The Tribune Book,* by Frank B. Goodrich, page 112.

[3] Goodrich says that "the first subscription-list to which the Rebellion gave birth," was signed, at the head of thirty other names, by Moses H. Grinnell, in New York City, on the morning of the 17th of April, 1861. Each subscribed one hundred dollars. It was for the use of the Seventh (New York) Regiment. The first public subscription for the personal relief of the soldiers, was made in Lowell, on the following day, by Judge N. Crosby, who gave one hundred dollars, saying in the letter that bore it:—"Our men have left us at the tap of the drum, without wavering, and without preparation. They have left home without shutting their doors, friends without adieus, and their hammers upon their benches. We must comfort those friends, and prevent loss in their business. We *who stay at home,* can well afford to do all this for them, and make *our* sacrifices in money, and thus care for our country, our constitution and laws. The burden of this struggle must rest upon every man's shoulders, in some form." These expressions form the key-note to the feelings of the loyal people at that time.

On the 20th of April, three ladies and one gentleman of Philadelphia (Mrs. Israel Bissell, Miss Eliza Austin, Mrs. S. Calhoun, and Peter E. M. Harris) signed a notice of a meeting of the ladies of several churches in that city, to make arrangements for providing hospital materials, which was read by the Rev. Dr. Taylor, from the pulpit of the Third Reformed Dutch Church of that city, on the next afternoon. This led to the formation of the "Ladies' Aid Society" of Philadelphia, which, during the war, collected and distributed money and supplies of the value of over three hundred thousand dollars. The "Ladies' Association for Soldiers' Relief," was formed in Philadelphia the next year, with Mrs. Mary A. Brady at its head. Many other associations were organized in Philadelphia for kindred purposes. Indeed, that city seemed to be a vast benevolent institution, during the whole war. It is believed that one of its citizens was the first person who left his home to visit the soldiers in camp, for the purpose of affording them comforts. That was the excellent Joseph Patterson, afterward the treasurer of the *United States Christian Commission.* He left Philadelphia for the purpose, on the morning of the 24th of April, and visited the camps at Havre de Grace, Annapolis, and Washington City.

[4] See page 575, volume I.

ciation for Relief. Its constitution was drawn up by Dr. Bellows. Auxiliary associations were formed, and after much difficulty an organization

was made on a far more extended and efficient plan, which contemplated the co-operation of the association with the Medical Department of the army, under the sanction of the Government, in the care of the sanitary interests of the soldiers. Miss Dix, as we have seen, had already done much in that direction. Dr. Bellows and his associates now endeavored to do much more, and their efforts were rewarded with success. On the 9th of June, 1861, the Secretary of War issued an order, appointing Henry W. Bellows, D. D., Professor A. D. Bache, LL. D. (Chief of the Coast Survey), Professor Jeffries Wyman, M. D., W. H. Van Buren, M. D., R. C. Wood,

HENRY W. BELLOWS.

Surgeon-General of the United States Army, G. W. Cullum, of General Scott's staff, and Alexander Shiras, of the United States Army, in conjunction with such others as they might associate with them, "A Commission of Inquiry and Advice, in respect of the Sanitary Interests of the United States Forces." They were to serve without pay from the Government, and were to have a room for their use in the city of Washington. "They were to direct their inquiries," says the historian of the Sanitary Commission,[1] "to the principles and practice connected with the inspection of recruits and enlisted men; the sanitary condition of volunteers; to the means of preserving and restoring health, and of securing the general comfort and efficiency of the troops; to the proper provision of cooks, nurses, and the hospitals, and to other subjects of a like nature."[1] They were to correspond freely with the War Department, and with the Medical Bureau. The Surgeon-General issued a circular, announcing the creation of the Commission.

The persons named in the Secretary's order proceeded[a] to organize a board of managers, with Dr. Bellows, who may be regarded as the founder of the Commission, at its head. He submitted a plan of organization, which was adopted. On the following day[b] the Commission waited on the President and Secretary of War, who gave their sanction to Dr. Bellows's plan by affixing their signatures to it, and it became the Constitution of the Commission. Its seal bore the style and the date of creation of the organization; also a shield bearing the figure of Mercy, winged, with the symbol of Christianity upon her bosom, and a cup of consolation in her hand, coming down from

[a] June 12, 1861.

[b] June 13.

---

[1] To Charles J. Stillé, of Philadelphia, one of the members of the Commission, was assigned the duty of preparing a general history of its organization and work. This was given, soon after the close of the war, in a volume of 550 pages, entitled, *History of the United States Sanitary Commission: being a General Report of its Work during the War of the Rebellion.* It is presented in three distinct parts: (1) A general history of the Commission's origin, purposes, and methods of operation; (2) a narrative of its special relief service; and (3) an account of the organization and practical workings of its supply system.

History of the Sanitary Commission, page 63.

the clouds to visit wounded soldiers on the battle-field. Such was the origin of the *United States Sanitary Commission.* Frederick Law Olmsted was chosen to be the Resident Secre-tary, which was a post of the highest importance, for that offi-cer was really the General Man-ager of the affairs of the Com-mission.[1]

SEAL OF THE SANITARY COMMISSION.

We may not here give the details of the workings of the Sanitary Commission. The read-er is referred to Mr. Stillé's His-tory for that information. Its labors were confined to the avowed object of its organiza-tion. It was not intended to substitute itself for any organ-ization of the Government, such as the Medical Bureau, nor to interfere with the duties and responsibilities of any Govern-ment officer. It was only to supplement Government deficiencies. This was well understood. The Commission appealed to the people, and was met by a most liberal response. Supplies and money flowed in in suffi-cient volume to meet all its demands. All over the country, men, women, and children, singly and collectively, were working for it and contributing to it. Fairs were held in large cities, which turned immense sums of money into its treasury.[2] Branches were established; agents were employed; corps of nurses were organized; ambulances, army wagons and steamboats of its own were employed in the transportation of the sick and wounded, and sup-plies. It followed the armies closely in all campaigns. Its vigilant ear list-ened for the sounds of battle everywhere, and before the smoke of conflict had fairly been lifted from the battle-field, there was the Sanitary Commis-sion, with its wagons, supplies, tents and nurses, ready to afford instant relief. It was like a guardian angel to the soldier—always at his side in mo-ments of greatest need.[3] When the war ceased and the record of the

---

[1] Its first officers were Rev. Henry W. Bellows, D. D., *President;* Professor A. D. Bache, LL.D., *Vice-President;* Elisha Harris, M. D., *Corresponding Secretary;* George W. Cullum, Alexander E. Shiras, Robert C. Wood M. D., Wolcott Gibbs, Cornelius R. Agnew, M. D., George T. Strong, Frederick Law Olmsted, Samuel G. Howe, M. D., and J. S. Newberry, M. D., *Commissioners.* To these were subsequently added, Horace Binney, Jr., Right Rev. Thomas M. Clark, D. D., Hon. Joseph Holt, R. W. Burnett, Hon. Mark Skinner, Rev. John H. Heywood, Pro-fessor Fairman Rogers, Charles J. Stillé, and J. Huntington Wolcott. There were about five hundred associate members, in all parts of the country. It is due to Mr. Olmsted, to say, that to his extraordinary powers of organ-ization must be attributed a large share of the success which attended the Commission. He gave his time wholly to that work. Dr. Bellows was its faithful and untiring chief from the beginning to the end.

[2] Fairs for the benefit of soldiers and their families were held in Lowell, Chicago twice, Boston, Rochester, Cincinnati, Brooklyn, Albany, Cleveland, Poughkeepsie, New York, Pittsburg, Philadelphia, Dubuque, St. Paul, St. Louis, and Baltimore, in the order here named. In a single fair, in the city of New York, the net receipts, over the expenses, were $1,181,500. In other places the receipts were in equal proportion to the population. In the little city of Poughkeepsie, on the Hudson, whose population was then about 16,000, the net profits of the fair were over $16,000.

[3] The Government supplied all regular rations, hospital stores, et cetera, to the full extent of its power. The Sanitary Commission supplied the sick and wounded with delicacies, ice, stimulants, fruits, &c., in abundance, with trained nurses, which the Government could not well supply.

work of the Sanitary Commission was made plain, it was found that the loyal people of the land had given to it supplies valued at *fifteen million dollars* and about *five million dollars in money.*

The *United States Christian Commission,* a kindred organization, working in harmony with the Sanitary Commission, performed mighty labors for

the spiritual and temporal good of the soldiers, and scattered blessings whose value may not be measured by any standard of Time. Of its history and noble work, we may speak only with brevity. It, too, had its historian in the Rev. Lemuel Moss, of the University of Pennsylvania, who made a complete record of its origin and work in a volume entitled *Annals of the United States Christian Commission.*[1] That organization had its origin in the Young Men's Christian Association of New York City, and was first suggested by Vincent Colyer,[2] an earnest worker in useful fields, who, with Frank W. Bal-

VINCENT COLYER.

lard, and Mrs. Dr. Harris, who represented the Ladies' Aid Society of Philadelphia, went to Washington City immediately after the first battle of Bull Run,[a] to do Christian

[a] July, 1861.

labor in the hospitals and camps there. Mr. Colyer remained. The Government, through General Scott, gave him every facility for visiting the Union camps, and even a permission to go to the Confederate camps if they would allow him to do so. He distributed Bibles, tracts, and hymn-books among the soldiers, held prayer-meetings, and labored most zealously in many ways for their spiritual good. At length, feeling the comparative inefficiency of separate societies, laboring apart, he suggested,[b]

[b] August 22.

soon after he began his labors in the army, the combination of all the Young Men's Christian Associations of the land, in the formation of a society similar in its organization to that of the Sanitary Commission. The suggestion was acted upon, and at a meeting of the Young Men's Christian Association, held in New York, on the 23d of September, a committee was appointed, with Mr. Colyer as its Chairman, to conduct the correspondence and make arrangements for holding a National Convention of such associations. So the work was begun; and on the first of October, Mr. Colyer wrote an earnest letter, setting forth the necessity for immediate associated effort. A convention was called. It assembled in the city of New York, on the 14th of November,[c] when the

[c] 1861.

United States Sanitary Commission was organized with the ever active and ever faithful philanthropist, George H. Stuart, of Philadelphia,[3] at its head. Its specific work was to be chiefly for the moral and religious wel-

---

[1] This volume contains 750 octavo pages, with several illustrations.   [2] See page 309, volume II.

[3] The officers were George H. Stuart, *Chairman;* Rev. W. E. Boardman, *Secretary;* Joseph Patterson, *Treasurer;* and George H. Stuart, Rev. Bishop E. S. Janes, D.D., Charles Demond, John P. Croser, and Jay Cooke. *Executive Committee.*

fare of the soldiers and sailors, conducted by means of oral instruction and the circulation of the Bible and other proper books, with pamphlets, newspapers, &c., among the men in hospitals, camps, and ships.

And so it was that the Christian Commission, of which Mr. Colyer was the real founder,[1] was organized and made ready for work, on the same general plan pursued by the Sanitary Commission. Its labors were not wholly confined to spiritual and intellectual ministrations, but, also, to the distribution of a vast amount of food, hospital stores, delicacies, and clothing. It, too, followed the great armies, and was like a twin angel of mercy with the Sanitary Commission. It co-operated efficiently with the chaplains of the army and navy, by supplying the soldiers and sailors with the Scriptures, and a large variety, and vast number of other good books, which not only instructed and amused them, but kept many of the former from indulgence in the vices of camp life.[2] Chapels for religious worship were erected at permanent camps;[3] and in many ways there was cast about the soldier a salutary hedge of Christian influence. The money and supplies for the purpose, came to the Commission as a free-will offering from the patriotic people, mostly collected by the women of various denominations of the Christian Church, and amounted in value to *six million dollars.* The labors of the Commission can not be estimated by computation. "Doubtless," said a contemporary writer, "there are, though removed from human eyes, tabular views kept in another way, and for other ends; and when the scroll shall be unrolled, those permitted to read it, will see that where we write Dollars, the recording angel has written Immortal Souls."[4]

While the two great organizations we have just considered were working with immense power, others, in large numbers, but less conspicuous, were laboring for the same end, some in the form of associations for the relief of soldiers and sailors; others for the relief of freedmen, in which the Friends or Quakers took the most conspicuous part; and others in the form of committees, and city, county, and State legislative bodies, working for the promotion of enlistments of men for the military and naval service. The grand example of Philadelphia in the establishment of Volunteer Refreshment Saloons,[5] was followed elsewhere, on a smaller scale. Indeed, every loyal

---

[1] Mr. Colyer was one of the most earnest and disinterested of workers in his Master's service. He labored for full sixteen months, without compensation, giving up his business for the purpose. His was a free-will offering. He worked among the soldiers continually. He was agent for the Young Men's Christian Association of Brooklyn, and for the Ladies of St. George's Church, New York, of which he was a member. During his term of service, he distributed over $27,000 worth of hospital stores, food, books, &c., besides being employed, on several occasions, in important services for the Government.—[See Moss's *History*, &c., page 101. We have noticed some of Mr. Colyer's labors at New Berne, under Burnside.—See page 309, volume II.

[2] The following statement, drawn from the records of the Commission, showing its work for the first year will give an idea of the extent of its operations. There were employed at the seat of war, and with army committees in home work, 1,069 Christian ministers and laymen. There were 3,945 meetings held with soldiers and sailors, in camps and hospitals, exclusive of those held at the seat of war, and 188 public meetings in their behalf. During that first year, were distributed 102,560 Bibles and Testaments; 115,757 miscellaneous books; 34,653 magazines and pamphlets; 130,697 soldiers' and sailors' hymn and psalm books; 384,781 newspapers; 10,953,706 pages of tracts; 300,000 temperance documents, and 3,691 boxes and barrels of stores and publications. There were 23 libraries supplied to hospitals.

[3] The interior of one of these is delineated on page 586. [4] Goodrich.

[5] In the first volume of this Chronicle (page 576) is given a brief sketch of the history and working of two free refreshment saloons for soldiers in Philadelphia, in which, according to statements since made to the author, there was an error as to the relative time of the opening of the two saloons, and an omission of three or four names, in the list of managers of one of them. These omissions have been supplied in the Second Edition. It is asserted by the managers of the " Union Volunteer Refreshment Saloon," that it was the first to give food to the pass'ng; diers, and that it was opened on the same day that the " Cooper-shop Refreshment Saloon " was,

head, and heart, and hand, in the land, became engaged in the holy work of
saving the Republic from destruction.[1] The mites of widows and the
abundance of the rich fell into the great treasury of Patriotism, in profusion.
A Michigan soldier put in a cent, with an expressed desire that it might
" grow." It did so, and yielded more than twenty-four thousand dollars.[2]
Cornelius Vanderbilt, an humble New York boatman fifty years earlier, presented to his Government a fully equipped steam-ship-of-war, worth nearly
one million dollars. To associations, and for special objects, about one hundred million dollars were contributed, of which public reports were made.
In every way, and for every object, already alluded to, in bounties for
soldiers and sailors,[3] and in private and isolated contributions, exclusive of
heavy taxes freely paid for the support of the Government, the loyal people
of the Republic gave for its ransom not less than *five hundred million dollars*.

Here we will close our Chronicle of the Civil War, waged on the battle-
field. It was a war begun by an oligarchy of Slave-holders, against the
great body of the people of the Commonwealth, for the perpetuation of the
system of slave-labor, which was rapidly sapping the moral and material
foundations of the Republic, and threatening its ruin. It was a war waged
by a narrow Oligarchy, striving for power by the reduction of the Union, in
theory and practice, to the perilous condition of a league of petty sovereign-
ties, against an enlightened Democracy, determined to maintain in its dignity,

---

but at an earlier hour. That is a question of little moment, compared to the vital one of the relative amount of
good performed by the two establishments, which, as we have observed, worked in generous rivalry. The work of
the " Union" was evidently far more extended than that of the "Cooper." Its receipts during the war in cash
($87,000) and supplies ($30,000), amounted to $117,000. The receipts of the "Cooper" in cash ($58,000) and
supplies ($20,000) amounted to $78,000, making a grand total, contributed by the citizens of Philadelphia for the
relief of passing soldiers, of $195,000.

One of the most active of the managers and friends of the Union Volunteer Refreshment Saloon, during the
entire period of the war, was Samuel B. Fales, a wealthy and benevolent gentleman of Philadelphia, to whom
was applied the deserved title of " The Soldiers' Friend." So untiring were his labors, and so munificent his
gifts in connection with that establishment, that after it was closed, the Committee of Management presented him
with a beautifully wrought testimonial in the form of an engrossed preamble and resolutions, in which were expressed their appreciation of his services as their General Financial Agent and Corresponding Secretary. These
resolutions were surmounted by the portrait of Mr. Fales, over which hovered an eagle. On one side was represented soldiers in the dining-hall, and on the other soldiers on the battle-field. Below the writing was a view
of the exterior of the saloon as it was after it was enlarged, when it had a much more imposing appearance than
in its original form given on page 578, volume I.

[1] For a detailed account of the labors and munificence of the loyal people the reader is referred to a superb
illustrated volume, entitled, *The Tribute Book: a Record of the Munificence, Self-sacrifice, and Patriotism of
the American People during the War for the Union*. By Frank B. Goodrich.

[2] Goodrich relates (*Tribute Book*, page 374) that some Sabbath-School children in Kalamazoo, Michigan,
were in the habit of meeting in their chapel, called " The Bird's Nest," on Sunday. In February, 1864, they
were visited by a soldier from a camp near by, who listened to an address to the children, and when a
collection-plate was passed round, he put in one cent, saying, " Here is a penny I found in the bottom of
my pocket, and it won't grow there ; now, I want to deposit it with ' The Bird's Nest,' and see if it will
grow *there*." The teacher held up the penny, and repeating the soldier's words, said, " Now, we will
see if we can put this into a soil where it can take root and grow." The mother of one of the children
gave ten cents. This was the first subscription to the stock of " The Bird's Nest Bank," which was
organized, the shares being ten cents each, and it was resolved that eight-tenths of all subscriptions should
be appropriated to the relief of the Freedmen, and two-tenths for the benefit of " The Bird's Nest." The
children devoted their leisure to selling shares. Very soon there were subscriptions from every State in the
Union, but two; also in Canada, England, Scotland, and Germany. In one year from its foundation, the
bank had sold 2,400 shares. The founder had then been in the grave several months. Such was the growth
of that little seed, in the rich soil of American hearts.

[3] All but a very small portion of the Union soldiers and sailors were volunteers, and very few of them
were mustered out of the service without having received a bounty from the General Government, the State
Governments, or from counties, towns, and cities, varying in amount, from $100 to $1,200, each. A large
number of the families of those volunteers and others, were supported, in a great degree, by contributions;
and it has been estimated that in the payment of these bounties, and subsistence, there were disbursed
about $300,000,000. This amount must be reckoned among the free-will offerings of the people, for it was as
much such, in voting to tax themselves for the purpose, as in making direct gifts of money and supplies

strength, and splendor, the nationality of that Union. It was a struggle between ideas of the dead past and those of the living present—between wrong and right in their broadest and most conspicuous aspects. It resulted in the utter extinction of slavery, and in the establishment of the Republic, with a Constitution purified and strengthened, upon the eternal foundations of Truth and Justice.

The Civil War produced a radical revolution, social and political; and the adjustment of the functions of society to the demands of the new order of things introduced by that revolution, was a task imperatively imposed upon the people. It remains for us now to give, as briefly as perspicuity will allow, the salient points in the history of that *reorganization*, not *reconstruction*, for no institution worthy of preservation had been destroyed. No State, as a component part of the Republic, had been annihilated. Those in which rebellion had existed were simply in a condition of suspended animation. They were all equal, living members of the Commonwealth, incapacitated by derangements for healthful functional action, and awaiting resuscitation at the hands of the only healer, the National Government. To that resuscitation—that reorganization, and fitting for active life, the Government was now called upon to employ its powers.[1]

A preliminary step toward reorganization was taken by the President on the 29th of April, 1865, when he proclaimed the removal of restrictions on commercial intercourse with the inhabitants of States in which rebellion had existed. A month later,[a] he issued a proclamation, stating the terms by which the people of the paralyzed States, with specified exceptions, might receive full amnesty and pardon, and be reinvested with the right to exercise the functions of citizenship. This was followed by the appointment, by the President, of provisional governors for seven of those States, namely, North Carolina, South Carolina, Georgia, Florida, Alabama, Mississippi, and Texas, clothed with authority to assemble citizens in convention, who had taken the amnesty oath, with power to reorganize State Governments, and secure the election of representatives in the National Congress. The plan was to restore to the States named, their former position in the Union without any provision for securing to the freedmen the right to the exercise of citizenship, which the Amendment to the National Constitution, then before the State Legislatures, would justly entitle them to.[2] The reorganized State Governments were bound only to respect their freedom.

[a] May 29, 1865.

This total disregard of the highest interests of the freedmen, who, by the Amendment would be made citizens, and the fact that the President was making haste to pardon a large number of those who had been active in the rebellion and would exercise a controlling influence in the States which he was equally in haste to reorganize on his plan, startled the loyal men of the country, and made them doubt the sincerity of his vehement declarations of intention to punish traitors and to make treason odious.[3] They felt that

---

[1] The sketch here given of the measures taken for the reorganization of the disordered State Governments, is substantially the same as that given by the author in his *Pictorial History of the United States, from the earliest Period to the Present Time*, published by Mr. Belknap, simultaneously with this work.

[2] See page 453.

[3] In addition to what the President said before his inauguration, it is proper here, to quote his threatening words immediately afterward, to a delegation from New Hampshire, who waited upon him. He said: "Treason

Justice, not Expediency, should be the rule in the readjustment of the affairs of the Republic; and it was demanded, as an act of National honor, that the freedman, when made a citizen by the Constitution, should have equal civil and political rights and privileges with other citizens, such as the elective franchise, and the use of courts of justice.

It soon became evident that the President was willing to take issue, upon vital points of principle and policy, with the party which had carried the country triumphantly through the great Civil War, and had given him the second office, in the Republic.[1] And, at the close of the year, it was plain to sagacious observers that the Chief Magistrate was more friendly to the late enemies of his country than consistency with his profession, or the safety of the Republic, would allow. As a consequence of that friendliness, it was perceived that the politicians who had worked in the interest of the rebellion, and newspapers which had advocated the cause of the Conspirators, had assumed a belligerent tone toward Congress and the loyal people, which disturbed the latter by unpleasant forebodings. Meanwhile measures for perfecting peaceful relations throughout the Republic had been taken. The order for a blockade of the Southern ports was rescinded;[a] more of the rigid restrictions on internal commerce were removed;[b] State prisoners were paroled,[c] and the act suspending the privilege of the writ of *Habeas Corpus* was annulled.[d]

[a] June 23, 1865.
[b] Aug. 29.
[c] Oct. 12.
[d] Dec. 1.

The provisional governors appointed by the President were diligent in carrying out his policy of reorganization, and before Congress met, in December, conventions in five of the disorganized States had ratified the Amendment of the Constitution concerning slavery, formed new Constitutions for their respective States, and caused the election of representatives in Congress. The President had hurried on the work by directing the provisional governors of the five States to resign their power into the hands of others elected under the new Constitutions. Some of the latter had been active participants in the rebellion, and some of the Congressmen elect, in those States, had been hard workers, it was said, in the service of the enemies of the Republic. The loyal people were filled with anxiety because of these events, and the assumptions of powers by the President in doing that which, as prescribed by the Constitution, belongs exclusively to the representatives of the people to do. Yet they waited with the quieting knowledge that

---

is a crime, and must be punished as a crime. It must not be regarded as a mere difference of political opinion. It must not be excused as an unsuccessful rebellion, to be overlooked and forgiven. It is a crime before which all other crimes sink into insignificance." Similar, and even severer language toward those who had lately tried to destroy the Republic, was used by him at that time.

[1] So early as August, or about four months after his accession to the Presidency, Mr. Johnson manifested an unfriendly feeling toward the most earnest men of the Republican party, and who had been most zealous supporters of the Government during the war. In a telegraphic dispatch to Mr. Sharkey, whom he had appointed Provisional Governor of Mississippi, he recommended[a] the extension of the elective franchise to all persons of color in that State who could read the National Constitution, or possessed property valued at $250. This would affect but very few people of that class, who, in that State, were kept enslaved and poor by the laws. His sole motive for the recommendation, as appears in the dispatch, was expressed in these words: "Do this, and as a consequence, the radicals, who are wild upon negro franchise, will be completely foiled in their attempt to keep the Southern States from renewing their relations to the Union." More than a year before, Mr. Lincoln had suggested similar action to the Governor of Louisiana, but with a different motive. "They would probably help," he said, almost prophetically, "in some trying time to come, *to keep the jewel of Liberty in the family of Freedom.*"—*Letter to Michael Hahn*, March 13, 1864.

[a] Aug. 15.

Congress had a right to judge of the qualifications of its members, and with the belief that disloyal men would not be allowed to enter that body over the bar of a test oath prescribed by law.[1]

When Congress assembled,[a] the subject of reorganization was among the first business of the session, and by a joint resolution a committee of fifteen was appointed[2] to make inquiries and report. This was known as the "Reconstruction Committee." This action offended the President. It was an interference of the representatives of the people with his chosen policy of reorganization, and hostility to Congress was soon openly manifested by him. This was vehemently declared by the President in a speech to the populace in front of the Presidential Mansion on the 22d of February[b]—a speech which Americans would gladly blot from the record of their country—in which, forgetting the dignity of his position and the gravity of the questions at issue, he denounced, by name, leading members of Congress, and the party which had given him their confidence. The American people felt humiliated by this act, but it was a small matter when compared with what occurred later in the year,[c] when the President and a part of his Cabinet, with the pretext of honoring the deceased Senator Douglas by being present at the dedication of a monument to his memory at Chicago, on the 6th of September, made a journey to that city and beyond. He harangued the people in language utterly unbecoming the chief magistrate of a nation, and attempted to sow the dangerous seeds of sedition by denouncing Congress as an illegal body, deserving of no respect from the people, and the majority of its members as traitors, "trying to break up the Government." That journey of the President, so disgraceful in all its features—its low partisan object, its immoral performances, and its pitiful results—forms a dark paragraph in the history of the Republic.[3]

[a] Dec. 4, 1865.

[b] 1866.

[c] August and September.

---

[1] By an act passed on the 22d of July, 1862, Congress prescribed that every member should make oath that he had not "voluntarily borne arms against the United States since he had been a citizen thereof," or "voluntarily given aid, countenance, counsel, or encouragement to persons engaged in hostility thereto," and had never "yielded voluntary support to any pretended government, authority, power, or constitution within the United States, hostile or inimical thereto."

[2] On the first day of the session, the House of Representatives, by a vote of 133 against 36, proposed and agreed to a joint resolution to appoint a joint committee, to be composed of nine members of the House and six of the Senate, to "inquire into the condition of the States which formed the so-called Confederate States of America, and report whether they, or any of them, are entitled to be represented in either House of Congress, with leave to report at any time, by bill or otherwise; and until such report shall have been made and finally acted upon by Congress, no member shall be received in either House from any of the so-called Confederate States; and all papers relating to the representatives of the said States, shall be referred to the said committee." The resolution was adopted by the Senate on the 14th. The House appointed Messrs. Stevens, Washburne, Morrill, Grider, Bingham, Conkling, Boutwell, Blow, and Rogers, as its representatives in the committee, and the Senate appointed Messrs. Fessenden, Grimes, Harris, Howland, Johnson, and Williams.

[3] A convention had just been held[d] in Philadelphia, composed chiefly of men who had been engaged in the rebellion, and the enemies of the Republican party, for the purpose of organizing a new party, with President Johnson as its standard-bearer. So discordant were the elements there gathered, that no one was allowed to debate questions of public interest, for fear of producing a disruption and consequent failure of the scheme. It utterly failed. A convention of loyal men from the South was held in Philadelphia soon afterward, in which representatives of the Republican party in the North participated. The President's journey being wholly for a political purpose, members of the latter convention followed in his track, making speeches in many places in support of the measures of Congress for effecting reorganization.

[d] Aug. 14.

So disgraceful was the conduct of the President at Cleveland and St. Louis, in the attitude of a mere demagogue making a tour for partisan purposes, that the common council of Cincinnati, on his return journey, refused to accord him a public reception. The common council of Pittsburg, in Pennsylvania, did the same. When, on the 15th of September, the erring President and his traveling party returned to Washington, the country felt a relief from a sense of deep mortification.

Having laid aside the mask of assumed friendship for those who had labored most earnestly for the suppression of the rebellion and for the freedmen, the President used his veto power to the utmost in trying to thwart the representatives of the people in their efforts to reorganize the disorganized States, and to quickly secure a full and permanent restoration of the Union on the basis of equal and exact justice.[1] He made uncompromising war upon the legislative branch of the Government, and caused members of his Cabinet, who could not agree with him, to resign, with the exception of the Secretary of War. The friends of the Republic urged that officer to remain, believing his retention of his bureau at that critical period in the life of the nation would be for the public benefit. He did so, and became the object of the President's hatred.

On the 2d of April,[a] the President, by proclamation, declared the Civil War to be at an end. Congress, meanwhile, was working assiduously in perfecting its plans for reorganization. Tennessee was formally restored to the Union by that body on the 23d of July, and on the 29th of that month, after a long and arduous session, Congress adjourned. Meanwhile, notable events in the foreign relations of the Government had occurred. The Emperor of the French had been informed that the continuation of French troops in Mexico was not agreeable to the United States, and on the 5th of April,[b] Napoleon's Secretary for Foreign Affairs gave assurance to our Government that those troops should be withdrawn within a specified time. This was done, and the Archduke Maximilian, of Austria, whom Louis Napoleon had placed on a throne in Mexico, with the title of Emperor, was deserted by the perfidious ruler of France, and after struggling against the native Republican Government for awhile, was captured and shot.[2]

a 1866.

b 1866.

The State elections held in the autumn of 1866 indicated the decided approval by the people, of the reorganization plans of Congress as opposed to that of the President, who was now openly affiliated with the Democratic party and the late enemies of the Government, in the South and elsewhere. The majority in Congress felt strengthened by the popular approval of their course, and went steadily forward in perfecting measures for the restoration of the Union. They took steps for restraining the action of the President, who, it was manifest, had determined to carry out his own policy in defiance of that of Congress. And as an indication of the general policy of the latter, concerning suffrage, a bill was passed [December 14] by a large majority of both Houses for granting the elective franchise in the District of Columbia, over which Congress has direct control, to persons, " without any distinction on account of color or race." The President vetoed this bill,[c] when it was re-enacted by the constitutional vote of two-thirds of the members of both Houses in its favor.

c January 7, 1867.

The steady opposition of the President to the measures for reorganization

---

[1] On the 19th of February, 1866, he vetoed the act for enlarging the operations of the Freedmen's Bureau, established for the relief of freedmen, refugees, and abandoned lands. On the 27th of March he vetoed the act known as the Civil Rights Law, which was intended to secure to all citizens, without regard to color or a previous condition of slavery, equal civil rights in the Republic. This Act became a law, after it was vetoed by the President, by the vote of a constitutional majority, on the 9th of April.

[2] See note 1, page 48.

adopted by Congress, and the uniform interposition of his veto, seemed so factious in intent, that on the day when he vetoed the District of Columbia Suffrage Bill, Mr. Ashley, Representative from Ohio, arose in his seat and charged " Andrew Johnson, Vice-President, and Acting-President of the United States, with the commission of acts which, in the estimation of the Constitution, are high crimes and misdemeanors, for which he ought to be impeached." He offered specifications and a resolution instructing the Committee on the Judiciary to make inquiries on the subject.[1] The resolution was adopted by a vote of one hundred and thirty-seven to thirty-eight, forty-five members not voting. This was the first public movement in the matter of the impeachment of the President, which resulted in his trial, in April, 1868.

At a former session of Congress, bills were passed for the admission of the Territories of Colorado and Nevada, as States of the Union. The President interposed. Now similar bills were passed, prescribing as a preliminary to admission, a provision in their constitutions granting impartial suffrage to their citizens, and the ratification of the Amendment to the Constitution. The President vetoed them, when that for the admission of Nevada was passed over his veto. That Territory became a State on the first of March, making the thirty-seventh. A bill limiting the authority of the President in making official appointments and removals from office, known as the "Tenure-of-Office Act," was passed, and was vetoed by the President, when it was passed over the veto.[2] Another bill was passed, vetoed, and passed over the veto, repealing so much of an act of July 17, 1862, as gave the President power to grant amnesty and pardon to those who had been engaged in the Rebellion. A bill was also passed, with the same opposition from the President, for the military government of the disorganized States.[3]

The Thirty-Ninth Congress closed its last session on the 3d of March, and the Fortieth Congress began its first session immediately thereafter. In view of the conduct of the President, which threatened the country with revolution, this action of the National Legislature was necessary for the

---

[1] Mr. Ashley presented the following: " I do impeach Andrew Johnson, Vice-President, and Acting-President of the United States, of high crimes and misdemeanors. I charge him with usurpation of power and violation of law, (1) In that he has corruptly used the appointing power; (2) In that he has corruptly used the pardoning power; (3) In that he has corruptly used the veto power; (4) In that he has corruptly disposed of public property of the United States; and (5) In that he has corruptly interfered in elections, and committed acts which, in contemplation of the Constitution, are high crimes and misdemeanors."

On the 14th of January, Representative Loan, from Missouri, in the course of a debate concerning the duty of the House to proceed to the impeachment of the President, said that the leaders of the rebellion comprehended the advantages of having such a man as the then incumbent, in the Presidential chair. "Hence," he said, "the assassination of Mr. Lincoln. The crime was committed. The way was made clear for the succession. An assassin's hand, wielded and directed by rebel hand, and paid for by rebel gold, made Andrew Johnson President of the United States of America. The price that he was to pay for his promotion was treachery to the Republic, and fidelity to the party of treason and rebellion." Mr. Loan was called to order. The Speaker decided that he was not out of order, the subject of debate being the charges against the President, of "high crimes and misdemeanors," a member having the right, on his own responsibility, to make a specific charge. This decision was appealed from, when the Speaker was sustained by a vote of 101 to 8.

[2] It took from the President, among other things, the power to remove a member of his cabinet, excepting by permission of the Senate, declaring that they should hold office "for and during the term of the President by whom they may have been appointed, and for one month thereafter, subject to removal by and with the consent of the Senate." The act was passed over the veto by a vote in the Senate of 35 to 11, and in the House of 131 to 37.

[3] Those States were divided into five military districts, and the following commanders were appointed: *First District*, Virginia, General J. M. Schofield; *Second District*, North and South Carolina, General D. E. Sickles; *Third District*, Georgia, Florida and Alabama, General J. Pope; *Fourth District*, Mississippi and Arkansas, General E. O. C. Ord; *Fifth District*, Louisiana and Texas, General P. H. Sheridan.

public good. It adjourned on the 31st of March, to meet on the first Wednesday in July. It assembled accordingly on the 4th of that month, and on the 20th adjourned to meet on the 21st of November. The chief business of the short session was to adopt measures for removing the obstructions cast by the President in the way of a restoration of the disorganized States. A bill supplementary to the one for the military government of those States was passed over the usual veto of the President, and it was believed that the Chief Magistrate would refrain from further acts calculated to disturb the public peace. Not so. Immediately after the adjournment of Congress, he proceeded, in defiance of that body, and in alleged violation of the Tenure-of-Office Act, to remove the Secretary of War (Mr. Stanton), and to place General Grant in his place. The President first asked[a] the Secretary to resign. Mr. Stanton refused.[1] A week later the President directed General Grant to assume the duties of Secretary of War. Grant obeyed. Stanton retired, under protest, well satisfied that his office was left in the hands of a patriot whom the President could not corrupt, nor unlawfully control.

[a] Aug. 5, 1867.

The removal of the Secretary of War was followed by the removal of General Sheridan from the command of the Fifth District, and General Sickles from that of the Second District, by which the country was notified that the most faithful officers, who were working with the representatives of the people for the proper and speedy restoration of the Union, would be deprived of power to be useful. General Grant protested against these acts, but in vain. The country was greatly excited, and the loyal people waited with impatience the reassembling of Congress, upon which they relied in that hour of seeming peril to the Republic. That body met at the appointed time, and on the 12th of December the President sent to the Senate a statement of his reasons for removing the Secretary of War. They were not satisfactory, and on the 13th of January[b] the Senate reinstated Mr. Stanton, and General Grant retired from the War Department.[2] Already Congress had made much progress toward the restoration of the disorganized States to the Union, by providing for conventions for framing constitutions and electing members of Congress; and a few days after the restoration of Mr. Stanton, a new bill for the further reorganization of those States was passed by the House of Representatives, in which larger powers were given to the General-in-Chief of the armies in their military government, and depriving the President of all power to interfere in the matter.

[b] 1868.

On the 21st of February,[c] the President caused a new and more intense excitement throughout the country, by a bolder

[c] 1868.

---

[1] The President addressed a note to the Secretary, in which he said, "Grave public considerations constrain me to request your resignation as Secretary of War." The Secretary replied: "Grave public considerations constrain me to continue in the office of Secretary of War until the next meeting of Congress." It is believed that the President was then contemplating a revolutionary scheme, in favor of the late enemies of the country, and was seeking to use the army for that purpose.

[2] The President was angry with General Grant for quietly giving up the office to Stanton, at the bidding of the Senate, and he charged the General-in-Chief with having broken his promises, and tried to injure his reputation as a soldier and a citizen. A correspondence ensued, which speedily found its way to the public. It assumed the form of a question of veracity between the President and the General-in-Chief. Finally, Grant felt compelled to say to the President: "When my honor as a soldier, and integrity as a man, have been so violently assailed, pardon me for saying that I can but regard this whole matter, from beginning to end, as an attempt to involve me in the resistance of law, for which you hesitated to assume the responsibility in orders, and thus to destroy my character before the country." The President did not deny this charge.

step in opposition to the will of Congress than he had hitherto ventured to take. On that day he issued an order to Mr. Stanton, removing him from the office of Secretary of War, and another to Lorenzo Thomas, the Adjutant-General, appointing him Secretary of War, *ad interim*. These orders were officially communicated to the Senate, whereupon that body passed a resolution that the President had no authority under the Constitution and laws to remove the Secretary of War. In the mean time, Thomas had appeared at the War Department and demanded the position to which the President had assigned him, when Mr. Stanton, his superior, refused to yield it, and ordered him to return to his proper office. The President being satisfied that he would not be permitted to use military force in the matter, did not attempt to eject Mr. Stanton by force, and so that officer retained his place. This action of the President was so manifestly in violation of law, that on the following day*ª* the House of Representatives, by a vote of   *ª Feb. 22, 1868.* 126 to 47,[1] "Resolved that Andrew Johnson, President of the United States, be impeached of high crimes and misdemeanors."[2] On the 29th,*ᵇ* a committee of the House, appointed for the purpose,[3] pre-   *ᵇ February.* sented articles of impeachment, nine in number, and these, with slight alterations, were accepted on the 2d of March.[4] The House then proceeded to the appointment of Managers, to conduct the business before the

---

[1] This was an almost strictly party vote. Only two Republicans (Cary of Ohio, and Stewart of New York) voted in the negative, while all the Democrats voted against the resolution.

[2] We have seen (page 617) that the subject of the impeachment of the President was referred to the Committee on the Judiciary. That Committee submitted reports,*ᶜ* which were acted upon on the 7th of December, when the House of Representatives, taking into consideration the gravity of such   *ᶜ Nov. 25, 1867.* a proceeding, and indulging a hope that the President would cease making war upon Congress, and attend to his legitimate duties as simply the executor of the people's will, expressed by their representatives, refused, by a large majority, to entertain a proposition for impeachment. Now, so flagrant was the act of the President, that the Republican members were eager to place him upon trial, and several who were not present when the vote recorded in the text was taken, afterward entered their votes in favor of impeachment.

[3] The committee consisted of Messrs. Boutwell, Stevens (who made the motion for impeachment), Bingham, Wilson, Logan, Julian and Ward. Messrs. Stevens and Bingham were appointed a committee to announce to the Senate the action of the House. This they did on the 25th of February, when the Senate, by unanimous vote, referred the subject to a select committee of seven to consider it.

[4] The following is a brief summary of the charges in the Articles of Impeachment:—Article 1. Unlawfully ordering the removal of Mr. Stanton as Secretary of War, in violation of the provisions of the Tenure-of-Office Act. Article 2. Unlawfully appointing General Lorenzo Thomas as Secretary of War, *ad interim*. Article 3. Substantially the same as Article 2, with the additional averment that there was at the time of the appointment of General Thomas, no vacancy in the office of Secretary of War. Article 4. Conferring with one Lorenzo Thomas, and other persons to the House of Representatives unknown, to prevent, by intimidation and threats, Mr. Stanton, the legally appointed Secretary of War, from holding that office. Article 5. Conspiring with General Thomas and others to hinder the execution of the Tenure-of-Office Act, and in pursuance of this conspiracy, attempting to prevent Mr. Stanton from acting as Secretary of War. Article 6. Conspiring with General Thomas and others to take forcible possession of the property in the War Department. Article 7. Repeated the charge of conspiring to hinder the execution of the Tenure-of-Office Act, and prevent Mr. Stanton from executing the office of Secretary of War. Article 9. Charged that the President called before him the commander of the forces in the Department of Washington and declared to him that a law, passed on the 30th of June, 1867, directing that "all orders and instructions relating to military operations, issued by the President or Secretary of War, shall be issued through the General of the Army, and in case of his inability through the next in rank," was unconstitutional, and not binding upon the commander of the Department of Washington; the intent being to induce that commander to violate the law, and to obey orders issued directly from the President.

On the 3d of March, the managers presented two additional articles, which were adopted by the House. The *first* charged that the President had, by inflammatory speeches, during his journey from Washington to Chicago, already mentioned (page 615), attempted, with a design to set aside the authority of Congress, to bring it into disgrace, and to excite the odium and resentment of the people against Congress and the laws it enacted. The *second* charged that in August, 1866, the President, in a public speech at Washington City, declared that Congress was not a body authorized by the Constitution to exercise legislative powers; and then went on to specify his offenses in endeavoring by unlawful means, to prevent the execution of laws passed by Congress. These formed the 10th and 11th Articles of Impeachment.

Senate,[1] when the Democratic members of the House, to the number of forty five, entered a formal protest against the whole proceedings.

On the 5th of March,[a] the Senate was organized as a jury for the trial of the President. Chief-Justice Salmon P. Chase presided.[2] On the 7th the President was summoned to appear at the bar; and on the 13th, when the Senate formally reopened, he did so appear, by his counsel, who asked for a space of forty days wherein to prepare an answer to the indictment. Ten days were granted, and on the 23d the President's counsel presented an answer. The House of Representatives, the accuser, simply denied every averment in the answer, when the President's counsel asked for a postponement of the trial for thirty days. They allowed seven days, and on Monday, the 30th of March, the trial began. The examination of witnesses was closed on the 22d of April, and on the following day the arguments of counsel began. These closed on the afternoon of Wednesday, the 6th of May, when the case was submitted to the judgment of the Senate. Its decision was given on the 26th of the same month. Every member of the Senate was present, and voted. Thirty-five pronounced the President guilty, and nineteen declared him not guilty. He escaped legal conviction by one vote.[3]

While the unseemly controversy between Congress and the President was going on, the work of reorganization, in accordance with the plans of Congress, was in steady motion, in spite of the interference of the Chief Magistrate; and at a little past midsummer,[b] a Fourteenth Amendment of the Constitution, which formed an important feature in the so-called "reconstruction" measures, was ratified by the requisite number of State Legislatures, and became a part of the "supreme law of the land."[4]

a 1868.

b 1868.

[1] The following members of the House of Representatives were chosen to be managers, on its part, of the impeachment case: Thaddeus Stevens, of Pennsylvania; Benjamin F. Butler, of Massachusetts; John A. Bingham, of Ohio; George S. Boutwell, of Massachusetts; James F. Wilson, of Iowa; Thomas Williams, of Pennsylvania, and John A. Logan, of Illinois. The chief management of the case, on the part of the House, as prosecutor, was intrusted to Mr. Butler.

[2] See clause 6, section 3, article I., of the National Constitution.

[3] The vote of the Senate was as follows:—

For Conviction—Messrs. Anthony, Cameron, Cattell, Chandler, Cole, Conkling, Conness, Corbett, Cragin, Drake, Edmunds, Ferry, Frelinghuysen, Harlan, Howard, Howe, Morgan, Morrill of Vermont, Morrill of Maine, Morton, Nye, Patterson of New Hampshire, Pomeroy, Ramsey, Sherman, Sprague, Stewart, Sumner, Thayer, Tipton, Wade, Willey, Williams, Wilson and Yates. These were all "Republicans."

For Acquittal—Messrs. Bayard, Buckalew, Davis, Dixon, Doolittle, Fessenden, Fowler, Grimes, Henderson, Hendricks, Johnson, McCreery, Norton, Patterson of Tennessee, Ross, Saulsbury, Trumbull, Van Winkle and Vickers. Eight of these, namely: Bayard, Buckalew, Davis, Hendricks, Johnson, McCreery, Saulsbury and Vickers, were elected to the Senate as "Democrats." The remainder were elected as "Republicans."

[4] This Amendment was a part of the "reconstruction" plan of the committee mentioned in note 2, page 615, and was first submitted to the lower house of Congress, in a report of that committee, on the 30th of April, 1866. It was amended by the Senate, and passed that body by a vote of 33 to 11, on the 8th of June. The House passed it on the 13th, by a vote of 120 yeas to 32 nays. The following is a copy of the Fourteenth Amendment to the Constitution:—

"ARTICLE XIV., SECTION 1.—All persons born or naturalized in the United States and subject to the jurisdiction thereof, are citizens of the United States and of the State wherein they reside. No State shall make or enforce any law which shall abridge the privileges or immunities of citizens of the United States; nor shall any State deprive any person of life, liberty, or property, without due process of law; nor deny to any person within its jurisdiction the equal protection of the laws.

"SEC. 2. Representatives shall be apportioned among the several States, according to their respective numbers, counting the whole number of persons in each State, excluding Indians not taxed; but when the right to vote at any election for the choice of electors for President and Vice-President of the United States, Representatives in Congress, the executive and judicial officers of a State, or the members of the Legislature thereof, is denied to any of the male inhabitants of such State (being 21 years of age and citizens of the United States), or in any way abridged, except for participation in rebellion or other crime, the basis of representation therein shall be reduced in the proportion which the number of such male citizens shall bear to the whole number of male citizens twenty-one years of age in said State.

Seven of the disorganized States ratified it, and having by that act, by the adoption of State Constitutions approved by Congress, and by the election of National Senators and Representatives, complied with the prescriptions of Congress, they took their places as resuscitated members of the Union.[1]

Although the country for a considerable time was agitated by the throes of civil war, peace, quiet and unexampled prosperity abound. The Republic has entered upon a new and more glorious era. In its dealings with its domestic enemies, the Government, conscious of its strength, has been lenient and magnanimous beyond all precedent, toward those who attempted to destroy the Union, and has thereby won the applause and admiration of civilized men. Of the thousands of the citizens of the Republic, who consciously and willingly committed "treason against the United States," according to the prescriptions of the Constitution,[2] only one had been punished for the crime,[3] and one other (Jefferson Davis) had been indicted when this record was closed.[4]

The developed and undeveloped resources of the country, and its actual visible wealth, are evidently so abundant and available, and the irrepressible energies of the people are so great, that the enormous debt created by the business of suppressing the Rebellion is not regarded as a very serious burden upon the industry of the nation. That debt amounts, in round numbers, to almost two thousand five hundred million dollars—a debt not nearly so large, in proportion to the population, as the inhabitants of the thirteen original States were subjected to at the close of the old War for Independence, when the resources of the country were almost undeveloped and unknown. It will be cheerfully paid by a grateful people, in accordance with the pledges given in the name of the Republic.[5] The nation having been purified and strengthened by the Civil War and its results, and placed upon the sure foundations of Truth and Justice, may we not reasonably believe that the fiat has gone forth from God, ESTO PERPETUA?

"SEC. 3. No person shall be a Senator, or Representative in Congress, or Elector of President or Vice-President, or hold any office, civil or military, under the United States, or under any State, who, having previously taken an oath as a member of Congress, or as an officer of the United States, or as a member of any State Legislature, or as an executive or judicial officer of any State, to support the Constitution of the United States, shall have engaged in insurrection or rebellion against the same, or given aid or comfort to the enemies thereof; but Congress may, by a vote of two-thirds of each House, remove such disability.

"SEC. 4. The validity of the public debt of the United States, authorized by law, including debts incurred for payment of pensions and bounties for services in suppressing insurrection or rebellion, shall not be questioned: but neither the United States nor any State shall assume or pay any debt or obligation incurred in aid of insurrection or rebellion against the United States, or any claim for the loss or emancipation of any slave. But all such debts, obligations, and claims shall be held illegal and void.

"SEC. 5. The Congress shall have power to enforce, by appropriate legislation, the provisions of this Article."

[1] These were North Carolina, South Carolina, Georgia, Alabama, Mississippi, Louisiana, and Arkansas.

[2] See clause 1, section 3, article III.

[3] Mumford, hung by Butler, at New Orleans. See page 351, volume II.

[4] See page 579.

[5] On the first of August, 1865, the actual debt of the Republic, considering back pay, bounties, overdue contracts, transportation, and a variety of other expenses incident to the closing of the war, since liquidated and unliquidated, amounted to $3,287,733,329. At the end of the last fiscal year (June 30, 1868), the National Debt was $2,488,000,000, showing the remarkable fact, that in the space of about three years since the close of the war, that debt had been reduced $802,733,329, or more than one-fourth of its full amount. At that rate of reduction, the entire debt may be paid off in the space of ten years.

INDEX.

A.

628 INDEX.

East Tennessee, cruel treatment of Unionists in, ii. 36–39; minor military movements in, iii. 281; journey of the author in, in 1866, iii. 283, 287.

Edenton, N. C., capture of, ii. 176.

Elizabeth City, N. C., capture of, ii. 174.

ELLET, Col. C. L., exploits of in the "*Queen of the West*," ii. 589.

ELLET, Gen. A., in the Red River expedition, iii. 253.

Ellison's Mill, skirmish at, ii. 404; battle at, ii. 419.

ELLSWORTH, Col. E. E., death of, i. 483.

Emancipation, first act of Congress concerning, ii. 29; consideration of in Congress and by Lincoln, ii. 554–558; the Chicago memorial in relation to, ii. 558; preliminary proclamation of, ii. 558; definitive proclamation of, ii. 559.

Emancipation Proclamation, effect of on the Confederates, iii. 229; firm stand of President Lincoln in relation to, iii. 230.

EMORY, Gen., at battle of Pleasant Grove, ii. 258.

ERICSSON, Capt. JOHN, the "*Monitor*" built by, ii. 360.

Europe, Confederate emissaries at the courts of, i. 565; attitude of sovereigns of in 1861, i. 570; effect in of the news of the battle of Bull's Run, ii. 19.

EWELL, Gen., surrender of at Sailor's Creek, iii. 554.

EWING, Gen. HUGH S., his defense of Pilot Knob against Price, iii. 277.

F.

Fairfax Court-House, Lieut. Tomkins's dash upon, i. 487; McDowell's advance on, ii. 586; Col. Stoughton carried off from by Moseby, ii. 21; Hooker at, iii. 52.

Fair Oaks Station, battle near, ii. 410; second battle near, ii. 412; visit of the author to in 1866, ii. 439.

Falling Waters, battle at, i. 524.

Falmouth, Hooker's head-quarters near, iii. 24.

FARRAGUT, Admiral DAVID G., his passage of the forts below New Orleans, ii. 331–336; panic at New Orleans on the approach of his fleet, ii. 342; his reply to Mayor Monroe, ii. 343; his bombardment of the batteries at Vicksburg, ii. 526; operations of against the Mobile forts, iii. 439–444.

Fast-Day, proclaimed by Buchanan, i. 77.

FAULKNER, CHARLES J., mischievous influence of in Europe, i. 565.

Fayetteville, Ark., repulse of Confederates at by Col. Harrison, iii. 213; relieved by Gen. Curtis, iii. 280.

Fayetteville, N. C., arsenal at seized by State troops, i. 386; Sherman at, iii. 497.

FELTON, S. M., his account of the first assassination plot (note), iii. 565.

Fernandina, occupation of by Nationals, ii. 321.

FERRERO, Gen., services of at Knoxville, iii. 173.

Finances, Confederate, schemes in relation to, i. 544; bad condition of in 1863 and 1864, iii. 227, 228.

Finances, national, condition of at the close of 1860, i. 115; toward the close of Buchanan's term, i. 297; and in 1863 and 1864, iii. 226.

"*Firing the Southern heart*," i. 41.

Fisher's Hill, battle of, iii. 366.

Five Forks, battle of, iii. 542.

Flag, national, General Dix's telegram in relation to, i. 185; shot away at Fort Sumter, i. 326; torn down in New Orleans after being raised by Farragut, ii. 343; but raised again permanently, ii. 344; raised again at Fort Sumter by Gen. Anderson, iii. 465.

Floating battery at Charleston, i. 312.

Florida, secession movements in, i. 60; conventions in, i. 165; operations of Dupont and Wright on coast of, ii. 320; expedition of Gen. Seymour to, iii. 466–469.

"*Florida*," Confederate cruiser, career of, iii. 433.

FLOYD, JOHN B., secret treachery of, i. 45; national arms transferred to the South by, i. 121; implicated in the Indian Trust Fund robbery, i. 144; his flight to Richmond, i. 146; flight of after the battle of Carnifex Ferry, ii. 97; flight of from New River, ii. 102; in command at Fort Donelson, ii. 210; flight of under cover of night, ii. 219.

Folly Island, batteries erected on by Vogdes, iii. 201.

FOOTE, Commodore ANDREW H., flotilla under the command of, ii. 198; operations of on the Cumberland River, ii. 232; death of, iii. 200.

FORREST, Gen. N. B., his capture of Murfreesboro' and approach to Nashville, ii. 501; routed at Parker's Cross-Roads, ii. 552; raid of in Tennessee as far as Jackson, iii. 237; escape of into Mississippi, iii. 238; repulses Gen. W. S. Smith at West Point and Okolona, iii. 239; raid of through Tennessee into Kentucky, iii. 243; his capture of and massacre at Fort Pillow, iii. 244–246; defeated at Tupelo by Gen. A. J. Smith, iii. 248; his dash into Memphis, iii. 248; repulsed by Gen. Rousseau at Pulaski, iii. 416.

Fortifications in Charleston harbor, description of, i. 117; anxiety of conspirators respecting, i. 120.

Fort Anderson, capture of, iii. 492.

Fort Barlow, capture of, ii. 173.

Fort Beauregard, capture of, ii. 120.

Fort Blunt, Confederates repulsed at, iii. 213.

Fort Clark, capture of, ii. 108.

Fort Clinch, found abandoned by Dupont, ii. 320.

Fort de Russy, capture of, iii. 254.

Fort Donelson, siege of, ii. 206–219; battle of, ii. 215; surrender of, ii. 220; effect of the fall of at home and abroad, ii. 222; the author's visit to in 1866, ii. 226; attempt of Wheeler to recapture, iii. 116.

Fort Fisher, expedition against under Gens. Butler and Weitzel and Admiral Porter, iii. 476–481; second and successful expedition against, iii. 484–489; visit of the author to in 1866, iii. 481.

Fort Gaines, seizure of, i. 175; recapture of, iii. 443.

Fort Hatteras, capture of, ii. 108.

Fort Henry, operations of Grant and Foote against, ii. 200–202; battle of, ii. 203; capture of, ii. 205.

Fort Hindman, capture of, ii. 581.

Fort Jackson, surrender of to Captain Porter, ii. 339.

Fort Jefferson, re-enforcements thrown into, i. 363.

Fort McAllister, bombardment of by Dupont, iii. 190; capture of by Gen. Hazen, iii. 412.

Fort Macon, capture of, ii. 312; visit of the author to in 1864, ii. 313.

Fort Marion, capture of, ii. 322.

Fort Morgan, seizure of by State troops, i. 174; surrender of to Farragut, iii. 443.

Fort Moultrie, description of, i. 117; garrisons of transferred to Fort Sumter by Major Anderson, i. 129; seizure of by South Carolina troops, i. 187.

Fort Norfolk, seizure of by insurgents, i. 398.

Fort Pemberton, Ross's expedition against, ii. 587.

Fort Pickens, attempt to seize frustrated by Lieut. Slemmer, i. 167; surrender of demanded by insurgents, i. 173; siege of, i. 363–371; Pensacola navy-yard and Confederate forts bombarded from, ii. 111.

Fort Pillow, evacuation of by Confederates, ii. 298; capture of by Forrest, iii. 245; cruel massacre of negro and white troops at, iii. 246.